FROMMER'S

COMPREHENSIVE TRAVEL GUIDE

FLORIDA '94

by Rena Bulkin,
Dan Levine & Nicole Faff,
Patricia Tunison Preston & John J. Preston,
Florence Lemkowitz

PRENTICE HALL TRAVEL

NEW YORK • LONDON • TORONTO • SYDNEY • TOKYO • SINGAPORE

FROMMER BOOKS

Published by Prentice Hall General Reference
A division of Simon & Schuster Inc.
15 Columbus Circle
New York, NY 10023

ISBN 0-671-84919-0
ISSN 1044-2391

Design by Robert Bull Design
Maps by Geografix Inc.

Frommer's Editorial Staff
Editorial Director: Marilyn Wood
Editorial Manager/Senior Editor: Alice Fellows
Senior Editors: Lisa Renaud, Sara Hinsey Raveret
Editors: Charlotte Allstrom, Thomas F. Hirsch, Peter Katucki, Theodore Stavrou
Assistant Editors: Margaret Bowen, Christopher Hollander, Alice Thompson, Ian Wilker
Editorial Assistants: Gretchen Henderson, Bethany Jewett
Managing Editor: Leanne Coupe

Special Sales
Bulk purchases (10+ copies) of Frommer's Travel Guides are available to corporations at special discounts. The Special Sales Department can produce custom editions to be used as premiums and/or for sales promotion to suit individual needs. Existing editions can be produced with custom cover imprints such as a corporate logo. For more information write to: Special Sales, Prentice Hall Travel, 15 Columbus Circle, New York, New York 10023.

CONTENTS

5 WHAT TO SEE & DO IN MIAMI 100

6 THE FLORIDA KEYS 137

7 THE GOLD COAST 165

8 INDIAN RIVER COUNTRY 210

9 ORLANDO & WALT DISNEY WORLD 225

LIST OF MAPS

FLORIDA

MIAMI

TAMPA/ST. PETERSBURG

REGIONAL & CITY MAPS

INVITATION TO THE READERS

In researching this book, we have come across many wonderful establishments, the best of which we have included here. We are sure that many of you will also come across appealing hotels, inns, restaurants, guesthouses, shops, and attractions. Please don't keep them to yourself. Share your experiences, especially if you want to comment on places that have been included in this edition that have changed for the worse. You can address your letters to the appropriate author (see inside back cover for a list):

Frommer's Florida '94
c/o Prentice Hall Travel
15 Columbus Circle
New York, NY 10023

A DISCLAIMER

Readers are advised that prices fluctuate in the course of time and travel information changes under the impact of the varied and volatile factors that affect the travel industry. Neither the authors nor the publisher can be held responsible for the experiences of readers while traveling. Readers are invited to write to the publisher with ideas, comments, and suggestions for future editions.

SAFETY ADVISORY

Whenever you're traveling in an unfamiliar city or country, stay alert. Be aware of your immediate surroundings. Wear a moneybelt and keep a close eye on your possessions. Be particularly careful with cameras, purses, and wallets, all favorite targets of thieves and pickpockets.

CHAPTER 1

GETTING TO KNOW FLORIDA

Lured by the promise of sunny skies and sandy beaches, millions of visitors each year flee bleak northern winters to bask in Florida's warmth. But though thousands of miles of pristine shoreline are its undeniable drawing card, America's Sunshine State offers much more than just a beach vacation.

Its lush tropical landscape, dotted with fish-filled lakes and springs, abounds in wildlife that will thrill the naturalist in you. Unspoiled marshes, mangroves, and mud flats provide habitats for great egrets, wood storks, ibis, bald eagles, flamingos, roseate spoonbills, pelicans, hawks, and herons among other shore birds; dolphins, otters, and manatees frolic in diverse waterways; and in the summer months, huge loggerhead turtles lumber ashore to lay their eggs in the sand. Dense forests of cypress draped in Spanish moss contrast with gracefully swaying palms and displays of brilliant bougainvillea, azaleas, hibiscus, crape myrtles, and fragrant jasmine and magnolias. Southwest of Miami is a vast primeval prairie that sweeps across 2,100 square miles of spectacular wilderness—Everglades National Park. The Keys, a string of coral reef islets, offer topography ranging from upland jungle and mangrove swamp to a 21-mile underwater garden filled with over 600 species of tropical fish. The world's largest stand of sand pines is in Ocala National Forest, a 366,000-acre wilderness. Citrus groves line the banks of Indian River. And Sanibel Island, which along with nearby Captiva Island comprises a National Wildlife Refuge, is considered one of the world's best shelling sites.

Sports fans can cheer their favorite major-league baseball teams as they head into each season with spring training here, while thousands of football fans descend on Miami for the Orange Bowl each year and on Jacksonville for the Gator Bowl. And that's just the beginning. Florida offers every manner of spectator sport, from major golf and tennis tournaments to such local favorites as jai alai and greyhound racing. And, of course, there's Daytona Beach, mecca for auto-racing enthusiasts. In addition, it would be hard to name an active sport not readily available in the Sunshine State. You'll find details in each chapter.

Finally, Florida is America's most popular family vacation destination, offering a host of kid-pleasers—most notably Walt Disney World, but also including water parks such as Wet 'n Wild, alligator and crocodile parks, Universal and Disney-MGM Studios, Busch Gardens, Sea World and Marineland, and Lion Country Safari.

DATELINE

- **1513** Ponce de León makes landfall near Cape Canaveral, becoming first European to step on Florida soil.
- **1565** Pedro Menéndez de Avilés establishes St. Augustine.
- **1566–1703** Scores of Franciscan missions dot interior Florida.
- **1586** Sir Francis Drake sacks St. Augustine.
- **1695** St. Augustine's Castillo de San Marcos completed.
- **1763** Under the terms of the Treaty of Paris, Spain relinquishes Florida to the British.
- **1784** Florida reverts to Spanish control after the American Revolution.
- **1813** Gen. Andrew Jackson drives British from Pensacola in War of 1812.
- **1818** First Seminole War; Jackson leads U.S. troops into Florida on punitive raids against the native peoples.
- **1821** Florida becomes U.S. territory.
- **1823** Tallahassee selected as territorial capital.
- **1835–42** Second Seminole War, bloodiest and costliest of all U.S.–Indian conflicts.

(continues)

1. HISTORY

THE FLOWERY LAND On April 2, 1513—more than a century before the Pilgrims landed at Plymouth Rock—Juan Ponce de León, in search of the fabled "fountain of youth," spied the beaches and lush greenery of Florida's Atlantic coast. The conqueror and colonial governor of Puerto Rico laid anchor just south of present-day Cape Canaveral, rowed ashore, and confidently claimed the land for the Spanish crown. Observing that the land was "very pretty to behold with many refreshing trees," he named it La Florida, or "the Flowery Land."

Eight years later, with a fighting force of 200 conquistadors, missionary priests, and a writ from the Spanish king promising him de facto ownership of any profits his endeavor might produce, he returned to conquer and colonize Florida. His party landed at Charlotte's Bay, near present-day Fort Myers, said a prayer of thanksgiving, and began building homes. But the fledgling settlement's prayers went unanswered. It was ferociously attacked with arrows and stones by hostile indigenous tribes. Ponce de León was wounded by an arrow and, along with other survivors, retreated to Cuba where he died. He was buried in Puerto Rico. Ponce de León's fate proved a harbinger of the difficulties the Spanish would encounter in Florida. Over the next 50 years, five expeditions pursuing rumors of golden cities attempted and failed to establish a colonial foothold on the peninsula.

It wasn't until 1565 that Pedro Menéndez de Avilés, arriving with 1,000 settlers and a priest, established St. Augustine, the first permanent European settlement in North America. In the years that followed, Franciscan friars created a chain of missions on Native American lands throughout Florida. Though the missions' ostensible aim was converting the tribes and instructing them in European trades and agricultural methods, they only succeeded in wreaking havoc among them. Many tribesmen died taking up primitive arms against Spanish steel and firepower, and many more were drafted into slavery. But the greatest toll was in deaths from European infectious diseases against which Native Americans had no immunities. By the middle of the 16th century, three-quarters of Florida's original inhabitants had been wiped out.

THE BRITISH ARE COMING Though their colony survived, life was difficult for the Spanish settlers who were beset by the same combination of harsh climate (those Florida hurricanes), hostile natives, famine, fire, and disease that undid earlier expeditions. St. Augustine was attacked time and again by pirates and armies of the rival French and British empires. Florida gained importance in the defense of Spain's commercial coastal route, but it never produced bounteous wealth for Spain as settlements in Mexico, the Caribbean, and South America had done. When the British captured the important Spanish port of Havana, Cuba, in the French and Indian War (1754–63), they offered to exchange Havana for the rights to Florida. Forced to choose, the Spanish reluctantly agreed.

During their two decades as stewards of Florida (1763–84), the British brought zeal and resources to the territory's development that far exceeded Spanish efforts. They began establishing Florida as a major agricultural center. Stately plantations, producing indigo, rice, and oranges, rose up along the Atlantic coast and the St. Johns River. St. Augustine bustled with activity. East Florida British Gov. James Grant captured the upbeat tenor of the times in a letter to a friend: "There is not so gay a Town in America as this is at present, the People [are] Musick and Dancing mad."

Bolstered by stipends from the British Parliament, Florida remained loyal to King George III during the American Revolution and, in fact, became a haven for Tories from the northern colonies. But when the newborn United States prevailed over England in 1783, the Treaty of Paris acknowledged Spain's wartime assistance by returning Florida to Spanish control.

SPANISH SETTLEMENT, SEMINOLE WARS & STATEHOOD Florida remained in Spanish hands for the next four decades (1784–1821), but it was clear from the beginning that this regime was living on borrowed time. To attract settlers, the Spanish offered land grants to anyone willing to immigrate to the colony, and as English-speaking homesteaders from the United States began to stream into Florida, its Spanish character underwent a subtle shift. In 1791, Thomas Jefferson wrote cagily to President Washington: "I wish 10,000 of our inhabitants would accept the invitation. It would be a means of delivering to us peacably what must otherwise cost us a war. In the meantime, we may complain of the seduction of our inhabitants just enough to make the Spanish believe it is a very wise policy for them."

This maneuvering over control of Florida between the two nations broke into open conflict with the outbreak of the War of 1812 and the First Seminole War of 1818. Andrew Jackson's unopposed marches through Florida during these two conflicts convinced Spain that it had no choice but to negotiate a graceful departure. In 1821, Spain ceded Florida to the United States.

The new territorial government aggressively set about encouraging the growth of its charge. Tallahassee, once a thriving Apalachee settlement, was chosen as the capital. Streets were laid in Cowford, a cattle crossing on the St. Johns River, and the village was renamed Jacksonville in honor of "Old Hickory." Florida's population, numbering 8,000 in 1821, had quadrupled by the 1830s. But one major obstacle to settlement yet remained—the Seminoles.

The Seminoles had migrated into the peninsula from Georgia toward the end of the 18th century, and by the 1820s, much of Florida's richest farmland—which the territorial government was eager to open to white homesteaders—lay in their hands. After a series of compromise treaties that left both sides dissatisfied, the federal government threw down the final gauntlet with the Indian Removal Act of 1830, stipulating that all eastern tribes be

DATELINE

- **1845** Florida becomes 27th state admitted to the Union.
- **1861** Florida secedes from the Union, joins the Confederate States of America.
- **1864** Battle of Olustee, lone major engagement of the Civil War to take place in Florida.
- **1887** Florida legislature passes Jim Crow measures mandating separation of races.
- **1895** Henry Morrison Flagler's Florida East Coast railroad incorporated; catastrophic freeze forces citrus industry to move south.
- **1912** Flagler's railroad reaches Key West.
- **1915** Miami Beach incorporated.
- **1925** Miami's population explodes to 300,000 as real estate boom peaks.
- **1926–29** Collapse of land boom, two destructive hurricanes, fruit-fly infestation, and national stock-market crash leaves Florida's economy in ruins.
- **1942** German U-boats sink U.S. ships off Florida coast throughout the summer; thousands of servicemen arrive in Florida's new military bases.

(continues)

DATELINE

- **1950** Booming tourism brings 4.5 million visitors to the state; first rocket launched from Cape Canaveral.
- **1959** Cubans fleeing Castro begin arriving in Florida.
- **1964** Civil rights protests rock St. Augustine.
- **1969** *Apollo XI*'s historic journey to the moon launched from Kennedy Space Center.
- **1971** Walt Disney World opens.
- **1974** Big Cypress Swamp National Preserve created, a harbinger of Florida's growing environmental awareness.
- **1982** EPCOT Center (Experimental Prototype Community of Tomorrow) opens at Walt Disney World.
- **1990** Universal Studios, theme park and working film studio, opens its doors.
- **1992** Hurricane Andrew slams into the Gold Coast, causing $1 billion in damages.

removed to reservations west of the Mississippi. The spark that ignited the Second Seminole War (1835–42) was provided by a young warrior named Osceola. At a treaty conference at Payne's Landing in 1832, he strode up to the bargaining table, slammed his knife into the papers on it, and pointing to the quivering blade, proclaimed, "The only treaty I will ever make is this!" Guerilla warfare thwarted the U.S. Army's attempts to remove the Seminoles for almost eight years. But finally, the Seminole population in Florida dwindled to fewer than 100 survivors who took refuge deep in the impenetrable swamps of the Everglades, where some of their descendants still live today. With the Seminoles out of the way, the Territorial General Legislature petitioned Congress for statehood, and on March 3, 1845, President John Tyler signed a bill making Florida the 27th state in the Union.

Florida grew rapidly over the next 15 years. Cotton, cattle ranching, and forest industries thrived; railroads began to appear; and visitors from the north arrived to enjoy the state's sunny winters. By 1860, Florida's population had jumped to 140,000, 40% of whom were slaves. Then came the Civil War.

REBELS & RECONSTRUCTION In 1861, Florida became the third state to secede from the Union, and the modest progress it had achieved as a state came to a standstill. The stars and bars flew from every flagpole. Only one major battle of the Civil War was fought on Florida soil, however, when Confederate forces met federal troops seeking to advance on and destroy Florida farms at Olustee, on February 20, 1864. The Rebels routed the Yanks, and, in the months that followed, continued to successfully defend interior Florida against Union attack. When Robert E. Lee surrendered at Appomattox, Tallahassee was the only southern capital still in Confederate hands, but this was little consolation to Floridians, who had lost some 5,000 of their own during the strife.

Florida's fledgling cities and industries emerged from the Civil War relatively unscathed, but residents did not escape the social and political turmoil of Reconstruction. The Emancipation Proclamation released nearly half of Florida's population from slavery, and intense wrangling ensued between northern reformers and Floridians over the role blacks would play in postwar society. Blacks enjoyed some initial gains. Local elections of 1868 saw 19 blacks ride the Union victory to seats in the Florida legislature, and schools for black children were founded. But as elsewhere in the South, the traditional political power base of white Democrats soon regained the upper hand.

THE GILDED AGE Florida emerged from the rigors of Reconstruction to rebuild the state's economy and usher in an era of rapid growth and development. North-central Florida enjoyed the benefits of a booming citrus industry. Cigar factories sprang up in Tampa. Large tracts of swamp in the peninsula's interior were drained for agricultural use, and this newly arable land was sold to eager arriving immigrants. Many of these arrivals were recently freed African Americans, who by the 1890s accounted for 47% of the state's population. State planners recognized that the expansion of the railroads was the requisite catalyst for economic growth. Industrialists Henry Plant and William Chipley built railroads that connected Tampa and Pensacola to the developed regions in Florida's northeast. To ensure the profitability of their new railroads, both men invested heavily in the isolated cities at the end of the line. Plant's posh Tampa Bay Hotel still graces the city's skyline as the home of the University of Tampa.

But the man who revolutionized Florida tourism was the flamboyant Henry Morrison Flagler, a partner in John D. Rockefeller's Standard Oil Company. Visiting Florida in the early 1880s, he envisioned the sunny Atlantic coast state as a winter playground for millionaires—a southern Newport. He bought up and knit together the short rail lines that extended south from Jacksonville and laid track as far as West Palm Beach, incorporating it all under the Florida East Coast Railway Company. In 1896, Flagler's trains chugged into the infant hamlet of Miami, and by 1912 the rail line extended south to Key West. In Palm Beach, Flagler built his own mansion, Whitehall, as well as two palatial hotels, the Poinciana and the Breakers. And in St. Augustine, his fabulous Ponce de Leon Hotel (today Flagler College), complemented by two other deluxe hostelries, the Alcazar and the Cordova, also drew moneyed visitors.

THE 20TH CENTURY: FLORIDA BOOMS . . . Florida entered the 20th century with a diversified economy centered on ranching, citrus, timber, and tourism. Prosperity was everywhere. The expanded rail system vastly improved mail service around the state; telephones and electricity reached most of rural Florida; a crude passenger airline began operating flights between St. Petersburg and Tampa, the first such outfit in the world; and an extensive road system accommodated the rapid growth of the automobile.

Congress passed the Eighteenth Amendment in 1919, and the Florida legislature, reflecting the staid attitudes of the rural population, quickly made Prohibition Florida law. But no such attitude ruled the increasingly cosmopolitan and sophisticated Gold Coast. People arrived in droves for holidays in Palm Beach and Miami, and illegal speakeasies rose up to serve them. Wild chases between lawmen and "rum runners" became commonplace. Florida quickly became one of the loosest environments of the Roaring '20s. The state was in a celebratory mood. As Henry Flagler had envisioned decades earlier, real estate was going through the roof. Millions of immigrants, speculators, and builders descended on the state, and new communities sprang up seemingly overnight. Miami Beach, for example, went from a barren strip of sand to a sprawling resort city with over 50 hotels in a decade. Land that had been available free to anyone who wanted it after the city's incorporation in 1915 was going for tens of thousands of dollars in 1925. The mayors of Miami, Miami Beach, Hialeah, and Coral Gables proclaimed their county "The most Richly Blessed Community of the most Bountifully Endowed State of the most Highly Enterprising People of the Universe."

. . . AND GOES BUST Quite suddenly the bubble burst. A July 1926 issue of the *Nation* provided the obituary for the land boom: "The world's greatest poker game, played with building lots instead of chips, is over. And the players are now . . . paying up." Construction stopped dead, and many newcomers who had arrived in Florida to jump on the bandwagon returned to their homes in the north. Two hurricanes, the first to hit the state in over a decade, pummeled the Gold Coast in 1926 and 1928, catastrophically damaging both the resort areas and the interior farmlands of the southern peninsula. A fruit-fly infestation crippled the citrus industry. The 1929 stock market crash that precipitated the Great Depression seemed almost an afterthought to Florida's ruined economy. Within a few years, the announcers at Tampa radio station WDAE were giving wry notice of the state's suffering by changing the station's slogan "Wonderful Days and Evenings" to "We Don't Always Eat."

President Franklin D. Roosevelt's New Deal programs helped the state begin to climb back on its feet. The Works Progress Administration (WPA) put 40,000 unemployed Floridians back in the labor force building the automobile causeway from the mainland to Key West and a bridge across the Panhandle's Ocklockonee Bay, among other public projects. By 1936 the tourist trade had revived somewhat, and the state began attracting a broader range of visitors than ever before. But the event that finally lifted Florida—and the nation—out of the Depression was World War II. Following the Japanese attack on Pearl Harbor in 1941, scores of army bases and training facilities were expanded or opened all over Florida. Thousands of U.S. servicemen did part of their hitch in the state, and hotels were filled to capacity with military personnel. The war came right to Florida's shores—in 1942, German subs sank a U.S. tanker, the *Pan Massachusetts,* and over two dozen other Allied ships in plain sight of Florida's beaches. When the war ended, many soldiers returned to settle in the Sunshine State, and in the 1940s Florida's population nearly doubled.

POSTWAR PROSPERITY Florida shared the bullish economy of the 1950s with the rest of the nation. Its population grew a whopping 78.7% during the decade, making it America's 10th most populous state, and tourists came in droves, nearly 4.5 million in 1950 alone. One reason for the influx was the advent of the air conditioner, which made life in Florida infinitely more pleasant.

A brand-new industry came into being at Cape Canaveral in 1950—the government-run space program. Cape Canaveral became NASA's headquarters for the Apollo rocket program that eventually blasted Neil Armstrong heavenward toward his famous "great step"—a happening in bizarre accordance with sci-fi writer Jules Verne's 1865 novel, *From the Earth to the Moon,* which foretold that mankind would first reach for the moon from this latitude of Florida.

Beginning in 1959, great numbers of Cuban immigrants fleeing Fidel Castro's socialist revolution began arriving on Florida's shores. Most of these exiles had led middle- or upper-class lives in Cuba, and collectively they created a remarkable American success story, planting an indelible stamp on the business and cultural life of the city. Other exile communities, most notably Haitians, have been arriving in Florida's cities in recent years and are jostling for a piece of the economic pie. But the state's most important new arrival since Flagler was a cute rodent, in 1971.

THE MOUSE THAT ROARED In the 1960s, Walt Disney began secretly buying up central Florida farmland and laying plans for the world's most spectacular theme park. Walt Disney World would soon turn the sleepy citrus-growing town of Orlando into the fastest-growing city in the state and attract so many visitors that they would outnumber residents. WDW continued to grow and expand, adding EPCOT Center, Disney-MGM Studios, and other adjuncts (described in detail in Chapter 9). Today, not just Orlando but the entire state abounds in theme parks.

Florida has become the state "where everyone is from somewhere else"—even Mickey came from California. At the forefront of this influx of outsiders are retirees. A steady stream of seniors from the Northeast have settled in the Miami area, while an equally large contingent from the Midwest has made the lower Gulf Coast its home. In nearly a third of Florida's 67 counties, seniors now account for more than a third of the population. Silver-haired politicians have organized their peers into a force to be reckoned with in state politics and have won seniors a level of social services rarely found elsewhere. Elderly newcomers have plunged into Florida retirement with youthful enthusiasm, returning to school, taking up sports again (as in the Kids and Kubs Senior Baseball League), and enjoying Florida's balmy air and sunshine.

IMPRESSIONS

The commodities of this land [Florida] are more than are yet knowen to any man. . . . it flourisheth with meadow, pasture ground, with woods of Cedar and Cypres, and other sorts, as better can not be in the world.

—Voyage of Sir John Hawkins, 1565, quoted by Richard Hakluyt

. . . with the approach of the long and bitter winter, I could see why Florida is a golden word. . . . I found that more and more people lusted toward Florida and that thousands had moved there and more and more thousands wanted to and would . . . the very name Florida carried the message of warmth and ease and comfort. It was irresistible.

—John Steinbeck, *Travels with Charley,* 1962

In the 1990s, Floridians have taken steps to protect their state's natural beauty and resources, including major initiatives to protect the Everglades and control the spread of tacky commercial districts. As they deal with challenges to Florida's continuing vitality—challenges both man-made and natural (such as 1992's Hurricane Andrew, which nearly annihilated South Dade County and left 250,000 homeless)—there is every reason for optimism. Florida's siren song beckons us to its shores throughout our lives. We come as children to the Magic Kingdom, return as young adults for spring break shennanigans and to view baseball spring training, as adults with our own children in tow, and finally as retirees.

2. THE REGIONS IN BRIEF

Northeastern Florida The northeast section of the state contains the oldest permanent settlement in America—St. Augustine, where Spanish colonists arrived and settled more than four centuries ago. Its history comes to life in a quaint historic district. St. Augustine is bordered to the north by Jacksonville, an up-and-coming sunbelt metropolis with miles of oceanfront beach and beautiful marine views along the St. Johns River. And to the south is Daytona Beach, home of the Daytona International Speedway and spring break mecca for the college crowd.

The Panhandle Sand beaches, historic homes, small farm towns, and acres of sea oats and pine trees are the defining features of the Panhandle. This region, which encompasses the cities of Pensacola, Panama City, and Tallahassee, has a distinctly southern flavor—not surprising since it borders Alabama and Georgia. In the last few years, it has begun attracting some of the spring break crowd that traditionally frequents Fort Lauderdale and Daytona Beach.

Central Florida Once a flat expanse of farmland, citrus groves, and scrub pine forests, Central Florida was transformed forever when Walt Disney World came to town in 1971. Today it's the state's theme park hub (what Anaheim is to California) and Orlando its fastest-growing city. Another brand of excitement is offered at the Kennedy Space Center, launch site for all manned U.S. space missions since 1968.

The West Coast Halfway down the west coast of Florida lies Tampa Bay, lined with miles of sandy beaches. Beside the bay flourishes one of the fastest-growing metropolitan areas in the country, Tampa and St. Petersburg. Just south lies Bradenton, where you'll find the headquarters of the world's most famous orange juice company (Tropicana), and Sarasota, the winter home of the Ringling Brothers and Barnum & Bailey Circus.

The Shell Coast Fort Myers and Naples occupy the southwestern corner of the state, and offshore lie the tranquil islands of Sanibel and Captiva, where you can indulge in one of life's quieter pleasures—searching for seashells on a white sand beach.

Indian River Country Just north of glittering Palm Beach, a sleepy atmosphere prevails in towns like Jupiter, Port St. Lucie, and Vero Beach. Nature lovers will enjoy the area's citrus groves and unspoiled beaches, still bypassed for the most part by developers.

The Southeast Coast The palm-dotted sands of Florida's "Gold Coast" are lined with beachfront hotels and posh resorts. Just north of Miami, the coast extends through Fort Lauderdale, Boca Raton, and Palm Beach, which has been famous for many years as a playground for the rich and famous.

Miami and Miami Beach Long a resort haven, Miami is a sophisticated, cosmopolitan city that boasts striking art deco architecture, gorgeous beaches, and glittering nightlife. It's also a major population center for Latin American immigrants, especially a thriving Cuban community. Southwest of the city lie the vast swamplands of Everglades National Park, teeming with unusual wildlife.

The Keys From the southern tip of Florida, U.S. 1 travels through a

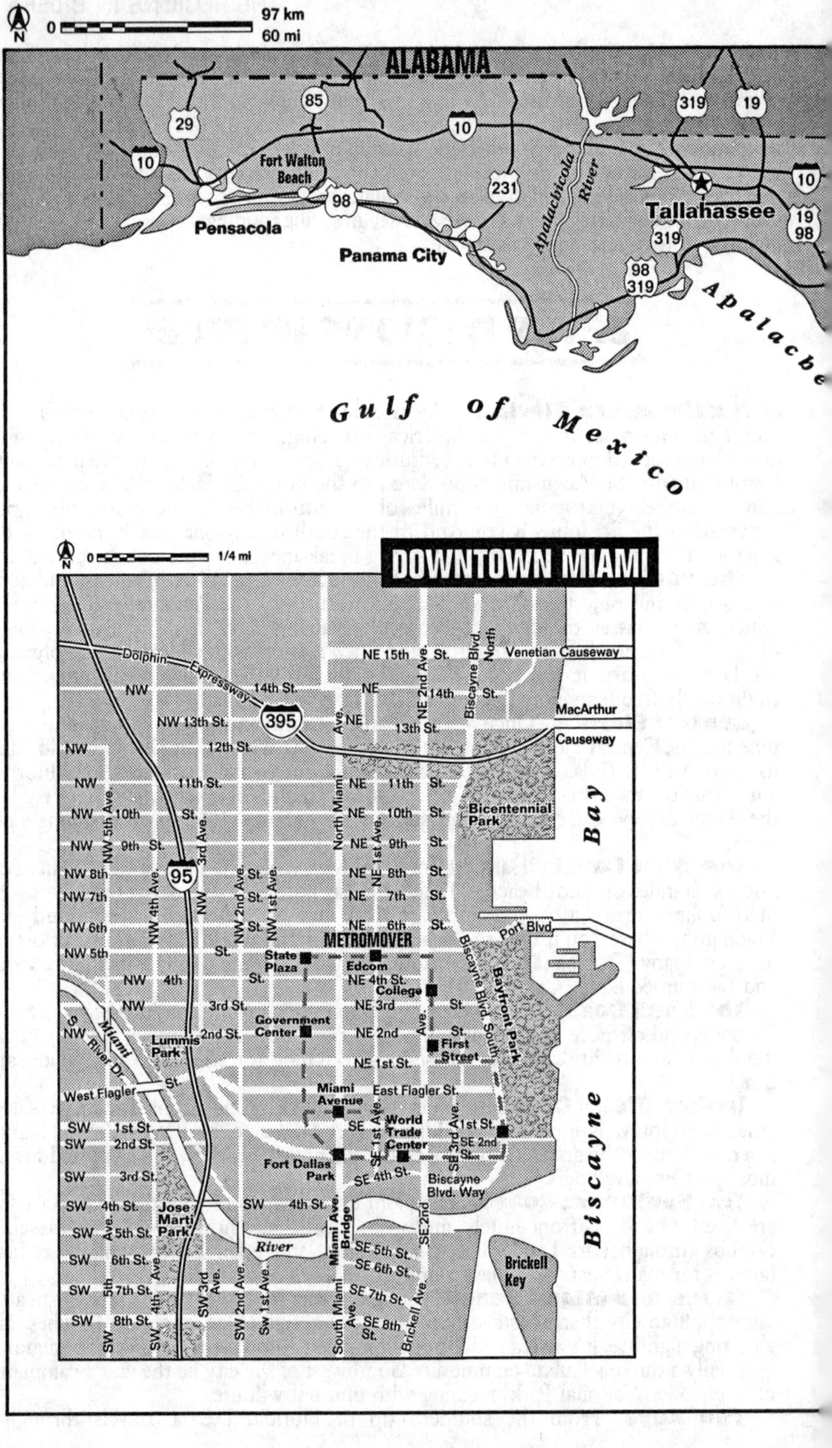

0 97 km 60 mi

ALABAMA

29 85 10 10 231 98 319 19 10 19 98 319 98 319

Fort Walton Beach

Pensacola

Panama City

Apalachicola River

Tallahassee

Apalachee

Gulf of Mexico

0 1/4 mi

DOWNTOWN MIAMI

Dolphin Expressway
395
95
NE 15th St.
Venetian Causeway
NW 14th St.
NE 14th St.
NW 13th St.
NE 13th St.
MacArthur Causeway
NW 12th St.
NW 11th St.
NE 11th St.
NW 10th St.
NE 10th St.
NW 9th St.
NE 9th St.
NW 8th St.
NE 8th St.
NW 7th St.
NE 7th St.
NW 6th St.
NE 6th St.
NW 5th St.
NW 4th St.
NE 4th St.
NW 3rd St.
NE 3rd St.
NW 2nd St.
NE 2nd St.
NE 1st St.
West Flagler St.
East Flagler St.
SW 1st St.
SE 1st St.
SW 2nd St.
SE 2nd St.
SW 3rd St.
SW 4th St.
SE 4th St.
SW 5th St.
SE 5th St.
SW 6th St.
SE 6th St.
SW 7th St.
SE 7th St.
SW 8th St.
SE 8th St.
NW 5th Ave.
NW 4th Ave.
NW 3rd Ave.
NW 2nd Ave.
NW 1st Ave.
North Miami Ave.
NE 1st Ave.
NE 2nd Ave.
Biscayne Blvd. North
Biscayne Blvd. South
Biscayne Blvd. Way
SE 1st Ave.
SE 3rd Ave.
SE 2nd
Brickell Ave.
South Miami Ave.
Sw 1st Ave.
SW 2nd Ave.
SW 3rd Ave.
SW 4th Ave.
SW 5th Ave.
S. River Dr.
Miami River
Miami Ave. Bridge
Port Blvd.
METROMOVER
State Plaza
Edcom
College
Government Center
First Street
Miami Avenue
World Trade Center
Fort Dallas Park
Lummis Park
Jose Marti Park
Bicentennial Park
Bayfront Park
Brickell Key
Biscayne Bay

FLORIDA

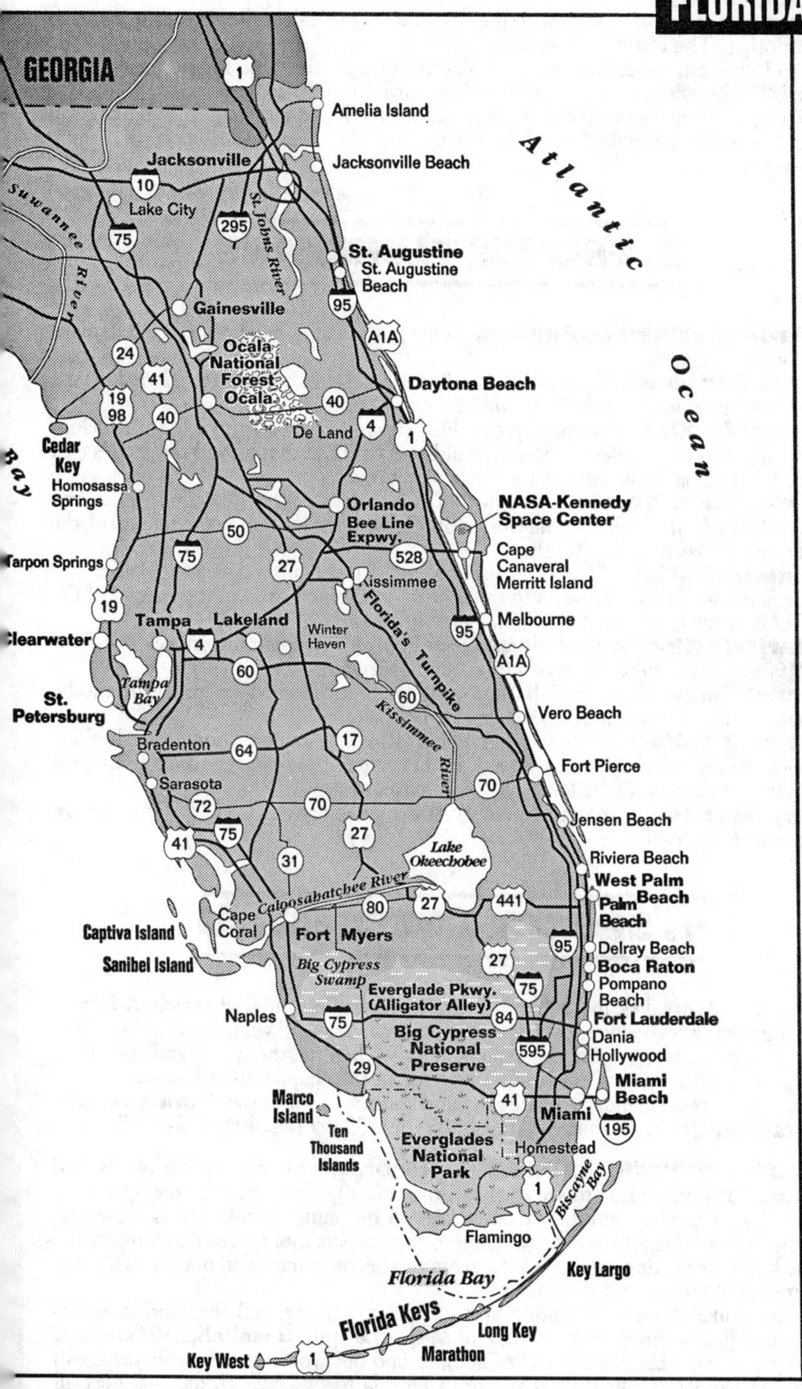

GEORGIA
Amelia Island
Jacksonville
Jacksonville Beach
Atlantic Ocean
Suwannee River
Lake City
St. Johns River
St. Augustine
St. Augustine Beach
Gainesville
Ocala National Forest
Ocala
Daytona Beach
De Land
Cedar Key
Bay
Homosassa Springs
Orlando
Bee Line Expwy.
NASA-Kennedy Space Center
Cape Canaveral
Merritt Island
Tarpon Springs
Kissimmee
Florida's Turnpike
Melbourne
Tampa
Lakeland
Winter Haven
Clearwater
Tampa Bay
St. Petersburg
Kissimmee River
Vero Beach
Bradenton
Fort Pierce
Sarasota
Jensen Beach
Lake Okeechobee
Riviera Beach
West Palm Beach
Palm Beach
Caloosahatchee River
Cape Coral
Captiva Island
Fort Myers
Delray Beach
Sanibel Island
Boca Raton
Big Cypress Swamp
Pompano Beach
Everglade Pkwy. (Alligator Alley)
Naples
Fort Lauderdale
Big Cypress National Preserve
Dania
Hollywood
Miami Beach
Marco Island
Miami
Ten Thousand Islands
Everglades National Park
Homestead
Biscayne Bay
Flamingo
Key Largo
Florida Bay
Florida Keys
Long Key
Key West
Marathon

hundred-mile string of islands with the Atlantic on one side and the Gulf of Mexico on the other. The chain extends down from Key Largo and John Pennecamp State Park to Key West, which lies only 90 miles from Cuba and is the southernmost point in the U.S. Though many of the islands don't have spectacular beaches, the Keys offer other visitor attractions—excellent deep-sea fishing and snorkeling, blazing tropical sunsets, a wildlife refuge full of tiny deer, and Key West's laid-back, bohemian atmosphere.

3. FAMOUS FLORIDIANS

Marjory Stoneman Douglas One of the state's most respected historians and conservationists.

Faye Dunaway Winner of the 1976 Best Actress Oscar for *Network,* she also starred in *Bonnie and Clyde* and *Mommie Dearest.*

Henry Flagler Railroad tycoon Flagler was largely responsible for developing Florida as a tourist destination by building a railroad that served the state's east coast and erecting luxurious resort hotels along it.

Zora Neale Hurston Author of *Their Eyes Were Watching God* and *Jonah's Gourd Vine,* this Florida-born novelist was one of the major talents of the Harlem Renaissance in the 1920s.

Sidney Poitier One of America's most distinguished actors, Poitier has appeared in such films as *Guess Who's Coming to Dinner?;* he was the winner of the 1963 Best Actor Oscar for his role in *Lilies of the Field.*

Marjorie Kinnan Rawlings Her Pulitzer Prize–winning novel *The Yearling* (1939) captured the flavor of life in rural Florida.

Janet Reno President Bill Clinton named this former Miami prosecutor to be the nation's first female attorney general in 1993.

John Ringling Circus entrepreneur Ringling built a home overlooking Sarasota Bay, and the area has served as the winter headquarters of the Ringling Brothers and Barnum & Bailey Circus ever since.

Ben Vereen A major Broadway star, Vereen won a 1973 Tony for his performance in *Pippin.*

4. SPORTS & RECREATION

With thousands of lakes, more than 100 rivers, and endless miles of coastline, Florida offers opportunities galore for fishing, sailing, canoeing, diving, waterskiing—just about any sort of water sport you can imagine. We'll detail the sports and recreation highlights of each city and town that's covered in the chapters that follow.

For brochures, calendars, schedules, and guides, contact the **Florida Sports Foundation,** 107 W. Gaines St., Tallahassee, FL 32399 (tel. 904/488-8347).

BASEBALL: SPRING TRAINING In February and March, throngs of baseball fans head down to Florida to see their favorite teams getting ready for the upcoming season. Teams used to return year after year to the same Florida towns for spring training, but as "Grapefruit League" games have become more lucrative, competition for the honor of hosting a major-league team has become fierce and many clubs are in the process of choosing new venues.

If you'd like to plan a vacation around spring training, call the Florida Sports Foundation (listed above) or main office of **Major League Baseball,** 350 Park Ave., New York, NY 10022 (tel. 212/339-7800), to find out where your favorite team will be playing. And don't wait until you're in Florida to purchase tickets—almost all games sell out weeks in advance.

5. FOOD & DRINK

A BOUNTY OF SEAFOOD Just a glance at a map will show you that Florida has hundreds of miles of coastline, so it should come as no surprise that seafood is a major attraction all across the state. Some waterfront restaurants even operate their own fishing boats, so you're guaranteed super-fresh offerings. You'll feast on snapper, swordfish, pompano, grouper, clams, gulf shrimp, oysters, and sweet deep-sea scallops.

Some of Florida's abundant seafood specialties will be new to your palate. The local **lobsters** are smaller and sweeter than the Maine variety, with most of their meat concentrated in the body rather than in the claws. You should also try **conch,** a chewy shellfish that's often served in deep-fried fritters, in chowder, or in a spicy salad marinated in lime juice. And you're sure to fall in love with the taste of Florida's succulent **stone crabs.** The claws are the only part of the animal you actually eat; harvesters just clip each crab's claws and toss it back into the ocean to grow a new one.

If you have the chance to eat in a **fish camp,** don't pass it up. These rustic, informal eateries are usually located right on the river or ocean and serve the very freshest of fish at unbelievably low prices.

CITRUS FRUITS & OTHER PRODUCE Florida's farms and citrus groves produce billions of dollars' worth of oranges, grapefruit, and tangerines each year. Bags of grapefruit and fresh, sweet oranges are sold at roadside stands throughout the state. But that's not all. Tomatoes, coconuts, kumquats, and tangy lemons and limes grow here, along with more exotic fruits like mangoes, hearts of palm, and papaya. Florida chefs are adept at using local produce in creative sauces and garnishes. A favorite regional dish is **key lime pie,** made with the tiny yellowish limes that grow only in Florida. It's best when it's made with an old-fashioned graham cracker crust and served chilled.

AND OTHER CUISINES Southern and Cajun culinary influences have found their way into Florida's kitchens, so you may find traditional favorites like catfish, hush puppies, frogs' legs, Créole-style blackened fish, gumbo, and southern fried chicken on many menus. As Florida's Asian population has increased, so has the number of restaurants across the state offering authentic Chinese, Thai, Japanese, Indian, and Vietnamese dishes. And Caribbean specialties have become popular too, from Bahamian conch fritters to fruity cocktails made with rum from the islands.

But Latin American and South American cuisines have had the most profound effect on Florida. Especially if you're visiting Miami, you should try one of the Cuban restaurants in Little Havana, which serve specialties like *pan cubano* (crusty white Cuban bread), *arroz con pollo* (succulent roast chicken served with yellow rice), roast suckling pig, plantains, and *café cubano,* rich (and very strong) black coffee served Cuban style in thimble-size cups. If Cuban and Spanish foods are a new taste for you, find a place that serves *tapas,* Spanish-style appetizers served in small portions, and try several dishes at once.

6. RECOMMENDED BOOKS & FILMS

BOOKS

GENERAL

Allman, T. D. *Miami: City of the Future* (Atlantic Monthly Press, 1987).

Buchanan, Edna. *The Corpse Had a Familiar Face: Covering Miami, America's Hottest Beat* (Random House, 1987).

Capitman, Barbara Baer. *Deco Delights: The Beauty and Joy of Miami Beach Architecture* (Dutton, 1988).
Didion, Joan. *Miami* (Simon & Schuster, 1987).
Douglas, Marjory Stoneman. *The Everglades: River of Grass* (Pineapple Press, 1988).
Hatton, Hap. *Tropical Splendor: An Architectural History of Florida* (Knopf, 1987).
Pulitzer, Roxanne. *The Prize Pulitzer: The Scandal That Rocked Palm Beach* (Random House, 1988).
Rieff, David. *Going to Miami: Exiles, Tourists, and Refugees in the New America* (Little, Brown, 1987).

HISTORY

Muir, Helen. *Miami, USA* (Banyan Books, 1987).
Rothchild, John. *Up for Grabs: A Trip through Time and Space in the Sunshine State* (Viking, 1985).

FICTION

Hemingway, Ernest. *To Have and Have Not* (Macmillan, 1988).
Hiaasen, Carl. *The Tourist Season* (Putnam Publishing Group, 1988).
Hurston, Zora Neale. *Their Eyes Were Watching God* (University of Illinois Press, 1978).
Pratt, Theodore. *The Barefoot Mailman* (Mockingbird Books, 1980).
Rawlings, Marjorie Kinnan. *The Yearling* (Macmillan, 1985) and *Cross Creek* (Macmillan, 1987).
Willeford, Charles. *Miami Blues* (Ballantine, 1987).

FILMS

Dozens of films have been set in Florida. A few of the very best are the 1964 James Bond thriller *Goldfinger,* part of which was filmed in the spectacular Fontainebleau Hilton in Miami Beach; *Body Heat,* starring William Hurt and Kathleen Turner; Jonathan Demme's *Married to the Mob;* and of course, the steamy classic *Key Largo,* with legendary screen stars Bogart and Bacall.

CHAPTER 2

PLANNING A TRIP TO FLORIDA

After you've chosen the Sunshine State as your destination, you'll find that doing a little homework before you go can save a lot of time and trouble later. This chapter pulls it all together for you: information sources, the best time of year to go, how to get there, and selecting an itinerary—all the advance-planning details that can help you plan and enjoy a smooth, successful trip.

1. INFORMATION & MONEY

INFORMATION Contact the **Florida Department of Commerce, Division of Tourism,** 126 W. Van Buren St., Tallahassee, FL 32399-2000 (tel. 904/487-1462), whose helpful staff will gladly answer your questions. Be sure to ask for their *Florida Vacation Guide,* a free guide to all the state's attractions that can help you choose which area of the state you want to visit.

For the lowdown on Walt Disney World, call or write **Walt Disney World Company,** P.O. Box 10000, Lake Buena Vista, FL 32830-1000 (tel. 407/ 824-4321).

Once you've chosen a specific destination within Florida, get in touch with the local visitor information office or chamber of commerce. I've listed each of the local offices in the chapters that follow.

MONEY Vacationers on a tight budget have always known that Florida offers some terrific travel bargains, especially in the off-season. (See "When to Go," below, for details.)

WHAT THINGS COST IN MIAMI	U.S. $
Taxi from the Miami airport to a downtown hotel	16.00
Local telephone call	.25

	US$
Double room at the Grand Bay Hotel (deluxe)	265.00
Double room at the Cavalier Hotel (moderate)	120.00
Double room at the Driftwood Resort Motel (budget)	65.00
Lunch for one at the Caribbean Room (moderate)	13.75
Lunch for one at the News Café (budget)	8.50
Dinner for one, without wine, at the Pavilion Grill (deluxe)	45.00
Dinner for one, without wine, at Thai Toni (moderate)	23.00
Dinner for one, without wine, at Versailles (budget)	12.00
Pint of beer	2.75
Coca-Cola in a restaurant	1.25
Cup of coffee	.85
Roll of ASA 100 film, 36 exposures	5.65
Admission to Miami Metrozoo	8.25
Movie ticket	7.00

Traveler's Checks If you don't want to carry large sums of cash with you, traveler's checks are a good bet. They are accepted by most hotels, restaurants, and shops, and can be exchanged for cash at any bank. **American Express** (tel. toll free 800/221-7282) traveler's checks are widely accepted and can be purchased at many banks across the country. The company charges a 1% commission fee, but checks are free for members of AAA. **Citicorp** (tel. toll free 800/645-6556) and **Bank of America** (tel. 415/624-5400; collect calls are accepted) are other major issuers of traveler's checks. Record the number of each check you purchase, and ask these companies about refund hotlines; you'll be able to recover your money if your checks are lost or stolen.

2. WHEN TO GO — CLIMATE & EVENTS

You'll find that a Florida vacation offers terrific value for your money, especially if you time your visit so that it doesn't coincide with the peak tourist season.

For the southern half of the state, the high season is October through May; each winter countless visitors migrate south to escape northern winters. If you're willing to brave the humidity of a South Florida summer, you'll be rewarded with incredible bargains on accommodations and smaller crowds of tourists. In northern Florida, the reverse is true: Tourists flock here in the summer.

If you want to time your visit to Walt Disney World to avoid crowds, keep in mind that Orlando area attractions are packed during any holiday (especially Christmas) and when school is not in session during the summer. See Chapter 9 on Orlando for details.

CLIMATE Odds are, whenever you visit Florida, you're going to find sunny skies and warm temperatures.

Spring brings tropical showers and the first waves of humidity. **Summer** is hot and *very* humid, so if you're in an inland city you may not want to schedule anything too taxing when the sun is at its peak. Coastal areas, however, reap the benefits of ocean breezes.

Fall is a great time to visit—the really hottest days are behind you and the crowds have thinned out a bit. August through November is, however, tropical storm season—you may remember Hurricane Andrew, the August 1992 storm that caused billions of dollars' worth of damage to South Florida. But be assured that it's highly improbable you'll be in any danger from such a storm. The National Weather Service tracks hurricanes and gives local residents ample warning if there's any need to evacuate coastal areas.

Winter gets a bit nippy in northern Florida—although snow is pretty rare, a flake or two has been known to fall in the Panhandle—but it's the peak season for the southern half of the state. When the rest of the country is bracing itself for icy winds, "snowbirds" are heading for Miami, Palm Beach, and the Keys to bask in the sun.

Average Temperatures (°F) in Selected Florida Cities

	Jan	Feb	Mar	Apr	May	Jun	July	Aug	Sept	Oct	Nov	Dec
Key West	69	72	74	77	80	82	85	85	84	80	74	72
Miami	69	70	71	74	78	81	82	84	81	78	73	70
Tampa	60	61	66	72	77	81	82	82	81	75	67	62
Orlando	60	63	66	71	78	82	82	82	81	75	67	61
Tallahassee	53	56	63	68	72	78	81	81	77	74	66	59

FLORIDA CALENDAR OF EVENTS

JANUARY

✪ ***THE ORANGE BOWL*** *Featuring two of the year's toughest college teams, this football match kicks off the month with a game in the stadium of the same name. Other activities include a marathon, a powerboat regatta, and the Three Kings Parade.*

Where: *Miami* ***When:*** *New Year's Day* ***How:*** *Tickets are available starting March 1, through the Orange Bowl Committee, Box 350748, Miami, FL 33135 (tel. 305/371-4600).*

- ☐ **Hall of Fame Bowl.** Two of the nation's top college teams meet at Tampa Stadium in this highly rated annual football game. Call 813/874-2695 for details. January 1.
- ☐ **Florida Citrus Bowl Football Classic.** This annual college game takes place at the Citrus Bowl Stadium in Orlando, 1 Citrus Bowl Place, at Church Street and Orange Blossom Trail (Hwy. 441). Call 407/423-2476 for information, 407/839-3900 for tickets. January 2.
- ☐ **Circus Festival.** In Sarasota, this is a giant salute to the circus at the Ringling Complex, with performers, arts and crafts, and music. Call 813/957-1877 for details. First week of January.
- ☐ **Art Deco Weekend.** Held along Miami's beach between 8th and 13th streets, this festival celebrates the whimsical architecture that has made South Beach one of America's most unique neighborhoods with bands, food stands, and other festivities. A weekend mid-month.
- ☐ **Taste of the Grove Food and Music Festival.** This Miami festival is an excellent chance for visitors to sample menu items from some of the city's top restaurants. The party is a fund-raiser held in the Grove's Peacock Park. For details, call 305/444-7270. A weekend mid-month.
- ☐ **Manatee Country Fair.** A week-long celebration and sampling of the Braden-ton area's produce—from citrus fruits and tomatoes to ornamental plants, cattle,

and seafood—held in Palmetto at Manatee County Fairgrounds. Call 813/722-1639 for details. Third week of January.

✪ ***SPEEDWEEKS*** *Sixteen days of events get underway with the* ***Rolex 24*** *(a 24-hour endurance road race for sports cars) which draws international entries. Following that, top names in NASCAR stock-car racing compete in the Busch Clash, Arca 200, Gatorade Twin 125-mile Qualifying Races, International Race of Champions (IROC), Florida 200, and Goody's 300, culminating in the Daytona 500 by STP which is always held on the Sunday before the third Monday in February.*

Where: *Daytona International Speedway, 1801 W. Intl. Speedway Boulevard (US 92), Daytona Beach.* ***When:*** *Late January/mid-February.* ***How:*** *Call 904/253-7223 for ticket information. For the Daytona 500, especially tickets must be purchased far—even as much as a year—in advance. They go on sale January 1 of the prior year.*

☐ **The Key Biscayne Art Festival** brings more than 200 artists together in a high quality, adjudicated show—all for charity. It is held in Cape Florida State Park. Call 305/361-0775 for more information. Late January.

FEBRUARY

☐ **Edison Pageant of Light.** Arts and crafts shows, a five-kilometer marathon, pageants, and a spectacular finale, the Parade of Lights in Fort Myers. Call the Pageant line directly, 813/334-2550 or the Lee County Visitors and Convention Bureau, 1-800/237-6444 for more information. First two weeks in February.

✪ ***GASPARILLA PIRATE INVASION AND PARADE*** *Ever since 1904, this has been Tampa's number-one annual event. In a spirit akin to Mardi Gras, the city's leading business executives don the pirate garb of José Gaspar—the legendary rogue of the high seas—and sail into the harbor on a triple-masted galleon flanked by a flotilla of 2,000 escort boats. This signals the start of a month-long program of parades, concerts, fiestas, races, and art festivals.*

Where: *Downtown Tampa, Bayshore Boulevard, and Harbour Island.* ***When:*** *Early February.* ***How:*** *Contact the Tampa/Hillsborough Convention & Visitors Association, 111 Madison Street, Tampa, FL 33602-4706 (tel. 813/223-1111 or toll free 800/44-TAMPA).*

✪ ***FLORIDA STATE FAIR*** *Just about anything that grows under the sun in Florida's 67 counties—from blue-ribbon livestock to fine foods and wines—is on display at this gathering, along with craft demonstrations, circus acts, carnival rides, horse shows, rodeos, alligator wrestling, and entertainment by top country-western stars.*

Where: *Florida State Fairgrounds, 4800 US Highway 301, Tampa.* ***When:*** *Second week of February.* ***How:*** *Contact the Florida State Fair Authority, P.O. Box 11766, Tampa, FL 33680 (tel. 813/621-7821).*

☐ **GTE Suncoast Classic.** The top players on the Senior PGA tour tee off for this tournament in Tampa at Cheval Polo and Golf Club. Call 813/971-1726 for details. Mid-month.

✪ ***MIAMI FILM FESTIVAL*** *This festival has made an impact as an important screening room for Latin American cinema. Fashioned after the San Francisco model, this annual event is relatively small, well priced, and easily accessible to the general public.*

Where: *Miami* ***When:*** *10 days in mid-February* ***How:*** *Contact the Film Society of Miami, 7600 Red Rd., Miami, FL 33157 (tel. 305/377-FILM).*

- ☐ **Coconut Grove Art Festival.** This is the state's largest art festival, and the favorite annual event of many locals. Almost every medium is represented including, unofficially, the culinary arts. For details call 305/447-0401. Mid-month.
- ☐ **The Grand Prix of Miami.** An auto race that rivals the big ones in Daytona this is a high-purse, high-profile event that attracts the top Indy car drivers and large crowds. For information and tickets contact Miami Motorsports, 7254 SW 48th St., Miami, FL 33155 (tel. 305/662-5660). Late February.
- ☐ **Bike Week/Camel Motorcycle Week.** This Daytona Beach event is the rallying point for an international gathering of motorcycle enthusiasts. Major races (featuring road racers, motocrossers, and dirt trackers) at the Speedway include the Daytona 200 by Arai Motorcycle Classic, the Daytona Supercross by Honda, and the Camel Pro Grand National Kickoff. Call 904/253-7223 for details. Late February/early March for 10 days.

MARCH

✪ ***FLORIDA STRAWBERRY FESTIVAL AND PARADE.*** *If strawberry shortcake, milkshakes, sundaes, and cobblers tempt your sweet tooth, don't miss this one. Held annually since 1930, it also offers music by top country stars, rides, and amusements. Plant City is the "winter strawberry capital of the world."*

Where: *Florida Strawberry Festival Fairgrounds, FL 574, off exit 10 of I-4 in Plant City, 25 miles east of Tampa.* ***When:*** *First week of March.* ***How:*** *Contact the Florida Strawberry Festival, P.O. Drawer 1869, Plant City, FL 34289-1869 (tel. 813/752-9194).*

- ☐ **Central Florida Fair,** Orlando. This takes place at the Central Florida Fairgrounds for 11 days. There are rides, entertainers, livestock exhibits, a monkey show, and lots of food booths. Call 407/295-3247 for details. Early March.

✪ ***SANIBEL SHELL FAIR*** *A four-day celebration on Sanibel Island for seashell lovers and collectors, held since 1937. The fair features exhibits of seashells from around the world along with related activities and sale of unusual shell art.*

Where: *Sanibel Community Center* ***When:*** *Early March* ***How:*** *Fair is open to the public free; admission is charged to the Shell Show. For more information, call Lee Island Coast Visitor and Convention Bureau, 1-800/733-7935.*

- ☐ **Nestlé Invitational.** Arnold Palmer hosts this seven-day PGA Tour event at the Bay Hill Club, 9000 Bay Hill Boulevard, Orlando. Daily admission is $25, week-long admission $50. Call 407/876-2888 for details. Mid-month.
- ☐ **River Run.** This annual 15K race in Jacksonville draws international participants. This event begins downtown and crosses two city bridges. Call 904/630-0837 for details. Mid-month.

✪ ***SPRINGTIME TALLAHASSEE*** *One of the south's largest celebrations, this festival features parades, arts and crafts, balloon rallies, food festivals, road races, and bluegrass to blues live music.*

Where: *Tallahassee* ***When:*** *March 16 to April 9, 1994* ***How:*** *For more information, call Betty Barnawell, Convention Chair for 1994, at 904/224-5012.*

- ☐ **Medieval Fair.** Held at the Ringling Museum, Sarasota, this three-day event features arts and crafts, street music, jousting, and a live chess match. Call 813/355-5101 for details. Early March.
- ☐ **Sidewalk Art Festival.** This major arts festival in Winter Park, drawing artists

and artisans from all over North America, takes place along Park Avenue. Call 407/623-3234 or 407/644-8281 for details. Third weekend in March.

✪ ***FESTIVAL OF THE STATES.*** *For more than 70 years, this festival has been considered "the South's largest civic celebration," as St. Pete plays host to award-winning high school bands from around the country. Other events include a windsurfing competition, fishing tournament, regatta, air show, jazz fest, and antique car rally.*

Where: *Downtown St. Petersburg.* ***When:*** *For 17 days during late March and early April.* ***How:*** *Contact the Suncoasters of St. Petersburg, Inc., P.O. Box 1731, St. Petersburg, FL 33731 (tel. 813/898-3654).*

- ☐ **The Players Championship (TPC).** This major golf event takes place at the posh Marriott Sawgrass Resort, 103 TPC Boulevard, Ponte Vedra Beach. The course is the toughest on the PGA tour, and its 17th hole, located on an island, is the most photographed hole in golf. Average attendance is 150,000. Call 904/285-7888 for details. Late March.
- ☐ **Spring Speedway Spectacular.** This car show and swap meet at the Daytona International Speedway features a wide variety of collector vehicles. In addition, displays include automotive toys and memorabilia, auto-themed art, and a crafts sale. Admission is charged. Call 904/255-7355 for details. Late March.
- ☐ **Dade County Youth Fair and Exposition.** Miami's huge, 2-week carnival-style romp, featuring dozens of rides, over 100 food booths, and more than 350 shows including dancers, magicians, and clowns. For more information call 305/223-7060. Late March.
- ☐ **Calle Ocho Festival.** One of the world's biggest block parties and Miami's answer to Carnival. Over one million people attend this salsa-filled blowout which is held along 23 blocks of Little Havana's SW 8th Street. For information call 305/644-8888.

APRIL

- ☐ **The Arts & Crafts Spring Festival on Palm Sunday.** A juried show in the downtown plaza of St. Augustine. Call 904/829-8175 for details.
- ☐ **Blessing of the Fleet and Parade de los Caballos y Coches.** This annual St. Augustine Easter celebration includes the blessing of the city's fishing fleet by the Bishop of the Diocese and a parade of horses and coaches complete with bonneted beauties, a drill team, and more. Call 904/829-5681 for details. Palm Sunday.
- ☐ **Easter Sunrise Service,** Orlando. An interdenominational service, with music, is presented at the Atlantis Theatre at Sea World, 7007 Sea World Drive. It is hosted by a well-known person each year. Admission is free. Call 407/351-3600 for details.
- ☐ **Easter Parade,** St. Augustine. The town's "Royal Family" portrays the Royal Family of Spain, riding on floats and in decorated horse-drawn carriages. Marching bands, too. Call 904/692-1032 for details.
- ☐ **The St. Augustine Passion Play,** St. Augustine. This 10-day event during the Easter holiday takes place in the St. Augustine Amphitheatre on A1A South. Call 904/471-1965 for details.
- ☐ **Jazz Festival.** This is a gathering in Sarasota of international jazz greats. Call 813/366-1552 for details. First week in April.
- ☐ **DeSoto Celebration.** This event commemorates the discovery of Bradenton, with parades and exhibits downtown and in DeSoto Park. Call 813/747-1998 for details. First two weeks in April.
- ☐ **Fort Walton Beach Seafood Festival.** An annual seafood eating frenzy. For more information call the Emerald Coast Convention and Visitors Bureau, 1-800/322-3319. Mid-April.
- ☐ **Fun 'n Sun Festival.** A tradition in Clearwater since 1953, this festival includes a

band competition, parades, boat regatta, and sportsfest. Call 813/462-6531 for details. Last two weeks in April.

- ☐ **Great Indian River Festival.** This river celebration in Titusville, highlighted by the Great Indian River Raft Race (only homemade craft allowed), includes an antique car show, boat show, arts and crafts booths, live entertainment, food, and carnival rides. Call 267-3036 for details.
- ☐ **Eglin Air Show.** An aviation spectacular at Eglin Air Force Base, Fort Walton Beach. The date varies from year to year, but usually is sometime in April. Call the Emerald Coast Convention and Visitors Bureau, 1-800/322-3319 for more information.

MAY

- ☐ **Riverwalk Arts & Crafts Festival.** This is a Jacksonville biggie with lots of food and crafts booths and live entertainment. Admission is free. Call 904/396-4900 for details. Mother's Day.
- ☐ **Greater Daytona Beach Striking Fish Tournament.** Some 250 boats from all over the southeast compete for more than $75,000 in cash and prizes in seven fishing categories. Call 904/255-0415 for details. Memorial Day Weekend.
- ☐ **Artworks!,** St. Petersburg. Held throughout the month, this event includes live theater, art shows, antique auto shows, outdoor concerts, and Fiesta de la Riba, a Spanish-themed festival commemorating Salvador Dali's birthday. Call 813/821-4069 for details.
- ☐ **The Miami International Festival.** Food, folklore, and dance from around the world are featured. Coconut Grove's Exhibition Center. Call 305/279-1538 for more information.

JUNE

- ☐ **Fiesta of Five Flags and the DeLuna Landing Festival.** Pensacola's annual extravaganza combines a commemoration of the Spanish Conquistador's arrival in 1559 with parades, a Spanish fiesta, a children's treasure hunt, a billfish tournament and much, much more. For more information call the Fiesta Office at 904/433-6512. June 3–12 in 1994.
- ☐ **Billy Bowlegs Festival.** An annual week-long party at Fort Walton Beach, named for William Augustus Bowles, self-proclaimed "King of Florida" and notorious buccaneer with a pirate flotilla, treasure hunts, fishing competitions, and contests for kids. For more information call the Emerald Coast Convention and Visitors Bureau, 1-800/322-3319. Early June.

✪ ***COCONUT GROVE GOOMBAY FESTIVAL*** *A Bahamian bacchanalia with dancing in the streets, this bash is billed as the largest black-heritage festival in America. It celebrates Miami's Caribbean connection.*

Where: *Coconut Grove, Miami* ***When:*** *Early June.* ***How:*** *Call 305/372-9966 for festival details.*

- ☐ **Music Festival.** Sarasota's music festival is a world-class presentation of chamber and symphony music. Call 813/953-4252 for details. First three weeks of June.
- ☐ **Silver Spurs Rodeo.** This major event on the professional rodeo circuit takes place at the Silver Spurs Arena, Kissimmee, on U.S. 192. Call 847-5000 for details, 407/847-5118 for tickets. Late June/early July.

✪ ***CROSS & SWORD*** *Florida's Official State Play tells the story of the founding of St. Augustine using drama, dance, music, stage combat, and spectacular special effects. Admission is $10 for adults, $8 for seniors, $4 for students, under 5 free.*

Where: *St. Augustine, in the 1,500-seat outdoor amphitheater of Anastasia State Park on A1A South.* ***When:*** *There are performances from* *about mid-June through late August at 8:30pm nightly except Sun.* ***How:*** *Call 904/471-1965 for details.*

- ☐ **Walt Disney World Wine Festival.** Over 60 wineries from all over the U.S. participate. Events include wine tastings, seminars, food, and celebrity chef cooking demonstrations. Call 407/827-7200 or 407/824-4321 for details.
- ☐ **Walt Disney World All-American College Orchestra and College Band.** The best collegiate musical talent in the country performs at EPCOT Center and the Magic Kingdom throughout the month. Call 407/824-4321 for details.

JULY

- ☐ **Independence Day.** July 4th is celebrated all over Florida. St. Augustine celebrates with fireworks over Castillo de San Marcos, barbecues, games, and concerts at the beach. There are exuberant celebrations with music and fireworks at Jacksonville Landing (call 904/353-1188 for details) and Jacksonville Beach (call 904/247-6236 for details). Sea World features a fireworks spectacular (call 407/351-3600 for information). Walt Disney World's Star-Spangled Spectacular brings bands, singers, dancers, and an unbelievable fireworks display to the Magic Kingdom (call 407/824-4321 for information).
- ☐ **Suncoast Offshore Grand Prix.** Held during the July 4th week in Sarasota, this boat-racing event brings powerboats, parades, live theater, boat shows, exhibits, and fireworks to the area. Call 813/955-9009 or 813/366-9255 for details. Early July.
- ☐ **Boca Grande Chamber Tarpon Tournament, World's Richest.** This two-day fishing contest, off the Lee Coast, has cash prizes totalling $175,000. Call the event hotline: 813/964-2995 or the Lee County Visitors and Convention Bureau, 1-800/237-6444. Early July.
- ☐ **Pepsi 400.** This race, marking the halfway point in the NASCAR Winston Cup Series for stock cars, is held at the Daytona International Speedway. Call 904/253-7223 for details. First Saturday in July.
- ☐ **Spanish Night Watch Ceremony.** Actors in period dress lead a torchlight procession through the Spanish Quarter of St. Augustine and reenact the closing of the city gates. Music and pageantry. Call 904/824-9550 for details. Third Saturday in July.

✪ ***FLORIDA INTERNATIONAL FESTIVAL.*** *This week-long musical event taking place every other year (in odd-numbered years), features concerts by major classical and pop musicians from all over the world—everything from the London Symphony Orchestra to Skitch Henderson, as well as pre-concert lectures, jazz bands, ballet, and special concerts for children.*

Where: *Daytona Beach. Peabody Auditorium, Ocean Center, and other local performance places.* ***When:*** *Late in July, possibly early August.* ***How:*** *Call 904/257-7790 for details and ticket information.*

AUGUST

- ☐ **Miami Reggae Festival.** Jamaica's independence is celebrated with a dozen top bands playing for much of the city's sizable Rastafarian community. The first Sunday in August.

SEPTEMBER

- ☐ **The Riverside Arts Festival.** Over 100 artists—sculptors, painters, wood carvers, ceramists, and others—set up booths at Riverside Park, 753 Park Street, Jacksonville, to sell their works. There are food vendors, too. This two-day event early in the month is free. Call 904/389-2449 for details.
- ☐ **The Miami Boat Show** draws almost a quarter of a million boat enthusiasts to

the Coconut Grove Convention Center, conveniently located right on the water. Call 305/579-3310 for details. Second or third week of September.

- ☐ **Festival Miami,** sponsored by the University of Miami, is a 3-week program of performing and visual arts centered in and around Coral Gables. For a schedule of events contact the University of Miami's School of Music, Box 248165, Coral Gables, FL 33124 (tel. 305/284-6477).
- ☐ **The King of the Beach Volleyball Tournament.** The action takes place in front of the Daytona Beach Marriott Hotel. The top eight male players in the world compete, and a 3,000-seat stadium is erected on the beach. Admission is charged. Call 904/255-0981 for details. Late September/early October.
- ☐ **Nights of Joy.** The Magic Kingdom is closed down for a festival of contemporary Christian music featuring top artists. It takes place over two weekends. This is a very popular event; obtain tickets early. Admission is about $25–$30 per night. Call 407/824-4321 for details.

OCTOBER

- ☐ **Walt Disney World Village Boat Show.** Central Florida's largest in-the-water boat show featuring the best of new watercraft takes place at the Village Marketplace over a three-day weekend. Call 407/824-4321 for details. Early October.
- ☐ **Jazz Festival.** This four-day extravaganza, held in Clearwater, features performances by top-name musicians. Call 817/461-0011 for details. Mid-October.
- ☐ **AMA/CCS Motorcycle Championship.** For three days, road-racing stars of tomorrow compete at the Daytona International Speedway. Events include a program of AMA/CCS "Races of Champions" National Championship Sprints for a variety of road racing classes, as well as the season-ending U.S. Endurance Championship event and the season finales for the Honda CBR 900RR Series and the Harley-Davidson Twin Sports Series. Call 904/253-7223 for details. Mid-October.
- ☐ **The Jacksonville Jazz Festival,** Jacksonville. This three-day nonstop-music event, featuring major artists and superstars, bills itself as the "world's greatest free jazz concert." Food and crafts booths, too. It takes place at Metropolitan Park, 1410 E. Adams Street. Call 904/242-7770 for details. Mid-October.
- ☐ **The Greater Jacksonville Agricultural Fair.** At Veterans Memorial Coliseum, 1145 E. Adams Street, the event features 11 days of live entertainment, animal displays, rides, food, and exhibits. Call 904/360-3900 for details. Third week in October.
- ☐ **Cracker Day.** This folksy event in St. Augustine includes a barbecue, a rodeo, horse shows, and entertainment (C&W bands) at St. John's County Fairgrounds on SR 207. Call 904/824-4564 for details. Third Saturday in October.
- ☐ **St. Augustine Folk Festival.** This lively festival features nationally known troubadours, storytellers, folk artists, and heritage crafts at the St. Augustine Amphitheatre on A1A South. Call 904/824-9550 for details. Fourth weekend in October.
- ☐ **Florida/Georgia College Football.** The annual football game between the University of Florida and the University of Georgia takes place at the Gator Bowl, 1400 E. Duval St. Call 904/630-3906 for information about the game, 904/353-3309 to charge tickets, 904/353-1188 to find out about related Jacksonville Landing festivities. Late October/early November.

✪ ***JOHN'S PASS SEAFOOD FESTIVAL.*** *This rustic waterfront village west of St. Petersburg hosts one of Florida's most popular seafood festivals—with music, arts and crafts, and enormous quantities of fresh fish and seafood.*

Where: *St. John's Pass Village and Boardwalk, Madeira Beach.* ***When:*** *Last weekend of October.* ***How:*** *Contact the Gulf Beaches Chamber of Commerce, 501 150th Avenue, Madeira Beach, FL 33108 (tel. 813/392-7373).*

- ☐ **Guavaween.** Ybor City's version of a Halloween parade, with costumes, music, food, and a giant street party. Call 813/248-3712. Last Saturday in October.
- ☐ **Halloween Horror Nights.** Universal Studios, 1000 Universal Studios Plaza, off Kirkman Road, Orlando, transforms its studios and attractions for a gigantic "spooktacular" Halloween nighttime party. Attractions include a haunted sound stage, a dungeon of terror, special shows, and ghouls and goblins roaming the studio streets. Special admission is charged. Call 407/363-8000 for details. Weekends up to October 31.
- ☐ **Destin Fishing Rodeo.** Celebrated annually, it proves why Destin is considered the "world's luckiest fishing village." Call the Emerald Coast Convention and Visitors Bureau, 1-800/322-3319 for more information. Month of October.
- ☐ **Walt Disney World Oldsmobile Golf Classic.** Top PGA tour players compete for a total purse of $1 million at the Palm, Lake Buena Vista, and Magnolia golf courses. The event is preceded by the world's largest golf tournament, the Oldsmobile Scramble, on the same courses. Admission for Scramble is free. For the Golf Classic, daily ticket prices range from $8 to $15. Call 407/824-4321 for details.

NOVEMBER

- ☐ **The Lincolnville Festival.** This St. Augustine event celebrates the city's black heritage with great jazz, blues, soul, and rock music. Food and crafts, too. Call 904/829-8379 for details. First weekend of November.
- ☐ **Fort Myers Beach Sand Sculpting Contest.** There are two divisions: the master, and a local competition that is broken down into family, business, etc., categories. Over 50,000 people attend this event which is spread out over four to six days. Call the contest line, 813/463-6451 for more information, or the Lee County Visitors and Convention Bureau, 1-800/237-6444. Early November.
- ☐ **Kahlua Cup International Yacht Races.** This Clearwater event, draws international craft. Call 813/447-6000 for details. Second weekend in November.
- ☐ **Walt Disney World Festival of the Masters.** One of the largest art shows in the south takes place at the Village Marketplace for three days. It features top artists, photographers, and craftspeople, winners of juried shows throughout the country. No admission. Call 407/824-4321 for details. Second weekend in November.
- ☐ **Florida Classic Football Game.** One of the longest-running college football competitions, in Tampa Stadium. Call 813/874-2695. Last weekend of November.
- ☐ **Daytona Beach Fall Speedway Spectacular.** Featuring the Annual Turkey Rod Run, this is the southeast's largest combined car show and swap meet, with thousands of street rods and classic vehicles on display and for sale. It takes place at the International Speedway. Admission is charged. Call 904/255-7355 for details. Weekend after Thanksgiving.
- ☐ **Blue Angels Air Show.** Thrilling, world-famous flight exhibitions at Pensacola Naval Air Station. Call the Public Affairs Office at 904/452-2583 at the air base for more information. Varies from year to year, but usually in November.
- ☐ **Miami Book Fair International.** One of the city's leading cultural attractions. Last year's show drew hundreds of thousands of visitors, including foreign and domestic publishers, and authors from around the world. For more information call 305/347-3000.

DECEMBER

- ☐ **Grand Illumination Ceremony.** A torchlight procession from St. Augustine's Government House through the Spanish Quarter features reenactments of British colonial customs. Call 904/824-9550 for details. First Saturday in December.
- ☐ **Second Christmas Reenactment.** Hernando DeSoto's first Christmas mass is commemorated on DeSoto State Archeological Site in Tallahassee. Call the Florida Park Service, 904/922-6007, for more information. Early December

- ☐ **Christmas Boat-A-Cade.** For over 25 years, this has been a holiday highlight in the St. Pete area at Madeira Beach, with lighted and decorated boats parading at night in Boca Ciega Bay. Call 813/392-0665 for details.
- ☐ **Hollywood Holidays.** Universal Studios, 1000 Universal Studios Plaza, off Kirkman Road, Orlando, celebrates the holiday season. The park is transformed into a winter wonderland, with carolers, parades, movie "snow," an outdoor ice show, and other attractions. Call 407/363-8000 for details. Throughout the month of December.
- ☐ **Sea World Holiday Events.** Sea World, 7007 Sea World Drive, features a special Shamu show and a luau show called *Christmas in Hawaii.* Call 407/351-3600 for details.
- ☐ **Walt Disney World Christmas Festivities.** EPCOT Center and MGM Studios offer special embellishments and entertainments throughout the holiday season. Holiday highlights include: Mickey's Very Merry Christmas Party, an after-dark ticketed event weekends at the Magic Kingdom with a traditional Christmas parade and a breathtaking fireworks display; The Glory and Pageantry of Christmas at the Walt Disney Village Marketplace, with several shows nightly, that tells the story of the birth of Jesus (free admission); and the Candlelight Procession along Main Street, when thousands of carolers proceed through the darkened Magic Kingdom. Call 407/824-4321 for details.
- ☐ **World Karting Association Enduro World Championships.** The biggest karting event in the country takes place at the Daytona International Speedway. Call 904/253-7223 for details. Between Christmas and New Year's.
- ☐ **WK Daytona Dirt Classic.** Held at Daytona Beach Municipal Stadium, 377 11th Street. Call 904/239-6565 or 904/253-7223 for details. Between Christmas and New Year's.
- ☐ **The Jacksonville Light Parade,** Jacksonville. The evening before the Gator Bowl game, boaters decorate their craft with colored lights and parade down the St. Johns River. This event also features fireworks, ice skating exhibitions, marching bands, and live entertainment. Call 904/396-4900 for details.
- ☐ **Gator Bowl.** The annual Gator Bowl game takes place at Jacksonville. Call 904/630-3906 for information about the game, 904/353-3309 to charge tickets, 904/353-1188 to find out about post-game festivities at Jacksonville Landing. Between Christmas & New Year's.
- ☐ **The King Mango Strut.** This Miami parade, from Commodore Plaza to Peacock Park in Coconut Grove, encourages everyone to wear wacky costumes and join the floats in a spoof on the King Orange Jamboree Parade, which is held the following night. Comedians and musical entertainment follow in the park. December 30.

✪ ***THE KING ORANGE JAMBOREE PARADE*** *Ending the year, this special New Year's Eve event may be the world's largest nighttime parade, and is followed by a long night of festivities.*

Where: *Along Biscayne Boulevard.* ***When:*** *December 31* ***How:*** *For information and tickets (which cost $7.50 to $13) call 305/642-1515 or contact the Greater Miami Convention and Visitors Bureau (see above).*

- ☐ **The Citrus Bowl Parade/New Year's Citrus Eve.** The impressive parade has lavish floats, some from Disney and Universal. Call 407/423-2476 for details. The official New Year's Eve celebration of the Citrus Bowl at Sea World, 7007 Sea World Drive, includes headliner concerts, a laser and fireworks spectacular, and special shows throughout the park. Admission is charged. Call 407/351-3600 for details. December 31.
- ☐ **Walt Disney World New Year's Eve Celebration.** The Magic Kingdom is open until 2am for a massive fireworks exhibition. Other New Year's festivities in the WDW parks include: a big bash at Pleasure Island featuring music headliners, a special Hoop-Dee-Doo-Revue show, and guest performances by well-known musical groups at MGM Studios. Call 407/824-4321 for details. December 31.

3. HEALTH & INSURANCE

HEALTH Florida doesn't present any unusual health hazards. The one thing you should protect yourself against is **sunburn,** and that's accomplished easily enough with a little common sense and a few precautions.

Don't underestimate the strength of the sun's rays down here, even in the middle of winter. Limit the amount of time you spend in the sun, especially in the first couple of days of your trip. Bring along sunscreen with a high protection factor and apply it liberally. Wear a hat when you're outside, drink lots of water, and try to avoid exposure to the sun from 11am to 2pm, when the sun's rays can really fry fair skin.

Pack an adequate supply of any prescription drugs you need in your carry-on luggage, and bring copies of your prescriptions with you. If you have a serious condition or allergy, consider wearing a Medic Alert identification bracelet; contact the **Medic Alert Foundation,** P.O. Box 1009, Turlock, CA 95381 (tel. toll free 800/432-5378), for details.

INSURANCE Before you leave home, call your credit card companies to investigate whether they offer any sort of travel coverage that's already free to you as a cardholder. Many companies offer personal accident insurance or rental-car insurance at no extra charge, and they may also be able to help you get refunds if there's a problem with an airline ticket or hotel room that's paid for with your credit card. Your current homeowners policy may offer you some protection against off-premises theft as well.

If you still feel that you need to purchase extra travel insurance, contact **Travel Guard International,** 1145 Clark St., Stevens Point, WI 54481 (tel. 715/345-0505, or toll free 800/826-1300), which offers policies that protect you against trip cancellation and include provisions for medical coverage and lost luggage as well. Prices start at $52 for one week of coverage.

Other companies to consider include **Travelers Insurance Co.,** 1 Tower Square, 10NB, Hartford, CT 06183-5040 (tel. 203/277-2318, or toll free 800/243-3174); and **Mutual of Omaha (Tele-Trip),** Mutual of Omaha Plaza, Omaha, NE 68131 (tel. toll free 800/228-9792), both of which offer similar protection.

4. WHAT TO PACK

It's not difficult to pack for a Florida vacation. Few places require jackets and ties; dress is casual in all but the poshest resorts and restaurants. (But bring at least one formal outfit for a special night out.) Light cotton clothing is the order of the day, so pack lots of T-shirts and shorts. Unless you're visiting in the hottest months of summer, bring along a couple of sweaters or a jacket to keep you warm if the nights get nippy—or if the ever-present Florida air conditioning gets to you.

Useful additions to any traveler's suitcase include a travel alarm, sunscreen, a fold-up umbrella, and a small plastic container of Woolite. And don't forget your bathing suit and sunglasses!

5. TIPS FOR THE DISABLED, SENIORS, SINGLES, FAMILIES & STUDENTS

FOR THE DISABLED The **Florida Department of Commerce, Division of Tourism,** Visitor Inquiry, 126 W. Van Buren St., Tallahassee, FL 32399 (tel.

904/487-1462), publishes the "Physically Challenged Guide to Florida," which offers valuable information on accessibility at tourist facilities throughout the state.

If you're eager to experience some of Florida's spectacular natural scenery firsthand, contact **Wilderness Inquiry,** 1313 5th St. SE (P.O. Box 84), Minneapolis, MN 55414 (tel. 612/379-3858, or toll free 800/728-0719). The company operates adventure tours for everyone, including people with disabilities, and sometimes offers tours of Florida's Everglades and Keys.

You can also contact the **Travel Information Service,** Moss Rehabilitation Hospital, 1200 W. Tabor Rd., Philadelphia, PA 19141 (tel. 215/456-9600). For a small fee, this organization will supply you with a travel packet providing information on the accessibility of hotels, restaurants, and attractions.

FOR SENIORS Florida has always been a popular destination for seniors, and all kinds of establishments all over the state offer senior-citizen discounts. Don't be shy about asking if these are available; mention the fact that you're a senior citizen when you first make your travel reservations. Always carry some kind of identification, such as a driver's license, that shows your birthdate.

Contact the **American Association of Retired Persons,** 601 E St. NW, Washington, DC 22049 (tel. 202/434-2277), which offers group travel opportunities, plus discounts on airfares, car rentals, and accommodations.

The **National Council of Senior Citizens,** 1331 F St. NW, Washington, DC 20005 (tel. 202/347-8800), is an advocacy group that charges $12 for annual membership. When you join, you'll receive a monthly newsletter that contains useful travel tips.

Saga International Holidays, 222 Berkeley St., Boston, MA 02116 (tel. toll free 800/343-0273), offers group tours designed for travelers over 60.

If you're looking for a travel experience that goes beyond the typical package tour, consider joining an **Elderhostel** program. Elderhostel's basic premise is to bring people together, sometimes on college campuses, for a one- to three-week course of study, with not-for-credit classes and plenty of time for relaxation and recreation. Prices include tuition, accommodations (usually in dormitories), and all meals. You must be at least 60 years old to register, although you can bring along an under-60 companion. Elderhostel publishes four catalogs per year describing their trips and courses. To find out about their current offerings in Florida and other destinations, write or call the main offices of Elderhostel, 75 Federal St., Boston, MA 02110 (tel. 617/426-8056).

FOR SINGLES Singles are often at a disadvantage when it comes to travel—just take a look at most travel advertisements, and you'll see how many offers are based on double occupancy. You can often get better deals when you travel with someone else, so consider contacting **Travel Companion,** P.O. Box P-833, Amityville, NY 11701 (tel. 516/454-0880), which matches single travelers with compatible partners. For a fee, you'll be listed in the organization's records, and you'll receive a list of potentional companions (you can request companions of the same sex or the opposite sex).

FOR FAMILIES Florida is a great family destination—and the presence of major kids' attractions like Walt Disney World means that most Florida hotels and restaurants are willing and eager to cater to families traveling with children. In the pages that follow, you'll find lots of recommendations for hotels with kids' programs and babysitting services—and many that let children under 18 stay free in their parents' room. If you call ahead before dining out, you'll see that most restaurants have some facilities for children, such as booster chairs and special kids' menus.

From the moment you begin planning your family's vacation to Florida, try to get your kids involved in and excited about the trip. (If you're headed to Walt Disney World, that shouldn't be too hard.) Set up ground rules before you leave about issues like bedtime and spending money.

Remember to pack a special toy or some other prized possession that will help your children feel at home even in strange surroundings. If you're traveling with an infant, pack enough baby food to last you through the trip and the first day or two until you've settled in and found the local supermarket.

Contact **Travel with Your Children,** 45 W. 18th St., New York, NY 10011 (tel. 212/206-0688), to subscribe to the *Family Travel Times,* a newsletter about traveling with children. It's packed with useful information, and readers can call in for advice during certain periods each week.

FOR STUDENTS It's worth your while to bring along your valid high school or college identification. Presenting it can open the door to discounted admission to museums and other attractions.

6. ALTERNATIVE/ADVENTURE TRAVEL

OUTDOOR ADVENTURES **All Florida Adventure Tours,** 8263B SW 107th Ave., Miami, FL 33173 (tel. toll free 800/33-TOUR-3), offers recreational and educational tours, including backpacking trips and ecotours, that emphasize local history and environmental education. Group tours can be tailored to suit special interests.

Another tour operator with a wild range of offerings—camping, canoeing, tubing, snorkeling, marine biology programs, and excursions into the Everglades, for example—is **Florida Outback Safaris,** 6446 SW 42nd St., Davie, FL 33314 (tel. 305/792-7393, or toll free 800/423-9944). Tours can be custom-designed for groups of 15 or more. The company's staff, which includes professional educators and naturalists, lead tours into some of Florida's most intriguing wilderness areas.

Rock Rest Adventures, Rte. 2, Box 424, Pittsboro, NC 27312 (tel. 919/542-5502), offers five- to seven-day canoeing and camping adventures in Florida's Everglades and Keys.

Camping, snorkeling, and other adventurous trips can be arranged through **Wilderness Southeast,** 711 Sandtown Rd., Savannah, GA 31410 (tel. 912/897-5108).

CYCLING TRIPS Cycling enthusiasts can tour the Sunshine State on two wheels with **Encompass Cycling Vacations,** P.O. Box 3461, Madison, WI 53704 (tel. toll free 800/236-4490), which specializes in fully supported biking tours for all ability levels. (They offer trips to many other destinations as well.)

Deluxe bike tours with leaders who give participants personal service are available for cyclists of all fitness levels from **VCC Four Seasons Cycling,** P.O. Box 145, Dept. 204, Waterbury Center, VT 05677 (tel. toll free 800/537-3850), which offers tours of Florida among its many other programs.

SWIMMING WITH DOLPHINS If you've ever dreamed of frolicking with Flipper, here's your chance. The **Dolphin Research Center,** Mile Marker 59, Overseas Highway, Grassy Key, FL 33050 (tel. 305/289-0002), is a not-for-profit educational and research facility with various offerings for visitors interested in learning more about these playful creatures.

Wednesday through Sunday, the center conducts hour-long educational walking tours; the cost is $7.50 for adults, $5 for children 4–12, and free for children 3 and under. There's also a "Dolphin Insight Program," held three times each week, that allows visitors to touch and interact with the dolphins, though they're not in the water with the animals. The cost is $65 per person; advance reservations are required and children must be at least 12 to participate. Occasionally the center also runs a week-long educational program that emphasizes the conservation of the dolphins' environment through lectures, seminars, and hands-on experience. Call the center for details.

The center's most popular offering is its "Dolphin Encounter," a limited program that allows visitors to actually swim with these gentle creatures. Advance reservations are required; the center starts taking reservations on the first day of the month for dates available in the following month (for example, if you want to participate in June, you should try to make reservations on May 1). The cost for the dolphin swim is $80 regardless of age; children must be at least 5 years old, and those under 12 must be accompanied in the water by a parent or guardian. Life jackets are available.

7. GETTING THERE

BY PLANE

THE MAJOR AIRLINES Most major carriers offer service into the Sunshine State, so taking the time to make a few phone calls and do some comparison-shopping can pay off—call all the airlines until you find the best deal available.

Delta Airlines (tel. toll free 800/221-1212), the official airline of Walt Disney World, offers more than 275 flights daily to 17 cities throughout the state, including Orlando (its Florida hub), Fort Lauderdale, Tampa/St. Petersburg, and Miami.

Other airlines serving the Sunshine State include: **American Airlines** (tel. toll free 800/433-7300), **Continental Airlines** (tel. toll free 800/525-0280), **TWA** (tel. toll free 800/221-2000), **United** (tel. toll free 800/241-6522), and **USAir** (tel. toll free 800/428-4322).

British Airways (tel. 081/897-4000 from within the U.K.) offers direct flights from London to Miami and Orlando, as does **Virgin Atlantic** (tel. 02/937-47747 from within the U.K.). Canadian readers might book flights with **Air Canada** (tel. toll free 800/776-3000), which offers service from Toronto and Montréal to Miami and Tampa.

AIRFARES Because Florida is such a popular destination, you'll have a wide choice of flights on many different carriers, and there's usually no shortage of promotional fares, especially in the off-season. Avoid flying during holiday periods, when fares can more than double from their usual levels.

Your best bet for securing a low fare is to book your flight well before your departure—you can often find great deals if you buy your ticket 30 days in advance. Ask the airline for the *lowest* fare, and *keep asking questions*. Find out if you can get a better deal by flying in midweek or staying over a Saturday night. Remember, too, that many of the best deals are nonrefundable, so you may have to stick with the travel dates you've chosen.

Consolidators act as clearinghouses for blocks of tickets that airlines discount and consign during their slow periods. You may be able to get discounted tickets by contacting **Travel Avenue,** 180 N. Des Plaines, Chicago, IL 60661 (tel. toll free 800/333-3335).

FROMMER'S SMART TRAVELER: AIRFARES

1. Call *all* the airlines that serve your destination to find the best fare.
2. Try to make your reservation 30 days in advance to take advantage of the lowest fares.
3. Keep checking fares as your departure date nears; airlines would rather fill a seat than have it fly empty, so they may cut fares dramatically in the days just before a flight leaves.
4. Investigate the cost of charter flights.
5. Avoid high-season travel, especially holidays. You can often get lower fares if you're willing to take midweek flights, too.
6. Always ask for the lowest fare, not just a discount fare.
7. Ask your airline about package deals that include accommodations and rental cars as well as airfare. Many of the major carriers have such deals, and most of them are excellent values.

BY TRAIN

Amtrak offers train service to Florida, with two daily trains that leave from New York, heading down the East Coast to Miami and Tampa—the ***Silver Meteor*** and the ***Silver Star.*** Travel time from New York is about 26 hours, but you can catch these trains as they make intermediate stops in Philadelphia, Washington, and Savannah. Depending on availability, round-trip fare from New York to Miami for midweek travel ranges from $160 to $230 and up.

If you want to travel to Florida by train while still bringing your own car, consider taking Amtrak's **Auto Train,** which runs daily from Lorton, Virginia, to Sanford, Florida (just northeast of Orlando). You'll travel in comfort while your car is secured in an enclosed car carrier. At press time, the fares for midweek travel were $175 for adults, $88 for children 15 and under, and $290 for a car.

In April 1993, Amtrak inaugurated regularly scheduled transcontinental rail service on the ***Sunset Limited,*** which runs three times weekly. The train leaves Los Angeles and crosses Arizona, New Mexico, Texas, Louisiana, Mississippi, and Alabama before it reaches its final destination in Florida 68 hours later. There are 52 stops along the way, including Orlando, Fort Lauderdale, and Miami. The train features reclining seats, a sightseeing car with large windows, and a full-service dining car. Round-trip coach fares begin at $287; sleeping accommodations are available for an extra charge.

For detailed information on schedules and fares (including Amtrak's "All Aboard America" fares), call Amtrak toll free at 800/USA-RAIL.

BY BUS

If you have the time for a leisurely trip, **Greyhound/Trailways** offers low-cost fares to a number of destinations in Florida. Service is available from almost anywhere in the country, and fares vary according to the point of origin. Discounted fares may be available if you can purchase your ticket in advance or if you travel in midweek.

Greyhound/Trailways no longer operates a single nationwide phone number, so consult your local directory for the office nearest you.

BY CAR

Countless visitors drive to Florida each year, and the state is easily reached by Interstate highway.

I-95 goes straight down the U.S. East Coast, from Maine down to Miami; it enters Florida just north of Jacksonville. **I-75** begins in northern Michigan and heads down through Ohio, Kentucky, Tennessee, and Georgia, before entering Florida; it then leads down to Tampa and other points on the southwestern coast of Florida. **I-10** traverses the southern part of the country, connecting southern California with Arizona, New Mexico, Texas, Louisiana, Mississippi, and Alabama before it enters Florida at the western end of the Panhandle. It then cuts across the northern part of the state, heading toward Jacksonville. If you enter the state on a major highway, you'll come across a state Welcome Center.

Before taking a major trip, have a mechanic check out your car to be sure it's in good shape. If you're a member of the **American Automobile Association (AAA),** call them and ask about travel insurance, towing services, and free trip-routing plans that are available to you with membership.

BY SHIP Premier is the official cruise line of Walt Disney World; it offers a "Cruise and Disney Vacation," including a three- or four-day Bahamas cruise and a three- or four-day stay at Disney World. Disney characters sail on every cruise. The package includes Premier's "All Three Parks Passports," with unlimited admission to Disney World. If you purchase tickets well in advance, fares start at $824 for adults, $579 for children. For a brochure and more information, write or call **Premier Cruise Lines,** P.O. Box 515, Cape Canaveral, FL 32920 (tel. toll free 800/473-3262).

Dozens of one- to four-day cruises sail from Miami to the Bahamas and other destinations. For information contact the Metro-Dade Seaport Department, 1015 North American Way, Miami, FL 33132 (tel. 305/371-7678). See Chapter 5, "What to See and Do in Miami" for details. Also see Chapter 7 for information on cruises from Palm Beach to the Bahamas.

PACKAGE TOURS

BY PLANE **Delta Airlines'** "Dream Vacations" offer hundreds of different ways to enjoy the Sunshine State. Packages usually include round-trip airfare, accommodations, and a rental car with unlimited mileage. For example, from May to early December 1993, you can book a seven-night package with accommodations at the Doral Ocean Beach Resort in Miami for just $729. Dozens of packages are available for stays in Orlando; early 1993 rates for four nights at the Dixie Landings resort in Walt Disney World, including round-trip airfare, a rental car with unlimited mileage, and a "Magic Passport" that offers unlimited admission to Disney attractions, were just $729. For specific information and current package prices, call Delta's Vacation Center (tel. toll free 800/872-7786).

Continental Airlines' "Grand Destinations" vacation packages, available for nine locations around Florida, all include round-trip airfare, hotel accommodations, and more. For more information and a free brochure, call toll free 800/634-5555. **American Airlines** (tel. toll free 800/433-7300) offers "Flyaway Vacations," which include airfare, hotel stays, and other amenities.

TWA Getaway Vacations (tel. toll free 800/GET-AWAY), **United Airlines** (tel. toll free 800/328-6877), and **American Express** (tel. toll free 800/241-1700) offer similar good-value packages. Your travel agent can also advise you of any other current packages that are available.

8. GETTING AROUND

BY PLANE Most major Florida cities are connected by intrastate airline routes, and fares for these short hops tend to be reasonable. Try the toll-free numbers listed in "Getting There," above, to book flights within Florida.

BY TRAIN You'll find that train travel from destination to destination isn't terribly feasible in Florida, and it's not a great deal less expensive than flying.

BY BUS Taking the bus, however, is fairly easy, as **Greyhound/Trailways** offers extensive service, even to the smaller cities and towns. Fares are reasonable, and bus travel is more comfortable than you might expect. Ask for a regional timetable at any local office.

BY RENTAL CAR Most visitors, however, opt for the freedom and flexibility of driving. If you're flying into Florida and want to rent a car, you'll have to sort out the maze of rental offers available.

Many packages are available that include airfare, accommodations, and a rental car with unlimited mileage. If you compare these prices with the cost of booking an airline ticket and renting a car yourself, you may find that these offers are a good deal. (See "Getting There," above, for more information on package tours.)

If you opt to rent a car on your own, call several rental companies to compare prices, since fare structures are complicated and promotional offers come and go frequently. Rental agents are less than helpful when it comes to finding the best rates, so keep asking questions. If you're a member of any organization (the AARP, for example), check to see if you're entitled to any discounts. Every major rental company is represented in Florida, including: **Alamo** (tel. toll free 800/327-9633), **Avis** (tel. toll free 800/831-2847), **Budget** (tel. toll free 800/527-0700), **Hertz** (tel. toll free

800/654-3131), **National** (tel. toll free 800/227-7368), and **Thrifty** (tel. toll free 800/367-2277).

As you're driving around the state, remember that the speed limit is 55 m.p.h. on state highways, and 55–65 m.p.h. on Interstate highways. Seat belts are required for all front-seat passengers. It's illegal to carry an open container of alcohol, and the police strictly enforce drunk-driving laws.

SUGGESTED ITINERARIES

IF YOU HAVE 10 DAYS IN SOUTHERN FLORIDA

Day 1: Tour Miami's art deco district. Then head downtown to stroll through Bayside Marketplace, a beautiful shorefront development full of retail shops and eateries.
Day 2: Visit the Miami Seaquarium and spend the rest of the day on the beach in Key Biscayne. Take in the sizzling Coconut Grove nightlife after dark.
Day 3: Head for Miami Metrozoo and Coral Castle, then treat yourself to an authentic Cuban dinner in Little Havana.
Day 4: Start out early in the morning and drive south of Miami to Everglades National Park. Tour the park and return to your Miami hotel for the night.
Day 5: Leave Miami and start heading south through the Keys. Pass through Key Largo, and visit John Pennekamp Coral Reef State Park, where you can go diving or take a glass-bottom-boat ride to view brilliantly colored tropical fish. Check into a hotel on Islamorada, 72 miles south of Miami.
Day 6: Enjoy a day of deep-sea fishing.
Day 7: Continue south to Key West and check into a hotel. Take the Conch Tour Train to get your bearings.
Day 8: Tour the Hemingway Home and Museum by day, and hit a few of the island's famous watering holes by night.
Day 9: Abandon yourself to the slow pace of Key West and relax.
Day 10: Drive back to Miami for your flight home.

IF YOU HAVE 10 DAYS IN CENTRAL FLORIDA

Day 1: Spend the day in the granddaddy of all Orlando attractions, the Magic Kingdom.
Day 2: Tour EPCOT Center, then dance your night away at Pleasure Island.
Day 3: Head for Universal Studios or Disney-MGM Studios and learn how movie magic is created.
Day 4: Take a day trip 40 miles east to tour the John F. Kennedy Space Center. Return to your Orlando hotel.
Day 5: Spend the day at Sea World.
Day 6: Leave Orlando, driving southwest. Stop and tour Cypress Gardens, near Winter Haven, before continuing on to your hotel in Tampa.
Day 7: Give yourself a break from all this structured sightseeing and hit the beach.
Day 8: Tour Busch Gardens, a 300-acre theme park designed to resemble turn-of-the-century Africa.
Day 9: Stroll around downtown Tampa, and take the People Mover to Harbour Island for shopping and waterfront dining.
Day 10: Take in the Salvador Dalí Museum in nearby St. Petersburg, and spend part of the day exploring Tampa's Latin Quarter, Ybor City.

9. WHERE TO STAY

For general information, get in touch with the **Florida Hotel/Motel Association,** 200 W. College Ave., Tallahassee, FL 32301 (tel. 904/224-2888).

IN WALT DISNEY WORLD Accommodations within Disney World range from the deluxe Grand Floridian Resort to the Fort Wilderness Campground. To find out about any of the Disney properties, contact the **Walt Disney World Central Reservations Office,** P.O. Box 10100, Lake Buena Vista, FL 32830-0100 (tel. 407/W-DISNEY).

CAMPING You can enjoy the great outdoors, keep accommodations costs down, and still stay near most of Florida's top attractions if you choose to stay at a KOA campground. RV sites are available, or you can pitch a tent; the campgrounds have restrooms, showers, food markets, and other facilities. For more information, contact **KOA Florida Camping,** P.O. Box 30558, Billings, MT 59114 (tel. toll free 800/848-1094).

For information on other campsites, write or call the **Florida Campground Association,** 1638 N. Plaza Dr., Tallahassee, FL 32308 (tel. 904/656-8878).

HOSTELS Membership in the American Youth Hostel organization is a great way to secure low-cost accommodations and discounts on other travel services. The properties in Florida include the St. Augustine AYH Hostel, located near the historic Spanish quarter; the Miami Beach International AYH Hostel, only two blocks from the beach in Miami's art deco district; and the Orlando International AYH Hostel at Plantation Manor, a Spanish-style hostel in downtown Orlando, overlooking Lake Eola and just minutes from Disney World. Rates at all three hostels are less than $15 per night. There are other hostels around the state as well; advance reservations are recommended at all hostels.

Contact the **Florida Council** office at P.O. Box 533097, Orlando, FL 32853-3097 (tel. 407/894-5872), or the national office of **American Youth Hostels (AYH)/Hostelling International,** 733 15th St. NW, Suite 840, Washington, DC 20005 (tel. 202/783-6161), for details. Annual membership is $25, $10 for those under 18, and $15 for those over 54.

FAST FACTS FLORIDA

Area Code For southern Florida (including Miami and Fort Lauderdale), it's 305; for central Florida (including Orlando and Melbourne), it's 407; for the west coast (including Tampa and Fort Myers), it's 813; and for northern Florida (including Jacksonville and Tampa), it's 904. If you have any doubt about which area code applies to a particular town, see the specific chapters that follow.

Banks Banks are usually open Monday through Friday from 9am to 3 or 4pm, though many have Automatic Teller Machines (ATMs) that offer 24-hour banking. If a particular bank is affiliated with the same ATM network that your local bank uses, you'll be able to get cash from your account. Each network has a toll-free number you can call to locate machines in a given city. The toll-free number for Cirrus, one of the most popular networks, is 800/424-7787.

Business Hours Most offices throughout the state are open Monday through Friday from 9am to 5pm. Shopping malls are generally open until 8 or 9pm Monday through Saturday.

Camera/Film You'll certainly want to take pictures on your trip to Florida, so don't forget to pack your camera and film (be sure to take film that will work well for outdoor shots). If you should find that you've forgotten film or that you need a few extra rolls, head for the nearest supermarket or drugstore, when you can find good prices on name brands. You'll spend a fortune if you buy film at shops or kiosks near major tourist attractions.

Car Rentals See "Getting Around," earlier in this chapter.

Climate See "When to Go," earlier in this chapter.

Drugstores Eckerd Drugs and Walgreens are two major chains; you'll see branches all over the state.

Emergencies Call **911** anywhere in the state to summon the police, the fire department, or an ambulance.

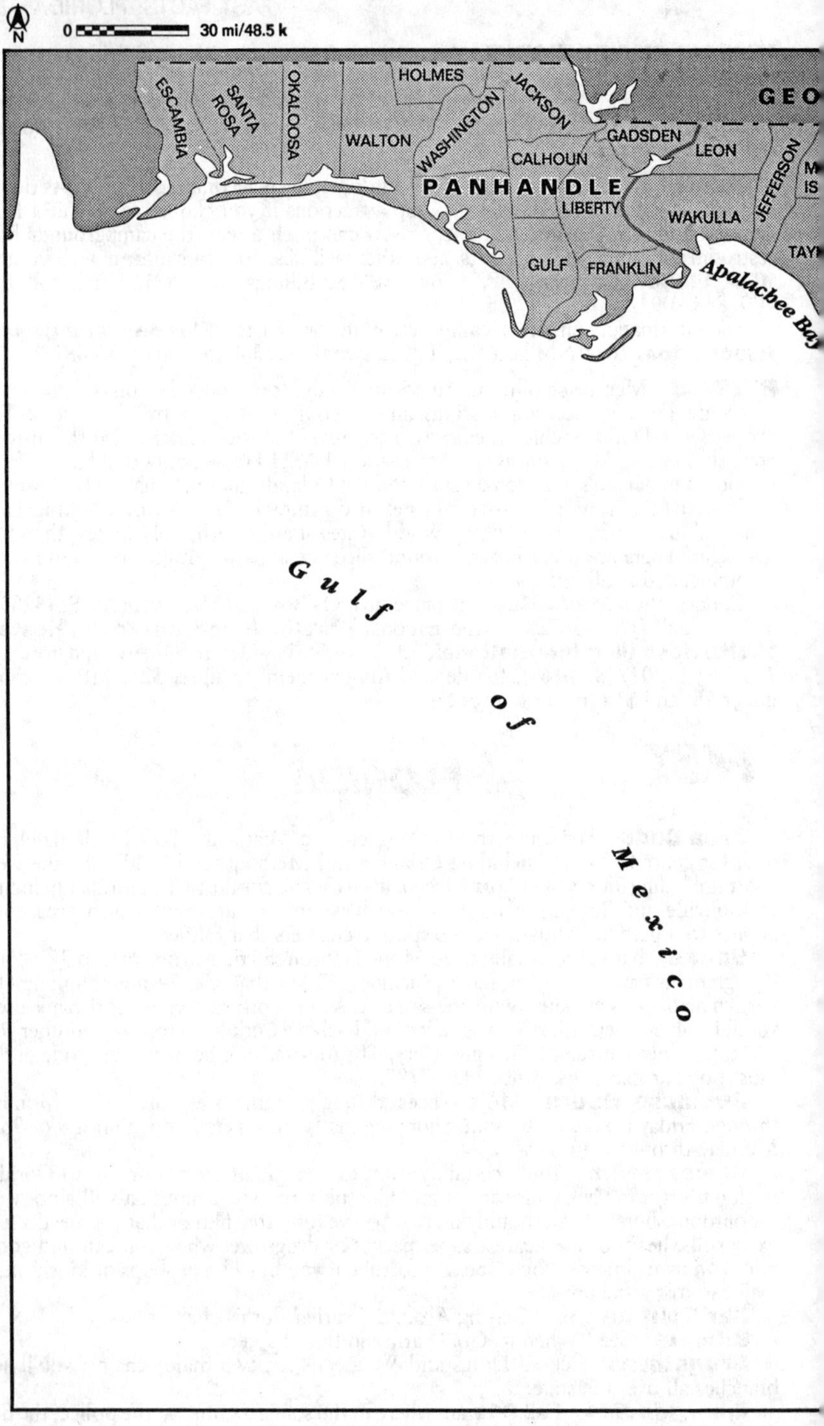

N

0 30 mi/48.5 k

HOLMES
ESCAMBIA
SANTA ROSA
OKALOOSA
WALTON
WASHINGTON
JACKSON
GEO
GADSDEN
LEON
CALHOUN
JEFFERSON
PANHANDLE
LIBERTY
WAKULLA
GULF
FRANKLIN
Apalacbee Ba

Gulf of Mexico

FLORIDA COUNTIES AND REGIONS

GIA
NASSAU
HAMILTON
COLUMBIA
BAKER
DUVAL
SUWANNEE
UNION
BRAD-
FORD
CLAY
ST. JOHNS
AFAYETTE
GILCHRIST
NORTH
FLORIDA
ALACHUA
PUTNAM
FLAGLER
DIXIE
LEVY
MARION
VOLUSIA
CITRUS
SUMTER
LAKE
SEMINOLE
HERNANDO
CENTRAL
FLORIDA
ORANGE
PASCO
PINELLAS
HILLSBOROUGH
POLK
OSCEOLA
BREVARD
Tampa
Bay
INDIAN
RIVER
MANTEE
HARDEE
OKEECHOBEE
ST.
LUCIE
SARASOTA
GULF
DE SOTO
HIGHLANDS
MARTIN
Lake
Okeechobee
GLADES
CHARLOTTE
PALM
BEACH
HENDRY
COAST
SOUTH FLORIDA
LEE
COLLIER
BROWARD
MONROE
DADE
Atlantic
Ocean
Florida Bay
FLORIDA KEYS

Liquor Laws You must be 21 to purchase or consume alcohol in Florida. This law is strictly enforced, so if you look young, carry some identification with you. Minors can usually enter bars where food is served.

Newspapers/Magazines Most cities of any size have a local daily paper, but the well-respected *Miami Herald* is generally available all over the state, with regional editions available in many areas.

Safety Whenever you're traveling in an unfamiliar city, state, or country, stay alert. Be aware of your immediate surroundings. Wear a moneybelt and keep a close eye on your possessions. Be particularly careful with cameras, purses, and wallets, all favorite targets of thieves and pickpockets. Always lock your car doors and the trunk when your vehicle is unattended, and don't leave any valuables in sight. See also the "Safety" section in the "For Foreign Visitors" chapter for specific information on car and driving safety.

Taxes Florida state sales tax is 6%. In addition, most municipalities levy a special tax on hotel and restaurant bills; see the individual city chapters that follow for details.

Telephone Beware of the astronomical cost of making phone calls—even local calls—from your hotel room. It's much safer to make collect calls, to use a credit card, or to go in search of a pay phone.

Time Most of Florida observes eastern standard time, but the section of the Panhandle west of the Apalachicola River is on central standard time, one hour behind the rest of the state.

Tipping Waiters and bartenders usually expect a 15% tip, and you might leave even more if you got exceptional service. Porters should be tipped about $1 per bag, taxi drivers get 10%–15%, and parking valets should get $1. Leave $1 or $2 in your hotel room for each day you've stayed for the housekeeping staff when you check out.

Tourist Information See "Information and Money," earlier in this chapter, for the tourist office serving the entire state; for local offices, which will have more detailed information on your particular destination, see the individual city chapters that follow.

CHAPTER 3

FOR FOREIGN VISITORS

Although American fads and fashions have spread across Europe and other parts of the world so that America may seem like familiar territory before your arrival, there are still many peculiarities and uniquely American situations that any foreign visitor will encounter.

1. PREPARING FOR YOUR TRIP

ENTRY REQUIREMENTS

DOCUMENTS Canadian nationals need only proof of Canadian residence to visit the United States. Citizens of Great Britain and Japan need only a current passport. Citizens of other countries, including Australia and New Zealand, usually need two documents: a valid **passport,** with an expiration date at least six months later than the scheduled end of their visit to the United States, and a **tourist visa,** available at no charge from a U.S. embassy or consulate.

To get a tourist or business visa to enter the United States, contact the nearest American embassy or consulate in your country; if there is none, you will have to apply in person in a country where there is a U.S. embassy or consulate. Present your passport, a passport-size photo of yourself, and a completed application, which is available through the embassy or consulate. You may be asked to provide information about how you plan to finance your trip or show a letter of invitation from a friend with whom you plan to stay. Those applying for a business visa may be asked to show evidence that they will not receive a salary in the United States. Be sure to check the length of stay on your visa; usually it's six months. If you want to stay longer, you may file for an extension with the Immigration and Naturalization Service once you are in the country. If permission to stay is granted, a new visa is not required unless you leave the United States and want to reenter.

MEDICAL REQUIREMENTS No inoculations are needed to enter the United States unless you are coming from, or have stopped over in, areas known to be suffering from epidemics, particularly cholera or yellow fever.

If you have a disease requiring treatment with medications containing narcotics or drugs requiring a syringe, carry a valid signed prescription from your physician to allay any suspicions that you are smuggling drugs.

CUSTOMS REQUIREMENTS Every adult visitor may bring in free of duty: one liter of wine or hard liquor; 200 cigarettes or 100 cigars (but no cigars from Cuba) or three pounds of smoking tobacco; $100 worth of gifts. These exemptions are offered to travelers who spend at least 72 hours in the United States and who have not claimed them within the preceding six months. It is altogether forbidden to bring into the country foodstuffs (particularly cheese, fruit, cooked meats, and canned goods) and plants (vegetables, seeds, tropical plants, and so on). Foreign tourists may bring in or take out up to $10,000 in U.S. or foreign currency with no formalities; larger sums must be declared to Customs on entering or leaving.

INSURANCE

There is no national health system in the United States. Because the cost of medical care is extremely high, we strongly advise every traveler to secure health coverage before setting out.

You may want to take out a comprehensive travel policy that covers (for a relatively low premium) sickness or injury costs (medical, surgical, and hospital); loss or theft of your baggage; trip-cancellation costs; guarantee of bail in case you are arrested; costs of accident, repatriation, or death. Such packages (for example, "Europe Assistance" in Europe) are sold by automobile clubs at attractive rates, as well as by insurance companies and travel agencies.

MONEY

CURRENCY & EXCHANGE The U.S. monetary system has a decimal base: one American **dollar ($1)** = 100 **cents** (100¢)

Dollar bills commonly come in $1 ("a buck"), $5, $10, $20, $50, and $100 denominations (the last two are not welcome when paying for small purchases and are not accepted in taxis or at subway ticket booths). There are also $2 bills (seldom encountered).

There are six denominations of coins: 1¢ (one cent or "penny"), 5¢ (five cents or "a nickel"), 10¢ (ten cents or "a dime"), 25¢ (twenty-five cents or "a quarter"), 50¢ (fifty cents or "a half dollar"), and the rare—and prized by collectors—$1 piece (both the older, large silver dollars and the newer, small Susan B. Anthony coin).

TRAVELER'S CHECKS Traveler's checks denominated in U.S. dollars are readily accepted at most hotels, motels, restaurants, and large stores. But the best place to change traveler's checks is at a bank. Do not bring traveler's checks denominated in other currencies.

CREDIT CARDS The method of payment most widely used is the credit card: VISA (BarclayCard in Britain), MasterCard (EuroCard in Europe, Access in Britain, Diamond in Japan), American Express, Diners Club, Discover, and Carte Blanche. You can save yourself trouble by using "plastic money" rather than cash or traveler's checks in 95% of all hotels, motels, restaurants, and retail stores (except for those selling food or liquor). A credit card can serve as a deposit for renting a car, as proof of identity (often carrying more weight than a passport), or as a "cash card," enabling you to draw money from banks that accept them.

Note: The "foreign-exchange bureaus" so common in Europe are rare even at airports in the United States, and nonexistent outside major cities. Try to avoid having to change foreign money, or traveler's checks denominated other than in U.S. dollars, at a small-town bank, or even a branch in a big city; in fact, leave any currency other than U.S. dollars at home—it may prove more nuisance to you than it's worth.

SAFETY

GENERAL While tourist areas are generally safe, crime is on the increase everywhere, and U.S. urban areas tend to be less safe than those in Europe or Japan. Visitors should always stay alert. This is particularly true of large U.S. cities. It is wise to ask the city's or area's tourist office if you're in doubt about which neighborhoods are safe. Avoid deserted areas, especially at night. Don't go into any city park at night unless there is an event that attracts crowds—for example, New York City's concerts in the parks. Generally speaking, you can feel safe in areas where there are many people, and many open establishments.

Avoid carrying valuables with you on the street, and don't display expensive cameras or electronic equipment. Hold on to your pocketbook, and place your billfold in an inside pocket. In theaters, restaurants, and other public places, keep your possessions in sight.

Remember also that hotels are open to the public, and in a large hotel, security may not be able to screen everyone entering. Always lock your room door—don't assume that once inside your hotel you are automatically safe and no longer need be aware of your surroundings.

DRIVING Safety while driving is particularly important. Question your rental agency about personal safety, or ask for a brochure of traveler safety tips when you pick up your car. Obtain written directions, or a map with the route marked in red, from the agency showing how to get to your destination. And, if possible, arrive and depart during daylight hours.

Recently more and more crime has involved cars and drivers. If you drive off a highway into a doubtful neighborhood, leave the area as quickly as possible. If you have an accident, even on the highway, stay in your car with the doors locked until you assess the situation or until the police arrive. If you are bumped from behind on the street or are involved in a minor accident with no injuries and the situation appears to be suspicious, motion to the other driver to follow you. *Never* get out of your car in such situations. You can also keep a pre-made sign in your car which reads: PLEASE FOLLOW THIS VEHICLE TO REPORT THE ACCIDENT. Show the sign to the other driver and go directly to the nearest police precinct, well-lighted service station, or all-night store.

If you see someone on the road who indicates a need for help, do *not* stop. Take note of the location, drive on to a well-lighted area, and telephone the police by dialing 911.

Park in well-lighted, well-traveled areas if possible. Always keep your car doors locked, whether attended or unattended. Look around you before you get out of your car, and never leave any packages or valuables in sight. If someone attempts to rob you or steal your car, do *not* try to resist the thief/carjacker—report the incident to the police department immediately.

The Crime Prevention Division of the Police Department, City of New York, publishes a "Safety Tips for Visitors" brochure. It is translated into French, Spanish, Hebrew, German, Japanese, Dutch, Italian, Russian, Chinese, Portuguese, and Swedish. For a copy, write to: Crime Prevention Division Office of D.C.C.A., 80-45 Winchester Blvd., Queens Village, NY 11427.

2. GETTING TO THE U.S.

Travelers from overseas can take advantage of the **APEX (Advance Purchase Excursion) fares** offered by all the major U.S. and European carriers. Aside from these, attractive values are offered by **Icelandair** on flights from Luxembourg to New York and by **Virgin Atlantic Airways** from London to New York/Newark.

British Airways (tel. 081/897-4000 from within the U.K.) offers direct flights from London to Miami and Orlando, as does **Virgin Atlantic** (tel. 02/937-47747 from within the U.K.). Canadian readers might book flights with **Air Canada** (tel. toll free 800/776-3000), which offers service from Toronto and Montréal to Miami and Tampa.

Some large American airlines (for example, TWA, American Airlines, Northwest, United, and Delta) offer travelers on their transatlantic or transpacific flights special discount tickets under the name **Visit USA,** allowing travel between any U.S. destinations at minimum rates. They are not on sale in the United States, and must, therefore, be purchased before you leave your foreign point of departure. This system is the best, easiest, and fastest way to see the United States at low cost. You should obtain information well in advance from your travel agent or the office of the airline concerned, since the conditions attached to these discount tickets can be changed without advance notice.

The visitor arriving by air, no matter what the port of entry, should cultivate patience and resignation before setting foot on U.S. soil. Getting through Immigration control may take as long as two hours on some days, especially summer weekends. Add the time it takes to clear Customs and you'll see that you should make very generous allowance for delay in planning connections between international and domestic flights—an average of two to three hours at least.

In contrast, travelers arriving by car or by rail from Canada will find border-crossing formalities streamlined to the vanishing point. And air travelers from Canada, Bermuda, and some places in the Caribbean can sometimes go through Customs and Immigration at the point of departure, which is much quicker and less painful.

For further information about travel to Florida, see "Getting There" in Chapter 2.

FOR THE FOREIGN TRAVELER

Automobile Organizations Auto clubs will supply maps, suggested routes, guidebooks, accident and bail-bond insurance, and emergency road service. The major auto club in the United States, with 955 offices nationwide, is the **American Automobile Association (AAA).** To join, call toll free 800/336-4357. Membership costs $55 for the first year, $35 for each consecutive year. The AAA can provide you with an **International Driving Permit** validating your foreign driving license. Members of some foreign auto clubs have reciprocal arrangements with AAA and enjoy its services at no charge. If you belong to an auto club, inquire about AAA reciprocity before you leave home.

Automobile Rentals To rent a car you need a major credit card, or you'll have to leave a sizable cash deposit ($100 or more for each day). A valid driver's license is required, and you usually need to be at least 25. Some companies do rent to younger people but add a daily surcharge. Be sure to return your car with the same amount of gas you started out with; rental companies charge excessive prices for gasoline. All the major car-rental companies are represented in Florida. (see "Getting Around" in Chapter 2).

Business Hours **Banks** are open weekdays from 9am to 3 or 4pm, although there's 24-hour access to the automatic tellers (ATMs) at most banks and other outlets. Generally, **offices** are open weekdays from 9am to 5pm. **Stores** are open six days a week, with many open on Sunday, too; department stores usually stay open until 9pm at least one day a week.

Climate See "When to Go" in Chapter 2.

Currency See "Money" in "Preparing for Your Trip," above.

Currency Exchange The very reliable **Thomas Cook Currency Services, Inc.,** in business since 1841, offers a wide variety of services. They handle about 130 currencies; sell commission-free foreign and U.S. traveler's checks, drafts, and wire transfers; and do check collections (including Eurochecks). Rates are competitive and service excellent. Always inquire at Thomas Cook about the optimum way to exchange your money on entering and leaving the United States or any country. They maintain an office at the JFK Airport International Arrivals Building in New York (tel. 718/656-8444, or toll free 800/582-4496). At this writing a new office is in the works at La Guardia Airport in New York (in the Delta terminal). Call the above toll-free number for information.

Currency Exchange You'll find currency-exchange facilities at the international airports in major Florida cities, including **BankAmerica International,** Concourse E, at Miami International Airport, which is open 24 hours; and **currency-exchange desks** in Orlando International Airport and Tampa International Airport.

Drinking Laws See "Liquor Laws" in "Fast Facts: Florida," Chapter 2.

Electricity The United States uses 110–120 volts, 60 cycles, compared to 220–240 volts, 50 cycles, as in most of Europe. In addition to a 100-volt converter, small appliances of non-American manufacture, such as hairdryers or shavers, will require a plug adapter, with two flat, parallel pins.

Embassies & Consulates All embassies are located in the national capital, Washington, D.C.; some consulates are located in major cities, and most nations have a mission to the United Nations in New York City. Foreign visitors can obtain telephone numbers for their embassies and consulates by calling "Information" in Washington, D.C. (tel. 202/555-1212).

The Canadian consulate closest to Florida is located at One CNN Center, Suite 400, South Tower, Atlanta, GA 30303 (tel. 404/577-6810). There's a British consulate located at 1001 S. Bayshore Dr., Miami, FL 33131 (tel. 305/374-1522).

Emergencies Call **911** to report a fire, call the police, or get an ambulance.

If you encounter traveler's problems, check the local directory to find an office of the **Traveler's Aid Society,** a nationwide, nonprofit, social-service organization geared to helping travelers in difficult straits. Their services might include reuniting families separated while traveling, providing food and/or shelter to people stranded without cash, or even emotional counseling. If you're in trouble, seek them out.

Gasoline [Petrol] One U.S. gallon equals 3.75 liters, while 1.2 U.S. gallons equals one Imperial gallon. You'll notice there are several grades (and price levels) of gasoline available at most gas stations. And you'll also notice that their names change from company to company. The unleaded ones with the highest octane are the most expensive (most rental cars take the least expensive "regular" unleaded) and leaded gas is the least expensive, but only older cars can take this any more, so check if you're not sure.

Holidays On the following legal national holidays, banks, government offices, post offices, and many stores, restaurants, and museums are closed:

January 1 (New Year's Day)
Third Monday in January (Martin Luther King Day)
Third Monday in February (Presidents Day, Washington's Birthday)
Last Monday in May (Memorial Day)
July 4 (Independence Day)
First Monday in September (Labor Day)
Second Monday in October (Columbus Day)
November 11 (Veteran's Day/Armistice Day)
Last Thursday in November (Thanksgiving Day)
December 25 (Christmas)

Also celebrated in some cities and states are the following:

February 12 (in the North) (Lincoln's Birthday)
March 17 (St. Patrick's Day)
April 19 (Patriot's Day)

Finally, the Tuesday following the first Monday in November is Election Day, and is a legal holiday in presidential-election years.

Languages Major hotels may have multilingual employees. Unless your language is very obscure, they can usually supply a translator on request. Especially in southern Florida, many people are fluent in Spanish.

Legal Aid The foreign tourist, unless positively identified as a member of the Mafia or of a drug ring, will probably never become involved with the American legal system. If you are pulled up for a minor infraction (for example, of the highway code, such as speeding), never attempt to pay the fine directly to a police officer; you may wind up arrested on the much more serious charge of attempted bribery. Pay fines by mail, or directly into the hands of the clerk of the court. If accused of a more serious offense, it's wise to say and do nothing before consulting a lawyer. Under U.S. law, an arrested person is allowed one telephone call to a party of his or her choice. Call your embassy or consulate.

Mail If you want your mail to follow you on your vacation, you need only fill out a change-of-address card at any post office. The post office will also hold your mail for up to one month. If you aren't sure of your address, your mail can be sent to you, in your name, **c/o General Delivery** at the main post office of the city or region where you expect to be. The addressee must pick it up in person and produce proof of identity (driver's license, credit card, passport, etc.).

Generally to be found at intersections, mailboxes are blue with a red-and-white stripe and carry the inscription U.S. MAIL. If your mail is addressed to a U.S. destination, don't forget to add the five-figure postal code, or ZIP (Zone Improvement Plan) Code, after the two-letter abbreviation of the state to which the mail is addressed (CA for California, FL for Florida, NY for New York, and so on).

Newspapers/Magazines National newspapers include the *New York Times, USA Today,* and the *Wall Street Journal.* National news weeklies include *Newsweek, Time,* and *U.S. News & World Report.* All over Florida, you'll be able to purchase the *Miami Herald,* one of the most highly respected dailies in the country.

Radio and Television Audiovisual media, with four coast-to-coast networks—ABC, CBS, NBC, and Fox—joined in recent years by the Public Broadcasting System (PBS) and the cable network CNN, play a major part in American life. In big cities, televiewers have a choice of about a dozen channels (including the UHF channels), most of them transmitting 24 hours a day, without counting the pay-TV channels showing recent movies or sports events. All options are usually indicated on your hotel TV set. You'll also find a wide choice of local radio stations, each broadcasting particular kinds of talk shows and/or music—classical, country, jazz, pop, gospel—punctuated by news broadcasts and frequent commercials.

Safety See "Safety" in "Preparing for Your Trip," above.

Taxes In the United States there is no VAT (Value-Added Tax) or other indirect tax at a national level. Every state, and each city in it, has the right to levy its own local tax on all purchases, including hotel and restaurant checks, airline tickets, and so on. In Florida, sales tax is 6%.

Telephone, Telegraph, Telex **Pay phones** are an integral part of the American landscape. You'll find them everywhere: at street corners; in bars, restaurants, public buildings, stores, service stations; along highways; and so on. Outside the metropolitan areas public telephones are more difficult to find. Stores and gas stations are your best bet.

Unlike the mail and the railroads, the telephone is not a public-service system. It is run by private corporations, which perhaps explains its high standard of service. In Florida, local calls cost 25¢.

For **long-distance** or **international calls,** stock up on a supply of quarters; the pay phone will instruct you when, and in what quantity, you should put them into the slot. For direct overseas calls, first dial 011, followed by the country code (Australia, 61; New Zealand, 64; United Kingdom, 44; and so on), and then by the city code and the number of the person you wish to call. For Canada and long-distance calls in the United States, dial 1 followed by the area code and number you want.

Before calling from a hotel room, always ask the hotel phone operator if there are any telephone surcharges. These are best avoided by using a public phone, calling collect, or using a telephone charge card.

For **reversed-charge or collect calls,** and for **person-to-person calls,** dial 0 (zero, *not* the letter "O") followed by the area code and number you want; an operator will then come on the line, and you should specify that you are calling collect, or person-to-person, or both. If your operator-assisted call is international, ask for the overseas operator.

For local **directory assistance** ("information"), dial 411; for **long-distance information,** dial 1, then the appropriate area code and 555-1212.

Like the telephone system, **telegraph** and **telex** services are provided by private corporations like ITT, MCI, and above all, Western Union, the most important. You can bring your telegram in to the nearest Western Union office (there are hundreds across the country), or dictate it over the phone (a toll-free call, 800/325-6000). You can also telegraph money, or have it telegraphed to you, very quickly over the Western Union system.

Telephone Directory See *"Yellow Pages,"* below.

Time The United States is divided into four **time zones** (six, if Alaska and Hawaii are included). From east to west, these are: eastern standard time (EST), central standard time (CST), mountain standard time (MST), Pacific standard time (PST), Alaska standard time (AST), and Hawaii standard time (HST). Always keep changing time zones in mind if you are traveling (or even telephoning) long distances in the United States. For example, noon in New York City (EST) is 11am in Chicago (CST), 10am in Denver (MST), 9am in Los Angeles (PST), 8am in Anchorage (AST), and 7am in Honolulu (HST).

Most of Florida observes eastern standard time, though the western part of the Panhandle region is on central standard time (its clocks are set an hour earlier). **Daylight saving time** is in effect from the last Sunday in April through the last Saturday in October (actually, the change is made at 2am on Sunday) except in Arizona, Hawaii, part of Indiana, and Puerto Rico. Daylight saving time moves the clock one hour ahead of standard time.

Tipping This is part of the American way of life, on the principle that you must expect to pay for any service you get. Here are some rules of thumb:

Bartenders: 10%–15%.
Bellhops: at least 50¢ per piece; $2–$3 for a lot of baggage.
Cab drivers: 15% of the fare.
Cafeterias, fast-food restaurants: no tip.
Chambermaids: $1 a day.
Checkroom attendants (restaurants, theaters): $1 per garment.
Cinemas, movies, theaters: no tip.
Doormen (hotels or restaurants): not obligatory.
Gas-station attendants: no tip.
Hairdressers: 15%–20%.
Redcaps (airport and railroad station): at least 50¢ per piece, $2–$3 for a lot of baggage.
Restaurants, nightclubs: 15%–20% of the check.
Sleeping-car porters: $2–$3 per night to your attendant.
Valet parking attendants: $1.

Toilets Foreign visitors often complain that public toilets are hard to find in most U.S. cities. True, there are none on the streets, but the visitor can usually find one in a bar, restaurant, hotel, museum, department store, or service station—and it will probably be clean (although the last-mentioned sometimes leaves much to be desired). Note, however, a growing practice in some restaurants and bars of displaying a notice that "toilets are for the use of patrons only." You can ignore this sign, or better yet, avoid arguments by paying for a cup of coffee or soft drink, which will qualify you as a patron. The cleanliness of toilets at railroad stations and bus depots may be more open to question, and some public places are equipped with pay toilets, which require you to insert one or two 10¢ coins (dimes) into a slot on the door before it will open.

Yellow Pages There are two kinds of telephone directories available to you. The general directory is the so-called **White Pages,** in which private and business subscribers are listed in alphabetical order. The inside front cover lists the emergency number for police, fire, and ambulance, and other vital numbers (like the Coast Guard, poison-control center, crime-victims hotline, and so on). The first few pages are devoted to community-service numbers, including a guide to long-distance and international calling, complete with country codes and area codes.

The second directory, printed on yellow paper (hence its name, ***Yellow Pages***), lists all local services, businesses, and industries by type of activity, with an index at the back. The listings cover not only such obvious items as automobile repairs by make of car, or drugstores (pharmacies), often by geographical location, but also restaurants by type of cuisine and geographical location, bookstores by special subject and/or language, places of worship by religious denomination, and other information that the tourist might otherwise not readily find. The *Yellow Pages* also include city plans or detailed area maps, often showing postal ZIP Codes and public transportation routes.

THE AMERICAN SYSTEM OF MEASUREMENTS

LENGTH

1 inch (in.)	=	2.54cm				
1 foot (ft.)	=	12 in.	=	30.48cm	=	.305m
1 yard	=	3 ft.	=	.915m		
1 mile (mi.)	=	5,280 ft.	=	1.609km		

To convert miles to kilometers, multiply the number of miles by 1.61 (for example, 50 mi. × 1.61 = 80.5km). Note that this conversion can be used to convert speeds from miles per hour (m.p.h.) to kilometers per hour (km/h).

To convert kilometers to miles, multiply the number of kilometers by .62 (for example, 25km × .62 = 15.5 mi.). Note that this same conversion can be used to convert speeds from kilometers per hour to miles per hour.

CAPACITY

1 fluid ounce (fl. oz.)	=	.03 liter		
1 pint	=	16 fl. oz.	=	.47 liter
1 quart	=	2 pints	=	.94 liter
1 gallon (gal.)	=	4 quarts	=	3.79 liter
	=	.83 Imperial gal.		

To convert U.S. gallons to liters, multiply the number of gallons by 3.79 (example, 12 gal. × 3.79 = 45.58 liters.)

To convert U.S. gallons to Imperial gallons, multiply the number of U.S. gallons by .83 (example, 12 U.S. gal. × .83 = 9.95 Imperial gal.).

To convert liters to U.S. gallons, multiply the number of liters by .26 (example, 50 liters × .26 = 13 U.S. gal.).

To convert Imperial gallons to U.S. gallons, multiply the number of Imperial gallons by 1.2 (example, 8 Imperial gal. × 1.2 = 9.6 U.S. gal.).

WEIGHT

1 ounce (oz.)	=	28.35 grams				
1 pound (lb.)	=	16 oz.	=	453.6 grams	=	.45 kilograms
1 ton	=	2,000 lb.	=	907 kilograms	=	.91 metric ton

To convert pounds to kilograms, multiply the number of pounds by .45 (example, 90 lb. × .45 = 40.5kg).

To convert kilograms to pounds, multiply the number of kilos by 2.2 (example, 75kg × 2.2 = 165 lb.).

AREA

1 acre	=	.41 hectare		
1 square mile (sq. mi.)	=	640 acres	=	2.59 hectares
	=	2.6km		

To convert acres to hectares, multiply the number of acres by .41 (example, 40 acres × .41 = 16.4ha).

To convert square miles to square kilometers, multiply the number of square miles by 2.6 (example, 80 sq. mi. × 2.6 = 208km²).

To convert hectares to acres, multiply the number of hectares by 2.47 (example, 20ha × 2.47 = 49.4 acres).

To convert square kilometers to square miles, multiply the number of square kilometers by .39 (example, 150km² × .39 = 58.5 sq. mi.).

TEMPERATURE

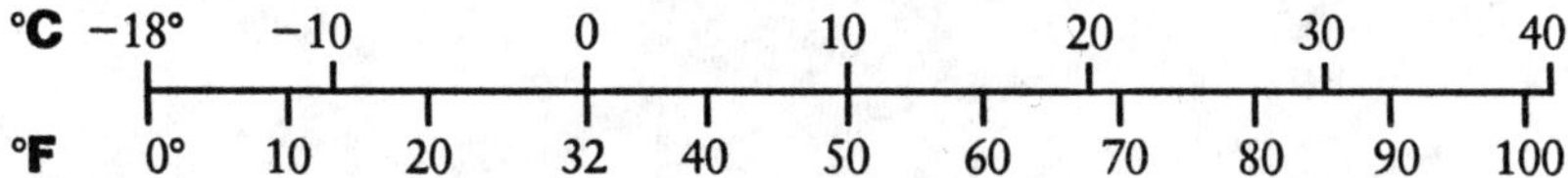

To convert degrees Fahrenheit to degrees Celsius, subtract 32 from °F, multiply by 5, then divide by 9 (example, 85°F − 32 × 5/9 = 29.4°C).

To convert degrees Celsius to degrees Fahrenheit, multiply °C by 9, divide by 5, and add 32 (example, 20°C × 9/5 + 32 = 68°F).

CHAPTER 4

SETTLING INTO MIAMI

Florida's second-largest city, with almost two million residents, and famous for its white sand beaches, glittering waters, and sun-filled days, Miami attracts more than eight million visitors annually. The unique influence of its complex mix of cultures creates exciting opportunities to explore.

The unofficial capital of the Gold Coast, the city is less than 100 years old. Until the end of the 19th century, much of the Florida peninsula had never even been surveyed, and Miami itself was nothing more than a small trading post and the ruins of a U.S. Army camp, once known as Fort Dallas. The arrival in 1891 of an adventurous widow from Cleveland, Julia Tuttle, changed all that. Sensing the potential of the area, she set out to create a full-blown town. Realization of her dream depended on access to the area, and at first the railroad magnates whom she approached were less than enthusiastic. However, in 1896, when Henry Flagler's first train steamed into town, Tuttle became the only woman in American history to have started a major city.

It wasn't long before Miami's irresistible combination of surf, sun, and sand prompted America's wealthy to build elaborate winter retreats overlooking Biscayne Bay. Miami became chic, and following World War I, middle-class interest in the region prompted spectacular growth; the population grew from 30,000 to 100,000 in just five years. The building boom of the Roaring Twenties is directly responsible for the city's distinctive neighborhoods of today.

During the last decade the city has experienced startling changes in demographics as well as a new spurt of economic growth. The influx of refugees, predominately from Cuba and Haiti, has swelled the city's Caribbean population and influenced all aspects of living, from art and architecture to food, music, and fashion.

Miami is a city still discovering its identity—a vibrant, brash young adult of a city. The air here is electric with the excitement of growth, change, and expansion.

1. ORIENTATION

ARRIVING

One hundred years ago Miami was a hard place to reach. But no longer: Today airlines fight perpetual price wars to woo tourists to the Sunshine State. In fact, fares are so

WHAT'S SPECIAL ABOUT MIAMI

Beaches

- ☐ Over a dozen miles of white sandy beaches, edged with coconut palms on one side and a clear, turquoise-blue ocean on the other.

Water Sports

- ☐ Parasailing, jet skiing, sailing, boating, windsurfing.

Nightlife

- ☐ Music—everything from rock to reggae, and irresistible Latin rhythms.

Festivals

- ☐ Party from Calle Ocho to Goombay.

Food

- ☐ America's freshest citrus and seafood.
- ☐ Miami Regional—the area's unique cuisine.

Architecture

- ☐ Miami Beach's art deco district—the largest collection of buildings on the National Register of Historic Places.
- ☐ The cityscape of downtown Miami, one of the prettiest in the world.

competitive that, unless you are visiting from an adjacent state, flying to Miami will almost always be your most economical option. But take a look at your alternatives, too. An overland journey to Florida's Gold Coast is both a more scenic and a more flexible way to travel. Greyhound/Trailways offers several types of bus passes, and Amtrak offers a host of rail services.

BY AIR Originally carved out of scrubland in 1928 by Pan American Airlines, **Miami International Airport (MIA)** has emerged as the 9th-busiest airport in the United States, and the 11th busiest in the world. It's also one of the most streamlined, making it a wonderful place to land. Since the airport is easy to negotiate, and located only six miles west of downtown, it's likely that domestic passengers can get from the plane to their hotel room in about an hour. International arrivals must pass through Customs and Immigration, a process that can double your time in the airport.

The route down to the baggage-claim area is clearly marked. You can change money or use your Honor or Plus System ATM card at Barnett Bank of South Florida, located near the exit.

Like most good international airports, MIA has its fair share of boutiques, shops, and eateries. Unless you're starving, or forgot to get a gift for the person picking you up, bypass these overpriced establishments. The airport is literally surrounded by restaurants and shops; if you can wait to get to them, you'll save a lot of money.

Note that if you're exiting Miami on an international flight, the excellent duty-free selection in the departure lounge shouldn't be missed.

If you're renting a car at the airport (see "Getting Around," below), you'll have to take one of the free shuttles to the rental site. Buses and vans, clearly marked with rental-car logos, circle the airport regularly, and stop at the wave of a hand. Signs at the airport's exit clearly point the way to various parts of the city.

Taxis line up in front of a dispatcher's desk outside the airport's arrivals terminals. Cabs are metered and will cost about $14 to Coral Gables, $16 to downtown, and $18 to South Miami Beach. Tip 10%–15%.

Group limousines (multipassenger vans) also circle the arrivals area looking for fares. Destinations are posted on the front of each van, and a flat rate is charged for door-to-door service to the area marked. SuperShuttle (tel. 871-2000) is one of the largest airport operators, charging between $10 and $17 per person for a ride within Dade County. Their vans operate 24 hours a day and accept American Express, MasterCard, and VISA.

Private limousine arrangements can be made in advance through your local travel agent. A one-way meet-and-greet service should cost about $50.

Public transportation is not a recommended way to get to your hotel, or anywhere, for that matter. Buses heading downtown leave the airport only once per hour (from the arrivals level), and connections are spotty at best.

BY TRAIN If you're traveling to Miami by train (see "Getting There," in Chapter 2), you will pull into Amtrak's Miami terminal at 8303 NW 37th Ave. (tel. 835-1205). Unfortunately, none of the major car-rental companies has an office at the train station; you'll have to go to the airport (see "Getting Around," below). Hertz (tel. toll free 800/654-3131) will reimburse your cab fare from the train station to the airport provided you rent one of their cars.

Taxis meeting each Amtrak arrival are plentiful. The fare to downtown is about $14; the ride takes less than 20 minutes.

BY CAR No matter where you start your journey, chances are you'll reach Miami by way of **I-95.** This north-south Interstate is the city's lifeline and an integral part of the region. The highway connects all of Miami's different neighborhoods, the airport, and the beach; and it connects all of South Florida to the rest of America. Every part of Miami is easily reached from I-95, and well-lit road signs clearly point the way. Take time out to study I-95's placement on the map. You'll use it as a reference point time and again. For a detailed description of the city's main arteries and streets, see "City Layout," below.

BY BUS Greyhound/Trailways buses pull into a number of stations around the city including: 99 NE 4th St. (downtown); 16250 Biscayne Blvd., North Miami Beach; and 7101 Harding Ave., Miami Beach. Consult your local directory for the office nearest you.

INFORMATION

In addition to the data and sources listed below, foreign visitors should see Chapter 3 for entry requirements and other pertinent information.

The **Greater Miami Convention and Visitors Bureau,** 701 Brickell Ave., Miami, FL 33131 (tel. 305/539-3063, or toll free 800/283-2707), is the best source of any kind of specialized information about the city. Even if you don't have a specific question, be sure to phone ahead for their free magazine, *Destination Miami,* which includes several good, clear maps. The office is open Monday through Friday from 9am to 5:30pm.

For information on traveling in the state as a whole, contact the **Florida Division of Tourism (FDT),** 126 W. Van Buren St., Tallahassee, FL 32399 (tel. 904/487-1462), open Monday through Friday from 8am to 5pm. Europeans should note that the FDT maintains an office in England at 18/24 Westbourne Grove, 4th Floor, London W2 5RH (tel. 071/727-1661).

In addition to information on some of South Miami Beach's better hotels, the **Miami Design Preservation League,** 1244 Ocean Dr. (P.O. Bin L), Miami Beach, FL 33119 (tel. 305/672-2014), offers a free, informative guide to the art deco district, and several books on the subject. They're open Monday through Saturday from 10am to 7pm.

Greater Miami's various chambers of commerce also send maps and information about their particular parcels. These include: **Coconut Grove Chamber of Commerce,** 2820 McFarlane Rd., Miami, FL 33133 (tel. 305/444-7270); **Coral Gables Chamber of Commerce,** 50 Aragon Ave., Coral Gables, FL 33134 (tel. 305/446-1657); **Florida Gold Coast Chamber of Commerce,** 1100 Kane Concourse (Bay Harbor Islands), Miami, FL 33154 (tel. 305/866-6020), which represents Bal Harbour, Sunny Isles, Surfside, and other North Dade waterfront communities; **Greater Miami Chamber of Commerce,** Omni International, 1601 Biscayne Blvd., Miami, FL 33132 (tel. 305/539-3063, or toll free 800/283-

2707); and **Miami Beach Chamber of Commerce,** 1920 Meridian Ave., Miami Beach, FL 33139 (tel. 305/672-1270).

The following organizations represent dues-paying hotels, restaurants, and attractions in their specific areas. These associations can arrange accommodations and tours, as well as provide discount coupons to area sights: **Miami Beach Resort Hotel Association,** 407 Lincoln Rd., Miami Beach, FL 33139 (tel. 305/531-3553, or toll free 800/531-3553), and **Sunny Isles Beach Resort Association,** 3909 Sunny Isles Blvd., Suite 307, Sunny Isles, FL 33160 (tel. 305/947-5826, or toll free 800/327-6366).

CITY LAYOUT

Miami may seem confusing at first, but it quickly becomes easy to negotiate. The small cluster of buildings that make up the downtown area is at the geographical heart of the city. You can see these sharp stalactites from most anywhere, making them a good reference point. In relation to Miami's downtown, the airport is west, the beaches are east, Coconut Grove and Coral Gables are south, and the rest of the country is north.

FINDING AN ADDRESS Miami is divided into dozens of areas with official and unofficial boundaries. To make map-reading easier, all the addresses listed in this book are followed by an area listing, indicating which part of the city it's in.

Street numbering in the **City of Miami** is fairly straightforward, but you must first be familiar with the numbering system. The mainland is divided into four sections—NE, NW, SE, and SW—by the intersection of Flagler Street and Miami Avenue. First Street and First Avenue begin near this corner, and, along with Places, Courts, Terraces, and Lanes, the numbers increase from this point. Hialeah streets are the exception to this pattern; they are listed separately in map indexes.

Establishment addresses are often descriptive; 12301 Biscayne Boulevard is located at 123rd Street. It's also helpful to remember that avenues generally run north-south, while streets go east-west.

Getting around the barrier islands of **Miami Beach** is somewhat easier than moving around the mainland. Street numbering starts with 1st Street, near Miami Beach's southern tip, and increases to 192nd Street, in the northern part of Sunny Isles. Collins Avenue makes the entire journey from head to toe. As in the City of Miami, some streets in Miami Beach have numbers as well as names. When they are part of listings in this book, both names and numbers are given.

You should know that the numbered streets in Miami Beach are not the geographical equivalents of those on the mainland. The 79th Street Causeway runs into 71st Street on Miami Beach.

MAPS It's easy to get lost in sprawling Miami, so a reliable map is essential. If you aren't planning on moving around too much, the tourist board's maps, located inside their free publication *Destination Miami,* may be adequate. But if you really want to get to know the city, it pays to invest in one of the large, accordion-fold maps, available at most gas stations and bookstores. The *Trakker Map of Miami* ($2.50) is a four-color accordion that encompasses all of Dade County, handy if you plan on visiting the many attractions in Greater Miami South.

Some maps of Miami list streets according to area, so you'll have to know which part of the city you're looking for before the street can be found. All the listings in this book include area information for just this reason.

NEIGHBORHOODS IN BRIEF

Much of Miami is sprawling suburbia. But every city has its charm, and aside from a fantastic tropical climate, and the vast stretch of beach that lies just across the bay, Miami's unique identity comes from extremely interesting cultural pockets within various residential communities.

Coral Gables Just over 70 years old, Coral Gables is the closest thing to "historical" that Miami has. It's also one of the prettiest parcels in the city. Created by George Merrick in the early 1920s, the Gables was one of Miami's first planned developments. Houses here were built in a "Mediterranean style" along lush tree-lined streets that open onto beautifully carved plazas, many with centerpiece fountains. The best architectural examples of the era have Spanish-style tiled roofs and are built of Miami oolite, a native limestone, commonly called "coral rock." Coral Gables is a stunning example of "boom" architecture on a grand scale—and a great area to explore. Some of the city's best restaurants are located here, as are top hotels and good shopping. See "Accommodations" and "Dining," below, for listings.

Coconut Grove There was a time when Coconut Grove was inhabited by artists and intellectuals, hippies and radicals. But times have changed. Gentrification has pushed most alternative types out, leaving in their place a multitude of cafés, boutiques, and nightspots. The intersection of Grand Avenue, Main Highway, and McFarlane Road, the area's heart, sizzles with dozens of interesting shops and eateries. Sidewalks here are often crowded with businesspeople, college students, and loads of foreign tourists—especially at night, when it becomes the best place to people-watch in all of South Florida.

Coconut Grove's link to The Bahamas dates from before the turn of the century, when the islanders came to the area to work in a newly opened hotel called the Peacock Inn. Bahamian-style wooden homes, built by these early settlers, still stand on Charles Street. Goombay, the lively annual Bahamian festival, celebrates the Grove's Caribbean link and has become one of the largest black heritage street festivals in America.

Miami Beach To tourists in the 1950s, Miami Beach *was* Miami. Its huge self-contained resort hotels were worlds unto themselves, providing a full day's worth of meals, activities, and entertainment.

In the 1960s and 1970s people who fell in love with Miami began to buy apartments rather than rent hotel rooms. Tourism declined and many area hotels fell into disrepair.

But since the late '80s Miami Beach has witnessed a tide of revitalization. Huge beach hotels are finding international tourist markets, and are attracting large convention crowds. New generations of Americans are discovering the special qualities that made Miami Beach so popular to begin with, and are finding out that the beach now comes with a thriving, international, exciting city.

Note: North Miami Beach is a residential area on the mainland near the Dade-Broward county line. It is in no way connected to Miami Beach.

Surfside, Bal Harbour, and Sunny Isles Lying just north of Miami Beach, on barrier islands, Surfside, Bal Harbour, and Sunny Isles are, for the most part, an extension of the beach community below it. Collins Avenue crosses town lines with hardly a sign, while hotels, motels, restaurants, and beaches continue to line the strip.

In exclusive Bal Harbour, fancy homes—tucked away on the bay—hide behind walls, gates, and security cameras. For tourists, it seems that—with some outstanding exceptions—the farther north you go, the cheaper lodging becomes. All told, excellent prices, location, and facilities make Surfside, Bal Harbour, and Sunny Isles attractive places to locate.

South Miami Beach—The Art Deco District Officially part of the city of Miami Beach, the Miami Beach Architectural District of South Miami Beach contains the largest concentration of art deco architecture in the world. South Beach, or SoBe, as it is known, is an exciting renaissance community with pensioners, soon-to-be-monied young investors, perpetually poor artists, and the usual Miami smattering of ethnic groups. Everywhere you go there's an air of excitement; hip clubs and cafés are filled with working models and their photographers, musicians and writers, and in-the-know locals, vacationers, and others.

Key Biscayne The first island in the Florida Keys chain is Miami's forested

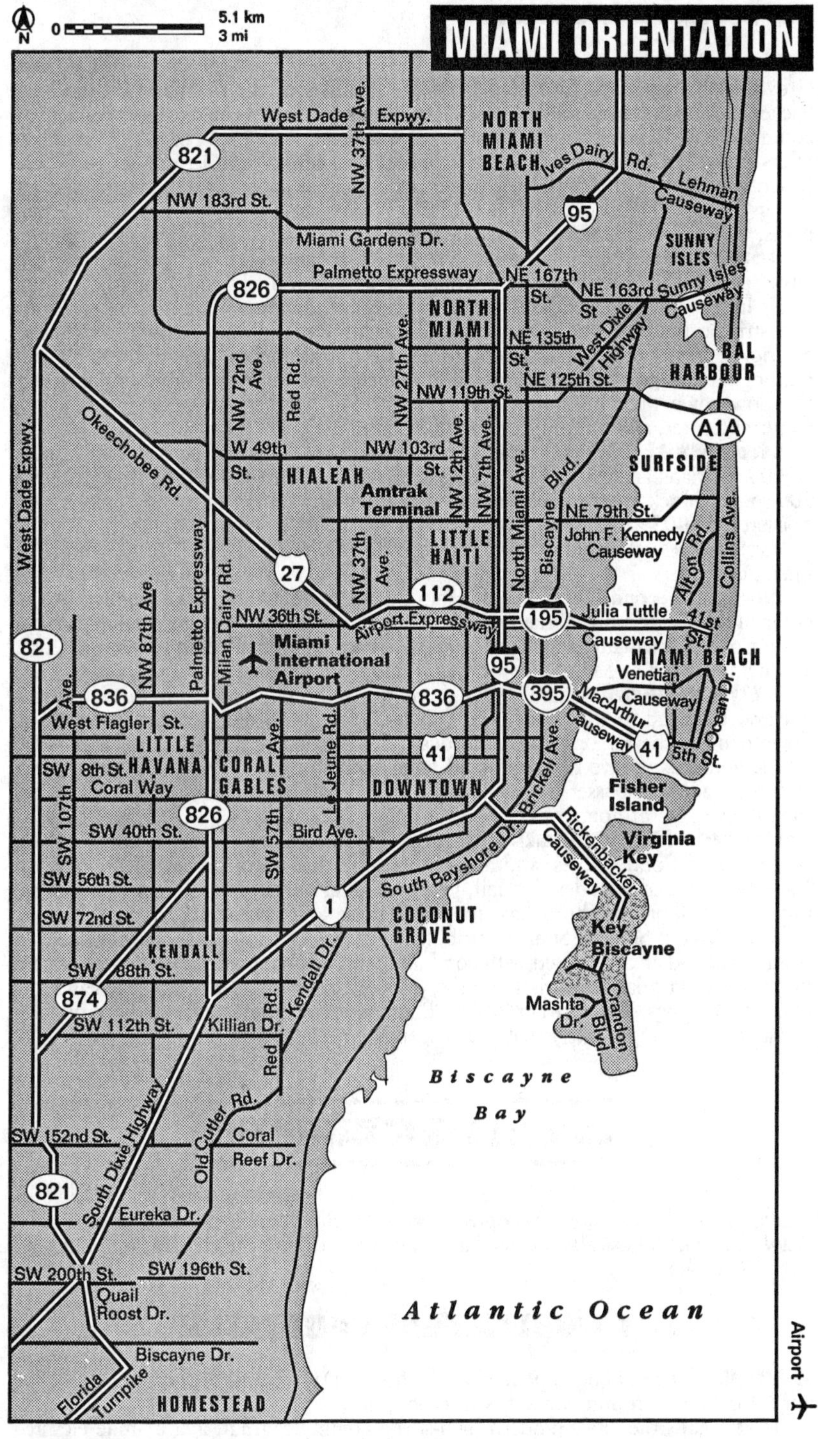

MIAMI ORIENTATION
N
0
5.1 km
3 mi
West Dade Expwy.
NORTH MIAMI BEACH
821
NW 37th Ave.
Ives Dairy Rd.
Lehman Causeway
NW 183rd St.
95
Miami Gardens Dr.
SUNNY ISLES
Palmetto Expressway
NE 167th St.
NE 163rd St
Sunny Isles Causeway
826
NORTH MIAMI
NW 27th Ave.
NE 135th St.
West Dixie Highway
BAL HARBOUR
NW 72nd Ave.
Red Rd.
NE 125th St.
NW 119th St.
A1A
Okeechobee Rd.
NW 12th Ave.
NW 7th Ave.
W 49th St.
NW 103rd St.
HIALEAH
SURFSIDE
North Miami Ave.
Biscayne Blvd.
Amtrak Terminal
NE 79th St.
West Dade Expwy.
Palmetto Expressway
LITTLE HAITI
John F. Kennedy Causeway
Alton Rd.
Collins Ave.
NW 87th Ave.
Milan Dairy Rd.
27
NW 37th Ave.
112
NW 36th St.
Airport Expressway
195
Julia Tuttle Causeway
41st St.
821
Miami International Airport
95
MIAMI BEACH
Venetian Causeway
Ave.
836
395
MacArthur Causeway
West Flagler St.
Ocean Dr.
LITTLE HAVANA
CORAL GABLES
Ave.
Le Jeune Rd.
41
5th St.
SW 8th St.
Coral Way
SW 107th Ave.
DOWNTOWN
Brickell Ave.
Fisher Island
826
SW 40th St.
SW 57th Ave.
Bird Ave.
Rickenbacker Causeway
Virginia Key
SW 56th St.
South Bayshore Dr.
1
SW 72nd St.
COCONUT GROVE
Key Biscayne
KENDALL
SW 88th St.
874
Kendall Dr.
Red Rd.
Mashta Dr.
Crandon Blvd.
SW 112th St.
Killian Dr.
Biscayne Bay
Old Cutler Rd.
South Dixie Highway
SW 152nd St.
Coral Reef Dr.
821
Eureka Dr.
SW 200th St.
SW 196th St.
Quail Roost Dr.
Atlantic Ocean
Airport
Biscayne Dr.
Florida Turnpike
HOMESTEAD

and fancy Key Biscayne. Located south of Miami Beach, off the shores of Coconut Grove, Key Biscayne is protected from the troubles of the mainland by the long Rickenbacker Causeway and a $1 toll. Key Biscayne is largely an exclusive residential community with million-dollar homes and sweeping water views. For tourists, this key offers great beaches, some top resort hotels, and several good restaurants. Hobie Beach, adjacent to the causeway, is the city's premier spot for sailboarding and jet skiing. On the island's southern tip is Bill Baggs State Park, offering great beaches, bike paths, and dense forests for picnicking and partying.

Downtown Miami's downtown boasts one of the world's most beautiful cityscapes. If you do nothing else in Miami, make sure you take your time studying the area's inspired architectural designs. The streets of downtown are unusually free of pedestrian traffic even during the height of lunch hour. You'll see plenty of stores and eateries here, but most sell discount goods and quick lunches. Unless you're bargain hunting for necessary items, there's not too much in the way of window-shopping. But the downtown area does have its mall (Bayside Marketplace), the Metro-Dade Cultural Center, and a number of good restaurants.

Little Haiti During a brief period in the late 1970s and early 1980s, almost 35,000 Haitians arrived in Miami. Most of the new refugees settled in a decaying 200-square-block area north of downtown. Extending from 41st to 83rd Streets, and bordered by I-95 and Biscayne Boulevard, Little Haiti, as it has become known, is a relatively depressed neighborhood with over 60,000 residents, 65% of whom are of Haitian origin.

Northeast Second Avenue, Little Haiti's main thoroughfare, is highlighted by the colorful new Caribbean Marketplace, located at the corner of 60th Street. Keep an eye out for one of the many Haitian religious shops selling aromatic herbs, roots, incense, and items related to Santería and other voodoo ceremonies.

Little Havana Miami's Cuban center is the city's most important ethnic enclave. Referred to locally as "Calle Ocho," SW 8th Street, located just west of downtown, is the region's main thoroughfare. Car-repair shops, tailors, electronic stores, and inexpensive restaurants all hang signs in Spanish. Salsa rhythms thump from the radios of passersby, while old men in guayaberas chain-smoke cigars over their daily game of dominoes.

Greater Miami South To locals, South Miami is both a specific area, southwest of Coral Gables, and a general region that encompasses all of southern Dade County and includes Kendall, Perrine, Cutler Ridge, and Homestead. For the purposes of clarity, this book has grouped all these southern suburbs under the rubric "Greater Miami South." Similar attributes unite the communities: They are heavily residential, and all are packed with condominiums and shopping malls as well as acre upon acre of farmland. Tourists don't stay in these parts, as there is no beach and few cultural offerings. But Greater Miami South does contain many of the city's top attractions, making it likely that you'll spend some time here during the day.

2. GETTING AROUND

Officially, Dade County has opted for a "unified, multi-modal transportation network," which basically means that you can get around the city by train, bus, and taxi. Here's how:

BY PUBLIC TRANSPORTATION

BY RAIL Two rail lines, operated by the Metro-Dade Transit Agency (tel. 638-6700 for information), run in concert with each other.

Metrorail, the city's modern high-speed commuter train, is a 21-mile elevated line that travels north-south, between downtown Miami and the southern suburbs. If you're staying in Coral Gables or Coconut Grove, you can park your car at a nearby station and ride the rails downtown. Unfortunately for visitors, the line's usefulness is limited. There are plans to extend the system to service Miami International Airport, but until those tracks are built, these trains don't go most places that tourists go. Metrorail operates daily from 6am to midnight. The fare is $1.25.

Metromover, a 1.9-mile elevated line, connects with Metrorail at the Government Center stop and circles the city's downtown area. Riding on rubber tires, the single-train car winds past 10 stations and through some of the city's most important office locations. Metromover offers a fun, futuristic ride. System hours are the same as Metrorail. The fare is 25¢.

BY BUS Miami's suburban layout is not conducive to getting around by bus. Lines operate, and maps can be had, but instead of getting to know the city, you'll find that relying on bus transportation will only acquaint you with how it feels to wait at bus stops. You can get a bus map by mail, either from the Greater Miami Convention and Visitors Bureau (see "Information" in "Orientation," above) or by writing the Metro-Dade Transit System, 3300 NW 32nd Ave., Miami 33142. In Miami, call 638-6700 for public transit information. The fare is $1.25.

BY TAXI

If you're not planning on traveling much within the city, an occasional taxi is a good alternative to renting a car. If you plan on spending your holiday within the confines of South Miami Beach's art deco district, you may also wish to avoid the parking hassles that come with renting your own car. The taxi's meter drops at $1.10 for the first one-seventh of a mile, and rises 20¢ for each additional seventh of a mile. An average cross-city ride will cost about $10.

Major cab companies include **Metro** (tel. 888-8888) and **Yellow** (tel. 444-4444).

BY CAR

Tales circulate about vacationers who have visited Miami without a car, but they are very few indeed. If you're counting on exploring the city, even to a modest degree, private motor transportation will be essential to your plans. Unless you're going to spend your entire vacation at a resort, or are traveling directly to the Port of Miami for a cruise, a car is a necessity. Miami's restaurants, attractions, and sights are far from one another and any other form of transportation is impractical.

When driving across a causeway, or through downtown, allow extra time to reach your destination because of frequent drawbridge openings. Bridges open about every half hour, stalling traffic for several minutes. Don't get frustrated by the wait. The bridges keep the city's pace from becoming too fast and frenetic.

RENTALS It seems as though every car-rental company, big and small, has at least one office in Miami. Consequently, the city is one of the cheapest places in the world to rent a car. Many firms regularly advertise prices in the neighborhood of $89 per week for their bottom-of-the-line tin can—not an unreasonable sum for seven days of sun and fun.

Most rental firms pad their profits by selling an additional Loss/Damage Waiver (LDW), which usually costs an extra $8–$10 per day. Before agreeing to this, however, check with your insurance carrier and credit-card companies. Many people don't realize that they are already covered by either one or both. If you're not, the LDW is a wise investment.

A minimum age, ranging from 19 to 25, is usually required of renters. Some rental agencies have also set maximum ages. If you are concerned that these limits may affect you, ask about rental requirements at the time of booking to avoid problems later.

National car-rental companies include: Alamo (tel. toll free 800/327-9633), Avis (tel. toll free 800/331-1212), Budget (tel. toll free 800/527-0700), Dollar (tel. toll free 800/822-1181), General (tel. toll free 800/327-7607), Hertz (tel. toll free

800/654-3131), National (tel. toll free 800/328-4567), and Thrifty (tel. toll free 800/367-2277). Literally dozens of other regional companies—some offering lower rates—can be found in the Miami *Yellow Pages* under "Automobile Renting and Leasing."

Finally, think about splurging for a convertible. Few things in life can match the feeling of flying along warm Florida freeways with the sun smiling on your shoulders and the wind whipping through your hair.

PARKING Always keep plenty of quarters, dimes, and nickels on hand in order to feed hungry meters. Parking is usually plentiful, but when it's not, be careful: Fines for illegal parking can be stiff.

In addition to parking garages, valet services are commonplace and often used. Expect to pay $3–$5 for parking in Coconut Grove and on South Miami Beach's Ocean Drive on busy weekend nights.

LOCAL DRIVING RULES Florida law allows drivers to make a right turn on a red light, unless otherwise indicated. In addition, all passengers are required to wear seat belts, and children under 3 years of age must be securely fastened in government-approved car seats.

BY BICYCLE

Miami's two best bicycling areas are vastly different from each other.

Miami Beach The hard-packed sand that runs the length of Miami Beach is one of the best places in the world to ride a bike. An excellent alternative to the slow pace of walking, biking up the beach is great for surf, sun, sand, exercise, and people-watching. You may not want to subject your bicycle to the salt and sand, but there are plenty of oceanfront rental places here. Most of the big beach hotels rent bicycles, as does **Beach Skates,** Ocean Drive at the 10th Street Bandshell (tel. 534-2252). Located in South Miami Beach, the shop rents mountain cruisers for $10 per hour. It's open daily from 11am to 8pm.

Coral Gables and Coconut Grove The beautiful and quiet streets of these neighborhoods beg for the attention of bicyclists. Old trees form canopies over wide, flat roads lined with grand homes and quaint street markers. Several bicycle trails are spread throughout these neighborhoods, including one that begins at the doorstep of **Dade Cycle,** 3216 Grand Ave., Coconut Grove (tel. 444-5997). It's open Monday through Saturday from 9:30am to 5:30pm and on Sunday from 10:30am to 5:30pm. MasterCard and VISA are accepted.

ON FOOT

With the exception of isolated pockets in Coconut Grove and South Miami Beach, Miami is not a walker's city. Because it is so spread out, most attractions are too far apart to make walking feasible. In fact, most Miamians are so used to driving that they drive even when going just a few blocks.

FAST FACTS: MIAMI

Airport See "Arriving" in "Orientation," above.

American Express For travel arrangements, traveler's checks, currency exchange, and other member services, Miami offices include: 330 Biscayne Blvd., downtown (tel. 358-7350); 9700 Collins Ave., Bal Harbour (tel. 865-5959); and 32 Miracle Mile, Coral Gables (tel. 446-3381). Offices are open Monday through Friday from 9am to 5pm and on Saturday from 9am until noon.

To report lost or stolen traveler's checks, call 800/221-7282.

Area Code The area code for Miami and all of Dade County is 305.

Babysitters Hotels can often recommend a babysitter or child-care service. If yours can't, try Central Sitting Agency, 1764 SW 24th St. (tel. 856-0550). Other child-minding agencies are listed in the *Yellow Pages* under "Sitting Services."

Bookstores Chain bookstores can be found in almost every shopping center in the city. A top bookseller in the city is Books & Books, 296 Aragon Ave. (tel. 442-4408), in Coral Gables.

Buses See "Getting Around," above.

Business Hours Banking hours vary, but most **banks** are open Monday through Friday from 9am to 3pm. Several stay open until 5pm or so at least one day during the week, and many banks feature Automated Teller Machines (ATMs) for 24-hour banking.

Most **stores** are open daily from 10am to 6pm; however, there are many exceptions. Shops in the Bayside Marketplace are usually open until 9 or 10pm, as are the boutiques in Coconut Grove. Stores in Bal Harbour and other malls are usually open one extra hour one night during the week (usually Thursday).

As far as **business offices** are concerned, Miami is generally a 9am-to-5pm town.

Car Rentals See "Getting Around," above.

Dentists The East Coast District Dental Society staffs an Emergency Dental Referral Service (tel. 285-5470). Michael H. Schenkman, D.D.S., in the Suniland Shopping Center, 11735 S. Dixie Hwy. (tel. 235-0020), features 24-hour emergency service and takes all major credit cards. All Dade Dental Associated, 11400 N. Kendall Dr., Mega Bank Building (tel. 271-7777), also offers round-the-clock care and accepts MasterCard and VISA.

Doctors In an emergency, call an ambulance by dialing 911 from any phone. No coins are required.

The Dade County Medical Association sponsors a Physician Referral Service (tel. 324-8717) Monday through Friday from 9am to 5pm.

In Miami, doctors still make house calls: 24 hours a day, seven days a week, a doctor will be sent to your hotel within an hour. The basic fee is $60. Call 945-6325.

Doctors' Hospital of Coral Gables, 5000 University Dr., Coral Gables (tel. 666-2111), is a 285-bed nonprofit hospital with a 24-hour physician-staffed emergency department.

Driving Rules See "Getting Around," above.

Drugstores Walgreens Pharmacies are all over town, including 8550 Coral Way (tel. 221-9271), in Coral Gables; and 6700 Collins Ave. (tel. 861-6742), in Miami Beach. Their branch at 5731 Bird Rd. (tel. 666-0757), is open 24 hours, as is Eckerd Drugs, 1825 Miami Gardens Dr. NE (185th Street), North Miami Beach (tel. 932-5740).

Embassies/Consulates See "Fast Facts: For the Foreign Visitor" in Chapter 3.

Emergencies To reach the police, ambulance, or fire department, dial **911** from any phone. No coins are needed. Emergency hotlines include: Crisis Intervention (tel. 358-4357), Poison Information Center (tel. toll free 800/282-3171), and Rape Hotline (tel. 549-7273).

Eyeglasses Pearle Vision Center, 326 Miracle Mile (tel. 448-3039), in Coral Gables, can usually fill prescriptions in about an hour.

Hairdressers/Barbers The chain, Supercuts, 9803 Bird Rd. (tel. 553-4965), offers one of the lowest-priced shears in the city, while the salon at the Grand Bay Hotel, 2669 S. Bayshore Dr., Coconut Grove (tel. 858-9600), boasts one of the most costly pamperings around. Many other major hotels also have hair salons.

Hospitals See "Doctors," above.

Information Always check local newspapers for special things to do during your visit. The city's highest-quality daily, the *Miami Herald,* is an especially good source for current-events listings, particularly the "Weekend" section in Friday's edition. For a complete list of tourist boards and other information sources, see "Information" in "Orientation," above.

Laundry/Dry Cleaning All Laundry Service, 5701 NW 7th St., west of downtown (tel. 261-8175), does dry cleaning and offers a wash-and-fold service by the pound in addition to self-service machines. It's open daily from 6am to midnight. Clean Machine Laundry, 226 12th St., South Miami Beach (tel. 534-9429), is convenient to South Beach's art deco hotels. It's open 24 hours daily. Coral Gables Laundry & Dry Cleaning, 250 Minorca Ave., Coral Gables (tel. 446-6458), has been dry cleaning, altering, and laundering since 1930. They offer a life-saving same-day service. Open Monday through Friday from 7am to 6:30pm and on Saturday from 8am to 3pm.

Libraries The Main Library in the Dade County system is located downtown at 101 W. Flagler St. (tel. 375-2665). It's open on Monday from 9am to 9pm, Tuesday through Saturday from 9am to 6pm, and on Sunday from 1 to 5pm.

Liquor Laws Only adults 21 years of age or older may legally purchase or consume alcohol in the state of Florida. Minors are usually permitted in bars that serve food. Liquor laws are strictly enforced; if you look young, carry identification. In addition to specialty shops, beer and wine are also sold in most supermarkets and convenience stores. The City of Miami's liquor stores are closed on Sunday. Liquor stores in the City of Miami Beach are open all week.

Lost Property If you lost it at the airport, call the Airport Lost and Found office (tel. 876-7377). If you lost it on the bus, Metrorail, or Metromover, call Metro-Dade Transit Agency (tel. 638-6700). If you lost it somewhere else, phone the Dade County Police Lost and Found (tel. 375-3366). You may also wish to fill out a police report for insurance purposes.

Luggage Storage/Lockers In addition to the baggage check at Miami International Airport (see "Arriving," in "Orientation," above), most hotels offer luggage-storage facilities. If you're taking a cruise from the Port of Miami, bags can be stored in your ship's departure terminal.

Mail Miami's Main Post Office, 2200 Milam Dairy Rd., Miami, FL 33152 (tel. 599-0166), is located west of Miami International Airport. Letters addressed to you and marked "General Delivery" can be picked up here. Conveniently located post offices include 1300 Washington Ave. (tel. 531-7306), in South Miami Beach; and 3191 Grand Ave. (tel. 443-0030), in Coconut Grove. Holders of American Express cards or traveler's checks can receive mail, free, addressed c/o American Express, 330 Biscayne Blvd., Miami, FL 33132.

Maps See "City Layout" in "Orientation," above.

Money In addition to paying close attention to the details below, foreign visitors should also see "Fast Facts" in Chapter 3 for monetary descriptions and currency exchange information.

U.S. dollar **traveler's checks** are the safest, most negotiable way to carry currency. They are accepted by most restaurants, hotels, and shops, and can be exchanged for cash at banks and check-issuing offices. For American Express offices, see "American Express," above.

Most banks offer **Automated Teller Machines (ATMs),** which accept cards connected to a particular network. Citicorp Savings of Florida, 8750 NW 36th St., and at other locations (tel. 599-5555), accepts cards on Cirrus, Honor, and Metroteller networks. Southeast Bank, N.A., 1390 Brickell Ave., and at other locations (tel. 599-2265), is on line with the Plus network. For additional bank locations, dial toll free 800/424-7787 for the Cirrus network, toll free 800/843-7587 for the Plus network.

Banks making **cash advances** against MasterCard and VISA cards include Barnett Bank (tel. toll free 800/342-8472), Florida National Bank (tel. 593-6200), and NCNB National Bank (tel. toll free 800/524-8114).

Newspapers/Magazines The well-respected *Miami Herald* is the city's best-selling daily. It is especially known for its mammoth Sunday edition, and its excellent Friday "Weekend" entertainment guide. There are literally dozens of specialized Miami magazines geared toward tourists and natives alike. Many are free, and can be picked up at hotels, restaurants, and in vending machines all around town. The best entertainment freebie is the weekly tabloid *New Times*. But keep an eye out for *Welcome, Key, Miami Beach News, Coral Gables News, Florida Sports,* and others. *South Florida* is the area's best glossy for upscale readers.

Photographic Needs Drugstores and supermarkets are probably the cheapest places to purchase film. You'll pay loads more for the same product at specialized kiosks near tourist attractions. One Hour Photo in the Bayside Marketplace (tel. 377-FOTO) charges $16 to develop and print a roll of 36 pictures. Open Monday through Saturday from 10am to 10pm and on Sunday from noon to 8pm. Coconut Grove Camera, 2911 Grand Ave. (tel. 445-0521), features 30-minute color processing and maintains a huge selection of cameras and equipment. They rent, too.

Police For emergencies, dial 911 from any phone. No coins are needed. For other matters, call 595-6263.

Radio/TV About five dozen **radio** stations can be heard in the Greater Miami area. On the AM dial, 610 (WIOD), 790 (WNWS), 1230 (WJNO), and 1340 (WPBR) all specialize in news and talk. WDBF (1420) is a good Big Band station, and WPBG (1290) features golden oldies. The best rock stations on the FM dial include WZTA (94.9), WGTR (97.3), and the progressive rock station WVUM (90.5). WKIS (99.9) is the top country station, and public radio (PBS) can be heard either on WXEL (90.7) or WLRN (91.3).

In addition to cable **television** stations, available in most hotels, all the major networks and a couple of independent stations are represented. They include: Channel 4, WTVJ (NBC); Channel 6, WCIX (CBS); Channel 7, WSVN (Fox); Channel 10, WPLG (ABC); Channel 17, WLRN (PBS); Channel 23, WLTV (independent); and Channel 33, WBFS (independent).

Religious Services Miami houses of worship are as varied as the city's population and include: St. Hugh Catholic Church, 3460 Royal Rd., at the corner of Main Highway (tel. 444-8363); Temple Judea, 5500 Granada Blvd., Coral Gables (tel. 667-5657); Bryan Memorial United Methodist, 3713 Main Hwy. (tel. 443-0880); Christ Episcopal Church, 3481 Hibiscus St. (tel. 442-8542); Plymouth Congregational Church, 3400 Devon Rd., at Main Highway (tel. 444-6521).

Restrooms Stores rarely let customers use the restrooms, and many restaurants offer their facilities for customers only. Most malls have bathrooms, as do many of the ubiquitous fast-food restaurants. Many public beaches and large parks provide toilets; in some places you have to pay, or tip an attendant. Most large hotels have clean restrooms in their lobbies.

Safety Whenever you're traveling in an unfamiliar city or country, stay alert. Be aware of your immediate surroundings. Wear a moneybelt and don't sling your camera or purse over your shoulder. It's your responsibility to be aware and alert, even in the most heavily touristed areas. See also "Safety" in Section 1 of Chapter 3.

Shoe Repair There are dozens of shoe- and leather-repair shops around the city. Check the Miami *Yellow Pages* for the location nearest you, or visit Miller Square Shoe Repair, 13846 SW 56th St. (tel. 387-2875). It's open Monday through Friday from 9am to 7pm and on Saturday until 6pm.

Taxes A 6% state sales tax is added on at the register for all goods and services purchased in Florida. In addition, most municipalities levy special taxes on restaurants and hotels. In Surfside, hotel taxes total 8%; in Bal Harbour, 9%; and in the rest of Dade County, a whopping 11%.

In Miami Beach, Surfside, and Bal Harbour, the resort (hotel) tax also applies to restaurants with liquor licenses.

Taxis See "Getting Around," above.

Telephone, Telex, and Fax Find out how much it costs to use the direct-dial telephone in your hotel room before you pick up the receiver. Hotel surcharges are often astronomical, and even a local call can cost 75¢ or more! You can often save yourself a lot of money by using one of the hotel's public telephones in the lobby.

Most large Miami hotels have telex and/or facsimile (fax) machines; their numbers are included in this book with the appropriate listings. You should know that many hotels charge several dollars per page even to *receive* fax messages! Beware of the Hotel Copy service, and other high-price fax services.

Time Miami, like New York, is in the eastern standard time zone. Between April and October, eastern daylight saving time is adopted, and clocks are set one hour ahead. America's eastern seaboard is five hours ahead of Greenwich mean time. To find out what time it is, call 324-8811.

Tipping Waiters and bartenders expect a 15% tip, as do taxi drivers and hairdressers. Porters should be tipped 50¢–$1 per bag, and parking valets should be given $1. It's nice to leave a few dollars on your pillow for the hotel maid, and lavatory attendants will appreciate whatever change you have.

Transit Information For Metrorail or Metromover schedule information, phone 638-6700. See "Getting Around," above, for more information.

Weather For an up-to-date recording of current weather conditions and forecast reports, dial 661-5065.

3. ACCOMMODATIONS

Miami is chock-full of hotels. Whether you're looking to locate on a quiet strip of beach or right in the heart of the hustle, accommodation possibilities seem endless. Hotels here offer a huge variety of locations and services, and they appeal to a multiplicity of personalities and pocketbooks.

You may already know that South Florida's tourist season is well defined, beginning in mid-November and lasting through Easter. From the season's commencement, hotel prices escalate until about February, after which they again begin to decline. During the off-season, hotel rates are typically 30%–50% lower than their winter highs. Oceanfront rooms are also more accessible between Easter and November, as are shops, roads, and restaurants.

But timing isn't everything. In many cases, rates will also depend on your hotel's proximity to the beach and how much ocean you can see from your window. Small motels, a block or two from the water, can be up to 40% cheaper than similar properties right on the sand. When a hotel *is* right on the beach, it is probable that its oceanfront rooms will be significantly more expensive than similar accommodations in the rear. Still, despite their higher prices, oceanfront rooms can often be hard to get; if you desire one, a reservation is definitely recommended.

There are so many hotels in Miami—in every price range—that few regularly fill to capacity. Even during the height of the tourist season, you can usually drive right into the city and find decent accommodations fairly quickly. But be careful. If you have your sights set on one particular hotel, if you have to have an oceanfront room, or if you want to stay in an area where accommodations are not particularly plentiful, you should reserve your room in advance.

Hotel toll-free telephone numbers will save you time and money when inquiring about rates and availability. Some of the larger hotel reservations chains with properties in the Miami area include: Best Western (tel. toll free 800/528-1234), Days Inns (tel. toll free 800/325-2525), Holiday Inn (tel. toll free 800/465-4329), Howard Johnson (tel. toll free 800/228-9000), Quality Inns (tel. toll free 800/228-5151), Ramada Inns (tel. toll free 800/272-6232), and TraveLodge (tel. toll free 800/255-3050).

If, after inquiring about room availability at the hotels listed in this book, you still come up empty-handed (an extremely unlikely prospect), look for an availability along Miami Beach's Collins Avenue. There are dozens of hotels and motels on this strip—in all price categories—so a room is bound to be available.

To help you decide on the accommodations option that's best for you, hotels below are divided first by area, then by price, using the following guide: "Expensive," more than $130; "Moderate," $80–$130; and "Budget," less than $80. Prices are for an average double room during the high season. Read carefully. Many hotels also offer rooms at rates above and below the price category they have been assigned. Most hotel rates are significantly lower between Easter and Thanksgiving.

Prices listed below *do not include state and city taxes,* which, in most parts of Miami, total 11% (see "Fast Facts: Miami," above). Be aware that many hotels make additional charges for parking and levy heavy surcharges for telephone use. Some, especially those in South Miami Beach, also tack on an additional service charge. Inquire about these extras before committing. Room rates include breakfast where noted.

MIAMI BEACH

You probably have never seen more hotels than the solid wall of high-rises that seems to go on forever along Collins Avenue. The buildings are so effective at blocking the ocean from the view of passersby that you hardly know you're driving along the coast. But reserve a room at one of these behemoths and you'll have some of the world's best beach at your doorstep.

Most of these big beach resorts are so encompassing that it's possible to spend your entire stay on the premises of a single hotel. But when you're ready to explore, Miami Beach is within easy reach of the art deco district and the mainland just across the bay.

EXPENSIVE

THE ALEXANDER ALL-SUITE LUXURY HOTEL, 5225 Collins Ave., Miami Beach, FL 33140. Tel. 305/865-6500, or toll free 800/327-6121. Fax 305/864-8525. Telex 808172. 150 suites. A/C MINIBAR TV TEL

$ Rates: Dec 17–Easter, $205–$415 one-bedroom suite; $295–$550 two-bedroom suite. Easter–Dec 16, $270–$540 one-bedroom suite; $370–$750 two-bedroom suite. Additional person $25 extra. Children under 18 stay free in parents' room. Packages available. AE, CB, DC, MC, V. **Parking:** $8.

One of the nicest offerings on Miami Beach, the Alexander is an all-suite hotel, featuring spacious one- and two-bedroom mini-apartments. All suites have a living room, a fully equipped kitchen, two bathrooms, and a balcony. The hotel itself is well decorated with fine sculptures, paintings, antiques, and tapestries, most of which were garnered from the Cornelius Vanderbilt mansion. The pretty hotel's two oceanfront pools are surrounded by lush vegetation; one of the "lagoons" is also fed by a cascading waterfall.

Dining/Entertainment: Dominique's, a gourmet restaurant for a top-drawer dinner, offers French cuisine featuring seafood, rack of lamb, rattlesnake, and Everglades alligator. There's also a piano lounge and a pool bar.

Services: Valet/laundry service, room service, turn-down service, currency exchange.

Facilities: Two heated freshwater swimming pools, four Jacuzzis, Sunfish and catamaran rentals; gift shop.

DORAL OCEAN BEACH RESORT, 4833 Collins Ave., Miami Beach, FL 33140. Tel. 305/532-3600, or toll free 800/223-6725. Fax 305/534-7409. 293 rms, 127 suites. A/C MINIBAR TV TEL

$ Rates: Dec 21–Apr, $180–$285 single or double; from $290 suite. May–Dec 20, $120–$200 single or double; from $240 suite. Additional person $20 extra. Weekend and other packages available. AE, CB, DC, DISC, MC, V. **Parking:** $9.

The 18-story Doral Resort stands guard over Collins Avenue with the proud self-confidence of a truly grand hotel. This is one of the beach's famous "big boys," and it's one of the city's luxury leaders. For an oceanfront resort, the hotel is relatively

3.2 km
2 mi
N
0
5424
FLORIDA
Miami
Alexander All-Suite Luxury Hotel 14
Avalon Hotel 28
Cavalier Hotel 22
Clay Hotel & Youth Hostel 21
Colonnade Hotel 36
Coronado Motel 9
Desert Inn 5
Dezerland Surfside Beach Hotel 11
Doral Ocean Beach Resort 15
Doubletree Hotel at Coconut Grove 38
Driftwood Resort Motel 6
Eden Roc Hotel and Marina 16
Essex House 27
Fontainebleau Hilton 17
Golden Sands 13
Grand Bay Hotel 37
Hilyard Manor Oceanfront Suites 8
Hotel Inter-Continental
Biscayne Canal
95
NORTH MIAMI
Opa-Locka Airfield
NE 6th Ave.
NW 135th St.
NE 135th St.
BAL HARBOUR
NE 125th St.
Miami Blvd.
Broad Causeway
96th St.
Gratigny Dr.
Red Rd.
1
Biscayne Park
A1A
Opa-Locka Canal
NW 103rd St.
NE 103rd St.
Collins Ave.
HIALEAH
NW 95th St.
Biscayne Blvd.
SURFSIDE
Amtrak Terminal
W 29th St.
E 8th Ave.
E 25th St.
NW 27th Ave.
NW 22nd Ave.
NW 79th St.
NE 79th St.
J.F. Kennedy Causeway
71st St.
LITTLE HAITI
NW 17th Ave.
W 4th Ave.
Palm Ave.
E 4th Ave.
NW 7th Ave.
North Miami Ave.
Alton Rd.
E 9th St.
NW 62nd St.
NE 2nd Ave.
Morningside Park
Hialeah Dr.
NW 54th St.
Okeechobee Rd.
Airport Expressway
112
Julia Tuttle Causeway
41st St.
27
NW 36th St.
195
Miami International Airport
NW 20th St.
MIAMI BEACH
1 2 3 4 5 6 7 8 9 10 11 12 13 14 15 16 17 18 19

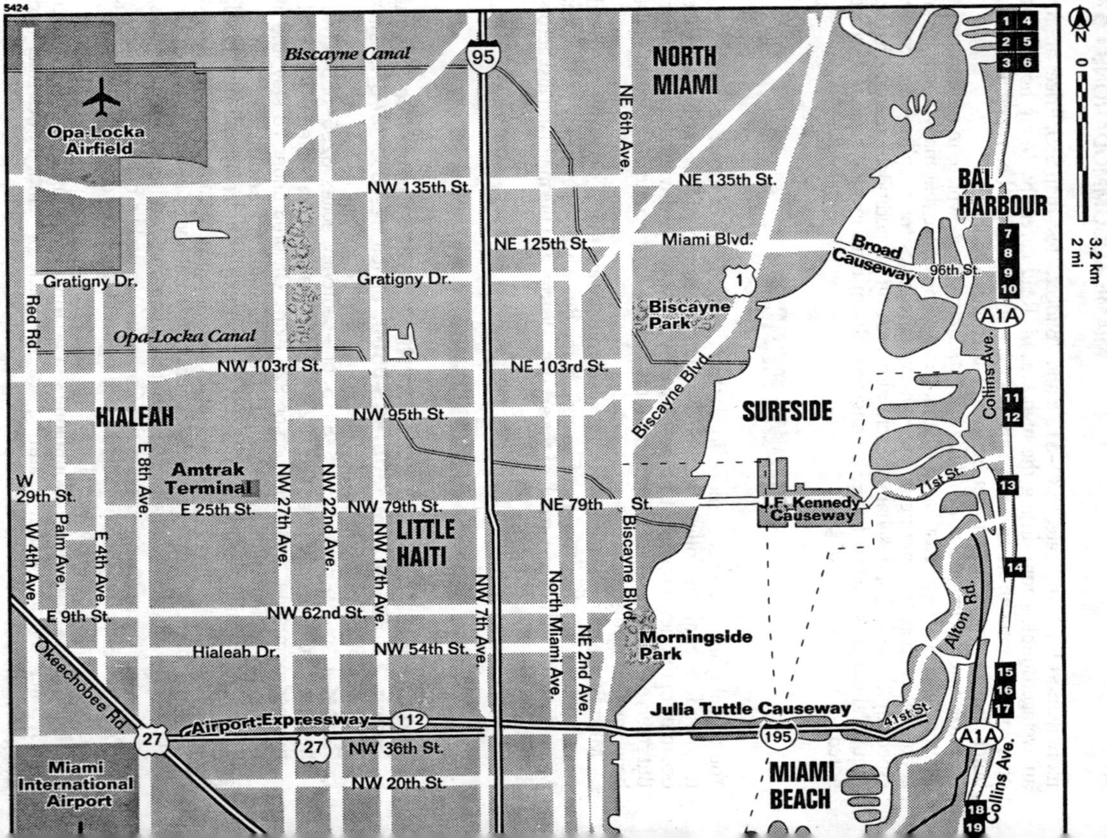

MIAMI AREA ACCOMMODATIONS

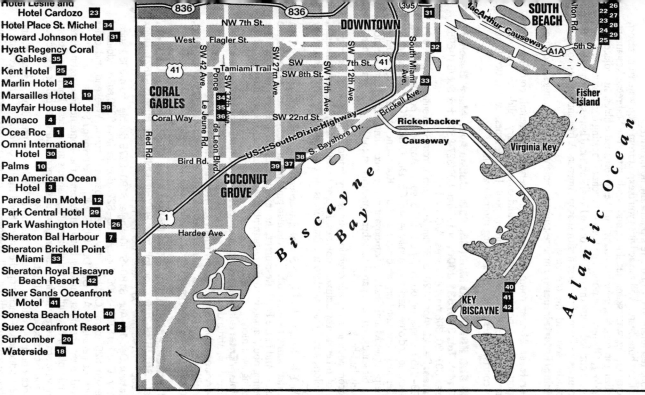

Hotel Leslie and Hotel Cardozo 23
Hotel Place St. Michel 34
Howard Johnson Hotel 31
Hyatt Regency Coral Gables 35
Kent Hotel 25
Marlin Hotel 24
Marsailles Hotel 19
Mayfair House Hotel 39
Monaco 4
Ocea Roc 1
Omni International Hotel 30
Palms 10
Pan American Ocean Hotel 3
Paradise Inn Motel 12
Park Central Hotel 29
Park Washington Hotel 26
Sheraton Bal Harbour 7
Sheraton Brickell Point Miami 33
Sheraton Royal Biscayne Beach Resort 42
Silver Sands Oceanfront Motel 41
Sonesta Beach Hotel 40
Suez Oceanfront Resort 2
Surfcomber 20
Waterside 18

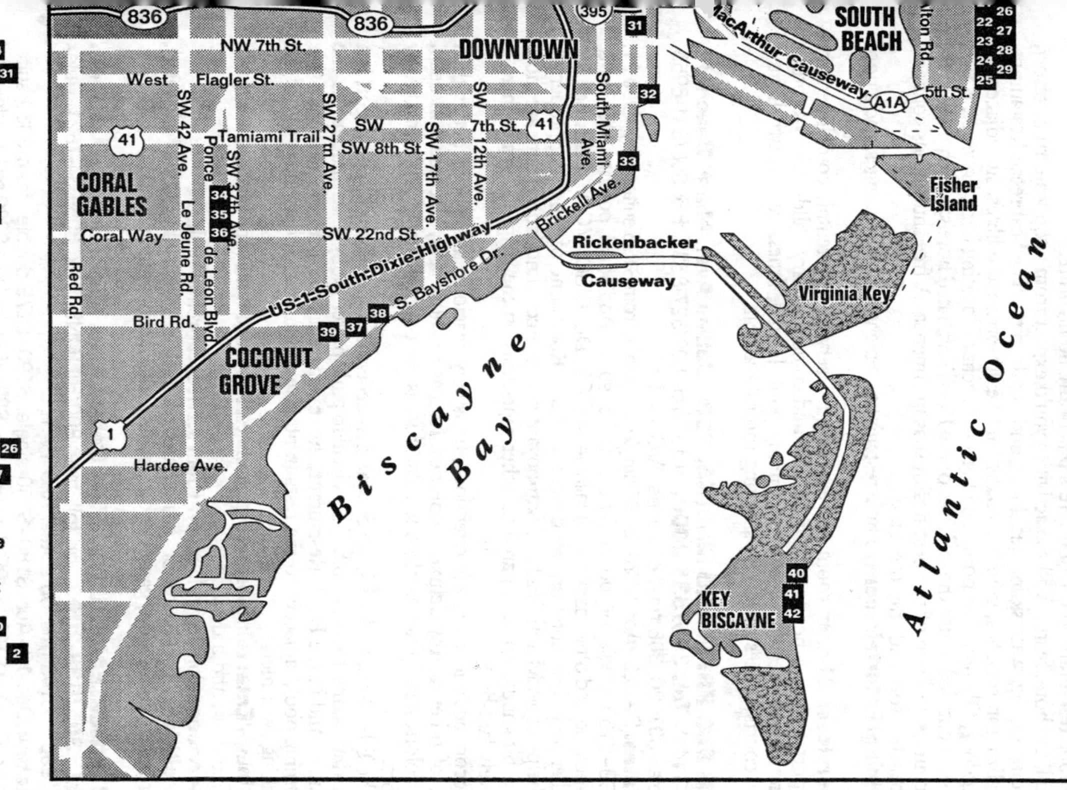

quiet. Its immediate neighbors are private apartment buildings and, except for its 18th-floor restaurant, the Doral offers practically no nightlife.

Still, the hotel features all the activities you'd expect from a top waterfront resort, including sailing, waterskiing, jet skiing, and windsurfing. The Seabreeze Restaurant, specializing in stir-fries, gourmet pizzas, and health-oriented edibles, sits adjacent to an outdoor, Olympic-size pool. The biggest benefit of locating here, however, is that guests are entitled to use the facilities of the Doral's affiliated hotels, which include six golf courses and one of the best health spas in America. A free shuttle bus connects this beach resort with the others.

Dining/Entertainment: Three restaurants, a nightclub, two lounges, and a pool bar.

Services: 24-hour room service, laundry service, car rental, complimentary transportation to other resorts, child care and complimentary child-activity center.

Facilities: Heated outdoor swimming pool, Jacuzzi, fitness center, two lighted tennis courts, games room; no-smoking rooms available.

EDEN ROC HOTEL AND MARINA, 4525 Collins Ave., Miami Beach, FL 33140. Tel. 305/531-0000, or toll free 800/327-8337. Fax 305/531-6955. Telex 807120. 306 rms, 45 suites. A/C TV TEL

$ Rates: Dec 22–Apr, $120–$185 single or double; from $195 suite. May–Dec 21, $99–$160 single or double; from $175 suite. Additional person $15 extra. Weekend and other packages available. AE, CB, DC, DISC, MC, V. **Parking:** $8.

Another long-time hotel on the beach, the Eden Roc is one of those big properties that helped give Miami Beach its flamboyant image. Accommodations here are more than a bit gaudy, but compared to other monoliths on the strip, the atmosphere is relatively laid-back.

Accommodations are unpretentious, unusually spacious, and priced better than those of other nearby deluxe properties. Rooms are alternately decorated in deep, dark colors, and lighter earth tones. Bathrooms are covered with marble and pretty mirrors.

The Eden Roc, with its huge crystal chandeliers and marble-and-brass decor, is a hotel that wants to show off. The circular pink pastel lobby is as fanciful as the entrance. And in the Porch Restaurant, the transparent glass sides of the lounge-side swimming pool, adjacent to the restaurant, give drinkers an underwater view of the frolicking swimmers.

Dining/Entertainment: Three lounges, two restaurants (one fancy, one casual), a coffee shop, and a deli.

Services: Concierge, laundry, room service, car-rental desk.

Facilities: Two outdoor swimming pools (one freshwater, one saltwater), water-sports concession, games room, beauty salon, shopping arcade.

FONTAINEBLEAU HILTON, 4441 Collins Ave., Miami Beach, FL 33140. Tel. 305/538-2000, or toll free 800/HILTONS. Fax 305/534-7821. Telex 519362. 1,143 rms, 63 suites. A/C TV TEL

$ Rates: Dec 16–Apr, $180–$250 single; $190–$275 double; from $330 suite. May–Dec 15, $130–$205 single; $150–$225 double; from $300 suite. Additional person $20 extra. Children stay free in parents' room. Weekend and other packages available. AE, CB, DC, DISC, MC, V. **Parking:** $8.

Far and away the most famous hotel in Miami, the Fontainebleau (pronounced "fountain-blue") has built its reputation on garishness and excess. For most visitors, the massive structure with its free-form swimming pool and waterfall, is a spectacle more tourist attraction than hotel.

Since opening its doors in 1954, the hotel has hosted presidents, pageants, and movie productions—including the James Bond thriller *Goldfinger.* The sheer size of the Fontainebleau, with its full complement of restaurants, stores, recreational facilities, and over 1,100 employees, makes this a perfect hotel for conventioneers. Unfortunately, the same recommendation can not be extended to individual travelers. It's easy to get lost here, both physically and personally. The lobby is terminally crowded, the staff is overworked, and lines are always long. Still, this is the one and only Fontainebleau, in many ways the quintessential Miami hotel. Facilities are terrific and, for all its shortcomings, this is one place you'll never forget.

Dining/Entertainment: Four large restaurants include the flagship Dining Galleries, featuring continental cuisine, and Chez Bon Bon, which serves breakfast, lunch, and dinner. There are a half dozen or so other cafés and coffee shops (including two by the pool), as well as a number of cocktail lounges, including the Poodle Lounge, which offers live entertainment and dancing nightly. Club Tropigala (see "Evening Entertainment" in Chapter 5), just off the lobby, features a "Las Vegas-style" floor show with dozens of performers and not one, but two orchestras.

Services: Room service, house doctor, limousine service, complimentary child care during holidays and summer, laundry service.

Facilities: Shopping arcade with 28 shops, games room, two outdoor swimming pools (one freshwater, one saltwater), three whirlpool baths, seven lighted tennis courts, award-winning health spa, special activities for children; no-smoking rooms available.

MODERATE

DEZERLAND SURFSIDE BEACH HOTEL, 8701 Collins Ave., Miami Beach, FL 33154. Tel. 305/865-6661, or toll free 800/331-9346, 800/331-9347 in Canada. Fax 305/866-2630. Telex 4973649. 225 rms. A/C TV TEL

$ Rates: Dec 26–Mar, $85–$125 single or double; Apr–Dec 25, $60–$75 single or double. Additional person $8 extra. Children under 19 stay free in parents' room. Special packages and group rates available. AE, CB, DC, MC, V. **Parking:** Free.

Designed by car enthusiast Michael Dezer, Dezerland is an unusual place—part hotel and part 1950s automobile wonderland. Visitors are welcomed by a 1959 Cadillac stationed by the front door, and a '55 Thunderbird hardtop sits in the lobby. A dozen other mint-condition classics are scattered about the floors, while walls are decorated with related '50s and '60s memorabilia.

Billed as "America's largest '50s extravaganza," this unique Quality Inn member features rooms that are named after some of Detroit's most famous models. Dezerland is located directly on the beach and features a mosaic of a pink Cadillac at the bottom of its surfside swimming pool.

Dining/Entertainment: American Classics restaurant and a lobby lounge with nightly entertainment.

Services: Laundry, babysitting.

Facilities: Adjacent tennis courts, gift shop featuring '50s memorabilia; no-smoking rooms available.

BUDGET

THE GOLDEN SANDS, 6910 Collins Ave., Miami Beach, FL 33141. Tel. 305/866-8734, or toll free 800/932-0333, 800/423-5170 in Canada. Fax 305/866-0187. Telex 6974107. 80 rms, 20 efficiencies. A/C TV TEL

$ Rates: Dec–Mar, $50–$60 single; $57–$77 double; $80 efficiency. Apr–Nov, $43 single; $47–$57 double; $60 efficiency. Additional person $10 extra. Children stay free in parents' room. AE, MC, V. **Parking:** $5.

Furnishings and decor are a bit dated in this 1950s-era hotel, but excellent rates and good services make the Golden Sands one of the best deals in Miami Beach. Located on the corner of 69th Street, right on the ocean, the hotel sports a large pool, an indoor lounge, and an inexpensive restaurant catering to a primarily German clientele.

PARADISE INN MOTEL, 8520 Harding Ave., Miami Beach, FL 33141. Tel. 305/865-6216. Fax 305/865-9028. 48 rms, 48 efficiencies. A/C TV TEL

$ Rates: Dec 21–Jan 23 and Mar 6–Apr 15, $40 single; $44 double. Jan 24–Mar 5, $44 single; $48 double. Apr 16–June and Sept–Dec 20, $28 single; $32 double.

FROMMER'S SMART TRAVELER: HOTELS

1. Always remember that at any time of year a hotel room is a perishable commodity: If it's not sold, the revenue is lost forever. Therefore, it is a fact that rates are linked to the hotel's occupancy level. If it's 90% occupied, the price goes up; if it's 50% occupied, the price goes down. So always try negotiating by stating *your* price.
2. In summer, ask about summer discounts. At this time of year, hotels in Miami are very negotiable. Downtown hotels are less elastic.
3. Many hotels offer big discounts or package rates on weekends (Friday to Sunday night). If you're staying on a weekend, always ask about these. Downtown hotels are more elastic.
4. Before selecting a hotel, always ask about parking charges. Charges can be as much as $10—a big difference if you're planning on staying a while.

July–Aug, $30 single; $34 double. Add $31 per person for efficiencies. Additional person in efficiencies $3 extra. Children under 13 stay free in parents' room. AE, CB, DC, DISC, MC, V.

It's amazing how inexpensive simple, clean, and perfectly acceptable accommodations can be just one block from the ocean in Miami Beach. Nothing fancy here, but all rooms in this cedar-roofed motel have color television and air conditioning. The motel features free parking and laundry facilities, and it's a two-minute walk from public tennis courts and the huge beachfront North Shore Park. Harding Avenue runs parallel to Collins Avenue.

THE WATERSIDE, 2360 Collins Ave., Miami Beach, FL 33139. Tel. 305/538-1951. Fax 305/531-3217. 100 rms. AC TV TEL

$ **Rates:** Dec 16–Apr, $75–$90 single or double; May–Dec 15, $40–$60 single or double. Additional person $10 extra. Children stay free in parents' room. AE, DC, MC, V.

Across Collins Avenue from the beach, the Waterside is a medium-size bilevel motel popular with European tourists. The new owners, French-born Gérard and Maryse Meulien, recently sold their hotel in Marseille to give their full attention to the completely renovated Waterside. This blue-and-white motel wraps around a large swimming pool and features simple, well-kept rooms with free parking and excellent rates.

SOUTH MIAMI BEACH

I love to stay in South Miami Beach. Hotels here are not stuffy, nor are they too fancy. They are well located, pretty, and surrounded by well-priced restaurants and some of Miami's best nightlife options.

Ocean Drive, an inviting 10-block strip inside Miami's historic art deco district is, hands down, the beach's best esplanade. Fronting the Atlantic Ocean, this historic street is lined with squat, ice cream–colored hotels and coconut palms taller than most of the buildings.

Collins Avenue, just one block back, runs parallel to Ocean Drive. This pretty stretch of the street is not on the water, but staying here—or even farther from the beach—usually means lower room rates and easier parking.

EXPENSIVE

THE MARLIN, 1200 Collins Ave., South Miami Beach, FL 33139. Tel. 305/673-8770. Fax 305/673-9609. 10 rms, 7 suites. A/C TV TEL

$ **Rates:** Dec–Apr, $170 studio; $185 one-bedroom suite; $205 deluxe one-bedroom suite; $250 two-bedroom suite. May–Nov, $95 studio; $105 one-bedroom suite; $125 deluxe one-bedroom suite; $150 two-bedroom suite. AE, CB, DC, DISC, MC, V.

Opened in early 1992 after extensive renovations and a complete exterior make-over, this hotel is visually one of the most outstanding on the beach. The hotel's proprietor, former Island Records owner Chris Blackwell, has attracted a rock-and-roll clientele that has made an instant hit out of the high-profile Marlin. The hotel's beautifully lit powder-blue exterior gives way to a far less grand interior filled with gaily painted but rather small and simple rooms and suites.

Although the relatively high prices might not be warranted by the quality of the rooms themselves, contemporary touches and an in-the-know staff give guests a sense of being someplace special. In addition to a kitchenette, every Jamaican-style room is outfitted with a TV, VCR, CD player, and a host of tropical toiletries. Deluxe one-bedroom suites have two bathrooms. Room service is provided by Shabeen, the hotel's in-house Caribbean restaurant.

MODERATE

AVALON HOTEL, 700 Ocean Dr., Miami Beach, FL 33139. Tel. 305/538-0133, or toll free 800/933-3306. Fax 305/534-0258. 60 rms. A/C TV TEL

$ **Rates** (including continental breakfast): Oct 15–May 15, $85–$135 single or double. May 16–Oct 14, $55–$110 single or double. Additional person $10 extra. 10% discount for stays of seven days or more. Weekly packages available. AE, MC, V. **Parking:** $6.

The Avalon is an excellent example of classic art deco digs right on the beach. Occupying a pretty parcel that wraps around the corner of 7th Street, the hotel is striking both inside and out. Rooms are well decorated in traditional '30s style, and all are equipped with compact refrigerators, cable televisions, and individually controlled air conditioning. The hotel's modest lobby is occupied by a casual restaurant, best for sandwiches at lunch either inside or on the outdoor patio.

The experienced management, known for their excellent inns in Newport, Rhode Island, run this hotel with an even hand. If the Avalon is full, don't hesitate to accept a room in their other property, the Majestic, located across the street.

Dining/Entertainment: The lobby restaurant is a top pick in the area for an informal lunch or a relaxing snack. By night, the menu gets fancier, prices get higher, and the cozy bar becomes a romantic place to pass the time.

Services: Like other hotels on the strip, reception can arrange car rental, babysitting, hairstyling, and other services.

CAVALIER HOTEL AND CABANA CLUB, 1320 Ocean Dr., Miami Beach, FL 33139. Tel. 305/534-2135, or toll free 800/338-9076. Fax 305/531-5543. Telex 204978. 43 rms, 2 suites. A/C TV TEL

$ **Rates** (including continental breakfast): Oct 16–Apr 14, $105–$135 single or double; $175 suite. Apr 15–Oct 15, $65–$120 single or double; $150 suite. All rates subject to 10% service charge. AE, DC, DISC, MC, V.

This architectural masterpiece, built in 1936, was one of Ocean Drive's first art deco renovations. Completely restored in 1987, the Cavalier now sports central air conditioning, beautifully restored period furnishings, and an ultra-contemporary atmosphere recalling less-hurried times.

Popular with fashion photography crews, rooms here are luxuriously carpeted, and guests are pampered with fluffy towels, fresh mineral water, and a newspaper every morning. Still, this place is no stuffed shirt. Like other area hotels, there are no parking attendants, no porters, and not a single tie in sight. The Cavalier is on the best strip on the beach, within walking distance to area's most noted restaurants and clubs. Still, it's easy to get a quiet night's sleep here as the lobby is devoid of bars, bands, or restaurants.

A full continental breakfast buffet, including fresh fruit and croissants, is served in the breakfast room each morning.

Services: Reception can make arrangements for hair cutting, massage, limousine, and laundry services.

ESSEX HOUSE, 1001 Collins Ave., Miami Beach, FL 33139. Tel. 305/534-2700, or toll free 800/55-ESSEX. Fax 305/532-3827. 38 rms, 12 suites. A/C TV TEL

$ **Rates** (including continental breakfast): Oct–May 1, $100–$145 single or double; $155–$185 petite suite; $205–$310 grande suite. May 2–Sept, about 20% lower. 10% service charge additional. Two-night minimum on weekends, three nights on holidays. AE, MC, V.

This art deco delight is one of South Beach's plushest gems. Now a TraveLodge affiliate, the pretty Essex House is the result of a painstaking restoration, a textbook example of the famous "Streamline Moderne" style, complete with large porthole windows, original etched glasswork, ziggurat arches, and detailed crown moldings. The solid oak bedroom furnishings are also original and, like many other details in this special hotel, were painstakingly restored.

Murphy's homey, personal touches include teddy bears on the beds, "touch-sensitive" lamps, and an extremely attentive staff. The Essex also features 24-hour reception, a high-tech piano in the lobby/lounge, and a state-of-the-art security system.

Located just one block from the ocean, this hotel is both romantic and spick-and-span clean. Smoking is not permitted in any of the rooms and, according to the hotel staff, children are "inappropriate" here.

Dining/Entertainment: The hotel's lobby/lounge is sort of an all-purpose room serving light lunches, afternoon tea, and evening cocktails. Pianists sometimes entertain.

Services: Limousine, babysitting, laundry service, evening turn-down.

HOTEL LESLIE and HOTEL CARDOZO, 1244 and 1300 Ocean Dr., Miami Beach, FL 33139. Tel. 305/534-2135, or toll free 800/338-9076. Fax 305/531-5543. Telex 204978. 69 rms, 8 suites. A/C TV TEL

$ **Rates** (including continental breakfast): Oct 16–Apr 15, $105–$135 single or double; $175 suite. Apr 16–Oct 15, $65–$120 single or double; $150 suite. All rates subject to 10% service charge. AE, DC, DISC, MC, V.

Operated by Tecton Management, the Leslie and the Cardozo were among the first properties on Ocean Drive to undergo extensive renovation.

Designed by noted architect Albert Anis in 1937, the Leslie is one of the area's smallest and quietest hotels. The light and airy beds and bureaus that dominate the hotel's art nouveau interior are a departure from the building's distinct art deco design. Still, the modern furniture and whimsical wall hangings look right in place.

The 40-room Cardozo is equally cozy but, by contrast, contains original walnut furniture and a new, as yet unnamed lobby restaurant and bar. It was here that Frank Sinatra filmed the 1950s movie *Hole in the Head;* today the hotel's soft pastels still grace the background of many fashion shoots.

These hotels are among the best in Miami. Guests in each are pampered with free morning newspapers and a hearty continental breakfast buffet.

Services: Reception can make arrangements for hair cutting, massage, babysitting, limousine, and laundry services.

PARK CENTRAL HOTEL, 640 Ocean Dr., Miami Beach, FL 33139. Tel. 305/538-1611. Fax 305/534-7520. 80 rms. A/C TV TEL

$ **Rates** (including continental breakfast): Dec–Apr, $75–$135 single or double. May–Nov, $55–$110 single or double. Additional person $10 extra. Senior discounts available. AE, DISC, DC, MC, V.

The Park Central is an architectural masterpiece, and one of the prettiest art deco hotels on the beach. Built in 1937, and reestablished 50 years later by New York developer Tony Goldman, the hotel competently combines the sophisticated style of a bygone era with the excitement and services of a modern-day hotspot. The smallish rooms are comparable, both in size and appointments, to others on the block, all with color TVs and direct-dial phones.

Dining/Entertainment: The Borroco restaurant, in the lobby's rear, serves competent Italian food at moderate to high prices. Sip a cocktail in the lobby; it's a great place to see and be seen, especially on weekend nights when it's quite crowded.

Services: If you're staying in the hotel, Borroco delivers. Limousine, laundry, and other services can be arranged at reception.

BUDGET

CLAY HOTEL & YOUTH HOSTEL, 1438 Washington Ave., Miami Beach, FL 33139. Tel. 305/534-2988. Fax 305/673-0346. 180 beds.

$ **Rates:** $21–$23 single; $25–$29 double; $10–$13 per person in a multishare. Sheets $2 extra; $3 per night extra for non-IYHF members. Weekly rates available. MC, V.

A member of the International Youth Hostel Federation (IYHF), the Clay occupies a beautiful 1920s-style Spanish Mediterranean building at the corner of historic Espanola Way. Like other IYHF members, this hostel is open to all ages and is a great place to meet like-minded travelers. The usual smattering of Australians, Europeans, and other budget travelers make this place the best clearinghouse of "inside" travel information in Miami. Even if you don't stay here, you might want to check out the ride board and make some friends.

Understandably, rooms here are basic. Reservations are recommended from December through April, and the above rates reflect accommodations with and without air conditioning.

KENT HOTEL, 1131 Collins Ave., Miami Beach, FL 33139. Tel. 305/531-6771. Fax 305/531-0720. 56 rms. A/C TV TEL

$ **Rates** (including continental breakfast): Dec 15–Easter, $50–$60 single or double. Easter–Dec 14, $40–$50 single or double. Weekly discounts available. AE, MC, V.

The well-located Kent is an excellent example of the way hotel prices drop dramatically when you get away from Ocean Drive. Typically art deco, the squat Kent is not fancy, and is elegant only in a historical kind of way. Still, the hotel is comfortable and full of character. Breakfast is served both inside and on the porch, and street parking is always available.

MARSEILLES HOTEL, 1741 Collins Ave., Miami Beach, FL 33139. Tel. 305/538-5711, or toll free 800/327-4739. Fax 305/673-1006. Telex 441106. 94 rms, 6 suites. A/C TV TEL

$ **Rates** (including continental breakfast): Dec 21–Easter, $65–$70 single or double, $70 single or double with kitchenette; $75 suite. Easter–Dec 20, $45–$50 single or double, $50 single or double with kitchenette; $55 suite. Additional person $5 extra. Children under 8 stay free in parents' room. AE, DC, MC, V. **Parking:** $4.

A skyscraper by area standards, this pretty and basic hotel is not one of the area's fanciest, but it is well located, well run, and extremely well priced. The hotel's furnishings are outdated but functional, and all rooms come equipped with a refrigerator and remote-control television. The Marseilles's lobby café, a casual eatery with light American food, is welcoming, but a short walk in almost any direction will put you right in the middle of some of the area's hottest nightspots and eateries.

PARK WASHINGTON HOTEL, 1020 Washington Ave., Miami Beach, FL 33139. Tel. 305/532-1930. Fax 305/672-6706. 35 rms, 15 suites. A/C TV TEL

$ **Rates:** Nov–Apr, $49 single; $69 double; $129–$170 suite. May–Oct, $39 single; $59 double; $119–$160 suite. Additional person $10 extra. Children stay free in parents' room. AE, MC, V.

The Park Washington, a newly refurbished, large hotel offers some of the best values in South Beach. Located three blocks from the ocean, this hotel is trying to make a name for itself by offering good-quality accommodations at incredible prices. It's not too fancy here. But unlike many other hotels in the area that accept long-term residents, this hostelry is strictly geared toward tourists.

Originally designed in the 1930s by Henry Hohauser, one of the beach's most famous architects, the new Park Washington reopened only in 1989. Most of the rooms do not have original furnishings, but they do include color TVs, direct-dial telephones, refrigerators, and individual air conditioning and heating.

THE SURFCOMBER, 1717 Collins Ave., Miami Beach, FL 33139. Tel. 305/532-7715, or toll free 800/336-4264. Fax 305/532-7280. 194 rms. A/C TV TEL

$ Rates (including continental breakfast): Dec 15–Easter, $60–$80 single or double. Easter–June 19, $50–$70 single or double. June 20–Dec 14, $45–$65 single or double. Kitchenettes $5 per day extra. Children under 15 stay free in parents' room. Monthly and seasonal rates, and senior discounts available. AE, CB, DISC, DC, MC, V.

Family-owned since 1949, the Surfcomber has been one of the art deco district's traditional standbys since the beginning. Well located and fronting 150 feet of beach, the hotel has been undergoing continual renovations for years. Some rooms are definitely more desirable than others, but all feature direct-dial phones and in-room movies. Refrigerators are available upon request.

Hotel services include a coffee shop, a gift shop, a health-food restaurant, and an outdoor bar alongside an Olympic-size heated swimming pool.

SURFSIDE, BAL HARBOUR & SUNNY ISLES

The residents of Surfside, Bal Harbour, and Sunny Isles like to think of their towns as more exclusive and sedate than the overpopulated, frenetic Miami Beach to the south. In reality, though, these towns are so similar to Miami Beach that most of their hotels use Miami Beach in their addresses. However, they're significantly farther than Miami Beach from Coconut Grove and downtown. On the plus side, the beaches here are just as good as Miami Beach's, and hotel prices are some of the lowest in Miami.

EXPENSIVE

PAN AMERICAN OCEAN HOTEL, 17875 Collins Ave., Sunny Isles, FL 33160. Tel. 305/932-1100, or toll free 800/327-5678. Fax 305/935-2769. Telex 6812038. 138 rms, 4 suites. A/C MINIBAR TV TEL

$ Rates: Dec 24–Apr, $139–$185 single or double; from $185 suite. May–Oct, $85–$125 single or double; from $130 suite. Nov–Dec 23, $99–$145 single or double; from $140 suite. Additional person $15 extra. Children under 17 stay free in parents' room. Weekend and other packages, and senior discounts available. AE, CB, DC, DISC, MC, V. **Parking:** Free.

A Radisson Resort, the Pan American is situated on the waterfront and is a good choice for businesspeople as well as tourists. Located close to the Broward County line, the hotel is minutes from the exclusive Bal Harbour shops, and it's equidistant from Miami and Fort Lauderdale airports.

Each room offers twice-daily maid service, ceiling fans, and complimentary morning newspaper. Most have an ocean view and overlook a lively pool area. The Pan American is not deluxe, but accommodations are high quality and offer all the necessary amenities—and more. The staff is exceedingly friendly, and a full schedule of guest activities is scheduled daily.

Dining/Entertainment: The Ocean Terrace, an attractive dining room and lounge, is complemented by the less formal Terrace Café and (weather permitting) a poolside grill. There are bars inside and out. Entertainment varies seasonally, but there's often a solo pianist in the lounge.

Services: Room service, complimentary afternoon tea, coin-operated laundry machines, scheduled guest activities, daily transportation to local shops and racetrack.

FROMMER'S COOL FOR KIDS: HOTELS

Doral Ocean Beach Resort *(see p. 57)* The Doral provides child care and a complimentary children's activity center.

Fontainebleau Hilton Hotel *(see p. 60)* Offering play groups and child care during holiday periods, the Fontainebleau has a waterfall swimming pool that's a child's dream come true.

Sonesta Beach Hotel *(see p. 70)* The Sonesta offers a "Just Us Kids" program and a free, supervised play group for children 5–13. Experienced counselors lead morning field trips as well as daily beach games and evening activities.

Facilities: Swimming pool, nine-hole putting green, four tennis courts, games room, gift shop, hair salon.

SHERATON BAL HARBOUR, 9701 Collins Ave., Bal Harbour, FL 33154. Tel. 305/865-7511, or toll free 800/325-3535. Fax 305/864-2601. Telex 519355. 625 rms, 50 suites. A/C MINIBAR TV TEL

$ Rates: Dec 16–Easter, $225–$310 single or double; from $415 suite. Easter–Dec 15, $155–$235 single or double; from $315 suite. Additional person $25 extra. Children under 18 stay free in parents' room. Weekend and other packages, and senior discounts available. AE, CB, DC, DISC, MC, V. **Parking:** $9.

This hotel has the best location in Bal Harbour, on the ocean and across the street from the swanky Bal Harbour Shops. It's one of the nicest Sheratons I've seen, with large, well-decorated rooms and a two-story glass-enclosed atrium lobby. A spectacular staircase wraps itself around a cascading fountain full of wished-upon pennies.

One side of the hotel caters to corporations, complete with ballrooms and meeting facilities, but the main sections of the hotel are relatively uncongested and removed from the convention crowd. A full complement of aquatic playthings can be rented on the beach, including sailboats and jet skis.

Dining/Entertainment: Seven restaurants and lounges including a pool bar and grill.

Services: Room service, laundry, currency exchange.

Facilities: Two swimming pools, two tennis courts, water-sports concession, gift shop; no-smoking rooms available.

MODERATE

THE PALMS, 9449 Collins Ave., Surfside, FL 33154. Tel. 305/865-3551, or toll free 800/327-6644, 800/843-6974 in Canada. Fax 305/861-6596. 120 rms, 50 efficiencies. A/C TV TEL

$ Rates: Dec 16–Easter, $90–$110 single or double; from $135 suite. Easter–Dec 15, $70–$85 single or double; from $90 suite. Efficiencies $10 extra. Additional person $10 extra. Children stay free in parents' room. Weekly rates available. AE, MC, V. **Parking:** Free.

The Palms is stereotypical Miami Beach. The majority of the guests here are retired. The lobby activity board advertises times for the day's shuffleboard tournaments, and nightlife usually centers around a singer who performs Eddie Fisher standards.

The hotel's management is intent on widening the hotel's popularity, and staying here can be really fun. Rooms are basic but comfortable; many have balconies overlooking the large pool and adjacent waterside bar. Located in the Surfside/Bal Harbour area of Miami Beach, the Palms is recommended for any traveler who wants to stay on the ocean—but still stay on a budget.

BUDGET

CORONADO MOTEL, 9501 Collins Ave., Surfside, FL 33154. Tel. 305/866-1625. 41 rms. A/C TV TEL

$ **Rates:** Dec 15–Jan 15 and Mar 15–Apr, $54–$70 single or double. Jan 16–Mar 14, $64–$80 single or double. May–Dec 14, $39–$59 single or double. Additional person $8 extra in winter, $5 extra in summer. Children stay free in parents' room. AE, CB, DISC, DC, MC, V.

Just one block from the Bal Harbour shops, the Coronado offers good budget accommodations with an excellent oceanfront location. The freshwater pool is heated in the winter, and there is a color TV and refrigerator in every room. The motel is on the corner of 95th Street.

DESERT INN, 17201 Collins Ave., Sunny Isles, FL 33160. Tel. 305/947-0621, or toll free 800/327-6361, 800/223-5836 in Canada. 54 rms, 50 efficiencies. A/C TV TEL

$ **Rates:** Dec 19–Jan 5, $51–$75 single or double. Jan 6–31, $41–$65 single or double. Feb–Apr 6, $60–$85 single or double. Apr 7–30, $41–$65 single or double. May–Dec 18, $38–$54 single or double. Efficiencies $10 extra. Additional person $10 extra. Children under 16 stay free in parents' room. AE, CB, DC, MC, V.

A member of the Friendship Inn chain, the Desert Inn stands out for its life-size horse-drawn covered wagon sculpture in front and its free tennis court out back. In between are a king-size swimming pool, laundry facilities, a dining room, patio bar, and large, clean rooms and efficiencies. There's also an outdoor beach shower, and a children's pool.

DRIFTWOOD RESORT MOTEL, 17121 Collins Ave., Sunny Isles, FL 33160. Tel. 305/944-5141, or toll free 800/327-1263. 118 efficiencies. A/C TV TEL

$ **Rates:** Dec 20–Jan 7, $50–$80 single or double. Jan 8–Feb 4, $43–$70 single or double. Feb 5–Apr 1, $68–$90 single or double. Apr 2–22, $38–$70 single or double. Apr 23–Dec 19, $32–$62 single or double. Additional person $10 extra. Children under 12 stay free in parents' room. AE, DC, MC, V.

The Driftwood's dated but clean rooms are all efficiencies, equipped with either stoves or microwaves, and utensils. Plenty of tiki grass hangs over the motel's entranceway and the large poolside bar. The motel's blue-and-white rooms are just steps from two shuffleboard courts, laundry facilities, a restaurant/lounge, and the parking lot. The motel is located smack in the middle of Motel Row; its pool, surrounded by plenty of lounge chairs, directly overlooks the ocean.

HILYARD MANOR OCEANFRONT SUITES, 9541 Collins Ave., Surfside, FL 33154. Tel. 305/866-7351, or toll free 800/327-1413, 800/453-4333 in Canada. Fax 305/864-3045. Telex 808165. 2 rms, 28 suites. A/C TV TEL

$ **Rates:** Dec 18–Jan 18 and Mar 20–Apr 20, $64–$83 single or double. Jan 19–Mar 19, $75–$92 single or double. Apr 21–June 22 and Sept 6–Dec 17, $43–$65 single or double. June 23–Sept 5, $48–$68 single or double. Additional person $8 extra. Children under 13 stay free in parents' room. AE, CB, DISC, DC, MC, V.

This U-shaped motel, complete with outdated furnishings and decor, is typical of the area in price and architecture. Atypical, however, is the emphasis on well-stocked suites, complete with bedroom, kitchen, living room, and dining area. The units are well equipped with plates, pots, a toaster, and even an ironing board. Oceanfront corner room no. 36 is best. There is a heated swimming pool and laundry facilities.

THE MONACO, 17501 Collins Ave., Sunny Isles, FL 33160. Tel. 305/932-2100, or toll free 800/227-9006. Fax 305/931-5519. Telex 529400. 74 rms, 39 efficiencies. A/C TV TEL

$ Rates: Dec 18–Jan 5, $65–$75 single or double. Jan 6–31, $55–$65 single or double. Feb–Apr 14, $70–$80 single or double. Apr 15–30, $50–$60 single or double. May–Dec 17, $50–$67 single or double. Efficiencies $5–$7 extra. Additional person $7 extra. Children under 16 stay free in parents' room. AE, CB, DISC, DC, MC, V.

The Monaco is one of the largest motels on the beach, encompassing a restaurant, oceanfront bar, and dozens of balconied rooms surrounding a large kidney-shaped pool. As usual, nothing fancy here, but the motel's yellow-and-white decor is complemented by a large grassy area and a wide swath of beach.

OCEAN ROC, 19505 Collins Ave., Sunny Isles, FL 33160. Tel. 305/931-7600, or toll free 800/327-0553. Fax 305/866-5881. 70 rms, 25 efficiencies. A/C TV TEL

$ Rates: Jan 15–Mar 15, $60 single or double. Mar 16–Apr 15 and Dec 15–Jan 14, $42–$56 single or double. Apr 16–Dec 14, $32–$40 single or double. Efficiencies $6 extra. Additional person $6 extra. Children stay free in parents' room. Special rates for longer stays. AE, CB, DC, MC, V. **Parking:** Free.

The Ocean Roc is the last motel on Collins Avenue before the Dade County line. Its simple rectangular shape allows for only eight oceanfront rooms, while the others have ocean views and sweeping parking-lot vistas. No-smoking rooms are available. In the 1960s, the motel's angled exterior lines probably looked futuristic. Today it's a bit outdated, but the prices can hardly be beat. In addition to an obligatory pool (with a shallow children's area), a coffee shop and laundry facilities are on the premises.

SUEZ OCEANFRONT RESORT, 18215 Collins Ave., Sunny Isles, FL 33160. Tel. 305/932-0661, or toll free 800/327-5278. Fax 305/937-0058. Telex 518883. A/C TV TEL

$ Rates: Dec 22–Apr, $55–$89 single or double. May–Dec 21, $40–$60 single or double. Add $12 for kitchenettes. Additional person $5 extra. Children under 16 stay free in parents' room. AE, DC, MC, V.

Guarded by an undersized replica of Egypt's famed Sphinx, the campy Suez offers nice rooms and lounges and some of the best motel facilities on the beach, all at highly competitive rates. Following a fairly strict orange-and-yellow motif, the motel is more reminiscent of a fast-food restaurant than ancient Egypt. The grass umbrellas over beach lounges add to the confused decor. The motel also offers three shuffleboard courts, two large swimming pools, one lighted tennis court, and half a basketball court. There's also a kiddy pool and a beachfront children's playground. The motel's large restaurant overlooks the ocean and features a nightly $16 all-you-can-eat buffet.

KEY BISCAYNE

This first island in Florida's Keys chain is the water-sports capital of Miami. Palms sway over busy beaches while windsurfers, jet-skiers, and sailboats ply the waters just off shore. There are only a handful of hotels here, though several more are planned. All are on the beach, and room rates are uniformly high. There are no budget listings here, but if you can afford it, Key Biscayne is a great place to stay. The island is far enough from the mainland to make it feel like a secluded tropical paradise, yet close enough to downtown to take advantage of everything Miami has to offer.

EXPENSIVE

SHERATON ROYAL BISCAYNE BEACH RESORT & RACQUET CLUB, 555 Ocean Dr., Key Biscayne, FL 33149. Tel. 305/361-5775, or toll free 800/325-3535. Fax 305/361-0360. Telex 518802. 171 rms, 21 suites. A/C TV TEL

$ Rates: Dec 17–Easter, $160–$240 single or double; from $270 suite. Easter–Dec 16, $95–$155 single or double; from $225 suite. Additional person $20 extra. Weekend and other packages, and senior discounts available. AE, CB, DC, MC, V **Parking:** Free.

This squat, three-story beachfront hotel is loaded with Caribbean character and Miami delights. Tropical birdcalls combine with wicker furniture to create an atmosphere worthy of any one of the islands it imitates. Although this older hotel is lacking in contemporary design, the Royal Biscayne boasts one of the best spots in Miami. Room windows are well placed and large enough to let in large gulps of the city's freshest air.

Dining/Entertainment: The hotel's two restaurants, two pool bars, and lounge offer top-quality dining and low-key entertainment.

Services: Room service, laundry service, car rental.

Facilities: Water-sports concession, two outdoor heated swimming pools, 10 tennis courts (4 lighted), bicycle rentals, hair salon, gift shop, guest laundry room; no-smoking rooms available.

SILVER SANDS OCEANFRONT MOTEL, 301 Ocean Dr., Key Biscayne, FL 33149. Tel. 305/361-5441. 50 efficiency apts, 4 cottages. A/C TV TEL

$ **Rates:** Oct 22–Dec 17, $79–$149 standard apt. Dec 18–Apr 22, $115–$139 standard apt. Apr 23–Sept 3, $79–$89 standard apt. Sept 4–Oct 21, $72–$89 standard apt. Year-round, $149–$215 oceanfront apt. Additional person $10 extra. AE, MC, V. **Parking:** Free.

The modest Silver Sands motel seems out of place on its million-dollar parcel, sandwiched between two luxury high-rises. The owners know this is a special place, so room rates are not particularly low. Still, they are priced well below the name-brand accommodations next door.

Accommodations here are basic; they probably haven't changed much since the 1960s. The standard efficiency apartments have small kitchenettes, and visitors can decide between a room facing the courtyard or one overlooking the parking lot (there's no view from either). The oceanfront apartments are some of the most sought-after rooms in Miami, popular with those in-the-know. Although they are not particularly cheap, they are as close to the ocean as you can get without getting wet, and the whispering surf assures a good night's sleep. The motel's duplex cottages offer more room and larger kitchens. They are a nice alternative to regular hotel rooms, but pale next to the oceanfront accommodations.

Dining/Entertainment: The Sandbar Restaurant, with a deck right on the beach, is one of Miami's most attractive hidden treasures.

Facilities: Olympic-size heated swimming pool.

SONESTA BEACH HOTEL, 350 Ocean Dr., Key Biscayne, FL 33149. Tel. 305/361-2021, or toll free 800/SONESTA. Fax 305/361-3096. Telex 519303. 269 rms, 16 suites, 15 villas. A/C MINIBAR TV TEL

$ **Rates:** Dec 18–Apr, $245–$285 single or double; from $550 suite. June–Sept, $155–$225 single or double; from $465 suite. May and Oct–Dec 17, $205–$260 single or double; from $505 suite. Year-round, $395–$900 villa (five night minimum). Additional person $35 extra. Children stay free in parents' room. Packages available. AE, CB, DC, DISC, MC, V. **Parking:** $4.50.

The Sonesta's dominating modern oceanfront pyramid is the sort of structure most communities tend to protest against when building plans are put forward, since it permanently changes the nature of the town. But now that it's done, enjoy! This place is definitely deluxe, and its balconied beachfront rooms are some of the best in Miami. Accommodations are excellent, but it's the hotel's spectacular location that justifies its high prices.

Services aside, the nicest thing about the Sonesta is its lack of pretension. No one ever forgets that this is a beach resort, lending these lodgings a sort of casual luxuriousness.

The hotel's luxurious villas come with a full kitchen (complete with beverages and breakfast foods), laundry facilities, daily chamber service, and a large, private heated pool. Parents with kids will appreciate the hotel's "Just Us Kids" program, a free, supervised play group for children 5–13. Experienced counselors lead morning field trips as well as daily beach games and evening activities.

Dining/Entertainment: The hotel's four restaurants include the Rib Room, and Two Dragons, with Japanese and Chinese cuisine, plus a snack shop/deli. Desires nightclub features daily happy hours, and dancing at night.

Services: Room service, laundry service, currency exchange, car rental, complimentary children's programs.

Facilities: Olympic-size heated swimming pool, 10 tennis courts (3 lighted), water-sports concession, bicycle rentals, beauty salon, three gift shops, travel agency, health club (with Jacuzzi, sauna, and steam rooms).

COCONUT GROVE

This intimate enclave hugs the shores of Biscayne Bay just south of U.S. 1. The Grove offers ample nightlife, excellent restaurants, and beautiful surroundings. Unfortunately, all the hotels are expensive. But even if you don't stay here, you'll surely want to spend a night or two exploring the area.

EXPENSIVE

DOUBLETREE HOTEL AT COCONUT GROVE, 2649 S. Bayshore Dr., Coconut Grove, FL 33133. Tel. 305/858-2500, or toll free 800/528-0444. Fax 305/858-5776. 172 rms, 18 suites. A/C TV TEL

$ Rates: Jan–Mar, $120 single; $130 double; from $170 suite. Apr–Dec, $100 single; $120 double; from $150 suite. Additional person $10 extra. AARP and AAA discounts; weekend and other packages available. AE, CB, DISC, DC, MC, V. **Parking:** $7.

Doubletree hotels are known as business hotels. And although this property is a good choice for working travelers, its superior location and relatively reasonable rates make it an excellent choice for vacationers as well.

Standard rooms are not particularly fancy, but they are more than adequate. Suites are large and pretty and feature floor-to-ceiling windows. On higher floors, guests are treated to sweeping views of Biscayne Bay and Coconut Grove.

Dining/Entertainment: The Café Brasserie, just off the lobby, offers an excellent breakfast buffet and relaxed all-day dining. There are bars both inside and poolside.

Services: Laundry service, complimentary welcoming chocolate-chip cookies, complimentary van service to local shops.

Facilities: Outdoor heated swimming pool, two lighted tennis courts; sailing, fishing, and boat docks just across the street.

GRAND BAY HOTEL, 2669 S. Bayshore Dr., Coconut Grove, FL 33133. Tel. 305/858-9600, or toll free 800/327-2788. Fax 305/858-1532. Telex 441370. 132 rms, 49 suites. A/C MINIBAR TV TEL

$ Rates: Oct–May, $220–$275 single or double; from $300 suite. June–Sept, $175–$245 single or double; from $300 suite. Additional person $15 extra. Packages available. AE, CB, DC, MC, V. **Parking:** $8.

The Grand Bay opened in 1983 and immediately won praise as one of the fanciest hotels in the world. Designed by the Nichols Partnership, a local architectural firm, and outfitted with the highest-quality interiors, this stunning pyramid-shaped hotel is a masterpiece both inside and out.

Rooms are luxurious, featuring high-quality linens; comfortable, overstuffed love seats and chairs; a large writing desk; and all the amenities you would expect in deluxe accommodations. Bathrooms have hairdryers, robes, telephones, and more towels than you know what to do with. Original art and armfuls of fresh flowers are generously displayed throughout.

There is no check-in counter here; guests are escorted to a goldleaf-trimmed antique desk and encouraged to relax with a glass of champagne while they fill out the forms. The Grand Bay consistently attracts wealthy high-profile people, and it basks in its image as a rendezvous for royalty, socialites, and superstars. Indeed, the list of rich and famous who regularly walk through the lobby is endless. Guests come here to be pampered, to see and be seen.

Dining/Entertainment: The hotel's Grand Café is one of the top-rated restaurants in Miami. Drinks are served in the Ciga Bar and the Lobby Lounge, where a traditional afternoon tea is served from 3 to 6pm. Regine's, the top-floor dance club, offers cocktails and dancing Thursday through Saturday from 10pm to 5am.

Services: 24-hour room service, 24-hour concierge, complimentary welcoming champagne, limousine service, same-day laundry and dry cleaning.

Facilities: Outdoor freshwater pool, health club, beauty salon, gift shop; no-smoking rooms available.

MAYFAIR HOUSE HOTEL, 3000 Florida Ave., Coconut Grove, FL 33133. Tel. 305/441-0000, or toll free 800/433-4555. 182 suites. A/C MINIBAR TV TEL

$ Rates: Dec 16–May, $230–$525 single or double; from $600 penthouse. June–Dec 15, $180–$445 single or double; from $600 penthouse. Additional person $35 extra. Packages available. AE, DC, DISC, MC, V. **Parking:** $9.50.

Situated inside Coconut Grove's posh Mayfair Shops complex, the all-suite Mayfair House is about as centrally located as you can get. Each guest room has been individually designed, and no two are identical. All are extremely comfortable, and some suites are even opulent. Most of the more expensive accommodations include a private, outdoor, Japanese-style hot tub. Top-floor terraces offer good views, and all are hidden from the street by leaves and latticework.

The hotel contains several no-smoking suites and about 50 rooms with antique pianos. Since the lobby is in a shopping mall, recreation is confined to the roof, where a small swimming pool, sauna, and snack bar is located.

Dining/Entertainment: There is a relaxed café in the lobby. The Mayfair Grill is more formal, and there's also a rooftop snack bar.

Services: 24-hour room service, twice-daily maid service, complimentary glass of champagne upon arrival, discount shopping card for stores below, laundry service, child care.

Facilities: Rooftop pool and Jacuzzi, beauty salon, travel agency, shopping arcade.

CORAL GABLES

Coconut Grove eases into Coral Gables, which extends north toward Miami International Airport. The Gables, as it's affectionately known, was one of Miami's original planned communities, and it's still one of the city's prettiest. Staying here means being close to the shops along Miracle Mile as well as to some of Miami's nicest homes. Like other wealthy communities, Coral Gables doesn't offer much in the way of budget accommodations, but if you can afford it, hotels here are great places to stay.

EXPENSIVE

COLONNADE HOTEL, 180 Aragon Ave., Coral Gables, FL 33134. Tel. 305/441-2600, or toll free 800/533-1337. Fax 305/445-3929. 140 rms, 17 bilevel suites. A/C MINIBAR TV TEL

$ Rates: Apr 16–Sept, $170–$209 single or double; from $280 suite. Oct–Apr 15, $215–$255 single or double; from $295 suite. Packages available. AE, CB, DC, DISC, MC, V. **Parking:** $8.50.

The Colonnade occupies part of a large, historic building, originally built by Coral Gables's inventor, George Merrick. Faithful to its original style, the hotel is a successful amalgam of new and old, with emphasis on the former. An escalator brings guests from street level to the hotel's grand rotunda entrance. The lobby is just down the hall, but pause for a moment and admire the pink-and-black marble floor, domed roof, and stylish column supports. This is the most eye-catching feature of Mr. Merrick's original building.

Guest rooms are outfitted with historic photographs, marble counters, gold-finished faucets, and understated furnishings worthy of the hotel's rates. Champagne upon arrival and morning coffee or tea are complimentary.

Dining/Entertainment: The Aragon Café is one of the area's most celebrated restaurants, while the hotel's Doc Dammers Saloon is probably the best happy-hour haunt for the 30-something crowd. There is frequent live entertainment.

Services: 24-hour room service, child care, car rental, complimentary shoe shine, same-day dry-cleaning and laundry service, evening turn-down service.

Facilities: Heated outdoor swimming pool, Jacuzzi, hot tub, and rooftop fitness center; no-smoking rooms available.

HYATT REGENCY CORAL GABLES, 50 Alhambra Plaza, Coral Gables, FL 33134. Tel. 305/441-1234, or toll free 800/233-1234. Fax 305/443-7702. Telex 529706. 192 rms, 50 suites. A/C MINIBAR TV TEL

$ Rates (including breakfast buffet): $175–$225 single; $195–$245 double; from $200 suite. Additional person $25 extra. Packages and senior discounts available. AE, CB, DISC, DC, MC, V. **Parking:** $8.50.

High on style, comfort, and price, this Hyatt is part of Coral Gables's Alhambra, an office-hotel complex with a Mediterranean motif. The building itself is gorgeous, designed with pink stone, arched entrances, grand courtyards, and tile roofs. Inside you'll find overstuffed chairs on marble floors, surrounded by opulent antiques and chandeliers. The hotel opened in 1987, but like many historical buildings in the neighborhood, the Alhambra attempts to mimic something much older, and much farther away.

Rooms are a good size and are well appointed, outfitted with everything you'd expect from a top hotel—terry robes and all. Most furnishings are antique.

Dining/Entertainment: A restaurant serving decent, high-priced food is augmented by a good lounge and nightclub.

Services: 24-hour room service, laundry service, babysitting on request.

Facilities: Health club with Nautilus equipment, heated outdoor swimming pool, Jacuzzi, two saunas, gift shop; no-smoking rooms available.

MODERATE

HOTEL PLACE ST. MICHEL, 162 Alcazar Ave., Coral Gables, FL 33134. Tel. 305/444-1666, or toll free 800/247-8526. Fax 305/539-0074. Telex 4951356. 24 rms, 3 suites. A/C TV TEL

$ Rates (including continental breakfast): Nov 16–Easter, $100 single; $115 double; $150 suite. Easter–Nov 15, $85 single; $95 double; $110 suite. Children under 12 stay free in parents' room. Additional person $10 extra. Senior discounts available. AE, CB, DC, MC, V. **Parking:** $3.

It's always a pleasure to stay in this unusual cultured gem in the heart of Coral Gables. The accommodations and hospitality are straight out of old-world Europe, complete with dark wood-paneled walls, cozy beds, beautiful antiques, and a quiet elegance that seems startlingly out of place in hip, future-oriented Miami. Everything here is charming, from the parquet floors to the paddle fans; one-of-a-kind furnishings make each room special. Guests are treated to fresh fruit baskets upon arrival, evening turn-down service, and complimentary continental breakfast each morning.

Hotel Place St. Michel is small, but in no way is it insignificant. Popular with visiting literati and cognoscenti, the hotel may well be the most romantic spot in the region. The ground-floor restaurant has an equally committed clientele and is widely regarded as one of Miami's finest French restaurants.

DOWNTOWN

Understandably, most downtown hotels cater primarily to business travelers. But this hardly means that tourists should overlook these well-located, good-quality accommodations. Miami's downtown is small, so getting around is relatively easy. Locating here means staying between the beaches and the Grove, and being within minutes of the Bayside Marketplace and the Port of Miami.

Although business hotel prices are often high, and less prone to seasonal markdowns, quality and service are also of a high standard. Look for weekend discounts, when offices are closed and rooms often go empty.

EXPENSIVE

HOTEL INTER-CONTINENTAL MIAMI, 100 Chopin Plaza, Miami, FL 33131. Tel. 305/577-1000, or toll free 800/332-4246. Fax 305/577-0384. Telex 153127. 612 rms, 34 suites. A/C MINIBAR TV TEL

$ Rates: Jan 16–Apr 20, $180–$240 single; $200–$260 double; from $450 suite. Apr 21–Sept, $150–$210 single; $170–$230 double; from $450 suite. Oct–Jan 15, $160–$220 single; $180–$240 double; from $450 suite. Additional person $20 extra. Weekend and other packages available. AE, CB, DC, MC, V. **Parking:** $10.

The Hotel Inter-Continental Miami is both an architectural masterpiece and, arguably, the financial district's swankiest hotel. Both inside and out, the hotel boasts more marble than a mausoleum. The five-story lobby features a marble centerpiece sculpture by Henry Moore and is topped by a pleasing skylight. Plenty of plants, palm trees, and brightly colored wicker chairs add charm and enliven the otherwise stark space. Brilliant building and bay views add luster to already posh rooms that are outfitted with every convenience known to hoteldom.

Dining/Entertainment: The hotel's three restaurants cover all price ranges and are complemented by two full-service lounges.

Services: 24-hour room service, laundry service, currency exchange, mobile phone, car rental.

Facilities: Heated outdoor swimming pool, access to an off-premises health spa, jogging track, gift shop, travel agency, guest laundry room; no-smoking rooms available.

OMNI INTERNATIONAL HOTEL, 1601 Biscayne Blvd., Miami, FL 33132. Tel. 305/374-0000, or toll free 800/THE-OMNI. Fax 305/374-0020. Telex 515005. 489 rms, 46 suites. A/C MINIBAR TV TEL

$ Rates: Jan–Apr 15, $130–$150 single; $145–$165 double; from $185 suite. Apr 16–Dec, $120–$140 single; $135–$155 double; from $175 suite. Additional person $20 extra. Senior discounts, weekend and other packages available. AE, CB, DISC, DC, MC, V. **Parking:** $8.50.

One of downtown's best-known megahotels, this glass-and-chrome structure offers contemporary accommodations overlooking the Venetian Causeway and Biscayne Bay. Built in 1977 atop a large multistory shopping mall, the hotel has undergone several renovations and is still one of the luxury leaders in Miami's ever-growing hotel marketplace.

Rooms are traditionally decorated with modest but comfortable furnishings and deluxe fittings like bathroom telephones. But the Omni's most important asset is the 150-plus shopping complex below, a convenience that includes a popular multiplex cinema.

Dining/Entertainment: The Fish Market, the hotel's flagship lobby-level restaurant, is an excellent, elegant place for seafood. A coffee shop offers simpler meals and snacks. Lobby and poolside lounges are also offered.

Services: 24-hour room service, child care, currency exchange, car rental, laundry, free beach shuttle, turn-down service.

Facilities: Fifth-floor heated outdoor pool, beauty salon, gift shop; shopping mall below; no-smoking rooms available.

SHERATON BRICKELL POINT MIAMI, 495 Brickell Ave., Miami, FL 33131. Tel. 305/373-6000, or toll free 800/325-3535. Fax 305/374-2279. Telex 6811701. 584 rms, 14 suites. A/C TV TEL

$ Rates: Jan–Apr 14, $135–$155 single; $155–$175 double; from $295 suite. Apr 15–Dec, $119–$129 single; $129–$149 double; from $275 suite. Additional person $20 extra. Children under 18 stay free in parents' room. Senior discounts, weekend and other packages available. AE, CB, DISC, DC, MC, V. **Parking:** $7.50.

This downtown hotel's waterfront location is its greatest asset. Nestled between Brickell Park and Biscayne Bay, the Sheraton is set back from the main road and surrounded by a pleasant bayfront walkway.

Just as clean and reliable as other hotels in the Sheraton chain, the Brickell Point has a pretty location and good water views from most of the rooms, as well as all the amenities you'd expect from a hostelry in this class. The dozens of identical rooms are both well furnished and comfortable.

Dining/Entertainment: Ashley's serves continental and American cuisine overlooking Biscayne Bay. The Coco Loco Club is an indoor/outdoor bar with a good happy-hour buffet and comedy nights.

Services: Room service, car rental, weekday laundry service.

Facilities: Outdoor heated swimming pool, gift shop; no-smoking rooms available.

MODERATE

HOWARD JOHNSON HOTEL, 200 SE Second Ave., Miami, FL 33131. Tel. 305/374-3000, or toll free 800/654-2000. Fax 305/374-3000, ext. 1504. 254 rms, 2 suites. A/C TV TEL

$ Rates: Dec–Feb and July–Sept, $80 single; $90 double. Mar–June and Oct–Nov, $90 single; $100 double. Year-round $175–$250 suite. Additional person $10 extra. Children under 18 stay free in parents' room. AE, CB, DISC, DC, MC, V. **Parking:** $5.

One of the best-priced downtown hotels is this excellently located property, right in the heart of the city. Guest rooms feature modern decor and are sparkling clean, but they're a far cry from luxurious. No-smoking rooms are available. Facilities include a games room, seventh-floor pool and sun deck, and the American Café, a moderately priced restaurant.

CAMPING

LARRY AND PENNY THOMPSON PARK, 12451 SW 184th St., Miami, FL 33177. Tel. 305/232-1049.

$ Rates: $14 per site (for up to four people).

This inland park encompasses over 270 acres and includes a large freshwater lake for swimming, fishing, and boating. Laundry facilities and a convenience store are also on the premises. The tent area is huge, and not separated into tiny sites.

From downtown, take U.S. 1 south to SW 184th Street. Turn right and follow the signs for about four miles. The park entrance is at 125th Avenue.

LONG-TERM STAYS

If you plan on visiting Miami for a month, a season, or more, think about renting a room in a long-term hotel in South Miami Beach, or a condominium apartment in Miami Beach, Surfside, Bal Harbour, or Sunny Isles. Rents can be extremely reasonable, especially during the off-season. And there's no comparison to a tourist hotel in terms of the amount of space you get for the same buck. A short note to the chamber of commerce in the area where you're looking will be answered with a list of availabilities (see "Information" in "Orientation," above).

Many area real estate agents also handle short-term (minimum of one month) rentals. These include: **Century 21 Realty,** 3100 NW 77th Court, Miami, FL 33122; and **Keys Company Realtors,** 100 N. Biscayne Blvd., Miami, FL 33152 (tel. 305/371-3592).

4. DINING

One of the best things about traveling is finding new restaurants and sampling new foods. Packed with an enormous array of foreign and inventive restaurants, Miami will not disappoint. Dozens of different specialty kitchens represent a world of cuisines, and all are available in a variety of price ranges. In addition to Chinese, French, Thai, and Italian eateries, there are, not surprisingly, many area dining rooms specializing in Cuban, Caribbean, and Latin American food. In fact, Miami boasts some of the best cooking those regions have to offer; high demand and good prices attract some of the world's best chefs and ingredients.

Be sure to sample Miami's own regional American fare. Based on the California model, these inventive dishes rely heavily on seafood and citrus and are exemplified by creative recipes and fresh, local ingredients.

Keep an eye out for flavorful tropical fruits like mangoes, papayas, and Surinam cherries. Shellfish, including rock shrimp, clams, oysters, and bay and deep-sea scallops (the former are smaller and sweeter) are also regular menu items.

Most hotels in Miami do not include breakfast in their room rates, but many in South Miami Beach do. These are usually good-sized buffets with fresh fruit, cold cuts, rolls, croissants, coffee, and fresh-squeezed orange juice. At lunch, many business-oriented restaurants offer entrees priced well below those served at dinner. Restaurants often serve dinner until midnight or later.

To help you choose where to eat, restaurants below are divided first by area, then by price, using the following guide: "Very Expensive," more than $40 per person; "Expensive," $30–$40 per person; "Moderate," $20–$30 per person; "Inexpensive," $10–$20 per person; and "Budget," less than $10 per person.

These categories reflect the price of the majority of dinner menu items and include an appetizer, main course, coffee, dessert, tax, and tip. Wine is not included. Whenever a special lunch menu is available—typically half the price of a full-course dinner—I have noted it in the heading of each listing.

MIAMI BEACH

VERY EXPENSIVE

THE DINING GALLERIES, in the Fontainebleau Hilton Hotel, 4441 Collins Ave. Tel. 538-2000.

Cuisine: CONTINENTAL. **Reservations:** Recommended.

$ Prices: Appetizers $5–$9; main courses $19–$27. AE, CB, DC, MC, V.

Open: Daily, 6:30am–2am.

Ensconced deep inside Miami Beach's most showy hotel, the Dining Galleries' overindulgence seems somehow appropriate. This restaurant is a pleasant and surprising treat, featuring fine food and tasteful, if overdone, decor. There are plenty of statuary and antique objets d'art and a soothing piano/violin duo.

Nothing here is basic. Soups include pheasant consommé and fresh lobster bisque, and the appetizer list includes shrimp, salmon, and Beluga caviar. The disciplined kitchen regularly turns out beautifully arranged main dishes that look like still-lifes, such as tender steak sautéed in herbed butter with medallions of lobster, quail egg, and brandied lobster bisque. It's really quite a mouthful. The menu is heavy on meat and fish—all dressed to the nines—and features the restaurant's flagship crown roast of lamb with fried pears and a homemade Florida citrus chutney.

DOMINIQUE'S, in the Alexander All-Suite Luxury Hotel, 5225 Collins Ave. Tel. 865-6500.

Cuisine: FRENCH/CONTINENTAL. **Reservations:** Recommended, especially at dinner.

$ Prices: Appetizers $8–$11; main courses $20–$30. AE, CB, DC, MC, V.

Open: Breakfast Mon–Sat 7–11:30am; lunch Mon–Sat 11:30am–3pm; dinner Sun–Thurs 5:30–11pm, Fri–Sat 5:30pm–midnight; brunch Sun 11:30am–3:30pm during winter only.

Dominique's is one of Miami Beach's best restaurants. Exorbitant and elegant, with heavy antique furniture and Oriental rugs, it boasts a good view of the Atlantic.

The menu spotlights a variety of wild-game appetizers that are not just novel, but tasty, too. They include such unusual dishes as buffalo sausage, tender alligator scaloppine, and fresh diamondback rattlesnake salad. Still, it's the more traditional dishes like marinated rack of lamb chops and prime steak that keeps the regulars returning. Service is good, and the heavy French food, the menu's main feature, is consistently excellent. Jackets are requested for men at dinner.

THE FORGE RESTAURANT, 432 Arthur Godfrey Rd. (41st St.). Tel. 538-8533.

Cuisine: AMERICAN. **Reservations:** Required.
$ **Prices:** Appetizers $6–$9; main courses $18–$25. AE, DC, MC, V.
Open: Dinner only, Sun–Thurs 5–11:30pm, Fri–Sat 5pm–1am.

English oak paneling and Tiffany glass suggest high prices and haute cuisine, and that's exactly what you can expect from the remodeled Forge. Each elegant dining room possesses its own character, and features high ceilings, ornate chandeliers, and high-quality, conservative European artwork.

The Forge's huge American menu has a northern Italian bias, evidenced by a long list of creamy pasta appetizers. Equal attention is given to fish, veal, poultry, and beef dishes, many of which are prepared on the kitchen's all-important oak grill. Look for appetizers like oak-grilled tomatoes with mozzarella, or a simple oak-grilled main course of meat or fish. Finally, it's important to note that the Forge has one of Miami's best wine lists, encompassing about 280 pages selected from the on-premises wine cellar.

EXPENSIVE

AMERICAN CLASSICS, in the Dezerland Surfside Beach Hotel, 8701 Collins Ave. Tel. 865-6661.

Cuisine: AMERICAN. **Reservations:** Not required.
$ **Prices:** Main courses $11–$20; lunch about a third less. AE, MC, V.
Open: Daily 7am–11pm.

Like the hotel in which it's located, American Classics is a theme restaurant, planned around vintage cars and '50s memorabilia. Overlooking the hotel's pool, and the ocean beyond, diners sit at tables and booths made of dismantled Fords and Buicks, and order from a high-priced, like-minded menu. Simple seafood specials are given fancy names like shrimp scampi Duesenberg and American Graffiti surf and turf.

FROMMER'S SMART TRAVELER: RESTAURANTS

1. Go ethnic—the city has some great inexpensive ethnic dining.
2. Eat your main meal at lunch when prices are lower—and you can taste the cuisine at the gourmet hot spots for a fraction of the dinner prices.
3. Watch the booze—it can add greatly to the cost of any meal.
4. Look for early-bird specials, which are commonplace in and around the city.
5. Keep an eye out for fixed-price menus, two-for-one specials, and other money-saving deals.

Chicken and steak round off the main dishes, which can then be followed by assorted desserts, or "tailgaters," as they're called. Meals here are competently prepared and presented, but like the hotel, American Classics appeals primarily to enthusiasts.

PLACE FOR STEAK, 1335 79th St. Causeway. Tel. 758-5581.
Cuisine: AMERICAN. **Reservations:** Not required.
$ Prices: Appetizers $6–$8; main courses $17–$25. AE, CB, DC, MC, V.
Open: Mon–Thurs 5–11pm, Fri–Sat 5pm–midnight, Sun 5–11pm. **Closed:** July–Aug.

Place for Steak is known for huge portions of prime aged New York sirloin steak and other heavy foods served in a dark, richly decorated dining room. Appetizers include shrimp cocktail, clams casino, and a platter containing whitefish salad, chopped herring, nova and cream cheese, gefilte fish, and chopped chicken liver. Best, perhaps, is the restaurant's nightly 58-foot hot-and-cold buffet—available from 5 to 10pm—that includes roast beef, rôtisserie chicken, shrimp, fish, soups, salads, and dozens of other items. The spread is hard to beat at any price. The restaurant is located in North Bay Village, on the 79th Street Causeway between Miami Beach and the mainland.

MODERATE

YO-SI PEKING, in the Eden Roc Hotel, 4525 Collins Ave. Tel. 532-9060.
Cuisine: KOSHER CHINESE/THAI. **Reservations:** Recommended; required for Friday dinner.
$ Prices: Appetizers $4–$12; main courses $11–$25. AE, MC, V.
Open: Lunch Sat–Thurs noon–2:30pm, Fri noon–3pm; dinner Sun–Thurs 4–10:30pm.

Only in Miami. Well, maybe Miami, New York, and Israel. Yo-Si Peking is a *glatt kosher* (very kosher), Thai-influenced, gourmet Chinese restaurant. It's both expensive and elegant (jackets are recommended for men), featuring black lacquer tables with mother-of-pearl inlays, and custom-made silk-covered chairs imported from Hong Kong.

The cooking here is of the highest quality. Needless to say there are no pork dishes on the menu, a category that is substituted for by creative veal selections. Unusual Thai twists include a boneless sautéed chicken curry, marinated and grilled beef satay, and a cold shredded chicken salad appetizer, fried in a spicy garlic sauce. Most of the other meals are traditional Chinese favorites, and all the dishes are untraditionally oil free. The Eden Roc Hotel is on the ocean at 45th Street.

INEXPENSIVE

PINEAPPLES, 530 Arthur Godfrey Rd. Tel. 532-9731.
Cuisine: AMERICAN. **Reservations:** Not accepted.
$ Prices: Salads and sandwiches $5–$6; main courses $8–$10. AE, MC, V.
Open: Daily 11am–10pm.

Half health-food store, half restaurant, Pineapples serves fresh juices, sandwiches, and a variety of menu items, either to take out or eat in. In the busy dining section, an overworked staff distributes huge menus to patrons sitting at the half dozen or so plain wooden tables set atop a clean red-tile floor. Both appetizers and main courses include a combination of American and Japanese-style foods, like buffalo chicken wings, miso soup, and California sushi rolls. Steamed vegetables and stir-fries are especially emphasized, as are meal-sized salads including vegetable, chicken, pasta, pineapple, and more. The restaurant is located in the middle of a row of boutiques on the south side of bustling Arthur Godfrey Road.

BUDGET

CURRY'S, 7433 Collins Ave. Tel. 866-1571.
Cuisine: AMERICAN. **Reservations:** Not accepted.
$ Prices: Meal $8–$11. AE, MC, V.
Open: Dinner only, Mon–Sat 4:30–9:30pm, Sun 4–9:30pm.

Established in 1937, this large dining room on the ocean side of Collins Avenue is one of Miami Beach's oldest restaurants. Neither the restaurant's name, nor the Polynesian wall decorations are indicative of the menu's offerings, which are straightforwardly American and reminiscent of the area's heyday. Broiled and fried fish dishes are available, but the best selections, including steak, chicken, and ribs, come off the open charcoal grill perched by the front window.

Prices are incredibly reasonable here, and all include an appetizer, soup, or salad, as well as a potato or vegetable, dessert, coffee or tea.

MIAMI BEACH PIZZA, 6954 Collins Ave. Tel. 866-8661.

Cuisine: ITALIAN.

$ **Prices:** Large cheese pizza $9.50; pasta $5–$6. MC, V.

Open: Mon–Thurs 11am–midnight, Fri–Sat 11am–1am, Sun noon–midnight.

New York–style pizza is delivered free to most Miami Beach hotels. The cheesy pies are inexpensive and good. Other menu items include veal parmigiana, chicken cacciatore, meatball sandwiches, beer, and soda.

SOUTH MIAMI BEACH — THE ART DECO DISTRICT

EXPENSIVE

CAFE DES ARTS, in the Locust Hotel, 918 Ocean Dr. Tel. 534-6267.

Cuisine: MEDITERRANEAN. **Reservations:** Recommended.

$ **Prices:** Appetizers $6–$7; main courses $14–$24. AE, DC, MC, V.

Open: Dinner only, Sun–Thurs 6–11:30pm, Fri–Sat 6pm–midnight. **Closed:** Two weeks in Aug.

Nestled among two of Ocean Drive's best examples of the art deco period, and in one of the oldest Mediterranean buildings in the district, Café des Arts has the distinction of being one of the first restaurants to open in this newly revitalized area.

The lighthearted art gallery/restaurant offers contemporary renditions of old favorites, like crabmeat ravioli and baked salmon with pink grapefruit, delivered to your table by artsy waiters. The Mediterranean menu is well planned, apropos of the Venetian Gothic architecture, and features creative selections of fish, pastas, and meats. Especially good is the chef's suggestion, ravioli Véronique, a crabmeat-stuffed ravioli bathed in a tangy, smooth seafood-grape sauce. Other dishes make liberal use of porcini (mushrooms), sun-dried tomatoes, cilantro, Dijon mustard, and other tasty and trendy ingredients.

F FROMMER'S COOL FOR KIDS: RESTAURANTS

American Classics *(see p. 77)* This is a theme restaurant, planned around vintage cars and '50s memorabilia. If you think your child would like to eat dinner inside a 1950s automobile, this is the place to go. The "surf and turf" menu is rounded off by a good assortment of desserts, or "tailgaters."

The Melting Pot *(see p. 92)* In this fondue joint diners dip chunks of bread into pots of sizzling cheese. It's definitely a fun way to eat, for kids as well as adults. But save room for dessert—chunks of pineapple, bananas, apples, and cherries are served with a creamy chocolate fondue for dipping.

Señor Frog's *(see p. 97)* This place is both fun and filling, featuring a house mariachi band and excellent food. The restaurant is right in the heart of Coconut Grove, so you can walk around and see the sights before or after dinner.

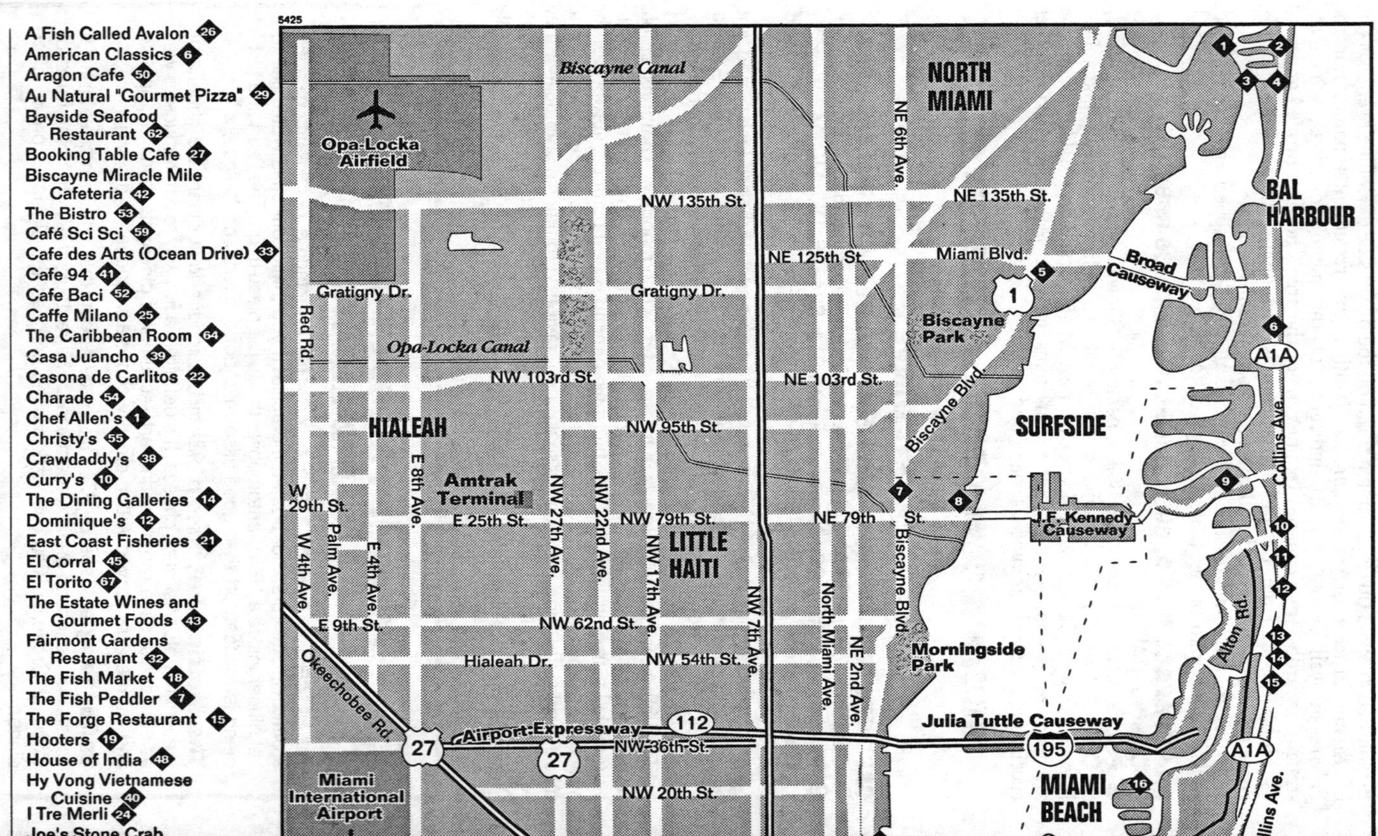

A Fish Called Avalon 26
American Classics 6
Aragon Cafe 50
Au Natural "Gourmet Pizza" 29
Bayside Seafood Restaurant 62
Booking Table Cafe 27
Biscayne Miracle Mile Cafeteria 42
The Bistro 53
Café Sci Sci 59
Cafe des Arts (Ocean Drive) 33
Cafe 94 41
Cafe Baci 52
Caffe Milano 25
The Caribbean Room 64
Casa Juancho 39
Casona de Carlitos 22
Charade 54
Chef Allen's 1
Christy's 55
Crawdaddy's 38
Curry's 10
The Dining Galleries 14
Dominique's 12
East Coast Fisheries 21
El Corral 45
El Torito 67
The Estate Wines and Gourmet Foods 43
Fairmont Gardens Restaurant 32
The Fish Market 18
The Fish Peddler 7
The Forge Restaurant 15
Hooters 19
House of India 48
Hy Vong Vietnamese Cuisine 40
I Tre Merli 24
5425
N
0
3.2 km
2 mi
Opa-Locka Airfield
Biscayne Canal
NORTH MIAMI
BAL HARBOUR
NW 135th St.
NE 135th St.
NE 6th Ave.
NE 125th St.
Miami Blvd.
Broad Causeway
Gratigny Dr.
Gratigny Dr.
Red Rd.
Biscayne Park
Opa-Locka Canal
NW 103rd St.
NE 103rd St.
A1A
HIALEAH
NW 95th St.
Biscayne Blvd.
SURFSIDE
Collins Ave.
Amtrak Terminal
W 29th St.
E 8th Ave.
NW 27th Ave.
NW 22nd Ave.
E 25th St.
NW 79th St.
NE 79th St.
J.F. Kennedy Causeway
LITTLE HAITI
NW 17th Ave.
W 4th Ave.
Palm Ave.
E 4th Ave.
NW 7th Ave.
North Miami Ave.
Biscayne Blvd.
Alton Rd.
E 9th St.
NW 62nd St.
Hialeah Dr.
NW 54th St.
NE 2nd Ave.
Morningside Park
Okeechobee Rd.
Airport Expressway
112
27
27
NW 36th St.
Julia Tuttle Causeway
195
A1A
Miami International Airport
NW 20th St.
MIAMI BEACH
Collins Ave.

Kaleidoscope
LB's Eatery 66
Le Festival 43
Mark's Place 5
The Melting Pot 3
Mezzanotte 31
Miami Beach Pizza 11
Mike Gordon's 8
Monty's Bayshore Restaurant 56
Mr. Pizza 2
News Cafe 35
Pavillon Grill 20
Pineapples 16
Pita and Eats 57
Place for Steak 9
Restaurant St. Michel 47
Ristorante Tanino 51
Rusty Pelican 61
The Sandbar 65
Señor Frog's 58
The Strand 36
Sundays on the Bay 63
Thai Toni 34
Tijuana Joe's 28
Toni's New Tokyo Cuisine and Sushi Bar 30
Versailles 44
Wolfie Cohen's Rascal House 4
Wolfie's 23
Yo-Si Peking 13
YUCA 49
Zum Alten Fritz 17

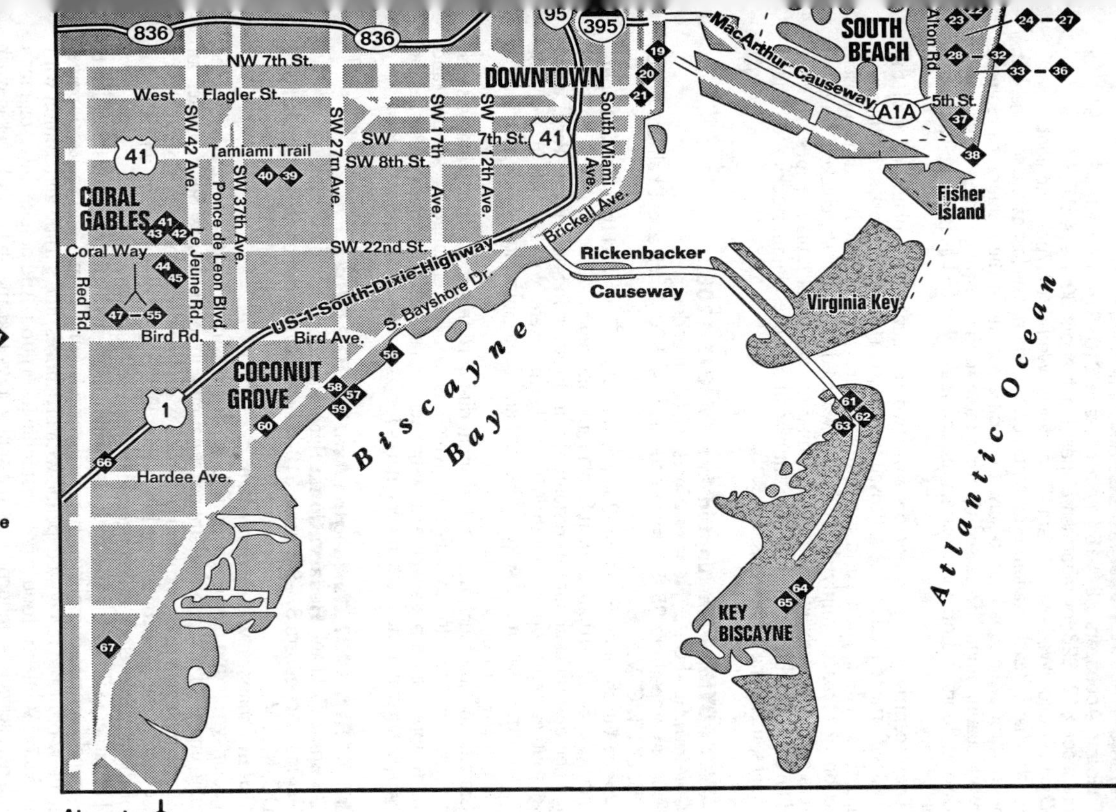

CAFFÈ MILANO, 850 Ocean Dr. Tel. 532-0707.

Cuisine: ITALIAN. **Reservations:** Recommended.

$ **Prices:** Appetizers $8–$15; main courses $10–$15 for pasta, $11–$14 for carpacci, $12–$23 for meat/fish dishes; lunch about 30% less. AE, MC, V.

Open: Lunch Wed–Mon 11am–5pm; dinner Wed–Mon 7pm–midnight.

In South Miami Beach, Italian restaurants seem to change as fast as the seasons, but, hopefully, the Milano is here to stay. Even on a nice night the restaurant's requisite sidewalk seating might be passed up for a table in the bustling dining room where hardwood floors and original abstract art can make you feel as if you're eating in a Soho gallery.

The eccentric young proprietors own two restaurants in Milan, and staff this kitchen with trained Italian chefs. Prosciutto, bresaola (air-dried beef), and other meat antipasti precede a good pasta menu (tortelli are recommended) and an unusual selection of carpacci (thinly sliced raw or warmed meats). Fish, chicken, and veal entrees are conservatively prepared according to traditional Italian recipes.

The pretty marble bar that lines an entire wall of the restaurant stocks a full line of beverages, including 15 grappas.

CRAWDADDY'S, 1 Washington Ave. Tel. 673-1708.

Cuisine: SEAFOOD. **Reservations:** Recommended.

$ **Prices:** Appetizers $5–$9; main courses $14–$20; lunch about half price. AE, CB, DC, MC, V.

Open: Lunch Mon–Fri 11am–3pm; dinner Mon–Thurs 5–11pm, Fri–Sat 5pm–midnight, Sun 5–10pm, brunch Sun 11am–3:30pm.

The best thing about this restaurant is its location in South Pointe Park, at the southernmost tip of South Miami Beach. Here you can sit in front of Government Cut and watch the cruise and cargo ships slowly ease their way in and out of the Port of Miami.

Crawdaddy's is casual, with several small dining rooms and lots of window seats. Appetizers include Florida alligator (which is not an endangered species) and bacon-wrapped shrimp, as well as raw-bar selections. Fish, in various guises, is the house specialty, but the kitchen gets marks for its tender steak and veal, too.

I TRE MERLI, 1437 Washington Ave. Tel. 672-6702.

Cuisine: ITALIAN. **Reservations:** Recommended.

$ **Prices:** Appetizers $7–$9; pasta $10–$12; meat/fish dishes $16–$20. AE, CB, DC, MC, V.

Open: Dinner only, daily 6pm–1am.

Immediately trendy upon opening in 1982, South Miami Beach's I Tre Merli is the spitting image of its popular sibling restaurant in New York's Soho. Under an unusually high ceiling are exposed red-brick walls lined with thousands of bottles of house-label wine. A second-floor loft overlooks the main dining room, where about 20 of the most coveted (and congested) tables are located.

The rather mainstream, strictly Italian menu augments all the traditional highlights like gnocchi (potato dumplings), spaghetti vongole (with clams), and veal scaloppine, with a few offbeat offerings like penne with artichokes, and shrimp and salmon with caviar sauce. While the food is not outstanding, it's good. And despite the restaurant's popularity, service is unhurried, as the staff knows that the ability to linger is what ultimately lures the patrons.

JOE'S STONE CRAB RESTAURANT, 227 Biscayne St. Tel. 673-0365.

Cuisine: SEAFOOD. **Reservations:** Not accepted.

$ **Prices:** $31.95 for jumbo crab claws, $23.95 for large claws. AE, CB, DC, MC, V.

Open: Lunch Tues–Sat 11:30am–2pm; dinner daily 5–10pm (until 11pm on Miami Heat home-game nights). **Closed:** Late May to early Oct.

Open since 1913 and steeped in tradition, this restaurant may be the most famous in Florida, as evidenced by long lines to get in. Other menu items are available, but to go to Joe's and not order stone crab is unthinkable. In fact, the restaurant is so identified with this single crustacean that it closes for the six months that the crabs are out of season. Stone crabs are available at other restaurants around Miami, but they just don't seem to taste as good as they do at the place where they were invented. If jumbo claws are available, splurge. Be warned: The wait can be long, and many readers have complained that the host gives preference to those who "tip" in advance. Lines are shortest Monday through Wednesday. The restaurant is at the corner of Biscayne Street and Washington Avenue. No shorts allowed.

MEZZANOTTE, 1200 Washington Ave. Tel. 673-4343.

Cuisine: ITALIAN. **Reservations:** Recommended.

$ Prices: Appetizers $7; main courses $12–$14 for pasta, $15–$25 for meat and fish. AE, CB, DC, MC, V.

Open: Dinner only, Sun–Thurs 6pm–midnight, Fri–Sat 6pm–2am.

Papparazzo charm is in full swing at this trendy-to-the-max corner bistro. Who cares if better food can be had at any number of places up the street? This is the place where the fashionable can see and be seen. The food is decent; traditional antipasti are followed by good veal chops, competent pastas, and simple meat dishes.

The large room is undivided for the best sightlines and easy table-hopping. An entire wall is mirrored so that no one's back is to the crowd, and a whip of neon around the ceiling keeps everyone bright enough to be seen. You might pass on dessert, but order a cappuccino; it's a small price to pay to linger.

MODERATE

CASONA DE CARLITOS, 2232 Collins Ave. Tel. 534-7013.

Cuisine: ARGENTINEAN. **Reservations:** Not required.

$ Prices: Appetizers $7–$9; main courses $8–$10 for pasta, $9–$16 for meat and fish; lunch about half price. AE, CB, DC, DISC, MC, V.

Open: Sun–Thurs noon–midnight, Fri–Sat noon–1am.

Except for its unusually large size, the outside of this corner storefront is rather unassuming. The dining room inside is not very fancy either, opting instead for a casual atmosphere that complements the unpretentious, traditional kitchen. Menus are available in English, Spanish, German, French, and Portuguese, and they contain dozens upon dozens of traditional dishes.

Shrimp ceviche and a delicately marinated eggplant are two of the more unusual appetizers. These can be followed by baked fish smothered in a bleu-cheese sauce, chicken oreganato in wine sauce, or any one of a number of grilled meats and homemade pastas. The restaurant is located on the corner of 23rd Street, across from the Holiday Inn.

FAIRMONT GARDENS RESTAURANT, in the Fairmont Hotel, 1000 Collins Ave. Tel. 531-0050.

Cuisine: ITALIAN/CONTINENTAL. **Reservations:** Recommended, especially on weekends.

$ Prices: Appetizers $4–$6; main courses $10–$12 for pasta, $14–$16 for meat and fish; brunch buffet $13. AE, CB, DC, MC, V.

Open: Dinner daily 6pm–midnight; brunch Sun 11am–2:30pm (happy hour Mon–Fri 4–7pm).

The Fairmont's fancy, tropical outdoor courtyard is adjacent to a far less extravagant hotel, one block from the ocean in the art deco district. Brightly colored angled canvas canopies provide a light and airy roof over a multilevel, pastel-colored dining area. Indoor tables are also available, but are far less desirable on warm nights.

Traditional hot and cold appetizers are bolstered by island-inspired selections like hearts of palm salad and a house lobster ravioli. Main dishes are equally adventurous, highlighted by boneless chicken served with sweet red pimientos and flamed in cognac and cream, conservatively prepared steaks, and a variety of fresh fish and pasta dishes. The Fairmont features live music (often calypso) nightly.

A FISH CALLED AVALON, in the Avalon Hotel, 700 Ocean Dr. Tel. 532-1727.

Cuisine: MIAMI REGIONAL. **Reservations:** Recommended.
$ Prices: Appetizers $6–$10; main courses $14–$22. AE, MC, V.
Open: Dinner only, Sun–Thurs 6–11pm, Fri–Sat 6pm–1am.

There's something about this well-placed Ocean Drive restaurant that's almost surreal; dramatic paintings are softened by intimate specular light, and mellow pastels counterpoint huge, imposing windows. White linen cloths and matching chair covers highlight each table's centerpiece—a single tropical Siamese fighting fish swimming around in a small glass bowl.

Chef Gillian Lowe changes the menu nightly, but the emphasis is always on fresh local fish, grilled or roasted, served with creative seasonal sauces. Steak and chicken are always on the menu, as are soups like chilled mango-peach and cream of carrot.

The Avalon's bar, a dramatically beautiful, intimately low-key lounge gets marks as one of the best little places to drink on the strip.

THE STRAND, 671 Washington Ave. Tel. 532-2340.

Cuisine: AMERICAN. **Reservations:** Recommended on winter weekends.
$ Prices: Appetizers $4–$7; main courses $5–$9 for burgers and sandwiches, $9–$18 for meat and fish; three-course pretheater menu (6–7pm) $10. MC, V.
Open: Dinner only, Sun–Thurs 6pm–midnight, Fri–Sat 6pm–2am.

Not just another hot spot for trendies and young professionals, the Strand actually has culinary integrity, offering a well-planned menu punctuated by high-quality and fresh ingredients. Candlelit tables and a large, open-room layout are conducive to both intimate dining and table-hopping. And, happily, this old standby is still a good place to see and be seen. The menu changes nightly, but both food and service are very consistent, and a number of well-priced and light items are always on offer and excellent homemade mousses and cakes are always freshly prepared. The house wine list contains some good vintages, including several selections below $15.

THAI TONI, 890 Washington Ave. Tel. 538-8424.

Cuisine: THAI. **Reservations:** Recommended on weekends.
$ Prices: Appetizers $6–$7; main courses $7–$13 ($15–$18 for fish). AE, MC, V.
Open: Dinner only, Sun–Thurs 5:30–11pm, Fri–Sat 5:30pm–midnight.

One of the best restaurants in Miami, Thai Toni sparkles with ultra-contemporary decor, traditional service, and really top-notch food. The most spectacular item on the menu, to both eye and palate, is the hot-and-spicy fish, a whole snapper fileted tableside and fried with a bold, spicy red sauce. Other top picks have tropical twists, like beef curry with coconut milk and avocado, and a tender, boneless crispy duck served with mushrooms, baby corn, water chestnuts, cashews, and a light wine sauce.

The casual atmosphere is complemented by taped jazz and the option of floor-cushion seating at traditional low tables.

TONI'S NEW TOKYO CUISINE AND SUSHI BAR, 1208 Washington Ave. Tel. 673-9368.

Cuisine: JAPANESE. **Reservations:** Not required.
$ Prices: Appetizers $4–$6; main courses $8–$14; deluxe sushi combination $12. AE, MC, V.
Open: Dinner only, Sun–Thurs 6–11pm, Fri–Sat 6pm–midnight.

The same owners of Thai Toni, four blocks away, have created a modern restaurant that has become Miami's latest "in" spot for sushi. In addition to partaking of the usual Japanese staples, South Miami Beach models, millionaires, and wanna-bes can also enjoy New Tokyo Cuisine, a combined Japanese and European cooking, exemplified at Toni's by such appetizers as sushi pizza, and main dishes like pasta with stir-fried shrimp and vegetables.

The single most important thing about sushi is freshness, and although cuts here are not unusually generous, high turnover assures top quality. The sushi bar, which is backed by a colorful, contemporary three-dimensional mosaic, features Miami specials like conch and crab nigiri and a "bagel roll" made of smoked salmon, cream cheese, and scallions.

INEXPENSIVE

BOOKING TABLE CAFE, 728 Ocean Dr. Tel. 672-3476.

Cuisine: INTERNATIONAL. **Reservations:** Not accepted.

$ Prices: Salads and sandwiches $5–$7; meat/fish dishes $9–$11; breakfast $3–$6. AE, MC, V.

Open: Daily 8am–2am.

Unlike many Ocean Drive restaurants, which seem to put more emphasis on style than substance, this indoor/outdoor café next to the Colony Hotel boasts some of the best food on the strip. Despite the glass brick and European-style marble tables, the Booking Room's decor is considerably more low-key than its neighbors.

The colorful menu has everything from soups, sandwiches, and salads to lobsters and steaks. Breakfasts are popular, and include anything from a simple croissant to eggs, waffles, and quiche. The fish is particularly recommended during lunch and dinner, and like most of the other offerings, it's extremely well priced. Cappuccino, drinks, and a small, well-chosen list of wines are also available.

TIJUANA JOE'S, 1201 Lincoln Rd. Tel. 674-1051.

Cuisine: MEXICAN. **Reservations:** Not accepted.

$ Prices: $5–$14. AE, MC, V.

Open: Sun–Thurs noon–11pm, Fri–Sat noon–midnight.

South Beach's best Mexican restaurant is not a phony American margarita chain, it's this simple corner Tex-Mex cantina. There is no separate bar here, just a dozen or so plastic tablecloth-topped tables, with white wooden chairs and a traditional menu. It's often crowded, as the place has caught on. Fajitas are the house specialty, and there is live Mexican music Tuesday through Saturday.

WOLFIE'S, 2038 Collins Ave. Tel. 538-6626.

Cuisine: JEWISH DELICATESSEN.

$ Prices: Omelets and sandwiches $4–$6, other dishes $5–$12. MC, V.

Open: Daily 24 hours.

Wolfie's originally opened in 1947 and quickly became a popular spot. The decor is simple—two wood-paneled rooms, lined on one side by a glass-enclosed display case—and the food is New York traditional. The bowl of pickles and basket of assorted rolls and miniature danishes on each table tells you this is the real thing. Meals include cold smoked-fish platters, overstuffed sandwiches, stuffed cabbage, chicken-in-a-pot, and other favorites. Wolfie's is a relic of the past, but like other South Beach monuments, it has recently received a lease on life from the area's fashionable late-night crowd.

BUDGET

AU NATURAL "GOURMET" PIZZA, 1427 Alton Rd. Tel. 531-0666.

Cuisine: PIZZA.

$ Prices: Large pizza $9–$19. No credit cards.

Open: Sun–Thurs 11am–midnight, Fri–Sat 11am–1am.

California-style pizza has reached the glitterati of South Miami Beach, with concoctions like pesto-and-ricotta, or smoked-salmon and cream cheese. Other designer pies include the Mediterranean, with sautéed eggplant, artichoke hearts, and prosciutto, and barbecued chicken with marinated mesquite-smoked poultry. Au Natural also delivers pints of Brices Yogurt and Ben & Jerry's ice cream.

NEWS CAFE, 800 Ocean Dr. Tel. 538-NEWS.

Cuisine: AMERICAN.

$ Prices: Continental breakfast $2.75; salads $4–$8; sandwiches $5–$7. AE, MC, V.

Open: Daily 24 hours.

Of all the chic spots around trendy South Miami Beach, the News Café is tops. Excellent and inexpensive breakfasts and café fare are served at about 20 perpetually congested tables. Most of the seating is outdoors, and terrace tables are the most coveted. This is the meeting place for Ocean Drive's multitude of fashion photography crews and their models—who, incidentally, also occupy most of the area's hotel rooms. Delicious, often health-oriented dishes include yogurt with fruit salad, various green salads, imported cheese and meat sandwiches, and a choice of quiches. Coffee (including espresso) and a variety of black and herbal teas are also available.

SURFSIDE, BAL HARBOUR & SUNNY ISLES

INEXPENSIVE

WOLFIE COHEN'S RASCAL HOUSE, 17190 Collins Ave. Tel. 947-4581.

Cuisine: JEWISH/DELICATESSEN

$ **Prices:** Omelets and sandwiches $4–$6; other dishes $5–$10.

Open: Daily 7am–1:45am.

Almost 40 years young and still going strong, this historic, nostalgic culinary extravaganza is one of Miami Beach's greatest traditions. Simple tables and booths as well as plenty of patrons fill the airy, 425-seat dining room. The menu is as huge as the portions, which include corned beef, schmaltz herring, brisket, kreplach, chicken soup, and other authentic Jewish staples. Take-out service is available.

BUDGET

MR. PIZZA, 18120 Collins Ave., Sunny Isles. Tel. 932-6915.

Cuisine: ITALIAN

$ **Prices:** Sandwiches $3.50–$4.50; pastas $4–$6; large pizza $8. AE, CB, MC, V.

Open: Daily 11:30am–2am.

Darkwood walls and red-and-white-checked tablecloths surround the restaurant's open kitchen. Mr. Pizza specializes in New York–style Sicilian and Neapolitan pies. Good pastas, subs, and calzones are also available. Best of all, they deliver—from 71st Street to the Dade County line—for $1.

KEY BISCAYNE

EXPENSIVE

RUSTY PELICAN, 3201 Rickenbacker Causeway. Tel. 361-3818.

Cuisine: CONTINENTAL. **Reservations:** Recommended.

$ **Prices:** Appetizers $4–$8; main courses $16–$20; lunch about half price. AE, CB, DC, MC, V.

Open: Lunch Mon–Sat 11:30am–4pm; dinner Sun–Thurs 5–11pm, Fri–Sat 5pm–midnight; brunch Sun 10:30am–4pm.

The Pelican's private tropical walkway leads over a lush waterfall into one of the most romantic dining rooms in the city, located right on beautiful blue-green Biscayne Bay. The restaurant's windows look out over the water onto the sparkling stalactites of Miami's magnificent downtown. Inside, quiet wicker paddle fans whirl overhead and saltwater fish swim in pretty tableside aquariums.

The restaurant's surf-and-turf menu features conservatively prepared prime steaks, veal, shrimp, and lobster. The food is good, but the atmosphere is even better, especially at sunset when the western view is especially awesome.

SUNDAYS ON THE BAY, 5420 Crandon Blvd. Tel. 361-6777.

Cuisine: AMERICAN. **Reservations:** Recommended for Sun brunch.

$ **Prices:** Appetizers $6–$7; main courses $15–$24; lunch about half price; Sun brunch $15.95. AE, CB, DC, MC, V.

Open: Lunch Mon–Sat 11:30am–5pm; dinner Sun–Wed 5pm–2am, Thurs–Sat 5pm–2:30am; brunch Sun from 10:30am.

Steak, chicken, pasta, veal—it's all on the menu here. But fish is the specialty, and all the local favorites—grouper, tuna, snapper, and so on—are broiled, boiled, or fried to your specifications. Competent renditions of classic shellfish dishes such as oysters Rockefeller, shrimp scampi, and lobster Fra Diavolo are also recommendable. Sunday is a fantastically fun tropical bar, with an upbeat, informal atmosphere. Sunday brunches are particularly popular, when a buffet the size of Bimini attracts the city's late-rising in-crowd.

The lively bar stays open all week until 2:30am, and live reggae music is featured Thursday through Saturday from 9pm and all day Sunday.

MODERATE

THE CARIBBEAN ROOM, in the Sheraton Royal Biscayne Hotel, 555 Ocean Dr. Tel. 361-5775.

Cuisine: SEAFOOD/TROPICAL. **Reservations:** Recommended for Fri dinner.

$ **Prices:** Appetizers $3–$7; main courses $13–$16; Fri night all-you-can-eat $25. AE, MC, V.

Open: Dinner only, daily 6–11pm.

A good pick any night of the week, the Caribbean Room becomes the find of the city every Friday, when it features a truly fantastic seafood extravaganza. On this night the restaurant features an all-you-can-eat fin-and-claw buffet, complete with mussels, clams, oysters, lobsters, shrimp, and other seafood delights. A roast is also on the table for landlubbers, as is a good selection of vegetables and homemade breads. The all-inclusive price includes dessert.

INEXPENSIVE

BAYSIDE SEAFOOD RESTAURANT AND HIDDEN COVE BAR, 3501 Rickenbacker Causeway. Tel. 361-0808.

Cuisine: SEAFOOD. **Reservations:** Not accepted.

$ **Prices:** Raw clams or oysters $7 per dozen; appetizers, salads, and sandwiches $4.50–$6; platters $7–$13. AE, MC, V.

Open: Sun–Thurs noon–11pm, Fri–Sat noon–midnight.

Known by locals as "The Hut," this ramshackle restaurant and bar is a laid-back eating and drinking place with an especially pleasant outdoor tiki hut and terrace. Good soups and salads make heavy use of local fish, conch, clams, and other seafood. Chicken wings, hamburgers, and sandwiches are also available, as is a long list of finger foods to complement the drinks and the view. On weekends, the Hut features their house band playing live reggae and calypso.

THE SANDBAR, in the Silver Sands Motel, 301 Ocean Dr. Tel. 361-5441.

Cuisine: AMERICAN. **Reservations:** Not accepted.

$ **Prices:** Main courses $7–$11; lunch about half price. AE, MC, V.

Open: Breakfast Sat–Sun 8–11am; lunch daily 11:30am–3:30pm; dinner daily 5–10pm.

★ The Sandbar is a Miami institution, boasting Key Biscayne's best beach location at any price. Situated oceanfront, in a motel that would hardly get a second look if it were anywhere else, the restaurant features fish, burgers, and salads, and a deck right on the beach. Extremely informal, patrons regularly dine barefoot, having just come off the beach. Eggs and omelets are served for breakfast on the weekends; otherwise, grouper sandwich, the house specialty, should be ordered.

DOWNTOWN

VERY EXPENSIVE

PAVILLON GRILL, in the Inter-Continental Hotel, 100 Chopin Plaza. Tel. 577-1000.

Cuisine: MIAMI REGIONAL. **Reservations:** Recommended.

$ **Prices:** Appetizers $7–$12; main courses $18–$24. AE, CB, DC, MC, V.

Open: Dinner only, Mon–Sat 6–11pm.

Private club by day, deluxe restaurant by night, the Pavillon Grill maintains its air of exclusivity, with leather sofas and an expensive salon setting. Dark-green marble columns divide the spacious dining room, while well-spaced booths and tables provide comfortable seating and a sense of privacy. The menu features both heavy club-room fare and lighter dishes prepared with a masterful Miami Regional hand. Prices here are rounded off to the highest dollar and spelled out in lieu of numerals—a practice that seems a touch pretentious, until your food arrives.

Standouts include the chilled trout appetizer, stuffed with seafood and basil, and an unusual grilled shrimp cocktail with pineapple relish and a citrus-flavored lobster mayonnaise. Skillfully prepared, adventurous dishes include boneless quail Louisiana, stuffed with oysters and andouille sausage. Meat, fish, and chicken dishes are abundant, as are a host of creative pastas, including an artichoke, garlic, truffles, and a cheese-stuffed ravioli that redefines the limits of these Italian tiny turnovers. The Hotel Inter-Continental is located adjacent to the Bayside Marketplace.

EXPENSIVE

THE FISH MARKET, in the Omni International Hotel, 1601 Biscayne Blvd. Tel. 374-0000.

Cuisine: SEAFOOD. **Reservations:** Recommended.

$ **Prices:** Appetizers $6–$8; main courses $17–$22. AE, CB, DC, MC, V.

Open: Lunch Mon–Fri 11:30am–2:30pm; dinner Mon–Sat 6:30–11pm.

One of the city's most celebrated seafood restaurants is this understated, elegant dining room right in the heart of the city. Located in an unassuming corner, just off the Omni International Hotel's fourth-floor lobby, the restaurant is both spacious and comfortable, featuring high ceilings, reasonable prices, and a sumptuous dessert-table centerpiece.

Don't overlook the appetizers here, which include a meaty Mediterranean-style seafood soup and a delicate yellowfin tuna carpaccio. Local fish, prepared and presented simply, is always the menu's main feature; sautéed or grilled, it's this guide's recommendation. The Omni International Hotel is just north of downtown at the corner of 16th Street.

MODERATE

EAST COAST FISHERIES, 360 W. Flagler St. Tel. 373-5516.

Cuisine: SEAFOOD. **Reservations:** Recommended.

$ **Prices:** Appetizers and grazing $4–$8; main courses $9–$15, most under $14; lunch from $7. AE, DISC, MC, V.

Open: Daily 10am–10pm.

East Coast Fisheries is a no-nonsense retail market and restaurant, offering a terrific variety of the freshest fish available. The dozen or so plain wood tables are surrounded by refrigerated glass cases filled with snapper, salmon, mahi mahi, trout, tuna, crabs, oysters, lobsters, and the like. The menu is absolutely huge, and features every fish imaginable, cooked the way you want it—grilled, fried, stuffed, Cajun style, Florentine, hollandaise, blackened. It's a pleasure to walk around and ask questions about the many local fish before choosing. Service is fast. But good prices and an excellent product still mean long lines on weekends. Highly recommended. The restaurant is located on the Miami River, at the edge of West Flagler Street.

LAS TAPAS, in the Bayside Marketplace, 401 Biscayne Blvd. Tel. 372-2737.

Cuisine: SPANISH. **Reservations:** Not required.

$ **Prices:** Tapas $4–$7; main courses $12–$19; lunch about half price. AE, CB, DC, DISC, MC, V.

Open: Sun–Thurs 11:30am–midnight, Fri–Sat 11:30am–1am.

Occupying a large corner of downtown's Bayside Marketplace, glass-wrapped Las Tapas is a pretty and fun place to dine in a laid-back, easy atmosphere.

Tapas, small dishes of Spanish delicacies, are the featured fare here. Good chicken, veal, and seafood main dishes are on the menu, but it's more fun to taste a variety of the restaurant's tapas. The best include: shrimp in garlic, smoked pork shank with Spanish sausage, baby eel in garlic and oil, and chicken sauté with garlic and mushroom.

An open kitchen in front of the entrance greets diners with succulent smells. The long dining room is outlined in red Spanish stone and decorated with hundreds of hanging hams. Bayside Marketplace is on Biscayne Bay in the middle of downtown.

ZUM ALTEN FRITZ, 1840 NE Fourth Ave. Tel. 530-8640.

Cuisine: GERMAN. **Reservations:** Not required.

$ Prices: Appetizers $3–$8; main courses $8–$17; half liter of beer $5. CB, DC, MC, V.

Open: Lunch Mon–Fri 11am–3pm; dinner Mon–Sat 5–11pm.

Offering a veritable survey of authentic German cooking, this excellent *essenhaus* (literally "eating house") is known for its homemade wursts and its on-site brewery (which operates during the winter months). The wieners, flavored with veal, paprika, or garlic, are all served with homemade sauerkraut, mashed potatoes, and a hearty German mustard. A number of schnitzels are also available, including an unusual vegetarian cheese variety.

Live oom-pah music is performed every Wednesday, Friday, and Saturday night (see "Evening Entertainment" in Chapter 5 for more information). The restaurant is located one block east of Biscayne Boulevard, three blocks north of the Omni International Hotel.

BUDGET

HOOTERS, in the Bayside Marketplace, 401 Biscayne Blvd. Tel. 371-3004.

Cuisine: AMERICAN. **Reservations:** Not accepted.

$ Prices: Meals $5–$12. AE, MC, V.

Open: Mon–Thurs 11am–midnight, Fri–Sat 11am–1am, Sun 11am–10pm.

Hooters' hiring policy seems to mean buxom waitresses in midriff tops, giving it a reputation as one of the most sexist restaurants in Florida. Despite this (or because of it, depending on your perspective), the casual second-floor restaurant does offer good, inexpensive meals, and a great terrace overlooking the Bayside Marketplace and Biscayne Bay. Large chicken, fish, and meat burgers are served with massive quantities of beer. Local fraternity brothers are a common sight here, huddled around mountains of chicken wings and full pitchers. Hooters is on the second floor of the Marketplace's north pavilion.

There is a second location in Coconut Grove's Cocowalk, 3015 Grand Ave. (tel. 442-6004).

LITTLE HAVANA

Southwest 8th Street, also known as Calle Ocho, is the center of Little Havana, home to a large number of Cuban immigrants. In addition to shops and markets, this area contains some of the world's best Cuban and Latin American restaurants, treasures that help make the city a wonderful place to visit.

Most restaurants list menu items in English for the benefit of "norteamericano" diners. Here's a sample of what you can expect:

Arroz con pollo: Roast chicken served with pimento-seasoned yellow rice.

Picadillo: A rich stir-fry of ground meat, brown gravy, peas, pimentos, raisins, and olives.

Platanos: A deep-fried, soft, mildly sweet banana.

Pan cubãno: This is the famous long, white crusty Cuban bread that should be ordered with every meal.

Ropa vieja: Literally meaning "old clothes," this is a delicious stringy beef stew.

Cafe cubano: Very strong black coffee, served in thimble-size cups with lots of sugar—a real eye-opener.

Palomilla: Similar to American minute steak, thinly sliced beef usually served with onions, parsley, and a mountain of french fries.

Camarones: Shrimp.

Paella: A Spanish dish of chicken, sausage, seafood, and pork mixed with saffron rice and peas—very good.

Fabada asturiana: A hearty black-bean and sausage soup.

Tapas: A general name for Spanish-style hors d'oeuvres; served in grazing-size portions.

MODERATE

CASA JUANCHO, 2436 SW 8th St. Tel. 642-2452.

Cuisine: SPANISH/CUBAN. **Reservations:** Recommended; not accepted Fri–Sat after 8pm.

$ **Prices:** Tapas $6–$8; main courses $11–$20; lunch about half price. AE, CB, DC, MC, V.

Open: Mon–Fri noon–midnight, Sat–Sun noon–1am.

Casa Juancho offers an ambitious menu of excellently prepared main dishes and tapas. Except for a few outstanding entrees like roast suckling pig, baby eels in garlic and olive oil, and Iberian-style snapper, diners would be wise to stick exclusively to tapas, smaller dishes of Spanish "finger food." Some of the best include mixed seafood vinaigrette, fresh shrimp in hot garlic sauce, and fried calamari rings.

The several dining rooms are decorated with traditional Spanish furnishings and are enlivened nightly by strolling Spanish musicians.

INEXPENSIVE

HY VONG VIETNAMESE CUISINE, 3458 SW 8th St. Tel. 446-3674.

Cuisine: VIETNAMESE. **Reservations:** Not required.

$ **Prices:** Appetizers $2–$3.50; main courses $8–$12. No credit cards.

Open: Dinner only, Tues–Sun 5:30–10:30pm. **Closed:** Two weeks in Aug.

Similar in style, if not taste, to Thai food, Vietnamese cuisine combines the best of Asian and French cooking with spectacular results. The food at Hy Vong is terrific. Appetizers include small, tightly packed Vietnamese spring rolls, and kimchee, a spicy, fermented cabbage. Star entrees include pastry-enclosed chicken with a watercress cream-cheese sauce, and fish in a tangy mango sauce.

The dining room itself is just a small, sparsely decorated, wood-paneled room. Located in the heart of Little Havana, it attracts an interesting and mixed crowd.

BUDGET

VERSAILLES, 3555 SW 8th St. Tel. 444-0240.

Cuisine: CUBAN. **Reservations:** Not accepted.

$ **Prices:** Soup and salad $2–$5; main courses $5–$8. DC, MC, V.

Open: Mon–Thurs 8am–2am, Fri 8am–3:30am, Sat 8am–4:30am, Sun 9am–2am.

Versailles is the area's most celebrated diner, especially after 10pm. The restaurant sparkles with glass, chandeliers, and mirrors, and moves at a quick pace to please patrons at tables and counters and in take-out lines. If you want inexpensive, authentic Cuban cuisine, look no further. Nothing fancy here, just straightforward food from the home country. The menu is a veritable survey of Cuban cooking and includes specialties like Moors and Christians (flavorful black beans with white rice), ropa vieja, and fried whole fish.

NORTH DADE

VERY EXPENSIVE

CHEF ALLEN'S, 19088 NE 29th Ave., North Miami Beach. Tel. 935-2900.

Cuisine: MIAMI REGIONAL. **Reservations:** Not required.

$ **Prices:** Appetizers $7–$10; main courses $20–$27. AE, MC, V.

Open: Dinner only, Sun–Thurs 6–10:30pm, Fri–Sat 6–11pm.

If one needs any evidence that Miami Regional cuisine is strongly influenced by California cooking, look no further than Chef Allen's. Owner/chef Allen Susser, of New York's Le Cirque fame, has built a classy but relaxed restaurant with art deco furnishings, a glass-enclosed kitchen, and a hot-pink swirl of neon surrounding the dining room's ceiling.

The delicious homemade breadsticks are enough to hold you, but don't let them tempt you away from an appetizer that may include lobster and crab cakes served with strawberry ginger chutney, or baked Brie with spinach, sun-dried tomatoes, and pine nuts. Served by an energetic, young staff, favorite main dishes include crisp roast duck with cranberry sauce, and mesquite-grilled Norwegian salmon with champagne grapes, green onions, and basil spaetzle. Local fish dishes, in various delectable guises, and homemade pastas are always on the menu. An extensive wine list is well chosen and features several good buys. The restaurant is on the mainland at 190th Street, near the Dade County Line.

EXPENSIVE

MARK'S PLACE, 2286 NE 123rd St., North Miami. Tel. 893-6888.

Cuisine: MIAMI REGIONAL. **Reservations:** Recommended.

$ Prices: Appetizers $6–$9, main courses $10–$15 for pasta and pizza, $16–$20 for meat and fish; lunch about half price. AE, MC, V.

Open: Lunch Mon–Fri noon–2:30pm; dinner Mon–Thurs 6–10:30pm, Fri–Sat 6–11pm, Sun 6–10pm.

Attracting an upscale but leisurely crowd, this restaurant's claim to fame is its owner/chef, Mark Militello, an extraordinarily gifted artist who works primarily with fresh, natural, local ingredients. A smart, modern bistro, Mark's Place shines with off-white walls, an aquamarine ceiling, contemporary glass sculptures, and a friendly, open kitchen. Each table has its own pepper mill, and fresh, home-baked bread.

Mark's inspired food is often unusual, and rarely misses the mark. Appetizers include oak-grilled mozzarella and prosciutto, curry-breaded fried oysters, and an unusual petite pizza topped with smoked chicken and Monterey Jack cheese. The best main dishes are braised black grouper, Florida conch stew, or flank steak in a sesame marinade. Try one of Mark's suggestions. Desserts like Icky Sticky Coconut Pudding are equally unusual, and baked with the same originality as the rest of the menu.

MODERATE

THE FISH PEDDLER, 8699 Biscayne Blvd. Tel. 757-0648.

Cuisine: SEAFOOD. **Reservations:** Not required.

$ Prices: Appetizers $2–$4; main courses $9–$15. AE, MC, V.

Open: Dinner only, Tues–Sun 5–10pm.

If it were owned and managed by anyone else, this modest restaurant would hardly deserve a second look. But seafood-king Mike Gordon has made the Fish Peddler his latest hobby, and it's one of the tastiest restaurants around. There's no view and little atmosphere, but knowledgeable locals still pack the place nightly. Dinners are prepared in an open, diner-style kitchen, and served by friendly, similarly styled waitresses. Appetizers include some excellent chowders (black grouper included) and fresh clam dishes. Whole fish are regularly available, and everything is fresh and cooked to order right before your eyes. Say "hi" to Mike—he's the oldest and most energetic man in the place, and always on the premises.

MIKE GORDON'S, 1201 NE 79th St. Tel. 751-4429.

Cuisine: SEAFOOD. **Reservations:** Not accepted.

$ Prices: Appetizers $3–$6; main courses $13–$17; lunch about half price. AE, CB, DC, MC, V.

Open: Daily noon–10pm.

Over 40 years have passed and this Miami institution is now managed by Mike Gordon's sons, but it still offers seafood as fresh as the fish market next door. This is a traditional pier restaurant in a Cape Cod kind of way, with dark-wood beams, ceiling fans, and pelicans playing on the docks outside. The huge menu features lobsters, crabs, and an usual array of meaty local fish, traditionally prepared and served with drawn butter and french fries. The best part of this dining experience is the restaurant's interesting location, directly on the Intracoastal Waterway. Even if you have reservations, it's likely you'll have to wait for a table. But the bar is long, and there are few better places in Miami to pass the time. The restaurant is located at the foot of the mainland side of the 79th Street Causeway.

A second restaurant has opened in the Four Ambassadors building, 801 S. Bayshore Dr., Coconut Grove (tel. 577-4202).

INEXPENSIVE

THE MELTING POT, in Sunny Isles Plaza shopping center, 3143 NE 163rd St., North Miami Beach. Tel. 947-2228.

Cuisine: FONDUE. **Reservations:** Not required.

$ Prices: Main courses $9–$10 for cheese fondue, $11–$16 for meat and fish fondues. AE, MC, V.

Open: Dinner only, Sun–Thurs 5:30–11pm, Fri–Sat 5:30pm–midnight.

Dipping your own chunks of bread into pots of sizzling cheese is certainly a different dining experience. This traditional dish is supplemented by combination meat-and-fish dinners, which are served with one of almost a dozen different sauces. The Melting Pot's variation on Swiss fondue is a good alternative dinner decision. But best, perhaps, is dessert: chunks of pineapple, bananas, apples, and cherries that you dip into a creamy chocolate fondue. No liquor is served here, but the wine list is extensive, and beer is available. The restaurant is located on the north side of 163rd Street, between U.S. 1 and Collins Avenue.

A second Melting Pot is located at 9835 SW 72nd St. (Sunset Drive), Kendall (tel. 279-8816).

CORAL GABLES & ENVIRONS

VERY EXPENSIVE

CHRISTY'S, 3101 Ponce de Leon Blvd. Tel. 446-1400.

Cuisine: AMERICAN. **Reservations:** Required.

$ Prices: Appetizers $4–$7; main courses $17–$25; lunch about half price. AE, CB, DC, MC, V.

Open: Lunch Mon–Fri 11:30am–4pm; dinner Sun–Fri 4–10:45pm, Sat 5–11:45pm.

Decorated in an elegant, Victorian style, Christy's is one of Coral Gables's most expensive trendy establishments. Frequented by a power-tie crowd, this New American eatery is known primarily for its generous cuts of thick, juicy steaks and ribs. "Big" appears to be the chef's chief instruction—the prime rib is so thick even a small cut weighs about a pound. New York strip, filet mignon, chateaubriand . . . it's all on the menu here, and all steaks are fully aged without chemicals or freezing. Entrees are served with a jumbo Caesar salad and a baked potato. Seafood, veal, and chicken dishes are also available.

EXPENSIVE

ARAGON CAFE, in the Colonnade Hotel, 180 Aragon Ave. Tel. 448-9966.

Cuisine: MIAMI REGIONAL. **Reservations:** Recommended.

$ Prices: Appetizers $6–$8; main courses $15–$22; lunch about half price. AE, DC, MC, V.

Open: Breakfast daily 6:30–10am; lunch Mon–Fri 11:30am–3pm; dinner Mon–Sat 6–11pm.

Like the hotel itself, the handcrafted mahogany and marble Aragon Café exudes a quiet elegance with an international flair. The 85-seat restaurant features period furniture and a formal atmosphere that's as elegant as the cuisine.

Appetizers include such delicacies as blue-crab cakes with fried and shredded leeks and radicchio-wrapped lobster. Seafood is the house specialty, and salmon is the fish of choice; several gutsy preparations each claim completely individual flavors. Other main choices include Muscovy duck with duck sausage and various veal selections. For dessert, a lemon torte with raspberry sauce literally takes the cake. The Aragon Café isn't cheap, but it's highly recommended as one of the best restaurants of its kind in Miami.

THE BISTRO, 2611 Ponce de Leon Blvd. Tel. 442-9671.

Cuisine: FRENCH. **Reservations:** Not required.

$ Prices: Appetizers $5–$10; main courses $16–$26; lunch $4–$14. AE, CB, DC, MC, V.

Open: Lunch Tues–Fri 11:30am–2pm; dinner Tues–Thurs 6–10:30pm, Fri–Sat 6–11pm.

The Bistro's intimate atmosphere is heightened by soft lighting, 19th-century European antiques and prints, and an abundance of flowers atop crisp white tablecloths.

Co-owners Ulrich Sigrist and André Barnier keep a watchful eye over their experienced kitchen staff, which regularly dishes out artful French dishes with an international accent. Look for the terrine maison, a country-style veal-and-pork appetizer that's the house specialty. Common French bistro fare like escargots au Pernod and coquilles St-Jacques are prepared with uncommon spices and accoutrements, livening a rather typical continental menu. Especially recommended is the roast duck with honey-mustard sauce and the chicken breasts in a mild curry sauce, each served with fried bananas and pineapple.

CAFFÈ BACI, 2522 Ponce de Leon Blvd. Tel. 442-0600.

Cuisine: ITALIAN. **Reservations:** Recommended for dinner.

$ Prices: Appetizers $6–$7; main courses $12–$13 for pasta, $14–$19 for meat and fish; lunch about half price. AE, CB, DISC, DC, MC, V.

Open: Lunch Mon–Fri 10:30am–2:30pm; dinner Sun–Thurs 6–11pm, Fri–Sat 6–11:30pm.

The most stylish bistro in Miami comes in the form of this tiny, classy restaurant with great food at reasonable prices. Soft pink pastel walls, covered with Roman architectural prints, reflect off a pretty, tin-can-shaped gold-metal ceiling. A typical meal, served by courteous, professional waiters, might start with fresh tuna carpaccio, or a marinated medley of artichoke hearts, mushrooms, tomatoes, and zucchini. Main courses include homemade pastas with sweet Italian sausages, porcini (mushrooms), basil and tomato sauces, as well as a number of succulent, marinated meats and fish topped with tomato and cream sauces and any number of aromatic herbs.

If you have difficulty choosing from the terrific menu—and you will—trust suggestions made by the boisterous proprietor, Domenico Diana.

CHARADE, 2900 Ponce de Leon Blvd. Tel. 448-6077.

Cuisine: FRENCH/SWISS. **Reservations:** Recommended.

$ Prices: Appetizers $5–$7; main courses $15–$20; lunch about half price. AE, CB, DC, MC, V.

Open: Lunch Mon–Fri 11:30am–3pm; dinner Sun–Thurs 6–11pm, Fri–Sat 6pm–midnight.

A historic Coral Gables low-rise is the setting for this restaurant with soft piano music, a romantic courtyard, and excellent French/Swiss cuisine. More formal than Kaleidoscope, its cousin in Coconut Grove (see below), Charade has a gentleman's club feel with wooden ceilings and furniture and old-world portraits on the walls.

Like many imaginative continental restaurants, eating here is a real culinary experience. Masterful entrees include shrimp-and-chicken jambalaya; duckling with orange, kiwi, ginger, and Grand Marnier; and chateaubriand.

LE FESTIVAL, 2120 Salzedo St. Tel. 442-8545.

Cuisine: FRENCH. **Reservations:** Required for dinner.

$ Prices: Appetizers $5–$8; main courses $16–$20; lunch about half price. AE, CB, DC, MC, V.

Open: Lunch Mon–Fri 11:45am–2:30pm; dinner Mon–Thurs 6–10:30pm, Fri–Sat 6–11pm. **Closed:** Sept–Oct.

Le Festival's contemporary, sharp pink awning hangs over one of Miami's most traditional Spanish-style buildings, hinting at the unusual combination of cuisine and decor that awaits inside. In fact, the snazzy, modern dining rooms, which are enlivened with New French features and furnishings, belie the traditional features that are the highlights of a well-planned menu.

Shrimp and crab cocktails, fresh pâtés, and an unusual cheese soufflé are star starters. Both meat and fish are either simply seared with herbs and spices, or doused in the wine-and-cream sauces that have made the French famous. Dessert can be a delight with a modest amount of foresight. Grand Marnier and chocolate soufflés are individually prepared, and must be ordered at the same time as the entrees. A wide selection of other homemade sweets should also entice you to leave room for dessert.

Le Festival is located five blocks north of Miracle Mile, in an area slightly removed from other Coral Gables restaurants.

RESTAURANT ST. MICHEL, in the Hotel Place St. Michel, 162 Alcazar Ave. Tel. 444-1666.

Cuisine: FRENCH/MEDITERRANEAN. **Reservations:** Recommended.

$ Prices: Appetizers $6–$8; main courses $14–$16 for pasta, $18–$22 for meat and fish. AE, CB, MC, V.

Open: Lunch Mon–Sat 11am–4pm; dinner Sun–Thurs 6–10:30pm, Fri–Sat 5–11:30pm; brunch Sun 11am–2:30pm.

One of the most subtly sensuous restaurants in Miami is, quite appropriately, located in the city's most romantic hotel. Art deco chandeliers, hardwood floors, delicate antiques, and flowers re-create the feeling of a quaint 1930s Parisian café.

The creative menu complements the artful decor with its metropolitan French coast cuisine. Scallop ceviche and grilled, marinated lamb highlight the hors d'oeuvres, while prosciutto-stuffed veal chops, and an excellent couscous lead the winning entrees. Goose, rabbit, venison, and other unusual meats often grace the tables, topped with tangy fruit sauces and spicy wine creations. A special six-course dinner is prepared and priced nightly.

YUCA, 148 Giralda. Tel. 444-4448.

Cuisine: CUBAN/AMERICAN. **Reservations:** Recommended.

$ Prices: Appetizers $5–$7; main courses $15–$20. AE, CB, DISC, DC, MC, V.

Open: Lunch Mon–Fri noon–2:30; dinner daily 6–11pm.

One of Miami's most celebrated ethnic eateries, Yuca features an exciting menu that combines traditional Cuban ingredients with the latest international influences. Fun is always the dish of the day, and not just because of the restaurant's catchy name, an anagram for Young Upscale Cuban-American. While the kitchen is strictly gourmet, one can't help but think that the colorful menu and decor were created with tongue firmly in cheek. Star entrees include barbecued ribs with a tangy guava sauce, and grilled kosher chicken with garlic, lime, and thyme. A rear-wall mural of smartly dressed young professionals looks down at diners, who sit in a small, busy room at simple round tables atop clean tile floors.

MODERATE

EL CORRAL, 3545 Coral Way. Tel. 444-8272.

Cuisine: NICARAGUAN. **Reservations:** Not required.

$ Prices: Appetizers $3–$5; main courses $9–$15 (served two for the price of one Mon–Thurs 5–7pm). AE, MC, V.

Open: Mon–Thurs 11:30am–11pm, Fri 11:30am–midnight, Sat noon–midnight, Sun noon–11pm.

This untraditional Nicaraguan steakhouse serves punchy marinated beef filets, along with plantains, rice, and beans from the barrio. Antojitos, Nicaragua's answer to appetizers, include homemade sausages with salad and plantains, fried pork with Créole sauce, and a wonderful deep-fried cheese. Aside from a couple of obligatory fish and chicken listings, the long entree menu focuses strictly on beef in various guises. Tender filet tips are served under a sauce of butter, brandy, cream, and Roquefort cheese. And a center cut tenderloin is matched with pickled onions and marinara sauce.

Most Nicaraguans don't even think of eating dinner before 9 or 10pm, so El Corral entices hungry others with a great two-for-the-price-of-one entree "early-bird" special, Monday through Thursday from 5 to 7pm. It's a good deal for vacationing carnivores on a budget.

RISTORANTE TANINO, 2312 Ponce de Leon. Tel. 446-1666.

Cuisine: ITALIAN. **Reservations:** Not required.

$ Prices: Main courses $5–$8 at lunch, $7–$8 at dinner for pasta, $9–$16 for meat, fish, and poultry. AE, CB, DC, DISC, MC, V.

Open: Lunch Mon–Fri 11:30am–3pm; dinner daily 6–11pm.

Restaurants in the Gables come and go. But, hopefully, Ristorante Tanino is here to stay. The beautiful, petite exterior houses an equally intimate dining room, where great Italian cuisine is remarkably underpriced. Lunch offers the best deals, with daily $6 specials that include a saucy manicotti, a robust lasagne, and a particularly well-done penne with eggplant and tomato sauce. All are served with soup or salad. Specials would easily sell for twice the price in New York. Dinner is à la carte, and the well-chosen menu is also kindly priced. Pastas, like fettuccine Alfredo with smoked salmon, are as good as or better than similar dishes served elsewhere at twice the cost. Most of the other meals are more traditionally prepared, like chicken parmigiana, veal marsala, and saltimbocca, representing both good cooking and good value.

INEXPENSIVE

HOUSE OF INDIA, 22 Merrick Way. Tel. 444-2348.

Cuisine: INDIAN. **Reservations:** Not required.

$ Prices: Appetizers $1–$5; main courses $7–$10, lunch buffet (served Mon–Fri 11:30am–3pm and Sat noon–3pm) $6.95. AE, MC, V.

Open: Mon–Thurs 10:30am–10pm, Fri–Sat 11:30am–11pm, Sun 5–10pm.

The House of India's curries, kormas, and kebabs are some of the city's best, but the restaurant's well-priced all-you-can-eat lunch buffet is unsurpassed. All the favorites are on display, including tandoori chicken, naan bread, and various meat and vegetarian curries, as well as rice and dal (lentils). If you've never had Indian food before, this is an excellent place to experiment, since you can see the food before you choose it. Veterans will know that this is high-quality cooking from the subcontinent.

The restaurant is not fancy, but nicely decorated with hanging printed cloths, and traditional music. It's located one block north of Miracle Mile.

BUDGET

BISCAYNE MIRACLE MILE CAFETERIA, 147 Miracle Mile, Coral Gables. Tel. 444-9005.

Cuisine: SOUTHERN AMERICAN. **Reservations:** Not accepted.

$ Prices: Main courses $3–$4. No credit cards.

Open: Lunch Mon–Sat 11am–2:15pm; dinner Mon–Sat 4–8pm, Sun 11am–8pm.

No bar, no music, and no flowers on the tables—just great southern-style cooking at unbelievably low prices. The menu changes, but roast beef, baked fish, and barbecue ribs are typical entrees, few of which exceed $4.

As the name says, food is picked up cafeteria style and brought to one of the many unadorned Formica tables. The restaurant is always busy.

CAFE 94, 94 Miracle Mile. Tel. 444-7933.

Cuisine: CUBAN.

$ Prices: Breakfast/lunch $2–$5. No credit cards.

Open: Mon–Sat 7am–4pm.

This Cuban coffee shop is a great place to try the island's specialties. Daily lunch specials cost less than $5 and usually include grilled chicken or steak, rice, black beans, and plantains. Cuban-style sandwiches are also available, as are hearty American-style breakfasts. Café 94 occupies a narrow storefront in the heart of the Gables' main shopping thoroughfare.

ESTATE WINES & GOURMET FOODS, 92 Miracle Mile. Tel. 442-9915.

Cuisine: POLISH/AMERICAN.

$ **Prices:** $4–$6. No credit cards.

Open: Mon–Fri 10am–8pm, Sat 10am–6pm.

This storefront, in the heart of Coral Gables main shopping strip, is primarily a wine shop. But Magdalena A. von Freytag, one of the friendliest storekeepers in Miami, also serves gourmet meals to a handful of lucky lunchers. Deliciously thick soups are served with pâtés, salads, and sandwiches around an overturned barrel that can only accommodate a handful of diners. I hesitate to write about this find for fear of spoiling it. Magdalena's only advertisement is word of mouth, and knowledgeable locals are her dedicated regulars.

COCONUT GROVE

EXPENSIVE

CAFE SCI SCI, 3043 Grand Ave. Tel. 446-5104.

Cuisine: ITALIAN. **Reservations:** Not required.

$ **Prices:** Appetizers $7–$9; main courses $11–$13 for pasta, $16–$23 for meat and fish; lunch about half price. AE, MC, V.

Open: Lunch Tues–Sun noon–4pm; dinner Sun–Thurs 5:30pm–12:30am, Fri–Sat 5:30pm–1am.

The original Sci Sci café (pronounced "shi shi") was a turn-of-the-century Naples eatery and a meeting place for international artists and intellectuals. That restaurant also claims it was the site where gelato—the silky-smooth Italian ice cream—was perfected. Like its namesake, Café Sci Sci in the Grove is also an inviting place to lounge and linger. Their solid marble floors and columns combine with ornate decor and furnishings to create one of the area's most stunning European-style cafés. Visually and gastronomically, this restaurant is a pleasing combination of old and new.

The large menu offers both hot and cold antipasti, including carpaccio, sautéed mussels, ham and melon, and fried mozzarella with marinara sauce. Pasta entrees feature such winning combinations as homemade black fettuccine with vodka, tomato, cream, and black pepper; tortellini filled with smoked cheese in Gorgonzola sauce; and papardella rustiche-wide noodles with shrimp, saffron, peas, and cream. Meat, fish, and chicken dishes also combine traditional and contemporary styles. The pace here is relaxed, as every order is freshly prepared. The restaurant is at the Groves' primary intersection, at the top of Main Highway.

KALEIDOSCOPE, 3112 Commodore Plaza. Tel. 446-5010.

Cuisine: CONTINENTAL. **Reservations:** Recommended.

$ **Prices:** Appetizers $6–$9; main courses $12–$15 for pasta, $14–$18 for meat and fish; lunch about half price. AE, CB, DC, DISC, MC, V.

Open: Lunch Mon–Fri 11:30am–3pm; dinner Mon–Sat 6–11pm, Sun 5:30–10:30pm.

Kaleidoscope is one of the few restaurants in the heart of Coconut Grove that would still be recommended if it were located somewhere less exciting. The atmosphere is elegantly relaxed, with attentive, low-key service, comfortable seating, and a well-designed terrace overlooking the busy sidewalks below. Dishes are well prepared and pastas, topped with meaty sauces like seafood and fresh basil, or pesto with grilled yellowfin tuna, are especially tasty. The linguine with salmon and fresh dill is perfection. The appetizers are tempting, but even hearty eaters should be warned that entrees are large, and all are preceded by a house salad.

MODERATE

MONTY'S BAYSHORE RESTAURANT, 2560 S. Bayshore Dr. Tel. 858-1431.

Cuisine: SEAFOOD. **Reservations:** Not required.
$ Prices: Chowder $3; appetizers and sandwiches $6–$8; platters $7–$12; main courses $15–$20. AE, CB, DC, MC, V.
Open: Daily 11am–3am.

Monty's comes in three parts: a lounge, a raw bar, and a restaurant. Between them, they serve everything from steak and seafood to munchies like nachos, potato skins, and buffalo chicken wings. This is a fun kind of place, usually with more revelers and drinkers than diners. Sitting at the outdoor dockside bar can be a pleasant way to spend an evening. There's live music nightly, as well as all day on the weekends (see "The Bar Scene" in "Evening Entertainment," in Chapter 5).

SEÑOR FROG'S, 3008 Grand Ave. Tel. 448-0999.

Cuisine: MEXICAN. **Reservations:** Recommended on weekends.
$ Prices: Main courses $9–$12. AE, CB, DC, MC, V.
Open: Dinner only, Mon–Thurs 5pm–1am, Fri 5pm–2am, Sat 2pm–2am, Sun 2pm–1am.

You know you're getting close to Señor Frog's when you hear laughing and singing spilling out of the restaurant's courtyard. Filled with the college-student crowd, this restaurant is known for a raucous good time, its mariachi band, and powerful margaritas. The food at this rocking cantina is as good as its atmosphere, featuring excellent renditions of traditional Mexican-American favorites. The mole enchiladas, with 14 different kinds of mild chiles mixed with chocolate, is as flavorful as any I've tasted. Almost everything is served with rice and beans and, like all good Mexican places, portions are so large, few diners are able to finish.

SOUTH MIAMI

INEXPENSIVE

EL TORITO, in The Falls shopping center, 8888 Howard Dr. Tel. 255-6506.

Cuisine: MEXICAN. **Reservations:** Not required.
$ Prices: Appetizers $4–$5.50; main courses $6–$9. AE, MC, V.
Open: Daily 11am–11pm.

Red clay tile, Mexican artifacts, and three-dimensional murals create an authentic south-of-the-border atmosphere only found in American restaurant chains. It's nice though. And seeing how it's pretty difficult to mess up Mexican "cuisine," especially when it's prepared by authentic Latinos, the food is pretty good too. All the hits are here, including enchiladas, tacos, chimichangas, and tostadas. It's pretty cheap, and very unlikely that you'll leave hungry.

A second El Torito is located in the Miami International Mall, 10633 NW 12th St. (tel. 591-0671).

BUDGET

LB'S EATERY, 5813 Ponce de Leon Blvd. Tel. 661-8879.

Cuisine: AMERICAN.
$ Prices: Salads and sandwiches $3–$4.50; main courses $5–$8. DISC, MC, V.
Open: Mon–Thurs 11am–10pm, Fri–Sat 11am–11:30pm.

High-quality, low-priced meals are served cafeteria style in this popular, no-nonsense eatery. A good selection of salads include chicken, tuna-apple, and a variety of green combinations. Sandwiches are built on breads or croissants, and include almost every known variation. For an entree, look for lasagne, chicken, roast beef, and vegetarian selections like ratatouille. Five nightly dinner specials include entree, salad, and garlic bread, and start under $5. There are no waiters here—order at the counter, and wait to be called. Despite its listing in this category, LB's is technically in Coral Gables, a half block from the University of Miami stadium, across from the Metrorail tracks.

SPECIALTY DINING

HOTEL DINING

The **Aragon Cafe** in the Colonnade Hotel (tel. 448-9966) is highly recommended as one of the best restaurants of its kind in Miami, with an atmosphere as elegant as the cuisine (see entry under "Coral Gables and Environs," above). In the Fontainebleau Hilton, the **Dining Galleries** (tel. 538-2000) has a pleasantly overdone decor and a menu emphasizing meat and fish (see the entry under "Miami Beach" above). The elegant and opulent **Dominique's** (tel. 865-6500), in the Alexander All-Suite Luxury Hotel, spotlights a variety of wild game appetizers such as alligator scaloppini as well as such entrees as tender, marinated rack of lamb and prime steak (see entry under "Miami Beach"; jackets required for men).

In the downtown area are two excellent choices. Just off the Omni International's fourth-floor lobby is **The Fish Market** (tel. 374-0000), with one of the best seafood menus in town. The **Pavillion Grill** (tel. 577-1000), in the Inter-Continental is a deluxe restaurant with an imaginative and adventurous cuisine. (See entries under "Downtown," above.) For a more laid-back choice, try the **Restaurant St. Michel** (tel. 444-1666) in the Hotel Place St. Michel, where a creative French coast cuisine is complemented by an artful deco decor (see entry under "Coral Gables and Environs," above).

BREAKFAST/BRUNCH

The Fontainebleau Hilton's famous Sunday brunch is served in The **Dining Galleries** (tel. 538-2000). Eggs cooked to order, carved meats, and fresh-baked breads served buffet style ensures that no one leaves hungry. Right in the heart of South Miami's art deco district, the **Fairmount Gardens Restaurant,** 1000 Collins Ave. (tel. 531-0050), in the Fairmount Hotel, features traditional dishes such as eggs Benedict and florentine served with fruit-flavored buns and well-prepared potatoes in a tropical outdoor courtyard setting. Near the same area, the **News Cafe,** 800 Ocean Dr. (tel. 538-NEWS) offers an inexpensive and excellent breakfast of both traditional and health-oriented yogurt dishes. **Sundays on the Bay,** 5420 Crandon Blvd. (tel. 361-6777) in Key Biscayne is a fun, tropical eatery with an upbeat, informal atmosphere. Sunday brunch here is highly popular, so reservations are recommended, but still expect a wait.

LATE NIGHT

Most (but not all) **7-Eleven** food stores are open around the clock, including the downtown store at 2 SE 7th St. (tel. 358-5409), and the South Miami Beach branch at 1447 Alton Rd. (tel. 672-1520), and the store at 51 Harbor Dr., Key Biscayne (tel. 361-6857).

In South Miami Beach, the **News Cafe** (tel. 538-NEWS), and **Wolfie's** (tel. 538-6626), both stay open until the wee hours (see entries under "South Miami Beach," above). **Versailles** (tel. 444-0240) is Little Havana's most celebrated diner, busy and brisk until 2am (see entry under "Little Havana," above).

DINING COMPLEXES

The **Bayside Marketplace Food Court,** 401 Biscayne Blvd. (tel. 577-3344), is not a single eatery. It's a restaurant shopping mall with more than 30 stalls and stands to choose from, representing a myriad of international cuisine. Choices range from bagel sandwiches and burgers to grilled chicken, Chinese stir-fry, Créole conchs, and Middle Eastern kebabs. Few dishes top $7. Plenty of public tables means that your entire party can be satisfied by different delights and still eat together.

Many of the counters here specialize in dessert, including Bimini Bay Brownies, the Cookie Bar, Everything Yogurt, and The Fudgery, making the Food Court an excellent stop, even if it's not mealtime. For more information on stores in the Bayside Marketplace, see "Savvy Shopping," in Chapter 5. The Food Court is located on the entire second level of the Marketplace's main pavilion. It's open Monday through

Saturday from 10am to 10pm and on Sunday from noon to 8pm. Some eateries open later.

PICNIC FARE

Publix is one of Miami's largest supermarket chains, with locations that include 18330 Collins Ave., Sunny Isles (tel. 931-9615); 2551 LeJeune Rd., Coral Gables (tel. 445-2641); and 4870 Biscayne Blvd., Greater Miami North (tel. 576-4318). Small groceries can be very convenient, and are literally located all over Miami. Ask at your hotel for the closest.

Because of the "immigrant" nature of the city, Caribbean staples can be found in even the most conservative supermarkets. Look for unusual sauces and dressings, as well as tropical fruits like guava and papaya. **One Man and His Dog,** 834 NE 183rd St. (tel. 770-1558), is a grocery in the heart of Miami's Jamaican community. Here you can pick up Rasta staples like jerk sauce, lime pepper, yam flour, extra-hot meat patties, and Red Stripe beer. A real find.

CHAPTER 5

WHAT TO SEE & DO IN MIAMI

1. **THE TOP ATTRACTIONS**
2. **MORE ATTRACTIONS**
- **FROMMER'S FAVORITE MIAMI EXPERIENCES**
3. **COOL FOR KIDS**
4. **ORGANIZED TOURS**
5. **SPORTS & RECREATION**
6. **SAVVY SHOPPING**
7. **EVENING ENTERTAINMENT**
8. **NETWORKS & RESOURCES**
9. **EASY EXCURSIONS FROM MIAMI**

Many of Miami's attractions were built in the 1940s and 1950s, designed to cash in on the growing tourist-oriented economy. Like the Fontainebleau hotel along Collins Avenue, the city's still-extant showplaces are time capsules—relics of an earlier age.

With few exceptions, Miami's best sights are outdoors. The city's beautiful buildings and beaches tend to be far away from each other, so driving is definitely in order. Miami is relatively easy to negotiate; you can't get too lost.

Miami has always been a city of dreams, a place for tourists to relax and recuperate. Miami's single most common attribute is its ability to entertain. The city's top tourist destinations highlight curiosities in architecture, plants, animals, and human beings. And leaping lizards! They're extremely entertaining.

SUGGESTED ITINERARIES

IF YOU HAVE ONE DAY In the morning, drive to Miami Beach's art deco district and take an informal tour of the area. Spend some time on the beach along Ocean Drive, and eat lunch in a nearby café. In the afternoon, head to Miami's Seaquarium, on Key Biscayne, then drive through the sparkling city at sunset.

IF YOU HAVE TWO DAYS Spend the first day as outlined above. Miami's art deco district, in particular, should not be missed.

On your second day, drive down to Greater Miami South to visit one or more of the attractions listed below, such as Monkey Jungle or Coral Castle. Alternatively, visit the Miami Metrozoo, or go downtown to shop and stroll in the Bayside Marketplace.

IF YOU HAVE THREE DAYS Spend your first two days as outlined above.

On your third day visit historical Miami. Start with a tour of Villa Vizcaya, one of the city's first estates. Visit the Barnacle in Coconut Grove, then drive through Coral Gables, and stroll around the grounds of the grand Biltmore Hotel and the Venetian Pool. If there's time, head north to the Spanish Monastery Cloisters, America's oldest standing structure.

IF YOU HAVE FIVE OR MORE DAYS Spend Days 1–3 as outlined above.

On your fourth and fifth days, take time out from sightseeing and head for the beach. Play golf or tennis, fish, sail, waterski, or even place a bet at the horse or dog races. Relax at a sidewalk café in Coconut Grove, or spend an evening dining in an elegant restaurant or dancing into the wee hours. With an extra day, you can drive up to Fort Lauderdale, down to the Everglades (see "Easy Excursions from Miami," below), visit Key West (see Chapter 6), or even hop on a one-day cruise to Freeport or Nassau in the Bahamas (see "Easy Excursions from Miami," below).

1. THE TOP ATTRACTIONS

CENTRAL MIAMI

THE ART DECO DISTRICT

Miami's best sight is not a museum or an amusement park, but a part of the city itself. Located at the southern end of Miami Beach, the art deco district is a whole community made up of outrageous, fanciful 1920s and 1930s architecture that shouldn't be missed.

MIAMI METROZOO, SW 152 St. and SW 124th Ave., south of Coral Gables. Tel. 251-0400.

Rarely does a zoo warrant mention as a city's "Top Attraction," but Miami's Metrozoo is different. This huge 290-acre complex is completely cageless; animals are kept at bay by cleverly designed moats. Star attractions include two rare white Bengal tigers. Especially appealing for both adults and children is PAWS, a newly designed petting zoo. The elephant ride is particularly fun.

Admission: $5 adults, $2.50 children 3–12, free for children under 3. Reduced rates for Florida residents.

Open: Daily 9:30am–5:30pm (ticket booth closes at 4pm). **Directions:** From U.S. 1, take the SW 152nd Street exit west three blocks to the Metrozoo entrance.

MIAMI SEAQUARIUM, 4400 Rickenbacker Causeway (south side), Key Biscayne. Tel. 361-5705.

Visitors walk around the 35-acre oceanarium, admiring the various mammals' beauty, creativity, and intelligence. One entertaining exhibit stars Flipper, the original dolphin from the television series. Other performances are highlighted by the antics of a trained killer whale.

Miami Seaquarium is a profit-making enterprise and admission is steep. Still, their shows are entertaining, and they help visitors gain insight into these interesting marine mammals.

Admission: $17.95 adults, $14.95 seniors over 65, $12.95 children under 13.

Open: Daily 9:30am–6pm (ticket booth closes at 4:30pm). **Directions:** From downtown Miami, take I-95 south to the Rickenbacker Causeway.

VILLA VIZCAYA, 3251 S. Miami Ave., just south of the Rickenbacker Causeway, north Coconut Grove. Tel. 579-2708.

You already know that South Florida is wacky, and this place proves it. Sometimes referred to as the "Hearst Castle of the East," this magnificent villa was built in 1916 as a winter retreat for James Deering, former vice-president of International Harvester. The industrialist was fascinated by 16th-century art and architecture, and his ornate mansion—which took 1,000 artisans five years to build—became a celebration of these designs.

Pink marble columns, topped with intricately designed capitals, reach up toward hand-carved European-style ceilings. Antiques decorate 34 of the 70 rooms, which are filled with baroque furniture and Renaissance paintings and tapestries. The spectacularly opulent villa wraps itself around a central courtyard. Outside, lush formal gardens, accented with statuary, balustrades, and decorative urns, front an enormous swath of Biscayne Bay.

Admission: $8 adults, $4 children 6–12, free for children under 6.

Open: Daily 9:30am–5pm; gardens open until 5:30pm (ticket booth closes at 4:30pm). **Closed:** Christmas Day. **Directions:** Take I-95 south to Exit 1 and follow the signs to Vizcaya.

GREATER MIAMI SOUTH

Many of Miami's tourist attractions are located in Howard, Perrine, Homestead, and other communities south of downtown. The best way to visit these attractions is via U.S. 1, a major highway that extends all the way down into the Keys. You can't get

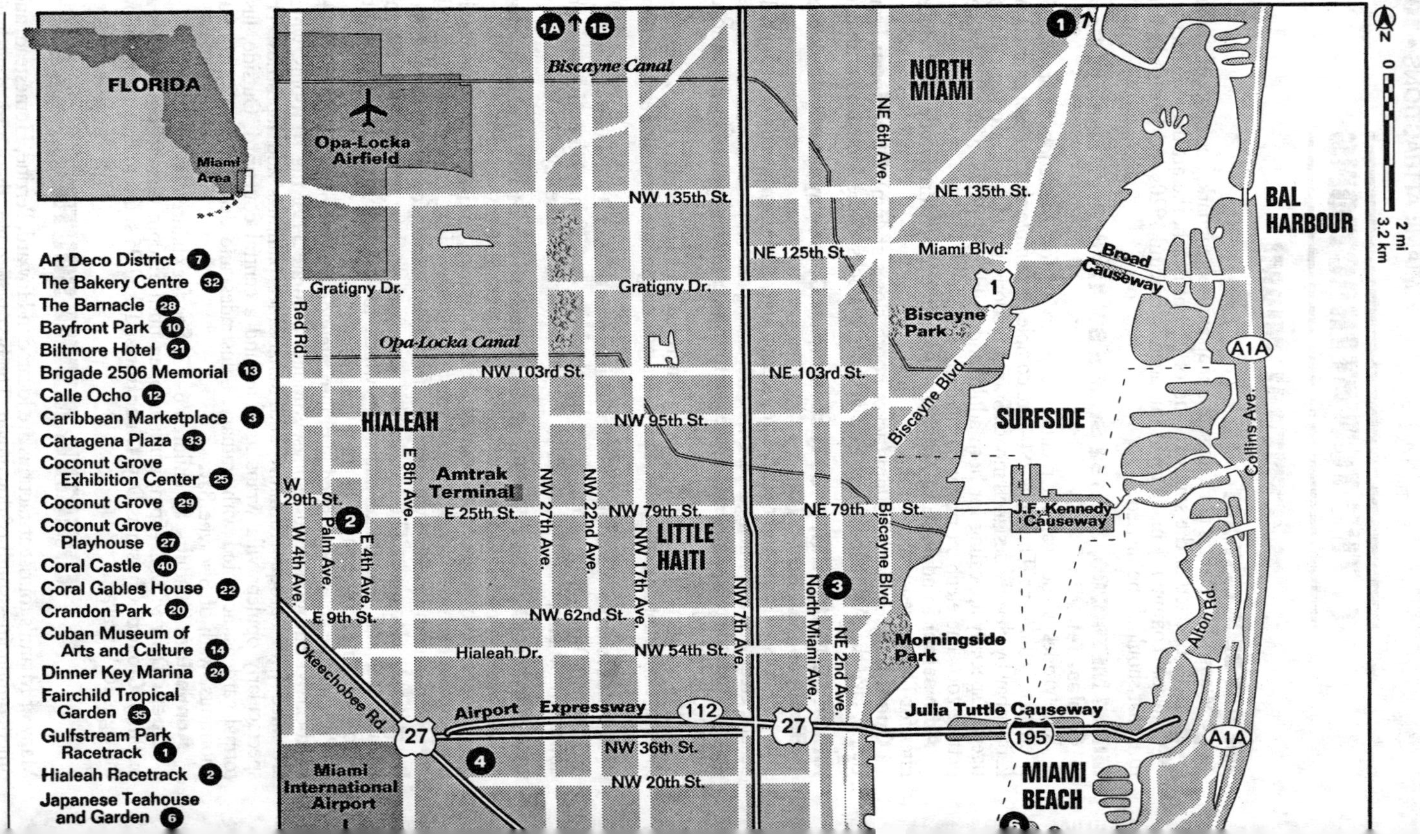

Art Deco District 7
The Bakery Centre 32
The Barnacle 28
Bayfront Park 10
Biltmore Hotel 21
Brigade 2506 Memorial 13
Calle Ocho 12
Caribbean Marketplace 3
Cartagena Plaza 33
Coconut Grove Exhibition Center 25
Coconut Grove 29
Coconut Grove Playhouse 27
Coral Castle 40
Coral Gables House 22
Crandon Park 20
Cuban Museum of Arts and Culture 14
Dinner Key Marina 24
Fairchild Tropical Garden 35
Gulfstream Park Racetrack 1
Hialeah Racetrack 2
Japanese Teahouse and Garden 6

FLORIDA
Miami Area

0 2 mi
3.2 km
N

Opa-Locka Airfield
Biscayne Canal
Opa-Locka Canal
NORTH MIAMI
BAL HARBOUR
SURFSIDE
HIALEAH
LITTLE HAITI
MIAMI BEACH
Biscayne Park
Morningside Park
Amtrak Terminal
Miami International Airport
NW 135th St.
NE 135th St.
NE 125th St.
Miami Blvd.
Broad Causeway
Gratigny Dr.
Red Rd.
NW 103rd St.
NE 103rd St.
NW 95th St.
Biscayne Blvd.
NE 6th Ave.
Collins Ave.
A1A
W 29th St.
E 25th St.
NW 79th St.
NE 79th St.
J.F. Kennedy Causeway
E 8th Ave.
NW 27th Ave.
NW 22nd Ave.
NW 17th Ave.
NW 7th Ave.
North Miami Ave.
NE 2nd Ave.
W 4th Ave.
Palm Ave.
E 4th Ave.
E 9th St.
NW 62nd St.
Hialeah Dr.
NW 54th St.
Alton Rd.
Okeechobee Rd.
Airport Expressway
112
27
Julia Tuttle Causeway
195
NW 36th St.
NW 20th St.
1A 1B
1

MIAMI AREA ATTRACTIONS

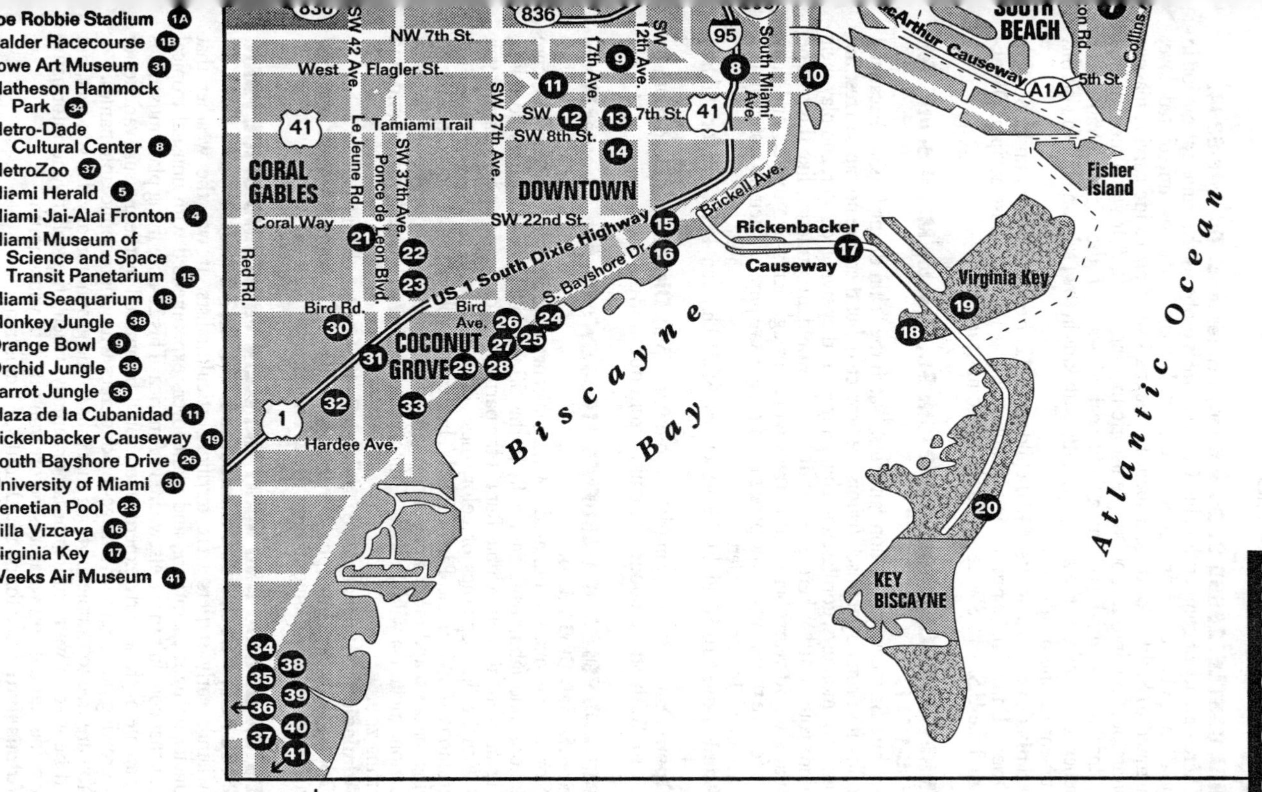
Joe Robbie Stadium 1A
Calder Racecourse 1B
Lowe Art Museum 31
Matheson Hammock Park 34
Metro-Dade Cultural Center 8
MetroZoo 37
Miami Herald 5
Miami Jai-Alai Fronton 4
Miami Museum of Science and Space Transit Panetarium 15
Miami Seaquarium 18
Monkey Jungle 38
Orange Bowl 9
Orchid Jungle 39
Parrot Jungle 36
Plaza de la Cubanidad 11
Rickenbacker Causeway 19
South Bayshore Drive 26
University of Miami 30
Venetian Pool 23
Villa Vizcaya 16
Virginia Key 17
Weeks Air Museum 41
Atlantic Ocean
Biscayne Bay
SOUTH BEACH
MacArthur Causeway
A1A
5th St.
Collins
Fisher Island
Virginia Key
Rickenbacker Causeway
KEY BISCAYNE
DOWNTOWN
CORAL GABLES
COCONUT GROVE
NW 7th St.
West Flagler St.
Tamiami Trail
SW 8th St.
SW 7th St.
SW 22nd St.
Coral Way
SW 42 Ave.
Le Jeune Rd.
Ponce de Leon Blvd.
SW 37th Ave.
SW 27th Ave.
17th Ave.
SW 12th Ave.
South Miami Ave.
Brickell Ave.
US 1 South Dixie Highway
S. Bayshore Dr.
Bird Ave.
Bird Rd.
Red Rd.
Hardee Ave.
836
95
41
1
Airport

lost—blaring billboards point the way to all attractions listed. Think about combining several of the following sights, put your car's top down, turn the music up, and prepare yourself for wacky times!

CORAL CASTLE, 28655 S. Dixie Hwy., Homestead. Tel. 248-6344.

There's plenty of competition, but Coral Castle is probably the zaniest attraction in Florida. In 1917, the story goes, a crazed Latvian, jilted by unrequited love, immigrated to South Florida and spent the next 25 years of his life carving massive amounts of stone into a roofless, prehistoric-looking "castle." It was a monumental task, that may remind you, in a light-hearted way, of the Great Pyramids or Stonehenge. If you're in the area, especially with kids in tow, take an hour to visit this monument of one man's madness.

Admission: $7.75 adults, $4.50 children 6–12, free for children under 6.

Open: Daily 9am–6pm, except Thanksgiving when they close at 5pm. **Directions:** Take U.S. 1 to SW 286th Street in Homestead.

MONKEY JUNGLE, 14805 SW 216th St., Greater Miami South. Tel. 235-1611.

See rare Brazilian golden lion tamarins! Watch the "skin diving" Asian macaques! Yes folks, it's primate paradise! Visitors are protected, but there are no cages to restrain the antics of monkeys, gorillas, and chimpanzees as they swing, chatter, and play their way into your heart! Where else but in Florida would an attraction like this still be popular after 50 years? Screened-in trails wind through acres of "jungle," and daily shows feature the talents of the park's most progressive pupils. Their newest exhibit is an Enchanted Topiary Garden.

Admission: $10.50 adults, $9.50 seniors, $5.35 children 4–12, free for children under 4.

Open: Daily 9:30am–6pm (tickets sold until 5pm). **Directions:** Head south on U.S. 1 to 216th Street, about 20 minutes from downtown.

PARROT JUNGLE AND GARDENS, 11000 SW 57th Ave., Greater Miami South. Tel. 666-7834.

Not just parrots, but hundreds of magnificent macaws, prancing peacocks, cute cockatoos, and fabulous flamingos fly in this 50-year-old park. Alligators, tortoises, and iguanas are also on exhibit. But it's the parrots you came for, and it's parrots you get! With brilliant splashes of color, these birds appear in every shape and size. Continuous shows in the Parrot Bowl Theater star roller-skating cockatoos, card-playing macaws, and more stunt-happy parrots than you ever thought possible! New attractions include a wildlife show, Primate Experience, a children's playground, and a petting zoo.

Admission: $10.50 adults, $7 children 3–12, free for children under 3.

Open: Daily 9:30am–6pm. **Directions:** Take U.S. 1 south, turn left onto SW 57th Avenue, and continue straight for 2½ miles.

PRESTON B. BIRD AND MARY HEINLEIN FRUIT AND SPICE PARK, 24801 SW 187th Ave., Homestead. Tel. 247-5727.

Miami's early settlers were terrific horticulturalists. It was the weather that originally brought them here, and plant lovers experimented with unusual tropical breeds that couldn't thrive elsewhere in America. This 20-acre living plant museum is an example of these early experiments. You'll be amazed by the unusual varieties of fruit growing on dozens of strange-looking trees with unpronounceable names.

You are free to sample anything that falls to the ground on any day you visit, but you'd be wise to wait until Saturday or Sunday, when an excellent and informative tour guide can tell you what it is before you put it in your mouth.

Admission: Free. Tours, $1.50 adults, $1 children.

Open: Daily 10am–5pm; tours given Sat–Sun at 1 and 3pm. Access for the disabled. **Directions:** Take U.S. 1, turn right on SW 248th Street, and go straight for five miles to SW 187th Avenue.

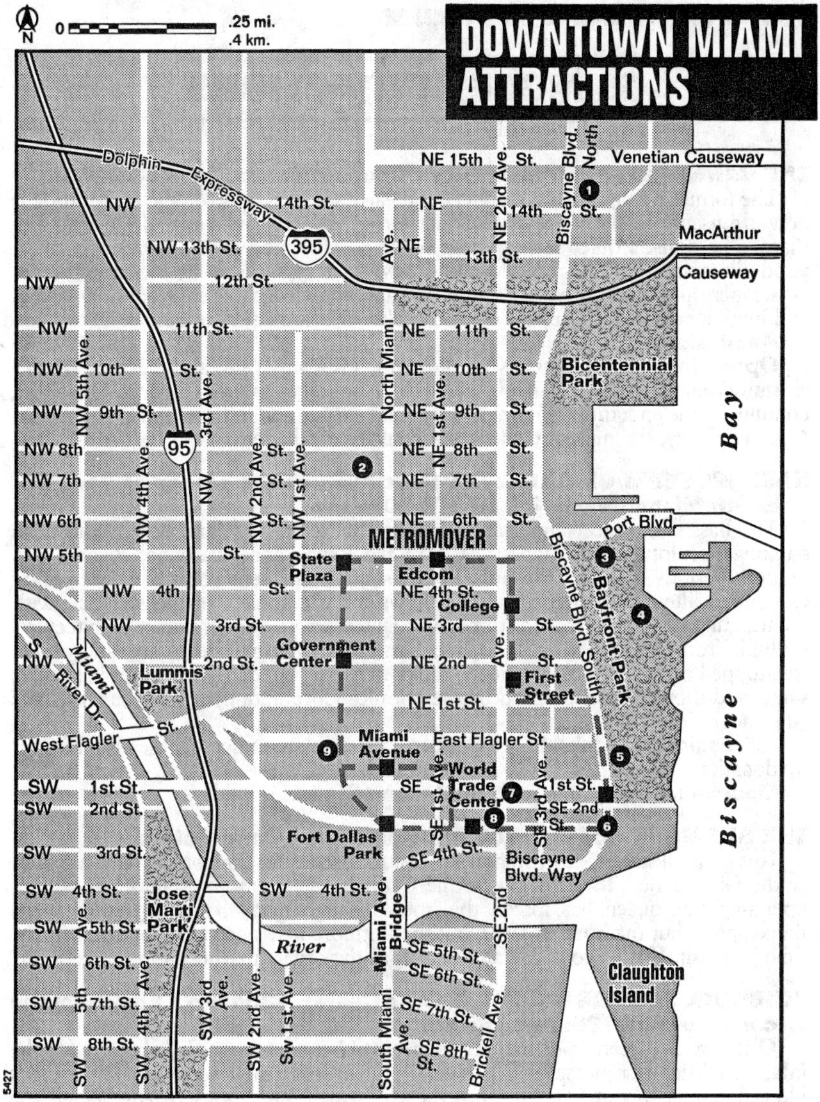

DOWNTOWN MIAMI ATTRACTIONS

N
0 .25 mi.
.4 km.

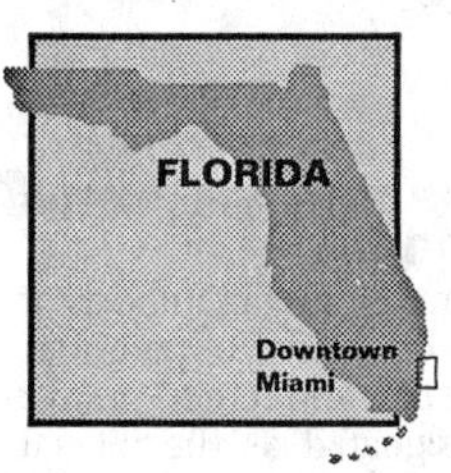

- Bayfront Park 3
- Bayside Marketplace 4
- Challenger Seven Memorial 5
- CenTrust Tower 8
- Gusman Philharmonic Hall 7
- Metromover 6
- Miami Arena 2
- Omni Shopping Mall 1
- Metro-Dade Cultural Center 9

2. MORE ATTRACTIONS

THE BARNACLE, 3485 Main Hwy., Coconut Grove. Tel. 448-9445.

The former home of naval architect and early settler Ralph Middleton Munroe is now a museum in the heart of Coconut Grove, two blocks south of Commodore Plaza. The house's quiet surroundings, wide porches, and period furnishings are a good illustration of the way Miami's privileged class lived in the days before skyscrapers and luxury hotels. Enthusiastic and knowledgeable state park employees and innumerable period objects offer a wealth of historical information.

Admission: $2.

Open: Tours given Thurs–Mon at 10am, 11:30am, 1pm, and 2:30pm. **Directions:** From downtown Miami, take U.S. 1 south to South Bayshore Drive and continue to the end; turn right onto McFarlane Avenue and left at the traffic light onto Main Highway; the museum is five blocks along on the left.

BASS MUSEUM OF ART, 2121 Park Ave., at the corner of 21st St., South Miami Beach. Tel. 673-7530.

The Bass is the most important visual arts museum in Miami Beach. European paintings, sculptures, and tapestries from the Renaissance, baroque, rococo, and modern periods make up the bulk of the small permanent collection. Temporary exhibitions alternate between traveling shows and rotations of the Bass's stock, with themes ranging widely, from 17th-century Dutch art, to contemporary architecture.

Built from coral rock in 1930, the Bass sits in the middle of six landscaped, tree-topped acres. Be sure to visit the funky outdoor fountain made up of bath tubs, sinks, and shower bases donated by the Formica Corporation, one of the museum's latest acquisitions.

Admission: $2 adults, $1 students, free for children under 16. Tues admission is by donation.

Open: Tues–Sat 10am–5pm, Sun 1–5pm. **Closed:** Holidays.

THE BILTMORE HOTEL, 1200 Anastasia Ave., Coral Gables.

This grand hotel is one of Miami's oldest properties. Its 26-story tower is a replica of the Giralda Bell Tower of the Seville Cathedral in Spain. The enormous cost of operating this queen has forced the hotel through many hands in recent years. Bankruptcy shut the hotel in 1990, but the Biltmore may once again be open by the time you visit. If it is, go inside and marvel at the ornate marble and tile interior.

CRIMINAL JUSTICE BUILDING, Civic Center, 1351 NW 12th St., at the corner of NW 13th Ave., downtown. Tel. 547-4888.

Okay, you've seen it in the newspaper, you've seen it on TV, but so far the infamous Miami crime scene has eluded you. If you really want to see the city's judicial system in process, stop into the city's main courthouse, right behind the Miami city jail, for some real-life drama. You're free to come and go as you wish, so check out a few courtrooms before settling on a case.

Admission: Free.

Open: Mon–Fri 9am–4:30pm.

CUBAN MUSEUM OF ARTS AND CULTURE, 1300 SW 12th Ave., at the corner of SW 13th St., Little Havana. Tel. 858-8006.

This unique museum displays significant works of art and memorabilia important for the promotion and preservation of the Cuban culture. The collection of paintings and drawings only adds up to about 200, but they are well selected, and representative of a wide range of styles. The museum has also been designated as the official repository for the mementos of Agustino Acosta, the famous Cuban poet.

Admission: $2 adults, $1 students and seniors.

Open: Wed–Sun 1–5pm. **Directions:** From downtown, head west on SW 7th Street and turn left on 12th Avenue; the museum is six blocks ahead on right.

FROMMER'S FAVORITE MIAMI EXPERIENCES

Airboat Through the Everglades You've seen these wide, flat boats driven by huge fans in the rear. Airboat rides, offered by the Miccosukee Indian Village (see "Easy Excursions from Miami," below) and other organizations, are fantastic half-hour, high-speed tours through some of America's most pristine lands. Birds scatter as the boats approach, and when you slow down, alligators and other animals appear.

Bayside Marketplace Miami's best shopping mall is this outdoor Rouse Company development, located on the water in the heart of the city's downtown. About 100 shops and carts sell everything from plastic fruit to high-tech electronics (see "Savvy Shopping," below). Upstairs, a mammoth fast-food eating arcade is a great place for a meal or snack (see "Dining" in Chapter 4).

Coconut Grove at Night The intersection of Grand Avenue, Main Highway, and McFarlane Road is the heart of Coconut Grove, a sedate village by day and a busy meeting place by night. Sizzling with dozens of interesting cafés, boutiques, and nightspots, the Grove's sidewalks are crowded with businesspeople, students, and tourists. On weekends, sidewalk tables stay occupied until long after midnight.

Little Havana Miami's Cuban center is the city's most important ethnic enclave. Located just west of downtown, Little Havana is centered around "Calle Ocho," SW 8th Street. This busy street is exciting and warrants exploration. Car-repair shops, tailors, electronics stores, and restaurants all hang signs in Spanish, salsa rhythms thump from the radios of passersby, and old men in guayaberas chain-smoke cigars over their daily game of dominoes. Little Havana is also home to some of the city's best ethnic restaurants (see "Dining" in Chapter 4).

Ocean Drive The beauty of the celebrated art deco district in South Miami Beach culminates on the 15-block beachfront strip known as Ocean Drive. Most of the buildings on this stretch are hotels that were built in the late 1930s and early 1940s. Even if you're not staying here, take a stroll along this colorful street.

The View from the Rickenbacker Causeway Almost every building in Miami's sleek, 21st-century skyline is a gem. The best view of this spectacular cluster is from the causeway that connects mainland Miami with Key Biscayne. You'll have to pay a toll of $1 for the privilege, but it's worth it.

FAIRCHILD TROPICAL GARDENS, 10901 Old Cutler Rd., Coral Gables. Tel. 667-1651.

These large botanical gardens feature both rare and exotic plants. Tropical cycads, palms, and other unique species create a scenic, lush environment. On the hourly tram tour you can learn what you always wanted to know about the various flowers and trees.

Admission (including tram tour): $7 adults, free for children under 13.

Open: Daily 9:30am–4:30pm. **Directions:** From U.S. 1 south, turn left on LeJeune Road, follow it straight to the traffic circle, and take Cutler Road 2½ miles to the park.

METRO-DADE CULTURAL CENTER, 101 W. Flagler St., downtown.

In addition to the Dade County Public Library, the Metro-Dade Cultural Center houses both a historical museum and a fine arts center.

The primary exhibit at the **Historical Museum of Southern Florida** (tel. 375-1492) is "Tropical Dreams," a state-of-the-art, chronological history of the last 10,000 years in South Florida. The hands-on displays, audiovisual presentations, and hundreds of artifacts are really quite interesting.

The **Center for Fine Arts** (tel. 375-1700) features an eclectic mix of modern and contemporary works by such artists as Eric Fischl, Max Beckman, Jim Dine, and Stuart Davis.

Admission (to both museums): $5 adults, $2.50 seniors 65 and over, $2 children 6–12, free for children under 6.

Open: Tues–Sat 10am–5pm (Thurs to 9pm), Sun noon–5pm. **Directions:** From I-95 north, take the NW 2nd Street exit, turn right, and continue east to NW Second Avenue; turn right and park at the Metro-Dade Garage (50 NW Second Ave.). From I-95 south, exit at the Orange Bowl–NW 8th Street exit and continue south to NW 2nd Street; turn left onto NW 2nd Street and go 1½ blocks to NW Second Avenue, turn right, and park at the Metro-Dade Garage (50 NW Second Ave). Bring the parking ticket to the lobby for validation.

SPANISH MONASTERY CLOISTERS, 16711 W. Dixie Hwy., at the corner of 167th St., North Miami Beach. Tel. 945-1462.

Did you know that the oldest building in the western hemisphere dates from A.D. 1141 and is located in Miami? It's true! The Spanish Monastery Cloisters were first erected in Segovia, Spain. Purchased by newspaper magnate William Randolph Hearst, the building was brought to America in pieces, and reassembled in 1954 on its present site!

Admission: $4 adults, $2.50 seniors, $1 children 7–12, free for children under 7.

Open: Mon–Sat 10am–5pm, Sun noon–5pm. **Directions:** From downtown, take U.S. 1 north and turn left onto 163rd Street; make the first right onto West Dixie Highway and the Cloisters are three blocks ahead on right.

3. COOL FOR KIDS

Florida's vacationland has always been family oriented, and offers a host of programs and activities exclusively for children. Several beachfront resort hotels provide excellent supervised activities for kids, including the Sonesta Beach Hotel on Key Biscayne, and the Fontainebleau and Doral hotels in Miami Beach (see "Accommodations" Chapter 4). Information on these and other family packages is available from the Miami Convention and Visitors Bureau (see "Information" in "Orientation," in Chapter 4).

TOP CITY ATTRACTIONS

For details of attractions listed here, see "The Top Attractions," above.

The Miami Metrozoo This completely cageless zoo offers such star attractions as a monorail "safari" and a newly designed petting zoo. Especially fun for kids are the elephant rides.

Monkey Jungle A zoo filled with monkeys, gorillas, and chimpanzees. Special shows are offered daily.

Parrot Jungle For its roller-skating cockatoos, card-playing macaws, and lots of stunt-happy parrots.

Miami Seaquarium Especially for performances given by Flipper, the original dolphin from the television series.

MORE ATTRACTIONS

MIAMI MUSEUM OF SCIENCE AND SPACE TRANSIT PLANETARIUM, 3280 S. Miami Ave., Coconut Grove. Tel. 854-4247 for general information, 854-2222 for planetarium show times.

The Museum of Science features over 150 hands-on exhibits which explore the mysteries of the universe. Live demonstrations and collections of rare natural-history specimens make a visit here fun and informative.

The adjacent Space Transit Planetarium projects astronomy and laser shows. Most interesting, perhaps, is the in-house observatory, free and open and to the public on weekend evenings.

Admission: Science museum, $6 adults, $4 children 3–12 and seniors, free for children under 3; planetarium, $5 adults, $2.50 children and seniors; combination ticket, $8.50 adults, $5 children and seniors.

Open: Science museum, daily 10am–6pm. Call for planetarium show times. **Closed:** Thanksgiving and Christmas Days. **Directions:** Take I-95 south to Exit 1 and follow the signs; alternatively, ride the Metrorail to the Vizcaya Station.

VENETIAN POOL, 2701 DeSoto Blvd., at Toledo St., Coral Gables. Tel. 442-6483.

Miami's most unusual swimming pool, dating from 1924, is hidden behind pastel stucco walls, and is honored with a listing in the National Register of Historic Places. The free-form lagoon is fed by underground artesian wells and shaded by three-story Spanish porticos, and features both fountains and waterfalls. During the summer months, the pool's 800,000 gallons of water are drained and refilled nightly, ensuring a cool, clean swim. Visitors are free to swim and sunbathe here, year-round, just as Esther Williams and Johnny Weissmuller did decades ago.

Admission: $4 adults, $3.50 children 13–17, $1.60 children under 13.

Open: June–Aug, Mon–Fri 11am–7:30pm, Sat–Sun 10am–4:30pm, Sept–Oct and Apr–May, Tues–Fri 11am–5:30pm, Sat–Sun 10am–4:30pm; Nov–Mar, Tues–Fri 11am–4:30pm, Sat–Sun 10am–4:30pm.

4. ORGANIZED TOURS

Like the tourist attractions, many of Miami's organized tours are interestingly offbeat. They are also fun and generally well priced. Always call ahead to check prices and times. Reservations are usually suggested.

WALKING TOURS

MIAMI DESIGN PRESERVATION LEAGUE, in the Leslie Hotel, 1244 Ocean Dr., South Miami Beach. Tel. 672-2014.

If you're lucky enough to be in Miami on a Saturday, don't miss this fascinating inside look at the city's historic art deco district. Tourgoers meet at South Beach's Welcome Center (address above) for a 1½-hour walk through some of America's most exuberantly architectured buildings. The Design Preservation League led the fight to designate this area a National Historic District, and is proud to share the splendid results with visitors.

Admission: $6 adults and children.

Schedule: Tours depart Sat at 10:30am.

BUS TOURS

OLD TOWN TROLLEY OF MIAMI. Tel. 374-8687.

Old Town's distinctive red-and-green "trolley" buses cruise the city's streets and causeways in a continuous 90-minute loop. You can stay aboard for the entire trip, or disembark at any one of a half dozen stops, and reboard at your convenience. Trolleys depart every 30 minutes, and tickets are valid all day. Tours are completely narrated. Departure points include the Bayside Marketplace and a dozen other locations. Call for information.

Admission: $14 adults, $5 children.

Schedule: Daily 10am–4pm.

BOAT TOURS

HERITAGE MIAMI II TOPSAIL SCHOONER, Bayside Marketplace Marina, 401 Biscayne Blvd. (downtown). Tel. 442-9697.

More adventure than tour, this relaxing ride aboard Miami's only tall ship is a fun way to see the city. Two-hour cruises pass by Villa Vizcaya, Coconut Grove, and Key Biscayne, and put you in sight of Miami's spectacular skyline. Cruises are offered September through May only. Call beforehand to make sure the ship is running on schedule.

Admission: $10 adults, $5 children under 12.

Schedule: Departures daily at 1:30 and 6:30pm; Sat–Sun also at 11am and 9pm.

BISCAYNE NATIONAL PARK TOUR BOATS, east end of SW 328th St., Homestead. Tel. 247-2400.

Biscayne National Park includes almost 200,000 acres of mangrove shoreline, barrier islands, and living coral reefs, which are all protected by the federal government. Tours of the area, aboard a 52-foot glass-bottom boat, cross the aquatic wilderness for a fish-eye view of some of America's most accessible coral reefs. Family snorkeling and canoe rentals are also offered.

Admission: $16.50 adults, $8.50 children under 13.

Schedule: Tours daily at 10am and 1:30pm. Reservations required.

***RIVER QUEEN* SIGHTSEEING, Eden Roc Yacht & Charter Center, 4525 Collins Ave., at 45th St., Miami Beach. Tel. 538-5380.**

The *River Queen,* an authentic Mississippi River–style paddlewheel boat, cruises up Indian Creek and out into Biscayne Bay. There are three daily sightseeing tours.

Admission: $10 adults, $5 children under 12.

Schedule: Tours daily at 10am, 1pm, and 4pm. Hotel pickup is available.

HELICOPTER

DADE HELICOPTER, 950 MacArthur Causeway. Tel. 374-3737.

Miami by helicopter is the ultimate photo opportunity! Rides range in length from 7 to 20 minutes, and cost $50–$120 per person. There's a two-person minimum, and children under 12 ride for half price. The helipad is located on the south side of the MacArthur Causeway, between the mainland and Miami Beach.

5. SPORTS & RECREATION

SPECTATOR SPORTS

Miami's spectacular sports scene includes several major professional franchises, including football and basketball, and an eclectic variety of international games including cricket, soccer, and jai alai. Check the *Miami Herald*'s sports section for a daily listing of local events, and the paper's Friday "Weekend" section for comprehensive coverage and in-depth reports.

BASEBALL

BALTIMORE ORIOLES SPRING TRAINING, Miami Stadium, 2301 NW 10th Ave. Tel. 643-7100.

From mid-February until the season opener, Baltimore's best can be seen training in Miami. Practices are relaxed, fun, and free.

UNIVERSITY OF MIAMI HURRICANES, Mark Light Stadium, on the U of M's Coral Gables Campus. Tel. 284-2655, or toll free 800/GO-CANES in Florida.

UM's baseball Hurricanes play about 50 home games in their 5,000-seat stadium on the Coral Gables campus. The season lasts from February to May with both day and evening games scheduled.

Admission: $3–$10.

Open: Box office, Mon–Fri 8am–6pm, Sat 8am–2pm.

BASKETBALL

MIAMI HEAT, Miami Arena, 721 NW First Ave. Tel. 577-HEAT.

The Heat made their debut in 1988, and are one of the newest entries in the National Basketball Association. Predictably, they are also one of Miami's hottest tickets. The approximately 41-home-game season lasts from November to April, with most games beginning at 7:30pm.

Admission: $9–$29.

Open: Box office, Mon–Fri 10am–4pm (until 8pm on game nights). Tickets also available through Ticketmaster (tel. 358-5885).

DOG RACING

Greyhound racing is Miami's most popular spectator sport. The dogs circle the oval at speeds averaging 40 miles per hour. Similar to the horsetrack, betting is simple and track workers are willing to give you a hand. Note that racing is during winter months only.

FLAGLER GREYHOUND TRACK, 401 NW 38th Court, at NW 33rd St. Tel. 649-3000.

This fun, high-stakes track features some of America's top dogs, with racing six days a week. The track hosts the $110,000 International Classic, one of the richest races on the circuit.

Admission: $1 general, $3 clubhouse; parking 50¢.

Post Times: Mon–Sat at 7:45pm; matinees Tues, Thurs, and Sat at 12:30pm.

HOLLYWOOD GREYHOUND TRACK, 831 N. Federal Hwy., at Pembroke Rd., Hallandale. Tel. 758-3647.

An average crowd of 10,000 fans wager a collective $1 million nightly at this track, considered by experts to be one of the best in the country. If you've never been to the dog track before, arrive a half hour early for a quick introduction to greyhound racing, shown on the track's television monitors.

Admission: 50¢ general, $1.50 clubhouse; parking $1.

Post Times: Late Dec to late Apr, Mon–Sat at 7:30pm, Sun at 7pm; matinees Mon, Wed, and Sat at 12:30pm.

FOOTBALL

MIAMI DOLPHINS, Joe Robbie Stadium, 2269 NW 199th St. (Greater Miami North). Tel. 620-5000.

The city's National Football League franchise is Miami's most recognizable team and followed by thousands of "dolfans." About six home games are played during the season, most starting at 1pm.

Admission: About $30.

Open: Box office, Mon–Fri 10am–6pm. Tickets also available through Ticketmaster (tel. 358-5885).

UNIVERSITY OF MIAMI HURRICANES, Orange Bowl Stadium, 1501 NW 3rd St. Tel. 284-2655, or toll free 800/GO-CANES in Florida.

The U of M football Hurricanes play at the famous Orange Bowl from September through November. The stadium is seldom full, and games here are really exciting. If you sit high up, you'll have an excellent view over Miami. Call for the schedule.

Admission: $5–$12.

Open: Box office, Mon–Fri 8am–6pm and prior to all games.

HORSE RACING

GULFSTREAM PARK, U.S. 1 and Hallandale Beach Blvd., Hallandale. Tel. 944-1242.

Wrapped around an artificial lake, this suburban course is both pretty and popular. Large purses and important races are commonplace, and the track is often crowded.

Admission: $2 grandstand, $4.50 clubhouse. Parking $1 and up.

Post Times: Jan 13–Mar, Tues–Sun at 1pm.

HIALEAH PARK, grandstand entrance at E. Second Ave. and 32nd St., Hialeah. Tel. 885-8000.

You've seen the park's pink American flamingos on "Miami Vice," and indeed, this famous colony is the largest of its kind. This track, listed on the National Register of Historic Places, is one of the most beautiful in the world, featuring old-fashioned stands and acres of immaculately manicured grounds.

Admission: $2 grandstand, $4 clubhouse; children under 18 free with adult. Parking $1.50 and up.

Open: Races mid-Nov to mid-May. Call for post times. Open year-round for sightseeing Mon–Sat 10am–4pm.

JAI ALAI

Jai alai, sort of a Spanish-style indoor lacrosse, is popular around these parts, and regularly played in two Miami-area frontons. Players use woven baskets, called cestas, to hurl balls, pelotas, at speeds that sometimes exceed 170 miles per hour. Spectators, who are protected behind a wall of glass, place bets on the evening's players.

MIAMI JAI ALAI FRONTON, 3500 NW 37th Ave., at NW 35th St. Tel. 633-6400.

America's oldest jai-alai fronton dates from 1926 and schedules 13 games per night.

Admission: $1 grandstand, $5 clubhouse.

Open: Year-round, except for a four-week recess in the fall. First game Mon–Sat at 7:10pm; matinees Mon, Wed, and Sat at noon.

SOCCER

MIAMI FREEDOM, Milander Stadium, 4800 Palm Ave., Hialeah. Tel. 446-3136.

Representing yet another attempt to make soccer a viable spectator sport, Miami Freedom has recently become incorporated. Games are played April through August, but as of this writing the schedule has not yet been set.

Admission: $8.50 adults, $3 children under 15.

Open: Box office, Mon–Fri 9am–5pm.

RECREATION

The climate in this southern city is perfectly suited for recreation, and there are a host of opportunities.

It should come as no surprise that the lion's share of participatory sports options here are water related. **Penrod's Beach Club,** 1 Ocean Dr. (tel. 538-1111), in South Miami Beach, offers a pool, a Jacuzzi, and a full day of activities for $39. This single, reasonable price includes use of beach bicycles, kayaks, windsurfers, rafts, snorkeling equipment, "muscle beach" free weights, and fishing gear. It also includes continental breakfast, lunch, and three drinks. It's open Sunday through Thursday from 10am to 2am and Friday and Saturday from 10am to 5am.

BEACHES

In short, there are two distinct beach alternatives: Miami Beach and Key Biscayne. It's all explained below.

MIAMI BEACH'S BEACHES Collins Avenue fronts 10 miles of white sandy beach and blue-green waters from 1st to 192nd Streets. Although most of this stretch is lined with a solid wall of hotels, beach access is plentiful, and you are free to frolic along the entire strip. There are lots of public beaches here, complete with lifeguards, toilet facilities, concession stands, and metered parking (bring lots of quarters). Miami Beach's beaches are both wide and well maintained. Except for a thin strip close to the water, most of the sand here is hard-packed—the result of a $10-million Army Corps of Engineers Beach Rebuilding Project meant to protect buildings from the effects of eroding sand.

In general, the beaches on this barrier island become less crowded the farther north you go. A wooden boardwalk runs along the hotel side of the beach from 21st to 44th Streets—about 1½ miles—offering a terrific sun and surf experience without getting sand in your shoes. Aside from the "Best Beaches" listed below, Miami Beach's public, lifeguard-protected beaches include: 21st Street, at the beginning of the boardwalk; 35th Street, popular with an older crowd; 46th Street, next to the Fontainebleau Hilton Hotel; 53rd Street, a narrower, more sedate beach; 64th Street, one of the quietest strips around; and 72nd Street, a local old-timers spot.

KEY BISCAYNE'S BEACHES If Miami Beach is not private enough for you, Key Biscayne might be more of what you had in mind. Crossing Rickenbacker Causeway ($1 toll) is almost like crossing into The Bahamas. The five miles of public beach here are blessed with softer sand, and are less developed and more laid-back than the hotel-laden strips to the north.

THE "BEST BEACHES" The following are the "best" beaches for various recreational activities.

Best Picnic Beach Bill Baggs Cape Florida State Park, on the south end of Key Biscayne, has barbecue grills and picnic tables shaded by a tall forest of trees. On weekends, the place really hops, primarily with partying families playing games, listening to music, and cooking up a storm. The adjacent, narrow, soft-sand beach is home to the picturesque Cape Florida Lighthouse, which has operated here since 1825. Admission is $2 per vehicle, $1 per passenger.

Best Surfing Beach The 1st Street Beach, at the bottom of Ocean Drive in South Miami Beach, has Miami's "gnarliest" waves. No lifeguard.

Best Party Beach Crandon Park Beach, on Crandon Boulevard in Key Biscayne, has three miles of oceanfront beach, 493 acres of park, 75 grills, three parking lots, several soccer and softball fields, and a public 18-hole championship golf course. The beach is particularly wide and the water is usually so clear you can see to the bottom. Admission is $2 per vehicle. It's open daily from 8am to sunset.

Best Swimming Beach The competition is fierce, but my favorite is the chic Lummus Park Beach, which runs along Ocean Drive from about 6th to 14th Streets in South Miami Beach's art deco district. It's pretty, has plenty of metered parking, and is close to a number of restaurants with excellent happy hours.

Best Windsurfing Beach Hobie Beach, beside the causeway leading to Key Biscayne, isn't really a beach, but a quiet inlet with calm winds and a number of windsurfer-rental places.

Best Shell-hunting Beach Bal Harbour Beach, Collins Avenue at 96th Street, is just a few yards north of Surfside Beach. There's a vita course, good shade, and usually plenty of colorful shells. No lifeguard.

BOATING/SAILING

Sailboats and catamarans are available through the beachfront concessions desk of several top resorts. They are listed under the appropriate hotels in Chapter 4. Other private rental places include:

BEACH BOAT RENTALS, 2380 Collins Ave., Miami Beach. Tel. 534-4307.

These 50-horsepower, 18-foot powerboats rent for some of the best rates on the beach. Cruising is exclusively in and around Biscayne Bay, as ocean access is prohibited. Renters must be over 21 years old, and must present a current passport or driver's license. The rental office is at 23rd Street, on the inland waterway in Miami Beach.

Rates: $45 for one hour, $120 for four hours, $175 for eight hours. AE, MC, V.

Open: May–Oct, daily 9am–6pm; Nov–Apr, daily 9am–5pm (weather permitting).

CLUB NAUTICO OF COCONUT GROVE, 2560 S. Bayshore Dr., Coconut Grove. Tel. 858-6258.

High-quality powerboats are rented for fishing, waterskiing, diving, and cruising in the bay or ocean. All boats are Coast Guard equipped with VHF radios and safety gear.

Two other locations include the Biscayne Bay Marriott Hotel, 1633 N. Bayshore Dr. (downtown (tel. 371-4252); and the Miami Beach Marina, Pier E, 300 Alton Rd., South Miami Beach (tel. 673-2502).

Rates: From $150 for four hours, from $249 for eight hours.

Open: Daily 8am–5:30pm (weather permitting).

FISHING

Bridge fishing is popular in Miami; you'll see people with poles over most every waterway.

Some of the best surf casting in the city can be had at **Haulover Beach Park,** at Collins Avenue and 105th Street, where there's a bait-and-tackle shop right on the pier. **South Pointe Park,** at the southern tip of Miami Beach, is another popular fishing spot, and features a long pier, comfortable benches, and a great view of the ships passing through Government Cut. A number of deep-sea fishing opportunities are also on offer, including:

KELLEY FISHING FLEET, Haulover Marina, 10800 Collins Ave., at 108th St., Haulover (Miami Beach). Tel. 945-3801.

Half-day, full-day, and night fishing aboard diesel-powered "party boats" lure in fish like snapper, sailfish, and mackerel. The fleet's emphasis on drifting is geared toward trolling and bottom fishing. Reservations recommended.

Cost: Half-day and night fishing, $18.75 adults, $11.75 children; full-day fishing, $28.75 adults, $17.50 children; rod and reel rental, $3.75.

Schedule: Half day, daily 9am–12:30pm and 1:45–5:30pm; full day, Wed and Sat–Sun 9am–4pm; nightly, 8pm–midnight.

CHARTER BOAT *HELEN C*, Haulover Marina, 10800 Collins Ave., Haulover (Miami Beach). Tel. 947-4081.

Although there's no shortage of private charter boats here, Capt. John Callan is a good pick, since he puts individuals together to get a full boat. His *Helen C* is a twin-engine 55-footer, equipped for big-game "monster" fish like marlin, tuna, dolphin, and bluefish. Call for reservations.

Cost: $60 per person.

Schedule: Daily 8am–noon or 1–5pm.

GOLF

There are dozens of golf courses in the Greater Miami area, many of which are open to the public. Contact the Greater Miami Convention and Visitors Bureau (see "Information" in "Orientation," Chapter 4) for a complete list of courses and costs.

BAYSHORE GOLF COURSE, 2301 Alton Rd., Miami Beach. Tel. 532-3350.

This Miami Beach park has an 18-hole green and a lighted driving range for night swings.

Admission: $25 per person during the week, $15 after 4pm; $26 per person on weekends, $20 after 4pm; Florida residents $5 less.

Open: Daily 6:30am–dusk.

KEY BISCAYNE GOLF COURSE, 6700 Crandon Blvd., Key Biscayne. Tel. 361-9129.

The Key Biscayne Golf Course is the number-one ranked municipal course in the state, and one of the top five in the country. The park is situated on 200 bayfront acres, and offers a pro shop, rentals, lessons, carts, and a lighted driving range.

Admission: Thanksgiving–Easter, $55–$60 per person; Easter–Thanksgiving, $35 per person. Carts ($25 for two people) are required until 1pm.

Open: Daily dawn–dusk.

HEALTH CLUBS

BARCADO BEACH CLUB GYMNASIUM, on the ground floor of Roney Plaza, 2377 Collins Ave., between 23rd and 24th Sts., Miami Beach. Tel. 531-7357.

Although there are some bicycles and Universal-type pulley systems here, the Barcado's workout room is primarily a free-weight facility. Not fancy, but well equipped, and visitors have free access to a nearby swimming pool.

Admission: $6 per day.

Open: Mon–Fri 7am–10pm, Sat 9am–8pm, Sun 9am–1pm.

JET SKIS

Tony's Jet Ski Rentals, 3601 Rickenbacker Causeway, Key Biscayne (tel. 361-8280), rents jet skis, Yamaha waverunners, and Kawasaki two-seaters. This is the city's largest rental shop, located on a private beach in the Miami Marine Stadium lagoon. The cost is from $45 per hour; waverunners rent for $60 per hour. It's open daily from 11am to dusk.

SCUBA DIVING/SNORKELING

In 1981, the government began a wide-scale project designed to increase the number of habitats available to marine organisms. One of the program's major accomplishments has been the creation of nearby artificial reefs, which have attracted all kinds of tropical plants, fish, and animals. An excellent reef guide is available free from Biscayne National Park, P.O. Box 1369, Homestead, FL 33090 (tel. 247-2044).

Several dive shops around the city offer organized weekend outings, either to these reefs, or to one of over a dozen old shipwrecks around Miami's shores. Check "Divers" in the *Yellow Pages* for rental equipment, and for a full list of undersea tour operators.

Anything Underwater Dive Charters, 3391 SW 25th Terrace, Miami 33133 (tel. 445-4930 or 478-2885) offers regularly scheduled full- and half-day dives. Experienced guides and quality equipment are provided to adventurers. Reservations are required. You pay $35 per person and rentals are additional. Call for sail times.

TENNIS

In addition to hotel tennis facilities, about 500 public courts are available free or for a minimal charge. Some of the best tennis courts are located in Miami Beach. For information on courts closest to you, contact the **Metro-Dade County Parks and Recreation Department** (tel. 579-2676), weekdays between 8am and 5pm.

The **Flamingo Park Center,** 1245 Michigan Ave., at 12th Street, South Miami Beach (tel. 673-7761), is the city's largest facility, with 20 clay courts. Open Monday through Friday from 9am to 8pm and on Saturday and Sunday from 9am to dusk. The

Bayshore Golf Course, 2301 Alton Rd., Miami Beach (tel. 532-3350), has two hard courts and is open daily during daylight hours.

WINDSURFING

Sailboards Miami, Rickenbacker Causeway, Key Biscayne (tel. 361-SAIL), operates out of big yellow trucks on Hobie Beach (see "Beaches," above), the most popular windsurfing spot in the city. Rentals are by the hour or day, and lessons are given throughout the day. You pay $15 per hour, $45 per day; a two-hour lesson and rental package is $39. It's open daily from 9am to 6pm.

6. SAVVY SHOPPING

With few exceptions, Miami's main shopping areas are not streets, but malls—a reminder of the city's strong suburban bent. Most, like Dadeland Mall and The Mall at 163rd Street, are unabashedly straightforward about their identities; others, like the Bal Harbour Shops and Bayside Marketplace, are more coyly named, as they shy away from the "mall's" middle-class connotations. South Florida's gaggle of galleries has created stiff competition, a situation that keeps shoppers happy with good values and lots of choices.

THE SHOPPING SCENE

SHOPPING AREAS Almost every major street in Miami is lined with an infinite variety of small stores, restaurants, motels, and fast-food joints. Some of the city's best shops and shopping areas are outlined below under "Shopping A to Z," but you're bound to make your own finds. Keep your eyes open and stop at shops that interest you.

Coconut Grove Downtown Coconut Grove is one of Miami's few pedestrian-friendly zones. Centered around Main Highway and Grand Avenue, and branching onto the adjoining streets, the Grove's wide, café- and boutique-lined sidewalks provide hours of browsing pleasure. You can't escape Miami's ubiquitous malls, however—there's one near this cozy village center (see "Mayfair Shops," below). Coconut Grove is best known for its dozens of avant-garde clothing stores, funky import shops, and excellent sidewalk cafés.

Coral Gables—Miracle Mile Actually only a half mile, this central shopping street was an integral part of George Merrick's original city plan. Today, the strip's importance seems slightly more historical than commercial. Lined primarily with small, '70s storefronts, the Miracle Mile, which terminates at the Mediterranean-style City Hall rotunda, also features several good and unusual restaurants (see "Dining" in Chapter 4), and is worth a stop on your tour of Coral Gables.

South Miami Beach—Lincoln Road The Lincoln Road Mall is an eight-block pedestrian zone, near the north end of Miami Beach's art deco district. The hip but struggling area stretches from Washington Avenue to Alton Road, and is the center of the city's most exciting art scene. The buildings that are not empty contain a unique assortment of art galleries, antiques stores, and furniture shops, as well as the studios of the Miami City Ballet. Surrounding streets, including Washington and Collins Avenues, are rife with funky thrift stores, eateries, and T-shirt shops.

HOURS, TAXES & SHIPPING For most shops around the city **open hours** are Monday through Saturday from 10am to 6pm and on Sunday from noon to 5pm. Many stay open late (usually until 9pm) one night of the week (usually Thursday). Shops in trendy Coconut Grove are open until 9pm Sunday through Thursday, and even later on Friday and Saturday nights. Department stores and shopping malls keep longer hours, staying open from 10am to 9 or 10pm Monday through Saturday and noon to 6pm on Sunday.

The 6% Florida state **sales tax** is added to the price of all nonfood purchases.

Most Miami stores can wrap your purchase and **ship** it anywhere in the world via the United Parcel Service (UPS). If they can't, you can send it yourself, either through UPS (tel. 238-0134) or through the U.S. Mail (see "Fast Facts: Miami" in Chapter 4).

BEST BUYS Locally produced and widely distributed goods are easily Miami's best buys. Not surprisingly, local seafood and citrus products are some of the city's most important exports. Other high-quality items are available in Miami, but fruit and fish are the region's specialties, and nowhere will you find them fresher.

Downtown Miami is the best district to visit for discounts on all types of goods, from watches and jewelry, to luggage and leather. Inexpensive electronics and discount clothing can also be found, often from shops with a heavy Hispanic influence. Look around Flagler Street and Miami Avenue for all kinds of cluttered bargain stores. Most of the signs around here are printed in both English and Spanish, for the benefit of locals and tourists alike.

Citrus Fruit There was a time when it seemed as though almost every other store was shipping fruit home for tourists. Today such stores are a dying breed, but a few high-quality operations still send the freshest oranges and grapefruit. **Todd's Fruit Shippers,** 221 Navarre Ave. (tel. 448-5215), can take your order over the phone, and charge it to American Express, MasterCard, or VISA. Boxes are sold by the bushel or fraction thereof, and start at about $17.

Seafood East Coast Fisheries, 360 W. Flagler St., downtown (tel. 373-5516), a retail market and restaurant (see "Dining" in Chapter 4), has shipped millions of pounds of seafood worldwide from its own fishing fleet. They're equipped to wrap and send 5- or 10-pound packages of stone crab claws, Florida lobsters, Florida Bay pompano, fresh Key West shrimp, and a variety of other local delicacies to your door via overnight mail.

Miami's most famous restaurant is **Joe's Stone Crab,** located at 227 Biscayne St., South Miami Beach (tel. 673-0365, or toll free 800/780-CRAB). Joe's makes overnight air shipments of stone crabs to anywhere in the country. Joe's is only open during crab season (from October through May).

SHOPPING A TO Z

ART & ANTIQUES

The best collection of antiques shops in the city is located in the art deco district of South Miami Beach. They are usually open Tuesday through Saturday afternoons. A full list of offerings with their specific operating hours can be obtained free from the **South Beach Welcome Center,** in the Leslie Hotel, 1244 Ocean Dr., South Miami Beach (tel. 672-2014). Good choices are:

DECOLECTABLE, 233 14th St., South Miami Beach. Tel. 674-0899.

This store sells art deco furniture, radios, clocks, and lighting.

GALLERY ANTIGUA, Boulevard Plaza Building, 5318 Biscayne Blvd. Tel. 759-5355.

One of the more unusual specialty shops, featuring African-American and Caribbean art, Gallery Antigua frequently offers individual original works as well as complete art installations.

ONE HAND CLAPPING, 432 Espanola Way, South Miami Beach. Tel. 532-0507.

This is another excellent find, featuring a broad range of art, antiques, and collectibles from this and previous centuries.

BEACHWEAR

In addition to stores in all of the area shopping malls, try the following:

TOO COOL OCEAN DRIVE, 504 Ocean Dr., South Miami Beach. Tel. 538-5101.

If it has to do with the beach, it's here: swimsuits, T-shirts, shorts, thongs, floats, beach chairs, towels, umbrellas, tanning lotions, and more.

BOOKS

B. DALTON, in the Bayside Marketplace, 401 Biscayne Blvd., downtown. Tel. 579-8695.

Like others in the chain, this B. Dalton has a wide selection of general-interest books.

A second bookshop is located in the Omni International Mall, 1601 Biscayne Blvd., downtown (tel. 358-1895).

BOOKS & BOOKS, 296 Aragon Ave., Coral Gables. Tel. 442-4408.

This is one of the best book shops to be found anywhere. It's not particularly big, but B&B stocks an excellent collection of new, used, and hard-to-find books on all subjects. They have a particularly strong emphasis on art and design, as well as alternative literature, and the shop hosts regular, free lectures by noted authors and experts. For a recorded listing of upcoming events, dial 444-POEM.

A second Books & Books is located at 933 Lincoln Rd. in South Miami Beach (tel. 532-3222).

BOOKWORKS II, 6935 Red Rd. Tel. 661-5080.

This is one of Miami's most upscale bookshops, located between Coconut Grove and Coral Gables. Bookworks has long featured works from both national and local publishers.

DOUBLEDAY BOOK SHOP, in the Bal Harbour Shops, 9700 Collins Ave. Tel. 866-2871.

Located in one of the city's most upscale shopping centers, this Doubleday is known for its good variety of titles, and a particular emphasis on books of local interest.

DOWNTOWN BOOK CENTER, 247 SE 1st St., downtown. Tel. 377-9939.

Downtown Books is the city's best commercial area store, and is a great place to browse. This long established shop is known for both its good service and wide selection.

They have a second location at 215 NE Second Ave. (tel. 377-9938).

WALDENBOOKS, in the Omni International Mall, 1601 Biscayne Blvd. Tel. 358-5764.

Waldenbooks is a good place for the latest titles, as well as good classics and light beach reading.

DEPARTMENT STORES

Department stores are often the primary "anchors" for Miami's many malls. The biggest include:

BURDINES, 22 E. Flagler St., downtown. Tel. 835-5151.

One of the oldest and largest department stores in the state, Burdines specializes in high-quality, middle-class home furnishings and fashions.

Additional stores are located in the Dadeland Mall and at 1675 Meridian Ave. in Miami Beach. All stores can be reached at the number above. Check the telephone directory for additional locations.

SEARS ROEBUCK & COMPANY, in the Aventura Mall, 19505 Biscayne Blvd., Aventura. Tel. 937-7500.

This common store has all the usual fashions and furnishings, plus appliances, insurance, and financial services.

It's also located at 3655 Coral Way (tel. 460-3400), next to the Miracle Center just east of Coral Gables.

DISCOUNT STORES & OUTLETS

FASHION Over 100 retail outlets are clustered in Miami's mile-square Fashion District just north of downtown. Surrounding Fashion Avenue (NW Fifth Avenue), and known primarily for swimwear, sportswear, high-fashion children's clothing, and glittery women's dresses, Miami's fashion center is second in size only to New York's. The district features European- and Latin-influenced designs with tropical hues and subdued pastels. Most stores offer high-quality clothing at a 25%–70% discount and on-site alterations. Most are open Monday through Friday from 9am to 5:30pm.

HOUSEWARES Miami's design district shops are also some of the best in the country. Strongly influenced by Latin American markets, outlets feature the latest furniture and housewares, all at discount prices. Not all stores are open to the public, but those that are offer incredible bargains to the savviest of shoppers. The district runs north along NE Second Avenue, beginning at 36th Street.

ELECTRONICS

BEYOND, in the Bayside Marketplace, 401 Biscayne Blvd. Tel. 592-1904.

Beyond features the latest in consumer electronics. Futuristic portable stereos, televisions, telephones, and the like are all offered at reasonable rates.

Other stores are located at Cocowalk, Dadeland, Aventura, and The Falls shopping malls.

SPY SHOPS INTERNATIONAL, INC., 2900 Biscayne Blvd. Tel. 573-4779.

Farther up the street, this store sells real-life James Bond–style gadgets like night-vision binoculars, bulletproof briefcases, "bug" detectors, and other expensive gizmos. This is a serious store, not a museum, so look like you intend to buy.

FOOD & DRINK

EPICURE MARKET, 1656 Alton Rd., South Miami Beach. Tel. 672-1861.

This is the place to go for prime meats, cheeses, and wines. Cooked foods include strictly gourmet hors d'oeuvres, pâtés, and desserts. The shop also sells homemade breads and soups, along with a variety of freshly made hot items that are ready to eat.

THE ESTATE WINES & GOURMET FOODS, 92 Miracle Mile, Coral Gables. Tel. 442-9915.

This exceedingly friendly storefront in the middle of Coral Gables's main shopping street offers a small but well-chosen selection of vintages from around the world. Every Thursday from 5 to 8pm, the store's knowledgeable owner hosts a wine tasting and lecture, at which vineyard representatives are present. Tastings cost $5, and are open to the public.

GIFTS & SOUVENIRS

DAPY, in the Bayside Marketplace, 401 Biscayne Blvd., downtown. Tel. 374-3098.

Gift shops are located all over town and in almost every hotel, but Dapy's tops if you're in the market for high-tech watches, rubber coasters, Technicolor trash cans, oversize calculators, Lucite televisions, and the like. If it's cool, it's here. New Wave Japanese and European fads and gifts cost from just a few cents to hundreds of dollars.

JEWELRY

THE SEYBOLD BUILDING, 3601 NE 1st St., downtown. Tel. 377-0122.

This is the best place in Miami for discount diamonds and jewelry. The building is located right in the middle of downtown, and houses a large variety of retail shops.

LINGERIE

LINGERIE BY LISA, 3000 McFarlane Rd., Coconut Grove. Tel. 446-2368.

Coconut Grove's best lingerie shop features a huge selection of bras, panties, teddies, and camisoles. Located on the corner of Main Highway, this store includes lots of items you'll never see in a national catalog. On weekends, a live model poses in the window.

LUGGAGE

BENTLEY'S, in the Bayside Marketplace, 401 Biscayne Blvd., downtown. Tel. 372-2907.

Carrying a large selection of luggage and travel-related items, this store also features leather cases and business accessories. Bentley's also makes expert repairs.

MALLS

There are so many shopping centers in Miami that it would be impossible to mention them all, but here's a list of the biggest and the best:

AVENTURA MALL, 19501 Biscayne Blvd., Aventura. Tel. 935-4222.

Enter this large, insulated indoor mall, located at Biscayne Boulevard and 197th Street near the Dade-Broward county line, and it's easy to imagine you're on the outskirts of Omaha—or anywhere else in America for that matter. Over 200 generic shops are complemented by the megastores JC Penney, Lord & Taylor, Macy's, and Sears. Parking is free.

BAL HARBOUR SHOPS, 9700 Collins Ave., Bal Harbour. Tel. 866-0311.

There's not much in the way of whimsy here, just the best quality goods from the fanciest names. Ann Taylor, Fendi, Krizia, Rodier, Gucci, Brooks Brothers, Waterford, Cartier, H. Stern, Tourneau . . . the list goes on and on. The Bal Harbour Shops are the fanciest in Miami. With Neiman Marcus at one end and Saks Fifth Avenue at the other, the mall itself is a pleasant open-air emporium, with covered walkways and lush greenery. The Bal Harbour shops are located at 97th Street, just opposite the tall Sheraton Bal Harbour hotel. Parking is $1.

BAYSIDE MARKETPLACE, 401 Biscayne Blvd., downtown. Tel. 577-3344.

Miami's successful Rouse Company development has taken over a stunning location—16 beautiful waterfront acres in the heart of downtown—and turned it into a lively and exciting shopping place. Downstairs, about 100 shops and carts sell everything from plastic fruit to high-tech electronics (some of the more unique specialty shops are listed in this section). The upstairs eating arcade is stocked with dozens of fast-food choices, offering a wide variety of inexpensive international eats (see "Dining" in Chapter 4). Some restaurants stay open later than the stores, which close at 10pm Monday through Saturday and at 8pm on Sunday. Parking is $1 per hour.

DADELAND MALL, 7535 N. Kendall Dr., Kendall. Tel. 665-6226.

The granddaddy of Miami's suburban mall scene, Dadeland features more than 175 specialty shops, anchored by five large department stores—Burdines, JC Penney, Jordan Marsh, Lord & Taylor, and Saks Fifth Avenue. Sixteen restaurants serve from the adjacent Treats Food Court. The mall is located at the intersection of U.S. 1 and SW 88th Street, 15 minutes south of downtown. Parking is free.

THE FALLS, 8888 Howard Dr., in the Kendall area. Tel. 255-4570.

Tropical waterfalls are the setting for this outdoor shopping center with dozens of moderately priced, slightly upscale shops. Miami's only Bloomingdale's is here, as are Polo Ralph Lauren, Godiva, Caswell-Massey, and over 60 other specialty shops. The Falls is located at the intersection of U.S. 1 and 136th Street, about three miles south of Dadeland Mall. Parking is free.

THE MALL AT 163RD STREET, 1421 NE 163rd St., North Miami Beach. Tel. 947-9845.

This aptly named three-story megamall, between U.S. 1 and I-95, in Greater Miami North, is protected by the world's first Teflon-coated fiberglass roof. Beneath it are 150-plus middle American shops including Burdines, Mervyn's, and Marshalls department stores. Parking is free.

MAYFAIR SHOPS IN THE GROVE, 2911 Grand Ave., Coconut Grove. Tel. 448-1700.

The small and labyrinthine Mayfair Shops complex, just a few blocks east of Commodore Plaza, conceals several top-quality shops, restaurants, art galleries, and nightclubs. The emphasis is on chic, expensive elegance, and intimate, European-style boutiques are featured. Valet parking is $5.

MARKETS

THE OPA-LOCKA/HIALEAH FLEA MARKET, 12705 NW 42nd Ave. (LeJeune Rd.), near Amelia Earhart Park. Tel. 688-0500.

Featuring over 1,000 merchants, this flea market sells everything from plants and pet food to luggage and linen. This indoor/outdoor weekend market is one of the largest of its kind in Florida. There are no real antiques here. Almost everything is brand new (of suspect quality and origin) and dirt cheap.

It's open from 5am to 6pm Friday through Sunday. Admission and parking are free.

PERFUMES & BEAUTY SUPPLIES

PERFUMANIA, in the AmeriFirst Building, 1 SE Third Ave., downtown. Tel. 358-3224.

Perfumania sells skin products, as well as designer fragrances, at 10%–60% below normal retail prices. The shop is in the heart of downtown Miami.

Other locations include 223 Miracle Mile, Coral Gables (tel. 529-0114); and 1604 Washington Ave., South Miami Beach (tel. 534-7221).

TOYS

FUNWORLD TOYS & HOBBIES, 145 E. Flagler St., downtown. Tel. 374-1453.

This large store features all the hits, including Legos, Sega electronics, Mattel cars and toys, and remote-control boats, cars, and airplanes. Fisher Price and other toddlers' toys are also available.

7. EVENING ENTERTAINMENT

One of the most striking aspects of the city is the recent growth of world-class music, dance, and theater. Miami proudly boasts an opera company and a symphony orchestra, as well as respected ballet and modern dance troupes.

South Florida's late-night life is abuzz, with South Miami Beach at the center of the scene. The **art deco district** is the spawning ground for top international acts including Latin artist Julio Iglesias, controversial rappers 2 Live Crew, jazz man Nestor Torres, and rockers Expose, Nuclear Valdez, and of course Gloria Estefan and the Miami Sound Machine. It's no secret that Cuban and Caribbean rhythms are extremely popular, and the sound of the conga, incorporated into Miami's club culture, makes dancing irresistible.

If you're not sure where to spend an evening, you can't go wrong by heading into downtown **Coconut Grove.** In the heart of this otherwise quiet enclave, music clubs blast their beats, and sidewalks are perpetually crowded with outdoor café tables. There's not a lot of professional entertainment in the Grove; the main show is always on the street, where crowds gather to see and to be seen.

New Times is the most comprehensive of Miami's free weekly newspapers. Available each Wednesday, this newspaper prints articles, previews, and advertisements on upcoming local events. Several **telephone hotlines**—many operated by local radio stations—give free recorded information on current events in the city. These include: WTMI Cultural Arts Line (tel. 550-9393), Love 94 Concert Hotline (tel. 654-94FM), PACE Free Concert (tel. 237-1718), Song & Dance Concerts (tel. 947-6471), 24-Hour Cosmic Hotline (tel. 854-2222), and the UM Concert Hotline (tel. 284-6477). Other information-oriented telephone numbers are listed under the appropriate headings, below.

THE PERFORMING ARTS

Where noted, tickets can be purchased by phone through **Ticketmaster** (tel. 358-5885). The company accepts all major credit cards, and has phone lines open 24 hours. If you want to pick up your tickets from a Ticketmaster outlet, call for the location nearest you. Outlets are open Monday through Saturday from 10am to 9pm and on Sunday from noon to 5pm. There's a small service charge.

MAJOR PERFORMANCE HALLS

COLONY THEATER, 1040 Lincoln Rd., South Miami Beach. Tel. 674-1026.

After years of decay and a $1-million face-lift, the Colony has become an architectural showpiece of the art deco district. This multipurpose 465-seat theater stages performances by the Miami City Ballet and the Ballet Flamenco La Rosa, as well as various special events.

DADE COUNTY AUDITORIUM, 2901 W. Flagler St., downtown. Tel. 545-3395.

Performers gripe about the lack of space, but for patrons, this 2,500-seat auditorium is comfortable and intimate. It's home to the city's Greater Miami Opera, and stages productions by the Miami Ballet Company and the Concert Association of Greater Miami.

GUSMAN CENTER FOR THE PERFORMING ARTS, 174 E. Flagler St., downtown. Tel. 372-0925.

Seating is tight, but sound is good at this 1,700-seat downtown theater. In addition to providing a regular stage for the Philharmonic Orchestra of Florida and the Ballet Theatre of Miami, the Gusman Center also features pop concerts, plays, film festival screenings, and special events.

The auditorium itself was built as a movie palace, the Olympia Theater, in 1926,

---

MAJOR CONCERT & PERFORMANCE HALL BOX OFFICES

Colony Theater, 1040 Lincoln Rd., South Miami Beach (tel. 674-1026).
Dade County Auditorium, 2901 W. Flagler St., downtown (tel. 545-3395).
Gusman Center for the Performing Arts, 174 E. Flagler St., downtown (tel. 372-0925).
Gusman Concert Hall, 1314 Miller Dr., Coral Gables (tel. 284-2438).
Jackie Gleason Theater of the Performing Arts (TOPA), 1700 Washington Ave., South Miami Beach (tel. 673-8300).

---

and its ornate interior is typical of the era, complete with fancy columns, a huge pipe organ, and twinkling "stars" on the ceiling.

GUSMAN CONCERT HALL, 1314 Miller Dr., Coral Gables. Tel. 284-2438.

Not to be confused with the Gusman Center, above, this roomy 600-seat hall gives a stage to the Miami Chamber Symphony and a varied program of university recitals.

JACKIE GLEASON THEATER OF THE PERFORMING ARTS (TOPA), 1700 Washington Ave., South Miami Beach. Tel. 673-8300.

It has become tradition for the American Ballet Theatre to open its touring season here during the last two weeks of January, after which TOPA is home to big-budget Broadway shows, classical music concerts, opera, and dance performances. This 2,705-seat hall has been newly renovated in order to improve the acoustics and sightlines.

MIAMIWAY THEATER, 12615 W. Dixie Hwy., North Miami. Tel. 893-0005.

Owned by actor Philip Michael Thomas of "Miami Vice" fame, this high-tech performing arts complex features a state-of-the-art sound system in a 435-seat theater. Although the stage is often dark, keep an eye out for interesting alternative productions as well as various live performances.

Admission: Depends on the production.

MINORCA PLAYHOUSE, 232 Minorca Ave., Coral Gables. Tel. 446-1116.

The Florida Shakespeare Theater calls Minorca "home." At other times, traveling dance and theater companies perform here. Performances are usually held Tuesday through Saturday evenings, as well as Wednesday, Saturday, and Sunday matinees throughout the year. The box office is open Monday through Saturday from 10am to 8pm and on Sunday from noon to 4pm.

Admission: Tickets, $18 and $20, $10 and $15 for students and seniors.

THE RING THEATRE, on the University of Miami Campus, 1380 Miller Dr., entrance no. 6, Coral Gables. Tel. 284-3355.

The university's Department of Theater Arts uses this stage for advanced student productions of comedies, dramas, and musicals. Faculty and guest actors are regularly featured, as are contemporary works by local playwrights. Performances are usually scheduled Tuesday through Saturday during the academic year only. The box office is open Monday through Friday from 9am to 5pm, and before show time.

Admission: Tickets, $3–$10.

THEATER

ACME ACTING COMPANY, 955 Alton Rd., Miami Beach. Tel. 531-2393.

Miami's closest approximation to New York's Off Off Broadway is embodied in this single local troupe. Lively productions of contemporary plays are most often performed at the Colony Theater in South Miami Beach. Performances are Wednesday through Saturday at 8:15pm and on Sunday at 7:15pm.

Admission: Tickets, $15 Wed–Fri and Sun, $17 Sat, $13 students and seniors.

COCONUT GROVE PLAYHOUSE, 3500 Main Hwy., Coconut Grove. Tel. 442-4000.

The Grove Theater, as it was originally called, opened as a movie house in 1927. Thirty years later, real estate developer George Engle bought this beautiful Spanish rococo palace and, after a $1-million renovation, staged one of the first major productions of Tennessee Williams's *A Streetcar Named Desire*.

Today this respected playhouse is known for its original and innovative staging of both international and local plays. Dramas and musicals receive equal attention on the theater's main stage, while the house's second, more intimate Encore Room is well suited to alternative and experimental productions.

The theater's play season lasts from October through June. The box office is open Tuesday through Saturday from 10am to 9pm and on Sunday and Monday from 10am to 6pm; tickets are also available through Ticketmaster. Main stage performances are Tuesday through Saturday at 8:15pm, with matinees on Wednesday, Saturday, and Sunday at 2pm. Encore Room performances are Tuesday through Saturday at 8:30pm, with matinees on Wednesday, Thursday, and Sunday at 2:15pm. Schedules differ during previews.

Admission: Tickets, $8–$35.

CLASSICAL MUSIC & OPERA

In addition to the local orchestras and operas described below, each year brings with it a slew of special events and touring artists. One of the most important and longest-running series is produced by the **Concert Association of Florida (CAF),** 555 17th St., South Miami Beach (tel. 532-3491). Known for almost a quarter of a century for their high-caliber, star-packed schedules, CAF regularly arranges the best classical concerts for the city. Season after season the schedules are punctuated by world-renowned dance companies and seasoned virtuosi such as Itzhak Perlman, and Andre Watts.

CAF does not have its own space. Performances are usually scheduled either in the Dade County Auditorium or the Jackie Gleason Theater of the Performing Arts (see "Major Performance Halls," above). The performance season lasts from October through April, and ticket prices range from $15 to $52.

GREATER MIAMI OPERA ASSOCIATION, 1200 Coral Way, Coral Gables. Tel. 854-1643.

The 50th anniversary of the Miami Opera was in 1991. It regularly features singers from America's and Europe's top houses. All productions are sung in their original language and staged with projected English supertitles. Tickets become scarce when Plácido Domingo or Luciano Pavarotti (who made his American debut here in 1965) come to town.

The opera's season runs roughly from January through April only, with performances four days per week. Most productions are staged in the Dade County Auditorium (see "Major Performance Halls," above).

Admission: Tickets, $13–$50; student and senior discounts available.

THE NEW WORLD SYMPHONY, 541 Lincoln Rd., South Miami Beach. Tel. 673-3331.

Alternating performances between downtown's Gusman Center for the Performing Arts and South Beach's Lincoln Theatre, this 5-year-old advanced-training orchestra is a major stepping-stone for gifted young musicians seeking a professional career. Accepting artists on the basis of a three-year fellowship, and led by artistic advisor Michael Tilson Thomas, the orchestra specializes in ambitious, innovative, energetic performances, and often features guest soloists and renowned conductors. The symphony's season lasts from October through April.

Admission: Tickets, $10–$40; student and senior discounts available.

FLORIDA PHILHARMONIC ORCHESTRA, Dade County Office, 836 Biscayne Blvd., downtown. Tel. toll free 800/226-1812.

South Florida's premier symphony orchestra, under the direction of James Judd, presents a full season of mainstream and pops programs interspersed with several childrens' and contemporary popular music dates. The Philharmonic performs downtown in the Gusman Center for the Performing Arts, the Jackie Gleason Theater, and the Dade County Auditorium (see "Major Performance Halls," above).

Admission: Tickets, $11–$35.

MIAMI CHAMBER SYMPHONY, 5690 N. Kendall Dr., Kendall. Tel. 662-6600.

Renowned international soloists regularly perform with this professional orchestra. The symphony performs October through May, and most concerts are held in the Gusman Concert Hall, on the University of Miami campus (see "Major Performance Halls," above).

Admission: Tickets, $12–$25.

DANCE

Several local dance companies train and perform in the Greater Miami area. In addition, top visiting troupes regularly pass through the city, stopping at the venues listed above. Keep your eyes open for special events and guest artists.

BALLET FLAMENCO LA ROSA, 1008 Lincoln Rd., South Miami Beach. Tel. 672-0552.

This year marks the ballet's fourth season in their home in South Miami Beach. Although other styles are danced, the company is primarily influenced by the flamenco and Latin style.

In addition to performances, which are held primarily in South Beach's Colony Theater, the Flamenco La Rosa also offers dancing lessons. They cost $8 each, and are held at their Lincoln Road studio. The ballet season runs from March through October.

Admission: Tickets, $15–$20.

MIAMI CITY BALLET, 905 Lincoln Rd. Mall, South Miami Beach. Tel. 532-4880.

Headquartered behind a storefront in the middle of the art deco district and directed by Edward Villella, this 7-year-old Miami company has quickly emerged as an important troupe, performing a repertoire of classical and contemporary works. The artistically acclaimed and innovative company features a repertoire of more than 60 ballets, many by George Balanchine, and more than 20 world premieres. The City Ballet season runs from October through March, with performances both at the Dade County Auditorium and in South Beach at the Lincoln Theater (see "Major Performance Halls," above).

Admission: Tickets, $17–$44.

MIAMI BALLET COMPANY (MBC), 2901 W. Flagler St. Tel. 667-5985.

Because MBC is an amateur troupe, performers put forth a lot of energy, fueled by the dream of going pro. Established in 1951, the company has a reputation for working with talented underage performers as well as guest dancers from around the world. Miami performances are in October, November, January, and May. MBC usually performs in the Dade County Auditorium (see "Major Performance Halls," above).

Admission: Tickets, $11–$38.

BALLET THEATRE OF MIAMI, 1809 Ponce de Leon Blvd., Coral Gables. Tel. 442-4840.

The Ballet Theatre is a professional troupe, under the artistic direction of Lizette Piedra and Tony Catanzaro, formerly of the Boston Ballet. Beautifully staged performances of traditional and avant-garde dances have earned critical acclaim. Performances are held from October through June in the Gusman Center for the Performing Arts (see "Major Performance Halls," above).

Admission: Tickets, $12–$40.

THE CLUB & MUSIC SCENE

COMEDY CLUBS

COCONUTS COMEDY CLUB, in the Peacock Café, 2977 McFarlane Rd., Coconut Grove. Tel. 446-2582.

Coconuts, which opened in spring 1990, has quickly become Miami's premier comedy room, mostly because of its great location. Like other Coconuts clubs, this one has become a major stop on the comedy circuit, showcasing all the names you might very well see on television. Obviously, acts vary. Shows are Sunday through Thursday at 9pm, and on Friday and Saturday at 8 and 11pm. Reservations are recommended.

Admission: $6 Wed–Sun, $10 Fri–Sat, plus a two-drink minimum.

LIVE REGGAE

Lots of local clubs regularly feature live and recorded reggae. Some are authentic Jamaican joints, while others play the music to round out their island motifs. Check the local listings for the latest.

THE HUNGRY SAILOR, 3064½ Grand Ave., Coconut Grove. Tel. 444-9359.

This small, wood-paneled, English-style "pub" has Watneys, Bass, and Guinness on draft, and reggae regularly on tap. The club attracts an extremely mixed crowd. There's a short British menu and high-quality live music Tuesday through Saturday. It's open Sunday through Thursday from noon to midnight and on Friday and Saturday from noon to 2:30am.

Admission: Free Sun–Thurs, $2 Fri–Sat.

SUNDAYS ON THE BAY, 5420 Crandon Blvd., Key Biscayne. Tel. 361-6777.

Terrific happy hours are followed by dockside disco nights. Sundays has a great party atmosphere, fantastic water views, and good tropical food (see "Dining" in Chapter 4). Open Sunday through Wednesday from 11am to 2am and Thursday through Saturday from 11am to 2:30am.

Sundays' sibling restaurant, Salty's (tel. 945-5115), also occupies a terrific location, in Haulover Park at Collins Avenue and 108th Street in Miami Beach.

Admission: Free.

ROCK/COUNTRY/FOLK

Rock clubs often overlap with dance spots (see below) which also sometimes offer live rock bands. For up-to-date listings, check the papers, **WGTR-FM Concertline** (tel. 284-6477), and the **ZETA Link** (tel. 620-3600). Along with the venues listed below, free rock concerts are held every Friday throughout the winter in South Miami Beach's South Pointe Park. The shows feature the best local bands and start at 8pm.

Many area clubs book country bands and folk musicians, but not regularly enough to be included here. Check the **Folk Hotline** (tel. 531-3655), scan the free weekly *New Times,* and keep your eyes and ears open for current happenings.

CACTUS CANTINA GRILL, 630 6th St. (just west of Washington Ave.), South Miami Beach. Tel. 532-5095.

This Los Angeles–style cantina is one of South Beach's hottest finds. Gritty to the max, the Cactus features music that's live and loud almost every night. Styles range from jazz and blues to country, rockabilly, and soul. A huge, excellent, and inexpensive Cal-Mex menu is complemented by killer margaritas and a well-stocked tequila bar. Highly recommended. Open daily from 5pm to 5am.

Admission: Free, except for occasional special events.

FIREHOUSE FOUR, 1000 S. Miami Ave., downtown. Tel. 379-1923.

Miami's oldest fire station is now a popular restaurant and club. Live new rock music is featured on Friday or Saturday, and there's usually a spirited crowd nightly. The club sometimes hosts folk artists on Thursday. Open Monday through Thursday from noon to midnight, and on Friday and Saturday from noon to 3am. (See "Happy Hours," below.)

Admission: Free–$5.

PENROD'S, 1 Ocean Dr., South Miami Beach. Tel. 538-1111.

South Miami Beach's jack-of-all-trades also books bands. On weekends, there is straightforward rock music all day. Drink and snack specials are common in this multilevel, sports-oriented club. It's open Sunday through Thursday from 10am to 2am, and on Friday and Saturday from 10am to 5am.

Admission: Free before 10pm, $3–$6 after 10pm.

THE SPOT, 218 Espanola Way, South Miami Beach. Tel. 532-1682.

Brand new and red-hot, Mickey Rourke's Spot is yet another celeb-owned spot in the city's trendiest quarter. Lines can be vicious, especially on weekends, but once inside, the crowd is mellower and surprisingly unpretentious. The large drinking room features a full bar and good music that's often even danceable. Open daily from 9pm to 5am.

Admission: Free.

WASHINGTON SQUARE, 645 Washington Ave. (between 6th and 7th Sts.), South Miami Beach. Tel. 534-1403.

Rock, blues, jazz, and DJ's all converge on this small, hip club in the heart of the art deco district. Washington Square has a stage at one end, an island bar in the middle, and an artsy late-night crowd all around. Open daily from 10pm to 5am.

Admission: Free–$3.

THE WHISKEY, 1250 Ocean Dr., South Miami Beach. Tel. 531-0713.

Sure it's got a good beachfront location, but it's the reputation of co-owner Matt Dillon that helps pack 'em into this rather regular pool table/jukebox drinking bar. Live bands sometimes perform. It's a worthy part of any Ocean Drive crawl. Open daily from 9:30pm to 2am.

Admission: Free–$10.

JAZZ/BLUES

South Florida's jazz scene is very much alive with traditional and contemporary performers. Keep an eye out for guitarist Randy Bernsen, vibraphonist Tom Toyama, and flutist Nestor Torres, young performers who lead local ensembles. The **University of Miami** has a well-respected jazz studies program in their School of Music (tel. 284-6477), and often schedule low- and no-cost recitals. Frequent jazz shows are also scheduled at the **Miami Metrozoo** (see "The Top Attractions," above). The lineup changes frequently, and it's not always jazz, but the quality is good and concerts are included in the zoo admission.

Additionally, many area hotels feature cool jazz and light blues in their bars and lounges. Schedules are listed in newspaper entertainment sections. Finally, some of the rock clubs listed above also feature blues bands. Try calling the **Blues Hotline** (tel. 666-MOJO), and the **Jazz Hotline** (tel. 382-3938) for the most up-to-date bookings in Miami's jazz rooms.

Perhaps because the area itself is reminiscent of the Jazz Age, the bulk of the listings below are clustered in the art deco district of South Miami Beach, making it easy to plan an evening walking tour of some of the city's best clubs.

5TH STREET, 429 Lenox St., at the corner of 5th St., South Miami Beach. Tel. 531-1910.

The deco district's best alternative video and dance club is also the premier place to listen and dance to jazz, reggae, calypso, house, and blues. Often packed into the wee hours, 5th Street features live music six nights a week, and a moderately priced southern-style menu which includes jerk chicken wings, blackened dolphin, collard greens, and black-eyed peas. Reservations are sometimes necessary on special nights. The club is open Wednesday through Sunday from 9pm to 4am, and every other Monday from 8 to 11:30pm.

Admission: Free–$10.

CAFE AVALON, in the Avalon Hotel, 700 Ocean Dr., at the corner of 7th St., South Miami Beach. Tel. 538-0133.

One of the beach's most stunning art deco hotels has jazz and other live music Thursday through Sunday in their lobby restaurant/bar. The café is open daily from dawn to midnight or 2am.

Admission: Free.

CLEVELANDER RESTAURANT, in the Clevelander Hotel, 1020 Ocean Dr., at 10th St., South Miami Beach. Tel. 531-3485.

Offering live jazz, rock, or reggae most nights, the Clevelander is another good choice along South Beach's most popular strip. It's open daily from 5pm to 3am.

Admission: Free.

LET'S MAKE A DAIQUIRI, in the Bayside Marketplace, 401 Biscayne Blvd., downtown. Tel. 372-5117.

Right smack in the middle of the mall is this outdoor bar with one of the best views in town. Live jazz, rock, reggae, and calypso are featured almost nightly, and you don't even have to order a drink. It's open Sunday through Thursday from 9am to midnight, and on Friday and Saturday from 9am to 2am. The music ends an hour before closing.

Admission: Free.

SCULLY'S TAVERN, 9809 Sunset Dr., South Miami. Tel. 271-7404.

Excellent local bands, most often jazz and blues oriented, frequent Scully's, a sports-type bar, with pool tables and television monitors. There's live music every night except Monday. Open Sunday through Wednesday from 11am to 11pm, on Thursday from 11am to midnight, and on Friday and Saturday from 11am to 3am.

Admission: Free.

TOBACCO ROAD, 626 S. Miami Ave., downtown. Tel. 374-1198.

Featuring live music nightly, Tobacco Road sports an eclectic menu of new and local jazz, rock, and blues. On weekends, two stages, one up and one down, heat up simultaneously. This is a great place to dance. It's open daily from noon to 5am.

Admission: Free–$6.

DANCE CLUBS

In addition to quiet cafés and progressive poolside bars, Miami Beach pulsates with one of the liveliest night scenes in the city. Several loud dance clubs feature live bands as well as DJ dancing.

FACADE, in the Intracoastal Mall, 3509 NE 163rd St. (just east of U.S. 1), North Miami Beach. Tel. 948-6868.

Modern and classical designs are so deftly styled here that even the American Society of Interior Designers called it "spectacular." Ultra-flashy features include contemporary lines adjacent to ancient Grecian murals, as well as floor-to-ceiling steel and stone columns around an immense sunken dance floor. Pop dance disks are regularly interrupted for performances by the club's 10-piece band and professional dancers. Expect the usual million-dollar light show. Open Tuesday through Sunday from 9pm to 6am.

Admission: Free–$15.

THE ISLAND CLUB, 701 Washington Ave., at 7th St. South Miami Beach. Tel. 538-1213.

Located on one of Miami's most progressive corners, this local tavern attracts chic visitors from the city's "underground." The club is unusually lively on Monday nights when the DJ kicks in and the Ping-Pong table is put away to accommodate the crowds. Open daily from 8pm to 4am.

Admission: Free.

THE KITCHEN CLUB, CLUB BEIRUT, AND REGGAE DIRECTORY, 100 21st St. at the beach, South Miami Beach. Tel. 538-6631.

The same space adopts different personas on alternate nights of the week. The Kitchen is a DJ dance joint featuring the newest wave grooves. Beirut is generally a live-music venue where cutting-edge bands are given a stage. Reggae Directory features new Jamaican sounds. Call for times and schedules.

Admission: Free–$10.

STUDIO ONE 83, 2860 NW 183rd St., Carol City. Tel. 621-7295.

This African-American–oriented disco with occasional Caribbean bands also features live jazz in the Jazz Room daily. Special live concerts are also booked. It's open daily from 5pm to 5am; there's a happy hour daily from 5 to 8pm.

Admission: Free–$5.

VAN DOME, 1532 Washington Ave., South Miami Beach. Tel. 534-4288.

South Beach's current star of the moment is an impressive New York–style dance club, located behind the carved stone walls of a former Jewish synagogue. Gothic styling and a wrap-around second-floor ambulatory have attracted trendies, while an excellent sound system, late-night snack/raw bar, and quiet-enough tables combine to give this place some staying power. It's open Thursday through Saturday from 10pm to 5am.

Admission: $5–$15.

THE BAR SCENE

In addition to the many music clubs listed above, Miami's bars and lounges are noted for their spirited happy hours. In addition, several unique "theme" bars offer fun and adventure.

HAPPY HOURS

Miami is a happy-hour heaven. For tourists and locals alike, few things are more relaxing than sitting down with food, drinks, and friends, in a casual atmosphere.

Most hotel bars and many restaurants—especially in South Miami Beach and Coconut Grove—offer discounted drinks and food, served just around sunset. Some are in sight of spectacular waterfront views. Many establishments offering special happy hours are listed with the restaurants in Chapter 4. Others are listed in this section under various club headings, and the rest are listed below.

ALCAZABA, in the Hyatt Regency Hotel, 50 Alhambra Plaza, Coral Gables. Tel. 441-1234.

The Hyatt's Top-40 lounge exudes a Mediterranean atmosphere that mixes fantasy with reality. Tropical drinks and authentic tapas are on the menu. Happy hour, Wednesday through Friday from 5 to 7pm and on Saturday from 9 to 11pm, offers half-price beer, wine, and well drinks plus a free buffet.

COCO LOCO'S, in the Sheraton Brickell Point Hotel, 495 Brickell Ave., downtown. Tel. 373-6000.

Coco's offers one of the best happy-hour buffets in town, with hot hors d'oeuvres like chicken wings and pigs-in-blankets. On Friday there's an extra special buffet. There is a $1 plate charge. Happy hour is Monday through Friday from 5 to 8pm.

CRAWDADDY'S, South Pointe Park, 1 Washington Ave., South Miami Beach. Tel. 673-1708.

The mood is casual, and the scenery breathtaking with views overlooking the Atlantic Ocean and Government Cut. This is a great place to "kick back," especially on Friday when the cruise ships pass by on their way out to sea. Happy hour is Monday through Friday from 5 to 7pm. There's a free buffet.

DOC DAMMERS SALOON, in the Colonnade Hotel, 180 Aragon Ave., Coral Gables. Tel. 441-2600.

A well-stocked mahogany bar and an easygoing 1920s motif are the hallmarks of this 30-something hangout. The light menu features dozens of upscale appetizers, gourmet pizzas, and alligator burgers. Happy hour is Monday through Friday from 5 to 8pm. Specials include $2.50 beer, wine, and drinks, plus a free buffet on Friday; look for $1-drink "Ladies' Nights."

FIREHOUSE FOUR, 1000 S. Miami Ave., downtown. Tel. 379-1923.

Burgers, fries, and crunchy conch fritters make great beer companions (see "Rock/Country/Folk," above). Happy hour is Monday through Friday from 5 to 8pm. Specials include $2 drinks and a free hot buffet.

MONTY'S RAW BAR, 2560 S. Bayshore Dr., Coconut Grove. Tel. 858-1431.

This tropical-looking, outdoor, pier-top bar offers the Grove's most swinging happy hour, with beautiful sea views and rocking island music. Fresh oysters, chowders, and fritters are available. Happy hour is Monday through Friday from 4 to 8pm.

TOBACCO ROAD, 626 S. Miami Ave., downtown. Tel. 374-1198.

Home of Miami's first liquor license, Tobacco Road still offers good music, great burgers (cheese, mushroom, chili), and wonderful homemade ice cream. Happy hour is Monday through Friday from 5 to 8pm. Specials include drink discounts and $1 appetizer plates.

THEME BARS

MIAMI BREWPUB, in Zum Alten Fritz Restaurant, 1840 NE Fourth Ave., downtown. Tel. 538-8640.

It's Oktoberfest nightly at the city's only brewpub, an establishment that makes its own barley malt right on the premises. The beer is the freshest in Miami, and several varieties (including Miami Weiss) are really top-notch. The restaurant is also worth visiting (see "Dining" in Chapter 4). Open Monday through Thursday from 11am to 10pm, on Friday from 11am to midnight, Sunday from 3pm to midnight.

Admission: Free.

PENROD'S BEACH CLUB, 1 Ocean Dr., South Miami Beach. Tel. 538-1111.

Earning a listing here for its party-happy evenings and frequent special events, Penrod's is always chock-full of surprises. Almost every night it has a featured attraction, like drink and food specials, dance and bathing-suit contests, barbecues, laser shows, and live bands. Open Sunday through Thursday from 10am to 3am, and on Friday and Saturday from 10am to 5am.

Admission: Free before 10pm, $3–$6 after 10pm.

MORE ENTERTAINMENT

SUPPER CLUBS

Since their heyday in the 1950s, Miami's many dinner shows fell upon difficult times. Today, however, they are experiencing a renaissance. Meals are served at all the establishments listed below, but you don't have to eat. After paying the cover charge, you can decide to just have drinks or coffee and dessert. Reservations are always recommended.

CLUB TROPIGALA, in the Fontainebleau Hilton Hotel, 4441 Collins Ave., Miami Beach. Tel. 538-2000.

Extravagant costumes on shapely showgirls are the hallmark of this glitzy hotel's tropical-theme nightclub. Musical reviews change, but all include huge casts, overdone production numbers, and two orchestras, on opposite sides of the room, alternating between Latin and Top-40 music. Shows are given on Wednesday, Thursday, and Sunday at 9pm, and on Friday and Saturday at 8 and 10pm. Jackets are required for men.

Admission: $10.

LES VIOLINS SUPPER CLUB, 1751 Biscayne Blvd., downtown. Tel. 371-8668.

What Club Tropigala is to the North American "snowbirds," Les Violins is to the Latin community. Garish, lavish, and utterly formal, the entertainment here features glittery costumes, spectacular floor shows, and strolling violinists. Somehow, however, it seems as though Les Violins is not fake or contrived. Rather, the club's intricately staged entertainment is performed with an entirely straight face. The dances amuse, and the sets are truly stunning. Except for Cuban desserts and Spanish wines, the cuisine is strictly continental. Highly recommended.

Shows are on Tuesday, Wednesday, and Sunday at 7 and 10:30pm; and Thursday through Saturday at 7pm, 10:30pm, and 12:30am. Jackets are required for men.

Admission: $10.

SEVEN SEAS DINNER SHOW, at the Holiday Inn Newport Pier Resort, 16701 Collins Ave., Sunny Isles. Tel. 940-7440.

It's not exactly the South Seas, but it's Miami's only Polynesian dinner theater, complete with live music, hula girls, and fire dancers. This all-inclusive tropical luau features an all-you-can-eat three-course meal with a heavy Chinese influence, tax, tip, and a souvenir island necklace. Shows are Wednesday through Sunday at 8:30pm.

Admission: $26–$28 for dinner and show.

MOVIES

Except for the annual Miami Film Festival (see "Florida Calendar of Events," in Chapter 2), foreign and independent screenings in the city are almost nonexistent. Most of Miami's libraries show classic films one day during the week (usually Wednesday), and are listed in the weekly *New Times,* and the *Miami Herald*'s Friday magazine section. Hollywood-oriented cinemas are commonplace, and are located in all the malls. Some of the larger and better-located multiplexes include:

Bay Harbor 4 (tel. 866-2441), at 96th Street west of Collins Avenue in Miami Beach.

Cinema 10 (tel. 442-2299), in the Miracle Center, 3301 Coral Way, just east of Coral Gables.

Movies at The Falls (tel. 255-5200), U.S. 1 and SW 136th Street, in The Falls shopping center in Greater Miami South.

Omni 10 (tel. 358-2304), 1601 Biscayne Blvd., inside the Omni International Mall at 16th Street (downtown).

8. NETWORKS & RESOURCES

FOR STUDENTS Located in south Coral Gables, the large main campus of the **University of Miami** encompasses dozens of classrooms, a huge athletic field, a large lake, a museum, a hospital, and more. For general information, call the university (tel. 372-0120).

The school's main student building is the **Whitten University Center,** 1306 Stanford Dr. (tel. 284-2318). Social events are often scheduled here, and important information on area activities is always posted. The building houses a recreation area, a swimming pool, a snack shop, and a Ticketmaster outlet.

The **Ring Theatre,** on the University of Miami Campus, 1380 Miller Dr. (tel. 284-3355), is the main stage for the Department of Theater Arts' advanced student productions. Faculty and guest actors are regularly featured, as are contemporary works by local playwrights. See "The Performing Arts" in "Evening Entertainment," above, for more information.

The **Gusman Concert Hall,** 1314 Miller Dr. (tel. 284-2438, or 284-6477 for a recording), features performances by faculty and students of the university's School of Music, as well as concerts by special guests. The auditorium is also home to the Miami Chamber Symphony. See "Major Performance Halls" in "Evening Entertainment," above, for more information, and call for schedules and tickets.

For tickets to Miami Hurricanes basketball, football, and baseball home games, call the **U of M Athletic Department** (tel. 284-3822, or toll free 800/GO-CANES in Florida). See "Sports and Recreation," above, for more information.

The university's **Beaumont Cinema** (tel. 284-2211) features new and classic films. Call for ticket prices and screening schedules.

FOR GAY MEN & LESBIANS Miami has a significant gay community, supported by a wide range of services.

The **Gay and Lesbian Community Hotline** (tel. 759-3661), an interactive recording that can be reached with a pushbutton phone, lists 14 categories of information of interest to the gay community. These include political issues, gay bars, special events, support groups, businesses serving the gay community, doctors and lawyers, help wanted, and others.

The **Gay Community Bookstore,** 7545 Biscayne Blvd. (tel. 754-6900), features quality literature, newspapers, videos, music, cards, and more. It's open Monday through Saturday from 11am to 9pm and on Sunday from noon to 6pm.

The *Weekly News* is the best local gay publication. It's available free at bookstores and gay bars throughout South Florida. Other local literature to look for include the magazines *David* and *Hot Shots.*

9. EASY EXCURSIONS FROM MIAMI

Miami's scenic surroundings make a short excursion a great idea. Whether you'd like to tour Everglades National Park, hop aboard a Caribbean cruise, or just relax on a beach in Key West (see Chapter 6), all are easily accessible to you. For information about the Greater Miami area, contact the **Greater Miami Convention and Visitors Bureau,** 701 Brickell Ave., Miami, FL 33131 (tel. 305/539-3063, or toll free 800/283-2707). The offices are open Monday through Friday from 9am to 5:30pm.

EVERGLADES NATIONAL PARK

Encompassing more than 2,000 square miles and 1.5 million acres, Everglades National Park covers the entire southern tip of Florida, and is one of America's most unusual regions. Unlike Yosemite or Grand Canyon National Parks, the Everglades' awesome beauty is more subtle. In fact, it is not its geological grandeur that, in 1947, led lawmakers to preserve this remarkable place. Rather, the Everglades is a wildlife sanctuary, set aside for the protection of its delicate plant and animal life. Don't misunderstand, this park is gorgeous—but its beauty may not be immediately obvious. At first glance, the Glades appear only to be a river of saw grass dotted with islands of trees. But stand still and look around: You'll notice deer, otters, and great white egrets. Follow a rustle and a tiny tree frog appears. Hawks and herons flutter about, while baby—and bigger—alligators laze in the sun. You're in one of the world's most unusual jungles; the longer you stay, the more you perceive. But beware of mosquitos! Wear protective clothing and don't forget your repellent.

INFORMATION

Part of the park was damaged by Hurricane Andrew in August 1992 and will remain closed indefinitely. For general information, as well as specific details, direct your inquiries to the Park Superintendent, Everglades National Park, P.O. Box 279, Homestead, FL 22020.

The **South Dade Visitors Information Center,** 160 U.S. 1, Florida City, FL 33034 (tel. 305/245-9180 or toll free 800/388-9669), is located at the turnoff from U.S. 1 to the main entrance to the park. You can pick up information about the surrounding area plus a good map. Open daily from 8am to 6pm.

GETTING THERE

From Miami, there are two ways to approach the park: either from the east, through the Main Visitor Center, or from the north, via the Tamiami Trail (U.S. 41).

The Main Visitor Center (tel. 305/242-7700) is located on the east side of the park, about 45 miles south of downtown Miami. From downtown Miami, take U.S. 1

south about 35 miles. Turn right (west) onto Fla. 9336 (follow the sign) and continue straight for about 10 miles to the park entrance. This is the park's official headquarters. There's a small building which houses audiovisual exhibits on the park's fragile ecosystems. It's open daily 8am to 5pm, and admission is $5 per car to enter the park, $3 per person by bus.

The Tamiami Trail (U.S. 41), runs east-west from downtown Miami to the Gulf of Mexico, and follows the northern edge of the Everglades into Big Cypress National Preserve. Along the way you'll pass a number of concerns offering airboat and other rides through the saw grass of the Everglades.

WHAT TO SEE & DO

If you just have one day to tour the park, take the single road that winds its way for about 38 miles from the **Main Visitor Center** at the park's entrance (see above) to the **Flamingo Visitor Center** in the southwest corner of the state. This scenic drive provides a beautiful introduction to the park. Along the way you'll pass through a half dozen distinct ecosystems, including a dwarf cypress forest, endless saw grass, and dense mangroves. Well-marked winding trails and elevated boardwalks are plentiful along the entire stretch; all contain informative signs.

At the **Royal Palm Visitor Center,** just beyond the main entrance, you'll come to two of the park's most famous paths: the Anhinga boardwalk, and the Gumbo Limbo Trail. You will see snakes, fish, alligators, and a cross section of the park's unusual offerings. The center itself is open daily from 8am to 4:30pm.

A visit to the Everglades through the park's northern entrance offers an extremely scenic, but slightly more superficial tour of the wetlands. However, approaching from this angle is recommended if you want to take advantage of the two excellent tours listed below. It's also shorter than the all-day trip to Flamingo (see above). To reach the park's northern edge, follow the scenic Tamiami Trail (U.S. 41) for about 35 miles to Shark Valley, or the Miccosukee Indian Reservation, just beyond. Along the way you'll see several signs advertising airboat rides and other tourist-oriented attractions.

In addition to a small visitor center and bookstore, **Shark Valley** (tel. 305/221-8455) offers an elevated boardwalk, hiking trails, bike rentals, and an excellent tram tour that delves 7½ miles into the wilderness to a 50-foot observation tower. Built on the site of an old oil well, the tower gives visitors sweeping views of the park, including endless acres of saw grass. Tours run regularly, year-round, from 9am to 4pm. Reservations are recommended from December to March. The cost is $7 for adults, $3.50 for children, and $6.25 for seniors.

At the **Miccosukee Indian Village** (tel. 305/223-8380), you can take a half-hour, high-speed airboat tour through the rushes. Birds scatter as the boats approach, and when you slow down, alligators and other animals appear. This thrilling "safari" through the Everglades is one you will not soon forget—highly recommended. Rides are offered daily from 9am to 5pm, and cost just $6.50.

FLAMINGO The Everglades' main road, which begins at the Main Visitor Center, terminates in the tiny "town" of Flamingo. This is the jumping-off point for a number of sightseeing excursions including the **White Water Bay Cruise** and the **Florida Bay Cruise.** Operated from the Flamingo Lodge Marina (tel. 305/253-2241), these boat tours cruise nearby estuaries and sandbars for an in-depth look at native plant and animal life. The White Water tour lasts about two hours and costs $10.50 for adults and $5 for children 6–12; free for children under 6. The Florida Bay Cruise, which goes out into open water, lasts an hour and a half, and costs $7.75 for adults and $3.75 for children 6–12. Tours run regularly year-round and, although reservations are not required, they are suggested from December to March. Phone for tour times.

The **Wilderness Tram Tour** also departs from the Flamingo Lodge, and winds its way through mangrove forests and tropical rushes. The two-hour tour operates from November to April only, and is sometimes stalled by flooding or particularly heavy mosquito infestation. The cost is $7 for adults, $3.50 for children 6–12. Phone for tour times.

WHERE TO STAY

Since the Everglades is so close to Miami, most visitors return to their city hotel rooms at night. If you want to stay in the park, however, Flamingo is not only the best, it's the *only* place. **Camping** is a good option here, though in the summer a ton of mosquito repellent is required gear. There are 235 sites made for cars and tents, and RVs. There is no electricity and showers are cold. Permits cost $4–$8 per site from November to April and it's free the rest of the year. Checkout time is 10am.

FLAMINGO LODGE MARINA & OUTPOST RESORT, P.O. Box 428, Flamingo, FL 33030. Tel. 305/253-2241. Fax 305/695-3921. 102 rms, 24 cottages. AE, CB, DC, DISC, MC, V.

$ Rates: Nov–Apr, $69–$95 single or double; from $62 cottage. May–Oct, $50–$70 single or double; from $62 cottages.

An attractive, well-appointed, and spacious motel, the Flamingo is located right in the center of the action. It's also the only lodging inside the Everglades park. Rooms are relatively simple and clean and overlook the Florida Bay. Lodge facilities include a restaurant and bar, freshwater swimming pool, gift shop, and coin-op laundry.

WHERE TO DINE

FLAMINGO RESTAURANT, in the Flamingo Visitor Center. Tel. 253-2241.

Cuisine: AMERICAN. **Reservations:** Not required.

$ Prices: Main courses $10–$15. AE, MC, V.

Open: Nov–Apr, breakfast daily 7–10:30am; lunch daily 11:30am–2:30pm; dinner daily 5:30–9pm. May–Oct, buffet dining 11:30am–9pm.

This is one of the best restaurants in South Florida, and the only one in the Everglades park area. The view from this multilevel eatery overlooking the Florida Bay is spectacular. The menu features several meat and poultry dishes, but is noted for its well-prepared fresh fish selections.

CRUISING THE CARIBBEAN

Most people think that taking a cruise means spending thousands of dollars, and booking a ship far in advance. It's true that some unusually big trips require serious advance planning, but most of the Caribbean-bound ships, sailing weekly out of the Port of Miami, are relatively inexpensive, can be booked without advance notice, and make for an excellent excursion. Usually all-inclusive, cruises offer exceptional value and unparalleled simplicity compared to other vacation options.

All the shorter cruises are well equipped for gambling, and casinos open as soon as the ship clears U.S. waters, typically 45 minutes after the ship leaves port. Usually, four full-size meals are served daily, with portions so huge they're impossible to finish. Games, movies, and other on-board activities ensure that you are always busy. Passengers can board up to two hours prior to departure for meals, games, and cocktails.

There are dozens of cruises to choose from. A full list of options can be obtained from the **Metro-Dade Seaport Department,** 1015 North America Way, Miami, FL 33132 (tel. 305/371-7678).

Most of the ships listed below offer two- and three-day excursions to The Bahamas. Cruise ships usually depart Miami on Friday night and return Monday morning. If you want more information, contact **The Bahamas Tourist Office,** 255 Alhambra Circle, Suite 425, Coral Gables, FL 33134 (tel. 305/442-4860). All passengers must travel with a passport or proof of citizenship for reentry into the United States.

CARNIVAL CRUISE LINES, 3655 NW 87th Ave., Miami, FL 33178. Tel. 305/599-2200, or toll free 800/327-9501.

One of the largest cruise ships in the world, Carnival's *Fantasy* made its debut in 1990. Several swimming pools, games rooms, and lounges surround a spectacular multistory foyer. The 70,000-ton ship can accommodate up to 2,600 passengers. The

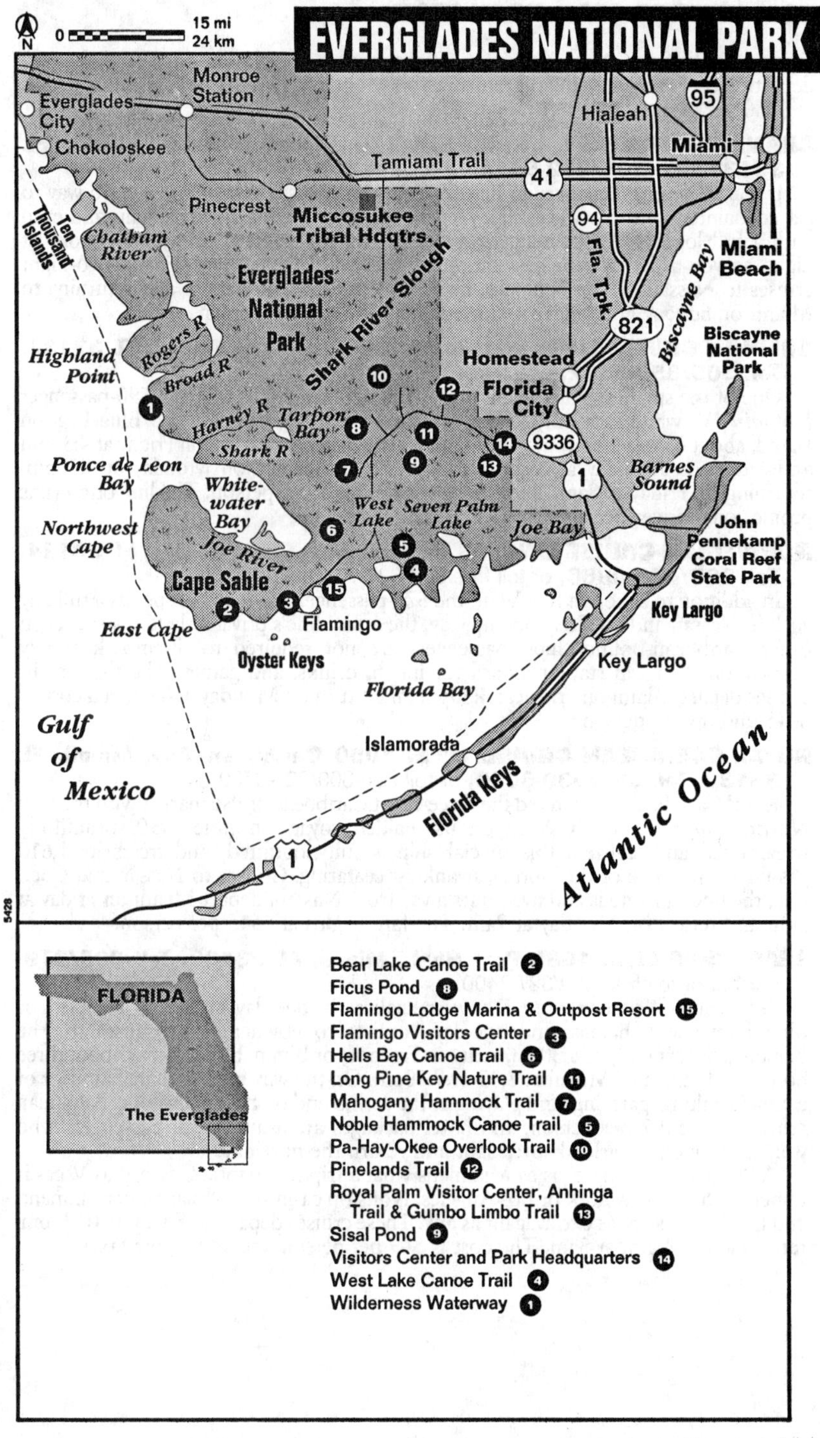
EVERGLADES NATIONAL PARK
N
0
15 mi
24 km
Everglades City
Monroe Station
Chokoloskee
Hialeah
95
Miami
Tamiami Trail
41
Pinecrest
Miccosukee Tribal Hdqtrs.
94
Ten Thousand Islands
Chatham River
Everglades National Park
Shark River Slough
Fla. Tpk.
Biscayne Bay
Miami Beach
821
Rogers R
Broad R
Highland Point
Homestead
Florida City
Biscayne National Park
Harney R
Tarpon Bay
Shark R
9336
Ponce de Leon Bay
White-water Bay
1
Barnes Sound
Northwest Cape
Joe River
West Lake
Seven Palm Lake
Joe Bay
John Pennekamp Coral Reef State Park
Cape Sable
Flamingo
Key Largo
East Cape
Oyster Keys
Key Largo
Florida Bay
Gulf of Mexico
Islamorada
Florida Keys
Atlantic Ocean
1
FLORIDA
The Everglades
Bear Lake Canoe Trail 2
Ficus Pond 8
Flamingo Lodge Marina & Outpost Resort 15
Flamingo Visitors Center 3
Hells Bay Canoe Trail 6
Long Pine Key Nature Trail 11
Mahogany Hammock Trail 7
Noble Hammock Canoe Trail 5
Pa-Hay-Okee Overlook Trail 10
Pinelands Trail 12
Royal Palm Visitor Center, Anhinga Trail & Gumbo Limbo Trail 13
Sisal Pond 9
Visitors Center and Park Headquarters 14
West Lake Canoe Trail 4
Wilderness Waterway 1

Fantasy sails from Miami on three-night cruises to Nassau in The Bahamas, departing on Friday at 4pm and returning on Monday at 7am. The cruise cost begins at $360 per person.

CHANDRIS FANTASY CRUISES, 4770 Biscayne Blvd., Miami, FL 33137. Tel. 305/262-5411, or toll free 800/437-3111.

If you've never taken a cruise before, Chandris Cruises' *Britanis* is a good way to get acquainted with the waves. It's very inexpensive, the food is excellent, and even with a full load of 922 passengers, it doesn't seem crowded. All sailing is done at night, so you arrive at your destination well rested. The *Britanis* sails on two-night cruises to Nassau in The Bahamas, departing on Friday at 4:30pm and returning to Miami on Sunday at 8am. This cruise begins at $220 per person.

DOLPHIN CRUISE LINE, 901 South American Way, Miami, FL 33132. Tel. 305/358-5122, or toll free 800/222-1003.

One of the smallest ships sailing from Miami is Dolphin's intimate 590-passenger *Dolphin IV,* which not only sails to Nassau but also to uncrowded Blue Lagoon Island, about 45 minutes away. Three-night cruises depart Miami on Friday at 4:30pm and return on Monday at 8am; four-night cruises depart on Monday at 4:30pm, returning on Friday at 8am. The charge is from $289 per person. The line often runs promotional price specials. Contact the line for details.

NORWEGIAN CRUISE LINE, 95 Merrick Way, Coral Gables, FL 33134. Tel. 305/445-0866, or toll free 800/327-7030.

In addition to a stop in Key West, the 676-passenger *Sunward II* spends a full day each in Nassau and on Great Stirrup Cay, the cruise line's private island resort. As on other Caribbean-bound ships, passengers are not required to disembark at any destination. You can stay on board for lunch, drinks, and games. The three-night cruises depart Miami on Friday at 4:30pm and return on Monday at 8am, at a cost of $415 and up per person.

ROYAL CARIBBEAN CRUISE LINE, 1050 Caribbean Way, Miami, FL 33132. Tel. 305/539-6000, or toll free 800/327-6700.

Royal Caribbean has entered the three-night Caribbean cruise market with the new *Nordic Empress,* which sailed on its maiden voyage in June 1990. Beautifully streamlined and stylized, this special ship is fully outfitted, and treats its 1,610 passengers to some of the world's swankiest seafaring. Cruises to Nassau and Coco Cay, the line's private island five hours away from Nassau, depart Miami on Friday at 5pm and return on Monday at 9am. The fare begins at $515 per person.

SEAESCAPE LTD., 1080 Port Blvd., Miami, FL 33132. Tel. 305/379-0000, or toll free 800/327-7400.

SeaEscape's *Scandinavian Dawn* specializes in one-day cruises to Freeport or Bimini in The Bahamas, and one-day "cruises to nowhere." Its cruises to The Bahamas depart daily at 8:30am, arrive in Freeport or Bimini by 2pm, stay about three hours, and return to Miami at 8:30 or 9:30pm. On the way is a bacchanalian orgy of eating, drinking, partying, and playing at the casino and on the dance floor. Bahamian cruises cost $107 per person, and hotel packages are available for passengers who want to stay on the islands overnight and return the next day.

A "cruise to nowhere" is to Miamians what a trip to Atlantic City or Las Vegas is to people from New York or Los Angeles. Nonstop casinos, on-board entertainment, and lavish meals are as extravagant as any. These cruises depart on Friday at 10:30pm, returning to Miami at 3am. The cost is $49 per person, including port taxes.

CHAPTER 6

THE FLORIDA KEYS

- **WHAT'S SPECIAL ABOUT THE FLORIDA KEYS**
- **1. THE UPPER KEYS: KEY LARGO TO MARATHON**
- **2. THE LOWER KEYS: BIG PINE KEY TO COPPITT KEY**
- **3. KEY WEST**

Although the Keys appear not to have had any permanent inhabitants during early times, several native groups visited the area, including Calusas, Seminoles, and the warlike Caribs. Juan Ponce de León, the Spanish explorer who is credited with "discovering" Florida, found the Keys in 1513—he called them Los Martieres (The Martyrs) because they looked like men in distress. The Keys remained largely undeveloped until Florida was "transferred" from Spain to the United States in 1819. The entire island of Key West was purchased by an American promoter, John W. Simonton, and developed into a mercantile and "wrecking" center, luring fishermen and shipwreck salvagers; by 1825, 28 salvage vessels were operating. By 1874, Key West had become the largest city in the state of Florida, attracting Bahamians, Cubans, and migrating North Americans. The establishment of iron-pile lighthouses from Key Largo to Key West, as well as better navigational methods, were a blow to Island wreckers/salvagers.

Before the new century was very old, Key West's fortunes began to wane, but with the extension of Henry Flagler's railroad to Key West in 1912 came an economic resurgence. Trade and tourism thrived until 1935, when a powerful hurricane in the Middle Keys destroyed the rail line.

The Overseas Highway (U.S. 1) was completed in 1938 on the old railroad bed. Soon after, President Franklin Roosevelt ordered the other Keys made more habitable. The Civilian Conservation Corps (CCC), a Depression-era WPA organization that was not conservation-minded at all was put in charge, and the Keys were opened to development with a "dredge and fill" philosophy that is anathema to today's ecological thinking. Inland waterways were created and sanctioned, allowing otherwise landlocked homeowners to dock their boats in their backyards. Chemical-based mosquito-abatement programs were instituted, coral reefs were slashed, trees were chopped, and towns began to sprout up along the hundred-mile highway.

Luckily, modern-day environmental activism and governmental protection has saved most of the Keys from this kind of devastating development. Surrounding what are known as the "Mainland" Keys, through which the Overseas Highway runs, are dozens of small islands known locally as the "Backcountry." Largely uninhabited, most of these islands are federally protected National Wildlife Refuges. Other areas are under the protection of a private organization, the Nature Conservancy. A rich variety of indigenous plants and animals live here, including many endangered species. Eagles, egrets, and Key deer are some of the most visible, as are gumbo limbo trees (with peeling red bark), mangroves, royal poincianas, banyans, and aloe.

The Florida Keys are surrounded by the world's third-largest barrier reef, precious living corals that support a complex and delicate ecosystem. About three miles wide, the reef contains a unique variety of stony and soft corals that can take years to grow just one inch. They are home to a variety of interdependent species including sponges, anemones, jellyfish, crabs, rays, sharks, turtles, snails, lobsters, and of course, thousands of varieties of fish.

WHAT'S SPECIAL ABOUT THE FLORIDA KEYS

Celebrations

- ☐ Sunsets are celebrated each evening in Key West's Mallory Square, where tourists and locals join with jugglers, artists, acrobats, vendors, and mimes to herald in the evening.
- ☐ Big-game fishing in Islamorada is ritualized with tournaments, held several times a year.
- ☐ Old Island Days, a full schedule of special events that lasts all summer long, makes Key West even more special.

Natural Habitats

- ☐ Key deer, three-foot tall miniatures, are unique to Big Pine Key, where they enjoy protected status from the U.S. government.
- ☐ The coral reef that surrounds the Keys, the third-largest barrier reef in the world, supports a dazzling array of life, including sharks, rays, lobsters, and seemingly endless varieties of fish.
- ☐ Indian Key and Lignumvitae Key, two small islands a mile from the Islamorada developments, allow tourists a glimpse of the "real" Keys, before "modernization." Now state botanical sites, the Keys sustain a complex and diverse ecosystem that is as fragile as it is unusual.

Unfortunately, the Key's reefs and the wildlife that inhabits them are in danger of destruction both from pollution washing down through the Everglades and from the garbage, anchors, and lines of unaware tourists and boaters. When you visit the Keys, do your part to save them; be environmentally conscious of this vulnerable habitat. Don't disturb nesting birds or feed any animals. Fishermen should catch and release, and divers and snorkelers should be aware that simply touching coral can damage and even kill it. I am convinced that the Keys are one of America's greatest treasures, and feel certain that if you take your time exploring these extraordinary gems, you, too, will become their advocate.

SEEING THE FLORIDA KEYS

Sure, you can fly to Key West from Miami (costing anywhere from $99 to $298 round-trip), but one of the best things about the Florida Keys is the car journey there. Unless you're really pressed for time, driving is the way to go. U.S. 1 (the Overseas Highway) skips over 42 bridges and across 31 islands through some of the most beautiful terrain in the world. Separating the Gulf of Mexico from the Atlantic Ocean, much of the stretch is wide, with water vistas where on either side you can see as far as the horizon. At other times the road is clogged with shopping centers and billboards advertising restaurants, rest stops, and attractions. A good portion of U.S. 1 is a narrow, two-lane highway; some sections open up to four lanes. The legal speed limit is 55 m.p.h. (35 m.p.h. in commercial areas), and on a good day you can make the trip to Key West from Miami in four hours. But don't rush. The scenery is beautiful, and there are plenty of places to stop along the way.

You should know that gasoline prices rise rapidly the farther south you go, but then descend slightly when you arrive on Key West. If you can, fill up in Miami.

FINDING AN ADDRESS Along the way, you'll find that most addresses are given by Mile Marker (MM), small green signs on the right side of the road that announce the distance from Key West. The markers begin with number 126, just south of the Florida mainland. The zero marker is in Key West, at the corner of Whitehead and Fleming Streets. Listings in this chapter are organized first by price, then by location,

THE FLORIDA KEYS

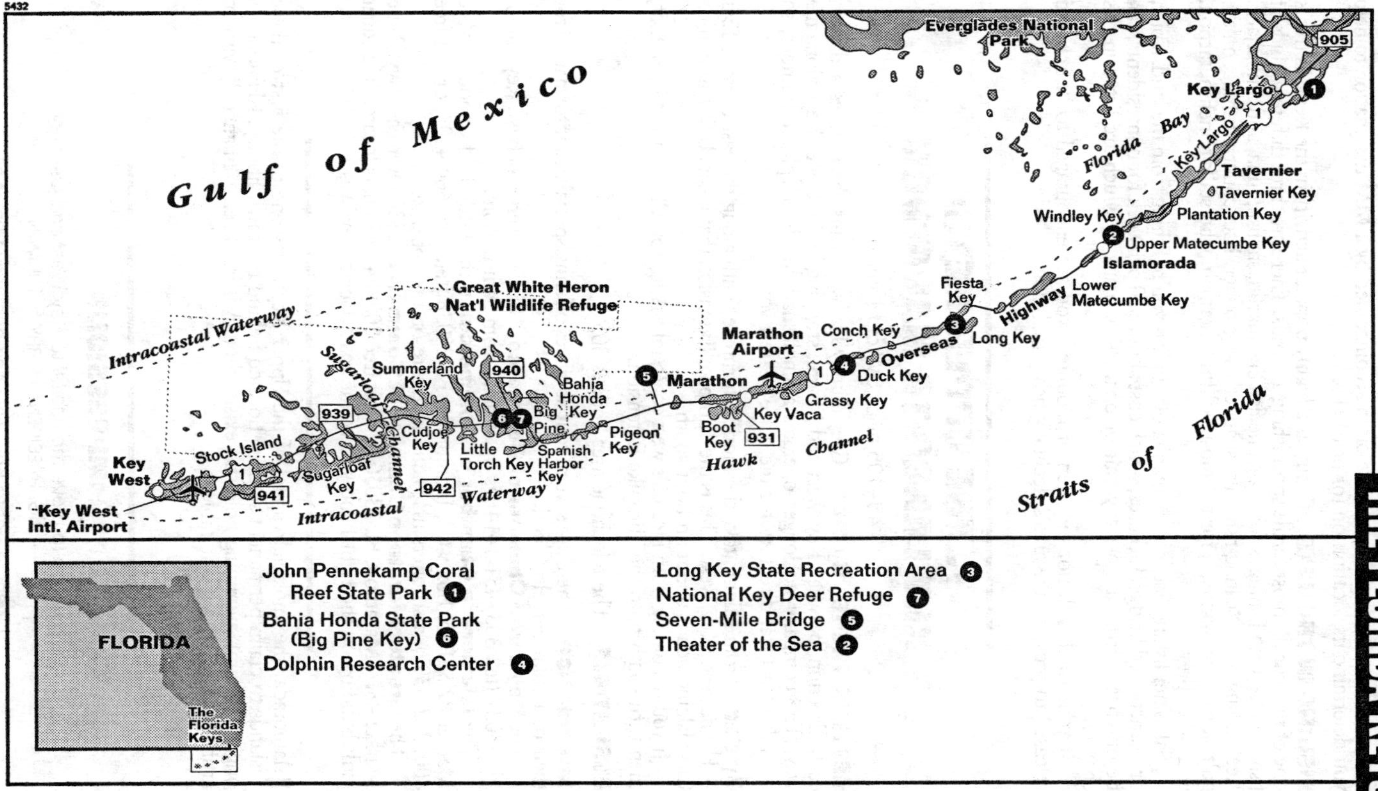

John Pennekamp Coral Reef State Park 1
Seven-Mile Bridge 2
Long Key State Recreation Area 3
Dolphin Research Center 4
National Key Deer Refuge 5
Bahia Honda State Park (Big Pine Key) 6
Theater of the Sea 7

Gulf of Mexico
Straits of Florida
Florida Bay
Hawk Channel
Sugarloaf Channel
Intracoastal Waterway
Everglades National Park
Great White Heron Nat'l Wildlife Refuge
Overseas Highway
Key Largo
Tavernier
Tavernier Key
Plantation Key
Windley Key
Upper Matecumbe Key
Islamorada
Lower Matecumbe Key
Fiesta Key
Long Key
Conch Key
Duck Key
Grassy Key
Marathon Airport
Marathon
Key Vaca
Boot Key
Pigeon Key
Bahia Honda Key
Big Pine Key
Spanish Harbor Key
Little Torch Key
Summerland Key
Cudjoe Key
Sugarloaf Key
Stock Island
Key West
Key West Intl. Airport
FLORIDA
The Florida Keys
905
1
931
940
942
939
941
9 mi
14 km
N
5432

from north to south. Addresses are often accompanied by a MM designation to help you determine its location on (or near) U.S. 1.

FISHING IN THE KEYS Fishing is a highly popular activity in the Keys, as this is one of the world's most fertile sportfishing grounds. There are three different kinds of fishing: Deep-sea fishing is for big-game fish like marlin, sailfish, tuna, and amberjack. Reef fishing is for "eating fish" like snapper and grouper. Backcountry fishing, on the gulf side of the islands, is for the most skillful fishermen, who stalk bonefish, tarpon, and other prey.

Saltwater fishing licenses are mandatory, unless you're fishing from the land, a pier, or a sanctioned bridge. Licenses, which cost about $20 per week for nonresidents, can be purchased from almost any bait or boat shop, many of which are listed in this chapter.

If your catch will not be eaten or mounted, you are encouraged to "catch and release" to preserve the area's declining fish population.

1. THE UPPER KEYS: KEY LARGO TO MARATHON

48–105 miles SW of Miami

GETTING THERE **By Bus** Greyhound/Trailways runs three buses a day, in each direction, between Key West and Miami, stopping in the Upper Keys along the way. The company no longer operates a single nationwide telephone number, so consult your local directory for the office nearest you.

By Car From Miami, take the Florida Turnpike south along the east coast to Exit 4, Homestead/Key West. This is the Turnpike Extension that meets U.S. 1 in Florida City. Islamorada is about an hour south.

If you're coming from Florida's west coast, take Alligator Alley to the Miami Exit, then turn south onto the Turnpike Extension.

ESSENTIALS The telephone area code is 305.

Information There are several tourist offices offering specialized information for their particular parcel of land.

The **Key Largo Chamber of Commerce,** 105950 Overseas Hwy., Key Largo, FL 33037 (tel. 305/451-1414), is open daily from 9am to 6pm.

The **Islamorada Chamber of Commerce,** in the Little Red Caboose, Mile Marker 82.5 (P.O. Box 915), Islamorada, FL 33036 (tel. 305/664-4503, or toll free 800/322-5397), also offers maps and literature on the upper keys.

The **Greater Marathon Chamber of Commerce,** 3330 Overseas Hwy., Mile Marker 48.7, Marathon, FL 33050 (tel. toll free 800/842-9580), is located in a squat pink building on the right-hand side of the road (facing Key West).

Islamorada, the unofficial capital of the Upper Keys, was one of the first of these islands to claim permanent settlers. Located behind the town library, Islamorada's original natural swimming hole still exists, though it has been "enhanced" with an artificial beach and picnic tables.

IMPRESSIONS

I've a notion to move the capital to Key West and just stay.
—U.S. President Harry S Truman

I want to get to Key West and get away from it all.
—Ernest Hemingway

Marathon, the Upper Keys' other main population center, began in 1908 as the construction headquarters for the overseas railroad. Located just north of the world-famous Seven-Mile Bridge, right in the middle of the key chain, Marathon is a curious mixture of modern tract-home community, tourist resort, and old fishing village.

In between Islamorada and Marathon are about 35 miles of highway, alternating between wetlands, strip malls, nesting grounds, resort hotels, blue waters, and billboards.

WHAT TO SEE & DO

SIGHTS & ATTRACTIONS

JOHN PENNEKAMP CORAL REEF STATE PARK, U.S. 1, Mile Marker 102.3, Key Largo. Tel. 451-1202.

The Keys' largest and most popular park is chock-full of activities, and definitely worth a stop on your way down the coast. In addition to camping (see "Where to Stay," below), visitors can participate in a plethora of daytime activities, such as swimming, sailing, and canoeing. The 188-square-mile park has dozens of winding nature trails where self-guided walkers can explore forests of mangroves and subtropical hardwoods. A boardwalk trail leads to an observation tower. Canoe trails wend their way through mangroves and natural tidal creeks, and a special snorkeling area is made even more distinctive by an authentic reconstruction of an early Spanish shipwreck.

The park's visitor center houses a 30,000-gallon saltwater marine aquarium surrounded by various educational exhibits. There are a few beach areas where visitors can sunbathe and swim, and a dive shop offering daily scuba and snorkeling reef excursions and boat rentals. They also rent scuba gear, sailboats, windsurfers, and canoes. Two-hour glass-bottom-boat tours take riders over coral reefs.

Admission: $3.25 per vehicle, $1 per pedestrian or bicyclist; glass-bottom-boat tours, $14 adults, $7.50 children under 12; sailing and snorkeling tours, $38 per person, including equipment; scuba dives, $32.50 per person, not including equipment; reef boat rental, $22–$30 per hour.

Open: Daily 8am–5pm; phone for tour and dive times.

THEATER OF THE SEA, Overseas Hwy., Mile Marker 84.5, Islamorada. Tel. 664-2431.

Established in 1946, the Theater of the Sea is one of the world's oldest marine zoos. Although facilities here seem a bit tired, and sea mammal acts have fallen from political correctness, the theater's dolphin and sea lion shows can be both entertaining and informative, especially for children. Sharks, sea turtles, and other local creatures are also on display. Under the pretense of "education," the park offers visitors the opportunity to swim with the dolphins in their supervised oceanwater lagoon. Reservations for this pricy "Dolphin Adventure" must be made in advance.

Admission: $11.25 adults, $5.75 children; Swim with the Dolphins, $65 per person.

Open: Daily 9:30am–4pm.

INDIAN KEY AND LIGNUMVITAE KEY, off Indian Key Fill, Overseas Hwy., Mile Marker 79. Tel. 664-4815.

Most of the Florida Keys that are not connected by the Overseas Highway are protected as wildlife preserves and closed to casual visitors. Indian Key and Lignumvitae Key are two worthy exceptions, which allow tourists a glimpse of the "real" keys, before modern development. These two small islands, preserved and managed by the Florida Department of Natural Resources, are located about one mile from the Islamorada highway. Named for the lignum vitae ("Wood of Life") trees found there, Lignumvitae Key supports a virgin tropical forest that's typical of the kind of vegetation that once thrived on most of the Upper Keys. Now a state botanical site located on the gulf side of Islamorada, the key sustains a complex and diverse ecosystem that's as fragile as it is unusual.

Indian Key, located on the Atlantic side of Islamorada, is a 10-acre historic site that was occupied by native Americans for thousands of years. It was also the original seat of Dade County before the Civil War. An 1840 rebellion by Native Americans almost wiped out the island's once-growing population, leaving the ruins to posterity.

Three-hour boat tours to these islands depart Indian Key Fill Thursday through Monday at 8:30am for Indian Key and at 1:30pm for Lignumvitae Key. In summer, tours operate Friday through Sunday only. The tour fee for each island is $7 for adults and $3 for children under 12. Reservations are suggested.

LONG KEY STATE RECREATION AREA, Overseas Hwy., Mile Marker 68, Long Key. Tel. 664-4815.

Located just north of Marathon Key, this is a great place to explore the natural habitats of the Upper Keys. Unique nature trails lead hikers through miles of wilderness where indigenous flora and fauna flourish. A specially marked canoe trail is particularly fun, guiding explorers through wild wetlands. Boat rentals are available in the park. In addition, the recreational area also offers a clean beach for year-round swimming and fishing, and several picnic areas.

DOLPHIN RESEARCH CENTER, Overseas Hwy., Mile Marker 59, Marathon Shores. Tel. 289-0002.

This nonprofit organization, dedicated to the increased understanding and appreciation of marine mammals, runs regularly scheduled tours to help visitors learn about and interact with dolphins and other sea creatures. In the basic tour, visitors can see families of dolphins, imprisoned in natural saltwater lagoons, respond to human commands and perform various tricks. The more in-depth DolphInsight program—a half-day presentation offered Wednesday, Saturday, and Sunday afternoons—includes a guided tour of the facility and open-air workshops on dolphin physiology and basic training techniques. Visitors are given the opportunity to touch and communicate with dolphins using a variety of hand signals. The center also operates a swim-with-the-dolphins program, called Dolphin Encounter, for which reservations are required up to a month in advance.

Admission: $7.50 adults, $5 children 4–12. DolphInsight Program, $65 per person; Dolphin Encounter, $80 per person.

Tour times: Daily 10am, 12:30pm, 2pm, and 3:30pm.

MUSEUM OF NATURAL HISTORY, Overseas Hwy., Mile Marker 50.5, Marathon. Tel. 743-9100.

Located at Crane Point Hammock, a woody park directly across from the K-Mart shopping center, this small museum displays dozens of local historical artifacts, including shell tools and pottery from pre-Columbian native tribes and booty from one of America's oldest shipwrecks. Other exhibits focus on the Keys' natural habitats, including a coral-reef tank, where visitors can see sharks, lobster, and tropical fish, and a touch tank, where you can handle rays, starfish, and other safe sea creatures. A special children's section of the museum has several informative interactive displays, including tropical aquariums, a miniature railway station, and a small saltwater lagoon. Outside, visitors are encouraged to wander through the museum's quarter-mile nature trail which winds through rare tropical palm hammock.

Admission: $5 adults, $2.50 seniors 65 and older, $1 students, free for children 12 and under.

Open: Mon–Sat 9am–5pm, Sun noon–5pm.

SEVEN-MILE BRIDGE, Overseas Hwy., Mile Markers 40–47.

The Keys' most celebrated span rests on 546 concrete piers, and rises to a 72-foot crest, the highest point in the Keys. The first bridge was constructed here in 1910, built to carry Henry Flagler's railroad track that ran all the way to Key West. Most of the bridge blew away in a hurricane on September 2, 1935; you can still see portions of the original trackbed running for miles adjacent to the modern span, which was constructed 10 years later.

Heading south on the Overseas Highway, slow down just before the bridge and turn right off the road, onto the unpaved parking lot at the foot of the bridge. From here you can walk along the old bridge that goes for almost four miles before abruptly dropping off into the sea. The first half mile of this "ghost bridge" is popular with area fishermen who use shrimp as bait to catch barracuda, yellowtail, and a host of other fish. Near the end of the bridge is the University of Miami's Institute of Marine Science, a research facility that's not open to the public.

ORGANIZED TOURS

BY BOAT Traveling aboard the 39-foot sailing yacht *Amantha,* built in 1946, is one of the best ways to see Florida Bay. The daily four-hour tour circumnavigates several uninhabited keys, passes under the old Seven-Mile Bridge, and skirts the historic buildings of Pigeon Key. Captains Ken Carter and Joan Pellegrino not only point out the sites, they also show you the rigging of their ship, offer sailing tips, and let first-timers try their hand at the sails. Contact **Sail *Amantha,*** Overseas Highway, Mile Marker 48, Marathon (tel. 743-9020), for departure times. Tour Prices are $30 for adults, $15 for children under 16.

BY PLANE The **Flight Department,** 9850 Overseas Hwy., Marathon Airport, (tel. 305/743-4222, or toll free 800/359-3711), has half-hour tours over the reef that give you a bird's-eye view of the islands and the coral that surrounds them. Passengers can choose their itinerary from several different flight plans. Tours cost $75 per flight for up to three passengers.

FISHING CHARTERS Located at the south end of the Holiday Isle Docks (see "Where to Stay," below), **Robbie's,** Overseas Highway, Mile Marker 84.5, on Islamorada (tel. 664-8070 or 664-4196), offers day and night deep-sea and reef-fishing trips on 60- and 70-foot party boats. Big-game-fishing charters are also available, and "splits" are arranged for solo fishermen. Party-boat fishing costs $25 for a half day, $40 for a full day, and $30 at night. Charters run $375 for a half day, $550 for full day; splits begin at $65 per person.

One of the largest marinas between Miami and Key West, **Bud n' Mary's Fishing Marina,** Overseas Highway, Mile Marker 79.8, on Islamorada (tel. 305/664-2461, or toll free 800/742-7945), is packed with sailors offering guided Backcountry fishing charters. Stalking tarpon, bonefish, trout, redfish, snook, and snapper is not for impatient novices. Deep-sea and coral-fishing trips are also arranged. The marina also offers snorkel and scuba trips to nearby Alligator Reef, as well as glass-bottom-boat tours.

Charters cost $350–$400 for a half day, $550–$600 for a full day, and splits begin at $100 per person. Snorkel and scuba trips run $20–$35; the glass-bottom-boat tour, $15.

The ***Bounty Hunter,*** 9500 Overseas Hwy., Mile Marker 48, Marathon (tel. 743-2446), offers full-day reef and Everglades trips to Florida's most deserted beaches. For years Capt. Brock Hook's huge sign has boasted NO FISH, NO PAY. You're guaranteed to catch *something.* Shark, barracuda, sailfish, and other trips are arranged.

WHERE TO STAY

VERY EXPENSIVE

JULES' UNDERSEA LODGE, Overseas Hwy., Mile Marker 103.2 (P.O. Box 3330), Key Largo, FL 33037. Tel. 305/451-2353. 1 rm. A/C TV TEL

$ Rates (including dinner): $195–$295 per person double. DISC, MC, V.

Originally built as a research lab in the 1970s, this small underwater compartment opened as a single-room hotel in November of 1986. As expensive as it is unusual, the lodge is popular with diving honeymooners and other active and romantic couples. You don't need to be a scuba specialist to stay here; guests use tethered breathing lines in lieu of air tanks. The underwater suite consists of a bedroom and galley, and sleeps up to six. Facilities include a stereo and VCR, and dinner (which is included) is delivered to your door in a waterproof container. Needless to say, this novelty is not for everyone. Phone for further information and a brochure.

CHEECA LODGE, Overseas Hwy., Mile Marker 82 (P.O. Box 527),

Islamorada, FL 33036. Tel. 305/664-4651, or toll free 800/327-2888. Fax 305/664-2893. 203 rms, 22 suites. A/C MINIBAR TV TEL

$ Rates: Dec 21–May 2, $200–$475 single or double; from $275 suite. May 3–Dec 20, $125–$325 single or double; from $200 suite. AE, CB, DC, DISC, MC, V.

Cheeca's blue-and-white plantation-style buildings surround Islamorada's most lushly landscaped gardens, tennis courts, pools, and golf courses. Located on 27 beachfront acres, this well-maintained resort offers guests a full range of activities and a high standard of accommodation.

While the guest rooms are not particularly plush, they are roomy, with large, comfortable beds, contemporary baths, VCRs, and balconies, many of which overlook the water. The resort works hard to educate their guests about environmental issues, and takes pains to protect their particularly lovely parcel. A unique kids' program, led by specially trained counsellors, combines nature lessons with fun activities that sometimes include parents as well.

Dining/Entertainment: The Atlantic's Edge restaurant is well known in these parts for excellently prepared seafood served in elegant surroundings. The more casual Ocean Terrace Grill has indoor and outdoor seating overlooking the pool and ocean. The Light Tackle Lounge is open daily and offers live entertainment on weekends.

Services: Room service, concierge, children's programs, free snorkeling lessons, water aerobics, massages.

Facilities: Six lighted tennis courts, nine-hole golf course, water-sports rentals, ocean beach, two swimming pools, saltwater lagoon, 525-foot fishing pier, sports shop, boutique, diving and fishing trips, four hot tubs, nature trail, champagne and sunset cruises, parasailing, bicycle rentals.

MODERATE

FARO BLANCO MARINE RESORT, Overseas Hwy., Mile Marker 48.5, Marathon, FL 33050. Tel. 305/743-9018, or toll free 800/759-3276. 170 rms, 20 condos. A/C TV TEL

$ Rates: Dec 20–Apr, $65–$119 single or double in the cottages, $95–$175 single or double on a houseboat, $175 single or double in the lighthouse; $225 condominium. May–Dec 19, $55–$99 single or double in the cottages, $75–$135 single or double on a houseboat, $135 single or double in the lighthouse; $198 condominium. Additional person $10 extra. AE, MC, V.

Spanning both sides of the Overseas Highway, and all on waterfront property, this huge, two-shore marina and hotel complex offers something for every taste. Camp-style cottages, each with a small bedroom and kitchen, are the least expensive accommodations; they're very basic, most with two single beds and slightly fading interiors. The rectangular houseboats, which float in a relatively quiet marina, look like buoyant mobile homes and are uniformly clean, fresh, and recommendable. The complex's large, first-class condominium apartments, located in a cluster of tall towers, each have three bedrooms, two baths, a living room, and a fully stocked kitchen. Finally, there are two unusual rental units located in a lighthouse on the pier; circular staircases, unusually shaped rooms and showers, and nautical decor make this quite an unusual place to stay, but some guests might find that it literally cramps their style.

There are several restaurants on the property, including Kelsey's, the resort's top eatery, which serves seafood, beef, veal, and poultry dishes. The Upper Deck Restaurant, which overlooks the bay, is a good choice for an afternoon snack or cocktail. Angler's serves burgers, sandwiches, and salads but is best known for its weekday-afternoon happy hours and nightly live entertainment.

INEXPENSIVE

HOLIDAY ISLE RESORT, Overseas Hwy., Mile Marker 84, Islamorada, FL 33036. Tel. 305/664-2711 or 305/664-3611, or toll free 800/327-7070. 180 rms, 19 suites.

$ Rates: Dec 18–Apr 17, $80–$150 single or double; from $120 suite. Apr 18–Sept 6, $65–$110 single or double; from $100 suite. Sept 7–Dec 17, $55–$110 single or double; from $80 suite. AE, DC, DISC, MC, V.

A huge resort complex encompassing five restaurants, lounges, and shops, and four distinct, if not distinctive hotels, the Holiday Isle is one of the biggest resorts in the Keys. The company's marketing strategy is decidedly downscale, attracting a spring break–style crowd year-round. Their Tiki Bar claims the invention of the Rum Runner drink (151-proof rum, blackberry brandy, banana liquor, grenadine, and lime juice), and there's no reason to doubt it. Hordes of partiers are attracted to the resort's almost nonstop merrymaking, live music, and beachfront bars. As a result, some of the accommodations here can be noisy—a plus to some.

El Captain and Harbor Lights, two of the least expensive hotels on the property, are both austere and basic. The Holiday Isle Hotel is located near the Tiki Bar at ground zero, while Howard Johnson's, which is a little farther from the action, is a shred more civilized. Small efficiency kitchens are available in most of the hotels.

BREEZY PALMS RESORT, Overseas Hwy., Mile Marker 80 (P.O. Box 767), Islamorada, FL 33036 Tel. 305/664-2361 or 664-2371. Fax 305/664-2572. 39 rms, 23 efficiencies.

$ Rates: Dec 16–Apr 20, $75–$85 single or double; from $105 apt. Apr 21–Dec 15, $65–$75 single or double; from $95 apt. Efficiencies available. Additional person $10 extra. AE, DISC, MC, V.

Family owned and operated, this simple, shingle-roofed, pastel motel gets mention for its ideal location, directly on the beach. It offers modest accommodations, a large swimming pool, a sheltered harbor with plenty of dock space, a boat ramp, volleyball and shuffleboard courts, and barbecue pits on the beach. Complimentary coffee is served each morning.

BUDGET

OCEAN VIEW, Overseas Hwy., Mile Marker 84, Islamorada, FL 33036. Tel. 305/664-2321. 6 rms. TV

$ Rates: Dec 18–Apr 17, $55–$60 single or double. Apr 18–Sept 6, $45–$50 single or double; Sept 7–Dec 17, $35–$40 single or double.

Located across from the Holiday Isle Resort, this place is as basic as can be, but it's also the least expensive you'll find. Units have small kitchenettes, and are located adjacent to a sports bar and package store.

CAMPING

JOHN PENNEKAMP CORAL REEF STATE PARK, Overseas Hwy., Mile Marker 102.3 (P.O. Box 487), Key Largo, FL 33037. Tel. 305/451-1202. 47 campsites.

$ Rates: $25 per site. MC, V.

One of Florida's most celebrated state parks (see "What to See and Do," above), Pennekamp offers 47 relatively secluded campsites, half available by advance reservation, the rest distributed on a first-come, first-served basis. Campers are not allowed to stay more than 14 days, and to hold reservations after 5pm the park must be notified of late arrival by phone on the check-in date. The park opens at 8am and closes at sundown, and pets are not allowed.

KOA FIESTA KEY RESORT, Overseas Hwy., Mile Marker 70, Long Key, FL 33001. Tel. 305/664-4922. 375 campsites.

$ Rates: $29–$32 per site, depending on location.

Although the campsites are too close to one another, the waterfront location is nice, as are the immaculately maintained grounds. Like most KOA campgrounds, this one is family oriented, offering many facilities and activities for children. In addition to ocean swimming, there is a recreation hall, shuffleboard courts, and a playground. There's also a restaurant and pub. The higher-priced camping spaces are wooded.

LONG KEY STATE RECREATION AREA, Overseas Hwy., Mile Marker 68 (P.O. Box 776), Long Key, FL 33001. Tel. 305/664-4815. 60 campsites.

$ Rates: $25 per site for one to four people. Additional person (over four) $1 extra.

One of the area's most popular camping grounds, we suggest reservations as far in advance as possible. Many sites are located oceanside, while others are farther from the tide.

WHERE TO DINE

VERY EXPENSIVE

ATLANTIC'S EDGE, in the Cheeca Lodge, Overseas Hwy., Mile Marker 82, Islamorada. Tel. 664-4651.

Cuisine: SEAFOOD. **Reservations:** Recommended.

$ Prices: Appetizers $4–$9; main courses $17–$32; fixed-price meals $25 and $29. AE, CB, DC, DISC, MC, V.

Open: Lunch daily 11am–3pm; dinner daily 5:30–10pm.

If you caught it, they'll cook it. If yours got away, the restaurant will prepare one of their fresh fish—blackened, grilled, braised, or steamed. One of the nicest restaurants in the Upper Keys, Atlantic's Edge offers elegant beachfront dining in a warm, window-wrapped dining room. Caribbean-influenced meals might start with a salad of avocado, grilled pineapple, black beans, and plantains, or a cup of roasted corn and stone crab soup. Onion-crusted Florida snapper (served with braised artichokes) and gulf shrimp on creamy polenta (with braised cabbage) are excellent examples of the kitchen's capabilities. There is also a well-stocked raw bar.

MODERATE

LAZY DAYS OCEANFRONT BAR AND SEAFOOD GRILL, Overseas Hwy., Mile Marker 80.5, Islamorada. Tel. 664-5256.

Cuisine: AMERICAN/SEAFOOD. **Reservations:** Not accepted.

$ Prices: Appetizers $4–$8; main courses $10–$13; lunch $5–$8. AE, DISC, MC, V.

Open: Tues–Sun noon–10pm.

It's hard to miss this Miami Vice–colored, glass-enclosed, rectangular restaurant on stilts. Located on your left (heading toward Key West), Lazy Days is set slightly back from the road behind willowy palms. Opened in 1992, the restaurant is refreshingly bright, boasting a single large dining room (with additional outdoor terrace seating), with blond-wood floors and the requisite mounted marlin.

Some of the more tempting appetizers include steamed clams with garlic and bell peppers; and nachos with seasoned beef, beans, cheese, and jalapeñas. Lunch selections include chowders, salads, and a large selection of sandwiches, including charcoal-grilled fish, spicy Caribbean jerk chicken, and sausages with green peppers and onions. Dinners rely heavily on fish, though Caribbean- and Italian-style foods are also served. Most entrees come with baked potatoes, vegetables, a tossed salad, and French bread.

MANNY & ISA'S KITCHEN, Overseas Hwy., Mile Marker 81.6, Islamorada. Tel. 664-5019.

Cuisine: SPANISH-AMERICAN. **Reservations:** Not accepted.

$ Prices: Appetizers $3–$4; main courses $9–$17; lunch $3–$8. AE, MC, V.

Open: Wed–Mon 11am–9pm.

I love this place. Opened a dozen or so years ago as a small shop selling key lime pies and conch chowder exclusively, this pint-size café-style restaurant has expanded its menu and become a very popular local hangout. There are fewer than 10 tables here, and a moderate-length menu packed with Florida-influenced Spanish-American specialties such as pork chops with black beans and rice, lobster enchiladas with lobster chunks in a Spanish sauce, and sandwiches. Of course they still serve conch chowder and key lime pie.

PAPA JOE'S, Overseas Hwy., Mile Marker 79.7, Islamorada. Tel. 664-8109.

Cuisine: AMERICAN. **Reservations:** Not required.

$ Prices: Appetizers $4–$8; main courses $10–$13; lunch $5–$8. AE, MC, V.

Open: Daily 11am–10:30pm.

From the road, this wooden landmark—under a big palm tree and yellow-and-white tiki-style sign—looks like the ultimate island eatery. It's well weathered and right on the water but, unfortunately, there are no outdoor tables. Inside, it's so dark that it feels like night even on the brightest days.

Whatever the fresh catch is, order it sautéed—on either a platter or a bun—and you won't be disappointed. The usual variety of burgers, salads, sandwiches, meat, and chicken are also available. The raw bar is particularly appealing, and a full range of drinks is served.

SID & ROXIE'S GREEN TURTLE INN, Overseas Hwy., Mile Marker 81.5, Islamorada. Tel. 664-9031.

Cuisine: SEAFOOD/AMERICAN. **Reservations:** Not required.

$ Prices: Appetizers $4–$6; main courses $10–$18; lunch $5–$11. AE, DC, DISC, MC, V.

Open: Tues–Sun noon–10:30pm.

An Islamorada landmark since 1947, the Green Turtle comes from an age when dark interiors were a mark of elegance. It's a family kind of place, where broiled surf-and-turf dinners come with soup, potatoes, and a salad. Soups, breads, and pies are all made on the premises, and served by career waitresses who have been here for years. In addition to prime beef and fresh-caught fish, the restaurant offers alligator steak, shrimp, and chicken dishes. Look for the giant turtle and you'll know you've found the place.

2. THE LOWER KEYS: BIG PINE KEY TO COPPITT KEY

110–140 miles SW of Miami

GETTING THERE By Bus Greyhound/Trailways runs three buses a day, in each direction, between Key West and Miami, stopping in the Lower Keys along the way. The company no longer operates a single nationwide telephone number, so consult your local directory for the office nearest you.

By Car From Miami, take the Florida Turnpike south along the east coast to Exit 4, Homestead/Key West. This is the Turnpike Extension that meets U.S. 1 in Florida City. Big Pine Key is about two hours south.

If you're coming from Florida's west coast, take Alligator Alley to the Miami exit, then turn south onto the Turnpike Extension.

ESSENTIALS The telephone area code is 305. The **Lower Keys Chamber of Commerce,** Overseas Hwy., Mile Marker 31, Big Pine Key, FL 33043 (tel. 305/872-2411, or toll free 800/872-3722), offers information on area sights, restaurants, and hotels.

Big Pine, Sugarloaf, Summerland, and the other Lower Keys are less developed and more inviting than their Upper Key neighbors. The Lower Keys have mercilessly been preserved for nature and, indeed, are one of the America's most important unaffected habitats—a last frontier that hopefully will always remain far from the reach of land developers and tourist-hungry profiteers. Unlike their neighbors to the north and south, the Lower Keys are devoid of rowdy spring break–style crowds, have few T-shirt and trinket shops, and fewer late-night bars. What they do have is a divine beauty that's truly awe-inspiring. Don't hurry to Key West. Stay overnight in the Lower Keys, rent a boat, and explore the reefs—you won't be disappointed.

WHAT TO SEE & DO

SIGHTS & ATTRACTIONS

LEDA-BRUCE GALLERYS, Overseas Hwy., Mile Marker 30.2, Big Pine Key. Tel. 872-0212.

A contemporary art gallery? Is this a sign that the Lower Keys are getting Hamptons hip? Well, not exactly. Owners Leda and Bruce Seigal are longtime residents of the Keys and famous in these parts for both their art and their eccentricities. In this concrete building, just past the island's only traffic light (when heading toward Key West), the couple displays some of the best works from the Keys' most important artists. In short, this is the finest gallery between Miami and Key West. It's a great place to browse, and the friendly owners are usually on hand to chat.

Admission: Free.

Open: Tues–Sat 10am–6pm.

NATIONAL KEY DEER REFUGE, Key Deer Blvd., near Mile Marker 30, Big Pine Key. Tel. 872-2411.

Speed-limit signs on Big Pine Key direct motorists to slow down to 35 m.p.h., a measure enacted to help preserve the key deer, a three-foot-tall miniature native to these woods, which are the only lands in the Keys that have fresh water. Except for their toy size and endangered status, these deer are much like their better-known mainland counterparts. They freeze when staring into headlights, and usually try to avoid the traffic on U.S. 1. You'll probably drive straight through Big Pine without spotting one of these cute creatures, unless you specifically look for them at the Deer Refuge, where there's a well-marked hiking trail.

When heading toward Key West, turn right at Big Pine Key's only traffic light onto Key Deer Boulevard (take the left fork immediately after the turn). The National Key Deer Refuge trailhead is about two miles ahead on your left.

BAHIA HONDA STATE PARK, Overseas Hwy., Mile Marker 29.5, Big Pine Key. Tel. 872-2353.

The best park in the Lower Keys, Bahia Honda rivals John Pennekamp Park (see "The Upper Keys," above) for facilities, character, and the sheer beauty of its wilderness. Spread out across 635 acres, the park offers large stretches of white sandy beach, deep waters close to shore that are perfect for snorkeling and diving, and miles of trails packed with unusual plants and animals. There are guided trail walks, fishing charters, daily snorkeling excursions, and shaded beachside picnic areas with tables and grills. Docking and camping facilities are available; see "Where to Stay," below, for complete information.

Admission: $3.25 per vehicle, $1 per pedestrian or bicyclist, free for children under 6; $2 boat-ramp fee.

SUGARLOAF BAT TOWER, next to Sugarloaf Airport by Mile Marker 17.

Standing silently alone—surrounded by nothing—the squat, wooden Sugarloaf Bat Tower was constructed in 1929 in an effort to attract bats that would in turn eat the ever-present mosquitoes that plague most of the keys. The bats never came, however, and the failed "Bat Motel" remains to beguile passersby who have no idea what it is.

To reach the tower, turn right at the Sugarloaf Airport sign and turn right again, onto the dirt road that begins just before the airport gate; the tower is about 100 yards ahead.

BOAT RENTALS

Several shops rent powerboats for fishing and reef exploring. Most also rent tackle, sell bait, and have charter captains available. Rental shops include **Bud Boats,** at the

Old Wooden Bridge Fishing Camp & Marina, Big Pine Key (tel. 743-6316); **Jaybird's Powerboats,** Overseas Highway, Mile Marker 33, Big Pine Key (tel. 872-4132, or 872-2351); and **T.J.'s Sugarshack,** at the Sugarloaf Lodge Marina, Overseas Highway, Mile Marker 17, Sugarloaf Key (tel. 745-3135).

ORGANIZED TOURS

Fantasy Dan's Airplane Rides, Overseas Highway, Mile Marker 17, Sugarloaf Key Airport (tel. 745-2217), offers 15-minute and half-hour rides over the reefs and keys. Tours usually include a buzzing of Key West, and the mangrove forests of uninhabited smaller islands. Flights require a minimum of two people and cost $25 per person for 15 minutes, $35 per person for a half hour.

WHERE TO STAY

VERY EXPENSIVE

LITTLE PALM ISLAND, Overseas Hwy., Mile Marker 28.5 (P.O. Box 1036), Little Torch Key, FL 33042. Tel. 305/872-2524, or toll free 800/343-8567. Fax 305/872-4843. 30 suites. A/C MINIBAR

$ Rates: Dec 21–Apr, $495–$795 double. July 8–Oct 19, $330–$695 double, the rest of the year, $395–$700 double. Special vacation packages available. AE, DC, MC, V.

Little Palm Island is the name of the resort that occupies the entire five acres of Little Munson Island, a former fishing camp that once accommodated Presidents Roosevelt, Truman, Kennedy, and Nixon, among other power elite. It's still an "in" spot; Vice-President Albert Gore stayed here during Thanksgiving 1991. The resort's top-of-the-line accommodations appeal to rich recluses—Hollywood glitterati need not apply. The island is only accessible by boat and privacy is the name of the game here, so much so that the resort's 30 secluded suites don't even have telephones (although that should hardly make a difference in this cellular world) or TVs.

The hotel's suites are well spaced about the property, hidden behind ample tropical plants and bushes including coconut palms, bougainvillea, oleander, and hibiscus, with private sun decks with hanging hammocks. Rooms are outfitted with ceiling fans, wicker and rattan furnishings, coffee makers, refrigerators, and outdoor showers. The Mexican-tile baths have whirlpool tubs and the contemporary amenities you'd expect from a top hotel.

Dining/Entertainment: The Little Palm Restaurant is a formal restaurant serving international cuisine. The Palapa Pool Bar offers refreshments and light snacks all day.

Services: Room service, laundry, massage, airport transportation.

Facilities: Swimming pool, complimentary water-sports rentals (including sailboats, windsurfers, canoes, kayaks, and snorkeling and fishing gear), sauna, boutique, fully equipped dive shop.

MODERATE

DEER RUN BED AND BREAKFAST, Long Beach Dr. (P.O. Box 431), Big Pine Key, FL 33043. Tel. 305/872-2015. 3 rms.

$ Rates (including breakfast): $85–$95 single or double.

Sue Abbott's small, smoke-free B&B is a real find, and a pleasure for those wanting an intimate look at the Lower Keys. Located directly on the beach, the neat three-room bed-and-breakfast is truly homey—the kind of a place where you'd stay if you had friends in the Keys. One upstairs and two downstairs bedrooms are comfortably furnished with queen-size beds, good closets, and touch-sensitive lamps. Breakfast, which is served in a pretty, enclosed deck, is cooked to order by Sue herself.

PARMER'S PLACE COTTAGES, Barry Ave., near Mile Marker 28.5, Little Torch Key (P.O. Box 445, Big Pine Key, FL 33043). Tel. 305/872-2157. 40 rms, 8 efficiencies.

$ Rates: Oct–Apr, $80–$85 single or double; $90 efficiency. May–Sept, $60–$65

single or double; $75 efficiency. Additional person $10 extra. AE, DISC, MC, V.
One of my favorite places in the Lower Keys, this downscale resort offers modest but comfortable cottages in a variety of configurations. Every unit is different: Some face the water while others are a few steps away. Some have small kitchenettes and others hold just a bedroom. Most cottages contain two separate units that can be combined into one for large families. Rooms are sparsely decorated and very clean, though guests who choose daily maid service will incur a small additional charge (otherwise there's only light housekeeping during your stay). Parmer's has been a fixture here for almost 20 years, and is well known for its charming hospitality and very informative staff.

SUGARLOAF LODGE, Overseas Hwy., Mile Marker 17 (P.O. Box 148), Sugar Loaf Key, FL 33044. Tel. 305/745-3211. 55 rms, 10 efficiencies. A/C TV TEL

$ Rates: Dec 19–Apr, $85–$95 single or double; $100 efficiency. May–Aug, $65–$80 single or double; $85 efficiency. Sept–Dec 18, $55–$65 single or double; $70 efficiency. Additional person $10 extra. AE, CB, DC, DISC, MC, V.
On one hand, this is just a motel: plain rooms, color TV, good parking, swimming pool—you get the idea. But its ideal location in the heart of the Lower Keys and its immediate proximity to the Backcountry reefs really make the Sugarloaf Lodge special. There are two wings to this sprawling property, which surround a lagoon where the motel's mascot dolphin lives. Efficiency rooms outfitted with small, fully equipped kitchenettes are also available. The motel is close to tennis courts and a miniature golf course, and adjacent to T.J.'s Sugarshack, an excellent marina from which you can fish or sightsee on the reef (see "Boat Rentals" in "What to See and Do," above). There's a restaurant and lounge serving meals and drinks all day.

CAMPING

BAHIA HONDA STATE PARK, Overseas Hwy., Mile Marker 29.5 (P.O. Box 782), Big Pine Key, FL 33043. Tel. 305/872-2353. 80 campsites, 6 cabin units.

$ Rates: Camping, $25 per site for one to four people; additional person (over four) $1 extra. Cabins, Dec 15–Sept 14, $125 per cabin for one to four people; Sept 15–Dec 14, $97 per cabin; additional person (over four) $6 extra.
One of the best parks in the whole state of Florida, Bahia Honda is as loaded with facilities and activities as it is with campers. Don't be discouraged by its popularity—this park encompasses over 600 acres of land, and some very private beaches. (see "What to See and Do," above, for complete information).

If you're lucky enough to get one, the park's cabins represent a very good value. Each holds up to eight guests, and comes complete with linens, kitchenettes, and utensils.

KOA CAMPGROUND, Overseas Hwy., Mile Marker 20, Sugarloaf Key (P.O. Box 469, Summerland Key, FL 33042). Tel. 305/745-3549. 200 campsites.

$ Rates: $30 per site. Additional person $7 extra.
Although it's a bit too popular with RV travelers, this campground offers excellent facilities for tent campers as well, including a large swimming lagoon, swimming pool, hot tub, pub, laundry facilities, and showers.

WHERE TO DINE

MODERATE

ISLAND REEF, Overseas Hwy., Mile Marker 31.3, Big Pine Key. Tel. 872-2170.

Cuisine: AMERICAN. **Reservations:** Not accepted.

$ Prices: Breakfast $3–$7; lunch $2–$8; dinner $9–$14. MC, V.

Open: Breakfast/lunch daily 6:30am–2:30pm; dinner daily 5–9:30pm.
This colorful ramshackle restaurant seems almost as old as the Keys themselves. It's

extremely popular with locals, and the conversations you'll overhear tend toward today's catch and tomorrow's weather. There are only about a dozen tables, as well as six stools at a small diner-style bar. Breakfasts tend toward fresh-fruit platters and French toast, while lunches mean simple sandwiches and tasty island chowders. Dinner specials change nightly; sometimes it's roast chicken with stuffing or leg of lamb, and other times it's prime rib or baked dolphin fish. It's always as good as the atmosphere.

BALTIMORE OYSTER HOUSE, Overseas Hwy., Mile Marker 30, Big Pine Key. Tel. 305/872-2314.

Cuisine: SEAFOOD. **Reservations:** Not required.

$ Prices: Appetizers $4–$10; main courses $6–$14. AE, MC, V.

Open: Mon–Sat noon–9pm.

Happily, the Baltimore Oyster House, which has had its ups and downs over the years, is up again. An old-timer on Big Pine, this house serves oysters, fresh shrimp, mussels, and clams, all priced by the pound. Crawdads (suck the head, dip the tail) are also available, as is fresh fish (like dolphin, salmon, and snapper), steak, chicken, and salads.

The restaurant's nautical-diner interior features fish nets on the ceiling and a full bar. The single-story, free-standing restaurant is located on your left (heading toward Key West), right in the middle of town.

MONTE'S, Overseas Hwy., Mile Marker 25, Summerland Key. Tel. 745-3731.

Cuisine: SEAFOOD. **Reservations:** Not accepted.

$ Prices: Appetizers $2–$4; main courses $9–$13; lunch $2–$7.

Open: Tues–Sat 10am–9:45pm, Sun noon–9pm. No credit cards.

If the food wasn't both excellent and fresh, then this place would close, because nobody goes to Monte's for its atmosphere: plastic place settings on plastic-covered picnic-style tables in a plastic-enclosed dining patio. Monte's has been open for 16 years because the food is very good and incredibly fresh; in fact, you can choose by sight the very fish you eat. Today's catch may include shark, tuna, lobster, stone crabs, and a variety of different size shrimp. In addition to grilling and frying fresh fish, the restaurant prepares several dishes including clam chowder, spiced crayfish pie, and even barbecued spareribs.

MANGROVE MAMA'S RESTAURANT, Overseas Hwy., Mile Marker 20, Sugarloaf Key. Tel. 745-3030.

Cuisine: SEAFOOD/AMERICAN. **Reservations:** Not accepted.

$ Prices: Appetizers $3–$9, main courses $12–$18; lunch $2–$9; brunch $5–$7. CB, DC, MC, V.

Open: Lunch daily 11:30am–3pm; dinner daily 5:30–10pm.

One of the few structures to survive the infamous 1935 hurricane, Mangrove Mama's (formerly Eddie's Fish Basket) is truly a Lower Keys institution. It's a dive, in the best sense of the word—a leap into another time, when the corner bar was the town's epicenter and "haute cuisine" was a foreign term. The restaurant is a mere shack that used to have a gas pump as well as a grill. A handful of simple tables, both inside and out, are shaded by trellises and often occupied by locals.

It's not surprising that fish is the menu's mainstay, though chowders, salads, and large omelets (including one filled with shrimp, scallops, and crabmeat) are also served. Grilled teriyaki chicken and club sandwiches are available, as are meatless chef's salad (with bleu cheese, boiled eggs, and vegetables), baked stuffed shrimp with crabmeat stuffing, and spicy barbecued baby back ribs.

BUDGET

MAXIMILLIONS DINER, at Sugarloaf Lodge, Overseas Hwy., Mile Marker 17, Sugarloaf Key. Tel. 745-3741.

Cuisine: AMERICAN. **Reservations:** Not accepted.

$ Prices: Breakfast $2–$5; lunch $4–$7; dinner $5–$8. AE, DC, DISC, MC, V.

Open: Breakfast/lunch daily 7:30am–2:30pm; dinner daily 5–9:30pm.

It's just a simple, small-town restaurant that could be anywhere—if it weren't for the mounted marlin and view of the dolphin pool. It's hard to believe that this huge dining room ever fills to capacity, though the adjacent wood-paneled bar is often hopping with local fishermen.

Breakfasts here include the usual variety of egg dishes, served with corned-beef hash, sausage, ham, or steak. Pancakes and French toast are also available. At lunch and dinner, you can get a variety of hot and cold sandwiches including chicken and steak, fish, burgers, and other traditional American foods. In deference to their dolphin, the diner never serves tunafish.

3. KEY WEST

150 miles SW of Miami

GETTING THERE **By Plane** Several major airlines fly nonstop from Miami to Key West, and charge $99–$298 round-trip, depending on date of travel and ticket restrictions. These include: **American Eagle** (tel. toll free 800/443-7300) and **USAir Express** (tel. toll free 800/251-5720). Planes fly into Key West International Airport, South Roosevelt Boulevard (tel. 305/296-5439), on the southeastern corner of the island.

By Bus Greyhound/Trailways runs three buses a day, in each direction, between Key West and Miami. The company no longer operates a single nationwide telephone number, so consult your local directory for the office nearest you.

By Car From Miami, take the Florida Turnpike south along the east coast to Exit 4, Homestead/Key West. This is the Turnpike Extension that meets U.S. 1 in Florida City. Key West is about 2½ hours south.

If you're coming from Florida's west coast, take Alligator Alley to the Miami exit, then turn south onto the Turnpike Extension.

The journey will take you across 42 toll-free bridges, including Seven-Mile Bridge, reputedly the longest segmental bridge in the world.

ESSENTIALS The telephone area code is 305.

The **Florida Keys & Key West Visitors Bureau,** P.O. Box 1147, Key West, FL 33041 (tel. 305/296-2228, or toll free 800/FLA-KEYS), offers a free vacation information kit for the asking. The **Key West Chamber of Commerce,** 402 Wall St. (P.O. Box 984), Key West, FL 33040 (tel. 305/294-5988, or toll free 800/527-8539), also offers general as well as specialized information and is open Monday through Friday from 8am to 5pm and on Saturday and Sunday from 8:30am to 5pm.

Key West is just four miles long and two miles wide, so getting around is easy. The "Old Town," centered around **Duval Street,** is the island's meeting ground and collective watering hole. It's also the location of most of the island's bars, restaurants, and sights. Many of the surrounding streets are filled with some of America's most beautiful Victorian/Bahamian-style homes.

Located about 150 miles from Miami, at the terminus of U.S. 1, Key West is the most distant member of Florida's key chain. Accessible only by boat until 1912, when Henry Flagler's railroad reached it, Key West's relative isolation from the North American mainland has everything to do with its charm.

During the first half of the 19th century, many locals made their living as "wreckers"—helping themselves to the booty of ships overturned in the shallows offshore. Since that time, the key has been home to an untold number of outlaws, drifters, writers, musicians, and other miscreants and eccentric types.

Today, in addition to artists and intellectuals, the island supports a healthy mix of Cubans and Caribbeans, and one of the largest gay populations in America. On Duval Street, smart boutiques stand next to old gin-joint dives and laid-back strollers fill the sidewalks. Key West is known for its terrific weather (about 10° cooler than Miami during the height of summer), quaint 19th-century architecture, and a friendly, easygoing atmosphere.

WHAT TO SEE & DO

Key West is famous for its relaxed atmosphere. Literally at the end of the road, this distant metropolitan hideaway has somehow eluded conventional domestication. Although it was tamed long ago by gourmet ice cream and chocolate-chip cookie shops, Key West has reached legend status for the way its residents jealously guard the island's independent identity. Tales of old-time pirating and modern-day renegades abound. And natives, who call themselves "conchs" (pronounced "conks"), have mockingly declared seccession from the United States in favor of their independent "Conch Republic."

Accordingly, the best thing to do on the island is to take a long stroll down Duval Street and stop in at the many open-air bars. Meet some locals, have a few drinks, and end up at the Mallory Docks by sunset. While strolling around, you might even want to visit some of the historical houses and fascinating museums below.

AUDUBON HOUSE AND GARDENS, 205 Whitehead St. Tel. 294-2116.

Named for the famous naturalist John James Audubon, who visited here in 1832, this restored three-story house features the master artist's original etchings and a large collection of lithographs. The house also holds a collection of Dorothy Doughty's porcelain birds and the period furnishings of its former owner, Capt. John Geiger, who was once one of the wealthiest men in Key West. Friendly docents are eager to answer questions, and admission includes a self-guided-tour brochure of the home and the lush tropical gardens that surround it.

Admission: $5 adults, $4 seniors, $1.50 children 6–12.

Open: Daily 9:30am–5pm.

THE CURRY MANSION, 511 Caroline St. Tel. 294-5349.

Built in 1855 by Florida's first millionaire, William Curry, this lovely conch-style mansion has been lovingly restored and filled with innumerable antiques. Listed in the National Register of Historic Places, the manor is a tribute to the early days of Key West. A self-guided tour of the house includes original parlors, several bedrooms, the dining room, and the carriage entrance. Also open to view is the master bedroom and dressing room, as well as the porches and surrounding grounds. Part of the mansion also operates as a bed-and-breakfast (see "Where to Stay," below, for complete information).

Admission: $5 adults, $1 children 4–12.

Open: Daily 10am–5pm.

EAST MARTELLO MUSEUM AND GALLERY, 3501 S. Roosevelt Blvd. Tel. 296-3913.

There are several museums in Key West dedicated to the island's history, but for variety, this is one of the best. Housed in a pre–Civil War fort that was built to protect the nation's southernmost flank, the museum exhibits various historical artifacts illustrating the Keys' history of shipwrecks, pirates, sponging, and cigar making.

In addition to displays of historical interest, the museum exhibits many works by local artists, including dozens by native Mario Sanchez, whose crude and colorful wood carvings depict scenes from his Key West boyhood.

Admission: $4 adults, $3 children 5–15.

Open: Daily 9am–5pm.

ERNEST HEMINGWAY HOUSE MUSEUM, 907 Whitehead St. Tel. 294-1575.

From 1931 to 1961 the author shared these quarters with 50-odd six-toed cats, and lived here while writing *For Whom the Bell Tolls, Death in the Afternoon,* and several other novels. Hemingway, it is said, usually awoke early and wrote in the loft of his poolhouse. If his work was progressing well, he would continue without a break for hours. "If the words are coming hard," Hemingway once said, "I often quit before noon."

Built in 1851, the writer's beautiful stone Spanish Colonial house was one of the first on the island to be fitted with indoor plumbing and a built-in fireplace. The house was opened to the public in 1963, two years after Hemingway's death, and contains many personal possessions, as well as dozens of six-toed feline descendants.

Admission: $6 adults, $1.50 children.

Open: Daily 9am–5pm.

KEY WEST CEMETERY, Margaret and Angela Sts.

Both old and picturesque, this 21-acre cemetery in the center of the island is a Key West original. The island's rocky geological makeup forced residents to "bury" their dead above ground, in stone-encased caskets. Many memorials are emblazoned with nicknames, which are popular on this informal island. Look for headstones labeled "The Tailor," "Bean," "Shorty," and "Bunny." Many other headstones also reflect residents' not-so-serious attitudes toward life. "I Told You I Was Sick" is one of the more famous epitaphs, as is a tongue-in-cheek widow's inscription "At Least I Know Where He's Sleeping Tonight."

KEY WEST LIGHTHOUSE MUSEUM, 938 Whitehead St. Tel. 294-0012.

Many locals mourned when the Key West Lighthouse was opened in 1848; its bright warning to ships also signaled the end of the island's profitable shipwrecking businesses. When the lighthouse keeper died in 1908, his wife, Mary Bethel, took his place, becoming the first and only female lighthouse keeper in America. The technical age of radar and sonar made the lighthouse obsolete; it was opened to tourists in 1972. Today, visitors can climb the 88 steps to the top for magnificent panoramic views of Key West and the ocean.

Admission: $4 adults, $3 children 5–15.

Open: Daily 9:30am–5pm.

MALLORY SQUARE SUNSET CELEBRATION.

Every evening, just before sunset, locals and visitors alike gather at the docks to celebrate the day gone by. This quaint Caribbean tradition is augmented by food vendors, jugglers, artists, acrobats, and mimes who compete for the attentions—and dollars—of tourists.

MEL FISHER'S TREASURE MUSEUM, 200 Greene St. Tel. 294-2633.

Some of the $400 million in gold and silver artifacts from the Spanish galleons *Atocha* and *Santa Margarita* are displayed in this tribute to treasure hunting. Many of the doubloons, emeralds, and solid gold bars are copies; but the cannons, historic weapons, and other less marketable finds are the real McCoy.

Admission: $5 adults, $1 seniors and children 6–12.

Open: Daily 9:30am–5pm.

ORGANIZED TOURS

The **Conch Tour Train** (tel. 294-5161) is not a train at all, but a series of tram cars pulled by a "locomotive." These canopied cars are a familiar sight around Key West, and represent a good way to see the island. The tour passes about 60 local sites, spread out over some 14 miles of road. Reservations are not necessary. Trains depart every few minutes from 3850 N. Roosevelt Blvd. (on U.S. 1, near the island bridge), and from Mallory Square (at the end of Duval Street). Tours cost $11 for adults and $5 for children under 16, and are given daily from 9am to 4pm.

I'll bet you didn't know that there were at least 100 interesting things to see and hear about in Key West. The 90-minute tour on the **Old Town Trolley,** 1910 N. Roosevelt Blvd. (tel. 296-6688), will point them all out. The trolley travels in a 30-minute loop around the island, allowing riders to get on and off at will, reboarding free of charge. Tours leave daily from 9am to 4pm and cost $11 for adults, $5 for children under 16.

SPORTS & RECREATION

BICYCLING Key West is a great place to see by bicycle. It's relatively small, the streets are safe, and the island is flat as a board. Several shops rent bikes for about $10 per day. They include **The Bike Shop,** 1110 Truman Ave. (tel. 294-1073); the **Moped Hospital,** 601 Truman Ave. (tel. 296-3344); **Bubba's Fun Rentals,** 705

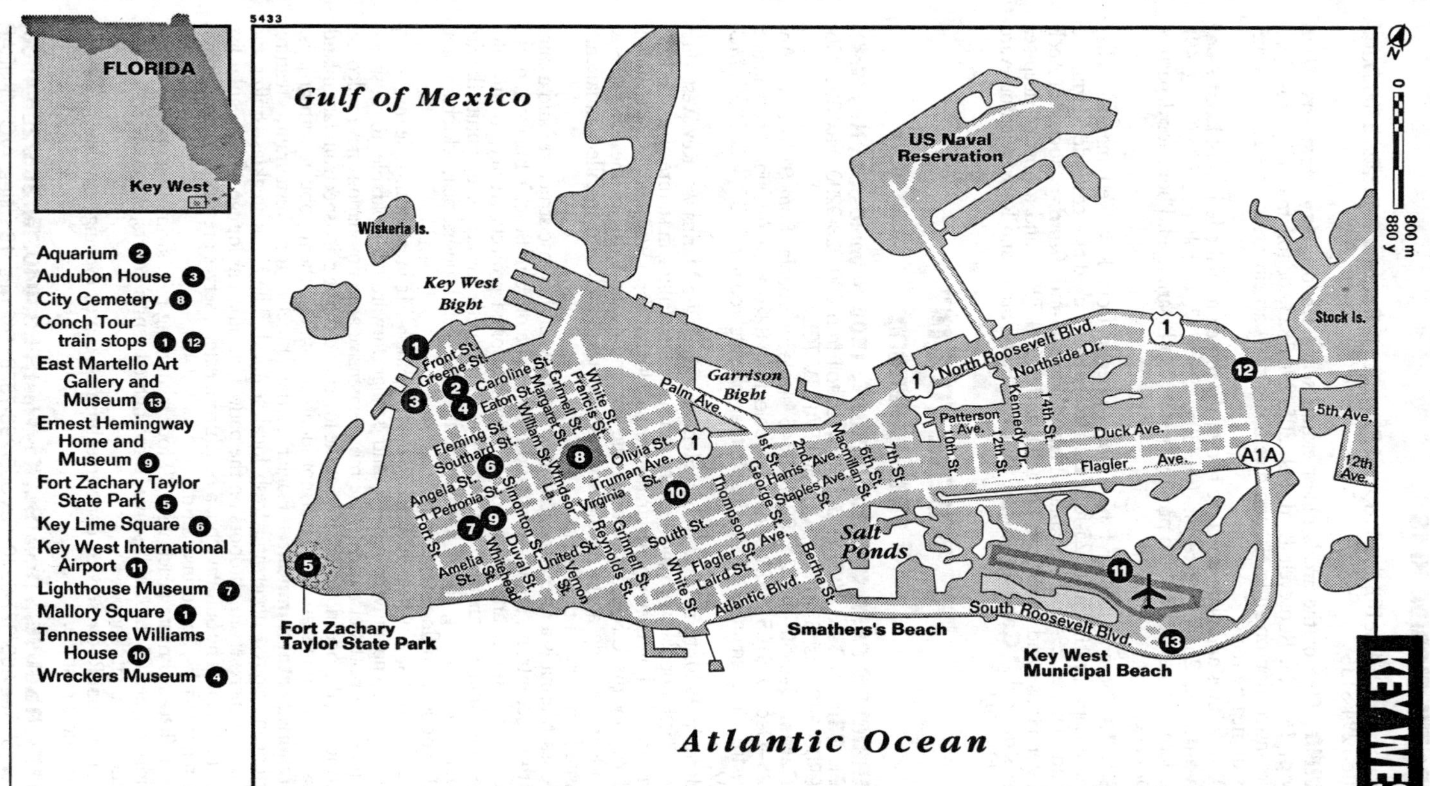

KEY WEST
FLORIDA
Key West
Aquarium 2
Audubon House 3
City Cemetery 8
Conch Tour train stops 1 12
East Martello Art Gallery and Museum 13
Ernest Hemingway Home and Museum 9
Fort Zachary Taylor State Park 5
Key Lime Square 6
Key West International Airport 11
Lighthouse Museum 7
Mallory Square 1
Tennessee Williams House 10
Wreckers Museum 4
0
800 m
880 y
Gulf of Mexico
Atlantic Ocean
US Naval Reservation
Wiskeria Is.
Key West Bight
Garrison Bight
Salt Ponds
Stock Is.
Fort Zachary Taylor State Park
Smathers's Beach
Key West Municipal Beach
Front St.
Greene St.
Caroline St.
Eaton St.
Fleming St.
Southard St.
Angela St.
Petronia St.
Fort St.
Amelia St.
Whitehead St.
Duval St.
Simonton St.
William St.
Margaret St.
Grinnell St.
Francis St.
White St.
Windsor La.
United St.
Vernon St.
Reynolds St.
Virginia St.
Truman Ave.
Olivia St.
Palm Ave.
South St.
Thompson St.
Flagler St.
Laird St.
Atlantic Blvd.
George St.
1st St.
Harris Ave.
2nd. Ave.
Staples Ave.
Macmillan St.
6th St.
7th St.
Bertha St.
Patterson Ave.
10th St.
12th St.
Kennedy Dr.
14th St.
North Roosevelt Blvd.
Northside Dr.
Duck Ave.
Flagler Ave.
South Roosevelt Blvd.
5th Ave.
12th Ave.
1
A1A
5433
Airport

Duval St. (tel. 294-2618); and **Tropical Bicycles & Scooter Rentals,** 1300 Duval St. (tel. 294-8136).

DIVING One of the area's oldest extant scuba schools, **Key West Pro Dive Shop,** 1605 N. Roosevelt Blvd. (tel. 305/296-3823, or toll free 800/426-0707), offers instruction on all levels, and dive boats take participants to scuba and snorkel sites on nearby reefs.

Wreck dives and night dives are two of the more unusual offerings of **Lost Reef Adventures,** 261 Margaret St. (tel. 305/296-9737, or toll free 800/952-2749). Regularly scheduled runs and private charters can be arranged. Phone for departure information.

FISHING Several charter fishing boats operate from Key West marinas. They include Capt. Jim Brienza's 25-foot ***Sea Breeze,*** docked at Oceanside Marina, 25 Arbutus Dr. (tel. 294-6027); Captain Henry Otto's 43-foot ***Sunday,*** docked at A&B Lobster House and Marina, 9 Geiger Rd. (tel. 294-7052), and a host of deep-sea vessels docked at **Garrison Bight Marina,** Eaton Street and Roosevelt Boulevard (tel. 296-9969).

WHERE TO STAY

VERY EXPENSIVE

MARRIOTT'S CASA MARINA RESORT, 1500 Reynolds St., Key West, FL 33040. Tel. 305/296-3535, or toll free 800/228-9290. Fax 305/296-9960. 312 rms, 63 suites. A/C MINIBAR TV TEL

$ Rates: Dec 20–Apr 24, $240–$345 single or double; from $345 suite. Apr 25–Dec 19, $165–$220 single or double; from $220 suite. Additional person $25 extra. Children under 18 stay free in their parents' room. AE, CB, DC, DISC, MC, V.

Built in the 1920s by railroad tycoon Henry Flagler, Casa Marina was Key West's first grand hotel, popular with movie stars and socialites. Falling in stature after the 1935 hurricane, the hotel was opened in the early 1940s to World War II military personnel, and run by the U.S. Navy. During the Cuban Missile Crisis in the early 1960s, President Kennedy again moved troops into the hotel, and installed antiaircraft missile launchers on the beach.

Casa Marina is a nice place, encompassing several low-rise structures and a huge swath of oceanfront, but it's not grand on the scale of Palm Beach's Breakers, or the Boca Raton Resort and Club—other Flagler-inspired projects created to lure film stars and land speculators. The lobby is the hotel's masterpiece, outfitted with saloon-style swinging doors, bronze paddle fans, French doors, peacock chairs, and dark woods from floor to ceiling.

Guest rooms, which are located in several Spanish-Mediterranean-style three-story wings, are comparatively modest and straightforward, comparable to business-oriented Marriott's elsewhere. The most expensive accommodations have balconies overlooking the ocean, while those at the lower end of the price spectrum face inland. Most of the rooms are similar, if not identical, making them popular with groups.

Dining/Entertainment: Flagler's, the hotel's top restaurant, features Caribbean-inspired decor and fresh local seafood. There's a breakfast buffet and Sunday brunch served outdoors on the patio. The adjacent lounge offers regular live entertainment. The Sun Pavilion, a beachfront eatery, serves breakfast, lunch, dinner, late-night snacks, and drinks all day.

Facilities: Private beach with 80-foot swimming pier, swimming pool, outdoor whirlpool, health club with sauna, three lighted tennis courts, water-sports center, beauty salon, gift shop.

Services: Room service, concierge, business center, evening turn-down, laundry, overnight shoeshine.

THE PIER HOUSE, 1 Duval St., Key West, FL 33040. Tel. 305/296-4600, or toll free 800/327-8340. Fax 305/296-7568. 142 rms, 13 suites. A/C MINIBAR TV TEL

$ Rates: Dec 21–Apr 19, $235–$375 single or double; from $450 suite; additional person $35 extra. Apr 20–Dec 20, $165–$285 single or double; from $295 suite; additional person $20 extra. AE, CB, DC, DISC, MC, V.

This is the best hotel in Key West, period. The Pier House's excellent location, at the foot of Duval Street just steps from Mallory Docks and stumbling distance from most every bar, is the envy of the island. Set back from the busy street, on a short strip of beach, the hotel is a welcome oasis of calm, offering luxurious rooms, top-notch service, and even a full-service spa.

Accommodations vary tremendously, from relatively simple business-class rooms to indulgently romantic guest quarters, complete with integrated stereo systems and whirlpool tubs. Every room has either a balcony or a patio.

Dining/Entertainment: Long a part of Key West history, it's said that Tennessee Williams was a frequent guest at the Pier House Restaurant, the hotel's primary eatery. As the name implies, the Roof Top Bar is a popular, elevated drinkery, with a large deck that wraps around the hotel and overlooks the water.

Services: Room service, concierge, laundry.

Facilities: Spa treatments, water-sports rentals, swimming pool, beach.

THE REACH, 1435 Simonton St., Key West, FL 33040. Tel. 305/296-5000. Fax 305/296-2830. 150 rms. A/C MINIBAR TV TEL

$ Rates: Dec 21–Apr 28, $220–$450 single or double. Apr 29–Nov, $125–$350 single or double. Dec 1–20, $120–$325 single or double. Additional person $25–$30 extra. AE, CB, DC, DISC, MC, V.

The colossal, labyrinthine, pastel-colored Reach is one of the few hotels on the island with its own strip of sandy beach. The ample surrounding grounds also encompass huge palms, a large pool with plenty of lounge chairs, and a private pier for fishing and suntanning. Rooms are relatively straightforward, in the Hilton or Sheraton mold. Most are identical, with small, well-equipped baths, double beds with brightly printed spreads, remote-control TVs, and fully stocked minibars. All rooms have sliding glass doors that open onto balconies, some with ocean views. The hotel is located a short walk from the "far" end of Duval Street—a 15-minute walk away from the center of the action.

Dining/Entertainment: The Ocean Club serves fresh local seafood in a Mediterranean seaside setting. The beachfront Sand Bar, a fish-and-burger place, is not known for its culinary prowess, but offers one of the best settings on the island. For a quick bite, stop by A Little Something, the resort's deli and French bakery. Nightfall, a rooftop bar, offers regular entertainment and good sunset views.

Services: Room service, concierge, laundry.

Facilities: Heated swimming pool, sauna, health spa, steam room, sailboats, windsurfers.

EXPENSIVE

THE CURRY MANSION INN, 511 Caroline St., Key West, FL 33040. Tel. 305/294-5349, or toll free 800/253-3466. Fax 305/294-4093. 21 rms. A/C MINIBAR TV TEL

$ Rates (including continental breakfast): Dec 22–May 1, $170–$200 single or double. June 2–Oct 1, $125–$160 single or double. The rest of the year, $140–$160 single or double. Additional person $25 extra. AE, MC, V.

Dating from 1899, and listed on the National Register of Historic Places, the Curry Mansion is a popular sightseeing destination as well as a notable bed-and-breakfast (see "What to See and Do," above, for complete information). The lobby has beautiful hardwood floors, a tiled fireplace, and copious antiques which are liberally spread throughout the house. Although the B&B's rooms—most of which are located in an adjacent annex—are not as luxurious as the inn's proprietors, Al and Edith Amsterdam, like to profess, they are of moderate standard, and in unusual turn-of-the-century surroundings. There's a small swimming pool on the property; guests are treated to complimentary afternoon cocktails and are entitled to use the facilities of the Pier House Beach Club, located just one block away.

MARQUESSA HOTEL, 600 Fleming St., Key West, FL 33040. Tel. 305/292-1919. Fax 305/294-2121. 15 rms. A/C TV TEL

$ Rates: Dec 21–Apr 11, $175–$200 single or double; from $235 suite. June–Oct 27, $110–$125 single or double; from $145 suite. The rest of the year, $130–$150 single or double; from $175 suite. Additional person $15 extra. AE, MC, V.

The Marquessa would be Key West's most luxurious bed-and-breakfast, if only they served breakfast. Food notwithstanding, however, everything about this finely restored Victorian home is very much like an elegant B&B—one of the nicest I've ever seen. Beautifully appointed rooms are carefully prepared with dozens of special touches and extra-plush furnishings. Every accommodation is different, though most have gilded mirrors, tropical accents, original contemporary art, and plenty of fresh flowers. There's a helpful concierge, and newspapers are delivered daily to each door.

Dining/Entertainment: The adjacent Café Marquessa is a great place for lunch or dinner. Trendy South Florida foods are served in equally faddish surroundings.

Services: Room service, concierge, evening turn-down.

Facilities: Swimming pool.

MODERATE

LA PENSIONE, 809 Truman Ave., Key West, FL 33040. Tel. 305/292-9923. Fax 305/296-6509. 7 rms. A/C

$ Rates (including continental breakfast): Dec 25–May 15, $128–$138 single or double. May 16–Dec 24, $68–$88 single or double. MC, V.

One of the island's newest bed-and-breakfasts, La Pensione opened in 1992, a lovely restoration of an 1891 Victorian home. Hoteliers Vince Cerrito and Joseph Rimkus have done a bang-up job creating a modestly priced charming inn that's thoroughly recommendable. Rooms are colorful and airy, featuring bright, flowery spreads and prints on well-chosen budget wicker and wood furnishings. There are big closets and clock radios, but no telephones or TVs—an attraction for some guests.

Breakfast, which includes waffles and fresh fruit, is served in a pleasing downstairs dining room, which is adjacent to an equally nice living room and porch which guests are encouraged to use.

THE MERMAID AND THE ALLIGATOR, 729 Truman Ave., Key West, FL 33040. Tel. 305/294-1894. Fax 305/296-5090. 5 rms.

$ Rates (including full breakfast): Dec 25–May 1, $95–$155 single or double. May 2–Dec 24, $65–$100 single or double. AE, MC, V.

One of the prettiest restored buildings on the street, this inspired, eccentric inn is packed with American amenities and European charm. Every room is different, but all have shiny hardwood floors and special touches that may include four-poster beds and large bay windows. A full breakfast is served outside on a lovely deck in back of the house. There's off-street parking and a heated swimming pool.

SOUTHERNMOST POINT GUEST HOUSE, 1327 Duval St., Key West, FL 33040. Tel. 305/294-0715. Fax 305/296-0641. 6 rms. A/C TV TEL

$ Rates (including continental breakfast): Dec 20–Apr, $80–$110 single or double; from $115 efficiency; from $130 suite. May–Dec 19, $55–$70 single or double; from $75 efficiency; from $95 suite. Additional person $5–$10 extra. AE, MC, V.

Built in 1885, this well-kept, architecturally stunning home pays tribute to the romantic charm of old Key West. The rather sparse and antiseptically clean rooms are not as fancy as the house's ornate exterior. Each offers basic beds and couches, and some are decorated with stuffed deer heads bagged by owner Mona Santiago. The hotel itself occupies a prime location, at the "far" end of Duval Street just one block from the beach.

INEXPENSIVE

WICKER GUESTHOUSE, 913 Duval St., Key West, FL 33040. Tel. 305/296-4275. 16 rms. A/C TV TEL

$ Rates: Dec–May, $69–$95 single or double. June–Nov, $40–$85 single or double. Additional person $10 extra. AE, MC, V.

Occupying three separate buildings overlooking busy Duval Street, the Wicker offers some of the best-priced accommodations on the island. Pretty porches outline the traditional "conch" houses, and the rooms are predictably sparse. This cozy hotel is a welcome option in tab-happy Key West.

BUDGET

KEY WEST INTERNATIONAL HOSTEL, 718 South St., Key West, FL 33040. Tel. 305/296-5719. Fax 305/296-0672. 80 beds.

$ Rates: $12 for IYHF members, $15 for nonmembers. MC, V.

It's not the Ritz, but it's cheap. Very busy with European backpackers, this place is just a hair above camping out.

WHERE TO DINE

EXPENSIVE

BAGATELLE, 115 Duval St. Tel. 296-6609.

Cuisine: SEAFOOD/TROPICAL. **Reservations:** Not required.

$ Prices: Appetizers $5–$9; main courses $15–$22; lunch $5–$13. AE, CB, DC, DISC, MC, V.

Open: Lunch daily 11:30am–4:30pm; dinner daily 5:30–10pm.

Resembling a Mediterranean mansion, Bagatelle has pretty, dark-wood floors, a beautiful upstairs dining room with wooden schoolhouse chairs at clothed tables, and outdoor dining on a great porch overlooking Duval Street. It's very romantic, and made even more fanciful by a keyboardist at the grand piano.

A large lunch selection includes blackened chicken breast sandwich with crumbled bleu cheese, a variety of grilled fish, and a salad of mixed greens combined with avocados, walnuts, raisins, cheeses, and scallions. Your dinner should begin with the herb-and-garlic-stuffed whole artichoke or the sashimilike seared rare tuna rolled in black peppercorns and served with garlic, soy, and sesame sauce. The best entrees are the local Florida fish selections such as shrimp-stuffed grouper crowned with shrimp and lobster-cream sauce, and garlic-herb pasta combined with shrimp, lobster, fish, and mushrooms. The best chicken and beef dishes are tropically treated, grilled with papaya, ginger, and soy.

THE BUTTERY, 1208 Simonton St. Tel. 294-0717.

Cuisine: FLORIDA REGIONAL. **Reservations:** Recommended.

$ Prices: Appetizers $7–$9; main courses $16–$24. AE, CB, DC, MC, V.

Open: Winter, dinner only, daily 6–10pm. Summer, dinner only, daily 7–10pm.

Now over a dozen years old, the Buttery was once one of Key West's brightest culinary stars. Its facade has faded, but the chefs still turn out consistently good dishes, even if their innovations have recently been eclipsed in younger kitchens.

The restaurant's surprisingly downscale, dark dining rooms have a 1970s steakhouse feel that's echoed by equally weighty preparations. Heavy creams douse tender steak filets, and local fruit sauces typically top the freshest of fish. Yellowtail is baked with sliced bananas, walnuts, and banana liqueur. Sea scallops are wrapped in bacon and brushed with roasted red-pepper hollandaise sauce. Some of the restaurant's more unusual appetizers include chilled spicy noodle salad with carrots, snow peas, shiitake mushrooms, and seafood; and pan-fried grouper with Chinese cabbage glazed with a combination of ginger, orange, and soy.

CAFE DES ARTISTES, 1007 Simonton St. Tel. 294-7100.

Cuisine: FRENCH. **Reservations:** Recommended.

$ Prices: Appetizers $5–$11; main courses $19–$25. AE, MC, V.

Open: Dinner only, daily 6–11pm.

Dark, quiet, and old-world elegant, the Café des Artistes has built quite a reputation in its 10 years of service. Parisian without pretension, the restaurant's beautiful surroundings include good-quality contemporary art, small shaded table lamps, and comfortable covered wooden chairs. During good weather you can choose to dine outside under the restaurant's retractable roof.

Cognoscenti suggest starting with chicken-liver pâté, made with fresh truffles, and old cognac or Maryland crabmeat served with an artichoke heart and herbed tomato confit. Entrees are no simpler, and include cognac-based lobster flambé with saffron butter, mango, and basil, and wine-basted lamb chops rubbed with rosemary and ginger. There's a good wine selection, including an inspired choice of specials by the glass.

LOUIE'S BACKYARD, 700 Waddell Ave. Tel. 294-1061.

Cuisine: CARIBBEAN CONTEMPORARY. **Reservations:** Required.

$ Prices: Appetizers $6–$10; main courses $17–$28; brunch $25. AE, CB, DC, MC, V.

Open: Lunch Mon–Sat 11:30am–2:30pm; dinner Mon–Sun 6–10:30pm; brunch Sun 11:30am–3pm.

Louie's Backyard has come under fire in recent years for being overpriced and uneven. And while both these accusations are true, when the weather is nice and the food is good, Louie's is unbeatable. The restaurant's multilevel rear deck is built directly over the water, offering the most comfortable and romantic dining experience on the island. While the inside dining room is less desirable, it's incredibly charming, with pastel colors and large paddle fans that complement an authentic "conch" house feel.

Asian, North African, and Latin American ingredients and preparations are combined into an interesting contemporary Caribbean cuisine. Sliced, grilled chicken breast is served atop a tangy mixture of black beans, Mexican slaw, sour cream, guacamole, and served with a crispy flour tortilla. Local shrimp are marinated in conch-Créole sauce and tossed with spinach pasta, and grilled veal chops, basted with a Spanish wine sauce, are coupled with artichokes, plum tomatoes, and onions. Sunday brunches offer equally engaging recipes, including gingerbread pancakes and poached eggs.

SQUARE ONE, 1075 Duval St. Tel. 296-4300.

Cuisine: AMERICAN. **Reservations:** Recommended.

$ Prices: Appetizers $4–$6.50; main courses $14–$20. AE, DISC, MC, V.

Open: Dinner only, daily 6:30–10:30pm.

When queried recently about their favorite restaurants in Key West, a number of knowledgeable local diners put Square One as their top spot. In its three short years of operation, this classy medium-sized Los Angeles–style restaurant has gained an excellent reputation for food, service, and surroundings. The single dining room, which also accommodates a small bar and grand piano, is stylish without being showy, while a few outdoor tables overlook a courtyard fountain.

The food here is sophisticated but not complicated. Baked garlic with puréed feta cheese makes an excellent start to a meal that might include sautéed duck breast with peppered pineapple sauce, or perfectly grilled mahimahi or salmon. The nightly pasta special can be anything from lobster ravioli to rigatoni with capers, olives, and sun-dried tomatoes—it's always recommendable.

MODERATE

ANTONIA'S, 615 Duval St. Tel. 294-6565.

Cuisine: ITALIAN. **Reservations:** Not required.

$ Prices: Appetizers $4–$9; main courses $11–$20. AE, DC, MC, V.

Open: Dinner only, daily 6–11pm.

It's hard not to like Antonia's, a festive Italian eatery that's fun and faithfully good. The Key West casual interior makes extensive use of aged woods that look as though they might have been culled from a turn-of-the-century sunken ship. Despite the restaurant's cordial, climate-controlled interior, large bay windows never let diners forget that bustling Duval Street is just a glance away.

Don't expect great Roman cooking and you won't be disappointed. Antonia's straightforward, down-home Italian-American cuisine is closer to Brooklyn than it is to Trastevere. Pastas include penne with eggplant and tomatoes, and spinach-and-ricotta-filled cannelloni. Deep-fried breaded veal chops are stuffed with fontina cheese and prosciutto and snapper is sautéed with shrimp and Italian greens, white wine, and olive oil. Good ports and sherries complement a small selection of wines.

CHARMS DINER, at La-Te-Da, 1125 Duval St. Tel. 294-8435.

Cuisine: ASIAN. **Reservations:** Not required.

$ Prices: Appetizers $3–$8; main courses $11–$19; brunch $3–$9. AE, MC, V.

Open: Brunch daily 8:30am–4pm; dinner Mon–Sat 6–11pm, Sun 6–9pm.

Once one of the town's most celebrated French dining rooms, this airy ground-floor restaurant now serves a contemporary Asian cuisine, combining fresh local ingredients with Oriental spices and creative know-how. Either inside, by the bar and grand piano, or outdoors, around the swimming pool, this beautiful spot is still one of the nicest places to dine in Key West.

Owner/chef Sin Svasti especially recommends the nightly dinner specials, which might include spicy Thai mussels steamed in a lime-scented broth with chili peppers and cilantro, or escargot-stuffed chicken wings baked in garlic-Pernod butter. Lighter starters include Chinese egg noodles tossed with vegetables, bean sprouts, and tangy sesame dressing; and a Thai-inspired salad of poached shrimp, pork, and chicken topping cucumbers and clear noodles. A selection of fresh seafood and imaginative pastas is always offered alongside a vegetarian entree made with grilled vegetables and parmesan potatoes.

I also endorse the restaurant's daily brunches that include eggs Blackstone: fried breaded tomatoes and poached eggs served on an English muffin and topped with hollandaise, crumbled bacon, and scallions.

THE TWISTED NOODLE, 628 Duval St. Tel. 296-6670.

Cuisine: ITALIAN. **Reservations:** Not required.

$ Prices: Appetizers $3–$5; main courses $6–$14. No credit cards.

Open: Dinner only, Fri–Wed 5–10pm.

This once-fading sanctuary of sanity in costly Key West received a new lease on life in 1992 when it was purchased by five young friends from Baltimore. The enthusiastic new owners are both friendly and knowledgeable about food. The chefs, who change the menu daily, might bake meat-stuffed artichoke hearts, or toss chilled noodles with sesame sauce. Spinach fettuccine may be topped with mushroom-Alfredo sauce, and a variety of seafood and vegetables are regularly paired with pastas. Only beer and wine are served.

The pastel-colored restaurant, which is set back about half a block from Duval Street, has only about a dozen tables, many of which are set out in front under the open sky.

YO SAKE, 722 Duval St. Tel. 294-2288.

Cuisine: JAPANESE. **Reservations:** Not required.

$ Prices: Sushi $2–$14; appetizers $5–$7; main dishes $12–$18. AE, DC, DISC, MC, V.

Open: Dinner only, daily 6–11pm.

A hip black-and-white dining room and a business steady enough to keep the fish fresh make Yo Sake Key West's most recommendable sushi room. A wall of sharply designed booths, and the long sushi bar that's planted opposite them, are the most important statements in the restaurant's Japanese pop interior. In addition to the usual sushi and sashimi selections, the kitchen prepares a number of noodle dishes (soba and udon), shrimp and vegetable tempura, and stir-fried gingered pork with vegetables.

INEXPENSIVE

HALF SHELL RAW BAR, 920 Caroline St. Tel. 294-7496.

Cuisine: SEAFOOD. **Reservations:** Not accepted.

$ Prices: Main courses $5–$10. No credit cards.

Open: Mon–Sat 11am–11pm, Sun noon–11pm.

Located at the foot of Margaret Street, the Half Shell is the best place on the island for inexpensive, fresh-as-can-be seafood, in an authentic dockside setting. Decorated with "vanity" license plates from every state in the Union, the restaurant features a wide variety of freshly shucked shellfish and daily catch selections. Beer is the drink of choice here, though other beverages and a full bar are available. Seating is either at indoor varnished wooden tables, or out on the small but pretty deck overlooking the piers.

JIMMY BUFFETT'S MARGARITAVILLE CAFE, 500 Duval St. Tel. 292-1435.

Cuisine: AMERICAN. **Reservations:** Not accepted.

$ Prices: Sandwiches $5–$6; fresh fish platter $10; margarita $4. AE, MC, V.

Open: Sun–Thurs 11am–2am, Fri–Sat 11am–4am.

This large, friendly, and easygoing restaurant/bar is heavy on soups, salads, sandwiches, and local catches. A long bar runs the length of the laid-back dining room, in clear sight of an adjacent gift shop which often seems as busy as the bar. Live bands regularly perform, and Mr. Buffett himself has even been known to take the stage on a whim. It's very touristy, but recommended.

SHALOM RESTAURANT, 601 Duval St. Tel. 294-3584.

Cuisine: ISRAELI. **Reservations:** Not accepted.

$ Prices: Breakfast $2.50–$3.50; lunch/dinner $8–$13.

Open: Sun–Thurs 8am–10pm, Fri 8am–4:30pm.

Opened in the fall of 1992, this small hole-in-the-wall is Key West's only kosher restaurant, serving Middle Eastern specialties like shwarma (sliced lamb), shish kebab (skewered beef), and falafel (fried chickpea) sandwiches. There's not much to the decor—a few red-and-white-checkered tablecloths and basement-style wood paneling—but the food is as good as it is in New York.

BUDGET

CROISSANTS DE FRANCE, 816 Duval St. Tel. 294-9148.

Cuisine: FRENCH.

$ Prices: Pastries $1–$3; lunch $3–$8. No credit cards.

Open: Thurs–Tues 7:30am–11pm (lunch served until 3pm).

One of the few true cafés on Duval Street, this pleasant restaurant more than adequately fills its niche. The unusual combination of French charm in a tropical setting works well here, where diners can eat fresh-baked breads, rolls, and croissants on a pleasant, plant-packed porch.

Breakfasts run the gamut from a simple croissant and coffee to a full European-style feast that includes breakfast with sliced ham, Swiss cheese, and French bread. Sandwiches, soups, salads, quiches, and crêpes are available until 3pm, after which only drinks and desserts are sold.

DUVAL DELI AND RESTAURANT, 724 Duval St. Tel. 294-3663.

Cuisine: CONTINENTAL.

$ Prices: Breakfast $3–$7; sandwiches $4–$6; pizza $6–$15. No credit cards.

Open: Daily 24 hours.

Locals swear by the Duval Deli, a great, bright and clean soup-and-sandwich spot that has a flair for style as well as substance. Despite hokey names like "sexy bagel" (served with cream cheese, red onion, tomato, smoked salmon, and a hard-boiled egg) and "Hollywood Bowl" (a fresh-fruit–topped bowl of granola), breakfasts and other meals are top-of-the-line. "Superstar" sandwiches include "Shirley Maclaine" (three kinds of cheese, veggies, and "Cosmic" dressing on a whole-wheat bun) and "Plain Jane" (peanut butter, jam, and banana). Gourmet pizzas are topped with tuna salad, peanut-and-ginger–marinated chicken, and other untraditionals. Coffee, wine, and beer are served. The restaurant offers a 10% discount to any diner sporting a nightclub handstamp.

SHOPPING

Without a doubt, **Duval Street** is *the* strip for Key West shopping. The island is hardly a shopper's paradise, but among the T-shirt shops that line this key's most touristy strip are several excellent boutiques that are well worth checking out. The island's best bets are shops selling men's fashions, including **Coco Ibiza,** 601 Duval St. (tel. 296-8348); **Swept Away for Men,** 605 Duval St. (tel. 296-6654); and **Zero for Men,** 624 Duval St. (tel. 294-3899). Most Duval Street shops are open daily from 11am to 8pm.

EVENING ENTERTAINMENT

THE PERFORMING ARTS

THE RED BARN THEATER, 319 Duval St. Tel. 296-9911.

Set back off Duval Street, the little red barn that now houses one of Key West's best stages was originally a carriage house connected to one of the island's oldest homes. The 100-seat Red Barn has gone through many changes since it was reborn in the 1940s as the home of the Key West Community Players. Renovated again in 1980, the theater now offers excellent local and visiting theatrical productions. Phone for current performance information.

Admission: Tickets, $13–$25.

WATERFRONT PLAYHOUSE. Mallory Square. Tel. 294-5015.

Larger and prettier then the Red Barn, the Waterfront Playhouse attracts a variety of theatrical performances, including musicals, plays, and other stage shows. Performances are usually held from December through April. Call for show times.

Admission: Tickets, $5–$15.

THE CLUB, MUSIC & BAR SCENE

Duval Street is the Bourbon Street of Florida. Between the T-shirt shops and clothing boutiques is bar after bar, serving stiff drinks to revelers who usually hop from one to another. Here's a run-down of the best.

CAPTAIN TONY'S SALOON, 428 Greene St. Tel. 294-1838.

Just around the corner from the beaten Duval path, Captain Tony's jealously retains its seasoned and quixotic pretourist ambience, complete with old-time regulars who really know what this island life is about. Smoky, small, and cozy, this saloon is owned by Capt. Tony Tarracino, a former Key West mayor who is well known in these parts for his acerbic wit and unorthodox ways. The bar is well supported by locals who say that Hemingway drank, caroused, and even wrote here.

CRAZY DAIZY'Z, in La Concha Hotel, 430 Duval St. Tel. 296-2991.

A full bar and short list of domestic and imported beers are served in plastic cups from a well-aged marble bar. There are two big-screen TVs, and occasional live music (usually on the weekends). The bar is well located, in the middle of the Duval Street action. Sandwiches and conch chowder are served.

DURTY HARRY'S, 208 Duval St.

One of Duval's largest entertainment complexes, Durty Harry's features live rock bands almost every night (and most afternoons, too), and several outdoor bars. Upstairs at Rick's is an indoor/outdoor dance club that's very popular almost every night. The Red Garter, yet another related business on this property, is a pocket-size strip club popular with local bachelor parties and the few visitors who know about it.

FAT TUESDAYS, 305 Duval St. Tel. 296-9373.

Over 20 colorful, slushy, frozen slightly chemically alcoholic concoctions swirl in special see-through tanks behind the bar of this lively outdoor bar. Located on an elevated deck near the busiest end of Duval, Fat Tuesdays features live music daily and is popular with a rowdy college-age crowd.

HAVANA DOCKS, at the Pier House Resort, 1 Duval St. Tel. 305/296-4600.

The huge outdoor, top-floor terrace of the Pier House, Key West's best hotel, is a natural for visitors looking to celebrate the sunset in style. Great water views and live music make this one of the most popular places to toast at twilight.

HOG'S BREATH SALOON, 400 Front St. Tel. 296-4222.

Except for the fact that they sell lots of T-shirts, there's no relationship between this bar and its namesakes in California and around America. Once you realize it's not part of a corporate chain—like Planet Hollywood or Hard Rock Café—the Hog's Breath becomes an inviting, fun place to hang out. Several outdoor bars, good live music, a raw bar, and decent food earn this place a top spot in this guide. There are daily happy hour specials from 5 to 7pm.

SLOPPY JOE'S, 201 Duval St. Tel. 294-5717.

Although this probably wasn't the place Ernest Hemingway made famous, the author figures prominently in this bar's logo. It can be debated whether Hemingway liked this place or not, but there's no argument that Sloppy Joe's turn-of-the-century wooden ceiling and cracked tile floors are Key West originals. Popular, loud, and rowdy, this large, raucous bar is crowded with tourists almost 24 hours a day. There's almost always live music, a full bar, and a rather uninspired selection of beers and wines.

208 TREE BAR, 208 Duval St.

Located right at the entrance to Durty Harry's (see above), this small, 12-seat bar only pours top-shelf liquors, and squeezes fresh limes and oranges into their margaritas and screwdrivers.

CHAPTER 7

THE GOLD COAST

The south-central coast of Florida, which is dominated by Palm Beach County, is one of the nation's richest residential regions. This "Gold Coast" is inhabited largely by wealthy retirees and other "snowbirds" from the north. Homes in Palm Beach are so grand, they are called "compounds." Residential sightseeing in Boca Raton is less satisfying, only because the nicest homes there are well hidden behind gates and shrubbery.

The region's recorded history dates back to 1835, when the U.S. Army cleared trails while battling native Seminole peoples. Few early settlers were attracted to these marshlands. Until the early 1870s, A. O. Lang, keeper of the Jupiter lighthouse, was the region's only known settler of European origin. Lang was later joined by a handful of families who, in 1878, planted thousands of coconuts which had been washed up on the shore by a wrecked Spanish ship.

The arrival of Henry Flagler's train in 1893 precipitated tremendous growth in the area. Along with architect Addison Mizner, who built one of the region's first hotels, Flagler parceled out much of southeastern Florida's land and encouraged the area's first developments.

SEEING THE GOLD COAST

All major tourist areas and roads along the Gold Coast hug the ocean, making it easy to navigate your way around. The closer you get to the water, the narrower and more picturesque the roads. Interstate 95 is a fast freeway, filled with commuters during rush hours. U.S. 1, which generally hugs the mainland side of the Intracoastal, is a narrower thoroughfare, choked with traffic lights and lined with an unending variety of shops and fast-food restaurants. Florida A1A, which is laid out over the barrier islands, is your best bet if you really want to see the various towns along the South Florida coast.

This chapter is arranged geographically from north to south. If you're driving up the coast from Miami, start with the last section.

1. JUPITER & NORTH PALM BEACH COUNTY

20 miles N of Palm Beach, 100 miles N of Miami

GETTING THERE **By Plane** **Palm Beach International Airport** (tel. 407/471-7420) serves this area. Volunteer "Airport Ambassadors," are nearly always on hand to help visitors with information. Major domestic carriers using the airport

WHAT'S SPECIAL ABOUT THE GOLD COAST

Palatial Homes

- ☐ The estates of Palm Beach and Boca Raton, some of the swankiest in the world—a cruise around these communities will make your jaw drop.

Historic Hotels

- ☐ The Breakers, the grand dame of South Florida hotels and a tourist attraction in its own right.
- ☐ The Spanish-Mediterranean–style main house of the Boca Raton Resort and Club, just the tip of a 350-acre complex that straddles both sides of the Intracoastal Waterway.

Top Shops

- ☐ A short stretch of Palm Beach's Worth Avenue, lined by some of the world's most exclusive shops, galleries, and restaurants (look for Louis Vuitton, Cartier, Chanel, and others).
- ☐ The Gardens Mall in Palm Beach Gardens, a 1.2-million-square-foot shopping complex boasting five major department stores and more than 200 other shops—a shopper's paradise.

Best Beaches

- ☐ Blowing Rocks Preserve, on Jupiter Island, just one of many wonderfully picturesque beaches here, made beautiful by a cluster of large rock formations.
- ☐ Dozens of swimming beaches from deserted to lively, guaranteeing plenty of sun, surf, and sand whatever your style.

---

include American (tel. toll free 800/433-7300), Continental (tel. 407/832-5200, or toll free 800/525-0280), Delta (tel. 407/655-5300, or toll free 800/221-1212), Northwest (tel. toll free 800/225-2525), TWA (tel. 407/655-3776, or toll free 800/221-2000), and United (tel. toll free 800/241-6522).

By Train Amtrak (tel. toll free 800/USA-RAIL) trains from New York stop in West Palm Beach on their way to Miami. The local station is at 201 S. Tamarind Ave., West Palm Beach (tel. 407/832-6169).

By Bus Greyhound/Trailways can get you to the Palm Beaches from almost anywhere. The company no longer operates a single nationwide telephone number, so consult your local directory for the office nearest you.

By Car If you're driving up or down the Florida coast, you'll probably reach the Palm Beach area on I-95, a highway that extends all the way from Maine to Miami. Visitors on their way to or from Orlando should take the Florida Turnpike, a toll road that runs almost directly from this county's beaches to Walt Disney World. Finally, if you're coming from Florida's west coast, you can take either Fla. 70, which runs north of Lake Okeechobee to Fort Pierce, or Fla. 80, which runs south of the lake to Palm Beach.

ESSENTIALS The telephone **area code** is 407. For information, maps, and an Arts and Attractions Calendar, contact the **Palm Beach County Convention and Visitors Bureau,** 1555 Palm Beach Lakes Blvd., Suite 204, West Palm Beach, FL 33401 (tel. 407/471-3995, or toll free 800/554-PALM).

Slate-blue water, warmed in winter and cooled in summer by the powerful Atlantic Gulf Stream, is North Palm Beach County's greatest asset. Like the rest of the county, North Palm is teeming with playful dolphins, majestic sea turtles, and giant marlin. Because it's farther from Miami, however, this region is less populated than areas to the south, offering welcome relief from crowded beaches and freeways. Several good hotels and restaurants make Jupiter and the surrounding area a happy medium between the barren lands to the north and the populous areas to the south.

WHAT TO SEE & DO

North Palm is best known for the giant **sea turtles** that lay their eggs on the sand from May through August. These endangered marine animals return here annually, from as far as South America, to lay their clutch of about 115 eggs each. Nurtured by the warm sand, but preyed upon by birds and other predators, only about one or two from each nest survive to maturity.

The **Gumbo Limbo Nature Center** (tel. 338-1473), which offers turtle expeditions in season, recommends that visitors take part in an organized program (rather than go on their own) in order to minimize any disturbance to the turtles. The Jupiter Beach Hilton (tel. 747-2511), the Jupiter Beach Resort (tel. 746-2511), and the Marinelife Center of Juno Beach (tel. 627-8280) also sponsor guided expeditions to the turtle egg-laying sites.

Actor Burt Reynolds is famous in Palm Beach County, and his name is associated with a number of businesses and attractions. You'll probably see advertisements for the **Burt Reynolds Ranch and Mini Petting Farm** (tel. 747-5390). However, this is a mediocre attraction where visitors can wander around old movie sets and see domesticated farm animals. The ranch is located two miles west of the Florida Turnpike on Jupiter Farms Road and is open daily from 10am to 4:30pm; admission is free, $10 for tours.

THE GARDENS MALL, PGA Blvd., Palm Beach Gardens. Tel. 622-2115.

South Florida is acquiring a reputation as the land of the "megamall," and this 1.2-million-square-foot shopping complex is one of the reasons why. Anchored by five major department stores—Macy's, Sears, Bloomingdale's, Burdines, and Saks Fifth Avenue—this two-story mammoth is rounded out by almost 200 other shops and decorated with marble floors, a glass ceiling, and art deco accents. The mall's fairly standard food court offers a large variety of world cuisines to suit many different tastes.

JUPITER INLET LIGHTHOUSE, U.S. 1 and Alternate Fla. A1A, Jupiter. Tel. 747-6639.

Owned by the U.S. Coast Guard, this is the oldest extant structure in Palm Beach County. Congress appropriated funds for its construction in 1853, and the lights went on in 1860. The Loxahatchee Historical Society sponsors tours of the lighthouse every Sunday, enabling visitors to explore the cramped interior, which includes a small museum in the structure's base.

Admission: $3, which includes entrance to the Historical Society Museum and Pioneer Home (see below).

Open: Sun 1–4pm only.

LOXAHATCHEE HISTORICAL SOCIETY MUSEUM, 805 U.S. 1 N., in Burt Reynolds Park, Jupiter. Tel. 747-6639.

The museum's primary exhibit, "History Shaped by Nature," consists of various historical artifacts from ancient times up to today relating to Jupiter and its vicinity. The displays are arranged chronologically, from Seminole Indian utensils to Burt Reynolds's boots.

There are also guided tours of nearby historical sites—ask for a current schedule.

Admission: $3 adults, $2 seniors, $1 children.

Open: Tues–Fri 10am–4pm, Sat–Sun 1–4pm.

MARINELIFE CENTER OF JUNO BEACH, Loggerhead Park, 1200 U.S. 1, Juno Beach. Tel. 627-8280.

An indoor/outdoor attraction located in a public beachfront park, the Marinelife Center is a combination ecology museum and nature trail, focusing on life in and close to the sea. Visitors can learn about the unique ecosystem of South Florida's shores through hands-on exhibits and informative placards. Outdoor trails wind through dune vegetation, and live (although endangered) sea turtles (which nest nearby during the summer) are always on display.

Admission: Free; donations accepted.

Open: Tues–Sat 10am–3pm.

BEACHES & PARKS

As you head north from populated Palm Beach, Jupiter and North Palm Beach are the first bits of land you encounter, where castles and condominiums give way to open space and public parkland.

BLOWING ROCKS PRESERVE, Fla. A1A, Jupiter Island.
This wonderfully picturesque beach owes its beauty to a cluster of large rock formations. Although swimming is not recommended, Blowing Rocks is popular for fishing. There's a small parking lot, but no beach facilities. The preserve is a 10-minute drive from downtown Jupiter.

BURT REYNOLDS PARK, U.S. 1 N., Jupiter.
Surrounded by the Intracoastal Waterway, this rocky beach is well known to boaters and water-sports enthusiasts. There are picnic shelters, as well as boat slips for short-term visitors.

CARLIN COUNTY PARK, State Rd. (Fla. A1A), Jupiter.
Located just north of Indiantown Road, this busy park has a large oceanfront area complete with picnic tables, restrooms, a snack bar, tennis courts, a fitness track, and hiking trails.

JOHN D. MACARTHUR BEACH STATE PARK, 10900 State Rd. (Fla. A1A), Singer Island.
One of the area's largest parks, MacArthur has more than 8,000 feet of oceanfront beach, a nature center, and acres of park overlooking bucolic Lake Worth Cove. To reach the park from the mainland, cross the Intracoastal on Blue Heron Boulevard and turn north.

SCUBA DIVING & SNORKELING

North Palm's year-round, warm, clear waters make this area great for scuba diving and snorkeling. Several coral reefs are accessible by swimming from the water's edge, while others, farther offshore, are accessible by means of boats that make daily dive runs. Diving equipment can be rented and information can be obtained on the area's reefs from several local dive shops, including: **Gulf Stream Diver,** 278 Sussex Circle, Jupiter (tel. 575-9800); **Seafari Sport and Dive Shop,** 304 N. Old Dixie Hwy., Jupiter (tel. 747-6115); and **Subsea Aquatics,** 1870 U.S. 1, Jupiter (tel. 744-6674).

WHERE TO STAY

VERY EXPENSIVE

PGA NATIONAL RESORT, 400 Ave. of the Champions, Palm Beach Gardens, FL 33418. Tel. 407/627-2000, or toll free 800/633-9150. Fax 407/622-0261. 335 rms, 59 suites. A/C TV TEL MINIBAR **Directions:** From I-95, exit onto PGA Boulevard west and continue for approximately two miles to the resort entrance.

$ Rates: Dec 24–Apr 16, $285–$350 single or double; from $500 suite. Apr 17–May 22 and Sept 26–Dec 23, $225–$290 single or double; from $425 suite. May 23–Sept 25, $125–$175 single or double; from $235 suite. AE, DC, DISC, MC, V.

★ A resort in the fullest sense of the word, the PGA National is a 2,340-acre estate that encompasses five golf courses, 19 tennis courts, five racquetball courts, three swimming pools, mineral spas, workout rooms, and a private beach fronting a 26-acre, water-sports-filled lake. Originally known for its well-conditioned 18-hole golf courses, the resort has since added a full-service spa, which offers a variety of pamperings, including massage therapies, algae wraps, and facials. Heated mineral pools contain healing salts from both the Pyrenees Mountains and the Dead Sea. Staff experts offer comprehensive fitness evaluations, as well as courses and lectures on menu planning and healthy living.

Other resort facilities include top-of-the-line exercise equipment, croquet, and tennis courts. Special children's programs are offered.

PGA's welcoming Mediterranean-style lobby features terra-cotta tile floors topped with large area rugs and light, plush furniture. The newly renovated guest rooms, which extend into three separate wings, are equally well furnished, with dark carpets, bright contemporary prints, crown moldings, and oak cabinets. Every room has a private terrace or balcony. Conveniences include soft terrycloth robes, in-room safes, hairdryers, and contemporary white tile and marble baths.

Dining/Entertainment: There are seven restaurants on the premises. The Citrus Tree, a casual eatery, specializes in low-calorie and low-fat spa cuisine, and offers both indoor and outdoor seating. The dark and richly decorated Explorers Restaurant is the resort's top dining room, open for dinner only. Legends Lounge offers nightly entertainment during the season and weekend entertainment in the off-season.

Services: 24-hour room service, concierge, evening turn-down, overnight shoeshine, laundry, car rental, babysitting service.

Facilities: Five 18-hole golf courses, 19 clay tennis courts (12 lighted), three swimming pools, private beach on a 26-acre lake, water-sports rentals, five indoor racquetball courts, aerobics studio, mineral spas, salon.

EXPENSIVE

JUPITER BEACH HILTON, 5 N. Fla. A1A (at Indiantown Rd.), Jupiter, FL 33477. Tel. 407/746-2511. Fax 407/744-3304. 176 rms, 18 suites. A/C MINIBAR TV TEL

$ Rates: Jan 1–15, $95–$275 single or double; Jan 16–Apr, $140–$305 single or double; May–Dec, $90–$240 single or double. Jan 1–Apr, from $325 suite, May–Dec, from $250 suite. Additional person $20–$30 extra. AE, DC, DISC, MC, V.

Just a few miles north of Palm Beach, this bright retreat is suitable for couples and families looking for a high-quality, beachfront vacation. Oceanfront accommodations are the most expensive, but on the other side one can enjoy beautiful sunsets. Nearly all rooms have two double beds, and all have private balconies, sheer drapes, and beds with rattan headboards and seashell spreads.

The lobby and public areas have a Mediterranean feel, decorated in green marble, and feature arched doorways, wooden chandeliers, and plush pastel furniture.

Dining/Entertainment: Sinclair's Restaurant, founded by restaurateur Gordon Sinclair, serves an eclectic mix of continental, southwestern, and Caribbean cuisine. Bananas, situated just off the lobby, features live entertainment several nights a week. Three other pool and beach bars serve snacks and refreshments throughout the day.

Services: Room service, concierge, supervised children's programs, evening turn-down, overnight shoeshine, laundry, free transportation to local shopping areas.

Facilities: Swimming pool, tennis court, exercise room, boutique, dive shop, water-sports rentals, coin laundry, games room.

INEXPENSIVE

BARREN'S LANDING MOTEL, 18125 Ocean Blvd. (Fla. A1A), Jupiter, FL 33477. Tel. 407/746-8757. 8 rms. A/C TV **Directions:** From U.S. 1, exit onto Ocean Boulevard (Fla. A1A) east, just south of the Jupiter inlet; The hotel is on your right, on the corner of Love Street.

$ Rates: Dec 15–Apr, $75 single or double. May–Dec 14, $45 single or double. No credit cards.

There are relatively few rooms in this single-story, Intracoastal-front motel, and many of them are rented to "snowbirds" for weeks or months at a time. Some rooms have twin beds, while others have doubles; most offer foldout sofas or daybeds for larger parties. Nearly all rooms have small kitchenettes, which include a refrigerator, sink, microwave, and dishes. There are no phones in the rooms. A swimming pool is available on the premises.

WELLESLEY INN, 34 Fisherman's Wharf, Jupiter, FL 33477. Tel. 407/575-7201, or toll free 800/444-8888. Fax 407/575-1169. 105 rms, 12 suites. A/C TEL TV

$ Rates: Dec 25–Apr 15, $70 single or double; from $90 suite. Apr 16–Dec 24, $40 single or double; from $50 suite. AE, CB, DC, DISC, MC, V.

Behind a neocolonial facade, complete with white columns, arched windows, and a tall, tiled fountain, are 105 modestly decorated guest rooms, each with plain bedspreads, small tables, and compact dressers. Some rooms do not have complete closets, but rather a small railing for hanging clothes and few amenities. The minisuites are actually large double rooms, while the larger maxisuites are outfitted with sofa beds, refrigerators, and microwave ovens. There's a small swimming pool on the premises. The inn is conveniently located—near the Intracoastal Waterway and Fla. A1A.

WHERE TO DINE

VERY EXPENSIVE

ST. HONORE, 2401 PGA Blvd., Palm Beach Gardens. Tel. 627-9099 or 627-5994.

Cuisine: FRENCH/CONTINENTAL **Reservations:** Recommended.

$ Prices: Appetizers $10–$22; main courses $22–$32; fixed-price meals $5–$26 at lunch, $45 at dinner. AE, CB, DC, MC, V.

Open: Lunch Mon–Sat noon–2:30pm; dinner daily 6–10:30pm.

A French restaurant with a continental flair, St. Honoré is located upstairs in the Harbour Shops, a small shopping center in Palm Beach Gardens. Picturesque and romantic, the restaurant's decor includes lovely wood-beamed ceilings, pastel-colored tablecloths, and comfortable, oversize old-fashioned chairs. There is an intimate bar lined with teak, rattan stools, and small, salmon-colored marble tables. Beyond the French doors is an outdoor patio with potted plants and covered with a wooden trellis.

Some of the more imaginative entrees include roasted salmon with pesto, seafood fettuccine, sautéed veal sweetbreads with candied ginger, and beef tenderloin in muscat-raisin sauce. A typical starter is lobster bisque made with mango. The restaurant makes its own pastries and desserts, and offers a nice wine list.

EXPENSIVE

BACKSTAGE, 1061 E. Indiantown Rd. (just west of U.S. 1), Jupiter. Tel. 747-9533.

Cuisine: AMERICAN. **Reservations:** Required.

$ Prices: Appetizers $5–$8; main courses $13–$22. AE, CB, DC, MC, V.

Open: Lunch Mon–Fri 11:30am–2:30pm; dinner Sun–Thurs 5–9:30pm, Fri–Sat 5pm–midnight.

Formerly owned by Burt Reynolds, Backstage is a rather formal dining spot featuring tiered seating and black lacquered tables illuminated by tiny stage lights. The walls are decorated with black-and-white photographs of film stars and media personalities.

The menu emphasizes such American-style dishes as blackened prime rib, herb-roasted chicken, Florida lobster, and veal in champagne sauce. Appetizers include Cajun fried shrimp, stuffed mushrooms, and frogs' legs. Live jazz is performed during most meals.

HARPOON LOUIE'S, 1065 Fla. A1A Service Rd., Jupiter. Tel. 744-1300.

Cuisine: SEAFOOD/TROPICAL. **Reservations:** Not required.

$ Prices: Appetizers $3–$9; main courses $14–$22; breakfast $3–$7; lunch $5–$7. AE, CB, DC, DISC, MC, V.

Open: Dec–Apr, daily 8am–10pm. May–Nov, Mon–Sat 11am–10pm, Sun 8am–10pm.

A tropical island-kind of eatery filled with low rattan tables and floral cushions, this is the kind of place found in southern Florida and southern California that may surprise tourists from other parts of the country. Somewhat fancy, but quite informal, this waterfront restaurant offers indoor dining as well as a large outdoor deck equipped with heatlamps and glass-topped tables—a beautiful place to enjoy a piña colada or a Palm Beach punch while relishing the majestic views of the lighthouse just across the water.

At lunch, you might want to choose only an appetizer, like smoked Irish salmon with brown bread, Jamaican chicken wings, or fried Florida alligator. There is also a selection of salads, soups, and seafood-topped pizzas. Jamaican-style chicken and pastas are available at dinner, but you would do better to choose one of the many seafood dishes like phyllo-wrapped grouper with lobster-basil sauce, fried coconut shrimp, or the fish of the day (grilled, broiled, or blackened).

MODERATE

LOG CABIN RESTAURANT, 631 N. Fla. A1A, Jupiter. Tel. 746-6877.

Cuisine: AMERICAN. **Reservations:** Not accepted.

$ Prices: Appetizers $1–$8; main courses $4–$16. AE, CB, DC, DISC, MC, V.

This restaurant is really housed in a log cabin. When you step up onto the wide porch and enter through the front door, you'll find yourself in a warm, snug home that is actually quite beautiful. Furnishings include antique clocks, sleds, framed yellowed newspaper articles, old bottles, and moonshine jugs, many of which hang from the vaulted ceiling. To reach the dining room, stay to the left; for the bar, go to your right.

Menu offerings include large portions of pit-smoked barbecued ribs, beef, and chicken, as well as deep-fried seafood. Standard favorites such as chili, beef stew, meatloaf, and burgers are also available. Traditional desserts—including pecan pie and sweet-potato pie—are homemade.

PARKER'S LIGHTHOUSE, in the Harbour Shops, 180 Rue de la Mer, Palm Beach Gardens. Tel. 627-0000.

Cuisine: SEAFOOD/CONTINENTAL. **Reservations:** Recommended.

$ Prices: Appetizers $3–$11; main courses $11–$20; lunch $5–$12. AE, DC, DISC, MC, V.

Open: Mon–Thurs 11:30am–10pm, Fri–Sat 11:30am–11pm; Sun brunch 11am–2:30pm, dinner 5–9pm (bar, Sun–Thurs until midnight, Fri–Sat until 1am).

Architecturally, this is one of the most unusual restaurants I've ever visited. Under a towering central skylight, designed to resemble a lighthouse, are three floors—the top two connected by a spiral staircase. The first floor contains the restaurant's glass-enclosed kitchen, fitted with red carpeting and nautical decor. The second floor, which is for dining, has tables situated next to glass walls; diners are treated to magnificent views of the luxury yacht harbor. The top floor has a wood-paneled lounge, built around a Z-shaped bar that serves drinks and snacks until late. Wrap-around windows offer panoramic harbor views.

The restaurant emphasizes fresh seafood appetizers and entrees, although Caesar salad with grilled chicken, prime rib, Thai-style chicken, and a small selection of sandwiches are also available.

SCHOONERS, 1001 N. Fla. A1A, at Love St. Jupiter. Tel. 746-7558.

Cuisine: SEAFOOD/AMERICAN. **Reservations:** Not required.

$ Prices: Appetizers $3–$7; main courses $11–$18; lunch $3–$10. AE, MC, V.

Open: Lunch daily 11am–4:30pm; dinner daily 5–9:30pm.

Schooners is especially recommended for warm afternoons when you can sit outside on the restaurant's large covered patio. Inside is a dark bar and dining room featuring such nautical decor as fish nets, boating lights, and schools of mounted fish.

The lunch menu includes burgers, deep-fried fish, and a large assortment of sandwiches. Dinners begin with an extensive choice of starters, from steamed mussels to honey-dipped chicken wings. An even longer list of entrees reads like a veritable survey of seaside American cooking, from fresh fish to pastas and prime New York strip steak.

Fishermen and other locals comprise most of the Schooners' clientele; they know a good and friendly place when they see one.

WATERWAY CAFE, 2300 PGA Blvd., Palm Beach Gardens. Tel. 694-1700.

Cuisine: SEAFOOD/AMERICAN. **Reservations:** Not required.

$ Prices: Appetizers $5–$9; main courses $11–$19; lunch $6–$8. AE, MC, V.

Open: Mon–Thurs 11:30am–10pm, Fri–Sat 11:30am–11pm, Sun 4–11pm (bar, open later).

Large, open, bright, and cheery, the Waterway Café is yet another good choice, overlooking the Intracoastal Waterway. Wooden crew boats, sporting Ivy League insignia, hang from the ceiling. Large, leafy plants, which adorn the well-polished light-wood floors, are highlighted by the sun that streams in through a domed skylight. Additional tables outdoors enable diners to see the restaurant's boat slips and floating tiki bar, which is equipped with lifevests for tipsy drinkers.

Raw oysters and clams are recommended for those who like them. Other good lunch choices include chilled poached salmon, crab cakes, and an assortment of sandwiches, salads, and pastas. Dinners are equally straightforward. Conch fritters and peel-and-eat shrimp make great starters, perhaps followed by shrimp, dolphin (fish), sea-scallop casserole, or stir-fried steak and shrimp. Pasta dishes are always available, as are salads and burgers. Plan to save room for the delectable Mississippi mud pie.

INEXPENSIVE

CHILI'S GRILL & BAR, 65 U.S. 1, at Indiantown Rd., Jupiter. Tel. 576-6900.

Cuisine: SOUTHWESTERN. **Reservations:** Not accepted.

$ Prices: Appetizers $4–$6; main courses $6–$15; lunch $3–$10. AE, DISC, MC, V.

Open: Sun–Thurs 11:30am–11pm, Fri–Sat 11:30am–midnight.

A chain restaurant in the Bennigan style, Chili's southwestern cuisine offers diners a welcome break from the usual Florida emphasis on fish. Brightly tiled table tops, copper lamps, green window shutters, and lots of plants hint at America's Southwest. But the enormous bar, which offers regular drink specials and televised sports, was clearly designed for the restaurant's local patrons.

The restaurant offers the same menu all day. The best appetizers are the fried mozzarella sticks, fried whole onions (served with an unusual seasoned sauce), and spicy buffalo chicken wings. Recommended main dishes include vegetarian soft tacos, shrimp Caesar salad, and fajitas (my favorite), which are served with an audible sizzle. Go elsewhere for dessert.

EVENING ENTERTAINMENT

THE PERFORMING ARTS

BURT REYNOLDS INSTITUTE FOR THEATER TRAINING, 304 Tequesta Dr., Tequesta. Tel. 746-8887.

Founded in 1979, this institute offers an apprenticeship program for promising young actors from across the country. Well-known professionals perform with the students in comedies, dramas, and musicals. There are both matinee and evening performances; call for a current schedule.

Admission: Tickets, $15–$20.

JUPITER DINNER THEATER, 1001 E. Indiantown Rd. at Fla. A1A, Jupiter. Tel. 746-5566.

Year-round productions include Broadway musicals and hit comedies. Original works are occasionally staged here, and top theater and film performers often appear in the cast. Dinner precedes the show; phone to find out what's on the menu.

Admission: Tickets, $40–$75.

THE CLUB & MUSIC SCENE

CLUB SAFARI, in the Marriott Hotel, 4000 RCA Blvd., Palm Beach Gardens. Tel. 662-8888.

I'm always skeptical about dance clubs in hotels, but this one is more hip than most, even if the safari theme is taken a bit too far. The huge, sunken dance floor is surrounded by vines and lanky, potted trees. Nearby, a large Buddha statue blows steam and smoke while waving its burly arms. Fake rocks are everywhere, sometimes concealing flame-shooting pots. There is DJ music, a large video screen, and a cover charge on the weekends. It's open Monday through Friday from 5pm to 3am and on Saturday and Sunday from 8pm to 3am.

Admission: Free Sun–Thurs, $5–$10 Fri–Sat.

JOX SPORTS CLUB, 200 N. U.S. 1, Jupiter. Tel. 744-6600.

The players are not just on television here—in this participatory-sports bar the patrons are encouraged to shoot hoops as well as pool. It's not just a jock joint, though. There's DJ dancing, several fully stocked bars, and a friendly atmosphere. Open Sunday through Thursday from 8pm to 2am and on Friday and Saturday from 8pm to 3am.

Admission: Free.

BACKSTAGE, 1060 E. Indiantown Rd. (just west of U.S. 1), Jupiter. Tel. 747-9533.

We recommended Backstage as a restaurant (see "Where to Dine," above), but it is also a good place for drinks and entertainment; live jazz is featured almost every night of the week. Open daily from 5pm to midnight.

Admission: Free.

WATERWAY CAFE, 2300 PGA Blvd., Palm Beach Gardens. Tel. 694-1700.

Two large bars inside and one floating on the water in back make the Waterway a great place for an afternoon or evening drink. There's usually live reggae every Sunday afternoon and Wednesday evenings (see "Where to Dine," above, for additional information). Open on Monday, Tuesday, and Thursday from 11:30am to 11pm; on Wednesday, Friday, and Saturday from 11:30am to 1am; and on Sunday from 4 to 11pm.

2. THE PALM BEACHES

26 miles N of Miami, 193 miles E of Tampa

GETTING THERE **By Plane** The **Palm Beach International Airport** (tel. 407/471-7420) is easy to negotiate and a pleasure to use. Volunteer "Airport Ambassadors," recognizable by their distinctive teal-green shirts and jackets, are nearly always on hand to help visitors with free information. Major domestic carriers using the airport include American (tel. toll free 800/433-7300), Continental (tel. 407/832-5200, or toll free 800/525-0280), Delta (tel. 407/655-5300, or toll free 800/221-1212), Northwest (tel. toll free 800/225-2525), TWA (tel. 407/655-3776, or toll free 800/221-2000), and United (tel. toll free 800/241-6522).

By Train Amtrak (tel. toll free 800/USA-RAIL) trains from New York stop in

West Palm Beach on their way to Miami. The local station is at 201 S. Tamarind Ave., West Palm Beach (tel. 407/832-6169).

By Bus Greyhound/Trailways can get you to the Palm Beaches from almost anywhere. The company no longer operates a single nationwide telephone number, so consult your local directory for the office nearest you.

By Car If you're driving up or down the Florida coast, you'll probably reach the Palm Beach area on I-95, a highway that extends all the way from Maine to Miami. Visitors on their way to or from Orlando should take the Florida Turnpike, a toll road that runs almost directly from this county's beaches to Walt Disney World. Finally, if you're coming from Florida's west coast, you can take either Fla. 70, which runs north of Lake Okeechobee to Fort Pierce, or Fla. 80, which runs south of the lake to Palm Beach.

ESSENTIALS The **telephone area code** is 407. The **Palm Beach County Convention and Visitors Bureau,** 1555 Palm Beach Lakes Blvd., Suite 204, West Palm Beach, FL 33401 (tel. 407/471-3995, or toll free 800/554-PALM), distributes an informative brochure, and will answer questions about visiting the Palm Beaches. Ask for a map as well as a copy of their Arts and Attractions Calendar, a day-by-day guide to art, music, stage, and other events in the county.

Palm Beach is an island, both literally and figuratively. Located just across the Intracoastal Waterway from West Palm Beach on the mainland, this area boasts one of the highest concentrations of expensive mansions and estates in the world. It is really astonishing to drive around Palm Beach and see so many elegant homes. Palm Beach has been the traditional winter home of America's super-rich—the Kennedys, the Rockefellers, the Trumps, well-to-do heirs and heiresses, and top-echelon CEOs. For tourists, a visit here means marvelous restaurants, great golfing, and spectacular sightseeing.

West Palm Beach, by contrast, is somewhat more work-oriented. With the exception of some wonderful (but expensive) golfing communities, the mainland is less extravagant and more commercial than its richer offshore counterpart.

WHAT TO SEE & DO

DREHER PARK ZOO, 1301 Summit Blvd., West Palm Beach. Tel. 533-0887.

More than 400 different animals inhabit this 25-acre zoo. Several endangered species are on display, including the Florida panther and the mouse-sized marmoset. It's worth going just for the unusual reptile exhibit.

Admission: $5 adults, $3.50 children, $4.50 seniors, free for children under 3.

Open: Daily 9am–5pm (last admission at 4:30pm).

HENRY MORRISON FLAGLER MUSEUM, Cocoanut Row, Palm Beach. Tel. 655-2833.

Henry Flagler probably had a greater influence on South Florida's development than any other individual. Cofounder of the Standard Oil Company, the future-oriented businessman built the railroad that would eventually link Jacksonville with Key West.

The museum that now bears his name was originally a mansion called Whitehall, built by Flagler in 1901 for his third wife, Mary Lily Kenan. In 1960 one of his granddaughters had the house restored to its original turn-of-the-century condition, including many of the home's original furnishings. "The Rambler," Mr. Flagler's beautifully outfitted personal railroad car dating from 1886, is also on display.

Admission: $5 adults, $2 children.

Open: Tues–Sat 10am–5pm, Sun noon–5pm.

LION COUNTRY SAFARI, Southernmost Blvd. W., West Palm Beach. Tel. 793-1084.

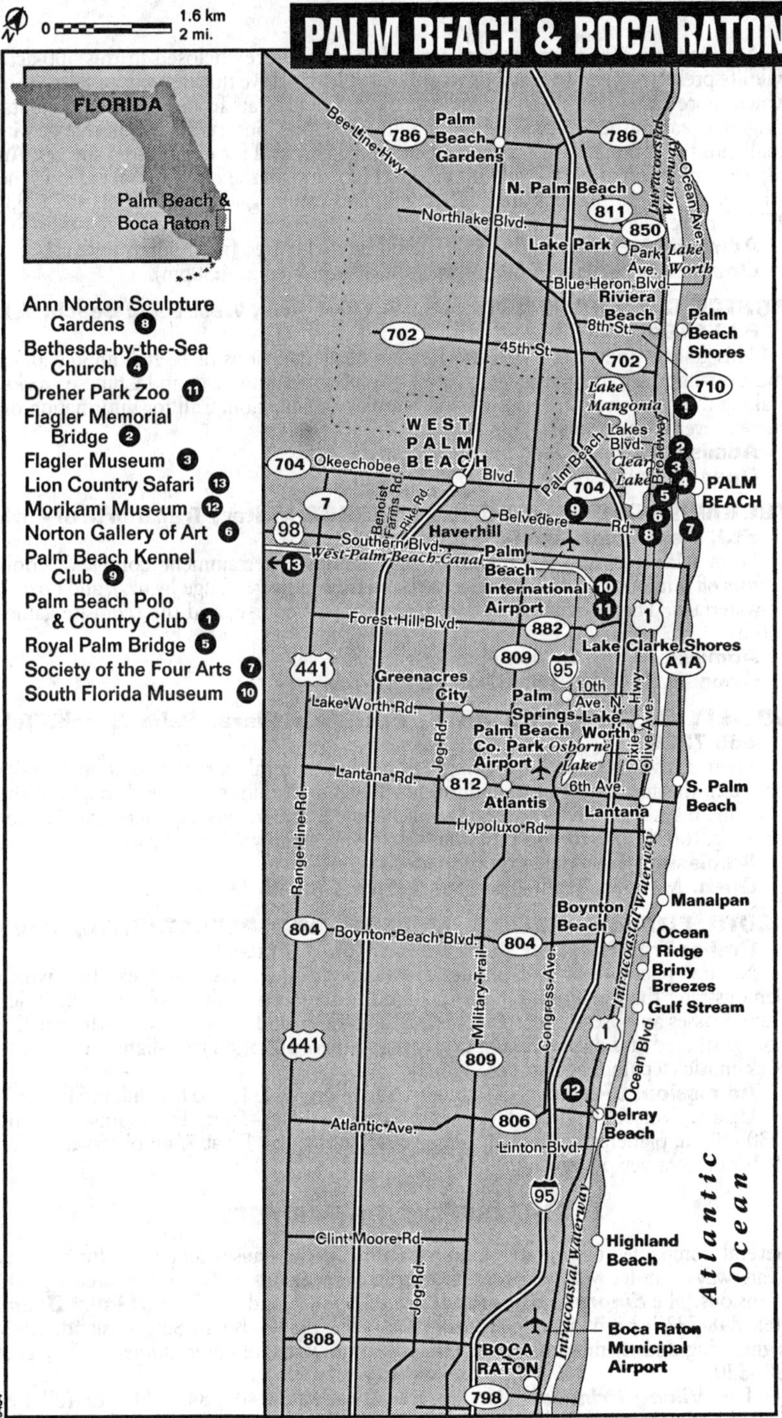

PALM BEACH & BOCA RATON
0
1.6 km
2 mi.
N
FLORIDA
Palm Beach & Boca Raton
Ann Norton Sculpture Gardens 8
Bethesda-by-the-Sea Church 4
Dreher Park Zoo 11
Flagler Memorial Bridge 2
Flagler Museum 3
Lion Country Safari 13
Morikami Museum 12
Norton Gallery of Art 6
Palm Beach Kennel Club 9
Palm Beach Polo & Country Club 1
Royal Palm Bridge 5
Society of the Four Arts 7
South Florida Museum 10
Bee Line Hwy
786
Palm Beach Gardens
N. Palm Beach
811
Northlake Blvd.
850
Lake Park
Park Ave.
Lake Worth
Intracoastal Waterway
Ocean Ave.
Blue Heron Blvd.
Riviera Beach
8th St.
Palm Beach Shores
702
45th St.
710
Lake Mangonia
Lakes Blvd.
Clear Lake
Broadway
Palm Beach
WEST PALM BEACH
704
Okeechobee Blvd.
PALM BEACH
7
Benoist Farms Rd
Pike Rd.
Belvedere Rd.
Haverhill
98
Southern Blvd.
West Palm Beach Canal
Palm Beach International Airport
13
Forest Hill Blvd.
882
1
Lake Clarke Shores
809
95
A1A
441
Greenacres City
Palm Springs
10th Ave. N.
Lake Worth
Lake Worth Rd.
Hwy
Dixie
Olive Ave.
Palm Beach Co. Park Airport
Osborne Lake
Lantana Rd.
812
Jog Rd.
6th Ave.
S. Palm Beach
Atlantis
Lantana
Hypoluxo Rd.
Range Line Rd.
Intracoastal Waterway
Manalpan
Boynton Beach
804
Boynton Beach Blvd.
Ocean Ridge
Briny Breezes
Military Trail
Congress Ave.
Gulf Stream
Ocean Blvd.
12
Delray Beach
806
Atlantic Ave.
Linton Blvd.
Atlantic Ocean
Clint Moore Rd.
Highland Beach
Jog Rd.
Boca Raton Municipal Airport
808
BOCA RATON
798
Airport
5434

More than 1,300 animals from around the world are enclosed in this 500-acre wildlife preserve. Keep your windows rolled up as you drive through this cageless zoo, which more or less faithfully reproduces the native habitats from various continents. Originally established to provide entertainment, Lion Country Safari has changed its goal with the times; now it's a protected breeding ground for endangered species. An adjacent amusement park is still intended as fun, and all the rides are included in the price of admission. Picnics are encouraged, and camping is available (tel. 407/793-9797 for overnight reservations).

Admission: $11.95 adults, $9.95 children 4–11, free for children under 4.

Open: Daily 9:30am–5:30pm (last vehicle admitted at 4:30pm).

NORTON GALLERY OF ART, 1451 S. Olive Ave., West Palm Beach. Tel. 832-5194.

This gallery houses one of Palm Beach's best collections of French impressionist and post-impressionist paintings, as well as renowned American and Chinese works, making the Norton an especially good rainy-day destination. Call for information on current events and shows.

Admission: Free; $5 donation suggested.

Open: Tues–Sat 10am–5pm, Sun 1–5pm.

THE RAPIDS GOLF, SLIDE AND BANKSHOT, Military Trail (north of 45th St.), West Palm Beach. Tel. 848-6272.

From March through September, this "family entertainment complex" cools visitors off with four gigantic water slides, an artificial river, a huge Jacuzzi, and dozens of waterfalls. There's also a 19-hole miniature golf course, and the requisite games room.

Admission: $13, $8 after 4pm.

Open: Daily 10am–8pm. **Closed:** Oct–Feb.

SOCIETY OF THE FOUR ARTS, Four Arts Plaza, Palm Beach. Tel. 655-7226.

There's always something going on in this cultural complex that includes a museum, theater, library, and auditorium. Local art exhibits change throughout the year, and plays and movies are regularly scheduled. The society's gardens are great for strolling, too. Phone to find out what's going on when you're in town.

Admission: Free; donation requested.

Open: Mon–Sat 10am–5pm, Sun 2–5pm. **Closed:** May–Nov.

SOUTH FLORIDA SCIENCE MUSEUM AND PLANETARIUM, 4801 Dreher Trail N., West Palm Beach. Tel. 832-1988.

Natural phenomena and physics are taught through hands-on exhibits which demonstrate the qualities of light, sound, energy, and the like. The complex encompasses an observatory, planetarium, aquarium, and a plant center, where native flora is studied and displayed. On Friday night, there are often laser-light shows set to rock music (separate admission).

Admission: $5 adults, $4.50 seniors, $2 children 5–11, free for children under 5.

Open: Museum, Tues–Thurs and Sat–Sun 10am–5pm, Fri 10am–5pm and 6:30–10pm; planetarium, shows Tues–Fri at 1 and 3pm, Fri at 7pm; observatory, Fri 8–10pm, weather permitting.

SIGHTSEEING/DAY CRUISES

Several companies offer water tours of Palm Beach, cruises along the Intracoastal Waterway that let you take an unobstructed peek at some of the area's grand mansions. The ***Empress Showboat*** (tel. 842-0882), and the ***Star of Palm Beach*** (tel. 848-7827) both operate from 900 E. Blue Heron Blvd., Singer Island. Daily sightseeing and theme cruises are offered, some with live entertainment. They cost $8–$30.

The ***Viking Princess,*** Port of Palm Beach (tel. 407/845-7447, or toll free 800/841-7447), offers half-day brunch and dinner ocean cruises, as well as one-day excursions to The Bahamas. A breakfast buffet and five-course dinner are served on the way to and from the island. Evening cruises cost $40–$50, brunch trips cost $60, and the Bahama island voyage costs $80.

SPORTS & RECREATION

Spectator Sports

GREYHOUND RACING Greyhounds, the world's fastest dogs, have been racing at the **Palm Beach Kennel Club,** 1119 N. Congress Ave., at Belvedere Rd., in West Palm Beach (tel. 683-2222), since 1932. Able to reach speeds of more than 40 miles an hour, the dogs chase a fake rabbit around the track while punters place bets to win, place, or show. There is racing year-round; call for post times. Admission is 50¢–$2, free on Sunday.

JAI ALAI Jai alai, a Spanish cross between lacrosse and handball, is popular in South Florida. Players use woven baskets, called cestas, to hurl balls, called pelotas, at speeds that sometimes exceed 170 miles per hour. Spectators, who are protected behind a wall of glass, place bets on the evening's players.

Games are played from September through July in West Palm Beach at the **Palm Beach Jai Alai Fronton,** 1415 45th St., in West Palm Beach (tel. 844-2444). Admission is 50¢–$5 and the games begin Tuesday at 6:30pm, Wednesday through Saturday at 1 and 6:30pm, and on Sunday at 1pm.

POLO The **Palm Beach Polo and Country Club,** 13198 Forest Hill Blvd., West Palm Beach (tel. 407/793-1440, or toll free 800/327-4204), is one of the world's premier polo grounds. This posh West Palm Beach club attracts some of this aristocratic sport's best players. Matches are open to the public and celebrities are often in attendance. Star-watchers have spotted Prince Charles, the Duchess of York, Sylvester Stallone, and Ivana Trump here, among others. General admission is $5; box seats cost $14. Matches are held on Sunday at 3pm, December to March.

Participatory Sports

BEACHES Most of Palm Beach's best beachfront real estate is now part of someone's private estate, raising the public beaches here to an almost sacred stature.

Palm Beach Municipal Beach, located on Fla. A1A, just south of West Palm's Royal Park Bridge, is small, undeveloped, and undercelebrated. **Phipps Ocean Park,** located on Ocean Boulevard between the Southern Boulevard and Lake Avenue causeways, is large and lively, encompassing over 1,300 feet of groomed and guarded oceanfront. There are picnic and recreation areas here as well as plenty of parking.

BICYCLING Palm Beach is great for biking. It's flat, and there are several trails that take you places that cars just can't go. The **Palm Beach Bicycle Trail Shop,** 223 Sunrise Ave. (tel. 659-4583), rents bicycles for $6.50 an hour or $20 a day, and they will be happy to direct you to the trails.

GOLF There's good golfing here, but many of the private club courses are maintained exclusively for the use of their members. Ask at your hotel, or contact the Palm Beach Convention and Visitors Bureau (tel. 407/471-3995) for information on which clubs are available for play.

From May to October or November, close to a dozen private golf courses open their greens to visitors who are staying in a Palm Beach County hotel. This "Golf-A-Round" program is free (carts are additional), and reservations can be made through most major hotels.

The **Palm Beach Public Golf Course,** 2345 S. Ocean Blvd. (tel. 407/547-0598), a popular public 18-hole course, is a par 58 with greens that are between 100 and 235 yards from the tee. Open at 8am, the course is run on a first-come, first-served basis. There are no club rentals. Green fees are $15.50 per person.

SCUBA DIVING & SNORKELING Year-round warm waters, barrier reefs, and plenty of wrecks make South Florida one of the world's most popular places for diving. One of the best-known artificial reefs in this area is a vintage Rolls-Royce Silver Shadow which was sunk offshore in 1985.

Several local dive shops rent equipment and dispense information on the area's reefs. They include: **Aqua Shop,** 505 Northlake Blvd., North Palm Beach (tel. 848-9042); **Atlantic Underwater,** 901 Cracker St., West Palm Beach (tel. 686-7066); **Dixie Divers,** 1401 S. Military Trail, West Palm Beach (tel. 969-6688); and **Ocean Sports Scuba Center,** 1736 S. Congress Ave., West Palm Beach (tel. 641-1144).

TENNIS Several places offer tennis courts on a first-come, first-served basis. All the following are in West Palm Beach:

Coleman Park, 1116 21st St. (tel. 688-6300), has just two courts, and although they're not lighted, they are free.

Currie Park, 2400 N. Flagler Dr. (tel. 688-6300), another public park, has three lighted hard courts. There is no charge for their use.

The nine hard courts in the **South Olive Tennis Center,** 345 Summa St. (tel. 582-7218), are all lighted and open to the public. The center is located close to Dixie Highway, just south of Forest Hill Boulevard. Courts cost $3 per person per hour.

WHERE TO STAY

VERY EXPENSIVE

BREAKERS HOTEL, 1 S. County Rd. Palm Beach, FL 33480. Tel. 407/655-6611, or toll free 800/833-3141. Fax 407/659-8403. 528 rms, 40 suites. A/C MINIBAR TV TEL **Directions:** From I-95, exit onto Okeechobee Boulevard east, and turn north onto South County Road; the hotel is just ahead on your right.

$ Rates: Dec 17–Apr 10, $280–$480 single or double; from $430 suite. May 28–Sept, $125–$270 single or double; from $255 suite. Apr 11–May 27 and Oct–Dec 16, $200–$440 single or double; from $360 suite. Additional person $15 extra. AE, CB, DC, DISC, MC, V.

The grand dame of South Florida hostelries, and a tourist attraction in its own right, the Breakers was Palm Beach's first major hotel, built by railroad magnate Henry Flagler in the early 1900s. After two fires, a couple of rebuilds, and a handful of additions and face-lifts, the hotel has been transformed into the celebrated structure you see today, complete with its trademark sandstone exterior and twin belvedere towers. Architect Leonard Schultze designed this elaborate masterpiece to resemble an Italian palace, crowned with hand-painted frescoed ceilings inside and a Florentine fountain out front. The grand gilded lobby, dripping with crystal chandeliers, is dressed with taffeta-and tapestry-covered furnishings, and features floor-to-ceiling French doors that open into a huge inner courtyard bubbling with its own fountains.

Although the hotel's guest rooms can't compare to the opulence of the public areas, accommodations are fine indeed, trimmed with little glass wall sconces and custom-framed artwork. In addition to the expected amenities, all accommodations include in-room safes and clock radios. The light marble bathrooms have a telephone, hairdryer, scale, and plush robes. There is also a separate vanity area.

Dining/Entertainment: There are six restaurants in the hotel. The window-walled Circle Dining Room serves breakfast daily in a beautiful setting with painted ceiling scenes of Italian cities and Monte Carlo and a huge, outstanding center skylight. The large Florentine Room has beamed ceilings and formal touches while live music plays to dinner guests. The Fairways Café and the Beach Club offer light snacks and refreshments. The Beach Club Patio surrounds an indoor (though unused) pool and serves meals all day as well as a Sunday buffet brunch attracting many locals.

Services: 24-hour room service, concierge, business center, evening turn-down, overnight shoeshine, massages.

Facilities: Two golf courses, 20 tennis courts (5 lighted), heated swimming pool, private beach, putting green, water-sports and bicycle rentals, children's playground, health club, shopping arcade, croquet, shuffleboard, beach volleyball courts.

THE OCEAN GRAND, 2800 S. Ocean Blvd., Palm Beach, FL 33480. Tel. 407/582-2800, or toll free 800/432-2335. Fax 407/547-1557. 210 rms, 14 suites. A/C MINIBAR TV TEL **Directions:** From I-95, take the Sixth Avenue exit east and turn left onto Big Sea Highway; then turn east onto Lake Avenue and north onto South Ocean Boulevard; and the hotel is just ahead on your right.

$ Rates: Dec 17–Apr 11, $290–$465 single or double; from $750 suite. May 28–Sept, $145–$225 single or double; from $500 suite. Apr 12–May 27 and Oct–Dec 16, $220–$380 single or double; from $600 suite. Additional person $25 extra. AE, MC, V.

Opened in 1990, this premier lodging is one of the newest additions to an ever-growing list of prestigious Palm Beach retreats. Guests are welcomed by an elegant cream-marble lobby tastefully decorated with antique European furnishings and original art. In both the lobby and the adjoining lounge, intimate tables and love seats are separated from one another by lofty palms and towering white columns.

Ocean views can be enjoyed from almost every guest room in the house. Each room has its own private balcony and is decorated in cool oceanic colors. Armoires hide a stereo system, TV, VCR, and minibar. Most rooms also have king-size beds and safes, with hairdryers, scales, and bathrobes in the good-size gray-and-white marble bathrooms. The hotel's "Club" rooms are a bit larger, and include access to a club lounge, where continental breakfast, afternoon refreshments, and evening cocktails are served gratis. Suites include an additional sitting room, oversize balconies, and two bathrooms.

A year-round "Kid's Club" offers supervised activities for children 3–12. In the morning, indoor and outdoor events include water sports, crab races, scavenger hunts, puppet shows, and arts and crafts. In the afternoon, the club opens up to the entire family, offering bike rides, fishing tournaments, and excursions to nearby Lion Country Safari (see "What to See and Do," above).

Dining/Entertainment: The hotel's signature restaurant, simply called "The Restaurant," serves an eclectic variety of dishes utilizing local ingredients and European cooking methods. The more casual Ocean Bistro serves breakfast, lunch, and dinner outdoors, overlooking the Atlantic. The elegant and comfortable Living Room lounge is one of the best places in town for an intimate cocktail. A live jazz trio performs here Friday and Saturday evenings, and a pianist plays every afternoon.

Services: 24-hour room service, concierge, evening turn-down, complimentary transportation to Worth Avenue, bicycle rentals, aerobics classes, overnight laundry and shoeshine, babysitting, massage.

Facilities: Three tennis courts, swimming pool, sauna, whirlpool, water-sports rentals, gym and health spa (offering body treatments and facials), beauty salon, gift shop.

RITZ-CARLTON, PALM BEACH, 100 S. Ocean Blvd., Manalapan, FL 33462. Tel. 407/533-6000, or toll free 800/241-3333. Fax 407/588-4555. 214 rms, 56 suites. A/C MINIBAR TV TEL **Directions:** From I-95, take Exit 45 (Hypoluxo Road) east; after a mile, turn left onto Federal Highway (U.S. 1), continue north for about one mile, and turn right onto Ocean Avenue; cross the Intracoastal Waterway, turn right onto South Ocean Boulevard, and the hotel is just ahead on your left.

$ Rates: Dec 13–Apr, $310–$500 standard single or double; $550–$600 Club-level single or double; from $860 suite. May 1–27, $220–$365 standard single or double; $415–$465 Club-level single or double; from $680 suite. May 28–Dec 12, $125–$230 standard single or double; $280–$330 Club-level single or double; from $525 suite. AE, DC, DISC, MC, V.

Like most of the members of the upscale Ritz-Carlton chain, the Palm Beach hostelry occupies an architecturally grand building with a prominent sandstone facade. Visitors enter an elegant and dramatic lobby dominated by a pink-marble fireplace. The lobby bar is outfitted with antique coffee tables, tapestry-covered furniture, and gold candelabra. Afternoon tea is served daily, but is best Wednesday through Saturday, when a jazz trio entertains.

Three towers of rooms are decorated in organic colors. Furnishings include marble writing desks and gilded mirrors; among other luxuries are marble baths with separate showers and tubs, double vanities, wall safes, three telephones, terrycloth robes, and private balconies. The hotel's Club level, popular with business travelers, offers concierge service and a lounge where complimentary continental breakfasts, midafternoon snacks, and evening cordials are served.

Dining/Entertainment: The elegant Dining Room serves continental-style dinners in ornate surroundings. Other restaurants on the property include the Grill, open for dinner only; the Restaurant, which serves all day; and the poolside Ocean Café and Bar, which is open from lunch until late. Cocktails are also served in the lobby lounge, and live entertainment is usually scheduled somewhere on the property every day of the week.

Services: 24-hour room service, concierge, complimentary airport transportation, evening turn-down, overnight laundry and shoeshine, babysitting, massage.

Facilities: Seven tennis courts, heated swimming pool, sauna, whirlpool, steam room, health club, scuba and snorkeling concessions, beauty salon, gift shop, bicycle rentals.

EXPENSIVE

CHESTERFIELD HOTEL DELUXE, 363 Cocoanut Row, Palm Beach, FL 33480. Tel. 407/659-5800, or toll free 800/243-7871. Fax 407/659-6707. 65 rms. A/C TV TEL **Directions:** From I-95, exit onto Okeechobee Boulevard east, cross the Intracoastal Waterway, and turn right on Cocoanut Row; the hotel is ahead, on your left, just past Australian Avenue.

$ Rates: Dec 14–Apr 2, $175–$250 single or double; from $375 suite. Apr 3–Dec 13, $75–$125 single or double; from $175 suite. AE, CB, DC, MC, V.

Less ostentatious than most of its expensive rivals, the intimate Chesterfield is packed with a discreet old-world charm. Its location, just one block from Worth Avenue, has made it popular with in-the-know visitors since the 1920s. Behind a light stucco exterior, enlivened with arched windows and colorful flags, is an overly designed lobby composed of contrasting furnishings and fabrics. The Chesterfield's English country manor style is evident in the wood-paneled library, just off the lobby. Dark wooden bookshelves filled with volumes are not just for show; guests are encouraged to browse and to borrow. Afternoon tea is served here daily from 3 to 5pm.

Lemon-yellow hallways with gold-leaf mirrors and ornately framed paintings lead to Laura Ashley rooms with brass knockers on the doors. Heavy wooden furniture and plush red carpets give each room a warm feeling. Baths are marble, and other pleasant touches such as thick terrycloth robes, armfuls of fresh flowers, and fluffy towels give the rooms a special homey feel.

Dining/Entertainment: Butler's, the hotel's primary dining room, serves respectable French favorites all day; reservations are essential for dinner. The Leopard lounge, named for the print that predominates here, serves light meals and cocktails throughout the day. There is live music here most evenings and on Sunday afternoons.

Services: 24-hour room service, concierge, complimentary transportation to local attractions, overnight laundry and shoeshine.

Facilities: Swimming pool, whirlpool.

PLAZA INN, 215 Brazilian Ave., Palm Beach, FL 33480. Tel. 407/832-8666, or toll free 800/233-2632. Fax 407/835-8776. 50 rms, 1 suite. A/C MINIBAR TV TEL **Directions:** From I-95, exit onto Okeechobee Boulevard east, cross the Intracoastal Waterway, turn right onto Cocoanut Row, then left onto Brazilian Avenue; the hotel is just ahead on your left.

$ Rates (including breakfast): Dec 15–Apr, $115–$165 single or double; from $195 suite. May–Dec 14, $65–$85 single or double; from $125 suite. Additional person $15 extra. AE, MC, V.

From the moment you arrive at this luxurious bed-and-breakfast, you are overcome with the feeling that you're visiting good friends at their summer home. A bright and shiny ground-floor entrance hall is made even warmer by a beautiful antique writing table, a grand piano, and lovely pastel wallcoverings.

Each and every individually decorated room exudes charm. Several contain carved four-poster beds, hand-crocheted spreads, lace curtains, and pastel-colored taffeta shower curtains; every room is dressed with the same meticulous attention to detail found throughout the inn.

Dining/Entertainment: A full cooked-to-order breakfast that includes fresh fruit, breakfast breads, and hot entrees, is served each morning in a delightful dining room designed with lace-covered tables, fresh flowers, and crystal chandeliers. Except for breakfast, no other meals are served in the hotel. The cozy Stray Fox Pub, a comfortable little bar with mahogany tables, serves cocktails throughout the evening.

Services: Concierge.

Facilities: Heated swimming pool, Jacuzzi.

MODERATE

BEACHCOMBER SEA CAY MOTER APARTMENTS, 3024 S. Ocean Blvd. (Fla. A1A), Palm Beach, FL 33480. Tel. 407/585-4646, or toll free 800/833-7122. Fax 407/547-9438. 46 rms, 4 suites. A/C TV TEL **Directions:** From I-95, exit onto Lake Worth Road east, stay to the right and take Lake Avenue over the Intracoastal Waterway, then turn right onto South Ocean Boulevard; the hotel is just ahead on your left.

$ Rates: Dec 20–Jan 14, $60–$100 single or double; from $110 suite. Jan 15–Apr 11, $75–$130 single or double; from $140 suite. Apr 12–Oct, $42–$68 single or double; from $75 suite. Nov–Dec 19, $45–$95 single or double; from $100 suite. Additional person $10 extra. Weekly rates available. AE, DISC, MC, V.

Because it's bright pink, this squat, two-story motel stands out among the high-rise buildings that surround it. For more than 35 years, the Beachcomber has been bringing sanity to tab-happy Palm Beach, offering a good standard of accommodation at reasonable prices. It's located directly on the beach, a short drive from Worth Avenue shops and local attractions.

Every room has two double beds, large closets, and distinctive furniture with tropical accents. The most expensive rooms have balconies overlooking the ocean, or contain small kitchenettes; suites have both. The motel offers coin-operated laundries, shuffleboard, a huge saltwater pool, and a sun deck overlooking the Atlantic Ocean.

HEART OF PALM BEACH HOTEL, 160 Royal Palm Way, Palm Beach, FL 33480. Tel. 407/655-5600, or toll free 800/523-5377. Fax 407/832-1201. 88 rms, 2 suites. A/C MINIBAR TV TEL **Directions:** From I-95, exit onto Okeechobee Boulevard east and continue over the Royal Park Bridge onto Royal Palm Way; the hotel is ahead, on your right, just past South County Road.

$ Rates: Dec 15–Apr, $99–$159 single or double; from $225 suite. May–Dec 14, $59–$99 single or double; from $99 suite. Additional person $10 extra. AE, CB, DC, MC, V.

Centrally located, the Heart of Palm Beach Hotel is within walking distance of Worth Avenue's shops and just half a block from the beach. Each of the hotel's two buildings is distinctively decorated: one with dark-wood furnishings and darker floral prints, the other with lighter, more modern furnishings and colorful, contemporary prints. Some rooms have balconies, some have patios, and all have clean, tiled baths with modern amenities. The hotel's staff is particularly outgoing when it comes to helping guests plan outings and itineraries.

Dining/Entertainment: The Town Tavern serves a selection of sandwiches, pastas, salads, and cocktails, and is open daily from morning to night.

Services: Room service, concierge.

Facilities: Heated swimming pool, complimentary covered parking.

PALM BEACH HAWAIIAN OCEAN INN, 3550 S. Ocean Blvd. (Fla. A1A), Palm Beach, FL 33480. Tel. 407/582-5631, or toll free 800/457-5631. Fax 407/582-5631. 58 rms, 8 suites. A/C MINIBAR TV TEL **Directions:** From I-95, exit onto Lantana Road east, turn right onto Federal Highway (U.S. 1) and then left onto Ocean Avenue; cross the Intracoastal Waterway, turn left onto Ocean Boulevard (Fla. A1A), and the inn is about a mile ahead, on your right.

$ Rates: Dec 15–Jan 14, $94–$100 single or double; from $109 suite. Jan 15–Apr, $98–$109 single or double; from $124 suite. May–Dec 14, $66–$74 single or double; from $89 suite. Additional person $5 extra. AE, CB, DC, DISC, MC, V.

This rather basic wooden motel is a good pick for those who want to save money, but still want to locate right on Palm Beach's beach. Most rooms have dark-wood paneling with pastel prints, two twin beds, and eclectic 1950s furnishings. Bathrooms are all covered with white tile and have standing showers instead of bathtubs.

Clearly, the best part about this place is its oceanfront swimming pool and large wooden sun deck that extends to the sand. Beach umbrellas and rafts are available for rent. The motel's restaurant, open for breakfast, lunch, and dinner, will deliver directly to your room.

INEXPENSIVE

HIBISCUS HOUSE, 501 30th St., West Palm Beach, FL 33407. Tel. 407/863-5633. 6 rms, 2 suites. A/C TV TEL **Directions:** From I-95, exit onto Palm Beach Lakes Boulevard east, continue for one mile, and turn left onto North Tamarind Avenue; turn right onto 25th Street, left onto Broadway, then right onto 30th Street; the hotel is at the end of the block, on your right.

$ Rates (including breakfast): Dec–Apr, $65–$75 single or double; $90 suite. May–Nov, $55–$65 single or double; $80 suite. No credit cards.

Inexpensive bed-and-breakfasts are truly a rarity in this part of South Florida, making the Hibiscus House a true find. Discreetly located a few miles inland in a quiet residential neighborhood, this 1920s-era B&B regularly hosts guests from around the world.

Each room is named for its predominant color scheme. Hence, the Red Room has cardinal walls and matching floral-print bedspreads and curtains; the Peach Room has a charming four-poster bed, 19th-century-style furniture, and polished pine floors. Every accommodation features its own private terrace or balcony. There are plenty of pretty public areas as well, many of which are filled with antiques. One little sitting room has walls of windows and comes complete with playing cards and board games for guests' use. The backyard has been transformed into a planted courtyard with a swimming pool and sun loungers.

A filling two-course breakfast is served each morning, either in the inside dining room or outside in the gazebo.

BUDGET

YWCA, 901 S. Olive Ave., West Palm Beach, FL 33401. Tel. 407/833-2439. 7 rms. A/C **Directions:** From I-95, exit onto Okeechobee Boulevard east, turn right onto Dixie Highway, take the first left onto Pembroke Place, then turn left again onto Olive Avenue; the YWCA is just ahead on your left.

$ Rates: $105 per bed per week with shared bath, $120 with private bath. No credit cards.

Only women are allowed to stay here, where they are provided with good, clean, but basic accommodations on a weekly basis. It's kind of an unusual set-up, but for the money, it's easily the best deal in town. There's a large kitchen for guests' use, along with separate dining and living rooms. There's also a community TV and VCR, as well as a public telephone where you can place free local calls. There's a swimming pool, coin laundry, in-room mini-refrigerators, no curfew, and 24-hour security.

WHERE TO DINE

VERY EXPENSIVE

CAFE L'EUROPE, in the Esplanade, 150 Worth Ave., Palm Beach. Tel. 655-4020.

Cuisine: CONTINENTAL. **Reservations:** Required.
$ **Prices:** Appetizers $7–$17; main courses $20–$32; lunch $7–$17. AE, CB, DC, MC, V.
Open: Lunch Mon–Sat 11:30am–3pm; dinner daily 6–10pm (the Caviar Bar stays open later).

It should come as no surprise that Palm Beach has several terrific restaurants, and this is definitely one of them. Located on the upper level of the Esplanade, a two-story Spanish-style shopping arcade, this formal restaurant is romantically decorated with tapestried café chairs surrounding the linen-topped tables set with crystal and china. Brick archways, wood-paneled walls, and terra-cotta floors are capped with lofty ceilings.

However, it's the food you've come for, and the chef won't disappoint. Lunch might include crispy, Chinese-style lettuce leaves wrapped around minced squab, water chestnuts, bamboo shoots, and rice; poached filet of salmon; Mediterranean salad (feta cheese, ham, Greek olives, eggs, and vegetables); or a giant bleu-cheese burger. Other dinnertime appetizers include snails in garlic butter, baked chèvre (goat cheese) salad with raspberry-walnut dressing, and chilled gazpacho with avocado. Main courses are equally as adventurous, and include salmon filet rolled in a pecan crust, grilled veal medallions rubbed with tarragon, and rack of lamb served with minted couscous. A pastry chef bakes chocolate cakes and fruit tarts here daily.

The Caviar Bar has five or more different caviars always available. Located adjacent to the dining room, it features a large marble bar and small European-style café tables. Visit it for light seafood dishes, dessert, and gourmet coffees.

EXPENSIVE

CHARLEY'S CRAB, 456 S. Ocean Ave., Palm Beach. Tel. 659-1500.
Cuisine: SEAFOOD. **Reservations:** Required.
$ **Prices:** Appetizers $5–$10; main courses $18–$25; lunch $6–$12. AE, DC, DISC, MC, V.
Open: Lunch Mon–Sat 11:30am–3pm; dinner daily 5–11pm; brunch Sun 10:30am–3pm.

Sort of legendary in these parts, Charley's Crab is well known as the place to go for the best and freshest local seafood. Price is as high as the quality, however, and unless you're prepared, you'll be thinking about this dinner bill all the way home.

All the usual fishes are served here—salmon, pompano, dolphin (fish)—as are baked clams, oysters Rockefeller, and mini crab cakes. Steak, lamb, and chicken dishes are also available. Entrees are accompanied with different side dishes each evening—if parmesan roasted potatoes are on today's menu, order them. The restaurant also features a good raw bar with a variety of shellfish, and a well-selected wine list with picks from California and around the world. There's live entertainment Wednesday through Saturday nights.

CHUCK & HAROLD'S CAFE, 207 Royal Poinciana Way, Palm Beach. Tel. 659-1440.
Cuisine: SEAFOOD/CONTINENTAL. **Reservations:** Recommended.
$ **Prices:** Appetizers $3–$8; main courses $14–$28; lunch $5–$12. AE, CB, DC, DISC, MC, V.
Open: Mon–Thurs 7:30am–midnight, Fri–Sat 8am–1am, Sun 8am–11pm.

Nestled between a popular row of restaurants and shops, this is one of the best places in town to people-watch. Chuck & Harold's serves consistently good food to a loyal clientele of both tourists and locals. Dining is either inside, in one of two spacious, palm-filled dining rooms, or outdoors on the patio, where reservations are essential.

When seated, diners are immediately presented with a basket of crispy crackers, served with a tangy hummus spread. Tuscan black-bean soup, chilled gazpacho, and pineapple, tomato, and Gorgonzola salad are the most recommendable appetizers. Entrees include fresh grilled or broiled fish, boiled lobster, and various pasta and chicken dishes. If you happen to visit during stone crab season, order them here.

Ecologically harvested, only one claw is removed from each crab; then it's returned to the ocean where it will grow another one. Crab claws are served steamed or chilled, and served with a traditional honey-mustard sauce.

One final hint: Unless you're still hungry, don't order dessert; complimentary cookies are served at the end of each meal.

TABOO, 221 Worth Ave., Palm Beach. Tel. 835-3500.

Cuisine: CONTINENTAL. **Reservations:** Recommended.

$ **Prices:** Appetizers $7–$11; main courses $7–$25; lunch $5–$15. AE, MC, V.

Open: Daily 11:30am–2am.

Kind of trendy, kind of classic, Taboo stands out among other snazzy Worth Avenue eateries, offering excellent food in pleasantly familiar surroundings. Lots of greenery, a glowing fireplace, and contemporary southwestern charm make Taboo as inviting and comfortable as its food is appealing. Variety is always the chef's special, with extensive lunch and dinner offerings that are often calorie- and cholesterol-conscious.

California-style individual-size gourmet pizzas are topped with delicacies like barbecued chicken, goat and mozzarella cheeses, and sweet roasted red peppers. Other lunch choices include scallops with roasted garlic, portobello mushrooms, and arugula; and a delicious sandwich of sweet peppers and goat cheese. The best dinner starter is fresh tuna marinated in ginger and lime, a sort of one-item ceviche. Dinner choices change nightly, and may include grilled swordfish topped with olive-caper sauce or sautéed chicken breast covered with green apples and a brandy-based cream sauce. Grilled veal served on the bone, Maine lobster, and various chicken dishes are also usually available. Desserts are made on the premises, and there's a nice wine selection.

MODERATE

BIMINI BAY CAFE, 104 Clematis St., West Palm Beach. Tel. 833-9554.

Cuisine: SEAFOOD/CONTINENTAL. **Reservations:** Not required.

$ **Prices:** Appetizers $3–$7; main courses $11–$17; lunch $3–$8. AE, DISC, MC, V.

Open: Sun–Thurs 10:30am–1am, Fri–Sat 10:30am–2am.

Popular with local, young urban professionals, Bimini Bay is busiest on weekdays soon after work lets out. From your table on the café's large wooden outdoor deck, you can see all the way across the Intracoastal Waterway to Palm Beach. The decor is *Casablanca* style; there are also lots of hanging plants, modern white-paper lamps, and neon lights.

Hot Maryland crab dip, baked Brie with fruit, and artichoke-spinach dip are the restaurant's specialty appetizers. Lunch here usually means soup, salad, or sandwiches; a good selection of each is always on offer. Dinner expands to include seafood entrees, pasta, chicken, and steak. Malibu mixed grill, which combines two fresh fish selections, is recommendable, as is the grilled chicken Alfredo with linguine. There's live music Thursday through Saturday nights.

CAFE PROSPECT, 3111 S. Dixie Hwy., West Palm Beach. Tel. 832-5952.

Cuisine: CONTINENTAL. **Reservations:** Recommended.

$ **Prices:** Appetizers $3–$9; main courses $14–$20; lunch $3–$8. MC, V.

Open: Lunch Tues–Fri 11:30am–2pm; dinner Tues–Sun 5–10pm.

You wouldn't expect to find such a charming restaurant located in an otherwise ordinary Dixie Highway strip mall. But Café Prospect is a pleasant surprise, with a smell of fresh garlic and spices, as arresting as the atmosphere of this relaxed, homelike place. The intimate restaurant has a pseudo–art deco decor with accents that include Asian-style screens, bright wall prints, ballooned floral drapes, and glass bricks. There's no printed menu; the day's offerings are marked on a chalkboard and usually include several fresh fish selections, soups, salads, and sandwiches. Every dish is made to order.

E. R. BRIDLE'S SALOON, 111 Bridle Place, at Royal Palm Way, Palm Beach. Tel. 833-3520.

Cuisine: AMERICAN. **Reservations:** Recommended.
$ Prices: Appetizers $2–$11; main courses $11–$17; lunch $4–$8. AE, MC, V.
Open: Mon–Fri 11am–3am, Sat–Sun 10am–3am.

Named after Edward Riley Bridle, an avid gambler who opened a casino here in 1898, this restaurant has just enough rough edges to keep it from seeming contrived. A bar runs the length of the restaurant, and just in case that's not enough, a second bar is located at the eatery's far end. Lattice ceilings are dotted with gently whirling fans. During warmer weather, there's outdoor dining at marble-top tables with woven placemats.

At lunch, you'd do well to stick with a meal of appetizers like baked Brie with bread and fruit, and a mountain of nachos served made with guacamole, cheese, and black beans. A variety of salads are available, as are unusually large sandwiches and burgers. The grilled fish and steaks are always available during dinner, but I suggest the manicotti, or the angel-hair pasta with shrimp and mussels. The restaurant is located on the corner of Royal Palm Way.

TESTA'S, 221 Royal Poinciana Way, Palm Beach. Tel. 832-0992.
Cuisine: CONTINENTAL. **Reservations:** Not required.
$ Prices: Appetizers $5–$12; main courses $11–$19; lunch $3–$13. AE, DC, DISC, MC, V.
Open: Daily 7am–midnight.

A family-owned restaurant, Testa's has been a Palm Beach fixture since 1921—an eon for a young city like this. A large outdoor patio, protected from passersby by a squat row of groomed hedges is a great spot for people-watching any time of the year. Inside, wooden booths with pink-clothed tables furnish the main room, while a second Garden Room is notable for its roof, which can be removed during fine weather.

The restaurant's friendly staff is one of the reasons for its continued success. The menu is vast, and the staff won't rush you into choosing—it really can be difficult to decide between appetizers like crabmeat- and cheese-stuffed potato skins, eggplant provençal, or just garlic bread. A long list of seafood, steak, chicken, and pasta entrees are available, as are a host of desserts. Especially if you're traveling with a family, Testa's is thoroughly recommendable.

INEXPENSIVE

HAMBURGER HEAVEN, 314 S. County Rd., Palm Beach. Tel. 655-5277.
Cuisine: AMERICAN. **Reservations:** Not accepted.
$ Prices: Salads and sandwiches $3–$6; burgers and dinners $5–$15; breakfast $3–$5. No credit cards.
Open: Daily 7:30am–8pm.

Hamburger Heaven hasn't changed much since it began flipping burgers in 1945. A central U-shaped bar, surrounded by low stools, is encircled by old-fashioned Formica booths which line the walls. A large sailboat-studded ocean mural covers one entire wall, a refreshing change from all the other overly decorated, and overpriced, restaurants in this area.

As you might have guessed, burgers are the main food sold here, but daily dinner specials widen the variety. Tuesday means chicken and dumplings, Friday is for pasta with tomato-basil sauce, and Saturday is homemade meatloaf day. Rice pudding, cakes, and pies are always available. A full egg menu is offered at breakfast.

NARCISSUS, 200 Clematis St., Palm Beach. Tel. 659-1888.
Cuisine: CONTINENTAL. **Reservations:** Not required.
$ Prices: Appetizers $3–$6; main courses $7–$12; lunch $5–$7. AE, MC, V.
Open: Lunch Mon–Fri 11am–3pm; dinner Mon–Thurs 4pm–midnight, Fri 4pm–1am; Sat–Sun noon–midnight.

This little restaurant always seems to be in vogue, popular with Palm Beach's younger set, who sit at tables on the front patio under yellow umbrellas. Inside, black lacquer-topped tables are matched with red café chairs, and booths are covered with contemporary geometric patterns.

A large selection of specialty salads and sandwiches includes Mandarin chicken salad and tuna pizza melt sandwich. Fresh snapper, grouper, swordfish, or tuna is always available, as are a selection of pasta dishes and homemade chicken pot pie. There's live entertainment here nightly during the high season.

BUDGET

GREEN'S PHARMACY, 151 N. County Rd., Palm Beach. Tel. 832-9171.
Cuisine: AMERICAN. **Reservations:** Not accepted.
$ Prices: Breakfast $2–$5; burgers and sandwiches $3–$5. AE.
Open: Mon–Sat 7:30am–5pm, Sun 7am–1pm.

This neighborhood corner pharmacy offers one of the best meal deals in Palm Beach. Both breakfast and lunch are served coffee-shop style, at a Formica bar above a black-and-white checkerboard floor.

Breakfast specials include eggs and omelets served with home-fries, bacon, sausage, or corned-beef hash. Cold cereal, oatmeal, and bagels are also available. At lunch, the grill serves up burgers and sandwiches, as well as ice-cream sodas and milkshakes.

SHOPPING

Palm Beach's **Worth Avenue** is a must, even if you have no desire to go shopping. The Rodeo Drive of the East Coast, Worth Avenue is lined with one of the world's most impressive collections of posh shops, interesting art galleries, and upscale restaurants. The four blocks between South Ocean Boulevard and Cocoanut Row, are home to the stores of Louis Vuitton, Cartier, Polo Ralph Lauren, and Chanel, among others. Victoria's Secret, The Limited Express, and several other less-impressive chains have snuck in here, too. Most of the street's stores are open Monday through Saturday from 10am to 5pm.

The Esplanade, 150 Worth Ave., Palm Beach, is a particularly nice mini-mall in the heart of the high-rent district. This two-story Spanish arcade is filled with specialty shops and restaurants. Big-name shops and department stores like Saks Fifth Avenue, Banana Republic, and Liz Claiborne surround Mediterranean-style gardens.

The **Palm Beach Mall,** Palm Beach Lakes Boulevard (tel. 683-9186), located just east of I-95, is where you go when you really need to buy something. Recently renovated with tropical fountains, plants, and skylights, this mall features several department stores, including Mervyn's, JC Penney, Sears, Burdines, and Lord & Taylor.

EVENING ENTERTAINMENT

There are several showrooms in the Palm Beaches, offering everything from live theater and classical concerts to heavy-metal rock. The **ArtsLine** (tel. 407/471-2901, or toll free 800/882-ARTS) offers up-to-date recorded information on cultural events and goings-on in Palm Beach County. Tickets to many area events can be charged to your credit card over the phone through Ticketmaster (tel. 966-3309).

THE MAJOR ALL-PURPOSE AUDITORIUMS

RAYMOND F. KRAVIS CENTER FOR THE PERFORMING ARTS, 701 Okeechobee Blvd., West Palm Beach. Tel. 833-8300. Fax 407/833-3901.

This stunning, $55-million center opened in late 1992. It's quite an architectural achievement, featuring a large, curved glass facade. Inside are three different performance spaces: The elegant, 2,200-seat main concert theater and adjacent 300-seat "black box" theater between them hold over 300 performances a year. Music, theater, and dance performances are staged almost every night of the week. Phone for a current schedule.

WEST PALM BEACH AUDITORIUM AND MUNICIPAL STADIUM, 1610 Palm Beach Lakes Blvd. Tel. 683-6012.

Many concerts, sporting events, and festivals are held here. Musical guests include popular rap stars and country greats. The complex is located half a mile east of Exit 53 off I-95, and on the corner of Congress Avenue.

THE PERFORMING ARTS

Theaters

QUEST THEATER INSTITUTE, INC., 444 24th St., at Spruce St., West Palm Beach. Tel. 832-9328.

Palm Beach's only African American–oriented theater is also one of the city's most active, offering a wide range of professional, multicultural works. Past performances have included *Ain't Misbehavin'* and *A Raisin in the Sun.* The theater operates year-round.

Admission: Tickets, $15 adults, $10 students and seniors, $5 children under 12.

ROYAL POINCIANA PLAYHOUSE, 70 Royal Poinciana Plaza. Tel. 659-3310.

Broadway and Off Broadway plays and musicals are staged here throughout the year. The playhouse promotes itself as "the most glamorous theater in the country," and this may be so. It's pretty, all right, and top names regularly perform. Musical concerts are produced here as well.

Admission: Tickets, $30–$45.

Classical Music, Opera, and Dance

FLORIDA PHILHARMONIC ORCHESTRA, at the Kravis Center, 701 Okeechobee Blvd., West Palm Beach. Tel. 659-0331.

The Kravis Center is the primary Palm Beach performance hall for the Florida Philharmonic (see "The Major All-Purpose Auditoriums," above). Under the baton of James Judd, this professional symphony orchestra performs from September through May.

Admission: Tickets, $15–$37.

GREATER PALM BEACH SYMPHONY, Royal Poinciana Playhouse, Palm Beach. Tel. 655-2703.

Performing throughout Palm Beach County, the symphony performs orchestra concerts and chamber music recitals in several area halls including the Breakers Hotel and the Kravis Center. The symphony usually plays 12–14 concerts from November through April.

Admission: Tickets, $25–$100.

PALM BEACH OPERA, 415 S. Olive Ave., West Palm Beach. Tel. 833-7888.

Three operas are performed each season, one each in December, January, and March. They're usually staged at the Kravis Center, and often feature world-famous soloists.

Admission: Tickets, $18.50–$75.

MIAMI CITY BALLET, West Palm Beach Auditorium, 1610 Palm Beach Lakes Blvd., West Palm Beach. Tel. 488-7134.

This young professional company regularly performs in four Florida cities. Works by resident choreographer Jimmy Gamonet de Los Heros are staged, as are the dances of George Balanchine, Martha Graham, and others. The season runs from July through April.

Admission: Tickets, $19–$50.

THE CLUB & MUSIC SCENE

AU BAR, 336 Royal Poinciana Way, Palm Beach. Tel. 832-4800.

Friends tell me that they never charged admission before William Kennedy Smith was accused of raping a girl he took home from here. Publicity from that affair was good for business, and now everyone knows about this luxurious bar that was once the mainstay of Palm Beach's young jet-set. Richly upholstered chairs and glass-top tables surround a tiny dance floor. The large marble-top bar is garnished with hanging crystal and a huge floral bouquet. Dress to kill. Au Bar is open Tuesday through Sunday from 8pm to 3am. Open Monday through Friday from 11am to 3am and on Saturday and Sunday from 10am to 3am.

Admission: $10.

CRUZANS, 2224 Palm Beach Lakes Blvd., West Palm Beach. Tel. 686-5613.

On the other end of the haughty spectrum from Au Bar, Cruzans is about as basic as it gets, looking like spring break all year long. It's huge, and has three bars, six pool tables, a large-screen TV, and even a hot tub. There are drink and theme specials every night of the week, including ladies' nights, bikini contests, miniskirt contests, and "red hot" male reviews. Music is not the only thing that throbs here. Open Monday through Wednesday from 5pm to 2am, on Thursday from 5pm to 3am, and Friday through Sunday from 5pm to 4am.

Admission: Varies depending on what's on. Call for the latest.

E. R. BRIDLE'S SALOON, 111 Bridle Place, Palm Beach. Tel. 833-3520.

Casual restaurant by day, busy bar by night, Bridle's is the kind of place where revelers literally dance on the bar—ducking to avoid the ceiling fans. A free happy hour buffet is offered Monday through Thursday from 4 to 6:30pm and on Friday and Saturday from 3 to 5pm. Bridle's is open Monday through Friday from 11am to 3am and on Saturday and Sunday from 10am to 3am.

RESPECTABLE STREET CAFE, 518 Clematis St., West Palm Beach. Tel. 832-9999.

This happening spot in downtown West Palm Beach has remained popular for over five years. The café's plain storefront exterior belies its funky high-ceilinged interior, decorated with large black booths, psychedelic wall murals, and a large checkerboard-tile dance floor. The young, alternative crowd dances to both live and recorded music. Open Tuesday through Saturday from 9pm to 4am.

Admission: $2–$5.

ROXY'S, 323 Clematis St., West Palm Beach. Tel. 833-1003.

It's one of the best neighborhood joints—complete with a long bar, low stools, a pool table, antique taps, and T-shirted locals. Go across the Intracoastal to mingle with the wannabe glitterati. Open daily from 9am to 3am.

3. BOCA RATON & DELRAY BEACH

26 miles S of Palm Beach, 38 miles N of Miami

GETTING THERE **By Plane** The **Palm Beach International Airport** (tel. 407/471-7420) serves the Boca Raton area, and is a pleasure to fly in or out of. Helpful "Airport Ambassadors" in their teal-green shirts and jackets, are on hand to offer information. Major domestic carriers servicing the airport include American (tel. toll free 800/433-7300), Continental (tel. 407/832-5200, or toll free 800/525-0280), Delta (tel. 407/655-5300, or toll free 800/221-1212), Northwest (tel. toll free 800/225-2525), TWA (tel. 407/655-3776, or toll free 800/221-2000), and United (tel. toll free 800/241-6522).

By Train Amtrak (tel. toll free 800/USA-RAIL) trains departing from New York stop in West Palm Beach on their way to Miami. The local station is at 201 S. Tamarind Ave., West Palm Beach (tel. 407/832-6169).

By Bus Greyhound/Trailways can get you to Boca from almost anywhere. The company no longer operates a single nationwide telephone number, so consult your local directory for the office nearest you.

By Car If you're driving up or down the Florida coast, you'll probably reach Boca Raton on I-95, a highway that runs all the way from Maine to Miami. Visitors on their way to or from Orlando should take the Florida Turnpike, a toll road that runs almost directly from this county's beaches to Walt Disney World. Finally, if you're coming from the state's west coast, you can either take Fla. 70, which runs north of Lake Okeechobee to Fort Pierce, or Fla. 80, which runs south of the lake to Palm Beach.

ESSENTIALS The **telephone area code** is 407. The **Palm Beach County Convention and Visitors Bureau,** 1555 Palm Beach Lakes Blvd., Suite 204, West Palm Beach, FL 33401 (tel. 407/471-3995, or toll free 800/554-PALM), distributes an informative brochure, and will answer your questions about visiting Boca Raton and Delray Beach.

Boca Raton was named by the Spanish conquistadors who landed here with Ponce de León—"Boca de Raton" means mouth of the rat. It is widely believed that the sailor's "rats" were actually the large and dangerous rocks that protrude from the water in Boca's protected harbor.

Not much happened here until the 1920s, when architect Addison Mizner built the Cloister Inn, a stunning Mediterranean Revival–style hotel that's still the architectural basis for all of Boca Raton. It wasn't until the 1960s that Boca really began to boom, growing around a new IBM manufacturing plant and other high-tech industries. The city's strict building codes and plethora of low-density developments make Boca popular with moneyed ex–New Yorkers.

Many of Boca's residents would shudder if you mention Delray Beach in the same breath, much less the same guidebook heading. Delray grew up completely separately, founded in 1894 by a midwestern postmaster who sold off five-acre lots through Michigan newspaper ads. Delray is named after a suburb of Detroit. For tourists, however, there's no reason why Boca and adjacent Delray should be explored independently. Budget-conscious travelers would do well to eat and sleep in Delray, and dip into Boca for sightseeing purposes only.

WHAT TO SEE & DO

BOCA RATON MUSEUM OF ART, 801 W. Palmetto Rd., Boca Raton. Tel. 392-2500.

In addition to a relatively small but well-chosen permanent collection that's strongest in 19th-century European oils, the museum stages a wide variety of temporary exhibitions by local and international artists. Lectures and films are offered on a fairly regular basis; phone for details.

Admission: Free; donations requested.

Open: Mon–Fri 10am–4pm, Sat–Sun noon–4pm.

CHILDREN'S SCIENCE EXPLORATORIUM, in the Royal Palm Plaza, Suite 15, 131 Mizner Blvd., Boca Raton. Tel. 395-8401.

Here, 30 interactive exhibits teach children—and elders—about how things work in the world we live in. There are displays on magnetic fields, bridge construction, gravitational forces, and computer technology. Even if you're not in a museum mood, you might want to visit the Exploratorium's unusual gift shop for freeze-dried astronaut food, hologram cards, and other unique presents you just can't get at home.

Admission: $2, free for children under 3.

Open: Tues–Sat 10am–5pm, Sun noon–5pm.

SPORTS & RECREATION

BEACHES Before South Florida was completely overrun with buildings, the state set aside lands dedicated to protection and preservation. Happily, many of these properties are on the waterfronts in Boca Raton and Delray Beach. Some are left alone and remain in a relatively natural state; others are groomed and lifeguarded.

The **Delray Beach Public Beach** is on Ocean Boulevard at the east end of Atlantic Avenue. This pretty beach is groomed and cleaned for the comfort of bathing and sunning beachgoers. There's limited parking along Ocean Boulevard.

At **Red Reef Park,** a fully developed 67-acre oceanfront park in Boca Raton, the beach has year-round lifeguard protection and good snorkeling around the rocks and reefs that lie just offshore. There's a small picnic area with grills, tables, and restrooms. The park is on Fla. A1A half a mile north of Palmetto Park Road, and is open daily from 8am to 10pm.

Spanish River Park, North Ocean Boulevard (Fla. A1A), Boca Raton, two miles north of Palmetto Park Road, is a huge oceanfront park that has a large grassy area, making it one of the best for picnicking. Facilities include picnic tables, grills, restrooms, and a bilevel 40-foot observation tower. Walk through tunnels under the highway to nature trails that wind through fertile grasslands.

GOLF From May to October or November, close to a dozen private golf courses open their greens to visitors who are staying in a Palm Beach County hotel. This "Golf-A-Round" program is free (carts are additional), and reservations can be made through most major hotels. Ask at your hotel, or contact the Palm Beach Convention and Visitors Bureau (tel. 407/471-3995) for information on which clubs are available for play.

The private 18-hole, par-61 course at the **Boca Raton Executive Country Club,** 7601 E. Country Club Blvd. (tel. 997-9410), is usually open to the public. A driving range is also on the property as well as a pro shop and a restaurant. A PGA professional gives lessons, and rental clubs are available. From Yamato Road east, turn left onto Old Dixie Highway; after about a mile, turn left onto Hidden Valley Boulevard, and continue straight to the club. Greens fees are $12–$23.

The **Boca Raton Municipal Golf Course,** 8111 Golf Course Rd. (tel. 483-6100), is located just north of Glades Road, half a mile west of the Florida Turnpike. This public 18-hole, par-72 course covers approximately 6,200 yards. There's a snack bar, and a pro shop where clubs can be rented. Greens fees are $10–$20 for 9 holes and $14–$21 for 18 holes.

TENNIS The snazzy **Delray Beach Tennis Center,** 30 NW First Ave. (tel. 243-7360), has been recently spruced up for a Virginia Slims tournament. There are 19 lighted courts. Phone for rates and reservations.

The 17 public lighted courts at **Patch Reef Park,** 2000 NW 51st St. (tel. 997-0881), are available on a first-come, first-served basis. It's recommended that you call ahead to see if courts are available. The fee for nonresidents is $5.75 per hour, per person. To reach the park from I-95, exit at Yamato Road west and continue past Military Trail to the park.

WHERE TO STAY

VERY EXPENSIVE

BOCA RATON RESORT AND CLUB, 501 E. Camino Real Dr. (P.O. Box 5025), Boca Raton, FL 33431. Tel. 407/395-3000, or toll free 800/448-8355. Fax 407/391-3183. 963 rms, 37 suites, 70 Golf Villa Apartments. A/C MINIBAR TV TEL **Directions:** From I-95 north, exit onto Palmetto Park Road east, turn right onto Federal Highway (U.S. 1), and then left onto Camino Real to the resort.

$ **Rates:** Jan–Apr, $210–$350 single or double; from $370 suite; from $350 golf villa apt. May 28–Sept, $105–$170 single or double; from $160 suite; from $145 golf villa apt. May 1–27 and Oct–Dec, $195–$305 single or double; from $300 suite; from $280 golf villa apt. AE, DC, MC, V.

The Spanish-Mediterranean–style main house of the Boca Raton Resort and Club used to be all there was to this now-grand retreat. Built in 1926, and originally named the Cloister Inn by southeastern Florida's seminal architect,

Addison Mizner, the hotel has grown substantially over the years. Today, Boca's best resort straddles both sides of the Intracoastal Waterway, occupying over 350 acres of land. Its romantic European architecture is mixed with modern buildings and additions.

Rooms in the historic Cloisters building have fine arched doorways, high beamed ceilings, refined wood furnishings, and Asian carpets covering terra-cotta floors. The Boca Beach Club building is the most contemporary in feel, with high glass walls, light marble floors, and pastel-and-white decor. Guests can also choose to lodge in one of three other structures: the modern, 27-story Tower; the service-oriented Palm Court Club, complete with its own private concierge service; or in the Golf Villas, which has patios and balconies overlooking the hotel's 18-hole golf course. Each building has its own charm and style, offering guests options for varying tastes.

Each room in every building comes with bathrobes, hairdryers, at least two phones, full-length mirrors, and in-room safes. Also, no matter where you stay here, you're guaranteed to receive top-notch service from an experienced and attentive staff.

Dining/Entertainment: Nine restaurants and three lounges are spread throughout the property. The Top of the Tower, a formal Italian restaurant, is located, appropriately enough, on the 27th floor of the Tower building, offering extraordinary views of Boca Raton and surrounding areas. Only dinner is served here. Nick's Fishmarket, located the Boca Beach Club, is known for excellently prepared seafood served in graceful surroundings. Or stop for an afternoon coffee at the Cappuccino Bar in the Cloister.

Services: 24-hour room service, concierge, business center, fitness classes, evening turn-down, laundry, overnight shoeshine.

Facilities: Three fitness centers, five swimming pools, two golf courses, 34 tennis courts (9 lighted), water-sports and bicycle rentals, snorkeling and scuba instruction, croquet, volleyball, basketball courts.

EXPENSIVE

SEAGATE HOTEL & BEACH CLUB, 400 S. Ocean Blvd., Delray Beach, FL 33483. Tel. 407/276-2421, or toll free 800/233-3581. Fax 407/243-4714. 70 suites. A/C TV TEL **Directions:** From I-95, exit onto Atlantic Avenue east, turn right onto Ocean Boulevard (Fla. A1A), and continue one block to the hotel.

$ Rates: Feb–Apr 18, $145–$241 one-bedroom suite; $285 two-bedroom suite; $425 penthouse. Apr 19–Nov 19, $59–$79 one-bedroom suite; $109 two-bedroom suite; $229 penthouse. Nov 20–Jan, $94–$145 one-bedroom suite; $190 two-bedroom suite; $299 penthouse. Additional person $15 extra. Children under 18 stay free in parents' room. AE, CB, DC, MC, V.

At the Seagate, an all-suite hotel, the ample rooms containing large kitchenettes are split between two adjacent buildings located directly across the street from the beach. Except for the fact that one of the buildings is closer to the swimming pool, it hardly matters which one you choose. Suites in both are painted in earthy pastels, and stocked with light-wood and wicker furniture; there are large closets, safes, and alarm clocks. Kitchenettes come chef-ready, prestocked with all the utensils and cookware you need. Fresh coffee, homemade muffins, and newspapers are available in the hotel's lobby every morning.

The Beach Club part of the hotel is located across the street. There are no accommodations here, just facilities that include a heated saltwater pool, chaise longues, towels, a restaurant, and cocktail service on the sand.

Dining/Entertainment: The Beach Club Restaurant, an American eatery, is open for lunch and dinner. There's a small bar here, too. The adjacent Patio Bar is far less formal, serving snacks, burgers, and drinks.

Services: Room service, children's activities during peak season, water aerobics.

Facilities: Water-sports rentals, locker rooms.

MODERATE

THE COLONY, 525 E. Atlantic Ave. (P.O. Box 970), Delray Beach, FL

33447. Tel. 407/276-4123, or toll free 800/552-2363. 93 rms. A/C TEL **Directions:** From I-95, exit onto Atlantic Avenue east; the hotel is about one mile ahead on your left.

$ Rates (including breakfast and dinner): Jan 10–Apr 5, $110–$180 single or double. Additional person $30 extra. AE, MC, V. **Closed:** May–Dec.

This three-story hotel, well located right on Delray's main street, is open during the "season" only. Not much has changed at the Colony since the hotel debuted in 1926; in fact, the furniture and decor may very well have been here since opening day. The spacious lobby is filled with rattan tables and chairs that often host senior-citizen card games. But the hotel is also popular with families who appreciate the many planned activities and meals that are offered here. Rooms are quite modest, and contain old-fashioned switchboard-type phones.

Guests have full access to the hotel's beachfront club, which offers a heated saltwater swimming pool, private beach, and various activities like putting and shuffleboard tournaments. Prices include both breakfast and dinner—not gourmet quality, but with good variety.

RAMADA INN, 2901 N. Federal Hwy., Boca Raton, FL 33431. Tel. 407/395-6850, or toll free 800/272-6232. Fax 407/368-7964. 100 rms, 32 suites. A/C TV TEL **Directions:** From I-95, exit onto Glades Road east; after two miles, turn left onto Federal Highway (U.S. 1) and the hotel is about a mile ahead on your left.

$ Rates: Dec 16–Apr, $75–$95 single or double; from $105 suite. May–July, $54 single or double; from $64 suite. Aug–Dec 15, $49 single or double; from $59 suite. AE, CB, DC, MC, V. **Parking:** Free.

Although the Ramada chain is most closely associated with business travel, this four-story pink concrete hotel is both well located and welcoming to vacationers. Rooms here are just as bright as the hotel's large, white marble lobby. There's nothing particularly fancy, but accommodations are both comfortable and modern. Suites are not much larger than regular rooms—the main difference is that they contain pull-out sofa beds. There's a large heated pool. The hotel's Garden Café, located adjacent to the lobby, serves lunch and dinner and offers live entertainment on weekends.

SHORE EDGE MOTEL, 425 N. Ocean Blvd. (Fla. A1A), Boca Raton, FL 33432. Tel. 407/395-4491. 16 rms. A/C TV TEL **Directions:** From I-95, exit onto Palmetto Park Road east, turn left onto Ocean Boulevard (Fla. A1A), and continue four blocks to the motel.

$ Rates: Jan–Feb, $75–$95 single or double. Mar, $65–$85 single or double. Apr and Dec, $55–$75 single or double. May–Nov, $40–$50 single or double. AE, MC, V.

Located slightly north of downtown Boca Raton, this is a great choice for those who wish to be near the beach, but want to avoid exorbitant resort rates. Despite its name, the Shore Edge is not on the sand, but across the street from a public beach. It's the quintessential South Florida motel: a small, pink, single-story structure surrounding a modest swimming pool and courtyard.

Although the rooms are a bit on the small side, they're very neat, outfitted with patterned curtains and framed artwork. The higher-priced accommodations are larger, and come with full kitchens. The motel's owners, Lauren and Don Manuel, are terrific hosts, and are more than willing to share their knowledge of the surrounding area with you.

INEXPENSIVE

RIVIERA PALMS MOTEL, 3960 N. Ocean Blvd., Delray Beach, FL 33483. Tel. 407/276-3032. 21 rms, 13 efficiencies. A/C TV

$ Rates: Dec 15–Jan, $50 single or double; from $55 efficiency. Feb–Apr 15, $60 single or double; from $65 efficiency. Apr 16–Dec 14, $40 single or double; from $45 efficiency. Weekly rates available. No credit cards.

In Florida, competition among hotels is tough, rates are competitive, and you usually get what you pay for. This place is no exception—it's plain, simple, and relatively inexpensive. Behind the motel's two-story, cream-colored exterior are large rooms filled with a mixed bag of 1950s-era furnishings. Efficiencies come with full kitchens complete with dishes and silverware. There are no phones in the rooms. A large swimming pool is surrounded by a nice courtyard with sunning lounges, patio tables, barbecue grills, and (of course) shuffleboard courts.

WHERE TO DINE

VERY EXPENSIVE

LA VIEILLE MAISON, 770 E. Palmetto Park Rd., Boca Raton. Tel. 391-6701 or 737-5677.

Cuisine: CONTINENTAL. **Reservations:** Required.

$ Prices: Appetizers $5–$13; main courses $18–$33; fixed-price dinner $48. AE, CB, DC, MC, V.

Open: Dinner only, daily 6–9:30pm (call for seating times).

In a rustic, old house with dark floral carpeting, French country crystal and silver, and original European art, lucky diners are treated to great food in a particularly romantic setting. Several small downstairs dining rooms, each with just one or two quiet tables, make you feel as if you're dining at home—if home is Versailles. Upstairs is larger and livelier, and the food is just as agreeable.

Begin with warm bell-pepper soup served with a dollop of sour cream, or an unusual open-face ravioli filled with duck confit and sage butter. You might choose to continue with salmon wrapped in rice paper, or try roast rack of lamb with thyme and goat cheese. Desserts are just as fine, and may include lemon crêpe soufflé with raspberry sauce, or crispy meringue with vanilla ice cream and chocolate sauce. The labels from the restaurant's vast, award-winning wine cellar could (and does) fill a thick book.

EXPENSIVE

BISTRO L'EUROPE, 346 Plaza Real, in Mizner Park, Boca Raton. Tel. 368-4488.

Cuisine: CONTINENTAL. **Reservations:** Recommended.

$ Prices: Appetizers $5–$9; main courses $17–$22; lunch $4–$13. AE, DC, MC, V.

Open: Lunch Mon–Sat 11:30am–3pm; dinner Mon–Thurs 6–10pm, Fri–Sat 6–11pm.

Although the restaurant is not small, it's somehow intimate, made cozy with a tricolored hardwood floor and fine wall murals of neighborhood scenes.

Tasty lunches run the gamut from Italian pastas to Mandarin-style stir-fries and healthful spa cuisine. A light Alfredo sauce is served over penne pasta with Gorgonzola cheese, asparagus, and mushrooms. Blackened chicken breast is served on toasted sourdough bread with mozzarella. And braised mahi-mahi is served with yellow squash and zucchini. Dinners, which are slightly more formal, might begin with tricolored caviar pie, or escargots in garlic-chablis butter. Entrees include sea shell pasta with pesto and chicken, and wienerschnitzel with potatoes and leaf spinach. A full range of desserts are also available, including fresh-baked fruit tarts, bread pudding, and mixed sorbets.

JOE MUER SEAFOOD, 6450 N. Federal Hwy., Boca Raton. Tel. 997-6688.

Cuisine: SEAFOOD. **Reservations:** Recommended.

$ Prices: Appetizers $4–$12; main courses $13–$24; lunch $4–$12. AE, MC, V.

Open: Lunch Mon–Fri 11:30am–3:30pm; dinner Sun–Thurs 4:30–9:30pm, Fri–Sat 4:30–10pm.

This enormous dining room seems to stretch on forever, interrupted only by a forest of flowers and plants. It tends to get a bit noisy here, but lots of diners seem to like it that way.

The restaurant has become justifiably famous for its oversize seafood dishes that are not just well prepared, but beautifully presented. The usual selection of ocean fish can be grilled, broiled, poached, sautéed, or blackened—any way you like it. Other fresh seafood choices include Michigan smelts, crabmeat-stuffed shrimp, and Lake Heron perch. Frogs' legs, filet mignon, and rack of lamb are also available. The nice wine list emphasizes California grapes.

MODERATE

BACI, 344 Plaza Real, in Mizner Park, Boca Raton. Tel. 362-8500.
Cuisine: ITALIAN. **Reservations:** Recommended.
$ **Prices:** Appetizers $5–$12; main courses $12–$17; lunch $5–$15. AE, MC, V.
Open: Lunch daily 11:30am–2:30pm; dinner Sun–Thurs 5:30–11pm, Fri–Sat 5:30pm–midnight.

Yet another good restaurant located in Mizner Park, Baci offers indoor and outdoor seating, as well as a huge bar for drinks and appetizers. White patio tables with black director's chairs surround a tiled fountain and tall Floridian palms. Inside, bulky matte-black modern furnishings and a massive granite bar create a curious art deco industrial look. A contemporary Italian-style café, this eatery is both loud and crowded on weekends, popular with Boca's see-and-be-seen crowd.

Lunch selections include a variety of salads like salmon, tuna, and sliced duck breast, most of which are made with designer greens like arugula, radicchio, and escarole. Pastas, pizza, and assorted sandwiches round out the rest of the menu. The gnocchi al verde (potato dumplings with spinach-pistachio pesto) is particularly recommendable, as are the individual-size gourmet pizzas, topped with oak-grilled chicken, goat cheese, and the like. The dinner menu includes many of the same lunch items as well as a special lasagne of the day (like whole-wheat pasta with broccoli, Italian sausage, and sun-dried tomatoes). The accede-roasted baby chicken with cornbread stuffing and the grilled rabbit with grappa-soaked cherries are also recommendable. There's a great selection of Italian wines.

BOSTON'S ON THE BEACH, 40 S. Fla. A1A, Delray Beach. Tel. 278-3364.
Cuisine: SEAFOOD/AMERICAN. **Reservations:** Not required.
$ **Prices:** Appetizers $3–$7; main courses $9–$18; lunch $3–$8. AE, MC, V.
Open: Mon–Sat 6:30am–1am, Sun 6:30am–midnight.

Somewhat of a legend in Delray Beach, Boston's is well known to regulars who have been coming here for years. Eclectic, low-budget wall decorations include street signs and framed sport prints. Informal and casual, the restaurant is most crowded around happy hour, daily between 4 and 6pm.

Omelets, pancakes, eggs Benedict, and French toast are served for breakfast, while traditional salads and sandwiches make up the bulk of the lunch selections. Some of the more unusual lunch and dinner offerings include bacon-wrapped scallops, smoked fish, and calamari topped linguine. Crab legs, shrimp, raw clams, and oysters are also always available, as are a host of steak and chicken dishes.

The restaurant is located across the highway from the Delray public beach. There is outdoor seating on a covered porch, and inside, around wooden tables.

MAX'S GRILL, 404 Plaza Real, in Mizner Park, Boca Raton. Tel. 368-0080.
Cuisine: AMERICAN. **Reservations:** Recommended.
$ **Prices:** Appetizers $5–$7; main courses $12–$20; lunch $5–$12. AE, CB, DC, MC, V.
Open: Lunch Mon–Sat 11:30am–2:30pm; dinner Mon–Thurs 5:30–10:30pm, Fri–Sat 5–11pm, Sun 5–10pm; brunch Sun 11:30am–3pm.

One of Mizner Park's best restaurants, Max's is Boca's quintessential contemporary Florida restaurant. Most everything on the menu is prepared with fresh, local ingredients, including meatloaf in a wild mushroom-cabernet sauce and grilled salmon with leek-cucumber glaze and tricolor spätzle. Lunch items include spinach salad with mushrooms, pistachio-goat cheese torta, and grilled yellowfin tuna sandwich.

Wrapped with enormous plate-glass windows that look out onto Mizner Park, the high-ceilinged dining room features black booths and tables with dark-wood accents and a large, open kitchen that welcomes the gaze of diners. Outdoor dining is also available on black tables with white plastic patio chairs.

INEXPENSIVE

BANANA BOAT RESTAURANT, 739 E. Ocean Ave., Boynton Beach. Tel. 732-9400.

Cuisine: SEAFOOD/AMERICAN. **Reservations:** Not required.

$ **Prices:** Appetizers $2–$7; main courses $11–$20; lunch $4–$11; weekend brunch $5–$7. AE, MC, V.

Open: Mon–Fri 11am–2am, Sat–Sun 9am–2am.

Skimpily clad waitresses serve lunch and dinner to frat boys and others in Mediterranean-style dining rooms. It's actually pretty nice both indoors and outside on a wooden patio that overlooks the Intracoastal Waterway. There's often a live band; if not, dance disks are spinning. The location, drinks, and entertainment are good; few people come here just for the food. In addition to a raw bar, chicken Caesar salads, fried fish, and a variety of sandwiches are always for sale. Hot dinner entrees include fresh fish, shrimp, and terriyaki steak. They also serve weekend brunch with omelets and waffles.

LUNCH ONLY

PATIO GARDEN CAFE, 303 Mizner Blvd., Boca Raton. Tel. 392-9444.

Cuisine: AMERICAN. **Reservations:** Not required.

$ **Prices:** Appetizers $2–$4; main courses $2–$6. AE, MC, V.

Open: Mon–Sat 11am–3pm.

Located adjacent to the Royal Palm Dinner Theater (see "Evening Entertainment," below), this restaurant serves dinner to theater guests only, but is open to the public for lunch. The dining room looks very much like a backyard patio, enclosed by large plate-glass windows protected by canvas awnings. A white trellis studded with silk flowers, and wicker chairs with pink and white cushions complete the effect. Outdoor seating is also available.

Lunches are good here, and include several salads, like fresh fruit, and crab Louie with asparagus tips and capers. A large and fancy sandwich selection is also available.

WOLLEY'S, 25 Royal Palm Plaza, Boca Raton. Tel. 392-2977.

Cuisine: AMERICAN. **Reservations:** Not accepted.

$ **Prices:** Main courses $3–$6. No credit cards.

Open: Mon–Sat 9am–6pm, Sun 11am–4pm.

This tiny café, rather sterile in atmosphere, but a good place to stop for a quick bite, serves well-prepared sandwiches and salads made fresh in their adjacent gourmet-food store. The eatery's little outdoor tables topped with large umbrellas are a pleasant place to sit. Try the frozen yogurt special: a whole baked apple topped with sliced bananas, frozen yogurt, and nuts; or perhaps toasted waffles topped with yogurt and fresh fruit.

SHOPPING

Mizner Park, on Federal Highway in Boca Raton (tel. 362-0606), is the area's most celebrated shopping arcade. There are just a handful of specialty shops here, nestled next to a few good restaurants. Each shopfront faces a grassy island with blue and green gazebos, potted plants, and garden benches. It's extremely popular with strollers who continue to stream in until late in the evening. The park entrance is between Palmetto Park Road and Glades Road.

Royal Palm Plaza, Federal Highway (U.S. 1), between Palmetto Park Road and Camino Real (tel. 392-8920), is another quaint Boca shopping center. Called the "Pink Plaza" for its distinctive architecture, Royal Palm features two-story buildings with terra-cotta roofs, central fountains, white stone benches, and large banyan trees. Specialty stores, boutiques, restaurants, and the Royal Palm Dinner Theater make this a popular place to shop.

A large number of antiques shops are clustered together on **Atlantic Avenue** in downtown Delray Beach. Most of the stores here are open Monday through Wednesday and on Friday and Saturday from 10am to 5pm, plus Thursday from 10am to 9pm. You can pick up the "Delray Beach Antique Shop Guide" at almost any of the stores on the street.

EVENING ENTERTAINMENT

THE PERFORMING ARTS

BOCA RATON SYMPHONIC POPS, 100 NE First Ave., Boca Raton. Tel. 393-7677.

This 85-member orchestra plays jazz, swing, pop, and classical music, often with well-known guest stars. During the winter months the Pops plays at Florida Atlantic University; in the summer, at the Boca Raton Hotel. Call for an events schedule.

Admission: Tickets, $10–$35.

CALDWELL THEATER COMPANY, 7873 N. Federal Hwy., Boca Raton. Tel. 832-2989 or 241-7380.

The resident company of this 305-seat theater presents professional-quality contemporary and classical plays, comedy, and musicals. There are usually four different productions staged between November and May.

Admission: Tickets, $20–$25.

DELRAY BEACH PLAYHOUSE, 950 NW 9th St., Delray Beach. Tel. 272-1281.

Plays and musicals performed by local amateurs are sometimes really quite good. There are usually six different productions in winter and one in the summer, often in July. Call to see what's on.

Admission: Tickets, $15–$18.

LITTLE PALM THEATER, 137 SE 1st St., Boca Raton. Tel. 394-0308.

Now in its 17th year, this popular children's theater performs every Saturday morning at 9:15am at the Royal Palm Dinner Theater (see below). Classic children's stories and fairy tales are the usual fare. Casts are composed of volunteer actors, both children and adults. Every six weeks the Little Palm takes its production to Boynton Beach at 128 E. Ocean Ave. Call for details. The box office is open only on Saturday from 8:30 to 9:15am.

Admission: $6 general admission.

ROYAL PALM DINNER THEATER, 303 Mizner Blvd., Boca Raton. Tel. 426-2211, 832-0262, or toll free 800/841-6765.

Hit Broadway musicals and comedies are the main fare at this shoebox-size dinner theater in Boca Raton. Music concerts are sometimes performed here as well. Dinner is eaten beforehand at the adjacent Patio Garden Café. Phone for prices and showtimes. The box office is open on Sunday and Monday from 10am to 5pm, and Tuesday through Saturday from 10am to 7pm.

THE CLUB & MUSIC SCENE

BOSTON'S ON THE BEACH, 40 S. Fla. A1A, Delray Beach. Tel. 278-3364.

One of the first places in the area to give reggae bands a stage, Boston's is still one of the best, especially on Monday nights when it gets quite crowded. It's not always Caribbean music, however, and the club's popularity on any given day depends on who's playing. Boston's is also a good choice for happy hour, Monday through Friday from 4 to 7pm. It's open Monday through Saturday from 6:30am to 1am and on Sunday from 6:30am to midnight.

CLUB BOCA, 7000 W. Palmetto Rd., Boca Raton. Tel. 368-3333.

Because it's a little far from the beach, Club Boca is relatively devoid of tourists, but extremely popular with those in-the-know. The club is huge, and features live music six nights a week. Food is available. It's open Monday to Thursday from 9pm to 3am and on Friday and Saturday from 10pm to 4am.

Admission: $5.

DIRTY MOE'S, 395 NE Spanish River Blvd., Boca Raton. Tel. 395-3513.

Big and casual, Moe's has been around for a while—and looks like it. There's a long wooden bar in each of two large rectangular rooms. One has a small elevated stage where bands usually perform Wednesday through Sunday. Glossy, wooden pizza-parlor tables are filled with beer drinkers who also hang around the bar's pool tables. The second room is quieter, and food is served. Open Sunday through Tuesday from 11:30am to midnight and Wednesday through Saturday from 11:30am to 2am.

Admission: $3–$5 when bands play.

PHOENIX, 6 S. Ocean Blvd., Delray Beach. Tel. 278-6082.

If you're attracted to the smell of patchoulli oil, you'll like Phoenix, where Grateful Dead–style bands perform for the tie-dye and Birkenstock crowd. The building is really quite ugly—behind a fake-rock facade—but there's usually a fun, dance-oriented crowd. Open daily from 11am to 2am.

4. FORT LAUDERDALE & ENVIRONS

10 miles N of Miami

GETTING THERE **By Plane** The **Fort Lauderdale/Hollywood International Airport** (tel. 305/357-6100) is small, extremely user-friendly, and located just 15 minutes from downtown. Major domestic carriers servicing the airport include American (tel. toll free 800/433-7300), Continental (tel. 407/832-5200, or toll free 800/525-0280), Delta (tel. 407/655-5300, or toll free 800/221-1212), Northwest (tel. toll free 800/225-2525), and United (tel. toll free 800/241-6522).

By Train Amtrak (tel. toll free 800/USA-RAIL) trains departing from New York do not stop in Fort Lauderdale. Passengers de-train in West Palm Beach, 201 S. Tamarind Ave. (tel. 407/832-6169), or in Miami.

By Bus Greyhound/Trailways can get you to Fort Lauderdale from almost anywhere in the country. The company no longer operates a single nationwide telephone number, so consult your local directory for the office nearest you.

By Car If you're driving up or down the Florida coast, you'll probably reach Fort Lauderdale on I-95, a highway that runs all the way from Maine to Miami. Visitors on their way to or from Orlando should take the Florida Turnpike, a toll road that runs from just north of Fort Lauderdale to Walt Disney World.

ESSENTIALS The **telephone area code** is 305. The **Greater Fort Lauderdale Convention & Visitors Bureau,** 200 E. Las Olas Blvd., Suite 1500, Fort Lauderdale, FL 33301 (tel. 305/765-4466), distributes an excellent visitors guide with information on events and sightseeing in Broward County.

Fort Lauderdale Beach, a two-mile strip along Fla. A1A, gained fame in the 1950s as a spring break playground for partying college students. Not amused, the city's elders have long since ushered the mayhem elsewhere, and continue to work hard to bolster the town's image among other, more respectable (and presumably, richer) visitors. Self-promoted as "The Venice of America," for its 300 miles of navigable waterways, Fort Lauderdale is riddled with artificial canals that permit thousands of residents to anchor boats in their backyards. Boating is not just a hobby in Fort

Lauderdale, it's a lifestyle—and the reason many residents have chosen to live here. Mega-yachts, unique to South Florida (and Monaco), are built here by Broward Marine, and the organizers of the Whitbread Round the World Race have chosen Fort Lauderdale as the April stop in their 1994 challenge.

Hollywood, founded in the 1920s as the "dream city" of developer Joseph Wesley Young, attracts an interesting mix of Montrealers and Manhattanites who speak in Québécois and New Yorkese. The city's three-mile paved beach Broadwalk is its greatest asset, and the strip around which most of the action occurs.

Several of the listings below are actually in Lauderdale-by-the-Sea, a charming little tourist village just north of Fort Lauderdale. Centered around an 876-foot fishing pier, and fronting a long strip of white sand, the hamlet has several hotels and restaurants in a small six-block area that's largely devoid of traffic.

WHAT TO SEE & DO

BONNET HOUSE, 900 N. Birch Rd., Fort Lauderdale. Tel. 563-5393.

Listed on the National Register of Historic Places, Bonnet House is a 35-acre plantation home and estate dating from the turn of the century. Located in the middle of a highly developed beach area, the house is still occupied by a member of the family that built it. It's open to the public by reservation only.

Admission: $7.50 adults, $5 seniors and students.

Open: Tours given May–Nov, Tues–Thurs at 10am and 1:30pm, Sun at 1:30pm.

BUTTERFLY WORLD, 3600 W. Sample Rd., Coconut Creek. Tel. 977-4400.

Truly a unique sightseeing destination, Butterfly World houses thousands of butterflies and moths in and around a screened aviary. Visitors can actually watch butterflies emerge from their cocoons, and see dozens of exotic live varieties. Dozens more are mounted in an adjacent museum. The gift shop sells butterfly-attracting plants.

Admission: $7.95 adults, $6.95 seniors, $5 children 3–12, free for children under 3.

Open: Mon–Sat 9am–5pm.

GOODYEAR BLIMP BASE, 1500 NE Fifth Ave., Pompano Beach. Tel. 946-8300.

One of only four blimp bases in operation around the world, this one offers free tours to visitors. Call for tour times and information.

HOLLYWOOD BEACH BROADWALK, Hollywood Beach from Sheridan St. to Georgia St.

If you want to get a quick feel for what South Florida means to millions of retirement-age "snowbirds," be sure to visit this lengthy paved beach path. Three miles long and 27 feet wide, the sandside Broadwalk is packed with French Canadians and others who take daily ritualistic strolls past the path's gift shops, cafés, and restaurants. Part of the pavement is dedicated to bicyclers who loudly proclaim their rights to wayward walkers.

INTERNATIONAL SWIMMING HALL OF FAME, 1 Hall of Fame Dr., Fort Lauderdale. Tel. 462-6536.

This huge, two-story ode to aquatics is the world's largest repository of swimming memorabilia, and includes films, books, interactive video displays, and seemingly endless archives relating to aquatic sports. A plethora of Olympic memorabilia from over 100 countries includes gold medals won by some of the sport's brightest stars. Home to the 1992 U.S. Olympic Diving Team, as well as a training facility for swimmers, the complex also houses two Olympic-size swimming pools. It's open year-round, daily from 9am to 7pm.

Admission: $3 adults, $2 students and seniors.

MUSEUM OF DISCOVERY & SCIENCE, 401 SW 2nd St., Fort Lauderdale. Tel. 467-MODS.

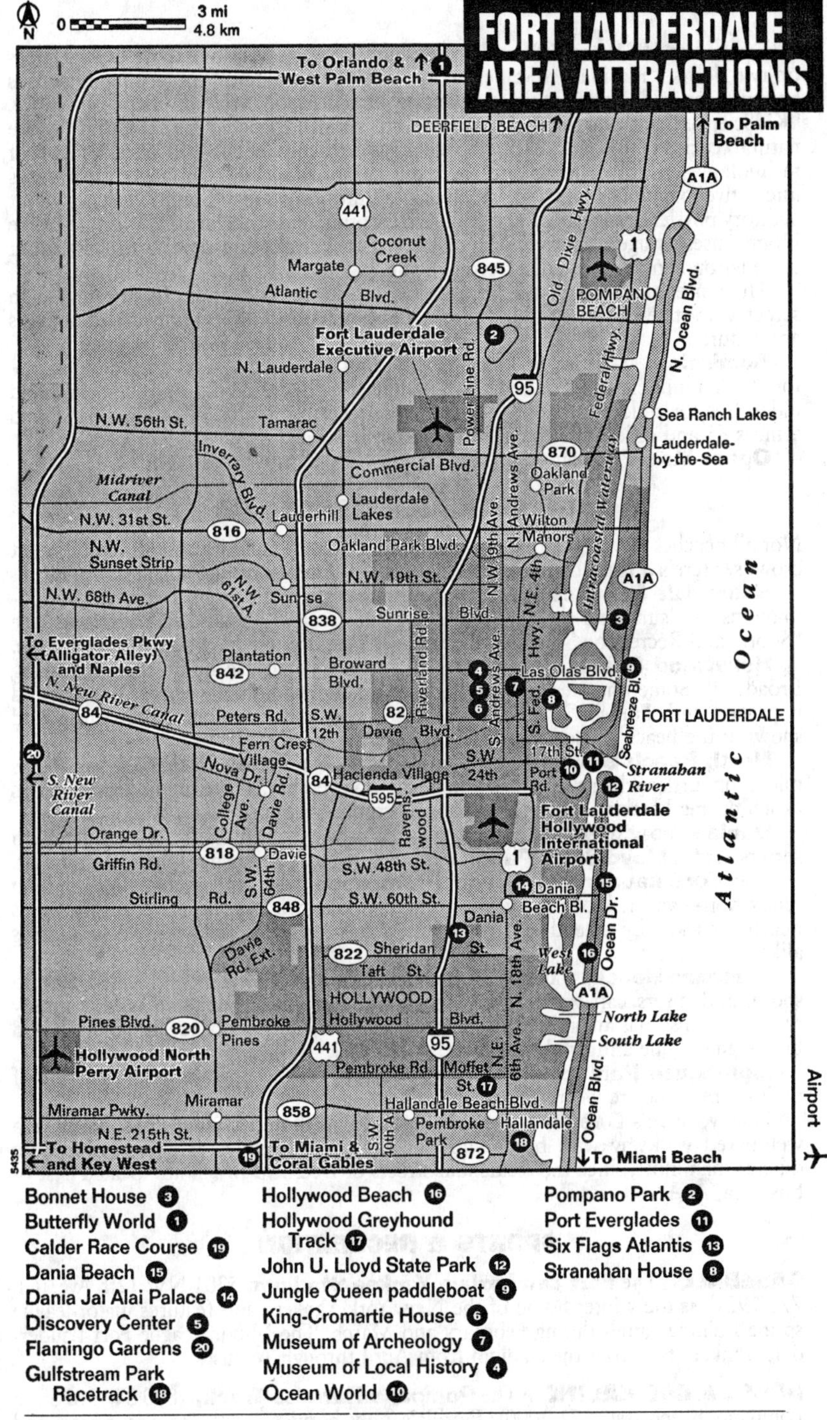
FORT LAUDERDALE AREA ATTRACTIONS
3 mi
4.8 km
To Orlando & West Palm Beach
DEERFIELD BEACH
To Palm Beach
Coconut Creek
Margate
Atlantic Blvd.
Old Dixie Hwy.
POMPANO BEACH
N. Ocean Blvd.
Fort Lauderdale Executive Airport
N. Lauderdale
Power Line Rd.
Federal Hwy.
Sea Ranch Lakes
Lauderdale-by-the-Sea
N.W. 56th St.
Tamarac
Inverrary Blvd.
Commercial Blvd.
Oakland Park
Midriver Canal
Lauderdale Lakes
Intracoastal Waterway
N.W. 31st St.
Lauderhill
Wilton Manors
N.W. Sunset Strip
Oakland Park Blvd.
N. Andrews Ave.
N.W. 9th Ave.
N.E. 4th Ave.
N.W. 61st A
Sunrise
N.W. 19th St.
N.W. 68th Ave.
Sunrise Blvd.
To Everglades Pkwy (Alligator Alley) and Naples
Plantation
Broward Blvd.
Riverland Rd.
S. Andrews Ave.
Hwy.
Las Olas Blvd.
Atlantic Ocean
N. New River Canal
Peters Rd.
S.W. 12th
Davie Blvd.
S. Fed.
Seabreeze Bl.
FORT LAUDERDALE
Fern Crest Village
S.W. 24th
17th St.
Stranahan River
S. New River Canal
Nova Dr.
Hacienda Village
Port Rd.
College Ave.
Davie Rd.
Ravenswood
Fort Lauderdale Hollywood International Airport
Orange Dr.
Griffin Rd.
Davie
S.W. 48th St.
S.W. 64th
Dania
Stirling Rd.
S.W. 60th St.
Beach Bl.
Ocean Dr.
Dania
Davie Rd. Ext.
Sheridan St.
N. 18th Ave.
West Lake
Taft St.
HOLLYWOOD
North Lake
South Lake
Pines Blvd.
Pembroke Pines
Hollywood Blvd.
Hollywood North Perry Airport
Pembroke Rd.
Moffet St.
N.E. 6th Ave.
Ocean Blvd.
Miramar
Miramar Pwky.
Hallandale Beach Blvd.
N.E. 215th St.
Pembroke Park
Hallandale
To Homestead and Key West
To Miami & Coral Gables
S.W. 40th A
To Miami Beach
Airport
Bonnet House 3
Butterfly World 1
Calder Race Course 19
Dania Beach 15
Dania Jai Alai Palace 14
Discovery Center 5
Flamingo Gardens 20
Gulfstream Park Racetrack 18
Hollywood Beach 16
Hollywood Greyhound Track 17
John U. Lloyd State Park 12
Jungle Queen paddleboat 9
King-Cromartie House 6
Museum of Archeology 7
Museum of Local History 4
Ocean World 10
Pompano Park 2
Port Everglades 11
Six Flags Atlantis 13
Stranahan House 8

Opened in 1991, this $32-million museum houses seven interactive exhibit areas on two floors. "Florida EcoScapes" is an "ecology mountain" comprising numerous aquaria, terraria, and simulated habitats demonstrating the diversity of nature. "KidScience," with its musical staircase and colorful carpeted maze, appeals to the natural curiosity of kids 3–5. "Space Base" teaches about the development of technology leading to flight and the exploration of space; "Choose Health" uses interactive exhibits to focus on wellness and nutrition issues; "Sound" teaches about auditory physical properties, as well as its reception and storage; and "No Place Like Home" uses a huge cutaway model of a house to increase consumer awareness about the environmental effects of everyday living.

The museum also contains the only IMAX theater in Florida. Its five-story-high screen with state-of-the-art sound shows specially produced short films about humans and nature.

Admission: Museum, $6 adults, $5 children 3–12 and seniors 65 and older, free for children under 3; IMAX theater, $5 adults, $4 children 3–12 and seniors 65 and older, free for children under 3; combination ticket, $8 adults, $7 children 3–12 and seniors 65 and older, free for children under 3.

Open: Mon–Fri 10am–5pm, Sat 10am–8:30pm, Sun noon–5pm.

PARKS & BEACHES

Not all beaches are created equal—they offer different facilities and attract different crowds. Here's a run-down on the county's best from south to north:

Hallandale Beaches attract the retirement-aged folks who live in the condominiums that surround them. Close to Gulfstream and Hallandale Racetracks (see "Sports and Recreation," below), the beaches here are less crowded after post time.

Hollywood Beach is really special, primarily because of its three-mile-long Broadwalk. Sometimes described as "Venice Beach without the weirdos," Hollywood is packed with French-Canadian vacationers who attend senior-citizen dances and shows at the beach's Theater Under the Stars.

North Beach State Park is known for its Sea Turtle Hatchery, which helps migrating turtles when they come ashore each November. There are no lights on this beach during hatching season so as not to confuse the turtles.

Dania's beaches have the best waves in the county, and are popular with surfers. **John Lloyd State Park** is best, as surf most everywhere else is usually flat.

The **Fort Lauderdale Beach Promenade** just underwent a $20-million renovation—and it looks marvelous. Once popular with spring break revelers, this beach is backed by an endless row of hotels and is popular with tourists and locals alike.

Pompano Beach is famous for fishing and diving. A coral reef is located close to shore, and divers can walk right to the dive site. While Pompano is very family oriented, it also has an authentic fishermen's charm. You kind of feel as if you should be hanging a line and drinking a beer.

Lighthouse Point and Hillsboro Beach are the upscale, pretty parcels of millionaires. They're worth a look.

Finally, there's **Deerfield Beach,** dotted with boulders and coves. There is a well-paved walkway with beach showers and good facilities. The sands here are quieter than most, since the residential streets of Deerfield Beach are located east of busy Fla. A1A.

SPORTS & RECREATION

BASEBALL The **Fort Lauderdale Yankee Stadium,** 5301 NW 12th Ave. (tel. 776-1921), is the winter home of the New York Yankees and features major-league spring training games during February and March. The Minor League Fort Lauderdale Yankees take over the stadium from April through August.

HORSE & DOG RACING The **Pompano Harness Track,** 1800 SW 3rd St. in Pompano Beach (tel. 972-2000), Florida's only harness track, features racing and betting from November to early April.

Greyhounds, the world's fastest dogs, reach speeds of more than 40 miles an hour while chasing a fake rabbit around a track. As with the horses, bettors can wager to win, place, or show. There is racing year-round at the **Hollywood Greyhound Track,** 831 N. Federal Hwy., Hallandale (tel. 454-9400). Call for post times.

There are lots of horse tracks in Florida, and while **Gulfstream Park,** 901 S. Federal Hwy. in Hallandale (tel. 454-7000), might not be the prettiest, it's one of the biggest and best-known thoroughbred tracks in the state.

JAI ALAI Jai alai, a Spanish cross between lacrosse and handball, is popular in South Florida. Players use woven baskets, called cestas, to hurl balls, called pelotas, at speeds that sometimes exceed 170 miles per hour. Spectators, who are protected behind a wall of glass, place bets on the evening's players. **Dania Jai-Alai,** 301 E. Dania Beach Blvd., Dania (tel. 428-7766), is one of the nicest frontons in the United States.

ORGANIZED TOURS

JUNGLE QUEEN CRUISES, Bahia Mar Yacht Center, Fla. A1A, Fort Lauderdale. Tel. 462-5596.

One of Fort Lauderdale's oldest attractions, this Mississippi River–style steamer is a sightseeing attraction in its own right, and a popular sight as it cruises up the New River. Each three-hour tour takes visitors past Millionaires' Row, Old Fort Lauderdale, the new downtown, and Port Everglades cruise-ship port.

Admission: $6.95 adults, $4.95 children.

Schedule: Tour given daily at 10am and 2pm.

SOUTH FLORIDA TROLLEY TOURS. Tel. 426-3044.

Visitors learn about historical and modern-day Fort Lauderdale aboard cute "old-style" trams. The trolleys pick up passengers at most major hotels. Phone for tour times.

Admission: $10 adults, $5 children 6–12.

WATER TAXI OF FT. LAUDERDALE. Tel. 565-5507.

Water taxis serve the dual purpose of transportation and entertainment around this city of canals. The service operates on demand, like a shared land taxi, carrying up to 27 passengers. Route maps are available from most area hotels. The service operates daily from 10am until midnight or 2am.

Admission: $4.50 per person per trip, or $12 for an entire day.

WHERE TO STAY

VERY EXPENSIVE

MARRIOTT'S HARBOR BEACH RESORT, 3030 Holiday Dr., Fort Lauderdale, FL 33316. Tel. 305/525-4000, or toll free 800/222-6543. Fax 305/766-6165. 624 rms, 35 suites. A/C TV TEL

$ Rates: Dec 13–Jan 2, $255–$350 single or double. Jan 3–May 1, $255–$320 single or double. May 2–July 10 and Sept 12–Dec 11, $190–$235 single or double. July 11–Sept 11, $150–$195 single or double. Year-round, suites from $500. AE, CB, DC, DISC, MC, V.

Located on 16 oceanfront acres, this premier resort features luxurious accommodations that are every bit as good as the hotel's ideal location. Every spacious room opens onto a private balcony, the most expensive of which overlook the hotel's exclusive strip of beach. Lavish gardens surround several bubbling fountains and an oversize 8,000-square-foot swimming pool.

Dining/Entertainment: Sheffield's, a classy continental restaurant, requires both jackets and reservations (see "Where to Dine," below). Kinoko is less formal, and serves Japanese hibachi-style dinners that are prepared at your table. The Oceanview,

Sea Breeze Grill, and Cascades are three other casual restaurants serving breakfast, lunch, dinner, and late-night drinks.

Services: 24-hour room service, concierge, complimentary golf at off-premises club, massage, babysitting.

Facilities: Swimming pool, five clay tennis courts, beach cabañas, whirlpool, sauna, exercise room, water-sports rentals.

EXPENSIVE

LAGO MAR, 1700 S. Ocean Lane, Fort Lauderdale, FL 33316. Tel. 305/523-6511, or toll free 800/255-5246. Fax 305/523-6511. 79 rms, 129 suites. A/C TV TEL **Directions:** From Federal Highway (U.S. 1), turn east onto the SE 17th St. Causeway, then right onto Mayan Drive; turn right again onto South Ocean Drive, left onto Grace Drive, and left again onto South Ocean Lane to the hotel.

$ Rates: Dec 16–Apr $150–$175 single or double; from $235 suite. May–Oct 25, $75–$105 single or double; from $115 suite. Oct 26–Dec 15, $95–$125 single or double; from $135 suite. AE, CB, DC, MC, V.

Lago Mar, Spanish for "lake to ocean," occupies its own little island between Lake Mayan and the Atlantic. The resort offers oversize rooms that are sparsely decorated with eclectic furnishings and textured wallpaper with pastel accents. In addition to balconies, all suites are equipped with either a full kitchen, or a microwave and a refrigerator. Newly remodeled Executive Suites are smarter and more modern than other rooms.

Dining/Entertainment: The Palm Garden Room serves three meals daily. Reservations are required for dinner and there's live entertainment six nights a week. The Sea Grape Terrace, also serving from morning to night, is less formal, and has a wonderful outdoor patio sheltered by white, vined trellises. The Soda Shop and Ocean Grill are open for lunch and snacks, while the Lago Mar Bar and Lounge and the Promenade Bar are open late for cocktails.

Services: Room service, concierge, supervised children's programs during holiday periods.

Facilities: Two swimming pools, four tennis courts, putting green, miniature golf course, children's playground, water-sports rentals, games room, apparel shops.

MODERATE

BANYAN MARINA APARTMENTS, 111 Isle of Venice, Fort Lauderdale, FL 33301. Tel. 305/524-4430. Fax 305/764-4870. 10 rms. A/C TV TEL

$ Rates: Dec–Apr, $75–$100 single or double; from $110 apt. May–Nov, $40–$55 single or double; from $70 apt. Weekly and monthly rates available. MC, V.

Peter and Dagmar Neufeldt's Banyan Marina Apartments represent one of the best accommodation values in South Florida. Wrapped around a 75-year-old banyan tree, this well-maintained two-story inn is located directly on an active waterway, halfway between Fort Lauderdale's downtown and the beach. The accommodations—standard hotel rooms, efficiencies, and one- and two-bedroom apartments—are all decorated differently. Some have modern art deco accents, some are outfitted with blond woods, and others have more contemporary ivory laminates and brass highlights. Livability is the key here. There's a small pool just off the center courtyard, and boat dockage for eight yachts.

LAUDERDALE COLONIAL, 3049 Harbor Dr., Fort Lauderdale, FL 33316. Tel. 305/525-3676. Fax 305/463-3787. 12 rms, 8 suites. A/C TV TEL

$ Rates: Dec 15–Apr, $85–$95 single or double; from $95 suite. May–Dec 14, $52–$62 single or double; from $64 suite. Additional person $15 extra. MC, V.

Listed here for its good Intracoastal waterfront location and above-average quality, this affordable motel is relatively straightforward, offering basic rooms, suites, and efficiencies surrounding a central courtyard. Although every room in this compact

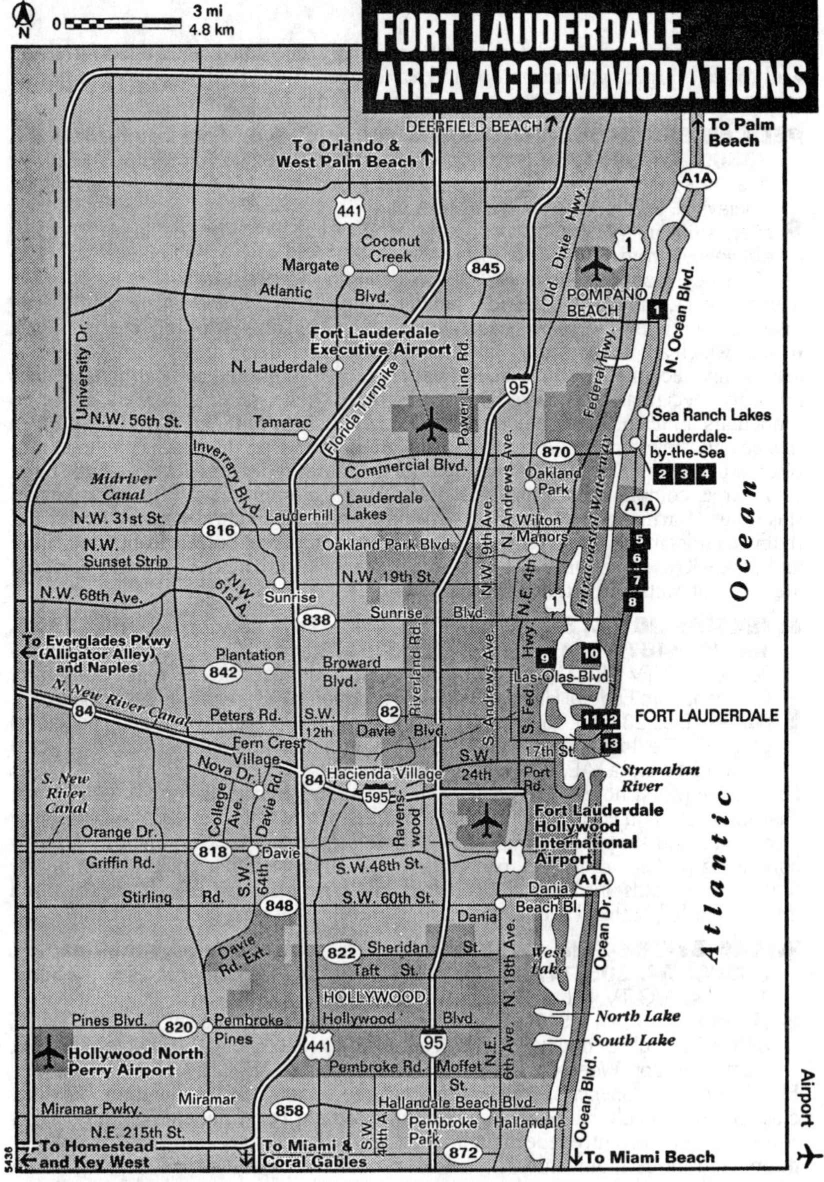

- Anacapri Inn 7
- Banyan Marina Apartments 10
- International House Hostel 6
- Lago Mar 13
- Lauderdale Colonial 11
- Marriott's Harbor Beach Resort 12
- Pelican Beach Resort 8
- Reef Motel 3
- Riverside Hotel 9
- The Ronny Dee Resort Motel 1
- Santa Barbara Motel 4
- Surf and Sun Hotel and Apartments 5
- Villas-by-the-Sea 2

black-and-white motel is different, all are simply decorated with light furniture, wall-to-wall carpeting, refrigerators, and tea/coffee-making facilities. There's a heated swimming pool, barbecue area, and laundry facilities for guest use.

PELICAN BEACH RESORT, 2000 N. Atlantic Blvd., Fort Lauderdale, FL 33305. Tel. 305/568-9431, or toll free 800/525-6232. Fax 305/565-2622. 47 rms, 12 suites. A/C TV TEL **Directions:** From Fla. A1A, turn east onto Atlantic Boulevard, just north of Sunrise Boulevard.

$ Rates (including breakfast): Dec–Apr, $85–$110 single or double; $110–$130 efficiency; from $140 suite. May–Nov, $50–$70 single or double; $65–$90 efficiency; from $85 suite. AE, CB, DC, DISC, MC, V.

The sprawling, family-owned and -operated Pelican Beach Resort encompasses seven dissimilar buildings, each of which possesses distinctive style and charm. Guest rooms, which are connected to one another by wooden decks and tropical walkways, are cleanly decorated with tile floors, pastel-colored walls, and vertical blinds. Suites are truly special, as they come with spa bathtubs, huge standing showers, and even binoculars. Efficiencies are equipped with small kitchens outfitted with dishes, coffee makers, and refrigerators. Although it's located directly on the beach, the hotel also offers a particularly striking swimming pool that glows by night with fiber-optic light.

A large, complimentary breakfast, served each morning from 7 to 10am, makes this hotel a particularly good value. Morning meals include hot oatmeal, fresh fruit, muffins, croissants, pastries, coffee, tea, and fresh juice. The hotel's proprietors, Steve and Jackie Kruse, are particularly helpful, and happy to share their knowledge of the area's restaurants and attractions.

RIVERSIDE HOTEL, 620 E. Las Olas Blvd., Fort Lauderdale, FL 33301. Tel. 305/467-0671, or toll free 800/325-3280. Fax 305/462-2148. 117 rms, 5 suites. A/C TV TEL **Directions:** From I-95, exit east onto Broward Boulevard, turn right onto Federal Highway (U.S. 1), and then go left onto Las Olas Boulevard.

$ Rates: Dec 23–Apr 15, $95–$110 single or double; from $175 suite; additional person $15 extra. Apr 16–Dec 22, $70 single or double; from $99 suite; additional person $10 extra. AE, CB, DC, MC, V.

One of the oldest hotels in South Florida, the 1936 Riverside is packed with prewar charm. Located on Fort Lauderdale's main street, sandwiched between contemporary restaurants and shops, the hotel is a welcome celebration of a bygone era. A lobby containing wicker furnishings, paddle fans, and a fireplace that crackles even on the hottest days leads into nicely decorated guest rooms with oak furnishings and intricately tiled baths. There is a concierge and evening turn-down service.

VILLAS-BY-THE-SEA, 4456 El Mar Dr., Lauderdale-by-the-Sea, FL 33308. Tel. 305/772-3550, or toll free 800/247-8963. Fax 305/772-3835. 148 rms. A/C TV TEL

$ Rates: Feb–Apr 11, $100–$130 single or double; from $145 apt. Apr 12–Dec 19, $65–$85 single or double; from $95 apt. Dec 20–Jan, $85–$115 single or double; from $130 apt. Weekly and monthly rates available. AE, CB, DC, MC, V.

Hotel rooms, efficiencies, and apartments are located in six different buildings clustered on a single block of this charming northern Fort Lauderdale village. Every room has been recently redecorated with light contemporary furniture, ceramic tile floors, and modern amenities. Each well-maintained pastel-colored building has its own small, tropical courtyard containing a swimming pool or sunbathing facilities.

There are five heated swimming pools on the grounds as well as a Jacuzzi, barbecue grills, and an outdoor fitness area. The hotel is justifiably popular with international tourists, many of whom stay here for months at a time.

INEXPENSIVE

ANACAPRI INN, 1901 N. Federal Hwy. (U.S. 1), Fort Lauderdale, FL 33305. Tel. 305/563-1111. Fax 305/568-3304. 120 rms. A/C TV TEL

$ Rates: Dec 15–Jan and Apr, $49–$59 single or double; from $95 suite. Feb–Mar, $54–$64 single or double; from $105 suite. May–Nov, $44–$49 single or double; from $95 suite. Additional person $10 extra. AE, MC, V.

Inside the large pink buildings that comprise the Anacapri are 10 dozen pleasant enough simply decorated rooms that are reliably comfortable and clean. Although the accommodations here won't win any awards for style, they are well located, within five minutes of most of the city's major attractions. There's a swimming pool and a café/bar offering happy hour specials on weekdays and live jazz on weekends.

REEF MOTEL, 4312 El Mar Dr., Lauderdale-by-the-Sea, FL 33308. Tel. 305/776-1164. 5 rms. A/C TV

$ Rates: Feb–Apr 1, $82–$87 single or double. May–Dec 14, $43–$46 single or double. Apr 2–30 and Dec 15–Jan, $62–$67 single or double.

We like this modest motel a lot. There's not much to this unassuming little green hostelry—no telephones, no swimming pool, and no special services—but the Reef is located directly on the ocean, there's a large sun deck, and owners Jim and Joan Smith keep their five 1950s-style rooms spic-and-span clean.

RONNY DEE RESORT MOTEL, 717 S. Ocean Blvd., Pompano Beach, FL 33062. Tel. 305/943-3020. 35 rms. A/C TV

$ Rates: Dec 16–Jan 7, $47–$55 single or double; from $65 apt. Jan 8–31 and Apr 1–15, $43–$50 single or double; from $60 apt. Feb–Mar, $56–$65 single or double; from $75 apt. Apr 16–Dec 15, $29–$32 single or double; from $37 apt. Additional person $6 extra. MC, V.

The bad news is that this family-owned motel is located on busy Fla. A1A; the good news is that it's just 100 yards from the beach, and amazingly inexpensive. Popular with European guests, this two-story yellow motel, wrapped around a central swimming pool, is outfitted with suburban-style wood-paneled guest rooms that are filled with an eclectic mix of furniture and small refrigerators. There are no in-room telephones; payphones are located in a public area, near a large games room that contains a pool table, a VCR, books, and assorted games. Ping-Pong and shuffleboard are also available.

Complimentary coffee and doughnuts are served each morning in the motel lobby.

SANTA BARBARA MOTEL, 4301 El Mar Dr., Lauderdale-by-the-Sea, FL 33308 Tel. 305/491-5211, 305/566-1164 at night. 13 rms. A/C TV

$ Rates: Dec 18–Jan 20, $40–$62 single or double; from $72 apt. Jan 21–Apr 10, $40–$72 single or double; from $82 apt. Apr 11–May 1, $36–$50 single or double; from $60 apt. May 2–Nov 1, $32–$36 single or double; from $42 apt. Nov 2–Dec 17, $36–$42 single or double; from $48 apt. MC, V.

One of the best values in Lauderdale-by-the-Sea, this small two-story motel offers little more than clean, basic, spacious, homey rooms, a small swimming pool, and cordial proprietors Bev and Gil Wilson.

SURF AND SUN HOTEL AND APARTMENTS, 521 N. Atlantic Blvd., Fort Lauderdale, FL 33304. Tel. 305/564-4341, or toll free 800/248-0463. Fax 305/564-4472. 23 rms. A/C TV TEL

$ Rates: Dec 21–Jan, $53 single or double; $66 efficiency; from $86 apt. Feb–Apr 19, $59 single or double; $74 efficiency; from $93 apt. Apr 20–Dec 20, $36 single or double; efficiency $42; from $53 apt. Additional person $6 extra. AE, DISC, MC, V.

Nobody stays here to lounge in the rooms, which tend to be a bit dark and musty. But you can't beat the location—directly across from Fort Lauderdale's brand-new $20-million beach promenade and within walking distance of several restaurants, bars, and shops. Accommodations are almost austere, though rooms do contain refrigerators. There's a small courtyard with wooden lounges for sunbathing.

BUDGET

INTERNATIONAL HOUSE HOSTEL, 3811 N. Ocean Blvd., Fort Lauderdale, FL 33308. Tel. 305/568-1615. 84 beds.

$ Rates: $15 per person.

Bare-bones budgeteers will appreciate this motel-style hostel, where international guests in their 20s share rooms by the half dozen. There are bunk beds and televisions in most rooms, and some come with kitchenettes. Private rooms are available for traveling couples. There's beach access across the street, a large swimming pool, and laundry facilities. Look for the colorful flags of the world flying outside the motel.

WHERE TO DINE

EXPENSIVE

CAFE ARUGULA, 3110 N. Federal Hwy., Lighthouse Point. Tel. 785-7732.

Cuisine: AMERICAN.
$ Prices: Appetizers $5–$8; main courses $15–$22. AE, MC, V.
Open: Dinner only, Sun–Thurs 5:30–10pm, Fri–Sat 5:30–10:30pm.

Celebrity restaurateur Dick Cingolani was one of the first to bring imaginative American "Cuisine" to Fort Lauderdale. Today, the Café Arugula remains one of the city's most celebrated restaurants. Amid comfortable surroundings which include soft lighting, plush furnishings, and properly distanced tables, both the kitchen and the dining room are clearly influenced by international trends that include the best of the Caribbean, California, and the Mediterranean. Mussels are wrapped with Cajun smoked ham, escargots mixed with chorizo (Mexican sausage), and red snapper is drenched with cilantro-lime butter and rolled in ground pecans. Desserts are equally interesting and inviting, and include such specialties as raspberry crème brûlée and bitter Mexican chocolate torte.

CHARLEY'S CRAB, 3000 NE 32nd Ave., Fort Lauderdale. Tel. 561-4800.

Cuisine: SEAFOOD. **Reservations:** Recommended.
$ Prices: Appetizers $5–$8; main courses $15–$22. AE, DC, DISC, MC, V.
Open: Lunch Mon–Sat 11:30am–3:30pm, Sun 11am–3:30pm; dinner Sun–Thurs 5–10pm, Fri–Sat 5–11pm.

The Fort Lauderdale outpost of this popular, upscale South Florida seafood chain is every bit as good—and almost as expensive—as its more celebrated Palm Beach sibling.

All the usual fish are served here—salmon, pompano, dolphin (fish)—as are baked clams, oysters Rockefeller, and mini crab cakes. Steak, lamb, and chicken dishes are also available. Entrees are accompanied by different side dishes each evening, and if parmesan roasted potatoes are on the day's menu, order them. The restaurant also features a good raw bar with a variety of shellfish, and a well-selected wine list with picks from California and around the world.

DOWN UNDER, 3000 E. Oakland Park Blvd., Fort Lauderdale. Tel. 564-6984.

Cuisine: CONTINENTAL. **Reservations:** Recommended.
$ Prices: Appetizers $5–$8; main courses $15–$22. DC, DISC, MC, V.
Open: Lunch daily 11am–2pm; dinner Mon–Sat 6–10:30pm, Sun 6–10pm.

There's nothing Australian about this superior, elegant riverside bistro that's named for its location—below an overpass that crosses the Intracoastal Waterway. Decorated with antiques, dark woods, and a jungle of hanging plants, the restaurant is much more appealing than its rather austere exterior would suggest.

While meals here were once thought refreshingly novel, the restaurant's California/Louisiana cuisine is no longer considered to be on the culinary edge. Chicken and fish in light spicy sauces are best bets and, together with a slightly sentimental atmosphere, make the Down Under one of the city's most romantic restaurants.

SHEFFIELD'S, in Marriott's Harbor Beach Resort, 3030 Holiday Dr., Fort Lauderdale. Tel. 525-4000.

Cuisine: CONTINENTAL. **Reservations:** Recommended.
$ Prices: Appetizers $8–$9; main courses $20–$30. AE, DC, DISC, MC, V.
Open: Dinner only, daily 5:30–10:30pm.

When you're ready to abandon South Florida's trendy light salads and rare braised fish, visit Sheffield's, a handsome, clubby, intimate restaurant inside an equally fancy but decidedly more casual hotel. Four small dark-wood dining rooms are decorated with plush heavy furnishings, etched-glass dividers, and plenty of cozy nooks. The restaurant's celebrated English manor house comfort is augmented by a conservative and knowledgeable career service staff and heavy continental menu.

Appetizers like escargots with garlic butter and Camembert cheese, French forest morels with brandied-cream sauce, and chilled roast duck medallions with pinot noir and currant sauce are sure to raise cholesterol levels, but at these prices, who's noticing? Entrees are just as divine, and include a classical beef Wellington, salmon with champagne beurre blanc, mesquite-grilled veal chops, Long Island duckling, and rack of lamb with mint-cabernet sauce. Desserts like chocolate pâté and Brie cheesecake don't disappoint either, but fitting it all in is another matter.

MODERATE

ARUBA BEACH CAFE, 1 Commercial Blvd., Lauderdale-by-the-Sea. Tel. 776-0001.

Cuisine: SEAFOOD/AMERICAN.

$ Prices: Appetizers $3–$7; main courses $7–$15; lunch $3–$10. AE, DC, DISC, MC, V.

Open: Daily 11am–2am (food served until 1am).

Brightly colored wicker chairs, a lively bar, indoor/outdoor seating, and large plate-glass windows overlooking a particularly beautiful stretch of beach combine to make this contemporary restaurant one of Fort Lauderdale's most atmospheric. The ambience is as easy as the menu, which is replete with salads, sandwiches, and the requisite local seafood offerings. Two of the best lunchtime entrees are blackened fish and herb-roasted chicken with new potatoes. Oversize evening entrees include coconut-fried shrimp served with yogurt-lime dipping sauce, grilled Cuban steak served with pickled onions, and seafood fettuccine marinara with shrimp, scallops, and swordfish. Any time of day you'd be well advised to start with the smoked fish dip served with seasoned flat bread, or a selection from the fresh raw bar.

BURT & JACK'S, Berth 23, Port Everglades. Tel. 522-5225.

Cuisine: AMERICAN. **Reservations:** Recommended.

$ Prices: Appetizers $7–$9; main courses $15–$22. AE, DC, DISC, MC, V.

Open: Dinner only, Sun–Thurs 5–10pm, Fri–Sat 5–11:30pm.

Despite the fact that this restaurant is partly owned by actor Burt Reynolds, it's not a celebrity glam spot filled with papparazzi and star seekers. Instead, Burt & Jacks is a highly respected surf-and-turf restaurant, serving excellent aged New York steaks, prime rib, Maine lobster, local fish, and large salads.

The restaurant is unusually located deep inside Fort Lauderdale's cruise-ship port; follow the signs to the ships.

FISHERMAN'S WHARF, 222 Pompano Beach Blvd., Pompano Beach. Tel. 941-5522.

Cuisine: AMERICAN. **Reservations:** Not required.

$ Prices: Appetizers $5–$9; main courses $11–$16; lunch $4–$7. AE, MC, V.

Open: Lunch daily 11am–2pm; dinner Sun–Thurs 4:30–10pm, Fri–Sat 4:30–11pm.

Fisherman's Wharf's casual atmosphere has everything to do with its location—on the sand, at the foot of Pompano Beach Pier. A double dining room outfitted with heavy wooden tables and chairs is centered around a busy bar, complete with a nonstop popcorn machine. The rear room, which looks very much like a glass box with good water views, holds a small stage where live bands perform every night but Sunday. Outside is separate tiki bar and barbecue shack.

Just as you'd expect, lunches include clam chowder, Cobb salad, blackened-fish sandwiches, burgers, and fresh fish selections. Dinner, which is more formal, adds filet mignon with mushroom caps, mussels marinara over linguine, and fancier fish dishes. Special children's selections are always available.

INEXPENSIVE

COUNTRY HAM N' EGGS, 4405 El Mar Dr., Lauderdale-by-the-Sea. Tel. 776-1666.

Cuisine: AMERICAN.

$ Prices: Breakfast $2.50–$3; lunch/dinner $5–$8.

Open: Daily 7am–9pm.

Europeans love this campy coffee shop, where breakfast is served all day at bright yellow booths and Formica tables. After 10:30am the menu is expanded to include a variety of sandwiches, homemade meatloaf, and burgers. The restaurant is located one block from the ocean in the cozy hamlet of Lauderdale-by-the-Sea.

PIER RESTAURANT, 2 E. Commercial Blvd, Lauderdale-by-the-Sea. Tel. 776-1690.

Cuisine: SEAFOOD/AMERICAN.

$ Prices: Sandwiches and burgers $3–$5.

Open: Daily 7am–4pm.

Located on the near end of the Lauderdale-by-the-Sea pier, this tiny eatery is little more than a luncheonette on the beach, occupying one of the region's most enviable locations. The built-in outdoor wooden picnic tables are the best seats, shaded from the sun but in full view of the suntanners. The menu, which is printed on wooden signs posted above the low Formica bar, features American standards like bacon and eggs, pancakes, patty melts, and milkshakes.

SHOPPING

There are three places every visitor to Fort Lauderdale should know about. The first is **Antique Row,** a strip of U.S. 1 around North Dania Beach Boulevard (in Dania, about one mile south of Fort Lauderdale/Hollywood International Airport) that holds about 200 antiques shops. Although most are a bit overpriced, if you're persistent, there are bound to be some good finds in furniture, silver, china, glass, linens, and more. The shops are closed Sunday.

The **Fort Lauderdale Swap Shop,** 3291 W. Sunrise Blvd. (tel. 791-7927), is one of the world's largest flea markets, containing endless acres of vendors as well as a mini–amusement park, a 12-screen drive-in movie theater, weekend concerts, and even a free circus complete with elephants, horse shows, high-wire acts, and clowns. This is truly one of the best flea markets anywhere. It's open daily and admission is free.

Sawgrass Mills, Sunrise Boulevard and Flamingo Road, Fort Lauderdale (tel. 846-2300), bills itself as the world's largest outlet mall, offering more than 225 brand-name off-price stores including Macy's, Saks Fifth Avenue, Ann Taylor, Spiegel, and Levi's. Merchandise is priced up to 75% below retail for discontinued or slightly irregular products. It's truly a unique shopping experience.

EVENING ENTERTAINMENT

THE PERFORMING ARTS

BROWARD CENTER FOR THE PERFORMING ARTS, 201 SW Fifth Ave., Fort Lauderdale. Tel. 522-5334.

Opened in 1991, this stunning new $52-million multitheater complex contains both a 2,700-seat auditorium and a smaller 595-seat theater. The center attracts top opera, symphony, dance, and Broadway productions, as well as more modest size shows.

OFF BROADWAY, on E. 26th St., Fort Lauderdale. Tel. 566-0554.

As the name says, this theater specializes in smaller, independent, and sometimes offbeat productions of contemporary plays. The stage operates year-round.

THE OPERA GUILD. Tel. 462-0222.

For more than 40 years this sometimes world-class society has been dazzling audiences with a wide-ranging series of shows that has featured such top names as

Pavarotti and Domingo. The season runs from December through April, usually in the Broward Center of the Performing Arts (see above).

PARKER PLAYHOUSE, 707 NE. 8th St. Tel. 764-0700.

Fort Lauderdale's best theater series, Parker productions regularly attract big-name shows with nationally known actors. This is a really good, "insider" kind of place, well supported by the community. It's small, and offers great sightlines from every seat.

PHILHARMONIC ORCHESTRA OF FLORIDA. Tel. 561-2997.

When this innovative South Florida–based company comes to Fort Lauderdale, they usually perform in the Broward Center for the Performing Arts (see above). Their season runs from October to May.

SINFONIA VIRTUOSI AND CHORUS OF FLORIDA. Tel. 561-5882.

Classical, romantic, baroque, and contemporary music is performed under the direction of James Brooks-Bruzzese. Individual tickets are usually available to the series which runs from November through May.

THE BAR, CLUB & MUSIC SCENE

CAFE 66, at the Pier 66 Resort and Marina, 301 SE 17th St. Causeway. Tel. 525-6666.

There's always something happening at this busy waterfront bar—sometimes it's live rock; sometimes a dance contest. Pier Top, a revolving restaurant and bar in the hotel's penthouse, attracts an older crowd that can appreciate a good sunset.

CROOCO'S, 3339 N. Federal Hwy., Oakland Park. Tel. 566-2406.

One of the largest bars in Florida, this giant sports disco and rock 'n' roll club encompasses numerous bars, several dance floors, a basketball court, a baseball batting cage, and one of the biggest TV screens you've ever seen.

DO DA'S AMERICAN COUNTY SALOON & DANCEHALL, 700 S. Fla. 7, Fort Lauderdale. Tel. 792-6200.

Line dancing is in, and this is where they do it best. Couples two-step till the wee hours on the large, polished dance floor. Free dance lessons are offered on Monday and Tuesday nights. It's open on Monday and Tuesday from 5pm to 2am, and Wednesday through Saturday from 5pm to 4am.

Admission: Free Mon–Thurs, $4 Fri–Sat.

ELBO ROOM, 241 Ocean Blvd.

This is the beachfront dive that was once almost synonymous with spring break. It's still a lively—and sometimes rowdy—place, packed with college kids and wet T-shirt contestants.

MAI-KAI, 3599 N. Federal Hwy., Fort Lauderdale. Tel. 305/563-3272, or toll free 800/262-4524.

Polynesian for "good food," Mai Kai is not just a touristy Hawaiian dinner show, it's a lively night of unusual entertainment and fun foods. Grass-skirted dancers have been hula-ing here twice nightly since time immemorial. Tropical drinks at the terrifically tacky Molokai bar are a bit pricy, but the selection is lengthy, and the "rain forest" atmosphere unparalleled. A la carte dinners are also served (steaks, ribs, seafood, and a variety of Polynesian pork dishes), and cost from $16 per person. Shows are given nightly at 7:15 and 10pm.

Admission: $8 per person.

SQUEEZE PROGRESSIVE DANCETERIA, 2 S. New River Dr. Tel. 522-2151.

A long-lasting club spinning straightforward dance beats to a twenty-something crowd, it's open Tuesday through Saturday from 9pm to 2am.

Admission: $5.

CHAPTER 8

INDIAN RIVER COUNTRY

The Intracoastal Waterway that runs between the Florida mainland and the barrier island, called Hutchinson Island, is known as the Indian River. The channel gives this area its name. You've probably heard of Indian River grapefruit, and indeed, this is one of the most fertile citrus-growing regions in the world. Indian River Country prides itself on environmentally conscious construction that's reminiscent of what so much of South Florida *used* to be. No massive growth here. Vast areas of pristine oceanfront remain undeveloped, with beautiful vistas that are unobscured by the condominiums, hotels, and other tropical skyscrapers that mar much of the lands to the south. This is the old Florida. Sandy stretches of coastline pay homage to bluff plants and native animals.

With that said, I must admit that Hutchinson Island, a 20-mile long barrier island just across the Intracoastal Indian River, is indeed dotted with a handful of high-rises (and pricy beach clubs), but there are not yet enough of them to spoil the wilderness. Here, you can expect to find relatively uncrowded beaches, where the tanners are locals and the tourists are few. Small-town museums and charming antiques shops compete with historical markers and unspoiled beaches for the attentions of visitors.

SEEING INDIAN RIVER COUNTRY

All the major roads in Indian River Country run north-south, making sightseeing easy. The best drive, either to or from Miami, is along Fla. A1A (also called the Dixie Highway), which hugs the ocean along most of the coast. U.S. 1 (also called Federal Highway), doesn't cross the Intracoastal to the barrier islands, making it a slightly faster (but less interesting) way to see Florida's east coast. It's hard to get too lost while wandering around the Indian River Country's roads; the ocean is always to the east.

1. STUART/JENSEN BEACH

130 miles SE of Orlando, 105 miles N of Miami

GETTING THERE **By Plane** The **Palm Beach International Airport** (tel. 407/471-7420), located about 25 miles to the south, is the closest gateway to the Stuart area. See Chapter 7 on the Gold Coast for complete information.

By Train Amtrak (tel. toll free 800/USA-RAIL) trains departing from New York stop in West Palm Beach, about 25 miles to the south, and in Okeechobee, about 30 miles to the west. The West Palm station is located at 201 S. Tamarind Ave., West Palm Beach (tel. 407/832-6169). The Okeechobee station is located at 801 N. Parrot Ave., off U.S. 441 N. (tel. 813/763-1114).

By Bus Greyhound/Trailways can get you to the Stuart area from almost anywhere. The company no longer operates a single nationwide telephone number, so consult your local directory for the office nearest you.

By Car If you're driving up or down the Florida coast, you'll probably reach the Stuart area on Interstate 95, a highway that runs all the way from Maine to Miami.

WHAT'S SPECIAL ABOUT INDIAN RIVER COUNTRY

Fishing

- ☐ Edible and game species that inhabit the ocean, rivers, inlets, and lakes, with world-class bottom fishing and inshore trolling.
- ☐ Big-game ocean fishing—so good here that the town of Stewart bills itself the "Sailfish capital of the World."

Water Sports

- ☐ Boating and sailing, popular activities year-round, as well as windsurfing at Sebastian Inlet State Park.
- ☐ Good snorkeling and diving at several offshore reefs and dive sites, with old wrecks make for particularly fine diving.

Beaches

- ☐ Over 26 miles of Atlantic coastline and an average year-round temperature of 73°, making this a great place for swimming and sunning.

Marine Marvels

- ☐ Endangered loggerhead turtles, crawling onto the sand from May through August to lay their eggs; local environmental groups lead educational "turtle watches."

Visitors on their way to or from Orlando should take the Florida Turnpike, a toll road that runs almost directly from this region's beaches to Walt Disney World. Finally, if you're coming from the state's west coast, you'll probably take Fla. 70, which runs north of Lake Okeechobee to Fort Pierce, located just up the road from Stuart.

ESSENTIALS The **telephone area code** is 407. The **Stuart/Martin County Chamber of Commerce,** 1650 S. Kanner Hwy., Stuart, FL 34994 (tel. 407/287-1088, or toll free 800/524-9704), is the region's main source for information. The **Jensen Beach Chamber of Commerce,** 1901 NE Jensen Beach Blvd., Jensen Beach, FL 34957 (tel. 407/334-3444), offers specialized information on their sparkling strip of sand.

The Stuart/Jensen Beach area has never been highly developed. From 1960 to the mid-1970s, the county's population swelled from a mere 6,000 residents to a whopping 37,000, evidence of South Floridians' desire to leave the metropolises of Miami and Palm Beach for quieter, less-known beaches. Despite the growth, it's still pretty quiet around these parts. Once populated primarily with pineapple plantations, the towns of Martin County—which include Stuart, Jensen Beach, Port Salerno, and Hobe Sound—are now home to citrus plantations, modest homes, and a handful of tourist-oriented hotels and sights. Strict building codes keep these communities free from high-rise condominiums and endless strip malls. Downtown Stuart has recently been spruced up with lovely landscaped walkways and attractive storefronts. Many historical buildings in both Stuart and Fort Pierce have been lovingly restored, making a stroll around these beachfront towns a worthy stop on your exploration of the Southeast Florida coast.

WHAT TO SEE & DO

MUSEUMS

COURTHOUSE CULTURAL CENTER, 80 E. Ocean Blvd., Stuart. Tel. 287-6676.

This historical former courthouse is now the region's principal center for the arts.

It functions primarily as a historical museum and art gallery with changing exhibitions, many of local interest. A helpful staff dispenses information on area events and activities.

Admission: Free.

Open: Mon–Fri 10am–4pm, Sat 11am–3pm.

ELLIOTT MUSEUM, 825 NE Ocean Blvd., Hutchinson Island, Stuart. Tel. 225-1961.

A treasure trove of early Americana, this museum was built by inventor Harmon Parker Elliott in 1961, in honor of his father and partner, Sterling Elliott. A series of tableaux illustrate life from the War of Independence to the Civil War. An apothecary, a barbershop, a blacksmith forge, a clock and watch shop, and other old-fashioned, life-size dioramas are displayed with collections of dolls, teas, spices, and even fishing tackle.

The inventor and his father claimed 222 patents between the two of them. Although none changed the world, a display dedicated to the Elliotts' inventions are the museum's highlight. They include an envelope-addressing machine and a mechanical knot-tier.

Admission: $2 adults, 50¢ children 6–13, free for kids under 6.

Open: Daily 1–4pm.

GILBERT'S BAR HOUSE OF REFUGE, 301 MacArthur Blvd., Stuart. Tel. 225-1875.

The oldest structure in this area dates from 1875, when it functioned as a rescue center, caring for shipwrecked sailors. Restored to its original splendor in 1975–76, Gilbert's is listed on the National Register of Historic Places, and operates as a historical museum displaying an unusual collection of marine artifacts, life-saving equipment, and related objects.

Admission: $1 adults, 50¢ children 6–13, free for kids under 6.

Open: Tues–Sun 11am–4:15pm.

STUART HERITAGE MUSEUM AT THE STUART FEED STORE, 161 NW Flagler Ave., Stuart. Tel. 220-4600.

In 1900, when the Stuart Feed Store was the territory's most important general store, the region's inhabitants would come from miles around to buy feed for their animals and supplies for themselves, as well as catch up on all the local news. Native Seminole peoples shopped and traded here as well Today, the former shop is a museum of local history, an ode to the pioneers who first worked the lands around Stuart.

Mrs. Catherine M. Lewis, the small museum's very friendly curator, is a storehouse of information and the museum's most valuable treasure. A member of the Stuart Heritage Committee, Mrs. Lewis loves to inform visitors about goings-on in this area, in the past and the present. Ask her about the museum's collection of antiques, which includes old soda fountains, meat grinders, and other settlers' tools.

Admission: Free.

Open: Mon–Sat 10am–4pm.

BEACHES & PARKS

Bathtub Beach, on Hutchinson Island, Stuart, is one of the best oceanside parks in the county. In addition to calm waters, protected by coral reefs, visitors can explore the region on dune and river trails. The reef here is very close to shore, and great for snorkeling. Bathtub Beach is popular with young families, especially on warmer weekends. To reach the park, cross the Intracoastal Waterway on Ocean Boulevard and turn right, onto MacArthur Boulevard. The beach is located about a mile ahead, on your left, just past the House of Refuge Museum.

Jaycee Park, on SE Ocean Boulevard, between Hutchinson Island and the mainland, is split between a picnic-area island, and a park that's popular with sports enthusiasts. When you cross the Intracoastal Waterway on Ocean Boulevard, the first island you reach is the picnic area. Continue over the next bridge to the park that's best known for fishing and windsurfing.

WHERE TO STAY

VERY EXPENSIVE

INDIAN RIVER PLANTATION, 555 NE Ocean Blvd., Hutchinson Island, FL 34996. Tel. 407/225-3700, or toll free 800/947-2148. Fax 407/225-3948. 200 rms, 54 suites. A/C TV TEL **Directions:** From U.S. 1, turn east onto Palm Beach Road, then right onto East Ocean Boulevard; the resort is located past the third bridge, on your right.

$ Rates: Feb 7–Apr 17, $185–$195 single or double; from $195 suite. May 31–Oct 2, $110–$130 single or double; from $125 suite. Apr 18–May 30 and Oct 3–Feb 6, $135–$150 single or double; from $150 suite. AE, CB, DC, DISC, MC, V.

The Indian River Plantation is the biggest thing ever to happen to this otherwise sleepy island. To those who don't care about the region's unadulterated natural habitats, this large resort appears to be southern Hutchinson Island's reason to be. Occupying a former pineapple plantation, the resort offers a multitude of family-oriented activities amid lush surroundings. The white lattice-and-wicker lobby is filled with a bountiful harvest of plants, and large windows that over look the hotel's swimming pool and tiki bar.

Generously sized standard rooms continue the floral motif, with colorful spreads and draperies. Simple rattan furnishings are enlivened with special extras that include clock radios, ceiling fans, two phones, small refrigerators, and contemporary bathrooms complete with hairdryers. All rooms, whether ocean-view or oceanfront, have large windows and balconies. Some come with complete kitchen facilities.

The resort's activities revolve around tennis, golfing, and boating. Sportsfishing, scuba diving, and various other water sports are also available. The Indian River Plantation is an excellent place for families with kids. The resort's Pineapple Bunch Children's Camp sponsors daily activities for children, teens, and families, like hayrides, bonfires, poolside games, marshmallow cookouts, golf and tennis lessons, arts and crafts, and beach walks. From May through August, sea turtles crawl onto the sand to lay their eggs, and local environmental groups lead educational "turtle watches."

Dining/Entertainment: Five restaurants, three lounges, and two tiki bars ensure that you'll never go hungry or thirsty. Scalawags, a seafood restaurant, is the resort's top dining room, and is popular with locals. The less-formal Emporium serves breakfast, lunch, and all-day snacks like frozen yogurt. There's live music nightly, in at least two bars.

Services: 24-hour room service, concierge, complimentary movie rentals, bicycle and sports-equipment rentals, overnight laundry and dry cleaning.

Facilities: 18-hole golf course, luxury sightseeing boat, full-service marina, 13 tennis courts (7 lighted), four heated swimming pools, two Jacuzzis, fitness center, shopping arcade.

MODERATE

HUTCHINSON INN, 9750 S. Ocean Dr. (Fla. A1A), Jensen Beach, FL 34957. Tel. 407/229-2000. A/C TV TEL **Directions:** From I-95 take the Stuart exit east to County Rd. 76 and continue to Fla. A1A north; the hotel is about four miles ahead on your right.

$ Rates (including continental breakfast): Dec–Apr, $80–$115 single or double; from $145 suite. May–Nov, $60–$85 single or double; from $125 suite. Additional person $20 extra. MC, V.

It may not look like much from the road, where only the tennis court is visible, but your entrance is soon greeted by striking white gazebos dotting thick green lawns and regal brick walkways leading to a proud, pastel two-story retreat. Located directly on the beach, the Hutchinson Inn is a quiet hideaway, a 15-minute drive from anywhere. It's hard to top it for charm, from its tiny lobby with its green canopy, to the little love birds that live below the stairs leading to your room.

Rooms are lightly decorated with rattan dressers, tables, and chairs. Most are good size and all have alarm clocks and tiled baths. Sofas convert into pull-out beds, and several rooms can be joined to accommodate large families.

Facilities and services are few, but there is a large pool and a good swimming beach, and freshly baked cookies are served each evening before bedtime. On Saturday afternoons, guests are invited to join in a complimentary barbecue.

WHERE TO DINE

MODERATE

ASHLEY RESTAURANT, 61 SW Osceola St., Stuart. Tel. 221-9476.

Cuisine: CONTINENTAL. **Reservations:** Not required.

$ Prices: Appetizers $2–$7; main courses $6–$14; breakfast $3–$5; lunch $4–$7. MC, V.

Open: Breakfast Sat 7:30–11:30am, Sun 8am–1pm; lunch Tues–Fri 11am–2:30pm; dinner Tues–Sat 5:30–10pm.

Fun and bright, the Ashley is an eclectic mix of tile, glass, and color. Ultra-contemporary wall prints hang under an unusual aqua-colored beamed ceiling, while stained-glass windows throw their colored light onto ornate gold bars that protect the kitchen from mealtime gazers.

Happily, the French-inspired food, accented with local citrus and seafood, is just as snappy as the surroundings. Simple lunches tend toward chicken, shrimp, and fruit crêpes; croissant sandwiches; and a variety of burgers. Dinner, the meal of choice here, might start with smoked salmon, crab-stuffed avocado, or escargots bobbing in burgundy. Imaginative pasta, meat, seafood, and poultry dishes might include duck breast in a caramel-orange sauce, or broiled local grouper.

Weekend breakfasts are especially recommended, when fresh fruit crêpes and homemade quiches tempt you away from your usual cereal and eggs.

ISLAND REEF, 10900 S. Ocean Dr., Jensen Beach, Hutchinson Island. Tel. 229-2600.

Cuisine: FLORIDA/CARIBBEAN. **Reservations:** Not required.

$ Prices: Appetizers $2–$8; main courses $8–$16; lunch $5–$11; brunch $2–$7. AE, DISC, MC, V.

Open: Lunch Mon–Sat 11:30am–2:30pm; dinner Sun–Thurs 5–9:30pm, Fri–Sat 5–10pm; brunch Sun 11:30am–2:30pm.

A wooden walkway over a tropics-inspired rock fountain transports you through a miniature fern gully into this beachfront restaurant. Fortunately, the handsome interior is not as calculated as the Disney-inspired entranceway. High wood-beamed ceilings and hardwood floors sandwich a well-stocked raw bar, and a wall of windows overlook a huge outdoor dune-top patio with the most coveted seats in the house.

The island-themed lunch menu features fresh fish covered with tropical spices and sauces—shrimp tempura with coconut butter and fruit juices is but one example. But wise diners would do well to ask for the sauce on the side, or stick to more traditional entrees like salads and sandwiches. The same goes for dinner, when you should enjoy reading the adventurous menu, then think of simpler things. The grouper baked in a banana leaf (sans curry-cream sauce) is very recommendable, as is the charcoal-grilled chicken with tropical fruit juices, cilantro, lemongrass, and salsa. But shrimp and scallops with angel-hair pasta in pepper-vodka-cream sauce and other complicated Caribbean-style preparations stretch the limits of the cooking staff.

Sunday brunches include many traditional North American plates with a twist. Try French toast topped with almond slivers or a breakfast burrito filled with eggs, chili beef, bell peppers, onions, cheese, and salsa.

INEXPENSIVE

CHINA STAR, 1501 S. Federal Hwy., Stuart. Tel. 283-8378.

Cuisine: CHINESE. **Reservations:** Not required.

$ Prices: Appetizers $1–$4; combination platters $5–$8; main dishes $4–$11. AE, DISC, MC, V.

Open: Mon–Thurs 11am–10pm, Fri–Sat 11am–11pm, Sun 11:30am–10pm.

China Star would look like a miniature White House misplaced on Federal Highway if it weren't for the telltale Chinese-red trim around the restaurant's doors and windows. There are few surprises inside, where red walls are adorned with the requisite Oriental prints and landscape murals. And why does almost every Chinese restaurateur decorate with fish tanks?

The food is straightforward and good—a rave from this spoiled New Yorker. A la carte selections are listed under the usual beef, poultry, pork, and seafood headings, and include jade scallop, moo goo gai pan, vegetable egg foo yung, and cashew chicken (my favorite). Combination platters come with fried rice, an eggroll, and wonton or egg drop soup.

BUDGET

NATURE'S WAY CAFE, 25 SW Osceola St., in the Post Office Arcade, Stuart. Tel. 220-7306.

Cuisine: VEGETARIAN. **Reservations:** Not accepted.

$ Prices: Sandwiches/salads \$3–\$6; juices/shakes \$1–\$3. No credit cards.

Open: Mon–Fri 10am–4pm, Sat 11am–3pm.

One large room with little tables, and a few strategically placed bar stools overlooking the sidewalk is all there is to this pleasantly decorated, white-tiled eatery. A sort of health-food deli, Nature's Way offers an assortment of prepared salads, make-your-own vegetarian sandwiches, and frozen yogurts. There's also a healthy assortment of shakes, fresh juices, and homemade muffins. If it's a particularly nice day, you might ask them to pack your lunch so you can picnic in a park or on the beach.

PICNIC SUPPLIES

In addition to **Nature's Way Café,** listed above, try **Plantation Pantry,** 650 NE Ocean Blvd., on Hutchinson Island, Stuart (tel. 225-1100), for some of the region's best take-away foods. Located across the road from the Indian River Plantation, and just behind a gas station, the shop looks much like any other quick-stop market. But usual it's not: In addition to a full deli making both hot and cold sandwiches, there's a large selection of gourmet treats such as smoked salmon and trout, homemade quiches, lasagnes, and freshly made jams and jellies. For dessert, get a piece of their locally produced fudge, which comes in an incredibly wide variety of flavors.

SHOPPING

You may have already realized that the Hutchinson Island area is no Paris or Milan, but that doesn't mean there's nothing to buy. This area's specialty is food, a tempting mix of tropical and southern flavors that, with surprisingly little effort, can be exported home.

The **Monterey Farmer's Market,** 642 SE Monterey Rd., in Bruner Plaza, Stuart (tel. 287-1588), sells all types of locally grown produce, including the famous Indian River grapefruit and oranges. They ship anywhere in North America.

Mrs. Peter's, at the Stuart Heritage Museum, 161 NW Flagler Ave., Stuart (tel. 407/220-4600), sells some of the most succulent smoked foods you've ever eaten. Their motto is "We Smoke Everything But Mermaids," and they've been doing so since 1931. Old-fashioned–style hand-smoked kingfish, amberhack, turkey breast, and other meats are sold and shipped from here. Order forms are available for other smoked specialties.

Mrs. Peter's has a second location at 1500 Fla. 707, Rio/Jensen Beach (tel. 334-2184).

EVENING ENTERTAINMENT

Even the tourist office of this relatively sleepy region refrains from boasting too loudly about Stuart's cultural evenings. Still, there *are* some things to do when the sun goes down; and you might be lucky enough to arrive on a particularly lively night. Phone the following listings to find out what's on.

THE PERFORMING ARTS

The Barn Theater, 2400 E. Ocean Blvd., Stuart (tel. 287-4884), is a good-quality community theater, presenting five shows per season, September to June.

The **Lyric Theater,** 216 SE Flagler Ave., Stuart (tel. 220-1942), a beautiful 1920s-era 600-seat hall, hosts a variety of shows throughout the year. Programs run the gamut from amateur plays to top-name theatrical shows and concerts, sometimes from the rock music world. Phone for the latest.

THE BAR SCENE

The bar at the **Ashley Restaurant,** 61 SW Osceola St., Stuart (tel. 221-9476), is one of the most "happening" places in town. Fun, bright, and colorful, the Ashley is an eclectic mix of styles. Loud, aqua-color ceiling beams, faux Tiffany glass lights, and stained-glass windows reflect off the restaurant's tiled floors and tables. Personally, I camp out on one of the vinyl stools by the dark-blue marble-top bar. On weekend nights, local musicians crowd onto a thumb-sized stage, and Rebecca, the fortune-teller, reveals patrons' futures for $5. The bar is open Tuesday through Thursday from 5:30 to 10pm and on Friday and Saturday from 5:30pm to midnight.

Higher rollers go to **Scalawag's Lounge,** 555 NE Ocean Blvd., at the Indian River Plantation, Stuart (tel. 225-3700), a fancy bar located inside the region's best hotel. The view from the upstairs lounge is so nice that you almost don't feel guilty about drinking so early in the afternoon. Stick around for the live musical entertainment that's offered almost every night.

2. PORT ST. LUCIE/FORT PIERCE

7 miles N of Stuart, 10 miles W of the ocean

GETTING THERE **By Plane** The **Palm Beach International Airport** (tel. 407/471-7420), located about 30 miles to the south, is the closest gateway to the Port St. Lucie/Fort Pierce area. See Chapter 7 on the Gold Coast for complete information.

By Train Amtrak (tel. toll free 800/USA-RAIL) trains departing from New York stop in West Palm Beach, about 30 miles to the south, and in Okeechobee, about 30 miles to the west. The West Palm station is located at 201 S. Tamarind Ave., West Palm Beach (tel. 407/832-6169). The Okeechobee station is located at 801 N. Parrot Ave., off U.S. 441 N. (tel. 813/763-1114).

By Bus Greyhound/Trailways can get you to the Port St. Lucie/Fort Pierce area from almost anywhere. The company no longer operates a single nationwide telephone number, so consult your local directory for the office nearest you.

By Car If you're driving up or down the Florida coast, you'll probably reach the Port St. Lucie/Fort Pierce area on Interstate 95, a highway that runs all the way from Maine to Miami. Visitors on their way to or from Orlando should take the Florida Turnpike, a toll road that runs almost directly from this region's beaches to Walt Disney World. Finally, if you're coming from the state's west coast, you'll probably take Fla. 70, which runs north of Lake Okeechobee right into Fort Pierce.

ESSENTIALS The **telephone area code** is 407. The **Stuart/Martin County Chamber of Commerce,** 1650 S. Kanner Hwy., Stuart, FL 34994 (tel. 407/287-1088, or toll free 800/524-9704), is the region's main source for information.

Port St. Lucie and Fort Pierce seem to thrive on sportfishing. Seemingly endless piers jut out along the Intracoastal Waterway and the Fort Pierce Inlet for both river and ocean runs. It's hard not to wax nostalgic about how Miami used to look when you drive along the region's relatively quiet streets, two-lane roads ruled by small pubs and raw bars. Here visitors can enjoy adventures like diving and snorkeling, as well as more passive pastimes like beachcombing and sunbathing.

Driving along Fla. A1A on Hutchinson Island, you'll discover several secluded beach clubs interspersed with 1950s-style homes, a few small inns, dozens of grungy single-story raw bars, and even a few high-rise condominiums. Much of this island is government-owned, kept undeveloped for the public's enjoyment. On the other side of the Intracoastal, along the road that hugs the river, you'll find attractive modest homes with small motorboats moored to private docks. Farther inland, fronting busy U.S. 1, are strip shopping malls and chain restaurants.

WHAT TO SEE & DO

Florida is full of unique museums, but none is more curious than the **UDT-Seal Museum,** 3300 N. Fla. A1A, Fort Pierce, on Hutchinson Island (tel. 489-3597 or 595-1570), a most peculiar tribute to the secret forces of the U.S. Navy—frogmen and their successors, the SEAL teams. Chronological displays trace the history of these clandestine divers, and detail their most important achievements. The best exhibits are those that display equipment used by the navy's most elite members. Needless to say, this is the only museum of its type in the world. Admission is $2 for adults, $1 for children, free for kids under 5. It's open Tuesday through Saturday from 10am to 4pm and on Sunday from noon to 4pm.

Jai alai, sort of a Spanish-style indoor lacrosse popular around South Florida, is regularly played in the **Fort Pierce Jai Alai Fronton,** Florida Service Road 713, Fort Pierce (tel. 407/464-7500, or toll free 800/524-2524 in Florida). Players use woven baskets (called *cestas*) to hurl balls (*pelotas*) at speeds that sometimes exceed 170 miles per hour. Spectators, who are protected behind a wall of glass, place bets on the evening's players. Games are played here from March through September. Admission is $3 for reserved seats, $1 for general admission. Games are played from March to September on Wednesday, Friday, Saturday, and Sunday at noon and 7pm, on Thursday at 7pm only.

WHERE TO STAY

EXPENSIVE

CLUB MED—THE SANDPIPER, 3500 Morningside Blvd., Port St. Lucie, FL 34952. Tel. 407/335-4400, or toll free 800/CLUB-MED. Fax 407/335-9497. 600 rms. A/C TV TEL **Directions:** From U.S. 1, turn west onto Westmoreland Boulevard, then turn left onto Pine Valley Road and the resort entrance is straight ahead.

$ Rates (including three meals per day): May–Dec 18, $145–$185 per person. Dec 19–25, $200–$240 per person. Dec 26–Jan 1 and Feb 13–19, $215–$255 per person. Jan 2–Feb 12, $155–$195 per person. Feb 20–27 and Apr 17–24, $170–$210 per person. Feb 28–Apr 16 and Apr 25–30, $185–$225 per person. All rates based on double occupancy. Weekly rates available. AE, MC, V.

Club Med, a pioneer of the all-inclusive resort, is represented in South Florida by this large, three-story lodge secluded on 500 acres on the shores of Port St. Lucie. To me, Club Med always conjures up images of a carefree paradise on a distant tropical island. Except for the fact that this place is not too far away, it very much lives up to my ideal. All meals and activities are included in the club's basic price, and guests are completely spoiled during their stay. This is not a singles' getaway. The resort is very family-oriented, and offers lots of programs just for children. In addition to golf and tennis, adults can waterski, sail, or cruise on the river. A free minibus shuttles guests 20 minutes to the beach.

The resort's simple rooms are decorated in bright ethnic colors, and feature small balconies, tiled floors, and modern amenities. All rooms come with in-room safes, large closets, and mini-refrigerators.

Dining/Entertainment: All-you-can-eat buffets are served in the main dining room three times a day. In addition, La Fontana restaurant serves late breakfasts and

Italian cuisine at dinner, and the French-style Riverside is open for dinner only. There's a variety of nightly entertainment around the resort.

Services: Room service, concierge, overnight laundry.

Facilities: Two golf courses, driving range, 19 tennis courts, waterskiing, volleyball courts, fitness center, water-sports rentals, billiards, five swimming pools, wading pool, aerobics classes, workshops, boutique, cinema.

MODERATE

HARBOR LIGHT INN, 1160 Seaway Dr., Fort Pierce, Hutchinson Island, FL 34949. Tel. 407/468-3555, or toll free 800/433-0004. 21 rms. A/C MINIBAR TV TEL

$ **Rates:** Dec 20–Apr, $75–$120 single or double. May–Dec 19, $55–$95 single or double. Additional person $10 extra. AE, CB, DC, DISC, MC, V.

Fronting the Intracoastal Waterway, the Harbor Light is a good choice for boating and fishing enthusiasts, offering 15 boat slips and two private fishing piers. The hotel itself carries on this nautical theme with pierlike wooden stairs, rope railings, and reinforced, waterproof exterior lighting. While not exactly captain's quarters, the rooms, simply decorated with pastel colors and small wall prints, are adequate. Higher-priced rooms either have waterfront balconies or small kitchenettes that contain a coffee maker, refrigerator, oven, and a toaster. The inn also offers a swimming pool with a large deck for sunbathing.

BUDGET

EDGEWATER MOTEL AND APARTMENTS, 1156 Seaway Dr., Fort Pierce, Hutchinson Island, FL 34949. Tel. 407/468-3555, or toll free 800/433-0004. 48 rms, 14 efficiencies. A/C TV TEL

$ **Rates:** Dec 20–Apr, $47 single or double; from $60 efficiency apt. May–Dec 19, $37 single or double; from $45 efficiency apt. Additional person $10 extra. Weekly rates available. AE, DC, MC, V.

This budget alternative to the Harbor Light Inn, next door, offers modestly decorated rooms garnished with an eclectic mix of furniture. There's a private swimming pool, and guests have access to the adjacent fishing pier and boat docks.

Efficiency apartments include small kitchens, and are available on a daily or weekly basis.

WHERE TO DINE

MODERATE

P.V. MARTIN'S, 5150 N. Fla. A1A, Fort Pierce. Tel. 456-7300 or 569-0700.

Cuisine: AMERICAN. **Reservations:** Recommended.

$ **Prices:** Appetizers $3.50–$8; main courses $9–$19; lunch $4–$11.

Open: Lunch Mon–Sat 11am–3:30pm; dinner Mon–Sat 5–10pm, Sun 3–10pm; brunch Sun 10:30am–2:30pm.

This relatively elegant eatery, with an eclectic American menu, is my top pick in Fort Pierce. The restaurant's wood floors, beamed ceilings, tiled-top tables, and rattan chairs would be nice anywhere, but here they look out through floor-to-ceiling windows onto sweeping ocean vistas. By night, the room is warmed by a huge central stone fireplace, and on weekends there's live entertainment in the adjacent bar.

Surf-and-turf dinners run the gamut from crab-stuffed shrimp and grouper baked with bananas and almonds, to Brie- and asparagus-stuffed chicken breast and barbecued baby back ribs. An excellent selection of appetizers includes escargots in mushroom caps and a succulent fried softshell crab (available in season).

Lunches can be lighter, and include sandwiches, burgers, and stuffed potato skins.

But prime rib, seafood-topped pasta dishes, and other meatier meals are always available.

INEXPENSIVE

CAFE COCONUTS, 4304 NE Ocean Blvd., Hutchison Island. Tel. 225-6006.
Cuisine: AMERICAN. **Reservations:** Not required.
$ Prices: Appetizers $4–$7; main courses $8–$15; lunch $3–$9. MC, V.
Open: Daily 11:30am–2am.

Located in the Island Shoppes shopping center on Fla. A1A, this large restaurant's three separate dining rooms are all packed with simple, pink-clothed tables. Pink and blue Miami Vice–toned walls are covered with oceanic prints and posters, as is the bar, which occupies much of the restaurant's principal room.

A wide variety of salads and sandwiches are matched by an equally extensive selection of meat and fish dishes, including seafood and steak, and chicken. Despite their healthfulness, the restaurant's "low-calorie suggestions" are also some of their tastiest. Try the charcoal-broiled chicken or the broiled fresh catch-of-the-day.

THEO THUDPUCKER'S RAW BAR AND SEAFOOD RESTAURANT, 2025 Seaway Dr., Fort Pierce. Tel. 465-1078.
Cuisine: SEAFOOD. **Reservations:** Not accepted.
$ Prices: Appetizers $2–$6; main courses $8–$14; lunch $4–$7. No credit cards.
Open: Mon–Thurs 11:30am–9:30pm, Fri–Sat 11:30am–11pm, Sun 1–9:30pm.

Nobody comes here for luxurious ambience. Located in a little building by the beach, wallpapered with maps and newspapers, Thudpucker's pretends only to be what it is: a straightforward fresher-than-now chowder bar. Prominently placed signs attest to the food's purity: "Both clams and oysters are packed with ice and are not opened until you place your order. Please be patient." Chowder and stews, often made with sherry and half-and-half, make excellent starters or light meals. The most recommendable (and filling) dinner entrees are sautéed scallops, onions, green peppers, and tomatoes; deviled crabs; and deep-fried Okeechobee catfish.

BUDGET

CAPTAIN'S GALLEY, 827 N. Indian River Dr., Fort Pierce. Tel. 466-8495.
Cuisine: SEAFOOD/AMERICAN. **Reservations:** Not accepted.
$ Prices: Appetizers $2–$3; main courses $9; breakfast/lunch $2–$5. MC, V.
Open: Breakfast/lunch Mon–Sat 7am–2pm, Sun 7am–noon; dinner Mon–Sat 5–9pm.

Anywhere else, this might be just another coffee shop. But here, just over the Intracoastal at the north end of Hutchinson Island, it's a local institution. Dressed up with printed window valances and hanging plants, the Captain's Galley is busiest during breakfast, when locals catch up on the previous day's events and plan for the coming one over eggs, toast, and home-fries. Lunch specials usually include a variety of burgers and a small selection of salads and sandwiches. And dinner is for seafood, when the Galley serves up scampied shrimp, the day's fish, or land specialties like strip steak and chicken française.

EVENING ENTERTAINMENT

Café Coconuts, 4304 NE Ocean Blvd. on Hutchison Island (tel. 225-6006), is recommended here for its bars and entertainment. There are three different drinking rooms: The circular bar downstairs is surrounded by televisions and has a kind of nautical theme. A second bar is more intimate, located on a small patio; and the third is upstairs, and outdoors, in a beach setting with high white bar tables that keep your feet off the floor. There's live music on the weekends. Admission is free, and it's open daily from 11:30am to 2am.

3. VERO BEACH

85 miles SE of Orlando, 175 miles N of Miami

GETTING THERE **By Plane** The **Palm Beach International Airport** (tel. 407/471-7420), located about 100 miles to the south, is the closest gateway to the Vero Beach area. See Chapter 7 on the Gold Coast for complete information.

By Train Amtrak (tel. toll free 800/USA-RAIL) trains departing from New York stop in West Palm Beach, about 30 miles to the south, and in Okeechobee, about 30 miles to the west. The West Palm station is located at 201 S. Tamarind Ave., West Palm Beach (tel. 407/832-6169). The Okeechobee station is located at 801 N. Parrot Ave., off U.S. 441 N. (tel. 813/763-1114).

By Bus Greyhound/Trailways can get you to the Vero Beach area from almost anywhere. The company no longer operates a single nationwide telephone number, so consult your local directory for the office nearest you.

By Car If you're driving up or down the Florida coast, you'll probably reach the Vero Beach area on Interstate 95, a highway that runs all the way from Maine to Miami. Visitors on their way to or from Orlando should take the Florida Turnpike, a toll road that runs almost directly from this region's beaches to Walt Disney World. Finally, if you're coming from the state's west coast, you'll probably take Fla. 70, which runs north of Lake Okeechobee right into Fort Pierce.

ESSENTIALS The **telephone area code** is 407. The **Indian River County Tourist Council,** 1216 21st St., Vero Beach, FL 32961 (tel. 407/567-3491), offers information on the entire county.

Vero Beach is located at the southern tip of the Indian River area. Much of the Vero Beach area belongs to the Indian River Citrus District and is responsible for 75% of the total grapefruit crop grown in the state of Florida. The warm climate that originally attracted so many citrus farms has also attracted many residents, and the area is growing. Native Floridians who want to escape from the intense development in the southern cities are moving north to Vero Beach. Residents who used to know Miami and Fort Lauderdale before the days of massive high-rises and overcrowding desire to reclaim the home-town feel they have lost. And that's exactly what you'll find in this area with its laid-back, relaxed atmosphere, nicely reflected in the moderate rates for accommodations just across from the beach. In addition, many water-sports enthusiasts are drawn to the area to enjoy offshore diving and snorkeling as well as surfing and windsurfing, and baseball buffs are drawn here in the summer to catch some action from the Vero Beach Dodgers as they participate in exhibition games during their spring training.

WHAT TO SEE & DO

MUSEUMS

McCLARTY CENTER MUSEUM, 13180 N. Fla. A1A. Tel. 589-2147.

When the treasure of a Spanish fleet that sank off this coast in 1715 was recovered, the hunters chose to cash in, leaving only replicas to this museum. So what if the gold and coins are not original? Suspend your disbelief and imagine what it must have been like to uncover this hoard of riches. Various Native American artifacts are also on display.

Admission: $1.
Open: Daily 10am–5pm.

FLORIDA EAST COAST RAILWAY DEPOT EXHIBITION CENTER, 2336 14th Ave. Tel. 778-3435.

Railroads built South Florida, and this station, established in 1903, was one of the first to be constructed in the area. From its pioneer-day beginnings through the Depression and two world wars, this depot welcomed thousands of passengers to this little piece of beachside paradise. Now no longer in use, the station house has been restored to its early condition, moved to the city-owned park, and opened as a museum. Inside are railroad artifacts, historical exhibits, and other displays of local interest. The museum also offers historical walking tours on most Wednesdays at 11am and 1pm; reservations are required.

Admission: Free.
Open: Wed 10am–3pm, Sat 10am–noon, Sun 2–4pm.

DODGERTOWN, 3901 26th St. (P.O. Box 2887), Vero Beach, FL 32960. Tel. 407/569-4900.

An entire sports and recreation complex has opened around the stadium that's the winter home of baseball's Los Angeles Dodgers. The 450-acre complex encompasses two golf courses, a conference center, country club, movie theater, and recreation room. Exhibition games are played here during the winter months at Holman's Stadium. If you want something more filling than a Dodger Dog, visit the Country Club Restaurant, where fans often report sightings of their favorite players.

Admission: Complex, free; stadium $5–$10.
Open: Daily 8am–11pm. **Directions:** From I-95, follow County Rd. 60 east for five miles to 43rd Avenue, turn left, continue to 26th Street, and turn right; the entrance is straight ahead.

SPORTS & RECREATION

BEACHES Most of Vero's beachfront is open to the public—an all too unusual situation that you should take advantage of. The beach at the end of Beachland Boulevard is one of the most popular and convenient. Others are best for sports and picnicking. Here's the lowdown:

Jaycee Beach Park, on Ocean Drive and Mango Road in Vero Beach, is a small park with a nice beach area, picnic facilities, public restrooms, showers, and even a restaurant.

Riverside Park, east of Barber Bridge at the end of Memorial Island Drive, is, appropriately enough, located directly on the Indian River. There are tennis and racquetball courts here, as well as a jogging course, boat ramps, and picnic pavilions.

South Beach Park, on South Ocean Drive, at the end of Marigold Lane, is a busy, developed beach with picnic tables, restrooms, and showers. This is one of the best swimming beaches, and lifeguards are on duty here.

GOLF There are two courses at **Dodgertown,** on the corner of 43rd Avenue and 26th Street (tel. 569-4800): an 18-hole championship course at the Dodger Pines Country Club, and a challenging 9-hole run located adjacent to the complex's baseball stadium. Club rentals are available and lessons are offered by PGA professionals. Greens fees are $11–$20.

The **Whisper Lakes** public course, at U.S. 1 and 53rd Street (tel. 567-3321), represents the best driving deal in town. Here you can play 9 or 18 holes of golf or just hit a practice bucket on the driving range. Clubs rent for $3; greens fees are $5 for 9 holes, $10 for 18 holes. Carts are an additional $7.

MINIATURE GOLF Duffers with kids in tow might visit **Safari Putting Golf n' Games,** 455 Oslo Rd. (tel. 562-6492), a deluxe miniature playland that offers not one, but two 18-hole miniature golf courses complete with waterfalls and castles.

There are also baseball and softball batting cages, as well as the requisite games room, outfitted with video games, billiards, and hard-to-find Skeeball and air-hockey games. Admission is $4.50 for adults, $3.50 children 5–12, free for kids 4 and under. It's open Monday through Thursday from 11am to 9:30pm, on Friday and Saturday from 11am to 11pm, and on Sunday from noon to 9:30pm.

TENNIS The 10 tennis courts (6 lighted) can each be rented for $3 per person per hour at the **Memorial Island Tennis Club,** on Royal Palm Boulevard at the east end of Barber Bridge (tel. 231-4787). Reservations are accepted up to 24 hours in advance. The club also has two racquetball courts at reasonable rates.

WHERE TO STAY

EXPENSIVE

GUEST QUARTERS SUITE RESORT, 3500 Ocean Dr., Vero Beach, FL 32963. Tel. 407/231-5666, or toll free 800/424-2900 or 800/841-5666. Fax 407/234-4866. 55 suites. A/C MINIBAR TV TEL

$ Rates: Dec 23–Apr, $175–$215 one-bedroom suite; $245 two-bedroom suite. May–Dec 22, $95–$125 one-bedroom suite; $145 two-bedroom suite. AE, CB, DC, DISC, MC, V.

Vero's best all-suite hotel is located directly on the beach, close to local restaurants and shops. First-class accommodations are located in a modern, pastel-colored, four-story building. What the nearly identical suites lack in character, they make up for in content. All are nicely decorated with pastel wallpapers and bedspreads. Rooms are equipped with small refrigerators and coffee makers, have two phones, and modern baths that include hairdryers.

Dining/Entertainment: The Lanai Room is open daily from 10am to 10pm, and serves breakfast, lunch, and dinner. The Seabreeze pool bar is open daily for snacks and cocktails.

Services: Room service, concierge, laundry.

Facilities: Swimming pool, whirlpool; tennis, golf, and racquetball are nearby.

MODERATE

ISLANDER MOTEL, 3101 Ocean Dr., Vero Beach, FL 32963. Tel. 407/231-4431, or toll free 800/952-5886. 16 rms. A/C TV TEL

$ Rates: Dec 19–Jan 22, $49–$59 single or double. Jan 23–Apr, $83–$94 single or double. May–Dec 18, $45–$49 single or double. Efficiency $10 extra; additional person $7 extra. AE, MC, V.

Resident owners Robert and Winifred Carter run one of the most comfortable and welcoming inns in the area. Well located in downtown Vero Beach, this aqua-colored motel is just a short walk to the beach, restaurants, and shops. Every guest room has either a king-size or two double beds and small refrigerators. Accommodations are outfitted in a Caribbean motif with brightly printed curtains, matching bedspreads, and white rattan furniture. There's a heated pool and a barbecue area in the handsomely landscaped central courtyard, along with a small, walk-up café.

VERO BEACH INN, 4700 N. Fla. A1A, Vero Beach, FL 32963. Tel. 407/231-1600, or toll free 800/227-8615 or 800/528-1234. 105 rms, 3 suites. A/C TV TEL **Directions:** From I-95, exit east on Fla. 60, continue all the way to the ocean and turn left onto Fla. A1A; the hotel is one mile ahead, on your right.

$ Rates: Feb 8–Apr 14, $90–$100 single or double; from $125 suite. Apr 15–Feb 7, $65–$75 single or double; from $90 suite. Additional person $6 extra. AE, CB, DC, DISC, MC, V.

One of my more unusual picks is this slightly eccentric inn located just north of downtown Vero Beach. Overgrown exterior plantings give this brick mansion a mildly mysterious look, intensified by tall white columns and red iron railings. The rooms are very comfortable, combining mauvey earthtones and modern amenities. I particularly like the inn's unusual swimming pool, which is partly enclosed by the hotel and partly open to the sky.

The hotel itself rests right on the beach, and is a short drive to nearby shops, restaurants, and attractions. Its restaurant, the Seagrape, has ocean and pool views, and Runyon's Lounge features live entertainment on the weekends.

CAMPING

SUNSHINE TRAVEL PARK, County Road 512 and I-95, Sebastian, FL 32978. Tel. 407/589-7828. 300 sites.

$ Rates: $18–$24.50 per site.

A kind of Club Med for campers, this tenting resort features a heated pool, shuffleboard, miniature golf, square dancing, and a full schedule of activities.

VERO BEACH KOA RV PARK, 8850 U.S. 1, Wabasso, FL 32970. Tel. 407/589-5665. 120 sites. **Directions:** From I-95, take County Road 512 east, then turn south on U.S. 1 to the campground.

$ Rates: $15.95–$18.95 per site.

This campground is two miles from the ocean and the Intracoastal Waterway. There's running water at most campsites, as well as showers and a shop, and hook-ups for RVs.

WHERE TO DINE

EXPENSIVE

THE BLACK PEARL, 1409 Fla. A1A. Tel. 234-4426.

Cuisine: CONTINENTAL. **Reservations:** Recommended.

$ Prices: Appetizers $3–$5; main courses $14–$17. AE, MC, V.

Open: Dinner only, daily 6–10pm.

It's unusual that such a small, unassuming little restaurant should handmake everything they serve, but that's exactly what they do here, where you can be wooed by seductive smells even before you walk through the front door. There's just a single, romantic dining room which features bright prints on crisply clean pastel walls. Full wine racks and black art deco accents round out the decor.

The restaurant's small list of appetizers may include feta cheese and spinach fritters, chilled leek-and-watercress soup, or oysters baked with crabmeat and butter. Equally creative entrees recently included Cajun pasta (topped with shrimp, scallops, and sausage), sautéed crabmeat-stuffed veal covered with hollandaise sauce, and rib-eye steak, blackened, with a crown of tomatoes. There's a good wine list, and a better dessert selection, baked daily in the restaurant's kitchen.

OCEAN GRILL, 1050 Sexton Plaza. Tel. 231-5409.

Cuisine: AMERICAN. **Reservations:** Recommended.

$ Prices: Appetizers $2–$9; main courses $11–$20; lunch $6–$11. AE, CB, DC, DISC, MC, V.

Open: Lunch Mon–Fri 11:30am–2:30pm; dinner daily 5:45–10pm.

The Ocean Grill was founded in 1941 by some of the area's earliest developers. Now something of a historical landmark in these parts, the restaurant is justifiably proud of its long service in South Florida. The grill's dark-wood interior and distinct musty aroma attest to its authenticity. The dining room is filled with Spanish antiques that include a massive iron chandelier that hangs above one of the world's largest solid, red mahogany tables. Winters are best, when a fire roars from an imposing stone fireplace. But summers are nice too, especially when you sit by the great glass windows that open onto the ocean.

It doesn't matter what main course you choose, as long as you accompany it with an order of onion rings. At lunch, it might be a deviled crab sandwich, hot thinly sliced roast beef on a toasted French roll, or spinach salad with hot bacon dressing. Dinners mean fresh fish, which is available broiled, fried, or Cajun style; grilled pork chops with homemade jalapeño applesauce; and a roast duckling that's deserving of the restaurant's self-congratulatory "gold seal."

MODERATE

CHARLIE BROWN'S, 1410 S. Fla. A1A. Tel. 231-6310.

Cuisine: AMERICAN. **Reservations:** Recommended.
$ Prices: Burgers and sandwiches $5–$9; main courses $10–$15. AE, MC, V.
Open: Dinner only, daily 5–10pm.

I'm usually not one for corporate restaurants, but this dark, wood-and-fern chain eatery gets high marks for its unusually large salad bar that rivals any I've seen. For a reason I don't quite understand, many diners order hot entrees to accompany the copious salad bar. Fish is blackened, baked, or charcoal-broiled; chicken is barbecued or grilled; and beef is served as prime rib, or shish kebab style on a skewer with onions, tomatoes, green peppers, and mushrooms.

SHOPPING

Ocean Boulevard and **Cardinal Drive** are Vero's two main shopping streets, both of which are near the beach and lined with specialty boutiques.

Some of the more distinctive shops in town include **Hale Indian River Groves,** 615 Beachland Blvd. (tel. 231-1752), a shipper of local citrus and jams since 1947; and **Bodi and Sol,** 3349 Ocean Dr. (tel. 231-5151), a shop selling contemporary women's clothing with pastel prints, and other tropical colors.

EVENING ENTERTAINMENT

CENTER FOR THE ARTS, 3001 Riverside Park Dr. Tel. 231-0707.

Vero Beach's boosters are justifiably proud of their newly completed cultural center. In addition to being beautifully designed and landscaped, the center actually attracts important events in its lecture hall, museum, and 250-seat Leohardt Auditorium. Volunteer docents give tours of the galleries Wednesday through Sunday from 1:30 to 3:30pm. Call for scheduled exhibitions and performances. The center is open October to April, Friday through Wednesday from 10am to 4:30pm and on Thursday from 10am to 8pm; May to September, on Tuesday, Wednesday, Friday, and Saturday from 10am to 4:30pm, on Thursday from 10am to 8pm, and on Sunday from 1 to 4:30pm.

Admission: Museum, free; auditorium prices vary, depending on the performance scheduled.

RIVERSIDE THEATER, on Riverside Park Dr., just past the drawbridge. Tel. 231-6990.

Plays, musicals, children's shows, summer workshops, and various celebrity events are scheduled here from October through May. During the summer months, there's usually only one major performance. Call for schedules and tickets.

Admission: Tickets, $5–$30.

CHAPTER 9

ORLANDO & WALT DISNEY WORLD

Orlando was a sleepy southern village ringed with sparkling lakes, pine forests, and citrus groves until Walt Disney waved his pixie-dusted paintbrush over 43 square miles of swampland in 1971 and turned it into a Magic Kingdom. He literally "animated" the area, sparking a building boom in hotels and restaurants to serve massive numbers of Walt Disney World visitors. And scores of additional attractions soon arose to take advantage of the tourist traffic Disney had generated. The world's most famous mouse has changed Central Florida forever. Many national firms have moved their headquarters to this thriving sunbelt region, and it has also become one of the fastest-growing high-technology centers in the country.

For the tourist, the city and its environs are so attraction-rich that unless you stay for several weeks, you can't possibly see everything in one trip. The original Magic Kingdom—a fantasyland of animated characters, rides, dazzling parades, and nightly fireworks—has been augmented by half a dozen additional Disney attraction areas and over 20 Disney resorts and official hotels. And scores of non-Disney attractions—most notably Sea World, Universal Studios, Cypress Gardens, and the Kennedy Space Center—also compete for your tourist dollar. This is one destination that requires advance planning for optimum enjoyment.

1. ORIENTATION

ARRIVING

BY PLANE The **Orlando International Airport** (tel. 407/825-2001), 25 miles from Walt Disney World, is a thoroughly modern and user-friendly facility with pleasant restaurants, shops, a 450-room on-premises Hyatt Regency Hotel, and centrally located information kiosks. Delta, the official airline of Walt Disney World, offers service from 200 cities and has a Fantastic Flyer program for kids. Other carriers include Aeropostal, Air Jamaica, All Nippon Airways, America West, American, American Trans Air, British Airways, ComAir, Continental, Icelandair, KLM, Kiwi, LTU, Mexicana, Northwest, Transbrasil, TWA, United, USAir, and Virgin Atlantic.

Since advance-purchase fares are almost always the lowest available, it's a good idea to book your flight as far in advance as possible.

When you call to reserve your flight, also inquire about **money-saving packages.** Delta has Walt Disney World Dream Vacations in several price ranges that include round-trip air transport, accommodations (state and hotel room tax included), an air-conditioned intermediate rental car with unlimited mileage or round-trip airport transfer, a "Magic Passport" which provides unlimited admission to all WDW parks for the length of your stay, one breakfast (which can be a character breakfast), and entry into a selected theme park one hour before regular opening time. Since the packages utilize Walt Disney World Resorts, you get all the advantages accruing to guests at these properties (see "Accommodations," below). If you put all those components together on your own, the cost would be much, much higher. Delta also has Orlando packages for which WDW tickets are optional. For details, call toll free 800/872-7786 or consult your local travel agent. Note: Delta is the only airline authorized to use Disney resorts in its packages.

BY TRAIN Amtrak trains (tel. toll free 800/USA-RAIL) pull into the station in Orlando at 1400 Sligh Blvd., between Columbia and Miller Streets, and in Kissimmee (about 15 miles from Walt Disney World) at 416 Pleasant St., between Dakin and Drury Avenues.

A limited number of discount-fare seats are set aside on each train; the sooner you reserve, the greater the savings. Many people reserve fares months in advance (they're almost always refundable). There may be some restrictions on travel dates for discounted fares around very busy holiday times.

To inquire about Amtrak's money-saving packages—including hotel accommodations, car rentals, tours, etc., with your train fare—call toll free 800/321-8684.

The Auto Train Amtrak's Auto Train offers the convenience of having a car in Florida without driving it there. The Auto Train begins in Lorton, Va. (about a four-hour drive from New York, two hours from Philadelphia) and ends up at Sanford, Fla. (about 23 miles northeast of Orlando). Once again, reserve early for the lowest fares. The Auto Train departs Lorton and Sanford at 4:30pm daily, arriving at the opposite destination at 9am the next morning. Note: You have to arrive one or two hours before departure time so they can board your car. Call toll free 800/USA-RAIL for details.

BY BUS Greyhound buses connect the entire country with Orlando. They pull into a terminal at 555 N. Magruder Blvd. (John Young Pkwy.), between West Colonial Drive and Winter Garden Road, a few miles west of downtown Orlando (tel. 407/292-3422), or in Kissimmee at 16 N. Orlando Ave., between Emmett and Mabbette Streets, about 14 miles from Walt Disney World (tel. 407/847-3911). There is van transport from the Kissimmee terminal to most area hotels and motels. The fare structure on buses tends to be complex, but the good news is that when you call to make a reservation, the agent will always give you the lowest-fare options. Once again, advance-purchase fares booked 3–21 days prior to travel represent vast savings. Check your phone book for a local Greyhound listing.

BY CAR Orlando is 436 miles from Atlanta, 1,312 miles from Boston, 1,120 miles from Chicago, 1,009 miles from Cleveland, 1,170 miles from Dallas, 1,114 miles from Detroit, 1,105 miles from New York City, and 1,261 miles from Toronto.

From Atlanta, take I-75 south to the Florida Turnpike to I-4 west. From Boston, New York, and other points in the Northeast, take I-95 south to I-4 west. From Chicago, take I-65 south to Nashville, then I-24 south to I-75 south to the Florida Turnpike to I-4 west. From Cleveland, take I-77 south to Columbia, S.C., then I-26 east to I-95 south to I-4 west. From Dallas, take I-20 east to I-49 south to I-10 east to I-75 south to the Florida Turnpike to I-4 west. From Detroit, take I-75 south to the Florida Turnpike to I-4 west. From Toronto, take Canadian Rte. 401 south to Queen Elizabeth Way south to I-90 (New York State Thruway) east to I-87 (New York State Thruway) south to I-95 over the George Washington Bridge, and continue south on I-95 to I-4 west. AAA and some other automobile club members can call local offices for maps and optimum driving directions.

TOURIST INFORMATION

Contact the **Orlando / Orange County Convention & Visitors Bureau,** 8445 International Dr. (in the Mercado Shopping Village), Orlando, FL 32819 (tel.

407/363-5871). They can answer all your questions and will be happy to send you maps, brochures (including the informative *Official Visitors Guide,* the *Area Guide* (to local restaurants), the *Official Accommodations Guide,* an events calendar, and the "Magicard" (good for discounts of 10%–50% on accommodations, attractions, car rentals, and more). Discount tickets to attractions other than Disney parks are sold on the premises, and the multilingual staff can also make dining reservations and hotel referrals. The bureau is open daily except Christmas from 8am to 8pm.

For general information about Walt Disney World, and a copy of the informative *Walt Disney World Vacation Guide,* write or call the **Walt Disney World Co.,** P.O. Box 10000, Lake Buena Vista, FL 32830-1000 (tel. 407/824-4321).

If you're driving, you can stop at a Walt Disney World information facility in Ocala, Fla., at the intersection of I-75 and Fla. 200, about 90 miles north of Orlando (tel. 904/854-0770). Here you can purchase tickets and Mickey ears, get help planning your park itinerary, and make hotel reservations.

And at the Orlando International Airport, arriving passengers can stroll over to Greetings from Walt Disney World (tel. 904/825-2301), a shop and information center on the third floor in the main lobby just behind the Northwest counter. This facility sells park tickets, makes dinner show and hotel reservations, and provides brochures and assistance. It's open daily from 7am to 10pm.

Also contact the **Kissimmee–St. Cloud Convention & Visitors Bureau,** 1925 U.S. 192 (P.O. Box 422007), Kissimmee, FL 34742-2007 (tel. 407/847-5000, or toll free 800/327-9159). They'll send maps, brochures, discount books, and the *Kissimmee–St. Cloud Vacation Guide* which details the area's accommodations and attractions.

CITY LAYOUT

Orlando's major artery is **I-4,** which runs diagonally across the state from Tampa to Daytona Beach. Exits from I-4 take you to Walt Disney World, Sea World, International Drive, U.S. 192, Kissimmee, Lake Buena Vista, Church Street Station, downtown Orlando, and Winter Park. The **Florida Turnpike** crosses I-4 and links up with I-75 to the north. **U.S. 192,** a major east-west artery, stretches from Kissimmee (along a major motel strip) to **U.S. 27,** crossing I-4 near the Walt Disney World entrance road. Farther north, a toll road called the **Beeline Expressway** (Fla. 528) goes east from I-4 past Orlando International Airport to Cape Canaveral.

Walt Disney World property is bounded roughly by I-4 and Fla. 535 to the east (the latter also north), World Drive (the entrance road) to the west, and U.S. 192 to the south. EPCOT Center Drive (Fla. 536, the south end of International Drive) and Buena Vista Drive cut across the complex in a more-or-less east-west direction; the two roads cross at Bonnet Creek Parkway. Excellent highways and explicit signs make it very easy to find your way around.

Note: The Disney parks are actually much closer to Kissimmee than to downtown Orlando.

NEIGHBORHOODS IN BRIEF

Walt Disney World A city unto itself, WDW sprawls over more than 26,000 acres containing theme parks, resorts, hotels, shops, restaurants, and recreational facilities galore (copious details below).

Lake Buena Vista On the eastern end of Disney property, Lake Buena Vista is a hotel village/marketplace owned and operated by Walt Disney World. However, though Disney owns all the real estate, many of the hotels, and some shops and restaurants, in this area are independently owned. It's a charming area of manicured lawns and verdant thoroughfares with traffic islands shaded by towering oak trees.

International Drive (Fla. 536) This attractive area extends 7–10 miles north of the Disney parks between Fla. 535 and the Florida Turnpike. It, too, centers—for a long way—on a wide thoroughfare with a tree-shaded traffic island. It contains numerous hotels, restaurants, shopping centers, and the Orange County Convention Center, and offers easy access to Sea World and Universal Studios. (*Note:* Locally, this road is always referred to as I-Drive.)

Kissimmee South of the Disney Parks, Kissimmee centers on U.S. 192/Irlo Bronson Memorial Highway, a strip as archetypical of American cities as Main Street. It's lined with budget motels, lesser attractions (such as Reptile World and the Elvis Presley Museum), and every fast-food restaurant you can name.

Downtown Orlando Reached via I-4 east, this burgeoning sunbelt metropolis is 17 miles northeast of Walt Disney World. Though many tourists never venture downtown, it does have a number of attractions, including noteworthy nightlife.

WHEN TO GO

Orlando is essentially a theme-park destination, and its busiest seasons are whenever kids are out of school—summer (early June to about August 20), holiday weekends, Christmas season (mid-December to mid-January), and Easter. Obviously, the whole experience is more enjoyable when the crowds are thinnest and the weather most temperate. Best times are the week after Labor Day until Thanksgiving, the week after Thanksgiving until mid-December, and the six weeks before and after school spring vacations. The worst time is summer, when crowds are very large and the weather hot and humid.

2. GETTING AROUND

FROM THE AIRPORT Orlando International Airport is 25 miles from Walt Disney World. **Mears Transportation Group** (tel. 407/423-5566) buses ply the route from the airport to all Disney resorts and official hotels, as well as most other area properties. The comfortable, air-conditioned shuttle vans operate around the clock, departing every 15–25 minutes. Rates vary with your destination: Round-trip cost for adults is $19 between the airport and downtown Orlando or International Drive, $23 for Walt Disney World/Lake Buena Vista, $35 for Kissimmee/U.S. 192. Children 4–11 pay $14, $17, and $28, respectively; children 3 and under ride free.

If you rent a car at the airport, take the Beeline Expressway (Fla. 528) toward Tampa to I-4 west and look for signs. It's a good idea to ask your hotel for explicit directions when you reserve.

BY BUS **Disney shuttle buses** serve all Disney resorts and official hotels, offering unlimited complimentary transportation via bus, monorail, ferry, and water taxi to all three parks from two hours prior to opening until two hours after closing; also to Disney Village Marketplace, Typhoon Lagoon, Pleasure Island, Fort Wilderness, and other Disney resorts. Disney properties offer transportation to other area attractions as well, though it's not complimentary. Almost all area hotels and motels also offer transportation to Walt Disney World and other attractions, but it can be pricey.

Mears Transportation Group (tel. 407/423-5566) operates buses to all major attractions, including Cypress Gardens, Kennedy Space Center, Universal Studios, Sea World, Busch Gardens (in Tampa), and Church Street Station, among others. Call for details.

BY TAXI Taxis line up in front of major hotels, and at smaller hostelries the front desk will be happy to call you a cab. Or call **Yellow Cab** (tel. 699-9999). The charge is $2.45 for the first mile, $1.40 per mile thereafter. A company called **Arco-Sun** (tel. 239-1616 in Orlando, 396-2071 in Kissimmee) operates on a zone basis, so you always pay a flat price, ascertained in advance. The minimum fare is $5 for up to five people in a cab. They have multilingual drivers and can put together sightseeing itineraries.

BY CAR Though you can get to and around Walt Disney World and other major attractions here without a car, it's always handy to have one. All the major car-rental

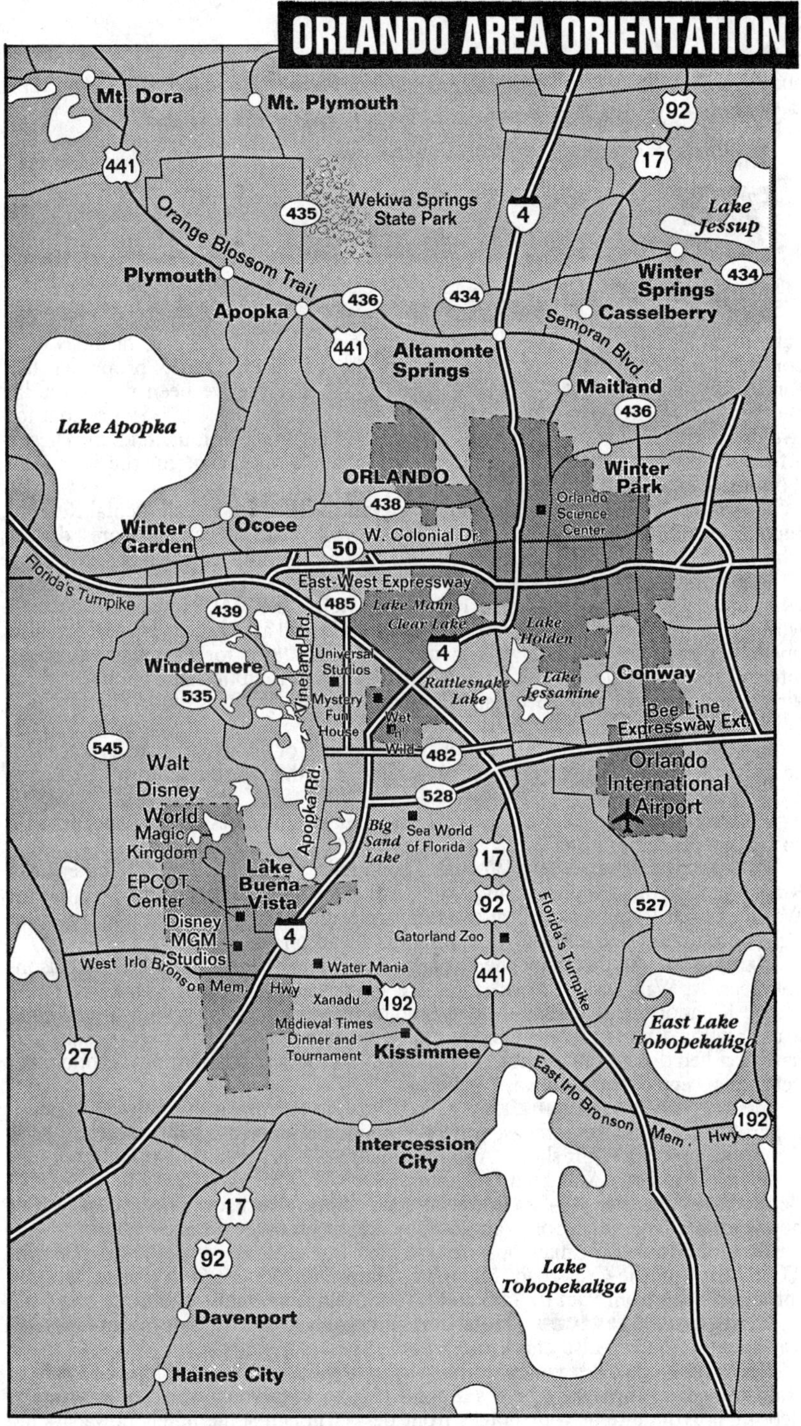
ORLANDO AREA ORIENTATION
Mt. Dora
Mt. Plymouth
92
17
441
Lake Jessup
Wekiwa Springs State Park
435
4
Orange Blossom Trail
Plymouth
Apopka
436
434
Winter Springs
434
Casselberry
Semoran Blvd.
441
Altamonte Springs
Maitland
436
Lake Apopka
Winter Park
ORLANDO
Orlando Science Center
438
Winter Garden
Ocoee
W. Colonial Dr.
50
Florida's Turnpike
East-West Expressway
485
Lake Mann
Clear Lake
439
Lake Holden
Windermere
Vineland Rd.
Universal Studios
4
Rattlesnake Lake
Lake Jessamine
Conway
535
Mystery Fun House
Wet 'n' Wild
Bee Line Expressway Ext.
545
482
Walt Disney World
Orlando International Airport
528
Apopka Rd.
Magic Kingdom
Big Sand Lake
Sea World of Florida
17
EPCOT Center
Lake Buena Vista
92
527
Disney MGM Studios
4
Gatorland Zoo
West Irlo Bronson Mem. Hwy
Water Mania
441
Florida's Turnpike
Xanadu
192
East Lake Tohopekaliga
Medieval Times Dinner and Tournament
Kissimmee
27
East Irlo Bronson Mem. Hwy
192
Intercession City
17
92
Lake Tohopekaliga
Davenport
Haines City

companies are represented here and maintain desks at the airport. Some handy phone numbers: **Alamo** (tel. toll free 800/327-9633), **Avis** (tel. toll free 800/331-1212), **Budget** (tel. toll free 800/527-0700), **Dollar** (tel. toll free 800/800-4000), **Hertz** (tel. toll free 800/654-3131), and **Thrifty** (tel. toll free 800/367-2277).

FAST FACTS ORLANDO

Area Code The telephone area code for most of Central Florida is 407.

Babysitters In this child-oriented town, almost every hotel provides babysitting services, and several hostelries have marvelous child-care facilities with counselor-supervised activity programs on the premises. Disney properties use KinderCare sitters (tel. 827-5444), so you can be sure they've been very carefully checked out. Rates for in-room service are $8 per hour for one child, $9 per hour for two children, $11 per hour for three children, $14 per hour for four children. There's a four-hour minimum, the first half hour of which is travel time for the sitter, and 24-hour advance notice is required.

Doctors and Dentists Inquire at your hotel desk, or call Dental Referral Service (tel. 628-4363), from 5:30am to 6pm daily; they can tell you the nearest dentist who meets your needs. Check the *Yellow Pages* for 24-hour emergency services.

Disney has first-aid centers in all three major parks. There's also a very good 24-hour service in the area called HouseMed (tel. 648-9234). HouseMed doctors, who can dispense medication, make "house calls" to all area hotels. HouseMed also operates the Medi-Clinic, a walk-in medical facility (not for emergencies) at the intersection of I-4 and U.S. 192, open daily from 9am to 9pm (same phone); call for directions from your hotel. See also "Hospital Emergency Wards" and "Pharmacies," below.

Emergencies Dial 911 to contact the police or fire department or to call an ambulance. The 24-hour emergency hotline for the Poison Control Center is 897-1940.

Hairdressers Many hotels have on-premises hairdressers. If yours doesn't, check out the better hotel listings below to find one.

Hospital Emergency Wards Sand Lake Hospital is at 9400 Turkey Lake Rd., about two miles south of Sand Lake Road (tel. 351-8550). Take Exit 27A (the Sea World exit) off I-4, make a left at the stop sign at the end of the exit ramp, and bear right onto Turkey Lake Road; the hospital is ahead on your left.

Kennels All the major theme parks offer animal-boarding facilities at reasonable fees. At Walt Disney World, there are kennels at Fort Wilderness, EPCOT, the Magic Kingdom, and Disney–MGM Studios. If you're traveling with a pet, don't leave it in the car, even with a window cracked, while you enjoy the park—many pets have perished this way in the hot Florida sun. Note: Where hotel listings mention that pets are accepted, there's always a charge.

Newspapers/Magazines The *Orlando Sentinel* is the major local newspaper, but you can also purchase papers of major cities (most notably the *New York Times)* in most hotel gift shops. Also informative is a city magazine called *Orlando.*

Pharmacies Walgreen Drug Store, 1003 W. Vine St. (U.S. 192), just east of Bermuda Avenue (tel. 847-5252), operates a 24-hour pharmacy. They can deliver to hotels for a charge ($10 from 7am to 5pm, $15 at all other times).

Post Office The main post office in Lake Buena Vista is at 12541 Fla. 535 near TGI Friday's in the Crossroads Shopping Center (tel. 828-2606). It's open Monday through Friday from 9am to 4pm and on Saturday from 9am to noon.

Religious Services Hotel desks invariably keep a list of local churches and synagogues. You can also check the *Yellow Pages.*

Safety Whenever you're traveling in an unfamiliar city, stay alert. Be aware of your immediate surroundings. It's a good idea to keep your valuables in a safety-deposit box (inquire at your hotel's front desk), though some hotels nowadays are equipped with in-room safes. Keep a close eye on your valuables when you're in a public place—restaurant, theater, even airport terminal. And don't leave valuables in your car, even in the trunk.

Tax Hotel tax in Orlando is 10% and in Kissimmee it's 11%, both including a state sales tax that's charged on all goods except most grocery-store items and medicines.

Time Call 646-3131 for the correct time and temperature.

Weather Call 851-7510 for a weather recording.

3. ACCOMMODATIONS

You'll find a wealth of hotel options in the Walt Disney World area. Stunningly landscaped multifacility resorts are the rule, but there's something to suit every taste and pocketbook. Do, of course, reserve as far in advance as possible—the minute you've decided on the dates of your trip.

In some hotel listings below, I've mentioned concierge levels. If you're not familiar with this concept, it involves a "hotel within a hotel" where guests enjoy a luxurious private lounge that's the setting for complimentary continental breakfast, hot and cold hors d'oeuvres at cocktail hour, late-night cordials and pastries, and other special services. Rooms are usually on high floors with upgraded decor.

Also mentioned under "Facilities" are counselor-supervised child-care/activity centers. These are, for the most part, creatively run facilities where kids enjoy Disney movies, video games, arts and crafts, and outdoor activities. Some centers provide meals and/or have beds where a child can go to sleep while you're out on the town. Check the individual hotel listings for these facilities and call to find out exactly what's offered.

Note: If you don't have a car, include the cost of shuttle buses to and from Disney and other theme parks in determining your hotel choice.

DISNEY HOSTELRIES & OFFICIAL HOTELS

There are 12 Disney-owned properties (hotels, resorts, villas, wilderness/homes, and campsites) and 9 privately owned "official hotels," a goodly selection of which are described in this section. All are within the Walt Disney World complex.

In addition to their proximity to the parks, there are a number of advantages to staying at a Disney property or official hotel. At all Disney resorts and official hotels these include:

- Unlimited complimentary transportation via bus, monorail, ferry, and water taxi to/from all three parks from two hours before opening until two hours after closing. Unlimited complimentary transport is also provided to/from Disney Village Marketplace, Typhoon Lagoon, Pleasure Island, Fort Wilderness, and other Disney resorts. Three hostelries—the Polynesian, Contemporary, and Grand Floridian—are stops on the monorail. This free transport can save a lot of money. It also means you're guaranteed admission to all parks, even during peak times when parking lots sometimes fill up.
- Reduced-price children's menus in almost all restaurants, and character breakfasts and/or dinners at many hostelries.
- TVs equipped with the Disney Channel and Walt Disney World information stations.
- A guest services desk where you can purchase tickets to all WDW theme parks and attractions and obtain general information.
- Use of—and in some cases, complimentary transport to—the five Disney-owned

golf courses and preferred tee times at them (these can be booked up to 30 days in advance).

- Access to most recreational facilities at other Disney resorts.
- Service by the Mears airport shuttle.

Additional perks at Disney-owned hotels, resorts, villas, and campgrounds (but not at "official" hotels) include charge privileges at restaurants and shops throughout Walt Disney World; early admission, prior to the public opening, to the Magic Kingdom on specific days; and dining and show reservations (including EPCOT restaurants) which can be made on the premises.

WALT DISNEY WORLD CENTRAL RESERVATIONS OFFICE To reserve a room at Disney hotels, resorts, and villas; official hotels; and Fort Wilderness homes and campsites, contact the Central Reservations Office, P.O. Box 10100, Lake Buena Vista, FL 32830-0100 (tel. 407/W-DISNEY), which is open seven days a week between 8:30am and 10pm. Have your dates and credit card ready when you call.

The CRO can recommend accommodations that will suit your specific needs as to price, location (perhaps you wish to be closest to EPCOT, Magic Kingdom, or Disney–MGM Studios), and facilities such as counselor-supervised child-care centers, on-premises sports and recreational facilities, a kitchen, and so on.

Be sure to inquire about their numerous package plans which include meals, tickets, recreation, and other features. The right package plan can save you both money and time, and a comprehensive plan is helpful in computing the cost of your vacation in advance.

The CRO can also give you information about various park ticket options and make dinner-show reservations for you at the *Hoop-de-Doo Revue,* the *Polynesian Revue,* and *Broadway at the Top* when you book your room.

OTHER RESERVATIONS & PACKAGES **Delta,** the official airline of Walt Disney World, is the only airline permitted to use Disney resorts and campgrounds in its packages. They offer accommodations in different price ranges at your choice of a number of resorts. For details, call toll free 800/872-7786.

American Express Vacations is also officially authorized to use Disney hostelries in its packages. For details, call toll free 800/241-1700.

Most **hotels** listed below also offer packages; inquire when you call. And **your travel agent** may also offer interesting packages.

DISNEY HOSTELRIES

Very Expensive

DISNEY'S BEACH CLUB RESORT, 1800 EPCOT Resorts Blvd. (P.O. Box 10100), Lake Buena Vista, FL 32830-0100. Tel. 407/W-DISNEY or 407/934-8000. Fax 407/354-1866. 584 rms, 24 suites. A/C MINIBAR TV TEL

$ **Rates:** $210–$290 single or double, depending on view and season. Additional person $15 extra; children under 18 stay free in parents' room. Inquire about packages. AE, MC, V. **Parking:** Free self- and valet parking.

With its pristinely white-trimmed sky-blue exterior, palm-fringed entranceway, sandy beach, and manicured gardens, the Beach Club evokes a luxurious Victorian Cape Cod resort. Charming rooms, furnished in bleached woods, are decorated in seafoam green with peach and coral accents. Beach umbrellas, seashells, and ocean waves adorn bedspreads, verdigris iron headboards, and a decorative frieze, and wall sconces are seahorse-shaped. Some rooms have widow's walk balconies. Amenities include ceiling fans, extra phones in the bath, remote-control cable TVs, clock radios, safes, and game tables. Note: The Beach Club is in walking distance of EPCOT Center.

Dining/Entertainment: The very elegant Ariel's, a seafood restaurant named for the *Little Mermaid* character, is open for dinner nightly (see "Dining," below, for details). Wines are also highlighted at the adjoining Martha's Vineyard Lounge, where international selections are offered by the glass. Ideal for family dining is the Cape

May Café, serving buffet character breakfasts hosted by Admiral Goofy, and authentic New England clambake buffet dinners in a charming dining room adorned with colorful beach umbrellas, sand sculpture displays, and croquet mallets. The Rip Tide Lounge, off the lobby, features an array of California wines, wine coolers, and frosty concoctions. Beaches & Cream, adjoining the video-games arcade and central to both the Yacht and Beach Clubs, looks like an old-fashioned ice-cream parlor, complete with an oldies-stocked Wurlitzer jukebox and marble pedestal tables; light fare, plus sundaes, floats, and shakes are featured. Also central to both properties, adjacent to Stormalong Bay, is Hurricane Hanna's Grill, for light fare, ice-cream sundaes, and specialty drinks.

Services: 24-hour room service, babysitting, guest services desk, nightly bed turn-down with chocolate mint, complimentary daily newspaper, boat transport to MGM theme park.

Facilities: Large secluded swimming pool, Jacuzzi, quarter-mile white sandy beach, boat rentals (pedalboats, sailboats, miniature speedboats, rowboats, pontoons, canopy boats), two hard-surface night-lit tennis courts, state-of-the-art health club, volleyball/croquet/bocci ball courts, two-mile jogging trail, coin-op washers/dryers, full-service unisex hair salon, shops, full business center, large video-games arcade, Sandcastle Club (a counselor-supervised child-care/activity center). Stormalong Bay, a 790,000-gallon free-form swimming pool-cum-waterpark, sprawls over three acres between the Yacht and Beach Clubs and flows into the lake; it includes a 150-foot serpentine water slide, a smaller slide for little kids, whirling waters, bubbling jets, shallow wading areas, and a sand strip.

DISNEY'S GRAND FLORIDIAN BEACH RESORT, 4401 Floridian Way (P.O. Box 10100), Lake Buena Vista, FL 32830-0100. Tel. 407/W-DISNEY or 407/824-3000. Fax 407/354-1866. 878 rms, 26 suites. A/C MINIBAR TV TEL

$ Rates: $230–$325 standard single or double, depending on view and season; $410–$440 single or double on the concierge floors; $500–$1,450 suite. Additional person $15 extra; children under 18 stay free in parents' room. Inquire about packages. AE, MC, V. **Parking:** Free self- and valet parking.

The Grand Floridian is magnificent from the moment you step into its opulent five-story lobby under triple-domed stained-glass skylights. The lacy white wrought-iron balustrades, plush furnishings, glittering chandeliers, white birdcage elevators, and Chinese Chippendale aviary are all reminiscent of a bygone era of luxury. A pianist entertains during afternoon tea, and an orchestra plays big-band music every evening from 5 to 10:30pm. Sunny rooms, some with dormer windows, are decorated in muted greens and pinks and furnished with Victorian-style convertible sofas and bleached oak two-poster beds made up with floral-chintz spreads. In-room amenities include remote-control cable TVs, safes, alarm-clock radios, and plantation-style ceiling fans. In the bath, you'll find a cosmetic mirror, extra phone, hairdryer, and terry robe. And private latticed balconies or verandas overlook formal gardens, the pool, or a 200-acre lagoon.

Dining/Entertainment: Victoria & Albert's, Orlando's finest restaurant, is described below (see "Dining"). The lovely Grand Floridian Café, with elegantly draped Palladian windows overlooking formal gardens, serves American fare from 7am to 11pm daily; southern specialties such as battered fried catfish are featured. The festive exposition-themed 1900 Park Fare is the setting for buffet character breakfasts and dinners. Entered via a Victorian rotunda, Flagler's has a 19th-century garden ambience. At dinner, the fare is northern Italian, and a strolling guitarist entertains. Weekends, the restaurant is used for buffet breakfasts. At the gazebolike Narcoossee's, overlooking the lagoon near the boat landing, grilled meats and seafood are prepared in an exhibition kitchen; it's open for lunch and dinner daily. The 24-hour Gasparilla Grill, adjoining the video-games arcade, offers sandwiches, snacks, and ice cream, as well as continental breakfasts, to Nintendo noshers. Cozily intimate and very Victorian, Mizner's Lounge offers an international selection of ports, brandies, and appetizers. The light and airy Garden View Lounge off the lobby is the setting for ultra-elegant afternoon teas; evenings, champagne cocktails are a specialty. And frozen drinks and snacks are available from the octagonal Summerhouse Pool Bar.

Services: 24-hour room service, nightly turn-down with Belgian chocolates, babysitting, on-premises monorail, boat transport to the Magic Kingdom and the Polynesian Resort, free trolley transport around the hotel grounds, shoeshine, massage, guest services desk, complimentary daily newspaper.

Facilities: Large swimming pool, children's wading pool, whirlpool, two night-lit clay tennis courts, boat rental (canopy boats, catamarans, Sunfish and cabin sailboats, Water Sprites), waterskiing, croquet, volleyball, children's playground, jogging trails, fishing excursions, white sand beach, full business center, full-service unisex hair salon, coin-op washers/dryers, shops, extensive state-of-the-art health club, videogames arcade, organized children's activities in summer and peak seasons, the Mouseketeer Clubhouse (a counselor-supervised child-care activity center).

DISNEY'S YACHT CLUB RESORT, 1700 EPCOT Resorts Blvd. (P.O. Box 10100), Lake Buena Vista, FL 32830-0100. Tel. 407/W-DISNEY or 407/934-7000. Fax 407/354-1866. 625 rms, 10 suites. A/C MINIBAR TV TEL

$ **Rates:** $210–$290 standard single or double, depending on view and season; $350–$390 single or double on the concierge level. Additional person $15 extra; children under 18 stay free in parents' room. Inquire about packages. AE, MC, V. **Parking:** Free self- and valet parking.

Legend has it that the ship of world traveler Old Stormalong went aground on a lagoon here, and the area was so beautiful that he decided to forsake adventuring and settle down. And beautiful it is! The Yacht Club shares a 25-acre lake, facilities, and gorgeous landscaping with the adjacent Beach Club. Grounds are planted with Japanese elms, Bradford pear trees, magnolias, crape myrtles, and lush tropical foliage; and gardenias and roses bloom in charming brick courtyards. The main five-story oyster-gray clapboard building evokes a luxurious turn-of-the-century New England yacht club. The nautical theme carries over to very inviting rooms, decorated in snappy blue and white, with brass sconces and ship lights, maps and paintings of ship's captains on the walls, and crisp floral-chintz drapes, valances, and bed ruffles. French doors open onto porches or balconies. Amenities include ceiling fans, extra phones in the bath, remote-control cable TVs, alarm-clock radios, safes, and game tables. The fifth floor is a concierge level.

Dining/Entertainment: The plush Yachtsman Steakhouse, open for dinner nightly, features an exhibition kitchen where select cuts of steak, chops, and fresh seafood are grilled over oak and hickory. The nautically themed Yacht Club Galley is the resort's comfortable family restaurant, offering American regional fare at all meals. The Crew's Cup Lounge, its pine-paneled walls hung with Ivy League rowing-team memorabilia, serves up light fare and frosted mugs of international ales and beers; sporting events are aired on the TV. The cozy Ale and Compass Lounge, a lobby bar with a working fireplace, features specialty coffees and cocktails. The seasonal Sip Ahoy Snack Bar serves the secluded pool. And a brass quartet entertains nightly on the mezzanine level. (See also the Beach Club restaurants and bars, above.)

Services: 24-hour room service, babysitting, guest services desk, nightly bed turn-down with chocolate mint, complimentary daily newspaper, boat transport to MGM theme park, tram transport to EPCOT Center.

Facilities: Yacht Club facilities are identical to those of the Beach Club (see above).

Expensive

DISNEY'S CONTEMPORARY RESORT, 4600 N. World Dr. (P.O. Box 10100), Lake Buena Vista, FL 32830-0100. Tel. 407/W-DISNEY or 407/824-1000. Fax 407/354-1866. 1,036 rms, 17 suites. A/C TV TEL

$ **Rates:** $189–$225 single or double standard/garden-view rooms, $215–$236 single or double lake-view rooms, $242–$263 single or double in the tower. Additional person $15 extra; children under 17 stay free in parents' room. Inquire about packages. AE, MC, V. **Parking:** Free self- and valet parking.

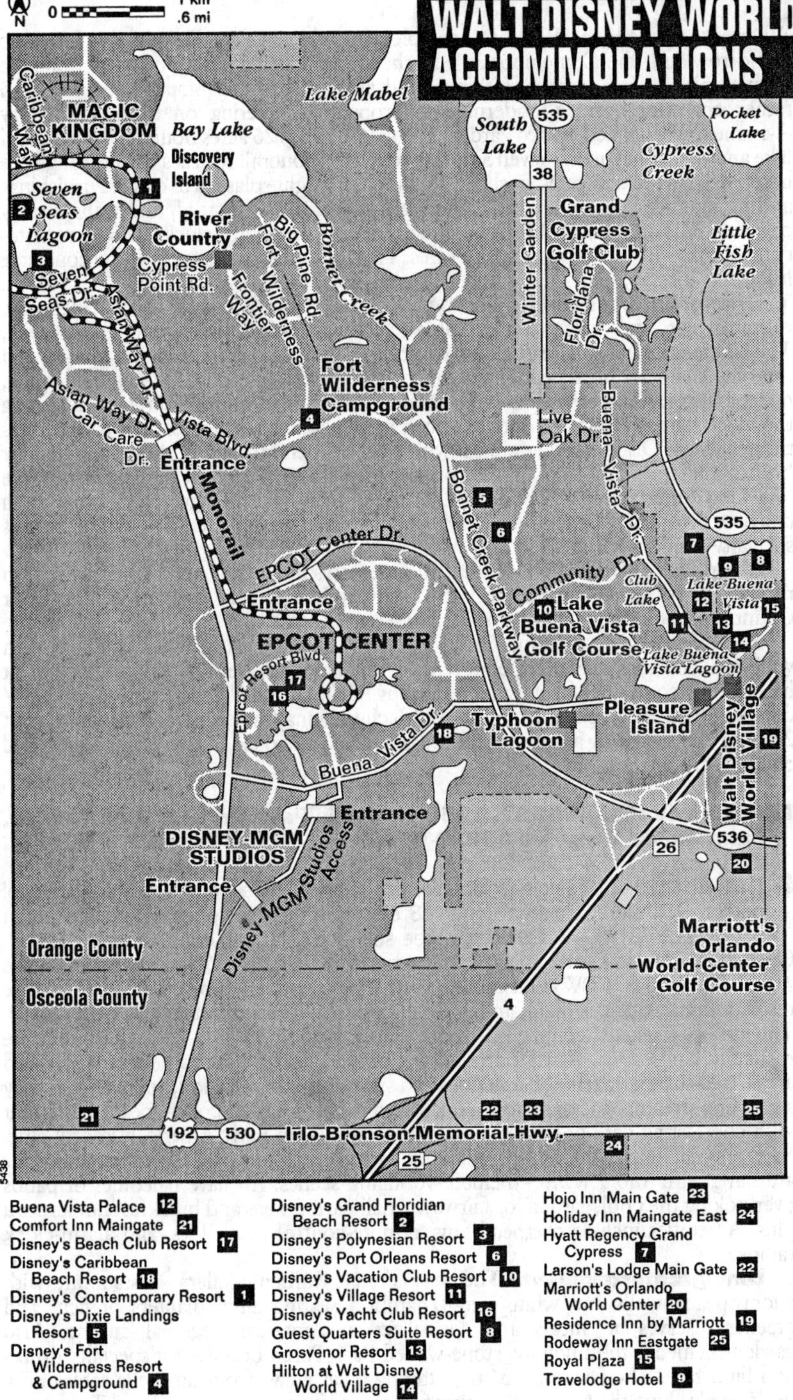
WALT DISNEY WORLD ACCOMMODATIONS
N
0
1 km
.6 mi
Lake Mabel
MAGIC KINGDOM
Caribbean Way
Bay Lake
Discovery Island
Seven Seas Lagoon
River Country
Cypress Point Rd.
Seven Seas Dr.
Asian Way Dr.
Big Pine Rd.
Fort Wilderness
Frontier Way
Bonnet Creek
South Lake
535
38
Pocket Lake
Cypress Creek
Grand Cypress Golf Club
Little Fish Lake
Winter Garden
Floridana Dr.
Fort Wilderness Campground
Asian Way Dr.
Car Care Dr.
Vista Blvd.
Entrance
Monorail
Live Oak Dr.
Buena Vista Dr.
Bonnet Creek Parkway
EPCOT Center Dr.
Entrance
EPCOT CENTER
Community Dr.
Club Lake
Lake Buena Vista Golf Course
Lake Buena Vista
Lake Buena Vista Lagoon
Epcot Resort Blvd.
Typhoon Lagoon
Pleasure Island
Walt Disney World Village
Buena Vista Dr.
Entrance
DISNEY-MGM STUDIOS
Entrance
Disney-MGM Studios Access
26
536
Orange County
Osceola County
Marriott's Orlando World Center Golf Course
4
192
530
Irlo-Bronson-Memorial-Hwy.
25
Buena Vista Palace 12
Comfort Inn Maingate 21
Disney's Beach Club Resort 17
Disney's Caribbean Beach Resort 18
Disney's Contemporary Resort 1
Disney's Dixie Landings Resort 5
Disney's Fort Wilderness Resort & Campground 4
Disney's Grand Floridian Beach Resort 2
Disney's Polynesian Resort 3
Disney's Port Orleans Resort 6
Disney's Vacation Club Resort 10
Disney's Village Resort 11
Disney's Yacht Club Resort 16
Guest Quarters Suite Resort 8
Grosvenor Resort 13
Hilton at Walt Disney World Village 14
Hojo Inn Main Gate 23
Holiday Inn Maingate East 24
Hyatt Regency Grand Cypress 7
Larson's Lodge Main Gate 22
Marriott's Orlando World Center 20
Residence Inn by Marriott 19
Rodeway Inn Eastgate 25
Royal Plaza 15
Travelodge Hotel 9
5438

When it opened in 1971 to complement the Magic Kingdom's futuristic Tomorrowland, the Contemporary's aesthetic was cutting-edge. Today its dramatic angular planes, free-form furnishings, and abstract paintings appear quaintly, and rather charmingly, retro-modern. The property—centering on a sleek 15-story A-frame tower flanked by two garden wings—occupies 26 acres bounded by a natural lake and the Disney-made Seven Seas Lagoon. The monorail whizzes right through the hotel. Rooms are decorated in shades of tan with bright splashes of color. Furnishings and lighting fixtures are art deco, there are ceiling fans overhead, and walls display cheerful Matisse prints. In-room amenities include alarm-clock radios, remote-control cable TVs, two phones, and safes. The 14th floor of the tower is the concierge level.

Dining/Entertainment: The Concourse Grill, with copper shoji screen–like room dividers and copper-topped tables, serves breakfast, lunch, and dinner daily. The Contemporary Café features all-you-can-eat prime rib/shrimp buffet dinners and morning character breakfasts. The Outer Rim, a bar/lounge overlooking the lagoon, offers piano bar and other live entertainment evenings. A no-frills cafeteria adjoining the video-games arcade on the first floor serves light fare; next to it is a children's theater where Disney movies are shown nightly. Open for nightly shows and Sunday brunch buffets, Top of the World, on the 15th floor, is a plush dinner theater (see "Evening Entertainment," below). Like its adjacent bar/lounge, open from noon daily, it provides a panoramic view. And in peak season the Sand Bar dispenses specialty drinks poolside.

Services: 24-hour room service; guest services desk; daily newspaper delivery to rooms; babysitting; boat transport to Discovery Island, Fort Wilderness, and River Country; direct monorail link to the Polynesian Resort.

Facilities: Two swimming pool, children's wading pool, white sand beach with volleyball court, shuffleboard, boat rentals, full-service unisex hair salon, six night-lit hard tennis courts (lessons available), shops, Delta Airlines desk, coin-op washers/dryers, full business center, extensive health club, sauna/massage/tanning rooms, vast 24-hour video-games arcade, the Mouseketeer Clubhouse (a counselor-supervised child-care/activity center).

THE DISNEY INN RESORT, 1950 Magnolia Palm Dr. (P.O. Box 10100), Lake Buena Vista, FL 32830-0100. Tel. 407/W-DISNEY or 407/824-2200. Fax 407/354-1866. 288 rms. A/C TV TEL

$ Rates: $180–215 single or double, depending on view and season. Additional person $15 extra; children under 18 stay free in parents' room. Inquire about packages. AE, MC, V. **Parking:** Free self- and valet parking.

Opened in 1973 as Disney's first golfing resort, this rambling 50-acre property is the site of the annual WDW/Oldsmobile Golf Classic, on the Pro-Am PGA Tour. The resort's Palm Course is rated among America's top 25 resort courses by *Golf Digest.* The inn has a relaxed countryside lodge theme, based on *Snow White.* Grounds are rustically landscaped. A walk around the property takes you past verdant wooded areas, tree-shaded gazebos, flamingoes and swans on tranquil lakes, and a grist mill by a gurgling stream. Spacious rooms, decorated in soft tones of cream, peach, and mint with contrasting dark-green carpeting, are furnished in Early American knotty pine. Beds are made up with floral-print cotton spreads with striped dust ruffles, and walls are hung with *Snow White*–themed woodland scenes. All have balconies or patios overlooking the pool, garden, or fairway. Small parlor areas and breakfast nooks are a plus. Amenities include overhead fans, remote-control cable TVs, and alarm-clock radios.

Dining/Entertainment: The very pretty Garden Gallery Restaurant, with adobe peach walls and white rattan/bamboo seating amid planters of ficus and greenery, serves all meals and specializes in American regional cuisine. Also garden-themed is the adjoining stone-walled Back Porch Lounge, for specialty drinks and light fare. The Diamond Mine, offering great views from umbrella tables on a deck overlooking the pool, serves light fare and soft drinks. And the Sand Trap serves light snacks and drinks poolside.

Services: Room service (7am–11pm), babysitting, guest services desk, complimentary daily newspaper.

Facilities: Two 18-hole championship golf courses, 9-hole walking course, golf and tennis pro shop/instruction, two hard-surface night-lit tennis courts, two large swimming pools, nice-sized children's wading pool in a magnolia courtyard, well-equipped health club, children's playground, jogging trail, coin-op washers/dryers, shops, video-games arcade.

DISNEY'S POLYNESIAN RESORT, 1600 Seven Seas Dr. (P.O. Box 10100), Lake Buena Vista, FL 32830-0100. Tel. 407/W-DISNEY or 407/824-2000. Fax 407/354-1866. 841 rms, 12 suites. A/C TV TEL

$ **Rates:** $195–$268 single or double, depending on view and season; $290–$310 single or double on the concierge floors; $342–$1,050 suite. Additional person $15 extra; children under 18 stay free in parents' room. Inquire about packages. AE, MC, V. **Parking:** Free self- and valet parking.

Designed to complement Adventureland in the Magic Kingdom, the 25-acre Polynesian Resort is fronted by lush tropical foliage, waterfalls, palms, and poi ponds. At night, lava rock walkways are illuminated by flaming torchiers. A private white sand beach—dotted with canvas cabañas, hammocks, umbrella tables, and large swings—looks out on a 200-acre lagoon. And the skylit lobby is a virtual rain forest of tropical plantings, with colorful resident macaws and a waterfall cascading into a stream stocked with goldfish. Large, beautiful rooms, all with balconies or patios, have canopied beds made up with gorgeous batik spreads, day-bed sofas strewn with batik pillows, bamboo and rattan furnishings, and walls hung with Gauguin prints. All overlook tropical gardens or the lagoon. In-room amenities include alarm-clock radios, remote-control cable TVs, and wood-bladed ceiling fans.

F FROMMER'S COOL FOR KIDS: HOTELS

All Disney properties and official hotels (*see pages 231–246*) offer many advantages for kids, including proximity to Walt Disney World parks, complimentary transportation between hotel and the parks, and reduced-price children's menus and Disney character appearances in hotel restaurants. Extensive facilities might include lakefront beaches, boating, waterskiing, bike rentals, playgrounds, video-games arcades, swimming pools with waterfalls and slides, and/or organized children's activities.

Disney's Fort Wilderness Resort and Campground (*see p. 241*) All of the above and more is offered here—plus you get to go camping.

Residence Inns (*see pp. 249 and 251*) Not only do they have swimming pools, children's playgrounds, and other recreational facilities but also accommodations with fully equipped kitchens—a potential money-saver for families. Rates include breakfast. The Meadow Creek Drive Residence Inn has an extensive recreation department offering free children's activities. The Lake Cecile hostelry has on-premises barbecue grills and picnic tables and offers boating and waterskiing on a scenic lake.

Holiday Inn Lake Buena Vista (*see p. 249*) This Holiday Inn has a special check-in desk for kids and on-premises mascots to welcome them. Rooms are equipped with kitchenettes. Kids under 12 eat free in their own restaurant where movies and cartoons are shown. Numerous organized children's activities are free.

Holiday Inn Maingate East (*see p. 250*) The children's facilities here are identical to those at the Lake Buena Vista counterpart.

Dining/Entertainment: The French Polynesian–themed Papeete Bay Verandah is the setting for Minnie's Menehune Character Breakfast (a daily buffet featuring Minnie and other Disney characters). It also serves à la carte Polynesian dinners (enhanced by a three-piece island band and dancer) and lavish buffet Sunday brunches. The exotic Tambu Lounge, specializing in Polynesian drinks and nightly piano bar music, adjoins. The Coral Isle Café serves American fare from 7am to 11pm. Captain Cook's Snack Bar, a classic ice-cream parlor, features an array of snack fare and a make-your-own-sundae bar. Tangaroa Terrace, a sunny plant-filled tropical dining room, serves à la carte and buffet breakfasts daily. Luau Cove is the setting for Mickey's Tropical Revue (a Polynesian/character show for children that takes place daily at 4:30pm) and the Polynesian Revue with shows at 6:45 and 9:30pm. Snack Isle, adjoining the video-games arcade, serves light fare (pizza, burgers, nachos). And the Barefoot Pool Bar, also featuring island drinks and light fare, has a beautiful setting on the beach overlooking the lagoon. A pianist entertains nightly on the second floor of the lobby.

Services: Room service (6:30am–1am), babysitting, on-premises monorail, boat transport (to Magic Kingdom, Discovery Island, Fort Wilderness, and River Country), guest services desk, complimentary daily newspaper.

Facilities: Two swimming pools (one of them immense, with waterfalls, grottoes, and a water slide), children's wading pool, boat rental, waterskiing, volleyball, children's playground, 1½-mile jogging trail, fishing excursions, unisex hair salon, coin-op washers/dryers, shops, large video-games arcade, the Neverland Club (a Peter Pan–themed counselor-supervised child-care/activity center).

DISNEY'S VILLAGE RESORT, 1901 Buena Vista Dr. (P.O. Box 10100), Lake Buena Vista, FL 32830-0100. Tel. 407/W-DISNEY or 407/827-1100. Fax 407/354-1866. 324 suites. A/C TV TEL

$ Rates: $185–$285 one-bedroom suites and villas; $295–$315 two-bedroom villas; $320–$342 three-bedroom villas; $760 two-bedroom Grand Vista homes; $840 three-bedroom Grand Vista homes. Rates are for any number of people. Range reflects view and season. Inquire about packages. AE, MC, V. **Parking:** Free self-parking.

Sprawled over 265 Arcadian acres of lakes, woodlands, and streams, the Village Resort is a great choice for golfers and families. Peacocks roam the grounds, and your accommodations might overlook a verdant golf course, a gurgling river, or a forest of towering pines, magnolias, cypress, and live oaks draped with Spanish moss. Octagonal Treehouse Villas, elevated on stilts à la Swiss Family Robinson, have large outdoor patios and balconies amid the treetops. Decorated in earth tones, with knotty-pine furnishings, beamed ceilings, and windows all around, these rustic two-story lodgings offer fully equipped kitchens, dining areas, full living rooms, three bedrooms, and two baths. Amenities include remote-control cable TVs and phones on each floor and AM/FM alarm-clock radios in all bedrooms. Similarly equipped two- and three-bedroom Fairway Villas, just off the golf course, are elegant ski-lodgey cedar town houses with rough-hewn slanted pine paneling and beamed cathedral ceilings. The most inexpensive accommodations are one-bedroom Club Suites. Bordering a lake, they're attractively decorated in forest green, rust, and tan, with cathedral ceilings, pine furnishings, and Ralph Lauren–look striped and plaid fabrics. They have kitchenettes and balconies or porches. One- and two-bedroom Vacation Villas are housed in gingerbread-trimmed two-story cottages fronted by small gardens and pots of geraniums. Big picture windows overlook woodlands or waterways, and Early American bleached-pine furnishings include spool beds and two-posters made up with pretty fabric spreads. All have country kitchens, dining areas, large living rooms with convertible sofas, and patios. And for total luxury there are two- and three-bedroom Grand Vista homes that sleep six to eight people. They're beautiful residential accommodations with full kitchens, two big screened porches (one set up for dining), upscale furnishings, marble whirlpool tubs in the bath, and homey touches such as live plants, shelves of books, and objets d'art. Each has its own electric golf cart, bicycles, and barbecue grill. Grand Vista guests also enjoy special services, such as nightly bed turn-down and daily newspaper delivery.

Dining/Entertainment: The *simpático* Lake Buena Vista Clubhouse Restaurant has windows all around overlooking the golf course and an awninged patio facing the pool. It's open for breakfast, lunch, Sunday buffet brunch, and dinner, the last meal featuring fresh Florida seafood, steaks, prime rib, and poultry dishes. A bar/lounge adjoins. The Snack Bar, next to the Clubhouse on the pool side, serves light fare and drinks in season. And a refreshment cart does the same on the golf course. Disney Village Marketplace restaurants are close by.

Services: Room service (7am–11pm), babysitting, guest services desk, free bus transport around the property, free grocery delivery from the Gourmet Pantry (meat, poultry, fresh vegetables, and more).

Facilities: 18-hole par-72 championship golf course, three hard-surface night-lit tennis courts, golf/tennis pro shops, electric cart rentals, six swimming pools, five whirlpool spas, kiddie pool, bicycle rental, eight miles of bike trails, boat rentals, health club, seven children's playgrounds, 3.4-mile jogging course with 32 exercise stations, coin-op washers/dryers, outdoor barbecue grills and picnic tables scattered throughout the property, two video-games arcades. A foot bridge connects to Disney's Village Marketplace.

Moderate

DISNEY'S CARIBBEAN BEACH RESORT, 900 Cayman Way (P.O. Box 10100), Lake Buena Vista, FL 32830-0100. Tel. 407/W-DISNEY or 407/934-3400. Fax 407/354-1866. 2,112 rms. A/C MINIBAR TV TEL

$ Rates: $94–$121 single or double. Additional person $12 extra; children under 17 stay free in parents' room. Inquire about packages. AE, MC, V. **Parking:** Free self-parking.

(S) Opened in 1988, the Caribbean Beach occupies 200 palm-fringed acres stunningly landscaped with lush tropical foliage. Upon registering in the Custom House lobby—where caged parakeets, potted palms, and overhead fans set the island mood—guests are issued helpful informational "passports." Accommodations are ranged around a large, duck-filled lake in five "villages," each with metal-roofed stucco buildings architecturally evocative of the Caribbean. Room interiors are charming, utilizing pleasing color schemes such as dusty rose and mint. All have attractive oak furnishings with pineapple motifs and exquisite floral-print cotton chintz bedspreads. In-room amenities include coffee makers, ceiling fans, and remote-control cable TVs. All rooms have verandas, many of them overlooking the lake. In addition, 16 beautifully landscaped public courtyards furnished with umbrella tables dot the property.

Dining/Entertainment: The festive Farmers Market Food Court, a garden setting with trellises and brightly colored Chinese kites overhead, has counters offering diverse fare—fresh-baked pastries, pizza, fajitas, chicken teriyaki, and more. Sporting events are aired on a large-screen TV in an adjoining bar/lounge called the Captain's Hideaway Tavern. And Banana Cabaña, featuring light snacks and frozen tropical drinks, serves the main pool.

Services: Room service (pizza only, noon–midnight), guest services desk, Mears airport shuttle, babysitting, complimentary shuttle around the grounds.

Facilities: Video-games arcade, shops, boat rentals, bicycle rental, coin-op washers/dryers in each village. The main swimming pool, in a central area called Old Port Royale, replicates a Spanish-style Caribbean fort with pirate's cannons and stone walls; it has a water slide, kiddie pool, and whirlpool. In addition, there are nice-sized pools, children's playgrounds, and lakefront white sand beaches in each village. A 1.4-mile promenade—popular for walking, jogging, and bicycling—circles the lake. An arched wooden bridge leads to Parrot Cay Island where there's a short nature trail, an aviary of tropical birds, a picnic area, and a playground.

DISNEY'S DIXIE LANDINGS RESORT, 1251 Dixie Dr. (P.O. Box 10100), Lake Buena Vista, FL 32830-0100. Tel. 407/W-DISNEY or 407/934-5000. Fax 407/354-1866. 2,048 rms. A/C TV TEL

$ Rates: $94–$119 for up to four people. Children under 18 stay free in parents' room. Inquire about packages. AE, MC, V. **Parking:** Free self-parking.

Nestled on the banks of the Disney-made Sassagoula River and dotted with bayous, Dixie Landings shares its magnificently landscaped 325-acre site with the Port Orleans Resort (described below). Themed after the Louisiana countryside, it's divided into "parishes" with accommodations housed in stately colonnaded plantation homes (fronted by brick courtyards and manicured lawns with vine-covered trellises) or rustic Cajun-style dwellings (set amid bayous and stands of towering cypress and pine). Rooms in the former are elegantly decorated in Federalist blue and gold, with brass-trimmed maple furnishings. Cajun rooms, on the other hand, feature bed frames made of bent branches, patchwork quilts, and calico-print drapes. In-room amenities throughout include remote-control cable TVs, ceiling fans, double sinks in the bath, and alarm-clock radios. Many accommodations offer river views.

Dining/Entertainment: Boatwright's Dining Hall, patterned after a 19th-century boat-building factory, serves Cajun fare at breakfast and dinner. The Colonel's Cotton Mill, a food court, occupies a rustic setting under a 50-foot massively beamed pine ceiling. The room centers on a cotton press powered by a gigantic water wheel. The fare runs the gamut from Tex-Mex to pizza and pasta, to po-boy sandwiches. Muddy Rivers, a poolside bar in a ramshackle structure, serves drinks and light fare; it has a very pleasant shaded porch cooled by ceiling fans. Off the lobby, the Cotton Co-op lounge, with its beautiful pressed-copper ceiling and plush leather couches before a blazing fireplace, is designed to suggest a cotton-trading commodity house. Monday-night football games are aired on a large-screen TV here, and Tuesday through Saturday comedians and singers entertain. Note: Bars here offer kiddie cocktails with names like Brer Rabbit.

Services: Room service (pizza only, noon–midnight), guest services desk, babysitting, boat transport (to Port Orleans, Village Marketplace, and Pleasure Island).

Facilities: Six large swimming pools, coin-op washers/dryers, children's playground, vast video-games arcade, bicycle rental, boat rentals, 1.7-mile riverfront jogging/biking path, Fulton's General Store. Ol' Man Island, a woodsy 3½-acre recreation area, centers on an ancient live oak tree with a 78-foot branch spread. On it are an immense rustically themed free-form pool with waterfalls cascading from a broken bridge and a waterslide entered via a pump house, a playground, children's wading pool, spa, sun deck, and fishin' hole (rent bait and poles and angle for catfish and bass).

DISNEY'S PORT ORLEANS RESORT, 2201 Orleans Dr. (P.O. Box 10100), Lake Buena Vista, FL 32830-0100. Tel. 407/W-DISNEY or 407/934-5000. Fax 407/354-1866. 1,008 rms. A/C TV TEL.

$ Rates: $94–$119 for up to four people. Children under 18 stay free in parents' room. Inquire about packages. AE, MC, V. **Parking:** Free self-parking.

This beautiful resort, themed after turn-of-the-century New Orleans, shares a site on the banks of the "mighty" Sassagoula River, with Dixie Landings, described above. The charming glass-walled lobby under a vaulted ceiling replicates a New Orleans mint; guests register at old-fashioned bank-teller windows. Cheerful three-story buildings, painted in variegated pastels with shuttered windows and lacy wrought-iron balconies, house lovely rooms. Decorated in mocha, rust, and teal, they have pretty cherrywood furnishings, swagged draperies, and art nouveau sconces. A handsome armoire conceals your remote-control cable TV, and in-room amenities include ceiling fans and alarm-clock radios. Accommodations buildings are fronted by lovely flower gardens (each unique to suggest individual lawns) opening onto fountained courtyards. Landscaping throughout the property is a delight, with stately oaks, formal boxwood hedges, azaleas, and jasmin. Charming stone and wooden bridges span the river.

Dining/Entertainment: The very New Orleansy Bonfamille's Café, enclosing a fountained courtyard, is open for breakfast (come by for beignets and café au lait) and dinner, the latter featuring Créole specialties. At the festive Sassagoula Floatworks and Food Factory, its ceiling festooned with whimsical Mardi Gras parade float props, food-court vendors serve up pizza, pasta, Créole specialties, spit-fried chicken, and more from 6am to midnight daily. Scat Cat's Club, a cocktail lounge off the lobby, features family-oriented live entertainment (rock, country, New Orleans jazz, sing-alongs). And the poolside Mardi Grog's offers cool and fruity libations and light snacks.

Services: Room service (pizza only, noon–midnight), guest services desk, babysitting, boat transport (to Port Orleans, Village Marketplace, and Pleasure Island).

Facilities: Six large swimming pools (including the free-form Olympic-size Doubloon Lagoon, which is surmounted by an enormous sea serpent–shaped water slide; a jazz band plays in a pink clam shell near the pool), whirlpool, children's wading pool, coin-op washers/dryers, children's playground, vast video-games arcade, bicycle rental, boat rentals (pedalboats, rowboats, float boats, canopy boats, and pontoons), 1.7-mile riverfront jogging/biking path, shops.

Villas

DISNEY'S VACATION CLUB RESORT, 1510 N. Cove Rd. (P.O. Box 10100), Lake Buena Vista, FL 32830-0100. Tel. 407/W-DISNEY or 407/827-7700. Fax 407/354-1866. 526 villas. A/C TV TEL

$ Rates: $180–$190 deluxe rooms; $230–$255 one-bedroom vacation home; $320–$340 two-bedroom vacation home; $725 three-bedroom Grand Villas. Rates are for any number of people. Range reflects high and low seasons. Inquire about packages. AE, MC, V. **Parking:** Free self-parking.

Its architecture evocative of Key West at the turn of the century, the Vacation Club is a time-share property. If you're interested in purchasing a vacation villa here, they'll be happy to give you a presentation. For non-owners, however, this is just like any other luxurious Disney resort—you rent accommodations when they're not in use by the owners. The 156-acre property is beautifully landscaped: Tree-lined brick walkways are edged by white picket fences, palms sway softly in the breeze, shore birds swoop lazily over lagoons, and the air is scented with honeysuckle. Accommodations, in two- and three-story tin-roofed clapboard buildings painted in pale pastels, offer lovely water, woodland, or fairway views. The architecture reflects the themed period with Victorian gingerbread trim and Queen Anne scalloped shingles. Gorgeous residential-style rooms offer home-away-from-home comfort. All but deluxe rooms have fully equipped kitchens and furnished patios, and amenities including bedroom ceiling fans, full laundry rooms (washers/dryers/ironing boards/irons), large-screen remote-control cable TVs with VCRs in the living room (smaller sets in the bedrooms), phones in each bedroom and living room, and AM/FM clock radios in all bedrooms. Many units contain whirlpool tubs in the master suite, and Grand Villas have stereo systems.

Dining/Entertainment: Olivia's Café, a pleasant plant-filled dining room, its pale-yellow walls hung with 19th-century Key West photographs and memorabilia, serves all meals; it offers al fresco seating on a patio overlooking the Trumbo Canal. At the Gurgling Suitcase pool bar (its name refers to liquor smuggling from Havana during Prohibition) you can sit out and watch the sunset over piña coladas. Good's Food, offering sandwiches and light fare to go, adjoins.

Services: Babysitting, guest services desk, ferry service to Disney Village Marketplace and Pleasure Island, free bus transport around the grounds; food shopping for a minimal charge.

Facilities: Two hard-surface night-lit tennis courts, white sand play area, boardwalk, three swimming pools, whirlpool, kiddie pool, bicycle rental, boat rentals (pedalboats, rowboats, float boats, canopy boats), children's playground, extensive health club, sauna, shuffleboard, horseshoes, volleyball, complementary use of washers/dryers, general store (groceries, resortwear, gifts, Disneyana, sundries), small video-games arcade. Conch Flats, a recreation center, shows Disney movies nightly and offers various activities.

A Disney Campground

DISNEY'S FORT WILDERNESS RESORT AND CAMPGROUND, 3520 N.

Fort Wilderness Trail (P.O. Box 10100), Lake Buena Vista, FL 32830-0100. Tel. 407/W-DISNEY or 407/824-2900. Fax 407/354-1866. 784 campsites, 408 wilderness homes. AC TV

$ Rates: $32–$49 campsite for up to 10 campers, depending on season, location, size (25–65 feet), and extent of hookup; $180–$195 wilderness home. Inquire about packages. AE, MC, V. **Parking:** Free self-parking at your campsite or wilderness home.

This woodsy 780-acre camping resort—shaded by towering pines and cypress trees and crossed by fish-filled streams, lakes, and canals—makes an ideal venue for family vacations. Secluded campsites—most set up for tent campers, the others for trailers—offer 110/220-volt outlets, barbecue grills, picnic tables, and children's play areas. Another option here is a wilderness home, a rustic one-bedroom cabin with a piney interior. Accommodating two adults and up to four children, these have cozy living rooms with Murphy beds, fully equipped eat-in kitchens, and on-premises picnic tables and barbecue grills. Amenities include remote-control cable TVs (with WDW information channels), phones, and clock radios. Guests here enjoy a lot of extras, including extensive recreational facilities and a nightly campfire program hosted by Chip 'n' Dale and featuring Disney movies, cartoons, and sing-alongs. A unique Fort Wilderness feature: Peacocks roam the grounds.

Dining/Entertainment: Trails End in Pioneer Hall, a rustic setting with log beams and wagon-wheel chandeliers overhead, is open for cafeteria-style breakfasts, lunches, and dinners daily (some noteworthy buffets here), and late-night pizza, with live entertainment (country and folk music) during the evening meal. Adjoining it is Crockett's Tavern, a cozy full-service restaurant filled with Davy Crockett memorabilia, even a stuffed "bar." It features Texas fare at dinner, after which you can "set" a while on rocking chairs out on the front porch. There's also a snack bar in the Meadow Recreation Complex adjacent to the video-games arcade, another near the beach. Guests enjoy a dazzling electrical water pageant from the beach here nightly at 9:45pm. And the rambunctious *Hoop-Dee-Doo Musical Revue* takes place in Pioneer Hall nightly (details in "Evening Entertainment," below).

Services: Guest services desk, babysitting, boat transport (to Discovery Island, Magic Kingdom, and Contemporary Resort).

Facilities: Comfort station in each campground area (with restrooms, private showers, ice machines, telephones, and laundry rooms), two large swimming pools, white sand beach, Circle D Ranch horseback riding (trail rides), petting farm, pony rides, fishing, three sand volleyball courts, ball fields, tetherball, shuffleboard, bike rentals, boat rentals (canoes, paddleboats, Water Sprites, pontoons), two-mile nature trail, two-mile jogging path with exercise stations, two night-lit hard tennis courts, shops, kennel, car-rental desk, two video-games arcades; adjacent 18-hole championship golf course.

LAKE BUENA VISTA / OFFICIAL HOTELS

These properties, designated "official" WDW hotels, are located on and around Hotel Plaza Boulevard, a delightful thoroughfare with a wide traffic island shaded by lofty oaks. Guests at these hotels enjoy many privileges (see above). And the location is a big plus—close to the Disney parks and within walking distance of Disney Village Marketplace and Crossroads shops and restaurants, as well as Pleasure Island nightlife.

Expensive

BUENA VISTA PALACE, 1900 Buena Vista Dr. (P.O. Box 22206), Lake Buena Vista, FL 32830. Tel. 407/827-2727, or toll free 800/327-2990. Fax 407/827-6034. 898 rms, 130 suites. A/C MINIBAR TV TEL

$ Rates: $130–$235 standard single or double, $219–$250 Crown Level single or double; $245–$290 one-bedroom suite; $390–$455 two-bedroom suite. Range reflects view and season. Additional person $15 extra; children under 18 stay free in parents' room. Inquire about packages and weekend rates. AE, CB, DC, DISC, MC, OPT, V. **Parking:** Free self-parking, $6 per night valet parking.

Entered via a balconied 15-story atrium lobby ascending to a stained-glass skylight, this 27-acre waterfront resort flies the flags of all EPCOT countries at its entrance. Rooms, in four handsome cream stucco towers, are decorated in earth tones with dark oak furnishings. All but a few have balconies or patios, many of them overlooking Lake Buena Vista. Amenities include remote-control cable TVs (with WDW and hotel-information channels and Spectravision movie options), alarm-clock radios, safes, bedroom and bath phones (the former a Mickey Mouse phone), and ceiling fans. Luxurious residential-style one- and two-bedroom suites—with living rooms, dining rooms, and private balconies or patios (microwave ovens and refrigerators are available on request)—are housed in a peach stucco art deco building on the property's Recreation Island; it connects to a tower building via tropically landscaped walkways. Crown rooms on the 10th floor comprise a concierge level.

Dining/Entertainment: Arthur's 27, offering breathtaking panoramic views of WDW parks and nightly fireworks from its 27th-floor location, is the hotel's elegant premier restaurant, serving continental fare at dinner enhanced by selections from a vast, award-winning wine cellar. An adjoining lounge offers live jazz and piano bar entertainment, dancing, hors d'oeuvres, and, of course, the view. The rustic Australian-themed Outback Restaurant, with rough-hewn paneling and a three-story indoor waterfall, specializes in steak, lobster, and fresh seafood grilled over an open pit; it's open for dinner only. Minnie, Goofy, and Pluto host Friday-night buffet dinners and Sunday-morning buffet breakfasts in the Watercress Café, a cheerful plant-filled eatery with large windows overlooking Lake Buena Vista. Open 6am to midnight daily, it specializes in Florida cuisine. The 24-hour Watercress Bake Shop, for incredible desserts, croissants, muffins, and Häagen-Dazs ice-cream sundaes, adjoins. The festive Laughing Kookaburra Good Time Bar boasts a selection of 99 beers and offers happy hour international hors d'oeuvres buffets and live bands for dancing nightly. The gazebo-style Lobby Lounge in the atrium serves cocktails, premium wines by the glass, gourmet teas and coffees, and pastries; come by for piano bar entertainment in the evening. The Recreation Island Pool Snack Bar offers light fare and tropical drinks to sunbathers. And Courtyard Pastries and Pizza, an outdoor ice-cream parlor/snack bar serves breakfast and light fare at umbrella tables on a fountained plaza where the shuttle buses to Disney parks pull up.

Services: 24-hour room service, babysitting, guest services desk (sells tickets, and arranges transportation to, all nearby attractions; tickets to WDW parks available at the Disney shop), complimentary newspaper at guest services, shoeshine/shoe repair, nightly bed turn-down, complimentary transport to/from all WDW parks, Mears airport shuttle.

Facilities: Two large swimming pools, whirlpool, children's wading pool, three night-lit hard-surface tennis courts, golf privileges at WDW courses, boat rentals on property and at nearby Disney Village Marina, three-mile jogging path, volleyball, children's playground, car-rental desk, full-service unisex beauty salon, massage, full business center, fully equipped health club, sauna, shops, coin-op washers/dryers, large video-games arcade, oversize speakerphone booths for family or group calls, Kids Stuff (a counselor-supervised child-care center, open summer and some major holidays only).

GUEST QUARTERS SUITE RESORT, 2305 Hotel Plaza Blvd., Lake Buena Vista, FL 32830. Tel. 407/934-1000, or toll free 800/424-2900. Fax 407/934-1008. 229 suites. A/C TV TEL

$ Rates: $139–$195 for one or two people in a one-bedroom suite (range depends on view and season; additional person $20 extra; children under 18 stay free in parents' suite); $325 two-bedroom suite year-round. Inquire about packages and rates including breakfast. AE, CB, DC, DISC, JCB, MC, OPT, V. **Parking:** Free self-parking.

Entered via a small skylit atrium lobby with ivied balconies and a large aviary of tropical birds, this seven-story all-suite hotel is a great choice for families. Large one-bedroom suites (643 square feet) which can sleep up to six people are delightfully decorated in teal, mauve, and peach, utilizing light wood furnishings and pretty floral-print fabrics. Accommodations include a full living room with a convertible sofa, dining area, and a bedroom with louver doors. Among the in-room amenities are a wet bar, refrigerator, coffee maker (free coffee and tea supplied), microwave oven, remote-control cable TVs with Disney information channels and pay-movie options in the living room and bedroom, a smaller black-and-white TV in the bath, two phones, an alarm clock radio, and a hairdryer.

Dining/Entertainment: Scoops & Games is an ice-cream parlor–cum–video-games arcade off the pool area. Parrot Patch, a tropically themed restaurant/lounge with upholstered bamboo furnishings and prints of parrots on the walls, serves American fare at all meals. There are umbrella tables on the terrace for outdoor dining at lunch. And at night, sporting events are aired on a large-screen TV in the bar. A pool bar serves the same menu as Parrot Patch.

Services: Room service (6:30am–11pm), babysitting, guest services desk (sells tickets to WDW parks and all other nearby attractions; also arranges transport to latter), complimentary transport to/from all WDW parks, Mears airport shuttle.

Facilities: Large swimming pool, whirlpool, children's wading pool with fountain, two night-lit hard-surface tennis courts, golf privileges at WDW courses, boat rental at nearby Disney Village Marina, jogging path, volleyball, children's playground, car-rental desk, exercise room, shops, coin-op washers/dryers, video-games arcade.

HILTON AT WALT DISNEY WORLD VILLAGE, 1751 Hotel Plaza Blvd., Lake Buena Vista, FL 32830. Tel. 407/827-4000, or toll free 800/782-4414. Fax 407/827-6380. 787 rms, 26 suites. A/C MINIBAR TV TEL

$ Rates: $159–$279 single or double (tower rooms $40 additional), depending on season. Additional person $20 extra; children of any age stay free in parents' room. Inquire about packages and weekend rates. AE, CB, DC, DISC, ER, JCB, MC, V.
Parking: Free self-parking, $6 per night valet parking.

Heralded by a palm-fringed circular driveway leading up to an imposing waterfall and fountain, the Hilton occupies 23 beautifully landscaped acres including two large lakes. Accommodations, in a vast 10-story main building with a plant-filled skylit lobby, are done up in soft earth tones with teal/mauve accents and floral-print bedspreads. Amenities include remote-control cable TVs with HBO and Spectravision movie options, alarm-clock radios, coffee makers, and phones with two lines. The 9th and 10th floors comprise the Towers, a concierge level.

Dining/Entertainment: The romantically candlelit American Vineyards serves American regional cuisine dinners enhanced by an extensive list of domestic wines; a pianist sings show tunes while you dine. The adjoining American Vineyard's Lounge is a *simpático* wine bar. Benihana Japanese Steakhouse, a stunning setting decorated with beautiful Japanese art and three aquariums of tropical fish, features teppanyaki dinners nightly; you can also enjoy appetizers such as calamari tempura, and/or tropical drinks, in the adjoining lounge. Fairground murals and striped awnings set the theme of County Fair, a cheerful coffee shop serving à la carte breakfasts, lunches, and dinners. The adjoining County Fair Buffeteria sets out a lavish buffet at breakfast. And the County Fair Terrace, with umbrella tables on a brick patio under a bright-yellow canopy, offers light al fresco breakfasts and lunches while you wait for the shuttle bus to WDW. Rum Largo Poolside Café & Bar provides snack/lunch fare and exotic tropical drinks to sunbathers. Cozy and elegant, John Ts Plantation Bar off the lobby evokes the antebellum South. It features light fare, exotic tropical drinks, and nighttime entertainment for dancing; major sporting events are aired on a large-screen TV. And kids love the Old Fashioned Soda Shoppe for pizzas, burgers, and hot dogs, not to mention malts, shakes, and sundaes; it even has video games. A cedar gazebo is the scene of frequent live poolside entertainment.

Services: Room service (6:30am–1am), babysitting, concierge (sells tickets and arranges transport to all other nearby attractions/airport; WDW tickets available at Walt Disney World men's shop on the lobby level), nightly bed turn-down on request, complimentary transport to/from all WDW parks.

Facilities: Two very large swimming pools, two-tiered whirlpool in tropical/rock garden setting, children's spray pool, two night-lit hard-surface tennis courts, golf privileges at (and free transportation to) WDW courses, boat rental at nearby

Disney Village Marina, 3½-mile jogging path, volleyball, water volleyball, badminton, children's playground, car-rental desk, full-service unisex beauty salon, full business center, fully equipped health club, sauna, shops, coin-op washers/dryers, large high-tech video-games arcade, Vacation Station Kids Hotel (a counselor-supervised child-care center).

Moderate

GROSVENOR RESORT, 1850 Hotel Plaza Blvd., Lake Buena Vista, FL 32830. Tel. 407/828-4444, or toll free 800/624-4109. Fax 407/827-6314. 625 rms, 5 suites. A/C MINIBAR TV TEL

$ Rates: $99–$160 for up to four people (range depends on view and season). Inquire about packages. AE, CB, DC, DISC, ER, JCB, MC, OPT, V. **Parking:** Free self-parking, $5 per night valet parking.

The British Colonial–themed Grosvenor, on 13 beautifully landscaped lakeside acres, centers on a 19-story peach stucco building fronted by towering palms. The recently renovated guest rooms have been attractively decorated in seafoam green or muted blue color schemes with splashy print bedspreads, light oak furnishings, and marble-top desks. Walls are adorned with decorative friezes and pleasant paintings of tropical resorts. Amenities include remote-control cable TVs with WDW and hotel information channels (VCRs and movie tapes can be rented), alarm-clock radios, coffee makers (tea and coffee supplied), safes, and hairdryers.

Dining/Entertainment: The rather elegant Baskervilles Restaurant, on the mezzanine, displays 19th-century Sherlock Holmes book illustrations on its walls and even has a Sherlock Holmes museum—and a re-creation of his Baker Street headquarters—on the premises. Windowed walls overlook the lake. Saturday nights, Baskervilles is the scene of mystery dinner theater productions. The restaurant also features buffet breakfasts and dinners (including a character breakfast every Saturday and Sunday and a character dinner every Wednesday night). A la carte American/continental selections are also an option at all meals. Moriarty's Pub, offering live entertainment in high season and a pool table, adjoins. Crumpets Café, a food court, is open 24 hours. Barnacles Pool Bar serves tropical drinks and light fare plus ice-cream sundaes. And at Cricket's Lounge, off the lobby, cappuccino and espresso are featured, and sporting events are aired on a large-screen TV.

Services: Room service (7am–midnight), babysitting, guest services (sells tickets and arranges transport to all nearby attractions; WDW park tickets are available at the Disney shop), free newspaper delivered to your room daily, free transport to/from all WDW parks, Mears airport shuttle.

Facilities: Two swimming pools, whirlpool, children's wading pool, two hard-surface night-lit tennis courts, golf privileges at (and free transportation to) WDW courses, boat rental at nearby Disney Village Marina, playground, lawn games, car-rental desk, business services, coin-op washers/dryers, shops, video-games arcade.

ROYAL PLAZA, 1905 Hotel Plaza Blvd., Lake Buena Vista, FL 32830. Tel. 407/828-2828, or toll free 800/248-7890. Fax 407/827-6338. 386 rms, 10 suites. A/C TV TEL

$ Rates: $97–$197 for up to four people; $304–$550 suite. Range depends on view and season. Inquire about packages. AE, Barclaycard, CB, DC, DISC, ER, JCB, MC, OPT, V. **Parking:** Free self- and valet parking.

The recently renovated 17-story Royal Plaza is a friendly little hotel with quite a few facilities. Rooms are decorated in teal, peach, and periwinkle, with grasspaper-covered walls and splashy print bedspreads. You can watch Magic Kingdom fireworks from your furnished balcony. Amenities include remote-control cable TVs with WDW channels, VCRs (movie tapes can be rented), alarm-clock radios, safes, and Mickey Mouse phones; refrigerators are available on request, and deluxe rooms have wet bars.

Dining/Entertainment: The plant-filled Plaza Diner, complete with old-fashioned Wurlitzer-style jukebox, serves American fare from 6am to midnight daily. The Giraffe Lounge is a lively disco, offering high-energy music for dancing nightly. It also features complimentary international happy hour buffets (Mexican, Cajun, etc.).

In the more sedate Intermissions Lounge, a pianist entertains nightly. And a pool bar is open in season.

Services: Room service (6am–midnight), babysitting, guest services (sells tickets and arranges transport to all nearby attractions; WDW park tickets are available at the Disney shop), free newspaper delivered to your room daily, free transport to/from all WDW parks, airport shuttle.

Facilities: Large L-shaped swimming pool, whirlpool, four hard-surface night-lit tennis courts, golf privileges at WDW courses, boat rental at nearby Disney Village Marina, children's playground, sauna, tanning salon, shuffleboard, Ping-Pong, car-rental desk, overnight film developing, video-camera rental, unisex hair salon, coin-op washers/dryers, shops, video-games arcade.

TRAVELODGE HOTEL, 2000 Hotel Plaza Blvd., Lake Buena Vista, FL 32830. Tel. 407/828-2424, or toll free 800/348-3765. Fax 407/828-8933. 321 rms, 4 suites. A/C MINIBAR TV TEL

$ Rates: $99–$159 for up to four people, depending on room size and season. Inquire about packages. AE, CB, DC, DISC, ER, JCB, MC, OPT, V. **Parking:** Free self-parking.

Following a major renovation in 1991, this 12-acre lakefront property is looking spiffy and immaculate—with rooms and public areas more upscale than you might expect at a Travelodge. This is the company's flagship hotel. Designed to evoke a Barbados plantation manor house, it has a Carribean resort ambience with tropical foliage and bright floral-print fabrics and carpeting. Rooms are particularly inviting, decorated in muted peach and beige with light bleached-wood furnishings. Walls are adorned with floral friezes and lovely framed botanical prints. All accommodations have furnished balconies, many of them overlooking Lake Buena Vista. Corner rooms, with king-size beds, chaise longues, and convertible sofas, are especially desirable. Amenities include remote-control cable TVs (with WDW and hotel-information channels and Spectravision movie options), alarm-clock radios, coffee makers (tea and coffee supplied), safes, and hairdryers. Free local phone calls are a plus.

Dining/Entertainment: Traders, with a wall of windows overlooking a densely wooded area, is open for breakfast and dinner, the latter featuring steak and seafood; a screened-in, plant-filled terrace adjoins. The Flamingo Cove Lounge, a cocktail bar where a pianist entertains at night, also has screened outdoor seating. The Parakeet Café, a casual cafeteria-style eatery open from 7am to midnight, serves pizza, croissant sandwiches, and salads. And on the 18th floor, Toppers, a beautiful nightclub with windows all around, offers magnificent views of Lake Buena Vista and beyond. It's a great vantage point for watching nightly laser shows and fireworks. A DJ or live band plays top-40s dance music.

Services: Room service (7am–midnight), babysitting, guest services (sells tickets and arranges transport to all nearby attractions; WDW park tickets are available at the Disney shop), free newspaper delivered to your room weekdays, free transport to/from all WDW parks, Mears airport shuttle.

Facilities: Large swimming pool, children's wading pool, golf privileges at WDW courses, boat rental at nearby Disney Village Marina, children's playground, car-rental desk, coin-op washers/dryers, shops, video-games arcade.

OTHER LAKE BUENA VISTA AREA HOTELS

All the hotels below are within a few minutes' drive of WDW parks.

VERY EXPENSIVE

HYATT REGENCY GRAND CYPRESS, 1 Grand Cypress Blvd., Orlando, FL 32836. Tel. 407/239-1234, or toll free 800/233-1234. Fax 407/239-3800. 675 rms, 75 suites, 146 villas. A/C MINIBAR TV TEL

$ Rates: $175–$310 for up to five people in a room; $350–$420 in the Regency Club; $150–$1,120 villa. Range reflects room size, view, and season. Inquire about packages. AE, CB, DC, DISC, ER, JCB, MC, V. **Parking:** Free self-parking, $7 per night valet parking.

This dazzling multifacility resort is in a class by itself. The tropical plantings of the atrium lobby comprise a small rain forest, with gurgling stone-bedded streams and live birds in brass cages. Outside, the Hyatt's gardeners have created an Edenic 1,500-acre botanic garden, dotted with babbling brooks, beautiful flower beds, charming outdoor sculpture, and rock gardens ablaze with bougainvillea and hibiscus. Colorful sailboats and swans glide serenely on 21-acre Lake Windsong. Thousands of palms sway in the breeze, and native oaks, pines, and cypresses create canopies of shade. Accommodations are deluxe, with grasspaper wall coverings and teal carpeting complemented by lovely cotton chintz bedspreads and curtains. Oak armoires house remote-control cable TVs with Spectravision movie options. Amenities include alarm-clock radios, ceiling fans, safes, and, in the bath, hairdryer, cotton robes, bathroom scale, and fine toiletries. Three floors comprise the Regency Club, a concierge level. And especially luxurious are one- to four-bedroom Mediterranean-style villas with fully equipped kitchens, patios, living rooms, and dining rooms. Many have working fireplaces and whirlpool bathtubs. Large picture windows overlook the golf course. Villa guests enjoy deluxe services and amenities.

Dining/Entertainment: The Key West–themed Hemingway's serves steaks and Florida seafood at lunch and dinner. The specialty at its on-premises Hurricane Bar is the "Papa Doble," a potent rum-and-fruit-juice concoction created by the legendary author himself. The Cascade Grill, down a brass spiral staircase, centers on a 35-foot sculpture of a bronze mermaid backed by a waterfall. American fare is served at all meals. La Coquina, with exquisitely appointed tables amid potted palms and splashing fountains, has a wall of two-story windows overlooking Lake Windsong. It serves classic French fare at dinner nightly; a harpist entertains. The gardenlike Palm Café, a self-service buffeteria with both indoor seating and umbrella tables on a poolside patio, offers traditional breakfast fare and an array of sandwiches, salads, entrees, and desserts at lunch; evenings, it's transformed into Papa Geppetto's, featuring California-style pizzas with gourmet toppings. The 19th-century western-motif White Horse Saloon specializes in aged Black Angus prime rib dinners; a country-western trio entertains while you dine. Swinging double doors lead to the White Horse Saloon. Papillon, a plush pool bar in a white canvas tent overlooking a lake, is a *simpático* setting for frosty drinks and snacks. Also wonderfully situated is On the Rocks, nestled in a rock cave surrounded by waterfalls, for specialty drinks, snack fare, and ice-cream concoctions. In the lobby "rain forest," set amid cascading waterfalls, is Trellises, a lobby bar where a jazz ensemble entertains evenings. The Rock Hyatt Club, adjoining the video-games arcade, offers movies, music, and games for teens 13–17. The *simpático* Black Swan, overlooking the golf course, serves contemporary American fare at dinner. Adjoining it is Fairways, a more casual venue with a working fireplace, open for all meals. And the Pool Snack Bar serves the pool by the villas.

Services: 24-hour room service, babysitting, concierge (sells tickets to WDW parks and other nearby attractions), nightly bed turn-down, free transportation around the grounds via shuttle buses and restored Victorian trolleys, hourly shuttle between the hotel and all WDW parks (round-trip fare is $4 per day), Mears airport shuttle.

Facilities: Half-acre lagoonlike swimming pool spanned by a rope bridge and flowing through rock grottoes (with 12 waterfalls and two steep water slides), three secluded whirlpools, white sand beach, 12 tennis courts (8 clay, 4 hard-surface, 6 lit for night play), award-winning 45-hole/par-72 Jack Nicklaus–designed golf course, 9-hole pitch-and-putt golf course, golf and tennis instruction/pro shops, equestrian center (lessons, trail rides), bicycle rental, boat rental (sailboats, sailboards, paddleboats, Suncats, canoes), 4.7-mile jogging path, 45-acre Audubon nature walk through pristine marshland with elevated boardwalks and descriptive signs, racquetball/volleyball/shuffleboard courts, croquet, children's playground, car-rental desk, full-service unisex beauty salon, full business center, state-of-the-art health club, shops, helicopter landing pad, large high-tech video-game arcade, counselor-supervised child-care center, teen activities program (inquire about additional children's activities).

EXPENSIVE

MARRIOTT'S ORLANDO WORLD CENTER, 8701 World Center Dr. (on Fl. 536 between I-4 and Fl. 535), Orlando, FL 32821. Tel. 407/239-4200, or toll free 800/621-0638. Fax 407/238-8777. 1,402 rms, 101 suites. A/C MINIBAR TV TEL

$ **Rates:** $150–$194 for up to five people in a room (range reflects season); pool-view rooms $10 additional per night (14-day advance-purchase rates $130–$157, subject to availability). $265–$2,400 suite. Inquire about packages and rates including full buffet breakfast. AE, CB, DC, DISC, ER, JCB, MC, OPT, V. **Parking:** Free self-parking, $8 per night valet parking.

This sprawling 230-acre resort, just two miles from WDW parks, is one of Florida's top venues for meetings and conventions. And the excellent service and array of facilities that make it so popular with corporate executives also make it a great choice for tourists. A grand palm-lined driveway, flanked by rolling golf greens, leads to the main building—a massive 27-story tower fronted by flower beds and fountains. In its 12-story atrium lobby, plants and palms flourish in sunlight streaming through a lofty skylight, museum-quality 16th- and 17th-century Chinoiseries and fine paintings set an elegant tone, and the sound of splashing fountains blends with soft piano music. The tower houses spacious guest rooms cheerfully decorated in pastel hues with bamboo and rattan furnishings. All have desks, sofa beds, and large closets (in which you'll find an iron and ironing board), and most have balconies. Amenities include alarm-clock radios, safes, remote-control cable TVs (with HBO, extensive pay movie options, and video account review/message retrieval), and hairdryers in the bath. Step outside the tower and you'll find magnificently landscaped grounds, punctuated by rock gardens, shaded groves of pines and magnolias, and cascading waterfalls; black and white swans and ducks inhabit over a dozen lakes and lagoons spanned by graceful arched bridges.

Dining/Entertainment: At the mahogany- and cherry-paneled Regent Court, the hotel's luxurious premier restaurant, 18th-century furnishings are enhanced by a 16th-century hand-painted Japanese screen and Louis Vuitton etchings. Haute-cuisine entrees are featured at dinner nightly. The Mikado Japanese Steak House is a serene setting for classic teppanyaki dinners overlooking rock gardens, reflecting pools, and a palm-fringed pond. The Garden Terrace, for family dining, is rather elegant with comfortable leather-upholstered furnishings amid lush tropical plantings and beautiful sienna lacquer paneling. It's open for breakfast, lunch, dinner, and Sunday buffet brunch. The Golf Grille is one of our favorite places in town for sun-dappled breakfasts and lunches on a screened balcony that yields breathtaking views of the lagoon and golf greens, or for cozy dinners in the rustic pine interior; the fare is American regional. Champion's, a *simpático* sports-themed bar, airs athletic events on 16 TV monitors and one large-screen TV; other amusements here include blackjack, pool tables, video games, air hockey, and, some nights, music for dancing. The Pagoda Lounge, offering nightly piano bar entertainment off the lobby, centers on an imposing Chinese black lacquer pagoda under a sloped skylight. You can relax over cocktails in plush armchairs or on a lovely outdoor veranda. Palm's serves drinks and light fare, including pizza, poolside. In high season it's augmented by the Shrimp Shack, vending peel-and-eat shrimp, and the hexagonal open-air Pavilion, overlooking a pool and waterfalls and serving frozen drinks and snacks. Stachio's, adjoining the video-games arcade, serves light fare throughout the day. (Several of the above-mentioned are further described in "Dining" or "Evening Entertainment," below.)

Services: 24-hour room service, babysitting, concierge, shoeshine, nightly bed turn-down on request, newspaper delivered to your room daily, Mears transportation/sightseeing desk (sells tickets to all nearby attractions, including WDW parks; also provides transport, by reservation, to WDW, other attractions, and the airport), one-hour film developing.

Facilities: Three swimming pools, four whirlpools, large children's wading pool, eight night-lit hard-surface tennis courts, 18-hole/par-71 Joe Lee–designed championship golf course, golf and tennis pro shops/instruction, 18-hole miniature golf course, two-mile jogging path, two volleyball courts, car-rental desk, full-service unisex beauty salon, extensive business center, state-of-the-art health club (offering sauna, massage therapy, and aerobics classes), coin-op washers/dryers, shops, video-games arcade, Lollipop Lounge (a counselor-supervised child-care/activities center). Inquire as well about organized children's activities—games, movies, nature walks, and more.

RESIDENCE INN BY MARRIOTT, 8800 Meadow Creek Dr., Orlando, FL 32821. Tel. 407/239-7700, or toll free 800/331-3131. Fax 407/239-7605. 688 suites. A/C TV TEL

$ Rates (including full breakfast): $150–$175 one-bedroom suite for up to four people; $180–$240 two-bedroom suite for up to six people. Range reflects season. Inquire about packages. AE, CB, DC, DISC, ER, JCB, MC, V. **Parking:** Free self-parking.

This delightful all-suite hostelry, a converted luxury apartment complex, occupies 50 magnificently landscaped acres, with neatly manicured lawns, duck-filled ponds, fountains, and flower beds shaded by tall palms, pine trees, live oaks, and magnolias. Guests enjoy a serene environment that offers the seclusion of a private community; you have to drive through a security gate to enter. In addition, they can avail themselves of the extensive facilities at the adjoining Marriott Orlando World Center (see details above) with room-charge privileges. A lighted walkway connects the two properties via a gorgeous golf course. Accommodations, housed in 86 two-story cream stucco buildings with Spanish-style terra-cotta roofs, are tastefully decorated in muted blue or green color schemes with soft peach and aqua accents. All offer fully equipped eat-in kitchens (some with washing machines and dryers), private balconies or patios, and large, comfortable living rooms with sleeper sofas. Amenities include remote-control cable TVs (with HBO, Spectravision movie options, and VCRs; movie tapes can be rented), alarm-clock radios, two phones (kitchen and bedroom), ceiling fans, and safes. Two-bedroom units have two baths.

Dining/Entertainment: A packaged breakfast, including your choice of entrees, is available in the gatehouse each morning. Many guests enjoy this meal al fresco on a covered open-air veranda overlooking the pool; others just take it to Walt Disney World and eat it while waiting for the parks to open. Local restaurants also deliver food (there are menus in each room), and, of course, there are quite a few restaurants at the Marriott.

Services: Guest services (sells tickets—most of them discounted—and provides transport to all nearby theme parks and attractions; round-trip to Disney parks costs $4.50), babysitting, complimentary daily newspaper, free shuttle transport around the grounds, same-day film developing, free food-shopping service, Mears airport shuttle.

Facilities: Three large swimming pools (one with a rock waterfall), two beautiful secluded whirlpools, sports court (basketball, badminton, volleyball, paddle tennis, shuffleboard), one night-lit hard-surface tennis court, children's playground, coin-op washers/dryers, shops, two small video-games arcades. A recreation department organizes numerous free children's activities—arts and crafts, puppet making, video game Olympics, outdoor sports, movies, and much more. These are on a daily basis in peak seasons, less frequently at other times. Note all the additional facilities available to guests here at the Marriott Orlando World Center (see above).

MODERATE

HOLIDAY INN LAKE BUENA VISTA, 13351 Fla. 535, Lake Buena Vista, FL 32821. Tel. 407/239-4500, or toll free 800/FON-MAXX. Fax 407/239-7713. 507 rms. A/C TV TEL

$ Rates: $75–$119 for up to four people, depending on season. Inquire about packages. AE, CB, DC, DISC, JCB, MC, V. **Parking:** Free self-parking.

Just 1½ miles from the park, this Holiday Inn caters to children in a big way. Kids "check in" at their own pint-size desk and receive a free fun bag containing a video-game token coupon, a lollipop, and a small gift; they're personally welcomed by animated raccoon mascots (Max and Maxine); and they can pick up a telephone receiver at Max's Magic Castle and listen to fairy tales. Camp Holiday activities—magic shows, clowns, Bingo, movies, sing-alongs, video games, arts and crafts, storytelling, and much more—are free of charge for kids 2–12. And parents can arrange (by reservation) for Max to come tuck a child into bed. Accommodations are decorated in aqua, peach, and teal, with bleached-oak furnishings, tropically themed paintings, and shell-motif lamps. All rooms have kitchenettes with refrigerators, microwave ovens, and coffee/tea makers. Amenities include remote-control cable TVs with local attraction-information channels, videocassette players (tapes can be rented), alarm-clock radios, hairdryers, and safes. Open-air hallways add to the resort ambience.

Dining/Entertainment: Maxine's, a pretty peach-walled dining room, is the setting for buffet and à la carte breakfasts and dinners, the latter featuring steak and seafood. The Coral Lounge, serving complimentary hot and cold hors d'oeuvres during happy hour, offers nightly Bingo (with prizes), and airs sporting events on a large-screen TV. Pinky's Diner, a skylit dining room with bamboo furnishings under canvas umbrellas, serves light fare (soup and salad bar, omelets, sandwiches, barbecued chicken and ribs); it's open from 6am (for breakfast fare) to midnight. Kids under 12 eat breakfast and dinner free, either in a hotel restaurant with their parents or in Kid's Kottage, a cheerful facility where movies and cartoons are shown on a large-screen TV and dinner includes a make-your-own-sundae bar. The Barefoot Bar and Grill serves snack fare (pizzas, nachos, burgers) and frozen drinks poolside.

Services: Room service (7am–2pm and 5pm–midnight), babysitting, guest services desk (sells tickets to all nearby attractions, including Walt Disney World parks), free scheduled transport to Magic Kingdom/EPCOT/Disney–MGM Studios (there's a charge for transport to other nearby attractions), telephone grocery shopping, Mears airport shuttle.

Facilities: Large free-form swimming pool with lovely palm-fringed sun deck, two whirlpools, children's wading pool, innovative children's playground, coin-op washers/dryers, shops, car-rental desk, video-games arcade, Camp Holiday (a counselor-supervised child-care/activity center for ages 2–12, open from 8am to midnight; parents can rent beepers to keep in touch with the kids).

INEXPENSIVE

COMFORT INN, 8442 Palm Pkwy., Lake Buena Vista, FL 32830. Tel. 407/239-7300, or toll free 800/999-7300. Fax 407/239-7740. 640 rms. A/C TV TEL

$ Rates: $39–$75 for up to four people, depending on season. Inquire about packages. AE, CB, DC, DISC, MC, V. **Parking:** Free self-parking.

This is an ideally located, large, and attractively landscaped property with two small man-made lakes amid expanses of manicured lawn and lush greenery. It offers great value for your hotel dollar, including free transport to/from Disney parks and free local phone calls. Immaculate rooms, tastefully decorated in shades of mauve or rust, are housed in two five-story stucco buildings, each with its own nice-sized swimming pool and sun deck. In-room amenities include cable TVs and safes. The Boardwalk Buffet, a sunny restaurant with windows all around, offers reasonably priced buffet meals at breakfast and dinner; kids under 12 eat free. The Comfort Zone, a bar/lounge, adjoins. And complimentary tea and coffee are served in the lobby every afternoon. The guest services desk sells tickets (most of them discounted) and provides transport to all nearby theme parks, dinner shows, and the airport. On-premises facilities include coin-op washers/dryers, a snack-vending machine area, a gift shop, and a video-games arcade. Pets are permitted.

ON U.S. 192/KISSIMMEE

This very American stretch of highway dotted with fast-food eateries isn't what you'd call scenic, but it does contain many inexpensive hotels within one to eight miles of WDW parks.

MODERATE

HOLIDAY INN MAINGATE EAST, 5678 Irlo Bronson Hwy. (U.S. 192),

Kissimmee, FL 34746. Tel. 407/396-4488, or toll free 800/FON-KIDS. Fax 407/396-8915. 670 rms. A/C TV TEL

$ Rates: $75–$95 for up to four people, depending on season. Inquire about packages. AE, CB, DC, DISC, JCB, MC, V. **Parking:** Free self-parking.

Just a mile from the entrance to the Magic Kingdom, the Holiday Inn Maingate, occupying 18 attractively landscaped acres, offers identical facilities to the Holiday Inn Lake Buena Vista (described above) including its own Camp Holiday and all the kid-pleaser features (here the welcoming mascots are Holiday and Holly Hound). There's even a small merry-go-round in the lobby. Accommodations, in two-story motel-style buildings enclosing courtyard swimming pools, are decorated in muted blue and peach. Once again, facilities and in-room amenities are identical to those at the Lake Buena Vista property. Pets are permitted here.

Dining/Entertainment: The Vineyard Café, decorated in grape purple and green, seats diners at canvas umbrella tables. Buffet and à la carte breakfasts and dinners are served, the latter featuring steak and seafood items. The Court Street Bar adjoins. The People's Choice, a food court, has six eateries, a pizza and pasta outlet, a deli, a soup and salad bar, and a bakery among them. Tropical Treasures Pool Bar, with seating on a wooden deck, serves up light fare and frozen tropical drinks. Kids under 12 eat breakfast and dinner free, either in a hotel restaurant with their parents or in the Gingerbread House, a cheerful facility where movies and cartoons are shown on a large-screen TV and dinner includes a make-your-own-sundae bar.

Services: Room service (7am–2pm and 5:30–10pm), babysitting, guest services desk (sells tickets to all nearby attractions, including Walt Disney World parks), free scheduled transport to the Magic Kingdom/EPCOT/Disney–MGM Studios (there's a charge for transport to other nearby attractions), telephone grocery shopping, Mears airport shuttle.

Facilities: Two Olympic-size swimming pools, two whirlpools, children's wading pool, two children's playgrounds, two night-lit hard-surface tennis courts, sand volleyball, basketball court, coin-op washers/dryers, shops, car-rental desk, two video-games arcades, Camp Holiday (a counselor-supervised child-care/activity center for ages 2–12, open from 8am to midnight; parents can rent beepers to keep in touch with the kids).

RESIDENCE INN BY MARRIOTT ON LAKE CECILE, 4786 W. Irlo Bronson Memorial Hwy., Kissimmee, FL 34746. Tel. 407/396-2056, or toll free 800/468-3027. Fax 407/396-2909. 159 suites. A/C TV TEL

$ Rates (including extended continental breakfast): $109–$115 studio for up to four people; $115–$119 studio double for up to four people; $149–$169 bilevel penthouse for up to six people. Range reflects season. Inquire about packages. AE, CB, DC, DISC, ER, JCB, MC, OPT, V. **Parking:** Free self-parking.

This all-suite hostelry has peacocks roaming its attractively landscaped grounds on the banks of beautiful 223-acre Lake Cecile. Like all Residence Inns, the accommodations here are in two-story residential-looking cream stucco buildings fronted by neatly manicured lawns. Suites, tastefully decorated in gray and mauve, have fully equipped eat-in kitchens and comfortable living room areas with sleeper sofas. All but studio doubles have wood-burning fireplaces (logs are supplied), and the cathedral-ceilinged penthouses have full baths upstairs and down. Many suites offer balconies overlooking the lake. Amenities include remote-control cable TVs with VCRs (movie tapes can be rented), alarm-clock radios, and in-room safes.

Dining/Entertainment: The lovely gatehouse lounge off the lobby, with a lofty peaked ceiling and big, comfy sofas facing a working fireplace, is the setting for an extended continental breakfast each morning. And an al fresco bar serves light fare and frosty drinks poolside on a canopied wooden deck with umbrella tables (drinks here are half price during happy hour). Local restaurants deliver food (there are menus in each room).

Services: Guest services (sells tickets—most of them discounted—and provides transport to all nearby theme parks and attractions; round-trip to Disney parks costs $7), complimentary daily newspaper, free food-shopping service, Mears airport shuttle.

Facilities: Small swimming pool, whirlpool, sports court (basketball, volleyball, badminton, paddle tennis), children's playground, coin-op washers/dryers, 24-hour food shop, picnic tables, barbecue grills. Lake activities include fishing, jet skiing, bumper rides, and waterskiing, and you can rent pedalboats, canoes, and sailboats.

INEXPENSIVE

COLONIAL MOTOR LODGE, 1815 W. Vine St. (U.S. 192), Kissimmee, FL 34741. Tel. 407/847-6121, or toll free 800/325-4348. Fax 407/847-0728. 83 rms, 40 apts. A/C TV TEL

$ **Rates** (including continental breakfast): $24–$42 for up to four people; $55–$80 two-bedroom apt. for up to six people. Range reflects season. AE, CB, DC, DISC, MC, V. **Parking:** Free self-parking.

This well-run motor lodge is entered via a white colonial-style building with peach columns and shutters and a Federalist eagle over the door. The pleasantly furnished lobby is the setting for a complimentary continental breakfast each morning. Standard motel rooms decorated in rust and tan with whitewashed pine-paneled walls offer remote-control cable TVs with HBO and alarm clocks. Two-bedroom apartments, in two-story white buildings fronted by small gardens, represent a good choice for families. In addition to two full bedrooms, they have living rooms and fully equipped eat-in kitchens.

Facilities include a large swimming pool. Adjacent to the Colonial are an International House of Pancakes and a shopping center with a dry cleaner and laundrette. The Black Angus, a steak and seafood restaurant, is across the street. And a supermarket, 7-Eleven, Hardy's, and Kentucky Fried Chicken are a block away. Guest services sells tickets to all Disney parks and nearby attractions (some of them discounted) and offers transportation to/from them and the airport. Transport to Disney parks is $9 per person round-trip.

COMFORT INN MAINGATE, 7571 W. Irlo Bronson Memorial Hwy. (U.S. 192), Kissimmee, FL 34747. Tel. 407/396-7500, or toll free 800/221-2222. Fax 407/396-7497. 281 rms. A/C TV TEL

$ **Rates:** $38–$74 single or double, depending on the season; garden rooms $6–$10 additional. Additional person $8 extra; children 18 and under stay free in parents' room. AE, CB, DC, DISC, ER, JCB, MC, V. **Parking:** Free self-parking.

Just one mile from Disney parks, this Comfort Inn houses clean, spiffy-looking standard motel accommodations in two-story peach stucco buildings. More upscale are the garden rooms, facing a lawn with a gazebo; decorated in teal, seafoam green, and peach, they're equipped with small refrigerators and hairdryers. The Royal Palms Restaurant on the premises serves low-priced buffets and à la carte meals. A comfortable bar/lounge adjoins. And right next door are a 7-Eleven and an International House of Pancakes. The guest services desk sells tickets (most of them discounted) and provides transport to all nearby attractions and the airport; round-trip to Disney parks costs $7. Facilities include a medium-sized swimming pool, children's playground, coin-op washers/dryers, and a small video-games arcade.

ECONO LODGE MAINGATE EAST, 4311 W. Irlo Bronson Memorial Hwy. (U.S. 192), Kissimmee, FL 34746. Tel. 407/396-7100, or toll free 800/ENJOY-FL. Fax 407/239-2636. 173 rms. A/C TV TEL

$ **Rates:** $33–$70 for up to four people, depending on the season. AE, CB, DC, DISC, MC, V. **Parking:** Free self-parking.

(S) At this attractively landscaped Econo Lodge, accommodations are set well back from the highway in rustic two- and three-story buildings with cedar balconies and roofing. Well-maintained standard motel rooms are equipped with cable TVs and safes; small refrigerators can be rented. Deli sandwiches, soups, pizza, yogurt, and Häagen-Dazs ice cream are sold in the lobby, and there's a microwave oven for guest use. In addition, the pool bar serves light fare, including full breakfasts and lunches at umbrella tables under towering live oaks. The guest services desk sells tickets (most of them discounted) and provides transport to all nearby attractions and the airport; round-trip to Disney parks costs $12. On-premises facilities include a large swimming pool, children's pool, volleyball, shuffleboard, horseshoes, coin-op washers/dryers, picnic tables, barbecue grills, and a small video-games arcade. This is one of six area hotels under the same ownership, all of which can be booked via the above toll-free number.

HOJO INN MAIN GATE, 6051 W. Irlo Bronson Memorial Hwy. (U.S. 192), Kissimmee, FL 34747. Tel. 407/396-1748, or toll free 800/288-4678. Fax 407/649-8642. 358 rms, 9 family suites. A/C TV TEL

$ Rates: $56–$76 for up to four people, depending on season, and children under 19 stay free in parents' room; add $10 for an efficiency unit with a kitchenette; $86–$106 family suite. Inquire about packages. AE, CB, DC, DISC, JCB, MC, V. **Parking:** Free self-parking.

This Howard Johnson's hostelry just two miles from the Magic Kingdom offers attractive accommodations housed in pristine white stucco two- and three-story buildings. Completely renovated in 1992, they're nicely decorated with quilted lavender bedspreads, royal-blue carpeting, and beach-themed paintings on the walls. In-room amenities include cable TVs with VCRs (movies can be rented in the lobby) and safes. Efficiency units have fully equipped kitchenettes with small refrigerators, two-burner stoves, and sinks. And family suites have both full kitchens and living rooms with convertible sofas.

Facilities here include a medium-size swimming pool, whirlpool, kiddie pool, children's playground, coin-op laundry, small 24-hour video-games arcade, car-rental desk, and pool table. A huge store next door sells resortwear, sundries, and Disneyana. Also adjoining the property is a large water park called Watermania and a particularly nice plant-filled International House of Pancakes open from 7am to 11pm. On the premises, a pool bar serves light fare and drinks, and complimentary coffee and tea are served in the very pleasant lobby throughout the day. Guest services sells tickets to all Disney parks and nearby attractions (some of them discounted) and offers transportation to/from them and the airport. Transport to Disney parks is $7 per person round-trip.

LARSON'S LODGE KISSIMMEE, 2009 W. Vine St. (U.S. 192), Kissimmee, FL 34741. Tel. 407/846-2713, or toll free 800/624-5905. Fax 407/846-8695. 200 rms. A/C TV TEL

$ Rates: $39–$69 for up to four people, depending on season; add $10 for an efficiency unit with a kitchenette. AE, CB, DC, DISC, MC, V. **Parking:** Free self-parking.

$ This friendly family-run hostelry just eight miles from Walt Disney World has been operated by the Larsons since 1976. Standard motel units decorated in teal and tan have a vaguely southwestern look. They're equipped with remote-control cable TVs and in-room safes. More upscale are cheerful peach-and-teal efficiency units which have living room areas and fully equipped kitchenettes with sinks, two-burner stoves, toasters, small refrigerators, microwave ovens, and coffee makers.

The guest services desk sells tickets to all nearby theme parks, including WDW (many of them discounted), and a shuttle bus plies the route between the hotel and all WDW parks at scheduled times throughout the day (round-trip fare is $10); transport is also available to other nearby attractions and the airport. On-premises facilities and amenities include a large V-shaped swimming pool, a smaller free-form pool, a kiddie pool, a whirlpool, an innovative children's playground, a night-lit hard-surface tennis court, a gift/sundries shop, coin-op washers/dryers, and a nice-size video-games arcade. Guests get free tickets to Watermania, the water park at Larson's Lodge Main Gate (see below). Pets are permitted. A shopping center is close by, and the Black Angus restaurant, serving all meals (dinner features steak and seafood), is on the premises; there's nightly entertainment in its adjoining western-motif lounge.

LARSON'S LODGE MAIN GATE, 6075 W. Irlo Bronson Memorial Hwy. (U.S. 192), Kissimmee, FL 34747. Tel. 407/396-6100, or toll free 800/327-9074. Fax 407/396-6965. 128 rms. A/C TV TEL

$ Rates: $39–$69 single or double, depending on season; add $15 for an efficiency unit with a kitchenette. Additional person $8 extra; children under 18 stay free in parents' room. AE, CB, DC, DISC, MC, V. **Parking:** Free self-parking.

With its large, on-premises water park (Watermania), children's playground, and poolside picnic tables and barbecue grills, Larson's Lodge is a good choice for families. It has a cheerful on-site Shoney's restaurant (open from 6am to midnight), and a HoJo is right next door. Accommodations are standard motel units attractively decorated in peach and seafoam green with bleached-oak furnishings. They're equipped with remote-control cable TVs (VCRs and movie tapes can be rented) and in-room safes. Efficiency units have fully equipped kitchenettes with sinks, two-burner stoves, small refrigerators, and microwave ovens. A supermarket is just a few minutes away by car.

The guest services desk sells tickets to all nearby theme parks, including WDW (many of them discounted), and a shuttle bus plies the route between the motel and all WDW parks at scheduled times throughout the day (round-trip fare is $7). Transport is also available to other nearby attractions and the airport. On-premises facilities include a large swimming pool and whirlpool, shops, coin-op washers/dryers, a small video-games arcade, and a pool table. Guests enjoy free use of a tennis court at Larson's Lodge Kissimmee and get free tickets to Watermania. Pets are permitted.

RODEWAY INN EASTGATE, 5245 W. Irlo Bronson Memorial Hwy. (U.S. 192), Kissimmee, FL 34746. Tel. 407/841-8541, or toll free 800/423-3864. Fax 407/396-0293. 200 rms. A/C TV TEL

$ **Rates:** $31–$55 for up to four people, depending on view and season. AE, CB, DC, DISC, ER, MC, V. **Parking:** Free self-parking.

The Rodeway's U-shaped configuration of two-story buildings, embellished with a blue-and-gray striped awning fringe, form an attractively landscaped courtyard around a large swimming pool. There are picnic tables and a children's playground on the lawn. Rooms are nicely decorated in teal, aqua, and mauve, with oak furnishings and grasspaper-look/bamboo-motif wall coverings.

The on-site Terrace Restaurant serves buffet breakfasts, and the comfy Half Time Lounge, where sporting events are aired on a seven-foot-square screen, has a pool table and dart boards. Other facilities include a small video-games arcade off the lobby, coin-op washers/dryers, and a shop selling gifts, sundries, and Disneyana. Guest services sells tickets to all Disney parks and nearby attractions (many of them discounted) and offers transportation to/from them and the airport. Transport to Disney parks is $7 per person round-trip.

INTERNATIONAL DRIVE

Properties listed here are 7 to 10 miles north of Walt Disney World parks and close to Universal Studios and Sea World.

EXPENSIVE

PEABODY ORLANDO, 9801 International Dr., Orlando, FL 32819. Tel. 407/352-4000, or toll free 800/PEABODY. Fax 407/351-0073. 835 rms, 57 suites. A/C MINIBAR TV TEL

$ **Rates:** $180–$220 for up to three people; $240 for Peabody Club; $375–$1,300 suite. Children under 18 stay free in parents' room; seniors 50 and over get a $1 discount per year of age. Rates May–Sept 15 slightly reduced. Inquire about packages. AE, CB, DC, DISC, ER, JCB, MC, V. **Parking:** Free self-parking, $6 per night valet parking.

This deluxe 27-story resort hotel—its porte-cochère facade fronted by splashing fountains, waterfalls, and lush tropical plantings—has some especially famous avian residents. Every morning at 11am, five fluffy ducks proudly parade along a red carpet to the beat of John Philip Sousa's *King Cotton* march, their journey culminating at a marble fountain in the lobby. They frolic there throughout the day, until the duckmaster directs them back to their "Royal Duck Palace" at 5pm. But ducks are just a fillip here. The Peabody, in the grand tradition, pampers guests with sumptuous surroundings and attentive service. Luxurious rooms have bamboo and bleached-wood furnishings and walls hung with quality artworks. Amenities include two phones (bedroom and bath) with two lines and modem capacity, remote-control cable TVs with Spectravision and laser-disc movie set-ups, and, in the bath, cosmetic lights, fine European toiletries, a hairdryer, and a small TV. The concierge-level Peabody Club occupies the top three floors. The Peabody is about 15 minutes by car from WDW parks and even closer to Sea World and Universal Studios.

Dining/Entertainment: Dux, the Peabody's elegant signature restaurant, features American regional cuisine dinners in a plush candlelit and crystal-chandeliered setting; it does not, however, serve duck. Capriccio, for sophisticated northern Italian fare, is open for dinner and champagne Sunday brunches. The B-Line Diner, a 24-hour art deco eatery in the nouvelle diner-chic tradition, dishes up American specialties such as turkey hash and barbecued beef sandwiches prepared with Culinary Institute panache. From the B-Line Express window, a 24-hour counter operation fronted by a tempting array of cakes and pastries, you can order take-out fare from the restaurant's menu. The Peabody Pool Bar serves cold, frothy specialty drinks and snacks. A singer and trio perform jazz, blues, and show tunes in the atrium Lobby Bar nightly from 7pm to 1am. The lobby is also the setting for weekday afternoon English teas. The adjoining Mallards Lounge is a cozy gathering place; sports events are aired on the TV over the bar. And al fresco jazz concerts take place on the fourth-floor recreation level spring and fall.

Services: 24-hour room service, babysitting, 24-hour concierge, shoeshine, nightly bed turn-down on request, free newspaper delivered to your room daily, "Double Ducker" shuttle bus making round-trip runs between the hotel and all WDW parks throughout the day (round-trip fare is $5), Mears transportation/ sightseeing desk (sells tickets to all nearby attractions, including WDW parks and dinner shows; also provides transport, by reservation, to attractions and airport).

Facilities: Double-Olympic-length swimming pool, indoor and outdoor whirlpools, large children's wading pool with waterfall fountain, four hard-surface night-lit tennis courts, golf privileges at four nearby courses, seven-mile jogging path, car-rental desk, Delta Airlines desk, full-service unisex beauty salon, full business center, state-of-the-art health club, shops, small video-games arcade, the Children's Hotel (a counselor-supervised child-care/activities center); hot-air balloon rides, deep-sea fishing, scuba lessons, and other amusements/excursions can be arranged.

MODERATE

SUMMERFIELD SUITES, 8480 International Dr., Orlando, FL 32819. Tel. 407/352-2400, or toll free 800/833-4353. Fax 407/352-4631. 146 suites. A/C TV TEL

$ **Rates** (including extended continental breakfast): $139–$159 one-bedroom suite for up to four people; $159–$199 two-bedroom suite for up to six people. Range reflects room size and season. Inquire about packages. AE, CB, DC, DISC, MC, V. **Parking:** Free self-parking.

(S) This delightful five-story cream stucco hotel is built around a nicely landscaped central courtyard. Open-air balconies adorned with potted plants serve as hallways, creating a welcoming resort ambience. Spacious, neat-as-a-pin residential-style suites, very attractively decorated in peach and teal with bleached-oak furnishings, contain fully equipped eat-in kitchens (the maid does your dishes), comfortable living rooms, big walk-in closets, and large dressing areas. Two-bedroom units have two baths. All bedrooms have doors (ensuring privacy), and you'll find a large desk in the master bedrooms. Amenities include irons and ironing boards, phones (with two lines, computer hookup, and voice-mail messaging) in each bedroom and the kitchen, remote-control satellite TVs (with free HBO, attraction-information station, and pay-movie options) in each bedroom and the living room (the latter with a VCR; rent your choice of 200 movies downstairs), and alarm-clock radios in each bedroom. A large shopping center is across the street, WDW parks are about 15 minutes away by car, Sea World and Universal Studios are even closer, and numerous restaurants are in the area. This is a great choice for families.

Dining/Entertainment: An extensive continental buffet breakfast—fresh-baked muffins, fruit, hard-boiled eggs, toast, applesauce, assorted cereals, juice, and coffee or tea—is served in a charming peach-walled dining room hung with delightful watercolors of tropical fish. The cozy lobby bar is a popular gathering place evenings. A cabaña bar offers drinks and snacks poolside. And local restaurants deliver food to the premises.

Services: Babysitting, concierge/tour desk (sells tickets to WDW parks and other nearby attractions), newspapers delivered to your room daily, transport between the hotel and all WDW parks (round-trip fare is $7), shuttle available to airport and nearby attractions, complimentary grocery shopping.

Facilities: Nice-size swimming pool with fountain and bilevel sun deck, whirlpool, children's wading pool, car-rental desk, full business services, exercise room, coin-op washers/dryers, 24-hour shop, small video-games arcade.

INEXPENSIVE

FAIRFIELD INN BY MARRIOTT, 8342 Jamaican Court, Orlando, FL 32819. Tel. 407/363-1944, or toll free 800/228-2800. Fax 407/363-1944. 135 rms. A/C TV TEL

$ Rates (including continental breakfast): $46–$62 single; $52–$67 double. Range reflects season. Additional person $7 extra; children under 18 stay free in parents' room. AE, CB, DC, DISC, ER, MC, V. **Parking:** Free self-parking.

Jamaican Court, in a secluded area off International Drive, is a neatly landscaped complex of hotels and restaurants, including this handsome three-story tan stucco hostelry with blue roofing and doors. It has spiffy-looking rooms decorated in rust, tan, and Federalist blue with oak furnishings. In-room amenities include remote-control cable TVs with free HBO and attractions-information channels, AM/FM radios, alarm clocks, and phones equipped with 25-foot cords and modem jacks. Guests enjoy a few thoughtful extras here: 100-watt bulbs in the lamps, candies on your pillow at check-in, complimentary daily newspapers, and free local calls. A continental breakfast of bagels, rolls, doughnuts, juices, fresh fruit, tea, and coffee is served in the lobby each morning. In addition, there are many free-standing and hotel restaurants right in Jamaican Court, and several local eateries deliver food (there are menus in each room).

The guest services desk sells tickets (most of them discounted) and provides transport to all nearby theme parks and attractions and the airport; round-trip to Disney parks costs $10. There's a small swimming pool on the premises, and the lobby has a microwave oven for guest use and a few video games.

4. DINING

Since most Orlando visitors spend the majority of their time in the Walt Disney World area, I'll concentrate on the best choices throughout that vast enchanted empire, then point out a few worthwhile choices beyond the realm. Parents will be pleased to note that just about every restaurant in town offers a low-priced children's menu and usually provides some kind of kid's activity (mazes, coloring, paper dolls) as well. See also the listings for dinner shows in "Evening Entertainment," later in this chapter.

AT WALT DISNEY WORLD

EPCOT CENTER

An ethnic meal at one of the World Showcase pavilions is part of the EPCOT experience. If you want to have lunch or dinner at a Future World or World Showcase restaurant, make reservations at Earth Center as soon as you enter the park in the morning. That will ensure optimum choice of dining time and cuisine. Guests at WDW-owned and official hotels can make reservations by phone up to three days in advance (ask the Central Reservations Office for details when you reserve, or call the guest services or concierge desk at your hotel). And during slower seasons, you can very often just walk up to an EPCOT restaurant and make a reservation on the spot. All the establishments listed below offer lunch and dinner daily, serve alcoholic beverages, are in the "Expensive" category, and take American Express, MasterCard, and VISA.

Note: In addition to the places listed below there are plenty of lower-priced walk-in eateries throughout the park that don't require reservations; check your *EPCOT Center Guidebook* for details.

World Showcase

UNITED KINGDOM The plank-floored **Rose & Crown,** entered via a cozy pub with a pungent aroma of ale, evokes Victorian England with servers in period costume, dark woods, stained glass, and English and Scottish folk music. It also offers outdoor seating at umbrella tables overlooking the lagoon. The menu features items like Scotch egg and Stilton cheese, fish and chips, steak-and-kidney pie, and sherry trifle. Traditional afternoon tea, with scones and finger sandwiches, is served daily at 4pm.

FRANCE **Chefs de France** is under the auspices of a world-famous culinary triumvirate: Paul Bocuse, Roger Vergé, and Gaston LeNôtre. A meal here might begin with a seafood cream soup with crab dumplings (Vergé), continue to an entree of broiled salmon in sorrel-cream sauce à la façon de Bocuse, and conclude with a soufflé Grand-Marnier (LeNôtre). The art nouveau/fin-de-siècle interior, under a coffered cherrywood ceiling, is agleam with etched glass, beveled mirrors, and brass candelabra chandeliers.

The ✪ **Bistro de Paris,** upstairs from Chefs de France and serving dinner only, offers similar fare in a more serene country French setting; I prefer it.

MOROCCO The palatial ✪ **Restaurant Marrakesh**—with its exquisitely carved faux-ivory archways, hand-set mosaic tilework, latticed teak shutters, and intricate cut-brass chandeliers suspended from a beamed ceiling painted with Moorish motifs—represents 12 centuries of Arabic design. Belly dancers perform to *oud, kanoun,* and *darbuka* music while you dine on dishes like lamb couscous, chicken bastilla (a sweet pastry flavored with chopped almonds and cinnamon), and shish kebab. The Moroccan diffa (traditional feast) that lets you sample a variety of dishes is recommended.

JAPAN The main dining area of the **Mitsukoshi Restaurant** is a teppanyaki steakhouse where diners sit at grill tables and white-hatted chefs perform samurailike culinary moves—rapidly dicing, slicing, stir-frying, and propelling the cooked food onto your plate with amazing dexterity. Entrees feature shrimp, scallops, lobster, steak, and chicken. It's great fun watching the chef wield his knife and utensils. Dining areas are divided by shoji screens. Since one shares a table with strangers, this makes for a convivial dining experience.

ITALY Patterned after Alfredo De Lelio's celebrated establishment in Rome, ✪ **L'Originale Alfredo di Roma Ristorante** evokes a seaside Roman palazzo with crystal candelabra chandeliers suspended from a high coffered ceiling and beautiful trompe-l'oeil frescoes of 15th-century patrician villas on the walls. Charming Italian waiters and exuberant strolling musicians create a festive ambience. De Lelio invented fettuccine Alfredo, and it remains an excellent choice here. Other recommendables are vodka-flavored ziti in a piquant tomato-cream sauce and chicken alla parmigiana served with an array of fresh vegetables. Don't pass up the sublime tira misu for dessert.

GERMANY Lit by streetlamps, **The Biergarten** simulates a Bavarian village courtyard at Oktoberfest with autumnal trees, a working waterwheel, and geranium-filled flower boxes adorning Tudor-style houses. Waiters are in lederhosen, waitresses in peasant dresses, and entertainment is provided by oom-pah bands, singers, dancers, and a strolling accordionist. Traditional fare includes goulash soup, sauerbraten with dumplings and red cabbage, and apple strudel for dessert. Wash it down with a 33-ounce stein of Beck's or a glass of Liebfraumilch.

CHINA One of the most attractive of the World Showcase restaurants, **Nine Dragons** has intricately carved rosewood paneling, lacquer screens embellished with cherry blossoms, and a beautiful dragon-motif ceiling. Window seats overlook the lagoon. You can choose Mandarin, Shanghai, Szechuan, Hunan, or Cantonese entrees ranging from Szechuan deep-fried shrimp in a Mao Tai liqueur-spiked fruit sauce to moo shoo pork. There are also dim sum appetizers and assorted Chinese pastries for dessert.

NORWAY **Akershus** re-creates a 14th-century castle fortress that stands in Oslo's harbor. Its pristine white stone interior, with glossy oak floors, lofty pine and beamed cherrywood ceilings, and leaded-glass windows, features intimate dining niches divided by Gothic stone archways. Soft lighting emanates from gas table lamps, brass candelabra chandeliers, and flickering sconces. The meal is an immense smörgåsbord including items like smoked pork with honey mustard, venison in cream sauce, gravlax, Norwegian tomato herring, cheeses, red cabbage, eggs nordique, cold meats, seafood, and salads. Order a "veiled maiden" for dessert and Norwegian beer.

MEXICO The ✪ **San Angel Inn** evokes a hacienda courtyard under a starlit sky in the shadow of a Yucatán pyramid, with the Popocatepetl volcano erupting in the distance. Tables are candlelit (even at lunch) and lighting is very low; it is nighttime. The fare is authentic and prepared from scratch. Order an appetizer of queso fundido (melted cheese with Mexican pork sausage, served with homemade corn or flour tortillas). Entree specialties include sautéed lobster (with tomatoes, onions, olives, and Mexican peppers in a white wine sauce), mole poblano (chicken simmered with more than 20 spices and a hint of chocolate), and combination platters of enchiladas, tacos, and chile relleños.

Future World

LIVING SEAS PAVILION Dine "under the sea" at the enchanting ✪ **Coral Reef,** where all seating rings a 5.6-million-gallon coral-reef aquarium inhabited by more than 4,000 denizens of the deep. The strains of Debussy's *La Mer* and Handel's *Water Music* playing softly in the background help set the tone. The menu features (what else?) seafood—oysters Rockefeller, lobster bisque, sautéed mahi-mahi in lemon-caper butter, Dover sole, and seafood fettuccine Alfredo, along with steak and chicken entrees. Dessert options include Belgian chocolate mousse cake and key lime pie.

THE LAND The revolving **Land Grille Room,** on the upper level of this pavilion, seats diners in comfortable semicircular velvet-upholstered booths lit by brass-shaded lamps. As you dine, your table travels past desert, prairie, farmland, and rain-forest environments. The fare is American. Dinner here might consist of an appetizer of spicy chicken wings with bleu cheese dressing, an entree of barbecued pork spareribs with a baked potato and corn on the cob, and angel-food cake with fresh berries for dessert. Many menu selections feature produce grown in the pavilion's greenhouses.

THE MAGIC KINGDOM

There are dozens of eateries throughout the Magic Kingdom, but I enjoy a quiet full-service meal. To dine at any of the establishments listed below, make reservations at the restaurant itself when you enter the park in the morning. Guests at WDW-owned and official hotels can make reservations by phone up to three days in advance (ask the Central Reservations Office for details when you reserve, or call the guest services or concierge desk at your hotel). All the establishments listed below take

American Express, MasterCard, and VISA. No Magic Kingdom restaurants serve alcoholic beverages.

FRONTIERLAND Highly recommended is the **Diamond Horseshoe Jamboree** in Frontierland, combining a light meal with a 40-minute western-themed musical revue (details in Section 5 of this chapter).

LIBERTY SQUARE The **Liberty Tree Tavern** is an 18th-century pub, with low beamed ceilings, peg-plank oak floors, displays of pewterware in oak hutches, and a vast brick fireplace hung with copper pots. The service staff is in period garb, background music is also appropriate to the period, and paintings on redwood illustrate historic scenes of Colonial America. Entrees range from New England pot roast served with mashed potatoes and vegetables to a traditional roast turkey dinner with all the trimmings. All-American desserts include apple pie topped with cinammon ice cream and red velvet cake. Open for lunch and dinner. Price range: Moderate to expensive.

CINDERELLA CASTLE **King Stefan's Banquet Hall** is a castle dining room complete with heraldic banners and candelabra chandeliers suspended from a vaulted ceiling. There are suits of armor and shields on display, and servers in 13th-century garb address guests as "Milord" and "Milady." Oak tables are candlelit. The only anachronistic note: The background music is from Disney movies. The menu features hearty cuts of steak and prime rib, along with chicken and seafood dishes. Open for lunch and dinner. Price range: Expensive.

MAIN STREET Inspired by the Disney movie *Lady and the Tramp*, **Tony's Town Square Restaurant** is Victorian plush, with rich cherrywood beams and paneling, stained glass, cut-glass mirrors, and globe lighting fixtures with dangling crystal pendants. Walls are hung with original cels from the movie. There's additional seating in a marble-floored, plant-filled solarium. The menu is Italian, featuring pastas, calzones, sandwiches, and antipastos at lunch, and entrees such as steak with lobster and linguine at dinner. Open for breakfast, lunch, and dinner. Price range: Moderate to expensive.

DISNEY–MGM STUDIOS

There are over a dozen eateries in this Hollywood-themed park with names like the Studio Commissary and Starring Rolls Bakery. The two listed below are my favorites. Both require reservations, which should be made at the restaurants themselves when you enter the park in the morning. Guests at WDW-owned and official hotels can make reservations by phone up to three days in advance (ask the Central Reservations Office for details when you reserve, or call the guest services or concierge desk at your hotel). Both serve lunch and dinner, have full bars, and take American Express, MasterCard, and VISA.

The **Hollywood Brown Derby,** modeled after the famed Los Angeles celebrity haunt where Loretta Parsons and Hedda Hopper held court, evokes its West Coast counterpart with interior palm trees, tables lit by small derby-shaded lamps, and mahogany-paneled walls hung with hundreds of caricatures—every major star from Barbara Stanwyck to Rin Tin Tin. Seating is in roomy semicircular leather booths. The Derby's signature dish is the Cobb salad, invented by owner Bob Cobb in the 1930s. A typical dinner: appetizer of pan-fried Maryland crabcakes served with spicy marinara sauce, entree of batter-fried lamb chops served with fresh vegetables, and bananas Foster for dessert. Price range: Expensive.

The **Sci-Fi Dine-In Theater Restaurant** replicates a 1950s Hollywood drive-in movie theater. Diners sit in flashy convertible cars (complete with fins and whitewalls) under a twinkling starlit sky, while friendly servers on roller skates bring complimentary popcorn and food. While you eat, you can watch the movie screen, where a mix of zany newsreels (like *News of the Future*) is interspersed with cartoons, horror movie clips (*Frankenstein Meets the Space Monster*), and coming attractions. Menu items have names like Terror of the Tides (broiled seasonal fish with orange-tamarind sauce, green beans, and potato) and Monster Mash (oven-roasted turkey with all the trimmings). Finish up with The Cheesecake That Ate New York. Your bill is presented as a speeding ticket. Price range: Moderate.

AT DISNEY RESORTS

Very Expensive

VICTORIA & ALBERT'S, in Disney's Grand Floridian Beach Resort, 4401 Floridian Way. Tel. 824-2383.

Cuisine: AMERICAN REGIONAL. **Reservations:** Required.

$ Prices: $80 per person prix fixe; $25 additional for the Royal Wine Pairing. AE, MC, V.

Open: Dinner only, daily, with seatings at 6–6:45pm and 9–9:45pm.

It's not often one describes a dining experience as flawless, but at Victoria & Albert's, the World's most elite restaurant (Walt Disney World, that is) I experienced nothing less than idyllic perfection. Entered via a plushly furnished lounge with a portrait of the eponymous monarchs surmounting the mantel of a blazing fireplace, the intimate dining room is girded by a circular colonnade. Tuscan-look faux-leather walls are hung with gilt-framed ink drawings, and an exquisite floral arrangement—above which a Chinoiserie chandelier is suspended from a beautifully painted dome—serves as an aesthetic centerpoint. Diners sit in leather-upholstered Louis XIII–style chairs at tables lit by silver-shaded Victorian lamps. A maid and butler provide deft and gracious service, and a harpist playing softly while you dine enhances the celestial ambience.

Dinner, a seven-course affair, is described in a personalized menu sealed with a gold wax insignia. The fare changes nightly. On a recent visit, I began with an hors d'oeuvre of Florida lobster tail with aioli on mitzuma lettuce. It was supplanted by a more formal appetizer, vermouth-poached jumbo sea scallops served in a crisp rice noodle basket on shallot-chive sauce and garnished with flying fish caviar and Chinese tat soi leaves. A shot of peppered vodka added piquancy to a velvety plum tomato bisque sprinkled with smoked bacon and lightly topped with pesto-cream sauce. For an entree I selected a fan of pinkly juicy sautéed Peking duck breast with wild rice and crabapple chutney. A salad of esoteric greens in an orange-sherry vinaigrette cleared the palate for the next course, English Stilton served with pine-nut bread, port wine, and a pear poached in burgundy, cognac, and cinnamon sugar. The conclusion: a sumptuous hazelnut and Frangelico soufflé, followed by coffee and chocolate truffles. This is a highly nuanced cuisine to be slowly savored. There is, of course, an extensive wine list. I suggest you opt for the Royal Wine Pairing, which pairs an appropriate wine with each course and lets you sample a variety of selections from the restaurant's distinguished cellars. Jackets are required for men, and no smoking is permitted. There is free self-parking and validated valet parking.

Expensive

ARIEL'S, at Disney's Beach Club Resort, 1800 EPCOT Resorts Blvd. Tel. 934-3357.

Cuisine: SEAFOOD. **Reservations:** Recommended.

$ Prices: Appetizers $4.25–$8.95; main courses $17.95–$24. AE, MC, V.

Open: Dinner only, daily 6–10pm.

Named for the *Little Mermaid* character, this exquisite restaurant overlooking Stormalong Bay is awash in seafoam green, peach, and coral. White-linened tables lit by shaded lamps are elegantly appointed with fish and seashell-motif china, a prismed 2,000-gallon coral-reef tank is filled with tropical fish, walls are hung with oil paintings of scenes from the movie, and whimsical fish mobiles and glass bubbles dangle from a vaulted ceiling. You'll feel like you're dining in an underwater kingdom.

Appetizers (which supplement a complimentary smoked clam dip) include scrumptious New England silver dollar crabcakes served with a spicy tartar sauce and a Cajun-style shellfish gumbo with chunks of shrimp, lobster, and smoky andouille sausage. Recommended seafood dishes here include a traditional paella and Maine lobster sautéed with shiitake mushrooms, lemon, and garlic and served atop a nest of tricolor angel-hair pasta with two sauces—a buttery lobster sauce (sauce américain) and herbed cream. A few nonseafood options are offered as well, among them oven-roasted boneless game hen stuffed with wild rice and lentils, served with a light pesto sauce. Desserts include a rich Chambord raspberry-chocolate cake, and an extensive award-winning wine list indicates which selections best complement your entree. There is free self- and valet parking.

Moderate

CAPE MAY CAFE, at Disney's Beach Club Resort, 1800 EPCOT Resorts Blvd. Tel. 934-8000.

Cuisine: CLAMBAKE BUFFET. **Reservations:** Not accepted.

$ **Prices:** Buffet, $16.95 adults, $8.95 ages 6–11, free for kids under 6. Lobster is additional. AE, MC, V.

Open: Dinner only, daily 5:30–9:30pm.

A hearty 19th-century-style New England clambake is featured nightly at this charming peach and seafoam-green restaurant, where sand sculptures, paintings of turn-of-the-century beach scenes, croquet mallets, and furled striped beach umbrellas evoke an upscale seaside resort. Diners sit in oversize chairs at birchwood tables covered by zany newspaper place mats filled with corny jokes, old-fashioned advertisements, and recipes. Large towel napkins are provided. Aromatic stews and chowders, steamed clams and mussels, corn on the cob, chicken, lobster, and redskin potatoes are cooked up in a crackling rockweed steamer pit that serves as the restaurant's centerpiece. And these traditional clambake offerings are supplemented by dozens of salads (pasta, seafood, fruit, vegetables), hot entrees (barbecued baby back ribs, smoked sausage, fried chicken, pasta dishes), and a wide array of oven-fresh breads and desserts. There's a full bar. There is free self- and valet parking.

WALT DISNEY WORLD VILLAGE MARKETPLACE / PLEASURE ISLAND

Located about 2½ miles from EPCOT Center off Buena Vista Drive, the Marketplace is a very pleasant complex of cedar-shingled shops and restaurants overlooking a scenic lagoon. Pleasure Island, a complex of nightclubs and shops, adjoins.

Note: You don't have to pay the entrance fee to Pleasure Island to dine at the Fireworks Factory or Portobello Yacht Club.

Expensive

PORTOBELLO YACHT CLUB, 1650 Lake Buena Vista Dr., Pleasure Island. Tel. 934-8888.

Cuisine: NORTHERN ITALIAN. **Reservations:** Not accepted (arrive early to avoid a wait).

$ **Prices:** Appetizers $5.95–$9.95; main courses $6.95–$8.95 at lunch, $12.95–$22.95 at dinner; pizzas $6.95–$7.95. AE, MC, V.

Open: 11:30am–midnight (dinner served from 4pm).

Not surprisingly, the Yacht Club is nautically themed, its interior, though casual, evoking a luxury cruise ship. It occupies a Bermuda-style house with high gables. Inside, robin's-egg-blue walls are plastered with photographs of racing yachts, navigational charts, and yachting flags, and shelves are lined with racing trophies. From the lively mahogany-paneled bar, you can watch oak-fired pizzas being prepared in an exhibition kitchen. Restaurant seating is on comfortable banquettes or al fresco on an awninged patio overlooking Lake Buena Vista.

Those oak-fired pizzas have crisply thin crusts and toppings such as quattro formaggi—mozzarella, romano, Gorgonzola, and provolone—with sun-dried tomatoes. At dinner, you might select an entree of charcoal-grilled half chicken marinated in olive oil, garlic, and fresh rosemary and served with oven-roasted potatoes and seasonal vegetables. Or choose a pasta dish such as bucatini with plum tomatoes, Italian bacon, garlic, and fresh basil. Entrees are served with sourdough bread and roasted spreadable garlic cloves. There's an extensive list of Italian and California wines (many of them hard-to-find vintages), supplemented by a selection of grappas, single-malt scotches, and cognacs. A dessert of crema bruccioto (white-chocolate custard with a caramelized sugar glaze) is recommended. There's free self-parking; valet parking is $4.

Moderate

CHEF MICKEY'S, at Walt Disney World Village. Tel. 828-3830.

Cuisine: AMERICAN **Reservations:** Recommended.

$ Prices: Appetizers $3.95–$6.95; main courses $5.75–$10.25 at lunch, $9.75–$15 at dinner; breakfast fare $1.95–$6.25. AE, MC, V.

Open: Breakfast 9–11am; lunch 11:30am–2pm; dinner 5–10pm.

Rustically attractive, Chef Mickey's plant-filled interior has ficus trees growing toward a skylight and exposed brick walls hung with signed photographs of Disney characters. About half the seats overlook Buena Vista Lagoon. One dining area has redwood-paneled walls and a beamed pine cathedral ceiling; another offers a view of white-hatted chefs at work in an exhibition kitchen. And should you have to wait for a table (only 20% of tables are alloted via reservations, with the rest reserved for walk-ins, but you can reserve up to 30 days in advance; walk-ins should arrive early to avoid a wait), you can do so in a lounge where kids can watch cartoons on a large-screen TV and adults can watch sporting events at the bar. Mickey turns out some pretty terrific food here, and, at dinner, he table-hops greeting patrons.

My favorite appetizer here is light and fluffy crabcakes Boca, to which nuances of Tobasco, cayenne, mustard, and Worcestershire sauce add zest. An excellent entree choice is the cheesy crisp-baked salmon lasagne served in a spinach/pine-nut sauce. Or you might opt for fork-tender barbecued ribs with grilled corn (served in the husk), a big slab of homemade cornbread, and fabulous coleslaw. Leave room for dessert—peach cobbler topped with vanilla bean ice cream or a very good key lime pie. There's a full bar and a low-priced menu for kids. Parking is free (use Lot A).

FIREWORKS FACTORY, 1630 Lake Buena Vista Dr., Pleasure Island. Tel. 934-8989.

Cuisine: AMERICAN REGIONAL. **Reservations:** Recommended.

$ Prices: Appetizers $4.95–$8.95; main courses $5.95–$9.95 at lunch, $13.95–$19.95 at dinner. AE, MC, V.

Open: 11:30am–11:30pm (dinner served from 4pm, with light fare and drinks served to 2am).

Housed in a high-ceilinged corrugated-tin warehouse, its exposed brick walls hung with neon beer signs and advertisements for fireworks, the Factory is an "explosively" exuberant setting for casual dining. Dozens of unopened boxes of beer are strewn around the floor, missile fireworks are prominently displayed, and the bar area offers a basketball set-up, a bowling machine, pinball, video games, and sporting events aired on TV monitors. Tables are covered with bright plaid plastic.

Lunch or dinner, you might start off with an order of spicy wings tossed in Louisiana hot sauce and served with bleu cheese dressing. Follow it up with a down-home barbecue trio: shredded pork loin, sliced brisket, and shredded chicken, served with corn on the cob and fries. And for dessert, a giant tollhouse cookie topped with vanilla ice cream and hot fudge. In addition to "dynamite" cocktails and wines, the Fireworks Factory offers over 45 varieties of domestic and imported beer, ale, and stout, including several microbrewery selections. There's free self-parking; valet parking is $4.

MEALS WITH DISNEY CHARACTERS

Especially for the 10-and-under set, it's a thrill to dine in a restaurant where costumed Disney characters show up to greet the customers, sign autographs, and pose in family photos. And for adults, it's lots of fun to watch the kids going nuts over Mickey or Donald. The following restaurants throughout the Walt Disney World complex offer character breakfasts and dinners. All accept American Express, MasterCard, and VISA.

FROMMER'S COOL FOR KIDS: RESTAURANTS

In a town where the major attractions are amusement parks, just about every restaurant is child-oriented. Some notables:

The Sci-Fi Dine-In Theater Restaurant *(see p. 259)* A drive-in movie theater where you sit in actual convertible cars and the servers are on roller skates. At Disney-MGM Studios.

Chef Mickey's *(see pp. 262 and 263)* Great food pleases mom and dad, and kids love the nightly appearances by Mickey Mouse. If you want to linger over dinner, the kids can retreat to a lounge where cartoons are shown.

Mickey's Tropical Revue *(see p. 264)* Not just a meal but a Polynesian floor show featuring Minnie, Mickey, Pluto, and Goofy along with a cast of South Sea Islanders. At Disney's Polynesian Resort in Luau Cove. Character breakfasts here, too.

Cape May Café Clambake Buffet *(see p. 263)* This old-fashioned nightly clambake at Disney's Beach Club Resort is fun for the whole family.

Hoop-Dee-Doo Musical Revue *(see p. 297)* I've never met anyone who didn't have a great time at this whoopin' and hollerin' country music dinner show in Fort Wilderness's Pioneer Hall.

CAPE MAY CAFE, at Disney's Beach Club Resort, 1800 EPCOT Resorts Blvd. Tel. 934-8000.

The Cape May Café, a delightful New England–themed dining room, serves lavish buffet character breakfasts daily. Food tables are laden with quiches, waffles, hot and cold cereals, egg dishes, roast beef hash, bread pudding, fruit fritters, cheese blintzes, bacon and cheese crêpes, biscuits with sausage gravy, fresh-baked pastries and muffins, and many other goodies. Admiral Goofy and his crew—Chip 'n' Dale, Pluto, Captain Hook, and Smee (exact characters may vary)—are hosts. Adults pay $12.95 and children 3–11 are charged $7.95; kids under 3 eat free. Reservations are not accepted; arrive early to avoid a wait.

CHEF MICKEY'S, at Walt Disney World Village. Tel. 828-3830.

At the very attractive Chef Mickey's, Mickey is on hand to greet dinner patrons each night from 5 to 10pm. Reservations are suggested, although only 20% of the tables are allotted via reservations, with the rest reserved for walk-ins. On the other hand, you can reserve up to 30 days in advance. Walk-ins should arrive early to avoid a wait. This is an especially appealing choice, since there's first-rate food for adults, and the menu also offers burgers, chicken bits, and other kid pleasers in the $3.25–$3.75 range.

THE CONTEMPORARY CAFE, at Disney's Contemporary Resort, 4600 N. World Dr. Tel. 824-1000.

The Contemporary Café—an indoor formal garden with faux topiary, trelliswork, planter dividers, and tables under bright-yellow canvas umbrellas—is the setting for buffet character breakfasts from 8 to 11am daily. On hand to meet, greet, and mingle with guests are Goofy, Pluto, Chip 'n' Dale, Tigger, and Prince John (from *Robin Hood*). The prix-fixe buffet ($10.95 for adults, $7.95 for children 3–9, free for kids under 3) features a wide array of breakfast foods: eggs, potatoes, French toast, pancakes, bacon and sausage, apple cobbler, bread pudding, and much more. Reservations are not accepted; arrive early to avoid a wait.

EMPRESS LILLY, at Walt Disney World Village. Tel. 828-3900.

Five opulently Victorian dining rooms aboard the *Empress Lilly*, a plushly furnished triple-decker paddlewheeler docked on Lake Buena Vista, are used for morning character breakfasts. There are two seatings daily, at 8:30 and 10am (arrive at least 20 minutes ahead of time). A prix-fixe menu ($10.95 for adults, $7.95 for children 3–9, free for kids under 3) features sausage and eggs and a Mickey-shaped waffle. Donald, Mickey, Minnie, and Pluto are on hand to greet the guests, and Disney movie music and friendly servers enhance the party atmosphere. The restaurant is amenable to menu substitutions for fussy kids, and adults who want a lighter meal can also ask for a fruit and yogurt plate. Reservations are essential, and can be made any time in advance; do so as soon as you decide the dates of your trip.

LUAU COVE, at Disney's Polynesian Resort, 1600 Seven Seas Dr. Tel. W-DISNEY.

Luau Cove, an exotic open-air facility, is the setting for an island-themed character show called *Mickey's Tropical Revue* daily at 4:30pm. It's an abbreviated verson of the Polynesian Luau Dinner Show described below in "Evening Entertainment," featuring Polynesian dancers along with Mickey, Minnie, Pluto, and Goofy. Your prix-fixe meal ($27 for adults, $21 for ages 12–20, $12 for ages 3–11, free for kids under 3) includes tropical fruit salad, a trio of entrees (seafood stir-fry, barbecued ribs, or teriyaki chicken), rice, coconut-almond bread with honey butter, and a Disney character ice-cream bar. Guests are presented with shell leis on entering. Reserve far in advance.

1900 PARK FARE, at Disney's Grand Floridian Beach Resort, 4001 Grand Floridian Way. Tel. 824-2383.

This exquisitely elegant Disney resort hosts character meals in the festive exposition-themed 1900 Park Fare, decorated with old-fashioned carved wooden merry-go-round animals, colorful flags and banners, antique toys, and circus-themed paintings. Big Bertha—a French band organ that plays pipes, drums, bells, cymbals, castanets, and xylophone—provides music. Mary Poppins, Winnie the Pooh, Goofy, Pluto, Chip 'n' Dale, and Minnie Mouse appear at elaborate buffet breakfasts served daily between 7:30am and noon. An assortment of fresh fruits, breakfast meats, egg dishes, home-fries, pancakes, French toast, waffles, fresh-baked pastries and muffins, bagels and creamcheese, hot and cold cereals, cheese blintzes, and fruit cobblers are featured. Adults pay $14.75, children 3–11 are charged $9.75; kids under 3 eat free.

Mickey and Minnie appear at nightly buffets (featuring prime rib, stuffed pork loin, fresh fish, and more) from 5 to 9pm. Adults pay $17.95, children 3–11 are charged $9.75, and kids under 3 eat free. Reservations are essential for both meals.

PAPEETE BAY VERANDAH, at Disney's Polynesian Resort, 1600 Seven Seas Dr. Tel. 824-1391.

The Polynesian Resort hosts Minnie's Menehune Character Breakfast buffets daily from 7:30 to 10:30am in the French Polynesian-themed Papeete Bay Verandah. A wide selection of hot and cold breakfast foods is featured: omelets, French toast, biscuits, cereals, fresh-baked pastries, fresh fruits, and more. Adults pay $10.95, children 3–11 are charged $7.95; kids under 3 eat free. Minnie, Goofy, and Chip 'n' Dale appear. Reservations are essential.

WATERCRESS CAFE, at the Buena Vista Palace, 1900 Buena Vista Dr. Tel. 827-2727.

The plant-filled Watercress Café—with paintings of parrots and flamingos adorning peach stucco walls and large windows overlooking Lake Buena Vista—is the setting for Sunday-morning character breakfasts and Friday-night character dinners featuring Minnie, Goofy, and Pluto. You can order à la carte or buffet meals. The dinner buffet (6:30 to 9pm) centers on prime rib, with pasta and salad bars, priced at $12.95 for adults, $5.95 for kids 4–12, and free for kids under 4. The breakfast buffet (8 to 10:30am) is $9.75 for adults, $4.95 for kids 4–12, and free for kids under 4. Reservations are not accepted; arrive early to avoid a wait.

INTERNATIONAL DRIVE: OUTSIDE WALT DISNEY WORLD

DUX, in the Peabody Hotel, 9801 International Dr. Tel. 345-4550.

Cuisine: AMERICAN REGIONAL. **Reservations:** Recommended.

$ Prices: Appetizers $5.50–$5.95 at lunch, $7.50–$13.25 at dinner; main courses $8.75–$12.50 at lunch, $22–$28.50 at dinner. AE, CB, DC, DISC, ER, JCB, MC, OPT, V.

Open: Lunch Mon–Fri 11:30am–2pm; dinner Mon–Sat 6–11pm.

Named for the hotel's signature ducks that parade ceremoniously into the lobby each morning to Sousa's *King Cotton* march, this is one of Central Florida's most highly acclaimed restaurants. Decorated in shimmery earth tones, it offers a deluxe setting, with ornate mirrors, soft lighting emanating from amber-shaded sconces, and textured gold walls hung with watercolors representing 72 ducks! Diners are comfortably ensconced in upholstered bamboo chairs and cushioned banquettes at candlelit, white-linened tables set with flowers. There's free self-parking and validated valet parking.

Chef Tom Condron maintains an herb garden on the premises, serves only free-range birds and veal, imports truffles from France and caviar from Russia, and pays local farmers to grow baby vegetables and other produce to his specifications. His menu changes seasonally. At a recent dinner, I started off with an appetizer of sautéed leeks, wild mushrooms, and sherried lobster meat wrapped in a phyllo-dough pocket, garnished with lobster slices and caviar, and finished with a buttery basil–white wine coulis. An entree of mesquite-grilled Gulf Coast snapper was served with applewood-roasted corn salsa, slices of grilled balsamic-marinated Chinese eggplant, and puréed Washington cherries in a red Zinfandel sauce. Another of baked Atlantic salmon came wrapped in a crispy grated-potato crust on a platter arrayed with haricots verts, ragoût of pearl onions, roasted garlic, wild mushrooms, and an edible flower garnish. Dessert was a sublime trilogy of crème brûlées: one topped with fresh raspberries and sprigs of mint, a second flavored with coffee beans, and a third with candied ginger. An extensive, award-winning wine list is available. Lunch here is a simpler affair, at which you might opt for a mesquite-grilled sirloin burger on a sourdough bun or a salad of smoked chicken and noodles in a spicy peanut dressing.

EXPENSIVE

MING COURT, 9188 International Dr., between Sand Lake Rd. and the Beeline Expwy., just across from the Peabody Hotel. Tel. 363-0338.

Cuisine: CHINESE REGIONAL. **Reservations:** Recommended.

$ Prices: Appetizers $4.50–$6.50; dim sum items $1.95–$3.50; main courses $3.95–$8.95 at lunch, $12.95–$18.95 at dinner. AE, CB, DC, DISC, JCB, MC, V.

Open: Lunch daily 11am–2:30pm; dinner daily 4:30pm–midnight.

I was thrilled to find an Orlando restaurant whose culinary offerings are on a par with the finest Chinese haute-cuisine bastions of New York and California. The Ming Court is fronted by a serpentine "cloud wall" crowned by engraved sea-green Chinese tiles (it's a celestial symbol; you dine above the clouds here, like the gods). Its candlelit interior is stunningly decorated in soft earth tones (subtle hues of rust, ochre, and tan) with unfinished oak wainscoting. Glass-walled terrace rooms overlook lotus ponds filled with colorful koi, a plant-filled area under a lofty skylight ceiling evokes a starlit Ming Dynasty courtyard, and an interior green-roofed gazebo that seats 8–10 people is perfect for small private parties. Beautiful Chinese paintings and pottery are on display, and between 7 and 10pm nightly a musician plays classical Chinese music on a *zheng* (a long zither). Self-parking is free.

The menu offers specialties from diverse regions of China, all of them uniquely spiced and sauced and prepared with the finest ingredients (including fresh Florida fish and seafood). Begin by ordering a variety of appetizers such as wok-charred Mandarin pot stickers, crispy spring rolls stuffed with wood ear cabbage, and wok-smoked shiitake mushrooms topped with sautéed scallions. Entrees will open up new culinary vistas to even the most sophisticated diners. Lightly battered deep-fried chicken breast is served with a delicate lemon-tangerine sauce. Szechuan charcoal-grilled filet mignon, marinated in olive oil and crushed herbs, is topped with a toasted onion/garlic/chili sauce and served with stir-fried julienne vegetables. Lamb chops, topped with finely chopped canteloupe, arrive atop broad rice noodles in coconut-cream/Madras-curry sauce studded with pine nuts. And crispy stir-fried jumbo Szechuan shrimp is enhanced by a light fresh tomato sauce nuanced with saké, ginger, chili oil, scallion, garlic, and cilantro. Saturday and Sunday at lunch, you can order from over 40 dim sum items in addition to menu offerings. An extensive wine list includes everything from Pouilly-Fuissé to Chinese rice wines, plum wines, and saké. And as a concession to Western palates, the Ming Court features sumptuous desserts such as a moist cake layered with Mandarin oranges, key lime, and fresh whipped cream in orange-vanilla sauce.

MODERATE

B-LINE DINER, at the Peabody Hotel, 9801 International Dr. Tel. 345-4460.

Cuisine: AMERICAN. **Reservations:** Not accepted.

$ Prices: Appetizers $5.50–$8.25; main courses $3.25–$8.25 at breakfast, $6.75–$9.50 at lunch, $7.25–$17.25 at dinner. AE, CB, DC, DISC, ER, JCB, MC, OPT, V.

Open: Daily 24 hours.

This popular local eatery is of the nouvelle art deco diner genre, which is to say that it's an idealized version of America's ubiquitous roadside establishments. A high-gloss peach-and-gray interior, with black-and-white tile floor, gleams with chrome edging that adorns everything from a cove ceiling to peach Formica tables. Seating is in comfortable leatherette booths or Breuer chairs, a jukebox plays oldies tunes, and a long black marble-top counter (with glass-top cake trays) faces an open kitchen. Just your average greasy spoon (not!).

The menu, in the shape of a Wurlitzer jukebox, offers sophisticated versions of diner food such as turkey meatloaf served with mashed potatoes, fresh vegetables, and cranberry relish; spicy Jamaican jerk chicken wings; a ham-and-cheese sandwich (on a baguette); and sautéed pork medallions with Thai sauce and papaya salsa. Other items—such as grilled tuna with vegetable couscous and red pepper coulis, classic French onion soup, and a falafel sandwich—bear no relation to traditional diner fare. You may have noticed a glass display case of scrumptious fresh-baked desserts when you came in, everything from banana cream pie to white-chocolate/Grand Marnier mousse cake. The dessert area adjoins B-Line Express, a 24-hour take-out counter. There's a full bar. And kids get their own low-priced menu, a coloring/activities book, and crayons. There's free self-parking and validated valet parking.

5. WALT DISNEY WORLD ATTRACTIONS

Walt Disney World, attracting more than 13 million visitors annually, is one of the world's most popular travel destinations. And why not? It provides a welcome retreat into a star-spangled all-American fantasyland where wonderment, human progress, and old-fashioned family fun are the major themes. And these themes are presented in spectacular parades, dazzling fireworks displays, 3-D and 360° movies, and adventure-filled journeys through time and space. Though it's not inexpensive, you'll seldom hear people complain about not getting their money's worth at WDW. Disney delivers!

The Magic Kingdom opened in 1971. Later additions include EPCOT Center, where guests take exhilarating voyages around the world and into the future; Disney–MGM Studios, centered on "Hollywood Boulevard" and providing a thrilling behind-the-scenes look at motion-picture and TV studios; Pleasure Island, an ongoing street festival in a six-acre complex of nightclubs and shops; the Walt Disney

Village Marketplace, a charming lakeside enclave of shops and restaurants; Typhoon Lagoon, a 56-acre water park where you can catch the world's largest man-made waves or plummet down steep water flumes; River Country, a smaller water park; and Discovery Island, an utterly delightful nature preserve and aviary.

WDW ORIENTATION

TIPS FOR PLANNING YOUR TRIP How you plan your time at Walt Disney World will depend on such factors as the ages of the children in your party, what you've seen on previous visits, your specific interests, and whether you're traveling at a peak time or off-season (when lines are shorter and you can cram more in). Planning, however, is essential. Unless you're staying for considerably more than a week, you can't possibly experience all the rides, shows, and attractions here, not to mention the vast array of recreational facilities. You'll only wear yourself to a frazzle trying—it's better to follow a relaxed itinerary, including leisurely meals and recreational activities, than to make a demanding job out of trying to see everything.

Information Call or write the **Walt Disney World Co.,** P.O. Box 10000, Lake Buena Vista, FL 32830-1000 (tel. 407/824-4321), for a copy of the very informative *Walt Disney World Vacation Guide,* an invaluable planning aid. Inquire about any special events that will be on during your stay. Once you've arrived in town, guest services and concierge desks in all area hotels—especially Disney properties and official hotels—have up-to-the-minute information about what's going on in the parks. Stop by to ask questions and pick up literature. If your hotel doesn't have this information, call 824-4321. There are also **information locations** in each park—at City Hall in the Magic Kingdom, Earth Station in EPCOT Center, and the Guest Services Building in Disney–MGM Studios.

Create an itinerary for each day Read the *Vacation Guide* and the detailed descriptions in this book of every nook and cranny of Walt Disney World, and plan your visit to include all shows and attractions that pique your interest and excitement. It's a good idea to make a daily itinerary, putting these in some kind of sensible geographical sequence so you're not zigzagging all over the place. Familiarize yourself in advance with the layout of each park. Schedule in sit-down shows, recreational activities (a boat ride or swim late in the afternoon can be wonderfully refreshing), and at least some unhurried meals. (My suggested itineraries are given below.)

Buy tickets in advance You can purchase four- or five-day passes (see details below) at the Orlando airport, at your hotel, or by contacting the Central Reservations Office (tel. 407/824-8000) prior to your trip (allow 21 days for processing your request). In the latter case there's a $2 postage-and-handling charge. Of course, you can always purchase tickets at any of the parks, but why stand on an avoidable line? Note: One-day tickets can be purchased only at park entrances.

In the Parks Upon entering any of the three major Disney parks, you'll be given an **entertainment schedule** and a comprehensive **park guidebook,** which contains a map of the park and lists all attractions, shops, shows, and restaurants. If by some fluke you haven't obtained these, they're available at the information locations mentioned above. If you've formulated an itinerary prior to arrival, you already know the major shows (check show schedules for additional ideas) you want to see during the day and what arrangements you need to make. If you haven't done this, use your early arrival time, while waiting for the park to open, to figure out which shows to attend, and, where necessary, make reservations for them as soon as the gates swing open. Some restaurant reservations also need to be made first thing in the morning (see "Dining" and "Evening Entertainment" in this chapter for details).

Leaving the Parks If you leave any of the parks and plan to return later in the day, be sure to get your hand stamped on exiting.

Best Days to Visit The busiest days at the Magic Kingdom and EPCOT Center are Monday through Wednesday; at Disney–MGM Studios, Wednesday through Friday. Surprisingly, weekends are the least busy at all parks. In peak seasons, especially, arrange your visits accordingly.

Arrive Early Always arrive at the parks a good 30–45 minutes before opening time, thus avoiding a traffic jam entering the park and a long line at the gate. Early arrival also lets you experience one or two major attractions before big lines form. In high season parking lots sometimes fill up and you may even have to wait to get in. Longest lines in all parks are between 11am and 4pm.

Parking Parking (free to guests at WDW resorts) otherwise costs $4 per day no matter how many parks you visit. Be sure to note your parking location before leaving your car. There are special lots for the handicapped at each park (call 824-4321 for details). Don't worry about parking far from the entrance gates; trams constantly ply the route.

The Easy Way Staying at Disney hostelries simplifies many of the above tasks and procedures. See the full list of perks for Disney and "official" hotel guests above under "Accommodations."

OPERATING HOURS Hours of operation vary somewhat throughout the year. The **Magic Kingdom** and **Disney–MGM Studios** are generally open from 9am to 7pm, with extended hours (sometimes as late as midnight) during major holidays and the summer months. **EPCOT Center** hours are generally 9am to 9pm, once again with extended holiday hours. **Typhoon Lagoon** is open from 10am to 5pm most of the year (with extended hours during some holidays), 9am to 8pm in summer. **River Country** and **Discovery Island** are open from 10am to 5pm most of the year (with extended hours during some holidays), 10am to 7pm in summer.

Note: EPCOT and MGM sometimes open a half hour or more before posted time. Keep in mind, too, that Disney hotel guests enjoy early admission to the Magic Kingdom on designated days for a full lineless hour.

TICKETS There are several ticket options. Most people get the best value from four- and five-day passes, which do not have to be used on consecutive days. Prices quoted below include sales tax, and kids under age 3 are admitted free to all parks.

The **Four-Day Super Pass** provides unlimited admission to the Magic Kingdom, EPCOT Center, and Disney–MGM Studios on any four days and includes unlimited use of the WDW transportation system. Cost is $132 for ages 10 and over, $103.50 for children 3–9.

The **Five-Day Super Duper Pass** provides unlimited admission to the Magic Kingdom, EPCOT Center, and Disney–MGM Studios on any five days and includes unlimited use of the WDW transportation system, *plus* unlimited admission to River Country, Typhoon Lagoon, Discovery Island, and Pleasure Island for a period of seven days beginning with the first date stamped. It costs $179.60 for ages 10 and over, $142.60 for children 3–9.

A **one-day, one-park ticket** for the Magic Kingdom, EPCOT Center, or Disney–MGM Studios is $35.90 for ages 10 and over, $28.50 for children 3–9.

A **one-day ticket to Typhoon Lagoon** is $21.75 for adults, $17.50 for children 3–9.

A **one-day ticket to River Country** is $14.05 for adults, $11.15 for children 3–9.

A **one-day ticket to Discovery Island** is $9 for adults, $5.05 for children 3–9.

A **combined one-day ticket for River Country and Discovery Island** is $17.75 for adults, $13 for children 3–9.

If you're staying at any Walt Disney World Resort or official hotel, you are eligible for a money-saving **Be Our Guest Pass** priced according to length of stay. It also offers special perks.

If you plan on visiting Walt Disney World more than one time during the year, inquire about a money-saving **annual pass.**

SUGGESTED ITINERARIES

You won't see all the attractions at any of the parks in a single day. Read through the descriptions, decide which are musts for you, and try to get to them. My favorite rides and attractions are starred. I stress once more—it's more enjoyable to keep a relaxed pace than to race around like a maniac trying to do it all.

A DAY IN THE MAGIC KINGDOM Get to the park well before opening time, tickets in hand. When the gates open, head for the kiosk just outside Disney Collectibles and make a reservation for a lunchtime show at the Diamond Horseshoe Jamboree. Then hightail it to Frontierland and ride Splash Mountain before long lines form. When you come off, it will still be early enough to beat the lines at another major attraction. Double back to Adventureland and do Pirates of the Caribbean. Then relax and take it slow. Complete whatever else interests you in Adventureland, and enjoy Frontierland attractions until it's time for your lunch show. After lunch, continue visiting Frontierland attractions as desired, or proceed to the Hall of Presidents and the Haunted Mansion in Liberty Square. By 2:30pm (earlier in peak seasons), you should snag a seat on the curb in Liberty Square along the parade route. After the parade, continue around the park taking in Fantasyland and Tomorrowland attractions. If SpectroMagic is on during your stay, don't miss it.

If you have little kids (age 8 and under) in your party, after making your lunch reservations for Diamond Horseshoe Jamboree, take the WDW Railroad from Main Street to Mickey's Starland to see the show. Work your way through Fantasyland until lunch. After lunch, visit the Country Bear Jamboree in Frontierland and proceed to Adventureland for the Jungle Cruise, Swiss Family Treehouse, and Tropical Serenade. Once again, stop in good time to get parade seats (in Frontierland). Little kids need to sit right up front to see everything. That's a long enough day for most little kids, and your best plan is to go back to your hotel for a nap or swim. If, however, you wish to continue, return to Frontierland and/or Fantasyland for the rides you didn't complete earlier.

A DAY IN EPCOT CENTER As above, arrive early, tickets in hand. Make your first stop at Earth Station to make lunch reservations at the San Angel Inn Restaurant in Mexico for about 1pm. If you like, also make dinner reservations at the World Showcase restaurant of your choice. (Note: Disney hotel guests can make these in advance.) Then head for the lagoon and take the launch to Germany. While cruising the lagoon, check your show schedule, and decide which shows to incorporate into your day. Don't stop in Germany. First take in Italy and the American Adventure (check show times for the latter) before working your way back counterclockwise through the Germany, China, and Norway pavilions. You should arrive in Mexico just about in time for a leisurely lunch, after which you can visit its attractions. After lunch, continue on the same side of the park, visiting World of Motion, Horizons, Wonders of Life, the Universe of Energy, and CommuniCore East in Future World. Frankly, unless crowds are very light, you can't see everything in all these showcase pavilions and themed areas in one day. So rather than do it all, hit the highlights you don't want to miss. If you have only one day at EPCOT, head over to the Odyssey Restaurant (or any other you like) for dinner and stay for IllumiNations (usually at 9pm, but check your schedule). Otherwise, leave the park, have dinner elsewhere (see "Dining" and "Evening Entertainment" for suggestions), and see IllumiNations your second night.

If You Have Two Days On your second day make your first stop at Earth Station to make dinner reservations for the World Showcase restaurant of your choice. Check your show schedule, and make your reservations early enough to allow time to find a seat on the lagoon at least a half hour before IllumiNations begins. Then take the launch across the lagoon to Morocco, walk to Japan, and after seeing its attractions (don't miss the show here), continue clockwise to Morocco, France, the United Kingdom, and Canada. Stop for a light early lunch at a casual restaurant, perhaps Au Petit Café in France or the Buffeteria in Canada (no reservations required at either). After lunch, visit Journey into Imagination, The Land, the Living Seas, Spaceship Earth, and CommuniCore West, have dinner, and watch IllumiNations.

A DAY AT DISNEY–MGM STUDIOS THEME PARK Since showtimes change seasonally, you may have to revise this itinerary a bit when you visit. Upon entering the park, stop at the Hollywood Brown Derby (details in "Dining") and make reservations for a 1pm lunch. Then, if the new Twilight Zone of Terror is open (it's scheduled for the summer of 1994) make a beeline for it, as it will no doubt have the longest lines as the day progresses. Otherwise, head over to the Magic of Disney Animation, followed by the Voyage of the Little Mermaid, the Backstage Studio Tour, and, if time allows, Inside the Magic, prior to lunch. After lunch, do the Great Movie Ride, Superstar

Television, the Monster Sound Show, Indiana Jones Epic Stunt Spectacular, Jim Henson's Muppet Vision 3D movie (not to be missed), and Star Tours, ending up at Beauty and the Beast in the Backlot Theater. You may have to make some adjustments to include the Aladdin's Royal Caravan parade (preferably in the afternoon); check your show schedule for times. In peak seasons, stay on for fireworks.

THE MAGIC KINGDOM

Centered around Cinderella's Castle, the Magic Kingdom occupies about 100 acres, with 45 major attractions and numerous restaurants and shops in seven themed sections or "lands." From the parking lot, you have to take a short monorail or ferry ride to the Magic Kingdom entrance. During peak attendance times, arrive at the Magic Kingdom no later than 8am to avoid long lines at these conveyances.

Upon entering the park, consult your ***Magic Kingdom Guidebook*** map to get your bearings. It details every shop, restaurant, and attraction in every land. Also consult your **entertainment schedule** to see what's on for the day.

If you have questions, all park employees are very knowledgeable, and **City Hall,** on your left as you enter, is both an information center, and, along with Mickey's Starland, a likely place to meet up with costumed characters. There's a stroller-rental shop just after the turnstiles to your right, and the Kodak Camera Center, near Town Square, supplies all conceivable photographic needs, including camera and Camcorder rentals and two-hour film developing.

MAIN STREET U.S.A.

Designed to replicate a typical turn-of-the-century American street, albeit one that culminates in a 13th-century castle, this is the gateway to the Kingdom. Don't dawdle on Main Street when you enter the park; leave it for the end of the day when you're heading back to your hotel.

WALT DISNEY WORLD RAILROAD & OTHER MAIN STREET VEHICLES You can board an authentic 1928 steam-powered railroad here for a 15-minute journey through Adventureland (en route to stations in Frontierland and Mickey's Starland) and on to Tomorrowland. There are also horse-drawn trolleys, horseless carriages, jitneys, omnibuses, and fire engines plying the short route along Main Street from Town Square to Cinderella's Castle.

MAIN STREET CINEMA Main Street Cinema is an air-conditioned hexagonal theater where vintage black-and-white Disney cartoons (including *Steamboat Willie* from 1928, in which Mickey and Minnie debuted) are aired continually on six screens. Viewers have to watch these standing—there are no seats.

PENNY ARCADE At this old-fashioned penny arcade, even the prices evoke nostalgia. Its 1¢ hand-cranked Cail-o-scopes, test-your-grip machines, old pinball games, Kiss-o-Meter, Gypsy fortune teller, and shooting gallery evoke pleasant childhood memories to those of a certain age and are a novelty to the Nintendo generation.

CINDERELLA'S CASTLE At the end of Main Street, in the center of the park, you'll come to a fairyland castle, 180 feet high and housing a restaurant (King Stefan's Banquet Hall) and shops. Mosaic murals inside depict the Cinderella story, and Disney family coats of arms are displayed. Cinderella herself, dressed for the ball, often makes appearances in the lobby area.

ADVENTURELAND

Cross a bridge to your left and stroll into an exotic jungle of lush tropical foliage, thatch-roofed huts, and carved totems. Amid dense vines and stands of palm and bamboo, drums are beating and swashbuckling adventures are taking place.

SWISS FAMILY TREEHOUSE This attraction is based on the 1960 Disney movie version of Johann Wyss's *Swiss Family Robinson,* about a shipwrecked family who created an ingenious dwelling in the branches of a sprawling banyan tree. Using materials and furnishings salvaged from their downed ship, the Robinsons created bedrooms, a kitchen, a library, and a living room. Visitors ascend the 50-foot tree for a close-up look into these rooms. Note the Rube Goldberg rope-and-bucket device with bamboo chutes that dips water from a stream and carries it to treetop chambers.

JUNGLE CRUISE What a cruise! In the course of about 10 minutes, your boat sails through an African veldt in the Congo, an Amazon rain forest, the Mekong River in Southeast Asia, and along the Nile. Lavish scenery, with ropes of hanging vines, cascading waterfalls, and lush foliage (most of it real), includes dozens of Audio-Animatronic™ birds and animals—elephants, zebras, lions, giraffes, crocodiles, tigers, even fluttering butterflies. On the shore you'll pass an Asian temple cave guarded by snakes and a jungle camp taken over by apes. But the adventures aren't all on shore. Passengers are menaced by everything from water-spouting elephants to fierce warriors who attack with spears.

PIRATES OF THE CARIBBEAN This is Disney magic at its best. You'll proceed through a long grottolike passageway to board a boat into a pitch-black cave where elaborate scenery and hundreds of Audio-Animatronic figures (including lifelike dogs, cats, chickens, and donkeys) depict a rambunctious pirate raid on a Caribbean town. To a background of cheerful "yo-ho-yo-ho" music, the sound of rushing waterfalls, squawking seagulls, and screams of terror, passengers view tableaux of fierce-looking pirates chasing maidens, swigging rum, looting, and plundering. This might be scary for kids under 5.

TROPICAL SERENADE In a large hexagonal Polynesian-style dwelling, 250 tropical birds, chanting totem poles, and singing flowers whistle, tweet, and warble songs such as "Let's All Sing Like the Birdies Sing." Highlights include a thunderstorm in the dark (the Gods are angry!), a light show over the fountain, and, of course, the famous "in the tiki, tiki, tiki, tiki, tiki room" song. You'll find yourself singing it all day. This is a must for young children.

FRONTIERLAND

From Adventureland, step into the wild and woolly past of the American frontier, where rough-and-tumble architecture runs to log cabins and rustic saloons, and the landscape is southwestern scrubby with mesquite, saguaro cactus, yucca, and prickly pear. Across the river is Tom Sawyer Island, reachable via log rafts.

SPLASH MOUNTAIN Themed after Walt Disney's 1946 film *Song of the South,* Splash Mountain is an enchanting journey in a hollowed-out log craft along the canals of a flooded mountain, past 26 brilliantly colored tableaux of backwoods swamps, bayous, spooky caves, and waterfalls. The music from the film forms a delightful audio backdrop. Your log craft twists, turns, and splashes—sometimes plummeting in total darkness—culminating in a thrilling five-story splashdown from mountaintop to briar-filled pond at 40 miles per hour!

BIG THUNDER MOUNTAIN RAILROAD This mining-disaster-themed roller coaster—its thrills deriving from hairpin turns and descents in the dark—is situated in a 200-foot-high redstone mountain with 2,780 feet of track winding through windswept canyons and bat-filled caves. You'll board a runaway train that careens through the ribs of a dinosaur, under a thundering waterfall, past spewing geysers and bubbling mudpots, and over a bottomless volcanic pool. Riders are threatened by flash floods, earthquakes, rickety bridges, and avalanches. Audio-Animatronic™ characters (such as the longjohn-clad fellow navigating the floodwaters in a bathtub) enhance the scenic backdrop, as does a wealth of authentic antique mining equipment.

DIAMOND HORSESHOE JAMBOREE This 40-minute show provides an opportunity to sit down in air-conditioned comfort and enjoy a rousing western revue. The "theater" is a re-creation of a turn-of-the-century saloon. Owner/bartender Sam plays the washboard, tells silly jokes, and shoots at the audience (with a water gun). Lily (a Mae West type) and her troupe of dancehall girls do a can-can (which Sam, in drag, joins in). And the cowboys perform feats of fast fiddling and foot-stomping acrobatic dances. There are five shows daily; plan on going around lunchtime so you can eat during the show. The menu features deli or peanut butter and jelly sandwiches served with chips. (Make reservations when you enter the park just outside Disneyana Collectibles on the east side of Main Street in Town Square.) Seating is reserved, so you can arrive shortly before showtime.

COUNTRY BEAR JAMBOREE Call us cornballs. I've always loved the Country Bear Jamboree, a 15-minute show featuring a troupe of fiddlin', banjo strumming', harmonica playin' Audio-Animatronics™ bears belting out rollicking country tunes and crooning plaintive love songs. The chubby Trixie, decked out in a frilly sundress and straw hat for a solitary picnic, laments lost love as she sings, "If heartaches were fried chicken, I could sell 'em by the pound." Teddi Barra, in raingear and galoshes, descends from the ceiling in a swing to perform "Singing in the Rain." A special holiday show plays throughout the Christmas season each year.

TOM SAWYER ISLAND Board Huck Finn's raft for a one-minute float across the river to the densely forested Tom Sawyer Island, where kids can explore the narrow passages of Injun Joe's Cave (complete with scary sound effects like whistling wind), a walk-through windmill, a serpentine abandoned mine, or Fort Sam Clemens. Narrow winding dirt paths lined with oaks, pines, and sycamores create an authentic backwoods island feel. You might combine this attraction with lunch at Aunt Polly's restaurant, which has outdoor tables on a porch overlooking the river.

FRONTIERLAND SHOOTIN' ARCADE Combining state-of-the-art electronics with a traditional shooting-gallery format, this vast arcade presents an array of 97 targets (slow-moving ore cars, buzzards, gravediggers) in a three-dimensional 1850s gold-mining town scenario. To keep the western ambience authentic, new-fangled electronic firing mechanisms loaded with infrared bullets are concealed in genuine Hawkins 54-caliber buffalo rifles. When you hit a target, elaborate sound and motion gags are set off. Here, 50¢ buys you 25 shots.

LIBERTY SQUARE

Serving as a transitional area between Frontierland and Fantasyland, Liberty Square evokes 18th-century America with Georgian architecture, Colonial Williamsburg–type shops, and neat flower beds bordering manicured lawns. You might encounter a fife-and-drum corps marching along Liberty Square's cobblestone streets.

THE HALL OF PRESIDENTS In this red-brick colonial hall, a giant bell suspended in its tower, all American presidents—from George Washington to Bill Clinton (actually, he's still being sculpted at this writing)—are represented by Audio-Animatronic™ figures that act out important events in the nation's history, from the signing of the Constitution through the space age. The show begins with a film, projected on a 180° screen, about the importance of the Constitution.

THE HAUNTED MANSION What better way to exhibit Disney special-effects wizardry than a haunted mansion? Its ambience enhanced by inky darkness, spooky music, eerie howling, and mysterious screams and rappings, this mansion is replete with bizarre scenes and objects: a ghostly banquet and ball, a graveyard band, a suit of armor that comes alive, cobweb-covered chandeliers, luminous spiders, a talking head in a crystal ball, weird flying objects, and much more. At the end of the ride, a ghost joins you in your car. The experience is more amusing than terrifying, so you can take small children inside.

BOAT RIDES A steam-powered sternwheeler called the *Richard F. Irvine* and two Mike Fink Keel Boats (the *Bertha Mae* and the *Gullywhumper*) depart from Liberty Square for scenic cruises along the Rivers of America. Both ply the identical route and make a restful interlude for foot-weary parkgoers.

FANTASYLAND

The attractions in this happy "land"—themed after such Disney film classics as *Snow White* and *Peter Pan*—are especially popular with young visitors. If your kids are 8 or under, you might want to make it your first stop in the Magic Kingdom. Note: Two rides here—Snow White's Adventures and Mr. Toad's Wild Ride—are a bit scary. If your under-5s frighten easily, skip them.

MAD TEA PARTY This is a traditional amusement park ride à la Disney with an *Alice in Wonderland* theme. Riders sit in oversize pink teacups on saucers that careen around a circular platform, tilt, and spin. Believe it or not, this can be a pretty wild ride or a tame one—it depends on how much you spin (a factor under your control via a wheel in the cup).

MR. TOAD'S WILD RIDE This ride is based on the 1949 Disney film *The Adventures of Ichabod and Mr. Toad*, which was itself based on one of my favorite stories, the divine *Wind in the Willows*. Riders navigate a series of dark rooms, hurtling into solid objects (a fireplace, a bookcase, a haystack) and through barn doors into a coop of squawking chickens. They're menaced by falling suits of armor, snorting bulls, and an oncoming locomotive in a pitch-black tunnel, and are sent to jail (for car theft), to hell (complete with pitchfork-wielding demons), and through a fiery volcano.

20,000 LEAGUES UNDER THE SEA Based on the Jules Verne classic, this submarine voyage travels beneath the waters of Fantasyland's lagoon. Via portholes, passengers observe undersea vegetation and creatures—talking fish, seahorses, mermaids, and sea serpents among them. You'll pass the classical remains of the lost continent of Atlantis and experience an underwater volcano and a storm at sea.

SNOW WHITE'S ADVENTURES You might not remember that *Snow White*, originally a Grimm's fairy tale, was a little scary, and this boat ride in the dark concentrates on some of its more sinister elements—the evil queen, the cackling witch offering a poisoned apple to Snow White, skeletons in cages, and a crocodile lurching at riders. Even the trees are menacing.

MAGIC JOURNEYS This 16-minute-long 3-D film beautifully utilizes the medium's potential. It's a dreamily delightful journey of the imagination seen through the eyes of five children who run through a meadow and blow dandelion spores toward the audience, fly a kite on the beach, swim underwater (3-D snorkeling), and soar over mountaintops. In a circus sequence, a lion jumps through a flaming hoop right at you and a magician releases a flock of doves. There's a preshow at this attraction—an early 3-D Donald Duck cartoon made in 1953 called *Working for Peanuts*.

CINDERELLA'S GOLDEN CAROUSEL It's a beauty, built by Italian wood carvers in the Victorian tradition in 1917 and refurbished by Disney artists who added scenes from the Cinderella story. The band organ plays Disney classics such as "When You Wish Upon a Star."

DUMBO, THE FLYING ELEPHANT This is a very tame kiddie ride in which the cars—baby elephants (Dumbos)—go around and around in a circle gently rising and dipping. But it's very exciting for wee ones.

IT'S A SMALL WORLD You know the song—and if you don't, you will. It plays continually as you sail "around the world" through vast rooms designed to represent different countries. They're inhabited by appropriately costumed Audio-Animatronic™ dolls and animals, all singing "It's a small world after all . . ." in tiny doll-like voices. This cast of thousands includes Chinese acrobats, Russian kazatski dancers, Indian snake charmers, singing geese and windmills in Holland, Arabs on magic carpets, mountain goats in the Swiss Alps, African drummers, a Venetian gondolier, and Australian koalas. Cute. Very cute.

PETER PAN'S FLIGHT Riding in Captain Hook's ship, passengers careen through dark passages while experiencing the story of *Peter Pan*. The adventure begins in the Darlings' nursery, and includes a flight over nighttime London to Nevernever Land, where riders encounter mermaids, Indians, a ticking crocodile, the lost boys, Tinkerbell, Hook, Smee, and the rest—all to the movie music "You Can Fly, You Can Fly, You Can Fly." It's fun.

SKYWAY Its entrance close to Peter Pan's Flight, the Skyway is an aerial tramway to Tomorrowland, which makes continuous round-trips throughout the day.

MICKEY'S STARLAND

This small land, adjacent to Fantasyland, with a topiary maze of Disney characters and a block of Duckburg architecture, is accessible from Main Street via the Walt Disney World Railroad. It includes a Walk of Fame à la Hollywood, with Disney character "voiceprints" activated when you step on a star; a hands-on fire station; storefronts that come alive at the push of a button; Grandma Duck's Farm (a petting zoo); funhouse mirrors; a treehouse; and an interactive video area. And Mickey's house is here too, complete with living room TV tuned to the Disney Channel and his familiar outfits hanging on a clothesline in the yard.

The main attraction is **Mickey's Starland Show,** which is presented on a stage behind his house. The show, a lively musical, features the Goof Troop, Chip 'n' Dale, a perky hostess named CJ, and a vocal computer-control system called Dude. The story line: The show is about to start, but Mickey is missing! While CJ frantically searches for him, Goofy and his son, Max, accidentally get locked in the house. But it all works out in the end. The cheerful cartoon-inspired scenery, audience participation, and dramatic special effects are all designed to appeal to young viewers. After the show there's an opportunity to meet Mickey backstage.

TOMORROWLAND

This futuristic land focuses on space travel and exploration, but its early 1970s architecture and vision of the future have become as retro-looking today as an old "Star Trek" episode. Don't think the folks at Disney haven't noticed. At this writing, they're revamping the land to reflect the future as a galactic, science fiction–inspired community inhabited by humans, aliens, and robots. New versions of Star Jets and the Carousel of Progress are in the works. And a major new attraction will soon replace Mission to Mars. Called **Alien Encounter,** it will have an interplanetary teleportation apparatus capable of beaming living things between planets light years apart. Disney publicists promise a shocking close encounter with an extraterrestial!

MISSION TO MARS This may be closed by the time you read this prior to its replacement by Alien Encounter. If not, a brief description: After a preflight briefing at Mission Control, you board a space vehicle that NASA helped develop for a voyage to the Red Planet. This being a Disney voyage, it offers both educational tidbits (you'll learn that Mars has no oxygen and its surface temperatures are far below zero) and thrills (hyperspace jumps over enormous distances, a view of Olumpus Mons—a volcano 2½ times higher than Mount Everest—and a meteor shower that briefly knocks the vehicle out of control!).

★ **AMERICAN JOURNEYS** This 360°, 20-minute Circle-Vision film celebrates the grandeur and diversity of America's scenery, people, and culture. You first see the American landscape through the eyes of pioneers journeying in stagecoaches. Moving into the present, the film projects an array of breathtaking images—the Staten Island Ferry chugging across New York Harbor, a New England fishing village, a bluegrass music festival, Louisiana bayous and Dixieland bands, a midwestern wheat farm, the Colorado Rockies, hot-air balloonists over the Grand Canyon, California's redwood forests, and much more—culminating with fireworks over the Statue of Liberty to the music of "God Bless America."

DELTA DREAMFLIGHT The history and wonder of aviation—from barnstorming to space shuttles—is captured in this whimsical fly-through adventure presented by the official airline of Walt Disney World. High-tech special effects and 70mm live-action film footage add dramatic 3-D–style verisimilitude. Guests travel from a futuristic airport up a hillside to witness a flying circus, parachutists, stunt flyers, wing walkers, crop dusters, and aerial acrobats. The action moves on to the ocean-hopping age of commercial flight, and finally your vehicle is pulled into a giant jet engine and sent into hypersonic flight through psychedelic tunnels of light for a journey to outer space at a simulated speed of 300 m.p.h.

STARJETS This is a tame, typical amusement-park ride. The "jets" are on arms attached to a "missile" and they move up and down while traveling in a circle. It's being revamped at this writing.

WEDWAY PEOPLEMOVER A futuristic means of transportation, the PeopleMover has no engine. It works by electromagnets, emits no pollution, and uses little power. Narrated by a computer guide named Horack I, it offers an overhead look at Tomorrowland, including a pretty good preview of Space Mountain. If you're only in the Magic Kingdom for one day, this can be skipped.

CAROUSEL OF PROGRESS This 22-minute show in a revolving theater features an Audio-Animatronic™ family in various tableaux demonstrating a century of development in electric gadgetry and contraptions. Like Starjets, it's being modernized at this writing.

SKYWAY Its Tomorrowland entrance just west of Space Mountain, this aerial tramway to Fantasyland makes continuous round-trips throughout the day.

SPACE MOUNTAIN In a precursor to the concept of preshows, Space Mountain entertains visitors on its long lines with space age music, exhibits, and meteorites, shooting stars, and space debris whizzing about overhead. These "illusioneering" effects, enhanced by appropriate audio, continue during the ride itself, which is something like a cosmic roller coaster in the inky starlit blackness of outer space. Your rocket climbs high into the universe, before racing—at what feels like breakneck speed—through a serpentine complex of aerial galaxies, making thrilling hairpin turns and rapid plunges. The exit to Space Mountain is a moving sidewalk, past scenes of Audio-Animatronic™ figures who demonstrate the future uses of electronic media.

GRAND PRIX RACEWAY This is a great thrill for kids (including teens still waiting to get their drivers licenses) who get to put the pedal to the metal, steer, and *vroom* down a speedway in an actual gas-powered sports car. Maximum speed on the four-minute drive around the track is about 7 m.p.h., and kids have to be four feet four inches tall to drive alone.

PARADES, FIREWORKS & MORE

You'll get an *Entertainment Show Schedule* when you enter the park, which lists all kinds of special goings-on for the day. These include concerts (everything from steel drums to barbershop quartets), encounters with Disney characters, holiday events, and the three major happenings listed below.

THE 3 O'CLOCK PARADE You haven't really seen a parade until you've seen one at Walt Disney World. The spectacular daily parade kicks off at 3pm year-round on Main Street and meanders through Liberty Square and Frontierland. The route is outlined on your *Entertainment Show Schedule*. The only problem: Even in slow seasons you have to snag a seat along the curb a good half hour before it begins, and even earlier during peak travel times. (That's a long time to sit on a hard curb; consider packing inflatable pillows.) But the parade is worth a little discomfort. Disney characters from Mickey Mouse to Roger Rabbit are represented by 40-foot Macy's-style balloon figures on an around-the-world journey with elaborate floats, costumes, special effects, and a captivating cavalcade of acrobats, court jesters, stilt-walking harlequins, Mardi Gras bands, and storybook characters. Great music, too.

SPECTROMAGIC Along a darkened parade route (the same one as above), 72,000 watts of dazzling high-tech lighting effects (including holography) create a glowing array of pixies and peacocks, seahorses and winged horses, flower gardens and fountains. Roger Rabbit is the eccentric conductor of an orchestra producing a rainbow of musical notes that waft magically into the night air. There are dancing ostriches from *Fantasia,* whirling electric butterflies, flowers that evoke Tiffany glass, bejewelled coaches, luminescent ElectroMen atop spinning whirlyballs, and, of course, Mickey, surrounded by a sparkling confetti of light. And the music and choreography are on a par with the technology. Once again, very early arrival is essential to get a seat on the curb. SpectroMagic takes place nightly in summer, on selected nights during Christmas and Easter vacation times, and during other special celebrations. Consult your *Entertainment Show Schedule* for details.

FIREWORKS Like SpectroMagic, Fantasy in the Sky Fireworks, immediately preceded by Tinker Bell's magical flight from Cinderella's Castle, take place nightly in summer, on selected nights during Christmas and Easter vacation times, and during other special celebrations. Consult your *Entertainment Show Schedule* for details. Suggested viewing areas are Liberty Square, Frontierland, and Mickey's Starland.

EPCOT CENTER

In 1982, Walt Disney World opened its second major attractions park, the World's Fair–like EPCOT Center (Experimental Prototype Community of Tomorrow). Its aims are described in a dedication plaque: "May EPCOT Center entertain, inform and inspire. And, above all . . . instill a new sense of belief and pride in man's ability to shape a world that offers hope to people everywhere." Ever growing, EPCOT Center today occupies 260 acres so stunningly landscaped as to be worth visiting for botanical beauty alone. There are two major sections, Future World and World Showcase.

EPCOT Center is huge, and walking around it can be exhausting (some people say its acronym stands for "Every Person Comes Out Tired"). Don't try to do it all in one day. Conserve energy by taking launches across the lagoon from the edge of Future World to Germany or Morocco. There are also double-decker buses circling the World Showcase Promenade and making stops at Norway, Italy, France, and Canada. Unlike the Magic Kingdom, EPCOT's parking lot is right at the gate. Stop by **Earth Station** (EPCOT's information center) when you come in to pick up an **EPCOT Guidebook** and **entertainment schedule,** and, if you so desire, make reservations for lunch or dinner. Many EPCOT restaurants are described in "Dining," earlier in this chapter. Strollers can be rented to your left at the Future World entrance plaza and in World Showcase at the International Gateway between the United Kingdom and France.

Since most people begin the day by touring Future World, the best way to beat the crowds is to head directly to World Showcase. As at the Magic Kingdom, arrive early, tickets in hand. Take a launch across to either side of the lagoon, and work your way down to the right or left, taking in World Showcase and Future World attractions on one side of the park. By the time you reach Future World in the afternoon, traffic there will be lighter. The second day, follow the same method and cover the other side of the park.

FUTURE WORLD

The northern section of EPCOT Center (where you enter the park) comprises Future World, centered on a giant geosphere known as Spaceship Earth. Future World's 10 themed areas, sponsored by major American corporations, focus on discovery, scientific achievements, and tomorrow's technologies in areas running the gamut from energy to underseas exploration.

SPACESHIP EARTH Spaceship Earth, housed in a massive silvery "geosphere," is EPCOT's most cogent symbol. Inside, a show narrated by Walter Cronkite takes visitors on a 15-minute journey through the history of communications. You board time-machine vehicles to the distant past, where an Audio-Animatronic™ Cro-Magnon shaman recounts the story of a hunt while others record it on cave walls. You advance thousands of years to ancient Egypt, where hieroglyphics adorn temple walls and writing is recorded on papyrus scrolls. By the 9th century B.C., the Phoenicians have developed a 22-letter alphabet, simplifying communications. The Greeks add vowels to the alphabet and refine its use as a tool to express new inner needs for speculative thought, art, and philosophy; the theater is born. Roman roads and the vast Islamic empire expand the network of communications, furthering knowledge of science, astronomy, and art. With the revolutionary development of the Gutenberg printing press in 1456, man's increasing ability to disseminate ideas becomes a catalyst for the Renaissance which, in turn, spawns the Age of Invention. Technologies develop at a rapid pace, enlarging our communications spectrum via steam power, electricity, the telegraph, telephone, radio, movies, and TV. It's but a short step to the age of electronic communications. You are catapulted into outer space to see "spaceship earth" from a new perspective, returning via a kaleidoscopic passageway for a dazzling finale.

As you leave Spaceship Earth, you'll enter **Earth Station,** an electronic information center with guest-relations booths and touch-sensitive video monitors (where you can make reservations for EPCOT restaurants). Staff here can answer all questions.

THE LIVING SEAS This United Technologies–sponsored pavilion contains the world's sixth "ocean," a 5.6-million-gallon saltwater aquarium (including a complete coral reef) inhabited by more than 4,000 sea creatures—sharks, barracudas, parrot fish, rays, and dolphins among them. While waiting on line, visitors pass exhibits tracing the history of undersea exploration, including a glass diving barrel used by Alexander the Great in 332 B.C. A 2½-minute multimedia preshow about today's tools of ocean technology is followed by a seven-minute film demonstrating the formation of the earth and seas as a means to support life.

After the film, visitors enter hydrolators for a rapid descent to the sunlit ocean floor. Upon arrival, they board Seacabs that wind around a 400-foot-long tunnel to enjoy stunning close-up views (through acrylic windows) of ocean denizens in a natural coral-reef habitat. The ride concludes in the Seabase Concourse, which is the visitors center of Seabase Alpha, a prototype ocean-research facility of the future. Here seven fascinating informational modules contain numerous exhibits focusing on ocean ecosystems, harvestable resources grown in controlled undersea environments, marine mammals, earth systems, the study of oceanography from space, undersea exploration, and life in a coral-reef community. Many of these exhibits are hands-on. You can step into a diver's JIM Suit and use controls to complete diving tasks, and expand your knowledge of oceanography via interactive computers.

THE LAND Sponsored by Kraft General Foods, this largest of Future World's pavilions highlights man's relation to food and nature in a variety of intriguing attractions.

Symbiosis: This 17-minute, 70mm motion picture explores the delicate balance between technological progress and environmental protection. Its message is stated in the narrator's first words: "Nothing in the universe exists alone." Dazzling cinematography ranges the world, capturing pristine scenery and wildlife. The movie demonstrates man's attempts throughout history to harness nature, from 3,000-year-old Philippine rice terraces to the Hoover Dam. You learn how unbridled enthusiasm for technology has engendered ecological disasters, but the film ends with a hopeful image—a vast fertile field that was once a dust bowl.

Listen to the Land: A 13-minute boatride takes you through three ecological environments—a rain forest, an African desert, and windswept American plains—each populated by appropriate Audio-Animatronic™ denizens. New farming methods are showcased in real gardens. If you'd like a more serious overview, take a 45-minute guided walking tour of the growing areas, offered every half hour between 9:30am and 4:30pm. Sign up at the Broccoli & Co. shop near the entrance to Kitchen Kabaret.

Kitchen Kabaret: This Audio-Animatronic™ musical revue—hosted by Bonnie Appetit and featuring the vaudeville team of Hamm 'n' Eggs, the Cereal Sisters, a trumpet-playing piece of toast, and a Mexican mariachi band made up of fruits and vegetables—takes a lighthearted look at nutrition. The action is set in a 1940s art deco kitchen, with a jazz age musical score.

JOURNEY INTO IMAGINATION In this wondrous pavilion, presented by Kodak, even the fountains are magical, with arching streams of water that leap into the air like glass rods. Its major attraction is:

Captain EO: This 17-minute 3-D, 70mm musical space adventure combines the creative talents of superstar Michael Jackson, directors George Lucas and Francis Ford Coppola, and Walt Disney imagineers! Michael (Captain EO) and a band of cute extraterrestrials discover a planet ruled by the Black Queen (Anjelica Huston) and her forces of darkness. It's a world devoid of happiness until Captain EO and his crew animate it with music, dance, and rainbows of light. The music and choreography are as dazzling as the special effects.

Journey into Imagination Ride: Visitors board moving cars for a 14-minute ride, hosted by a red-bearded adventurer named Dreamfinder and his sidekick, Figment, a mischievous baby dragon with a childlike ability to dream. After a simulated flight across the nighttime sky, you enter the "Imaginarium," where whimsical tableaux featuring Audio-Animatronic™ characters explore creativity in the fine arts, performing arts, literature, science, and technology. The ride culminates at:

Image Works, housing dozens of hands-on electronic devices and interactive computers. Here you can activate musical instruments by stepping on hexagons of colored light, participate in a TV drama, draw patterns with laser beams, operate a giant kaleidoscope, and conduct an electronic philharmonic orchestra.

COMMUNICORE WEST This crescent-shaped building to your right just beyond Spaceship Earth (remember, you're facing south as you enter the park) houses **Futurecom,** which offers, among other things, dozens of hands-on exhibits. Via interactive computers, you can compose music, try to match colors, test your memory, do electronic finger painting, or unscramble a kind of Rubik's Cube assemblage of your own face. Visitors can learn about American states via a computer with extensive informational menus, find out about future products such as 3-D viewer-participation TV programs, and get the lowdown on upcoming phone technologies (after all, this pavilion *is* sponsored by AT&T). And do try the **Phraser,** which repeats whatever you type on its keyboard in five different voices. The central exhibit is the **Fountain of Information,** representing the flood of communications data generated in a modern society via TV, print, advertising, films, laser discs, etc. CommuniCore West also houses **EPCOT Outreach,** a comprehensive research library that can answer questions about any aspect of WDW. If, for instance, you'd like to learn more about hydroponics after visiting The Land, they can print out an information sheet on it.

COMMUNICORE EAST The mirror-image of CommuniCore West, CommuniCore East offers a behind-the-scenes look at Walt Disney World operations in an attraction called:

Backstage Magic: A computer operator and her animated computergraphic sidekick, I/O (input/output), take you on a journey through computer history, from the old 30-ton electronic models of yesteryear to today's microchip miniatures. But the most fascinating aspect of this show is a backstage look at the massive electronic "brain" that runs everything at Walt Disney World—programming and controlling its thousands of Audio-Animatronic™ characters, making hotel reservations, operating lighting, and monitoring vehicles on high-speed thrill rides. The cute I/O zips across video terminals and over computer hardware to demonstrate the machines' speed and versatility. The 18-minute show (including a 7½-minute preshow) ends in a dazzling finale that brings all the computers to life in a burst of fiber optics, neon, and other special effects. Outside the theater, in Computer Central's main foyer, you can pit your wits against computers—including a little purple robot named SMRT-1—in a variety of innovative games.

Energy Exchange: Exxon sponsors this overview of tomorrow's alternative energy sources. It informs via touch-sensitive screens and interactive exhibits.

Person of the Century: Join this vast public-opinion poll to choose the individual who has made the greatest impact on the 20th century. Mixed in with major figures such as Picasso, James Joyce, and Gandhi are some rather odd choices, including Donald Trump, Pele, Andy Warhol, and Ray Croc!

WORLD OF MOTION Everything you always wanted to know about transportation—past, present, and future—is explored in this General Motors–sponsored vast wheel-shaped, gleaming stainless-steel pavilion.

World of Motion Show: The pavilion's highlight is this whimsical 15-minute ride that utilizes animated scenery, 70mm film, and a cast of 140 Audio-Animatronic™ characters to document civilization's eternal quest for movement. It begins with sore-footed cavemen, early attempts at riding animals (test-driving a zebra), and the invention of the wheel. Leonardo da Vinci is shown experimenting with ideas for flight, the era of railroads is represented by a train being held up by masked desperados, and an astonished horse looks on as a man cranks up a car. Just about every mode of transport is covered, from paddlewheelers to ocean liners, from wagon trains to barnstorming planes. You proceed—always to a cheerful background score called "It's Fun to Be Free"—to the widening travel opportunities presented by auto and air travel. And, this being WDW, the ride climaxes with a dizzying journey through computer-graphics space for a look at the future: spaceship transportation.

Transcenter: The other major attraction here is a behind-the-scenes look at General Motors' advanced engineering and manufacturing facilities, its prototype vehicles of the future, and its concerns in creating nonpolluting engines and fuel economy. Here you can test your knowledge of automotive signals, learn how robotics are used in automobile manufacturing (via a humorous show starring a wisecracking toucan and an assembly-line robot named Tiger), and sit down in the prototype models and examine the controls.

HORIZONS The theme of this General Electric–sponsored pavilion is the future, which presents an unending series of new horizons. In the line area, designed as a futuristic transportation center, a public address system pages passengers bound for exotic destinations. You board sideways-facing gondolas for a 15-minute journey into the next millennium. The first tableau honors visionaries of past centuries (like Jules Verne) and looks at outdated visions of the future and classic sci-fi movies. You ascend to an area where an IMAX film projected on two 80-foot-high screens presents a kaleidoscope of brilliant micro and macro images—growing crystals, colonies in space, solar power, a space shuttle launching, DNA molecules, and a computer chip. You then travel to 21st-century cityscapes, desert farms, floating cities under the ocean's surface, and outer-space colonies populated by Audio-Animatronic™ denizens who use holographic telephones, magnetic levitation trains, and voice-controlled robotic field hands. For the return to 20th-century earth, you can select one of three futuristic transportation systems: a personal spacecraft, a desert hovercraft, or a mini-submarine.

WONDERS OF LIFE Housed in a vast geodesic dome fronted by a 75-foot replica of a DNA molecule, this EPCOT Center pavilion offers some of Future World's most engaging shows and attractions. They include:

The Making of Me: Starring Martin Short, this captivating 15-minute motion picture combines live action with animation and spectacular in-utero photography to create the sweetest introduction imaginable to the facts of life.

Body Wars: You're miniaturized to the size of a single cell for a medical rescue mission inside the immune system of a human body. Your objective: to save a miniaturized immunologist who has been accidentally swept into the bloodstream.

This motion-simulator ride takes you on a wild journey through gale-force winds (in the lungs) and pounding heart chambers.

Cranium Command: In this hilarious multimedia attraction, Buzzy, an Audio-Animatronic™ brain-pilot-in-training, is charged with the seemingly impossible task of controlling the brain of a typical 12-year-old boy. Cranium Command is a training center for brain pilots, in which Buzzy has to prove his ability at the helm. The boy's body parts are played by Charles Grodin, Jon Lovitz, Bob Goldthwait, Kevin Nealon and Dana Carvey (as Hans and Franz), and George Wendt (Norm from "Cheers").

Fitness Fairgrounds: This large area is filled with fitness-related shows, exhibits, and participatory activities, including a film called *Goofy About Health* (Goofy has the "Unhealthy Livin' Blues" until he reforms) and Coach's Corner, where your tennis, golf, or baseball swing is analyzed by experts. You can also try working out on a video-enhanced exercise bike, get a computer-generated evaluation of your health habits, and take a video voyage to investigate the effects of drugs on your heart. There's much, much more. You could easily spend hours here.

UNIVERSE OF ENERGY Sponsored by Exxon, this pavilion, its roof glistening with solar panels, aims to better our understanding of America's energy problems and potential solutions via a 35-minute ride-through attraction with visitors seated in solar-powered "traveling theater" cars. The experience begins with an introductory kinetic multi-image preshow tracing our use of energy from primitive to modern times. On a massive screen in Theater I, an animated motion picture depicts the earth's molten beginnings, its cooling process, and the formation of fossil fuels. You move from Theatre I to travel back 275 million years into an eerie storm-wracked landscape of the Mesozoic Era, a time of violent geological activity. Here, you're menaced by giant Audio-Animatronic™ dragonflies, pteryodactyls, dinosaurs, earthquakes, and streams of molten lava before entering a steam-filled tunnel deep through the bowels of the volcano to emerge back in the 20th century in Theatre II. In this new setting, which looks like a NASA Mission Control room, a 70mm film projected on a massive 210-foot wraparound screen depicts the challenges of the world's increasing energy demands and the emerging technologies that will help meet them. Your moving seats now return to Theatre I where swirling special effects herald a film about how energy impacts our lives in areas such as mobility, communications, agriculture, health, education, and recreation. It ends on a dramatically upbeat note—a vision of an energy-abundant future.

WORLD SHOWCASE

Surrounding a 40-acre lagoon at the park's southern end is World Showcase, a permanent community of 11 miniaturized nations, all with authentically indigenous landmark architecture, landscaping, background music, restaurants, and shops. The cultural facets of each nation are explored in art exhibits, dance performances, and innovative rides, films, and attractions. And all employees in each pavilion are natives of the country represented.

CANADA Our neighbors to the north are represented by diverse architecture ranging from a mansard-roofed replica of Ottawa's 19th-century French-style Château Laurier (here called the Hôtel du Canada) to a British-influenced rustic stone building modeled after a famous landmark near Niagara Falls. A Native American village—complete with rough-hewn log trading post and 30-foot replicas of Ojibwa totem poles—signifies the culture of the Northwest, while the Canadian wilderness is reflected by a steep mountain (a Canadian Rocky), a waterfall cascading into a white-water stream, and a "forest" of evergreens, stately cedars, maples, and birch trees. Don't miss the stunning floral displays inspired by the Butchart Gardens in Victoria, B.C. The pavilion's highlight attraction is ***O Canada!***, a dazzling 360° Circle-Vision™ film that reveals Canada's scenic splendor from sophisticated Montréal to the thundering flight of thousands of snow geese near the St. Lawrence. Other scenes (there are over 50) depict a chuckwagon race in the Calgary Stampede, the pine-covered mountains of Banff National Park, a fishing village off the Newfoundland coast, herds of reindeer in the Northwest Territory, and an aerial view of the majestic snow-covered Rockies. The film is 18 minutes in length. Canada pavilion shops carry sandstone and soapstone carvings, snowshoes, lumberjack shirts, duck decoys, fur-lined parkas, toy tomahawks and teepees, a vast array of Eskimo stuffed animals and Native American dolls, turquoise jewelry, and, of course, maple syrup.

UNITED KINGDOM Centered on Brittania Square—a formal London-style park, complete with copper-roofed gazebo bandstand and a statue of the Bard—the U.K. pavilion evokes Merry Olde England. Four centuries of architecture are represented along quaint cobblestone streets, troubadours and minstrels entertain in front of a traditional British pub, and a formal garden replicates the landscaping of 16th- and 17th-century palaces. High Street and Tudor Lane shops display a broad sampling of British merchandise: toy soldiers, Paddington bears, hobby horses, personalized coats of arms, Scottish clothing (cashmere and Shetland sweaters, golf wear, tams, knits, and tartans), shortbreads, Royal Doulton china, and Waterford crystal. A tea shop occupies a replica of Anne Hathaway's thatch-roofed 16th-century cottage in Stratford-upon-Avon, while other emporia represent the Georgian, Victorian, Queen Anne, and Tudor periods. Background music ranges from "Greensleeves" to the Beatles.

FRANCE Focusing on La Belle Epoque (1870–1910)—a flourishing period for French art, literature, and architecture—this pavilion is entered via a replica of the beautiful cast-iron Pont des Arts footbridge over the "Seine." It leads to a park inspired by Seurat's painting, *A Sunday Afternoon on the Island of La Grande Jatte,* with pleached sycamores, Bradford pear trees, flowering crape myrtles, and sculpted parterre flower gardens. A one-tenth replica of the Eiffel Tower constructed from Gustave Eiffel's original blueprints looms above the grand boulevards, and period buildings feature copper mansard roofs and casement windows. The highlight attraction is ***Impressions de France.*** Shown in a palatial (mercifully sit-down) theater à la Fontainebleau, this 18-minute film is a breathtakingly scenic journey through diverse French landscapes projected on a vast 200° wraparound screen. Enhanced by music of French composers, it takes you from charming farm and fishing villages to the sophistication of Paris and the Côte d'Azur. You soar over the steep cliffs of Etretat in Normandy and the French Alps near Mont Blanc, attend a traditional Brittany wedding, visit Versailles, and see vineyards at harvest time. Emporia in the covered shopping arcade, with art nouveau Métro facades at either end, have interiors ranging from a turn-of-the-century bibliothèque to a French château. Merchandise includes French art prints, cookbooks, cookware, fashions, wines, pâtés, bonbons, berets, Madeline and Babar books and dolls, and perfumes. A marketplace/tourism center revives the defunct Les Halles, where Parisians used to sip onion soup in the wee hours. The heavenly aroma of a boulangerie penetrates the atmosphere, and mimes, jugglers, and strolling chanteurs entertain.

MOROCCO This exotic pavilion—its architecture embellished with intricate geometrically patterned tilework, minarets, hand-painted wood ceilings, and brass lighting fixtures—is heralded by a replica of the Koutoubia Minaret, the prayer tower of a 12th-century mosque in Marrakesh. The Medina (old city), entered via a replica of an arched gateway in Fez, leads to Fez House (a traditional Moroccan home) and the narrow winding streets of the *souk,* a bustling marketplace where all manner of authentic handcrafted merchandise is on display. Here you can peruse or purchase pottery, brassware, sheepskin bags, baskets, hand-knotted Berber carpets, colorful Rabat carpets, prayer rugs, and wall hangings. There are weaving demonstrations in the *souk* throughout the day. The Medina's rectangular courtyard centers on a replica of the ornately tiled Najjarine Fountain in Fez, the setting for musical entertainment. The pavilion's Royal Gallery contains an ever-changing exhibit of Moroccan art, and the Center of Tourism offers a continuous three-screen slide show.

JAPAN Heralded by a flaming red *torii* (gate of honor) on the banks of the lagoon and the graceful blue-roofed Goju No To pagoda (its five stories representing earth, water, fire, wind, and sky), this pavilion focuses on Japan's ancient culture. The pagoda, topped by a bronze spire with gold wind chimes and a water flame, was inspired by a shrine built at Nara in A.D. 700. In a traditional Japanese garden, cedars, yew trees, bamboo, "cloud-pruned" evergreens, willows, and flowering shrubs frame a contemplative setting of pebbled footpaths, rustic bridges, waterfalls, exquisite rock landscaping, and a pond of golden koi. The Yakitori House is based on the renowned 16th-century Katsura Imperial Villa in Kyoto, designed as a royal summer residence and considered by many to be the crowning achievement of Japanese architecture. Exhibits ranging from 18th-century Bunraki puppets to Samurai armor take place in the moated White Heron Castle, a replica of the Shirasagi-Jo, a 17th-century fortress overlooking the city of Himeji. And the Mitsukoshi Department Store (Japan's answer to Macy's) is housed in a replica of the Shishinden (Hall of Ceremonies) of the Gosho Imperial Palace built in Kyoto in A.D. 794. It sells lacquer screens, kimonos, kites, fans, collectible dolls in traditional costumes, origami books, tea sets, Samurai swords, Japanese Disneyana, incense burners, bonsai plants, pottery, even modern electronics. In the courtyard, artisans demonstrate the ancient arts of *anesaiku* (shaping brown rice candy into dragons, unicorns, and dolphins), *ikebana* (flower arranging), *sumi-e* (calligraphy), and *origami* (paper folding). Be sure to include a show of traditional Japanese music and dance at this pavilion in your schedule. It's one of the best in the World Showcase.

AMERICAN ADVENTURE Housed in a vast Georgian-style structure, ***The American Adventure*** is a 29-minute dramatization of U.S. history utilizing a 72-foot rear-projection screen, rousing music, and a large cast of lifelike Audio-Animatronic™ figures, including narrators Mark Twain and Ben Franklin. The "adventure" begsin with the voyage of the *Mayflower* and encompasses major historic events. You view Jefferson writing the Declaration of Independence, the expansion of the frontier, Mathew Brady photographing a family about to be divided by the Civil War, the stock market crash of 1929, Pearl Harbor, and the *Eagle* heading toward the moon. John Muir and Teddy Roosevelt discuss the need for national parks, Susan B. Anthony speaks out on women's rights, Frederick Douglass on slavery, Chief Joseph on the situation of Native Americans. While waiting for the show to begin, you'll be entertained by the wonderful Voices of Liberty Singers performing American folk songs in the Main Hall. Note the quotes from famous Americans on the walls here. Formally symmetrical gardens shaded by live oaks, sycamores, elms, and holly complement the pavilion's 18th-century architecture; ivy suspended from lampposts is shaped into Liberty Bells; and a rose garden includes varieties named for American presidents. A shop called Heritage Manor Gifts sells American food products, Coca-Cola memorabilia, patchwork baby quilts, Confederate and Davy Crockett hats, books on American history, historically costumed dolls, classic political campaign buttons, and vintage newspapers with banner headlines like "Nixon Resigns!" An artisan in the shop makes jewelry out of coins.

ITALY One of prettiest World Showcase pavilions, Italy lures visitors over an arched stone footbridge to a replica of Venice's intricately ornamented pink-and-white Doge's Palace (built between the 9th and 16th centuries), the 83-foot campanile (bell tower) of St. Mark's Square topped by a gold-leafed angel, Venetian bridges, Corinthian columns, and a central piazza enclosing a version of Bernini's Neptune Fountain with a delightful statue of the sea god flanked by water-spewing dolphins. A garden wall suggests a backdrop of provincial countryside, and Mediterranean citrus, olive trees, cypress, and pine frame a formal garden. Gondolas are moored on the lagoon. Shops—some of them in the Arcata d'Artigiani, a Tuscan-style open-air market—sell baskets, leather, Perugina chocolates, biscotti, cameo and filigree jewelry, Murano and Venetian glass, alabaster figurines, and inlaid wooden music boxes. A troupe of street actors perform a contemporary version of 16th-century Commedia del Arte in the piazza.

GERMANY Enclosed by towered castle walls, this festive pavilion is centered on a cobblestone *platz* with pots of colorful flowers girding a fountain statue of St. George and the Dragon. An adjacent clock tower is embellished with whimsical glockenspiel figures that herald each hour with quaint melodies. The pavilion's outdoor biergarten—where it's Oktoberfest all year long—was inspired by medieval Rothenberg. And 16th-century building facades replicate a merchant's hall in the

Black Forest (embellished with statues of three Habsburg emperors) and the town hall in Frankfurt's Romsburg Square. Shops here carry Hummel figurines, crystal, glassware, cookware, cuckoo clocks, cowbells, music boxes, pewterware, German wines and specialty foods, toys (German Disneyana, teddy bears, dolls, and puppets), Christmas ornaments, art reproductions, and books. An artisan demonstrates the molding and painting of Hummel figures; another paints exquisite detailed scenes on eggs. Background music runs the gamut from oom-pah-pah bands to Mozart symphonies.

CHINA Bounded by a serpentine wall that snakes around its outer perimeter, the China pavilion is entered via a vast triple-arched ceremonial gate inspired by the Temple of Heaven in Beijing, a summer retreat for Chinese emperors. Passing through the gate, you'll see a half-size replica of this ornately embellished red-and-gold circular temple, built in 1420 during the Ming Dynasty. Gardens simulate those in Suzhou, with miniature waterfalls, fragrant lotus ponds, groves of bamboo, stately pines, corkscrew willows, and weeping mulberry trees. The highlight attraction here is ***Wonders of China,*** a 20-minute, 360° Circle-Vision™ film that explores 6,000 years of dynastic and Communist rule and the breathtaking diversity of the Chinese landscape. Narrated by 8th-century Tang Dynasty poet Li Bai, it includes scenes of the Great Wall (begun 24 centuries ago!), a performance by the Beijing Opera, a Manchurian ice-sculpture festival, the Forbidden City in Beijing with 9,000 rooms in six palaces, Yangtze River gorges, rice terraces of Hunan Province, the Gobi Desert, and tropical rain forests of Hainan Island. Adjacent to the theater, an art gallery fronted by a hanging lotus gate and atrium courtyard houses changing exhibits of Chinese art. A bustling marketplace festooned with colorful streamers and banners offers an array of merchandise including silk robes, lacquer and carved-jade furniture, jade figures, cloisonné vases, paper umbrellas, silk rugs and embroideries, stuffed pandas, kites, dolls, fans, pottery, wind chimes, and Chinese clothing. Note the towering stone elephant nearby: Legend has it that if you throw a stone on its back and it remains there, luck will follow you the rest of your days. Artisans here paint wooden ducks and demonstrate calligraphy.

NORWAY Centered on a picturesque cobblestone courtyard, this pavilion evokes ancient Norway. A *stavekirke* (stave church), styled after the 13th-century Gol Church of Hallingdal, its eaves embellished with wooden dragon heads, houses changing exhibits. A replica of Oslo's 14th-century Akershus Castle, next to a cascading woodland waterfall, is the setting for the pavilion's featured restaurant. Other buildings simulate the red-roofed cottages of Bergen and the timber-sided farm buildings of the Nordic woodlands. There's a two-part attraction here. **Maelstrom,** a boatride in a dragon-headed Viking vessel, traverses Norway's fjords and mythical forests to the music of *Peer Gynt*—an exciting journey during which you'll be menaced by polar bears prowling the shore and trolls who cast a spell on the boat and propel it backward into raging rapids. The watercraft crashes through a narrow gorge and spins into the North sea where a violent storm, complete with crashing waves and lightning, is in progress. But the storm abates, and passengers disembark safely in a 10th-century Viking village to view the 70mm film ***Norway,*** which documents a thousand years of history. Featured images include *Oseberg bat* (a 1,000-year-old Viking ship), a fiery nighttime view of an oil rig silhouetted against 45-foot waves of the tumultuous North Sea, a small fishing village, festive national holiday celebrations in Oslo, and soaring jumps at the Holmenkollen ski resort. Shops feature hand-knit wool hats and sweaters, toys (Legos—there's a table where kids can play with them while you shop—troll dolls, children's books, Viking swords), pewterware, and jewelry made from Norwegian gemstones.

MEXICO You'll hear the music of marimba and mariachi bands as you approach the festive showcase of Mexico, fronted by a towering Mayan pyramid modeled on the Aztec Temple of Quetzalcoatl (God of Life) dating to the 3rd century A.D. It's adorned with fierce serpent heads, symbols of fertility and renewal, and surrounded by dense Yucatán jungle landscaping. Upon entering the pavilion, you'll find yourself in a museum of pre-Columbian artifacts. Down a ramp is a small lagoon, the setting for **El Rio del Tiempo** (River of Time), where visitors board boats for eight-minute cruises through Mexico's past and present. Dance performances focusing on the cultures of Mayan, Toltec, Aztec, and Colonial Mexico are presented in film segments and by a folk-costumed Audio-Animatronic™ cast in vignettes ranging from a Day of the Dead skeleton band to children breaking a piñata. The show culminates in a Mexico City fiesta with exloding fiber-optics fireworks. Shops in and around the Plaza de Los Amigos (a "moonlit" Mexican *mercado* with a tiered fountain and streetlamps) display an array of leather wallets and handbags, baskets, sombreros, big paper flowers, piñatas, pottery, embroidered dresses and blouses, maracas, papier-mâché birds, worry dolls, turquoise jewelry, carved onyx animals, cut-tin candle lamps, weavings, and blown-glass objects (an artisan gives demonstrations). La Casa de Vacaciones, sponsored by the Mexican Tourist Office, provides travel information.

ILLUMINATIONS & SHOWS

Shows, especially those in World Showcase, make up an important part of the EPCOT experience. Check your show schedule when you come in, and plan your day to include some of them.

A 16½-minute spectacular using high-tech lighting effects, darting laser beams, fireworks, strobes, and rainbow-lit dancing fountains, ✪ **IlluminNations** takes place nightly. A backdrop of classical music by international composers (representing World Showcase nations) enhances the drama. Each nation is highlighted in turn. Colorful kites fly over Japan, the giant Rockies loom over Canada, a gingerbread house rises in Germany, and so on. Find a seat around the lagoon about a half hour before show time.

DISNEY–MGM STUDIOS THEME PARK

In 1989, WDW premiered its third "magical kingdom," Disney–MGM Studios, offering exciting movie and TV-themed shows and behind-the-scenes "reel-life" adventures. Its main streets include Hollywood and Sunset Boulevards, with art deco movie sets evocative of Hollywood's glamorous Golden Age. There's also a New York street lined with Gotham landmarks (the Empire State, Flatiron, and Chrysler Buildings) and typical New York characters including peddlers hawking knock-off watches. More important, this is a working movie and TV studio, where shows are in production even as you tour the premises.

Arrive at the park early, tickets in hand. Unlike the Magic Kingdom and EPCOT, MGM's 110 acres of attractions can pretty much be seen in one day. The parking lot is right at the gate. If you don't get a ***Disney–MGM Studios Guidebook*** and/or **entertainment schedule** when you enter the park, you can pick them up at **Guest Services** (MGM's information center). First thing to do is check showtimes and work out an entertainment schedule based on highlight attractions and geographical proximity. My favorite MGM restaurants are described in the "Dining" section of this chapter. Strollers can be rented at Oscar's Super Service inside the main entrance.

✪ **THE MAGIC OF DISNEY ANIMATION** You'll see Disney characters come alive at the stroke of a brush or pencil as you tour actual glass-walled animation studios and watch artists at work. Walter Cronkite and Robin Williams explain what's going on via video monitors, and they also star in a very funny eight-minute Peter Pan-themed film about the basics of animation. You'll see original cels from famous Disney movies on display here. The tour also includes very entertaining video talks by animators and a grand finale of magical moments from such Disney classics as *Pinocchio, Snow White, Bambi,* and *Cinderella.* This very popular attraction should be visited early in the morning; long lines form later in the day.

BACKSTAGE STUDIO TOUR This 25-minute tram tour takes you behind the scenes for a close-up look at the vehicles, props, costumes, sets, and special effects used in your favorite movies and TV shows. You'll see costumers at work in wardrobe, the house facade of "The Golden Girls," and carpenters building sets. All very interesting until the tram ventures into Catastrophe Canyon, where an earthquake in the heart of desert oil country causes canyon walls to rumble and riders are threatened by a raging oil fire, massive explosions, torrents of rain, and flash floods! Then you're taken behind the scenes to see how filmmakers use special effects to create such disasters. Almost as interesting as the ride is the preshow, featuring video commentary by well-known actors and directors on overhead monitors; Tom Selleck and Carol Burnett are hosts.

VOYAGE OF THE LITTLE MERMAID Hazy light, creating an underwater effect in the reef-walled theater, helps set the mood for this charming musical spectacular based on the Disney feature film. The show combines live and Audio-Animatronic™ performers with over 100 puppets, movie clips, and innovative special effects—bubbles, mist, cascading water, lightning, laser beams, stage smoke, and fireworks. Sebastian sings the movie's Academy Award-winning song "Under the Sea"; the ethereal Ariel shares her dream of becoming human in a live performance of "Part of Your World"; and the evil, tentacled Ursula, 12 feet tall and 10 feet wide, belts out "Poor Unfortunate Soul" in which she tempts Ariel to part with her most precious possession, her voice. It all has a happy ending, as most of the young audience knows it will—they've seen the movie.

INSIDE THE MAGIC Movie and TV special effects and production facets are the focus of this behind-the-scenes walking tour of studio facilities. The tour is enhanced by entertaining videotaped narrations en route by Warren Beatty, Mel Gibson, Pee Wee Herman, George Lucas, R2-D2, and others. You'll see how a naval battle—complete with burning ships and undersea explosions—is created and how miniaturization was achieved in the movie *Honey, I Shrunk the Kids*. You'll also visit studio soundstages; view a short movie called *The Lottery* starring Bette Midler and learn how its special effects were achieved; and find out what goes on in video and audio post-production areas. The tour ends with a screening of coming Disney attractions in a sit-down theater.

JIM HENSON'S MUPPET VISION 3D This utterly delightful film starring Kermit and Miss Piggy combines Jim Henson's puppets with Disney Audio-Animatronics™ and special-effects wizardry, animation, 70 mm film, and cutting-edge 3-D technology. The coming-at-you action includes flying Muppets, cream pies, cannon balls, high winds, fiber-optic fireworks, bubble showers, even an actual spray of water. Statler and Waldorf critique the action (which includes numerous mishaps and disasters) from a mezzanine balcony, and Nicki Napoleon and his Emperor Penguins (a full Muppet orchestra) provide music from the pit. Kids in the first row interact with the characters. In the preshow area, guests view a hilarious Muppet video on overhead monitors and see an array of Muppet movie props.

THE BACKLOT THEATER This outdoor theater presents a 25-minute live Broadway-style production of *Beauty and the Beast* based on the Disney movie version. Musical highlights from the show range from the rousing "Be Our Guest" opening number (sung by a kitchen-full of dancing plates, a cup and teapot, colorful utensils, and swirling chefs) to the poignant title song featured in a romantic waltz-scene finale complete with the release of white doves. A highlight is "The Mob Song" scene in a dark forest, in which villagers armed with axes, hoes, and pitchforks set out on a rampage to "kill the beast," setting up the emotional climax: Belle speaks the three magic words that heal the beast's heart and transform him into a handsome prince. Sets and costumes are lavish, production numbers spectacular. Arrive early to get a seat.

STAR TOURS A wild galactic journey based on the *Star Wars* trilogy (George Lucas collaborated on its conception), this action-packed adventure uses dramatic film footage and flight-simulator technology to transform the theater into a vehicle careening through space. On a voyage to the Moon of Endor, you encounter robots, aliens, and droids, among them our inexperienced pilot, RX-24. No sooner has he extricated your spaceship from an asteroidlike tunnel of frozen ice fragments, than he's drawn into combat with a massive Imperial Star Destroyer. The ship lurches out of control, and passengers experience sudden drops, violent crashes, and oncoming laser blasts. The harrowing ride ends safely, and you exit into a "droid and baggage claim" area which leads to a *Star Wars* merchandise shop.

MONSTER SOUND SHOW Four volunteers are chosen from the audience to create sound effects for a hilarious mystery film starring Chevy Chase and Martin Short that includes thunder, rain, creaking doors, falling chandeliers, footsteps, ringing bells, and explosions. You see the film three times: first with professional sound, then without sound as volunteers frantically scramble to create an appropriate track, and finally with the sound effects they've provided. Errors in timing and volume make it all quite funny, as a knock at the door or crashing glass comes just a few seconds too late. David Letterman narrates a terrific video preshow, including one of his famous "top 10" lists, in this case "most entertaining sounds" (number 10: "a sweaty fat guy getting up out of a vinyl bean chair"). In a post-show area called Soundworks, guests can try their hand at creating sounds via interactive computers.

SUPERSTAR TELEVISION This 30-minute show takes guests through a broadcast day that spans TV history. During the preshow, "casting directors" choose volunteers from the audience to reenact 15 famous television scenes (arrive early if you want to snag a role). The broadcast day begins with a 1955 black-and-white "Today" show featuring Dave Garroway and continues through "Late Night with David Letterman," including scenes from "Howdy Doody," a classic "I Love Lucy" episode (the candy factory), "General Hospital," "Bonanza," "Gilligan's Island," "Cheers," and "The Golden Girls" among others. Real footage is mixed with live action, and though occasionally a star is born, there's plenty of fun watching amateur actors freeze up, flub lines, and otherwise deviate from the script.

THE GREAT MOVIE RIDE Audio-Animatronic™ replicas of movie stars enact some of the most famous scenes in filmdom on this thrilling ride through movie history: Bergman and Bogart's classic airport farewell in *Casablanca,* Rhett carrying Scarlett up the stairs of Tara for a night of passion, Brando bellowing "Stellllaaaa," Sigourney Weaver fending off slimy *Alien* foes, and many more. Action is enhanced by dramatic special effects. The setting for this attraction is a full-scale reproduction of Hollywood's famous Grauman's Chinese Theatre, complete with hand, foot, and paw prints (Mickey and Kermit) of the stars out front.

INDIANA JONES EPIC STUNT SPECTACULAR Visitors get an inside look at the world of movie stunts in this dramatic 30-minute show, which re-creates major scenes from the *Raiders of the Lost Ark* series. The show opens on an elaborate Mayan temple backdrop. Indiana Jones crashes dramatically onto the set in a free fall, and as he searches with a torch for the golden idol, he encounters booby traps, fire and steam, and spears popping up from the ground, before being chased by a vast rolling boulder! The set is dismantled to reveal a colorful Cairo marketplace where a swordfight ensues and the action includes jumps from high places, virtuoso bullwhip manoeuvers, lots of gunfire, and a truck bursting into flame. An explosive finale takes place in a desert scenario. Throughout, guests get to see how elaborate stunts are pulled off. Volunteers are chosen to participate as extras during the preshow.

THE TWILIGHT ZONE TOWER OF TERROR Under construction as we go to press, this white-knuckle thrill ride in a deserted Sunset Boulevard grand hotel is designed to pay tribute to the horror/science-fiction genre of films. Guests will enter a once-grand but now deserted (and haunted) Sunset Boulevard hotel and wend their way through a series of deceptive optical-illusion rooms to the ride vehicle—for a ride to "The Twilight Zone"! The climax: The hotel "elevator" malfunctions in descent, sending guests on a terrifying 13-story free-fall plunge.

PARADES, SHOWS, FIREWORKS & MORE A dazzling parade, **Aladdin's Royal Caravan,** based on the movie, takes place once or twice daily (check your entertainment schedule for route and times). Its exotic cast includes a 26-foot genie on a bejeweled float, brass bands, amazing acrobats, scimitar dancers, golden camels, a giant out-of-control ape, a rope climber, a fire eater, a snake charmer, magicians, a harem, and the grand entrance of Prince Ali and Princess Jasmine on

Abu (transformed from a monkey into an elephant), followed by Aladdin's old nemesis, the villainous Jafar, now reduced to pushing the honey bucket behind them. Don't miss it! Find a curbside seat (or grab a bench near the Monster Sound Show) along the parade route a half hour before it begins.

The ✪ **Sorcery in the Sky** fireworks show is presented nightly during summer and peak seasons. Check your entertainment schedule to see if it's on.

The **Star Today** program features frequent appearances by stars such as Betty White, Howie Mandel, and Sally Struthers. They visit attractions, record their handprints in front of the Chinese Theater, and appear at question-and-answer sessions with park guests. Check your entertainment schedule to see if it's on.

The **Teenage Mutant Ninja Turtles** emerge from the sewers to demonstrate their radical moves, sing, order pizza, and sign autographs in a "totally awesome" show on New York street several times each day. A similar show, **Jim Henson's Muppets on Location,** takes place outside the Muppet 3-D movie theater. Check your entertainment schedule for show times.

A movie set replica serves as a playground in the ***Honey, I Shrunk the Kids* Movie Set Adventure.** Outsize props include 30-foot blades of grass, giant Legos, and a sliding pond made from an immense film reel. And you might stop by **Studio Showcase** to see props and costumes from your favorite TV shows and movies—everything from Johnny Carson's desk to masks used in *Dick Tracy*.

TYPHOON LAGOON

Located off Lake Buena Vista Drive halfway between Walt Disney World Village and Disney–MGM Studios, this is the ultimate in water theme parks. Its fantasy setting is a palm-fringed tropical island village of ramshackle tin-roofed structures, strewn with cargo, surfboards, and other marine wreckage left by the "great typhoon." A storm-stranded fishing boat dangles precariously atop the 95-foot-high Mount Mayday, the steep setting for several major park attractions. Every half hour the boat's smokestack erupts, shooting a 50-foot geyser of water into the air. Colorful tropical birds enhance the island ambience. In summer, arrive no later than 9am to avoid long lines; the park is often filled to capacity by 10am and closed to later arrivals. Beach towels and lockers can be obtained for a minimal fee, and all beach accessories can be purchased at Singapore Sal's. Light fare is available at two restaurants, and there are picnic tables (consider bringing picnic fare; you can keep it in your locker until lunchtime). Guests are not permitted to bring their own flotation devices into the park.

TYPHOON LAGOON This large and lovely blue lagoon, the size of two football fields and surrounded by white sandy beach, is the park's main swimming area. Large surfing and bobbing waves crash against the shore every 90 seconds. A foghorn sounds to warn you when a wave is coming. Young children can wade in the lagoon's peaceful bay or cove.

CASTAWAY CREEK Hop onto a raft or inner tube and meander along this 2,100-foot lazy river. Circling the lagoon, Castaway Creek tumbles through a misty rain forest, past caves and secluded grottoes. It has a themed area called Water Works where jets of water spew from shipwrecked boats, and a Rube Goldberg assemblage of broken bamboo pipes and buckets spray and dump water on passersby. There are exits along the route where you can leave the creek; if you do the whole thing, it takes about a half hour.

WATER SLIDES Humunga Kowabunga consists of two 214-foot Mount Mayday water slides that drop you down the mountain before rushing into a cave and out again at 30 m.p.h. Three longer, but less steep slides—Jib Jammer, Rudder Buster, and Stern Burner—take you on a serpentine route through waterfalls and bat caves, and past nautical wreckage at about 20 m.p.h. before depositing you in a bubbling catch pool; each offers slightly different views and thrills.

WHITE-WATER RIDES Mount Mayday is also the setting for three white-water rafting adventures—Keelhaul Falls, Mayday Falls, and Gangplank Falls—all offering steep drops, coursing through caves, and passing lush scenery. Keelhaul Falls has the most winding spiral route, Mayday Falls the steepest drops and fastest water, while the slightly tamer Gangplank Falls uses large tubes so the whole family can ride together.

SHARK REEF Guests are given free snorkel equipment (and instruction) for a 15-minute swim through this 362,000-gallon simulated coral-reef tank populated by about 4,000 rainbow parrotfish, queen angelfish, yellowtail damselfish, rock beauties, and other colorful denizens of the deep. There's a rock waterfall at one end. If you don't want to get in the water, you can observe the fish via portholes in a walk-through area. Shark Reef is housed in a sunken upside-down tanker.

KETCHAKIDDIE CREEK Many of the above-mentioned attractions require guests to be at least four feet tall. This section of the park is a kiddie area exclusively for those *under* four feet. An innovative water playground, it has bubbling fountains to frolic in, mini-water slides, a pint-sized white-water tubing adventure, spouting whales and squirting seals, rubbery crocodiles to climb on, grottoes to explore, and waterfalls to loll under.

RIVER COUNTRY

One of the many recreational facilities at the Fort Wilderness Resort campground, this mini-water park is themed after Tom Sawyer's swimming hole. Kids can scramble over man-made boulders that double as diving platforms for a 330,000-gallon clearwater pool. Two 16-foot water slides also provide access to the pool. Attractions on the adjacent Bay Lake, which is equipped with ropes and ships' booms for climbing, include a pair of flumes—one 260 feet long, the other 100 feet—that corkscrew through Whoop-N-Holler Hollow; White Water Rapids, which carries inner tubers along a winding 230-foot creek with a series of chutes and pools; and the Ol' Wading Pool, a smaller version of the swimming hole designed for young children. There are poolside and beachside areas for sunning and picnicking, plus a 350-yard boardwalk nature trail. Beach towels and lockers can be obtained for a minimal fee. Light fare is available at Pop's Place.

To get here, take a launch from the dock near the entrance to the Magic Kingdom or a bus from its Transportation and Ticket Center.

DISCOVERY ISLAND

This lushly tropical 11-acre zoological sanctuary—just a short boat ride away from the Magic Kingdom entrance, the Contemporary Resort, or Fort Wilderness—provides a tranquil counterpoint to Disney World dazzle. Plan to spend a leisurely afternoon strolling its scenic mile-long nature trail which, shaded by a canopy of trees, winds past gurgling streams, groves of palm and bamboo, ponds and lagoons filled with ducks and trumpeter swans, a bay that's a breeding ground for brown pelicans, and colonies of rose-hued flamingos. Peacocks roam free, and aviaries house close to 100 species of colorful exotic birds. Discovery Island denizens also include Patagonian cavies (they're a kind of guinea pig), alligators and caimans, Galapagos tortoises, small primates, and Muntjac miniature deer from Southeast Asia. Two different bird shows and a reptile show are scheduled several times throughout the day; they take place outdoors with seating on log benches. Guests can also look through a viewing area to see the nursery complex of the island's animal hospital, where baby birds and mammals are often hand-raised.

6. TWO TOP ORLANDO ATTRACTIONS

SEA WORLD

This popular 175-acre marine-life park, at 7007 Sea World Dr. (tel. 407/351-3600), explores the mysteries of the deep in a format that combines entertainment with wildlife-conservation awareness. Its beautifully landscaped grounds, centering on a 17-acre lagoon, include flamingo and pelican ponds (over 1,500 birds, primarily water fowl, make their home in the park) and a lush tropical rain forest. Sea World's involvement in marine-life research, education, animal rescue and release programs, and preserving and breeding endangered species is impressive. Shamu, a killer whale, is the star of the park.

MAJOR ATTRACTIONS There are 10 major shows and attractions:

Mission: Bermuda Triangle Combining a high-definition underwater adventure film with state-of-the-art flight-simulator technology, this attraction takes visitors aboard a scientific research submarine. Your "mission": to explore the 444,000-square-mile expanse of the Atlantic Ocean known as the Bermuda Triangle, in which thousands of people and hundreds of ships and planes have vanished without a trace. It's all very rational and scientific . . . until an underwater earthquake threatens the expedition!

Terrors of the Deep This exhibit houses 220 specimens of venomous and otherwise scary sea creatures in a tropical-reef habitat. Immense acrylic tunnels provide close encounters with slithery eels and three dozen sharks. Barracudas, lionfish, and poisonous pufferfish are also on display. A theatrical presentation focusing on sharks puts across the message that pollution and uncontrolled commerical fishing make humankind the ultimate "terror of the deep."

Manatees: The Last Generation? Today the Florida manatee is in danger of extinction—just 2,000 remain. Underwater viewing stations, innovative cinema techniques, and interactive displays combine to create an exciting format for teaching visitors about the manatee and its fragile ecosystem. Also on display here are hundreds of other native fish as well as alligators, turtles, and shore birds, and there's a nursing pool for manatee mothers and their babies.

Sea World Theatre: Window to the Sea A multimedia presentation takes visitors behind the scenes at Sea World and explores a variety of marine subjects. These include an ocean dive in search of the rare six-gilled shark, a killer whale giving birth, babies born at Sea World (dolphins, penguins, walruses), dolphin anatomy, and underwater geology.

Shamu: New Visions Sea World trainers develop close relationships with killer whales, and in this partly covered open-air stadium, they direct performances that are extensions of natural cetacean behaviors—twirling, waving tails and fins, rotating while swimming, and splashing the audience (sit pretty far back if you don't want to get soaked). An informative video, narrated by James Earl Jones and projected on a vast 16- by 20-foot monitor, adds an underwater perspective to the show. The evening show here, called "Shamu: Night Magic," utilizes rock music and special lighting effects; I suggest attending it instead of the daytime show. It's a fun way to wind up your day at Sea World.

The Whale and Dolphin Discovery Show At Discovery Cove, a big partially covered open-air stadium, whales and Atlantic bottlenose dolphins perform flips and high jumps, swim at high speeds, twirl, swim on their backs, and give rides to trainers—all to the accompaniment of calypso music. Once again, these are extensions of natural behaviors which showcase the abilities of these creatures.

The Gold Rush Ski Show This wacky waterski exhibition features a cantankerous prospector and a talented team of cowboy waterskiers performing long-distance jumps, water ballet, flips, and backward and barefoot skiing. Their antics are accompanied by rollicking hoedown music and dance.

Penguin Encounter This display of hundreds of penguins and alcids (including adorable babies) native to the Antarctic and Arctic regions also serves as a living laboratory for protecting and preserving polar life. On a moving walkway, you'll view six different penguin species congregating on rocks, nesting, and swimming underwater. The attraction is augmented by video displays about penguins and an additional area for puffins and murres (flying Arctic cousins of penguins).

Hotel Clyde and Seamore Two sea lions, along with a cast of otters and walruses, appear in this fishy "Fawlty Towers" comedy with a conservation theme.

Shamu's Happy Harbor This innovative three-acre play area provides facilities for kids to climb a four-story net tower with a 35-foot crow's-nest lookout, fire water cannons, play steel drums, swing on tires, operate remote-controlled vehicles, and navigate a water maze.

ADDITIONAL ATTRACTIONS The park's other attractions include: **Pacific Point Preserve,** a 2½-acre naturalistic setting that duplicates the rocky northern Pacific Coast home of California sea lions and harbor and fur seals; a **Tide Pool of touchables,** such as sea anemones, starfish, sea cucumbers, and sea urchins; a 160,000-gallon man-made **coral-reef aquarium,** home to 1,000 brightly hued tropical fish displayed in 17 vignettes of undersea life; and **Stingray Lagoon,** where visitors enjoy hands-on encounters with harmless southern diamond and cownose rays.

A **Hawaiian dance troupe** entertains with island songs and dances in an outdoor facility at Hawaiian Village; if you care to join in, grass skirts and leis are available. You can ascend 400 feet to the top of the **Sea World Sky Tower** for a revolving 360° panorama of the park and beyond (there's an extra charge of $3 per person for this activity). And at the 5.5-acre **Anheuser-Busch Hospitality Center** you can try free samples of Anheuser-Busch beers and snacks and stroll through the stables to watch the famous Budweiser Clydesdale horses being groomed (Anheuser-Busch owns Sea World).

The **Aloha! Polynesian Luau Dinner and Show,** a musical revue featuring South Seas food, song, and fire dancing, takes place nightly at 6:30pm. Park admission is not required. The cost is $27.95 for adults, $18.95 for children 8–12, $9.95 for kids 3–7, and free for kids under 3. Reservations are required (tel. 407/363-2559, or toll free 800/227-8048).

There are, of course, numerous **restaurants,** snack bars, and food kiosks throughout the park, offering everything from chicken and biscuits to mesquite-grilled ribs. Dozens of **shops** carry marine-related gifts, as well as wilderness/conservation-oriented items.

And visitors can take 90-minute behind-the-scenes **tours** of the park's breeding, research, and training facilities and/or attend a 45-minute presentation about Sea World's animal behavior and training techniques. Cost for either tour is $5.95 for ages 10 and over, $4.95 for children 3–9, free for kids under 3.

ADMISSION A one-day ticket costs $31.95 for ages 10 and over, $27.95 for children 3–9; a two-day ticket is $36.95 for ages 10 and over, $32.95 for children 3–9; a one-year pass costs $54.95 for ages 10 and over, $44.95 for children 3–9; kids under 3 are free. There are discounts for seniors, military, AAA members, and the handicapped. Discounted admissions in conjunction with Cypress Gardens (see "Easy Excursions from Orlando;" below) and Busch Gardens in Tampa (see Chapter 12) are also available; call for details or inquire at the gate. Parking costs $4 per vehicle, $6 for RVs and trailers.

OPEN The park is open from 9am to 7pm 365 days a year, later during summer and holidays when there are also laser/fireworks spectaculars and additional shows at night. Call before you go.

DIRECTIONS Take I-4 to the Bee Line Expressway (Fla. 528) and follow the signs.

UNIVERSAL STUDIOS

Universal Studios Florida, 1000 Universal Studios Plaza (tel. 407/363-8000), is a working motion-picture and television production studio. As you stroll along "Hollywood Boulevard" and "Rodeo Drive," you'll pass more than 40 full-scale sets and large props from famous movies.

MAJOR ATTRACTIONS Thrilling rides and attractions utilize cutting-edge technology—such as OMNIMAX 70mm film projected on seven-story screens—to create unprecedented special effects. And on hand to greet visitors are Hanna-Barbera characters (Yogi Bear, Scooby Doo, Fred Flintstone, and others). While waiting on line, you'll be entertained by excellent preshows. There are six major attractions:

E.T. Adventure Visitors are given a passport to E.T.'s planet, which needs his healing powers to rejuvenate it. You'll soar with E.T. on a mission to save his ailing planet, through the forest and into space, aboard a star-bound bicycle—all to the accompaniment of that familiar movie theme music.

Back to the Future The year is 2015. The incompetent but evil Biff has penetrated Doc Brown's Laboratory of Future Technology, imprisoned Doc, and taken off in the DeLorean. On a mission to save the time machine from Biff, visitors blast through the space-time continuum, plummeting into volcanic tunnels ablaze with molten lava, colliding with Ice Age glaciers, thundering through caves and canyons, and are briefly swallowed by a dinosaur, in a spectacular multisensory adventure.

Kongfrontation It's the last thing the Big Apple needed. King Kong is back! As you stand in line in a replica of a grungy, graffiti-scarred New York subway station, CBS newsman Roland Smith reports on Kong's terrifying rampage. Everyone must evacuate to Roosevelt Island. So it's all aboard the Roosevelt Island tram. Cars collide and hydrants explode below, police helicopters hover overhead putting you directly in the line of fire, the tram malfunctions, and, of course, you encounter Kong—32 feet tall and 13,000 pounds. He emits banana breath in your face and menaces passengers, dangling the tram over the East River. A great thrill—or just another day in New York.

Earthquake, The Big One You board a BART train in San Francisco for a peaceful subway ride, but just as you pull into the Embarcadero station there's an earthquake—the big one, 8.3 on the Richter Scale! As you sit helplessly trapped, vast slabs of concrete collapse around you, a propane truck bursts into flames, a runaway train comes hurtling at you, and the station floods (60,000 gallons of water cascade down the steps).

Ghostbusters There are so many ghosts these days, Ghostbusters just has to sell franchises. Lewis Tully delivers a zany high-pressure sales pitch to the audience, and volunteers come up on stage and get slimed. Tully demonstrates flushing ghosts into the Ectoplasmic Container Chamber and discusses starter kits in three price ranges. But the ghosts, of course, break loose from Gozer's Temple and demons lunge at the audience.

Jaws You're in the charming New England town of Amity. Did you really think it was safe to go into the water? But you board a boat and put yourself in line for a series of terrifying attacks from a three-ton, 32-foot-long shark that tries to sink his teeth into the passengers.

ADDITIONAL ATTRACTIONS Other park attractions include: a **Wild West stunt show;** a **Rocky and Bullwinkle character show,** with those scheming no-goodnik spies, Boris and Natasha; the **Gory, Gruesome, & Grotesque Horror Makeup Show** for a behind-the-scenes look at the transformation scenes from movies like *The Fly* and *The Exorcist;* a **tribute to Lucille Ball,** America's queen of comedy; the **Beetlejuice Graveyard Revue,** a very funny rock-music show with pyrotechnic special effects and MTV-style choreography, starring Dracula, Wolfman, the Phantom of the Opera, Frankenstein and his Bride, and Beetlejuice; **Fievel's Playland,** an innovative western-themed playground based on the Spielberg movie *An American Tail;* ***"Murder She Wrote,"*** which puts you on the set with Angela Lansbury and lets you make post-production executive decisions via computer; **Alfred Hitchcock's 3-D Theatre,** a tribute to the "master of suspense" in which Tony Perkins narrates a reenactment of the famous shower scene from *Psycho,* and *The Birds,* as if it weren't scary enough, becomes an in-your-face 3-D movie; and the **FUNtastic World of Hanna-Barbera,** a motion-simulator ride that takes visitors careening through the universe in a spaceship piloted by Yogi Bear.

On the set of **Nickelodeon** kids get a chance to be on the show or in the audience. Descendants of Lassie, Benji, Mr. Ed, and other animal superstars perform their famous pet tricks in the **Animal Actors Show.** During **Screen Test Home Video Adventure,** a director, crew, and team of "cinemagicians" put visitors on the screen in an exciting video production. And **Dynamite Nights Stunt Spectacular,** a nightly show, combines death-defying stunts with a breathtaking display of fireworks.

Over 25 **shops** in the park sell everything from Lucy collectibles to Bates Motel towels, and **restaurants** run the gamut from Mel's Drive-In (of *American Graffiti* fame), to the Hard Rock Café, to Schwab's.

ADMISSION A one-day ticket costs $34 for ages 10 and over, $27 for children 3–9; a two-day ticket is $53 for ages 10 and over, $42 for children 3–9; an annual pass (admission for a full year) is $85 for ages 10 and over, $67.50 for children 3–9; ages 2 and under enter free. Parking costs $4 per vehicle, $6 for RVs and trailers.

OPEN The park is open 365 days a year. Hours are basically 9am to 7pm, extended during summer and holidays. Call before you go.

DIRECTIONS Take I-4 east, making a left on Sand Lake Road, then a right onto Turkey Lake Road, and follow the signs.

7. MORE ORLANDO ATTRACTIONS

GATORLAND, 14501 S. Orange Blossom Trail (U.S. 441), between Irlo Bronson Memorial Hwy. (U.S. 192) and Fla. 536. Tel. 855-5496.

Founded in 1949 with a handful of alligators living in huts and pens, Gatorworld today features 5,000 alligators and crocodiles on a 55-acre spread. Breeding pens, nurseries, and rearing ponds are situated throughout the park, which also displays monkeys, snakes, deer, goats, birds, Galapagos tortoises, and a bear. A 2,000-foot boardwalk winds through a cypress swamp and a 10-acre breeding marsh with an observation tower. Or you can take the Gatorland Express Train around the park. There are three shows scheduled throughout the day: gator wrestling, gator jumping, and an informative snake show. An open-air-restaurant, shop, and picnic facilities are on the premises.

Admission: $10.55 adults, $7.35 children 3–11, free for kids under 3. Parking is free.

Open: Daily 8am–dusk.

ORLANDO MUSEUM OF ART, 2416 N. Mills Ave., in Loch Haven Park off U.S. 17/92. Tel. 896-4231.

Founded in 1924, the Orlando Museum of Art displays its permanent collection of 19th- and 20th-century American art, pre-Columbian artifacts dating from 1200 B.C. to A.D. 1500, and African objects on a rotating basis. These holdings are augmented by long-term loans focusing on Mayan archeology (recently discovered ceramics, sculptured stucco, and jade pieces from Belize) and arts of the African sub-Saharan region (cast bronze works, intricate beaded objects, and wood figures from the ancient kingdoms of Yoruba and Benin). Inquire about guided tours, children's workshops, gallery talks, workshops, and other activities. A restaurant and museum shop are on the premises.

Admission: $4 adults, $2 children 4–11, free for kids under 4. Parking is free.

Open: Tues–Sat 9am–5pm, Sun noon–5pm. **Directions:** Take I-4 to Exit 43 (Princeton Street) and follow the signs.

WATER MANIA, 6073 W. Irlo Bronson Memorial Hwy. (U.S. 192), just east of I-4 in Kissimmee. Tel. 396-2626.

This conveniently located 38-acre water park offers a variety of aquatic thrill rides and attractions. You can boogie-board or body-surf in continuous wave pools, float lazily along an 850-foot river, enjoy a white-water tubing adventure, and plummet down spiraling water slides and steep flumes. Or dare to ride the Abyss, an enclosed tube slide that corkscrews through 300 feet of darkness, exiting into a splash pool. There's a rain forest-themed water playground for children. A miniature golf course and wooded picnic area—with arcade games, a beach, and volleyball—adjoin.

Admission: $19.95 adults, $17.95 children 3–12, free for kids under 3. Parking is free.

Open: Daily. Hours vary seasonlly (call before you go). **Closed:** Nov 29–Dec 25.

WET 'N WILD, 6000 International Dr., between Sand Lake Rd. and Republic Dr. Tel. 351-WILD.

When temperatures soar, head for this 25-acre water park and cool off jumping waves, careening down steep flumes, and running rapids. Among the highlights: **Surf Lagoon,** a vast pool with four-foot ocean waves; **Bombs Bay** (enter a bomblike casing 76 feet in the air for a speedy vertical flight straight down to a target pool; **Black Hole** (enter a spaceship and board a two-person raft for a 30-second, 500-foot, twisting, turning, space-themed reentry through total darkness propelled by a 1,000-gallon-a-minute blast of water!); **Raging Rapids,** a simulated white-water tubing adventure with a waterfall plunge; and **Lazy River,** a leisurely float trip. There are additional flumes, a challenging children's water playground, a sunbathing area, and picnic area. Food concessions are located throughout the park, lockers and towels can be rented, and you can purchase beach accessories at the gift shop.

Admission: $21.15 adults, $17.95 children 3–9, free for kids under 3. Parking is free.

Open: Daily. Hours vary seasonally (call before you go).

8. SPORTS & RECREATION

In addition to the listings below, check out the Friday "Calendar" section in the *Orlando Sentinel.* It lists numerous outdoor activities in the Orlando area ranging from bass-fishing trips to bungee jumping.

SPECTATOR SPORTS

The Orlando Centroplex administers six public sports and entertainment facilities in the downtown area. These include three major sporting arenas: the Florida Citrus Bowl, the Orlando Arena, and Tinker Field.

FLORIDA CITRUS BOWL, 1610 W. Church St., at Tampa St. Tel. 849-2020 for information, 839-3900 to charge tickets.

The Florida Citrus Bowl seats 70,000 people for major sporting events including the annual New Year's Day Citrus Bowl classic, college football games, NHL exhibition games, mud and monster truck racing, motocross, and World Cup soccer games.

Admission: Ticket prices vary with the event. Parking is $5.

Open: Year-round. **Directions:** Take I-4 east to the East-West Expressway and head west to U.S. 441, make a left on Church Street and follow the signs.

ORLANDO ARENA, 600 W. Amelia St., between I-4 and Parramore Ave. Tel. 849-2020 for information, 839-3900 to charge tickets.

This 15,000-seat arena is the home of the NBA **Orlando Magic** basketball team during their October–April season, the NHL **Tampa Bay Lightning** hockey team (same season), and the **Orlando Predators** (arena football, May–August). The McDonald's American Cup Gymnastic Competition takes place here every March, and the National Championship Finals Rodeo every November. The arena also hosts five WWF wrestling matches annually. In the past it has also hosted key events such as the NCAA Basketball Championship and NBA All-Star Weekend. Call to find out what's on when you're in town.

Admission: Ticket prices vary with the event. Tickets to Orlando Magic games (about $10–$30) have to be acquired far in advance; they usually sell out by September before the season starts. Parking costs $4 (for up-to-the-minute parking information, tune your car radio to 1620 AM).

Open: Year-round. **Directions:** Take I-4 east to Amelia Avenue, turn left at the traffic light at the bottom of the off-ramp, and follow the signs.

TINKER FIELD, 287 S. Tampa Ave., between Colonial Dr. (Fla. 50) and Gore St. Tel. 872-7593 for information and to charge tickets.

From April to September, the **Orlando Cubs** (the Chicago Cubs Class AA

Southern League affiliate) play at Tinker Field, which adjoins the Citrus Bowl. Various other baseball and softball events take place here throughout the year. Call for details.

Admission: Tickets to Cubs games, $3–$5. Parking is $3.

Open: Year-round. **Directions:** Take I-4 east to the East-West Expressway, head west to U.S. 441, make a left on Church Street, and follow the signs.

RECREATION

Recreational facilities of every description abound in Walt Disney World and the surrounding area. These are especially accessible to guests at Disney-owned resorts, official hotels, and Fort Wilderness Resort and Campground, though many other large resort hotels also offer comprehensive facilities (see details in "Accommodations," above). The Disney facilities listed below are all open to the public, no matter where you're staying. For further information about WDW recreational facilities, call 407/824-4321. Guests at Disney properties can inquire when making hotel reservations or at guest services/concierge desks.

BIKING Bike rentals (single- and multispeed bikes for adults, tandems, and children's bikes) are available from the **Bike Barn** (tel. 824-2742) at Fort Wilderness Resort and Campground. Rates are $3 per hour, $8 per day ($1 additional for tandems).

BOATING At the **Walt Disney World Village Marketplace Marina** you can rent Water Sprites, canopy boats, and 20-foot pontoon boats. For information call 828-2204.

The **Bike Barn** at Fort Wilderness (tel. 824-2742) rents canoes ($4 per hour, $10 per day) and pedalboats ($5 per half hour, $8 per hour).

FISHING Fishing excursions on **Lake Buena Vista**—mainly for largemouth bass—can be arranged up to 14 days in advance by calling 407/934-6743. Equipment can be rented. No license is required. The fee is $70 for one person for two hours, $90 for two people, $110 for three to six people, $25 for each additional hour, those rates including gear, guide, and refreshments.

You can also rent fishing poles at the **Bike Barn** (tel. 824-2742) to fish in Fort Wilderness canals. No license is required.

GOLF Walt Disney World operates five championship 18-hole, par-72 golf courses and one nine-hole, par-36 walking course. All are open to the general public and offer pro shops, equipment rentals, and instruction. For tee times and information, call 407/824-2270 up to 7 days in advance (up to 30 days for Disney resort and "official-hotel" guests).

HAYRIDES The hay wagon departs from Pioneer Hall at **Fort Wilderness** nightly at 7 and 9:30pm for hour-long old-fashioned hayrides with singing, jokes, and games. The cost is $5 for adults, $4 for children 3–11, free for kids under 3. Children under 12 must be accompanied by an adult. No reservations—it's first-come, first-served.

HORSEBACK RIDING Disney's Fort Wilderness Resort and Campground offers 50-minute scenic trail rides daily, with four to six rides per day. The cost is $16 per person. Children must be at least 9 years old. For information and reservations up to five days in advance, call 407/824-2832.

TENNIS Nineteen lighted tennis courts are located throughout the Disney properties. Most are free and available on a first-come, first-served basis. If you're willing to pay for court time, courts can be reserved at two Disney resorts: the Contemporary (up to two weeks in advance; $10 per hour) and the Grand Floridian (up to a month ahead of time; $12 per hour). There's a large pro shop at the Contemporary where equipment can be rented. To reserve a court or lesson time with resident pros, call 824-3578 at the Contemporary, 824-2433 at the Grand Floridian.

WATER PARKS/SWIMMING See Walt Disney World listings for River Country and Typhoon Lagoon, as well as the parks listed in "More Orlando Attractions," above.

9. SAVVY SHOPPING

Just about every shop throughout Walt Disney World carries what I call "Disneyana": plush Mickey Mice, *Little Mermaid* T-shirts, etc. But you may be surprised at some of the other merchandise on display here.

THE MAGIC KINGDOM

Main Street Area Disneyana Collectibles carries limited-edition movie cels, antique Disney clocks and porcelain figures, collectible dolls, and items such as a 1947 Donald Duck cookie jar that today is worth $2,000! (Why did I ever let Mom throw out my old toys?)

In Town Square, **The Emporium** houses the park's largest selection of Disneyana, everything from Mickey-logo golf balls to Winnie the Pooh slippers. There's a wonderful collection of music boxes here. Note the Audio-Animatronic™ window displays.

Basically an old-fashioned candy store, **The Market House** also carries an interesting line of pipes and tobaccos. Disney-themed kitchenware too, including Mickey and Minnie corn picks, cupcake papers, ice-cube molds, and waffle irons.

Over at the **Harmony Barber Shop,** where nostalgic men's grooming items are sold (moustache wax, spice colognes, shaving mugs), a barbershop quartet performs on the hour between 9am and 4pm. **The House of Magic** is the place to acquire double-headed nickels, folding quarters, squirting calculators, invisible inks, and other items with which to amaze and impress your friends. And at the **Shadow Box** you can watch a silhouette artist create cut-out portraits of customers on black paper.

Adventureland Traders of Timbuktu carries carved verdite animals from Zimbabwe and carved wooden and soapstone animals and cowhide drums from Kenya, among other exotic wares. Safari-look clothing is available from **Elephant Tales.** The **Zanzibar Shell Shop** is the place for shell mobiles and hangings. The **House of Treasure** retails pirate merchandise: hats, Captain Hook T-shirts, ships in bottles, skull and crossbones keychains, and toy muskets and daggers. And rather fun is **Lafitte's Portrait Deck,** where you can have a costumed photo taken in any of six elaborate Disney sets.

Frontierland Mosey into the **Frontier Trading Post** for western-look leather items, cowboy boots, turquoise jewelry, western and Native American sculpture, toy pistols, and feather headdresses. Similar wares are found at **Prairie Outpost & Supply.**

Liberty Square Olde World Antiques is an actual antiques emporium selling items ranging from an 18th-century pine hutch to 19th-century Staffordshire Chinoiserie willow-pattern platters. The adjoining **Silversmith** carries Revere-style silver and pewter butter dishes, candlesticks, bowls, trays, and picture frames, along with such valuable items as a 46-piece set of Benjamin Franklin sterling silverware in a cherrywood chest ($3,500).

Over at **Heritage House** you can purchase parchment copies of famous American documents as well as actual historic framed letters (one signed by Andrew Johnson in 1864 was priced at $2,350).

Fantasyland It's always the holiday season at **Mickey's Christmas Carol,** supply central for Disney-motif ornaments, caroller dolls, stockings, and charming Christmas carousels. The **King's Gallery,** inside Cinderella's Castle, is cluttered with family crests, tapestries, suits of armor, and other medieval wares. An artisan demonstrates damascening, a form of metal engraving that originated in Damascus circa A.D. 600.

Tomorrowland Kids love browsing over **Space Port's** *Star Trek* and *Star Wars* merchandise and games, sonic-blaster guns, robots, alien masks, and astronaut-costumed Mickeys.

EPCOT CENTER

The most fascinating shops are found in **World Showcase** pavilions, which comprise an international bazaar selling everything from Berber rugs to Japanese kimonos.

In **Future World,** check out the **Centorium,** a vast Disneyana shop that also carries a wide variety of EPCOT souvenirs and memorabilia.

DISNEY–MGM STUDIOS

There's some really interesting shopping here. **Sid Cahuenga's One-of-a-Kind** sells autographed photos of the stars, original movie posters, and star-touched items such as a bracelet that once belonged to Joan Rivers, Richard Dreyfuss's director's chair from *Lost in Yonkers,* Cher's black spiked wig, and an original letter written by Tyrone Power. Over at **Cover Story** you can have your photograph put on the cover of your favorite magazine, anything from *Forbes* to *Psychology Today* to *Golf Digest.* Costumes are available.

Celebrity 5 & 10, modeled after a 1940s Woolworth's, has movie-related merchandise: *Gone With the Wind* memorabilia, MGM Studio T-shirts, movie posters, Elvis mugs, Humphrey Bogart ties, and more. And major park attractions all have complementary merchandise outlets selling Indiana Jones adventure clothing, *Little Mermaid* stuffed characters and logo-wear, *Star Wars* souvenirs, and so on.

DISNEY VILLAGE MARKETPLACE

Just 2½ miles from EPCOT Center, this complex of restaurants and shops on Buena Vista Lagoon makes for a very pleasant browse. About 20 shops, open daily from 9:30am to 10pm, carry a wide variety of giftware, Disneyana, resortwear (including many logo items), Christmas-year-round merchandise, jewelry, crystal, housewares, surfboarding gear, wines and spirits, and sports shoes. There's plenty of free parking.

10. EVENING ENTERTAINMENT

My hat's off to those of you who, after a long day of traipsing around amusement parks, still have the energy to venture out at night in search of entertainment. You'll find plenty to do. And this being kids' world, many evening shows are geared to families.

Check the "Calendar" section of Friday's *Orlando Sentinel* for up-to-the-minute details on local clubs, visiting performers, concerts, and events. It has hundreds of listings. A recent edition would have informed you of entertainment options including the Captain and Tenille, the Byrds, the Black Crowes, Itzhak Perlman, and Marie Osmond.

Tickets to many performances are handled by Ticketmaster. Call 839-3900 to charge tickets.

MAJOR CONCERT/PERFORMANCE HALLS

BOB CARR PERFORMING ARTS CENTRE, 401 W. Livingston St., between I-4 and Parramore Ave. Tel. 849-2020 for information, 839-3900 to charge tickets.

This 2,500-seat theater is the home of the Orlando Opera Company and the Southern Ballet Theater, both of which perform during October to May seasons here. The centre also offers concerts and comedy shows (a recent year's performers included Patti LaBelle, B.B. King, Manhattan Transfer, and Crosby, Stills, and Nash).

The Orlando Broadway Series here (September to May) features original-cast Broadway shows such as *Cats, Les Misérables,* the *Will Rogers Follies* (starring Keith Carradine), *Camelot* (starring Robert Goulet), and *The Magic of David Copperfield.*

Admission: Tickets, concert prices vary with performers; ballet, $12–$30; opera, $19–$41; Broadway Series, $20–$45. Parking costs $4 (for up-to-the-minute parking information, tune your car radio to 1620 AM).

Open: Year-round. **Directions:** Take I-4 east to Amelia Avenue, turn left at the traffic light at the bottom of the off-ramp, and follow the signs.

FLORIDA CITRUS BOWL, 1610 W. Church St., at Tampa St. Tel. 849-2020 for information, 839-3900 to charge tickets.

This 70,000-seat arena is the setting for major rock concerts starring such headliners as Paul McCartney, George Michael, Pink Floyd, Genesis, Guns n' Roses, and Metallica.

Admission: Ticket prices vary with the performer. Parking is $5.

Open: Year-round. **Directions:** Take I-4 east to the East-West Expressway, head west to U.S. 441, make a left on Church Street, and follow the signs.

ORLANDO ARENA, 600 W. Amelia St., between I-4 and Parramore Ave. Tel. 849-2020 for information, 839-3900 to charge tickets.

This 15,000-seat arena offers an array of family-oriented entertainment, including the Ringling Bros. and Barnum & Bailey Circus every January, the Tour of World Figure-Skating Champions in April or May, *Walt Disney's World on Ice* in September, and *Sesame Street Live* in October. It also hosts about 30 varied music and comedy concerts a year, featuring performers such as Elton John, Billy Joel, Bruce Springsteen, Amy Grant, Al Jarreau, and Clint Black. Call to find out who's on when you're in town.

Admission: Ticket prices vary with the event. Parking costs $4 (for up-to-the-minute parking information, tune your car radio to 1620 AM).

Open: Year round. **Directions:** Take I-4 east to Amelia Avenue, turn left at the traffic light at the bottom of the off-ramp, and follow the signs.

WALT DISNEY WORLD DINNER SHOWS

Three distinctly different dinner shows are hosted by Walt Disney World. Other nighttime park options include SpectroMagic, fireworks, and IllumiNations (details above in "Walt Disney World Attractions").

HOOP-DEE-DOO MUSICAL REVUE, Disney's Fort Wilderness Resort and Campground, 3520 N. Fort Wilderness Trail. Tel. W-DISNEY.

Fort Wilderness's rustic log-beamed Pioneer Hall is the setting for this two-hour foot-stompin', hand-clappin', down-home musical revue. Arrive a little early to catch the preshow entertainment on the porch. The Hoop-Dee-Doo troupe of Wild West performers makes a dramatic entrance, arriving in a stagecoach. It's a high-energy show, with 1890s costumes, corny vaudeville jokes, rousing songs, and lots of good-natured audience participation. And during the show, you'll chow down on an all-you-can-eat barbecue dinner including chips and salsa, salad, smoked ribs, country-fried chicken, corn on the cob, baked beans, loaves of fresh-baked bread with honey butter, and a big slab of strawberry shortcake for dessert. Beverages are included. Reservations required. If you catch an early show, stick around for the Electrical Water Pageant at 9:45pm, which can be viewed from the Fort Wilderness Beach.

Admission: $33 adults 21 and over, $25 ages 12–20, $17 children 3–11. Taxes and gratuities extra. Free self-parking.

Open: Daily, showtimes at 5, 7:15, and 9:30pm.

POLYNESIAN REVUE, at Disney's Polynesian Resort, 1600 Seven Seas Dr. Tel. W-DISNEY.

This delightful two-hour dinner show features a colorfully costumed cast of entertainers from New Zealand, Tahiti, Hawaii, and Samoa performing authentic hula, warrior, ceremonial, love, and fire dances on a flower-bedecked stage. There's even a Hawaiian/Polynesian fashion show. It all takes place in a heated open-air theater with candlelit tables and red-flame lanterns suggesting torchiers. The all-you-can-eat meal includes a marvelous tropical fruit-and-greens salad with creamy ranch dressing, a loaf of coconut-almond bread, fried rice with vegetables, seafood stir-fry, barbecued ribs, a flaming volcano ice-cream dessert, and beverages (non-alcoholic specialty cocktails are available for kids). Everyone is presented with a shell lei on entering. Reservations required. There's also a 4:30pm version daily (see "Meals with Disney Characters" in "Dining," above).

Admission: $31 adults 21 and over, $24 ages 12–20, $16 children 3–11. Taxes and gratuities extra. Free self- and valet parking.

Open: Daily, showtimes at 6:45 and 9:30pm.

TOP OF THE WORLD, at Disney's Contemporary Resort, 4600 N. World Dr. Tel. W-DISNEY.

High above the Kingdom, on the 15th floor of the Contemporary Resort, Top of the World is a posh dinner theater with windows all around offering panoramic nighttime vistas of the park and Seven Seas Lagoon. Diners are seated in plush semicircular booths at candlelit tables overlooking the stage and dance floor. The show, called *Broadway at the Top,* is a dazzling musical revue. A talented cast and a five-piece band perform over 50 hit songs from top Broadway musicals. The dinner menu offers several selections for each course. I began with an appetizer of tricolor ravioli served with marinara and pesto sauces, followed by grilled rainbow trout with brown rice and an array of fresh vegetables (other choices included chicken Kiev, shrimp primevara Alfredo over linguine, and roast prime rib). Dessert was white-chocolate mousse cake. Everything was very good. Coffee is included; wine and cocktails are extra. There's a children's menu, though I don't really think this is the ideal evening show for kids—it's more of a romantic evening. Jackets are requested for men. No smoking permitted. Reservations required.

Admission: $44.50 adults, $19.50 children 3–11. Taxes and gratuities extra. Free self- and valet parking.

Open: Daily, showtimes at 6 and 9:15pm.

ENTERTAINMENT COMPLEXES

PLEASURE ISLAND, in Walt Disney World, adjacent to Walt Disney World Village. Tel. 934-7781.

Opened in 1989, this Walt Disney World theme park is a six-acre complex of nightclubs, restaurants, shops, and movie theaters where, for a single admission price, you can enjoy a night of club-hopping till the wee hours. The park is designed to suggest an abandoned waterfront industrial district with clubs in "converted" ramshackle lofts, factories, and warehouses, but the streets are festive with brightly colored lights and balloons. Dozens of searchlights play overhead and rock music emanates from the bushes. You'll be given a map and show schedule when you enter the park; take a look at it and plan your evening around shows that interest you. The mood here is always festive. For one thing, every night at Pleasure Island is New Year's Eve, celebrated on the stroke of midnight with a high-energy street party, live entertainment, and a barrage of fireworks. You can feel perfectly secure sending your teenage kids here for the evening, though they must be 18 to get in unless accompanied by a parent or legal guardian. The on-premises clubs come and go. At this writing they include:

Mannequins Dance Palace: Housed in a vast dance hall with a small-town moviehouse facade, Mannequins is supposed to be a converted theatrical mannequin warehouse (remember, you're still in Disney World). It's a high-energy club with a large rotating dance floor. Three levels of bars and hangout space are festooned with elaborately costumed mannequins and moving scenery suspended from overhead rigging. A DJ plays contemporary tunes at an ear-splitting decibel level; high-tech lighting effects, with laser shows twice nightly, are part of the excitement. You must be 21 to get in, and they're very serious about it. They even carded me, and I learned to dance to the Platters.

Neon Armadillo Music Saloon: You guessed. This trilevel club is country, with neon beer signs, rustic tables mounted on beer barrels, walls hung with spurs and saddles, and a spur-shaped neon chandelier. Live country bands play nightly, and dancers whirl around the floor doing the Texas two-step or cotton-eyed Joe (lessons are given from 7 to 8pm). Sometimes name stars come in and take the stage, and one night actor John Goodman belted out a few songs. The staff is in cowboy/cowgirl garb. A specialty at the bar is Jell-O shooters—Jell-O cubes laced with rum, vodka, and other alcoholic beverages. You can also order southwestern fare such as chili and fajitas.

Adventurers Club: The most unusual of Pleasure Island's clubs—and my personal favorite—occupies a multistory building that, according to Disney legend, was designed to house the vast library and archeological trophy collection of Island founder and compulsive explorer Merriweather Adam Pleasure. It's also headquarters for the Adventure Club, which Pleasure headed until he vanished at sea in 1941. The plushly furnished club is chock-full of artifacts: early aviation photos, hunting trophies, shrunken heads, Buddhas, Indian goddesses, spears, and a mounted "yakoose" (half yak, half moose) who occasionally speaks. He's not the only one. In the eerie Mask Room, strange sounds are often heard, and over 100 masks move their eyes, jeer, and make odd pronouncements. Also on hand are Pleasure's zany band of globe-trotting friends and club servants. Played by skilled actors who interact with guests and always stay in character, they include the Colonel (a British pukka sahib), Pamelia Perkins (the stuffy upper-class club president), Otis T. Wren (a curmudgeonly ichthyologist, oft seen racing up the stairs muttering about being forced to mix with riffraff), Hathaway Brown (dashing aviator; "the earth was no magnet for him, the skies beckoned"), Emile Bleehall (pigeon trainer and country hick from the Sandusky, Ohio, chapter of the club), Mandora (leopardskin-clad adventuress), and Graves (the lugubrious butler). Improvisational comedy shows take place throughout the evening in the main salon, and diverse 20-minute cabaret shows in the library (during which "volunteers" are dragooned from the audience). You could easily hang out here all night imbibing potent tropical drinks in the library and at the bar, where elephant-foot barstools rise and sink mysteriously!

Comedy Warehouse: Housed in the island's former power plant, the Comedy Warehouse—another of my favorites—has a rustic interior with tiered seating. A very talented troupe performs improvisational comedy based on audience suggestions. There are five shows a night, and bar drinks are available. Arrive early. Tickets are distributed 30 minutes before showtime, and lines soon form.

XZFR Rock & Roll Beach Club: Once the laboratory where Pleasure developed a unique flying machine, this three-story structure today houses a dance club where live bands play oldies and top-40 tunes nightly. There are bars on all three floors. The first level contains the dance floor. The second and third levels offer air hockey, pool tables, basketball machines, pinball, video games, blackjack tables, foosball, a bowling machine, and a pizza and beer stand.

8 TRAX: This tie-dye–decor 1970s-style club, with 170 TV monitors airing diverse shows and videos over the dance floor, occupies three levels, all with bars. A DJ plays disco music, and guests engage in games of Twister.

Other Attractions: In addition, **live bands**—including occasional big-name groups—play the West End Plaza outdoor stage and the Hub Stage; check your schedule for showtimes. You can star in your own music video at **SuperStar Studios.** And there are carnival games, a video game arcade, a Velcro wall, and an Orbitron (originally developed for NASA, it lets you experience weightlessness). **Shops and eateries** are found throughout the park. A jazz club is in the works.

Admission: $14.80. Admission is included in the Five-Day Super Duper Pass. There's no admission prior to 7pm, but you have to pay after that. Free self-parking; valet parking is $4.

Open: Clubs, daily 8pm–2am; shops, daily 10am–1am.

CHURCH STREET STATION, 129 W. Church St., off I-4 between Garland and Orange Aves. in downtown Orlando. Tel. 422-2434.

Though not part of Walt Disney World, Church Street Station in downtown

Orlando operates on a similar principle to Pleasure Island. Occupying a cobblestone city block lined with turn-of-the-century buildings—genuine ones—it, too, is a shopping/dining/nightclub complex offering a diverse evening of entertainment for a single admission price. There are 20 live shows nightly; consult your show schedule on entering. Stunning interiors are the rule here. It's worth coming by just to check out the magnificent woodwork, stained glass, and thousands of authentic antiques. And capitalizing on the traffic Church Street generates, many other clubs have opened in the immediate area, further enlarging your bar-hopping potential. Entry to restaurants, the Exchange Shopping Emporium, and the Midway game area is free. Highlights include:

Rosie O'Grady's Good Time Emporium: This 1890s saloon, with beveled- and leaded-glass panels, etched mirrors, and vast globe chandeliers suspended from a high pressed-tin ceiling, is filled with interesting antiques. The train benches came from an old Florida rail station, backbar mirrors from a Glasgow pub, and bank teller's cages from a 19th-century Pittsburgh bank. Dixieland bands, banjo players, singing waiters, and can-can dancers entertain nightly. Light fare is available. The house specialty drink is a rum-and-fruit concoction called the Flaming Hurricane (served in a souvenir glass).

Apple Annie's Courtyard: Adjoining Rosie's, this brick-floored establishment, domed by arched pine and cypress trusses from an early 19th-century New Orleans church, evokes a Victorian tropical garden. The room is further embellished by 12-foot hand-carved filigree mirrors created in Vienna circa 1740 and magnificent 1,000-pound chandeliers suspended from an ornate vaulted cherrywood ceiling. An 18th-century French communion rail serves as the front bar, and seating is in wicker peacock chairs at English pub tables. Patrons sip potent tropical fresh fruit and ice-cream drinks while listening to live folk and bluegrass music.

Lili Marlene's Aviator's Pub & Restaurant: Its plush oak-paneled interior is embellished with World War I memorabilia, stained-glass transoms, burnished brass railings, and accoutrements from an 1850 Rothschild town house in Paris. And eclectic seating ranges from hand-carved oak pews that came from a French church to a place at a large drop-leaf mahogany table where Al Capone once dined. Model airplanes and marvelous Victorian chandeliers are suspended from a beamed pine ceiling with a stained-glass skylight. The menu features premium aged steaks, prime rib, and fresh seafood.

Phineas Phogg's Balloon Works: This whimsical bar, with hot-air balloons and airplanes over the dance floor, is a high-energy club playing loud, pulsating music. It doubles as a virtual ballooning museum housing photographs and artifacts from historic flights, including those of Orlando native Joe Kittinger, the first man to cross the Atlantic in a gas balloon. Every Wednesday from 5:30 to 7pm, beers cost just 5¢ here. No one under 21 is admitted.

Cheyenne Saloon and Opera House: This stunning trilevel balconied saloon, crowned by a lofty stained-glass skylight, is constructed of golden oak lumber from a century-old Ohio barn. Quality western art is displayed throughout, including many oil paintings and 11 Remington sculptures. An 1885 solid rosewood pool table from San Francisco is on the upper tier, the three central chandeliers are from the home of St. Louis beer baron Joseph Schlitz, and six others (circa 1895) came from the Philadelphia Mint. Balcony seating, in restored church pews, overlooks the stage, the setting for entertainment ranging from country bands to clogging exhibitions. The menu features steaks, barbecued chicken and ribs, and hickory-smoked brisket, served with buttermilk biscuits and honey-and-bourbon baked beans.

The Orchid Garden Ballroom: This stunning space, with ornate white wrought-iron arches and Victorian lighting fixtures suspended from an elaborate oak-paneled ceiling, is the setting for an oldies dance club. A DJ plays rock 'n' roll classics like "Great Balls of Fire" and "Let's Go to the Hop."

Crackers Oyster Bar: Brick columns, oak paneling, and a gorgeous antique oak-and-mahogany bar characterize this cozy late 1800s-style dining room. A glass section of the Saltillo-tile floor provides a view of the wine cellar below. Fresh Florida seafood is featured, along with more than 50 imported beers. You can nibble on appetizers such as oysters Rockefeller, smoked fish dip served with carrot and celery sticks, and steamed mussels. Or opt for more serious entrees ranging from crabcakes remoulade to paella.

Other Attractions: In addition, the 87,000-square foot Exchange houses the carnivallike **Commander Ragtime's Midway of Fun, Food and Games** (including an enormous video-games arcade), a food court, and over 50 specialty shops. You can rent a **horse-drawn carriage** out front for a drive around the downtown area and Lake Eola. And **hot-air balloon flights** can be arranged (tel. 841-8787).

Admission: Free before 5pm, $16.90 after 5pm. There are several parking lots nearby (call for specifics); valet parking, at Church Street and Garland Avenue, is $5.

Open: Clubs, daily until 2am; shops, daily until 11pm. **Directions:** Take I-4 east to Exit 38 (Anderson Street), stay in the left lane, and follow the blue signs. Most hotels offer transportation to and from Church Street (and since you'll probably be drinking, I advise it).

TERROR ON CHURCH STREET, 135 S. Orange Ave., at Church St. in downtown Orlando, a block from Church Street Station. Tel. 649-FEAR or 649-1912.

This weird and spooky entertainment is a lot of fun. It incorporates a multimedia high-tech special effects and 23 highly theatrical sets on two floors. On a labyrinthine 25-minute tour of the darkened premises, guests are menaced by cleaver- and chain-saw-wielding maniacs, deranged mental patients, ghoulish monks, hunchbacks, Frankenstein, assorted cadavers, vicious dogs, Freddie Kruger, and Dracula, among others—many of them convincingly portrayed by live actors. Children under 8 are not admitted without an adult. A gift shop on the premises sells stick-on warts, burn scars, and the like.

Admission: $10 adults, $8 children under 17.

Open: Tues–Thurs and Sun 7pm–midnight, Fri–Sat 7pm–1am. **Directions:** Take I-4 east to Exit 38 (Anderson Street), stay in the left lane, and follow the blue signs to Church Street Station parking. Most hotels offer transportation to the area. There are several parking lots nearby (call for specifics); you can use Church Street Station's valet parking, at Church Street and Garland Avenue, for $5.

MOVIES

Pleasure Island AMC Theater, in Walt Disney World adjacent to the Pleasure Island nightclub complex (tel. 827-1300), a 10-screen AMC theater complex, is equipped with state-of-the-art Dolby-digital sound systems and 70mm projection capability. A bridge connects the theater complex with Pleasure Island clubs. New Disney films première here, and first-run films are shown.

Admission for matinees is $4.50 for adults, $3.75 for seniors and children 2–13; twilight shows (from 4:30 to 6pm) are $3.25 for all seats; and evening shows cost $6.50 for adults, $4.50 for students, $3.75 for seniors (over 55) and children 2–13. Kids under 2 always enter free.

Check the *Orlando Sentinel* for showtimes. Self-parking is free.

11. EASY EXCURSIONS FROM ORLANDO

Two of the Central Florida's major sights are within an hour's drive of the Disney parks.

CYPRESS GARDENS Founded in 1936, Cypress Gardens, Fl. 540 at Cypress Gardens Blvd., in Winter Haven (tel. 813/324-2111, or toll free 800/237-4826, 800/282-2123 in Florida), came into being as a 16-acre public garden along the banks of Lake Eloise, with cypress-wood-block pathways and thousands of tropical and subtropical plants. Today it has grown to over 200 acres, with ponds and lagoons, waterfalls, classic Italian fountains, topiary, bronze sculptures, manicured lawns, and—most notably—ancient cypress trees shrouded in Spanish moss forming a backdrop to ever-changing floral displays of 8,000 varieties of plants from 75 countries. Southern belles in Scarlett O'Hara costumes stroll the grounds or sit on benches under parasols in idyllic tree-shaded nooks. They symbolize Florida's old-fashioned southern hospitality. In the late winter and early spring, more than 40 varieties of bougainvillea, 60 of azalea, and 500 of roses burst into bloom. Crape myrtles, magnolias, and gardenias perfume the late-spring air, while brilliant birds of paradise, hibiscus, and jasmine brighten the summer landscape. And in winter, the golden rain trees, floss silk trees, and camellias of autumn give way to millions of colorful chrysanthemums and red, white, and pink poinsettias.

Strolling the grounds is, of course, the main attraction (there are over two miles of winding botanical paths, and half the park's acreage is devoted to floral displays), but this being Central Florida, it's not the only one. Four shows are scheduled several times each day. The world-famous **Greatest American Ski Team** performs daring free-style jumps, swivel skiing, barefooting, ski ballet, and slalom exhibitions on Lake Eloise in a show augmented by an awesome hang-gliding display. **Feathered Follies,** a bird show, features trained cockatoos, macaws, and other exotic members of the parrot family roller-skating, playing basketball, and otherwise mimicking humans. **Variété Internationale** features specialty acts from all over the world. And since visitors can't be here to observe all seasonal changes, a slide show called **Seasons of Cypress Gardens** provides an overview of the year's blooms.

And there's still more. An enchanting exhibit called **Wings of Wonder** surrounds visitors with hundreds of brightly colored free-flying butterflies (representing more than 50 species) in a 5,500-square-foot Victorian-style glass conservatory filled with tropical plantings, orchids, and waterfalls. **Electric boats** navigate a maze of lushly landscaped canals in the original botanical gardens area. You can ascend 153 feet to Kodak's **Island in the Sky** for a panoramic vista of the gardens and a beautiful chain of Central Florida lakes. **Carousel Cove,** with eight kiddie rides and arcade games, centers on an ornate turn-of-the-century–style carousel. It adjoins another kid pleaser, **Cypress Junction,** an elaborately landscaped model railroad (scenery includes everything from a burning house to Mount Rushmore) that travels over 1,100 feet of track with up to 20 trains moving at one time. **Cypress Roots,** a museum of park memorabilia, displays photographs of famous visitors (Elvis on waterskis, Tiny Tim tiptoeing through the roses) and airs ongoing showings of *Easy to Love* starring Esther Williams (it was filmed here). A **radio museum** commemorates the age of radio with a display of hundreds of vintage radios, radio memorabilia, and recordings of radio shows and music from the 1920s to the 1950s. Wind up your visit with a relaxing 30-minute narrated **pontoon cruise** on scenic Lake Eloise, past virgin forest, bulrushes, and beautiful shoreline homes (there's a $3.50-per-person charge).

Dining options range from a food court to the Crossroads Restaurant, a cheerful full-service facility serving American fare; the latter also offers al fresco seating at umbrella tables on a terrace. Fresh strawberries are sold throughout the park in season. And if you care to pack a basket, there are picnic tables. Over a dozen **shops** sell everything from quaint country-store merchandise to gardening books and paraphernelia.

Admission is $22.95 for ages 10 and over, $14.65 for children 3–9; ages 2 and under, free. There are discounts for seniors. Discounted admissions in conjunction with Sea World (see "Two Top Orlando Attractions," above) and Busch Gardens in Tampa (see Chapter 12) are also available; call for details or inquire at the gate. Parking is free.

Open: Cypress Gardens is open 365 days a year from 9:30am to 5:30pm, with extended hours during peak seasons.

Directions: Take I-4 west to U.S. 27 south, and proceed west on to Fla. 540. The park is 45 miles southwest of Orlando.

JOHN F. KENNEDY SPACE CENTER Operated by NASA, the Kennedy Space Center (tel. 407/452-2121) has been the launch site for all U.S. manned space missions since 1968. Astronauts departed earth at this site en route to the most famous "small step" in history—man's first voyage to the moon.

Nonoperational areas of the Kennedy Space Center are part of the 140,000-acre **Merritt Island National Wildlife Refuge** (tel. 407/861-0667). This pristine wilderness of dense woods, unspoiled beaches, crystal-clear waterways, and swampland provides refuge for over 500 species of native Florida wildlife, many threatened and endangered species. To find out about guided nature walks, interpretative programs, and self-guided hikes, call or visit the **Visitor Information Center,** which is four miles east of Titusville on Fla. 402, open Monday through Friday from 8am to 4:30pm and on Saturday from 9am to 5pm; closed all major holidays. (*Note:* You won't have time to tour nature trails and see the Space Center in the same day.)

At **Spaceport USA,** the visitor facility of the Kennedy Space Center, the past, present, and future of space exploration are explored on bus tours of the facility and in movie presentations and numerous exhibits. It takes at least a full day to see and do everything. Arrive early and make your first stop at Information Central (it opens at 9am) to pick up a schedule of events/map and for help in planning your day. Nearby are space-related exhibits and interactive computers at which you can access information about all 10 U.S. NASA centers.

On the two-hour **Red Tour** you'll board a double-decker bus to explore the complex. En route, your driver will point out significant buildings. At the first stop—in a simulated launch control firing room of the Flight Crew Training Building—visitors view a film about the *Apollo 11* mission. The countdown, launch, and planting of a flag on the moon are thrilling even at secondhand. In the adjoining room, related exhibits include an *Apollo 11* command service module (home for the three crew members during their round-trip) and a lunar module (their home on the lunar surface). The tour continues to Complex 39 Space Shuttle launch pads (where a stop is made for exploration) and the massive Vehicle Assembly Building where Space Shuttles are assembled. Nearby, visitors get a close-up look at an actual Apollo/Saturn V moon rocket, America's largest and most powerful launch vehicle. Also on view are massive six-million-pound Crawler Transporters that carry Space Shuttles to their launch pads. There are many photo opportunities, both on the tour and throughout the Spaceport complex. Tours depart at regular intervals beginning at 9:45am, with the last tour leaving two hours before dusk. Purchase tickets at the Ticket Pavilion as soon as you arrive. Note: Itinerary variations may occur subject to launch schedules.

Though most visitors are sated by the Red Tour, a second two-hour **Blue Tour** (same hours) visits Cape Canaveral Air Force Station. On this tour, you'll see where America's first satellites and astronauts were launched in the Mercury and Gemini programs, view launch pads currently being used for unmanned launches, visit the original site of Mission Control, and stop at the Air Force Space Museum which houses a unique collection of missiles and space memorabilia.

Satellites and You is a 50-minute voyage through a simulated future space station. In Disney-esque fashion, the attraction combines Audio-Animatronic™ characters with innovative audiovisual techniques to explain satellites and their uses.

In the **Galaxy Center** building, two spectacular IMAX films projected on 5½-story screens are shown continually throughout the day in twin theaters. In *The Dream Is Alive*—featuring in-flight footage from three Space Shuttle missions—viewers join astronauts in preflight training, aboard the Space Shuttle in orbit, and on a breathtaking launch and landing. The second film, *Blue Planet,* is an environmentally themed look at Spaceship Earth from the vantage point of outer space. The Galaxy Center also houses a NASA art exhibit; a walk-through replica of the future Space Station *Freedom,* a manned research laboratory that will be orbiting the earth by 1999; and an exhibit called Spinoffs from Space. This exhibit, hosted by hologram characters, displays some of the 30,000 spinoffs that have resulted from space program research, including improved consumer products ranging from football helmets to cordless tools.

The **Gallery of Spaceflight,** a large museum, houses hardware and models relating to significant space projects and offers interesting exhibits on lunar exploration and geology. You can view a moon rock and have a photograph taken of yourself in a Lunar Rover.

Spaceport Theater presents films on a variety of topical space-related subjects, such as what astronauts do inside the Space Shuttle, the evolution of the space program, and the history of Kennedy Space Center. The **Astronauts Memorial,** a 42.5- by 50-foot black granite "Space Mirror" dedicated May 9, 1991, honors the 16 American astronauts who have lost their lives in the line of duty. Aboard a full-size replica of a Space Shuttle orbiter, visitors can experience the working environment of NASA astronauts. And the **Rocket Garden** displays eight actual U.S. rockets.

Today a rocket soaring skyward is not an uncommon sight, but it's still one that fills most observers with awe. **If you'd like to see a launch,** call Spaceport USA (tel. 407/452-2121 for current launch information, ext. 260 to make reservations, or fax 407/454-3211). Tickets for viewing cost $7 for adults, $4 for children 3 to 11, free for kids under 3. You can reserve tickets up to seven days before a launch, but they must be picked up at least two days before the launch. A special bus takes observers to a site just six miles from the launch pad.

There are two **cafeterias,** the Orbit and the Lunch Pad, on the premises, though an organization capable of sending men to the moon should be able to create better food and a more pleasant dining environment. The **gift shop** carries a wide array of innovative space-related books, toys, games, videotapes, astronaut flight suits, NASA- and space-logo clothing, and more.

Admission is free. Tickets for either bus tour cost $7 for adults, $4 for children 3–11, free for kids under 3. IMAX film tickets are $4 for adults, $2 for children 3–11, free for kids under 3. Parking is free.

Open: The center is open daily from 9am to dusk; closed Christmas.

Directions: Take the Beeline Expressway (Fla. 528) east, and where the road divides, go left on Fla. 407, make a right on Fla. 405, and follow the signs.

CHAPTER 10

NORTHEAST FLORIDA

Few people realize that the first European settlements in America were not in Jamestown, Virginia (1607), or at Plymouth Rock (1620). Juan Ponce de León discovered and named the Florida coast in 1513, and by 1565 the Spanish had settled 1,000 people in St. Augustine and crushed a French attempt to stake a claim in nearby Jacksonville. In both of these popular beach-resort cities, you can visit sites that evoke the earliest European incursions into the New World. St. Augustine has a large and quaintly charming restored historic district and Spanish Quarter, where the lives of residents in centuries past is vividly evinced.

Jacksonville, with its abundance of shimmering blue waterways, reminds us of San Diego. If you love marine scenery, you'll be enchanted. To get a feel for a little-known facet of Florida history (a brief 16th-century French colony) and to explore beautiful unspoiled woodlands, tranquil marsh, and ancient Timucuan sites, be sure to visit Fort Caroline and take a guided nature walk through the adjoining Theodore Roosevelt Area.

Nearby Daytona Beach is famous for a more recent kind of history—automotive speed. It's the "World Center of Racing," home to the Daytona International Speedway. And, of course, the town is synonymous with spring break vacation frenzy. Pack your favorite wet T-shirt and party on.

---

1. JACKSONVILLE

35 miles S of Georgia, 160 miles NE of Orlando, 400 miles N of Miami

GETTING THERE **By Plane** American, Continental, Delta, TWA, United, and USAir fly into the spiffy-looking **Jacksonville International Airport** (recently renovated to the tune of over $100 million) on the city's north side, about 12 miles from downtown. The Convention and Visitors Bureau on the lower level (tel. 904/741-4902) is open daily from 8am to 10pm.

By Train There's an Amtrak station in Jacksonville at 3570 Clifford Lane, off U.S. 1, just north of 45th Street (tel. toll free 800/USA-RAIL).

By Bus Greyhound buses connect Jacksonville with most of the country. They pull into a terminal at 10 N. Pearl St., between Bay and Forsyth Streets in the heart of downtown (tel. 904/356-5521).

By Car If you're coming from north or south, take I-95. From points west, take I-10.

Boasting the largest land mass of any city in the continental United States (840 square miles), this sunbelt metropolis is on its way to becoming one of the nation's first-tier cities. An important Atlantic seaport, it's the insurance and banking capital of

WHAT'S SPECIAL ABOUT NORTHEAST FLORIDA

Architecture

- ☐ Historic houses, constructed of *tabby* (a kind of primitive concrete made of sand, water, and crushed oyster shells) and a similar but natural shell rock called *coquina*.

Florida Wilderness and Wildlife

- ☐ Dolphins and dozens of sea birds off-shore near St. Augustine.
- ☐ The Theodore Roosevelt Area at Fort Caroline National Memorial in Jacksonville.

Museums

- ☐ The Lightner Museum in St. Augustine, a vast collection of Victoriana in a converted turn-of-the-century Spanish-Renaissance-style hotel.
- ☐ The Cummer Gallery of Art in Jacksonville with a permanent collection comprising works from 2000 B.C. to the present.

Sports

- ☐ Daytona International Speedway, the "World Center of Racing."
- ☐ Dog races, an archetypical Florida experience, at the Daytona Beach Kennel.

For Kids

- ☐ Art Connections at the Cummer Gallery in Jacksonville, an innovative art-themed play area with holograms, computer art stations, and other hands-on exhibits.
- ☐ Jacksonville Museum of Science & History, focusing on science and North Florida history, with dozens of hands-on activities for children plus planetarium shows.
- ☐ Jacksonville Zoological Park, a lushly landscaped zoo.
- ☐ Marineland of Florida in St. Augustine, for close encounters with dolphins and other marine denizens.

---

the South and corporate headquarters to many Fortune 500 companies, with a downtown of gleaming glass skyscrapers stunningly mirrored on the waterfront. Rapid economic growth is bringing cosmopolitan trappings to town—good museums, fancy hotels, fine restaurants, and first-rate entertainment among them. But these urban advantages aside, Jacksonville will always have more to offer than big-city sophistication. In addition to 20 miles of pristine oceanfront beach, the St. Johns River bisects the city, creating breathtaking marine views against a landscape of pine wilderness and parkland. A downtown riverside "festival marketplace" called Jacksonville Landing is just one of many places where you can enjoy a passing parade of seagulls, sandpipers, pelicans, and boats over a leisurely lunch.

A BRIEF HISTORY In this modern city, you'll also learn about some of America's earliest history. The Timucuan peoples and their ancestors lived here peacefully from ancient times until 1562 when French admiral and Huguenot leader Jean Ribault sailed into the St. Johns River in search of wealth and religious freedom, and with the short-lived hope of challenging Spanish supremacy in Florida. Though the French did found a settlement here in 1564, it was destroyed by the Spanish a year later and the entire colony was massacred. Today you can visit a replica of the French fort. Spain and England spent the next few centuries battling over the area, until 1821 when Florida became a territory of the United States. At that time, this sleepy town had about two dozen residents and served merely as a cattle crossing where cows were ferried from one side of the St. Johns River to the other. By the 1840s, Jacksonville—named in 1822 for Florida's first territorial governor, Gen. Andrew Jackson—had established itself as a viable port town exporting cotton and timber. After the Civil War, it emerged as a winter resort, and by the end of the 19th century, with the arrival of a railway system, it was drawing 75,000 tourists to its beaches each year. The tourist boom was cut short by a yellow fever epidemic in 1888, followed by a massive fire in 1901 that destroyed 146 city blocks and 2,368 buildings, including most of the downtown district. A new town rose from the ashes, emerging briefly as a center of the movie industry. There were over 30 studios here in the early 20th century, and Oliver Hardy's first movie was shot in one of them. The industry had moved on to Los Angeles by the 1920s, but by this time World War I had brought a boom in shipbuilding and prosperity showed in the downtown skyline that was underway. After World War II, Jacksonville became a leading southern financial center. More recent developments, in the mid-1980s, include the creation of riverfront recreational areas such as Jacksonville Landing and the Riverwalk. Today Jacksonville is a thriving business center and tourist mecca—well worth a few days' visit.

ORIENTATION

INFORMATION Write, call, or visit the **Jacksonville and the Beaches Convention & Visitors Bureau,** 3 Independent Dr. (just north of Water Street, at Main Street), Jacksonville, FL 32202 (tel. 904/798-9148), for informative literature, maps, brochures, events calendars, and suggestions on accommodations, restaurants, and shopping. It's open Monday through Friday from 8am to 5pm.

CITY LAYOUT Jacksonville is bisected by the St. Johns River, so getting around will usually involve crossing a bridge or two. I-295 forms a beltway around the city, I-95 is the major north-south artery, and I-10, which forks into Atlantic and Beach Boulevards heading toward the ocean, is the major west-east artery. Florida A1A runs from Mayport south along Atlantic Beach, Neptune Beach, Jacksonville Beach, and Ponte Vedra Beach, all bordering the Atlantic Ocean. The Main Street bridge spans the St. Johns River leading to the heart of downtown at its northern end.

GETTING AROUND

ARRIVING Airport vans stop just outside the baggage-claim area; they charge fares of about $8 to downtown Jacksonville hotels, about $30 to beach hotels. A taxi will cost about $20 to downtown, about $40 to the beach hotels.

BY TAXI Taxis charge $1.25 when the meter drops, and $1.25 for each additional mile thereafter.

BY BUS The Jacksonville Transit Authority provides local bus service seven days a week from about 5am to 3am. The fare is 60¢ for adults, 45¢ for children under 17 with student ID, free for children under 42 inches accompanied by an adult and seniors. For route information, call 630-3100.

WHAT TO SEE & DO

ATTRACTIONS

ANHEUSER-BUSCH BREWERY, 111 Busch Dr. Tel. 751-8116.

On its free self-guided tours given throughout the day, Anheuser-Busch explains the beer-making process and traces the company's growth from its inception in 1852. You'll also learn about the history of beer (it was known to the Egyptians as early as 3000 B.C.), and about the famed Budweiser Clydesdales. From observation windows, you'll view all the steps in vast beer-making operation. Additional exhibits deal with the scope of AB's operation (the company owns the St. Louis Cardinals and several theme parks, as well as other business ventures). Along the tour route, you'll be serenaded by commercials for Busch products. And at the end, there's a brewski for you (two gratis 10-ounce cups, actually) and a bowl of Eagle brand pretzels which you can enjoy in a comfortable lounge. A gift shop carries a large variety of Anheuser-Busch and Clydesdale logo merchandise.

Admission: Free. Parking is free on the premises.

Open: Mon–Sat 9am–4pm. **Directions:** Take I-95 north to the Busch Drive exit.

CUMMER GALLERY OF ART, 829 Riverside Ave., between Post and Fisk Sts. Tel. 356-6857.

Founded in 1958 when Mrs. Ninah M. H. Cummer donated her art collection to the city, this stunning museum with its fountain courtyard has a permanent collection that encompasses works from 2000 B.C. to the present. It is especially rich in American impressionist paintings, while other highlights include a large collection of 18th-century Meissen porcelain and 18th- and early 19th-century Japanese Netsuke ivory carvings. American portrait and landscape artists of the 18th and 19th centuries include Thomas Sully, Gilbert Stuart, Thomas Cole, Winslow Homer, Thomas Eakins, John Singer Sargent, James McNeill Whistler, Frederic Remington, and Childe Hassam. Other galleries contain works from antiquity, and European painting.

Two additional galleries used for temporary exhibits have curved glass windows overlooking formal gardens. Take a stroll outside to view the Cummer's spectacular English, azalea, and Italian gardens, the last with beautiful fountains, reflecting pools, and statuary created after the famous garden of the Villa Gamberaia near Florence. The gardens are shaded by a 200-year-old live oak, and vine-covered brick archways frame a scenic vista of the St. Johns River beyond. Bring the kids—an extensive facility called Art Connections features child-size hands-on exhibits, including computer art stations where youngsters can experiment. The Cummer's gift shop is filled with objets d'art and jewelry. Two new gallery wings that will increase exhibition space by 7,000 square feet are in the works at this writing.

Admission: $3 adults, $2 seniors over 62, $1 students and children 5–18, free for children under 5. Parking is free in the lot across the street.

Open: Tues–Fri 10am–4pm, Sat noon–5pm, Sun 2–5pm. **Closed:** New Year's Day, Easter, July 4, Labor Day, Thanksgiving, Christmas Day; early closing day on New Year's Eve.

FORT CAROLINE NATIONAL MEMORIAL, 12713 Fort Caroline Rd., off Monument Rd. Tel. 641-7155.

This 16th-century fort on the St. Johns River was a French outpost in the European struggle for ascendancy in the New World. The French hoped to compete for gold and silver, and establish a haven for persecuted French Protestants (Huguenots). French admiral and Huguenot leader Gaspard de Coligny sent Jean Ribault on an exploratory expedition to the area in 1562. Ribault erected a column to claim the land for France and signify eventual return and settlement, then sailed home to gather colonists and supplies. He found France in the midst of a civil war, and, unable to secure support there, turned to Queen Elizabeth of England. At first she agreed to help him, but then changed her mind and threw him in jail. In 1564, while Ribault was still imprisoned, de Coligny sent René de Laudonnière to Florida with several hundred soldiers, artisans, and colonists. They founded a settlement here named La Caroline in honor of King Charles IX. The native Timucuans initially welcomed the colonists, but the relationship soon soured. By 1565, the settlers were discontented with their meager lifestyle, disappointed in their search for riches, and on the brink of starvation. They were ready to abandon the colony and return to France when Ribault sailed into the harbor that August with seven ships loaded with food, supplies, and 600 settlers. But the French colony's relief was short-lived.

Ribault's arrival was viewed with alarm by the Spanish throne, and Philip II sent Admiral Pedro Menéndez de Avilés to rout the French. Menéndez established a base of operations in nearby St. Augustine, and Ribault sailed down the coast to attack and destroy it. However, a hurricane devastated his fleet. Menéndez rushed to take advantage of the situation, storming the poorly guarded fort and massacring 140 settlers. Returning south with booty from Fort Caroline, Menéndez's troops encountered Ribault and the shipwrecked Frenchmen and slaughtered 350 of them. The French never again gained a foothold in Florida.

Today a replica of Fort Caroline near the original site is under the auspices of the

National Park Service, as is the nearby 600-acre **Theodore Roosevelt Area.** This beautiful woodland, rich in history and undisturbed since the Civil War, contains natural salt- and freshwater marsh and dune scrub. On a two-mile hike along a centuries-old park trail, you'll see a wide variety of birds (including bald eagles, wood storks, and pelicans), wildflowers, and maritime hammock forest. After the trail crosses Hammock Creek, you're in ancient Timucuan country, where their ancestors lived as far back as 500 B.C. Here, you're walking on vast shell mounds, 15–20 feet deep, resulting from the disposal of oyster shells which were a mainstay of this ancient people's diet. Farther along is a cabin in the wilderness that belonged to reclusive brothers Willie and Saxon Browne. They lived without electricity or running water, and supported their needs by hunting and fishing. Saxon died in 1953, and Willie stayed on alone. In 1969 he dedicated his property to the Nature Conservancy for safekeeping, so that people could come here and "learn about God." The land became part of the National Park System in 1988.

We strongly suggest the guided tours of the fort and Theodore Roosevelt Area; park rangers provide a wealth of fascinating information about history, flora, and fauna. Arrive at the fort early, allowing about half an hour to see two films on these attractions. If you can't fit a guided tour into your schedule, pick up trail maps and information at the Fort Caroline Visitor Center. Bring binoculars if you have them; hiking boots are recommended but not mandatory. There are picnic areas at the fort and the trailhead.

Admission: Free. Parking is free at both sites.

Open: Daily 9am–5pm; 30-minute ranger-guided tours of Fort Caroline given Sat–Sun at 1pm, followed by 1½-hour guided nature walks through the Theodore Roosevelt Area at 2:30pm. **Closed:** Christmas Day. **Directions:** Take Atlantic Boulevard east, make a left on Monument Road, and turn right on Fort Caroline Road. The Theodore Roosevelt Area is entered from Mt. Pleasant Road, about a mile southeast of the fort; look for an inconspicuous sign on your left that says TRAILHEAD PARKING and follow the narrow dirt road to the parking lot.

JACKSONVILLE ART MUSEUM, 4160 Boulevard Center Dr., between Beach and Atlantic Blvds. Tel. 398-8336.

Founded in 1924, this is Jacksonville's oldest museum. It moved to its current building in 1964 and was expanded in 1973. On permanent display is a notable pre-Columbian collection which spans a geographical range from northern Mexico to southern Peru and a time range from 3000 B.C. through A.D. 1500. Totally unrelated is the museum's collection of art from 1945 to the present, including works by Picasso, Louise Nevelson, Roy Lichtenstein, and other noted artists. An ongoing series of temporary exhibits ranges from a major Andrew Wyeth retrospective to "Annie Leibovitz: Photographs 1970–1990." Three Mayan stelae (monumental stones) from A.D. 849–870 grace the museum's outdoor sculpture garden which adjoins a pine-shaded picnic area.

Admission: Free. Parking is free on the premises.

Open: Tues–Wed and Fri 10am–4pm, Thurs 10am–10pm, Sat–Sun 1–5pm. **Closed:** New Year's Day, July 4, Thanksgiving, and Christmas Day.

JACKSONVILLE LANDING, 2 Independent Dr., between Main and Pearl Sts. on the St. Johns River. Tel. 353-1188.

This delightful six-acre dining/shopping/entertainment complex on the waterfront was developed by the Rouse Company in 1987. Its vast two-story Main Building adjoins other structures to form a semicircle facing the river and girding a central fountain courtyard. The Main Building entrance takes you into King's Road Market, where open-air stalls display an array of meats, cheeses, fresh seafood, baked goods, flowers, and produce. A cookie bakery here makes for a delightful aroma. Upstairs, a 10,000-square-foot facility called Ostrich Landing, houses video and arcade games, including a shooting gallery. At Dawson & Buckles Market, also upstairs, pushcart vendors hawk trendy wares. There are over 65 shops in the complex, including all the mall regulars—Laura Ashley, The Limited, The Gap, B. Dalton—and specialty emporia selling items like kitchenware, toys and games, and silk flowers. Diners have a choice of seven full-service restaurants. And Founders Food

Hall—a sunny second-floor fast-food court with indoor and outdoor seating overlooking the river—offers international specialties running the gamut from chicken teriyaki to Armenian lavash sandwiches. The Landing is the scene of hundreds of special events annually ranging from arts festivals to baseball-card shows. From March through the end of December, there are free outdoor rock, blues, country, and jazz concerts every Friday and Saturday night. Call the above number to find out what's going on at the Landing during your stay. Weather permitting, water taxis ply the route between Jacksonville Landing and the Riverwalk between about 11am and 10pm (hours vary a bit seasonally); the fare is $1.50 each way, $1 for children under 12.

Admission: Free. Parking is 35¢ per half hour for the first three hours, 70¢ each half hour thereafter, to a $7.50 maximum daily charge ($6 evenings after 6pm and Sat–Sun, and holidays).

Open: Mon–Sat 10am–9pm, Sun noon–5:30pm; restaurants and cafés may have later hours. **Closed:** Christmas Day. **Directions:** Take I-95 north, cross the Main Street bridge and make a right on Newnan Street, turn right again at Coastline Drive, and follow the purple signs to the parking lot.

JACKSONVILLE MUSEUM OF SCIENCE & HISTORY, 1025 Museum Circle (Gulf Life Dr.), on the Riverwalk between Main St. and San Marco Blvd. Tel. 396-7062.

This hands-on interactive children's museum focuses on science and northern Florida history. Kids are greeted by a mechanical green alien called MOSH (an acronym for the museum's name). Permanent exhibits on the first floor include a small aviary of Florida songbirds; a 10,000-gallon aquarium of Florida fish; and "Defense in a Boneless World," an exhibit on protective devices used by starfish, sea urchins, fiddler crabs, scorpions, and lizards. A sinuous pathway called "The Ribbon of Life" explores the history and ecology of the St. Johns River area, focusing on its wetlands and wildlife. Over 100 Florida animals and natural-history specimens can be seen in the Living World and Living Room. In Kidspace, an environment designed for children under 48 inches tall, activities include face painting, a play telephone system, a puppet theater, miniature cars and gas pumps, and a water table (kids can operate a water wheel, dam the water, and test items to see if they sink or float).

On the second floor are a number of interactive and historical exhibits. For example, kids can learn about such things as sound, electricity, and motion or find their pulse rates, reaction times, and muscle endurance. "Bridges, Bridges, Bridges" explores Jacksonville's many bridges; kids get to build a bridge as well as run cars over and steer boats under a video of one.

Planetarium shows for adults and children are scheduled daily (call ahead for show times, and at the same time, inquire about science demonstrations, workshops, and lectures). A pleasant window-walled cafeteria serves light fare and offers outdoor seating on a deck overlooking the Hixon Courtyard, a garden of native plants with a small stream running through it. Note the flock of exotic chickens that live just outside the museum on the Riverwalk.

Admission: $5 adults, $3 seniors and children 4–12, free for children under 4. Use the parking lot across San Marco Boulevard (it's free for up to two hours; if you need to stay longer, get a sticker at the museum).

Open: Mon–Fri 10am–5pm, Sat 10am–6pm, Sun 1–6pm, (Sept hours vary; call ahead for details). **Closed:** New Year's Day, Thanksgiving, and Christmas.

JACKSONVILLE ZOOLOGICAL PARK, 8605 Zoo Rd., off Heckscher Dr. Tel. 757-4462 or 757-4463.

This lushly landscaped zoo exhibits over 700 mammals, birds, and reptiles—many of them in large, natural enclosures that simulate native habitats. It participates in breeding programs involving such rare and endangered species as the Florida panther. Near the entrance is a free-flight aviary housing rare Pondicherry vultures and Marabou storks. Lions inhabit an African veldt setting in Mahali Pa Simba (it means "the place of the lion" in Swahili), with ostriches and various African antelopes as neighbors. Okavango Delta, a walk-through aviary of exotic birds on the St. Johns

River, adjoins the junglelike Okavango Village and is home to Nile crocodiles, blue duikers, Kirk's dik-diks, and South African crested porcupines; it also contains a petting zoo offering close encounters with such domestic African animals as pygmy goats, dwarf zebus, miniature horses, and Sardinian pygmy donkeys. At the Educational Center (open weekends and holidays only, from 10am to 4pm), hands-on exhibits offer the opportunity to examine birds' eggs and nests, peer at insects through a microscope, or touch a giraffe vertebra or tiger skull.

A 30-minute demonstration called "Elephant Encounter" takes place at 11:30am on weekdays, at noon and 2:30pm on weekends and holidays. In addition, from early March to the end of November, an ecologically oriented show called *Animals and Us*—starring an Andean condor—takes place on weekends and holidays at the Show Arena at 11am, 1:30pm, and 3:30pm. During warmer months visitors can view alligator and crocodile feedings on Saturday at 2pm. There's a large oak- and pine-sheltered picnic grove near the main gate, with some tables overlooking a waterfall, and two on-premises eateries—Botswana Burger and Kalahari Kooler—offer light meals and snack fare. Wheelchairs and strollers can be rented for $1.50. Inquire about special events—lectures, workshops, and storytelling. A train ride around the zoo costs $1.50; departures are from Livingstone Station near a gift shop called Zulu Trading Post.

Admission: $4 adults, $3 seniors 65 and over, $2.50 children 3–12, free for children under 3. Shows and parking are free.

Open: Daily 9am–5pm. **Closed:** New Year's Day, Thanksgiving, and Christmas Day. **Directions:** Take I-95 north to Heckscher Drive (Exit 124) and follow the signs.

RIVERWALK, on the south bank of the St. Johns River between Crawdaddy's Restaurant and the Friendship Fountain. Tel. 396-4900.

This 1.2-mile wooden zigzag boardwalk bordering the St. Johns River is one of Jacksonville's most popular recreational areas. Throughout the day it's filled with joggers, tourists, and folks sitting on benches watching the passing parade of riverboats and shore birds. Along the Riverwalk you'll pass the Navy Memorial, a bronze statue of a sailor peering out at the river; a memorial honoring the men and women of Desert Storm; dozens of exotic chickens in front of the Museum of Science & History; and a bust of Ponce de León. The Friendship Fountain at the west end is, at 200 feet in diameter, the nation's largest self-contained fountain; it's especially beautiful at night when illuminated by 265 colored lights. The Riverwalk is the scene of seafood fests, food tastings, parties, parades, and arts-and-crafts festivals. There are food vendors and restaurants along its route. Weather permitting, water taxis festooned with colored flags ply the route between the Riverwalk and Jacksonville Landing from about 11am to 10pm (hours vary a bit seasonally); the fare is $1.50 each way, $1 for children under 12.

Admission: Free. Parking is free at Crawdaddy's.

Open: Daily 24 hours. **Directions:** Take I-95 north to the Prudential Drive exit, make a right, and follow the signs; look for Crawdaddy's Restaurant on your left.

ZEPHANIAH KINGSLEY PLANTATION, 11676 Palmetto Ave., just off Fla. A1A. Tel. 251-3537.

A winding three-mile road under a canopy of trees, with lushly tropical foliage on either side, is what remains of an elegant palmetto drive that led to the 19th-century plantation of Zephaniah Kingsley. Here, on the banks of the Fort George River, Kingsley lived from 1813 to 1839 with his Senegalese wife, Anna Madgigaine Jai, whom he had originally purchased as a slave in Havana. A man of contradictions, he was a Quaker who believed that "the coloured race were superior to us, physically and morally," yet made a fortune in the slave trade and utilized over 200 slaves to tend his 30,000 acres of Sea Island cotton, sugar cane, sweet potatoes, corn fields, and citrus orchards. To motivate his work force, he instituted a system whereby each slave was assigned daily tasks, upon completion of which he or she could enjoy any remaining daylight hours. Ambitious slaves used the free time to grow their own crops, improve their dwellings, or moonlight for money. His will contained provisions to enable them to buy their freedom after his death. When Florida changed from a Spanish colony to an American territory in 1821, Kingsley was appointed to the Legislative Council by

President Monroe. In 1838, alarmed by rising sentiment against free blacks, he sent Anna and their four children to Haiti to live.

Visitors can tour the two-story residence, kitchen house, barn/carriage house, and the remains of 23 slave cabins made of tabby, a kind of primitive concrete composed of sand, water, and crushed oyster shells. In the kitchen house is a display of artifacts from Kingsley's era, which, though Kingsley claimed to treat his slaves humanely ("My object was to excite their ambition and attachment by kindness, not to depress their spirits by fear and punishment") include a pair of leg stocks. Today the plantation is under the auspices of the National Parks Service, and rangers provide very interesting tours.

Admission: Free; donations are appreciated. Parking is free on the premises.

Open: Daily 9am–5pm; 30-minute tours are scheduled throughout the day; call ahead for times. **Closed:** Christmas. **Directions:** Take I-95 north to Heckscher Drive and follow the signs.

SPORTS & RECREATION

Fish, swim, snorkel, sail, sunbathe, or stroll on the sand dunes along Jacksonville's ocean **beaches**—they're just 12–15 miles from downtown via Atlantic, Beach, or J. Turner Butler Boulevards. As home to the PGA Tour's world headquarters, the city has over a dozen major public **golf** courses, some of them top rated, and as home to the international Association of Tennis Professionals, it also abounds with high-quality **tennis** courts.

You can go **fishing** off the Jacksonville Beach Pier, just south of Beach Boulevard at Sixth Avenue (tel. 246-6001); rods, reels, and bait can be rented on the premises. Or fish for red snapper, grouper, sea bass, small sharks, and amberjack 15–25 miles offshore in the Atlantic Ocean aboard the *King Neptune,* a 65-foot deep-sea air-conditioned fishing boat. It departs at 8am daily from 4378 Ocean St., a half mile south of the Mayport Ferry (tel. 246-0104). The price is $35 per person, including all bait and tackle. Light fare can be purchased on board.

Sawgrass Stables, 23900 Marsh Landing Pkwy., off Fla. A1A in Ponte Vedra Beach (tel. 285-3791), offers daily trail rides and riding lessons. Call for details.

The gargantuan 85,000-seat **Gator Bowl,** 1400 E. Duval St., at Adams Street (tel. 360-3900 for information, 353-3309 to charge tickets), one of the nation's largest stadiums, is the site of the annual Florida/Georgia football game every October and the Gator Bowl every New Year's Eve. It hosts additional college football games September through December, NFL pre-season football games, fairs, rodeos, and motorsports events.

Adjacent to it, and under the same auspices, is the 10,600-seat **Jacksonville Veterans Memorial Coliseum,** 1145 E. Adams St. (same phone numbers), a venue for minor-league hockey games, NHL exhibition games, ice-skating exhibitions, wrestling matches, and gymnastics championships.

Gator Bowl tickets run $25–$35 and should be purchased as far in advance as possible. Tickets to the Florida/Georgia game are in the $20–$30 range. There's paid parking for ticketed events; rates vary with the event.

WHERE TO STAY

SOUTHPOINT/BAYMEADOWS

Moderate

RESIDENCE INN BY MARRIOTT, 8365 Dix Ellis Trail (off I-95 at the Baymeadows exit), Jacksonville, FL 32256. Tel. 904/733-8088, or toll free 800/331-3131. Fax 904/731-8354. 112 suites. A/C TV TEL

$ Rates (including full breakfast): Mon–Thurs, $95–$109 single; $100–$114 double; $100–$130 penthouse for four to six people. Fri–Sun, about 40% less, subject to availability. AE, DC, DISC, ER, MC, V. **Parking:** Free self-parking.

This home-away-from-home hotel chain was designed to meet the needs of travelers on extended visits, but it's marvelous even if you're only spending a single night. It's

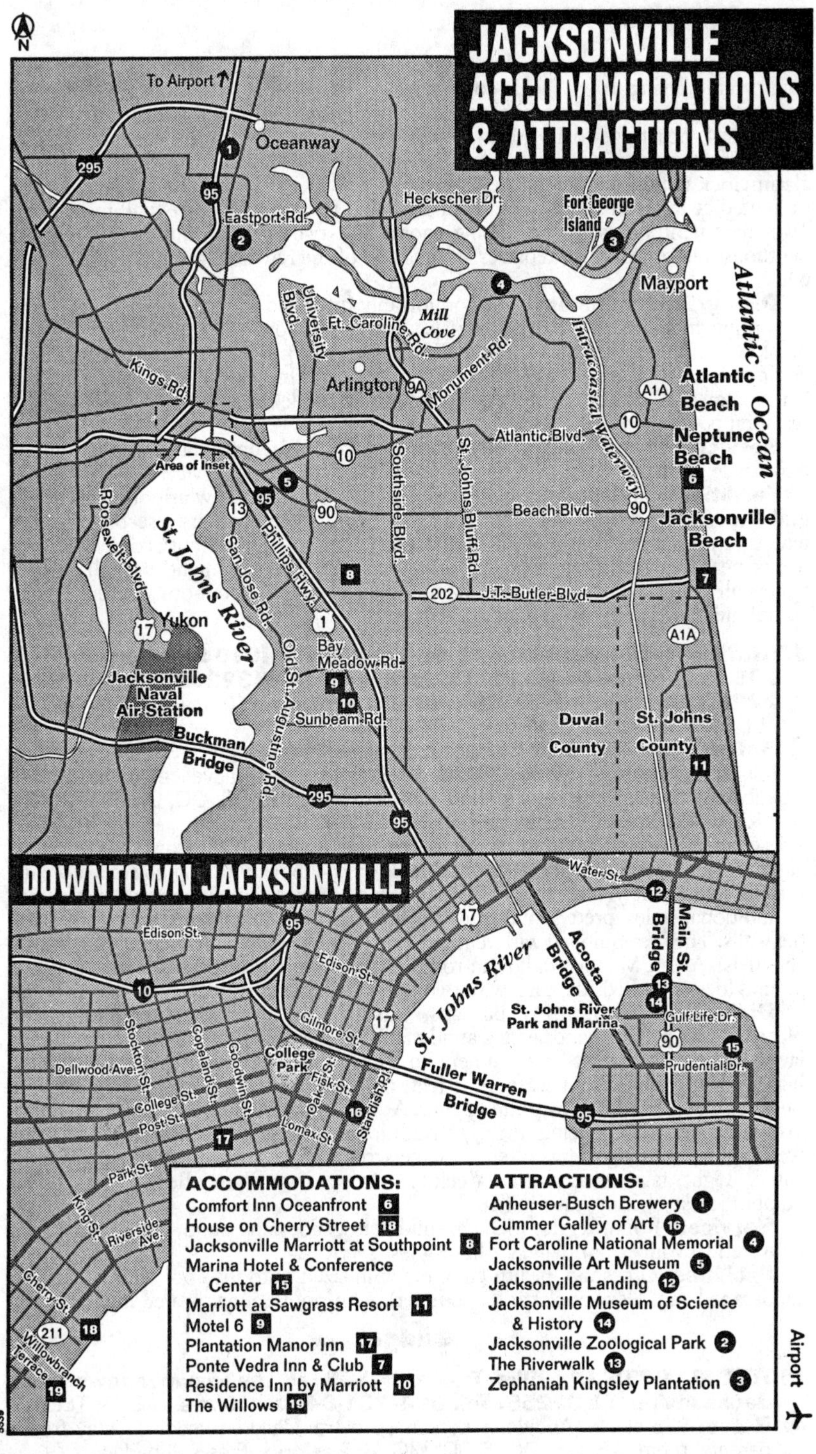
JACKSONVILLE ACCOMMODATIONS & ATTRACTIONS
DOWNTOWN JACKSONVILLE
ACCOMMODATIONS:
Comfort Inn Oceanfront 6
House on Cherry Street 18
Jacksonville Marriott at Southpoint 8
Marina Hotel & Conference Center 15
Marriott at Sawgrass Resort 11
Motel 6 9
Plantation Manor Inn 17
Ponte Vedra Inn & Club 7
Residence Inn by Marriott 10
The Willows 19
ATTRACTIONS:
Anheuser-Busch Brewery 1
Cummer Galley of Art 16
Fort Caroline National Memorial 4
Jacksonville Art Museum 5
Jacksonville Landing 12
Jacksonville Museum of Science & History 14
Jacksonville Zoological Park 2
The Riverwalk 13
Zephaniah Kingsley Plantation 3
To Airport
Oceanway
Heckscher Dr.
Eastport Rd.
Fort George Island
Mayport
Atlantic Ocean
Mill Cove
Ft. Caroline Rd.
University Blvd.
Monument Rd.
Kings Rd.
Arlington
Atlantic Beach
Atlantic Blvd.
Neptune Beach
Intracoastal Waterway
Area of Inset
St. Johns River
Roosevelt Blvd.
San Jose Rd.
Phillips Hwy.
Southside Blvd.
St. Johns Bluff Rd.
Beach Blvd.
Jacksonville Beach
J.T. Butler Blvd.
Yukon
Bay Meadow Rd.
Old St. Augustine Rd.
Jacksonville Naval Air Station
Sunbeam Rd.
Buckman Bridge
Duval County
St. Johns County
Water St.
Main St. Bridge
Edison St.
Acosta Bridge
St. Johns River Park and Marina
Gulf Life Dr.
Prudential Dr.
Stockton St.
Copeland St.
Goodwin St.
Gilmore St.
College Park
Dellwood Ave.
Fisk St.
Oak St.
Standish Pl.
Fuller Warren Bridge
College St.
Post St.
Lomax St.
Park St.
King St.
Riverside Ave.
Cherry St.
Willowbranch Terrace
Airport
5539

like having your own Jacksonville apartment, with a large fully equipped kitchen and comfortable living room area containing a convertible sofa, coffee table, and armchairs. Oak and bamboo furnishings, colorful floral-print fabrics, resort decorator colors (teal, peach, seafoam green), lamps shaped like fish or seashells, and beach-themed paintings give rooms a Florida look. In-room amenities include AM/FM alarm-clock radios, remote-control cable TVs with free HBO (VCRs and movies can be rented at the front desk), ironing boards, and phones with voice-mail messaging. Two-story penthouses feature dining rooms and two baths. Many rooms and all penthouses have working fireplaces. This is one of the few hotels in town that allows pets.

Dining/Entertainment: The comfortably furnished gatehouse—a lounge with a working fireplace, CD player, library, games, and toys—is the setting for daily breakfast buffets. Monday through Thursday, the gatehouse additionally offers complimentary evening buffets (changing nightly). In your room, you'll find a "cuisine-on-call" menu listing a wide selection of deliverable items from nearby restaurants.

Services: Complimentary daily newspaper, complimentary shuttle service within a five-mile radius of hotel, complimentary grocery-shopping service.

Facilities: Outdoor swimming pool and sun deck, three whirlpools, barbecue grills, sports court for volleyball and basketball, complimentary use of two very extensively equipped nearby health clubs (everything you could want), complimentary use of nearby night-lit tennis courts, guest activities (Monday-night football parties, volleyball games, Bingo nights, many holiday events), coin-op washer dryers, complimentary laptop computers on request.

JACKSONVILLE MARRIOTT AT SOUTHPOINT, 4670 Salisbury Rd. (off I-95 at J. Turner Butler Blvd.), Jacksonville, FL 32256. Tel. 904/296-2222, or toll free 800/228-9290. Fax 904/296-7561. 250 rms, 6 suites. A/C TV TEL

$ Rates: Sun–Thurs, $109 for up to four people in a room; Fri–Sat, $69 including full buffet breakfast for two; $175–$275 suite. Lower advance-purchase rates subject to availability. Inquire about golf packages. AE, CB, DC, DISC, ER, JCB, MC, V. **Parking:** Free self-parking.

This centrally located hotel, just minutes from the beach and downtown attractions, is entered via a plushly furnished marble-floored lobby with Chinoiserie accents. Rooms, handsomely decorated in celadon green or tan, feature mahogany furnishings in traditional styles, pretty floral-print bedspreads, and gilt-framed Oriental prints on the walls. They're equipped with remote-control cable TVs (with Spectravision movie channels), AM/FM clock radios, in-room irons and full-size ironing boards, and two phones (desk and bedside, each with two lines). "King-bed rooms" have sleeper sofas.

Dining/Entertainment: Banyans, a softly lit resort-style restaurant with bleached-oak paneling and seating amid many large plants, serves all meals, including lavish Sunday brunches (see "Where to Dine," below); American regional fare, highlighting fresh Florida seafood, is featured. Weather permitting, you can dine at outdoor tables bordered by potted palms. At the simpatico Beau's Lounge, a DJ plays Top-40 tunes for dancing nightly. Additional diversions include blackjack on weeknights, sporting events aired on large-screen TVs, and an interactive TV trivia game. Light fare is available. Weekdays from 5 to 8pm, Beau's puts out a complimentary happy hour buffet.

Services: Room service (6:30am–midnight), shoeshine stand, gratis *USA Today* delivered to your room daily, 24-hour guest services.

Facilities: Gift shop, health club, medium-sized outdoor pool with attractively landscaped sun deck, pool bar (in summer), whirlpool, sauna, heated indoor pool.

Budget

MOTEL 6, 8285 Dix Ellis Trail (off I-95 at the Baymeadows exit), Jacksonville, FL 32256. Tel. 904/731-8400. 109 rms. A/C TV TEL

$ Rates: $26 single. Additional person $6 extra. Children under 17 stay free in parents' room. AE, CB, DC, DISC, MC, V. **Parking:** Free self-parking.

$ Accommodations at this centrally located branch of the budget Motel 6 chain are far back from the highway, so there's no traffic noise. Clean, attractive standard motel units contain cable TVs with HBO movie stations. "King-bed rooms" have sofa beds. A small free-form pool is on the premises, a Denny's coffee shop is within walking distance, and dozens of restaurants are just a few minutes away by car. Pets are allowed.

ON THE RIVERWALK

Moderate

MARINA HOTEL & CONFERENCE CENTER, 1515 Prudential Dr. (on the Riverwalk), Jacksonville, FL 32207. Tel. 904/396-5100, or toll free 800/342-3605. Fax 904/396-7154. 307 rms, 18 suites. A/C TV TEL

$ **Rates:** Sun–Thurs, $79–$89 single; $99 double. Fri–Sat, $58 single; $68 double. $175–$365 suite. Additional person $10 extra. Children under 18 stay free in parents' room. High-end rates are for river views. Inquire about packages. AE, CB, DC, MC, V. **Parking:** Free self-parking.

This five-story hotel on the St. Johns River is appropriately nautical looking, from its ultramarine roofing to its enormous shiplike lobby with exposed pipes and corrugated-tin ceiling. Classical music is played in public areas. Rooms—half with river views—are very cheerful, with shell-motif bleached-oak furnishings, dusty-rose carpeting, Matisse-like paintings of beach scenes on the walls, and bright abstract bedspread fabrics. They're equipped with AM/FM alarm-clock radios and remote-control satellite TVs with Spectravision movie options.

Dining/Entertainment: The very pretty Café St. John, offering breakfast, lunch, and dinner, is festively decorated in bright colors with seating around a tiled fountain. It serves American fare, highlighting steaks and seafood. Equally pleasant is the lobby lounge, with indoor tables under white canvas umbrellas, where guests gather to watch Monday-night football; light fare and frozen tropical drinks are served.

Services: Room service (6:30am–midnight), complimentary *USA Today* at front desk, complimentary morning coffee in lobby, airport shuttle ($8 each way), travel agency (handles airline tickets and car rentals).

Facilities: Two hard-surface tennis courts lit for night play, medium-size swimming pool/sun deck, small videogame arcade with pool table, gift/sundries shop.

BED & BREAKFAST

These charming B&Bs, in the historic Riverside district, are 10 minutes from downtown attractions.

HOUSE ON CHERRY STREET, 1844 Cherry St. (on the St. Johns River), Jacksonville, FL 32205. Tel. 904/384-1999. Fax 904/981-2998. 4 rms (all with bath). A/C

$ **Rates** (including full breakfast): $70 single; $85 double. Additional person $15 extra. No small children accepted. No smoking on premises. MC, V. **Parking:** Free on premises.

This neatly painted colonial-style wood-frame house nestles in a tree-shaded cul-de-sac on the St. Johns River. The entrance hall is strewn with Persian rugs and centers on a piecrust table used for lavish floral displays; a collection of 19th-century woven wool coverlets adorns the walls. French doors open to a delightful screened-in back porch furnished with rocking chairs; it overlooks an expanse of tree-shaded lawn (where guests play croquet) leading to the river. A full breakfast—fresh-baked muffins, croissants or breads, an entree (perhaps Gouda soufflé or eggs Benedict), fresh fruit, juice, and coffee—is served daily in a pleasant dining room furnished with antiques.

Rooms are exquisitely decorated. You might select the lovely river-view Rose Room, with a canopied four-poster bed, late 18th-century walnut armoire, shelves displaying objets d'art, and pretty floral-print wallpaper and chintz curtains. A four-poster (with a hand-crocheted antique lace canopy) also graces the Duck Room, which has shelves of books, a beautiful wool-plaid-upholstered couch, and a bath with Victorian tub and duck-themed wallpaper. It, too, offers river views. Ducks are rather a theme here; hundreds of antique decoys are displayed in rooms and public areas. All accommodations offer adjacent sitting rooms, AM/FM alarm-clock radios, and ceiling fans, and one has a cable color TV. They're supplied with fresh flowers, books and magazines, and jars of mints.

Complimentary wine and hot and cold hors d'oeuvres are served daily at 6pm on the patio or in the dining room, and an upstairs refrigerator is stocked with free soft drinks, bottled water, and beer. There are bicycles for guest use. Genial owner/hosts Carol and Merrill Anderson are tennis buffs who referee U.S. Open matches. They keep a gentle pet greyhound—formerly a racing dog—named Streak.

PLANTATION MANOR INN, 1630 Copeland St. (between Oak and Park Sts.), Jacksonville, FL 32204. Tel. 904/384-4630. 8 rms (all with bath). A/C TV TEL

$ Rates (including full breakfast): $75 single; $85–$135 double. Additional person $10 extra. AE, MC, V. **Parking:** Free on premises.

This three-story plantation-style home, fronted by a spacious veranda with massive fluted Doric columns, was built for a real estate mogul in 1905. Its interior features glossy pine floors and gorgeous cypress paneling, wainscotting, and carved moldings. Breakfast—breakfast meats, eggs, fresh fruit, juice, fresh-baked muffins and breads, and coffee—is served in a lovely dining room with a crystal chandelier above a lace-clothed table, swagged mint-green draperies, and a working fireplace. Or, weather permitting, you might take the morning meal on an enclosed brick patio, a delightful setting with ivied walls, flower beds and pots of geraniums, outdoor statuary, and garden furnishings under the shade of a massive live oak tree. The patio also contains a lap pool and whirlpool spa. Another public area is a comfortable living room with a stunning cypress-framed ceramic-tile fireplace. And there's also a big furnished wraparound porch on the second floor with seating amid potted geraniums, hibiscus, and bougainvillea.

Accommodations are beautifully furnished with antiques. Yours might have an 1870s French bedroom suite, a king-size mahogany four-poster made up with a Laura Ashley rose-motif bedspread and ruffled pillow shams, an 18th-century Louis XVI–style bed with a lilac-motif spread, an Early American oak armoire and rolltop desk, Oriental silk rugs, or 19th-century cherrywood Mission pieces. There are wonderful curtain treatments throughout, all rooms are equipped with ceiling fans and clock radios, and residential touches include shelves of objets d'art, baskets filled with Victorian dried-flower arrangements, decorative fireplaces, and marvelous old paintings. Amenities include nightly turn-down with a chocolate mint and brandy, fresh fruit in every room, and a public refrigerator stocked with complimentary beer and soft drinks.

THE WILLOWS, 1849 Willow Branch Terrace (on the St. Johns River), Jacksonville, FL 32205. Tel. 904/387-9152 or 904/389-6394. 2 rms (both with bath). A/C MINIBAR TV TEL

$ Rates (including full breakfast): $65–$85 per room. No small children accepted. No smoking on premises. No credit cards. **Parking:** Free on premises.

This charming riverside B&B occupies an ivy-covered Mediterranean-style stucco house on a tranquil tree-lined street. Inside, guests have access to a vast terra-cotta-floored living room with a beamed pecky-cypress ceiling, serpentine Moorish furnishings, a hand-painted German piano, and a working fireplace flanked by brass torchiers; French tapestries adorn its white stucco walls. A lacy black wrought-iron gate heralds the dining room, which overlooks the river. Full breakfasts—fresh fruit, juice, breakfast meats, homemade muffins and biscuits, an entree (perhaps French toast or cheese soufflé), and coffee—are served here on a handsome oak table. The back lawn, which faces on the river and contains a 50-foot swimming pool, is planted with magnolias, palms, pines, and live oaks. Guests can sit out on a porch or balcony portico, sipping complimentary wine and watching boats gliding along the river.

The jade-and-cream bedroom downstairs is Asian themed, with a Chinese carpet, silk embroideries, and chairs upholstered in a pagoda motif. A nonworking fireplace is used to display an arrangement of silk and dried flowers. The other, more ornate accommodation has a dusty-rose velvet sofa with throw pillows, a French floral-pattern rug on an oak floor, a Venetian-style candelabra chandelier ornamented with ceramic roses, and a suite of bedroom furnishings embellished with ormulu floral decorations. French doors open to a private balcony with Moorish-style Corinthian columns framing arched windows—another setting in which to enjoy river views. Both rooms have beautifully tiled baths and refrigerators stocked with free beer, wine, and soft drinks. Charming hostess Mary Collins pampers guests with fruit, liqueurs, chocolates, and fresh flowers on arrival.

PONTE VEDRA BEACH RESORTS

Originally an executive retreat for a titanium-mining company, Ponte Vedra Beach is one of Florida's ritziest areas. Officially, it's part of St. Augustine, but since the deluxe resorts described here are closer to Jacksonville, I've listed them in this section.

Expensive

MARRIOTT AT SAWGRASS RESORT, 1000 TPC Blvd. (off Fla. A1A between U.S. 210 and J. Turner Butler Blvd.), Ponte Vedra Beach, FL 32082. Tel. 904/285-7777, or toll free 800/457-GOLF or 800/228-9290. Fax 904/285-0906. 324 rms, 214 suites/villas. A/C MINIBAR TV TEL

$ **Rates:** $105–$189 single or double in standard rooms and villa rooms (additional person $20 extra; Children under 17 stay free in parents' room); $175–$240 one-bedroom villa; $265–$440 two-bedroom villa; $325–$550 three-bedroom villa. Higher rates reflect peak season (mid-Feb to mid-Jun). Inquire about golf, tennis, and honeymoon packages. Lower advance-purchase rates subject to availability. AE, CB, DC, DISC, ER, JCB, MC, V. **Parking:** Free self-parking, $8 per night valet parking.

Entered via a towering skylit atrium lobby, with a waterfall cascading into a lush tropical garden, this stunning 4,800-acre resort occupies a verdant landscape of golf greens, waterfalls, lakes, and lagoons spanned by graceful wooden bridges. Forests of ancient oaks and magnolias and natural areas of sawgrass, palm, and bamboo form a backdrop for prim manicured lawns and flower beds. The grounds are home to hundreds of blue herons, egrets, and other shore birds.

Rooms in the main building are cheerfully decorated in teal hues, with birch furnishings and splashy floral prints adding peach, mauve, and lavender accents. All are equipped with bedside and desk phones, clock radios, and remote-control cable TVs (offering Spectravision movies, tourism information channels, account review, and video checkout/messaging). "King rooms" have sofas. One- and two-bedroom villas on or near a golf course are decorated in soft resort colors. These offer fully equipped kitchens, living rooms with ceiling fans, and large furnished patios or balconies. And especially luxurious are one- to three-bedroom beachfront villas furnished in residential style with huge kitchens, living rooms with working fireplaces, full dining rooms, and large screened wooden decks.

Dining/Entertainment: The ultra-elegant Augustine Room is the resort's gourmet dining room (see "Where to Dine," below). The country club–like Café on the Green, a lovely plant-filled restaurant with a picture window overlooking the golf course, serves breakfast, lunch, dinner, and Sunday brunch. Adjoining it is Cascades, a multilevel, tropically themed piano bar below an indoor waterfall. The upscale Cabana Club restaurant at the beach serves nouvelle cuisine; it has an outdoor patio and an adjoining lounge featuring nightly music for dancing. The 100th Hole, a poolside bar, serves light fare and frozen tropical drinks; it has open-air seating on a wooden deck with umbrella tables. Champs, an on-premises dance club, is described in "Evening Entertainment," below.

Services: Room service (6:30am–1am), concierge (7am–8pm), car-rental desk, complimentary shuttle to/from the beach and golf courses, newspaper delivery/nightly turn-down on request, airport transfer available.

Facilities: Three tropically landscaped swimming pools (one is Olympic size), kiddie pool, two secluded whirlpools, pool/beach accessories shop, 21 tennis courts on four different surfaces (Har-Tru, red clay, hard, grass), two first-rate health clubs, five championship golf courses (with 99 holes, Marriott at Sawgrass is America's second-largest golf resort; two of its courses are top-ranked), golf/tennis pro shop and teaching pros/clinics, four driving ranges, six putting greens, gratis use of 2½-mile private beach at the nearby Cabana Club, on-premises rentals (jet skis, windsurf boards, bicycles, fishing poles), lagoons stocked with wide-mouth bass for fishing, nature and biking trails, horseback riding, Sawgrass Village (a complex of boutiques and specialty shops), gift shop.

The Grasshopper Gang, a children's program, offers daily activities for ages 3–12, a recreation room, and a playground; open Mon–Sat 10am–3pm, it costs $20 per child, lunch included. There's also a teen program for ages 13–15.

PONTE VEDRA INN & CLUB, 200 Ponte Vedra Blvd. (off Fla. A1A), Ponte Vedra Beach, FL 32082. Tel. 904/285-1111, or toll free 800/234-7842. Fax 904/285-2111. 182 rms, 20 suites. A/C MINIBAR TV TEL

$ **Rates:** Dec–Feb, $95–$115 single or double. Mar–May, $175–$195 single or double. June–Aug, $125–$145 single or double. Sept–Nov, $145–$165 single or double. Suites $70–$100 extra. Additional person $8 extra; children under 12 stay free in parents' room. Highest rates for oceanfront views, lowest for golf course views. Inquire about golf, tennis, spa, and other packages. AE, CB, DC, DISC, MC, V. **Parking:** Free self- and valet parking.

Here's a chance to pamper yourself at a luxurious 300-acre private country club and spa that has been "enjoyed by some of this country's finest families" since 1928. The Ponte Vedra Inn is ultra-elegant from the moment you drive up to its manicured front lawn that doubles as a putting green. Inside, a charming lobby adjoins the lodgelike Great Lounge, a sedate precinct under a beamed cypress ceiling with overstuffed sofas and armchairs and massive fireplaces at either end.

Spacious rooms—all with furnished patios or balconies—are individually decorated in beachy pastel colors (aqua, peach, mauve) and furnished with bleached-wood pieces. They're enhanced by lovely fabrics and aesthetically pleasing valence and cornice treatments. Some have four-poster or sleigh beds. In-room amenities include wet bars, coffee makers, safes, ceiling fans, alarm-clock AM/FM radios, and remote-control cable TVs with free HBO. You'll find a hairdryer, scale, luxury bath products, and plush terry robe in the bath, a cosmetic mirror and double sink in your large dressing room. Microwave ovens and small refrigerators are available on request.

Dining/Entertainment: Breakfast and dinner are served in the formal Gourmet Room, a genteel setting with beautifully appointed white-linened tables, candlelit at night. A traditional continental menu features steaks, chops, and seafood. The adjoining Audubon Lounge offers nightly piano bar entertainment. Steak and seafood are also on the menu at the casual turquoise-and-peach Florida Room, open for dinner only. The Golf Club Restaurant, with picture windows overlooking the greens and a lagoon, serves reasonably priced American fare at lunch; a bar/lounge adjoins. The Surf Club, its entrance walls adorned with historic beach photos, is open for lunch only, March through October, offering salads, sandwiches, and frozen tropical drinks; it has outdoor seating at umbrella tables. And the elegant Seafoam Dining Room, with tiered ocean-view seating, serves American/continental lunches and dinners; a pianist entertains at dinner, and there's dancing on Friday and Saturday nights to a live trio in the adjoining Seahorse Lounge. The spa has its own little ocean-view restaurant serving light lunches to women enjoying "days of beauty." And the High Tides Lounge, with umbrella tables on a patio overlooking the ocean, serves light fare and frozen drinks.

Services: 24-hour room service, concierge, executive business center, nightly bed turn-down, shoeshine, complimentary newspaper each morning.

Facilities: Three outdoor swimming pools (one Olympic-size), children's wading pool, oceanfront whirlpool, two championship 18-hole golf courses, 15 Har-Tru tennis courts (many lit for night play), golf/tennis pro shops and instruction, upscale gift/resortwear shop, FTD-affiliated flower shop, the Surf Shop, beach equipment rentals, half a mile of beautiful private sand beach and boardwalk, extensive health club, sand volleyball court, library, planned activities for adults and children. A gorgeous on-premises spa offers all spa services—treat yourself to a "day of beauty." A child-care facility called the Nursery provides care and activities for children 6 months to 6 years for $3 per child ($1 per additional child); in summer there's a full youth camp program for children 4–12.

JACKSONVILLE BEACH

Inexpensive

COMFORT INN OCEANFRONT, 1515 N. 1st St. (off Fla. A1A), Jacksonville Beach, FL 32250. Tel. 904/241-2311, or toll free 800/654-8776. Fax 904/249-3830. 177 rms, 3 suites. A/C TV TEL

$ **Rates** (including continental breakfast): $59.50–$69.50 standard single or double, $65–$75 single or double with pool or ocean view, $75–$95 single or double oceanfront; $125–$135 suite. Additional person $10 extra. Children under 18 stay free in parents' room. AE, CB, DC, DISC, ER, JCB, MC, V. **Parking:** Free self-parking.

Fronted by 3,000 feet of pristine white sand beach, the Comfort Inn offers spiffy-looking accommodations and numerous facilities. Rooms are decorated in raspberry or seafoam-green color schemes, with bleached-wood or oak furnishings and paintings of beach scenes and shore birds on the walls. All have balconies (screened patios on the first level) and are equipped with remote-control cable TVs with pay movie options. Microwave/refrigerator units are available for $7 a night. An especially good deal here is a honeymoon suite with Jacuzzi tub, living room area, microwave oven (dishes and cooking utensils are supplied), refrigerator, and wet bar.

Dining/Entertainment: Continental breakfast and light fare (soups, sandwiches, salads) are served in Lite Bites, a small poolside eatery. Kokomo's, a beautiful pine-paneled lounge with a window wall overlooking the ocean, features live music for dancing nightly April through Labor Day, as well as a pool table and dart boards. Complimentary hors d'oeuvres are served weekdays at happy hour. In season you can order light fare at Kokomo's, and, weather permitting, there's outdoor seating at umbrella tables. An oceanside cabana bar is also operational in peak season.

Facilities: Large pool with rock waterfalls and palm-fringed sun deck, secluded grotto whirlpool, small fitness room, gift/sundries shop/convenience store, multicourt sand volleyball park (scene of major tournaments), rentals (summer only; surfboards, boogie boards, bicycles, kayaks, windsurfers, beach chairs and umbrellas).

WHERE TO DINE

VERY EXPENSIVE

THE AUGUSTINE ROOM, in the Marriott at Sawgrass Resort, 1000 TPC Blvd. (off Fla. A1A between U.S. 210 and J. Turner Butler Blvd.), Ponte Vedra Beach. Tel. 285-7777.

Cuisine: AMERICAN/CONTINENTAL. **Reservations:** Recommended.

$ **Prices:** Appetizers $7.95–$11.95; main courses $21.95–$31.95. AE, CB, DC, DISC, ER, JCB, MC, V.

Open: Dinner only, Tues–Sat 6:30–10pm.

The oak-paneled Augustine Room is Jacksonville's most formal dining room. Tables covered in ecru Belgian linen sparkle with fine china, crystal, silver, and vases of fresh flowers. Seating is in plush leather banquettes or Regency-style chairs, and ultra-suede walls are hung with hand-tinted etchings and lithographs of turn-of-the-century St. Augustine. Soft lighting emanates from graceful chandeliers and shaded candle lamps, and the background music is classical. Men are requested to wear jackets. Free parking is available on premises.

Freshly shucked baked oysters filled with backfin crabmeat and topped with mornay sauce and fresh-grated parmesan make a great beginning to your meal here.

Another possibility is an enchilada stuffed with julienne of Maine lobster served with a crisp-fried smoked scallop wonton and crisscrossed with a spicy tomato coulis. A dish of sautéed jumbo shrimp was served atop a bed of nutmeg-flavored spinach and angel-hair pasta garnished with roasted pine nuts in basil-cream sauce. Also excellent was the rack of lamb—a fan of slices served with orange marmalade sauce, dauphinois potatoes, and an array of vegetables including sun-dried tomatoes, fried onion rings, and snowpeas on red- and yellow-pepper coulis. Sorbet is served between courses, and coffee is accompanied by a silver tray laden with chocolate shavings, nutmeg, cinnamon sticks, brown sugar, orange rind, and fresh whipped cream. Desserts are fittingly sumptuous. You might opt for banana-strawberry mousse in a gingerbread-cinnamon horn served atop a strawberry-marbelized custard and garnished with rum-soaked strawberries and banana slices. The restaurant's extensive wine list is international in scope.

EXPENSIVE

THE CHART HOUSE, 601 Hendricks Ave., at Prudential Dr. (on the Riverwalk). Tel. 398-3353.

Cuisine: STEAK/SEAFOOD. **Reservations:** Recommended. **Directions:** Take I-95N and make a right at the Prudential Drive exit, a left at Hendricks Avenue, and a right into the Marina complex.

$ Prices: Appetizers $4.25–$7.95; main courses $12.95–$22.95. AE, CB, DC, DISC, MC, V.

Open: Dinner only, Sun–Thurs 5:30–10pm, Fri–Sat 5:30–11pm.

This beautiful restaurant, with a window wall overlooking the St. Johns River, was designed by a protégé of Frank Lloyd Wright named Kendrick Kellogg. Like Wright, Kellogg highlights natural elements—a stone waterfall at the entrance, an arched cypress ceiling crossed by rough-hewn beams, and seating in roomy circular booths enclosed by teakwood, amid ficus trees, ferns, and potted palms. Stone columns serve as a base for massive planters of cascading philodendrons. It's almost like dining outdoors. Candlelit tables are topped with laminated oak-framed world maps—a Chart House tradition. The Chart House is a national chain, but each location is different. There's free parking on premises.

There are few appetizers on the menu, because your main-dish price includes—along with a basket of hot fresh-baked sourdough and cakey brown squaw breads—unlimited selections from a very extensive salad bar. If you want something additional before your entree, try the New England clam chowder, a thick, creamy soup with big chunks of potato and clams. For a main course, we suggest baked grouper, lightly dredged in garlicky herbed breadcrumbs, or, if you're in a meatier mood, filet mignon with béarnaise butter. The Chart House serves fresh seafood and midwestern corn-fed Grade-A beef, aged and cut on the premises. Main courses are accompanied by a baked Idaho potato or yummy Chart House rice tossed with toasted almonds and bits of pimiento and pineapple. For dessert, indulge in ultra-creamy cheesecake on a graham cracker crust or decadent mud pie—coffee mocha ice cream on a buttery chocolate cookie crust topped with fudge sauce, real whipped cream, and butter-toasted almonds. There's a full bar, and a sizable wine list, with premium wines available by the glass. The service staff, festively attired in Hawaiian floral prints, proffers deft and friendly service.

SAND DOLLAR, 9716 Heckscher Dr., just north of the Maypont Ferry. Tel. 251-2449.

Cuisine: SEAFOOD. **Reservations:** Accepted only for large parties.

$ Prices: Appetizers $3.50–$6.95; burgers and sandwiches $3.95–$5.50; main courses $6.75–$10.95 at lunch, $11.95–$20.95 at dinner. All-you-can-eat specials $12.95 Mon–Thurs after 4pm. MC, V.

Open: Sun–Thurs 11am–10pm, Fri–Sat 11am–11pm.

This is the perfect place to stop for lunch en route to or from the Kingsley Plantation, the Jacksonville Zoo, or the Anheuser-Busch Brewery. The rustic interior, with rough-hewn pine dividers and overhead beams, is warmly inviting, and the view from a wall of windows—a passing parade of boats and shore birds along the St. Johns

River—is thrillingly scenic. Seating is in captain's chairs at pine tables with starfish, seahorses, and seashells embedded in laminated tabletops. All tables offer great water views, and in summer you can dine on a riverside wooden deck. Many boats dock here for meals.

Fried seafood—oysters, shrimp, and deviled crab—is the specialty. Order a combination plate with a baked potato and cole slaw. Another good choice is the Fort George roaster—grilled shrimp, served with new potatoes, fresh corn on the cob, and steamed cabbage. Or you might select a po-boy sandwich of fried shrimp or oysters on a hoagie bun with tartar sauce. Chicken, steaks, and burgers are available for non-seafood fanciers, and a children's menu offers $3.25 meals. The bar is a popular hangout for locals. Homemade desserts include mud and key lime pies.

MODERATE

CIAO GIANNI RISTORANTE, Jacksonville Landing. Tel. 353-2626.

Cuisine: ITALIAN. **Reservations:** Recommended; required at lunch.

$ Prices: Appetizers $4.95–$5.50 at lunch, $4.50–$10.50 at dinner; main courses $6.50–$8.95 at lunch, $10.95–$15.95 at dinner. AE, MC, V.

Open: Sun–Thurs 11am–10:30pm, Fri–Sat 11am–11pm (lunch menu available until 3:30pm).

This casual Jacksonville Landing restaurant is popular with locals, especially for dessert and espresso after shows at the nearby Civic Center (park in the Landing lot). Sunny during the day, candlelit at night, it has marble-top tables, cherrywood beams and columns, and interior leaded-glass windows. Owner/chef Giovanni Recupito, from Salerno, tosses pizzas and pastas in an open display kitchen. Italian music or light jazz enhance the ambience. In good weather, you can dine al fresco under a bright-yellow awning.

Appetizers of fried mozzarella, calamari, or zucchini come with chunky marinara sauce. Thin-crusted pizza—perhaps quatro formaggi, topped with meunster, mozzarella, fontina, and romano cheeses—is another good beginning. Or you might request a scrumptious starter salad of fresh mozzarella with roasted red and green peppers in herbed vinaigrette. Among the pasta dishes, I like the fettuccine San Remo, tossed in cream sauce with an array of fresh fish and seafood—calamari, scallops, shrimp, scungilli, clams, and mussels—served with fresh-grated parmesan. Entrees include a house salad and hot, garlicky herbed rolls. Non-pasta choices—such as grilled shrimp scampi or chicken sautéed with mushrooms, cream, and fresh tarragon—also include a side of pasta. You can get half orders of pasta for children, and lunch fare includes sandwiches such as eggplant parmigiana on Italian bread. There's a full bar, and the wine list highlights French and California selections, with house-label wines available by the glass. The dessert of choice is creamy zabaglione topped with fresh strawberries.

STERLING'S FLAMINGO CAFE, 3551 St. Johns Ave., between Talbot and Ingleside Aves. Tel. 387-0700.

Cuisine: INTERNATIONAL. **Reservations:** Recommended.

$ Prices: Appetizers $3.95–$7.95 at lunch, $7.95–$8.95 at dinner; main courses $6.25–$8.50 at lunch, $15.95–$19.95 at dinner; Sun brunch $10.75 prix-fixe. AE, CB, DC, DISC, MC, V.

Open: Lunch Mon–Sat 11am–2:30pm; dinner Mon–Thurs 5:30–10pm, Fri–Sat 5:30–11pm; brunch Sun 11am–2:30pm.

This charming restaurant has a gardenlike feel. The front room, hung with botanical prints, has forest-green carpeting, and baskets of flowers are perched on the sills of large, square windows. In the main dining room, peach walls are hung with prints of flamingos (the restaurant's signature), and beautifully appointed candlelit tables are graced by fresh flower arrangements. French doors lead to a lovely plant-filled patio under a striped awning. Soft jazz adds to Sterling's' simpatico ambience, and exquisite food presentations enhance its sophisticated cuisine.

Begin your dinner with a salad of lightly breaded pan-sautéed goat cheese atop mixed baby greens tossed with sun-dried tomatoes, hazelnuts, and fresh cilantro, in a basil vinaigrette. Pastas are available as appetizers or entrees. Among the non-pasta entrees are grilled filet mignon stuffed with roasted garlic cloves, served in a cabernet sauce topped with Gorganzola butter; grilled salmon and shrimp in a roasted red-pepper/hollandaise sauce with fried spinach; and a fresh catch (perhaps grouper) baked en papillote (in parchment) with an array of fresh herbs, white wine, lemon, and butter. Entrees are served with a side of pasta, rice, or potato du jour and fresh vegetables such as grilled asparagus. At lunch, you can opt for tasty salads and sandwiches, and both lunch and dinner menus are augmented by many specials. The prix-fixe Sunday brunch includes juice, fruit (perhaps broiled grapefruit), bacon or smoked sausage, cheese grits or home fries, and sweet rolls along with such dishes as banana bread French toast or smoked pork chop with sautéed apples. Sterling's offers a good selection of domestic and imported wines—many available by the glass—to complement your meal. And sumptuous desserts range from an ambrosial chocolate crème brûlée to a rich flourless Belgian chocolate cake served with vanilla Häagen-Dazs.

24 MIRAMAR, in the Miramar Shopping Center, 4446 Hendricks Ave., between Emerson St. and University Blvd. Tel. 448-2424.

Cuisine: UPSCALE CALIFORNIAN. **Reservations:** Recommended.

$ Prices: Appetizers $6.95–$8.50; main courses $14.75–$22.50. AE, CB, DC, DISC, MC, V.

Open: Dinner only, Mon–Thurs 5:30–10pm, Fri–Sat 5:30–11pm.

This elegant restaurant is the creation of Tim (he's the chef) and Barbara (pastry wizard) Felver, a couple with an impressive culinary résumé. They've worked with Wolfgang Puck in Los Angeles, cooked at Johnny Carson's house, prepared food for Madonna's wedding, and catered dinners for everyone from Philippe Rothschild to Nureyev. A postmodern art deco black-and-white background—checkerboard floor, black leather booths and banquettes, black-and-white photographs on gallery-white walls, and tables adorned with arrangements of white flowers in black vases on white linen—contrasts with a jade-green ceiling and colorful murals of fish, fruits, and vegetables. Soft lighting and New Age music set a mellow tone.

Food is aesthetically presented. Marvelous subtleties unfold as you savor appetizers such as chilled Apalachicola oysters topped with gazpacho and served with chorizo sausage and corn tamales filled with mashed stone-ground corn, jalapeños, and cilantro; and pan-fried herb-flavored crabcakes served with mango-tomatillo salsa and emulsified sun-dried tomato vinaigrette, garnished with finely shredded daikon radish sprinkled with black sesame seeds. An entree of angel-hair pasta, tossed with sautéed garlic and shrimp, chopped tomato, fresh basil, and soft crumbled goat cheese in virgin olive oil was unforgettable. Ditto the Thai shrimp served with lemongrass-butter sauce, spring vegetables, and a crisp pan-fried angel-hair pasta pancake with crunchy morsels of julienned leek, chili peppers, carrot, and squash. And one final dish we must mention is Norwegian smoked salmon served atop a crispy nest of very delicately shredded deep-fried potato, garnished with herbed crème fraîche, chives, and two caviars. Barbara bakes different breads each night. She might present you with a basket of oven-fresh foccacia topped with grilled tomatoes, basil, and goat cheese. And her desserts—such as a marscapone cheese tart on raspberry sauce topped with shavings of white chocolate and fresh blackberries—garner rave reviews. There's a carefully chosen list of American and imported wines, and service is excellent.

INEXPENSIVE

CAFE CARMON, 1986 San Marco Blvd., between Carlo St. and Naldo Ave. Tel. 399-4488.

Cuisine: AMERICAN. **Reservations:** Not accepted.

$ Prices: Appetizers $4.95–$7.95; main courses $5.95–$7.95 at lunch, $7.50–$14.95 at dinner. AE, DC, DISC, MC, V.

Open: Mon–Thurs 11am–11pm, Fri–Sat 11am–midnight; brunch Sun 11am–3pm.

This comfy and casual restaurant is located in the heart of the San Marco shopping district, an area filled with interesting bookstores, boutiques, and antiques shops. During the week it's a mecca for foot-weary shoppers, and on Friday and Saturday nights the place is jammed with post-movie and theatergoers who come in for cappuccino and dessert. Seating is out front on a terra-cotta patio or at a counter and banquettes inside. The interior is decorated in pristine black and white, with fans and schoolroom lights suspended from a lofty ceiling and an exposed-brick wall behind the bar. Stark gallery-white walls are hung with museum art posters.

At lunch or dinner, you can order delicious salads such as sautéed goat cheese with sun-dried tomatoes, toasted hazelnuts, cilantro, and mixed greens in a tangy vinaigrette. At dinner entrees include pastas, pon soo chicken breast (stuffed with caramelized ginger and garlic), and blackened filets of grouper with cumin butter, the latter dishes served with house salad, warm bread, and a side dish (perhaps red-skin potato salad or pasta primavera). Everything is made from scratch, and it's all first-rate. Leave room for dessert. The rich, moist carrot cake—a huge slab studded with raisins and walnuts, layered with praline cream, slathered with cream cheese icing, and topped with toasted coconut—is the *ne plus ultra* of its genre.

CHILI'S GRILL & BAR, in the Baymeadows Commons Shopping Center, 9500 Baymeadows Rd., just west of Southside Blvd. Tel. 739-2476.

Cuisine: SOUTHWESTERN. **Reservations:** Not accepted.

$ Prices: Appetizers $3.95–$5.95; main courses $4.75–$9.95. AE, CB, DC, DISC, MC, V.

Open: Sun–Thurs 11am–11pm, Fri–Sat 11am–midnight.

Chili's is a national chain, based in Texas, offering superior "bowls of red" and other southwestern specialties. This branch is sunny and plant-filled, with seating in comfortable upholstered booths. Hanging lamps made from old copper chili pots illuminate ceramic-tiled tables and slowly whirring fans are suspended from the forest-green ceiling. You can also eat in the lively bar area where the TV is tuned to sporting events. This is a great choice for family dining, and there's free parking, too.

The same menu is offered all day. Chili is, of course, a specialty, available with or without beans. Equally popular are fabulous half-pound burgers, made from fresh-ground beef. They come with home-style fries made from scratch, topped with cheese and chili if you wish. Another big item is fried chicken with country gravy, served with homemade mashed potatoes (with skins), corn on the cob, and Texas toast. And should you want something lighter, order a grilled tuna salad with greens, pico de gallo, sugary walnuts, and onions in a ranch dressing. Desserts run the gamut from frozen yogurt to a brownie topped with vanilla ice cream, hot fudge, chopped walnuts, and whipped cream. A children's menu lists full meals for just $2.45.

L&N SEAFOOD GRILL, Jacksonville Landing. Tel. 358-7737.

Cuisine: SEAFOOD/STEAK/PASTA. **Reservations:** Not accepted (but call ahead for preferred seating).

$ Prices: Appetizers $3.95–$6.95; main courses $4.50–$8.95 at lunch, $8.50–$15.95 at dinner. AE, CB, DC, DISC, MC, V.

Open: Lunch daily 11am–4pm; dinner Sun–Thurs 4–10pm, Fri–Sat 4–11:30pm.

A riverside seafood restaurant with wraparound windows offering scenic water views, L&N is a handsome place with seating in teak booths at crisply white-linened tables, lots of leafy plants, and wood-bladed fans suspended from a dark-green pressed-tin ceiling. A shiplike effect is enhanced by teak paneling and columns and walls pristinely adorned with nautically themed prints and scientific illustrations of fish. Soft lighting emanates from halaphane lamps and sconces. You can enjoy drinks and fresh-shucked oysters at a marble-top bar in the black-and-white–tiled lounge. And there's outdoor seating on an awninged brick terrace bordered by flowering plants. Many boaters tie up at a dock just outside the restaurant. Parking is in the Jacksonville Landing lot.

Begin your meal with a sharp seafood cheese dip loaded with shrimp and scallops and served with blue- and white-corn tortilla chips. Or opt for plump oysters

Rockefeller baked with a topping of herbed breadcrumbs, fresh spinach, garlic butter, and sherried cheese sauce. Dinner entrees include a crisp bottomless salad with homemade creamy ranch dressing and unlimited fresh-baked biscuits. Among your choices: baked shrimp stuffed with softshell crabmeat in a creamy mornay sauce, served with rice pilaf and crisply cooked fresh vegetables; wood-smoked chicken, tossed with penne pasta and slivers of sweet red peppers in a white wine–pesto sauce, topped with fresh-grated parmesan; and mesquite-grilled sirloin served with garlic butter and redskin potatoes. Most of the above items are also available at lunch. Also recommendable at either meal is blackened chicken salad with honey-mustard dressing. Desserts range from a light fresh lemon mousse to ultra-rich butterscotch-pecan pie served in caramel sauce and topped with vanilla ice cream.

BRUNCH

Banyan's, at the Jacksonville Marriott, 4670 Salisbury Rd., off I-95 at J. Turner Butler Boulevard (tel. 296-2222), offers a lavish buffet brunch, including unlimited champagne, every Sunday from 10:30am to 2pm. The table is laden with piles of peel-and-eat shrimp, assorted salads, broiled fresh fish, a chicken dish, breakfast meats, lyonnaise and new potatoes, pasta dishes, blintzes, bagels and lox, fresh fruits and vegetables, cheeses, juices, and tea and coffee. There's an omelet/waffle/French toast/pancake station, a roast meat–carving station, and a Caesar salad station. And the dessert display table offers homemade cobbler, ice cream, pies, cakes, and mousses. Banyan's is softly lit, with comfortable seating at white-linened tables, bleached-oak panels and columns, and many plants. Weather permitting, there are tables on a patio outside bordered by potted palms. A harpist entertains while you dine. The cost is $12.95 for adults, $10.95 for seniors 65 and over, $6.95 for ages 6–12, free for kids under 6. Reservations suggested.

EVENING ENTERTAINMENT

There's lots to do at night in this lively beach town. Check the papers for concerts and events at Jacksonville Landing and other entertainment venues.

THE PERFORMING ARTS

ALHAMBRA DINNER THEATRE, 12000 Beach Blvd., between Hodges and St. Johns Bluff Rds. Tel. 641-1212.

The Alhambra presents entertaining professional productions of Broadway shows—most of them musicals and many of them Neil Simon comedies. Recent productions have included *Greater Tuna, My Fair Lady, Hello Dolly, Biloxi Blues, Broadway Bound,* and *Brighton Beach Memoirs*. There are seven productions each year. The price of admission includes a full buffet dinner featuring a prime rib carving station, baked chicken entree, seafood Newburg, and an array of vegetables, salads, and desserts, as well as tea or coffee. A full bar and wine list are available. Tuesday through Sunday, the buffet dinner begins at 6:30pm, the show at 8:15pm; for the Saturday matinee, the buffet begins at 11:30am, the show at 1:15pm; and for the Sunday matinee, the buffet begins at 12:15pm, the show at 2pm.

Admission: Sun–Fri $27.50, Sat night $29.50, Sat–Sun matinees $24.50; seniors 55 and over and children under 17 pay $2 less except on Fri–Sat nights.

CIVIC AUDITORIUM, 300 Water St., between Coastline Dr. and Pearl St. Tel. 630-0700 for information, 353-3309 to charge tickets.

This 3,200-seat facility on the St. Johns River is used for symphony concerts, ballet performances, headliner concerts (Julio Iglesias, Liza Minnelli, Sade, the Black Crowes, Tom Jones), and theatrical productions. In addition to presenting Broadway shows such as *Cats* and *Les Misérables,* the Civic is the home of the acclaimed Jacksonville Symphony (in summer they do an outdoor series as well at Metro Park), and visiting performers have included everyone from flautist James Galway to violinist Itzhak Perlman. From the lobby, the waterfront setting provides a beautiful backdrop. Park in the adjacent lot; the charge varies with the event.

Admission: Ticket prices vary with the event.

ROCK, POP & FAMILY SHOWS

THE GATOR BOWL, 1400 E. Duval St., at Adams St. Tel. 360-3900 for information, 353-3309 to charge tickets.

This huge facility is the setting for major rock concerts featuring such superstars as Michael Jackson and the Rolling Stones.

Adjacent to it, and under the same auspices, is the 10,600-seat **Jacksonville Veterans Memorial Coliseum,** 1145 E. Adams St. (same phone numbers), another venue for many headliner concerts—Frank Sinatra, Garth Brooks, Van Halen, Jimmy Buffett, Alabama, Cure—as well as family shows such as the circus and *Disney on Ice*. There's paid parking for ticketed events; rates vary with the event.

Admission: Ticket prices vary according to the event.

THE CLUB & BAR SCENE

CHAMPS, at the Marriott at Sawgrass Resort, 1000 TPC Blvd., off Fla. A1A, Ponte Vedra Beach. Tel. 285-7777.

This handsome mahogany-paneled club is popular with locals and visitors alike. Plushly furnished, it has a wall of windows overlooking a lagoon and even offers outdoor seating on a flagstone patio. A live band plays Top-40 tunes for dancing Tuesday through Saturday nights. There's a nice-sized dance floor, and additional attractions include blackjack tables (you can't win money, but you can hone your skills). Champs serves complimentary hot and cold hors d'oeuvres weekdays during happy hour (5:30 to 7pm). At night it offers light fare—pizzas, quesadillas, blackened chicken salad—and a wide range of specialty drinks ranging from concoctions like a frozen sand castle (Kahlúa, cream of coconut, and pineapple juice) to liqueur-spiked coffees topped with whipped cream. It's open nightly until 12:30am. Parking is free on the premises.

Admission: Free.

CLUB CAROUSEL, 8550 Arlington Expressway (Hwy. 115/U.S. 90 Alt.), on the service road just south of Mill Creek Rd. Tel. 725-2582.

A 30,000-square-foot facility, with a 4,000-square-foot dance floor enhanced by high-tech laser/lighting effects and a revolving stage, the Club Carousel offers an eclectic mix of entertainment. At this writing the schedule is as follows: Monday and Wednesday nights a DJ plays country music from 7pm to midnight, with free line-dancing lessons offered from 7 to 9:30pm. Tuesday nights might feature live country, Top-40, or big-band concerts (hours vary, and sometimes the club is closed; call ahead). Thursday. Friday, and Saturday nights offer a mix of female impersonator shows, comedians, bands, and DJ music until about 3am. Sunday night entertainment varies, sometimes including non-alcoholic dance nights for teenagers with a DJ on hand. And the first and third Sunday of every month there's ballroom dancing here afternoons from 2 to 5pm. Walls are lined with carousel horses. There's a quiet bar up front, away from the dance/show area, where sporting events are aired on a large-screen TV. Adjoining it is a snack bar serving nachos, pizza, hot dogs, and burgers, which you can take into the club or eat at indoor umbrella tables adjoining. There are also bars—and pool tables—at either end of the club. You must be 18 to get in. There's free on-premises parking.

Admission: Usually $4, higher for some concerts and teenage nights.

THE COMEDY ZONE, in the Ramada Inn Conference Center, 3130 Hartley Rd., just above the junction of I-295 and San Jose Blvd. in Mandarin. Tel. 292-4242.

The Comedy Zone presents nationally known comics—the acts you see on comedy channels and the Leno and Letterman shows. Each show features three performers. Celebrity comics such as Marsha Warfield, Yakov Smirnoff, Judy Tenuda, Jeff Foxworthy, and Rita Rudner appear about one week out of every month, and the first Monday of every month is amateur night. Light fare—pizzas and sandwiches—is available. You must be 18 to get in. It's open nightly except Monday, with shows Tuesday through Thursday and Sunday at 8pm, on Friday and Saturday at 8 and 10:15pm, but show times and prices may change when there are special celebrity performances. To get there, take San Jose Boulevard south to Hartley Road and make a left. There's free parking on the premises.

Admission: $5 Tues–Thurs and Sun, $8 Fri–Sat, plus a one-drink minimum (average drink is $3.50; if you're under 21, you must purchase a $3 beverage coupon for soft drinks); amateur night, $2.

CRAZY HORSE SALOON, 5800 Phillips Hwy., a block south of University Blvd. Tel. 731-8892.

This large facility actually encompasses two clubs on its premises, the Crazy Horse and Masquerade. At the Crazy Horse—an archetypical urban cowboy club—a DJ plays country-western music, and every Tuesday night a cable show called "Hitkicker Country" is filmed on the dance floor. Neon beer signs adorn the walls; the crowd wears boots, jeans, and cowboy hats; and there are half a dozen pool tables off the dance floor. Lessons in the Texas two-step are given free to beginners on Monday and Thursday nights, while Tuesday nights there are lessons in western swing for more advanced dancers.

At Masquerade, a DJ plays Top-40 tunes and progressive rock. The club is the scene of frequent contests—hot buns, wet T-shirts, hot legs, and the like—most offering prizes. Dress is casual. You must be 21 to get into either part of the club.

Crazy Horse is open Monday through Saturday till 2am; Masquerade, Wednesday through Saturday till 2am. Parking is free on the premises.

Admission: $2, good for both clubs; Wed nights ladies are admitted free, and Thurs nights everyone is admitted free.

RAGTIME TAVERN AND TAPROOM, 207 Atlantic Blvd., off Fla. A1A. Tel. 241-7877.

This popular beach bar and restaurant features local groups playing live jazz and blues Thursday through Sunday nights. It's a simpatico setting, with a tongue-in-groove pine ceiling and exposed-brick walls hung, country-western style, with neon beer signs. Weekends, especially, the place is really jumping and the crowd is young, but it's lively rather than rowdy. Ragtime brews its own beers—lager, stout, red ale, and wheat beer—in a brewery on the premises. A fairly extensive menu highlights New Orleans specialties, but it also lists other items ranging from pasta dishes to fajitas. You must be 21 to get in Friday or Saturday after 11pm. There are other clubs on this corner, so you can begin an evening at Ragtime and go bar-hopping. It's open on Thursday and Sunday till 11pm, on Friday and Saturday till 1am, and there's free parking on the premises.

Admission: Free.

2. ST. AUGUSTINE

123 miles NE of Orlando, 344 miles N of Miami, 43 miles S of Jacksonville

GETTING THERE By Plane St. Augustine is about equidistant (a one-hour drive) from airports in Jacksonville and Daytona Beach.

By Train The closest Amtrak station (tel. 800/USA-RAIL) is in Jacksonville (see Section 1 of this chapter for details).

By Bus Greyhound buses connect St. Augustine with most of the country. They pull into a very centrally located terminal at 100 Malaga St., near King Street (tel. 904/829-6401).

By Car If you're coming from north or south, take I-95 to U.S. 1. From points west, take I-10 to I-95 South to U.S. 1.

With its 17th-century fort, horse-drawn carriages clip-clopping along narrow cobblestone streets, old city gates, and reconstructed 18th-century Spanish Quarter, St. Augustine seems more like a picturesque European village than a modern American city. This is an exceptionally charming town, replete, like other coastal

Florida destinations, with palm-fringed ocean beaches—but its primary lure is historic. Here Western civilization first took root in the New World.

A SHORT HISTORY The First Spanish Period Founded in 1565, 55 years before the Pilgrims landed at Plymouth Rock, St. Augustine was America's first city. Though Juan Ponce de León sighted—and named—the Florida coast as early as 1513, it was Pedro Menéndez de Avilés who established Spanish supremacy that lasted for two centuries. He arrived with some thousand settlers and a priest, and named the town St. Augustine in honor of the saint whose feast day—August 28—coincided with his first sighting of the Florida coast. The newcomers settled in a Timucuan village called Seloy—site today of the Fountain of Youth and Mission de Nombre de Dios—and set about routing the French from nearby Fort Caroline and converting the natives to Christianity. Later, for reasons of military strategy, the colony moved to higher ground about a mile south, near the bayfront. Life was not easy. The fledgling town was beset by famine, fire, hurricanes, plagues, and attacks by Native Americans, pirates, and the rival British Empire. But St. Augustine survived, and its importance grew as it became increasingly vital to Spain's defense of her commercial coastal route. Between 1672 and 1695 the colonists constructed an impregnable fort, the Castillo de San Marcos, out of a unique local material called coquina (ko-*kee*-nah), a natural stone made up of layers of tiny broken seashells and lime that didn't crumble under artillery fire. Though British troops attacked and burned the town in 1702 and 1740, the populace holed up in the Castillo and survived both onslaughts.

Briefly British In 1763, the British finally gained control of St. Augustine when Spain ceded all of Florida to them in exchange for Havana and other territorial possessions after the French and Indian War. Rather than become British subjects, most of the 3,000 Spanish inhabitants sailed to Cuba. In fact, only eight stayed on. During the American Revolution, St. Augustine remained loyal to the crown. The population increased in 1777 with the arrival of 1,400 Minorcan, Italian, and Greek indentured servants fleeing the tyranny of harsh servitude in New Smyrna, a town about 80 miles south of St. Augustine.

The Second Spanish Regime In 1784, the Treaty of Paris returned Florida to Spain as a reward for its aid during the American Revolution. Once again the population shifted, as many prior Spanish residents returned and most of the English left. The Minorcans—whose previously British Balearic Island country had come under Spanish rule by this time—stayed on. The British loyalists left the city in a shambles. The inhabitants valiantly tried to rebuild, but by the beginning of the 19th century the Spanish empire was already beginning to decline. When it became evident, after numerous incursions, that the Americans would eventually seize Florida anyway, the Spanish sensibly decided to sell it to them. The transfer took place peacefully in 1821, and the Spanish soldiers departed, never to return.

From the Territorial Era to the Gilded Age American rule got off to a shaky start, as a massive yellow fever epidemic decimated the population. Many of St. Augustine's buildings by this time were run-down or in ruins. Nine years after American occupation, there were only 1,700 residents, a third of them slaves. In 1835 the city suffered two major disasters—a freeze that destroyed the orange crop and the onset of a seven-year Seminole War, during which Native Americans struggled to regain control of Florida. But as the focus of hostilities moved away from St. Augustine, the town began to prosper by providing weapons and ships to its embattled neighbors. Roads were built with the profits, and the population grew, and with it the pressure for statehood. In 1845, Florida entered the Union as the 27th state.

During the early days of statehood, with the Seminole Wars over, seasonal visitors from the chilly north began arriving in Florida to enjoy its warm winters. This growth in tourism was interrupted by the Civil War. In March 1862, St. Augustine surrendered to Union forces, and the city remained occupied until the end of the conflict. But almost immediately after the war, the snowbirds began to return. A most important visitor arrived in 1883—Standard Oil magnate Henry M. Flagler. Taken with St. Augustine's Spanish antiquity and mellow charm, he determined to develop the area as a fashionable resort for the wealthy—a winter Newport in the South. By the turn of the century, Flagler had revolutionized the tourism industry throughout

Florida, building plush hotels and developing rail travel along its eastern coastline. Flagler spared no expense—his decorator was Louis Comfort Tiffany. Three of his deluxe hostelries—the Cordova (today the county courthouse), the Alcazar (today the Lightner Museum), and the Ponce de León (today Flagler College)—can still be seen.

St. Augustine Today It wasn't until well into the 20th century, however, that St. Augustine began to fully appreciate its unique heritage and architectural treasure trove. The Historic St. Augustine Preservation Board, formed in 1959, has been responsible for extensive restoration, preservation, and research into the city's past. Today's visitors can explore fascinating historic sites, relax on beautiful beaches, dine at waterfront fish camps and charming cafés, and reside in quaint antique-furnished bed-and-breakfast lodgings. Few places can offer more.

ORIENTATION

INFORMATION Before you go, write or call the **St. Augustine Chamber of Commerce,** 1 Riberia St., St. Augustine, FL 32084 (tel. 904/829-5681), which will send you a calendar of events, maps, and information on attractions, restaurants, and accommodations.

Upon arrival, make your first stop in town the **St. Augustine Visitor Information Center,** 10 Castillo Dr., at San Marco Avenue (tel. 904/825-1000). Here you can view an 18-minute film called *St. Augustine Adventure;* pick up brochures about accommodations, restaurants, sights, and shops; and—most important—obtain a combined three-day ticket for sightseeing trains and trolleys along with discount tickets to major attractions (for details, see "Getting Around," below). A knowledgeable staff can answer all your questions. There's inexpensive parking on the premises. The VIC is open daily (except Christmas Day) from 8:30am to 5:30pm.

CITY LAYOUT St. Augustine is quite a small town, and you'll easily find your way around. It's bounded to the west by U.S. 1, to the east (along the coast of the Intracoastal Waterway and Matanzas Bay) by Avenida Menendez. The North Bridge leads to Fla. A1A North and Vilano Beach, the beautiful Bridge of Lions to Fla. A1A South and Anastasia Island. Florida 16 on the north side of town provides access to I-95. The heart of town is still the original plaza laid out in the 16th century, bounded east and west by Charlotte and St. George Streets, north and south by Cathedral Place and King Street. The old Spanish Quarter is farther north on St. George Street, between Cuna and Orange Streets.

GETTING AROUND

BY SIGHTSEEING TROLLEYS & TRAINS St. Augustine provides excellent transportation, via sightseeing trolleys and trains, to its numerous historic sites and tourist attractions. These vehicles travel around town along seven-mile loop routes, stopping at or near all attractions. It's easier than using a car, because you never have to worry about parking, which can be difficult at times (you can leave your car at the trolley or train lot, or take advantage of complimentary pickup and return to and from local hotels). Entertaining and informative on-board narrations enhance your touring.

Trolleys and trains are run by two separate (and equally recommended) companies, and these two firms have collaborated to offer a truly great deal. If you purchase your tickets at the **Visitor Information Center** (see "Information," in "Orientation," above) you can get a three-day ticket for both trolleys and trains at the same price you'd pay elsewhere for either separately—$9 for adults, $4 for children 6–12, free for children under 6. Both trolleys and trains depart from the VIC as well. While you're there, inquire about trolley and train tickets that include discount admissions to the attractions. There are numerous plans.

St. Augustine Historical Tours, 167 San Marco Ave., at Williams Street (tel. 829-3800, or toll free 800/397-4071), operates San Francisco–style green-and-white open-air trolleys between 8:30am and 5pm daily. You can park your car at their headquarters, which is also a stop on the tour and site of two tourist attractions. There are 16 stops on the route, and for the price of your ticket you can get off at any stop, visit the attractions, and step aboard the next vehicle that comes along. Several trolleys make a continuous circuit along the route throughout the day; you won't ever have to wait more than 15–20 minutes for a trolley to come along. Or you can ride the entire route, which is enhanced by entertaining live narration. It takes about an hour to complete.

St. Augustine Sightseeing Trains, 170 San Marco Ave., at Fla. A1A (tel. 829-6545, or toll free 800/226-6545), is almost identical to the above, but takes a different route. Its vehicles are red-and-blue open-air trains.

BY HORSE-DRAWN CARRIAGE **Colee's Carriage Tours** (tel. 829-2818), operated by the Colee family, has been showing people around town in quaint surreys (some with fringed canopies), turn-of-the-century vis-a-vis, and broughams since 1877. Original owner Louis Colee took Henry Flagler on a sightseeing trip in a two-seater barouche when he first arrived in St. Augustine. The carriages line up at the bayfront, just south of the fort. Slow-paced, entertainingly narrated 45- to 50-minute rides (which include a 10-minute stop at Memorial Presbyterian Church) are offered from 9am to 9pm daily except Christmas. The cost is $9 per adult, $4 for children 5–11, free for kids under 5, with hotel and restaurant pickup available for an additional charge. Tours go past the Castillo, old town and Spanish Quarter sights, churches and historic homes, Flagler College, the Lightner Museum, and other notable landmarks and attractions. It makes for a delightful ride.

BY BOAT The Usina family has been running **St. Augustine Scenic Cruises** (tel. 824-1806) on Matanzas Bay since the turn of the century. They offer 75-minute narrated tours aboard the *Victory II* and *Victory III* (the original *Victory* was sold decades ago)—open-air sightseeing boats departing from the Municipal Marina just south of the Bridge of Lions. The tours are delightful. There are often dolphins cavorting on the bay, and you're likely to spot brown pelicans, cormorants, kingfishers, and other water birds. From the boat you'll see the Castillo, unspoiled saltwater marshes, oyster beds, the St. Augustine Lighthouse, the San Sebastian and North Rivers, the St. Augustine inlet to the Atlantic Ocean, and Vilano Beach waterfront homes, many of them with boats docked out front. Snacks and soft drinks are sold on board, and if the weather gets nippy outside you can retreat to enclosed seating below deck. Weather permitting, departures are at 11am, 1pm, 2:45pm, and 4:30pm daily except Christmas, with an additional tour at 6:15pm Labor Day to October 15 and April 1 to May 14; May 15 to Labor Day there are two additional tours, at 6:45 and 8:30pm. That's the current schedule, but call ahead—schedules can change. Adults pay $7.50, children 3–11 are charged $3, and kids under 3 ride free. If you're driving, allow a little time to find a parking space on the street.

WHAT TO SEE & DO

St. Augustine attractions are open seven days a week. In addition to over a dozen historic sites and museums, there's almost always some **special event** going on. It might be anything from a reenactment of Sir Francis Drake's raid on the town in 1586 to a very 20th-century beach festival.

There are numerous **golf** courses and 22 municipal **tennis** courts (inquire at the Visitor Information Center). The best **beaches** are St. Augustine Beach, about four miles out of town on Fla. A1A South (take the Bridge of Lions) and Vilano Beach on Fla. A1A North, right over the North Bridge. And the historic district is dotted with quaint shops.

AUTHENTIC OLD JAIL, 167 San Marco Ave., at Williams St. Tel. 829-3800.

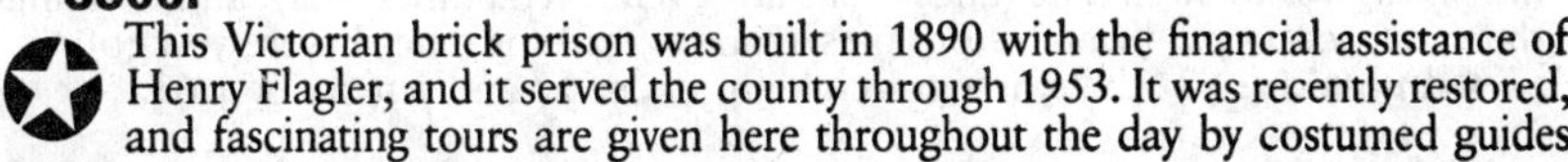

This Victorian brick prison was built in 1890 with the financial assistance of Henry Flagler, and it served the county through 1953. It was recently restored, and fascinating tours are given here throughout the day by costumed guides assuming the roles of Sheriff Joe Perry and his wife, Lulu. Perry, 6′6″ tall and weighing 300 pounds, was sheriff here for 25 years, earning a reputation as a fearless law enforcer. Visitors are shown the Perrys' living quarters and the kitchen where Lulu cooked for her family and the inmates. Downstairs are four spartan accommodations for women. On the same floor are a maximum-security cell where murderers, horse thieves, and those convicted of grand theft were confined; a cell housing prisoners condemned to hang (they could see the gallows being constructed from their window); and an especially grim solitary-confinement cell, a pitch-dark empty room with no windows, bed, or mattress. Minimum-security prisoners—bootleggers, debtors, petty thieves—were kept in upstairs quarters.

Additional exhibits include photographs of all the county's sheriffs from 1845 to the present, documentation of a 1908 hanging, early 20th-century newspaper articles, weapons seized from criminals, restraining devices, and an exact replica of the electric chair still used today in Florida.

Admission: $4.25 adults, $3.25 children 6–12, free for kids under 6. Parking is free on the premises.

Open: Daily 8:30am–5pm. **Closed:** Easter, Christmas Eve Day, and Christmas Day.

CASTILLO DE SAN MARCOS NATIONAL MONUMENT, 1 Castillo Dr., between Orange and Charlotte Sts. Tel. 829-6506.

In 1669—a year after English pirates had sacked St. Augustine—Mariana, Queen Regent of Spain, ordered colonists to construct an impregnable stone fort to stave off future British advances. The little town was of key importance to Spain in defending Florida's coastal commercial route along which its galleons, loaded with gold and silver from the mines of Mexico and Peru, sailed back to Cádiz. The Castillo, which took 23 years (1672–95) to build, was stellar in design, with a double drawbridge entrance over a 40-foot moat. The earth dug out from the moat created a small embankment, called a *glacis*, that prevented cannon balls from hitting the wall bases. Massive coquina (shell rock) walls enclosed a large courtyard lined inside with storage rooms, and diamond-shaped bastions in each corner—which enabled cannons to set up a deadly crossfire—contained domed sentry towers. Originally, the fort was painted red and white, the colors of the Spanish flag, so that passing ships could recognize its nationality.

The Castillo was never captured in battle, and its coquina walls did not crumble when pounded by enemy artillery. In 1702, the English occupied St. Augustine for 50 days, and though they burned the town, its 1,500 residents holed up in the fort and remained safe. The fort also held up during a 27-day British bombardment in 1740. The British only gained possession when Spain ceded Florida to them in return for Havana after the French and Indian War in 1763. They held the fort (renaming it Fort St. Mark) through the American Revolution for 21 years, after which the Treaty of Paris returned Florida to Spain. The Castillo, like the rest of Florida, came under American rule in 1821, and in 1824 its name was changed to Fort Marion in honor of a Revolutionary War general. It was used to house Native American prisoners during the Seminole War of 1835–42, occupied briefly by Confederate troops during the Civil War, and served as a military prison during the Spanish-American War. America's oldest—and best-preserved—masonry fortification was decommissioned as an active military base in 1900, designated a National Monument in 1924, and given back its original name in 1942.

Today the old storerooms house museum exhibits documenting the history of the fort, and visitors can also tour the vaulted powder magazine room, a dank prison cell, the chapel, and guard rooms. A walk around the upper-level gundeck is both historically evocative and scenic. Most of the copper and cast-iron cannons are at least 200 years old and could fire a ball over a mile. A self-guided tour map and brochure are provided at the ticket booth. In addition, subject to staff availability, interesting 20- to 30-minute ranger talks are given several times a day, and in summer there are occasional living-history presentations (call for times before you go).

Admission: $2 adults, free for children under 17 and seniors over 61.

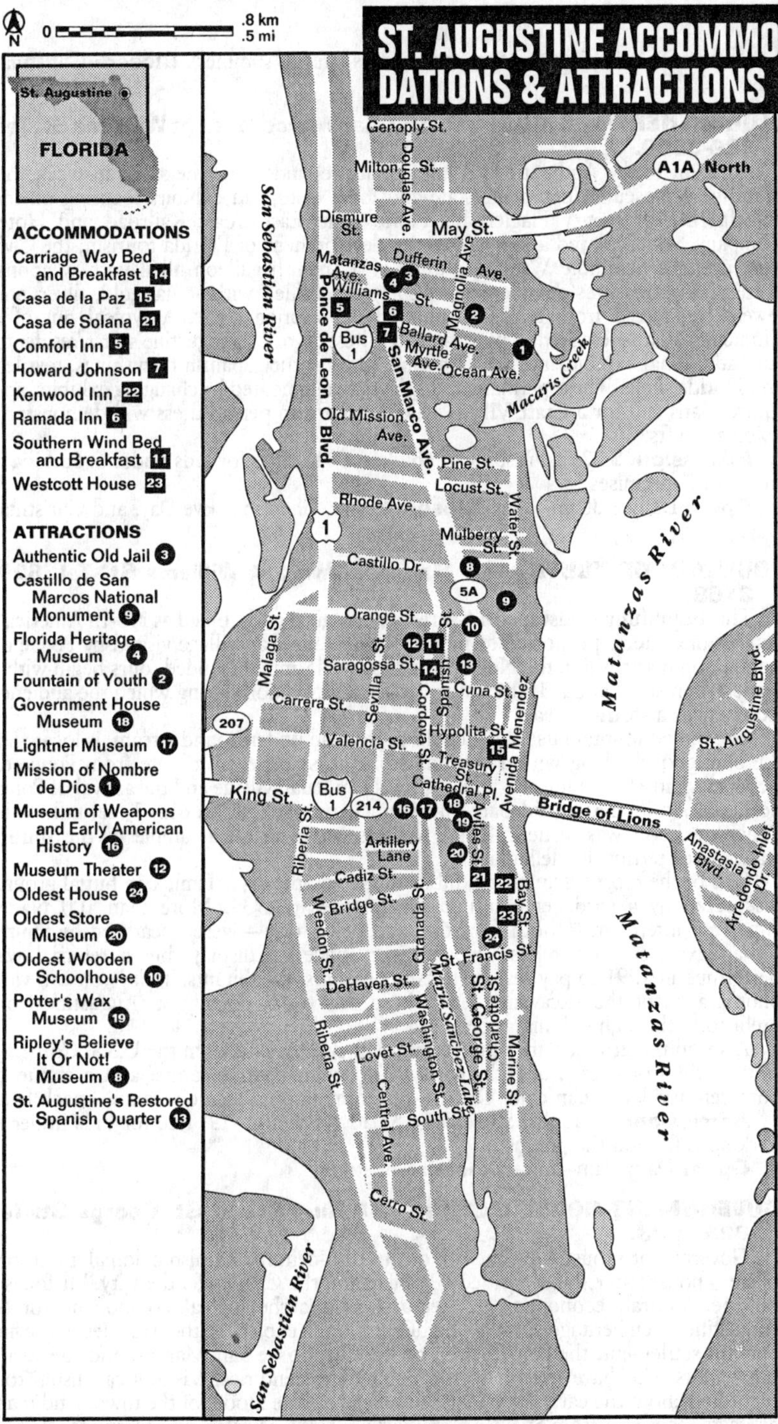
ST. AUGUSTINE ACCOMMODATIONS & ATTRACTIONS
0 .8 km .5 mi
N
St. Augustine
FLORIDA
ACCOMMODATIONS
Carriage Way Bed and Breakfast 14
Casa de la Paz 15
Casa de Solana 21
Comfort Inn 5
Howard Johnson 7
Kenwood Inn 22
Ramada Inn 6
Southern Wind Bed and Breakfast 11
Westcott House 23
ATTRACTIONS
Authentic Old Jail 3
Castillo de San Marcos National Monument 9
Florida Heritage Museum 4
Fountain of Youth 2
Government House Museum 18
Lightner Museum 17
Mission of Nombre de Dios 1
Museum of Weapons and Early American History 16
Museum Theater 12
Oldest House 24
Oldest Store Museum 20
Oldest Wooden Schoolhouse 10
Potter's Wax Museum 19
Ripley's Believe It Or Not! Museum 8
St. Augustine's Restored Spanish Quarter 13
Genoply St.
Milton St.
Douglas Ave.
A1A North
Dismure St.
May St.
Magnolia Ave.
Matanzas Ave.
Dufferin Ave.
Williams St.
Bus 1
Ballard Ave.
Myrtle Ave.
Ocean Ave.
Macaris Creek
San Sebastian River
Ponce de Leon Blvd.
San Marco Ave.
Old Mission Ave.
Pine St.
Locust St.
Rhode Ave.
Water St.
1
Mulberry St.
Castillo Dr.
5A
Matanzas River
Orange St.
Malaga St.
Sevilla St.
Saragossa St.
Spanish St.
Cuna St.
Cordova St.
Carrera St.
207
Hypolita St.
Avenida Menendez
Valencia St.
Treasury St.
St. Augustine Blvd.
Cathedral Pl.
King St.
214
Bridge of Lions
Aviles St.
Riberia St.
Artillery Lane
Anastasia Blvd
Arredondo Inlet Dr.
Cadiz St.
Bay St.
Bridge St.
Weedon St.
Granada St.
St. Francis St.
DeHaven St.
Charlotte St.
St. George St.
Maria Sanchez Lake
Washington St.
Marine St.
Lovet St.
Riberia St.
Central Ave.
South St.
Cerro St.
San Sebastian River
Matanzas River
5440

Open: Daily 8:45am–4:45pm (sometimes later in summer). **Closed:** Christmas Day.

FLORIDA HERITAGE MUSEUM, 167 San Marco Ave., at Williams St. Tel. 829-3800.

Adjacent to the Authentic Old Jail (see above) and under the same auspices, this brand-new museum documents state and local history in exhibits focusing on the colorful life of Henry Flagler; his Florida and East Coast Railroad and Hotel Company, which played a key role in the development of Florida tourism; the Civil War; and the Seminole Wars. A replica of a Spanish galleon filled with weapons, pottery, and treasures complements display cases filled with actual gold, silver, and jewelry recovered from galleons sunk off the Florida coast. A typical hut of a Timucuan in a forest setting illustrates the lifestyle of St. Augustine's first residents. And additional exhibits include 17th- and 18th-century Spanish furnishings, textiles, and Florida shells. These permanent displays are augmented by changing exhibits, and future plans call for a Craft Village where artisans in period dress will demonstrate colonial crafts.

Admission: $4.25 adults, $3.25 children 6–12, free for kids under 6. Parking is free on the premises.

Open: Daily 8:30am–5pm. **Closed:** Easter, Christmas Eve Day, and Christmas Day.

FOUNTAIN OF YOUTH, 155 Magnolia Ave., at Williams St. Tel. 829-3168.

This beautifully landscaped 14-acre archeological park, billed as North America's first historic site, is purported to be the Native American village visited by Ponce de León upon his arrival in the New World. Today, 45-minute guided tours begin with a planetarium show about 16th-century celestial navigation during which the audience experiences a storm at sea.

The famed fountain itself, which flows from an underground stream, is located in the Springhouse along with a coquina stone cross believed to date from Ponce de León's visit in 1513. Tableaux here depict a Timucuan village and the arrival of Ponce de León. An interesting sidebar: The Timucuans were giants, 6½–7 feet tall, while Ponce de León was a mere 4′11″. Visitors get to drink a sample of the sulfury water—not terrifically delicious.

One of the most fascinating exhibits in the complex is a Timucuan burial ground discovered by a gardener planting orange trees in 1934. More than 100 Native American interments—both Christian and prehistoric—were unearthed by Smithsonian experts. The skeletal remains were once on display, but a reburial was performed in 1991 to pay respect to America's first inhabitants. Today you can view photographs of the excavation. Murals in this room portray St. Augustine from prehistoric through colonial times.

Also on the grounds are historic cannons, such as one from the U.S.S. *Constitution* ("Old Ironsides"), a 16th-century Timucuan dugout canoe, and a statue of 16th-century Timucuan chief Oriba—not to mention a picnic area and snack bar.

Admission: $4 adults, $3 seniors, $1.50 children 6–12, free for kids under 6. Parking is free on the premises.

Open: Daily 9am–5pm. **Closed:** Christmas.

GOVERNMENT HOUSE MUSEUM, 48 King St., at St. George St. Tel. 825-5033.

Government House—on the site of the 16th-century Spanish colonial governor's office—houses an exhibit entitled "The Dream, the Challenge, the City." It focuses on the cultural, economic, architectural, and archeological components of St. Augustine's rich heritage. Displays highlight Florida explorers, the struggles of the first Spanish settlement, the construction of the Castillo de San Marcos, and the varied inhabitants who have lived here throughout the centuries. Visitors can listen to a recording about the early days while looking at a scale model of the town. And many artifacts recovered from Spanish shipwrecks—coins, jewelry, and weapons—are on display.

Admission: $2 adults, $1 students and children 6–12, free for kids under 6. Park in the lot at the Visitor Information Center at San Marco Avenue and Castillo Drive.

Open: Daily 10am–4pm. **Closed:** Christmas.

LIGHTNER MUSEUM, 75 King St., at Granada St. Tel. 824-2874.

Henry Flagler's opulent Spanish Renaissance-style Alcazar Hotel, built in 1889, closed during the Depression, and stayed vacant until Chicago publishing magnate Otto C. Lightner bought the building in 1948 to house his vast collection of Victoriana. The former hotel makes a gorgeous museum, centering on an open palm courtyard with an arched stone bridge spanning a fish pond. The first floor houses a Victorian village, with shopfronts representing emporia selling various wares. A Victorian Science and Industry Room displays shells, rocks, minerals, and Native American artifacts in beautiful turn-of-the-century cases. Other exhibits include stuffed birds, an Egyptian mummy from 500 B.C., Italian cameos, steam engine models, and amazing examples of Victorian glassblowing. A room of automated musical instruments on this floor—a self-playing violin, organ grinder's street piano, roller organ, music boxes, and an 1874 German orchestrion among them—are best seen during daily concerts of period music at 11am and 2pm, which are enhanced by docent lectures.

You'll find 18th- and 19th-century European porcelains, art nouveau glass by Louis Comfort Tiffany and contemporaries, and other decorative arts. You'll also see a malachite urn from the St. Petersburg Winter Palace of the tsar and a 19th-century Chickering grand piano that belonged to opera star Amelia Galli-Curci.

Victorian furnishings ranging from the British Raj to intricate Near Eastern mother-of-pearl inlay pieces are on the third floor, along with collections of buttons, stamps, coins, dolls, dollhouses, and textiles.

Take some time to look at the building itself, designed by Thomas Hastings and John Carrère, architects of the U.S. Senate Office building and the New York Public Library. It's listed in the National Register of Historic Places. And on your way out, check out the gift shop's 19th-century antique and reproduction objets d'art.

Admission: $4 adults, $1 college students with ID and children 12–18, free for children under 12. Parking is free on the premises.

Open: Daily 9am–5pm. **Closed:** Christmas.

MARINELAND OF FLORIDA, 9507 Ocean Shore Blvd. (Fla. A1A). Tel. 471-1111.

This beachfront marinelife park on the Atlantic Ocean came into being in 1938 as an underwater motion picture studio and tourist attraction. It was the first establishment to successfully maintain dolphins in a man-made environment and achieve a successful birth in captivity. In pre-Disney days, it was Florida's most popular commercial attraction. Today, Marineland features dolphin shows in a vast circular saltwater oceanarium as well as displays of other marine animals. A second oceanarium is home to thousands of marine specimens representing more than 125 species. A marine science exhibit, which incorporates a video and eight large aquariums, examines the biology of underwater creatures. Native Florida species (gar, largemouth bass, sunfish, and crappie) can be viewed in the 35,000-gallon Wonders of the Spring aquarium—the world's largest freshwater exhibit. Over 6,000 rare and beautiful sea shells are on display at the Margaret Herrick Shell Museum. And a 20-minute 3D film called *Sea Dream* is shown throughout the day in the Aquarius Theater. A full-service oceanfront restaurant, lounge, fast-food eatery, and snack bars are on the premises. And speaking of dining, you can view underwater feedings. Marineland is 18 miles south of St. Augustine.

Admission: $12.85 adults, $10.30 seniors 55 and over, $7.50 children 3–11, free for kids under 3. Parking is free.

Open: Daily 9am–5:30pm.

MISSION OF NOMBRE DE DIOS, San Marco Ave. and Old Mission Rd. Tel. 824-2809.

This serene setting overlooking the Intracoastal Waterway is believed to be the site of the first Indian Mission in the United States, founded in 1565. An arched bridge spans a lagoon, leading to a statue of Fr. Francisco López de Mendoza Grajales, chaplain of Menéndez de Avilés's fleet and founding pastor of the parish. A towering 208-foot gleaming stainless-steel cross—illuminated at night to create a "beacon of faith" visible to ships at sea—marks the site where the first Christian cross was planted in the New World. Also on the grounds are a charming old mission-style vine-covered chapel built in 1915, the Shrine of Our Lady of La Leche, on the site of an original 1613 chapel. The mission is a popular destination of religious pilgrimages. Whatever your beliefs, it's a beautiful tree-shaded spot, ideal for quiet meditation.

Admission: Free; donations appreciated. Parking is free on the premises.

Open: Daily 7am–6pm.

MUSEUM OF WEAPONS AND EARLY AMERICAN HISTORY, 81-C King St., between Sevilla and Cordova Sts. Tel. 829-3727.

An eclectic assortment of historic artifacts and weapons from 1500 to 1900 are displayed in this small private museum. Exhibits include Native American war clubs, spears, and arrowheads; 19th-century pistols, rifles, and muskets; a miniature Austrian pistol (about 1½ inches long) that really works; and Kentucky rifles that helped open the frontier. Among many Civil War items are an array of Confederate weapons, money, belt buckles, and buttons; a bible that stopped a bullet; a Florida Confederate flag that was taken in the Battle of Fredericksburg in 1862; and a Vicksburg, Mississippi, newspaper printed on the back side of wallpaper in 1863 during a paper shortage. Related antiques and reproductions and books on the Civil War are sold in the adjoining gift shop. Parking is free on the premises.

Admission: $2.50 adults, $2 seniors 62 and over, 50¢ children 6–12, free for kids under 6.

Open: Daily 9:30am–5pm. **Closed:** Christmas Day.

MUSEUM THEATER, 5 Cordova St., at Tolomato Lane. Tel. 824-0339.

A 52-minute film called *Dream of Empire* has continuous daily showings here every hour on the hour. Using film shot locally and in Spain, it relates the early history of St. Augustine as experienced by one 16th-century colonial family. This is a good orientation for visiting historic sites. Exhibits in the lobby further elucidate the period.

Admission: $3 adults, $1.50 children 6–15, free for kids under 6. Parking is free on the premises.

Open: Daily 9am–5pm. **Closed:** Christmas Day.

THE OLDEST HOUSE, 14 St. Francis St., at Charlotte St. Tel. 824-2872.

Archeological surveys indicate that a dwelling stood on this site as early as the beginning of the 17th century. Like the rest of the town, it was probably burned by the British in 1702. What you see today, called the Gonzáles-Alvarez House (for two of its prominent owners), evolved from a two-room coquina dwelling built between 1702 and 1727. Rooms are furnished to evoke various historical eras. There are several abandoned wells on the site, and Native American, Spanish, and British artifacts (some of them discovered in those wells) are displayed.

Tomás Gonzáles, a colonist from Tenerife in the Canary Islands, lived here with his fourth-generation St. Augustine wife, Francisca, from about 1727 through 1763, when Florida became a British colony and the town's 3,000 Spaniards were ordered to leave. Tomás worked as an artilleryman at the Castillo, supplementing his meager salary by fishing, hunting, and tending fruit trees and a vegetable garden out back. The Gonzáleses had 10 children, 6 of whom survived infancy. One of the original two rooms is simply furnished to represent this period. Possessions are scant (sleeping pallets and a chest or two), and artifacts include a few native clay bowls and olive jars used for cooking and storage; a brazier provided heat and served as a deterrent to mosquitoes (carriers of the dread yellow fever).

After the Gonzáleses' departure for Havana, Mary and Joseph Peavett (he was a paymaster for the British garrison; she a widow from South Carolina) took possession. They added a second story, a fireplace, and glass window panes. The ambitious Mary operated a store and tavern on the premises, and she also worked as a midwife. In 1783, Florida became Spanish once again and now the British were forced to leave unless they publicly professed conversion to Catholicism. Joseph Peavett was already a Catholic, and Mary converted at the age of 56, shortly after Joseph's death in 1786. That same year she remarried, this time to 28-year-old John Hudson. Deemed a "profligate wastrel," Hudson ran up outrageous debts and got himself arrested for tearing down a government edict and making "the indecent gesture of wiping his backside" with it. After serving time in the Castillo, he was banished from St. Augustine and died in exile at the age of 33. A room upstairs with a tea-tray ceiling evokes the era of Mary's tenancy.

In 1790 the house was auctioned to pay the Hudsons' debts, and it became the property of Gerónimo Alvarez, a Spanish immigrant who owned a store and bakery close by. His wife, Antonia, died at the age of 25 in 1798 after bearing five children, only two of whom survived. Alvarez and his son Antonio went on to become important figures in local politics. The family and its descendants lived in the house for almost a century. A kitchen such as they would have had occupies the second room downstairs, and a dining room of their period is re-created upstairs.

Admission also entitles you to explore the adjacent **Museum of Florida's Army,** which occupies a mid-18th-century building and details the state's military history from the days of the conquistadors to the present. And you can also check out exhibits in the **Manucy Museum of St. Augustine History,** where artifacts, maps, and photographs document the founding of St. Augustine, European struggles for supremacy in the New World, lifestyles of local inhabitants, the British and second Spanish periods, and the Flagler era.

Admission: $5 adults, $4.50 seniors 55 and over, $2.50 students, free for children 6 and under; $10 families. Parking is free on the premises.

Open: Daily 9am–5pm; tours depart on the hour and half hour, with the last tour leaving at 4:30pm. **Closed:** Christmas Day.

THE OLDEST STORE MUSEUM, 4 Artillery Lane, between St. George and Aviles Sts. Tel. 829-9729.

The C. F. Hamblen General Store was St. Augustine's one-stop shopping center from 1835 to 1960, and the museum on its premises today replicates the emporium at the turn of the century. On display are over 100,000 items sold here in that era, many of them gleaned from the store's attic. They include such diverse items as red-flannel underwear, high-button shoes, lace-up corsets, butter churns, gramophones, spinning wheels, sewing machines, coffee grinders, barrels of dill pickles (you can purchase one), and medicines that were 90% alcohol! Some 19th-century brand-name products shown here are still available today, among them Hershey's chocolate, Ivory soap, and Campbell's soups. A harness-maker's shop, blacksmith, gunmaker, cobbler, and ship's chandlery were on the premises, and vehicles sold here ran the gamut from steam-driven tractors to Model-T Fords. Itinerant dentists and doctors treated patients at the store as well. It all makes for fascinating browsing. Visitors are greeted by guides in 19th-century dress, and recordings at various exhibits provide a self-guided tour. An adjoining gift shop carries old-time merchandise.

Admission: $3.50 adults, $3 for seniors 55 and over, $1.50 children 6–12, free for kids under 6.

Open: Mon–Sat 9am–5pm, Sun noon–5pm (in summer, Sun 10am–5pm). **Closed:** Christmas Day.

THE OLDEST WOODEN SCHOOLHOUSE, 14 St. George St., at Orange St. Tel. 824-0192.

This red cedar and cypress structure, held together by wooden pegs and handmade nails, is more than two centuries old, with hand-wrought beams still intact. Its original hand-split cypress roof shingles were replaced by cedar ones after a hurricane. The floor is composed of tabby, an oyster shell–based concrete. Minorcan immigrant Juan Genoply purchased the house in 1780. He lived upstairs with his wife and three children and ran a school downstairs. His classroom is re-created today with animated pupils and teacher (a typical lesson is shown), complete with a dunce and a below-stairs "dungeon" for unruly children. There's a display of old schoolroom artifacts. Rules for teachers from 1872 state that although "men teachers may take one evening each week for courting purposes . . ." "women teachers who marry or engage in unseemly conduct will be dismissed." Visitors can see a kitchen outbuilding where teachers prepared their meals and a kitchen garden where they grew produce. Also on the grounds are the old school bell, an outhouse, and a wishing well under the shade of an ancient pecan tree. The last class was held here in 1864.

Admission: $1.50 adults, 75¢ children 6–12, free for kids under 6. Park in the lot on the corner of Orange Street and Avenida Menéndez.

Open: Daily 9am–5pm. **Closed:** Christmas Day.

POTTER'S WAX MUSEUM, 17 King St., between Aviles and St. George Sts. Tel. 829-9056.

Over 170 wax figures are on display at Potter's, among them not only key figures in local Florida history (Ponce de León, Pedro Menéndez de Avilés, and Seminole leader Osceola) but international religious leaders, kings and queens, presidents and premiers, military leaders, writers, artists, composers, poets, and explorers. The features of each wax figure have been carefully researched at the British Museum in London, and equal effort was spent determining authentic costuming. Francis Drake and de Soto, for instance, are clad in actual armor from their eras. It's fun putting faces to famous names you've heard all your life—everyone from Catherine de Medici to Omar Khayyam.

Wax figures are also incorporated into a 12-minute film presentation shown continually throughout the day. And in a workshop up front, you can see a craftsperson at work on wax figures.

Admission: $4.50 adults, $4 for seniors 55 and over, $2.50 children 6–12, free for kids under 6.

Open: Daily 9am–5pm (to 8pm June 15–Labor Day). **Closed:** Christmas Day.

RIPLEY'S BELIEVE IT OR NOT! MUSEUM, 19 San Marco Ave., at Castillo Dr. Tel. 824-1606.

Housed in a converted 1887 Moorish Revival residence known as Warden Castle—complete with battlements, massive chimneys, and rose windows—this massive display comprises hundreds of curiosities and fascinating artifacts from faraway places. Financed by Hearst's King Features Syndicate, Robert Ripley spent a lifetime traveling the world (he visited 198 countries) in search of bizarre items. He showed his ever-burgeoning collection—ranging from shrunken heads to medieval torture instruments—in traveling shows nationwide. After his death in 1949, the collection was catalogued, and, with later additions, it has filled more than 20 museums worldwide.

Many exotic items are on display here as well as exhibits utilizing mannequins, such as a woman who sat on a nest of eggs until they hatched. Videos and a film at various points document amazing people tricks (such as a man who can completely rotate his head), weird human activities (like the man who bangs nails into wood planks with his hands and pulls them out with his teeth). And one intriguing exhibit features a mysterious disappearing naked lady (hint: they do it with mirrors).

Admission: $7.50 adults, $4.25 children 5–12, free for kids under 5. Parking is free on the premises.

Open: Daily 9am–6pm (to 9pm mid-June to Labor Day).

ST. AUGUSTINE ALLIGATOR FARM, 999 Anastasia Blvd. (Fla. A1A), at Old Quarry Rd. Tel. 824-3337.

A St. Augustine attraction since 1893, the Alligator Farm today houses the world's most complete collection of crocodilians, a category that includes alligators, crocodiles, caymans, and gavials. To celebrate its 100th birthday in 1993, the farm opened a new exhibit called "Crocodilians of the World." Encompassing all 22 species—and most of the 28 subspecies—it is arranged zoogeographically, by continent.

Another notable exhibit is Gomek, at 1,800 pounds and almost 18 feet in length, the largest crocodile in captivity in the western hemisphere. His species (*Crocodylus porosus*) has been known to attack, kill, and devour humans. Housed in a setting that simulates his native New Guinea habitat, Gomek can be viewed both above and below water. In addition to alligators and crocs, other creatures on display here include geckos, prehensile-tailed skinks, lizards, snakes, tortoises, Australian wallabies and joeys, spider monkeys, macaws, cockatoos, mynahs, kookaburras, and toucans. There are ponds filled with a variety of ducks, geese, and swans, as well as a petting zoo with Nubian goats, Mouflon sheep, and Fallow deer. And in addition to official residents, numerous shore birds—herons, egrets, wood storks, white ibis, and roseate spoonbills—nest and feed in the park's natural tropical foliage and alligator-filled lagoon. The birds seek out roosts above the alligators, because they afford them protection from tree-climbing predators.

There are entertaining and very educational 20-minute alligator and reptile shows throughout the day, and spring through fall you can often see narrated feedings (the menu highlights nutria, which are large muskrats); be sure to check the show and feeding schedule when you enter the park.

The Alligator Farm makes for a delightful and informative outing. The grounds are beautiful, the animal inhabitants are treated with respect and dignity, and environmental awareness is stressed. For many years the farm has been involved in breeding endangered crocodilians. It also maintains a habitat planted with southern red cedars for the endangered Sweadner's hairstreak butterfly.

Admission: $7.95 adults, $7.20 seniors 65 and over, $5.25 children 3–10, free for kids under 3. Parking is free.

Open: Daily 9am–5pm (to 6pm June–Labor Day).

ST. AUGUSTINE'S RESTORED SPANISH QUARTER, entrance on St. George St., between Cuna and Orange Sts. Tel. 825-6830.

This two-block area south of the City Gate is St. Augustine's most comprehensive historic section, where the city's colonial architecture and landscape has been re-created. Docents and craftspeople in 18th-century attire are on hand to interpret the life of early inhabitants. It wasn't until 1959 that a commission was established to restore and preserve the city's heritage. What you see today is the result of extensive research and archeological investigation under the auspices of the Historic St. Augustine Preservation Board. About 90% of the buildings in the area are reconstructions, with houses named for prominent occupants. Unless otherwise indicated, the buildings described below date to the mid-18th century, the period re-created here. Highlights include:

The Spanish Colonial-style **Triay House**—with its highly pitched shingled gable roof and grape arbor overhanging the patio—belonged to Minorcan settlers, Francisco and María Triay. The property remained in their family through 1834. Today it serves as an orientation center, where visitors learn about area history and archeological studies and view many of the artifacts uncovered in local digs.

The **Gómez House** was the home of Lorenzo Gómez, a foot soldier, and his Native American wife, Catalina. They lived in this sparsely furnished one-room cypress A-frame with three children, and supplemented Lorenzo's meager income by operating a store and part-time tavern on the premises. Some of the items they would have sold, such as wine, blankets and fabrics, rosin (used heated for caulking), beans, jars of olives, and tobacco—can be seen here. There's a sleeping loft upstairs where the children slept in cold weather on straw-filled mattresses. Generally, whole families slept in the same room; privacy was not an issue for them. Like most people of this era, the Gómez family had little furniture. It all had to be handcrafted, which took time, and it was difficult to gather the requisite wood because of the danger of native tribe attack. Cooking was done in the yard outdoors, where you'll also see a square coquina well (the family's water source) and a typical vegetable garden. Most residents of this old garrison town raised much of their own food.

The **Gallegos House,** built in 1720, was home to Martín Martínez Gallegos and his wife, Victoria, who lived here with three children and Juan Garcia, a retired infantryman in his 60s. The Gallegos family was more affluent than the Gómez family. Martín was an officer—an artillery sergeant stationed at the Castillo. Their two-room tabby (oyster-shell concrete) home has a built-in interior masonry stove, though most cooking was still done outside over a wood fire. A thatch-roofed pole shed over this outdoor fire protected the cooking space from the elements. An outdoor wooden trough served the Gallegos family as a sink, washing machine, and bathtub, with whelk shells used for dippers. In the yard is a three-barrel well (people dug a hole until they hit water and then inserted as many barrels as necessary to form a well). In addition to fruit trees, vegetables, and herbs, there's aloe growing in the walled garden; it was used for healing purposes. A craftsperson on the premises demonstrates lace making. Note the swinging rat shelf used to store food over the table; its motion scared rats away. Outside is a *matate* made of volcanic rock as well as a mortar and pestle—all used for grinding corn. It may interest you to know that hand-grinding corn for three hours produces enough for just one loaf of bread!

Nearby is a **blacksmith shop** where a craftsman turns out hand-wrought hardware using 18th-century methods. He can tell you about his work, his life (he lives above the shop), and everyday expressions deriving from his craft, such as "strike when the iron is hot."

The rectangular **Gonzáles House,** home of cavalryman Bernardo Gonzáles, is larger than many of its neighbors, indicating a prosperous owner. The architecture is typical of the first Spanish Period, with a flat roof constructed of hand-hewn boards laid across hand-hewn rafters. The house is used for spinning and weaving demonstrations utilizing a 1797 loom. Here you'll see the exquisite natural yarn colors created from berries, carrots, onionskins, plants like marigold and indigo, and even crushed insects. The vegetable garden is supplemented by plants used for dyes.

The tabby **Geronimo de Hita y Salazar House** was home to a soldier with a large family. Here a woodworker demonstrates how typical items—such as furniture, wooden kitchen implements like eggbeaters and mallets, and religious artifacts—were made in the 18th century, using a manual lathe to turn wood.

The **DeMesa-Sánchez House** exemplifies two periods. Two rooms date to the residence of shore guard Antonio de Mesa in the late 1700s, while a second story was added in the 19th century. Furnishings reflect the comfortable lifestyle of Charles and Mary Jane Loring, who lived here during the American Territorial Period (1821–45). They even had a bathtub in the kitchen, the practice of bathing having recently come into vogue. The Lorings had servants and slaves to do rough work, and, unlike earlier residents, enjoyed some leisure. Mr. Loring might have used this time to attend horse races or pursue real estate interests; his wife might have played an instrument or done needlework. The house is made of coquina, which has been plastered over and painted white.

The **José Peso de Burgo and Francisco Pellicer House,** a wooden structure dating from the British Period (1763–83), was shared by two families. Peso de Burgo, a Corsican, was a merchant and shopkeeper; Francisco Pellicer, a Minorcan carpenter. The families had separate kitchens. Today a shop occupies the house, selling books and gift items relating to the period. Outbuildings here were used as slave quarters and for storage.

After you've left the Spanish Quarter, explore the quaint narrow streets nearby. They also contain many reconstructed and original historic buildings (indicated by markers), as well as charming boutiques and antique shops.

Admission: Ticket for all exhibit buildings, $5 adults, $3.75 seniors, $2.50 students 6–18, free for kids under 6, $10 maximum per family. Park in the lot at the Visitor Information Center at San Marco Avenue and Castillo Drive.

Open: Daily 9am–5pm. **Closed:** Christmas.

WHERE TO STAY

St. Augustine's accommodations include lovely bed-and-breakfast lodgings, most of them in beautifully restored historic homes. Generally, the B&Bs don't take young children. For families, I recommend a beach hotel or a motel with a swimming pool.

HOTELS AT THE BEACH

LA FIESTA OCEANSIDE INN, 3050 Fla. A1A S. (at F St.), St. Augustine, FL 32084. Tel. 904/471-2220, or toll free 800/852-6390. Fax 904/471-0186. 36 rms. A/C TV TEL

$ Rates: Labor Day to early Feb, $35–$40 single or double; $60 ocean-view room or bridal suite. Early Feb to Labor Day, $60–$70 single or double; $90 ocean-view room or bridal suite. Additional person $5 extra. A three-bedroom house with complete kitchen sometimes available for $800 a week. AE, CB, DC, DISC, MC, V. **Parking:** Free.

La Fiesta's cheerful beachfront accommodations are housed in two-story tan stucco buildings with Spanish-style terra-cotta roofs and fragrant Confederate jasmine climbing the columns. They're decorated in soft, beachy hues, with white furnishings and prints of beach scenes adorning stucco walls. Eight offer ocean views, and two are ocean-view bridal suites equipped with extra-large tubs (ample for two), wet bars, small refrigerators, and king-size beds. The latter have very nice rattan and bamboo furnishings. All rooms are equipped with remote-control cable TVs with tourism-information stations.

Dining/Entertainment: The sunny Beachhouse Café serves breakfast daily from 7am to noon, with options ranging from hotcakes to eggs scrambled with sharp Cheddar and ham served with home-fries or grits and homemade biscuits. You can also get sandwiches and award-winning Minorcan clam chowder here, and if you sample the alligator salad, you're given a certificate of membership in the Alligator Eating Society of America.

Facilities: Coin-op laundry, children's playground, beach, 60-foot pool, 18-hole beachfront miniature golf course (it's designed to look like St. Augustine in old Spanish days, with a pirate galleon, waterfalls, and cave), small video-game room, hair salon, open-air picnic area with barbecue grill.

OCEAN GALLERY, 4600 Fla. A1A S. (between Dondonville Rd. and Trade Winds Lane), St. Augustine, FL 32084. Tel. 904/471-6663, or toll free 800/940-6665. 200 condo apts. A/C TV TEL

$ **Rates** (per week, one-week minimum): Mar–Aug, $375 one-bedroom/one-bath apt; $400 two-bedroom/one-bath apt; $425–$610 two-bedroom/two-bath apt; $500–$735 three-bedroom/two-bath apt. Jan–Feb, $275 one-bedroom/one-bath apt; $300 two-bedroom/one-bath apt; $325–$475 two-bedroom/two-bath apt; $400–$600 three-bedroom/two-bath apt. Sept–Dec, $275 one-bedroom/one-bath apt; $295 two-bedroom/one-bath apt; $315–$435 two-bedroom/two-bath apt; $375–$535 three-bedroom/two-bath apt. Reduced monthly rates. Maid service $35–$40 extra for length of stay. MC, V. **Parking:** $10 length-of-stay charge.

Set on 44 attractively landscaped acres with gardens, lakes, and lagoons, the Ocean Gallery offers beautiful vacation homes with access to 17 miles of palm-fringed, white sandy beach. All its condos are decorated in upscale resort styles, complete with such residential touches as shelves of knickknacks; some have VCRs and/or CD and cassette players. Units offer fully equipped kitchens (including dishwashers, washer/dryers, and refrigerators with ice makers), full living and dining areas, and furnished balconies or patios. About half have beach views, but keep in mind that the more stunningly beautiful your ocean view, the higher the price. These are very spacious living quarters; one-bedroom units are 1,110 square feet, two-bedroom units 1,156–1,320 square feet, three-bedroom units 1,450–1,627 square feet.

Book as far in advance as possible; the Ocean Gallery is very popular.

Dining/Entertainment: There are no restaurants on the premises, since most guests do their own cooking (a Publix supermarket is a few minutes away by car), but there are barbecue grills and picnic tables at the Clubhouse, and some units have their own outdoor grills. Restaurants are nearby. January through March, an on-premises social director organizes daily activities such as walks, bridge games, Bingo, crafts, aqua-robics, dancing, and cocktail parties.

Facilities: Five swimming pools, five whirlpools, four hard-surface tennis courts (lit for night play), two racquetball courts, two shuffleboard courts, exercise room, two saunas, small video-game room, clubhouse (equipped with games and a library), storage lockers.

A RESORT HOTEL

PONCE DE LEÓN GOLF & CONFERENCE RESORT, 4000 U.S. 1 N., St. Augustine, FL 32095. Tel. 904/824-2821, or toll free 800/228-2821. Fax 904/829-6108. 169 rms, 24 minisuites, 7 suites. A/C TV TEL

$ Rates: $75 single; $85 double; $85 minisuite for one, $95 for two; $135 suite for one, $145 for two. $10 higher June–Aug. Additional person $10 extra; children under 18 stay free in parents' room. Inquire about golf packages. AE, CB, DC, DISC, ER, JCB, MC, V. **Parking:** Free.

This lovely 350-acre resort—with a beautiful championship golf course bordering a large saltwater marsh/bird sanctuary—has been a St. Augustine tradition since 1916 when Henry Flagler built it to serve his ultra-luxurious in-town hotels. President Warren G. Harding came here to relax on the greens before his inauguration in 1921, and many famous golfers have played the course. Resort accommodations were added in 1952. The grounds, shaded by palms, magnolias, and centuries-old live oaks, vary neat flower beds with duck-filled lagoons and clumps of sawgrass. Traditionally furnished rooms are large and cheerful, with white faux-moiré silk wall coverings; teal, mauve, or raspberry carpeting; and pretty floral-print bedspreads in complementary colors. All feature furnished patios or balconies overlooking the golf course, and in-room amenities include remote-control cable TVs (with 35 channels). Minisuites additionally offer small sitting rooms separated from sleeping areas by trellises, clock radios, and in-room coffee makers.

The hotel is just a 10-minute drive from the historic district. Rooms and public areas are being renovated at this writing, and landscaping is also being upgraded.

Dining/Entertainment: Michael's, an attractive cathedral-ceilinged restaurant with a working fireplace and a wall of windows overlooking the golf course, serves American/continental à la carte and buffet meals at breakfast, lunch, and dinner. A lavish prime rib and seafood buffet is featured every Saturday night, an extensive champagne buffet brunch every Sunday. The adjoining bamboo-furnished Bogie Lounge, also with golf course views, offers complimentary happy hour hors d'oeuvres, nightly piano bar entertainment, and light fare; patio seating is a plus in good weather.

Facilities: Donald Ross–designed par-72 championship golf course, 18-hole poolside putting green, golf pro shop, six hard-surface tennis courts (lit for night play), large cloverleaf-shaped swimming pool, sand volleyball court, shuffleboard, croquet, bocci ball, basketball, horseshoes, jogging trails, coin-op laundry, planned activities for children in summer.

MOTEL ACCOMMODATIONS

COMFORT INN, 1111 Ponce de Leon Blvd. (U.S. 1 N., at Old Mission Rd.), St. Augustine, FL 32084. Tel. 904/824-5554, or toll free 800/228-5150. Fax 904/829-2948. 78 rms, 6 suites. A/C TV TEL

$ Rates (including continental breakfast): $42–$79.95 single or double Sun–Fri, $89 Sat, $99.95 during special events and holidays. Suites $10 extra; additional person $5 extra; children under 18 stay free in parents' room. AE, CB, DC, DISC, ER, JCB, MC, V. **Parking:** Free.

Housed in a two-story tan stucco building with a terra-cotta roof and mission-style facade, the Comfort Inn offers attractive rooms decorated in dark teal and peach. They're looking very spiffy after a recent renovation, with new oak furnishings, grasspaper-look wall coverings, and pretty tropical-print bedspreads. Remote-control cable TVs offer tourism-information channels. Large suites feature dressing rooms with double sink vanities and parlor areas with extra TVs and pull-out sofas.

Continental breakfast—toast, danish, fresh fruit, juice, coffee, tea—is served in a pleasant wicker- and bamboo-furnished room with windows overlooking the pool. There's no on-premises restaurant, but several fast-food restaurants are across the street. Other facilities include a nice-size swimming pool/whirlpool and coin-op laundry. The property is two minutes from the historic district.

HOWARD JOHNSON, 137 San Marco Ave. (between Sebastian/Myrtle Aves. and Sanchez Ave.), St. Augustine, FL 32084. Tel. 904/824-6181, or toll free 800/654-2000. Fax 904/824-4743. 70 rms, 7 suites. A/C TV TEL

$ Rates (including continental breakfast): $39–$59 for up to four Sun–Thurs, $59–$89 Fri–Sat, $99.95 during special events and holidays; $159 suite Sun–Thurs, $199 Fri–Sat. Additional person $5 extra; children under 18 stay free in parents' room. AE, CB, DC, DISC, ER, JCB, MC, V. **Parking:** Free.

HoJo's terra cotta–roofed mission-style building evokes the Spanish colonial period. The theme is further reflected in the cozy lace-curtained lobby which has a Saltillo tile floor and a mural of the Spanish Quarter behind the registration desk. Standard motel rooms—decorated in teal and peach with bleached-wood furnishings—offer remote-control TVs with tourism-information channels; most have extra sinks in the dressing area. Three suites have in-room Jacuzzis, and all offer second bedrooms with their own TVs.

On-premises facilities include a medium-size swimming pool and whirlpool surrounded by flower beds and partly shaded by a tall pecan tree. Landscaping, generally, is a plus here; a garden courtyard planted with palms and hibiscus centers on a massive 500-year-old live oak draped in Spanish moss. A morning meal of toast, danish, bagels, juice, and coffee or tea is served in a pleasant breakfast nook off the lobby. HoJo is just a few minutes from the historic district.

RAMADA INN, 116 San Marco Ave. (at Old Mission Rd.), St. Augustine, FL 32084. Tel. 904/824-4352, or toll free 800/228-2828. Fax 904/824-2745. 100 rms. A/C TV TEL

$ Rates: $39.95–$79 single or double Sun–Thurs, $54.95–$89 Fri–Sat, $99.95 during special events and holidays. Additional person $7 extra; children under 18 stay free in parents' room. AE, CB, DC, DISC, ER, JCB, MC, V. **Parking:** Free.

Across the street from the Mission del Dios (site of religious pilgrimages), the Ramada is appropriately housed in a pale-pink stucco building with a mission facade, arched entranceway, terra-cotta Spanish-style roofing, and a ceramic tile fountain out front. It's just minutes from the historic district. Rooms are standard motel units decorated in peach and teal with oak furnishings. They're equipped with remote-control cable TVs with tourism-information channels. An on-premises restaurant called the Sea Port Café specializes in steaks and seafood; it's open for breakfast, lunch, and dinner. A bar/lounge adjoins. The Ramada also features a medium-size swimming pool and whirlpool, and there are snack-vending machines off the lobby.

BED & BREAKFAST

Expensive

CASA DE SOLANA, 21 Aviles St. (at Cadiz St.), St. Augustine, FL 32084. Tel. 904/824-3555. 4 suites (all with bath). A/C TV

$ Rates (including full breakfast): $125 single or double. No children under 12 accepted. AE, DISC, MC, V. **Parking:** Free at the Oldest House Museum a block away.

This charming dormer-windowed colonial house was built in 1763 for Don Manuel Solana—a Spanish soldier who became wealthy in the import-export business. Like all of St. Augustine's early buildings (this is the city's seventh-oldest house), it was constructed of coquina stone, but in the mid-1800s the exterior was covered over with the pale-pink stucco you see today. The house is fronted by a lovely walled garden planted with jasmine and trumpet vines. And since it has been under the rule of three governments, British, Spanish, and American flags fly from the balcony.

Hostess Faye McMurry has been running a B&B in these historic precincts since 1982. Her homemade breakfasts—an egg dish (perhaps a quichelike sausage-and-cheese casserole), delicious fresh-baked muffins and breads, fruit juices, grits, and gourmet teas and coffees—are served in an elegant crystal-chandeliered dining room with Williamsburg-blue wainscotting and dark-wood beams overhead. Faye dons colonial dress for the occasion and sets her table with fine china and silver.

Rooms are nicely decorated with antique pieces, such as white wicker furnishings. Yours might have a four-poster, brass, art deco, or mahogany-rice bed, perhaps made up with a ribbon-and-lace quilt and pillow shams. Attractive window treatments (cornices, balloon curtains) and doors hung with vine wreaths enhance the homey ambience, as do decorative fireplaces. All accommodations are equipped with cable color TVs, radios, and clocks (a public phone is in the hallway), and you'll find a welcoming crystal decanter of sherry in your room on arrival. Three suites have full living rooms (the fourth has a small parlor), and one has a balcony. Faye wants her guests "to feel at home without the cares of being at home." Bicycles are available free of charge. And there's a baby grand in the dining room, scene of occasional impromptu nighttime singalongs. No smoking is permitted in the house.

WESTCOTT HOUSE, 146 Avenida Menendez (between Bridge and Francis Sts.), St. Augustine, FL 32084. Tel. 904/824-4301. 8 rms (all with bath). A/C TV TEL

$ Rates (including continental breakfast): $95–$135 single or double Sun–Thurs, $135 Fri–Sat. AE, MC, V. **Parking:** On street or free in a nearby lot.

Its bayfront location would make Wescott House a winner, even if it were not for its pristine and exquisitely furnished rooms. Everything here just gleams. Another of St. Augustine's elegant 19th-century houses, this two-story Victorian/Queen Anne wood frame is neatly painted pale peach with white trim and gray-blue shutters. A porch and second-story veranda—both furnished with white wicker rockers and hung with plants—overlook the boat-filled Matanzas Bay, as does a coquina-walled brick courtyard with ornate white garden furnishings under shade trees. All these make delightful venues for breakfast, which here consists of croissants and danish, fresh fruit, juices, bagels and cream cheese, dry cereal, and tea or coffee.

As for the above-mentioned rooms—some with bay windows and/or working fireplaces—they're simply stunning. A typical unit has a brass bed made up with a white quilt and lace dust ruffle, pretty floral-print wallpaper, and kelly-green chintz balloon curtains. Another, painted pale pink with plum trim, has Victorian furnishings, a fan chandelier overhead, a highly polished pine floor strewn with area rugs, and walls hung with attractive artwork and vintage photographs. And all offer in-room hairdryers, clocks, and remote-control cable TVs (discreetly concealed in armoires). On-premises amenities include a barbecue grill in the courtyard and bicycles for rent. Complimentary fresh fruit and peach or apricot brandy are available all day in the parlor, and guests are cossetted with terry bathrobes and fruit brandies and chocolates at nightly turn-down. Smoking is not permitted in the house.

Moderate

CARRIAGE WAY BED AND BREAKFAST, 70 Cuna St. (between Cordova and Spanish Sts.), St. Augustine, FL 32084. Tel. 904/829-2467. 9 rms (all with bath) A/C TEL

$ Rates (including full breakfast): $59–$95 single or double Sun–Thurs, $69–$105 Fri–Sat. No children under 8 accepted. DISC, MC, V. **Parking:** Free on premises.

Occupying an 1883 Victorian wood-frame house fronted by roses and hibiscus, the Carriage Way is in the heart of the historic district. Its rooms—charmingly decorated in soft pastel colors like pale peach, powder blue, and mint green—are furnished with quality antiques. One unit has an oak four-poster bed with carved pineapple posts made up with a white comforter, lacy dust ruffle, and eyelet-trimmed pillow shams. Others have brass, wicker, or even canopy beds. Accommodations are enhanced by beautiful dried-flower arrangements and wreaths, lovely curtains and window treatments, and aesthetically pleasing paintings. One guest room features a converted wood-burning fireplace (it burns Sterno); another, a cathedral ceiling with high triangular windows. Baths throughout have clawfoot tubs and are papered in pretty floral prints. In-room amenities include clocks and terry bathrobes.

A console TV, books, magazines, and games are provided in a comfortable cedar-paneled parlor. And a second-story veranda offers a nice view of the picturesque area (horse-drawn carriages frequently pass by). Breakfast, served in the dining room or al fresco on the front porch, includes eggs, breakfast meats, homemade fruit breads and muffins, fresh fruit, juice, and beverage. Hospitable owner/hosts Bill and Diane Johnson offer many complimentary extras: bicycles for touring the area; tea and coffee set out all day long in an upstairs alcove hung with an antique patchwork quilt; decanters of crème de menthe, red wine, and sherry ever available on a buffet table in the entrance hallway; and a refrigerator stocked with iced glasses, beer, and soft drinks. A basket of complimentary sundries—toothpaste, sewing kit, razor—is available, and guests can also utilize the Johnsons' washer and dryer at no charge. On request, you can arrange romantic extras such as long-stemmed roses and/or champagne in your room, breakfast in bed, or a gourmet picnic lunch. No smoking is permitted in the house.

CASA DE LA PAZ, 22 Avenida Menendez (between Hypolita and Treasury Sts.), St. Augustine, FL 32084. Tel. 904/829-2915. 4 rms, 2 suites (all with bath). A/C TV

$ Rates (including full breakfast): $70–$85 single or double Sun–Thurs, $85–$110 Fri–Sat. Additional person $10 extra. No children under 8 accepted. AE, DISC, MC, V. **Parking:** Free behind house and nearby.

This bayfront white stucco Mediterranean Revival B&B offers up an alluring package. Its exquisite country French rooms and public areas are *Architectural Digest* caliber, and owner/hostess Sandy Upchurch proffers warm hospitality. The inn (built in 1915) is entered via a lovely sun-drenched parlor furnished in white wicker, with thriving plants hanging in arched windows and potted palms adding Victorian nuance. French doors lead to a pristinely charming dining room—very 18th century, with white-trimmed, pale yellow walls, a Federalist mirror, and a Georgian-style chandelier over the table. Full breakfasts are served here each morning—marvelous egg casseroles, hot croissants, bagels, fresh-baked fruit breads and muffins, juice, platters of fresh-cut fruit, and tea or coffee. Guests can relax in the living room, where comfortable overstuffed furnishings (covered in gorgeous French floral chintzes) are ranged around a wood-burning fireplace, and a large picture window overlooks Matanzas Bay. Water views can also be enjoyed from a second-story veranda. And there's a charming walled garden behind the house planted with palms, camellias, gardenias, jasmin, roses, and pots of geraniums; a golden rain tree blooms in the fall.

Rooms furnished with antiques are delightfully decorated in pastel colors such as eggshell green, pale yellow, and lavender. Glossy pine floors are strewn with rag rugs, lacy metal beds are made up with snowy white quilts set off by charming floral chintz pillow shams and dust ruffles, walls are hung with framed botanical prints and gorgeous dried-flower wreaths, and windows are adorned with white lace and swagged curtains. Live plants and ficus trees enhance the residential ambience. A remote-control cable TV is discreetly concealed in an armoire, and a clock is available. One suite has a working fireplace. Sandy stocks her guest rooms with an assortment of books and magazines, a decanter of sherry, and chocolates. Complimentary wine and champagne are available on request, and iced tea and cookies are served on weekend afternoons in summer. There's a washer/dryer for guest use. No smoking permitted in the house.

SOUTHERN WIND BED AND BREAKFAST, 18 Cordova St. (between Saragossa and Orange Sts.), St. Augustine, FL 32084. Tel. 904/825-3623. Fax 904/825-0360. 7 rms (all with bath). A/C TV

$ Rates (including full breakfast): $60–$105 single or double. Additional person $8 extra. Rooms on boat $150 per night, with a two-night minimum. AE, DISC, MC, V. **Parking:** Free on premises.

Dennis and Jeanette Dean, originally from Los Angeles, were cruising on their yacht in 1988, docked in St. Augustine, fell in love with the town (this happens frequently here), and decided to stay on. Hence, the Southern Wind (it was the name of the boat), a charming two-story colonnaded house fronted by a flower-bordered lawn. A plant-filled porch and second-story veranda are furnished with white wicker rockers and armchairs. Inside, a cozy parlor with a lace-curtained bay window has wing chairs and sofas facing a fireplace. The eclectically furnished rooms are homey, offering a mix of antiques and flea-market finds. They have glossy pine floors, beds made up with ruffled pillow shams, and attractive window treatments such as balloon curtains. Most desirable is the Honeymoon Suite, which, like the parlor downstairs has a bay window. Guests are cosseted with fresh flowers and chocolates on arrival, and wine is served in the parlor every afternoon. Classical music is played in public areas.

Breakfast consists of fresh fruit, fresh-baked fruit breads and muffins, bagels and cream cheese, juice, and a hot dish—perhaps baked eggs with ham and spices. Bicycles can be rented.

The Deans also rent two staterooms with private bath—each accommodating up to three people—on their 76-foot sailing yacht docked on Matanzas Bay. Guests on board also have use of a main salon with a working fireplace. When the boat is not rented out, Dennis Dean, Jr.—manager and host at Southern Wind—offers sunset dinner cruises on it.

The Deans also have another B&B close by, the Family Inn, 34 Saragossa St. (same phone and rates), a vine-covered cottage with a white picket fence. Rooms here offer wet bars, small refrigerators, coffee makers, and microwaves; dishes and utensils are supplied.

Inexpensive

THE KENWOOD INN, 38 Marine St. (at Bridge St.), St. Augustine, FL 32084. Tel. 904/824-2116. 10 rms, 4 suites (all with bath). A/C

$ Rates (including continental breakfast): $45–$65 single; $55–$85 double; $125 three-room suite for one or two. Additional person $10 extra. No children under 8 accepted. DISC, MC, V. **Parking:** On street or free in a nearby lot.

The delightful Kenwood Inn wins points with me by playing classical music in its public areas. Originally built as a summer residence, this hip-roofed Victorian wood-frame house with graceful verandas—today invitingly painted in pale peach with white trim—has served as a boarding house or inn since the late 19th century. It is on the National Register of Historic Places.

Each room is uniquely decorated. The Colonial Room, for instance, is painted in Williamsburg blue and furnished with a canopied mahogany bed, a beautiful oak armoire, and rocking chairs. The very feminine Classic Rose Room has mint walls and white iron beds made up with rose-motif bedspreads, ruffled curtains, and pillow shams. Navy-blue paisley fabrics, an antique steamer trunk, a ship's desk, and nautical prints set the theme for the Captain's Room. Chintz plaids, balloon curtains, wing chairs, a king-size mahogany bed, and a working fireplace are assets of the Old English Room. The exquisite Country French Room (my favorite) has an 18th-century reproduction headboard and sofas upholstered in striped chintz. And you don't have to be a newlywed to rent the lovely 1,000-square-foot Honeymoon Suite offering bay views along with an eat-in kitchen and separate living and sitting rooms. Throughout, highly polished pine-plank floors are strewn with Chinese and Persian rugs, fans whirr slowly overhead, and decorative touches include framed vintage photographs, botanical prints, dried-flower wreaths, and charming hand-painted fireplace screens. A private wraparound veranda with cushioned white wicker furnishings and rocking chairs is a plus for residents of two rooms upstairs.

Breakfast—coffee, juice, and freshly baked muffins, fruit breads, cinnamon strudels, and cakes—can be enjoyed in a lovely parlor with lace-curtained bay windows and a working fireplace; in a wicker-furnished sun room equipped with books, games, and a TV; or on the front porch. A small swimming pool, its sun deck planted with hibiscus, is a plus. And guests can also retreat to a secluded garden courtyard which has a fishpond and neat flower beds under the shade of a sprawling pecan tree. There's a refrigerator for guest use, and complimentary sherry, tea, and coffee are offered throughout the day. Smoking is not permitted in the house.

WHERE TO DINE

For a small town, St. Augustine has a lot of excellent restaurants, many of them featuring fresh seafood. Local specialties include red-hot datil peppers, Minorcan clam chowder, alligator, and oysters.

EXPENSIVE

CHART HOUSE, 46 Avenida Menendez, between Cathedral Place and Treasury St. Tel. 824-1687.

Cuisine: SEAFOOD/STEAK. **Reservations:** Recommended.

$ Prices: Appetizers $3.25–$7.75; main courses $12.95–$22.95; early-bird dinners $10.50–$14.95; children's dishes $3.25–$6.95. AE, CB, DC, DISC, MC, V.
Open: Dinner only, Sun–Thurs 5–10pm, Fri–Sat 5–10:30pm.

Housed in a charming gable-roofed Colonial Revival house (it dates to 1888) with dormer and Palladian windows, the Chart House is entered via an imposing coquina archway that's over two centuries old. Inside, a cozy fire blazes in the lounge, which adjoins an oyster bar and, via French doors, a plant-filled patio. The candlelit dining rooms upstairs and down are intimate venues with pristine white woodwork, lace-curtained multipaned windows, dozens of plants, and working fireplaces. Oak tables topped with laminated world maps, nautical prints, and boat models reflect the restaurant's marine theme, an effect enhanced when you're seated at window tables overlooking the bay.

Fresh-shucked Apalachicola oysters from Florida's northern Gulf Coast make a great appetizer. Order the combo, which gives you six oysters Rockefeller (broiled with butter, spinach, and a soupçon of anise, splashed with Pernod) and six oysters casino (broiled with butter, herbed breadcrumbs, and sherry, topped with crumbled bacon, parmesan, and bits of pimento). Recommended entrees include spicy Santa Fe chicken—rubbed with chili, charcoal-broiled, and served with bleu cheese dressing—and New Orleans shrimp skewered with lemon and lime and baked in herb butter with a touch of Tabasco. The gingery teriyaki shrimp is also excellent. All entrees come with a fabulous bottomless salad bowl, a basket of hot sourdough and seven-grain squaw bread (it's made with molasses), and a baked potato or Chart House rice—a melange of white and wild rice cooked in chicken broth and tossed with slivered almonds, pineapple, pimento, and green onions.

For dessert, the key lime pie is key lime pie at its very best. However, the creamy cheesecake is equally delicious. And the ultra-rich mud pie—coffee ice cream on a chocolate Oreo crust smothered in hot fudge and whipped cream and topped with toasted buttered almonds—is also not lacking in appeal. A selection of premium scotches, aged whiskeys, and cognacs supplements the wine list. An inexpensive early-bird dinner (a full meal) is offered from 5 to 6pm nightly. There's parking on the street or in the bank lot on Charlotte Street directly behind the restaurant.

MODERATE

FIDDLER'S GREEN, 2750 Anahma Dr., at Ferroll Rd. on Vilano Beach. Tel. 824-8897.

Cuisine: FLORIDIAN/SEAFOOD. **Reservations:** Recommended Sun–Fri, not accepted Sat. **Directions:** Head north on San Marco Avenue, cross the Vilano Bridge (Fla. A1A North), and bear right to Vilano Beach.
$ Prices: Appetizers $3.95–$5.50; main courses $8.95–$14.95. AE, CB, DC, MC, V.
Open: Dinner only, daily 5–10pm.

Situated right on the Atlantic Ocean, the shiplike Fiddler's Green is appropriately entered via a kind of gangplank. Inside, rustic elegance is the keynote, an effect achieved with pecky cypress and cedar paneling, a beamed knotty-pine ceiling, two blazing coquina stone fireplaces, and a profusion of hanging plants. There's a warren of five gorgeous dining rooms, each with unique decorator schemes. Most of the seating overlooks the grassy marsh and ocean beyond. Lighting is soft and romantic, and mellow jazz provides a simpatico musical backdrop.

Start your meal with peppery conch fritters fried in beer batter (ask for tarragon tartar sauce with them) or sautéed mushroom caps stuffed with finely chopped shrimp and artichokes in a brandied roasted red-pepper/cream sauce. For an entree, you can't go wrong with the Mariner—fresh catch of the day, lightly floured and sautéed in browned butter, lemon, and parsley. You can also order the daily catch crusted with sliced almonds and shredded coconut, baked, and topped with banana slices and creamy orange-curry sauce. Another noteworthy entree is chicken Anastasia, a roasted whole breast of chicken filled with a sherried apple/pecan/herb stuffing. This hearty dish is glazed with raspberry-port sauce and garnished with fresh mint. All entrees come with fresh vegetables and a starch—perhaps coarsely mashed dolloped potatoes (mixed with onion, sour cream, and parsley, topped with old English Cheddar, and oven browned) or brown rice tossed with crunchy bits of sautéed carrots, onion, and celery. You also get a very good house salad topped with kernels of popped wheat and a basket of fresh-baked squaw and sourdough breads. For dessert, try a "chimney sweep"—homemade espresso/chocolate-chip ice cream splashed with Kahlúa and crowned with fresh whipped cream. However, if the chocolate crème brûlée is on the menu, it's not to be missed. There's a carefully chosen and fairly extensive wine list. Free parking.

LA PARISIENNE, 60 Hypolita St., between Spanish and Cordova Sts. Tel. 829-0055.

Cuisine: FRENCH. **Reservations:** Recommended.

$ Prices: Appetizers $5.50–$6.50; main courses $4.80–$6.50 at lunch, $12–$16.50 at dinner; breakfast items 75¢–$1.50. AE, DISC, MC, V.

Open: Breakfast Sat–Sun 9am–11pm; lunch Tues–Sun 11am–3pm; afternoon tea Tues–Sun 3–4pm; dinner Tues–Sun 5:30–9pm (6–9pm May–Aug).

This quaintly charming little restaurant does indeed evoke Paris in both ambience and cuisine, and its location in the heart of the picturesque historic district further enhances the illusion that you're dining in Europe (there's metered parking in a lot across Cordova Street). A trellised plant-filled entranceway leads to a lovely dining room with a beamed pine ceiling, lace-curtained windows, and white stucco walls adorned with art nouveau posters and lithographs of Paris. Diners sit on wicker-seated ladderback chairs at white-linened tables (candlelit at night). Fresh-baked cakes, croissants, and breads are displayed at a counter up front. The restaurant is run by the Poncet family of Provence.

A typical dinner here features classic French menu items—appetizers such as escargots à la bourguignonne and soup à l'oignon, entrees like fresh fish meunière, steak au poivre in rich peppery cognac-cream sauce, and roast rack of lamb coated with Dijon mustard sauce and fresh garlic. The lunch menu offers traditional bistro fare—quiche Lorraine, croque monsieur (the Gallic answer to an American grilled ham-and-cheese sandwich), croissant sandwiches, and salade niçoise, among other selections. Fresh-baked baguettes are served with your meal, and an extensive wine list is available. Also visit La Parisienne for a delightful weekend breakfast of rich French coffee and flaky-buttery croissants—plain, almond, chocolate, or perhaps filled with cinnamon apples or apricots and crème pâtissière. Croissants and oven-fresh pastry is served at afternoon tea (or coffee).

RAINTREE, 102 San Marco Ave., at Bernard St. Tel. 824-7211.

Cuisine: CONTINENTAL. **Reservations:** Recommended. **Transportation:** A complimentary courtesy car provides transportation from/to local hotels; parking is free.

$ Prices: Appetizers $4.95–$7.95; main courses $8.95–$19.95; early dinner selections (served 5–6pm) $8.95–$10.95; children's dishes $5.95. AE, CB, DC, MC, V.

Open: Dinner only, daily 5–10pm.

Occupying an 1879 Victorian house, this is one of St. Augustine's most romantic restaurants. Bamboo furnishings, dozens of plants and ficus trees, and a red-and-white-striped canvas awning create a cozy garden ambience, and cut-crystal lamps cast a soft glow on red-linened tables. Classical music enhances the ambience. Some seating is upstairs in a charming plant-filled room with swagged damask curtains and stained-glass panels; a model of the Bequia whaling boat on which owners Tristan and Alex MacDonald sailed the Atlantic serves as a room divider. Another room has a working fireplace. And, weather permitting, you might opt for after-dinner drinks or dessert and coffee on the open-air porch, balcony, or lushly planted brick patio. Note the landscaping, which includes a gazebo, fountain, goldfish pond, and small aviary.

Truffle goose-liver pâté with toast points makes a heavenly appetizer, as does a smoked-salmon–filled crêpe topped with sour cream and caviar. You can, by the way, dine inexpensively by ordering a crêpe dish here, or in the same price category, a pasta dish such as linguine sautéed in herbed garlic butter tossed with sun-dried tomatoes, artichoke hearts, and black olives in sherry-cream sauce. More serious entrees include fresh fish of the day (I had grouper with sautéed mushrooms in a white wine–Dijon mustard–cream sauce), rack of lamb with port wine sauce, beef Wellington, and filet mignon béarnaise. All come with potatoes au gratin, fresh vegetables, a basket of hot fresh-baked breads, and a house salad of 17 varieties of leaf lettuce in a creamy Dijon vinaigrette. The menu is augmented by many daily specials and complimented by an extensive, award-winning wine list. Desserts range from crêpes Suzette to a sinfully rich chocolate mousse served in a white-chocolate cup.

INEXPENSIVE

CREEKSIDE DINERY, 160 Nix Boat Yard Rd., off U.S. 1 (turn at Long John Silver). Tel. 829-6113.

Cuisine: TRADITIONAL FLORIDIAN. **Reservations:** Not accepted.

$ **Prices:** Appetizers $2.75–$5; main courses $8–$14. MC, V.

Open: Dinner only, daily 5–10pm.

This cozy restaurant occupies a dormer-windowed white frame house fronted by live oak, pecan, and magnolia trees. Guests wait for tables on a rose vine-covered porch furnished with wicker rocking chairs. The rough-hewn cedar interior is equally charming, with curtained multipaned windows, numerous plants and ficus trees, and seating under a peaked cathedral ceiling with fishnet draped over white-painted beams. Each candlelit table has a different cloth, creating a cheerful variegated effect, while some seating is on a screened patio overlooking a creek and boatyard. And big-band music from the '30s and '40s creates a perfect acoustic backdrop.

A good beginning here is hot-and-spicy shellfish chowder—a rich seafood stew replete with scallops, shrimp, fish, oysters, and clams, as well vegetables and datil peppers to add considerable piquancy. The creamy chicken buttermilk bisque is also excellent. And I love garlicky, buttery oysters Creekside topped with oven-browned provolone cheese and herbed breadcrumbs. Among entrees, a superb specialty is the catch of the day (mine was a marvelously tender fresh flounder) baked on an oak plank and topped with crunchy breadcrumbs and horseradish-spiked mustard sauce. It came with roasted potatoes and fresh stringbeans and butter beans seasoned with herb-garlic butter. Also fabulous: sautéed fresh shrimp Sebastian, served with a cilantro-flavored garlic-cream sauce over angel-hair pasta. Steaks and chicken dishes (perhaps roast chicken glazed with rosemary-plum sauce) are also options. Entrees are served with a basket of soft garlicky breadsticks and a tasty house salad. The all-American wine list highlights selections from Florida vineyards. Leave room for a dessert called "the chocolate thing," basically an old-fashioned icebox cake made of chocolate cookie and whipped cream layers. Arrive early to avoid a wait.

GYPSY CAB COMPANY, 828 Anastasia Blvd. (Fla. A1A), between White and Comares Sts. Tel. 824-8244.

Cuisine: URBAN ECLECTIC. **Reservations:** Accepted at lunch only. **Directions:** Take the Bridge of Lions to Anastasia Boulevard; the restaurant is on your left after a short drive.

$ **Prices:** Appetizers $5–$7; main courses $5–$7 at lunch, $9–$15 at dinner. MC, V.

Open: Lunch Wed–Mon 11am–3pm; dinner Sun–Thurs 5:30–10pm, Fri–Sat 5:30–11pm.

The concept seems more New York than St. Augustine. Gypsy Cab is funky, comfortable, and eclectic. Its decor—already too grandiose a word to describe so casual a setting—consists of glossy pine tables (candlelit at night), a bit of glass brick, a bit of trellising, a few neon signs, and a changing art exhibit on the walls. It all reflects the personality of offbeat owner Ned Pollack, whose arrival in town was less than auspicious. Driving through Florida with no particular destination in mind, he hit a car full of nuns in St. Augustine. No one was hurt, but while Ned's truck was being repaired, he decided he liked the place and stayed on.

The menu changes nightly. On our last visit appetizers included cheese spedini (lightly herb-breaded Swiss cheese that's sautéed and finished with lemon, garlic, parsley, and butter), a hummus platter with pita bread, and a shrimp and black-bean tostada. An entree of blackened salmon with herbed citrus (lemon, lime, and orange) butter came with an array of fresh veggies (red cabbage, carrots, and broccoli) and sautéed rice tossed with minced onions, tomato, garlic, and herbs (you can, however, request homemade mashed potatoes instead). Other choices included New York strip steak with peppercorn Gorgonzola glaze and sautéed shrimp with fresh basil and artichoke hearts in a light, garlicky mornay sauce over angel-hair pasta. Lunch fare is similar, but offers sandwiches, salads, and egg dishes as well. There's a full bar, and rich fresh-baked desserts—such as creamy peanut butter pie on semisweet-chocolate crust—are topped with dollops of real whipped cream. Chocolate lovers can opt for something called "obscene cake."

OSCAR'S OLD FLORIDA GRILL, 614 Euclid Ave., off Fla. A1A on the Intracoastal Waterway. Tel. 829-3794.

Cuisine: OLD FLORIDA/SEAFOOD. **Reservations:** Not accepted, but you can call ahead for priority seating (that means you get the first table available when you arrive). **Directions:** Go over the Vilano Bridge, veer left on Fla. A1A north and drive about 2½ miles, turning left at Compton's.

$ Prices: Appetizers $2.50–$6.95; main courses $3.95–$10.95. MC, V.

Open: Wed–Thurs 5–9pm, Fri 5–10pm, Sat noon–10pm, Sun noon–9pm.

Boats have been docking here for grub since the late 19th century when Frank and Catherine Usina served up oyster roasts to Henry Flagler, his Vanderbilt pals, and other hungry sailors in palmetto-thatched huts. The Usinas' old fish camp is today Oscar's, a rustic eatery housed in a 1906 roadhouse with pine-plank floors and a steeply pitched tin ceiling, its rough-hewn rafters twined with philodendrons and strings of tiny lights. Tables are covered with green-and-white-checkerboard plastic cloths, the walls hung with neon beer signs. In this very casual setting (wear your jeans), the mood ranges from convivial (strangers talk to one another) to rollicking—especially on Wednesday and Thursday nights when live bluegrass and country music groups perform from 6 to 9pm. That's definitely the time to visit, though I also love weekend lunches here, when one can sit outside at riverside picnic tables shaded by a grove of live oaks. A bait shop adjoins, and people frequently fish from the dock after lunch. Parking is free.

Like the atmosphere and the music, the menu lacks nothing in old Florida authenticity. Order up a large bucket of steamed oysters or a platter of fried shrimp, fresh fish, oysters, clam strips, or crab patties—all accompanied by french fries *and* hush puppies, homemade cole slaw, and homemade sauces. These fried items are also available as sandwiches. Other good choices are crab Oscar (crabmeat baked in a rich cream sauce) and grilled fish of the day served with linguine and cheese toast. Some side dishes merit attention, among them red beans and rice with country sausage and scallions, pan bread (unsweetened southern-style cornbread served in a cast-iron skillet), Minorcan clam chowder (a local specialty), and cheese grits. Because the owners wanted Oscar's to be a family-oriented operation, not a rowdy fish camp bar, only beer and wine are served. The graham cracker–crusted key lime pie and the rich sweet-potato pie are great desserts.

SALT WATER COWBOY'S, 299 Dondanville Rd., off Fla. A1A. Tel. 471-2332.

Cuisine: OLD FLORIDA/SEAFOOD/BARBECUE. **Reservations:** Not accepted, so arrive early to avoid a wait. **Directions:** Go over the Bridge of Lions and follow Fla. A1A south for about 10 minutes; look for the restaurant's billboard, and make a right onto Dondanville Road just before you see a 7-Eleven store.

$ Prices: Appetizers $2.95–$6.95; main courses $7.95–$13.95. MC, V.

Open: Dinner only, daily 5–10pm.

Arrive early for dinner at Salt Water Cowboy's—not only because it's immensely popular and fills up quickly, but because you'll want to enjoy the spectacular view of the sun setting over a saltwater marsh. Designed to resemble a turn-of-the-century fish camp, this rambling Intracoastal Waterway restaurant has a rustic candlelit interior paneled with cedar lapwood and shingles. The unfinished wide-plank pine floors come from an old Jacksonville train station. And dozens of plants are suspended from rough-hewn cypress log beams overhead. A mix of dining areas ranges from intimate booths in alcoves lit by driftwood sconces to an outdoor plant-filled deck shaded by live oaks and illumined by tiki torches. One room has a hibiscus theme; another, flamingos. The background music is great—ragtime, Dixieland, and banjo tunes played at a low decibel level. And an attractive young staff offers friendly service. It's a casual place.

Like the ambience, the cuisine harks back to old Florida. Order up a smoked-fish appetizer with crackers and a glass of wine while you peruse the menu. For openers, there's a very rich and creamy chowder with big chunks of clam, potato, and celery. And garlicky oysters Dondanville are baked with a buttery topping of parmesan cheese and herbed breadcrumbs. An entree of fork-tender baby back ribs is a great choice; the ribs are smothered in a piquant barbecue sauce and served with fries and cole slaw. Another winner: oysters, scallops, or shrimp fried in light cornmeal batter. Scallops are also superb here, baked in a cream/shallot/white wine sauce and crisply gratinéed. And there's a first-rate spicy jambalaya served over seasoned rice with homemade cornbread. Entrees come with hot breads, a very good house salad, a baked potato, and a vegetable. Plan on dessert—creamy chocolate-almond pie on a chocolate cookie crust.

BUDGET

SCHMAGEL'S BAGELS, 69 Hypolita St., at Cordova St. Tel. 824-4444.

Cuisine: BAGEL SANDWICHES.

$ Prices: Sandwiches $1.75–$4.50. No credit cards.

Open: Mon–Sat 8am–2pm, Sun 9am–2pm.

On sunny mornings I just love to sit outdoors at one of Schamgel's umbrella-shaded patio tables and peruse the morning paper over oven-fresh bagels and steaming coffee. It's a perfectly peaceful setting in the heart of the historic district. But even when it rains and I have to sit in one of the Formica booths inside, I can't resist Schmagel's authentically plump New York–style bagels. They come in nine varieties—plain, whole wheat, sesame, onion, salt, cinnamon-raisin, blueberry, poppy seed, and garlic—or a combination of most of the above. Cream cheese spreads come mixed with scallions, vegetables, honey pecans, strawberries, or walnuts and raisins. Of course, you can always order a traditional cream cheese and Nova. The menu also lists fresh soups du jour, soft drinks, and fresh-baked fruit muffins. There's metered parking in a lot across Cordova Street.

EVENING ENTERTAINMENT

MILL TOP TAVERN, 19½ St. George St., at Fort Alley. Tel. 829-2329.

Housed in an 18th-century mill building (the water wheel is still outside), this rustic tavern has a woody interior—rough-hewn beams, pecky cypress walls, and pine plank floors. Weather permitting, it's an open-air space, with glassless windows overlooking the Castillo. If it gets cold, the windows are covered with plastic, and the room is heated. There's additional seating at picnic tables on an outdoor wooden deck and on a ground-floor patio shaded by live oak and palm trees. Every Sunday and Monday a classic rock guitarist performs. Tuesday is Ladies Night (discounted drinks for women) and the music is contemporary rock. On Wednesday, jazz and blues are featured; Thursday it's bluegrass. And Friday and Saturday varies bluegrass, rock, blues, and country rock. A full menu—burgers, sandwiches, salads—is served till 11pm Monday through Saturday, till 9pm on Sunday, and there's a large selection of specialty drinks with names like "Sex on the Beach" and "Beam Me Up Scotty." Most of the crowd is thirtysomething. You must be 21 to get in evenings. There's live entertainment from 1pm to 1am Monday through Saturday, from 1 to 10pm on Sunday. On-street parking is available.

Admission: Free Sun–Thurs, $1 Fri–Sat.

PASSPORT JOE'S, 2665 Fla. A1A S., at 4th St. Tel. 471-6722.

This is your classic funky beach bar, and it's always pulsing with activity. In addition to live entertainment, sporting events (such as Monday-night football) are aired on TV monitors over the bar and on a large-screen TV on the patio. There are pool tables and dart boards, weekly dance competitions, beer-chugging contests, trivia games, ladies' nights, and karaoke nights (Monday and Saturday). On Sunday the music is provided by an acoustic guitarist and/or live bands. On Monday an acoustic guitarist and singer perform. On Tuesday (the only night 18- to 20-year olds are allowed in) live progressive bands are featured, and there's free beer. On Wednesday, Thursday, and Saturday a DJ plays high-energy dance music. And on Friday live bands play oldies. There's a full restaurant menu featuring both snack fare (burgers, sandwiches, chicken wings, nachos) and full steak, seafood, Mexican, Caribbean, and pasta entrees. Dinner is served until midnight. Open nightly from 4pm to 1am, with live entertainment from 9pm. To get there, take the Bridge of Lions and follow Fla. A1A south for about four miles; it's on your right. There's free parking on the premises.

Admission: $1; Tues nights those under 21 pay $3 cover. Occasionally higher admission is charged for special events.

SCARLETT O'HARA'S, 70 Hypolita St., at Cordova St. Tel. 824-6535.

In the heart of St. Augustine's historic district, Scarlett O'Hara's offers a warren of cozy rooms with working fireplaces and shuttered windows in a rambling 19th-century wood-frame house. And if you want to get away from the crowd—and fairly loud music—you can sit out on rockers on the front porch or dine in a booth upstairs. Live rock, jazz, and R&B bands play Monday through Saturday, and though there's no dance floor, people get up and dance wherever. Sunday is karaoke night. Sporting events are aired on a TV in a room set up as an oyster bar. Sandwiches, seafood, southern specialties, and munchies on the order of nachos and buffalo wings are served nightly through midnight. You must be 21 to get in after 9pm. There's nightly entertainment from 9pm to 12:30am. Parking is free in a lot across Cordova Street.

Admission: Usually free; sometimes $1 Fri–Sat.

TRADE WINDS TROPICAL LOUNGE, 124 Charlotte St., between Cathedral Place and Treasury St. Tel. 829-9336.

Toni Leonard and her daughters, Janet and Julie, have been operating this funky-friendly local hangout for four decades. The ambience is nautical/tropical, with corrugated-tin roofing, a neon alligator and palm trees, bamboo wall coverings, a Gauguin-like mural, and a clutter of plants, seashells, buoys, and ship's lanterns suspended from fishnet overhead. The music is mostly oldies and country-western, occasionally jazz. Toni gets a kick out of telling how she fired Jimmy Buffet before he was famous because she didn't think he had any talent (they're still friends). Most of the groups playing Trade Winds are local, but well-known oldies groups like the Platters, the Coasters, the Drifters, and the Byrds do occasional gigs here. And on Palm Sunday every year, all the musicians who've ever played the club come back for a music marathon. Light fare—chili, smoked fish spread with crackers, croissant sandwiches, nachos, calzones—is available. You must be 21 to get in after 9pm. Trade Winds is also a simpatico spot for weekday happy hour from 5 to 8pm. There's live entertainment nightly from 9pm to 1am. Parking is on the street or in the bank lot next door.

Admission: Free Sun–Thurs, $1–$2 Fri–Sat.

WHITE LION, 20 Cuna St., between Charlotte and St. George Sts. Tel. 829-2388.

The White Lion is a cozy two-story British-style pub, with beamed ceilings, pine-plank floors, stained-glass windows, candlelit tables, and working fireplaces upstairs and down. Tuesday evenings an acoustical guitarist plays mellow rock from 7:30 to 10:30pm. On Friday and Saturday, jazz, rock, R&B, and bluegrass groups perform from 9:30pm to 1am. And weekends, weather permitting, a guitar player entertains on the large trellised outdoor patio. Even when there's no entertainment, this is a simpatico hangout. A full menu featuring steaks, burgers, sandwiches, chili, and fish and chips is offered through 9pm nightly. Frozen daiquiris and margaritas, draft beer, and potent tropical drinks are specialties. Drinks are half price during happy hour weekdays 4:30 to 7:30pm. You must be 21 to get in after 9:30pm. The White Lion is open Sunday through Thursday till about 11pm, on Friday and Saturday to 1am. Use the parking lot on Charlotte Street, less than half a block away.

Admission: Free Sun–Thurs, $1 Fri–Sat.

3. DAYTONA BEACH

50 miles NE of Orlando, 260 miles N of Miami, 89 miles S of Jacksonville

GETTING THERE **By Plane** American, Continental, Delta, and USAir fly into **Daytona Beach International Airport** (tel. 904/248-8030). A taxi from the airport to most beach hotels costs about $10.

By Train The closest Amtrak station (tel. 800/USA-RAIL) is in De Land, 23 miles southwest of Daytona.

By Bus **Greyhound** buses connect Daytona with most of the country. They pull into a very centrally located terminal at 138 S. Ridgewood Ave. (U.S. 1) between International Speedway Boulevard and Magnolia Avenue (tel. 904/253-6576).

From Orlando, **Daytona-Orlando Transit Service (DOTS)** (tel. 904/257-5411, or toll free 800/231-1965) provides van transport between the two cities. They offer about 10 round-trips daily. One-way fare is $26 for adults, $46 round-trip; children under 12 are charged half price. The service brings passengers to the company's terminal at 1598 N. Nova Rd., at 11th Street, or, for an $8–$21 fee, to beach hotels. In Orlando the vans depart from the airport.

By Car If you're coming from north or south, take I-95 and head east on International Speedway Boulevard (U.S. 92). From Tampa or Orlando, take I-4 east to U.S. 92. From northwestern Florida, take I-10 east to I-95 south.

The self-proclaimed "World's Most Famous Beach" is even more celebrated as the "Birthplace of Speed" and the "World Center of Racing." It has been a mecca for car-racing enthusiasts since the days when automobiles were called horseless carriages. Early automobile magnates Ransom E. Olds, Henry Ford, the Stanley brothers (of steamer fame), and Louis Chevrolet—along with motor-mad millionaires like the Vanderbilts, Astors, and Rockefellers—wintered in Florida and raced their vehicles on the hard-packed sand beach. The first competition, in 1902, was between Olds and gentleman racer Alexander Winton; they worked up to the then-impressive speed of 57 miles an hour. By 1904, a Daytona Beach event called the Winter Speed Carnival was drawing participants from all over the world, most of them wealthy sportsmen and financiers. Three years later, Fred Marriott wrapped a mile of piano wire around the boiler of his souped-up Stanley Steamer (to keep it from blowing up) and raced the course at a spectacular 197 m.p.h.! At the end of the stretch he crashed, just as spectacularly, into the pounding surf. He emerged uninjured, but after the accident the Stanley brothers quit racing their steam-driven cars, and gas engines became more prominent.

Many men who were to become famous for their skill with machinery first tested their ideas on the sands of Daytona Beach. Glenn Curtiss, the father of naval aviation, raced motorcycles here. And Sir Malcolm Campbell, a millionaire English sportsman, raced a car powered by an aircraft engine in 1928, reaching a speed of over 206 m.p.h.; in later years he set the ultimate beach speed record of 276.8 m.p.h. Most of these early beach events, by the way, were individual speed trials rather than actual races. The final speed trials were held in 1935.

The year 1936 ushered in the era of stock-car racing with a new beach racecourse, a host of daredevil drivers, and thousands of cheering fans. In 1947, driver and race promoter Bill France founded the National Association for Stock Car Auto Racing (NASCAR), headquartered at Daytona Beach. Today it's the world's largest motorsports authority, sanctioning the Daytona 500 and other major races at the International Speedway and tracks throughout the United States. The last stock-car race on the beach took place in 1958. A year later, France's dream of a multimotorsports facility, the Daytona International Speedway, was realized.

Of course you don't have to be a racing aficionado to enjoy Daytona. It has 23 miles of sandy beach, 500 feet wide at low tide (you can still drive and park—but not race—on the sand; maximum speed allowed is 10 m.p.h.). The town is mobbed with college students during spring break—the annual beach blanket Babylon—and during Bike Week in February thousands of leather-clad motorcycle buffs make the scene. But barring spring break and major speedway events, Daytona is a laid-back beach resort, offering boating, tennis, golf, water sports, and the opportunity to stroll the sands, swim, and soak up some sunshine.

ORIENTATION

INFORMATION **Destination Daytona,** at 126 E. Orange Ave., just west of the Silver Beach Bridge (P.O. Box 910), Daytona Beach, FL 32115 (tel. 904/255-0415, or toll free 800/854-1234), can help you with information on attractions, accommodations, dining, and events. Call in advance for maps and brochures, or visit their office when in town. They also maintain a branch at the Speedway.

CITY LAYOUT Daytona Beach is surrounded by water. The Atlantic Ocean borders its east coast and the Halifax River flows north to south through the middle of the city. There are actually four little towns along its beach—**Ormond Beach** to the north, the centrally located **Daytona Beach** and **Daytona Beach Shores,** and **Ponce Inlet** at the southern tip, just above New Smyrna Beach.

Florida A1A (Atlantic Avenue) runs along the beach north to south. **U.S. 1** runs inland paralleling the west side of the Halifax River, and I-95 vaguely parallels it still farther west. **International Speedway Boulevard** is the main east-west artery.

GETTING AROUND

BY TROLLEY & BUS VOTRAN, Volusia County's public transit system, runs **buses** throughout major areas of town Monday through Saturday between 6am and 7pm. Adults pay 75¢, children under 17 and seniors pay 35¢, and children under 6 accompanied by an adult ride free.

The company also operates free turn-of-the-century-style **trolleys** in the downtown area between 10am and 2pm weekdays, 8am to noon on Saturday. Trolleys also ply the route between Granada Boulevard and Dunlawton Avenue along Fla. A1A Monday through Saturday from noon to 12:30am; fares are the same as bus fares. Call 904/761-7700 for routing information.

BY CAR You can drive and park directly on the beach here. There's a $3 access fee between February 1 and Labor Day; the rest of the year it's free.

WHAT TO SEE & DO

In addition to the attractions listed below, the **Daytona Flea Market** is one of the world's largest, with 1,000 covered booths and over 100 antiques shops. Located on Tokoma Farms Road, a mile west of the Speedway at the junction of I-95 and U.S. 92 (tel. 252-1999), it is open year-round Friday through Sunday from 8am to 5pm (parking is free). And the **Dixie Queen Riverboat Company** (tel. 904/255-1997, or toll free 800/329-6225) offers year-round lunch, Sunday brunch, and dinner cruises—all with entertainment—as well as full-day trips to St. Augustine aboard a 150-passenger paddlewheeler.

BIRTHPLACE OF SPEED MUSEUM, 160 E. Granada Blvd., a block west of N. Atlantic Ave. Tel. 672-5657.

The history of beach racing is chronicled at this small Ormond Beach museum in displays of automotive memorabilia and photographs of vehicles, races, and famous drivers and auto pioneers. Antique cars on exhibit include a 1929 Model-A Ford woody wagon and a replica of the Stanley Steamer that Fred Marriott crashed into the ocean in 1907.

Admission: $1.

Open: Tues–Sat 1–5pm. **Closed:** Major holidays.

CASEMENTS, 25 Riverside Dr., at Granada Blvd. in Ormond Beach. Tel. 676-3216.

Casements (named for its casement windows) was the winter home of billionaire John D. Rockefeller, where he vacationed from 1918 to 1937. Today it serves as a cultural and civic center, and only one room is refurbished to evoke his era. Still, you might be interested in touring these once-posh precincts. Half-hour guided tours are given between 10am and 2:30pm weekdays, 10 and 11:30am on Saturday. There are historic photographs on display, as well as an art gallery, a large exhibit of Boy Scout memorabilia, and a room of Hungarian folk art and costumes.

Admission: By donation. Parking is free on the premises.

Open: Mon–Thurs 9am–9pm, Fri 9am–5pm, Sat 9am–noon.

DAYTONA BEACH KENNEL CLUB, 2201 W. International Speedway Blvd., just west of Fentress Blvd. Tel. 252-6484.

This is a pleasant way to spend a day or evening, especially if you opt to watch the races over lunch or dinner in the upstairs restaurant. There are a variety of ways to bet on the greyhounds; if you've never done it before, pick up a free brochure that explains how. You can also buy tip sheets recommending computer and expert picks. Each meet includes 14 races. You must be at least 18 years old to enter the betting area.

The moderately priced Pavilion Clubhouse Restaurant (lunch entrees are $5.95–$9.95; dinner entrees, $11.95–$17.95) has tiered seating, with big picture windows overlooking the track and TV monitors enhancing your view at higher tables. Tables are elegantly appointed with peach linen napery. At lunch you might order a Caesar salad, or a Reuben sandwich. A typical dinner might consist of French onion soup and an entree of prime rib or shrimp scampi. There's a full bar. Reservations are suggested; request a window seat.

Admission: $1 adults (seniors 55 and over free at matinees); grandstand seating, 50¢–$1.75; restaurant, $2. Parking is free on the premises; preferred parking (closer to entrance) is $1, and valet parking, $2.

Open: Night races Mon–Sat at 7:45pm; matinees Mon, Wed, and Sat at 1pm. Doors and restaurant open an hour before post time.

DAYTONA INTERNATIONAL SPEEDWAY, 1801 W. International Speedway Blvd. (U.S. 92). Tel. 253-RACE for tickets, 254-2700 for information.

★ Opened in 1959 with the first Daytona 500, this 450-acre "World Center of Racing" is practically the raison d'être for Daytona Beach—certainly the keynote of the city's fame. It presents about eight weekends of major racing events annually, featuring stock cars, sports cars, motorcycles, and go-karts, and is also used for automobile testing. Its grandstand, almost a mile long, seats 97,900.

Major annual races here include Speedweeks (16 days of stock- and sports-car racing in late January to mid-February, culminating in the Daytona 500 by STP), Bike Week (10 days of motorcycle events in late February or early March), Daytona Beach Spring Speedway Spectacular (car show and swap meet featuring collector vehicles, late in March), the Pepsi 400 (stock cars, in July), the AMA/CCS Motorcycle Championship (on a three-day weekend in mid-October), and the Daytona Beach Fall Speedway Spectacular (a car show and swap meet the weekend after Thanksgiving). For further information, write to Daytona International Speedway, P.O. Box 2801, Daytona Beach, FL 32120-2801.

To learn more about racing, head for the **Visitors' Center** at the west end of the Speedway and NASCAR office complex. Open daily from 9am to 5pm, the center is also the departure site for 30-minute guided van tours of the facility that provide a close look at the high-banked 2.5-mile trioval and 3.56-mile road courses, the

Winston Tower, the pit, and the garage area. Admission is $3 for adults, free for children 7 and under. Tours depart daily every half hour from 9am to 4:30pm, except during races, special events, or car testing. Also at the Visitors' Center are a large gift shop; the Gallery of Legends, where the history of motorsports in the Daytona Beach area is documented through photographs and memorabilia; and the Budweiser Video Wall, presenting a continuous showing of racing in the Daytona Beach area, tracing its history from the "Birthplace of Speed" to the World Center of Racing." The center also stocks information on area accommodations, restaurants, attractions, and nightlife.

Admission: Auto events, $30–$60; motorcycle events, $10–$35; go-kart events, under $10. Big events sell out months in advance, so plan far ahead and also reserve accommodations well before your trip. Parking is free for grandstand seating; infield parking charges vary with the event.

Open: Daily. **Closed:** New Year's and Christmas Days.

MUSEUM OF ARTS AND SCIENCES, 1040 Museum Blvd., off Nova Rd. Tel. 255-0285.

This rather eclectic museum, houses both art and natural science exhibits. In 1956, Cuban dictator Fulgencio Batista—a collector of Cuban art and a frequent visitor to Daytona Beach—donated his vacation home and his art collection to the city. In 1971, the Batista house and property were sold to finance the present building, and a decade later his collection—and other important Cuban art and artifacts donated since—were installed in their own 3,000-square-foot wing.

The collection spans two centuries of Cuban art—mostly paintings—from 1759 to 1959. Also on permanent display here is the Karshan Center of Graphic Arts, Fine and Decorative Arts from the Age of Napoleon, and the museum's vast Art in America Collection (1640–1910), as well as a pre-History of Florida section.

The most recent permanent display at the museum, "Africa: Life and Ritual," documents African peoples from over 30 cultures in 15 countries. Exhibits include *vigango* (tall wooden ancestral images from Kenya that serve as memorials to the dead), masks, rare Ashanti gold ornaments, fetishes, baskets, and vessels.

There's a contemporary sculpture garden on the grounds. Permanent exhibits are complemented by an ongoing schedule of concerts, lectures, and changing shows. And planetarium shows take place at 1 and 3pm daily.

Admission: Museum, $3 adults, $1 children and students with ID, free for kids under 6 (free for all on Fri); planetarium shows, $1. Parking is free on the premises.

Open: Tues–Fri 9am–4pm, Sat–Sun noon–5pm. **Closed:** Major holidays. **Directions:** Take International Speedway Boulevard west, make a left on Nova Road, and look for a sign on your right.

PONCE DE LEÓN INLET LIGHTHOUSE, 4931 S. Peninsula Dr., Ponce Inlet. Tel. 761-1821.

Built in the mid-1880s, this is, at 175 feet, the second-tallest lighthouse in the United States. And you'll find out just how high that is if you climb the 203 steel steps that spiral up its interior. The present beacon, visible for 10 nautical miles, flashes every 10 seconds.

In the 1970s this brick-and-granite coastal sentinel and its original outbuildings were restored and added to the National Register of Historic Places. The head lighthouse keeper's cottage—which was used as a barracks during World War II and later served as the first town hall of Ponce Inlet—today houses a museum of exhibits on navigational aids, marine biology, deep-sea fishing, and ocean exploration. The first-assistant keeper's house is furnished to reflect turn-of-the-century occupancy. And other historic buildings contain a museum of tools and artifacts involved in keeping the light burning, a picture gallery of lighthouses of the world, and a theater, where a 12-minute video on the history of this particular lighthouse is shown continually throughout the day (visit it first). On display in the boatyard is the 46-foot oak-and-cypress *F. D. Russell* Tug Boat, built in 1938, which you can board and explore. A gift shop on the premises sells lighthouse- and Florida-related items. There's an adjoining playground and picnic area with tables and barbecue grills.

Admission: $3 adults, $1 children under 12. Parking is free on the premises.

Open: May–Aug, 10am–9pm; Sept–Apr, 10am–5pm (last admission an hour before closing). **Closed:** Christmas. **Directions:** Follow Atlantic Avenue (Fla. A1A) south, make a right on Beach Street, and follow the signs.

SPECIAL EVENTS

Besides the events at the International Speedway (see above), Daytona hosts the **Florida International Festival** annually in July and August. The festival is the "summer home" of the London Symphony Orchestra (LSO). Michael Tilson Thomas is the orchestra's principal conductor, and concerts feature such guest artists as conductor Gennadi Rozhdestvensky and soloists Vladimir Feltsman and Elmar Oliveira. The festival also features a chamber music series; a pop series by the orchestra; and jazz, rock and roll, folk, and country concerts by such performers as Skitch Henderson and the Dukes of Dixieland. For information, write or call the Florida International Festival, P.O. Box 1310, Daytona Beach, FL 32115 (tel. 904/257-7790.)

SPORTS & RECREATION

DEEP-SEA FISHING If you're interested in deep-sea fishing and/or whale-watching, contact **Critter Fleet,** 4950 S. Peninsula Dr., Ponce Inlet (tel. 767-7676), or **Sea Love Marina,** 4884 Front St., Ponce Inlet (tel. 767-3406).

GOLF There are a dozen golf courses within 25 minutes of the beach, and most hotels can arrange starting times for you. The **Daytona Beach Golf Course,** 600 Wilder Blvd. (tel. 258-3119), is the city's largest, with 36 holes.

HORSEBACK RIDING **Shenandoah Stables,** 1759 Tomoka Farms Rd., off U.S. 92 (tel. 257-1444), offers daily trail rides and horseback-riding lessons between 10am and 5pm.

WATER SPORTS **Jet Ski Headquarters,** 3537 Halifax Dr., just northwest of the Dunlawton Bridge (tel. 788-4143), rents waverunners, sailers, Hobie Cats, and Sunfish; it's open Monday through Friday from 10am to 6pm and on Saturday from 10am to 2pm. Additional water-sports equipment, as well as bicycles, beach buggies, and mopeds, can be rented along the beach in front of major hotels. A good place to look is in front of the Marriott at 100 N. Atlantic Ave.

WHERE TO STAY

Daytona Beach hotels fill to the bursting point during major races at the Speedway and other special events, and whenever college students are on break. At these times room rates skyrocket, if you can find a room at all, and there's often a minimum-stay requirement. If you're planning to be in town at one of these busy times (see the "Calendar of Events" in Chapter 2), reserve far in advance. All the accommodations listed below are on or near the beach and close to the Speedway.

AT THE BEACH

Expensive

MARRIOTT, 100 N. Atlantic Ave. (between Earl St. and Auditorium Blvd.), Daytona Beach, FL 32118. Tel. 904/254-8200, or toll free 800/228-9290. Fax 904/253-8841. 377 rms, 25 suites. A/C MINIBAR TV TEL

$ **Rates:** $170 single or double ($235–$250 during special events, when there's also a seven-night minimum stay); $198 single or double on the Executive Level ($250–$265 during special events); $250–$750 suites. Children under 18 stay free in parents' room; additional person $20 extra. AE, CB, DC, DISC, MC, V. **Parking:** Free in lot across the street; valet parking $8 per night.

This is Daytona's most luxurious—and most central—beachfront hotel, designed so that every room offers a gorgeous ocean view. It's right at the clock tower and bandshell, and, in season, its beach and boardwalk are the site of concessions offering parasailing, bicycle rentals, motorized four-wheelers, pedal carts, surfboards, boogie boards, cabanas, and umbrellas. Accommodations are decorated in pleasing resort colors—mauve, peach, and light turquoise—with bleached-oak furnishings. Lovely watercolors of underwater scenes with seahorses and tortoises are a nice touch. In-room amenities include alarm-clock radios and remote-control cable TVs with Spectravision movie stations. Rooms on the Executive Level (16th floor) feature king-size beds, pullout sofas and armchairs, ceiling fans, VCRs, and, in the baths, black and white TVs, hairdryers, and extra phones. Executive Level guests receive a welcome gift on arrival and have use of a private ocean-view lounge with a console TV and games.

Dining/Entertainment: The Marriott has two full-service restaurants. The very pretty plant-filled Parkside Oceanfront Café, with swagged floral-print curtains framing picture windows overlooking the beach, serves moderately priced breakfasts, lunches, and dinners daily. Weather permitting, you can sit outside at umbrella tables. Early-bird dinners here, served from 5 to 7pm daily, are a great bargain.

Coquinas is the hotel's plush premier dining room, with candlelit, peach-clothed tables amid massive oak columns, Louis XV–style chairs, and mirrored walls embellished with frosted-glass swans. Gourmet steak and seafood dinners are featured (specialties range from Norwegian salmon en papillote to filet mignon), and there's an extensive wine list.

Splash, an attractive poolside bar with Saltillo-tile floors, pots of ferns, and palm trees, serves light fare and specialty drinks; it has indoor and outdoor seating. Also on the beach is a complex of small restaurants with outdoor café seating, serving international fare—everything from souvlaki to cheese steaks. There's a lively on-premises high-energy dance club called Waves, and the sophisticated Clock Tower Lounge offers live jazz (see "Evening Entertainment," below).

Services: Concierge, room service (7am–11pm), free newspapers at bell desk.

Facilities: Indoor/outdoor swimming pool, two whirlpools, steam and sauna, kiddie pool, vast palm-fringed sun deck, sand volleyball court, playground, video-game arcade, full-service unisex hair and beauty salon (also offers massage), coin-op washer/dryers, complete health club ($5 charge per visit or $10 per length of stay), business services, florist, camera shop, an arcade of shops; Memorial Day–Labor Day, free activities for children 5–12 (arts and crafts, sports, etc.); a small amusement park adjoins the hotel, and there are cable-car rides on the pier.

Moderate

ACAPULCO INN, 2505 S. Atlantic Ave. (between Dundee Rd. and Seaspray St.), Daytona Beach, FL 32118. Tel. 904/257-1950, or toll free 800/874-7420. Fax 904/253-9935. 42 rms, 91 suites. A/C TV TEL

$ **Rates:** $78–$100 single or double; $84–$116 efficiency suite. Children under 18 stay free in parents' room; additional person $6–$10 extra. Monthly rates available. Inquire about golf and honeymoon packages. AE, CB, DC, DISC, MC, V. **Parking:** Free on the premises.

One of five beachfront properties here under the auspices of a company called Oceans Eleven, the Acapulco Inn is fronted by festive Mayan symbols that comprise something of a local landmark when lit up at night. Resort-style balconied rooms are decorated in teal, mauve, and peach, with grasspaper-look wall coverings and tropically themed paintings on the walls. All are equipped with small refrigerators, in-room safes, and remote-control cable TVs with HBO, Spectravision pay movies, and tourist-information channels. Efficiency units, most with ocean views, offer fully equipped eat-in kitchens. Higher rates reflect high season and ocean view.

Dining/Entertainment: The many-windowed Fiesta Restaurant, which overlooks the ocean and offers outdoor seating at umbrella tables, serves all meals. Typical American fare is featured. Prices are reasonable, and there's a children's menu. In summer, the Fiesta offers poolside waiter service. The comfortable Sombrero Lounge adjoins.

Note: All Oceans Eleven hotels are good bets for families, offering beachfront accommodations, organized resort activities, and opportunities for socializing with your fellow guests. You can reserve at any of them via the above toll-free number, and

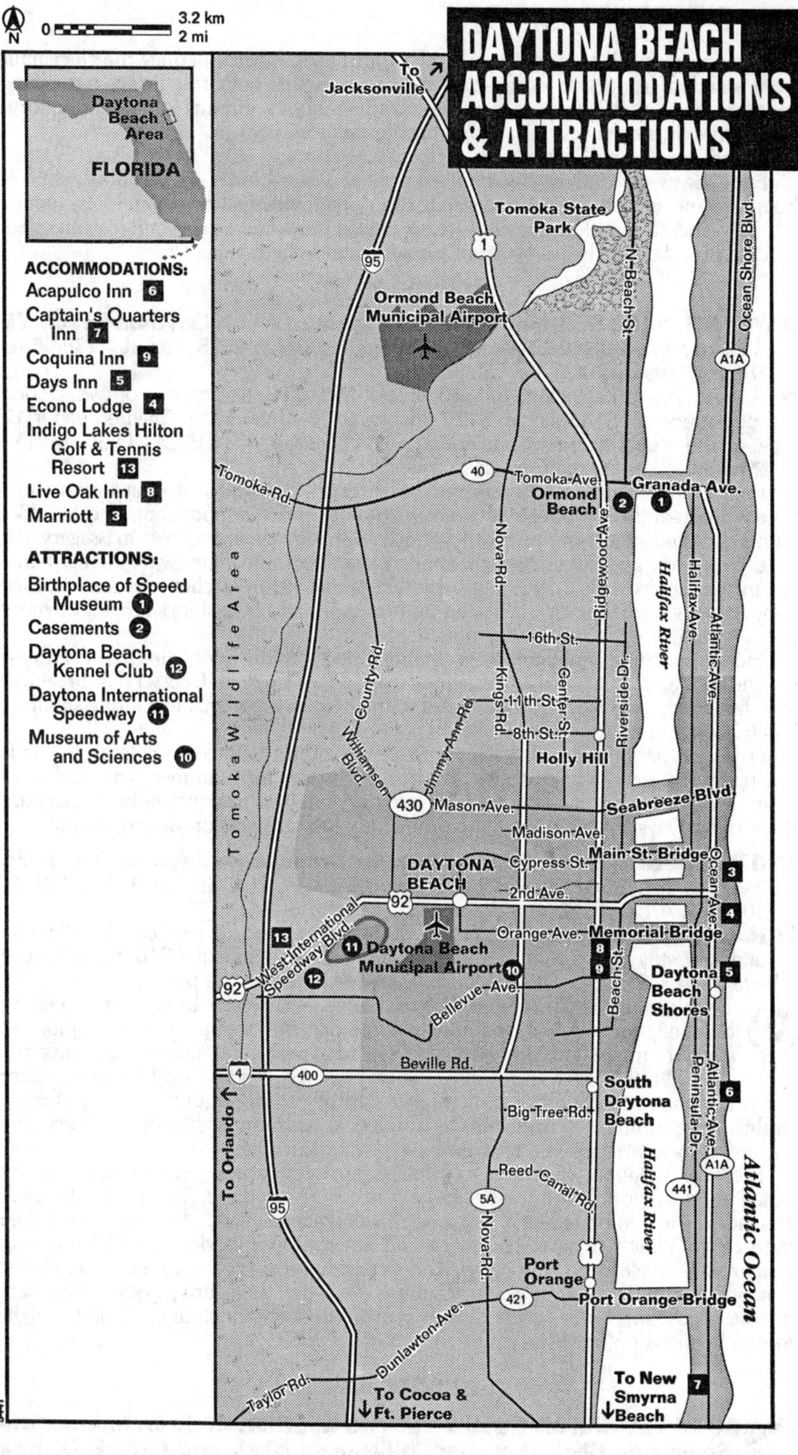
DAYTONA BEACH ACCOMMODATIONS & ATTRACTIONS
3.2 km
2 mi
N
Daytona Beach Area
FLORIDA
ACCOMMODATIONS:
Acapulco Inn 6
Captain's Quarters Inn 7
Coquina Inn 9
Days Inn 5
Econo Lodge 4
Indigo Lakes Hilton Golf & Tennis Resort 13
Live Oak Inn 8
Marriott 3
ATTRACTIONS:
Birthplace of Speed Museum 1
Casements 2
Daytona Beach Kennel Club 12
Daytona International Speedway 11
Museum of Arts and Sciences 10
To Jacksonville
Tomoka State Park
Ormond Beach Municipal Airport
N. Beach St.
Ocean Shore Blvd.
Tomoka Rd.
Tomoka Ave.
Granada Ave.
Ormond Beach
Tomoka Wildlife Area
Nova Rd.
Ridgewood Ave.
Halifax River
Halifax Ave.
Atlantic Ave.
16th St.
County Rd.
Williamson Blvd.
Jimmy Ann Rd.
Kings Rd.
Center St.
Riverside Dr.
11th St.
8th St.
Holly Hill
Mason Ave.
Seabreeze Blvd.
Madison Ave.
Main St. Bridge
Cypress St.
DAYTONA BEACH
2nd Ave.
Ocean Ave.
Orange Ave.
Memorial Bridge
West International Speedway Blvd.
Daytona Beach Municipal Airport
Daytona Beach Shores
Bellevue Ave.
Beach St.
Beville Rd.
South Daytona Beach
To Orlando
Big Tree Rd.
Peninsula Dr.
Reed Canal Rd.
Atlantic Ocean
Port Orange
Port Orange Bridge
Dunlawton Ave.
Taylor Rd.
To Cocoa & Ft. Pierce
To New Smyrna Beach
5441

the operator can tell you which best suits your needs. Their offerings run the gamut from standard rooms to ocean-view penthouse suites with full living and dining rooms. Guests at all properties receive coupon books offering discounts at local sports-equipment concessions, shops, and restaurants.

Services: Complimentary newspaper in restaurant.

Facilities: Oceanfront swimming pool, two whirlpools, kiddie pool, shuffleboard, picnic area, coin-op laundry, gift shop, small video-game room, lobby lounge with TV and card tables. Like all Oceans Eleven properties, the Acapulco Inn offers an extensive daily activities program for adults and children.

Inexpensive

DAYS INN, 1909 S. Atlantic Ave. (at Flamingo Ave.), Daytona Beach, FL 32118. Tel. 904/255-4492, or toll free 800/325-2525. Fax 904/238-0632. 188 rms, 8 suites. A/C TV TEL

$ Rates: $35–$50 single; $45–$60 double; $55–$75 suite for one or two. During special events, $125 single; $130 double; $125–$150 suite. Children under 12 stay free in parents' room; additional person $5 extra. AE, CB, DC, DISC, MC, V. **Parking:** Free on the premises.

At this recently renovated beachfront hotel, every room provides an ocean view. Pretty peach-and-teal rooms with oak furnishings offer remote-control cable TVs with HBO and visitor-information channels, in-room safes, and bed massagers. All have balconies, and some contain small refrigerators and microwave ovens. Large oceanfront suites with fully equipped kitchens and eat-in kitchenettes are ideal for families; they have king-size beds and pullout sofas, and furnishings are a little more upscale than those in standard rooms.

Facilities include a medium-size swimming pool/kiddie pool/sun deck overlooking the beach, an on-premises restaurant called the Tropical Tree serving breakfast and dinner, coin-op washer/dryers, and a small video-game arcade. During summer, lunch is offered at a pool bar.

Days Inns nationwide offer a Super Saver rate of just $29–$49 single or double if you reserve 30 days in advance via the above toll-free phone number. This deal is, of course, subject to availability, but it's worth a try. If you can't get in here, there are three other Days Inns in town, all conveniently located beachfront properties.

ECONO LODGE, 301 S. Atlantic Ave. (at Broadway), Daytona Beach, FL 32018. Tel. 904/255-6421, or toll free 800/76-LODGE. Fax 904/252-6195. 100 rms. A/C TV TEL

$ Rates: $38–$78 single or double, $90–$150 during special events. Children under 17 stay free in parents' room; additional person $5 extra, $10 during special events. AE, CB, DC, DISC, MC, V. **Parking:** Free on the premises.

(S) This very centrally located Econo Lodge occupies a beachfront five-story building, with half of its rooms overlooking the ocean. Accommodations—standard motel units attractively decorated in peach and mauve—are equipped with cable TVs that offer visitor-information channels. A good deal for families are the reasonably priced suites (at the higher end of the rates quoted above) offering sizable living room areas with sofas in addition to bedrooms, plus small refrigerators and microwave ovens; some of these have private balconies.

Facilities include a very large swimming pool with a sun deck overlooking the beach (there's a pool bar in season, and a concession called the Tiki Hut vends beach accessories), a coin-op laundry, and a small video-game arcade. A casual hotel coffee shop called Time Out serves breakfast and lunch. Room service is available during restaurant hours (6am to 2pm daily). And a cozy on-premises pub called the Hole Bar is a popular local hangout featuring music (live or DJ) nightly, pool tables, dart boards, foosball, video games, and sporting events—including Monday-night football—aired on large-screen TV.

A RESORT HOTEL

INDIGO LAKES HILTON GOLF & TENNIS RESORT, 2620 W. International Speedway Blvd. (between Williamson Blvd. and I-95; P.O. Box

10859), Daytona Beach, FL 32120. Tel. 904/258-6333, or toll free 800/874-9918. Fax 904/254-3698. 147 rms, 64 suites. A/C TV TEL

$ **Rates:** $75–$99 single; $85–$109 double; $120–$165 executive king room; $145–$185 one-bedroom suite. Children of any age stay free in parents' room; additional person $10 extra. Inquire about golf, tennis, and honeymoon packages. AE, CB, DC, DISC, MC, V. **Parking:** Free on the premises.

This multifacilitied 250-acre resort is very close to the Speedway and a five-minute drive from the beach. The property is beautifully landscaped with verdant lawns and duck-filled lakes and lagoons spanned by arched bridges. Handsome accommodations, housed in two-story tan stucco buildings, are attractively decorated in earth tones with grasspaperlike wall coverings and dark oak furnishings. Each room is equipped with an alarm-clock radio, coffee maker (and complimentary coffee), and remote-control TV with HBO, Spectravision pay movies, an extensive roster of cable stations, and a tourist-information channel. Most rooms contain small refrigerators, and all have patios or balconies. Large executive king rooms are especially luxurious and offer parlor areas. And gorgeous residential-style one-bedroom suites—many overlooking the golf course—offer additional TVs, radios, and phones in the extra bedroom and also include fully equipped kitchens, baths with whirlpool tubs, and large, plushly furnished living/dining room areas.

Dining/Entertainment: A branch of Red Hot & Blue, the barbecue restaurant chain founded by the late Lee Atwater, is on the premises (see "Where to Dine," below, for details).

Major Moultries is the elegant plant-filled golf-course restaurant with a wall of windows overlooking the greens and lagoons. It serves American regional fare at breakfast and lunch, and dinner in high season. A bar/lounge adjoins, as does a snack bar with umbrella tables.

Services: Room service (7am–11pm), complimentary newspaper daily, complimentary van to/from the golf course, tennis and golf instruction from resident pros, complimentary airport shuttle.

Facilities: Two swimming pools (one Olympic-size), 18-hole/par-72 Lloyd Clifton–designed championship golf course (ranked 19th in the state) with putting green and pro shop, volleyball, shuffleboard, horseshoes, basketball, 10 lighted hard-surface tennis courts with pro shop, 1½-mile jogging trail, health club ($5 a day charged for use), massage, business center, gift/sundry shop, coin-op washer/dryers, Budget car-rental desk.

BED & BREAKFAST

CAPTAIN'S QUARTERS INN, 3711 S. Atlantic Ave. (about a quarter mile south of Dunlawton Ave.), Daytona Beach, FL 32127. Tel. 904/767-3119, or toll free 800/332-3119. Fax 904/760-7712. 26 suites. A/C TV TEL

$ **Rates** (including full breakfast): $75–$95 single or double, $110–$145 ocean-view penthouse suite. During special events, $90–$140 single or double; $130–$195 ocean-view penthouse suite. Additional adult $10 extra, $5 for children under 17. Lower rates available for weekly and monthly stays. AE, DISC, MC, V. **Parking:** Free.

This five-story beachfront inn offers large and lovely suites, most with ocean or river views. They have living/dining room areas, fully equipped kitchens, and country-look bedrooms furnished in oak antique reproductions. Residential decorator schemes utilize charming floral-print wall coverings and fabrics, balloon curtains, dried-flower wreaths, and framed botanical prints. French doors open onto balconies or patios furnished with wooden rockers.

Accommodations are equipped with clock radios and remote-control cable TVs with HBO, and penthouse suites have fireplaces, spa tubs, and big picture windows overlooking the ocean. On-premises facilities include a country crafts/gift shop off the lobby, a heated swimming pool, coin-op washer/dryers, and the Galley Restaurant, which has an outdoor deck overlooking the ocean. Open for breakfast and lunch daily, it serves scrumptious fresh-baked cakes, cinnamon buns, and danish, as well as homemade soups, salads, and sandwiches on homemade breads. It's worth stopping by even if you're staying elsewhere. Other pluses: free transport to and from the airport, complimentary daily newspapers, wine and cheese at check-in, chocolate mints on your night table, and a full breakfast of eggs, bacon, grits or home-fries, juice, and coffee served each morning in your room or the Galley. Owner Becky Sue Morgan provides warm hospitality.

COQUINA INN, 544 S. Palmetto Ave. (at Cedar St.), Daytona Beach, FL 32114. Tel. 904/254-4969, or toll free 800/727-0678. 4 rms (all with bath). A/C

$ Rates (including full breakfast): $70–$105 single or double, $115–$140 during special events; $195 suite. Additional person $10 extra, $30 during special events. No children accepted. MC, V. **Parking:** Free on the premises.

This charming terra-cotta–roofed coquina and cream stucco house sits on a tranquil tree-shaded street half a block west of the Halifax River and Harbor Marina. Guests can relax before a working fireplace in a lovely parlor furnished with leather wing chairs, a comfortable sofa, and a baby grand piano. Baskets of magazines, books, and games, and a TV are in the adjoining sunroom, which has terra-cotta–tile floors and cheerfully upholstered white wicker furnishings. An Oriental rug graces the highly polished oak floor of the dining room, which also features French doors, casement windows, and a crystal chandelier. Breakfast—elegantly served by candlelight on Lenox and Rosenthal china—includes an entree such as eggs Benedict or French toast stuffed with cream cheese, bananas, and pecans; fresh fruit; fresh-ground coffee; and homemade breads and muffins. Classical music is played in public areas.

Each room is exquisitely decorated, most with area rugs strewn on oak floors and ceiling fans overhead. The Jasmine Room, painted adobe peach, features a working coquina fireplace and a canopied mahogany bed. In the Hibiscus Room, decorated in soft greens and pinks, a black iron bed embellished with gold leaf is made up with a pretty floral chintz spread. French doors lead to a private plant-filled balcony (pots of geraniums, hibiscus, gardenias, and hydrangeas) overlooking an ancient live oak draped with Spanish moss. Painted in raspberry with a floral frieze, the sunny Azalea Room has light streaming in from corner windows. It's furnished with a mahogany waterfall bed (a Victorian teddy bear sits amid its throw pillows), white wicker chairs, and an antique Governor Winthrop desk; since its bath is detached, robes are provided for occupants. And the Magnolia Room, its mint stucco walls hung with framed botanical prints, contains a shell-shaped sink and a hand-carved mahogany four-poster bed and white iron day bed, both made up with beautiful floral chintz bedspreads and ruffled pillows. The Jasmine and Hibiscus Rooms can be combined to create a two-bedroom/two-bath suite. All rooms have clock radios and are provided with bubble bath and candles. Portable phones and TVs are available on request. Complimentary tea and sherry are served in the parlor throughout the day. Also gratis—10-speed bicycles and use of an Olympic-size pool at the nearby YWCA. During busy seasons, a two-night minimum stay is required.

LIVE OAK INN, 448 S. Beach St. (at Loomis Ave.), Daytona Beach, FL 32114. Tel. 904/252-4667. Fax 904/255-1871. 4 rms (all with bath). A/C TV TEL

$ Rates (including extended continental breakfast): $60 single or double Mon–Thurs, $99 Fri–Sun. Additional person $6 extra. Rates higher during peak events. Packages including dinner, golf, and other extras also available. AE, MC, V. **Parking:** Free.

Occupying a restored 19th-century house, this charming B&B hostelry is surrounded by centuries-old live oaks hung with Spanish moss. An inviting front porch with white wicker rocking chairs faces the street. Inside are a parlorlike lobby and two beautiful plant-filled dining areas.

The guest rooms—three with private sun porches or balconies—are exquisitely decorated. Yours might be painted pale peach with pristine white trim, furnished with an Eastlake bed and matching marble-top dresser and upholstered white wicker chairs and chaise longue. Or perhaps you'll get a Victorian sleigh bed with a patchwork quilt and throw pillows and a private plant-filled sun porch furnished with Adirondack chairs. Rooms look out on the Halifax Harbor Marina or a delightful garden. Baths have Victorian soaking tubs or Jacuzzis, TVs are concealed in old-fashioned radio and Victrola cabinets (you may find a VCR or cassette player as well), area rugs are strewn on highly polished oak floors, and wood-bladed fans whirr slowly overhead. Live plants, old family photographs, and baskets of potpourri add to the residential ambience. All rooms are stocked with books and magazines and equipped with alarm-clock radios.

The lobby bar is open throughout the day, and the in-house restaurant is first-rate (see "Where to Dine," below). Other amenities include a croquet set on the front lawn, a washer/dryer and copy machine for guest use, a complimentary drink when you check in, a fruit basket and flowers in your room on arrival, terry robes, afternoon tea and cocktails, free transport to/from the beach, free airport shuttle, and room service during restaurant hours. Guests can also use an Olympic-size swimming pool at the YWCA four doors down. A delicious breakfast is served daily. The good news is that the owners have purchased a similar 19th-century building next door and plan to add 12 more rooms. No smoking is permitted in the house.

WHERE TO DINE

EXPENSIVE

LIVE OAK INN, 448 S. Beach St., at Loomis Ave. Tel. 252-4667.

Cuisine: AMERICAN/CONTINENTAL. **Reservations:** Recommended.

$ Prices: Appetizers $3.50–$4.25; main courses $3.75–$5.50 at lunch, $14–$17 at dinner. AE, MC, V.

Open: Lunch Mon–Fri 11:30am–1:30pm; dinner daily 5–9:30pm.

The restaurant at this charming B&B (see "Where to Stay," above) has two plant-filled dining rooms, one with high windows and dark-stained pine walls, the other with white stucco walls and lace-curtained windows. French doors open onto an enclosed porch. Elegantly appointed candlelit tables are covered with mauve linen cloths draped over white, furnishings include a Victorian oak organ used as a sideboard and a marble-top Victorian oak buffet, and classical music enhances the romantic ambience.

The menu changes frequently. On a recent visit my party enjoyed appetizers of creamy roasted corn and crab chowder and baked mushrooms stuffed with proscuitto, herbed breadcrumbs, and smoked Cheddar. Entrees—served with a delicious Caesar salad, twice-baked potatoes au gratin, and a medley of fresh vegetables—included grilled filet mignon with mushroom-cabernet sauce and sautéed grouper with black-bean chili salsa. And for dessert there was a rich terrine of chocolate with vanilla sauce. The Live Oak offers a small but well-chosen list of California wines. The lunch menu features croissant sandwiches and a marvelous salad niçoise with chunks of grilled fresh tuna on a bed of greens, tossed with new potatoes, hard-boiled egg, and tomatoes in a balsamic vinaigrette.

MODERATE

ANNA'S ITALIAN TRATTORIA, 304 Seabreeze Blvd., at Peninsula Dr. Tel. 239-9624.

Cuisine: ITALIAN. **Reservations:** Recommended.

$ Prices: Appetizers $4.25–$13.95; main courses $7.95–$15.50; early-bird pasta dinners (served 5–6:30pm) $5.95. AE, MC, V.

Open: Dinner only, daily 5–10pm.

This charming little family-run restaurant, operated by the Triani family from Sicily, is pristinely decorated in pale pink, peach, and gray, with ceiling fans overhead and soft lighting from brass oil lamps and sconces. Everything here is homemade, from the creamy Italian dressing on your house salad to the basket of hot crusty bread that accompanies all entrees. That bread comes in handy for soaking up the dressing of a scungilli salad appetizer here—extra-virgin olive oil with pieces of celery, slivers of fresh garlic, lemon, parsley, and oregano. An order of lightly breaded fried calamari with a piquant marinara sauce is also a good starter. Two irresistible pasta dishes are the fettuccine alla campagniola (pasta tossed with strips of sautéed eggplant and chunks of sausage in tomato-cream sauce flavored with a soupçon of crushed red pepper and romano cheese) and rigatoni siciliana (tubular pasta with sautéed broccoli, garlic, and pine nuts in a fresh tomato sauce). Nonpasta recommendables include Anna's chicken and shrimp scampi (sautéed in garlic butter, mushrooms, sherry wine, and lemon) and grouper genovese (sautéed filet in a light marinara and dry white wine sauce with black olives, capers, and thinly sliced onions).

Portions are hearty. Entrees come with soup or salad and a side dish of angel-hair pasta or a vegetable. Take the pasta and order a vegetable side dish as well—perhaps asparagus, escarole, or broccoli sautéed in oil and garlic. Lime sorbet is served between courses, and there's a nice selection of Italian wines to complement your meal. The tira misu for dessert is a must. There's free parking in a lot across Peninsula Drive.

AUNT CATFISH'S, 4009 Halifax Dr., at the west end of the Port Orange Bridge. Tel. 767-4768.

Cuisine: SOUTHERN/SEAFOOD. **Reservations:** Not accepted, but you can—and should—call ahead for priority seating (that means you get the first table available when you arrive).

$ Prices: Appetizers $2.90–$4.95; main courses $5–$8 at lunch, $8–$13 at dinner; early-bird dinners $7–$10.50. Reduced prices for children and seniors. Sun brunch $9 for adults, $5.50 for children 4–12, free for kids under 4. AE, DC, DISC, MC, V.

Open: Mon–Sat 11:30am–9:30pm, Sun 9am–9:30pm (brunch Sun 9am–2pm; early-bird dinners daily noon–6:30pm). **Closed:** Christmas.

Aunt Catfish was the nickname of a gruff-voiced local character whom owner Jim Galbreath knew as a kid. She fished all day, drove around in a black Cadillac, and ate dinner every night in a restaurant owned by Jim's parents. Her namesake restaurant abounds in southern-cracker ambience. Tables are topped with laminated horse-feed sacks, and weathered-looking rough-hewn wood-paneled walls are hung with historic photographs of the Daytona Beach area. During the day, ask for a window seat overlooking the Halifax River. Parking is free.

The food is great, and there's plenty of it. No way will you finish everything you order. For one thing, all entrees include hush puppies, a chunk of watermelon, unbelievable yummy hot cinnamon rolls, a side dish (perhaps Cajun rice or baked Mexican potato skins with melted Cheddar, salsa, and sour cream), and unlimited helpings from an extensive salad bar, which in addition to salads is laden with such down-home fare as cheese grits, cinnamon apples, fresh-baked cornbread, and hominy. A great entree choice is the Florida cracker sampler platter—a spit-roasted quarter chicken with cranberry-orange relish, crabcakes served in hollandaise sauce, fried shrimp, and fried catfish fingerlings. Lightly breaded fried oysters here are also highly recommendable. Beverage options include house wines, bar drinks, bottomless pitchers of iced tea, and fresh-squeezed lemonade. For dessert, split a boatsinker fudge pie with Häagen-Dazs coffee ice cream dipped in a coat of hardened chocolate and topped with whipped cream. Aunt Catfish's key lime and raspberry pies are also first-rate.

Sunday brunch provides an opportunity for overindulgence. A buffet meal, it includes all the salad bar items, plus an omelet station, pancakes, French toast, hot entrees, fresh-baked muffins and pastries, and more—all for under $10! Lunch choices include burgers, sandwiches, and a soup and salad buffet in addition to ribs, chicken, and seafood entrees.

JULIAN'S, 88 S. Atlantic Ave., one block south of Granada Blvd., Ormond Beach. Tel. 677-6767.

Cuisine: STEAK/SEAFOOD. **Reservations:** Not accepted.

$ Prices: Appetizers $1.75–$4.50; main courses $7.45–$14.45. Reduced prices for children. AE, CB, DC, MC, V.

Open: Dinner only, daily 4–11pm.

Extremely popular locally, Julian's is one of a kind. Designed after the Tropicana nightclub in Miami, its interior might be described as "bizarre Polynesian mission church." Creating this admittedly unlikely ambience is an organist who plays skating rink–style music Monday through Saturday nights in front of a vast mural depicting outrigger canoes with hula dancers and a village of thatched huts. Lighting fixtures are painted with Polynesian totem symbols. In contrast, rough-hewn wood paneling, red carpeting, and white linen tablecloths draped over red ones evoke a traditional steakhouse. Parking is free.

And this is, by the way, a good place to order steak—charcoal-broiled USDA prime western filet mignon, T-bone, or New York sirloin. Other good choices are fried oysters and charcoal-broiled lamb chops with mint jelly. Entrees come with baked potato and salad, but for an extra $1.50 you get a full dinner that also includes a relish tray, black-bean soup, vegetable, dessert, and tea or coffee. Bread baskets yield hot dinner rolls and cinnamon buns. There's a full bar, and inexpensive desserts include fresh-baked pies and eclairs.

RED HOT & BLUE, 2620 W. International Speedway Blvd., between Williamson Blvd. and I-95 at the Indigo Lakes Hilton. Tel. 258-PORK.

Cuisine: BARBECUE. **Reservations:** Not accepted.

$ Prices: Appetizers $2.25–$4.95; sandwiches/salads $3.95–$5.95; main courses $8.95–$14.95. AE, CB, DC, DISC, MC, V.

Open: Daily 11:30am–10pm.

The late Lee Atwater created this restaurant chain which takes its Memphis-style barbecue seriously. "Southern barbecue," says the menu, "is inexorably linked to politics, to churches, to civic clubs, to Friday night drive-ins and Sunday potluck suppers. . . . Question a Southern man's patriotism before you question his choice of barbecue." Named for the Memphis radio show that introduced Elvis Presley and Jerry Lee Lewis, it's an immense eatery with seating in comfortable upholstered booths. Walls are hung with blues memorabilia—photographs, posters, musical instruments, and record album covers of Aretha Franklin, T-Bone Walker, John Lee Hooker, B. B. King, and others, not to mention a logo of Blues Brothers pigs in dark glasses strumming neon-stringed guitars. The background music, of course, is blues. Parking is free on the premises.

Barbecued pork—smoked 12–14 hours over hickory wood and pulled fork tender from the bone—is the house specialty, served on a bun with sauce, slaw, and barbecued beans. Homemade chili here is chunky with smoked beef brisket and topped with Cheddar and onions. On the other hand, you might opt for Tijuana taco salad topped with chili and beef or smoked chicken. And dinner entrees include smoked prime rib, pork chops, T-bone steak, and grilled fresh fish—served with new potatoes, fresh veggies, and a salad. There's a good choice of beers to wash it all down, a full bar is on the premises, and dessert options include pecan, apple, fudge, and key lime pies. Kids 6 and under eat free from the children's menu.

RICCARDO'S, 610 Glenview Blvd., at Fla. A1A. Tel. 253-3035.

Cuisine: ITALIAN. **Reservations:** Recommended.

$ Prices: Appetizers $3.75–$4.95; main courses $7.75–$14.95. Reduced prices for children 12 and under. AE, CB, DC, MC, V.

Open: Dinner only, daily 5–10pm.

The Segale family has owned this casual Daytona Beach restaurant since 1972. It has a cozy candlelit interior with white stucco walls, dark-wood beams, stained-glass panels, and framed art prints (Monet, van Gogh, Cézanne, Degas) adorning arched cork panels. A warm glow emanates from wrought-iron lighting fixtures with amber glass. There's free parking in an adjoining lot.

A nice feature here is a large complimentary antipasto salad—lettuce, cheeses, Italian salami, tomato, black olives, and garlicky marinated vegetables dressed with herb-seasoned olive oil. If you want an appetizer as well, order up the stuffed calamari served with chunky fresh tomato sauce. A pasta dish of sausage and roast peppers over homemade spaghetti in a rich tomato sauce is recommended. And a house specialty is shrimp Riccardo—shrimp sautéed in garlic butter and served on fettuccine with lemon wedges. Note that Riccardo's tends to cook pasta thoroughly, so if you want it al dente be sure to mention this when you order. I like to get a side dish of fresh spinach or asparagus sautéed in oil and garlic (once again, request this prepared heavy on the garlic if you like it that way). Portions are large, everything is made from scratch, and there's a full bar. Homemade desserts, such as rum cake with fresh whipped cream, change daily.

ST. REGIS RESTAURANT, 509 Seabreeze Blvd., between Wild Olive and Grandview Aves. Tel. 252-8743.

Cuisine: AMERICAN/CONTINENTAL. **Reservations:** Recommended.

$ Prices: Appetizers $2.50–$6.95; sandwiches/salads $4.95–$8.50; main courses $9.95–$13.95. MC, V.

Open: Lunch Mon–Fri 11:30am–2pm; dinner Mon–Sat 5:30–10pm.

Housed in a late Victorian home (it was a boarding house and B&B for over a century), the St. Regis is heralded by a burgundy canopy and an old-fashioned front porch. Its three downstairs dining rooms evoke a cozy plant-filled parlor, with lace-curtained windows, Oriental rugs on oak-plank floors, ornately gilt-framed mirrors and tapestries, and corner cupboards used to display decorative china. Tables covered in peach linen cloths are lit by oil candles at night. An awninged open-air patio contains a bar, and there are lovely private dining rooms upstairs furnished in opulent Victoriana.

The cuisine is eclectic. Appetizer choices, for instance, include such diverse offerings as blue crab and artichoke bottoms garnished with hard-boiled egg slices and topped with sauce Louis; roasted garlic with sun-dried tomatoes; and blackened Cajun chicken bits served with cream cheese and horseradish. Try the creamy oyster stew served with seasoned croutons. A St. Regis salad—avocado, artichokes, tomatoes, cucumbers, greens, and mushrooms—comes with a choice of delicious homemade dressings such as bleu cheese and pepper parmesan. Sandwich offerings range from cheeseburgers to Italian sausage with peppers and onions on a toasted garlic roll. And you can opt for serious entrees such as steak au poivre in cognac-cream sauce or sautéed boneless pork loin medallions with sherry-drenched prunes, apples, pears, and pecans. Fresh vegetables and a potato or rice dish accompany these entrees. There's an extensive wine list, and desserts are superb; I had a scrumptious pumpkin cheesecake with a brown-sugary graham cracker crust.

SOPHIE KAY'S TOP OF DAYTONA, 2625 S. Atlantic Ave., at Florida Shores Blvd. Tel. 767-5791.

Cuisine: CONTINENTAL/STEAK/SEAFOOD/PASTA. **Reservations:** Recommended.

$ Prices: Appetizers $3.95–$6.95; main courses $9.95–$16.95. Reduced prices for children under 12. AE, CB, DC, MC, V.

Open: Dinner only, Mon–Thurs 5–10pm, Fri–Sat 5–11pm.

At 29 stories the tallest oceanfront restaurant on the Florida coast, Sophie Kay's offers panoramic 360° beach and city views. Early arrivals enjoy spectacular sunsets. Sophie herself is author of a dozen cookbooks and she does a cooking segment on an Orlando-based news show. Her elegant circular restaurant is the Daytona Beach venue for celebrity bashes. Local resident John Travolta celebrated his mother's birthday here, Carol Channing threw a dinner party, and Tom Jones liked the place so much he had Sophie send him food on the road. The ambience is romantic, with candlelit white-linened tables, live piano music nightly, and baskets of philodendrons strung with tiny lights looping the inner dining room. Ask for a window seat when you reserve; parking is free.

An appetizer of buttery baked mushrooms stuffed with marsala wine- and herb-flavored crabmeat makes an excellent beginning, as does traditional French onion soup au gratin. Sophie is a great hand with pasta (she's written an entire book on the subject), and her primavera—ziti tossed with broccoli, onions, and mushrooms in a delicate white sauce—is a tasty example. It comes with a dinner salad. Another very popular entree here is Sophie's Choice—fresh large shrimp sautéed with mushrooms, chopped tomatoes, shallots, and garlic in a seasoned butter-wine sauce and served over a bed of linguine. And many people come here for steak, prime rib, beef Wellington, and surf-and-turf combinations. For dessert, don't pass up Sophie's delicious twice-baked cheesecake on a brown-sugary graham cracker crust—one of the best of its genre. You'll also find a goodly selection of wines, cordials and cognacs, and after-dinner cocktails here.

INEXPENSIVE

DOWN THE HATCH, 4984 Front St., Ponce Inlet. Tel. 761-4831.

Cuisine: SEAFOOD. **Reservations:** Not accepted, but call ahead for priority seating (that means you get the first table available when you arrive). **Directions:** Take Fla. A1A south, make a right on Beach Street, and follow the signs.

$ Prices: Appetizers $2.75–$5.95; main courses $7.95–$12.95; sandwiches $3.25–$5.25. Reduced prices for children. AE, MC, V.

Open: Daily 11:30am–10pm. **Closed:** Thanksgiving and Christmas.

Occupying a half-century-old fish camp on the Halifax River, Down the Hatch is a cozy, candlelit restaurant serving up fresh fish and seafood (note their shrimp boat docked outside). During the day, picture windows provide scenic views of a passing parade of boats and shore birds—blue herons, egrets, pelicans, and cormorants—and you might even see dolphins frolicking. At night, arrive early to catch the sunset over the river, and also to beat the crowd at this very popular place. Inside, rough-hewn cypress walls are hung with hundreds of photographs of the Daytona Speedway and the old fish camp, and the nautical ambience is enhanced by a clutter of mounted fish trophies, ship models, harpoons, hurricane lamps, and antique bottles. In summer, light fare is served outside on an awninged wooden deck. Parking is free.

Start your meal with an order of buffalo shrimp—tiny shrimp quick-fried in hot oil, finished with a piquant Louisiana hot sauce, and served with chunky homemade bleu cheese dressing. Raw oysters served with cocktail sauce and horseradish are tasty. Entrees include fried or broiled fresh fish such as red snapper or grouper, and there's an excellent crab Imperial—crabmeat broiled in a tarragon-mayonnaise sauce and garnished with chopped green peppers. If seafood isn't your thing, filet mignon is aged on the premises. All entrees are served with hush puppies and a choice of baked potato, salad, cole slaw, and fries. There's a full bar; desserts include mud cake, key lime pie, and cheesecake.

SOPHIE KAY'S COFFEE TREE FAMILY RESTAURANT, 100 S. Atlantic Ave., at Bosarvey Dr., Ormond Beach. Tel. 677-0300.

Cuisine: AMERICAN. **Reservations:** Not accepted.

$ Prices: Appetizers $1.95–$3.50; main courses $5–$9; breakfast items mostly under $5. Reduced prices for children and seniors over 55. AE, MC, V.

Open: Daily 7am–10pm.

This casual coffee shop, with sunshine streaming in through numerous windows, is a cheerful spot for inexpensive meals. You can sit in a comfy booth or at a counter facing an open kitchen hung with copper pots. Food is served on colorful Fiestaware dishes.

The same menu—including breakfast fare—is served all day, with specials such as homemade meatloaf, lasagne, and stuffed cabbage offered at lunch and dinner. You might begin the day here with thick slabs of Texas-style French toast, Belgian waffles dusted with powdered sugar, or eggs Benedict. The rest of the day, choices include deli sandwiches, burgers, salads, and entrees ranging from fried shrimp to roast turkey served over sage dressing with cranberry sauce, either including cole slaw, mashed potatoes, and a fresh vegetable. For dessert, try the ultra-rich chocolate suicide cake. Everything is fresh and well prepared. This is food like Mom's. And parking is free.

SPRING GARDEN RANCH, 900 Spring Garden Ranch Rd., DeLeon Springs. Tel. 985-0526.

Cuisine: AMERICAN. **Reservations:** Required. **Directions:** Take International Speedway Boulevard to U.S. 92W, turn right at Rte. 1792 (Woodland Boulevard), stay on your left, and take U.S. 17 to Spring Garden Ranch Road; look for the sign on your right and go to Gate 3.

$ Prices: Breakfast fare $1.95–$6.95; breakfast buffet $4.95 for adults, $3.50 for children under 10; lunch fare $2–$5.50. MC, V.

Open: Daily 6am–2pm. **Closed:** Easter, Thanksgiving, and Christmas.
This is more than a meal, it's an outing. Spring Garden Ranch is a 148-acre training center for harness race horses, and from its trackside restaurant you can watch pacers and trotters being schooled through large picture windows. The surroundings are scenic, and, all in all, this is nice way to start your day. After you eat, you can go look at the horses.

Breakfast choices include a hearty buffet—eggs, biscuits and gravy, pancakes, sausage patties and bacon, home-fries, grits, and citrus fruits. Or you might order steak and eggs à la carte. Lunch fare includes sandwiches, salads, burgers, and entrees like southern fried chicken, with fruit cobbler à la mode for dessert. Ask for a window seat when you reserve; parking is free.

EVENING ENTERTAINMENT

THE PERFORMING ARTS

At the 2,552-seat **Peabody Auditorium,** 600 Auditorium Blvd., between Noble Street and Wild Olive Avenue (tel. 255-1314), Daytona Beach's Civic Ballet performs *The Nutcracker* every Christmas and sponsors another ballet every spring. The Daytona Beach Symphony Society arranges a series of six classical concerts between December and April. During the same season, Concert Showcase features pop artists such as Liza Minnelli, Tony Bennett, Steve Lawrence and Eydie Gorme, Victor Borge, and Rita Moreno, as well as full Broadway-cast stage shows like *Cats* and *Grand Hotel.* And the London Symphony Orchestra has been performing here for over 25 years during the semiannual Florida International Festival.

Under the same city auspices is the **Oceanfront Bandshell** (tel. 258-3169), on the boardwalk next to the Marriott Hotel. The city hosts a series of free big-band concerts at the Bandshell every Sunday night from early June through Labor Day. And during spring break MTV hosts a series of free rock, comedy, and rap music concerts at the Bandshell featuring major performers like the Black Crowes, Run DMC, and Squeeze.

Prices at both venues vary with the performances. Parking is $3 in an adjacent lot.

THE CLUB & BAR SCENE

CLOCK TOWER LOUNGE, in the Marriott Hotel, 100 N. Atlantic Ave., between Earl St. and Auditorium Blvd. Tel. 254-8200.

This sophisticated bar lounge, with bamboo furnishings and palm trees growing toward a skylight ceiling, offers piano-bar music Monday through Thursday and excellent live jazz (piano, sax, and vocalist) on Friday and Saturday. There's a small dance floor, and in addition to drinks you can order interesting light-fare items such as smoked-salmon mousse with crackers or black lobster ravioli with light cream sauce. This is one of Daytona's most romantic settings. Make a night of it, and dine earlier in Coquinas, the Marriott's elegant steak and seafood restaurant. It's open nightly from 8pm to midnight. Parking is free in a lot across the street; valet parking is $3.

Admission: Free.

COLISEUM, 176 N. Beach St., just west of the International Speedway Blvd. bridge. Tel. 257-9982.

Heralded by a pedimented Doric colonnade, this upscale Roman-theme dance club occupies a converted movie theater. Inside, a raised dance floor is flanked by Ionic columns, and Roman-style bas-reliefs and sculpture adorn the walls. A DJ plays alternative/progressive dance music, with occasional lapses into Top-40 tunes; four big movie screens project music and ambience videos; and there are nightly laser light shows. The crowd is mostly twentysomething with occasional glitterati; Tom Cruise partied here during the filming of *Days of Thunder*. During spring break there are live concerts and special events.

At this writing the management is completing an art deco sports bar next door which will offer pool tables, dart boards, video games, and an indoor basketball court. There will be no cover or minimum, and a finger-food menu is planned. A DJ will play country, jazz, rock, blues, and oldies, and major sporting events will be aired.

The Coliseum is open from 9pm to 3am, nightly from February to October, and Thursday through Sunday the rest of the year. Parking is free across the street and behind the club; usually there's ample street parking as well.

Admission: $5–$6.

RAZZLES, 611 Seabreeze Blvd., between Grandview and S. Atlantic Aves. Tel. 257-6236.

At this large and popular dance club, a DJ plays progressive and Top-40s music till 3am nightly. The setting is archetypical, with lots of neon tubing, the requisite monitors flashing music videos, and sophisticated lighting effects over the dance floor. A magician frequently entertains in the lobby, and there are four pool tables, a blackjack table, and a few video games. An awninged patio out front provides a place for quiet conversation. The crowd is young—early 20s. Street parking only.

Admission: Before 10pm, $6–$8 with free drinks; after 10pm, $5 for 18- to 20-year-olds, $3 for those 21 and over.

701 SOUTH, in the Texan Hotel, 701 S. Atlantic Ave., between E. International Speedway Blvd. and Orange Ave. Tel. 255-8431.

This is a high-energy club, with a big dance floor, two giant matrix (multiscreen) video walls, 13 bartenders (overseeing 8,000 square feet of bar area), and sexy "shooter" girls in leotards offering shots of a drink called Sex on the Beach—a mix of cranberry and orange juices, peach schnapps, and vodka—to willing customers. Monday through Saturday a DJ and live bands alternate, playing progressive music and rock 'n' roll; Sunday there's a DJ only. Big-name acts have played here, among them Paula Abdul, Samantha Fox, Red Hot Chili Peppers, Marky Mark, and Naughty by Nature. When you weary of dancing, you can play pool, darts, foosball, or air hockey, or retire to an umbrella table at the oceanfront oyster bar. Light fare is available. It's open nightly from 8pm to 3am, and the action gets underway about 11pm. Parking is free on the premises.

Admission: $6 ages 18–20, $4 for those 21 and over, higher when big-name bands play.

CHAPTER 11

FLORIDA'S PANHANDLE

- **WHAT'S SPECIAL ABOUT FLORIDA'S PANHANDLE**

1. **PENSACOLA**
2. **FORT WALTON/ DESTIN & THE EMERALD COAST**
3. **PANAMA CITY/ PANAMA CITY BEACH**
4. **TALLAHASSEE**

One glance at the map of Florida and it's easy to see why this northwest area is known as the Panhandle. Bordered by Alabama, Georgia, and the Gulf of Mexico, the Panhandle is definitely the "Deep South," notable for gracious antebellum mansions, farms that were vast plantations, old cemeteries dotted with the graves of Confederate soldiers, tranquil towns graced by oak-shaded streets, and old-fashioned gardens flaunting azaleas and camellias. In this languid atmosphere, southern accents prevail and the southern hospitality is truly genuine.

Mother Nature certainly blessed the Panhandle with extraordinary beauty—countless acres of fragrant, green pine forests; crystal-clear rivers; spring-fed lakes and streams; soft white sand beaches with towering dunes and lacy, golden sea grasses.

Because the lifestyle is slow-paced, emphasis is on family activities in the great outdoors and enthusiastic participation in a variety of amusing annual festivals, such as the Boggy Bayou Mullet Fry in Niceville, the Watermelon Seed Spittin' Contest in the "watermelon capital" of Monticello, and the Wausau 'Possum Festival. It's fun to exit the superhighways and explore the colorful towns.

Fascinating history abounds in the Panhandle. Archeological sites and massive Native American mounds are interesting to tour. In the early 17th century, Spanish conquistador Hernándo de Soto set up camp one winter, before marching onward in his futile search for gold. During that time a Spanish mission was established to convert Native Americans, who seemed to be utilizing the Spaniards for target practice. Centuries later, the Seminoles were residents of the Panhandle until Gen. Andrew Jackson and early plantation owners greedily decided that all this rich farmland should be theirs. By hiding in the limestone cavern at Marianna, about 60 miles northwest of Tallahassee, many Seminoles were fortunate enough to escape the general's attacks but they lost their land.

Serendipity plays a big part in a Panhandle vacation. Would you ever have expected to encounter a French influence here? The Marquis de Lafayette owned a plantation in the Panhandle; Congress awarded him 23,040 acres for his heroic service in the Revolutionary War. Lafayette did not approve of slavery, so he persuaded French farmers to migrate to the Panhandle to work his land.

The Panhandle was also distinguished by French royalty. Prince Achille Murat, son of the King of Naples and nephew of Napoléon Bonaparte, was an enthusiastic Panhandle plantation owner. His wedding in 1826 to George Washington's grand-niece, Catherine Gray, in Tallahassee was an international high-society event. Smitten by Catherine's beauty, the prince had wooed her by sipping champagne from her dainty slipper. The fun-loving prince and the new princess hosted many soirees at their plantation home, and because they loved Tallahassee so much, the royal couple were buried in St. John's Cemetery.

The wide diversity of the Panhandle, from the simplicity of peaceful rivers and historic towns to the sophistication of Florida's capital city, makes this multifaceted area one of the most fascinating in Florida.

WHAT'S SPECIAL ABOUT FLORIDA'S PANHANDLE

Ace Attractions

- ☐ Eglin Air Force Base, Fort Walton Beach, where World War II hero Gen. Jimmy Doolittle's Raiders trained.
- ☐ Fort Pickens, a spectacular setting in Gulf Islands National Seashore, where Apachee Chief Geronimo was imprisoned.
- ☐ Lake Jackson Mounds, Tallahassee, an 81-acre settlement dating to A.D. 1200.
- ☐ San Luis Archeological Site, Tallahassee, an Apalachee tribal village and 17th-century Spanish mission.
- ☐ Seville Preservation District, Pensacola, with 10 historic buildings and museums, plus a shopping and dining complex.

Museums and Archives

- ☐ Black Archives Research Center and Museum, on the Florida A&M University campus, Tallahassee, with the world's second-largest collection on African American history.
- ☐ National Museum of Naval Aviation, at Pensacola U.S. Naval Air Station, one of the world's largest aerospace museums.
- ☐ Indian Temple Mound and Museum, Fort Walton Beach, with the world's largest collection of prehistoric southeastern Native American ceramics (6,000+ pieces).

Parks and Gardens

- ☐ Edward Ball Wakulla Springs State Park, near Tallahassee, one of the world's deepest freshwater springs.
- ☐ Alfred B. Maclay State Gardens, Tallahassee, with more than 300 acres of gorgeous magnolias, camellias, and azaleas, plus the restored Maclay House.
- ☐ St. Marks Wildlife Refuge and Lighthouse, south of Tallahassee, 64,000 acres with more bird species than anywhere else in Florida except the Everglades.

Architecture

- ☐ Seaside, east of Grayton Beach, a unique resort community built in 1981 and acclaimed one of the top U.S. architectural achievements.
- ☐ Eden State Gardens and Mansion, north of Grayton Beach, a restored 1898 Greek Revival southern mansion.
- ☐ Florida State Capitol, Tallahassee, a modern legislative center.
- ☐ Old State Capitol, Tallahassee, a restored 1902 white-columned American Renaissance building.

Beaches

- ☐ Gulf Islands National Seashore, 150 miles of dazzling white sand and rolling dunes, stretching from Pensacola Beach to Fort Walton Beach.
- ☐ Grayton Beach, considered one of the best beaches in the continental U.S.

SEEING THE PANHANDLE

Visiting the Panhandle can best be done by car, as distances are great and public transportation is not available in most areas. Superhighways lead to major destinations with state roads and backroads offering photogenic scenery surrounding charming small towns.

The easy route between Tallahassee and Pensacola, east to west, is I-10. The stretch of Fla. 90 leading northeast from Pensacola toward Tallahassee was designated an Official Scenic Route of Florida. Fla. 90 also leads to Marianna and Florida Caverns State Park and Maclay Gardens State Park.

Five old scenic secondary roads from Tallahassee, once Native American paths that became Spanish trails, are known as "canopy roads." These two-lane routes are lined with ancient live oaks dripping with Spanish moss, their branches reaching high above to form a canopy.

The coastal route, U.S. 98, ribbons along the Gulf of Mexico, south of Tallahassee all the way to Pensacola. Here, Fla. 399, leading to Santa Rosa Island and the Gulf Islands National Seashore, is a very scenic drive.

PANHANDLE HOTEL TIP Hotel and motel reservations are necessary from May to Labor Day, when Alabama and Georgia vacationers flock to the nearby Panhandle beaches. Summer rates are always highest. Winter is off-season, because temperatures are much cooler than on Florida's southeast and southwest coasts.

1. PENSACOLA

200 miles W of Tallahassee, 375 miles W of Jacksonville

GETTING THERE **By Plane** The **Pensacola Regional Airport** (tel. 904/435-1746) is served by American, Continental, Delta, Northwest, and USAir.

By Train Amtrak began service to Pensacola in April 1993 with the *Sunset Limited,* which departs from Los Angeles and travels to Miami with stops along the way at Pensacola, Chipley, Crestview, and Tallahassee. Passengers can also connect from Jacksonville and New Orleans. Pensacola's Amtrak train station is located at 940 E. Heinberg St, near the bayfront. For information and reservations, call Amtrak (tel. toll free 800/TEL-TRAK).

By Car On Florida's westernmost tip, Pensacola is located off I-10; just follow the signs.

Pensacola's turbulent past has all the elements of an exciting movie, but no Hollywood producer could ever imagine a scenario so complicated—the region has seen more than a dozen conquerors, and five different flags have been unfurled here.

It all began with the native tribes who lived in the area centuries ago and who left behind evidence of their sojourn in the pottery shards and artifacts discovered in the sand dunes. In 1559 King Philip II of Spain commissioned Tristan De Luna to colonize the coastal territory. But the ill-fated settlement survived only two years before De Luna and his settlers returned to Spain. Spain was more successful on the second try, when Capt. Jordan de Reina colonized Pensacola in 1698. Pensacola has had a long-time friendly feud with St. Augustine as to which city was the nation's first settlement—St. Augustine, founded in 1564, can claim to be the nation's first permanent settlement.

Important because of its strategic deep harbor, subsequent events led to takeovers of Pensacola by the French, the British, the United States, and the Confederacy. Pensacola's colorful history is just one reason why the city is so fascinating—it has the atmosphere of Old Spain, a romantic French influence reminiscent of New Orleans, and there remain the magnificent mansions built by the wealth of the lumber barons after Britain initiated that industry in the area.

The sophistication of the city leads to the simplicity of sun, sand, and sea just across the causeway where miles of platinum white beaches are splashed by the Gulf of Mexico. Two of the Pensacola area's beaches are among America's top 10—Perdido Key, rated no. 3, and eastern Perdido Key, rated no. 7 by Dr. Stephen Leatherman of the University of Maryland's Laboratory for Coastal Research.

And there is yet another facet of Pensacola. A short drive from downtown, the U.S. Naval Air Station provides a glimpse into the high-tech future with thrilling exhibitions by the Blue Angels pilots, the epitome of expertise in the skies.

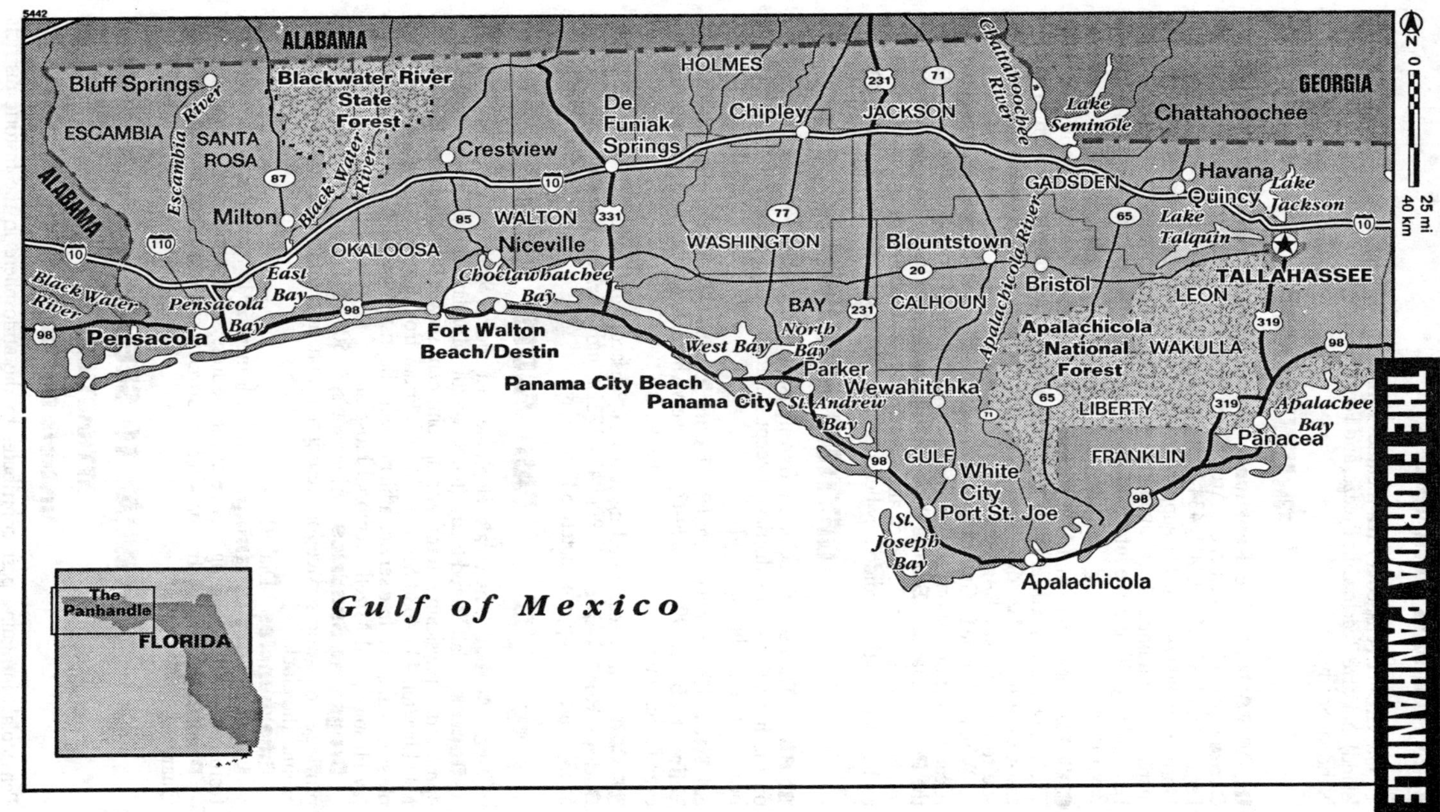

THE FLORIDA PANHANDLE
25 mi
40 km
N
ALABAMA
GEORGIA
Gulf of Mexico
Bluff Springs
Blackwater River State Forest
HOLMES
De Funiak Springs
Chipley
JACKSON
Chattahoochee River
Lake Seminole
Chattahoochee
ESCAMBIA
SANTA ROSA
Escambia River
Black Water River
Crestview
Milton
WALTON
Niceville
OKALOOSA
WASHINGTON
GADSDEN
Havana
Quincy
Lake Jackson
Lake Talquin
TALLAHASSEE
Blountstown
Apalachicola River
Bristol
LEON
East Bay
Choctawhatchee Bay
Pensacola Bay
Pensacola
Fort Walton Beach/Destin
BAY
CALHOUN
North Bay
West Bay
Parker
Panama City Beach
Panama City
St. Andrew Bay
Wewahitchka
Apalachicola National Forest
WAKULLA
LIBERTY
Apalachee Bay
Panacea
GULF
White City
Port St. Joe
FRANKLIN
St. Joseph Bay
Apalachicola
The Panhandle
FLORIDA

The Greater Pensacola Area includes Pensacola, Pensacola Beach (on Santa Rosa Island), Navarre Beach, Gulf Breeze, and Perdido Key (all the way west at Gulf Islands National Seashore).

ORIENTATION

INFORMATION The **Pensacola Convention and Visitor Information Center** (part of the Pensacola Area Chamber of Commerce), 1401 E. Gregory St., Pensacola, FL 32501 (tel. 904/434-1234, or toll free 800/874-1234, 800/343-4321 in Florida; fax 904/432-8211), supplies detailed descriptive brochures and very helpful maps for self-guided tours, including the Naval Air Station. When you drive into Pensacola, you'll find the information center at the foot of the three-mile Pensacola Bay Bridge.

CITY LAYOUT I-10 and U.S. 90 lead into downtown Pensacola from the north. The major north-south artery is **Palafox Street,** which goes through town. The east-west artery is **Garden Street,** which becomes **Navy Boulevard** and takes you to the U.S. Naval Air Station.

When you drive to Gulf Islands National Seashore and the beaches, travel south on Alcaniz Street or east on Garden Street to Gregory. After driving east on Gregory, take the **Pensacola Bay Bridge** (U.S. 98), leading directly to the beaches. Follow signs to Fla. 399 for Pensacola Beach and Navarre Beach; follow signs to County Road 292 to drive west to the Perdido Key beaches, also part of Gulf Islands National Seashore.

GETTING AROUND

BY BUS The Escambia County Transit System (tel. 904/436-9383) schedules buses on the hour to various districts, except for the beaches (buses don't go near the beaches at all). The fare is $1.

BY TAXI Taxi service includes **Airport Express Taxi** (tel. 904/572-5555) and **Yellow Cab** (tel. 904/433-1143). As everywhere, taxis are expensive, costing well over $1 per mile.

BY CAR Major car-rental agencies in Pensacola are **Avis** (tel. 904/433-5614), **Budget Rent-A-Car** (tel. 904/474-3721), and **Thrifty Rental** (tel. 904/477-5553). Rates are approximately $30 per day.

FAST FACTS

Area Code Pensacola's telephone area code is 904.

Doctor Call Sacred Heart (tel. 474-5700 Monday through Friday from 8am to 4pm), a free physician referral and appointment service with access to 200 doctors. MD Line (tel. 434-4080 Monday through Friday from 9am to 5pm) has access to 100 physicians and is a free service affiliated with Baptist Hospital, Gulf Breeze Hospital, Jay Hospital, and Mizell Memorial Hospital.

Drugs and Sundries Albertson's, at 5055 N. Ninth Ave. (tel. 476-7700), provides a one-stop service for prescriptions, pharmaceuticals, groceries, and liquor around the clock.

Emergencies Dial 911.

Laundry/Dry Cleaning Vick's Cleaners, 2915 Navy Blvd. (tel. 432-8351), features same-day cleaning service at this address and several more locations.

Parking There is free parking on Government Street, just beyond the Seville Quarter.

WHAT TO SEE & DO

ATTRACTIONS

Historic Districts

Pensacola's intriguing past contributes to the atmosphere in the historic districts, where cobblestone streets are shaded by majestic live oaks and flowering, in season, magnolias. Old-world-style gaslight street lamps, wrought-iron balconies, and elaborate architecture recall the days when Pensacola was a prized pawn in the struggle between Spain and Britain. After Spain ceded western Florida and its capital, Pensacola, to Britain in 1763, the British carefully mapped out the city's streets. When Spain regained Pensacola in 1781, the British street names became Spanish again; for example, George Street, a main thoroughfare, became Palafox in honor of Spanish hero Gen. José de Palafox.

For **information** about the historic districts, call 444-8905.

SEVILLE HISTORIC DISTRICT & HISTORIC PENSACOLA VILLAGE One of your first stops should be the Seville Historic District, which includes Seville Square. Listed on the National Register, this impressive downtown district has some of Florida's oldest homes, along with charming boutiques and interesting restaurants.

Historic Pensacola Village, a living-history community, offers an interesting glimpse back into the past as you observe costumed "living history" characters go about their daily chores and demonstrate old crafts.

Among the landmarks to visit are the Museum of Industry, the Museum of Commerce, the French Créole–style Charles Lavalle House, the elegant Victorian Dorr House, the French colonial-Créole Quina House, St. Michael's Cemetery (land was deeded by the king of Spain), and Old Christ Church (one of Florida's oldest), housing the Pensacola Historical Museum. Unfortunately, the ornate mansion where Gen. Andrew Jackson and his wife, Rachel, stayed in 1821 burned down in 1831. And the very grand Opera House, where world-famous celebrities appeared, including actress Sarah Bernhardt, was destroyed in the 19th century. One of the most interesting sites is the **Julee Cottage Black History Museum.** Julee Cottage, built around 1790, was owned by Julee Panton, a freed black slave, who ran her own business, invested in real estate, and loaned money to slaves so they could buy their freedom. Today the museum recalls her life and deeds, as well as the achievements of other African Americans with Pensacola associations.

A combination ticket to Historic Pensacola Village and the T. T. Wentworth, Jr., Florida State Museum costs $5.50 for adults, $4.50 for senior citizens and military, $2.25 for children 4–16, free for children under 4. Tickets, good for an entire week, may be purchased at the Museum of Industry, at the corner of Zaragoza and Terragona Streets, Monday through Saturday from 10am to 4pm.

THE PALAFOX HISTORIC DISTRICT The Palafox Historic District, formerly Old Pensacola's harborfront commercial center, features beautiful Spanish Renaissance–style buildings. At one time the area had such outstanding hotels as the San Carlos, considered one of the South's finest. The Mediterranean Revival–style hotel at Palafox and Garden Streets remains, but has been closed for many years. In the good old days, more than a dozen foreign consulates were located here. Many structures, including the ornate Saenger Theatre, have been restored to their original beauty, including the New Orleans–style wrought-iron balconies.

The two-story Mission Revival building that once housed the Pensacola City Jail and City Court is now home to the Pensacola Museum of Art. Also located here is the T. T. Wentworth, Jr., Florida State Museum, a beautiful example of Renaissance Revival design and formerly Pensacola's City Hall (see "Museums," below).

Plaza Ferdinand VII, a National Historic Landmark and part of Pensacola's first settlement, is a Palafox district highlight. In a ceremony at the Plaza in 1821 Gen. Andrew Jackson formally accepted Florida into the United States, and his statue commemorates the event.

THE NORTH HILL PRESERVATION DISTRICT The 50-block North Hill Preservation District, listed on the National Register of Historic Places, is just north of the Palafox Historic District. Descendants of early settlers still live in some of the more than 500 homes, and family backgrounds include Spanish nobility, timber barons, British merchants, French Créoles, buccaneers, and Civil War veterans. At one time, Spain and Britain had forts in this area; residents still occasionally find a cannonball or two, while working in their gardens.

The private homes are not open to the public, but are a bonanza for anyone interested in architecture. Various home designs include Mediterranean Revival, Queen Anne, Tudor Revival, neoclassical, art moderne, Victorian, Craftsman Bungalow, and more. The North Hill district includes Lee Square at Palafox and Gadsden Streets, where Union troops erected a fort in 1863. In 1891, Lee Square was dedicated to the Confederacy, complete with a 50-foot-high obelisk and sculpture based on John Elder's painting *After Appomattox.*

Museums

CIVIL WAR SOLDIERS MUSEUM, 108 S. Palafox St. Tel. 469-1900.

This museum houses life-size dioramas, paintings, letters, and artifacts dealing with the Civil War. Notable is the museum's bookstore, with more than 500 books dealing with the Civil War, as well as art prints, period music, and such souvenirs as Confederate soldier's caps.

Admission: $3 adults, $1.50 children 6–12, free for children under 6.

Open: Mon–Sat 10am–4:30pm. **Closed:** Major holidays.

NATIONAL MUSEUM OF NAVAL AVIATION, U.S. Naval Air Station. Tel. 452-3604.

One of the world's largest aerospace museums is located on the world's largest air station. Naval aviation history, complete with exhibits of 100 aircraft, is traced from its very beginnings to the Space Age and Desert Storm. The museum's hands-on displays for both children and adults include sitting at the controls of a jet trainer, and an immense re-creation of an aircraft carrier deck.

When the U.S.S. *Forrestal,* an enormous aircraft carrier, is at home, it's docked at the station and open to the public.

Admission: Free.

Open: Museum, daily 9am–5pm; U.S.S. *Forrestal,* Sat–Sun and holidays 9am–3pm. Phone the public affairs office (tel. 452-2311) or inquire at the gate for visitor passes.

PENSACOLA HISTORICAL MUSEUM, 405 S. Adams St. Tel. 433-1559.

In the old Christ Church, built in 1823, the museum has just about everything pertaining to the city's history, from Native American artifacts to a library with more than 2,000 volumes.

Admission: $2 adults, $1 children 4–16, free for children under 4.

Open: Mon–Sat 9am–4:30pm. **Closed:** Holidays.

PENSACOLA MUSEUM OF ART, 407 S. Jefferson St. Tel. 432-6247.

A Palafox Historic District landmark, the museum showcases permanent art and sculpture collections as well as art on loan. Shows range from avant-garde works by Andy Warhol to classic European masterpieces. The museum is a splendid building in itself.

Admission: Free.

Open: Tues–Fri 10am–5pm, Sat 10am–4pm.

T. T. WENTWORTH, JR., FLORIDA STATE MUSEUM, 330 S. Jefferson St. Tel. 444-8586.

The museum houses exhibits of western Florida's history, and has a special hands-on Discovery Museum for children on the third floor. Located in the Palafox Historic District, the building is an architectural highlight.

Admission: Included in the ticket to Historic Pensacola Village, $5 adults, $4 seniors and military, $2 children 4–6, free for children under 4.

Open: Daily 10am–4pm; closed holidays.

Attractions Nearby

If you want to see the Panhandle's answer to King Kong, visit **The Zoo,** where Colossus, one of the largest lowland gorillas in captivity, is the star of the show, although at least 600 more animals roam freely in landscaped natural habitats. Two rare white tigers are also a main attraction, but there are other show-stoppers too: elephant shows, bird shows, a giraffe-feeding station, a petting zoo. The Safari Line Limited train is the fun way to travel around the animals' free-roaming area. The 50 acres include botanical gardens, an authentic Japanese garden, a lakeside restaurant, and a gift shop. The Zoo, which claims to be the "World's Friendliest Zoo," is located about 10 miles east of Gulf Breeze on U.S. 98. Open daily from 9am to 4pm, The Zoo also offers children's rides during summer months. Admission is $7.50 for adults, $4.50 children ages 3–11, free for tots under 3. Call 932-2229 for information and current show schedules.

Now part of Gulf Islands National Seashore, **Fort Barrancas** was originally built by the Spanish in the 16th century and has been restored. In true ancient Spanish style, access to the fort is possible only by drawbridge across the moat. No admission is charged to tour the fort, to picnic in the surrounding area, or to stroll along the nature trails. The fort is open daily from 10:30am to 4pm. Guided tours are offered daily: at 11am and 2pm from June to September, and at 2pm the remainder of the year.

A short distance south of Fort Barrancas and near the National Museum of Naval Aviation, the photogenic **Lighthouse** has been operating since 1825. Its beam is visible for hundreds of miles across the gulf.

Fort Pickens, at Gulf Islands National Seashore, across the bay from Fort Barrancas, was constructed in the 1830s to protect Pensacola Harbor. Apache Chief Geronimo was imprisoned here. Located in a gorgeous seaside setting amid towering sand dunes, the fort also includes areas for swimming, scuba diving, fishing, picnicking, hiking, and camping. For information about rangers' guided tours, call 934-2600. Fort Pickens is open daily (except Christmas Day). The Gulf Islands National Seashore Information Center is close by.

East of Gulf Breeze is the 1,378-acre **Naval Live Oaks Plantation** (tel. 932-9994), where the strong-as-iron live oak trees have been protected since 1828. It was this wood that gave the old warship U.S.S. *Constitution* the name "Old Ironsides." According to artifacts discovered in the area, prehistoric tribes settled here 10,000 years ago. In this area of great primitive beauty, popular activities are birdwatching, hiking, and camping. It's easy to visit this site en route to Gulf Islands National Seashore, via the three-mile Pensacola Bay Bridge (see "Nature Trails and Coastal Parks," below).

Nature Trails and Coastal Parks

At the **Edward Ball Nature Walk,** located on the campus of the University of West Florida, there are 2½ miles of boardwalk around a shaded bayou—take along some dry bread to feed the turtles and fish. The nature trail is free and open daily. During the week, guided tours are offered by the Delta Tau Delta Fraternity (tel. 474-3000 or 474-2425). The trail is on the northwest side of the outstanding 1,000-acre campus, where the wetlands and woodland have been left in their natural state. The trail was named in honor of Edward Ball, a Florida millionaire who donated much of his fortune to preserving Florida's wildlife.

Bay Bluffs Park, located on the corner of Scenic and Summit, offers rustic boardwalks and 20 acres of nature trails maintained by the city of Pensacola. This is part of the Scenic Highway, where U.S. 90 heads northeast to Tallahassee, an official Florida Scenic Route. The park's elevated boardwalk descends Florida's only scenic bluffs, a prehistoric formation dating back 20,000 years. From the unique, towering red bluffs, the views of Pensacola Bay can only be described as "breathtaking."

Across the Bob Sikes Bridge (named for a Florida governor) is **Santa Rosa Island,** bordered by the Gulf Islands National Seashore. On Santa Rosa Island are Pensacola Beach and Navarre Beach, with Fort Pickens State Park at the western tip.

Stretching the 150 miles between Gulfport, Mississippi, and Destin, Florida, the unbelievably white sands and rolling sand dunes of ✪ **Gulf Islands National Seashore** comprise one of the world's most gorgeous beaches, most of which is located in Greater Pensacola. Established in 1971 to conserve and protect the beaches, the national seashore area is a natural environment for at least 280 different species of birds. Visitors enjoy swimming, boating, fishing, scuba diving, camping, ranger-supervised tours, and visiting historic forts. Along the hiking and dune nature trails, Native American tribes and Spanish conquistadors once walked. For advance information, contact the Gulf Islands National Seashore, 1801 Gulf Breeze Pkwy., Gulf Breeze, FL 32561 (tel. 904/934-2600).

Wildlife Rescue and Sanctuary Park, about 10 miles east of Gulf Breeze on U.S. 98, saves injured wildlife and birds so that after recuperation they can return to their habitats. Creatures that could not survive again in the wild live happily ever after in the sanctuary. The facility is open Tuesday through Sunday from 10am to 4pm and admission is free.

Approximately 10 miles southwest of Pensacola via County Road 292A, the **Big Lagoon State Recreation Area** offers an outstanding beach for swimming, boating, picnicking, camping, and fishing. At the east beach area, the observation tower provides panoramic views of the Big Lagoon and Gulf Islands National Seashore across the Intracoastal Waterway. The salt marshes here attract brown thrashers, nuthatches, cardinals, and many other species of birds, as well as such wading birds as great blue herons. For advance information, contact Big Lagoon State Recreation Area, 12301 Gulf Beach Hwy., Pensacola, FL 32507 (tel. 904/492-1595).

While in this locale, visit the **Perdido Key State Recreation Area,** about 15 miles southwest of Pensacola (access via Fla. 292). The spectacular ultra-wide, sparkling white sand beaches, undulating sand dunes, and golden sea oats have gained awards in the top 10 listing of best beaches in the nation. Swim, picnic, or just relax and watch the many varieties of shore birds. For more information, call 492-1595 or write to the Perdido Key State Recreation Area, c/o Big Lagoon State Recreation Area (same address as above).

SPORTS & RECREATION

DOG RACING The **Pensacola Greyhound Track,** 951 Dog Track Rd. (tel. 455-8598), features races year-round at 7:30pm Tuesday through Saturday, 1pm on Friday, Saturday, and Sunday. Admission is $1. For an excellent view of the action, there's a $2.50 charge for the Kennel Club, which also has a pleasant restaurant. Matinees are free for seniors, active military personnel, and tourists who show their hotel or motel key.

FISHING Red snapper, grouper, mackerel, tuna, and billfish are abundant. Anglers congregate along the Pensacola Bay Bridge Fishing Pier (which claims to be the world's longest), the Bob Sikes Bridge Fishing Pier, and also on the Fort Pickens Fishing Pier and Navarre Beach Pier. For information about the piers' hours of operation and fishing license information, contact the Visitor Information Center (tel. 434-1234).

Fishing charter services are offered by **Scuba Shack/Charter Boat *Wet Dream*,** 719 S. Palafox St. (tel. 433-4319). **Dolphin Marine/AAA Charter Service,** at Pitt Slip Marina in downtown Pensacola's Harbour Village (tel. 438-3242), offers deep-sea fishing charters, sailing charters, sunset cruises, and more. ***Chulamar*,** on Pensacola Beach at the Bob Sikes Bridge (tel. 434-6977), features one of the area's best fishing boats and also makes arrangements for bottom fishing, trolling, and bay fishing, and is open 24 hours. **Lo-Baby Charters,** 142 Highpoint Dr. (tel. 934-5285) can make arrangements for deep-sea fishing, diving, sightseeing, and sunset excursions.

GOLF Among the 18-hole championship courses are **Creekside Golf Course,** 2355 W. Michigan Ave. (tel. 944-7969); **Marcus Pointe Golf Course** (site of the Ben Hogan PGA Tour, Pensacola Open, and American Amateur Classic), 2500 Oak Pointe Dr. (tel. 484-9770); **Perdido Bay Golf Resort,** One Doug Ford Dr. (tel. 492-1223); **Osceola City Municipal Golf Course,** 300 Tonawanda (tel. 456-2761); **Tiger Point Golf Course and Country Club** (36 holes!), 1255 Country Club Rd. overlooking Santa Rosa Sound (tel. 932-1330); and **Hidden Creek Golf Course,** 3070 PGA Blvd. in Navarre (tel. 939-4604). Reasonably priced golf packages can be arranged at local hotels and motels.

SAILING & SURFBOARDING **Surf & Sail Boardsailing** (tel. 932-SURF) on

Pensacola Beach rents surfboards and offers instruction. **Key Sailing Center,** 289 Pensacola Beach Rd. (tel. 932-5550), rents Hobie Cats, jet skis, and windsurfing boards.

SCUBA DIVING & SNORKLING Visibility in the waters around Pensacola can range from 30 to 50 feet inshore to 100 feet just 25 miles offshore. The battleship U.S.S. *Massachusetts,* submerged in 30 feet of water, is one of the interesting artificial reefs where you can sight loggerhead turtles.

Gulf Coast Pro Dive, 7203 U.S. 98 West (tel. 456-8845), is considered the area's scuba specialist, offering rentals, all levels of instruction, and diving excursions. There's another branch in Gulf Breeze (tel. 934-8845). **Scuba Shack/Charter Boat *Wet Dream*,** 719 S. Palafox St. (tel. 433-4319), located at the waterfront, is Pensacola's oldest dive shop, offering rentals and NASDS classes. ***Chulamar*** (tel. 434-6977) at Pensacola Beach makes diving arrangements, and **Lo-Baby Charters,** 142 Highpoint Dr. (tel. 934-5285), also makes arrangements for diving excursions.

SPEED CAR RACING **Five Flags Speedway,** 7450 Pine Forest Rd. (tel. 944-0466), spotlights thrilling action Friday nights on one of the fastest half-mile tracks in the country. Top race-car drivers, such as Darrell Waltrip and Rusty Wallace, varoom around the course for the prize money. Admission fees are $7 for adults, $5 for active military, $4 for children 6–12, free for children under 6. Call ahead for the schedule and program.

TENNIS The **Bayview Recreation Center,** 20th St. and Lloyd St. (tel. 435-1788), offering six hard courts, is open free to the public daily from 9am to 5pm; **Gulf Breeze Recreation Center,** Sunset and Shoreline Drive in Gulf Breeze (tel. 934-5140 or 934-5141), with six hard courts, is also open free to the public, Monday to Saturday from 8am to 9pm and on Sunday from 1 to 6pm. **Scott Tennis Center,** 4601 Piedmont (tel. 432-2939), is the area's largest tennis facility, and offers 18 hard courts at a low daily rate. It is open Monday to Friday from 8am to 10pm; Saturday and Sunday from 9am to 6pm. See "Where to Stay," below, for hotels and motels with tennis courts.

SPECIAL EVENTS

The **Fiesta of Five Flags** is Pensacola's annual June extravaganza. It combines with the DeLuna Landing Festival, commemorating the Spanish conquistador's arrival in 1559, and is celebrated with parades, a Spanish fiesta, a children's treasure hunt, a sand sculpture contest, a billfish tournament, and much, much more.

The **Blue Angels Air Show,** a thrilling, world-famous flight exhibition, takes place at the Pensacola Naval Air Station. It's usually scheduled in July and November.

First Spanish Settlement Walk is featured in October, and the **Christmas Walk in Old Seville** is a joyous, historic experience every December.

WHERE TO STAY

The greater Pensacola area, which includes the city, Pensacola Beach, Gulf Breeze, Navarre Beach, and Perdido Key, offers reasonably priced, attractive hotels. Several well-known chains are represented—Best Western, Days Inn, Howard Johnson, Holiday Inn, Ramada, and Quality, just to name a few.

Of course, sun worshippers will want to stay on the beaches, notable for very pleasant hotels, motels, and condominium apartments. Should you want to rent a condominium apartment, the Visitor Information Center (tel. 904/434-1234, or toll free 800/874-1234, 800/343-4321 in Florida) will send a list of real estate contacts in advance; for Pensacola Beach, call the Pensacola Beach Chamber of Commerce (tel. 904/932-1500), and for Perdido Key, contact the Perdido Key Area Chamber of Commerce, 15500 Perdido Key Dr. (P.O. Box 34052), Pensacola, FL 32507 (tel. 904/492-4660).

The peak season in the Panhandle, when rates are highest, is from the end of May to September. This is also the time of year when hotels, motels, and condominium apartments are usually booked to capacity. Therefore, make reservations well in advance.

DOWNTOWN

Moderate

NEW WORLD LANDING, 600 S. Palafox St., Pensacola, FL 32501. Tel. 904/432-4111. Fax 904/435-8939. 14 rms, 2 suites. A/C TV TEL

$ Rates: $70–$80 double; $85–$100 suite. AE, CB, DC, DISC, MC, V.

Near the scenic bay and in the historic district, this outstanding inn is enhanced by flower gardens adorned with splashing fountains. From the pretty lobby, a grand staircase leads to high-ceilinged, artistically decorated spacious rooms with interesting antiques. The lovely accommodations depict Pensacola's rich history; for example, four rooms flaunt Spanish decor, four rooms are très chic French style, four rooms portray Early Americana, and four focus on Oulde England. The adjoining New World restaurant and pub is popular for local seafood.

PENSACOLA GRAND HOTEL, 200 E. Gregory St., Pensacola, FL 32501. Tel. 904/433-3336, or toll free 800/348-3336. Fax 904/432-7572. 200 rms and suites. A/C TV TEL

$ Rates: $90–$100 double. Ask about special single rates, suite rates, corporate rates, convention rates, Concierge Club rates, and honeymoon packages. AE, DC, DISC, MC, V.

On the site of the old L & N Railroad depot in the Seville Historic District, this unique hotel incorporates the antiquated station into the grand lobby, the Lobby Bar, restaurants, lounges, meeting rooms, and the new library-museum area. It's well worth a visit to the beautifully restored lobby (especially if you're a railroad buff) just to admire the wealth of turn-of-the-century accoutrements: the ornate railroad clock, the original oak stair rails, the imported marble, the fancy ceramic mosaic tile floors, and the old-fashioned carved furniture. Formerly the Pensacola Hilton, the hotel is now privately owned and has undergone a $2-million renovation. A two-story glass Galleria links the historic depot to the modern 15-story guest-room tower. New amenities include attractive bathrobes in every room. On the 14th and 15th concierge floors, accessible by special elevator key only, guest rooms are exceptionally attractive and provided with extra amenities and services. Should you not be a hotel guest, you're welcome to relax with a drink in the plush Lobby Bar or dine in one of the interesting restaurants, such as The 1912.

RESIDENCE INN BY MARRIOTT, 7230 Plantation Rd., Pensacola, FL 32504. Tel. 904/479-1000. Fax 904/477-3399. 64 suites. A/C TV TEL

$ Rates: $79–$105 suite for two. AE, DC, DISC, MC, V.

These very pleasant suite accommodations have fireplaces and kitchenettes, certainly a bargain at these rates. A swimming pool, whirlpool, sports court, and restaurant are on the premises. For people who love to shop, the hotel is next door to University Mall.

Budget

DAYS INN DOWNTOWN, 710 N. Palafox St., Pensacola, FL 32501. Tel. 904/438-4922, or toll free 800/325-2525. 150 rms, 2 suites. A/C TV TEL

$ Rates: $39–$50 double; $65 suite. Inquire about special group and weekly rates. AE, CB, DC, MC, V.

A very convenient place to stay, this friendly hotel has nicely decorated guest rooms, a restaurant, a cocktail lounge with a wide-screen TV, meeting facilities, a swimming pool, a coin laundry, and movie rentals. There is no charge for local phone calls. Complimentary transportation is available to and from Pensacola Regional Airport.

Another 80-room Days Inn North is at 7051 Pensacola Blvd. (tel. 904/476-9090).

HAMPTON INN–UNIVERSITY MALL, 7330 Plantation Rd., Pensacola, FL 32504. Tel. 904/477-3333, or toll free 800/HAMPTON. Fax 904/474-0100. 124 rms. A/C TV TEL

$ Rates (including continental breakfast): Summer, $47–$63 double. Winter, $39–$56 double. Inquire about discount rates for seniors. AE, DC, DISC, MC, V.

Surrounded by beautiful shade trees in a landscaped setting, this award-winning inn is conveniently located next to the mall. The complimentary breakfast, free local telephone calls, and complimentary airport transportation certainly help the vacation budget.

SEVILLE INN, 223 E. Garden St., Pensacola, FL 32501. Tel. 904/433-8331, or toll free 800/277-7275. 120 rms. A/C TV TEL

$ Rates: Summer, $39–$79 double. Winter, $30–$59 double. AE, DC, MC, V.

If you plan to do lots of sightseeing, shopping, and taking in evening entertainment, you couldn't do better than this inn conveniently located at the entrance to the downtown Seville Historic District, adjacent to the Garden Street Antique Village, across the street from the Civic Center, and about four blocks from the Saenger Theatre. Two swimming pools are on the premises and a coffee shop is open for breakfast only. As part of the hospitality at this 20-year-old inn, guests receive complimentary passes to the Pensacola Greyhound track—who knows, you might win enough money to pay for the room.

PENSACOLA BEACH

Expensive

CLARION SUITES RESORT & CONVENTION CENTER, 20 Via de Luna Dr., Pensacola Beach, FL 32561. Tel. 904/932-4300, or toll free 800/874-5303. 125 suites. A/C TV TEL

$ Rates (including continental breakfast): $99 suite Sun–Wed, $119 Thurs–Sat. Children under 18 stay free in parents' suite. Corporate, group, honeymoon, and sports packages available. AE, DC, DISC, MC, V.

Newly opened in the summer of 1993, this beachfront resort's 86 one-bedroom suites can accommodate up to four people. The attractively decorated, spacious accommodations include a living room, dining room, bathroom (the 39 bilevel loft suites have 1½ bathrooms), and kitchen with refrigerator, microwave, toaster oven, all utensils, and china. It's nice to have two televisions—one in the living room, one in the bedroom—and two telephones. A complimentary continental breakfast is served every morning, if you wish. On the premises, are a swimming pool, a fitness center, a children's play area, a beach pavilion, and a dunes crosswalk. As soon as you walk into the atrium lobby, you just know a most enjoyable beach vacation awaits.

HOLIDAY INN PENSACOLA BEACH, 165 Fort Pickens Rd., Pensacola Beach, FL 32561. Tel. 904/932-5361, or toll free 800/465-4329. 150 rms. A/C TV TEL

$ Rates: Apr–Sept, $90–$110 double. Nov–Feb, $60–$90 double. Mar and Oct, $70–$80 double. Ask about senior citizen discounts. AE, DC, DISC, MC, V.

Just outside the national park entrance, this gulf-front eight-story hotel boasts one of the area's most beautiful white sand beaches. Views are terrific from the Penthouse Lounge and the Gulf Front Café. From Memorial Day to Labor Day, Beach Bunch children's programs are offered. Amenities include four lighted tennis courts, two racquetball courts, a volleyball area, a swimming pool, and rental boats. Arrangements can be made for fishing and surfing. The pleasant dining room is open from 6:30am to 10pm.

Moderate

BARBARY COAST MOTEL, 24 Via de Luna Dr., Pensacola Beach, FL 32561. Tel. 904/932-2233. 24 rms and suites. A/C TV TEL

$ Rates: Summer, $70–$110 double. Winter, $45–$65 double. Monthly and weekly rates available. MC, V.

Although an older motel, the Barbary Coast has a great Gulf of Mexico location, complete with beautiful sand dunes. Guest rooms have been refurbished with a tropical decor. Some of the less expensive rooms do not have kitchenettes but the larger double rooms have cooking facilities. For families, suites will accommodate four to six people in two bedrooms plus the convertible sofa in the living room. In addition to the beach and swimming pool, the covered picnic area with a barbecue pit is fun. A very friendly atmosphere prevails here.

BEST WESTERN PENSACOLA BEACH, 16 Via De Luna Dr., Pensacola Beach, FL 32561. Tel. 904/934-3300, or toll free 800/528-1234. 62 rms. A/C TV TEL

$ Rates (including continental breakfast): Summer, $85–$95 double. Winter, $45–$59 double. AE, DC, DISC, MC, V.

New on the gulf-front, this small, casual hotel is notable for extra-spacious accommodations, complete with refrigerators, coffee makers, microwaves, and wet bars. The swimming pool and Cabana Bar are on the beachfront. Rental bikes are available to explore the scenic area. Inquire about the golf packages and deep-sea fishing trips.

THE DUNES, 333 Fort Pickens Rd., Pensacola Beach, FL 32561. Tel. 904/932-3536, or toll free 800/83-DUNES. 140 rms and penthouse suites. A/C TV TEL

$ Rates: Mid-May to Labor Day, $75–$110 double. Labor Day to mid-May, $59–$92 double. Special vacation and golf packages available. AE, DISC, MC, V.

Families enjoy staying here because of the spacious accommodations and the children's activities program that runs from late May to early September. There are two swimming pools (one heated), a jogging trail, a bicycle path, a volleyball area, and miles of white sand beach for strolling, sunning, and swimming. For refreshments and food, the Gulf Front Lounge & Café is a casual rendezvous. From the moderately priced penthouse suites, the beach panorama is spectacular.

Budget

FIVE FLAGS MOTEL, 299 Fort Pickens Rd., Pensacola Beach, FL 32561. Tel. 904/932-3586. 49 rms. A/C TV TEL

$ Rates: Summer, $59–$69 double. Winter, $40–$59 double. MC, V.

At this friendly, cozy motel, big picture windows look out to the undulating dunes and the gorgeous white sand beach. The swimming pool is beautifully bordered by the photogenic dunes, which are covered with golden sea oats swaying in the refreshing breezes. Although the accommodations are small, every room has a splendid view of the gulf—and the rates are a bargain. Also, the friendly management will accept small pets.

SANDPIPER INN, 23 Via de Luna Dr., Pensacola Beach, FL 32561. Tel. 904/932-2516. 26 rms, 6 cottages. A/C TV TEL

$ Rates: Summer, $49–$120 double. Winter, $29–$89 double. Inquire about special weekly rates and other discounts. AE, MC, V.

Should you prefer preparing some of your meals, ask for one of the 10 rooms with kitchenettes. The swimming pool may be small, but the large private sun deck on the water is delightful. Floor-to-ceiling picture windows make up for the rather small accommodations; however, every room is beautifully maintained. Restaurants and shops are conveniently nearby.

GULF BREEZE

Moderate

HOLIDAY INN–BAY BEACH, 51 Gulf Breeze Pkwy., Gulf Breeze, FL 32561. Tel. 904/932-2214, or toll free 800/HOLIDAY. Fax 904/932-2214. 168 rms. A/C TV TEL

$ Rates: May–Sept 1, $67–$110 double. Sept 2–Apr, $50–$71 double. AE, DISC, MC, V.

On a private bayside beach, this pleasant hotel offers complimentary coffee and newspaper with your morning wake-up call and complimentary drinks served every evening in the special cocktail suite—a nice way to become acquainted with other hotel guests. In addition to fun on the beach, there's a swimming pool plus a wading pool for the kids. Several rooms have refrigerators, which you may request. From the guest rooms, the scenic bay views are beautiful. The Bon Appetit Café serves breakfast, lunch, and dinner, opening at 6:30am (closed from 3 to 5pm in between lunch and dinner). Pensacola Beach is a very short drive to the south with Navarre Beach to the east and Perdido Key beaches to the west.

Budget

GULF COAST INN MOTEL, 843 Gulf Breeze Pkwy. (U.S. 98), Gulf Breeze, FL 32561. Tel. 904/932-2222. 33 rms. A/C TV TEL

$ Rates: Summer, $38–$48 double. Winter, $28–$40 double. Weekly rates available. AE, DISC, MC, V.

Since this nice motel is such a short drive to Pensacola Beach to the south, you may want to be budget-wise and stay on quiet Pensacola Bay, closer to Pensacola's downtown historic districts. Rooms have kitchenettes, which is another advantage.

NAVARRE BEACH

Moderate

HOLIDAY INN NAVARRE BEACH, 8375 Gulf Blvd., Navarre Beach, FL 32569. Tel. 904/939-2321, or toll free 800/465-4329. Fax 904/939-4768. 254 rms. A/C TV TEL

$ Rates: Apr to mid-Sept, $70–$120 single or double. Mid-Sept to Mar, $50–$98 single or double. AE, DC, DISC, MC, V.

Secluded among the sand dunes and on a tranquil white sand gulf beach, the resort is a perfect "get-away-from-it-all" vacation spot. Super-size guest rooms look out to outstanding gulf views. For tennis buffs, four lighted courts await. The outdoor swimming pool is probably upstaged by the indoor pool's tropical ambience. Should you indulge in the Ice Cream Parlor, just work off the calories in the Health Spa. A good restaurant, two bars, a movie theater, and a gift shop are also on the premises. During the summer, the Beach Brigade Children's Program keeps the kids entertained.

PERDIDO KEY

Moderate

COMFORT INN, 13585 Perdido Key Dr., Pensacola, FL 32507. Tel. 904/492-2755. 100 rms. A/C TV TEL

$ Rates (including continental breakfast): May–Sept 4, $54–$78 double. Sept 5–Apr, $49–$58 double. Family rates available. AE, DC, DISC, MC, V.

At this moderately priced motel, in addition to the beautiful white sand beach a short walk away, there's a swimming pool on the premises and an indoor hot tub. Since this motel is so family-oriented, another plus factor is the children's playground. If you want to do some deep-sea fishing, inquire at the desk and arrangements will be made.

PERDIDO BAY RESORT, One Doug Ford Dr., Pensacola, FL 32507. Tel. 904/492-1214, or toll free 800/874-5355. 37 rms in 9 cottages. A/C TV TEL

$ Rates: Summer, $58–$83 double. Winter, $48–$73 double. AE, MC, V.

Because of the well-known par-72 golf course here, most people call this the "Perdido Bay Golf Resort." The course is open to the public—just call ahead to reserve a tee time. The tennis courts, however, are for guests only. There's a swimming pool, two restaurants, and two cocktail lounges. The two- and four-bedroom cedar-and-brick cottages are clustered around the golf course. Individual rooms may be rented, should you not require the entire cottage, and the charge for the kitchenette is an additional $25. Incidentally, Pensacola is less than a 20-mile drive away, east of Perdido Key.

CAMPING

Big Lagoon State Park (Perdido Key), Fla. 292A off U.S. 98 West, Pensacola, FL 32507 (tel. 904/492-1595), is open from 8am to sunset year-round. From March to September, camping sites with electricity cost $16 ($14 without electricity); from October to February, rates are $10 with electricity, $8 without. Facilities include restrooms, boat ramp and launch, picnic area, nature trails, and hiking trails. Gasoline, groceries, and a laundry are within a quarter mile of the park.

Island View Campground, 7420 Gulf Blvd., Navarre Beach, FL 32566 (tel. 904/939-3399), features full hookups, electricity, water, and sewage. The rate is $16 for two people (if you stay six days, the seventh day is free).

Mayfair RV Park, 4540 Mobile Hwy., Pensacola, FL 32506 (tel. 904/455-8561), offers RV and tent camping. Sites for two people cost $12 with electricity, $9 without electricity. The campsite is within walking distance of shopping malls and grocery stores and is close to restaurants, service stations, the Naval Air Station, and the Pensacola Greyhound track.

Timberlake, 2600 W. Michigan Ave., Pensacola, FL 32505 (tel. 904/944-5487), offers RV camping only, for $15 per day, or $206 per month. Facilities include a swimming pool and clubhouse courts for tennis, basketball, and volleyball. There's also a lake for fishing and an adjoining golf course. The beach is less than a 15-mile drive away.

Adventures Unlimited, Route 6 (Box 283), Milton, FL 32570 (tel. 904/623-6197), offers 14 waterfront cottages and group cabins on Coldwater Creek, less than an hour's drive north of Pensacola. The company also arranges canoeing, kayaking, rafting, and tubing. It's open daily year-round. Rates are $25–$65 a day, $150–$320 a week (five cabins have fireplaces). Call for directions.

WHERE TO DINE

Most Greater Pensacola restaurants are unpretentious and specialize in good southern-style cooking. Best of all, the price of main dishes usually includes salad, a choice of vegetables, and coffee or tea. In the historic districts, dining is delightful in small, atmospheric restaurants housed in restored landmarks. Beach restaurants are very casual but popular for great seafood.

DOWNTOWN

Expensive

JAMIE'S, 424 E. Zaragoza St. Tel. 434-2911.

Cuisine: CONTINENTAL. **Reservations:** Recommended.

$ **Prices:** Main courses $5–$10 at lunch, $15–$25 at dinner. AE, DC, MC, V.

Open: Lunch Tues–Sat 11:30am–2:30pm; dinner Mon–Sat 6–10pm.

Very intimate and chic, Jamie's is Pensacola's classiest and most romantic restaurant. In a restored Victorian home in the Seville Historic District, dinners are enhanced by glowing fireplaces, soft candlelight, gleaming antiques, and subdued background music. Popular with Pensacola residents who enjoy fine food or are celebrating a special occasion, Jamie's features a gourmet menu. Among the favorites are grilled lamb chops subtly laced with a fresh mint-mustard sauce, and broiled just-caught snapper lightly topped by a piquant herb-butter sauce and garnished with Brie. Freshly baked breads are irresistible, and try the authentic French onion soup. Among the luscious desserts, the white-chocolate Grand Marnier mousse is wonderful. As you would anticipate, the wine list is extensive, featuring at least 200 imported and domestic choices. Every year, Jamie's is rated among Florida's Top 100 Restaurants.

Moderate

BACK DOOR CAFE, 1010 N. 12th Ave. Tel. 469-0055.

Cuisine: AMERICAN. **Reservations:** Not required.

$ **Prices:** Main courses $10–$15. MC, V.

Open: Mon–Thurs 11am–10pm, Fri–Sat 11am–11pm.

Enjoy lunch or dinner in the old-fashioned courtyard or the dining room, depending on the weather, of course. An Old Pensacola atmosphere prevails in this pleasant restaurant. For lunch, Greek salads and Caesar salads are popular with those who prefer lighter meals. The dinner menu highlights a variety of pasta dishes; try the fettuccine with seafood. There are also beef kebabs and thick steaks. Different specials are featured every day. There's a good wine list, too.

CAP'N JIM'S, 905 E. Gregory St. Tel. 433-3562.

Cuisine: SEAFOOD/STEAK. **Reservations:** Recommended.
$ Prices: Main courses $6–$20. AE, MC, V.
Open: Mon–Sat 11am–9:45pm.

At the foot of Pensacola Bay Bridge and overlooking scenic water views, this popular restaurant is noted for a lengthy menu listing deliciously prepared seafoods, great steaks, and crisp salads. The freshwater catfish and barbecued big shrimp are southern-style favorites. Although this friendly, family restaurant is so casual, white linens on the table are a nice touch. And kids enjoy making their own selections from the children's menu.

HALL'S CATFISH & SEAFOOD, 916 E. Gregory St. Tel. 438-9019.

Cuisine: SEAFOOD. **Reservations:** Not accepted.
$ Prices: Main courses $9–$15. MC, V.
Open: Sun–Thurs 11am–9pm, Fri–Sat 11am–10pm.

At least seven all-you-can-eat seafood selections are on the menu. Of course, there are many other choices, such as freshwater catfish, broiled snapper, sautéed flounder, a variety of shrimp dishes, oysters on the half shell, hearty sandwiches, fresh salads, and grilled steaks—all at moderate prices. Senior citizens are given the choice of 21 all-you-can-eat platters. The scenic location at the foot of Pensacola Bay Bridge is conducive to dining on seafood.

MCGUIRE'S IRISH PUB, 600 E. Gregory St. Tel. 433-6789.

Cuisine: AMERICAN/IRISH. **Reservations:** Not accepted.
$ Prices: Main courses $10–$20. AE, DC, MC, V.
Open: Mon–Sat 11am–2am, Sun 11am–1am (11am–4pm for brunch).

Every day is St. Patrick's Day here with corned beef and cabbage, Irish stew, Irish seafood platters, and much more. In addition, there are such hybrids as Seafood O'Fettuccine. Super-size hamburgers, peppercorn steak, grilled fish, beer-batter shrimp, barbecued ribs, hearty bean soup, salads, nachos, and other treats are also on the menu. This is Pensacola's oldest brewery (great beer!). The Irish entertainment is considered the best south of Boston. It's more than just the luck o' the Irish that McGuire's is rated in the list of Florida's Top 100 Restaurants.

Other McGuire-related Pensacola restaurants include Flounder's Chowder and Ale House and Zapata's Tex-Mex Joint.

MESQUITE CHARLIE'S, 5901 N. "W" St. Tel. 434-0498.

Cuisine: STEAK. **Reservations:** Not required.
$ Prices: Main courses $20. MC, V.
Open: Dinner only, Sun–Thurs 5–10pm, Fri–Sat 5–11pm.

When you crave delicious Wild West grub, Mesquite Charlie's is the right place. Cowboy and cowgirl steaks are seasoned with Charlie's own blend of natural spices and grilled to order over mesquite charcoal. Chicken, seafood, and baby back ribs are also grilled over mesquite and basted with Charlie's secret sauce. Putting on the feedbag here is great fun for little cowpokes too, who feel right at home on the range with the special children's menu.

NEW WORLD LANDING RESTAURANT, in the New World Landing Inn, 600 S. Palafox St. Tel. 434-7736.

Cuisine: CONTINENTAL/SEAFOOD. **Reservations:** Recommended.
$ Prices: Main courses $8–$18. AE, MC, V.
Open: Breakfast daily 7–9:30am; lunch daily 11am–2pm; dinner daily 5:30–9:30pm. **Closed:** Major holidays and often Sun.

Recalling the colorful historic past, this charming restaurant honors Spain with a

Barcelona Room, spotlights French history in a Marseilles Room, and gives tribute to the city itself in the very special Pensacola Room. Sparkling chandeliers, antique furnishings, and rich wood paneling lend a very special atmosphere whether you're enjoying a casual breakfast or lunch, or a memorable dinner. Fresh seafood is a specialty, but the menu also features excellent steaks, prime rib of beef, tender veal, and more. Favorite cocktails are expertly mixed and there's a good wine list. If you're a history buff, note the enlarged old photographs of Pensacola.

THE YACHT RESTAURANT AND LOUNGE, 600 S. Barracks St., Slip no. 1. Tel. 432-3707.

Cuisine: SEAFOOD/STEAK. **Reservations:** Recommended.

$ Prices: Main courses $6–$19. MC, V.

Open: Lunch Tues–Sat 11:30am–2:30pm; dinner Tues–Sun 6–10pm; brunch Sun 11am–2pm.

Welcome aboard Pensacola's only shipboard restaurant, docked across from the historic downtown area. The spectacular panorama of Pensacola Bay adds to the enjoyable dining experience. Locally caught fish is prepared many delicious ways, from poached to Louisiana-style blackened. Shrimp, prepared with tasty sauces or simply grilled, is a favorite. Tender steaks are broiled to your taste. There's something very glamorous about dining aboard a yacht.

Budget

E. J.'S RESTAURANT, 232 E. Main St. Tel. 432-5886.

Cuisine: AMERICAN. **Reservations:** Not accepted.

$ Prices: Main courses $3–$7. MC, V.

Open: Lunch only, Mon–Fri 11am–2:30pm.

A long-time favorite with local residents, E. J.'s is conveniently situated in the Seville Historic District and was originally the First Southeastern Baptist Church. A warm, homey atmosphere is accented by lace curtains, paddle fans, and checkered tablecloths. Favorite homemade specialties are the pecan-chicken salad sandwiches and the fried oysters-in-a-basket. Every day a different special is featured in addition to the regular menu. Selections from the salad bar could be a meal in itself. If you want to picnic in Seville Square or anywhere else, the restaurant will package your take-out order.

HOPKINS' BOARDING HOUSE, 900 N. Spring St. Tel. 438-3979.

Cuisine: AMERICAN. **Reservations:** Not accepted.

$ Prices: Main courses less than $7 at dinner. No credit cards.

Open: Breakfast Tues–Sat 7–9:30am; lunch Tues–Sat 11am–2pm, Sun noon–2pm; dinner Tues–Sat 5:15–7:30pm.

There's a delicious peek into the past when you dine at this real boarding house, popular for authentic southern specialties since 1949. Shaded by beautiful trees, the house is surrounded by a veranda with old-fashioned rocking chairs. Indoors, the parlor is decorated with all sorts of ornaments collected by the Hopkins family through the years. Lacy curtains on the window are another touch of nostalgia. Everyone sits together to enjoy a real family-style meal. Platters are piled high with good food. Most vegetables and seasonal fruits are from nearby farms. The bountiful breakfast will "stick to your ribs" for a good part of the day (try the true southern grits). And you haven't lived until you've tasted real southern fried chicken or fried catfish here. And yes, there really is a Hopkins family, and they're still actively involved with the boarding house.

JERRY'S STEAM SHACK RESTAURANT AND MARINA, 3050 Barrancas Ave. Tel. 457-1612.

Cuisine: SEAFOOD. **Reservations:** Not accepted. AE, MC, V.

$ Prices: Main courses $6–$15 at dinner.

Open: Lunch Mon–Fri 11am–2pm; dinner Sun–Thurs 5–9pm, Fri–Sat 5–10pm.

Since Jerry's also sells shrimp (from their very own boats) to customers who want to cook a special dish at home, you just know that the seafood served here is as fresh as can be. Of course, the menu highlights seafood steamed to order—the natural flavor is wonderful. Another specialty is the healthful steamed vegetables, served separately or with your order. For those who prefer seafood raw, broiled, or fried, many other choices are on the menu, including locally caught fish.

MARINA OYSTER BARN, 505 Bayou Blvd. Tel. 433-0511.
Cuisine: SEAFOOD. **Reservations:** Not accepted.
$ Prices: Main courses $7–$12. DISC, MC, V.
Open: Tues–Thurs 11am–8:45pm, Fri–Sat 11am–9:45pm.
At the Johnson-Rooks Marina, this rustic restaurant has been a favorite with seafood lovers since 1969. As you'd expect, freshly shucked oysters are the delicious attraction. Locally caught fish is deliciously prepared, either broiled or fried. It's a nice surprise to find that the shrimp tempura is among the best this side of Tokyo. Daily luncheon specials are offered from 11am to 2pm. Glorious sunsets are another daily feature.

ZAPATA'S! A TEX-MEX JOINT, in the Cordova Mall, 5100 N. Ninth Ave. Tel. 479-1991.
Cuisine: TEX-MEX. **Reservations:** Not required.
$ Prices: $5–$12. AE, MC, V.
Open: Daily 11am until very late.
The very name of Pensacola's only Tex-Mex restaurant gives a good clue that this is a very lively place—and it is. Mariachis play favorite south-of-the-border songs (you're welcome to sing along) and the daily margarita happy hour is indeed happy. This is one of the three action-filled restaurants under the McGuire banner (McGuire's Irish Pub and Flounder's are the other two). Lunch, dinner, and late-night snacks don't cost much for authentic Tex-Mex favorites, such as sassy beans and rice, guacamole, burritos, nachos, quesadillas, piquantly seasoned beef, and more.

PENSACOLA BEACH

Expensive

JUBILEE RESTAURANT, 400 Quietwater Beach Rd., Pensacola Beach. Tel. 934-3108.
Cuisine: SEAFOOD/STEAK/POULTRY. **Reservations:** Not required.
$ Prices: Main courses $4.95–$13.50 at lunch, $12–$20 at dinner. AE, DC, DISC, MC, V.
Open: Mon–Thurs 11:30am–10pm, Fri–Sat 11:30am–11pm, Sun 9am–3pm (champagne brunch) and 5–9pm (dinner).
At this beachside restaurant complex, complete with Island Bar and cocktail lounge, most dining is very casual. An exception is the five-star Topside Restaurant, where gourmet dinners are a highlight and the chef excels in the preparation of local fish and shellfish. Shrimp scampi with fettuccine is a favorite, as is a fish sampler, featuring grilled catch-of-the-day, served with sautéed julienned vegetables. Chicken de Luna, topped by sautéed fresh chunks of crabmeat, is deliciously different. Juicy steaks are mesquite grilled. Lunch is served in the Beachside Restaurant, offering a varied menu of fish and deli sandwiches, seafood combinations, just-shucked oysters, nachos, all sorts of great salads, chicken marsala, pastas, softshell crabs (in season), and more. In summer there are live bands for dancing under the stars, and indoor entertainment year-round.

Moderate

FLOUNDER'S CHOWDER AND ALE HOUSE, 800 Quietwater Beach Rd., Pensacola Beach. Tel. 932-2003.
Cuisine: SEAFOOD. **Reservations:** Not accepted.
$ Prices: Main courses $10–$18. AE, DC, DISC, MC, V.
Open: Daily 11am–2am (brunch Sun 11am–3pm).
Of course, the big specialty is flounder, baked and stuffed. Grilled swordfish, shrimp fettuccine, blackened red snapper, and broiled lobster tail are among the many selections on the menu. Since this is a fun place under the McGuire banner (McGuire's Irish Pub is a Pensacola favorite), you can expect a "bottomless" glass of champagne with your eggs Benedict during the sumptuous Sunday brunch. In

addition to the scenic Santa Rosa Sound panorama, take notice of the stained-glass windows from an old New York convent and the confessional booth walls. At night, dance to live music on Flounder's beach.

NAVAL AIR STATION
Budget

LIGHTHOUSE POINT, Radford Blvd., Naval Air Station. Tel. 452-3251.
Cuisine: AMERICAN. **Reservations:** Not required.
$ Prices: $2–$5. MC, V.
Open: Lunch only, Mon–Fri 10:30am–2pm.
Especially if you're visiting the outstanding National Museum of Naval Aviation, this casual restaurant is the perfect oasis, located just across the street. At present, one of the terrific bargains is the all-you-can-eat sandwich bar, where you can select from a variety of breads and rolls, sliced meats, cheeses, and more for a mere $4. Usually, the soup of the day is included. Healthful salads are very popular. If it's on the menu, try the flavorful chicken gumbo soup. Homemade chocolate cake, cheesecake, and apple pie are among the favorite daily desserts. By the way, the views of the bay are exceptionally beautiful from this very friendly restaurant.

SHOPPING

Shopping and sightseeing can be combined very easily in downtown Pensacola's interesting Palafox and Seville Historic Districts. Many shops are housed in renovated centuries-old buildings, stocked with everything from artwork to fashions and unusual gifts. And, of course, you'll find modern shopping malls.

ANTIQUE MALL, 380 N. Ninth Ave. Tel. 438-3961.

A grand variety of merchandise is tempting in approximately 25 stalls, filled with crystal, china, glassware, baseball cards, old-fashioned toys and dolls, costumes, and much more. Open Monday through Saturday from 10am to 5pm and on Sunday from noon to 5pm.

BAYOU COUNTRY STORE, 823 E. Jackson St., at Ninth Ave. Tel. 432-5697.

Nostalgia permeates this store specializing in old-time dolls, colorful quilts, braided and hooked rugs, fabrics with matching wallpaper, furniture, pottery, and just about everything for provincial decor.

CORDOVA MALL, 5100 N. Ninth Ave. Tel. 477-7562.

Pensacola's premier mall boasts 140 specialty shops and such well-known department stores as Dillards and Montgomery Ward. The Palm Court contains a variety of eateries. Movie buffs can catch the latest films in the theaters here. Open Monday through Saturday from 10am to 9pm and on Sunday from 12:30 to 5:30pm.

J. W. RENFROE PECAN CO., 2400 W. Fairfield Dr. Tel. 432-2083, or toll free 800/874-1929.

Satisfy your sweet tooth here with fresh pecans, homemade fudge, assorted roasted nuts, and a variety of goodies—free samples, too. Unusual gift items are also offered. This is headquarters for their popular mail-order company. Open Monday through Friday from 9am to 5pm and on Saturday from 9am to 1pm.

QUAYSIDE ART GALLERY, 15-17 E. Zaragoza St. Tel. 438-2363.

This is one of the nation's largest art-gallery cooperatives—the works of approximately 200 artists are featured here. Many of the regional artists have concentrated on painting the beautiful local seascapes. Jewelry, figurines, pottery, and batik are designed by local artists, also. Open Monday through Saturday from 10am to 5pm and on Sunday from 1 to 5pm.

QUAYSIDE MARKET, 712 S. Palafox St. Tel. 433-9930.

In a handsomely restored, century-old brick warehouse is a veritable bazaar with shops galore, featuring a wealth of collectibles, rare books, colorful Depression glass, antique jewelry, china, old-fashioned linens, and gourmet coffees, too. This quaint waterfront market also houses pleasant little restaurants and bars. As a side note, the ballast from sailing vessels was unloaded in this area centuries ago, which created the ground under your feet.

UNIVERSITY MALL, 7171 N. Davis Hwy. Tel. 478-3600.

This popular mall features 100 stores, including JC Penney, Sears, and the new Foodworks. Open Monday through Saturday from 10am to 9pm and on Sunday from 12:30 to 5:30pm.

EVENING ENTERTAINMENT

THE PERFORMING ARTS

PENSACOLA CIVIC CENTER, 201 E. Gregory St. Tel. 433-6311.

This 10,000-seat multipurpose facility hosts a variety of entertainment: touring productions of Broadway plays and musicals, rock groups, famous bands, family shows, sporting events, and much, much more. Call ahead for the current schedule.

Admission: Tickets, $10–$20.

PENSACOLA LITTLE THEATER, 186 N. Palafox St. Tel. 432-2042.

For more than 50 years, the performances here have delighted audiences. Both drama and comedy are spotlighted in each season's nine productions. By the time you read this, the Pensacola Little Theater will be settled in its new home in the new Pensacola Cultural Center. Incidentally, this is the Southeast's oldest continuing community theater. Call in advance for current schedules.

Admission: Tickets, $8–$12.

PENSACOLA SYMPHONY ORCHESTRA. Tel. 435-2533.

Considered the oldest continuous symphonic organization on the Gulf Coast, the Pensacola Symphony has performed for more than 65 years. Once a year there's a very special performance with the city's Choral Society. Call ahead to find out where the Symphony Orchestra is performing during the time you're in town.

SAENGER THEATER, 118 S. Palafox Place. Tel. 444-7686.

A masterpiece of Spanish baroque architecture, this ornate theater has been lovingly restored, including the original bricks salvaged from the old Pensacola Opera House. The variety of presentations spotlighted here include the Pensacola Opera Company, the Pensacola Symphony, the First City Dance Company, visiting magician David Copperfield's astounding shows, and a 50th Anniversary showing of the great film classic *Gone with the Wind*. Current programs are published in the local newspapers.

Admission: Tickets, $5–$35.

UNIVERSITY OF WEST FLORIDA, on U.S. 90A. Tel. 474-2696.

A six-story center for fine and performing arts, the UWF Art Gallery presents University Theater performances. Theater experts conduct seminars and preside at discussions here. Call for information.

PENSACOLA JAZZ SOCIETY.

Jazz musicians are invited to perform at local venues and this organization is the primary supporter of the annual Jazz Fest, a major local event. For information, contact the Visitor Information Center (tel. 434-1234).

THE BAR SCENE

Seville Quarter, in the Seville Historic District, is downtown Pensacola's prime entertainment-dining complex, with eateries and small lounges for relaxing with a drink. In the various courtyards, musicians entertain with everything from bluegrass to country-western. If you want to stop for a late-night snack, visit the **Palace Oyster Bar,** 130 E. Government St. (tel. 434-6211), open from 11am to 2am daily. Two of the favorites are Aunt Jessie's seafood gumbo and the Nassau grits.

FLORA-BAMA LOUNGE. Tel. 904/492-0611.

A favorite with the "Redneck Riviera" set. Here, country music sets the tempo, especially during the special jam sessions from noon until way past midnight on Saturday and Sunday. Because original music is in the limelight, Flora-Bama sponsors an International Song Writer's Festival every November. And if you've never attended an Interstate Mullet Toss, catch the fun during the last weekend in April. The raw oyster bar is popular all the time. Take in the great gulf views from the Deck Bar. This is Pensacola's answer to the Grand Ol' Opry in Nashville. It's open seven days a week from 9am until the wee hours, and is on the gulf at the Florida-Alabama state line.

FLOUNDER'S CHOWDER AND ALE HOUSE, 800 Quietwater Beach Rd., Pensacola Beach. Tel. 932-2003.

Dancing to a live reggae band on Flounder's beach keeps night owls happy until the wee hours seven days a week. For recharging the batteries, the special drink, Diesel Fuel (sipped from a Mason jar), keeps everyone in good spirits.

JUBILEE, on the Boardwalk at Pensacola Beach. Tel. 934-3108.

Live entertainment is in the spotlight at the Beachside Restaurant in this popular dining complex. When weather permits, there's dancing on the open-air deck. By the way, their beautiful Topside Restaurant is highly rated.

MCGUIRE'S IRISH PUB, 600 E. Gregory St. Tel. 433-6789.

If your mother comes from Ireland, you may want to leave an autographed dollar bill or an autographed drinking mug for the collection of more than 35,000 bills and 3,000 mugs contributed by customers who love the Irish fun here. Every night is party night. While quaffing beer from McGuire's very own brewery, you can enjoy Irish specialties, super-size sandwiches, and munchies. The Irish entertainment makes any other pub green with envy. Open Monday through Saturday from 11am to 2am and on Sunday from 4pm to 1am.

ZAPATA'S! A TEX-MEX JOINT, in the Cordova Mall, 5100 N. Ninth Ave. Tel. 479-1991.

The fiesta never stops at Zapata's, where mariachi bands blare out until the wee hours. A south-of-the-border café atmosphere prevails. It seems that the margarita happy hour continues around the clock. Áficionados of Tex-Mex food congregate at Zapata's soon after the restaurant opens at 11am.

COMEDY CLUBS & DISCOS

At the **Coconuts Comedy Club,** in the Holiday Inn at University Mall, 7171 N. Davis Hwy. (tel. 484-NUTS), different comedians appear at five weekly shows. The first performance is usually at 8:30pm, but the current schedule may change.

Disco fans may want to check out **Sam's,** 4520 Mobile Hwy. (tel. 453-6223), a video dance club with live disc jockeys. Call ahead for days and hours of operation.

AN EASY EXCURSION

Less than an hour's drive northeast of Pensacola, Milton, "The Canoe Capital of Florida," is a change of pace from the beach scene. The spring-fed wilderness streams of the Coldwater and Blackwater Rivers and Sweetwater/Juniper Creek meander through state forests and are perfect for canoeing, kayaking, tubing, rafting, and paddle-boating. The Blackwater River, at **Blackwater River State Park,** is considered one of the world's purest sand-bottom rivers and has retained its primitive beauty. Along the nature trails, plant life and wildlife may be closely observed.

Facilities for fishing, picnicking, camping, and cabin stays are provided. Blackwater is also Florida's largest state forest, with about 183,000 acres of oak, pine, and juniper.

Start your canoeing adventure at Milton, less than a half-hour drive northeast of Pensacola. Milton, once known as Scratch Ankle, celebrates its heritage every year with the Scratch Ankle Festival in March, the Milton Riverfest in June, and the Blackwater Heritage Tour in December.

Adventures Unlimited, Route 6, Milton (tel. 623-9197), can make advance arrangements for canoeing, kayaking, rafting, and paddle-boating in Blackwater State Park and surrounding rivers. Meandering along waterways surrounded by some of

Florida's most gorgeous scenery is a memorable experience—special arrangements are made for novices.

2. FORT WALTON/DESTIN & THE EMERALD COAST

50 miles E of Pensacola, 160 miles W of Tallahassee

GETTING THERE **By Plane** The **Okaloosa County Airport,** near Fort Walton Beach (tel. 904/651-0822) is served by American, Delta, Northwest, and USAir.

By Train Amtrak's *Sunset Limited* transcontinental service from Los Angeles (launched in April 1993) now stops at Pensacola and Tallahassee (with intermediate stops at Crestview, north of Fort Walton Beach, and Chipley, north of Panama City). For Amtrak information, call toll free 800/TEL-TRAK.

By Bus The Greyhound bus station is located at 105 Chestnut Ave., Fort Walton (tel. 904/243-1940).

By Car I-10 crosses the Panhandle going east-west. From I-10, exit via Fla. 85 and drive directly south to Fort Walton Beach. Driving east via U.S. 98 leads to Destin and the beaches of South Walton. The new bridge from the north shore of Choctawhatchee Bay (near Bluewater Bay) to the southern shore joins the Emerald Coast Parkway near Matthew Boulevard. The city of Niceville is less than five miles from Destin.

Widely ribboned by the exquisitely white sand of gulf beaches and sun-sparkled emerald-green waters, the Fort Walton/Destin area flaunts the new name of "The Emerald Coast." The neighboring beaches, stretching for 26 miles between Destin and Panama City, are blessed by equally gorgeous white sand beaches and iridescent emerald waters but are grouped under the banner "The Beaches of South Walton" and encompass 18 seaside communities.

Fort Walton Beach and Destin are in Okaloosa County and the Beaches of South Walton are in Walton County. Regardless of their area names, this entire beach vacation paradise is located about halfway between Pensacola's old-fashioned charm and the razzle-dazzle of Panama City Beach. The shimmering green gulf waters are reminiscent of the Caribbean and the Mediterranean along the Aga Khan's Costa Smeralda (Emerald Coast). Towering ivory-white sand dunes, some as high as river bluffs, contribute to the beaches' dramatic beauty. Seashell hunters might like to know that these beaches are rated among the world's top five shelling destinations. For fishing enthusiasts, the bays and gulf are an angler's dream, and the area has Florida's largest charter-fishing-boat fleet. This beach world is delightfully slow-paced, yet activities include 225 holes of championship golf to play, plenty of tennis courts (grass courts, too), all water sports, biking, and more—or you can just unwind and relax.

ORIENTATION

INFORMATION There are two separate tourist information offices, one for Fort Walton and Destin and one for the South Walton beaches. For brochures and maps covering Fort Walton Beach and Destin, contact the **Emerald Coast Convention and Visitors Bureau,** 348 Miracle Strip Pkwy. (P.O. Box 609), Fort Walton Beach, FL 32549-0609 (tel. 904/651-7131, or toll free 800/322-3319). The **Visitor Information Center** for the Fort Walton area is located at the Paradise Village Office Complex in Fort Walton Beach. The **Destin Chamber of Commerce** (tel. 904/837-6241) provides free information for Destin.

For the Beaches of South Walton, contact the **South Walton Tourist Development Council,** Santa Rosa Beach, U.S. 98, in the Emerald Coast Plaza, Unit 37 (tel. toll free 800/822-6877, a 24-hour, daily service), and request the free lodging directory, listing the area's resorts, condominiums, cottages, and the real estate agency contacts. The office is open Monday through Friday from 8am to 4:30pm.

AREA LAYOUT U.S. 98, running east and west along the Emerald Coast beaches is actually "main street." Addresses west of U.S. 98 usually have a "W" for west, and addresses in Destin are given as U.S. 98E for east. The Miracle Strip Parkway is another address name for U.S. 98.

GETTING AROUND

BY TAXI OR LIMO For a taxi, call **Veterans Cab Co.** (tel. 244-6666). **Continental Limousine** (tel. 651-5868) will drive you around in style.

BY RENTAL CAR The only convenient way to get around is by car. Rental-car agencies include **Avis** (tel. 651-0822), **Economy Rent-A-Car** (tel. 678-6223), **Budget** (tel. 651-9600 at the airport, 244-5800 downtown), **Hertz** (tel. 651-0612), and **Sears** (tel. 651-9999 at the airport, 244-1970 downtown).

FAST FACTS

Area Code The telephone area code for all of this region is 904.
Emergencies Dial 911 for the police, fire department, and an ambulance.
Medical Assistance Humana Hospital in Destin (tel 654-7680) sponsors a free physician-information service during business hours.

WHAT TO SEE & DO

ATTRACTIONS

DESTIN FISHING MUSEUM, Moreno Plaza, 35 U.S. 98E, Destin. Tel. 654-1011.

Dedicated anglers will want to visit this museum, with finny friends from the "World's Luckiest Fishing Village." World-record trophies for red snapper to state-record trophies for blue marlin are displayed, as well as a variety of maritime memorabilia. There's also a hands-on tidal pool and a dry walk-through aquarium where the sand bottom exhibits sponges, sea fans, coral reefs, sea turtles, and other marine life.

Admission: $1, free for children under 12.
Open: Call for schedule information.

EGLIN AIR FORCE BASE. Tel. 882-3933.

This is the world's largest air force base, encompassing more than 700 square miles. Free tours include demonstrations of the world's largest environmental test chamber, McKinley Climatic Laboratory; a look into the 33rd Tactical Fighter Wing (the "Top Guns" of Desert Storm); and more. World War II's historic Doolittle's Tokyo Raiders trained at the base. Interesting bus tours of the base are offered in the summer months.

The **U.S. Air Force Armament Museum** (tel. 882-4189), the only U.S. museum highlighting air force armament, has 25 reconnaissance, flighter, and bomber planes, including the SR-71 Blackbird Spy Plane. The fighter-cockpit simulator spans developments from World War II through the Korean and Vietnam Wars to the Persian Gulf. Also exhibited are war films, photographs, rockets, bombs, missiles, and more.

The base is located less than 10 miles north of U.S. 98 on Fla. 85, and the museum is just outside the west gate. Bus tours depart from the Officer's Club parking lot.

Admission: Free.

Open: Museum, daily 9:30am–4:30pm (closed major holidays). Base tours given three days a week in summer at 9:30am; call for the schedule.

EDEN STATE GARDENS AND MANSION, Point Washington. Tel. 231-4214.

These splendid gardens and the Wesley Mansion should not be missed. The magnificent 1895 Greek revival mansion has been lovingly restored and richly furnished. It stands overlooking scenic Choctawhatchee Bay, surrounded by immense moss-draped oak trees. The gorgeous gardens are resplendent with camellias, azaleas, and other typical southern flowers. Picnicking is allowed on the plantation grounds. The gardens and mansion are a short drive north of Grayton Beach.

Admission: $1.50 for mansion and gardens.

Open: Gardens, daily 8am–sunset. Call for information about guided tours of the mansion.

FOCUS CENTER, 139 Brooks St., Fort Walton Beach. Tel. 664-1261.

This children's museum appeals to kids by stimulating the imagination with interactional fun and fantasy. It has such attractions as a reflecting Castle of Mirrors, an electrifying Illuma Storm, colossal bubble makers, and much more.

Admission: $2 adults and children over 2.

Open: Mon–Fri 9–12am; Sat and Sun 1–5pm.

GULFARIUM, U.S. 98E. Tel. 244-5169.

This is one of the nation's original marine parks. It features on-going shows with dolphin performers, and also shows off its California sea lions, Peruvian penguins, and Ridley turtles. There are at least 14 fascinating exhibits, including the Living Sea, with special windows that provide viewing of undersea life.

Admission: $12 adults (discounts for seniors), $8 children 4–11, free for children under 4.

Open: Daily 9am–dusk.

INDIAN TEMPLE MOUND AND MUSEUM, 139 Miracle Strip Pkwy. Tel. 243-6521.

This ceremonial mound, one of the largest ever discovered, dates back to A.D. 1400. The museum, located next to it, showcases ceramic artifacts from southeastern Native American tribes. The largest such collection, it contains at least 6,000 items. Exhibits depict the lifestyles of the four tribes that lived in the Choctawhatchee Bay region for 10,000 years.

Admission: 75¢ adults, free for children under 12.

Open: Oct–May, Mon–Sat 11am–4pm; June–Sept, Mon–Sat 9am–4pm.

Parks & Beaches

The area's beautiful gulf-front parks offer much to see and do. Just east of Destin on U.S. 98, **Henderson Beach State Recreation Area** provides miles of sugar-white sand and remarkably clear emerald waters. Boardwalks allow easy access to the beach without endangering the towering dunes and fragile vegetation. Swimming, sunning, surf fishing, picnicking, and seabird-watching are part of the fun. The 208-acre park is a natural environment for magnolias, scrub oaks, sand pines, and a variety of wildflowers. For information, contact Henderson Beach State Recreation Area, 17000 Emerald Coast Pkwy., Destin, FL 32541 (tel. 904/837-7550).

Also east of Destin, in the Beaches of South Walton district, the 356-acre **Grayton Beach State Recreation Area,** P.O. Box 6600, Santa Rosa Beach, FL 32549 (tel. 904/231-4210), has an outstanding beach adorned with lofty sand dunes and swaying sea oats. The park also contains pine forests and the scenic Western Lake, complete with boat ramp. Hookups are provided for camping vehicles, as well as campsites for tents. Swimming, fishing, and picnicking are permitted. There's a self-guided tour leaflet for the Nature Trail.

And there's more to see. North of Destin, across Choctawhatchee Bay, the **Fred Gannon Rocky Bayou State Recreation Area** in Niceville (tel. 904/833-2144) encompasses 357 acres for camping, swimming, fishing, boating, picnicking, and enjoying Mother Nature's beauty.

SPECIAL EVENTS

The area celebrates more than 20 annual festivals, some of them outstanding.

The **Fort Walton Beach Seafood Festival,** an annual April celebration, is a virtual seafood-eating frenzy.

The **Eglin Air Show,** an aviation spectacular at Eglin Air Force Base, Fort Walton Beach, varies in time from year to year, but often takes place in April. Call the Emerald Coast Convention and Visitors Bureau (tel. toll free 800/322-3319) for information.

The **Billy Bowlegs Festival,** an annual week-long party in June at Fort Walton Beach, is named for William Augustus Bowles, self-proclaimed King of Florida who became a notorious buccaneer known as Capt. Billy Bowlegs. A pirate flotilla, treasure hunts, fishing competitions, kids' contests, and amusing races are part of the fun.

The **Destin Fishing Rodeo,** celebrated annually all of October, proves why Destin is considered "World's Luckiest Fishing Village" and "Billfish Capital of the Gulf." The **Destin Seafood Festival** is also in October.

Other festivals in Destin are the **International Golf Tournament** in October, the **Boggy Bayou Mullet Festival** in October, and the **Christmas Boat Parade** in December. For the exact dates and the festival programs, call the Visitor Information Center (tel. 651-7131).

The Beaches of South Walton feature many cultural and fun events, including the annual **Grayton Beach Fine Arts Festival** in May (tel. 267-1216, or toll free 800/822-6877); the **National and U.S. Open Water Ski Tournament** in August (same phone numbers); the annual **South Walton Sportsfest Weekend** in November (tel. toll free 800/822-6877); the **PGA Pro Am/Pro-Pro Tournament** at the Sandestin Resort, also in November (tel. 267-8000); and dazzling **Christmas celebrations** lighting up the entire area.

Don't miss the annual **Winter Visitors' Appreciation Tea Dance,** usually held in February and sponsored in part by the Beaches of South Walton Tourist Development Council (tel. 267-1216, or toll free 800/822-6877).

SPORTS & RECREATION

BOAT RENTALS Hobie Cat and small craft rentals are available from many marinas, fringing the gulf beaches, as well as from several beachfront resorts. For sailing charters and excursions, contact the ***Flying Eagle*** (tel. 837-4986 or 837-3700), located behind Capt. Dave's on the Harbor Restaurant, about a quarter mile east of Destin Bridge. Rates aboard this authentic gaff-rigged, tops'l schooner are $25 for adults, $15 for children 3–10, free for tots under 3.

Party Pontoons, located dockside at the A. J. Seafood and Oyster Bar, just east of the Destin Bridge (tel. 837-2222), offer pontoon boats for a relaxing sojourn on the gulf; barbecue grills are available on board. Rates are $30 per hour, $110 for a half day, $175 for a full day.

Atlantic Cruise Lines (tel. 837-6811 or 267-7777) has a fleet of 17- to 28-foot powerboats for rent at the Baytowne Marina at Sandestin, the Destin Yacht Club, and Pelican Point on Destin Harbor. Best to call ahead for reservations. Also inquire about Atlantic Cruise's rental of waverunners, Jet-N-Cat, tandem cruisers, and paddleboats.

CANOEING Canoeing lazily along crystal-clear rivers, bordered by scenic woodlands, is especially enjoyable in **Blackwater River State Park,** less than an hour's drive northwest of Fort Walton Beach (see "An Easy Excursion" in the Pensacola section for information about Adventures Unlimited in Milton, the "Canoeing Capital of the World)."

CRUISES Nature cruises are offered by **Atlantic Cruise Lines** (tel. 837-6811 or 267-7777) along Choctawhatchee Bay's Cypress River and Swamp (departure from Baytowne Marina at Sandestin). Dinner cruises aboard a 150-passenger, two-deck boat including dancing are also offered.

FISHING Destin is known as the "World's Luckiest Fishing Village," but most anglers call it "Fishing Heaven." Almost every month, a different kind of fishing competition pays off with big money for the big ones. In fact, comedian Bob Hope won first prize with a big white marlin when he first visited the area.

Bottom fishing in the gulf offers grouper, amberjack, and snapper. **Inshore trolling** provides king and Spanish mackerel, cobia, and more. Serious sports-fishermen hook sailfish, wahoo, tuna, and blue marlin. In the **bays and bayous,** you can catch trout, bass, sheepshead, bluefish, and buckets of blue crab. Less than an hour away, **freshwater fishing** is terrific in the Blackwater, Shoal, and Yellow Rivers, teeming with bass, bream, and catfish. The enormous Hurricane Lake in Blackwater River State Park abounds in large-mouth bass, catfish, bluegill, and more.

Destin also claims Florida's largest charter-boat fleet, with more than 140 vessels from party boats to private charters. To name just one of the many fishing charters, **Backdown Fishing Service** (tel. 837-9551) is located behind A. J.'s Restaurant, about a quarter mile east of the Destin Bridge at Harbor Cove. Captain Gary Jarvis provides plenty of fishing information. The **Destin Chamber of Commerce** (tel. 837-6241) provides a list of fishing boats and captains.

Anglers also like to fish along the 1,200-foot **Okaloosa Pier,** which is illuminated at night. The 3,000-foot **Destin Bridge Catwalk** is another popular fishing spot.

For guided fishing excursions in lakes and Choctawhatchee Bay (groups up to six), contact **Elrod's Fish Camp,** on Mack Bayou Road (tel. 267-2318), about a five-minute drive from the Sandestin Resort.

GOLF The area takes great pride in its 10 courses—225 holes of golf altogether—designed by such well-known architects as Dye, Fazio, and Cupp. For advance information on all area courses, contact the **Emerald Coast Golf Association,** in the Sandestin Beach Resort, 1040 U.S. 98E (P.O. Box 304), Destin, FL 32540 (tel. 904/654-7086).

Open to the public, the **Fort Walton Beach Golf Course,** on Lewis Turner Boulevard (tel. 862-3314), is an 18-hole, par-72 course, complete with pro shop. Greens fees are about $15 (carts around the same price), with discounted rates for after-4pm tee-off in summer. The **Santa Rosa Golf & Beach Club,** off U.S. 98E (turn right on County Road 30A to Dune Allen; tel. 267-2229), open to the public, offers a challenging 18-hole course through tall pines looking out to vistas of the gulf. The club has a pro shop, Beach Club restaurant and lounge, and also tennis courts. The **Sandestin Beach Resort,** on U.S. 98E (tel. 267-8000), offers 45 holes on two outstanding championship golf courses open to the public (see "Where to Stay," below). The **Seascape Resort & Conference Center,** 100 Seascape Dr. (tel. 837-9181), features an 18-hole course, where the public is invited to play. Another beautiful 18-hole public golf course is at the **Emerald Bay Golf Club,** 40001 Emerald Coast Pkwy. (tel. 837-4455). Nonguests may play golf (36 holes) or tennis (21 courts) at the **Bluewater Bay Resort** in Niceville (tel. 897-3613), only a 15-minute drive via the new Mid-Bay Bridge. Call ahead for reservations and fees.

HORSEBACK RIDING The **Brand'n Iron Corral,** on County Road 1 in Santa Rosa Beach (tel. 267-2433), features guided tours on horseback (safe for inexperienced riders, too) on trails winding through Santa Rosa's forests and around Choctawhatchee Bay.

Fort Walton stables include **Sleepy Oaks** (tel. 863-2919) and the **Equestrian Center** (tel. 863-3295).

MINIGOLF The **Magic Carpet Golf,** 1320 U.S. 98E, Fort Walton Beach (tel. 243-0020), has a course amusingly decorated with statues of kooky characters. Where else could you get a magic carpet ride for about $7? Summer hours are 10am to 9pm. The Magic Carpet usually doesn't fly from October to February (could be closed in colder months).

SNORKELING & SCUBA DIVING At least a dozen dive shops are located along the beaches. Considered one of the best, **Scuba Tech-Sea Cobra Diving Charters** has two locations: at 312 U.S. 98E in Destin (tel. 837-1933) and 5371 U.S.

98E (tel. 837-2822), about a half mile west of the Sandestin Beach Resort. Beginner and advanced diving instruction classes are offered. Aboard the 45-foot dive boat *Sea Cobra,* a four-hour/two-tank reef or wreck dive (about 65–90 feet in depth) costs $40, a six-hour/two-tank reef or wreck dive (down to 110 feet in depth) costs $55, the eight-hour/three-tank dive costs $65, and the one-tank night reef or wreck dive costs $40. Equipment is not included in these prices.

Kokomo Snorkeling Adventures (tel. 837-9029) specializes in snorkeling only and takes you aboard the 50-foot custom-built *Kokomo* for snorkeling excursions into the Gulf of Mexico and Choctawhatchee Bay. Gear is included for a 2½-hour excursion at $20 per person.

TENNIS Have a smashing time at the **Fort Walton Beach Municipal Tennis Center,** 45 W. Audrey Dr. (tel. 243-8789), featuring 12 lighted courts, a clubhouse, lounge, lockers, and showers. Rates are approximately $3 per day. The **Sandestin Beach Resort,** U.S. 98E (tel. 837-2121), offers 16 courts open to the public, including hard, clay, and grass. *Tennis* magazine designated Sandestin as one of the nation's top 50 tennis resorts and the only ranked resort with natural grass courts. The **Seascape Resort & Conference Center,** 100 Seascape Dr. (tel. 837-9181), has eight courts open to the public. The **Destin Racquet & Fitness Center,** at 995 Airport Rd. (tel. 837-7300), provides six Rubico tennis courts. You do have to phone ahead for reservations; also inquire about the very special rate of $6 per person per day to play tennis or racquetball, or participate in the activities here.

WATERSKIING Arrangements can be made at **Club Nautico,** Baytowne Marina at Sandestin Beach Resort. The fee includes rental gear and ski boats.

WHERE TO STAY

FORT WALTON BEACH

The western end of the Beaches of South Walton area has superstar beach resorts among the best anywhere. On the eastern end are casual accommodations and more secluded beaches. From U.S. 98, turn off on County Road 30A for the scenic beach route through tranquil gulf-front communities, such as Grayton Beach, one of Florida's oldest townships; the highly acclaimed Seaside; Seagrove Beach; and more; offering an excellent choice of interesting places to stay. The various chambers of commerce would be pleased to provide you with lodging lists and realtor contacts for condominium apartments, private beach houses, and cottages.

Remember that summer is the peak season and rates really go down in winter. Reservations are essential between Easter and Labor Day.

Expensive

HOLIDAY INN, 1110 Santa Rosa Blvd., Fort Walton Beach, FL 32548. Tel. 904/243-9181, or toll free 800/732-4853. Fax 904/664-7652. 385 rms. A/C TV TEL

$ Rates: Summer, $95–$125 double. Off-season, $65–$105 double. Inquire about special vacation rates. AE, DC, DISC, MC, V.

Situated on an outstanding Gulf of Mexico beach, the resort keeps guests active with three swimming pools (two are heated), a wading pool for the kids, two lighted tennis courts, and an exercise room for working out. For early birds, the restaurant is open for breakfast at 6am, and serves lunch until 2pm and dinner from 5:30 to 10pm. The cocktail lounge is a friendly rendezvous. An activities program for children is available for those who would like to participate.

RAMADA BEACH RESORT, U.S. 98 (Miracle Strip Pkwy.), Fort Walton Beach, FL 32548. Tel. 904/243-9161, or toll free 800/447-0010. Fax 904/243-2391. 454 rms, 4 suites. A/C TV TEL

$ Rates: Summer, $90–$135 double; $185–$235 suite. Winter, $65–$90 double; $125–$175 suite. AE, CB, DC, MC, V.

This privately owned showplace resort is not a Ramada hotel franchise. Considered Fort Walton Beach's prime hotel, the resort boasts one of the most beautiful swimming pool–patio areas anywhere, with waterfalls cascading over lofty rocks and a romantic grotto bar. Rooms are tastefully furnished, painted with wall murals and carpeted. Views look out to the beach, pool, or courtyard (rooms with beach views are the most expensive). Some suites have kitchenettes and separate bedrooms. The Pelican's Roost features casual seafood favorites, such as just-shucked oysters and crab claws. And the lobster dinners in the Lobster House are a treat. Calories can be worked off in the Healthy Habit Spa and there's dancing in the Bubbles Lounge.

SHERATON CORONADO BEACH RESORT, 1325 Miracle Strip Pkwy. (U.S. 98), Fort Walton Beach, FL 32548. Tel. 904/243-8116, or toll free 800/874-8104. Fax 904/244-3064. 154 rms. A/C TV TEL

$ Rates: Summer, $95–$120 double. Off-season, $70–$93 double.

Accommodations are very spacious, decorated with vivid, tropical colors and enhanced by beautiful views of the gulf and gardens. Many rooms have refrigerators and kitchenettes. Amenities include a heated swimming pool, whirlpool, exercise room, dining room, and cocktail lounge. There's plenty of fun on the beautiful beach at this gulf-front resort.

Moderate

CAROUSEL BEACH RESORT, 571 Santa Rosa Blvd., Fort Walton Beach, FL 32548. Tel. 904/243-7658, or toll free 800/523-0208. Fax 904/243-7658. 105 rms. A/C TV TEL

$ Rates: Mar–Sept, $65–$100 double. Oct–Feb, $50–$80 double. AE, DC, DISC, MC, V.

At this friendly motel with apartments, families like the spacious accommodations. Rooms with kitchenettes cost more (usually $89 in summer for a beachfront view, but $80 for side view of the gulf); in winter, a standard motel room can be priced as low as $45. Rooms that have balconies overlook towering sand dunes on the sparkling white sand beach. Two swimming pools are on the premises. Overlooking the shimmering green gulf waters, the fourth floor Stowaway Lounge is a delightful oasis for cocktails. A good Italian restaurant is next door.

MARINA BAY RESORT, 80 Miracle Strip Pkwy. (U.S. 98), Fort Walton Beach, FL 32548. Tel. 904/244-5132. 120 rms. A/C TV TEL

$ Rates: Summer, $50–$120 double. Off-season, $44–$99 double ($35 studio Nov–Feb except holidays). AE, DC, DISC, MC, V.

On the Intracoastal Waterway, this resort sports a dock, its own fishing pier, a volleyball court, a swimming pool, a whirlpool, a putting green, shuffleboard, and an exercise room and sauna. More than half the guest rooms are equipped with kitchenettes (request one, if that's your preference). The big bargain here is the special off-season $35 rate for studio accommodations.

Budget

CONQUISTADOR INN, 847 Venus Court, Fort Walton Beach, FL 32548. Tel. 904/244-6155, or toll free 800/824-7112. 31 rms, 56 suites. A/C TV TEL

$ Rates: Mar–Sept, $65 double; $80–$175 suite; $175 penthouse. Oct–Feb, $30 double; $45–$55 suite; $80 penthouse. Children under 12 stay free in parents' room. AE, DISC, MC, V.

Overlooking a towering ivory-white sand dune, the inn is a friendly place to stay. Though standard motel rooms are available, the suites are an excellent choice, with one or two bedrooms, nice kitchens, plenty of space in the living-dining area, and balconies or patios. The penthouse is exceptionally lovely, with great gulf views. All the accommodations were freshly painted recently in colors inspired by the blue-greens of the gulf. A swimming pool is on the premises and there are boardwalks for crossing the dunes.

HOWARD JOHNSON LODGE, 314 Miracle Strip Pkwy. SW (U.S. 98), Fort Walton Beach, FL 32548. Tel. 904/243-6162, or toll free 800/654-2000. 138 rms, 2 suites. A/C TV TEL

$ Rates: Summer, $50–$60 double, suites $104–$115. Winter, $45–$50 double, suites $95–$115. AE, CB, DISC, MC, V.

Beautifully located on the Intracoastal Waterway, this pleasant hotel is only a 2-mile drive to the beach and conveniently only 10 miles from Eglin Air Force Base. Majestic oak trees and lovely magnolia trees grace the courtyard. Here's a tip: Request a room that overlooks the courtyard with its large swimming pool. The hotel's Waffle House (now you know what to order for breakfast) is open 24 hours.

DESTIN

Privately owned secluded beach cottages, seaside bungalows, condominium apartments, and penthouse suites comprise more than 3,000 room selections in Destin. In addition to the local **Destin Chamber of Commerce** (tel. 904/837-6241) which will supply a lodging list, **Abbott Realty Services** provides a 24-hour central reservations line (tel. 904/837-4774 or 904/837-0805, or toll free 800/336-GULF) and a brochure of their many accommodations in Destin, Fort Walton Beach, and the South Walton beaches—everything from condominiums to cottages to resorts.

Destin's newest (on the Abbott Realty list) is **Water's Edge,** a tiny Victorian village of pastel "gingerbread"-trimmed, three-bedroom cottages on scenic U.S. 98 East. All are fully furnished with complete kitchens, two or three bathrooms, fireplaces, porches, and paths leading to the beach. Rates range from $140 to $325 per day, with special weekly and monthly packages.

Expensive

HENDERSON PARK INN, 2700 U.S. 98E, Destin, FL. Tel. 904/837-4853, or toll free 800/336-4853. 19 suites, 18 villas. A/C TV TEL

$ Rates (including buffet breakfast): Summer, $195 per night, $812 per week. Off-season, $175 per night, $721 per week. Special honeymoon, family, and business meeting packages. DISC, MC, V.

Bordered by a mile-long spectacular dune-topped white sand beach and emerald gulf waters, this is definitely a romantic, get-away-from-it-all hideaway. Nestled in a tranquil cul-de-sac on the undeveloped eastern edge of Henderson Beach Park, the Victorian-designed new inn sports a beachside veranda complete with old-fashioned rocking chairs to sit in and admire the glorious sunsets. The adjacent villas are designed as old-style summer beach cottages, furnished with Queen Anne reproductions. No two accommodations are alike. Several suites feature high ceilings, fireplaces, canopied beds, Victorian wicker furniture, and gulf views from the whirlpool baths. Every designer-decorated room has a private balcony looking out to the scenic gulf.

Dining/Entertainment: All rates include complimentary daily buffet breakfast in the restaurant and complimentary cocktails at the nightly before-dinner social hour. Reservations are required for the gourmet-style dinners in the classy restaurant.

Services: Arrangements are made for golf, tennis, scuba, snorkeling, sailing, and fishing; children's programs available.

Facilities: Heated swimming pool, beachside sun deck, complimentary beach umbrellas and chairs, a beach gazebo, grills for barbecuing.

HOLIDAY INN OF DESTIN, 1020 U.S. 98E, Destin, FL 32541. Tel. 904/837-6181, or toll free 800/HOLIDAY. 230 rms. A/C TV TEL

$ Rates: Summer, $85–$250 double. Off-season, $75–$225 double. Inquire about special vacation packages and discounts for seniors.

This attractive, circular gulf-front resort features two swimming pools (one heated) and a wading pool for the kids. During the summer, a children's activities program is offered, plus an adult's recreation program, for those who wish to participate. An exercise room and sauna help guests keep fit. The beach here is exceptionally beautiful. Rooms are nicely decorated and spacious, and have balconies for admiring the views. For early-risers, the restaurant opens for breakfast at 6:30am; lunch is served until 2pm, and dinner, from 5:30 to 10pm.

SANDESTIN BEACH RESORT, 5500 U.S. 98E, Destin, FL 32541. Tel. 904/267-8000, or toll free 800/277-0800. Fax 904/267-8197. 400 units, including rooms, suites, condominium apartments, and villas.

$ Rates: Summer, $155–$300 unit for two (rates higher on some villas). Variety of off-season rates and vacation packages. AE, DISC, MC, V.

A superstar resort, situated on 2,600 acres complete with a spectacular beach, Sandestin is a vacation wonderland. The array of handsomely decorated accommodations overlook the gulf or Choctawhatchee Bay, the golf fairways, lagoons, or a nature preserve—just state your preference. All accommodations—junior suites, condominium apartments, villas, and three-bedroom penthouses—are complete with kitchen, living room, and patio or balcony. Don't worry about getting around the resort. Most amenities are a short walk or bike ride away. A tram shuttles around the resort and a tunnel runs under U.S. 98 connecting Sandestin's gulf and bay areas.

Dining/Entertainment: Waterfront restaurants include the casual Seafood House. The exotically decorated Elephant Walk is romantic for dinner, gleaming with candlelight and overlooking the shimmering gulf panorama. Overlooking Choctawhatchee Bay, the Sunset Bay Café (formerly Babe's Seafood House) serves breakfast, lunch, dinner, and Leonardo's famous pizzas. (See "Resort Dining" in "Where to Dine," below, for more on these restaurants.)

Services: Free shuttle tram around the resort.

Facilities: Kids' Crew is the summer children's program for ages 3–13. For teenagers, the resort offers a junior's academy for both tennis and golf. Guests may rent bikes, boats, and water-sports equipment. Fishing is arranged in Sandestin's stocked lakes, abundant with large-mouth bass, or arrangements can be made for deep-sea-fishing charters from nearby Destin.

Club Nautico at Sandestin's Baytowne Marina charters excursions or you can captain your own vessel. Eleven tennis courts offer hard and Rubico surfaces at the beach or bayside tennis centers, plus the Wimbledon-style grass tennis courts for a different experience; there's a tennis clinic also. Forty-five holes of championship golf include links along Choctawhatchee Bay: the Dunes (splendid gulf views), the Harbor, and the new Troon course with a unique island green. The fully equipped Sports/Spa & Clinic is highly acclaimed. There are nine swimming pools, three wading pools, a playground for kids, a conference center, and the Market at Sandestin with 30 shops (Chico's, Benetton, La Bonbonière with Godiva chocolates, Zoo Gallery, Islander's Surf and Sport, and Jamaica Joe's, to name just a few).

SANDESTIN BEACH HILTON GOLF & TENNIS RESORT, 5540 U.S. 98E, Destin, FL 32541. Tel. 904/267-9500, or toll free 800/HILTONS. Fax 904/267-3076. 400 junior suites. A/C TV TEL

$ Rates: Summer, $180–$230 suite. Off-season, $100–$150 suite. AE, CB, DC, DISC, MC, V.

Actually, the resort is nicely situated on the grounds of the Sandestin Beach Resort. The very family-oriented Hilton features spacious accommodations, including a special area for childrens' bunk beds (kids love this set-up). Another family convenience is the dressing room with sink outside the bathroom (sink inside, too). And there's plenty of closet space, a wet bar, in-room refreshment center, refrigerator, and small hotplate. Balconies look out to splendid gulf views.

Dining/Entertainment: The multilevel Sandcastles Restaurant and Lounge (see "Resort Dining" in "Where to Dine," below) features a moderately priced menu. The Italian Café is the place for pastas, the Beach Club Grill is enjoyably casual, and the Ice Cream Shop features sweet treats. For indoor or outdoor dining, the exotic Elephant Walk restaurant is nearby (see the entry for the Sandestin Beach Resort, above).

Services: 24-hour room service, guest services director, babysitting, summer program for children, youth program.

Facilities: Outdoor swimming pool, heated indoor pool, whirlpool spa and saunas, 16 tennis courts, 45 holes of USGA championship golf, sailing, windsurfing, charter fishing, games room, shops, meeting rooms.

TOPS'L BEACH AND RACQUET CLUB, 5550 U.S. 98E, Destin, FL 32541. Tel. 904/267-9222, or toll free 800/476-9222. Fax 904/476-2955. 57 apts. A/C TV TEL

$ Rates: Summer, Beach Manor, $250–$350 apt; Tennis Village, $215–$298 apt. Bargain rates in spring, fall, and winter. Inquire about mini-week and weekly special prices. AE, MC, V.

Rated as one of the nation's top 50 tennis resorts, Tops'l is also notable for very fashionably decorated and spacious town houses in the Tennis Village and outstanding, classy apartments in gulf-front Beach Manor—two- and three-bedroom units with fully equipped kitchens. Larger accommodations are comfortable for six to eight people.

Dining/Entertainment: Delicious meals are served in the Centre Court Dining Room, Tops'l Beach Pavilion, and the Ocean Club Restaurant and Bar, if you want a break from cooking in your apartment.

Services: A free tram shuttles around the resort.

Facilities: 12 tennis courts, three racquetball courts, a 1.7-mile lighted jogging and walking path, Nautilus and aerobics center, steam room with saunas, whirlpool, indoor/outdoor swimming pools, a variety of beach activities (including sailing), Tops'l Center (with fashion boutiques, a liquor store, and a beauty salon).

Moderate

FRANGISTA BEACH INN, 4150 Old U.S. 98E, Destin, FL 32541. Tel. 904/654-5501. 19 rms, 2 suites. A/C TV TEL

$ Rates: Summer, $74–$135 double. Off-season, $50–$80 double. Weekly and monthly special rates available. MC, V.

Located directly on the beautiful white sand gulf beach, the inn was built in 1939. The original owner was from Frangista, Greece, so the inn and its stretch of beach bear the unusual name. The inn was tastefully refurbished and renovated in 1989: The white stuccoed walls, terra-cotta-tile floors, and pastel prints combine the relaxed feeling of the Greek islands and the Caribbean. Most rooms have kitchenettes, and there's one two-bedroom suite and one three-bedroom suite. Ask if you prefer a room with bathtub, as many units have only shower facilities. Definitely a delightful place to stay!

Budget

VILLAGE INN, 215 U.S. 98E, Destin, FL 32541. Tel. 904/837-7413, or toll free 800/821-9342. Fax 904/654-3394. 100 rms. A/C TV TEL

$ Rates: May 28–Sept 6, $50–$60 double. Sept 7–Oct, $40 double. Nov–Mar 4, $30 double. Mar 5–May 27, $40 double. Weekly rates are lower. Children under 18 stay free in parents' room. AE, DC, DISC, MC, V.

Directly across the street from the charter fishing fleet, this friendly hotel features oversize rooms with a choice of two queen-size beds or one king-size bed; some rooms have refrigerators. A swimming pool is on the premises. The drive to the gulf beaches is only five minutes; restaurants, shopping, golf, and some attractions are within a two-mile radius. Next door, the Waffle House restaurant is open 24 hours.

BED & BREAKFAST

A HIGHLANDS HOUSE, P.O. Box 1189, Santa Rosa Beach, FL 32459. Tel. 904/267-0110. 3 rms (all with bath). A/C

$ Rates (including breakfast): Mar–Nov, $75 single or double; $95 Carriage House. Dec–Feb, $50 single or double; $70 Carriage House. Additional person $10 extra; children under 10 stay free in parents' room. No credit cards.

Beautifully situated on Dune Allen Beach in the Beach Highlands area, A Highlands House was built in 1991 by Joan and Ray Robins, who are the proud innkeepers. The architecture reproduces the kind of luxurious 18th-century summer homes that Old South plantation owners once built for family beach vacations to escape the inland summer heat. The Robinses furnished their dream inn with four-poster "rice beds," comfy wingback chairs, and antique accoutrements. Wicker furniture inspires relaxation on the extra-wide porch. The formal parlor is lovingly decorated. In the cheerful dining room, delicious breakfasts are served—one favorite is the mile-high brandy-battered French toast, heaped with strawberries and cream. Joan's freshly baked coffee cakes are irresistible. Mother Nature provides delightful music in the sound of the gulf surf splashing against the sugar-white beach.

A NEARBY GOLF & TENNIS RESORT

BLUEWATER BAY RESORT, 1950 Bluewater Blvd., Niceville, FL 32578. Tel. 904/897-3613, or toll free 800/874-2128. Fax 904/897-2424. 98 rms. A/C TV TEL

$ Rates: Summer, $80–$135 double. Off-season, $65–$105 double. Weekly and monthly rates and vacation packages available. AE, MC, V.

For golfers, 36 holes await and tennis buffs can play on 21 tennis courts (10 clay, 9 hard, 2 Rubico—12 lighted). (Nonguests are welcome to play golf or tennis at the resort; just call in advance about hours and fees.) And if you want more sports action, there are four racquetball courts, four swimming pools, rental boats at the bay marina, rental bikes, and more. In summer, a children's program is offered and a playground is on the premises. For families, the three-bedroom apartments are comfortable; many rooms have kitchenettes or fully equipped kitchens. Two restaurants and a cocktail lounge are on the landscaped grounds. The resort is only a 15-minute drive from Fort Walton/Destin via the new Mid-Bay Bridge.

CAMPING

Campgrounds

Emerald Coast RV Resort, on Dune Allen Beach (tel. 904/267-2808, or toll free 800/232-2478), offers 43 campsites on 90 acres, shaded by beautiful trees. Secluded from heavy traffic, the resort is about a quarter mile off U.S. 98, on County Road 30A, near the Sandestin Beach Resort and east of Seaside. In addition to full RV hookups, the resort offers a putting green, fishing lakes, hiking and nature trails, a clubhouse, outdoor games area, a heated swimming pool, picnic facilities, a beach shuttle, and more. Of course, laundry rooms and cable television are provided. The landscaped site is guarded around the clock to ensure camping safety. Daily, weekly, and monthly rates are offered (rates are around $27 a day in summer, $24 a day in winter). The office is open from 7am to 7pm daily. No tents or pop-ups are allowed. For advance information, write to Emerald Coast RV Resort, Rte. 1, Box 2820, Santa Rosa Beach, FL 32459.

Holiday Travel Park, on the gulf side of U.S. 98 near Sandestin Beach Resort (tel. 837-6334), is the area's largest and oldest campground, offering 250 campsites, many right on the beach. In addition, the travel park has a bunkhouse that sleeps 40, three bath houses, picnic tables, a fishing pond, grocery store, and gift shop. Call for rates information.

Other campgrounds to contact are the **Playground RV Park,** 777 Beal Pkwy., Fort Walton Beach (tel. 904/862-3513); **Bayview Camping,** 749 Beach Dr., Destin (tel. 904/837-5085); **Crystal Beach Campground,** 2825 U.S. 98E, Destin (tel. 904/837-6447); **Destin Campgrounds,** 209 Beach Dr., Destin (tel. 904/837-6511); **Destin RV Resort,** 3175 Cobia St., Destin (tel. 904/837-6215); and **Gibson's Destin KOA,** 3175 Cobia St., Destin (tel. 904/837-5698).

Parks

Grayton Beach State Recreation Area, on Grayton Beach (tel. 904/231-4210), offers hookups for camping vehicles as well as primitive campsites in this beautiful 356-acre park. Campfire interpretive programs are available to campers (call for the current schedule). Also request the free self-guiding leaflet for the Nature Trail. A boat ramp is available on the park's Western Lake. Swimming and surf fishing are permitted in the park; there are good picnic facilities, too. Camping fees are around $14 from March to September, and less than $10 a night from October to February;

fees are subject to change without notice. For advance information, write to Grayton Beach State Recreation Area, Route 2, Box 6600, Santa Rosa Beach, FL 32459.

About an hour's drive northwest of Fort Walton Beach, **Blackwater River State Park,** Rte. 1, Box 57C, Holt, FL 32564 (tel. 904/623-2363), provides campsites at a cost of $10 per night year-round. Blackwater River is terrific for canoeing, and swimming, fishing, boating, picnicking, and walking along nature trails are enjoyable here.

WHERE TO DINE

FORT WALTON BEACH

Moderate

BACK PORCH, 1740 U.S. 98E, Fort Walton Beach. Tel. 837-2022.

Cuisine: SEAFOOD. **Reservations:** Not accepted.

$ Prices: Main courses $5–$15. AE, MC, V.

Open: Daily 11am–11pm.

A cedar-shingled seafood shack with glorious beach views, this popular restaurant originated charcoal-grilled amberjack (a favorite local fish). Additional charcoal-grilled varieties of fish and seafood are now on the menu, also charcoal-grilled chicken and juicy hamburgers. Seafood lovers go for the Commodore's Basket (softshell crab, shrimp, scallops, fish, clams, oysters) or the Beach Party (crab claws, shrimp, scallops, smoked fish dip, plus a cup of soup). Great sandwiches, salads, and veggie platters, too! And there's a children's menu. Beer, wine, and cocktails are served. My favorite frozen libation is the Key Lime Freeze, a drink that tastes like key lime pie (best when sipped watching the spectacular sunset).

JEREMIAH'S, 203 SE Brooks Blvd., Fort Walton Beach. Tel. 664-6666.

Cuisine: STEAK/SEAFOOD. **Reservations:** Recommended. **Directions:** Take U.S. 98 to Brooks Bridge, turn right to cross the bridge, then turn right through the parking lot and take another right under the bridge to Brooks Boulevard.

$ Prices: Main courses $13–$18. AE, MC, V.

Open: Dinner only, daily 5–10pm.

Away from "the madding crowd," rustic Jeremiah's is secluded on a private peninsula's tip, which juts into Santa Rosa Sound. Decorated with interesting antiques and a profusion of leaded glass, the waterside restaurant specializes in succulent frogs' legs and seafood; but the 20-ounce steak, personally selected from the glass showcase, is the conversation piece. Jeremiah's attentive staff is very helpful about wine recommendations to enhance the appetizers and entrees you order. In the very spacious bar, the water views are exceptionally beautiful.

PANDORA'S RESTAURANT, 1120 Santa Rosa Blvd., Fort Walton Beach. Tel. 244-8669.

Cuisine: STEAK/SEAFOOD. **Reservations:** Not required.

$ Prices: Main courses $10.95–$19.95. AE, DC, DISC, MC, V.

Open: Dinner only, daily 5–10pm (lounge open until 2am). **Closed:** Sun–Mon Sept–Apr.

Although Pandora gained its reputation as a steakhouse, freshly caught local fish and shellfish are among the seafood choices. But steaks remain the top favorite. The tender beef is cut on the premises and grilled to perfection. Pandora's setting is unusual; the restaurant is housed in a beached yacht on Okaloosa Island. It's relaxing to sip a drink in the main-deck lounge before proceeding downstairs to the beamed-ceilinged dining room, aglow with lights from copper chandeliers. Delicious breads and pies are homemade. Because of the high quality of the steaks and seafood, Pandora's is the place to indulge in surf-and-turf combinations such as steak with lobster, crab legs, or gulf shrimp. Live entertainment and dancing are an added attraction in the lounge; call in advance for the current schedule.

PERRI'S ITALIAN RESTAURANT, 300 Eglin Pkwy., Fort Walton Beach. Tel. 862-4421.

Cuisine: ITALIAN. **Reservations:** Not required.
$ Prices: Main courses $8–$16. MC, V.
Open: Dinner only, Tues–Thurs 5–10pm, Fri–Sat 5–11pm. **Closed:** Dec 19–Jan 4.

Mama mia, the saltimbocca alla romana and the chicken alla bolognese rival the restaurants in Italy! For many, many years, the Perri family has maintained their restaurant's popularity with recipes that have been handed down for generations. A variety of veal dishes and sauces for pastas are lovingly prepared. Fettuccine replete with shellfish is a favorite with seafood lovers. This attractive restaurant also offers a children's menu. The wine list features good vinos from Italy. Many patrons like to relax with a drink before or after dinner in the cocktail lounge.

THE SOUND, 108 SW Miracle Strip Pkwy. (U.S. 98). Tel. 243-2722.
Cuisine: SEAFOOD. **Reservations:** Not required.
$ Prices: Main courses $10–$18. AE, DC, MC, V.
Open: Daily 11am–10pm. **Closed:** New Year's Day, Thanksgiving, and Christmas Day.

Just like dining in a friend's cozy waterside home, the Sound is notable for real southern hospitality—and, of course, deliciously prepared fish and shellfish. If you have rented a boat, dock alongside the private waterway wharf. Sensational views of Santa Rosa Sound are part of the enjoyable dining experience here. Local fish and seafood may be ordered simply steamed, broiled with lemon and butter, or combined with gourmet sauces. "Early-bird" dinners are featured at special prices. For the little ones, there's a children's menu. During the peak summer season, live entertainment is spotlighted in the cocktail lounge.

STAFF'S SEAFOOD RESTAURANT, 24 Miracle Strip Pkwy. (U.S. 98), Fort Walton Beach. Tel. 243-3526.
Cuisine: SEAFOOD. **Reservations:** Not accepted.
$ Prices: Main courses $11.95–$25. AE, MC, V.
Open: Dinner only, daily 5–11pm.

Considered the first Emerald Coast restaurant, Staff's is a 1913 barrel-shaped warehouse with the original pressed-tin ceiling. Among the display of memorabilia are an old-fashioned phonograph lamp and a 1914 cash register. All entrees are served with heaping baskets of hot, home-baked wheat bread from Pop Staff's 70-year-old secret recipe. One of the favorite main dishes is the Seafood Skillet, sizzling with broiled yellowfin tuna, shrimp, scallops, and crabmeat stuffing, drenched in butter and sprinkled with cheese. Tangy seafood gumbo and creamy oyster stew have also gained fame for this casual, historic restaurant. Many celebrities have dined here, including Hollywood's Bob Hope and the former First Lady Rosalyn Carter.

Budget

HOSER'S, 1225 Santa Rosa Blvd., Fort Walton Beach. Tel. 664-6113.
Cuisine: AMERICAN. **Reservations:** Not accepted.
$ Prices: $4–$9. AE, DISC, MC, V.
Open: Mon–Sat 11am–4am, Sun noon–4am.

For those who dreamed of being firefighters when they grew up, Hoser's is filled to the brim with firefighting memorabilia, from boots to hats and hoses to hydrants. Naturally, the most popular dish on the menu is Three Alarm Chili, a spicy secret recipe garnished with jalapeños and grated cheese. If your taste buds catch fire, douse the flame with any of 80 imported cold beers, including Thai Singha, Mexican Chihuahua, German Bitburger, and English Oatmeal Stout, to name just a few. Super-size hamburgers, stacked-high sandwiches, and other favorites are on the menu. Night owls love to roost at Hoser's, where the action is nonstop.

DESTIN

Moderate

AJ'S SEAFOOD & OYSTER BAR, 116 U.S. 98E, Destin. Tel. 837-1913.
Cuisine: SEAFOOD. **Reservations:** Not accepted.

$ Prices: Main courses $5–$15. MC, V.
Open: Daily 11am–10pm (later on weekends).
On the picturesque Destin Harbor docks, where fishing boats unload the daily catch, tiki-topped AJ's is popular for fried blue crab claws, spicy steamed shrimp, fried seafood in baskets, charcoal-grilled local fish (and chicken, too), steamed Dungeness crab, hearty fish and seafood sandwiches, delicious seafood salads, Cajun crayfish fettuccine, and seafood gumbo. Yes, you can get a charcoal-grilled hamburger here too, and even buffalo hot wings. For the kids, there's a special menu. Monday through Friday, the Oyster Happy Hour lasts for hours—11am to 6pm. On Sunday, the Crayfish Boil attracts the crowds. On the second level, Club Bimini features a hibachi menu. Live entertainment spotlights reggae music and limbo contests on Thursday, Friday, Saturday, and Sunday, often beginning at 3pm. AJ's also delivers menu items (call 678-FOOD).

CAPTAIN DAVE'S ON THE HARBOR, U.S. 98, Destin Harbor. Tel. 837-6357.
Cuisine: SEAFOOD. **Reservations:** Not accepted.
$ Prices: Main courses $12–$20. No credit cards.
Open: Dinner only, daily 4:30–10pm.
While the movie *Jaws II* was being filmed on the photogenic beaches in this area, Captain Dave's was a mealtime rendezvous for the actors and film crew. The fishing fleet docks at the restaurant so you can be assured of the freshest seafood. In addition to a variety of fish and seafood, prepared just the way you like it, prime rib and chicken are also on the menu. Captain Dave's Oar Oyster Bar is right next door, serving lunch daily from 10am to 3pm (oysters and clams are the big favorites).

HARBOR DOCKS, U.S. 98E in Destin, one mile east of Destin Bridge. Tel. 837-2506.
Cuisine: CAJUN/THAI. **Reservations:** Not accepted.
$ Prices: $6.95–$19.95. MC, V.
Open: Lunch/dinner daily 11:30am to late night.
You can't miss the three tiki-style thatched roofs of this casual restaurant, where harbor views are spectacular from indoors or outdoors. The splendid hand-carved wood-and-marble bar dates back to 1890. Luncheon specialties include Gulf Coast seafood gumbo, red beans and rice, fried triggerfish, charcoal-grilled amberjack sandwich, and big hamburgers. Several Thai dishes are on the menu, served with a typical egg roll. Appetizers on the dinner menu include smoked yellowfin tuna with mustard sauce and shrimp nachos. Favorite entrees are charcoal-grilled filet of cobia in a delicate dill sauce, broiled filet of grouper stuffed with crabmeat, grilled filet mignon, and charcoal-grilled marinated chicken breast. For the kids, there's a special menu. Everyone loves Annie's homemade pies for dessert. Live entertainment every night and different bands weekly keep the action going on the outdoor deck. Harbor Docks delivers menu items: Call 678-FOOD.

MARINA CAFE, on the second floor of the Destin Yacht Club, 320 U.S. 98E. Tel. 837-7960.
Cuisine: ITALIAN/LOUISIANNE. **Reservations:** Recommended.
$ Prices: Main courses $8–$25. AE, MC, V.
Open: Dinner only, daily 5–10pm (later on weekends).
Overlooking the multi-million-dollar fleet of the prestigious Destin Yacht Club, the Marina Café provides a classy penthouse atmosphere with soft candlelight, subdued music, and formally attired waiters. It's so pleasant to dine on the outdoor balconied deck, or perhaps sip drinks and nibble on crisply fried calamari prior to dining indoors, where the window wall looks out to the shimmering waters. Pastas are prepared with a special flair, especially the fettuccine combined with andouille sausage, shrimp, crayfish tails, and a piquant tomato-cream sauce. Among the chef's creative dishes is grilled yellowfin tuna steak with bronzed jumbo sea scallops and a jalapeño vinaigrette. Grilled prime steaks, sautéed veal medallions, grilled chicken, and crisply roasted boneless duckling are favorites always. And you don't have to be a vegetarian to enjoy the eggplant lasagne, served with grilled vegetables, savory black

beans, and roasted garlic. A talented pianist performs at the Piano Bar Wednesday through Saturday from 7pm, which inspires romantically minded couples to dance.

SCAMPI'S, U.S. 98E, Destin. Tel. 837-7686.

Cuisine: SEAFOOD. **Reservations:** Not accepted.

$ Prices: Main courses $11.95–$23.95. AE, MC, V.

Open: Dinner only, daily 4:30–9:30pm.

Constructed from the historic pilings of the old Destin Bridge, this two-level restaurant is especially popular for the bountiful seafood buffet. From an entire amberjack, stuffed and baked, to Louisiana Cajun étoufée, this is a veritable fish and shellfish "groaning board." From the regular menu, you can begin with just-shucked oysters (or crayfish in season). The steaming hot bowl of piquant seafood gumbo is almost a meal in itself, accompanied by freshly baked French bread. Just about all your piscine preferences can be satisfied in this casual, friendly restaurant. The lengthy bar and cocktail lounge are a local rendezvous.

Budget

BUSTER'S OYSTER BAR AND SEAFOOD RESTAURANT, in Delchamps Plaza, on U.S. 98E one mile before the Sandestin Beach Resort. Tel. 837-4399.

Cuisine: SEAFOOD. **Reservations:** Not required.

$ Prices: $4–$12. DISC, MC, V.

Open: Dinner only, 5–9:30pm.

A local favorite, Buster's claims that more than two million oysters have been shucked here. A fun place, Buster's likes to add something outrageous to the menu, such as "a toasted sea spider sandwich." Kids enjoy the Playground Menu and the family atmosphere. Fish and seafood dinners are deliciously prepared to order—and try the award-winning seafood gumbo. Cocktails are served here, also. If you want any of the menu items delivered, just call 678-FOOD.

THE DONUT HOLE, 635 U.S. 98E, Destin. Tel. 837-8824.

Cuisine: AMERICAN. **Reservations:** Not accepted.

$ Prices: $3.50–$6. No credit cards.

Open: Daily 24 hours.

While vacationing, isn't it great to know that breakfast can be enjoyed any time of the day or night? No matter what the hour, breakfast is a special treat in this rustic "hole-in-the-wall." Who could resist luscious freshly made doughnuts and crullers, hot-from-the-oven breads and muffins, light-as-a-feather pecan waffles, Old South–style cheese grits, fluffy omelets, or rich eggs Benedict? And there's nothing like a real good cup of just-brewed hot coffee to go with these goodies. In addition to the great breakfasts, hearty sandwiches on bakery-fresh bread are served for lunch, and country-style dinners are the evening specials.

By popular demand, there's a Donut Hole II Café and Bakery, also on U.S. 98E, just two miles east of the Sandestin Beach Resort (tel. 267-3239), but open only from 6am to 8pm.

HARRY T'S, 320 U.S. 98E, Destin. Tel. 654-6555.

Cuisine: AMERICAN. **Reservations:** Not required.

$ Prices: $4–$12. AE, MC, V.

Open: Daily 4pm–2am (lunch served certain months—check ahead).

The family of big top trapeze artist "Flying Harry T" opened this casual restaurant to honor his memory. Standing guard is Stretch, Harry's beloved giraffe, now duly stuffed for posterity. Circus memorabilia adorns this fun place. Also note the interesting items from the luxury cruise ship *Thracia,* which sank off the Emerald Coast in 1927. Harry T personally led the heroic rescue of the more than 2,000 passengers, and was presented the ship's salvaged furnishings and fixtures. As for the menu, at least 100 items are listed, such as Mexican chimichangas, Cajun-style burgers, blackened grouper sandwich, Harry's Boathouse Salad, charcoal-grilled pork chops, and buffalo wings (Harry was a Buffalo native so the recipe is authentic). Key lime pie and strawberry cheesecake are two favorite desserts.

SANTA ROSA BEACH

Moderate

BAYOU BILL'S CRAB HOUSE, U.S. 98 at Santa Rosa Beach, and on County Rd. 30A, three miles east of Seagrove Beach. Tel. 267-3849 and 231-1400.

Cuisine: SEAFOOD. **Reservations:** Not required.

$ Prices: $5–$14. MC, V.

Open: Dinner only, Tues–Sun 5–10pm.

At two locations, Bayou Bill's features nightly chalkboard specials with a variety of chowders, salads, sandwiches, smoked entrees, buckets of steamed garlic crabs, steamed shrimp, combination seafood buckets, and charcoal-grilled and fried fish. In season, the sautéed alligator is a big favorite.

The Santa Rosa Beach location is notable for rustic, tropical decor plus outdoor dining in the Garden Room. At the Seagrove Beach location, nestled in native hardwood hammocks, the restaurant features a covered walkway, where local artisans ply their special crafts. Inside, the colorful 12-foot-wide crab-and-lobster mobile adds fun to the decor. You'll find the same interesting menus at both locations.

GOAT FEATHERS, County Rd. 30A, Santa Rosa Beach. Tel. 267-1273.

Cuisine: SEAFOOD. **Reservations:** Not accepted.

$ Prices: Main courses $6–$14. MC, V.

Open: Thurs–Tues 11:30am–9pm.

This casual small restaurant, decorated with nautical antiques, offers a raw bar and indoor and outdoor dining (the outside deck and bar are covered). The gulf views are absolutely gorgeous. Try the tasty deep-fried oysters wrapped in shrimp and bacon—something different. The popular seafood platters are heaped high with shrimp, scallops, local fish, oysters, and more. No need to dress up here—cover-ups and cutoffs are permitted.

NENA'S, Kreig Rd. (off U.S. 98), Santa Rosa Beach. Tel. 267-3663.

Cuisine: STEAK/CONTINENTAL. **Reservations:** Recommended.

$ Prices: Main courses $8–$25. MC, V.

Open: Dinner only, 5–9:30pm.

A romantic atmosphere prevails in this attractively decorated, chic restaurant, enhanced by a large fireplace and luxuriant plants in pretty clay pots. Nena is rightfully proud of her reputation for serving superior steaks, tender veal, and the freshest of seafood. One of her innovations is the Fiesta Dinner, a delicious array of New York strip steak, medallions of veal, stuffed shrimp, grilled fish, crabmeat-filled tomatoes, twice-baked stuffed potatoes, and asparagus, all served beautifully on a silver platter for two—perfect for romantic gourmets! Nena bakes her own tasty breads and tempting pies daily. The New York and Hollywood expression for complimenting food, "It's to die for," describes the irresistible Nena's Millionaire Pie, a luscious blending of pecans, chocolate, and caramel topped with rich ice cream. In one word, it's yummy.

GRAYTON BEACH

Moderate

CRIOLLA'S, 1267 County Rd. 30A, Grayton Beach. Tel. 267-1267.

Cuisine: LOUISIANA CREOLE/CARIBBEAN. **Reservations:** Recommended.

$ Prices: Main courses $12.95–$25. MC, V.

Open: Apr–Sept, dinner only, Mon–Sat 6–10pm; Mar and Oct–Nov, dinner only, Tues–Sat 6–10pm; Feb, dinner only, Thurs–Sat 6–10pm. **Closed:** Dec–Jan.

One of Florida's Top 10 Golden Spoon Award winners, this charming restaurant derives its name from the archaic word *criollo,* signifying persons of pure Spanish descent born in the New World. The attractive decor, combining New Orleans atmosphere with the Caribbean, features a soft pink and vivid turquoise color scheme, enormous potted palms, whirling ceiling paddle fans, and tropical island paintings on the walls. Many of the unusual dishes are Chef Johnny Earles's old family recipes, such as crabmeat louisianne and snapper butter pecan. The restaurant is also famed for sautéed or wood-grilled tuna, red snapper, pompano, lamb, and game. From the extensive list, wines may be ordered by the bottle or glass. Homemade sweets and plantation coffees top off a memorable meal.

RESORT DINING

Because friendly southern hospitality prevails in this beach vacation area, you don't have to be a resort guest to dine in any of their restaurants—everyone is welcome.

At the Sandestin Beach Resort, the romantic ✪ **Elephant Walk** restaurant (tel. 267-4800) is more glamorous than ever, after a million-dollar renovation. The story behind it begins in Ceylon, when a defiant tea plantation owner, John Whiley, built his huge home to block the elephant herd's path to the river and prevent damage to his land. In 1890, when the elephants became desperately thirsty, their stampede toward the river devastated the plantation home. After Whiley saw his property reduced to rubble, he vowed never to return. For 30 years he roamed the globe, buying treasures and yearning for a new home. Then he discovered the white sands and green waters of the Panhandle and decided to settle down. Whiley's treasures are displayed in the Elephant Walk restaurant, designed as a Ceylon tea plantation home. Overlooking shimmering waters, the candlelit room features an entirely different dinner menu, highlighted by the chef's prize-winning shellfish ragoût. The ice cream drink menu offers exotic refreshment.

Sandestin's other new restaurant is the **Sunset Bay Café** (formerly Babe's Seafood House; tel. 267-7108), with a Jamaican villa motif and many Caribbean specialties on the menu. Open for breakfast, lunch, and dinner, Sunset Bay overlooks Choctawhatchee Bay. Order the savory gumbo, which won an award at a recent cook-off. Leonardo's homemade pizzas can also be ordered at Sunset Bay, usually open until 10pm.

Sandcastles is the beautiful dining room in the Sandestin Beach Hilton Golf & Tennis Resort (tel. 267-9500), open for breakfast, lunch, and dinner. Among the dinner specialties are grilled grouper, grilled snapper, stuffed shrimp, and veal scaloppine. The casual atmosphere is also enjoyable for family dining.

Seascape's Courtyard Restaurant (tel. 837-9181) is a golfer's favorite as it's located next to the pro shop and overlooks the challenging golf course at the Seascape Resort. Open daily for breakfast and lunch, the restaurant is noted for the selection of omelets, club sandwiches, steak and prime rib sandwiches, and the crispy chef salads.

The **Viewpoint Café** (tel. 837-4700) at the Surfside Resort attracts families with a reasonably priced menu at breakfast, lunch, and dinner. There's no extra charge for the spectacular gulf views. Hot dogs, hamburgers, prime rib, and seafood are always popular here. And isn't it nice that the kids are able to order half portions of any entree at half price?

The **Seagrove Wheelhouse** (tel. 231-4205), adjoining the 30-unit Seagrove Villas in Seagrove Beach, is well known to locals for the very economical luncheon buffet, which includes all-you-can-eat soup, salad, three different entrees, and six choices of veggies.

EVENING ENTERTAINMENT

THE PERFORMING ARTS

The area is proud of its **Okaloosa Symphony Orchestra,** the **Stage Crafters Community Theater,** and the ballet and choral groups. Presentations are scheduled mostly in the winter months. Contact the individual beach chambers of commerce or inquire at your hotel for the current programs.

THE CLUB, MUSIC & BAR SCENE

Most resorts spotlight live entertainment during the summer season, including the Ramada Beach Resort, Sandestin Beach Resort, the Sandestin Hilton, and the Seascape. It's a good idea to inquire ahead to make sure entertainment is scheduled when you plan to be at a particular lounge or restaurant.

The Piano Bar at the **Marina Café** in the Destin Yacht Club is a popular rendezvous, Wednesday through Saturday nights beginning at 7pm.

The Down Under Bar at Fudpucker's Beachside Bar & Grill in Destin (tel. 654-4200), is double the fun with two different stages, one on the scenic deck and the other in the Down Under Bar. Seven nights a week, live music plays on with everything from classic rock to jazz and reggae. There's also a lively Fudpucker's Beachside Bar & Grill on Fort Walton Beach (tel. 243-3833) to extend the fun-filled night.

On Grayton Beach (on County Road 30A), **Palapa's** is named for its thatched palapa roof. The late-night menu and lively entertainment in the Great Australian Beach Bar lures the night owls. During daytime hours, Palapa's serves delicious crab cakes, fresh seafoods, a variety of pastas, prime rib, veal Oscar, and a children's menu, too.)

Hog's Breath Saloon 1230 Seibert St. (tel. 244-2199), a lively late-night spot, actually opens for lunch at 11am but the real action doesn't begin until nighttime and continues until the wee hours. From this intriguingly named rustic saloon, you can bar-hop to neighboring **Hoser's,** 1225 Santa Rosa Blvd. filled with firefighting memorabilia, and other adjacent bars, which comprise "Shanty Town." Block bashes have been known to last until 4am on mellow summer nights.

Three different bars are under one roof at sprawling **Nightown,** 140 Palmetto St. in Destin (tel. 837-6448), which includes a terrific dance club, a rowdy saloon, and a Jimmy Buffet–style reggae bar. Nightown has gained fame in top magazines, acclaiming the live entertainment, disco, games room, and the outdoor deck.

The dockside **AJ's Club Bimini,** 116 U.S. 98E in Destin (tel. 837-1913), offers live entertainment (lots of reggae music) on weekend nights. If you dare, try the Bimini Bash, a potent concoction of pineapple, orange, and cranberry juices plus five different rums. **Fish Heads,** 414 U.S. 98E in Destin (tel. 837-4848), features the Big Red Snapper, a lethal mixture of vodka, rum, and more. At **The Deck** at Harbor Docks, overlooking Destin Harbor (tel. 837-2506), musical entertainment is in the limelight nightly with a different band weekly.

EASY EXCURSIONS

SEASIDE

Less than a half hour's scenic coastal drive east of Destin (via County Road 30A), Seaside is one of the world's most beautiful beach towns, described as a "Downhome Utopia" by *Time* magazine, and "extraordinary" by Britain's Prince Charles. The American Institute of Architects has designated Seaside as one of the decade's top architectural masterplans, and the beachside town has received worldwide acclaim as well as many awards for its combination of creative architecture, urban planning, and ecological cooperation with Mother Nature. Yet despite its world fame, Seaside retains an atmosphere of secluded tranquility and a sense of solitude on its long stretch of gorgeous beach.

Built in the early 1980s on 80 acres of beach property, Seaside is a masterpiece of architectural style, inspired by Victoriana's distinctive charm, and artistic planning. Every individually designed home is painted in pastel sunrise colors and adorned with an old-fashioned porch, gazebo, and garden. Secret, winding paths and streets lead to charming beach pavilions, which are gateways to the superb white sands splashed by the gulf's emerald waters. In addition to a Mediterranean-style open market, the village of Seaside is notable for interesting shops, fine art galleries, delightful restaurants, small hotels, and a postcard-pretty post office.

Imbued with nostalgia and with a most relaxing slow pace, Seaside provides a memorable day trip. Should you wish to stay longer (and you probably will), fabulous homes and cottages may be rented by the day, week, or month and include the use of Seaside's swimming pool, tennis courts, croquet lawn, and more. Since Seaside was planned specifically for strolling around in the old-fashioned way, without a car, the village is a delight to explore on foot, or you may want to rent a bike.

Seaside also offers an eclectic schedule of **special events** throughout the year. In the Seaside Meeting Hall, the free architectural lectures are fascinating (tel. 231-4224 for information). In April, merchants usually sponsor a food, wine, and music festival, and there are always special Easter weekend activities. July 4th is celebrated with old-fashioned parades and fireworks. During September's concert series, international performers are in the spotlight. The Annual Wine-Jazz Festival is an October event. During the holiday season, Seaside is an extravaganza of Christmas lights. For information about Seaside's events and the current schedule, call 231-4224.

Where To Stay

JOSEPHINE'S BED & BREAKFAST, 101 Seaside Ave., Seaside, FL 32459. Tel. 904/231-1939, or toll free 800/848-1940. 7 rms, 2 suites. A/C TEL TV

$ Rates (including gourmet breakfast): $120–$200 unit for two. Weekly rates available. MC, V.

Reminiscent of an elegant Virginia inn with its six large Tuscan columns framing the front entrance, Josephine's recalls the romantic Old South with mahogany four-poster beds, Battenburg lace comforters, rich furnishings, and fancy bathrooms with marble bathtubs; most guest rooms also have fireplaces. Enjoy your sumptuous breakfast beside the fireplace or on your private veranda or in the gracious dining room. It's nice to have some modern conveniences too, such as a wet bar, microwave, coffee maker, and small refrigerator neatly designed so as not to conflict with the nostalgic charm. Guest rooms are named for southern flowers: Peony, Marigold, Amaryllis, Lily, Narcissus, Chrysanthemum, Hibiscus. The Guest House offers two suites: Rose on the first floor and Dianthus upstairs with a gulf view (perfect for a honeymoon). Each lovely suite includes a living room, dining room, master bedroom with fireplace, kitchen, and full bath. Josephine's beautiful dining room is open to the public for dinner, by reservation only.

SEASIDE MOTOR COURT, County Rd. 30A, Seaside, FL 32459. Tel. 904/231-1320. 7 rms. A/C TV TEL

$ Rates: Approximately $100 double. MC, V.

Reminiscent of the one-story motels of the 1940s, the Seaside has standard rooms furnished with the tasteful Seaside designer decor. However, don't expect the usual porches and furbelows of Seaside's architecture. The motel rooms are perfect for staying overnight at an excellent rate for Seaside.

Long-Term Rentals

Whether you want to rent a beautifully furnished home or a hideaway cottage, **Seaside Rental,** P.O. Box 4730, Seaside, FL 32459 (tel. 904/231-1320, or toll free 800/635-0296), will assist you. During the peak summer season, a three-day or one-week minimum stay may be required. As an example of rates, from May through August a two-bedroom house costs around $260–$300 per night, or about $1,250–$1,400 for a week. Three- and four-bedroom homes are in the $340–$460 range per night or about $1,650–$2,300 for a week. Prices go down after Labor Day.

Seaside Rental's Honeymoon Cottages are romantic bungalows with gulf-view porches and screened-in decks with whirlpools that rent for approximately $300 per night from May through August. Dreamland Heights has spacious two-story loft suites.

Monarch Realty, which also operates as **B & B Resorts,** P.O. Box 4767, Seaside, FL 32459 (tel. toll free 800/475-1841), handles the 22 outstanding Executive Cottages, such as Sunset Dreams, Pirate's Penthouse, and Southern Comfort. Rates range from $125 per night for a one-bedroom to $975–$2,295 per week for a four-bedroom. During summer, the minimum stay is one week.

Where To Dine

BASMATI'S, at the Seaside Motor Court, County Rd. 30A. Tel. 231-1366.

Cuisine: ASIAN. **Reservations:** Recommended.

$ Prices: Main courses $8.95–$20. No credit cards.
Open: Lunch Thurs–Tues 11am–3pm; dinner Thurs–Tues 5:30–9:30pm.
The cozy restaurant is owned by Charles Bush and his wife, Shueh Mei Pong. She is the talented chef and the cuisine reflects her Thai heritage. Among the specialties are honey-roasted duckling, piquantly spiced beef wrapped in Chinese pancakes, and curried chicken. Veggies Asian style take on new life. The house drink is an interesting blend of sake and plum wine. Or try the refreshing exotic juices, such as mango, papaya, and guava. Asian beers, such as Asahi and Tsing Tao, are also served. Since the restaurant seats only 22, a few outdoor tables are added in warm weather.

BUD AND ALLEY'S, on the beach at Seaside. Tel. 231-5000.
Cuisine: MEDITERRANEAN. **Reservations:** Recommended.
$ Prices: Main courses $16–$25. MC, V.
Open: Lunch Wed–Mon 11:30am–3pm; dinner Wed–Mon 6–9:30pm.
Still Number One to the steady patrons, this was Seaside's very first restaurant. The freshest of seafoods can be selected from the Raw Bar. Delicious pastas are a specialty, as well as osso buco and the crostini of chopped chicken livers combined with onion confit. You can dine indoors or outdoors on the screened veranda, where you hear the waves splashing against the white sands. Usually on weekends, jazz is in the spotlight. On New Year's Eve, everyone in town and from miles around celebrate in Bud and Alley's.

JOSEPHINE'S DINING ROOM, 101 Seaside Ave. Tel. 231-1939.
Cuisine: GOURMET SOUTHERN/FRENCH. **Reservations:** Required.
$ Prices: Main courses $14.95–$25. MC, V.
Open: Dinner only, Mon–Sat 5:30–9:30pm
(If a major holiday falls on a Sunday, Josephine's is open, but check ahead).
In this southern plantation-style dining room, with rich mahogany furniture and a wealth of period accoutrements, the stage is set for a romantic dinner. Glowing with candlelight, the intimate room seats only 20 people. Josephine's chef de cuisine creates innovative dishes based on traditional southern recipes, such as piquantly seasoned sautéed softshell crab and French-style sauces to enhance beef, seafood, veal, and chicken. One of the favorites is a succulent rack of lamb. Rhett Butler and Scarlett O'Hara would fall in love again if they dined here.

SHADE'S, Seaside Town Square & Markets, Seaside. Tel. 231-1950.
Cuisine: AMERICAN. **Reservations:** Not required.
$ Prices: Main courses $10–$20. MC, V.
Open: Lunch/dinner daily 11:30am–9pm.
In another life, this was a rustic house built around the mid-1900s in the small town of Chattahoochee. Over 70 years later the house was moved to Seaside's Town Square to be born again as quaint Shade's restaurant. Stacked-high sandwiches are popular for lunch and there are wings and hamburgers, too. At dinner, the bountiful fried seafood platter is a big favorite. In addition to reasonable prices, the service is very friendly.

Also in Seaside Town Square & Markets, Sip & Dip serves hearty sandwiches, freshly squeezed lemonade, and rich ice cream. Dawson's Yogurt is popular for flavorful yogurt in homemade cones topped by fresh fruit.

Shopping

It's fun to browse through the Mediterranean-style **Seaside Market,** where you will find **Per-spi-Cas-ity** (yes, that's how it's spelled), which claims some of the most unusual gift and fashion items south of Bloomingdale's.

In Seaside's Town Square, **Modica Market** will remind you of a European food hall, where a great array of gourmet groceries and outstanding deli goodies are stocked—and there are café tables for relaxing with a cup of richly brewed coffee. **Azure d'Mare** specializes in casual beachwear for men. **L. Pizitz & Co.** is the place for decorative home furnishings and distinctive housewares. For a good read, **Sundog**

Books has everything under the sun, from kids' classics to trashy novels to read under a beach umbrella. For art, visit **Gallery Expose** and **Papyrus Posters & Prints.**

DEFUNIAK SPRINGS

For a giant step into the Victorian past in a lakeside setting of magnificent oak trees bearded with Spanish moss, a day trip to DeFuniak Springs is truly out-of-this-world. Less than 35 miles north of Grayton Beach or Seaside, via U.S. 331 and just three miles off I-10, DeFuniak Springs is Old Florida and on the National Register of Historic Places. Along Circle Drive, a one-mile road encircling the perfectly round lake, are some of the most magnificent ✪ **Victorian homes** with ornate turrets and fancy "gingerbread" trimmings. Inside, all are as elegantly furnished as when these prestigious residences were built in the 1880s. If you happened to visit the architectural wonder of Seaside before your day trip, you may wonder if Seaside's designers and developers were inspired by DeFuniak Springs. At certain times of the year, the historic homes are open for touring.

DeFuniak Springs also boasts **Florida's oldest library,** which was established by women and also contains a surprising collection of weaponry, some dating back to the Crusades.

Should you be interested in wines, you're in for a pleasant surprise at **Chautauqua Vineyards,** DeFuniak Springs (tel. 904/892-5887), Florida's largest winery. Yes, there are wines to please the connoisseur, which are offered for tasting during the free daily tours. Usually a wine festival is celebrated here in early Sept. The vineyard is at the intersection of I–10 and Fla. 331. Take exit 14; there are signs on the interstate.

During the Chautauqua era, from 1885 to 1929, DeFuniak Springs was considered the cultural center of Florida and now the programs have been revived with International Elderhostel seminars in February, April, and October.

If you like **antique-ing,** visit Marie's Hitching Post, Bell's Bargain Box, The Doll House, and Cate Craft (for miniature dollhouses).

A variety of **special events** are scheduled throughout the year, including the Chautauqua Festival (usually in late April), featuring sports activities, cultural programs, arts and crafts, and fireworks. The American Indian Fall Festival (usually in November) is a colorful Creek tribal event held at the E-Chota Cherokee Reservation in Mossy Head, a short drive east of DeFuniak Springs. Native American arts and crafts, traditional food, and intertribal dancing are among the highlights. In December, the Annual Victorian Ball is splendid, with everyone wearing authentic costumes. Hollywood costume designer Armand Coutu, now a resident here, owns Edwardian Enterprises and creates many of the gorgeous fashions for the gala. Most guests arrive in horse and carriage.

By the way, **horse-and-carriage tours** clip-clop around the historic district on weekends.

The sports-minded may **rent a bike** at King Hardware (tel. 892-3711), **jog** along the 1-mile lakeside trail, or drive about 10 miles east to Vortex Springs at **Ponce de Leon Springs State Recreation Area,** which includes Florida's largest driving facility.

WHERE TO STAY A few of the historic homes are now interesting bed-and-breakfast inns. **Sunbright Manor** (tel. 904/892-0656) is a very ornate Queen Anne mansion adorned with priceless antiques; **Live Oaks** (tel. 904/892-0849) is shaded by gorgeous oak trees; and the **Biselli Doll House** (tel. 904/892-7665), decorated with antique dolls, is also known for its "doll hospital."

WHERE TO DINE Among the friendly restaurants to choose from are Mom and Dad's Italian Restaurant; Lowe's Restaurant and Oyster Bar, Rick's Café, and the DeFuniak Springs Country Club (the dining room is open to the public). For a refresher, relax in Mia's Tea Room in the historic district. And for a quick snack, stop at H&M's Hot Dogs.

INFORMATION For more information, contact Diane Pickett, Founder, **The**

Turn Around Society, Rt. 8, Box 912, DeFuniak Springs, FL 32433 (enclose a self-addressed stamped envelope for your reply) or call her at 904/892-4300. Or write the **Walton County Chamber of Commerce,** P.O. Box 29, DeFuniak Springs, FL 32433 (tel. 904/892-3191). Information about Vortex Springs is available from **Ponce de Leon Springs State Recreation Area,** c/o Falling Waters State Recreation Area, Rte. 5, Box 660, Chipley, FL 32445 (tel. 904/836-4281).

3. PANAMA CITY / PANAMA CITY BEACH

100 miles E of Pensacola, 100 miles SW of Tallahassee

GETTING THERE **By Plane** American, Delta, Northwest, and USAir commuter planes fly into the **Panama City / Bay County Regional Airport** (tel. 904/763-6751).

By Train Amtrak's *Sunset Limited* transcontinental service from Los Angeles to New Orleans and Miami (launched in April 1993) stops at Pensacola and Tallahassee, with intermediate stops at Crestview, north of Fort Walton Beach, and Chipley, north of Panama City. For Amtrak information, call toll free 800/TEL-TRAK.

By Bus The Greyhound depot is located at 917 Harrison Ave. (tel. 904/785-7861).

By Car Interstate 10 runs east-west, just 30 miles to the north, and then you can take U.S. 231 leading south to the beach; and Fla. 77 and Fla. 79 also connect the city to I-10. U.S. 98, another main east-west artery, also leads to Panama City. Panama City and Panama City Beach are connected by the Hathaway Bridge across St. Andrews Bay on the south and North Bay on the north.

Although Panama City and Panama City Beach are usually considered one and the same, each has its own separate identity. They are linked by the toll-free three-mile Hathaway Bridge, which spans St. Andrews Bay.

Centuries ago, Native Americans lived in this remarkably beautiful coastal area. In the 16th century, Spanish conquistadors sailed from the Gulf of Mexico directly into St. Andrews Bay and what is now Panama City, but their obsession for gold was not fulfilled here. Finally, in 1765, the British, impressed by the strategic harbor, founded the first settlement. During ensuing centuries, Panama City was considered just a sleepy fishing village. How times have changed! Now the popular resort city is one of the state's leading ports and an industrial center. Since boating and charter-boat fishing are favorite sports, the attractive city is fringed by a 400-slip marina located where Harrison Avenue culminates at St. Andrews Bay. Because of the many sunken shipwrecks, the scuba diving is great here, offering a variety of underwater sites to explore.

For many years, Panama City Beach has attracted vacationers from nearby states (at one time it was affectionately known as "The Redneck Riviera"). But now vacationers from around the nation flock to the miles of brilliant white sand beaches, splashed by the jewel-green gulf waters. Panama City Beach has also been compared to New York's Coney Island because of the razzle-dazzle amusement parks, with screaming crowds on the wild roller coasters. For vacationers who prefer lots of action, Panama City Beach is the liveliest vacation destination along the Panhandle—and the most crowded, especially in summer.

The super-wide Panama City Beach, rated among the nation's best, is notable for unbelievably white, soft sands, and is attributed to a special variety of quartz, which has become very finely ground and polished through the centuries. There's exciting surf too, caused by offshore formations. The same phenomena have encouraged the abundant growth of exotic marine life, especially along the gulf's natural reef system only a few miles offshore, which is perfect for snorkeling, scuba diving, spearfishing, lobstering, and shelling.

Both Panama City and Panama City Beach radiate a very friendly, casual atmosphere. The southern hospitality in hotels, motels, and restaurants, plus the reasonable prices, appeal to families. Newer, luxurious hideaway resorts, wonderful seafood, the sports activities, and fabulous beaches bring more and more vacationers and honeymooners to "discover" the area.

ORIENTATION

INFORMATION The **James I. Lark, Sr., Visitors Information Center,** 12015 Front Beach Rd., Panama City Beach, FL 32407 (tel. 904/234-3193), is conveniently across from Miracle Strip Park and provides recommendations on accommodations, restaurants, and attractions in Panama City Beach. The visitor information center is affiliated with the Panama City Beaches Chamber of Commerce (same address; same telephone number). Information is also supplied by the **Panama City Beach Convention & Visitors Bureau,** 415 Beckrich Rd., Suite 205 (P.O. Box 9473), Panama City Beach, FL 32407 (tel. 904/233-6503, or toll free 800/PC-BEACH).

The **Bay County Chamber of Commerce** offers assistance to tourists interested in Panama City and is located at 235 W. 5th St., Panama City, FL 32407 (tel. 904/785-5206).

CITY LAYOUT Leading into the city from the east or west, **U.S. 98** becomes **Business 98** to enter the small downtown area. **Alternate 98** is lined with most of the hotels, motels, restaurants, and attractions along the beach. Since this scenic road runs parallel also to Business 98, just make sure that you're on 98A for any beach destination. Here's a tip: As you drive west on 98A, the address numbers get higher. Don't worry should you have to exit at any time—there are 14 exits and connections between 98 and 98A.

GETTING AROUND

At the airport, some of the top **rental-car companies** have offices and there is also taxi or limousine service. Most hotels will make rental-car arrangements with Avis, Hertz, Dollar, National, etc. However, during the peak summer vacation time, it's best to make advance reservations by calling one of the major car rentals (all have nationwide toll-free numbers).

Yellow Cab (tel. 763-4691) charges by the zone and rates vary.

Bike rentals are available at the Marriott Bay Point Resort (tel. 234-6911) for under $20 per day.

FAST FACTS

Area Code The telephone area code is 904.

Convenience Store At the Shoppes at Edgewater, on Front Beach Road at Edgewater Beach Road on Panama City Beach, (tel. 234-7915), there's a Food World, open around the clock.

Emergencies For police and medical help, dial 911.

Flags Pay attention to the beach flags: A **blue** flag signifies that the gulf is calm; **yellow** cautions about an undertow; the **red** flag announces that the undertow is dangerous. Lifeguards also have the daily report about gulf conditions.

Medical Assistance A physician is always on duty and no appointment is required at the Bay Walk-in Clinic, at the corner of 23rd Street and Fla. 77, across from the mall (tel. 763-9744); another location is at 8811 W. U.S. 98A (tel. 234-8511).

Newspapers/Magazines The *Panama City News-Herald* prints the latest information, including tourist attraction schedules and rates, etc. Also take a look at the free *See* magazine with lots of information about restaurants and attractions.

Pharmacy Eckerd Drugs is located in the Shoppes at Edgewater (see "Convenience Store," above).

WHAT TO SEE & DO

ATTRACTIONS

Museums

JUNIOR MUSEUM OF BAY COUNTY, 1731 Jenks Ave., Panama City. Tel. 769-6128.

An educational experience for young people and adults too, the museum displays Native American artifacts from nearby archeological digs (a life-size teepee can be explored, too). A re-created 1880s farm where chickens and ducks can be fed by visitors, a Nature Trail meandering through three northwest Florida–type environments, puppet shows, science exhibits, concerts, and more offer a variety of interests for the entire family.

Admission: Free.

Open: Tues–Fri 9am–4:30pm, Sat 10am–4pm. **Closed:** New Year's Day, July 4, Labor Day, Thanksgiving, and Christmas Day. Check ahead for any schedule changes.

MUSEUM OF MAN IN THE SEA, 17314 Back Beach Rd., Panama City Beach. Tel. 235-4101.

Owned by the Institute of Diving and the Panama City Marine Institute, this unusual museum exhibits relics from the first days of scuba diving, historical displays of the underwater world (dating back to 1500), and treasures recovered from shipwrecks, including artifacts from the Spanish galleon *Atocha* (a 25-minute video shows Mel Fisher discovering the *Atocha*). Visitors learn about marine life sciences, astronauts' training underwater, oceanography, underwater archeology, and much more.

Admission: $4 adults, $1.50 children 6–16, free for children under 6.

Open: Daily 9am–5pm.

Amusement Parks

MIRACLE STRIP AMUSEMENT PARK, 12000 Front Beach Rd. Tel. 234-5810.

The exciting roller coaster, towering up to 2,000-feet high, defies the laws of gravity on the thrilling downward trip. This is just one of the 30 rides in the park. If you dare, ride the 40-foot-high Sea Dragon, designed like a Viking ship, which rocks passengers up to 70-feet in the air. Little ones love the traditional carousel. Marvelous at night, when everything is gaudily illuminated, this landmark amusement park is one of Florida's top 10 attractions. Nine acres of fun include nonstop entertainment and snackeries with great junk food.

Admission (including all rides): Less than $20 adults, less than $15 children under 11. (You may pay a gate admission and buy a coupon rides booklet, but not that many dollars are saved.)

Open: June–Labor Day, Mon–Fri 5–11:30pm, Sat–Sun 1–11:30pm; mid-Mar to May, Sat–Sun 1–11:30pm. **Closed:** Labor Day to mid-Mar.

SHIPWRECK ISLAND WATER PARK, 12000 Front Beach Rd. Tel. 234-0368.

Encompassing six landscaped acres of water rides and picnic areas, Shipwreck Island Water Park features the 1,600-foot winding Lazy River for tubing and the daring 35-m.p.h. Speed Slide. For adventure, try the Rapid River Cascades or the White Water Tube Trip. From young children to adults, there's a variety of fun things to enjoy in the water. Lounge chairs, umbrellas, and inner tubes are free, and a lifeguard is on duty.

Admission (including all rides): Less than $15 adults, around $11 children under 10.

Open: April–Sept, daily 10:30am–6pm. **Closed:** Oct–Mar.

More Attractions

GULF WORLD, 15412 Front Beach Rd. Tel. 234-5271.

This landscaped tropical garden marine showcase spotlights shows with talented porpoises, sea lions, penguins, and more. Not to be upstaged, parrots perform daily, too. Sea turtles, alligators, ducks, and other critters call Gulf World home. Scuba demonstrations, shark feeding, and underwater shows keep the crowds entertained.

Admission: $13.95 adults, $7.95 children 5–12, free for children under 5.

Open: Summer, daily 9am–7pm.

ST. ANDREWS STATE RECREATION AREA, 4415 Thomas Dr. Tel. 233-5140.

With more than 1,000 acres of dazzling white sand, topped by towering sand dunes that look like lofty snowdrifts, this is beachcombers' heaven. Lacy, golden sea oats sway in the refreshing gulf breezes. Fragrant rosemary grows wild on the more inland dunes near pine-tree woodland. Picnicking is delightful on either the gulf beach or the Grand Lagoon. Showers are conveniently located to refresh yourself after a swim. For anglers, there are two fishing piers, jetties, and a boat ramp. Along the Nature Trail, it's fun to watch the wading birds and perhaps sight an alligator or two. Overnight camping is permitted. Take a look at the historic turpentine still on display; it was formerly utilized by lumbermen, who drew resin from the pine trees, then brewed it in the still to make turpentine and also rosin, important for caulking the old wooden ships. The park is beautifully located right on the gulf at the tip of County Road 392, only three miles east of Panama City Beach.

Admission: $3.25 per car (maximum of eight people).

Open: Daily 8am–sunset.

ZOO WORLD ZOOLOGICAL & BOTANICAL PARK, 9008 Front Beach Rd. Tel. 230-0096.

More than 100 species of animals live in re-created natural habitats. An active participant in the Species Survival Plan (SSP), which helps protect the world's endangered species with specific breeding and housing programs, Zoo World has many rare and endangered animals. Orangutans and other primates, big cats, reptiles, and other creatures provide an educational and entertaining experience here. Also included are a walk-through aviary and a petting zoo.

Admission: $8.95 adult, $7.95 senior, $6.50 children 3-11, free for children under 3.

Open: Daily 9am–sunset.

A Day Trip to Shell Island

Accessible by boat only, Shell Island is a 7½-mile-long, 1-mile-wide barrier island off the coast of St. Andrews State Recreation Area. The uninhabited natural preserve is great for shelling, and also fun for swimming, suntanning, or just relaxing. At least six cruise boats offer day-trip excursions to Shell Island from Panama City Beach marinas (lunch is included on some boats). One of the most popular is the double-decker sailing daily at 9am and 1pm from Captain Anderson's Marina at Grand Lagoon Drive (tel. 234-3435). The excursion costs about $8 for adults, $4 for children. Or request a Shell Island boat list from the visitors information center (tel. 234-3193).

SPECIAL EVENTS

The annual **Gulf Coast Offshore Powerboat Races** at St. Andrews Marina are the main event in April. In late June, the **Annual Ladies Billfish Tournament** is held at Bay Point Marina. The weekend after July 4, the **Bay Point Billfish Invitational** is one of the nation's most prestigious ($300,000 in cash prizes!).

Mid-September begins the **Annual Panama City Beach Fishing Classic,** which continues to the end of September; the annual **Treasure Island King Mackerel Tournament,** at Treasure Island Marina, is a late September event.

The annual **Indian Summer Seafood Festival,** in Panama City Beach, takes place in Aaron Z. Bessant Wayside Park (across from the Dan Russell Fishing Pier). Celebrated the second week of October, this is one of the South's top events, with continuous entertainment by famous performers, an amazing abundance of seafood to enjoy, and at least 100 arts and crafts vendors.

Important golf tournaments and sports competitions are also on the schedule. For current information, contact the visitors information center (tel. 234-3193).

In nearby Marianna, an important **Civil War battle** fought there in 1864 is reenacted, usually annually in October. For information call 904/482-8061. From Panama City, take U.S. 231 north and follow the signs to Marianna.

SPORTS & RECREATION

The **Panama City Parks and Recreation Department** (tel. 872-3005) sponsors 20 tennis courts, 12 nature parks, and several community centers (including Noah's Ark, for activities-oriented senior citizen vacationers). Call for current information about these very inexpensive or free city-operated places.

BOAT RENTALS A grand variety of boats are available from the following marinas: **Bay Point Yacht & Country Club,** 100 Dellwood Beach Rd. (tel. 234-0220); **Capt. Anderson Davis Marina,** 5550 N. Lagoon Dr. (tel. 234-3435, or toll free 800/874-2415); **Panama City Boat Yard,** 5323 N. Lagoon Dr. (tel. 234-3386); **Passport Marina,** 5325 N. Lagoon Dr. (tel. 234-5609); **Pirates Cove Marina,** 3901 Thomas Dr. (tel. 234-3839); **Port Lagoon Yacht Basin,** 5201 N. Lagoon Dr. (tel. 234-0142); **Rude Roy's Marina,** 6400 W. U.S. 98 (tel. 234-0609); and **Treasure Island Marina,** 3605 Thomas Dr. (tel. 234-6533).

CRUISES Daily sightseeing trips sail out from Capt. Anderson's Marina (tel. 234-3425) and dinner-dance cruises are offered from Memorial Day through Labor Day. The Captain Davis Queen Fleet is popular for the dolphin-feeding cruises aboard the glass-bottom boat (tel. 234-3435). Capt. Davis excursions sail out from Capt. Anderson's Marina, 5550 N. Lagoon Dr., at Thomas Drive, Panama City Beach. Also inquire about Capt. Anderson's Shell Island cruises and the Gospel Music Cruise.

Hydrospace (tel. 234-3063 or 234-9063) has a popular three-hour snorkeling and dolphin-watching excursion daily, a fun trip for the entire family.

DOG RACING The **Ebro Greyhound Park,** just a 15-minute drive north of Panama City via Fla. 79 to Ebro, offers exciting greyhound racing and the opportunity to win some money (over a million dollars is won every week). From March until September greyhound racing begins Monday through Saturday at 7:30pm, with races every 15 minutes; matinees are scheduled on Wednesday and Saturday at 1pm. Hot dogs and snacks can be purchased trackside, or you can dine in the clubhouse dining room (open from 6pm), where seafood and prime rib are specialties. Children are welcome if accompanied by an adult. During off-season months, satellite wagering is popular on thoroughbred races and harness races. Call 234-3943 for information, current post times, and dining room reservations. Note: From March through mid-May, there's no live greyhound racing on Tuesday.

FISHING Close to a quarter million visitors come just to fish in the bountiful waters. Anglers catch Spanish mackerel, flounder, redfish, bonito, sea trout, bluefish, amberjack, sailfish, marlin, and many more. Panama City Beach boasts three fishing piers—the **Dan Russell Municipal Pier** is the longest, stretching 1,642 feet into the gulf.

From March through November, charter-fishing-boat trips depart daily for trips of 4–12 hours (the longer the trip, the larger total catch and bigger the fish). A deep-sea fishing boat fleet operates from the **Capt. Anderson Pier,** 5500 N. Lagoon Dr. (tel. 234-3435). Charter-fishing boats are operated also from **Treasure Island Deepsea Fishing Charter,** 3605 Thomas Dr. (tel. 234-8944).

GOLF Thirty-six holes of championship golf are offered at **Marriott's Bay Point Resort,** 100 Delwood Beach Rd. in Panama City Beach (tel. 234-3307). The "Lagoon Legend" course challenges with "monster hazards." Greens fees range from $45 to $75, depending on the season and day of the week. Or tee off at the **Holiday Golf Course and Country Club,** 100 Fairway Blvd., Panama City Beach (tel. 234-1800), an 18-hole, par-72 course; **The Hombre,** 120 Coyote Pass, Panama City Beach (tel. 234-3573), where the 18-hole course is a venue for golf tournaments; **Signal Hill,** 9516 N. Thomas Dr., Panama City Beach (tel. 234-3218); or the

Edgewater Beach Resort, 11212 U.S. 98A (tel. 235-4044). Reservations for tee times are recommended.

MINIATURE GOLF Six minigolf courses await, each a fantasy of waterfalls, luxuriant landscaping, and such themes as pirate ships, jungle adventures, and castles. Among the courses to choose from are **Coconut Creek Mini Golf and Gran Maze** (tel. 234-2625); **Emerald Falls Raceway and Fantasy Golf** (tel. 234-1049); **Goofy Golf** (tel. 234-6403); **Hidden Lagoon Super Golf & Racetrack** (tel. 234-9289); **Pirate Island Adventure Golf** (tel. 235-1171); and **Skull Island Miniature Golf** (tel. 235-8877). Call the courses in advance for current schedules and prices.

SNORKELING & SCUBA DIVING **Marriott's Bay Point Resort,** off Thomas Drive at Grand Lagoon (tel. 234-3307), rents catamarans, waverunners, windsurfing boards, and snorkeling equipment, and arranges snorkel and scuba trips. **Hydrospace Dive Shop** has two full-service shops on Panama City Beach (tel. 234-3063 or 234-9063) and professionally trained staffs, offering a good opportunity to take snorkeling or scuba lessons aboard any of their six customized dive boats. Four-, six-, or eight-hour dive trips, 2–20 miles offshore in 60–100 feet of water are priced from $38 per person.

Scuba diving is especially interesting offshore of Panama City, with more than 50 artificial reefs and shipwrecks to explore, such as *The Grey Ghost, Empire Mica, The Chippewa,* and the S.S. *Tarpon.* Brochures on exciting underwater trips can be obtained from the Panama City Beach Chamber of Commerce, 12015 Front Beach Rd. (tel. 235-1159).

TENNIS & RACQUETBALL **Sports Park,** 15238 Front Beach Rd. (tel. 235-1081), features tennis courts and racquetball courts at reasonable prices. Nautilus workout equipment, aerobics classes, a whirlpool, and sauna are offered in the fitness center.

Large resorts and hotels have excellent tennis programs for their guests. Call the **Panama City Recreation Department** (tel. 872-3005) for information about the municipal courts.

WHERE TO STAY

In the Panama City/Panama City Beach area, hotels, motels, and condominiums offer an extensive variety of accommodations, from luxurious suites to very reasonably priced places to stay. Rental condominium apartments are a smart vacation buy: They can be shared by families or groups of friends, and offer the advantage of fully equipped kitchens. In addition, most have recreation areas with tennis courts, swimming pools, games rooms, etc. One of the many agencies offering one-, two-, three-, and four-bedroom gulf-front, fully furnished condominium apartments is **Condo World,** 8815-A Thomas Dr. (P.O. Box 9456), Panama City Beach, FL 32408 (tel. 904/234-5564, or toll free 800/232-6636). Since there are thousands of rental condominium apartments, contact the **Panama City Beaches Chamber of Commerce,** 12015 Front Beach Rd., Panama City Beach, FL 32407 (tel. 904/234-2193), to obtain a listing.

Prices are most reasonable in Panama City, where a double room in summer costs no more than $55, and the very best accommodations for two run about $70. Among the most popular are the **Best Western Bayside Inn** (tel. 904/763-4622); **Comfort Inn** (tel. 904/769-6969); **Days Inn Panama City** (tel. 904/784-1777); **Holiday Inn–Mall** (tel. 904/769-0000); and the **Ramada Inn on the Bay** (tel. 904/785-0561).

PANAMA CITY BEACH

Expensive

EDGEWATER BEACH RESORT, 11212 Front Beach Rd., Panama City Beach, FL 32407. Tel. 904/235-4044, or toll free 800/874-8686. Fax 904/233-7599. 510 apts.

$ Rates: Spring, $100–$240; summer, $150–$325; winter, $65–$130. Weekly rates available. DC, DISC, MC, V.

One of the Panhandle's largest condominium resorts, the beautiful beachfront location and garden landscaping with palm trees conjures thoughts of Polynesia. The spectacular swimming lagoon with cascading waterfalls includes an island in the center.

Tropically decorated, spacious one- to three-bedroom apartments feature fully equipped kitchens, living and dining areas, and the convenience of your own washer and dryer. Views look out to the gulf, swimming lagoon, or the fairway, whichever you prefer.

Dining/Entertainment: Breakfast is served in Bimini, a casual lunch in Palapa, and delicious dinners in the Upstairs Clubhouse, all on the premises. There's also a poolside bar.

Services: Shuttle service around the resort, children's program, airport transportation.

Facilities: Pool, whirlpools, 12 tennis courts (6 lighted); nine-hole Hombre Golf Club a quarter mile north; rental sailboats and bikes; arrangements for parasailing.

HOLIDAY INN BEACHSIDE, 11127 Front Beach Rd., Panama City Beach, FL 32407. Tel. 904/234-1111, or toll free 800/633-0266. Fax 904/235-1907. 342 rms. A/C TV TEL

$ Rates: Summer, $100–$140 double. Off-season, $55–$138 double. Weekly and monthly rates available; discount for seniors. AE, DC, DISC, MC, V.

Designed in a dramatic curve, this 15-story resort hotel has won architectural awards. Very attractive, spacious guest rooms feature private balconies and gulf views. Each has a full-size icemaker-refrigerator, which makes the accommodations suitable for a family vacation. The hotel is one of Holiday Inn's top 20 and has won the corporation's Quality Excellence and Torch Bearer awards.

Dining/Entertainment: Charlie's Grill, on the poolside deck, is enjoyable for lunch. For breakfast and dinner, the Blue Marlin features good food at moderate prices. A lively rendezvous, the Starlight Lounge serves drinks until late and usually offers entertainment during the peak summer season.

Facilities: Large swimming pool, whirlpool, exercise room.

MARRIOTT'S BAY POINT RESORT, 100 Delwood Beach Rd., Bay Point, FL 32407. Tel. 904/234-3307, or toll free 800/874-7105. Fax 904/233-1308. 378 rms, suites, and villas. A/C TV TEL

$ Rates: May–Sept, $144–$195 double; up to $275 suite. Winter rates much less. Variety of vacation packages year-round. AE, DC, DISC, MC, V.

Ranked among the nation's top 25 golf and tennis resorts and named as one of America's favorite family resorts, this vacation mini-world encompasses 1,100 landscaped acres with 32 ponds and a beach. Secluded on a tropical wildlife preserve peninsula bordering St. Andrews Bay and Grand Lagoon, the hideaway resort complex overlooks the Gulf of Mexico—the best of all worlds! The outstanding, multilevel, vivid coral stucco hotel is surrounded by gardens, palm trees, oaks, and magnolias. In the glamorous three-story lobby, the window walls look out to scenic water views. The romantic atmosphere also attracts honeymooners.

Dining/Entertainment: No one could ever be hungry or thirsty here—the resort features seven restaurants and four lounges. Fiddler's Green is a favorite, open daily for dinner at 6pm, and also serves a Friday seafood buffet from 5 to 9pm and a Sunday brunch from 10am to 1:30pm. Luscious chocolate key lime pie is the signature dessert. Teddy Tucker's Back Bay Beach Club serves delicious sandwiches and tropical drinks. Stormy's has salads, pizza, and sandwiches, and makes the best homemade ice cream. Terrace Court, overlooking the marina, is notable for French-style tableside service at dinner. Live entertainment is spotlighted in some of the lounges; check with the concierge for current schedule.

Services: Concierge, fax and secretarial services.

Facilities: There are 36 holes of championship golf on the Lagoon Legend Course (second most difficult in the U.S.) and the Club Meadows Course, each with its own clubhouse, putting green, driving range, clinic, and private instruction with video analysis. The Point Tennis Center features 12 clay courts (4 lighted), tennis shop, tennis clinics, and private lessons. The Bay Point Yacht Club, with a 145-slip marina, is in a 12-acre protected cove. At the water-sports center, snorkeling, scuba, waterskiing, sailing, and parasailing can be arranged (or you can take lessons), and free sailing and windsurfing clinics are offered. Play beach volleyball or front lawn croquet. The kids' activities program, the Alligator Point Gang, is for ages 5–12 (great fun!). The Island Queen Riverboat takes guests to Shell Island for delightful excursions. Six swimming pools (one indoor) are on the resort's premises; poolside and beach activities are scheduled daily for all guests. Rental boats, rental bikes, and fishing arrangements are offered, and sunset cruises can be arranged. The resort also has outstanding conference and meeting facilities. Marriott's Bay Point Resort Health Club and the new Club Meadows Health Club are on the premises. For shoppers, five boutiques and Bay Town shops await. Among the resort's special events, the Bay Point Billfish Invitational in July is an exciting celebration, which includes the country's largest billfish award—$350,000!

MOONSPINNER CONDOMINIUMS, 4425 Thomas Dr., Panama City Beach, FL 32408. Tel. 904/234-8900, or toll free 800/223-3947. Fax 904/233-0719. 115 units. A/C TV TEL

$ Rates: May–Sept, $800–$1,065 per week apt. Off-season, $450–$600 per week apt. Daily and monthly rates available. MC, V.

"Next door" to beautiful St. Andrews State Park, these gulf-front two-bedroom/two-bath and three-bedroom/three-bath fully furnished condominium apartments with completely equipped kitchens are tropically decorated and have such advantages as full-size washers and dryers and cable television with HBO. From your private balcony, enjoy the glorious gulf sunsets. When you're not in the mood to cook, good restaurants are nearby.

Services: Free local telephone calls.

Facilities: Wide white sand beach, large swimming pool, wading pool for the kids, hot tub, two tennis courts (lighted for night play), exercise room, saunas, video-games room with a pool table.

PINNACLE PORT, 23223 Front Beach Rd., Panama City Beach, FL 32407. Tel. 904/234-8813, or toll free 800/874-8823. Fax 904/233-2634. 200 apts. A/C TV TEL

$ Rates: May 15–Sept 7, $115–$180 apts. Sept 8–Mar 14, $80–$105 apt. Mar 15–May 14, $105–$150 apt. Weekly and monthly rates available. MC, V.

On at least a half mile of gulf beach, this condominium complex has a hideaway atmosphere and likes to call itself a "peninsula paradise." One-, two-, and three-bedroom units sport Caribbean decor and have kitchens and balconies looking out on the gulf panorama. Among the amenities are two swimming pools (one indoor heated), saunas, four lighted tennis courts, a children's playground, boat dock, and more.

Moderate

FLAMINGO DOME BY THE SEA MOTEL, 15525 Front Beach Rd., Panama City Beach, FL 32413. Tel. 904/234-2232, or toll free 800/828-0400. 67 units. A/C TV TEL

$ Rates: Summer, $60–$100 unit. Off-season, $32–$70 unit. AE, DISC, MC, V.

This friendly, family-owned motel takes great pride (and rightfully so) in the gorgeous tropical garden under the dome—an exotic paradise of palms, hibiscus, ferns, and flamboyant flowers that's cool for strolling in no matter how hot the summer's day. Bordering the garden, the swimming pool and large sun deck overlook the shimmering gulf. Brightly decorated rooms with kitchenettes sleep two to six people. Across the street from the beach, the kitchenette rooms accommodate six to eight. Budget-conscious families will like the low-priced rooms with small refrigerators, accommodating two to four. The famous fishing pier is only half a mile west of the Flamingo, and a casual seafood restaurant is also nearby. From a poolside lounge chair, you can sit back and admire a fabulous sunset daily.

GEORGIAN TERRACE, 14415 Front Beach Rd., Panama City Beach, FL 32413. Tel. 904/234-2144 or 904/234-8413. 28 apts. A/C TV TEL

$ Rates: Mid-May to mid-Sept, $75–$85 single or double. Off-season $44–$73 single or double. AE, DISC, MC, V.

A two-level apartment-motel right on the beach, the Georgian Terrace is family-owned and family-operated. All apartments overlook the beach and all have full kitchens, separated by room dividers. Cheerfully decorated, the rooms are cozily paneled with knotty pine. The homey decor is extended to private enclosed sunporches with each apartment. The pool area is exceptionally beautiful, surrounded by a colorful garden and attractive lounge chairs.

HORIZON SOUTH, 17462 Front Beach Rd., Panama City Beach, FL 32413. Tel. 904/234-6663, or toll free 800/476-6458. 75 apts. A/C TV TEL

$ Rates: Summer, $65–$120 apt for two. Off-season rates much less. Daily, weekly, and monthly rates available. AE, DISC, MC, V.

Directly across the street from the wide expanse of gulf beach, most of these one-, two-, and three-bedroom town houses are equipped with washers and dryers, and all have full kitchens and cable television with HBO. Private patios or sun decks are a nice touch. The resort community features three swimming pools (one is heated), a wading pool for the kids, a whirlpool hot tub, lighted tennis courts, an 18-hole miniature golf course, a games room, and much more.

Horizon South II (tel. 904/234-8329) is part of this same resort community and offers one- and two-bedroom condominium apartments with slightly lower rates.

Tip: When making reservations in this resort community, check to find out if your accommodations are located one or three blocks from the beach.

RAMADA INN BEACHSIDE RESORT, 12907 Beach Front Rd., Panama City Beach, FL 32407. Tel. 904/234-1700. Fax 904/235-2700. 147 rms. A/C TV TEL

$ Rates: Summer, $90 double. Off-season, $52 double. AE, DC, DISC, MC, V.

With a great location on the beach, all accommodations look out to the gulf. There's also a very pleasant swimming pool area. On the premises, the restaurant is open for breakfast, lunch, and dinner, from 6:30am to 10pm, and the menu is very reasonably priced. At night the fifth-floor Crow's Nest Lounge, which overlooks the gulf panorama, is very lively (open until 4am in summer).

RENDEZVOUS BEACH RESORT, 17281 Front Beach Rd., Panama City Beach, FL 32407. Tel. 904/234-8841, or toll free 800/874-6617. 66 rms, 6 suites. A/C TV TEL

$ Rates: Summer, $75–$105 single or double; $110 suite. Winter, $40–$45 single or double; $75 suite. AE, MC, V.

A relaxing island atmosphere prevails at this fun resort, directly on the gulf. Rooms are attractively decorated in pastel hues with white rattan furniture and balconies look out to beautiful gulf views. In addition to the outstanding swimming pool and its cascading waterfalls, there's a Jacuzzi. The U-Turn Sunburn Beach Club is popular for live country music, when entertainment is spotlighted in summer months. From the Beach Bar, the views are splendid at any time of the year. The highly acclaimed Boar's Head Restaurant is across the street (see "Where to Dine," below).

Budget

FIESTA MOTEL, 13623 Front Beach Rd., Panama City Beach, FL 32413. Tel. 904/235-1000, or toll free 800/833-1415. Fax 904/233-1677. 150 rms, 34 suites. A/C TV TEL

$ Rates: Summer, $50–$90 room or suite. Children 17 and under stay free in parents' room. AE, MC, V.

A friendly beachfront motel, the Fiesta has a Spanish-Mediterranean touch. Rooms are neat with wall-to-wall carpeting and most have balconies or patios to enjoy views of the gulf. The two-bedroom family suites have paneled-wood kitchens supplied with utensils. The palm-tree fringed swimming pool is right next to the beach.

LA BRISA INN, 9424 Front Beach Rd., Panama City Beach, FL 32404. Tel. 904/235-1122, or toll free 800/523-4369. 60 rms. A/C TV TEL

$ Rates: Summer, $50–$57 double. Off-season, $30–$40 double. Weekly and monthly rates available. AE, DC, DISC, MC, V.

A good vacation buy for families, the inn has rooms with a king-size or two double beds, and many have kitchenettes. Cribs are supplied for the little ones. Every morning, complimentary coffee and doughnuts are served, and local telephone calls are free.

There's another La Brisa Inn in the Tyndall Air Force Base area at 5711 E. U.S. 98, Panama City, FL 32404 (tel. 904/871-2345).

MARK II QUALITY INN, 15285 Front Beach Rd., Panama City Beach, FL 32413. Tel. 904/234-8845, or toll free 800/874-7101. 122 rms. A/C TV TEL

$ Rates (including continental breakfast): Summer, $85 double, $95 with kitchenette. Off-season, $52 double, $60 with kitchenette. AE, MC, V.

In 1993, Quality Inns took over the Mark II Beach Resort and renovated everything. All guest rooms are gulf-front, with balconies for enjoying glorious views. On a quarter mile of pure white sand private beach, the property also includes a swimming pool, super sun deck, a water-sports center for renting waverunners, windsurfer boards, jet skis, and sailboats. Arrangements can be made for fishing or parasailing. Due to popular demand, Sharky's beachfront restaurant and tiki bar have not been changed by the renovation. Across the street, the inn's Sports Park Fitness Center offers workout equipment, tennis and racquetball courts, and an indoor pool.

SUNSET INN, 8109 Surf Dr., Panama City Beach, FL 32407. Tel. 904/234-7370. 50 units. A/C TV TEL

$ Rates: Summer, $55–$90 unit. Off-season, $40–$70 unit. Weekly, monthly and family rates available. AE, MC, V.

This very well maintained, two-level inn accommodates families in one- and two-bedroom carpeted units with kitchens. Directly on the white sand beach, the inn sports a large swimming pool and a spacious sun deck overlooking the gulf.

SUGAR SANDS MOTEL, 20723 Front Beach Rd., Panama City Beach, FL 32413. Tel. 904/234-8802, or toll free 800/367-9221. 50 rms, 4 suites. A/C TV TEL

$ Rates: Summer, $50–$80 double; $95 suite. Off-season, $35–$45 double; $55 suite. AE, DISC, MC, V.

On what is considered the family-oriented beach area, all but one of the Sugar Sands buildings are gulf-side. The swimming pool is nestled in a pretty courtyard, complete with gazebo. There's also a picnic area and grills to barbecue hot dogs or steaks. The motel's beach service will make arrangements for boat rentals and water-sports gear. Volleyball and shuffleboard courts are on the premises. A grocery store and a gift shop are across the street. Three 18-hole golf courses are a short drive away. The family-operated motel likes to say that Sugar Sands is the sweetest deal on Panama City Beach.

ACCOMMODATIONS NEARBY

Budget

GULFVIEW INN, 21722 W. U.S. 98A (P.O. Box 199), Sunnyside, FL 32461. Tel. 904/234-6051. 5 rms (all with bath), 1 suite, 1 apt. A/C TV TEL

$ Rates (including special continental breakfast): April 1–Labor Day, $50 single; $60 double; $75 suite; $650 per week apt. Monthly rates available off-season. No credit cards.

This is probably the only bed-and-breakfast in the beach area. Less than five miles west of Panama City Beach, the unusually designed, new two-story beach house is painted Cape Cod blue with cream-colored lattice trim. Guest quarters have private entrances. Hosts Raymond and Linda Nance invite you to enjoy breakfast on the upstairs sun deck, overlooking Gulf of Mexico views. The home-baked breakfast breads and homemade jellies are a treat. Beautiful Sunnyside Beach is just 200 feet across the road, and there are outdoor hot and cold showers to refresh yourself after a wonderful time on the beach.

EL GOVERNOR MOTEL, U.S. 98 (P.O. Box 13325), Mexico Beach, FL 32410. Tel. 904/648-5757. Fax 904/648-5754. 120 rms, suites, and townhouse apts. A/C TV TEL

$ Rates: Apr–Sept, $70 double; $120 suite; $115–$125 apt. Oct–Mar, $55 double; $100 suite; $110 apt. AE, MC, V.

Spacious, beachfront rooms, complete with kitchenettes or fully equipped kitchens and private balconies, make for one of the best bargains in the area. The beautiful two- and three-bedroom townhouse apartments are exceptionally nice places to stay. There's a swimming pool and poolside bar on the premises, tiki huts for cook-outs, and a gift shop and store to buy groceries, liquor, etc. The Top of the Gulf Restaurant & Lounge, owned by the motel, is nearby at U.S. 98 at 42nd St. (tel. 648-5275), open from 4 to 10pm.

Across from the motel, El Governor Campground (tel. 904/648-5432) features tent and camper sites, full hookups, showers, picnic tables, laundry facilities, and free beach access.

CAMPING

The **St. Andrews State Recreation Area,** at the end of County Road 392 (tel. 904/233-5140), is beautifully located on the Gulf of Mexico. Encompassing 1,063 acres of dune-studded beach (some sand dunes are amazingly high), woodland, and marshes, the park offers one of the most outstanding camping sites anywhere. Park entrance fees are $3.25 for everyone in the car. From March to September, camping fees are $15 a night, only $8 a night from October to February. The park is open year-round from 8am to sunset. For information, write to St. Andrews State Recreation Area, 4415 Thomas Dr., Panama City Beach, FL 32407.

The **Long Beach Camp Inn,** 10496 W. U.S. 98A, Panama City Beach, FL 32407 (tel. 904/234-3584), is right on the gulf and offers almost 200 hookups for $25–$40 per night.

The **Panama City Beach Campground and RV Resort,** 11826 W. U.S. 98, Panama City Beach, FL 32407 (tel. 904/235-1643), has approximately 200 rentals, ranging from $12 to $35 per night. There's also a swimming pool here.

Venture Out at Panama City Beach, 4345 Thomas Dr., Panama City Beach, FL 32407 (tel. 904/234-2247), features more than 725 hookups and two swimming pools; rates are approximately $25 for two people.

There are at least a dozen more camping/RV parks on the beach; a list is available from the **Panama City Beach Visitors' Information Center** (tel. 904/234-3193).

WHERE TO DINE

In most restaurants, just-caught local fish and shellfish predominate on the reasonably priced menus. Most places are very casual, and just about every restaurant features a children's menu.

PANAMA CITY BEACH

Expensive

THE TERRACE COURT, at Marriott's Bay Point Resort, 100 Delwood Beach Rd. Tel. 234-3307.

Cuisine: INTERNATIONAL. **Reservations:** Recommended.

$ Prices: Main courses $14.95–$22.50. AE, DC, DISC, MC, V.

Open: Dinner only, Wed–Thurs 6–9:30pm, Fri–Sat 6–10pm.

Although the Terrace Court is the most expensive Panama City Beach restaurant (men are required to wear jackets), the dining experience is worth the splurge. Overlooking the marina, the handsomely decorated private yacht club glows with romantic candlelight. The chef's seafood specialties include grouper Santa Rosa. For couples celebrating a special occasion, the menu features chateaubriand for two and rack of lamb for two. Sautéed chicken prepared with fresh figs in a subtle madeira wine sauce, and veal scaloppine with champagne sauce are just two of the gourmet offerings. Steaks are grilled to perfection. As you would anticipate, the wine list is extensive. Breads and pastries are baked in the restaurant's special kitchen. Irresistible desserts are highlighted by the praline mousse and the fresh fruit crêpes.

The less formal Fiddler's Green restaurant, overlooking the Grand Lagoon, is also on the Marriott's Bay Point Resort premises.

Moderate

ANGELO'S STEAK PIT, 9527 Front Beach Rd. Tel. 324-2531.

Cuisine: STEAK. **Reservations:** Not accepted.

$ Prices: Main courses $8–$20. AE, MC, V.

Open: Mar 15–May and Sept, dinner only, Mon–Sat 5–10pm; June–Aug, dinner only, daily 4:30–10pm. **Closed:** Oct–Mar 15.

You can't miss enormous super-steer Big Gus standing guard at the entrance, a landmark since 1957. Family-owned Angelo's is one of the area's most popular restaurants. Western decor provides the colorful ambience for enjoying hickory-pit barbecued steaks, beef, and chicken—hearty portions for cowboys and cowgirls. A big baked potato accompanies your order, plus a choice of crispy salad or savory soup. Next door, the Longhorn Saloon is the place to belly up to the bar or relax at a table with your favorite western brew.

BOAR'S HEAD RESTAURANT, 17290 Front Beach Rd. Tel. 234-2239.

Cuisine: AMERICAN. **Reservations:** Recommended.

$ Prices: Main courses $12–$20. AE, DC, DISC, MC, V.

Open: Dinner only, daily 5–10pm. **Closed:** Mon off-season.

This interesting restaurant and tavern with its impressively beamed ceiling and stone walls provides a very different type of atmosphere from the usual beach-area dining spots. The Merry Oulde England decor, complete with fireplaces, presents a classy setting for a delightful dinner. Among the specialties are prime rib of beef with Yorkshire pudding (of course), coquilles St.-Jacques, charcoal-grilled grouper, angel-hair pasta combined with shellfish and a delicate sauce, oysters baked with artichoke hearts, shrimp Grecian style, and tender baby back pork ribs. The wine list has won awards. A favorite for more than 15 years, the Boar's Head is also notable for luscious desserts, such as macadamia nut cheesecake.

CAPTAIN ANDERSON'S RESTAURANT, 5551 N. Lagoon Dr. Tel. 234-2225.

Cuisine: SEAFOOD. **Reservations:** Not accepted.

$ Prices: Main courses $10–$29. AE, DC, DISC, MC, V.

Open: Jan 16–Oct, dinner only, Mon–Sat 4–10pm (or later). **Closed:** Nov–Jan 15.

Overlooking the Grand Lagoon, this famous restaurant attracts early diners so that they can watch the fishing fleet unload the catch-of-the-day. For more than 25 years, Captain Anderson's has been so popular that sometimes there's almost a two-hour wait for a table during the peak summer vacation time. But here's a tip: Just relax with a drink in the air-conditioned lounge or admire the views from the open-air top deck. One of Florida's top 10 restaurants and one of the nation's top 50, Captain Anderson's is noted for charcoal-grilled local fish, crabmeat-stuffed jumbo shrimp, a heaped-high seafood platter, and much more. The Greek salad accompanying dinners is a favorite (and there's also a choice of potato and home-baked rolls). Especially for the first-time visitor, Captain Anderson's is a "must."

CAPTAIN DAVIS DOCKSIDE RESTAURANT, 5550 N. Lagoon Dr. Tel. 234-3608.

Cuisine: SEAFOOD/STEAK. **Reservations:** Recommended.

$ Prices: $8–$20. MC, V.

Open: Dinner only, Thurs–Tues 4–10pm.
Overlooking the Grand Lagoon and the deep-sea-fishing fleet, Captain Davis's features deliciously prepared seafood as well as grilled steaks and juicy prime rib of beef. A family atmosphere prevails and the kids are not the only ones who like to watch the waterfront action from the window walls. Cocktails are served, too. Families like to dine here either before or after Captain Davis's glass-bottom boat sails out on the daily dolphin-feeding cruise (5:15–6:30pm). The restaurant was renovated after the great March storm of 1993.

JP'S RESTAURANT AND BAR, 617 Azalea St. at the west end of Middle Beach Rd. Tel. 234-7147.
Cuisine: SEAFOOD/STEAK. **Reservations:** Recommended.
$ Prices: Main courses $8.95–$18.95. AE, DISC, MC, V.
Open: Mon–Sat 11am–10pm (bar open later, especially on weekends).
There's a new Gulf-view second-story deck at this lively, casual restaurant. The chef specializes in sautéed and Cajun blackened fresh fish and seafood. Thick, tender steaks are hand cut and charbroiled to your preference. Homemade pastas are delicious, especially the fettucini combined with shellfish. Savory soups and chowders are homestyle, great for lunch with a salad and homebaked bread. Delicious pies are featured on the dessert list. JP's has another restaurant and bar in Panama City, just a half mile east of the Hathaway Bridge on 4701 W. Hwy. 98 (tel. 769-3711). Both locations spotlight live entertainment during summer.

Budget

BILLY'S, 3000 Thomas Dr. Tel. 235-2349.
Cuisine: SEAFOOD. **Reservations:** Not accepted.
$ Prices: Main courses $5–$10. MC, V.
Open: Daily 11am–9pm.
A favorite for many years, family-owned Billy's has one of the most popular oyster bars in town. You can get the bivalves raw, steamed, or baked. Lobster, crayfish, clams, and local fish are prepared to your preference. And if you just want a big juicy hamburger or a heaped-high sandwich, Billy's will accommodate you. Beer and wine are served. Billy's is still very proud of the complimentary review they received in the *New York Times* a few years ago.

CAJUN INN, 477 Beckrich Rd. Tel. 235-9987.
Cuisine: LOUISIANA CAJUN. **Reservations:** Not accepted.
$ Prices: Main courses $5–$11. MC, V.
Open: Daily 11am–9:30pm.
Near the Edgewater Beach Resort, this restaurant brings the Big Easy to the gulf. If you liked the chicory café au lait and beignets in New Orleans, you'll love this strong, special coffee and the light-as-a-feather pastries in the Cajun Inn. Louisiana's famous Cajun chef Paul Prudhomme would approve of the restaurant's Bayou Têche jambalaya and the seafood étouffée. Overstuffed hoagie sandwiches, known as po'boys and muffalettas, are also specialties at the restaurant. The "Big Mamou" burger with lots of grilled onions could make you forget the Big Mac.

MARINER RESTAURANT, 9104 Front Beach Rd. Tel. 234-8450.
Cuisine: AMERICAN. **Reservations:** Not accepted.
$ Prices: Breakfast/lunch buffet under $5; dinner buffet $15. AE, DISC, MC, V.
Open: Breakfast buffet Wed and Fri–Sun 8–10:30am; lunch buffet daily 11am–2:30pm; dinner buffet daily 5–10pm. **Closed:** Holidays.
Although the restaurant's claims to fame are the bountiful buffets, there's also a full-service menu, featuring steaks, seafood, poultry, and more. The home-style breakfast buffet includes fresh fruits, scrambled eggs, smoked sausage, bacon, steak nuggets, grits, hash browns, spicy rice, French toast, biscuits and gravy, and assorted pastries. At lunch, the buffet selections feature salads, seafoods, a variety of meats, breads, desserts, and much more. The Super Seafood Buffet at night is a delicious array of steamed and fried shrimp, broiled and fried grouper, Alaskan snow crab legs, fried clam strips, stuffed crab, Cajun crayfish, fried oysters, six vegetables, an

enormous salad bar, two types of meat, desserts—and an ice-cream bar. Children up to 12 years old pay half price; tots under 3 years old are free. If you want window seating to enjoy the view, call before 5pm.

The Mariner Restaurant West is at 15519 Front Beach Rd. (tel. 234-7773), across from Gulf World.

MONTEGO BAY SEAFOOD HOUSE & OYSTER BAR, Thomas Dr. Tel. 234-8686.

Cuisine: SEAFOOD. **Reservations:** Not required.
$ Prices: Main courses $4–$11. MC, V.
Open: Daily 11am–10pm.

Especially popular with families, the Montego Bay restaurants are locally famous for the $3.95 lunch specials and the dinnertime Captain's Catch Seafood Platter, stacked high with a variety of favorites and served with a savory hot gumbo and a crisp salad, all for $9.95. Paneled walls and tropical greenery are part of the pleasant atmosphere.

There are four other locations: Edgewater (tel. 233-6033), West End (tel. 233-2900), Middle Beach (tel. 235-3585), and downtown (tel. 872-0098).

PANAMA CITY

Moderate

HARBOUR HOUSE, in the Ramada Inn–Panama City, 3001A W. 10th St. Tel. 785-9053.

Cuisine: STEAK/SEAFOOD. **Reservations:** Not accepted.
$ Prices: Main courses $10–$18. AE, DC, DISC, MC, V.
Open: Daily 6am–10pm. **Closed:** Christmas Day.

On the historic St. Andrews Bay waterfront, the Harbour House is a long-time favorite. Regular patrons begin with breakfast and return for the sumptuous buffet lunch and popular early-bird dinner. During the usual dining hours, the menu highlights prime rib, charcoal-broiled steaks, and delicious gulf seafood. Usually, live entertainment is scheduled in the cocktail lounge, a friendly rendezvous. With great views, good food, and reasonable prices, the Harbour House has a winning combination.

Budget

AEGEAN RESTAURANT, 1031 W. 15th St. Tel. 769-5514.

Cuisine: GREEK/AMERICAN. **Reservations:** Recommended.
$ Prices: Main courses $5–$12. MC, V.
Open: Lunch Mon–Sat 11am–2:30pm; dinner Mon–Sat 5–9pm. **Closed:** Major holidays.

As friendly and casual as a taverna on a Greek island, the Aegean features Greek-style seafood, prepared with sautéed onions, green peppers, tomatoes, feta cheese, and subtle seasonings. Or you can have your fresh fish filet simply broiled. Mousakka is a favorite, prepared with seasoned ground beef, eggplant, and the traditional delicate sauce. Wonderful breads and desserts are homemade. At lunch, the hearty Greek salad is a meal in itself. There's a children's menu, too. And cocktails are served in this hospitable restaurant.

SPECIALTY DINING

The Treasure Ship, Treasure Island Marina, 3605 S. Thomas Dr. (tel. 234-8881), overlooks the Grand Lagoon with sensational sunsets. Even if you have only a drink on board, the Treasure Ship must be seen to be believed with its amazing two acres of ship space. The Treasure Ship claims to be the world's largest land-based Spanish galleon, an authentic replica of the three-masted sailing ships, which carried priceless loot from the New World to Spain in the 16th and 17th centuries. You can get anything from an ice cream cone to peel-it-yourself shrimp to a sophisticated dinner on board in the various dining rooms and eateries. The Wharf Galley deli restaurant, for example, serves a nice lunch and sandwiches at reasonable prices from 11am to

5pm. Seafood specialties are highlighted in the Treasure Ship Dining Room, open Monday through Saturday from 4 to 10pm; dinner prices range from about $12 to $20. In the Captain's Quarters, live entertainment and dancing continue until the wee hours. Two cocktail lounges, games rooms, and boutiques are on board. Admission is free to the Treasure Ship, and take along your camera. It's a good idea to call ahead for current dining hours in the various restaurants, as at least two require reservations.

For a mini–Love Boat experience, **Captain Anderson's dinner-dance cruises** are romantic, available from Memorial Day through Labor Day. Boarding is at Capt. Anderson's Marina at 5550 N. Lagoon Dr. (tel. 234-5940) at 6:30pm Monday through Saturday. Steak dinners are usually featured, but check ahead. The ticket costs about $25 per adult, about $20 for children under 12 (tips are included). Live entertainment is always on the program. The triple-decker fun boat is so popular that it's a good idea to make reservations well in advance (weeks ahead, should you be celebrating a special occasion and want to make sure you can be accommodated).

SHOPPING

Alvin's Island Tropical Department Store, at Panama City Beach (tel. 234-8897), specializes in beachwear, T-shirts, and a hot selection of swimsuits. Joke gifts and souvenirs can be outrageous. Alvin's Island is also an attraction, with tropical birds plus daily feedings of sharks and alligators. It has to be seen to be believed.

The **Shoppes at Edgewater,** on Front Beach Road at Edgewater Beach Road, Panama City Beach (tel. 234-7915), features men's and women's designer fashions, colorful resortwear, swimwear, gifts, and more. There's a 24-hour grocery here too, and an Eckerd Pharmacy. For film buffs, the mini-mall has six theater screens.

The **Panama City Mall,** just east of the Hathaway Bridge in Panama City (tel. 785-9587), boasts more than 80 specialty stores and department stores such as Sears and JC Penney. Centered around a fountain-splashed garden courtyard, the mall has everything from books to beach supplies, restaurants, movie theater, and two family-style games rooms. It's open Monday through Saturday from 9:30am to 9pm and on Sunday from 12:30 to 6pm.

Manufacturer's Outlet Center, 105 W. 23rd St., Panama City, claims that you can save up to 70% in such designer factory stores as London Fog, Capezio, Van Heusen, Corning Revere, Publishers Warehouse, Aileen Sportswear, and many more. Open seven days a week.

EVENING ENTERTAINMENT

THE PERFORMING ARTS

Yes, there *is* life after the beach. The **Marina Civic Center,** 8 Harrison Dr., Panama City (tel. 763-4696), features a variety of performances throughout the year. Among the presentations last season were the musicals *The Buddy Holly Story* and *The Music Man,* performed by Broadway touring companies. The amazing magician David Copperfield was also in the spotlight, just one of the celebrities who stage special shows here.

The **Kaleidoscope Theater,** 201 E. 24th St., Panama City (tel. 265-3226), is a community theater that offers presentations of dramas, musicals, and comedies.

THE CLUB & MUSIC SCENE

At least three romantic lounges are in the limelight for both live entertainment and dancing: **The Treasure Ship,** 3605 S. Thomas Dr. (tel. 234-8881); **The Boar's Head,** 17290 W. U.S. 98A (tel. 234-6628); and **Captain Anderson's,** dockside at the Grand Lagoon (tel. 234-2225). Call in advance for current schedules (hours vary according to season).

Good old-fashioned country comedy and country music are featured in the **Ocean Opry Show,** 8400 W. U.S. 98 (tel. 234-5464), starring the Rader family and a cast of 20. This is Panama City Beach's answer to Nashville and to Branson, Missouri. The air-conditioned theater, seating 1,000, is open year-round. Nashville country music stars are usually spotlighted October through March; June through

August, there's a show nightly at 7:30pm, but the schedule varies in other months. Popcorn, hot dogs, and soft drinks are sold at the theater. The two-hour show costs about $12 for adults, about $6 for children (prices vary for special shows). The box office opens at 9am and reservations are necessary for the Opry Show, which is a long-time favorite.

For more than 20 years, **The Breakers,** 12627 Front Beach Rd. (tel. 234-6060), has been a popular night owls' roost. The nightclub recently was rebuilt with special tiered seating for better viewing of the terrific show (and the gulf). It's the place to dance all night, see a special show, and enjoy food and drinks.

Sharky's, at the Mark II Best Western, 15201 Front Beach Rd. (tel. 235-2420), is also a favorite for dancing and live entertainment (good food here, too).

The young late-night crowd likes open-air **Schooners,** 5121 Gulf Dr. (tel. 235-9074). Just-shucked oysters and grilled seafood are menu favorites. Every table has a gulf view, perfect for relaxing with a drink. There is good music for dancing, and Schooners describes itself as "the last local beach club, somewhere near the east end of Thomas Drive, right on the beach."

Spinnaker, 8795 Thomas Dr. (tel. 234-7882), is another action-filled restaurant-club, staying open until 4am. The band plays on and on for dancing and listening.

THE BAR SCENE

Especially in summer, almost every hotel and restaurant in Panama City Beach offers entertainment. For peace and quiet with cocktails, relax in the **Magnolia Court** in Marriott's Bay Point Resort, 100 Delwood Beach Rd. (tel. 234-3307). Soft piano music creates a romantic atmosphere in this southern-style lounge. Dancing and live entertainment are often scheduled in all the restaurants and lounges at Marriott's Bay Point, so check ahead.

The Ramada Beachside Resort, 12907 Beach Front Rd. (tel. 234-1700), offers a fifth-floor panoramic view in the **Crow's Nest Lounge,** a popular rendezvous for drinks and music (until 4am on weekends in summer).

Pineapple Willie's Lounge, 9900 S. Thomas Dr. (tel. 235-0928), is open from 11am until the wee hours, serving Australian-style fun food, such as koala wings, and spotlighting live entertainment. Dancing includes everything from "Waltzing Matilda" to reggae.

EASY EXCURSIONS

★ Three miles north of Marianna, **Florida Caverns State Park,** 3345 Caverns Rd., Marianna, FL 32446 (tel. 904/482-9598), is well worth the approximately one-hour drive from Panama City. Sprawling underground for at least 10 acres, the intriguing series of caves is resplendent with stalagmites, limestone stalactites, columns, and veritable "draperies" sculpted in stone by Mother Nature. Centuries-old formations decorate the ornate wedding-cake appearance of the Wedding Chapel—where many a wedding ceremony has taken place—and the Cathedral Room. The guided ranger tours (about $4) include half a mile of illuminated passageways through this underground fantasy. Spelunkers may request further exploration. During the Seminole Wars, many caves were hideaways for the Native Americans, seeking refuge from banishment to the West. Best months to visit the caves are May through February (March and April could be wet).

Since the park encompasses 10,000 acres, take some time to observe nature along the hiking trails. Or you can swim, fish, or go horseback riding (stables are available). Take along a picnic lunch. Overnight camping is also permitted. Should you want to paddle a canoe along scenic waters, the 50-mile Chipola River Canoe Trail begins in the park (this is part of the state's excellent canoe trail system). The park is open daily from 8am to sunset; admission is $3.25 for everybody in the car.

Falling Waters State Recreation Area, Rte. 5, Box 660, Chipley, FL 32428 (tel. 904/638-6130), three miles south of Chipley, off Fla. 77A, a pleasant drive east of Marianna, is named for the impressive 67-foot waterfall. The Falling Waters Sink is a 100-foot-deep, 20-foot-wide round pit into which the water drops 67 feet to the bottom; so far, nobody has figured out the water's final destination. Certainly this is one of the state's most notable geological attractions. Open daily from 8am to sunset, the park offers picnicking, hiking, swimming, and overnight camping.

A short drive east of Panama City, the scene changes considerably at **Dead Lakes State Recreation Area,** P.O. Box 989, Wewahitchka, FL 32465 (tel. 904/639-2702), one mile north of Wewahitchka off Fla. 71, near the Appalachicola River and the Apalachicola National Forest. The park is named for a geological phenomenon said to have been formed when sand bars, created by the Apalachicola River's currents, blocked the Chipola River. The resulting high water evidently killed thousands of trees, hence the name "Dead Lakes." Along the nature trails, pines, magnolia, and cypress trees border wetlands where you can spot some alligators and other critters. Fishing, boating, and overnight camping are available.

South of Panama City, along scenic coastal U.S. 98, it's a lovely drive to Port St. Joe. Beautifully situated on St. Josephs Bay, Port St. Joe, then St. Joseph, was the site of Florida's first constitutional convention and the capital of the Florida Territory. The Constitution Convention State Museum is located in **St. Joseph Peninsula State Park,** and has exhibits that date back to the 1830s. Dioramas tell the story of St. Joseph and its later devastation by hurricanes and yellow fever.

The 2,516-acre park offers boating, fishing, swimming, picnicking, and overnight camping. There are snack bars here, too. A super-wide dune-studded beach extends for at least 20 miles, with the gulf on the west and the bay on the eastern side. Surf-tipped beach and green pine woodland combine for a scenic collage. The park is great for birdwatching; sightings of more than 209 species are on record. In summer, guided nature walks are offered and campfire nature programs are scheduled. For information, contact St. Joseph Peninsula State Park, Star Rte. 1, Box 200, Port St. Joe, FL 32456 (tel. 904/277-1327).

4. TALLAHASSEE

200 miles W of Jacksonville, 200 miles E of Pensacola, 250 miles NW of Orlando

GETTING THERE By Plane The **Tallahassee Regional Airport** (tel. 904/891-7800), 10 miles from downtown, is served by American Eagle, Comair, Delta, USAir, and various charter flights.

By Train Amtrak began service to Tallahassee in 1993 with the *Sunset Limited* from Los Angeles through New Orleans, Jacksonville, and Orlando to Miami. Other new Panhandle stops are Chipley, Crestview, and Pensacola. Tallahassee's railroad station is at 918 Railroad Ave. For information or reservations, call Amtrak (tel. toll free 800/TEL-TRAK).

By Bus The Greyhound bus depot is at 112 W. Tennessee St. (tel. 904/222-4240).

By Car Four major highways lead to Tallahassee. From the east and west, highway access is Interstate 10 and U.S. 90. From the north and south it's U.S. 27 and U.S. 319.

Since 1824, Tallahassee has been the capital of Florida, selected for its midpoint location between St. Augustine and Pensacola, which were the state's major cities at that time. An Old South atmosphere prevails in this slow-paced area, dotted with lovingly restored antebellum mansions, plantations, beautiful lakes and streams, towering pine and cypress trees, richly scented magnolias, and colorful azaleas. In true southern style, tradition and history are highly important, and many of the city's historic homes and buildings have been preserved, especially along Park Avenue and Calhoun Street.

Nestled in the first foothills of the Appalachian Mountains, the environs of Tallahassee offer many picturesque drives. Majestic live oaks draped with Spanish moss canopy the old secondary roads—veritable green "tunnels" are formed by the leafy branches of trees joining together from both sides of the road. There are five official Canopy Roads (see "What to See and Do," below), lined with historic plantations, ancient Native American settlement sites and mounds, gorgeous gardens, quiet parks with picnic areas, and lakes for bass fishing. The blissful solitude is a rare experience in today's lifestyle. Indeed, Tallahassee is an unusual city, combining modernity with the elegance of a bygone era.

ORIENTATION

INFORMATION For free assistance with area accommodations, or self-guided tour maps, an attractions list, suggestions on where to dine, and a variety of helpful brochures, visit the **Tallahassee Area Convention and Visitors Information Bureau,** New Capitol Building, West Plaza Level, North Duval Street, Tallahassee, FL 32302 (tel. 904/681-9200, or toll free 800/628-2866). The center is open Monday through Friday from 8am to 5pm, and on Saturday, Sunday, and holidays from 8:30am to 4:30pm.

The **Visitor Information Center,** 200 W. College Ave. (P.O. Box 1369), Tallahassee, FL 32302 is part of the helpful Tallahassee Area Convention and Visitors Bureau, and uses the same telephone numbers.

Another good information source is the **Tallahassee Chamber of Commerce,** located in the historic home The Columns, 100 N. Duval St., Tallahassee, FL 32302 (tel. 904/224-8116), open Monday through Friday from 9am to 5pm.

Check the Tallahassee telephone directory's informative blue pages, (included there are football stadium seating diagrams for Florida A&M University and Florida State University).

CITY LAYOUT It's easy to get around Tallahassee's downtown area, accessible via U.S. 27 (also known as the Apalachee Parkway), leading to the Capitol Complex. U.S. 90, which is also Tennessee Street, leads to Florida State University. U.S. 98 joins Fla. 61, becoming Monroe Street and traversing the center of the city. Calhoun Street runs parallel to Monroe, and you will find the historic districts here within a compact area. For further sightseeing, Tallahassee is within a 30-minute drive south to the Gulf of Mexico, via U.S. 319 to U.S. 98.

GETTING AROUND

BY PUBLIC TRANSPORTATION The bright-red **Old Town Trolley** (tel. 574-5200), complete with authentic cable-car gong, harks back to the days when a simple mule-drawn rail trolley connected Tallahassee and St. Marks. Among the Town Trolley's stops are Adams Street Commons, the Old and New Capitol buildings, the Museum of Florida History, and the Union Bank—and it's free.

Taltran is the city bus service (tel. 574-5200—same as the Old Town Trolley), the fare is 75¢. For route information and schedules, give them a call.

BY TAXI & LIMO One of the taxi services is **Yellow Cab** (tel. 222-3070). **Capital Limousine** (tel. 574-4350) provides both limousine and taxi service.

BY RENTAL CAR Major car-rental agencies are at the airport and downtown offices. Among the many to contact are **Alamo** (tel. toll free 800/327-9633), **Avis** (tel. toll free 800/331-1212), **Budget** (tel. toll free 800/527-0700), **Dollar** (tel. toll free 800/800-4000), and **Hertz** (tel. toll free 800/654-3131). Best to reserve in advance, especially when the legislature is in session.

FAST FACTS

Area Code The telephone area code is 904.

Doctor The Patients First Medical Center (tel. 562-2010, 878-8843, or 668-3380) offers three locations, open Monday through Friday from 8am to 8pm and on Saturday and Sunday from 9am to 6pm. Or contact the Tallahassee Community Hospital, 2626 Capital Medical Blvd. (tel. 656-5000, or toll free 800/882-4556); or the Tallahassee Memorial Regional Medical Center, Magnolia and Miccosukee (tel. 681-1155).

Drug Stores and Convenience Stores Tallahassee Sing Stores are open 24 hours, seven days a week, at 14 different locations. Two convenient ones are at 2849 Apalachee Pkwy. (tel. 877-3053) and 3510 Thomasville Rd. (tel. 893-6616). In addition to convenience items, they sell gasoline. Albertson's super market, 1925 N. Monroe St. (tel. 386-7135), usually open around the clock, has a pharmacy, open from 9am to 9pm.

Emergencies Dial 911.

24-Hour Restaurant Popi's, in the Days Inn Downtown, 722 Apalachee Pkwy. (tel. 224-8181), and the Waffle House, at the Hampton Inn, 3210 N. Monroe St. (tel. 562-4300), never close.

Weather Call 422-1212.

WHAT TO SEE & DO

ATTRACTIONS

The Capitol Complex

Number one on your must-see Tallahassee list should be the Capitol Complex, dominating the downtown area. The **New Capitol Building,** a $43-million skyscraper, was built in 1977 to replace the Old Capitol, which dates back to 1845. Inside the New Capitol, laws are made for the more than 15 million people in this fastest-growing state. The Chambers of the House and the Senate have public viewing galleries; legislators convene from February to April.

At any time of the year, the highlight is the spectacular view from the 22nd-floor **observatory.** On a clear day you can see the St. Marks Lighthouse and the Tallahassee–St. Marks Historic Railroad Trail (now popular for hiking, biking, and horseback riding). Vistas extend from rolling green hills all the way to the sun-sparkled Gulf of Mexico. Should you plan to drive along the Canopy Roads, take along a map so that you can identify the five routes from the observatory.

The New Capitol is also noteworthy for its interior decor. Located on South Adams Street, it's is open Monday through Friday from 8am to 5pm (closed major holidays). Guided tours (tel. 488-6167) are scheduled Monday through Friday from 9am to noon and on Saturday and Sunday from 1 to 4pm. Weekend visitors must take a guided tour.

The strikingly white **Old Capitol** with its majestic dome is known as "The Pearl of Capitol Hill," and has been restored to its original beauty. An eight-room exhibit entitled "A View from the Capitol," portrays Florida's political history. Turn-of-the-century furnishings, cotton gins, and other artifacts are also of interest. For information, call 487-1902. Admission is free to both the Old and New Capitols.

Facing the Old Capitol are the twin granite towers of the **Vietnam Veterans Memorial,** honoring Florida's Vietnam veterans.

Historic Districts

The **Adams Street Commons,** 200 S. Adams St., is a one-block winding brick and landscaped area, retaining an old-fashioned southern town-square atmosphere. Restored buildings include the Governor's Club, a 1900s Masonic Lodge, and Gallie's Hall. Built in 1874, Gallie's Hall is listed on the National Register of Historic Places and is important to African American history. Florida's first five African American college students received their diplomas here in 1892, after graduating from Florida A&M University. You can take a self-guided historic downtown walking tour. Restaurants, shops, and Gallie Alley are also in the Adams Street Commons. Tour maps are free at the Pensacola Convention and Visitor Information Center, 1401 East Gregory St. (tel. 434-1234).

The **Calhoun Street Historical District,** affectionately called "Gold Dust Street" in the old days, was once a status-symbol address. The elaborate homes, built by prominent citizens, date back to the era between 1830 and 1880. Among the most outstanding are the Bloxham House, the Elizabeth Cobb House, the Bowen House, the Towle House, and the Randall-Lewis House. For tour information, call the Historic Preservation Board (tel. 488-3901).

The **Park Avenue Historic District** is a lovely promenade of beautiful trees, gardens, and outstanding old mansions. Park Avenue was originally named 200 Foot

Street and then McCarty Street. However, it was renamed Park Avenue to satisfy a snobbish society matron's desire for a very sophisticated address to be imprinted on her son's wedding invitations.

Among the historic homes open to the public are the Knott House (see "Historic Sites and Buildings," below), the Murphy House, the Shine-Chittenden House, and the Wood House. For information about visiting these elaborate homes, call the Historic Preservation Board (tel. 488-3901).

The **Walker Library,** 209 E. Park Ave. (tel. 224-5012), was Florida's first library. The handsomely furnished library dates back to 1884. Admission is free, and it's open Monday through Friday from 9am to 1pm.

Historic Sites and Buildings

BROKAW-MCDOUGALL HOUSE, 329 N. Meridian. Tel. 488-3901.

Constructed in 1856, this magnificent house with six impressive Corinthian columns is considered a superb example of Italianate and Classical Revival architecture. The landscaping is gorgeous and was designed when the house was built. The Historic Preservation Board is housed here, a perfect setting. It's also available for special meetings and tours.

Admission: Free.

Open: Mon–Fri 8am–5pm.

THE COLUMNS, 100 N. Duval St. Tel. 224-8116.

The city's oldest surviving building, this beautiful mansion was the private residence of banker William "Money" Williams and his family of 10 children. The white-columned brick home was built in the 1830s on land purchased for $5 by Mr. Williams, who was president of the Bank of Florida. According to legend, there's a nickel embedded in every brick. The Columns now houses the Tallahassee Chamber of Commerce.

Admission: Free.

Open: Mon–Fri 9am–5pm.

FIRST PRESBYTERIAN CHURCH, 110 N. Adams St. Tel. 222-4504.

Built in 1838, this is Tallahassee's oldest church. During the Seminole raids of 1838 and 1839, local residents sought refuge beneath the church steeple. The church is also important to African American history: Slaves were always welcome to worship here as independent members, with or without their "master's" consent.

FLORIDA GOVERNOR'S MANSION, 700 N. Adams St. Tel. 488-4661.

Florida's First Family lives in this lovely Georgian-style mansion, enhanced by a portico patterned after Andrew Jackson's columned antebellum home, the Hermitage. Giant magnolia trees shade the landscaped lawns. Visitors are welcome to tour five of the rooms, furnished with 18th- and 19th-century antiques, and displaying such collectibles as the holloware from the battleship U.S.S. *Florida.* Paintings by Renoir, Modigliani, and other famous artists adorn the walls. A collection of books by Florida authors is also displayed.

Adjacent to the Governor's Mansion, the plantation home The Grove was home to Ellen Call Long, known as "The Tallahassee Girl," the first child born after Tallahassee was settled.

Admission: Free.

Open: Sept–May, Mon, Wed, and Fri 10am–noon. **Closed:** June–Aug. Check ahead for current schedule, as it varies.

KNOTT HOUSE MUSEUM ["THE HOUSE THAT RHYMES"], 301 E. Park Ave. Tel. 488-3901.

Adorned by a columned portico, this stately 1843 mansion is furnished with Victorian elegance and boasts the nation's largest collection of 19th-century gilt-framed mirrors. The most unusual feature is the eccentric rhymes written by Mrs. Knott and attached by satin ribbons to tables, chairs, and lamps. Her poems comment upon 19th-century women's issues, plus the social, economic, and political events of the era. The house is in the Park Avenue Historic District, and is listed in the National Register of Historic Places.

Admission (includes one-hour tour): $3 adults, $1.50 children under 18.
Open: Wed–Sat 10am–4pm, but call ahead for current schedule.

OLD CITY CEMETERY AND EPISCOPAL CEMETERY, Park Ave. and Bronough St. Tel. 545-5842.

These adjacent cemeteries contain the graves of Prince Achille Murat, Napoleon's nephew, and Princess Catherine Murat, his wife and George Washington's grand-niece. Also buried here are two governors and numerous Confederate and Union soldiers who died at the Battle of Natural Bridge during the Civil War. The cemeteries are important to African American history since a number of slaves and the first African American Florida A&M graduates are among those buried here.

UNION BANK, 295 Apalachee Pkwy. Tel. 487-3803.

The Union Bank with its columned portico is Florida's oldest surviving bank, built in 1841. The building is an excellent example of architectural restoration. Once a "planter's bank" for cotton plantation owners and then a Freedman's Bank for emancipated slaves, the bank now presents the history of territorial-period banking. The bank is only one block south of the Capitol Complex, directly across from the Old Capitol.

Admission: Free.
Open: Tues–Fri 10am–1pm, Sat–Sun 1–4pm.

Museums

BLACK ARCHIVES RESEARCH CENTER AND MUSEUM, on the Florida A&M University campus, between Gaines St. and Orange Ave., off Monroe St. Tel. 599-3020.

Housed in the columned library built by Andrew Carnegie, this fascinating research center and museum displays one of the nation's most extensive collections of African American artifacts as well as such treasures as the 500-piece Ethiopian cross collection. Most important, however, the archives contain one of the world's largest collections on African American history. It's interesting to listen to tapes of elderly people reminiscing about the past. There are also tapes of gospel music. The Florida Agricultural and Mechanical University (FAMU) was founded in 1887, primarily as a black institution. Today it is acclaimed for its business, engineering, and pharmacy schools.

Admission: Free. A visitor parking permit is available at the security office.
Open: Mon–Fri 9am–4pm. **Closed:** Major holidays.

FOSTER TANNER FINE ARTS GALLERY, Florida A&M University. Tel. 599-3334.

The focus in this gallery is on works by African American artists, with a wide variety of paintings, sculptures, and more. Exhibits change monthly, with local, national and international artists in the limelight.

Admission: Free.
Open: Mon–Fri 9am–5pm.

FLORIDA STATE UNIVERSITY GALLERY AND MUSEUM, 250 Fine Arts Building, at Copeland and Call Sts. on the FSU Campus. Tel. 644-6836.

A permanent art collection features 16th-century Dutch paintings, 20th-century American paintings, Japanese prints, pre-Columbian artifacts, and much more. Every three or four weeks, touring exhibits are displayed.

Admission: Free.
Open: Mon–Fri 9am–5pm.

LEMOYNE ART FOUNDATION, 125 N. Gadsden St. Tel. 222-8800 or 224-2714.

A restored 1852 antebellum home is the lovely setting for this collection of art. The building (known as the George Meginniss House) is listed on the National Register of Historic Places. The art foundation is named in honor of Jacques LeMoyne, a member of a French expedition to Florida in 1564. LeMonyne, commissioned to depict the natives' dwellings and map the sea coast, was the first artist known to have visited North America.

Exhibits include permanent displays by local artists, traveling exhibits, sculpture, pottery, photography—everything from traditional to avant-garde. The gardens with an old-fashioned gazebo are spectacular during the Christmas holiday season. During the year, the schedule also includes programs of classical music combined with visual arts. Check in advance for the current schedule.

Admission: Free.

Open: Tues–Sat 1–5pm, Sun 2–5pm.

MUSEUM OF FLORIDA HISTORY, in the R. A. Gray Building, 500 S. Bronough St. Tel. 488-1484 or 488-1673.

Herman, a skeletal prehistoric mastodon, which originally weighed in at five tons (when he prowled around Wakulla Springs), is the museum mascot. Ancient artifacts from Native American tribes are exhibited, plus such relics from Florida's exciting past as the treasures of 16th- and 17th-century sunken Spanish galleons. Climb aboard a reconstructed steamboat (sorry, Herman cannot be a passenger) to recapture the good old days. Inquire about guided tours and educational programs. There's an interesting museum gift shop, too.

Admission: Free.

Open: Mon–Fri 9am–4:30pm, Sat 10am–4:30pm, Sun noon–4:30pm. **Closed:** Holidays.

TALLAHASSEE MUSEUM OF HISTORY AND NATURAL SCIENCES (formerly the Tallahassee Junior Museum), 3945 Museum Dr. Tel. 576-1636.

From tots to adults, there's something of interest here for all ages. Along a winding trail through a 55-acre natural woodland habitat, the wildlife includes alligators, red wolves, Florida panthers, and a variety of other animals. Farm animals roam around the re-creation of an 1880s farm. There are special programs demonstrating butter churning, syrup making, blacksmithing, sheep shearing, spinning, weaving, and quilt making. Other exhibits feature science and history displays, a restored one-room schoolhouse, a gristmill, an old church, and a railroad caboose. Bellevue, the restored plantation home of Princess Murat, was moved here in 1967 (100 years after her death) and is listed on the National Register of Historic Places. Special events are always scheduled, from arts and crafts shows to wildflower walks. Picnic facilities, a snack bar, and a gift shop are on the premises.

Admission: $5 adults, $4 senior citizens, $3 children 3–15, free for children under 3.

Open: Tues–Sat 9am–5pm, Sun 12:30–5pm.

Archeological Sites

DE SOTO ARCHEOLOGICAL AND HISTORICAL SITE, 1022 DeSoto Park Dr. Tel. 922-6007 or 925-6216.

During the winter of 1539, Spanish conquistador Hernándo de Soto, his troops and friars, set up an encampment here before continuing their ill-fated search for gold. The friars celebrated the first Christmas mass in North America with de Soto and his entourage. An archeologist searching for Spanish mission ruins in 1986 discovered the de Soto encampment site. Rare copper coins, armor fragments, and a fossilized pig's jaw were unearthed. In the 1930s, when former Gov. John Martin built his English hunting lodge–style home at the site, he had no idea de Soto had camped here. His home is planned as a museum for exhibiting the artifacts. In December a colorful pageant-drama re-enacting the first Christmas is presented, beginning at 9am and continuing to 8pm. Check ahead for the exact date and program schedule. The admission is free.

Because the archeological site is being excavated and the home is under restoration, only the Christmas pageant is open to the public at present.

LAKE JACKSON MOUNDS STATE ARCHEOLOGICAL SITE, 1313 Crowder Rd. Tel. 562-0042.

Artifacts discovered on this 18-acre excavation have revealed that tribes settled on the shores of Lake Jackson centuries ago. (Could they have been lured by the lake's abundant bass? This is still one of the nation's best bass fishing spots.) Evidently this Southeastern Ceremonial Complex flourished around A.D. 1200. You'll see six earth temple mounds and a burial mound. Part of the village and plaza area and two of the largest mounds are within the state site. The largest mound is 36 feet high with a base that measures 278 by 312 feet. If you'd like a guided tour, call the above number.

Admission: Free.

Open: Daily 8am–sundown.

SAN LUIS ARCHEOLOGICAL AND HISTORIC SITE, 2020 Mission Rd. Tel. 487-3711.

Located high on a hilltop west of downtown Tallahassee is this important Apalachee tribal settlement. A Spanish Franciscan mission was set up here in 1656. San Luis de Talimali, as it was called, soon included a tribal council house, a Catholic church, a Spanish fort, and many homes. In 1704 the inhabitants burned the town rather than submit to British invaders. The missions were destroyed and the Apalachees dispersed. Exhibits along the trails depict the San Luis story. Visitors are welcome to stroll around the area and to observe state archeologists uncover artifacts (in the spring season).

Admission: Free.

Open: Mon–Fri 9am–4:30pm, Sat 10am–4:30pm, Sun noon–4:30pm. Public tours Sun at 2pm (check the schedule to be sure there are no changes); group tours by appointment only. **Closed:** Thanksgiving and Christmas.

NEARBY ATTRACTIONS

The Canopy Roads

Graced by canopies of Spanish moss–draped oak trees and colorful flowers, the St. Augustine, Miccousukee, Meridian, Old Bainbridge, and Centerville Roads are the five official old canopy roads. Driving is slow on these winding, two-lane country roads, some of which are canopied for as much as 20 miles. Take along a picnic lunch; there are few places to eat in this tranquil setting. Here are highlights of each road.

The cotton harvest was piled on wagons, drawn by six-mule teams and transported along the **Centerville Road** to St. Marks to be loaded onto schooners. Plantation owners planted the majestic live oaks around 1800 to shade the mule teams. Stop at Bradley's Country Store for the area's best homemade sausage.

The only straight road in the group, the **Meridian Road** was built in 1825 according to a federal survey. However, the mule-drawn wagons made deep ruts and the packed clay on both sides created walls, now covered by lichen. From here, you can drive to Maclay Gardens or stop for bass fishing at Lake Jackson or at the picnic grounds on nearby Miller's Landing Road.

Originally, the **Miccousukee Road** was an early Native American trail. Driving north on Miccousukee, you reach the plantation town of Thomasville, Georgia, which has many beautiful antebellum homes as well as the All American Rose Test Gardens where 2,000 roses bloom from April to November.

The **Old Bainbridge Road** is considered the most scenic of the canopy roads. It leads to the Lake Jackson Indian Mounds State Archeological Site. Continuing on, about 15 miles north of Tallahassee you arrive at Havana, an old-fashioned typical southern town, known for good restaurants and antiques shops.

Other than the scenic beauty, and the pleasure of leisurely driving, there's not much to see or do along the **St. Augustine Road.** However, the road's history goes back to early Native American tribes and the subsequent Spanish invasion. Missions were established here in the mid-16th century by Spain's Franciscan friars, and according to records, about 15,000 Native Americans in this area were converted to Catholicism. Unfortunately, not one of the area's 20 missions remains—by the end of the 17th century they had all been destroyed in the battles between Spain and England.

For information and maps, contact the **Tallahassee Area Visitor Information Center,** New Capitol Building, West Plaza Level, North Duval Street (tel. 681-9200), open Monday through Friday from 8am to 5pm, and on Saturday, Sunday, and holidays from 8:30am to 4:30pm.

State Parks and Gardens

LAKE TALQUIN STATE RECREATION AREA, off Fla. 20 on Vause Rd. 20 miles west of Tallahassee. Tel. 922-6007.

When the Jackson Bluff Dam was constructed on the Ochlockonee River to produce hydroelectric power in the late 1920s, Lake Talquin was formed. Evidently, the fish love it, as records have been made in catching largemouth bass, speckled perch, and shellcracker. Along the nature trail, you may sight osprey, bald eagles, wild turkey, and deer. In addition to fishing, boating and picnicking are permitted. Thick pine forests, deep ravines, and rolling hills add to the park's scenic beauty.

Admission: $3.25 per car.

Open: Daily 8am–sunset.

MACLAY STATE GARDENS, 3540 Thomasville Rd. (U.S. 319). Tel. 487-4566.

New York financier Alfred B. Maclay and his wife, Louise, began planting this floral wonderland in 1923. The mansion was their winter home. After her husband's death in 1944, Louise Maclay continued his dream of an ornamental garden to delight the public. In 1953 the land was bequeathed to the state of Florida. The more than 300 acres of flowers feature at least 200 varieties; 28 acres are devoted exclusively to azaleas and camellias. The beautifully restored home contains a camellia information center. The surrounding park offers nature trails, canoe rentals, boating, picnicking, swimming, and fishing.

The gardens are located six miles north of the Florida State Capitol Complex. The high blooming season is from January to April 10; the floral peak is mid- to late March.

Admission: Park and garden, May–Dec, $3.25 per car load; Jan–Apr, $3 adults, $1.50 children under 12.

Open: Park, daily 8am–sunset; gardens, daily 9am–5pm; Maclay House, Jan–Apr, daily 9am–5pm.

Historic Sites

NATURAL BRIDGE BATTLEFIELD STATE HISTORIC SITE, National Bridge Rd., about 15 miles southeast of Tallahassee. Tel. 922-6007.

The park and monument commemorate the site where Confederate troops battled Union forces along the natural bridge spanning the St. Marks River. Union troops had planned to take Tallahassee by surprise during the last weeks of the Civil War. They were surprised by the Confederate troops and volunteers, who repelled the attackers and saved Tallahassee from capture. Picnic facilities are offered in the park. Every February, a costumed, reenactment of the battle takes place (check ahead for exact schedule).

Admission: Free.

Open: Daily 8am–sunset.

SAN MARCOS DE APALACHEE STATE HISTORIC SITE, St. Marks. Tel. 925-6216.

In 1528, Spanish conquistador Panfilo de Narvaez arrived here with a couple of hundred men after marching overland from the Tampa Bay area. At the strategic juncture of the Wakulla and St. Marks Rivers, de Narvaez and his men built and launched the New World's first ships, in which they planned to sail back to Spain. Spanish conquistador Hernándo de Soto and his men arrived in 1539 after following de Narvaez's overland route, and then marched onward. In 1679 the Spanish governor of Florida began construction of Florida's first fort which, three years later, was burned and looted by pirates. A second wooden fort was built in 1718 by Capt. José Primo de Ribera. Finally, in 1739 construction of a stone fort was begun, but before it was completed it was captured by the British in 1763. Spain regained the fort in 1787 but lost it in 1800 to Billy Bowlegs and his independent Creek Nation of 400 Indians. After five weeks, a Spanish flotilla of nine ships again regained the fort. General Andrew Jackson also invaded the fort for a short time, creating a diplomatic crisis between Great Britain and the young United States. However, after Florida was ceded to the United States in 1821, the fort eventually was presented to the Territory of Florida. During the Civil War, the Confederates renamed it Fort Ward.

The visitor center is a veritable museum, housing historic exhibits and artifacts excavated nearby. In fact, the center rests on the foundation of the federal marine hospital, built in 1857 utilizing stones from the Spanish fort. Hike along the Fort Wall Trail to observe the historic ruins and an old military cemetery. The park offers picnic facilities and a special viewing platform to observe Mother Nature's beauty.

For information, contact San Marcos de Apalachee State Historic Site, P.O. Box 27, St. Marks, FL 32355. The historic site and park are about a 25-mile drive south of Tallahassee.

Admission: Park, free; museum, $1 adults, free for children under 6.

Open: Thurs–Mon 9am–5pm. **Closed:** New Year's Day, Thanksgiving, and Christmas Day.

ST. MARKS LIGHTHOUSE AND NATIONAL WILDLIFE REFUGE, just south of San Marcos de Apalachee Historic Site, St. Marks. Tel. 925-6121.

Bordering Ochlockonee Bay and the Gulf of Mexico, the wildlife refuge encompasses more than 60,000 acres of very varied terrain. Stop first at the **visitor center** for an orientation and to view the bird, waterfowl, and wildlife habitat displays. The refuge contains more species of birds than anywhere else in Florida except the Everglades. During the autumn, flocks of Canadian geese are among the many species of waterfowl migrating here.

The visitor center has maps and an informative brochure; a booklet is available outlining a self-guiding, seven-mile driving tour of Lighthouse Road. Special stops are marked for observing plants, trees, wildflowers, wildlife, and birds. You can also bike along Lighthouse Road. For observing native plants and trees, stroll along the half-mile Plum Orchard Pond Trail behind the visitor center. The Mounds Nature Trail, about a mile long, crosses over a Native American mound dating back to A.D. 500, and ends at the still-functioning **St. Marks Lighthouse,** a National Historic Site, built in 1831. Picnic facilities are located next to Mounds Trail and at Otter Lake, where fishing is permitted. At the Lighthouse, the shore is popular for crabbing. From autumn through spring, hunting is permitted for resident game, but check ahead for regulations and exact dates.

Admission: $3.25 per car, $1 walk-ins and bicyclists.

Open: Park, daily sunrise–sunset; visitor center, Mon–Fri 8:15am–4:15pm, Sat–Sun 10am–5pm.

TALLAHASSEE–ST. MARKS HISTORIC RAILROAD STATE TRAIL, entrance on Fla. 363, just south of Tallahassee. Tel. 922-6007.

Constructed with the financial assistance of wealthy Panhandle cotton plantation owners and merchants, this was Florida's oldest railroad, functioning from 1837 to 1984. Cotton and other products were transported to the St. Marks port for shipment to other cities. After the tracks were removed in recent years, the historic trail was improved along 16 miles for joggers, hikers, bicyclists, and horseback riders. A paved parking lot is at the entrance.

SPECIAL EVENTS

Springtime Tallahassee, celebrated from mid-March to mid-April, is the main local event, a four-week jubilee featuring parades, festivals, arts and crafts, sports competitions, and much more. The Natural Bridge Battlefield Re-Enactment takes place in March, as does the competitive Bike Tour of Tallahassee; and the Summer Swamp Stomp is in July. In September comes the Native American Heritage Festival, and in October the Greek Food Festival and the 11-day North Florida Fair. Winter

Farm Days are celebrated in December, and the Winter Festival and Celebration of Lights marks the holiday season. The First Christmas Reenactment commemorates first Christmas Mass at Spanish Conquistador Hernando de Soto's encampment on the De Soto Archeological and Historical Site. For information about these and other area celebrations call the Tallahassee Area Convention and Visitors Bureau at 904/681-9200 or toll free 800/628-2866.

SPORTS & RECREATION

The football frenzy scores a touchdown when games are scheduled at **Florida State University** with their Seminoles team and at **Florida A&M University** when the Rattlers are cheered on by their high-stepping, world-famous Marching 100 Band. Both stadiums are packed to the rafters with the most enthusiastic fans in the football world. Movie buffs might like to know that Hollywood star Burt Reynolds was a great halfback at Florida State University, when he was a student there in 1957; he's very proud of his alma mater. FSU also features a terrific **Flying High Circus** (tel. 644-4874), with annual shows (free) in April. Both FSU and FAMU have a seasonal schedule of sports events, including basketball, baseball, tennis, and track. Call for schedules and tickets (tel. 644-1830 for FSU, 599-3230 for FAMU).

Tallahassee features at least eight **city parks,** offering a variety of recreational facilities, including A. J. Henry Park (tel. 891-3905); Dorothy B. Oven Park (tel. 891-3915); Forest Meadows (tel. 891-3920); Hilaman Park (tel. 891-3935); Lafayette Park (tel. 891-3946); Lake Ella (tel. 891-3866); Myers Park (tel. 891-3866); and Tom Brown Park (tel. 891-3966).

On the 100-acre **Seminole Reservation,** 3226 Flastacowo Rd. (tel. 644-5730), the multipurpose recreational facility includes sailing, canoeing, and waterskiing on Lake Bradford (rentals available), a volleyball court, a playground for the kids, and a picnic area.

BICYCLING **Cycleogical Bicycle Rentals & Touring,** 4780 Woodville Hwy., at the entrance of the 16-mile Tallahassee–St. Marks Historic Railroad Trail, offers a variety of rental bikes, off-road tours, cycling supplies, and in-line skate rentals (tel. 656-0001). Approximate bike-rental rates are $9 for two hours, $14 for four hours, and various rates for three to five bikes' rental for families and groups. Guide maps and refreshments are also on hand. Cycleogical is open daily; check on the special weekend hours.

BOATING & CANOEING Countless scenic waterways are enjoyable for boating and canoeing. Among the beautiful river recreation areas with boat and canoe rentals are **Three Rivers State Recreation Area** (tel. 482-9006), **Lake Bradford** on the Seminole Reservation (tel. 644-5730), the **Ochlockonee River** in Ochlockonee River State Park (tel. 962-2771), and the **St. Marks River** in the St. Marks National Wildlife Refuge (tel. 925-6121). All are within a 30- to 50-mile drive from Tallahassee.

FISHING Bass abound in Tallahassee area lakes. Record-size catches have been made in **Lake Jackson** and **Lake Talquin.** For a Tallahassee area guide to fishing camps and lodges, contact the **Tallahassee Visitor Information Center** (tel. 681-9200, or toll free 800/628-2866).

In the nearby gulf, deep-sea-fishing excursions are available for grouper, snapper, and king mackerel. Check with the marinas at **Shell Point, Alligator Point,** and **Panacea** (also known as "The Blue Crab Capital of the World).

GOLF & TENNIS Play golf and tennis at outstanding **Hilaman Park,** 2731 Blair Stone Rd., where the Hilaman Park Municipal Golf Course features 18 holes (par 72), a driving range, racquetball, squash courts, and a swimming pool. Rental equipment is at the club, and there's a restaurant, too (tel. 891-3935 for information and fees). The park also includes Jake Gaither Municipal Golf Course, at Bragg and Pasco Streets, with a 9-hole par-35 fairway and a pro shop (tel. 891-3942). Open daily from 7:30am to 7:30pm, the park also has tennis courts, which are lighted for night play. Tennis courts are also available at Lafayette Park, Tom Brown Park, Myers Park and Forest Meadows (the latter two have lighted courts).

The leading golf course is at **Killearn Country Club and Inn** (tel. 893-2186, or toll free 800/476-4101), home of the $750,000 PGA Centel Classic. Moss-draped oaks enhance the beautiful 27-hole championship course, which is for guests only. Killearn also offers four lighted hard tennis courts and four soft courts, and racquetball and handball courts, for guests only.

HIKING In addition to the 16-mile **Tallahassee–St. Marks Historical Trail** and numerous trails in state parks, the **Florida National Scenic Trail** meanders 110 miles through the Apalachicola National Forest and St. Marks National Wildlife Refuge. On the trail you will encounter sink holes, the Bradwell Bay Wilderness Area, Confederate salt evaporation ponds, and more. Eventually, the trail will be extended to span 1,300 miles across Florida. For information, call 488-7326.

HUNTING In the 1800s, wealthy plantation owners invited friends on hunting expeditions. The custom is maintained at **Myrtlewood Plantation,** P.O. Box 32, Thomasville, GA 31799 (tel. 912/228-6232), about 35 miles from Tallahassee. Special arrangements can be made in season to hunt ducks, white-tail deer, pheasant, and quail. The 3,300-acre plantation also offers attractive, comfortable accommodations and meals. Largemouth bass and bluegill bream are abundant in the four fishing lakes. For plantation deer hunts arranged by **Big Pine Hunting,** call 912/226-2541 or toll free 800/841-0001. For the plantation quail hunt, contact **Southern Style Hunting Preserve,** P.O. Box 199, Thomasville, GA 31799 (tel. 912/228-0987). Myrtlewood also has a championship sporting clays marksmanship course (tel. 912/228-0987).

At **St. Marks National Wildlife Refuge,** hunting is permitted only with such primitive weapons as cross-bows and muzzle-loading guns. For information, call 925-6121.

The **Apalachicola National Forest** is one of only two areas in the state where the American black bear may be hunted. For information, call 926-3561, 681-7265, or 670-8644.

WHERE TO STAY

Hotels are often completely booked when the legislature is in session (usually between February and May) and during the very popular universities' football games on weekends from September to December. Rates go up, too, so reserve well in advance or you may have to stay far from the city. Just about every hotel offers excellent meeting/convention facilities.

DOWNTOWN

Expensive

GOVERNORS INN, on Adams Street Commons, 209 S. Adams St., Tallahassee, FL 32301. Tel. 904/681-6855, or toll free 800/342-7717. Fax 904/222-3105. 32 rms, 8 suites. A/C MINIBAR TV TEL

$ **Rates** (including continental breakfast and evening cocktails): $119–$135 single or double; $160–$220 suites. AE, DC, DISC, MC, V.

One of the most elegant hotels anywhere, the award-winning Governors Inn was opened in 1984 by the son of Gov. Lawton Chiles (at the time, he was a senator and then became governor). Actually, the hotel was named in honor of Andrew Jackson, Florida's first military governor, known for his appreciation of the good life.

On a brick-paved historic street, just half a block from the Old Capitol, the richly furnished hotel was a livery stable long ago and part of the building's original architecture has been preserved, including the impressive beams. Guest rooms are distinctive with four-poster beds, black oak writing desks, rock maple armoires, and antique accoutrements. Suites, each one named for a Florida governor, are sumptuous, some with whirlpool bath or loft bedrooms with wood-burning fireplace. Among the amenities are comfy robes.

Dining/Entertainment: The pine-paneled Florida Room is the perfect retreat for enjoying the complimentary continental breakfast elegantly presented with a silver service, fine china, sparkling crystal, and lovely linens. Early-evening complimentary cocktails are also served in this handsome room. For lunch or dinner, the award-winning Golden Pheasant restaurant pleases the most discriminating gourmet.

Services: Valet parking, airline reservations, European turn-down service, limousine transportation within a five-mile radius, your choice of newspaper delivered daily to your door, same-day laundry service, shoeshines, room service, remote control TV with Movie Channel and ESPN, airport transportation, health club privileges.

SHERATON TALLAHASSEE HOTEL, 101 S. Adams St., Tallahassee, FL 32301. Tel. 904/224-5000, or toll free 800/325-3535. Fax 904/222-9216. 246 rms, 7 suites. A/C TV TEL

$ Rates: $70–$130 single; $90–$180 double; $175–$300 suites. Also special Concierge Level rooms and suites. AE, DC, DISC, MC, V.

A favorite with politicians and lobbyists, this outstanding hotel is usually booked solid during legislative sessions. Not only is the hotel only a block from the Capitol Building but it's also notable for spacious, attractive guest rooms and beautiful public rooms. And, of course, the rooms are stocked with all the amenities, Sheraton style.

Dining/Entertainment: Café in the Court, with its skylight ceiling and lush greenery, is a favorite rendezvous for the power breakfast, lunch, or dinner. When the political celebrities aren't here, they're in the Club Palm Beach library lounge.

Services: Room service, health club privileges, same-day laundry service, shoeshines, airport transportation, free or pay TV movies.

Facilities: Swimming pool (outdoor), beauty/barber salon, gift shop, garage, convention facilities.

Moderate

HOLIDAY INN UNIVERSITY CENTER DOWNTOWN, 316 W. Tennessee St., Tallahassee, FL 32301. Tel. 904/222-8000, or toll free 800/465-4329. 174 rms. A/C TV TEL

$ Rates: $60–$70 double. Corporate and government rates available. AE, DC, MC, V.

Distinguished by its cylindrical 12-story design, this is one of two Holiday Inns in Tallahassee. At this location, you are convenient to FAMU, FSU, the State Capitol, and the Governor's Mansion. All guest rooms overlook the city panorama or the rolling hills. If you stay in the higher-priced rooms on the concierge level, there's a private rooftop lounge. Especially during the football season, the Reflections cocktail lounge is very lively and so is the Windows restaurant (good steaks and seafood). The airport shuttle is complimentary.

RADISSON HOTEL, 415 N. Monroe St., Tallahassee, FL 32301. Tel. 904/224-6000, or toll free 800/333-3333. 116 rms, 8 suites. A/C TV TEL

$ Rates: $83–$125 double. AE, DC, DISC, MC, V.

About half a mile from the Capitol, the Radisson features cheerfully decorated guest rooms, a fitness facility with sauna and whirlpool, and facilities for the business executive. Complimentary airport transportation is provided. The pleasant Plantation Dining Room is open daily for breakfast, lunch, and dinner. The cocktail lounge is a friendly rendezvous.

Bed-and-Breakfast

RIEDEL HOUSE BED & BREAKFAST, 1412 Fairway Dr., Tallahassee, FL 32301. Tel. 904/222-8569. 2 rms.

$ Rates (including breakfast): $65 double. No credit cards.

Surrounded by majestic live oaks, pines, magnolias, and flowers, this white-brick Federal-style, two-story home was built in 1937 for the Cary D. Landis family (he was a former Florida attorney general). Talented artist and art teacher Carolyn Riedel, the gracious innkeeper, now owns the elegant house. From the beautiful foyer, the spiral staircase leads to the upstairs art gallery and bedrooms. Period furniture and antiques adorn the spacious guest rooms. The delicious continental breakfast is served in the lovely dining room overlooking terraced gardens. Located in the prestigious country club area, the Riedel House is just minutes away from Florida State University and the Capitol, and within walking distance of tennis courts and a golf course.

NORTH OF DOWNTOWN

Moderate

CABOT LODGE EAST, 1653 Raymond Diehl Rd., Tallahassee, FL 32308. Tel. 904/386-7500, or toll free 800/255-6343. 135 rms, 1 suite. A/C TV TEL

$ Rates (including continental breakfast buffet): $50–$83 double. AE, DC, DISC, MC, V.

One of the best bargains among the city's hotels, the Cabot Lodge East offers guests a complimentary continental breakfast buffet (fruit, yogurt, bagels, croissants, and more) from 6:30 to 10am daily in the lobby, as well as complimentary cocktails served daily from 5:30 to 7:30pm. The highest rates are for the 29 rooms and the one suite on the Executive Floor, complete with microwaves, refrigerators, and Jacuzzis. A fax, copier, and PC hookup are also on this floor. A swimming pool is on the premises of this hospitable five-story hotel, located less than five miles from the Capitol.

CABOT LODGE NORTH, 2735 N. Monroe St., Tallahassee, FL 32303. Tel. 904/386-8880, or toll free 800/223-1964. 160 rms. A/C TV TEL

$ Rates (including continental breakfast): $50–$75 double. AE, DC, DISC, MC, V.

This is the sibling hotel of the newer Cabot Lodge East, a very neat complex of five two-story buildings where you can park at your room location. A complimentary continental breakfast and early evening complimentary cocktails are served in the main building. Executives may use the copier and fax facilities. And there's a swimming pool here, too. This is also a hotel bargain, located about 3½ miles from the Capitol.

KILLEARN COUNTRY CLUB AND INN, 100 Tyron Circle, Tallahassee, FL 32308. Tel. 904/893-2186. Fax 904/668-7637. 39 rms, 4 suites. A/C TV TEL

$ Rates: $55–$75 single; $65–$90 double; $65 basic suite; Golf and vacation packages available. AE, DC, DISC, MC, V.

In the Lodge, newly renovated luxurious rooms include two double beds, a sitting area, and dressing rooms; some accommodations have a wet bar. Each room is individually decorated with attractive furnishings and spacious balconies overlooking the woodland-bordered golf course. Suites are flexible. To a basic large room with fridge, wet bar, and murphy bed, one to four bedrooms can be attached.

This is Tallahassee's leading golf course, staffed with PGA professionals and home of the $750,000 PGA Centel Classic. For tennis buffs, the resort offers four lighted hard courts and four soft courts; racquetball and handball courts are on the premises. The swimming pool is Olympic size. For keeping fit, there's a Hydra-Gym exercise facility plus miles of surrounding roads for jogging. Moderate prices prevail in the classy, beamed-ceiling Oak View restaurant. Live entertainment is spotlighted in the nightclub. This is one of the area's best resort bargains.

RAMADA INN TALLAHASSEE, 2900 N. Monroe St., Tallahassee, FL 32303. Tel. 904/386-1027, or toll free 800/228-2828. Fax 904/422-1025. 200 rms. A/C TV TEL

$ Rates: $65–$75 double. Two children under 18 stay free with existing bed space in parents' room. Special family rates available. AE, DC, DISC, MC, V.

On 13 landscaped acres, the Ramada Inn is located less than four miles from the Capitol. An outdoor swimming pool and jogging trail help keep guests fit. The tropically decorated lobby bar is relaxing for a drink. Breakfast, lunch, and dinner are served in the new Monroe Street Grill. Dooley's Australian Nightclub is the fun place at night. For the executive, there's a business center and conference rooms (facilities for handling meetings up to 500 people).

Budget

HAMPTON INN, 3210 N. Monroe St., Tallahassee, FL 32303. Tel. 904/562-4300, or toll free 800/HAMPTON. 92 rms. A/C TV TEL

$ Rates (including continental breakfast): $45–$55 double. Children stay free in parents' room. MC, V.

New in 1993, this attractive inn offers free local telephone calls. The inn is approximately a five-mile drive from the Capitol. Just next door, the Waffle House is open 24 hours, serving breakfast, lunch, dinner, and snacks (pecan waffles are a favorite).

SHONEY'S INN, 2801 N. Monroe St., Tallahassee, FL 32303. Tel. 904/386-8286, or toll free 800/222-2222. 112 rms, 26 townhouse suites. A/C TV TEL

$ Rates (including continental breakfast): $40–$88 double.

Formerly Las Casas Motor Inn, Shoney's has taken over this attractive, Spanish-style inn and completely remodeled the accommodations. The townhouse suites, especially, are a bargain. Guest rooms overlook pretty views of green lawns and moss-draped trees. A heated swimming pool is on the premises, also a Cantina cocktail lounge (restaurants are conveniently close by). Hospitality begins upon arrival, when a complimentary welcome cocktail is served. Complimentary airport shuttle service is offered from 7am to 10pm.

TALLAHASSEE MOTOR HOTEL, 1630 N. Monroe St., Tallahassee, FL 32303. Tel. 904/224-6183, or toll free 800/251-1962. 92 rms. A/C TV TEL

$ Rates: $32–$50 double. AE, DC, MC, V.

A landmark for more than 60 years, this hospitable hotel, complete with swimming pool, has a lovely setting on five acres of lawn, shaded by Spanish moss–draped oak trees.

Very small but pretty Lake Ella is across the way. For a water view, request the newer and more spacious accommodations overlooking the lake. Lorenzo's Lake Ella Café (tel. 681-3622) is next door at 1600 N. Monroe St., open from 6am to 10pm for breakfast, lunch, and dinner. Delicious pastas, veal specialties, traditional Italian dishes, and pizzas are very reasonably priced. There's outdoor seating too, and a children's menu. Beer and wine are served. The toll-free telephone number connects to the Master Host reservations system so don't think that you have the wrong number when you call for reservations.

ON APALACHEE PARKWAY

Moderate

HOLIDAY INN PARKWAY, 1302 Apalachee Pkwy., Tallahassee, FL 32301. Tel. 904/877-3141, or toll free 800/465-4329. Fax 904/877-3141. 167 rms. A/C TV TEL

$ Rates: $45–$55 single; $50–$60 double. AE, DC, DISC, MC, V.

Pleasant guest rooms encircle landscaped lawns, a courtyard, and a swimming pool. About a mile from the downtown area, the inn also provides complimentary greens fees at a nearby course and complimentary passes to a nearby fitness facility. On site, the International House of Pancakes is open 24 hours with a varied menu. There's a cocktail lounge, too. Meeting facilities are available.

Budget

BEST WESTERN PRIDE INN, 2016 Apalachee Pkwy., Tallahassee, FL 32301. Tel. 904/656-6312, or toll free 800/827-7390. Fax 904/942-4312. 78 rms, 30 suites. A/C TV TEL

$ Rates (including continental breakfast): $39–$60 double or suite. AE, DC, DISC, MC, V.

The friendly inn is within walking distance of the Governor's Square Mall for shopping and dining, and about two miles from the Capitol. Every evening, complimentary wine and cheese are offered. A small swimming pool and sunning patio are on the premises. Health club privileges can be arranged. There's a Shoney's Restaurant just steps away at 2014 Apalachee Pkwy. (tel. 878-3979), serving budget-priced breakfasts, lunches, and dinners, with specials for children and seniors.

STERLING INN, 2020 Apalachee Pkwy., Tallahassee, FL 32301. Tel. 904/877-4437, or toll free 800/253-4787. Fax 904/878-9964. 100 rms, 13 suites. A/C TV TEL

$ Rates (including continental breakfast): $40 double; $60–$120 suite. AE, DC, MC, V.

Reminiscent of an English country inn, there's more than just a touch of class here. Spacious, attractive guest rooms are tastefully furnished with sofa, wing chairs, king-size beds, desks, and night tables. The complimentary continental breakfast (delicious pastries!) is served in the cozy parlor, off the marble-lined lobby. Because the inn has no restaurant, cocktail lounge, or meeting rooms, the rates are lower than would be expected for such a pleasant place.

CAMPING

Bell's Trailer Park, 6401 W. Tennessee St. (U.S. 90) (tel. 904/575-5006), offers 62 RV and tent campsites (there's a lake for fishing, too). Rates are approximately $15 per night, and weekly rates are available.

At the **Seminole Reservation,** along Lake Bradford, 3226 Flastacowo Rd. (tel. 904/644-6892 or 644-5730), two primitive cabins can accommodate up to 20 people. There's also tent camping. Plenty of recreational opportunities are here.

The **Tallahassee East KOA Kampground** (tel. 904/997-3890), about 20 miles east of Tallahassee, offers rustic camping under 100-year-old oak trees as well as 39 RV sites with full hookups and two furnished cabins with air conditioning/heat and electricity. The park has a swimming pool, fishing pond, playground, games room, general store, and shower/bathroom facilities.

The **Tallahassee RV Park,** 6504 Mahan Dr. (tel. 904/878-7641), features 66 RV campsites with full hookups in a scenic setting of rolling hills.

Camping is also permitted in several state recreation areas (see "What to See and Do," above).

WHERE TO DINE

DOWNTOWN

Expensive

ANDREW'S 2ND ACT, 228 S. Adams St. Tel. 222-2759.

Cuisine: AMERICAN/INTERNATIONAL. **Reservations:** Recommended.

$ Prices: Main courses $15–$30. AE, MC, V.

Open: Lunch Mon–Fri 11:30am–1:30pm; dinner Mon–Thurs 6–10pm, Fri–Sat 6–11pm, Sun 6–9:30pm.

A consistent award winner, Andrew's 2nd Act is Tallahassee's premier restaurant, the dining rendezvous of gourmets, politicians, and lobbyists. In the labyrinth of intimate subterranean dining rooms, the old-world ambience is enhanced by stucco walls, paintings, and tiles. Tables are set with pretty linens, flowers, and candles. The tremendous wine cellar is notable for an amazing variety of wines; there's also a private wine-cellar room which diners may request. Favorites at lunch are stacked-high deli sandwiches, pastas, and seafood crêpes. Dinner specialties are superbly prepared, from puff pastry filled with escargots to succulent rack of lamb Dijon. Steaks, chops, veal, poultry, and seafood are always listed on the menu. Tableside cooking features steak Diane, expertly tossed Caesar salad, and flaming bananas Foster. Andrew's 2nd Act has won so much applause that the two encores (in the same building) are Andrew's Upstairs and Andrew's Adams St. Café (see below).

Moderate

CHEZ PIERRE, 115 N. Adams St. Tel. 222-0936.

Cuisine: FRENCH. **Reservations:** Recommended.

$ Prices: Main courses $5–$15. MC, V.
Open: Lunch Mon–Sat 11:30am–2:30pm; dinner Wed–Sat 5:30–9:30pm. Pastry shop, Mon–Sat 10am–4pm.

In this chic restaurant, you become an instant Francophile. Provincial French specialties are highlighted, such as pâtés, garlic-buttered escargots, onion soup, salade niçoise, croque monsieur sandwiches, just-baked croissants, and crusty French bread. Seafood lovers recommend crêpes fruits-de-mer, two light-as-a-feather crêpes filled with scallops, shrimp, and fish in a luscious lobster sauce. Roast duck and veal dishes are featured. French table wines are very moderately priced, and california house wines are also served. For dessert, the pastry tray, brought to your table, is an array of irresistible delights from Chez Pierre's pastry shop. And the delicious cheeses can also be purchased from their deli-case. Chez Pierre has a new wine and espresso bar.

Budget

ANDREW'S ADAMS STREET CAFE, 228 S. Adams St. Tel. 222-3444.
Cuisine: DELI. **Reservations:** Not accepted.
$ Prices: Main courses $3–$8. AE, MC, V.
Open: Lunch only, Mon–Fri 11:30am–2:30pm.

Enjoy dining on a high-backed banquette amid a decor of green plants, brass, and paneled wood walls. From the cafeteria-style selection, there's a delicious array of soups, salads, and sandwiches galore. The outdoor café area is directly on the Adams Street Commons, delightful in warm weather.

ANDREW'S UPSTAIRS, A BAR AND GRILLE, 228 S. Adams St. Tel. 222-3446.
Cuisine: NEW AMERICAN. **Reservations:** Recommended.
$ Prices: Main courses $6–$12. AE, DC, MC, V.
Open: Lunch Mon–Fri 11:30am–2pm; champagne brunch Sun 10:30am–2pm.

Another in the trio of Andrew Reiss's famous Tallahassee restaurants, Andrew's Upstairs is especially popular with business executives who prefer a quick but extra-special lunch. Steaks, chicken, and seafood from the mesquite grill are big favorites. The hot and cold all-you-can-eat buffet is perfect for those in a rush. Blue Plate Specials are featured daily. The varied menu also lists pastas, salads, and pizzas. From the dining room, there's a nice view of the Capitol Complex. The Sunday brunch is a veritable "groaning board." Monday through Friday, the happy hour brings in the happy crowds for discounted cocktails and the complimentary hors d'oeuvres.

NORTH OF DOWNTOWN

Expensive

ANTHONY'S, 1950 Thomasville Rd. Tel. 224-1447.
Cuisine: ITALIAN. **Reservations:** Recommended.
$ Prices: Main courses $14–$28. AE, MC, V.
Open: Dinner only, Mon–Thurs 5–10pm, Fri–Sat 5:30–10:30pm, Sun 5:30–9pm.

In this attractive downstairs dining room, locals come to see and be seen; therefore, sometimes there's a wait for a table. Among the specialties are pesce venezia, spinach fettuccine tossed in a wine-mushroom sauce with scallops, crabmeat, and fish. Chicken piccata and chicken San Marino are favorites. Of course, a thick, juicy steak is always popular with beefeaters. The wine list features nicely priced choices from Italy and the United States. The dessert menu is highlighted by espresso pie.

Moderate

ANNELLA'S, 1400 Village Square Blvd. Tel. 668-1961.
Cuisine: AMERICAN. **Reservations:** Recommended.
$ Prices: Main courses $7–$12. MC, V.
Open: Lunch Tues–Sat 11:30am–2:30pm; dinner Thurs–Sat 5:30–9:30pm. MC, V.

Food is served with a special flair in this stylish restaurant, noted for steaks, seafood, salads, and marvelous desserts such as French silk pie and peach cobbler with homemade peach ice cream. There's also a full bar, and live entertainment is featured (check ahead for the current schedule).

THE MELTING POT, 1832 N. Monroe St. Tel. 386-7440.

Cuisine: SWISS. **Reservations:** Recommended.
$ Prices: Main courses $10–$15. AE, MC, V.
Open: Dinner only, daily 6–10pm.

A romantic atmosphere prevails, especially for loving couples enjoying the beef or seafood fondue for two (whoever inadvertently drops the food from the fork into the pot is supposed to kiss the person sitting next to them). The bubbling hot cheese fondue is always a favorite, with chunks of French bread for dipping (the same kissing rule applies). Chocoholics love the rich chocolate fondue with strawberries and fresh fruit to dip and "to die for." There's also a full bar here.

MOBY DICK, 6703 Thomasville Rd. Tel. 893-0270.

Cuisine: SEAFOOD. **Reservations:** Recommended.
$ Prices: Main courses $8–$17. MC, V.
Open: Dinner only, Tues–Sat 5–11pm, Sun home-style buffet 11am–2:30pm.

Fried catfish and fried mullet are big favorites, accompanied by southern-style hush puppies. From the Captain's Grill, the charcoal-grilled grouper can be combined with charcoal-grilled chicken or ribeye steak à la surf-and-turf. Cheese grits accompany the entrees (unless you prefer potatoes), and the unlimited salad bar is also complimentary. Beer, wine, and cocktails are served. A special children's menu pleases the little ones.

ROOSTER'S, 2226 N. Monroe St. Tel. 386-8738.

Cuisine: STEAKS. **Reservations:** Recommended.
$ Prices: Main courses $7–$18. AE, MC, V.
Open: Dinner only, Mon–Sat 5pm–2am.

At this country-style hangout, the grilled steaks are something to crow about, especially if you select the 32-ounce sirloin. Grilled chicken is also on the menu, but everything seems to be upstaged by the steaks. Live bands are featured here every evening, attracting a lively crowd of night owls, who like to dance.

SILVER SLIPPER, 531 Scotty's Lane. Tel. 386-9366.

Cuisine: STEAK/SEAFOOD. **Reservations:** Recommended.
$ Prices: Main courses $9–$25. AE, DC, DISC, MC, V.
Open: Dinner only, Mon–Sat 5–11pm.

The oldest family-operated restaurant in Florida, the Silver Slipper has served thick, tender, juicy steaks to Presidents John F. Kennedy, Lyndon Johnson, Jimmy Carter, Ronald Reagan, and George Bush. As you would anticipate, the steaks are the very best Black Angus. From the award-winning menu, you can also select seafood dishes, lamb, veal, and quail; bacon-wrapped big shrimp are another favorite. A favorite of politicians and lobbyists, the Silver Slipper is always packed to the rafters, especially the cocktail lounge, open to midnight Monday through Thursday and to 2am on Friday and Saturday. Should you prefer privacy, curtained booths can be requested, rather than the dining room.

Budget

BARNACLE BILL'S, 1830 N. Monroe St. Tel. 385-8734.

Cuisine: SEAFOOD. **Reservations:** Recommended.
$ Prices: $5–$12. AE, MC, V.
Open: Lunch daily from 11:30am; dinner daily 5:30–11pm.

There's always plenty of action here, especially when everyone is watching sports events on the big screen TV. During summer, it's pleasant to dine outdoors and enjoy smoked fish and grilled or steamed seafood. For munchies, try the buffalo chicken wings. Freshly shucked oysters are served at the oyster bar. Among the menu favorites are the grilled fish platter, the shrimp Alfredo, and the Admiral (an enormous platter of oysters, shrimp, Alaskan crab, fish-of-the-day, fresh corn, potatoes, and salad). Each night a different special is offered. In addition, there are specials for the kids and for senior citizens. At lunch, the Fit & Trim Menu and a variety of sandwiches are popular. From the bar, margaritas are usually priced at only $1. Every weekend, live bands play in the cocktail lounge.

FOOD GLORIOUS FOOD, 1950-C Thomasville Rd. Tel. 224-9974.
Cuisine: AMERICAN/INTERNATIONAL. **Reservations:** Not required.
$ Prices: $4–$7. MC, V.
Open: Mon–Sat 11am–7pm.

Very unusual (but very healthy) sandwiches, salads, and pastas have made this café the talk of the town. Certainly the Tijuana lasagne is different, a tasty dish of layered baked polenta with piquantly spiced chicken, tomato-chile sauce, and a topping of Monterey Jack cheese. What might be called a mile-high carrot-Cheddar-chicken quiche measures at least six inches high. Shrimp and artichoke hearts are served over tricolored pasta for a delicious and colorful dish. The paella salad is a medley of yellow rice, chorizo sausage, and vegetables. Taste buds are tantalized by the grilled flank steak fajita salad with lime-cumin dressing. Desserts feature tempting pastries and cookies. Take-out food can also be ordered.

ON APALACHEE PARKWAY

Moderate

THE WHARF, 4141 Apalachee Pkwy. Tel. 656-2332 or 656-2395.
Cuisine: SEAFOOD. **Reservations:** Recommended.
$ Prices: Main courses $6–$15. AE, MC, V.
Open: Lunch Mon–Fri from 11am; dinner Sun–Thurs to 9pm, Fri–Sat to 10pm.

Notable for southern hospitality and southern home-style cooking, the Wharf is always filled to its 400-seat capacity. Fried fresh mullet and hush puppies are undoubtedly the best ever tasted. Grouper stuffed with deviled crab and sizzled to perfection on a cast-iron skillet would please any gourmet. Other favorites include the savory seafood gumbo and the broiled or fried heaped-high combination seafood platters (served with real southern cheese grits, of course). Sweet tooths are satisfied by homemade desserts, such as key lime pie (only freshly squeezed juice is used) and rich chocolate–peanut butter pie. For the kids, there's a special menu. You may bring your own bottle of preferred spirits (many regular patrons keep their bottles in a special room at the Wharf).

Budget

LUCY HO'S BAMBOO GARDEN, 2814 Apalachee Pkwy. Tel. 878-3366.
Cuisine: CHINESE/JAPANESE. **Reservations:** Not required.
$ Prices: Main courses $8–$12. AE, DC, MC, V.
Open: Mon–Thurs 11:30am–10pm, Fri 11:30am–11pm, Sat 5–11pm, Sun noon–10pm.

This exotic restaurant and cocktail lounge is a popular rendezvous. Authentic Japanese specialties are featured at the Sushi Bar and the Japanese Hibachi Steak and Tatami Room. The luncheon buffet is a great Chinese-style smörgåsbord, highlighting Cantonese and Szechuan cuisines. The classy Lucy Ho, married to a University of Florida professor, runs several very successful restaurants.

Another Lucy Ho's is located at 1700 Halstead Blvd. (tel. 893-4112).

MILL BAKERY, EATERY AND BREWERY, 2329 Apalachee Pkwy. Tel. 565-2867.
Cuisine: AMERICAN. **Reservations:** Not required.
$ Prices: $4–$7. MC, V.
Open: Daily 6am–midnight.

Where else would you find all salads served in edible bowls? Not only is the restaurant ecology-oriented but also very nutrition-conscious. The menu lists detailed information about calories, fat, and sodium for every dish. Sandwiches are prepared with home-baked breads; bran muffins are a specialty. If you don't care about splurging on calories, try the extra-special Mill Reuben sandwich? The veggie lasagne and traditional lasagne are delicious. Pizzas are very popular, including the Mill Max (with everything) and the Veggie Max. Homemade soups, especially the veggie-chili soup, are very tasty. As you can note from the wonderful fragrance at the Mill, pastries are also baked on the premises. From their brewery, try Gator Tail Ale and Seminole Gold beer. Don't miss the great breakfast buffet on weekends.

Another branch of the restaurant is at 2136 N. Monroe St. (tel. 386-2867).

MOM AND DAD'S, 4175 Apalachee Pkwy. Tel. 877-4518.

Cuisine: ITALIAN. **Reservations:** Not accepted.
$ Prices: Main courses $6–$12. AE, DC, MC, V.
Open: Dinner only, Sun and Tues–Thurs 5–10pm, Fri–Sat 6–11pm.

A long-time favorite, this cheerful restaurant is bright with red-and-white-checked tablecloths and the typical accoutrements of an Italian trattoria. Plates are piled high with pastas and sauces, the hearty portions that Mama Mia would serve to her family. Veal dishes are a specialty. And who could resist the homemade Italian desserts?

SPECIALTY DINING

Nearby Dining

NICHOLSON FARMHOUSE RESTAURANT, 15 miles north of Tallahassee, off Fla. 12 in Havana. Tel. 904/539-5931.

Cuisine: AMERICAN. **Reservations:** Recommended.
$ Prices: Main courses $8–$20. MC, V.
Open: Dinner only, Tues–Sat 4–10pm.

Talk to anyone in Tallahassee about where to dine and you will invariably be told, "You must have dinner at Nicholson Farmhouse." Built in 1828 by Dr. Malcolm Nicholson, the farmhouse has been occupied by succeeding generations. In fact, the current owner is the doctor's great-great-grandson. Varying only slightly from the original farmhouse, the hardwood floor, hand-hewn pine steps, front porch columns, and unusual curved ceiling are of architectural interest. The restaurant has been so successful that the outbuildings and two additional turn-of-the-century farmhouses have been converted into extra dining space. Especially aged steaks are a specialty (two ribeyes cut heart-shape are the popular "sweetheart steak"). Grilled chicken breasts, boneless grilled pork chops, shrimp "farmhouse style," and fish-of-the-day are among the deliciously prepared entrees, served in hearty portions with salad, baked potato, and hot freshly baked bread. There's a children's menu, too. You may bring your own bottle of favorite spirits.

Located between Quincy and Havana, the area around the restaurant is great for antique-ing and sightseeing.

Dining on the Coast

On weekends especially, Tallahassee residents enjoy driving to the coast for lunch or dinner in Spring Creek or Panacea. In addition to dining at Spring Creek, you can make arrangements for boating, sailing, and fishing at the Shell Point Marina, or at other nearby marinas.

Two restaurants that are favorites are described below. Other popular restaurants in the area are **Posey's Restaurant** in Panacea (tel. 984-5799), open Tuesday through Sunday, and the **Shell Point Restaurant** in Shell Point (tel. 926-7161), open daily.

ANGELO'S, U.S. 98, at the Panacea Bridge. Tel. 984-5186.

Cuisine: SEAFOOD. **Reservations:** Recommended.
$ Prices: Main courses $8–$22. MC, V.
Open: Dinner only, Mon and Wed–Thurs 4:30–10pm, Fri–Sat 4:30–11pm, Sun noon–10pm.

Built on historic pilings, this picturesque restaurant overlooks scenic Ochlockonee Bay. Family-owned and family-operated for more than 45 years, Angelo's is a consistent award winner and one of Florida's top 100 restaurants. Since Panacea is considered "The Blue Crab Capital of the World," you can expect the freshest and most deliciously prepared crustaceans here. (During the annual Blue Crab Festival, at least 20,000 crab lovers come to Panacea.) Broiled fish filets in a subtle butter-lemon sauce are another favorite in Angelo's. A variety of just-caught fish and shellfish are on the menu; there are also salads and sandwiches.

SPRING CREEK RESTAURANT, Route 2, Spring Creek. Tel. 926-3751.
Cuisine: SEAFOOD. **Reservations:** Not required.
$ Prices: Main courses $10–$20. MC, V.
Open: Wed–Fri 5–10pm, Sat noon–10pm, Sun noon–9pm.

Located in a quiet fishing village near the St. Marks Wildlife Refuge, the Spring Creek restaurant has the right rustic atmosphere, with knotty-pine paneling and a limestone fireplace. The owner's fishing boats bring in the catch of the day, which are prepared home-style. A very light batter enhances the super-size fried shrimp. Scamp, a fish related to grouper, is cut into thick steaks and broiled with lemon butter—delicious! Crisp mixed salad and real southern-style hush puppies accompany the entrees. For dessert, the famous homemade chocolate–peanut butter pie is luscious. To get there, from U.S. 27, drive south on Fla. 363 to U.S. 98. Take U.S. 98 west to Fla. 365 and follow 265 to Spring Creek.

EVENING ENTERTAINMENT

PERFORMING ARTS

The **Tallahassee-Leon County Civic Center,** 505 W. Pensacola St. (tel. 222-0400 or toll free 800/322-3602) features a Broadway play series, a concert series, performances by celebrity pop singers and much more.

Special concerts are presented by the **Tallahassee Symphony Orchestra** at **FSU Ruby Diamond Auditorium,** College Ave. and Copeland St. (tel. 224-0462). The **FSU Mainstage/School of Theatre,** Fine Arts Building, Call and Copeland Sts. (tel. 644-6500), presents excellent productions from classic dramas to comedies. The Tallahassee Little Theatre, 1861 Thomasville Rd. (tel. 224-8474), is noted for exceptional presentations.

THE NIGHTCLUB & BAR SCENE

Although Tallahassee is rather quiet, fun people and night owls will find some action. Most hotel and restaurant cocktail lounges present a variety of entertainment. **Rooster's,** 2226 N. Monroe St. (tel. 386-8738), features live bands and dancing every night, until 2am. Entertainment is spotlighted in **Andrew's Upstairs** cocktail lounge (see "Where to Dine," above). In La Quinta Inn, **Julie's Place,** 2901 Monroe St. (tel. 386-7181), is popular as a late-night lounge. **The Moon,** an upscale nightclub on 1105 E. Lafayette St. (tel. 222-6666), showcases name performers with music from the '50s to rhythm and blues. **Club Park Avenue,** on 115 E. Park Ave. (tel. 599-9143), offers two dance floors (the DJ selects the music).

A downtown pub, **Clyde's & Costello's,** 210 S. Adams St. (tel. 224-2173), is very popular, featuring dancing to music from the '40s. You can play pool here, too. Another favorite billiard room, **Halligan's Pub-N-Pool,** 1700 Halstead Blvd. (tel. 668-7665), also serves snacks and beer. **Dooley's Downunder** is a comedy club in the Ramada Inn, 2900 N. Monroe St. (tel. 386-1027). Entertainment, pool tables and a big screen television attract sports fans to **The Palace Saloon,** 1303 Jackson Bluff Rd. (tel. 575-3418). **Charley Mac's Restaurant & Lounge,** Oak Lake Village, on Capitol Circle N.E. (tel. 893-0522), has a daily Happy Hour in the lounge from 4pm (5pm on Saturday) until the wee hours (good food here, too).

SHOPPING

ANTIQUES If you like antique-ing, you may find just what you're searching for in Tallahassee's antiques shops. Three downtown shops are clustered together: **Forget-Me-Not** and **Mid-Century Collectibles** are both at 1318 N. Monroe St. (tel. 222-4833 for both), and **Old World Antiques** is at 929 N. Monroe St. (tel. 681-6986). Hours are Monday through Saturday from 10am to 4pm. **SK's Antiques and Collectibles,** 317 E. Park Ave. (tel. 224-1838), is another good source. **Pedlers**

Antique Mall, 600 Capital Circle NE (tel. 877-4674), is open Monday through Saturday from 10am to 5:30pm and on Sunday from 1 to 5pm. **B&C Trading Post,** 4213 Woodville Hwy. (tel. 656-3113), is open Tuesday through Sunday from 10am to 6pm.

A MARKET Shopping and sightseeing can be combined in historic downtown Tallahassee, where you'll find a variety of boutiques and shops. One interesting district is **All Around Town Art in Gallie's Alley,** at Adams Street and College Avenue (tel. 224-3252), an open-air market showcasing locally designed pottery, unusual jewelry, some fashions, and a variety of artwork. The market is open Tuesday through Friday from 9am to 5pm.

MALLS Should your shoes need repairing or you have to take clothes to the cleaners, you can shop and use the services in the **Parkway Center and Village,** at the corner of Apalachee Parkway and Magnolia, about half a mile east of the Capitol. In addition to fashion boutiques and a Bass shoe outlet, the mall includes a Walgreen drug store, the Parkway Suburban Beauty Salon, Blue Ribbon Cleaners, Superior Shoe Repair, Mick's Florist, Radio Shack, a walk-in clinic, Books-A-Million, Gold's Downtown Athletic Club, and such restaurants as the Olive Garden, Cabo's Tacos, and Little Caesar's Pizza.

The newly expanded **Governor's Square,** 1500 Apalachee Pkwy. (tel. 877-2186), features 150 specialty shops, pushcarts, the Food Court, and such major stores as Burdines, Dillards, JC Penney, and Sears. Only a mile east of the Capitol, the mall is open Monday through Saturday from 10am to 9pm and on Sunday from 12:30 to 5:30pm.

Recently remodeled and expanded, the **Tallahassee Mall,** 2415 N. Monroe St. (tel. 385-7145), has Parisian, Gayfers, and Montgomery Ward department stores, 60 new specialty stores, a new Food Court, and a movie theater. The mall is open Monday through Saturday from 10am to 9pm and on Sunday from 12:30 to 5:30pm.

SPECIALTY SHOPPING NEARBY **Bradley's Country Store,** on Centerville Road (tel. 893-1647 or 893-4742), one of the historic Canopy Roads, sells more than 80,000 pounds of sausage per year, both over the counter and from orders from around the country. Grandma Mary Bradley began the business in 1910, selling her homemade sausage from her kitchen. Her secret seasoning recipe is still used, without preservatives or additives (Bradley's describes its sausage as "a link to the past"). The rustic store is still Bradley-owned and -operated. Other country-style southern specialties produced and sold at Bradley's are coarse-ground grits, country-milled cornmeal, hogshead cheese, liver pudding, cracklings, and specially cured hams. On the National Register of Historic Places, the store is also a sightseeing attraction and everyone is welcome to stop in for a taste of the old-fashioned, friendly atmosphere. About a 12-mile scenic ride north of Tallahassee, Bradley's Country Store is open Monday through Saturday from 8am to 6pm.

Blackberry Patch home-cooked jellies, jams, and syrups, concocted from old and new southern recipes, are available at local stores or by contacting Blackberry Patch, P.O. Box 918C, Tallahassee, FL 32308 (tel. 893-3163). The famous **Whigham pecans,** deep-fried and rolled in cinnamon sugar, are produced nearby in Whigham, Georgia. If you want to take advantage of their pick-your-own-pecans bargain, contact the Whigham Chamber of Commerce, Whigham, GA 31797 (tel. 912/762-4215).

EASY EXCURSIONS

THE APALACHICOLA AREA

Sights and Attractions

★ **APALACHICOLA NATIONAL FOREST** This is the largest of Florida's three national forests, a varied woodland with lakes and streams, encompassing about 600,000 acres, which includes parts of four Panhandle counties. Picnic facilities include sheltered tables and grills. Stroll along nature trails to observe the flora and fauna (perhaps a bear!) or bike along the paths. The canoe trails along the Sopchoppy and Ochlockonee Rivers are popular, or you can do some boating. Camping is permitted—everything from RV hookups and cabins to tents. The Trout Pond is unique, offering especially designed recreational facilities for the physically handicapped, such as a swimming area, fishing pier, and an interpretive nature trail.

Free, helpful information is available from the district headquarters office at Crawfordville, south of Tallahassee. They will also give you opening and closing hours, as well as all the different fees. The forest is on U.S. 319; the closest entrance is approximately 20 miles south of Tallahassee (tel. 926-3561, 681-7265, or 670-8644).

The **Apalachicola Wildlife and Environmental Area** adjoins the forest. In season, hunting is allowed for duck and other waterfowl, wild turkey, white-tailed deer, wild hogs, etc. For information, call the above telephone numbers.

APALACHICOLA A scenic drive via U.S. 98 takes you to the fishing and oystering village of Apalachicola, about 80 miles south of Tallahassee. A bustling cotton port before the Civil War, the town is still highly photogenic, with its antebellum homes and colorful fishing fleet.

Although Apalachicola was always important to Florida's history, undoubtedly its major contribution was Dr. John Gorrie's invention of an early form of air conditioning during the early 1800s. Dr. Gorrie, who was also Apalachicola's postmaster, treasurer, councilman, and bank director, was so concerned with keeping his yellow fever patients cool that he created the mechanism that became the groundwork for modern air conditioning and refrigeration. A replica of his invention (which was the catalyst for tourism to Florida) is exhibited in the small John Gorrie State Museum on 6th Street (one block off U.S. 98), open daily from 9am to 5pm.

About 90% of Florida's oysters and more than half of Florida's shellfish come from Apalachicola. It's interesting to watch the oystermen at work when the oyster beds are most productive. Apalachicola's restaurants and bars serve just-shucked oysters, or you may want to buy a big bag for an oyster roast in one of the Panhandle parks (merely throw them on the grill and the bivalves open up for a taste treat).

Apalachicola's annual Seafood Festival (usually the first weekend in November) is a great experience. If you stay overnight during the festival, make hotel reservations well in advance.

FORT GADSDEN STATE HISTORIC SITE History buffs should visit this historic site, about 25 miles north of Apalachicola off Fla. 65. During the War of 1812, the fort was a British recruitment center for Native Americans and African Americans. Known at that time as Prospect Bluff, it served as a threat to supply ships headed to the U.S. territorial boundary, about 50 miles north. When U.S. gunboats with orders to destroy the fort opened fire, a shot hit the powder magazine and the fort exploded and killed all but 30 of the 300 people inside. Later the fort was renamed for James Gadsden, Gen. Andrew Jackson's aide-de-camp and hero of the Seminole Indian Wars. Gadsden County (which includes Quincy, Havana, and Chattahoochee) was also named in his honor.

The lovely park surrounding Fort Gadsden is delightful for a picnic (tables and benches are provided) and is open daily from 8am to sunset. For information, call 904/653-9347.

ST. VINCENT ISLAND NATIONAL REFUGE Birdwatchers will not want to miss this park in the Apalachicola area. The St. Vincent Island National Refuge attracts a great variety of sea birds because of the bountiful seafood in local waters. Located just west of Apalachicola, the refuge is reached by Fla. 30, which ribbons along the bay shores.

ST. GEORGE ISLAND STATE PARK Countless sea birds, such as terns, snowy plovers, and black skimmers, nest along St. George Island State Park. A network of trails and observation platforms allows for viewing. Swimming, fishing, camping, and hiking are also available in the 2,000-acre park, and the park's wide surf-tipped beach extends for at least 20 miles.

St. George Island is bordered by near-primitive beaches dotted by sand dunes, some almost 30 feet high. Legends claim that pirate treasure is buried on the island, or on Little George Island, which is accessible only by boat, and where a lighthouse more than 150 years old guards the secret. St. George Island and the state park are just south of Apalachicola via the toll bridge.

TORREYA STATE PARK The high bluffs along the Apalachicola River, some rising steeply 150 feet high, make Torreya State Park very special, as such lofty hills are indeed a rare sight in Florida. Another rarity is the Torreya tree, for which the park is named. This rare species grows only along the Apalachicola River bluffs (legend says that this tree grew in the Garden of Eden). You can hike along the seven-mile loop trail or enjoy a picnic in the park. Overnight camping is permitted. Ranger-guided tours will take you through the restored Gregory House.

About 50 miles west of Tallahassee, the park is located on Fla. 12, about 14 miles north of Bristol. For information, contact Torreya State Park, Rte. 2, Box 70, Bristol, FL 32321 (tel. 904/643-2674).

The park is open from 8am to sunset. Admission is $3.25 for a car load.

Where To Stay and Dine in the Apalachicola Area

GIBSON INN, 57 Market St., Apalachicola, FL 32320. Tel. 904/653-2191. 25 rms, 5 suites. A/C TV TEL

$ Rates: $65–$80 double; $110 suite. AE, MC, V.

Built at the turn of the century, the vivid blueberry-painted inn, a brilliant example of ornate Victorian architecture, is listed on the National Register of Historic Inns. An abandoned ruin, it was restored to its original splendor in 1985 by Michael and Neil Koun of Tallahassee. Overlooking Apalachicola Bay, the hospitable inn recalls the good old days, when the town was an important train stop, after the Lake Wimico & St. Joseph Railroad began service in 1879.

Gibson Inn guest rooms are richly furnished and decorated with a wealth of antiques. In the aristocratic dining room, moderately priced lunches and dinners are served daily (seafood is a specialty, of course). Nonguests are welcome to look around, or to dine in the restaurant. If you plan to stay for a weekend or during the seafood festival, make reservations well in advance.

ST. GEORGE INN, P.O. Box 222, St. George Island, Eastpoint, FL 32328. Tel. 904/670-2903. 8 rms. A/C TV TEL

$ Rates: $70–$90 double. MC, V.

In an idyllic setting, the St. George Inn is a delightful place to stay, complete with wide porches for admiring the views or reading a good book. Guest rooms are spacious and attractive. Glass French doors lead out to the double-decker porch. With its southern-style architecture and antique accoutrements, the inn conveys the lovely impression of an old-fashioned guesthouse, but it was built in the past decade. Much of the pottery and paintings adorning the inn were created by local artists. For meals and refreshments, the inn has a pleasant restaurant. The hospitable innkeepers will inform you about the variety of shells on the beach and the many species of sea birds.

WAKULLA SPRINGS

The 2,860-acre ✪ **Edward Ball Wakulla Springs State Park** (tel. 904/922-3632) is the location of the world's largest and deepest freshwater spring. Edward Ball was a financier who administered the DuPont estate; he turned the springs into a preservation area.

Glass-bottom boats transport visitors around the remarkably clear waters and to the cavern site, 120 feet below, where mastodon bones were discovered (including Herman, now in Tallahassee's Museum of Florida History). Diver-explorers have found caves 250 feet below the springs, which have been known to dispense an amazing 14,325 gallons of water per second at certain times.

A free orientation movie is offered at the park's theater. You can hike or bike along the nature trails, and swimming is allowed, but only in designated areas. It's important to observe swimming rules—alligators can be very curious. A 30-minute wildlife observation boat tour is also offered. The Tarzan movies, starring Johnny Weissmuller were filmed in this park.

The park is located 15 miles south of Tallahassee at the junction of Fla. 61 and Fla. 267. Both boat tours cost $5 for adults, half price for children. Entrance fees to the park are $5 for adults, $2.50 for children. The park is open daily from 8am to dusk.

Where to Stay and Dine

WAKULLA SPRINGS LODGE AND CONFERENCE CENTER, 1 Springs Dr., Wakulla Springs, FL 32305. Tel. 904/224-5950. Fax 904/561-7251. 27 rms, 3 suites. A/C TV TEL

$ Rates: $55–$85 double; from $240 suite. MC, V.

On the grounds of Wakulla State Park, the lodge is distinctive for its magnificent Spanish architecture and ornate old-world furnishings, such as rare Spanish tiles, black granite tables, marble floors, and ceiling beams painted with Florida scenes by a German artist, supposedly Kaiser Wilhelm's court painter. High-ceilinged guest rooms are beautifully furnished and have marble bathrooms.

You don't have to be a lodge guest to dine in the lovely Azalea Dining Room, enhanced by arched windows and an immense fireplace. Meals are moderately priced. Dining hours are 7:30 to 10am for breakfast, noon to 2pm for lunch, and 6:30 to 8:30pm for dinner. For snacks and light meals, the coffee shop is open from 8am to 5pm (there's a 60-foot-long marble soda fountain for old-fashioned ice-cream sodas).

CHAPTER 12

THE TAMPA BAY AREA

- **WHAT'S SPECIAL ABOUT THE TAMPA BAY AREA**
- **1. TAMPA**
- **2. ST. PETERSBURG**
- **3. SARASOTA**
- **4. BRADENTON**

Rimmed by the Gulf of Mexico in the heart of Florida's central west coast, the Tampa Bay area is often referred to as the "suncoast." The area not only boasts over 50 miles of white sandy beaches—from St. Petersburg, Treasure Island, Madeira, and Clearwater to Anna Maria Island, Longboat Key, Lido Key, and Siesta Key—but also a perpetually perfect climate, with temperatures averaging in the 70s and about 361 days of sunshine a year.

But the Tampa Bay area is more than sunshine, sand, and surf. It is also the cities of Tampa, St. Petersburg, Sarasota, and Bradenton—four historic and fast-growing urban centers.

First settled by Native Americans of the Tocobaga and Timucuan tribes, the Tampa Bay area was discovered by the Spanish in the 16th century when explorers Juan Ponce de León, Panfilo de Narvarez, and Hernándo de Soto came in search of gold but found a tropical paradise instead.

Travelers have been "discovering" the area's beauty ever since. In fact, in 1885, a prominent Baltimore physician presented a paper to the American Medical Society declaring the area "the healthiest place on earth."

The 1920s were boom years for Tampa and St. Petersburg. Henry B. Plant brought his narrow-gauge South Florida Railroad to the area and great hotels—the Tampa Bay Hotel, Belleview Biltmore, Don CeSar, and Vinoy—were built to accommodate the flow of movers and shakers who flocked to the area. Happily, all but the first have been restored to serve today's travelers (the Tampa Bay has been transformed into a university and museum). At the same time, south of the Bay in Sarasota, circus-master John Ringling built a new winter residence, modeled after a Venetian palace and still standing today for the enjoyment of visitors.

Though they're united by a common history and a stretch of beautiful beaches, the Tampa Bay cities of Tampa, St. Petersburg, Sarasota, and Bradenton are different individually.

Tampa, the business hub of the quartet, is the home of Busch Gardens, the number-one visitor attraction on the west coast of Florida, and Ybor City, an ethnic enclave rich in Spanish and Cuban architecture and tradition.

St. Petersburg, long known as a haven for seniors but growing fast with new younger residents, offers such one-of-a-kind attractions as the Pier, an inverted pyramid of shops, restaurants, and attractions on the bay; the Florida Suncoast Dome, a new stadium that's the largest of its type in the world; and the Salvador Dalí Museum, repository of the world's largest collection of works by the Spanish surrealist painter.

Sarasota, home of the Ringling Museum Complex, is the cultural capital of Florida's west coast, with an array of arts and theatrical centers including the Van Wezel Performing Arts Hall and the Asolo Theater.

The sweet aroma of citrus fills the air at Bradenton, headquarters of Tropicana.

WHAT'S SPECIAL ABOUT THE TAMPA BAY AREA

Beaches

- ☐ From the fun-seeking watersports activities at the St. Petersburg and Clearwater beaches to the sheltered "old Florida" ambience of Pass-A-Grille and the wide sandy strand of Treasure Island.
- ☐ Sarasota Keys, 20 miles of barrier island beaches, running from Longboat and Lido to St. Armands and Siesta Keys.
- ☐ Anna Maria Island at Bradenton, a 7.5-mile stretch of tree-shaded and sandy beaches.

Architectural Highlights

- ☐ The Pier, an "inverted pyramid" stretching out from downtown into Tampa Bay.
- ☐ The Suncoast Dome, a slant-roofed stadium that is the first cable-supported dome of its kind in the U.S. and the largest of its type in the world.
- ☐ Tampa's Hyde Park National Register Historic District, a showcase of American architecture from Colonial to Victorian.

Museums

- ☐ Salvador Dalí Museum in St. Petersburg, housing the world's largest collection of works by the surrealist Spanish artist.
- ☐ Ringling Museum Complex in Sarasota, onetime home of circus master John Ringling and now Florida's official state art museum.
- ☐ Museum of African-American Art in Tampa, the first of its kind in Florida and home of the U.S.'s foremost collection of African-American art.
- ☐ Museum of Science and Industry in Tampa, for a look at a simulated space shuttle operation, ham radio center, or weather station.

Events/Festivals

- ☐ Festival of the States, a winter celebration, with 17 days of parades, pageantry, and outdoor fun.
- ☐ Gasparilla Festival, Tampa's traditional annual frolic, with modern-day pirates, parades, concerts, and more.
- ☐ Florida State Fair, a two-week fest of all the best in Florida and Tampa.

Attractions

- ☐ Gamble Plantation, a 19th century antebellum plantation home and now the oldest structure on Florida's southwest coast.
- ☐ Busch Gardens, for up-close views of 3,000 animals in natural settings, and thrilling rides and activities.

Activities

- ☐ Swimming, sunning, shelling, or shore-walking along St. Petersburg's strip of sandy white beaches.
- ☐ Sailing aboard a ketch, sloop, yacht, or windjammer from St. Pete Beach or Clearwater Harbor.

This city offers a host of diverse attractions ranging from the South Florida Museum and Bishop Planetarium to Nick Bolletteri's Tennis Academy.

1. TAMPA

200 miles SW of Jacksonville, 254 miles NW of Miami, 63 miles N of Sarasota

GETTING THERE **By Plane** **Tampa International Airport,** off Memorial Highway and Fla. 60, Tampa (tel. 813/276-3400), five miles northwest of downtown Tampa, is the gateway for all scheduled domestic and international flights. Most major airlines fly into Tampa, including Air Canada, American, America Trans Air,

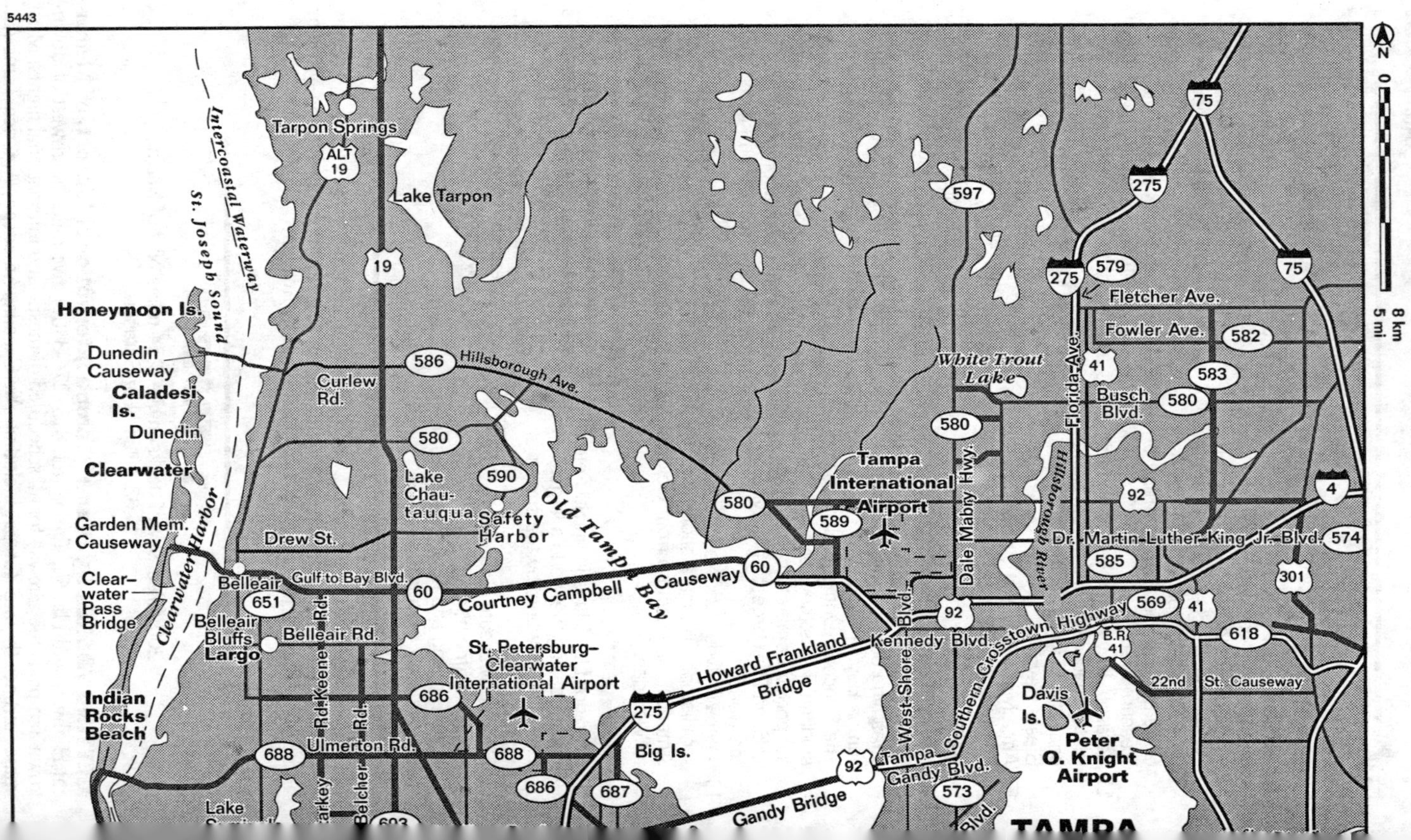
5443
N
0
8 km
5 mi
Tarpon Springs
Lake Tarpon
Intercoastal Waterway
St. Joseph Sound
Honeymoon Is.
Dunedin Causeway
Caladesi Is.
Dunedin
Clearwater
Garden Mem. Causeway
Clear-water Pass Bridge
Clearwater Harbor
Indian Rocks Beach
Belleair
Belleair Bluffs
Largo
Belleair Rd.
Gulf to Bay Blvd.
Drew St.
Curlew Rd.
Hillsborough Ave.
Lake Chautauqua
Safety Harbor
Old Tampa Bay
Courtney Campbell Causeway
St. Petersburg–Clearwater International Airport
Ulmerton Rd.
Keene Rd.
Belcher Rd.
Lake
Howard Frankland Bridge
Big Is.
Gandy Bridge
Gandy Blvd.
Tampa
West Shore Blvd.
Kennedy Blvd.
Southern Crosstown Highway
Tampa International Airport
Dale Mabry Hwy.
White Trout Lake
Hillsborough River
Florida Ave.
Fletcher Ave.
Fowler Ave.
Busch Blvd.
Dr. Martin Luther King Jr. Blvd.
22nd St. Causeway
Davis Is.
Peter O. Knight Airport
TAMPA
19
ALT 19
586
580
590
60
651
686
688
687
275
92
573
589
597
579
75
4
41
582
583
585
569
B.R. 41
618
301
574

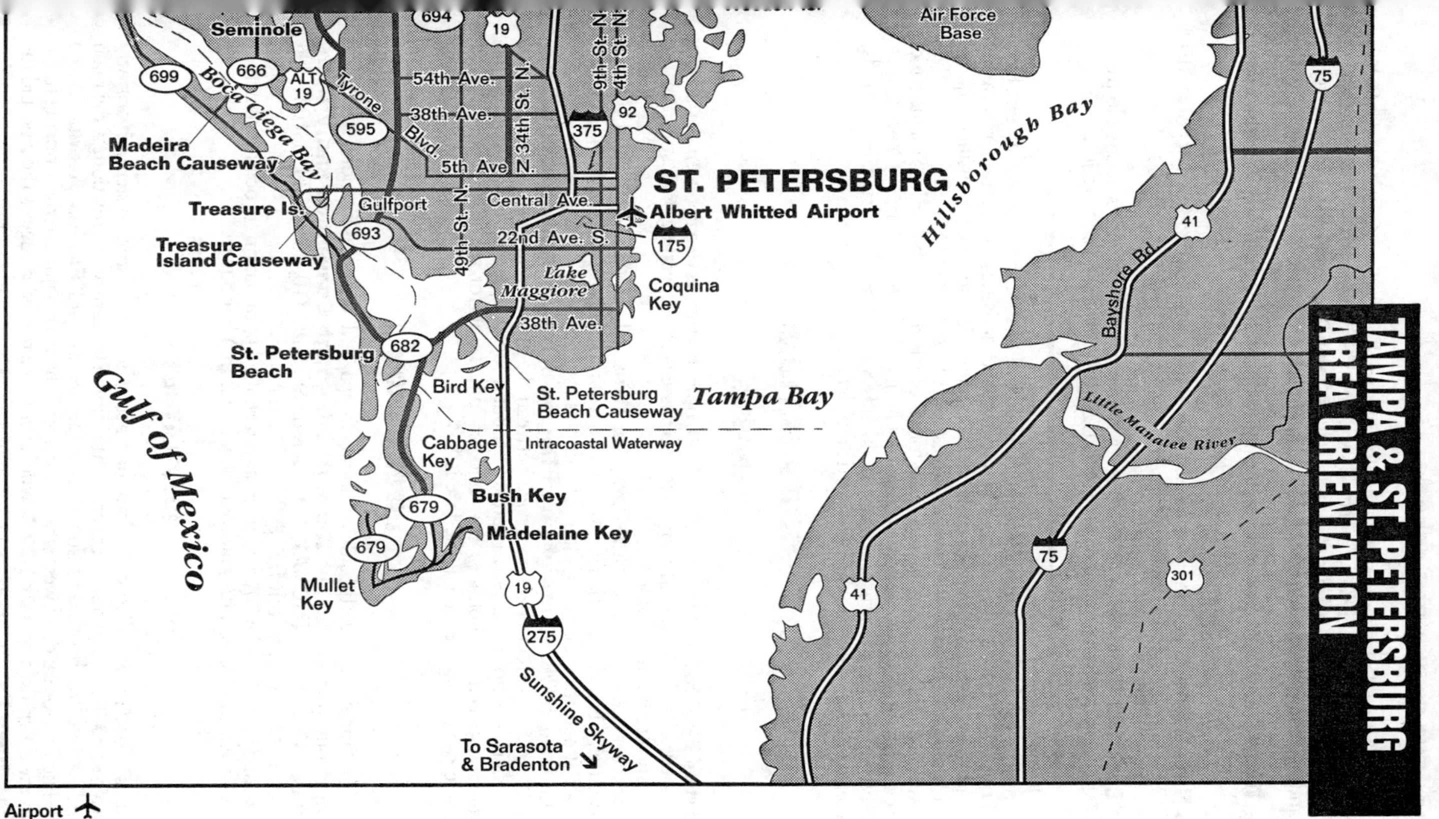

TAMPA & ST. PETERSBURG AREA ORIENTATION
Seminole
694
19
Air Force Base
699
666
ALT 19
Tyrone Blvd.
54th Ave.
38th Ave.
595
Boca Ciega Bay
Madeira Beach Causeway
5th Ave N.
34th St. N.
9th St. N.
4th St. N.
375
92
75
Hillsborough Bay
ST. PETERSBURG
Albert Whitted Airport
Treasure Is.
Gulfport
Central Ave.
693
22nd Ave. S.
175
Treasure Island Causeway
49th St. N.
Lake Maggiore
Coquina Key
38th Ave.
41
Bayshore Rd
682
St. Petersburg Beach
Gulf of Mexico
Bird Key
St. Petersburg Beach Causeway
Tampa Bay
Little Manatee River
Cabbage Key
Intracoastal Waterway
Bush Key
679
Madelaine Key
679
Mullet Key
75
301
41
19
275
Sunshine Skyway
To Sarasota & Bradenton
Airport

Cayman Airways, Canadian Airlines International, Condor, Continental, Delta, Martinair, Northwest, TWA, United, USAir, and USAir Express.

Peter O. Knight Airport, Davis Islands, Tampa (tel. 813/251-1717), serves as a landing strip for private planes.

By Train Amtrak trains arrive at the Tampa Amtrak Station, 601 Nebraska Ave. N., Tampa (tel. 813/221-7600).

By Bus Greyhound/Trailways buses arrive at the carrier's downtown depot at 610 Polk St., Tampa (tel. 813/229-2174).

By Car The Tampa area is linked to the Interstate system and is accessible from I-275, I-75, I-4, U.S. 19, U.S. 41, U.S. 92, U.S. 301, and many state roads.

Sitting on the Hillsborough River and rimmed by Hillsborough Bay and Tampa Bay, Tampa is a city of many waterfront views and activities—a natural mecca for vacationers. This metropolis of nearly 300,000 people is also a major business hub on Florida's west coast and the seventh-largest port in the United States.

Although Tampa's number-one draw for visitors is the Busch Gardens theme park, the city also offers many other attractions, including the historic charm of Ybor City, a recently rejuvenated ethnic enclave that blends Spanish architecture, Cuban foods, flamenco music, and a Soho-style artistic ambience.

ORIENTATION

ARRIVING

Central Florida Limo (tel. 813/276-3730) operates van service between the airport and hotels. The fare is $7–$15 for up to two passengers, depending on destination (for most downtown hotels it would be $11).

Taxi service is provided by **Yellow Cab Taxis** (tel. 813/253-0125) and **United Cabs** (tel. 813/253-2424). The average fare from the airport to downtown Tampa is $10–$12 and the ride takes about 15 minutes.

In addition, **Hillsborough Area Regional Transit Authority/HARTline** (tel. 813/254-HART) operates service between the airport and downtown on its no. 31 bus. This is not an airport express bus, but a local route that makes stops at the airport, between the hours of 6am and 8:15pm. Look for the HARTline bus sign outside each airline terminal; the fare is 85¢.

INFORMATION

For brochures and helpful advice about Tampa and hotel reservations before or during your visit, contact the **Tampa/Hillsborough Convention and Visitors Association, Inc. (THCVA),** 111 Madison St., Suite 110, Tampa, FL 33602-4706 (tel. 813/223-1111, or toll free 800/44-TAMPA).

In addition, the THCVA also maintains unstaffed information/brochure centers at the Convention Center, on Harbour Island, and in Ybor Square.

CITY LAYOUT

Tampa's downtown district is laid out according to a grid system. **Kennedy Boulevard** (Fla. 60), which cuts across the city in an east-west direction, is the main dividing line for north and south street addresses; and **Florida Avenue** is the dividing line for east and west street addresses. The two major arteries bringing traffic into the downtown area are **I-275,** which skirts the northern edge of the city, and the **Crosstown Expressway,** which extends along the southern rim.

All the streets in the central core of the city are one-way, with the exception of pedestrians-only Franklin Street. From the southern tip of Franklin, you can also board the People Mover, an elevated tram to Harbour Island.

Neighborhoods in Brief

Downtown The core of Tampa, this compact area is primarily a business and financial hub, where John F. Kennedy Boulevard (Fla. 60) and Florida Avenue intersect.

Ybor City East of downtown, this is Tampa's Latin Quarter, settled for more than 100 years by Cuban immigrants. Today it's home to many Spanish and Cuban restaurants, as well as local artists and craftspeople.

Harbour Island South of downtown, this small island is linked by an elevated People Mover to the mainland. It is the city's waterfront playground, with a marina and water-sports activities as well as a hotel, restaurants, shops, health center, and residential condominiums.

Hyde Park West of downtown, this is the city's classiest residential neighborhood, Tampa's answer to Beverly Hills, with many of its homes part of a National Register Historic District.

West Shore West of Hyde Park, this area runs from Tampa International Airport southward, particularly along Westshore Boulevard. It's a commercial and financial hub, with office buildings and business-oriented hotels.

Courtney Campbell Causeway This is a small beach strip, running west of the airport, as Kennedy Boulevard (Fla. 60) crosses Old Tampa Bay. It's a prime tourist area, with waterfront hotels, restaurants, and sports activities.

Busch Gardens North of downtown, this area surrounds the famous theme park of the same name. Busch Boulevard, which runs from east to west, is a busy commercial strip just south of the Busch Gardens entrance.

GETTING AROUND

BY PUBLIC TRANSPORTATION By Bus Hillsborough Area Regional Transit/HARTline (tel. 813/254-HART) provides regularly scheduled bus service between downtown Tampa and the suburbs. The service is geared mainly to commuters, although visitors staying at downtown hotels certainly can use a bus to get to the airport or major shopping centers.

Fares are 85¢ for local services, $1.50 for express routes; correct change is required. Many buses start or finish their route downtown at the Marion Street Transit Parkway, between Tyler and Whiting Streets. It provides well-lit open-air terminal facilities including 40-foot shelters with copper roofs, informational kiosks, benches, newspaper stands, landscaping, and 24-hour security.

The People Mover This motorized tram on elevated tracks connects downtown Tampa with Harbour Island. It operates from the third level of the Fort Brooke Parking Garage, on Whiting Street between Franklin Avenue and Florida Street. Travel time is 90 seconds, and service is continuous, Monday through Saturday from 7am to 2am and on Sunday from 8am to 11pm. The fare is 25¢ each way.

BY TAXI Taxis in Tampa do not normally cruise the streets for fares, but they do line up at public loading places, such as hotels, the performing arts center, and bus and train depots. If you need a taxi, call either **Yellow Cab** (tel. 813/253-0125) or **United Cab** (tel. 813/253-2424).

BY CAR Although the downtown area can easily be walked, it's virtually impossible to see the major sights and enjoy the best restaurants of Tampa without a car. Most visitors step off a plane and pick up a car right at the airport for use throughout their stay. Five major firms are represented on the grounds of Tampa International Airport: **Avis** (tel. 813/276-3500), **Budget** (tel. 813/877-6051), **Dollar** (tel. 813/276-3640), **Hertz** (tel. 813/874-3232), and **National** (tel. 813/276-3782). Most of these companies also maintain offices downtown and in other parts of Tampa such as the Busch Gardens area.

In addition, many smaller firms and local companies have premises just outside the airport. These firms, which provide van pickups to/from the airport and often post the most competitive rates, include **Alamo** (tel. 813/289-4323), **A-Plus** (tel. 813/289-4301), **Payless** (tel. 813/289-6554), **Thrifty** (tel. 813/289-4006), **USA** (tel. 813/286-7770), and **Value** (tel. 813/289-8870).

FAST FACTS

Area Code Tampa's area code is 813.

Business Hours Most businesses are open Monday through Friday from 9am to 5pm, with shops and stores open from 9am to 6pm or later. Banks are open Monday through Friday from 9am to 4pm; some banks are open on Friday until 6pm and others are open on Saturday morning.

Dentist For information about dentists in the area, call the Dental Referral Service Inc. (tel. 224-0073).

Doctor Most hotels have a doctor on call; if not, contact the Doctor Referral Service of the Hillsborough County Medical Association (tel. 253-0471) or the 24-hour Ask-A-Nurse/Physician Referral Service of St. Joseph's Hospital (tel. 870-4444).

Drugstores Eckerd Drugs is one of the leading pharmacy groups in the area, with over 35 stores throughout downtown and the suburbs, including a 24-hour branch at 11613 N. Nebraska Ave. (tel. 978-0775).

Emergencies Dial 911.

Hospitals If you need a hospital, try Doctors Hospital of Tampa, 4801 N. Howard Ave., Tampa (tel. 879-1550); St. Joseph's Hospital, 3001 W. Buffalo Ave. (tel. 870-4000); Tampa General Hospital, Davis Islands (tel. 251-7000); and University Community Hospital, 3100 E. Fletcher Ave. (tel. 971-6000).

Laundry/Dry Cleaning Most hotels supply same-day laundry and dry-cleaning service. Two local chains, each with several locations spread throughout the Tampa area, are Pioneer (tel. 253-3323) and Sterling (tel. 221-8055).

Libraries The main branch of the Tampa Public Library is downtown at 900 N. Ashley St. (tel. 223-8945), with a north branch at 8916 North Blvd. (tel. 932-7594).

Newspapers/Magazines The *Tampa Tribune* is the daily newspaper. The best periodical covering the area is *Tampa Bay*, a monthly magazine.

Photographic Needs Eckerd Express Photo offers one-hour processing at over half a dozen convenient Tampa locations, including one at 3714 Henderson Blvd., in the Henderson Boulevard Shopping Center (tel. 879-2020), and another at 2750 W. Hillsborough Ave. in the Hillsboro Plaza Shopping Center (tel. 875-8665). For equipment repairs, try the Camera Barn, 100 E. Hillsborough Ave., Tampa (tel. 237-4935), or VP Technical, 2316 N. Dale Mabry Hwy. (tel. 876-7099).

Post Office The main post office is at Tampa Airport, 5201 W. Spruce St. (tel. 879-1600), open 24 hours daily.

Shoe Repairs Try the Florida Shoe Hospital, 406 E. Zack St. (tel. 223-1020).

Taxes A 6.5% sales tax is applied to all purchases and the cost of restaurant meals. The local hotel-occupancy tax is 10.5%, added to the cost of your hotel room. There's also a $6 airport departure tax for international flights.

Transit Information For information on the local bus system, call 254-HART.

Weather Dial 622-1212.

WHAT TO SEE & DO

THE TOP ATTRACTIONS

BUSCH GARDENS, 3000 E. Busch Blvd. Tel. 987-5171.

★ Founded 30 years ago as a hospitality garden for the local Anheuser-Busch brewery, this 300-acre family entertainment center has grown to become the most popular attraction on Florida's west coast—and the second most popular in the state (after Walt Disney World). Designed to reflect the atmosphere of turn-of-the-century Africa, the park contains one of the largest collections of free-roaming wild animals in the United States, as well as live entertainment, restaurants, shops, and dozens of rides, including "Kumba," the largest steel roller coaster in the Southeast. The park is divided into eight distinct sections:

Timbuktu is an ancient desert trading center with African craftsmen at work, plus a sandstorm-style ride, boat-swing ride, roller coaster, and electronic games arcade.

Morocco, a walled city with exotic architecture, has Moroccan craft demonstrations, a sultan's tent with snake charmers, and the Moroccan Palace Theater.

Serengeti Plain is an open area that's home to hippos, buffalos, impalas, gazelles, reticulated giraffes, black rhinos, elephants, and zebras, as well as antelopes, crocodiles, dromedaries (camels), flamingos, and ostriches.

Nairobi is home to a baby animal nursery, as well as a petting zoo, reptile displays, and Nocturnal Mountain, where a simulated environment allows visitors to observe animals that are active in the dark.

Stanleyville, a prototype African village, has a shopping bazaar and live entertainment, as well as two water rides, the Tanganyika Tidal Wave and Stanley Falls.

The Congo features Claw Island, a display of rare white Bengal tigers in a natural setting, plus such man-made attractions as a 1,200-foot roller coaster, and white-water-raft rides.

Bird Gardens, the original core of Busch Gardens, offers rich foliage, lagoons, and a free-flight aviary for hundreds of exotic birds including golden and American bald eagles, hawks, owls, and falcons.

Crown Colony, the newest area of the park, is the home of a team of Clydesdale horses as well as the Anheuser-Busch hospitality center.

In total, there are more than 3,700 animals, birds, and reptiles and many types of live entertainment. And the Anheuser-Busch brewery tour (self-guided) allows the visitor to observe the beer-making process and gives an opportunity to sample the famous brews.

To get the most from your visit, arrive early and allow at least eight hours. Start the day by taking one or more of the rides that circle the park (the monorail, open-air skyride, or train) to get your bearings and acquaint you with the location of things.

Admission: $28.70 adults, $24.45 children 3–9, free for children 2 and under. Parking is $3.

Open: Daily 9am–6pm, with extended hours in summer and holiday periods. **Directions:** Take I-275 northeast of downtown to Busch Boulevard (Exit 33), and go east two miles to the entrance on 40th Street (McKinley Drive).

HENRY B. PLANT MUSEUM, 401 W. Kennedy Blvd. Tel. 254-1891.

Modeled after the Alhambra in Spain, with 13 silver minarets and distinctive Moorish architecture, this landmark is a stand-out along the Tampa skyline. It was originally built in 1891 as the 511-room Tampa Bay Hotel by railroad tycoon Henry B. Plant, who filled it with priceless art and furnishings from Europe and the Orient.

Although it ceased to operate as a hotel in 1927, the building was saved by the University of Tampa and was declared a National Historic Landmark in 1977. Today the ground-floor rooms have been converted into a museum, filled with elegant displays of Venetian mirrors, Wedgwood china, Louis XV and XVI furniture, and other original art objects and fashions that hark back to the hotel's heydey.

Admission: Free; suggested donation, $3 adults, $1 children 12 and under.

Open: Tues–Sat 10am–4pm. **Directions:** Take Fla. 60 west of downtown.

MUSEUM OF AFRICAN AMERICAN ART, 1308 N. Marion St. Tel. 272-2466.

Touted as the first of its kind in Florida, this museum is the home of the $7.5-million Barnett-Aden collection, considered the country's foremost collection of African American art. More than 80 artists are represented in the display, which includes sculptures and paintings that depict the history, culture, and lifestyle of African Americans from the 1800s to the present.

Admission: $2 suggested donation.

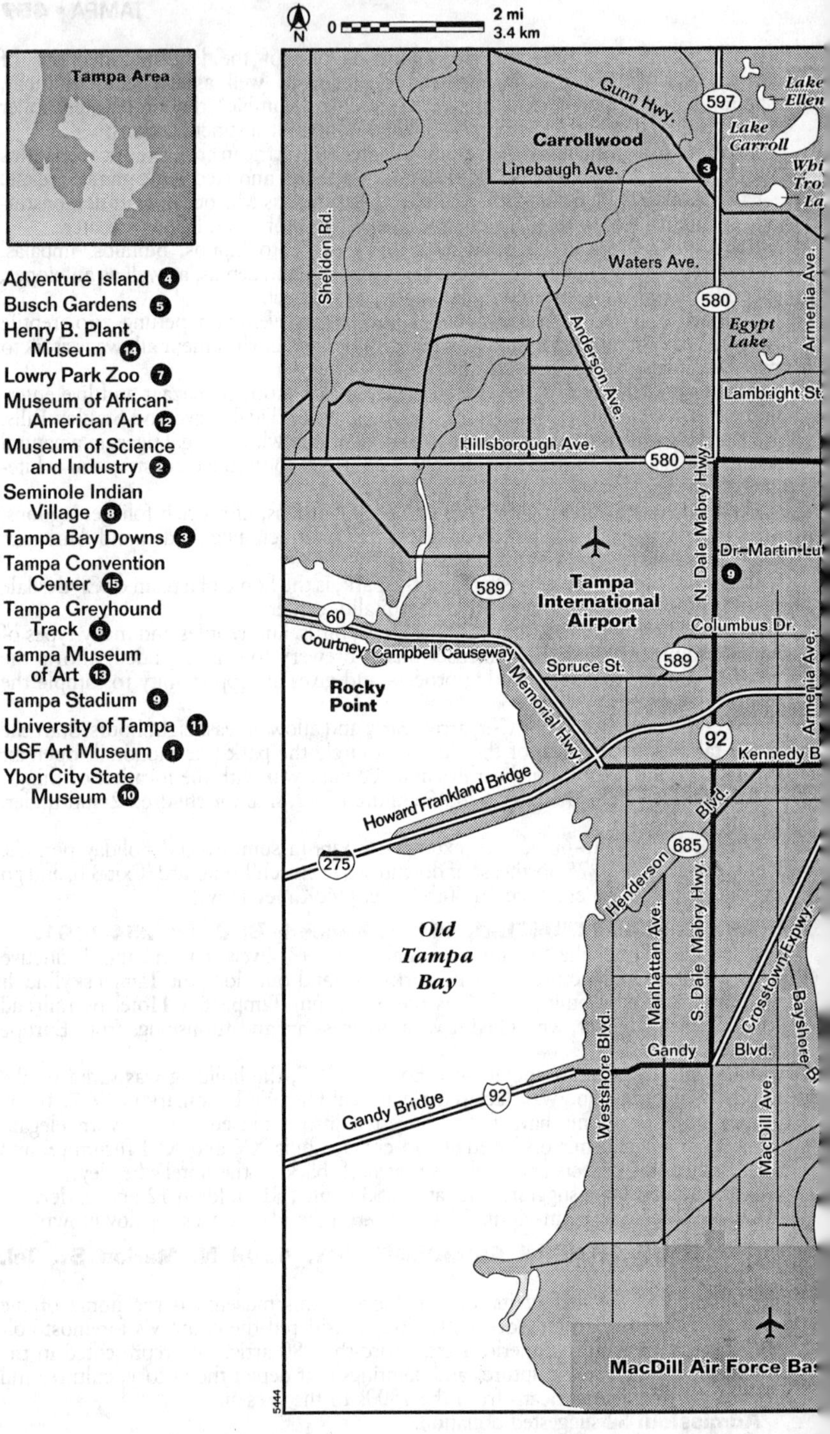

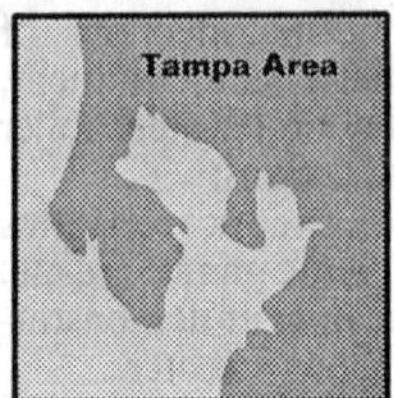

Adventure Island 4
Busch Gardens 5
Henry B. Plant Museum 14
Lowry Park Zoo 7
Museum of African-American Art 12
Museum of Science and Industry 2
Seminole Indian Village 8
Tampa Bay Downs 3
Tampa Convention Center 15
Tampa Greyhound Track 6
Tampa Museum of Art 13
Tampa Stadium 9
University of Tampa 11
USF Art Museum 1
Ybor City State Museum 10

N
0 2 mi
3.4 km

Gunn Hwy.
597
Lake Ellen
Lake Carroll
Carrollwood
Linebaugh Ave.
3
Sheldon Rd.
Waters Ave.
580
Egypt Lake
Armenia Ave.
Anderson Ave.
Lambright St.
Hillsborough Ave.
580
N. Dale Mabry Hwy.
Dr. Martin Lu
9
589
Tampa International Airport
60
Columbus Dr.
Courtney Campbell Causeway
Spruce St.
589
Rocky Point
Memorial Hwy.
Armenia Ave.
92
Kennedy B
Howard Frankland Bridge
Blvd.
685
Henderson
275
Old Tampa Bay
Manhattan Ave.
S. Dale Mabry Hwy.
Crosstown Expwy.
Bayshore B
Westshore Blvd.
Gandy
Blvd.
92
Gandy Bridge
MacDill Ave.
MacDill Air Force Bas
5444

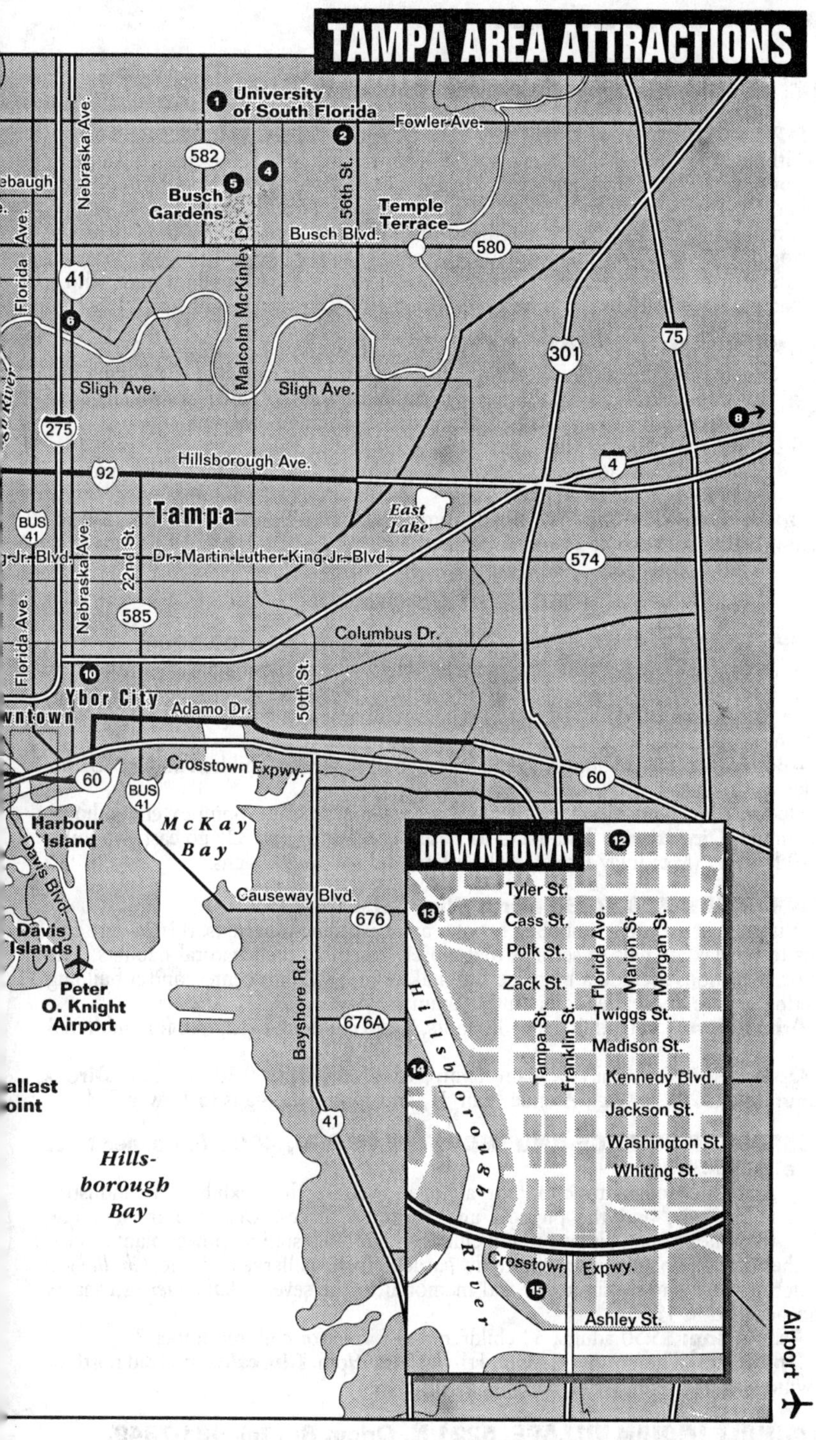
TAMPA AREA ATTRACTIONS
University of South Florida
Fowler Ave.
Busch Gardens
Temple Terrace
Busch Blvd.
56th St.
Nebraska Ave.
Florida Ave.
Malcolm McKinley Dr.
Sligh Ave.
Hillsborough Ave.
Tampa
East Lake
Dr. Martin Luther King Jr. Blvd.
22nd St.
Columbus Dr.
50th St.
Ybor City
Adamo Dr.
Crosstown Expwy.
Harbour Island
McKay Bay
Davis Blvd.
Causeway Blvd.
Davis Islands
Peter O. Knight Airport
Bayshore Rd.
Hills-borough Bay
DOWNTOWN
Tyler St.
Cass St.
Polk St.
Zack St.
Florida Ave.
Marion St.
Morgan St.
Tampa St.
Franklin St.
Twiggs St.
Madison St.
Kennedy Blvd.
Jackson St.
Washington St.
Whiting St.
Hillsborough River
Crosstown Expwy.
Ashley St.
Airport

Open: Tues–Sat 10:30am–4:30pm, Sun 1–4:30pm. **Directions:** Take Exit 26 off I-275; the museum is downtown, between Scott and Laurel Streets.

TAMPA CONVENTION CENTER, 333 S. Franklin St. Tel. 223-8511.

Although not technically open as a public attraction, this is the city's focal point for conventions, meetings, and occasional concerts. Even if you're not attending a function inside, it's worth a look at the impressive exterior of this $140-million building owned and operated by the City of Tampa. Situated on a 14-acre site overlooking the Hillsborough River and Harbour Island, it has 2,000 feet of riverfront views and lush landscape. In the front of the center is a $1.7-million park with a spectacular six-ton fountain, *Shamayim—Fire & Water* by Yaacov Agam.

TAMPA MUSEUM OF ART, 601 Doyle Carlton Dr. Tel. 223-8130.

Situated on the east bank of the Hillsborough River, south of the Tampa Bay Performing Arts Center, this fine arts complex offers six galleries with changing exhibits ranging from classical antiquities to contemporary art.

Tours are given Tuesday through Friday at noon and 1pm.

Admission: $3.50 adults, $3 seniors, $2 children 6–18, free for children under 6. Free for everyone Sat 10am–1pm.

Open: Tues, Thurs, and Sat 10am–5pm; Wed 10am–9pm; Sun 1–5pm. **Directions:** Take I-275 to Exit 25 (Ashley Street).

MORE ATTRACTIONS

ADVENTURE ISLAND, 4545 Bougainvillea Ave. Tel. 987-5600.

Adjacent to Busch Gardens, this is a separate 19-acre outdoor water theme park. A favorite with kids and teens, it has three swimming pools and water slides/play areas. There is also an outdoor café, picnic and sunbathing areas, games arcade, and dressing-room facilities. Wear a bathing suit and bring towels.

Admission: $16.95 adults; $14.95 children 3–9; free for children under 3; $1 for lockers.

Open: Mar–Oct, Mon–Fri 10am–5pm, Sat–Sun 9:30am–6pm; extended hours in summer. **Directions:** Take I-275 to Busch Boulevard (Exit 33); go east two miles to 40th Street (McKinley Drive), make a left, and follow the signs.

LOWRY PARK ZOO, 7530 North Blvd. Tel. 935-8552.

With lots of greenery, bubbling brooks, and cascading waterfalls, this 24-acre zoo aims to display animals in settings that closely resemble their natural habitats. The major attractions include a manatee hospital, aviary, wildlife center, and a building catering to rare and endemic nocturnal animals.

Admission: $5.50 adults, $4.50 seniors, $3.50 children 4–12, free for children 3 and under.

Open: Apr–Oct, daily 9:30am–6pm; Nov–Mar, daily 9:30am–5pm. **Directions:** Take I-275 to Sligh Avenue (Exit 31) and follow the signs to Lowry Park.

MUSEUM OF SCIENCE AND INDUSTRY (MOSI), 4801 E. Fowler Ave. Tel. 985-5531.

An educational attraction for all ages, MOSI offers exhibits on industry, technology, and the physical and natural sciences. Designed in a unique three-floor open-air layout, it includes a ham radio station, power plant model, weather station, planetarium, butterfly garden, fossil gallery, and the *Challenger* Center, a space shuttle simulator and memorial to the seven *Challenger* astronauts who perished in 1986.

Admission: $5.50 adults, $2 children 3–15, free for children under 3.

Open: Sun–Thurs 9am–4:30pm, Fri–Sat 9am–9pm. **Directions:** Head north of downtown, one mile east of Busch Gardens.

SEMINOLE INDIAN VILLAGE, 5221 N. Orient Rd. Tel. 621-7349.

Located on Tampa's Seminole Indian reservation, this museum is designed to trace that tribe's history in the area. The structures include "chickees," thatched huts built just as they were 150 years ago, which shelter skilled Seminole craftspeople as they practice bead-working, wood-carving, basket-making, and patchwork-sewing. Other more lively demonstrations include alligator wrestling and snake-handling.

Admission: $4.50 adults, $3.50 seniors, $3.75 children.

Open: Mon–Sat 9am–5pm, Sun noon–5pm. Tours given every hour on the half hour, with the last tour at 3:30pm. **Directions:** Take I-4 northeast of downtown to Exit 5.

USF CONTEMPORARY ART MUSEUM, Building FAM 101, University of South Florida, 4202 E. Fowler Ave. Tel. 974-2849.

On the western side of the campus, this 10,630-square-foot facility spotlights artists and artworks from throughout the world. In particular, there are valuable collections of pre-Columbian and African artifacts, as well as contemporary prints from the southeastern United States.

Admission: Free.

Open: Mon–Fri 10am–5pm, Sat 1–4pm. **Directions:** Head one block north of Busch Gardens, between Fowler and Fletcher Avenues.

YBOR CITY STATE MUSEUM, 1818 Ninth Ave., Ybor City. Tel. 247-6323.

The focal point of Ybor City, this museum is housed in the former Ferlita Bakery (1896–1973), a century-old yellow-brick building. Various exhibits in the museum depict the political, social, and cultural influences that shaped this section of Tampa, once known as "the cigar capital of the world." You can take a self-guided tour around the museum, which includes a collection of cigar labels, cigar memorabilia, and works by local artisans.

Adjacent to the museum is **Preservation Park,** the site of three renovated cigar workers' cottages, furnished as they were at the turn of the century.

Admission: Museum, $1 adults and children 6 and up, free for children under 6; tours of cigar workers' cottages, $1 extra per person.

Open: Tues–Sat 9am–noon and 1–5pm. **Directions:** Head northeast of downtown, between 18th and 19th Streets.

ORGANIZED TOURS

Water and Land Tours

GONDOLA GETAWAY CRUISES, The Waterwalk, Harbour Island. Tel. 888-8864.

See the skyscrapers and other downtown highlights as you float across the waters of Tampa Bay and the lower Hillsborough River via an authentic 70-year-old, 30-foot Venetian gondola. These narrated trips last 35–45 minutes and depart from the Waterwalk dock on Harbour Island, beneath the Columbia Restaurant.

Price: $20 per couple; additional people $5 each to a maximum of four per cruise.

Schedule: Mon–Sat 6pm–midnight, Sun noon–9pm; other times by appointment. Reservations accepted daily 9am–7pm.

YBOR CITY WALKING TOURS, Ybor Sq., 1901 N. 13th St., Ybor City. Tel. 223-1111, ext. 46.

Led by enthusiastic local volunteer guides, these tours are the ideal way to acquaint yourself with the highlights of Tampa's Latin Quarter. The route, which starts at Ybor Square and ends at Preservation Park, covers over three dozen points of interest and takes about 1½ hours; reservations are suggested.

Price: Free.

Schedule: June–Sept, Tues, Thurs, and Sat at 11am; Oct–May, Tues, Thurs, and

Sat at 1:30pm. **Directions:** Assemble at the Information Desk of Ybor Square, between Eighth and Ninth Avenues.

SPORTS & RECREATION

SPECTATOR SPORTS

BASEBALL About a half-hour drive from downtown Tampa, the **Plant City Stadium,** Park Rd., Plant City (tel. 752-7337), is the spring-training turf of the Cincinnati Reds. The season is from mid-February to April and admission is $4 to $7.

DOG RACING **Tampa Greyhound Track,** 8300 Nebraska Ave. (tel. 932-4313), features 13 races daily, with eight dogs competing in each. Races are from July–December on Monday and Wednesday to Saturday at 7:30pm, Monday, Wednesday and Saturday at noon, and Sundays at 1pm. It's closed the rest of the year. Admission is $1 to the grandstand, $2 to $3 to the clubhouse and parking is 50¢ to $1.

FOOTBALL, SOCCER & MORE Home to the Tampa Bay Bucaneers football team and the Tampa Bay Rowdies soccer team, ✪ **Tampa Stadium,** 4201 N. Dale Mabry Hwy. (tel. 872-7977) caters to sports events of all types, from the Super Bowl to horse shows, rodeos, motorcycle races, and tractor-pulling. Times and schedules vary. Admission ranges from $5 to $35 or higher, depending on the event.

HOCKEY **Tampa Bay Lightning,** P.O. Box 44, (tel. 813/229-8800), is Tampa's professional hockey team, and the southernmost National Hockey League franchise. Long range plans call for the construction of a new $97.5-million arena, the Tampa Coliseum, but at present the team plays at Exposition Hall at the Florida State Fairgrounds. The season is from October to mid-April and admission is $12 to $50.

HORSE RACING The only oval thoroughbred race course on Florida's west coast, ✪ **Tampa Bay Downs,** 12505 Racetrack Rd., Oldsmar (tel. 855-4401), is the home of the Tampa Bay Derby. The program features 10 races a day. Admission is $1.50 to the grandstand, $3 to the clubhouse; there is free grandstand admission for seniors on Wednesday and for women on Friday. Parking costs $1. From December to May, post time Monday to Tuesday and Thursday to Friday is 12:30pm; Saturday and Sunday, 1pm. The track is closed June to November.

JAI-ALAI Similar to racquetball, the Spanish game of Jai-Alai is considered the world's fastest ball game (the ball can go over 180 m.p.h.). At **Tampa Jai-Alai Fronton,** 5125 S. Dale Mabry Hwy. (tel. 831-1411), professional players volley the lethal *pelota* with a long, curved glove called a *cesta*. Admission is $1 to $3 and parking is $1 or free. From early November to late September, it's open Monday to Saturday at 7pm; Wednesday and Saturday at noon.

POLO Mallets swing at the **Cheval Polo Club,** 3939 Cheval Trail, Lutz (tel. 920-3873). This club, north of downtown, is open eight months of the year from October to May, Sundays at 10am and 3pm. There is an admission charge of $5 per person. In Plant City you can visit the **Tampa Bay Polo Club,** Walden Lake Polo and Country Club, 1602 W. Timberlane Dr., Plant City (tel. 223-2200). Polo is played regularly at this sylvan site east of Tampa. Each week a different local charity benefits from the proceeds. Admission is free, although parking is $5 to $7; it's open mid-January to May, Sundays at 2pm.

RECREATION

BOAT RENTALS Paddle downstream via a two-person canoe along a 20-mile stretch of the Hillsborough River amid 16,000 acres of rural lands in Wilderness Park, the largest regional park in Hillsborough County. The trips take two to four hours, covering approximately two to three miles per hour. **Canoe Escape,** 9335 E. Fowler Ave. (tel. 986-2076), charges $20 for two-hour trips, $25 for four-hour trips, and is open from Monday to Friday from 8am to 5pm, Saturday and Sunday from 8am to 6pm.

Club Nautico, The Waterwalk, Harbour Island (tel. 229-2107), lets you captain your own craft on the waters of Tampa Bay. This company rents boats, pontoons, ski motorboats, and wave-runners. Prices for half day rentals are from $79 to $169 for ski boats, $89 to $189 for powerboats, and $99 to $199 for pontoon boats; two seat wave-runners rent from $37.50 per half hour. It's open daily from noon to 6pm or later, depending on the season.

Jam 'n Dan's, off Rocky Point Drive, Courtney Campbell Causeway (tel. 286-SAND), rents wave-runners, jet skis, tubes, and other equipment. Prices are $25 per half hour for wave-runners, $35 per half hour for jet skis, and $10 per mile for tubes, and it's open daily from 10am to 6pm.

Trident Boat Rentals, The Waterwalk on Harbour Island (tel. 223-4168), rents small electric pedal boats and three-passenger electric boats to ply the waters of Garrison's Channel or the Hillsborough River around Harbour Island. Prices are $6 (two passengers) per half hour for pedal boats, $10 for electric boats. It's open Monday to Thursday noon to 10pm, Friday and Saturday noon to midnight, and Sunday noon to 9pm.

FISHING Tampa's opportunities for casting a line are confined primarily to lakes, rivers, and bays. There's good freshwater fishing for trout in **Lake Thonotosassa,** east of the city, or for bass along the **Hillsborough River.** Pier fishing on Hillsborough Bay is also available from Ballast Point Park, 5300 Interbay Blvd. (tel. 831-9585).

GOLF Situated north of Lowry Park, **Babe Zaharias Municipal Golf Course,** 11412 Forest Hills Dr. (tel. 932-8932), is an 18-hole, par-70 course. It has a pro shop, putting greens, and a driving range. Golf-club rentals and lessons are available. Prices range between $13.25 and $17.75; $11 to $22.25 with a cart. The course is open daily 7am to dusk.

You can literally step off the plane at Tampa Airport and play a round of golf at the 18-hole, par-72 course **Hall of Fame Golf Club,** 2222 N. Westshore Blvd. (tel. 876-4913). Facilities include a driving range and club rentals; lessons are also available. Prices, which include a cart, are from $12 to $22; it's open daily, 7am to dusk.

The **Rocky Point Golf Municipal Golf Course,** 4151 Dana Shores Dr. (tel. 884-5141), located between the airport and the bay, is an 18-hole, par-71 course, with a pro shop, practice range, and putting greens. Lessons and golf club rentals are available. Prices are $17.75 to $22.25, including a cart, and it's open daily, 7am to dusk.

On the Hillsborough River in north Tampa, the **Rogers Park Municipal Golf Course,** 7910 N. 30th St. (tel. 234-1911) is an 18-hole, par-72 championship course with a lighted driving and practice range. Lessons and club rentals are available. Prices, including cart, are $11 to $22.50. It's open daily, 7am to dusk.

University of South Florida Golf Course, 4202 Fowler Ave. (tel. 974-2071), is just north of the USF campus. This 18-hole, par-72 course is nicknamed "The Claw" because of its challenging layout. It offers lessons and club rentals. The charge is $18, $30 with a cart. It's open 7am to dusk.

RUNNING **Bayshore Boulevard,** a 7-mile stretch along Hillsborough Bay, is famous for its 6.3-mile sidewalk. Reputed to be the world's longest continuous sidewalk, it's a favorite for runners, joggers, walkers, and cyclists. The route goes from the western edge of downtown in a southward direction, passing stately old homes, condos, retirement communities, and houses of worship, ending at Gandy Boulevard.

For more information on other recommended running areas, contact the **Parks and Recreation Department,** 7225 North Blvd. (tel. 223-8230).

TENNIS The **City of Tampa Tennis Complex,** Hillsborough Community College, 4001 Tampa Bay Blvd. (tel. 870-2383), across from Tampa Stadium, is the largest public complex in Tampa, with 16 hard courts and 12 clay courts. It also has racquetball courts, a pro shop, locker rooms, showers, and lessons. Reservations are required. Prices range from $2 to $4.50 per person per hour. It's hours are Monday to Friday, 8am to 1pm, Saturday and Sunday, 8am to 6pm.

On the water and overlooking Harbour Island, **Marjorie Park,** 59 Columbia Dr., Davis Islands (tel. 253-3997), has eight clay courts. Reservations are required. The price is $4.50 per person per hour and it's open Monday to Friday, 8am to 9pm, and Saturday and Sunday, 8am to 6pm.

Harry Hopman/Saddlebrook International Tennis School, 5700 Saddlebrook Resort, Wesley Chapel (tel. 973-1111 or toll free 800/237-7519, 800/282-4654 in Florida), with its 37 tennis courts is a well-equipped school which caters to beginners as well as skilled players of all ages. A basic five-day, six-night package includes 25 hours (minimum) of tennis instruction, unlimited playing time, match play with instructors, audiovisual analysis, agility exercises, and accommodations at the Saddlebrook resort. Prices range from $630 to $1,035 per person, double occupancy.

At the north end of the University of Tampa, **Riverfront Park,** 900 North Blvd. (tel. 223-8602), offers 11 courts, and visitors are welcome to use it on a first-come, first-serve basis. The courts are lit until 10pm. All facilities are free, and it's open daily, 7am to 10pm.

WHERE TO STAY

Tampa is a city of relatively new hotels, all built in the last 25 years or so. Unlike many major cities, the downtown section of Tampa is not flush with hotels. Instead, the greatest concentration of hotels is near Tampa Airport, primarily along Westshore Boulevard and the Courtney Campbell Causeway. The next largest cluster of lodgings is north of downtown in the Busch Gardens area.

Price-wise, the high season is January through April, although rates don't vary dramatically throughout the year. The big price breaks come on weekends—all year long—when rates drop as much as 50%. The only exception to this rule is the Busch Gardens area, where rates don't dip on weekends, and can even be slightly higher for holiday weekends or special events.

VERY EXPENSIVE

HYATT REGENCY WESTSHORE, 6200 Courtney Campbell Causeway, Tampa, FL 33607. Tel. 813/874-1234, or toll free 800/233-1234. Fax 813/870-9168. 445 rms. A/C TV TEL

$ Rates: $155 single; $175 double. AE, CB, DC, DISC, MC, V.

Situated a mile west of Tampa Airport and overlooking Old Tampa Bay, this 14-story property is nestled on a 35-acre nature preserve, convenient to downtown and yet sequestered in a world of its own. Seashore colors and light woods grace the guest rooms, most of which provide expansive views of the bay and evening sunsets.

Dining/Entertainment: Armani's is a rooftop restaurant known for its fine Italian food and views. Behind the main hotel a 250-foot boardwalk leads to Oystercatchers, a Key West–style seafood eatery with indoor and outdoor seating overlooking the bay. For casual fare, there's Petey Brown's Café and the Bistro Bar.

Services: Airport courtesy shuttle, 24-hour room service, concierge, babysitting, valet laundry.

Facilities: Two outdoor heated swimming pools, two lighted tennis courts, whirlpool, saunas, health club, nature walks, and jogging trails.

SHERATON GRAND HOTEL, 4860 W. Kennedy Blvd., Tampa, FL 33609. Tel. 813/286-4400, or toll free 800/325-3535. Fax 813/286-4053. 350 rms. A/C TV TEL

$ Rates: $110–$140 single; $140–$160 double. AE, CB, DC, MC, V.

Located near the airport in the heart of the Westshore business district, this contemporary-style 11-story property is part of Urban Center, a financial office complex. In addition to a steady business clientele, it attracts vacationers who enjoy the panoramic views from the three glass elevators, and the bright atriums filled with greenery and cascading fountains. The guest rooms have soft-toned color schemes, traditional dark-wood furnishings, writing desks, easy chairs, full-length mirrors, built-in armoires, roomy closets, and marble-finished bathrooms. Rooms on the upper floors have views of Old Tampa Bay.

Dining/Entertainment: For continental recipes and fresh Florida seafood, try J. Fitzgerald's. There's also the Courtyard Café, for light meals in an indoor/outdoor setting, and the Grand Slam Sports Bar.

Services: Courtesy airport shuttle, 24-hour room service, concierge, valet laundry.

Facilities: Outdoor heated swimming pool, gift shop, florist, two banks, news/tobacco shop.

TAMPA AIRPORT MARRIOTT, Tampa International Airport, Tampa, FL 33607. Tel. 813/879-5151, or toll free 800/228-9290. Fax 813/873-0945. 296 rms. A/C TV TEL

$ Rates: $150 single; $160 double. AE, CB, DC, DISC, MC, V.

Wedged between the terminals, this is the only on-site hotel at Tampa's busy airport and a good specimen for those who thrive on the excitement of overnighting near the jetways. Guest rooms are well soundproofed, and decorated in contemporary style with dark woods and fabrics of cheery pastel tones.

Dining/Entertainment: An express elevator takes you to CK's, the hotel's revolving rooftop restaurant and lounge. On the lobby level is the Garden Café for light fare and the Flight Room for cocktails and a large-screen TV.

Services: Concierge, babysitting, valet laundry.

Facilities: Outdoor heated swimming pool, health club, gift shop.

WYNDHAM HARBOUR ISLAND HOTEL, 725 S. Harbour Island Blvd., Harbour Island, Tampa, FL 33602. Tel. 813/229-5000, or toll free 800/822-4200. Fax 813/229-5322. 300 rms. A/C MINIBAR TV TEL

$ Rates: $149–$189 single; $169–$209 double. AE, CB, DC, MC, V.

If location is everything, then this 12-story luxury property has a distinct advantage—it's just a minute or two from the bustle of downtown, yet it sits tranquilly on Harbour Island, surrounded by the channels linking the Hillsborough River and Bay. It's likewise connected to the shops and waterside activities of the Harbour Island complex, and offers customers all the perks of living on the island, including guest privileges at the Harbour Island Athletic Club. The bedrooms, all with views of the water, are furnished in dark woods and floral fabrics, and each has a well-lit marble-trimmed bathroom, executive desk, and work area.

Dining/Entertainment: Watch the yachts drift by as you dine at the Harbourview Room, or enjoy your favorite drink in The Bar, a clubby room with equally good views. Snacks and drinks are available during the day at the Pool Bar.

Services: Courtesy airport shuttle, room service, concierge, secretarial services, notary public, evening turn-down service, valet laundry.

Facilities: Outdoor heated swimming pool and deck, 50 boat slips, newstand/gift shop.

EXPENSIVE

CROWN STERLING SUITES HOTEL, 4400 W. Cypress St., Tampa, FL 33607. Tel. 813/873-8675, or toll free 800/433-4600. Fax 813/879-7196. 263 suites. A/C TV TEL

$ Rates (including full breakfast and evening cocktail party): $69–$139 single; $79–$149 double. AE, CB, DC, MC, V.

With an exterior of salmon-toned Spanish-style architecture, this eight-story building adds an old-world charm to the busy corridor beside the airport and Westshore Boulevard. The interior includes a plant-filled atrium with cascading

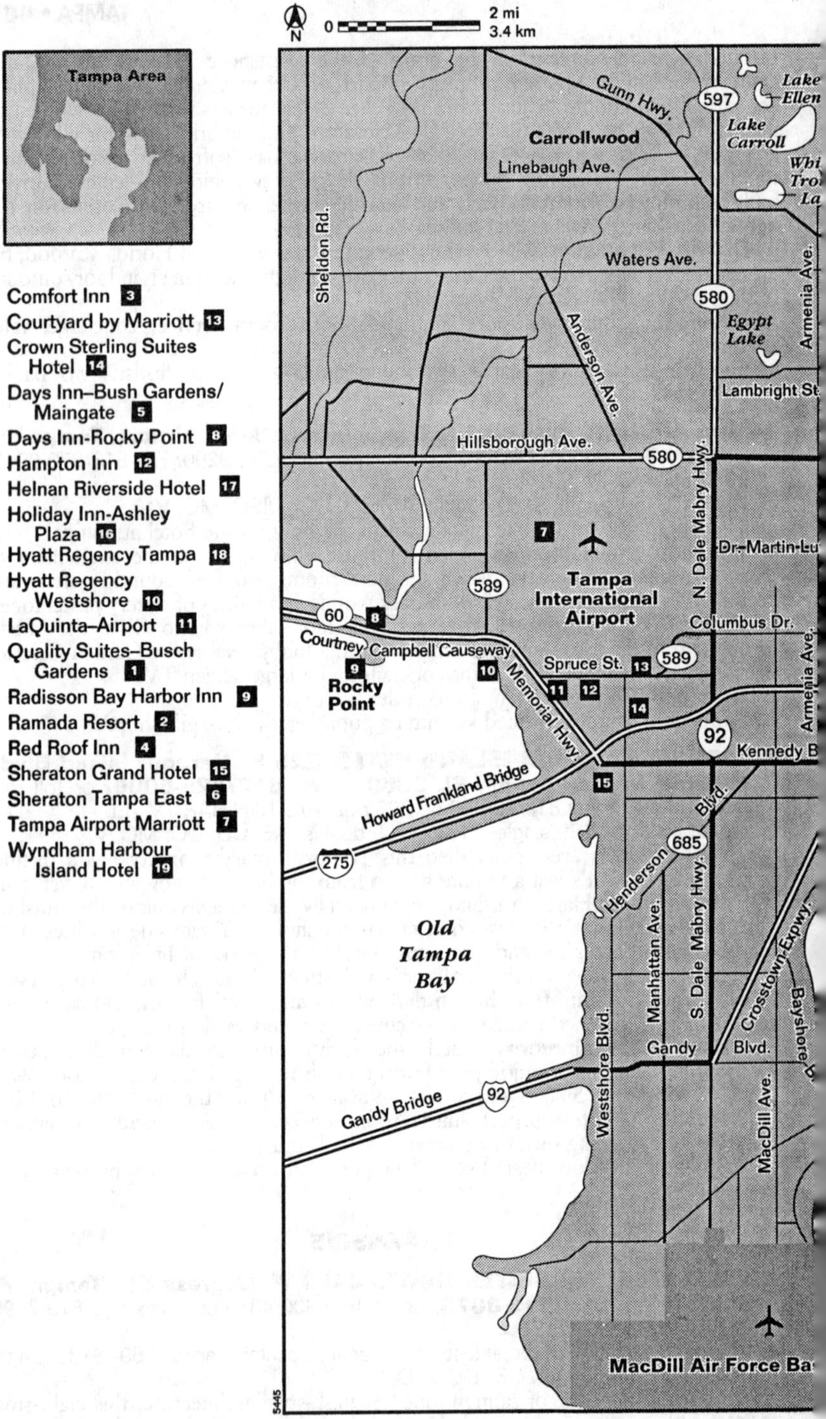

N
0 2 mi
3.4 km

Comfort Inn 3
Courtyard by Marriott 13
Crown Sterling Suites Hotel 14
Days Inn–Bush Gardens/ Maingate 5
Days Inn-Rocky Point 8
Hampton Inn 12
Helnan Riverside Hotel 17
Holiday Inn-Ashley Plaza 16
Hyatt Regency Tampa 18
Hyatt Regency Westshore 10
LaQuinta–Airport 11
Quality Suites–Busch Gardens 1
Radisson Bay Harbor Inn 9
Ramada Resort 2
Red Roof Inn 4
Sheraton Grand Hotel 15
Sheraton Tampa East 6
Tampa Airport Marriott 7
Wyndham Harbour Island Hotel 19

Gunn Hwy.
597
Lake Ellen
Carrollwood
Lake Carroll
Linebaugh Ave.
Sheldon Rd.
Waters Ave.
580
Egypt Lake
Armenia Ave.
Anderson Ave.
Lambright St.
Hillsborough Ave.
580
N. Dale Mabry Hwy.
7
Dr. Martin Lu
589
Tampa International Airport
60
8
Columbus Dr.
Courtney Campbell Causeway
9
Rocky Point
10
Memorial Hwy.
Spruce St.
13
589
11
12
14
Armenia Ave.
92
Kennedy B
15
Howard Frankland Bridge
275
685
Henderson Blvd.
Old Tampa Bay
Manhattan Ave.
S. Dale Mabry Hwy.
Crosstown Expwy.
Bayshore B
Westshore Blvd.
Gandy Blvd.
92
Gandy Bridge
MacDill Ave.
MacDill Air Force Ba
5445

TAMPA AREA ACCOMMODATIONS

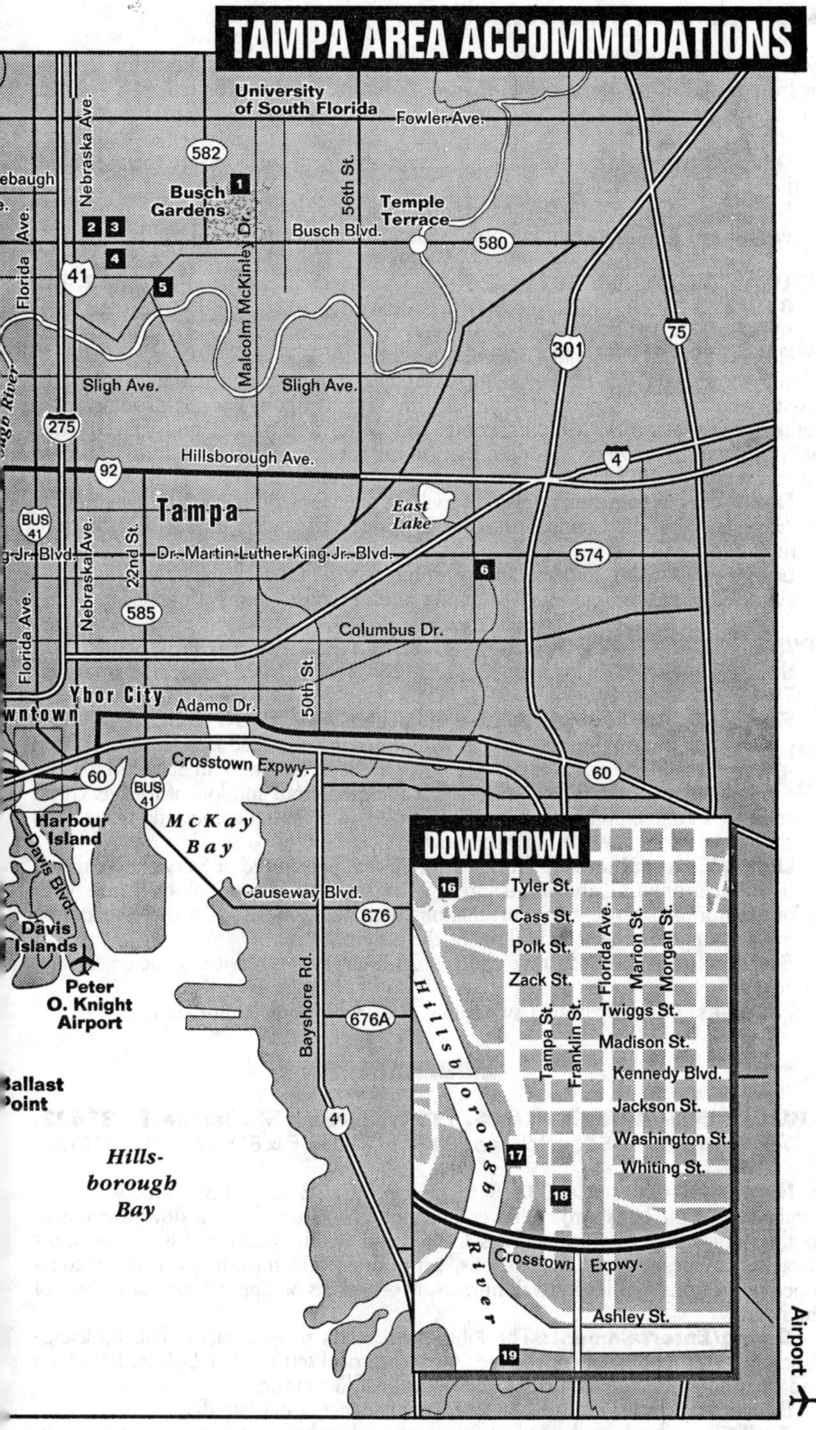

waterfalls and a tropical garden courtyard. The guest units are suites with separate bedrooms and living areas, contemporary furniture, muted color schemes, and wet bar, and most have sofa beds, microwave ovens, coffee makers, and private patios or balconies.

Dining/Entertainment: Regional dishes and local seafoods are the specialties at the St. James Bar & Grill.

Services: Airport courtesy shuttle, room service, valet laundry.

Facilities: Indoor swimming pool, sauna, steam room, gift shop.

HELNAN RIVERSIDE HOTEL, 200 N. Ashley Dr., Tampa, FL 33602. Tel. 813/223-2222, or toll free 800/AT-TAMPA. Fax 813/273-0839. 285 rms. A/C MINIBAR TV TEL

$ Rates: $99–$129 single; $115–$145 double. AE, CB, DC, MC, V.

Ideally located on the Hillsborough River near the new convention center, this six-story downtown property was formerly the Tampa Hilton. The guest rooms have a contemporary decor with blond woods and pastel tones; most units have private balconies with river views. Modern bathrooms have extra perks, such as a makeup mirror, hairdryer, and phone.

Dining/Entertainment: Choices include the Mermaid restaurant, overlooking the river; Septembers Lounge; and the Riverside Café, with indoor and outdoor seating.

Services: Airport courtesy shuttle, room service, valet cleaning (weekdays).

Facilities: Heated outdoor swimming pool, exercise room, gift shop.

HYATT REGENCY TAMPA, 211 N. Tampa St., Tampa, FL 33602. Tel. 813/225-1234, or toll free 800/233-1234. Fax 813/223-4353. 518 rms. A/C TV TEL

$ Rates: $115–$150 single; $120–$165 double. AE, CB, DC, DISC, MC, V.

Standing out on the city skyline, with a striking mirrored facade, this 17-story tower sits in the heart of downtown adjacent to the Franklin Street Mall. The eight-story atrium lobby boasts a cascading waterfall and lots of foliage. Guest rooms have a contemporary flair with light woods and coastal colors, and many units on the upper floors have bay or river views.

Dining/Entertainment: Florida-style cuisine is featured at Saltwaters Bar and Grille (lunch only). Light meals are on tap at Pralines, an all-day café with indoor/outdoor patio seating. For libations with piano music, take the escalator to Breeze's Lounge on the second floor of the atrium.

Services: Airport courtesy shuttle, 24-hour room service, concierge, valet laundry.

Facilities: Outdoor heated swimming pool, whirlpool, health club.

MODERATE

HOLIDAY INN—ASHLEY PLAZA, 111 W. Fortune St., Tampa, FL 33602. Tel. 813/223-1351, or toll free 800/ASK-VALUE. Fax 813/221-2000. 315 rms. A/C TV TEL

$ Rates: $65–$95 single; $85–$105 double. AE, CB, DC, DISC, MC, V.

Perched along the Hillsborough River, this modern 14-story hotel is downtown, next to the Tampa Bay Performing Arts Center and within walking distance of most attractions. Guest rooms are spacious, with dark-wood furnishings, rose or aqua-toned fabrics, and full-length wall mirrors. Most rooms on upper floors have views of the river.

Dining/Entertainment: The lobby level offers three choices: The Backstage Restaurant, for moderately priced meals in a theatrical setting; The Deli for light fare; and the Encore lounge for drinks and occasional live music.

Services: Airport courtesy shuttle, room service, valet laundry.

Facilities: Outdoor heated swimming pool, whirlpool, fitness room, coin-operated laundry, gift shop.

QUALITY SUITES—BUSCH GARDENS, 3001 University Center Dr., Tampa, FL 33612. Tel. 813/971-8930, or toll free 800/228-5151. Fax 813/971-8935. 150 suites. A/C TV TEL

$ Rates (including full breakfast and evening cocktail reception): $69–$109 single; $74–$114 double. AE, DC, DISC, MC, V.

This hacienda-style all-suite hotel sits directly behind Busch Gardens, although the entrance to the theme park is four blocks away. Each guest unit has a separate bedroom with built-in armoire and well-lit mirrored vanity area, a living/dining room with sofa bed, plus wet bar, coffee maker, microwave, and stereo/VCR unit. The decor relies heavily on art deco–style furnishings.

Services: 24-hour gift shop/food store, VCR rentals, valet laundry.

Facilities: Outdoor heated swimming pool, Jacuzzi, meeting rooms, coin-operated laundry.

RADISSON BAY HARBOR INN, 7700 Courtney Campbell Causeway, Tampa, FL 33607. Tel. 813/281-8900, or toll free 800/333-3333. Fax 813/281-0189. 257 rms. A/C TV TEL

$ Rates: $89–$129 single or double. AE, CB, DC, MC, V.

Situated on Old Tampa Bay, two miles west of the airport, this six-story property is one of the few hotels that actually has a sandy beach of its own. The guest rooms, all with views of the water, have a balcony or patio. The decor, which uses mostly pastel-toned fabrics, reflects art deco influences.

Dining/Entertainment: Views of the water and food are the prime attractions at the lobby-level Yankee Trader Restaurant and Lounge.

Services: Airport courtesy shuttle, valet laundry.

Facilities: Heated outdoor swimming pool, two lighted tennis courts, hair salons for men and women, gift shop.

RAMADA RESORT, 820 E. Busch Blvd., Tampa, FL 33612. Tel. 813/933-4011, or toll free 800/288-4011. Fax 813/932-1784. 255 rms. A/C TV TEL

$ Rates: $55–$75 single; $65–$85 double. AE, CB, DC, DISC, MC, V.

Attracting a business clientele as well as vacationers, this two- and four-story hotel is situated two miles west of Busch Gardens. The lobby leads to an enclosed skylit atrium-style courtyard with fountains, streetlights, benches, shops, café, bars, a pool, and other sports facilities. Guest rooms, which surround the courtyard, offer standard furnishings, enlivened by colorful, eye-catching fabrics.

Dining/Entertainment: Apricots Restaurant, off the lobby, features seafood dishes. Charades Nite Club offers live entertainment and the Atrium has a café, lounge, and coffee shop.

Services: Courtesy transport to Busch Gardens, concierge desk, secretarial services, valet laundry.

Facilities: Indoor and outdoor heated swimming pools, two Jacuzzis, sauna, four lighted tennis courts, tennis pro shop, exercise room, games room, coin-operated laundry, gift shop.

SHERATON TAMPA EAST, 7401 E. Hillsborough Ave., Tampa, FL 33610. Tel. 813/626-0999, or toll free 800/325-3535. Fax 813/626-0999, ext. 246. 156 rms. A/C TV TEL

$ Rates: $60–$75 single; $70–$85 double. AE, CB, DC, MC, V.

Ten minutes from downtown, this two-, three-, and six-story property is situated off I-4 in a palm-tree–shaded setting, close to the State Fairgrounds and an hour away from Orlando-area attractions. Guest rooms, many of which surround a central courtyard and pool area, are contemporary in decor, with dark woods, brass fixtures, pastel tones, and floral art. Most units have balconies or patios.

Dining/Entertainment: The lobby area has a lounge bar with an informal atmosphere; or follow a covered walkway to an adjacent building and the Cypress Landing Restaurant and Lounge.

Services: Airport courtesy shuttle, room service, valet laundry, secretarial services.

Facilities: Outdoor heated swimming pool, health club, gift shop.

INEXPENSIVE

COURTYARD BY MARRIOTT, 3805 W. Cypress St., Tampa, FL 33607. Tel. 813/874-0555, or toll free 800/321-2211. Fax 813/870-0685. 145 rms. A/C TV TEL

$ Rates: $56–$90 single or double. AE, CB, DC, DISC, MC, V.

With a fireplace glowing in the lobby, this contemporary four-story hotel is a quiet oasis tucked beside the busy Dale Mabry Highway, three miles from the airport. Like other properties of this chain, it follows the usual layout, with guest rooms surrounding a central courtyard. The rooms, which offer a choice of a king-size bed or two double beds, feature dark-wood furnishings and pastel-toned fabrics, and have in-room coffee makers. Facilities include a café/lounge, outdoor swimming pool, indoor whirlpool, exercise room, and guest laundry.

DAYS INN ROCKY POINT, 7627 Courtney Campbell Causeway, Tampa, FL 33607. Tel. 813/281-0000, or toll free 800/237-2555, 800/332-6688 in Florida. Fax 813/281-1067. 152 rms. A/C TV TEL

$ Rates: $50–$60 single; $55–$80 double. AE, DC, DISC, MC, V.

Set back from the main road two miles west of the airport, this motel-style property has a lovely waterfront setting on Old Tampa Bay, but no beach. The layout encompasses six two-story wings, surrounding an outdoor swimming pool with landscaped courtyard, so the bedrooms offer either bay-view or poolside views. The units have a cheery decor with basic light-wood furniture.

For dining or imbibing, try the Alessi Deli and Lagoon Saloon. Facilities include a heated outdoor swimming pool, two tennis courts, a shuffleboard court, horseshoes, badminton, a volleyball court, a children's playground, rentals for paddle boats, and a coin-operated guest laundry.

BUDGET

COMFORT INN, 2106 E. Busch Blvd., Tampa, FL 33612. Tel. 813/931-3313, or toll free 800/221-2222. Fax 813/933-8140. 50 units. A/C TV TEL

$ Rates: $31–$75 single; $36–$75 double; $40–$75 efficiency. AE, DISC, MC, V.

Situated about half a mile west of Busch Gardens, this three-story motor inn offers a choice of accommodations. Most rooms are standard doubles, and some have only a shower instead of a full bath. In addition, there are larger rooms with king-size beds and full baths; and over a third of the units are efficiencies outfitted with small kitchenettes. Facilities are limited, but there's an outdoor heated swimming pool.

DAYS INN–BUSCH GARDENS/MAINGATE, 2901 E. Busch Blvd., Tampa, FL 33612. Tel. 813/933-6471, or toll free 800/325-2525. Fax 813/931-0261. 179 rms. A/C TV TEL

$ Rates: $32–$59 single; $37–$64 double. AE, DC, MC, V.

Within walking distance of Busch Gardens, this two-story motel is popular with families. Although the registration office is just off the main thoroughfare, most of the guest rooms are set back in a quieter environment surrounding an outdoor swimming pool. Rooms offer standard furnishings, mostly with two double beds. There are no dining outlets on the premises, but a full-service 24-hour restaurant is adjacent. In addition to the pool, on-site facilities include a children's playground, games room, and coin-operated laundry.

HAMPTON INN, 4817 W. Laurel St., Tampa, FL 33607. Tel. 813/878-0778, or toll free 800/HAMPTON. Fax 813/287-0882. 134 rms. A/C TV TEL

$ Rates (including continental breakfast): $47–$54 single; $54–$61 double.

This six-story property offers good value along the busy corridor within a mile of the airport. Guest rooms are decorated with dark woods, set off by pink, peach, and beige tones. Some units offer king-size beds and extra work areas and 50% of the rooms are designated as no-smoking. Facilities are limited, but there is an outdoor heated swimming pool and a courtesy shuttle to the airport.

LA QUINTA–AIRPORT, 4730 W. Spruce St., Tampa, FL 33607. Tel. 813/287-0440, or toll free 800/531-5900. Fax 813/286-7399. 122 rms. A/C TV TEL

$ Rates: $58–$65 single; $66–$73 double. AE, CB, DC, DISC, MC, V.

Equally convenient to the airport and the Westshore business district, this two-story hacienda-style motel offers a homey alternative to the many sleek high-rise hostelries in this area. Guest rooms, which surround a central courtyard, are decorated in a southwestern motif, with light woods, pueblo art, and colorful fabrics. Public areas include a cozy lobby with a fireplace and a sundeck with sombrero-shaped umbrellas. There's a complimentary airport shuttle and an adjacent 24-hour restaurant.

RED ROOF INN, 2307 E. Busch Blvd., Tampa, FL 33612. Tel. 813/932-0073, or toll free 800/THE-ROOF. Fax 813/933-5689. 108 rms. A/C TV TEL

$ Rates: $33–$45 single; $39–$55 double. AE, CB, DC, DISC, MC, V.

Half a mile west of Busch Gardens, this two-story property is set back from the road in a well-landscaped, grassy setting. The layout consists of two adjacent wings with an outdoor pool and whirlpool in the center. The guest units are outfitted with bright checkered fabrics and standard furnishings.

WHERE TO DINE

Tampa offers a wide variety of fine restaurants, with menus ranging from typically American fare to regional southern dishes or Cajun Créole cooking, as well as more exotic offerings from Spain, France, Italy, Germany, Mexico, and the Orient. Most of all, the Tampa area is outstanding for seafood—delights fresh from nearby gulf waters and beyond. The port of Tampa is home to one of Florida's largest shrimp-boat fleets. Other local favorites include grouper, pompano, snapper, stone crabs, rock shrimp, and crayfish.

VERY EXPENSIVE

BERN'S STEAK HOUSE, 1208 S. Howard Ave. Tel. 251-2421.

Cuisine: AMERICAN. **Reservations:** Required.

$ Prices: Main courses $13.80–$41.50. CB, DC, MC, V.

Open: Dinner only, daily 5–11pm.

No visit to Tampa is complete without dinner at Bern Laxer's one-of-a-kind restaurant, an attraction in itself; indeed, many people make reservations weeks in advance. Started on a small scale in 1953, and still totally unpretentious on the outside, it has grown to a two-story, seven-room Tampa institution.

Above all, it's a temple of beef where the motto is "art in steaks"—you order a prime, well-aged steak according to the thickness and weight you prefer, which is then cut and broiled over charcoal to your specifications. If beef is not your fancy, perhaps the menu can tempt you with lamb, veal, chicken, and fish. Depending on the season, most vegetables served at Bern's are grown in the restaurant's own organic garden. All entrees come with onion soup, salad, baked potato, garlic toast, and onion rings. (*Note:* Smoking is prohibited in the main dining rooms).

CK's, 8th Floor in the Tampa Airport Marriott, Tampa International Airport. Tel. 879-5151.

Cuisine: CONTINENTAL/AMERICAN. **Reservations:** Recommended.

$ Prices: Main courses $15–$24.95. AE, CB, DC, MC, V.

Open: Lunch Mon–Sat 11:30am–2:30pm, Sun 10:30am–2:30pm; dinner Mon–Sat 5–11pm, Sun 5–10pm.

In the heart of the airport, this revolving rooftop restaurant is a one-of-a-kind in Tampa and an attraction in its own right. There is an ever-changing view from every table, spanning the adjacent jetways and more distant vistas of

Tampa Bay and the city skyline. The extensive dinner menu ranges from local seafoods to prime ribs, steaks, and rack of lamb. Specialties include seared pepper tuna, basil swordfish, shrimp scampi with tri-color linguine, spinach ravioli stuffed with crabmeat, and blackened breast of chicken. The "early bird" menu, available from 5 to 7pm, offers exceptional value.

DONATELLO, 232 N. Dale Mabry Hwy. Tel. 875-6660.

Cuisine: NORTHERN ITALIAN. **Reservations:** Recommended.

$ Prices: Main courses $15.95–$24.95. AE, CB, DC, MC, V.

Open: Lunch Mon–Fri noon–3pm; dinner daily 6–11pm.

With stucco arches, Italian tilework, and peach-colored linens, this romantic restaurant has a Mediterranean flair, artfully enhanced by soft individual table lighting, and an attentive tuxedoed waiting staff. Specialties include linguine with Maine lobster, breast of duck with Curaçao and orange sauce, veal "Dolce Vita" (with ham, mushrooms, and truffles), salmon Stromboli (with asparagus, shrimp, and creamy white wine sauce), and osso buco alla milanese.

EXPENSIVE

THE CASTAWAY, 7720 Courtney Campbell Causeway. Tel. 281-0770.

Cuisine: AMERICAN/POLYNESIAN/SEAFOOD. **Reservations:** Accepted for dinner, with seating at the first available table at the time requested.

$ Prices: Main courses $12.95–$19.95. AE, CB, DC, MC, V.

Open: Lunch Mon–Fri 11am–3pm, Sat–Sun noon–3pm; dinner Mon–Thurs 5–10pm, Fri–Sat 5–11pm, Sun 4–10pm.

Situated beside the Ben T. Davis Municipal Beach, this nautically themed spot bills itself as Tampa's only beachfront restaurant. The building rests on stilts over the waters of Old Tampa Bay, making the views hard to equal, especially at sunset time. The menu is a blend of seafaring specials with a Polynesian influence. Choices range from seafood brochettes, bouillabaisse, and stir-fry dishes to mahimahi macadamia, coconut shrimp, and scallops chardonnay. Non-seafood selections include Hawaiian chicken, pastas, and steaks.

SELENA'S, 1623 Snow Ave. Tel. 251-2116.

Cuisine: CAJUN/ITALIAN. **Reservations:** Recommended.

$ Prices: Main courses $8.95–$19.95. AE, CB, DC, MC, V.

Open: Mon 11am–10pm, Tues–Thurs 11am–11pm, Fri–Sat 11am–midnight, Sun 11am–2:30pm and 4:30–9pm.

Step inside this charming restaurant, in the Old Hyde Park shopping complex, and you'll feel like you're in the heart of New Orleans, whether you sit in the plant-filled Patio Room, the eclectic Antique Room, or the elegant linens-and-lace Queen Anne Room. Open the menu and you'll see an interesting blend of dishes, reflecting the owners' family backgrounds. Local seafoods, especially grouper and shrimp, top the menu at dinner, with many of the dishes served Créole style or blackened, as well as broiled and fried. Choices also include pastas, chicken, steaks, and veal. At night, jazz sounds enliven the proceedings, as musical groups perform in the upstairs lounge.

VILLANOVA BY LAURO, 4030 W. Waters Ave. Tel. 889-8800.

Cuisine: ITALIAN. **Reservations:** Recommended.

$ Prices: Main courses $12.50–$19.75. AE, CB, DC, MC, V.

Open: Lunch Mon–Fri 11:30am–2pm; dinner Mon–Sat 6–11pm.

With a classic decor, soft music, tuxedoed waiters, and a kitchen presided over by award-winning chef Lauro Medaglia, this restaurant is a little off the beaten track, but well worth a detour northwest of the airport, off the Dale Mabry Highway. The menu includes six different veal dishes; steak flamed in a cream sauce of brandy and green peppercorns; chicken breast with eggplant, mozzarella, and tomatoes; sweetbreads with prosciutto; and jumbo marinated grilled shrimp; as well as over a dozen freshly made pastas such as fettuccine Alfredo, cannelloni, tortellini, and gnocchi con Gorgonzola (potato dumplings with Gorgonzola cream cheese).

MODERATE

CAFE CREOLE AND OYSTER BAR, 1330 Ninth Ave., Ybor City. Tel. 247-6283.

Cuisine: CAJUN/CREOLE. **Reservations:** Recommended.

$ Prices: Main courses $8.95–$13.95. AE, CB, DC, MC, V.

Open: Mon–Thurs 11:30am–10pm, Fri–Sat 11:30am–11pm, Sun noon–4pm.

If you're curious about Ybor City history, the setting of this indoor/outdoor restaurant tells quite a tale. The building, dating back to 1896, was originally known as El Pasaje, the home of the Cherokee Club, a gentlemen's hotel and private club with a casino and a decor rich in stained-glass windows, wrought-iron balconies, Spanish murals, and marble bathrooms. During the Depression and the years following, the building was used variously as a political club, low-rent hotel, and WPA school of music, art, and dance. It was placed on the National Register of Historic Places in 1973 and new owners restored it in the 1980s.

Specialties include Louisiana-style dishes—red beans and rice with andouille sausage, blackened catfish, seafood gumbo, grouper Bienville, crayfish étouffé, and jambalaya. The oyster bar also offers Bajou country oysters from New Orleans served half a dozen ways.

THE COLONNADE, 3401 Bayshore Blvd. Tel. 839-7558.

Cuisine: AMERICAN/SEAFOOD. **Reservations:** Accepted only for large parties.

$ Prices: Main courses $7.95–$16.95. AE, DC, MC, V.

Open: Sun–Thurs 11am–10pm, Fri–Sat 11am–11pm.

Overlooking Hillsborough Bay and nestled in Hyde Park's palm-shaded residential neighborhood, this restaurant was established in 1935, and it has since become a local institution, winning special acclaim for fresh seafood. Specialties include grouper in lemon butter, crab-stuffed flounder, wild Florida alligator, Cajun catfish, broiled Florida lobster, and half a dozen varieties of shrimp (from batter-dipped or crabmeat-stuffed, to pecan-fried or scampi). Prime rib, steaks, and chicken are also available.

THE COLUMBIA, 2117 Seventh Ave. E., Ybor City. Tel. 248-4961.

Cuisine: SPANISH. **Reservations:** Recommended.

$ Prices: Main courses $10.95–$16.95. AE, CB, DC, MC, V.

Open: Daily 11am–11pm.

This is the Columbia that everyone talks about, dating back to 1905 and occupying a full city block in the heart of Ybor City. The decor throughout is graced with hand-painted tiles, wrought-iron chandeliers, dark woods, rich red fabrics, and stained-glass windows.

Among the tempting menu items are red snapper Alicante (baked in a casserole with Spanish onions and peppers, and topped with almonds, eggplant, and shrimp), filet mignon Columbia (wrapped in bacon, with mushrooms, ham, onions, peppers, in a tomato-and-burgundy sauce), traditional chicken and yellow rice, and three types of spicy paellas. All entrees come with Cuban bread and yellow rice or potato. A favorite starter is the "Original 1905 Salad"—lettuce, tomato, smoked ham, Swiss and Romano cheeses, olives, and more, with a house garlic dressing. Monday through Saturday, there's also a flamenco show at 8:30pm ($5 extra).

A second location, with water views, is at 601 S. Harbor Island Blvd., Harbour Island (tel. 229-2992). Other branches are in downtown St. Petersburg, Clearwater, and Sarasota.

CRAWDADDY'S, 2500 Rocky Point Dr. Tel. 281-0407.

Cuisine: REGIONAL/SEAFOOD. **Reservations:** Recommended.

$ Prices: Main courses $3.95–$7.95 at lunch, $10.95–$17.95 at dinner. AE, CB, DC, MC, V.

Open: Lunch Mon–Thurs 11am–3pm, Fri–Sat 11am–3pm; dinner Mon–Thurs 4:30–11pm, Fri–Sat 4:30pm–midnight, Sun 4–10pm.

Overlooking Old Tampa Bay near the airport off the Courtney Campbell Causeway,

- Bern's Steak House 12
- Cactus Club 13
- Cafe Creole & Oyster Bar 14
- Castaway 8
- Cha Cha Coconuts 22
- CK's 7
- Colonnade 19
- Columbia, Harbour Island 23
- Columbia, Ybor City 16
- Crabby Tom's 6
- Crawdaddy's 9
- Donatello 10
- Le Bordeaux 18
- Loading Dock 20
- Lucy Ho's Bamboo Garden 1
- Mel's Hot Dogs 3
- Mise en Place 21
- Parker's Lighthouse 24
- Rumpelmayer's 4
- Selena's 17
- Shells, Dale Mayby Hwy. 11
- Shells, 30th Street 2
- Silver Ring 15
- Villanova by Lauro 5

N
0
2 mi
3.4 km
Gunn Hwy.
597
Lake Ellen
Carrollwood
Lake Carroll
Linebaugh Ave.
Sheldon Rd.
Waters Ave.
580
Anderson Ave.
Egypt Lake
Armenia Ave.
Lambright St.
Hillsborough Ave.
N. Dale Mabry Hwy.
Dr. Martin Lu
589
Tampa International Airport
60
Columbus Dr.
Courtney Campbell Causeway
Rocky Point
Memorial Hwy.
Spruce St.
92
Kennedy B
Howard Frankland Bridge
Henderson Blvd.
685
275
Old Tampa Bay
Manhattan Ave.
S. Dale Mabry Hwy.
Crosstown Expwy.
Bayshore Bl
Westshore Blvd.
Gandy
Blvd.
Gandy Bridge
MacDill Ave.
MacDill Air Force Bas
5446

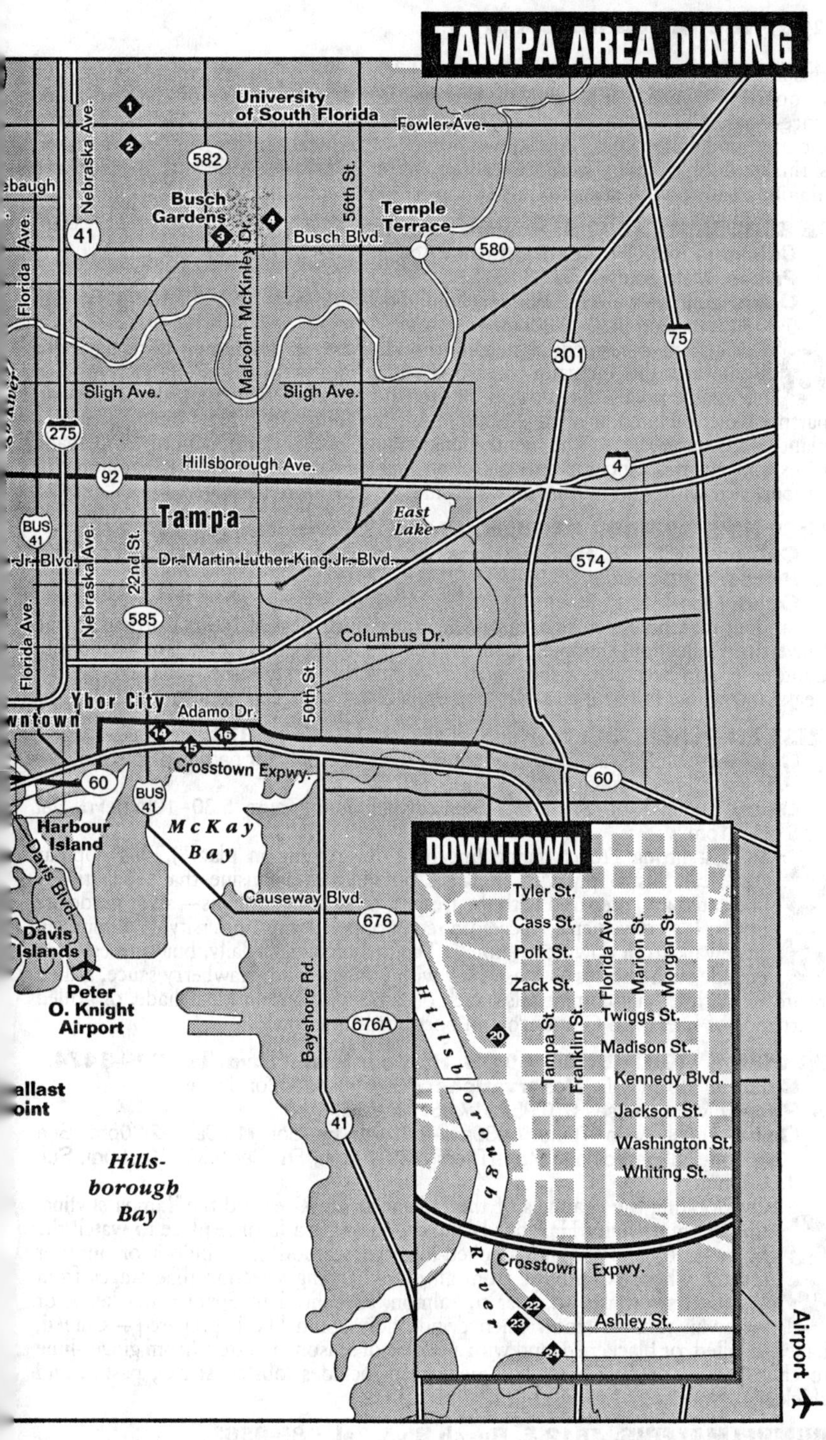

TAMPA AREA DINING
University of South Florida
Fowler Ave.
Nebraska Ave.
582
Busch Gardens
56th St.
Temple Terrace
Busch Blvd.
580
Malcolm McKinley Dr.
Florida Ave.
41
75
301
Sligh Ave.
Sligh Ave.
275
Hillsborough Ave.
92
4
Tampa
East Lake
BUS 41
Nebraska Ave.
22nd St.
Dr. Martin Luther King Jr. Blvd.
574
585
Columbus Dr.
Florida Ave.
50th St.
Ybor City
Adamo Dr.
Crosstown Expwy.
60
60
BUS 41
Harbour Island
McKay Bay
Davis Blvd.
Causeway Blvd.
676
Davis Islands
Peter O. Knight Airport
Bayshore Rd.
676A
Hills-borough Bay
41
DOWNTOWN
Tyler St.
Cass St.
Polk St.
Zack St.
Florida Ave.
Marion St.
Morgan St.
Twiggs St.
Madison St.
Tampa St.
Franklin St.
Kennedy Blvd.
Jackson St.
Washington St.
Whiting St.
Hillsborough River
Crosstown Expwy.
Ashley St.
Airport

this informal spot is named after Beauregard "Crawdaddy" Belvedere, a Roaring '20s tycoon. He owned a fish camp on this site and the decor has not changed much since—the seven dining rooms are all bedecked with Victorian furnishings, books, pictures, and collectibles. The "down home"-style menu ranges from beer-battered shrimp and fish camp fry (shrimp, scallops, and fresh fish, deep-fried in corn crisp and almond coating, with jalapeño hush puppies) to surf-and-turf, prime ribs, and steaks.

LE BORDEAUX, 1502 S. Howard Ave. Tel. 254-4387.

Cuisine: FRENCH. **Reservations:** Accepted for parties of six or more.
$ Prices: Main courses $7.95–$14.95. AE, DC, MC, V.
Open: Lunch Mon–Fri 11:30am–2pm; dinner Mon–Thurs 5:30–10pm, Fri–Sat 5:30–11pm, Sun 5:30–9:30pm.

Located in a residential neighborhood, west of downtown near Bayshore Boulevard, this bungalow/bistro is a real find, with first-rate French food at affordable prices. The domain of French-born chef/owner Gordon Davis and partner Colette Hatch, it offers seating in a living room–style main dining area or a plant-filled conservatory. The menu changes daily, but you can count on homemade pâtés and pastries, and the specials often include salmon en croûte, papillotte of halibut, veal with wild mushrooms, and filet of beef au roquefort.

LUCY HO'S BAMBOO GARDEN, 2740 E. Fowler Ave. Tel. 977-2783.

Cuisine: CHINESE. **Reservations:** Accepted only for parties of five or more.
$ Prices: Main courses $5.95–$15.95. AE, DC, MC, V.
Open: Mon–Sat 11:30am–10pm, Sun 11:30am–9pm.

A standout for Chinese cuisine, this restaurant is northwest of Busch Gardens, in the University Collection Shopping Center. The menu features a blend of Mandarin, Cantonese, and Szechuan dishes, such as Mongolian beef, cashew chicken, pepper steak, and whole fish Hunan style. Chinese alcohol and beer are also available.

MISE EN PLACE, 442 W. Kennedy Blvd. Tel. 254-5373.

Cuisine: AMERICAN. **Reservations:** Accepted only for parties of six or more.
$ Prices: Main courses $9.95–$15.95. MC, V.
Open: Lunch Mon–Fri 11am–3pm; dinner Tues–Thurs 5:30–10pm, Fri–Sat 5:30–11pm.

With a fitting French name (meaning "everything in place"), this popular American bistro puts its emphasis on innovative cuisine that's beautifully presented and prepared with the freshest of local ingredients—all at moderate prices. It's conveniently located directly opposite the University of Tampa, an easy walk from downtown hotels. The menu changes daily, but entrees often include such choices as roast duck with Jamaica wild strawberry sauce, grilled swordfish with tri-melon mint salsa, rack of lamb with hazelnut parsliade, or grilled tournedos of beef with Gorgonzola in port-bordelaise sauce.

PARKER'S LIGHTHOUSE, 601 S. Harbour Island Blvd. Tel. 229-3474.

Cuisine: SEAFOOD. **Reservations:** Recommended for dinner.
$ Prices: Main courses $10.95–$17.95. AE, MC, V.
Open: Lunch Mon–Thurs 11:30am–2:30pm, Fri–Sat 11:30am–2:30pm, Sun 10:30am–2:30pm; dinner Mon–Thurs 5:30–10pm, Fri–Sat 5:30–10:30pm, Sun 4:30–9pm.

Overlooking the channels of the Hillsborough River and the Tampa skyline, this bright and airy Harbour Island restaurant is a favorite place to watch the boats go by and to enjoy cooked-to-order seafood in an indoor or outdoor setting. Choose an entree from an ever-changing selection that ranges from shark to swordfish, snapper to salmon, sheephead to Spanish mackerel, or yellowfin tuna to trout. Then decide how you'd like it prepared—sautéed, baked, broiled, or blackened, and with a choice of seasoned butters (from ginger-lime to chive-parsley or pine nut). The menu also includes lobster, steaks, pastas, and chicken.

RUMPELMAYER'S, 4812 E. Busch Blvd. Tel. 989-9563.

Cuisine: GERMAN/EUROPEAN. **Reservations:** Recommended.

$ **Prices:** Main courses $7.50–$17.50. MC, V.
Open: Dinner only, Tues–Sun 5–10pm.

Here's a little bit of Bavaria just eight blocks from Busch Gardens. The menu presents tasty and traditional entrees ranging from haringsla (a cold plate of North Sea herring with red beets, apples, and onions), to assorted wursts, wienerschnitzel, sauerbraten, Hungarian stuffed cabbage, and Polish kolbassi. Seafood lovers take delight in the smoked mackerel from the North Sea, "Garnalen" (shrimp scampi with Moselle wine), and Dutch flounder sautéed in brown butter.

INEXPENSIVE

CRABBY TOM'S OLD TIME OYSTER BAR AND SEAFOOD RESTAURANT, 3120 W. Hillsborough Ave. Tel. 870-1652.
Cuisine: SEAFOOD. **Reservations:** Accepted only for parties of 10 or more.
$ **Prices:** Main courses $4.95–$15.95. DISC, MC, V.
Open: Mon–Thurs 11am–10pm, Fri–Sat 11am–11pm, Sun 4–9pm.

Although this spot lacks waterside views and an impressive decor, the seafood lovers dining here don't seem to mind. Sit back, relax, and crack open a pile of mild or spicy steamed blue crabs, stone crab claws, Alaska snow crab claws, or king crab legs. If you tire of crab, there's always a lobster from the tank or an array of other seafood, from grouper, flounder, and catfish to shrimp, scallops, smelts, and smoked mullet, as well as clams and oysters on the half shell. Chicken, pastas, and ribs are also offered.

BUDGET

CACTUS CLUB, 1601 Snow Ave. Tel. 251-4089.
Cuisine: MEXICAN/AMERICAN SOUTHWEST. **Reservations:** Not required.
$ **Prices:** Main courses $5.95–$11.95. MC, V.
Open: Mon–Sat 11:30am–midnight, Sun noon–midnight.

Big and brassy, yet casual and comfortable, this sometimes-noisy café radiates southwestern pizazz in the heart of the Old Hyde Park shopping complex. It's the place to be if you're in the mood for fajitas, tacos, enchiladas, chili, hickory-smoked baby back ribs, Texas-style pizzas, blackened chicken, or guacamole/green-chili burgers.

CHA CHA COCONUTS, 601 S. Harbour Island Blvd. Tel. 223-3101.
Cuisine: AMERICAN. **Reservations:** Not required.
$ **Prices:** Main courses $3.95–$7.95. AE, DC, MC, V.
Open: Mon–Thurs 11am–10pm, Fri–Sat 11am–midnight, Sun noon–9pm.

With indoor/outdoor seating and lovely views of Hillsborough Bay and downtown, this informal Harbour Island eatery is billed as a tropical bar and grill. Ideal for lunch or a light meal, the menu is simple—burgers, grouper sandwiches, chowders and chilis, and finger foods such as peel-and-eat shrimp, oysters on the half shell, and chicken wings. Live music is often on tap, and all items on the menu are also available on a "to go" basis. Also located in St. Petersburg, Clearwater, and Sarasota.

THE LOADING DOCK, 100 Madison St. Tel. 223-6905.
Cuisine: AMERICAN/DELI. **Reservations:** Not required.
$ **Prices:** Main courses $1.75–$4.95. No credit cards.
Open: Mon–Fri 8am–8pm, Sat 10:30am–2:30pm.

As its name implies, this downtown eatery occupies a vintage Tampa building that was once the city's main loading dock for wholesale groceries. The menu conveys a loading dock theme, with sandwiches such as the "union boss" (hot corned beef, Swiss, and sauerkraut), the "box car" (salami and provolone), and the "forklift" (all-beef knockwurst with sauerkraut and spicy mustard). Salads and soups are also featured.

MEL'S HOT DOGS, 4136 E. Busch Blvd. Tel. 985-8000.
Cuisine: AMERICAN. **Reservations:** Not accepted.

$ **Prices:** Main courses $1–$6. No credit cards.
Open: Mon–Sat 10am–10pm, Sun 11am–9pm.

If you crave an old-fashioned Chicago-style all-beef hot dog before or after a foray into Busch Gardens, look no further. Considered "the big daddy" of hot-dog eateries, this informal place offers everything from "bagel-dogs" to bacon-, cheddar-, or corndogs. All choices are served on a poppyseed bun and most come with french fries and a choice of cole slaw or baked beans. Even the decor is dedicated to weiners, with walls and windows lined with hot-dog memorabilia. And just in case hot-dog mania hasn't won you over, there a few alternative choices (sausages, chicken breast, and burgers).

SHELLS, 202 S. Dale Mabry Hwy. Tel. 875-3467.
Cuisine: SEAFOOD. **Reservations:** Not accepted.
$ **Prices:** Main courses $4.95–$12.95. MC, V.
Open: Dinner only, Sun–Thurs 5–10pm, Fri–Sat 5–11pm.

Shells is a local institution, synonymous with fresh seafood at low prices. Founded in 1985, it has a simple formula for success—a fresh seafood menu, no frills, no reservations, and, above all, no strain on the budget. You may have to wait at least a half hour to be seated, and then you'll eat at picnic-style tables with paper and plastic utensils—but the food is worth it. The menu features Alaskan king crab legs and claws, Dungeness crab clusters, snow crab, scallops, shrimp, grouper, cod, and pasta combinations such as shrimp and cheese tortellini. There are also a few beef and chicken choices.

Other Tampa locations are at 14380 N. Dale Mabry Hwy. (tel. 968-6686) and 11010 N. 30th St. (tel. 977-8456). Also located in St. Petersburg and Bradenton.

SILVER RING, 1831 E. Seventh Ave., Ybor City. Tel. 248-2549.
Cuisine: SPANISH/AMERICAN. **Reservations:** Not required.
$ **Prices:** Main courses $2.25–$4.95. No credit cards.
Open: Mon–Sat 6:30am–5pm.

Operating since 1947, this place is now an Ybor City tradition. The walls are lined with old pictures, vintage radios, a 1950s jukebox, fishing rods, and deer heads. Most of all, it's *the* place to get a genuine Cuban sandwich—smoked ham, roast pork, Genoa salami, Swiss cheese, pickles, salad dressing, mustard, lettuce, and tomato on Cuban bread. Other menu items include Spanish bean soup, deviled crab, and other types of sandwiches.

SHOPPING

MALLS & MARKETS

OLD HYDE PARK VILLAGE, 712 S. Oregon Ave., Hyde Park. Tel. 251-3500.

Located in one of the city's oldest and most historic neighborhoods, this is Tampa's "Rodeo Drive," a cluster of 50 upscale shops and boutiques in a village layout. The selection includes Brooks Brothers, Crabtree & Evelyn, Godiva Chocolatier, Laura Ashley, and Polo–Ralph Lauren. Open Monday through Wednesday and Saturday from 10am to 6pm, on Thursday and Friday from 10am to 9pm, and on Sunday from noon to 5pm.

THE SHOPS ON HARBOUR ISLAND, 601 S. Harbour Island Blvd., Harbour Island. Tel. 223-9898 or 228-7807.

Tampa's waterfront marketplace, on an island directly south of downtown, is well worth a day's outing. The 20 different shops include art galleries and fashion boutiques, as well as outlets for swimwear, sportswear, sunglasses, candies, collectibles, and Oriental treasures. Open Monday through Saturday from 10am to 9pm, and on Sunday from 11am to 6pm.

YBOR CITY FARMERS MARKET, Centennial Park, Ybor City. Tel. 248-5223.

This is a colorful open-air farmer's market in the heart of Tampa's historic Latin

Quarter, with a different seasonal theme each month. You might come away loaded down with fresh produce, pastries, flowers, wines, cheeses, coffee, antiques, or books. Open on the third Saturday of each month from 8am to 1pm.

YBOR SQUARE, 1901 13th St., Ybor City. Tel. 247-4497.

Listed on the National Register of Historic Places, this complex consists of three brick buildings (dating to 1886) that once comprised the largest cigar factory in the world, employing over 4,000 workers. Today it's a specialty mall, with over three dozen shops, selling everything from clothing, crafts, and jewelry to (of course) cigars. Open Monday through Saturday from 9:30am to 5:30pm and on Sunday from noon to 5:30pm.

SPECIALTY STORES

ADAM'S CITY HATTERS, 1621 E. Seventh Ave., Ybor City. Tel. 229-2850.

Established over 75 years ago and reputed to be Florida's largest hat store (with a mind-boggling inventory of more than 18,000 hats), this shop offers all types of headgear, from Stetsons and Panamas to top hats, sombreros, and caps. Open Monday through Friday from 9:30am to 5:30pm.

HEAD'S FLAGS, 1923 E. Seventh Ave., Ybor City. Tel. 248-5019.

Here you'll find colorful flags from all nations and all states, as well as banners, ethnic items, T-shirts, and hats. Open Monday through Friday from 9:30am to 5:30pm and on Saturday from 9:30am to 3pm.

MARTINEZ DE YBOR ART GALLERY, 2025 E. Seventh Ave., Ybor City. Tel. 247-2771.

Step inside this shop/studio and meet Arnold Martinez as he puts scenes of Tampa and Ybor City on canvas with his unique media—paints and acrylics made of Cuban coffee, tea pigments, and Tampa tobacco. Open Wednesday through Saturday from 11am to 4pm.

ONE WORLD GIFT SHOP, 412 Zack St. Tel. 229-0679.

Tucked into two rooms of the First Presbyterian Church, this downtown shop sells handcrafted clothes, jewelry, and gifts made by Third World artisans from Central and South America, Asia, India, and Mexico. Open Monday through Friday from 11am to 2pm.

THE PEN STORE, 404 Zack St. Tel. 223-3865.

The only store in the Southeast specializing in pens, this unique downtown shop stocks all the major brands of writing instruments, as well as desk sets and inks. Open Monday through Saturday from 9am to 5pm.

EVENING ENTERTAINMENT

Whether you're a fan of drama or dance, rock or reggae, comedy or the classics, chances are you'll find it in Tampa. To assist visitors, the Tampa/Hillsborough Arts Council maintains an **Artsline** (tel. 229-ARTS), a 24-hour information service providing the latest on current and upcoming cultural events.

THE PERFORMING ARTS

Major Concert/Performance Halls

TAMPA BAY PERFORMING ARTS CENTER, 1010 N. MacInnes Place. Tel. 221-1045, or toll free 800/955-1045.

With a prime downtown location on a nine-acre site along the east bank of the Hillsborough River, this huge three-theater complex is the focal point of Tampa's performing arts scene. It presents a wide range of classical, orchestral, and pop concerts, operas, Broadway plays, cabarets, and special events.

Admission: Tickets, $12.50–$45 evenings, $4–$25 matinees.

TAMPA STADIUM, 4201 N. Dale Mabry Hwy. Tel. 872-7977.

Home of Super Bowls XVIII and XXV and many other sporting events, this giant 74,296-seat stadium is frequently the site of world-class concerts.

Admission: Tickets, $10–$35 and up, depending on the event.

USF SUN DOME, 4202 S. Fowler Ave. Tel. 974-3002, or 974-3001 for recorded information.

On the University of South Florida (USF) campus, this arena hosts major concerts by touring pop stars, rock bands, jazz groups, and other contemporary artists.

Admission: Tickets, $12–$25, depending on the event.

Theaters

LOFT THEATER, 1441 E. Fletcher Ave. Tel. 972-3383 or 251-8964.

In the same neighborhood as Busch Gardens, this theater is an oasis for aspiring bay area artists and an active venue for alternative and contemporary works.

Admission: Tickets, $6–$12.

SPANISH LYRIC THEATRE, 1032 Coral St. Tel. 223-7341.

A mainstay for over 35 years, this theater presents major international musicals and operettas in Spanish and English, preserving the traditions of Tampa's early days.

Admission: Tickets, $12.50–$17.50.

TAMPA THEATRE, 711 Franklin St. Tel. 223-8981.

On the National Register of Historic Places, this restored 1926 theater presents a varied program of classic, foreign, and alternative films, as well as concerts and special events.

Admission: Tickets, $4.75 adults, $3.75 seniors, $2 children 2–12. Some special events cost $5–$10 or more.

THE CLUB & MUSIC SCENE

Comedy Clubs

THE COMEDY WORKS, 3447 W. Kennedy Blvd. Tel. 875-9129.

An ever-changing program of live comedy is on tap at this club west of downtown. Shows are Sunday and Tuesday through Thursday at 8:30pm and on Friday and Saturday at 8:30 and 10:45pm.

Admission: $5–$10.

SIDESPLITTERS COMEDY CLUB, 12938 N. Dale Mabry Hwy. Tel. 960-1197.

Located northwest of downtown, Sidesplitters presents professional stand-up comedians on most nights. Shows begin Tuesday through Thursday at 8:30pm, and on Friday and Saturday at 8 and 10:30pm.

Admission: $6–$8.

Jazz/Blues/Reggae

BLUES SHIP, 1910 E. Seventh Ave., Ybor City. Tel. 248-6097.

With a mural of a ship adorning the wall, this club presents live blues and reggae in an informal meeting-house atmosphere. Open from 5pm to 3am Thursday through Saturday, and 5pm to 2am on Tuesday, Wednesday, and Sunday.

Admission: $2–$5.

BROTHERS LOUNGE, 5401 W. Kennedy Blvd. Tel. 286-8882.

A jazz haven for 20 years, this lounge concentrates solely on jazz, seven nights a week. Open on Monday from 8:30pm to 12:30am, Tuesday through Thursday from 9:30pm to 1:30am, on Friday and Saturday from 9:30pm to 2:30am, and on Sunday from 8pm to midnight.

Admission: $1–$3.

SKIPPER'S SMOKEHOUSE, 910 Skipper Rd. Tel. 971-0666.
This is a prime spot for live reggae or blues, and "zydeco," the Créole-blues-soul sound from New Orleans. Open on Tuesday, Wednesday, Saturday, and Sunday from 6:30 to 11pm, and on Friday from 8 to 11pm.
Admission: $2–$6; special events, $10 and up.

Dance Clubs/Discos/Rock and Top 40s Music

CLUB 911, 911 N. Franklin St. Tel. 224-0911.
A DJ plays a blend of progressive and alternative dance music, enhanced by big-screen movie clips. Open on Wednesday and Thursday from 9:30pm to 3am, and on Friday and Saturday from 9:30pm to 5am.
Admission: $3–$5.

ROCK-IT CLUB, 5016 N. Dale Mabry Hwy. Tel. 879-3699.
This rock 'n' roll club presents live bands, including big-name recording artists. Open daily 9pm to 3am.
Admission: $4–$12.

STINGERS, 11921 N. Dale Mabry Hwy. Tel. 968-1515.
Stingers boasts 15 video screens, seven bars, and two dance floors. Music is mostly Top-40 hits and some oldies, played by a DJ. Open nightly from 5pm to 3am. Drinks run $2–$5.
Admission: Free.

THE RITZ, 1503 E. Seventh Ave., Ybor City. Tel. 247-3319.
Housed in a former theater, this progressive dance club features live rock bands and groups playing the latest alternative hits for a youngish, mostly 20s crowd. Next to the main theater is a smaller room called Apocalypse, a dance club with a DJ who spins alternative music. Open Monday through Saturday from 9pm to 3am.
Admission: $5–$15 for live music, $1–$3 for DJ music.

YUCATAN LIQUOR STAND, 4811 W. Cypress St. Tel. 289-8454.
This is as close as you can get to a beach bar without actually being on a beach—counters made of old surfboards, tiki-hut trim, mounted fish specimens, and tropically painted booths within. The music (live Wednesday through Friday) ranges from Top-40s to reggae, country, or progressive. Open Monday through Thursday from 4pm to 3am, on Friday from 3pm to 3am, and on Saturday and Sunday from 6pm to 3am. Drinks cost $1 and up.
Admission: Free.

2. ST. PETERSBURG

20 miles SW of Tampa, 289 miles NW of Miami,
84 miles SW of Orlando

GETTING THERE By Plane Tampa International Airport, off Memorial Highway and Fla. 60 in Tampa (tel. 813/870-8700), approximately 16 miles northeast of St. Petersburg, is the prime gateway for all scheduled domestic and international flights serving the area (see the Tampa section for a list of airlines).

St. Petersburg–Clearwater International Airport, Roosevelt Boulevard/ Fla. 686, Clearwater (tel. 813/535-7600), is approximately 10 miles north of St. Petersburg. Although primarily a charter facility, it's served by scheduled flights operated by USAir Express and SkyBus.

Albert Whitted Municipal Airport, 108 Eighth Ave. S., St. Petersburg (tel. 813/893-7654), located downtown on the bayfront, serves as a landing strip for private planes.

By Train Passengers heading for St. Petersburg arrive first at the Tampa Amtrak Station at 601 Nebraska Ave. N. in Tampa (tel. 813/221-7600), and are then transferred by bus to the St. Petersburg Amtrak Station, 33rd Street North and 37th Avenue North, St. Petersburg (tel. 813/522-9475).

By Car The St. Petersburg area is linked to the Interstate system and is accessible from I-75, I-275, I-4, U.S. 19, and Fla. 60.

By Bus Greyhound/Trailways buses arrive at the carrier's downtown depot at 180 9th St. N., St. Petersburg (tel. 813/895-4455).

Sitting on a sheltered curve of land between Tampa Bay and the Gulf of Mexico, St. Petersburg blends the pulse of a city with the heart of a resort. Sleek new office towers stand beside historic Spanish-style landmarks, and businesses hum while sailboats breeze by.

But St. Petersburg (pop. 238,629) is more than just a city—it's a city surrounded by some of the Gulf of Mexico's finest beaches. There's St. Petersburg Beach, a 7½-mile paradise of sun, surf, and sand, and the adjacent "Holiday Isles"—a cluster of a dozen other beaches, stretching from Treasure Island northward to Clearwater Beach. Altogether, the city plus its neighboring beach communities constitute this vibrant Gulf Coast resort.

ORIENTATION

ARRIVING

The Limo Inc., 11901 30th Court N., St. Petersburg (tel. 813/572-1111, or toll free 800/282-6817), offers 24-hour door-to-door van service between Tampa International or St. Petersburg/Clearwater Airport and any St. Petersburg area destination or hotel. No reservations are required on arrival; just proceed to any Limo desk outside each baggage-claim area. The flat-rate one-way fare is $11.75 from Tampa Airport and $9.25 from St. Petersburg/Clearwater Airport to any St. Pete or gulf beach destination.

Red Line Limo Inc. (tel. 813/535-3391, or toll free 800/350-5466) also provides a daily 24-hour van service from Tampa International or St. Petersburg/Clearwater Airport to St. Petersburg or any other destination in Pinellas County. The cost is $10.25 from Tampa Airport and $8 from St. Pete/Clearwater, and reservations are required 24 hours in advance.

Yellow Cab Taxis (tel. 813/821-7777) line up outside the baggage-claim areas; no reservations are required. Average fare from Tampa Airport to St. Petersburg or any of the gulf beaches is approximately $25–$35 per taxi (one or more passengers). The fare from St. Petersburg/Clearwater Airport is approximately $15–$20.

TOURIST INFORMATION

For information on St. Petersburg, St. Petersburg Beach, and the neighboring "Holiday Isles," contact the **St. Petersburg/Clearwater Area Convention & Visitors Bureau,** Florida Suncoast Dome, One Stadium Dr., Suite A, St. Petersburg, FL 33705-1706 (tel. 813/892-7892).

Specific information about downtown St. Petersburg is also available from the **St. Petersburg Chamber of Commerce,** 100 Second Ave. N., St. Petersburg, FL 33701 (tel. 813/821-4069). There are also walk-in **visitor information centers** at The Pier in downtown St. Petersburg, and at St. Petersburg Beach, Treasure Island, Madeira Beach, Indian Rocks Beach, Clearwater, and Clearwater Beach.

CITY LAYOUT

St. Petersburg is laid out according to a grid system, with streets running north to south and avenues running east and west. **Central Avenue** is the dividing line for north and south addresses.

With the exception of Central Avenue, most streets and avenues downtown are one-way. Two-way traffic is also permitted on boulevards, usually diagonal thoroughfares west or north of downtown, such as Tyrone Boulevard, Gandy Boulevard, and Roosevelt Boulevard.

St. Petersburg's **downtown** district sits between two bays—Tampa and Boca Ciega. The major focus is on the section lining Tampa Bay, known as the Bayfront. Here you'll find The Pier, major museums, and most downtown hotels. Fanning out from the Bayfront, the city is composed of various residential neighborhoods.

St. Petersburg Beach, west of downtown and between Boca Ciega Bay and the Gulf of Mexico is a 7½-mile stretch of beach. **Gulf Boulevard** is the main two-way north-south thoroughfare, and most avenues, which cross in an east-west direction, have two-way traffic.

The **Holiday Isles,** north of St. Petersburg Beach and west of downtown, include Treasure Island, 3½ miles in length; Sand Key Island, a 12-mile island composed of Madeira Beach, Redington Beach, North Redington Beach, Redington Shores, Indian Shores, Indian Rocks Beach, and Belleair Beach; and Clearwater Beach.

GETTING AROUND

BY PUBLIC TRANSPORTATION **By Bus** The **Pinellas Suncoast Transit Authority/PSTA** (tel. 813/530-9911) operates regular bus service. The fare is 90¢.

BATS City Transit, 6655 Gulf Blvd., St. Petersburg Beach (tel. 813/367-3086), offers bus service along the St. Petersburg Beach strip. The fare is 95¢.

Treasure Island Transit System, c/o City Hall, 120 108th Ave. (tel. 813/360-0811), runs along the Treasure Island strip. The fare is $1.

By Trolley The **Clearwater Beach Trolley** is operated by the PSTA (tel. 813/530-9911) in the Clearwater Beach area. The ride is free.

BY TAXI Call either **Yellow Cab** (tel. 813/821-7777) or **Independent Cab** (tel. 813/327-3444). Along the beach, the major cab company is **BATS Taxi,** 5201 Gulf Blvd., St. Petersburg Beach (tel. 813/367-3702).

BY CAR All major firms are represented at the airports and in the St. Pete area, including **Avis** (tel. 813/867-6662), **Dollar** (tel. 813/367-3779), **Hertz** (tel. 813/360-1631), and **National** (tel. 813/530-5491). Local car-rental companies include **Pinellas** (tel. 813/535-9891) and **Suncoast** (tel. 813/393-3133).

FAST FACTS

Area Code St. Petersburg's area code is 813.

Business Hours Most businesses are open Monday through Friday from 9am to 5pm; shops and stores are open from 9am to 6pm or later. Banks are open Monday through Friday from 9am to 4pm; some banks are open on Friday until 6pm and others are open on Saturday mornings.

Dentist For 24-hour emergency services or referrals, call the Pinellas County Dental Society (tel. 323-2992).

Doctor Most hotels have a doctor on call; if not, contact the Pinellas County Physician Information line (tel. 585-PHIL) or the Bayfront Medical Center Doctor Referral Service (tel. 893-6112).

Drugstores Eckerd Drugs is the leading pharmacy chain in the area, with many stores throughout downtown and the beaches, including a 24-hour branch at the Tyrone Gardens Shopping Center, 900 58th St. N. (tel. 345-9336).

Emergencies Dial 911.

Hospitals Two major facilities in St. Petersburg are the Bayfront Medical Center, 701 6th St. S. (tel. 823-1234), and St. Anthony's Hospital, 601 12th St. N. (tel. 825-1000).

Laundry/Dry Cleaning Most hotels supply same-day laundry and dry-cleaning service. Reliable local firms include Pillsbury Cleaners, 1800 4th St. N. (tel.

822-3456), and five other locations; and Rogers Cleaners and Laundry, 1700 Central Ave. (tel. 822-3869) and 2018 4th St. N. (tel. 894-0706).

Libraries The St. Petersburg Central Library is at 3745 Ninth Ave. N., St. Petersburg (tel. 893-7724), with five branches spread throughout the city.

Newspapers/Magazines The *St. Petersburg Times* is the city's award-winning daily newspaper; the best periodical covering the area is *Tampa Bay,* a monthly magazine.

Photographic Needs Eckerd Express Photo Services offers one-hour processing at several St. Petersburg area locations, including 7900 Gateway Mall, St. Petersburg (tel. 579-4257); Dolphin Village, 4685 Gulf Blvd., St. Petersburg Beach (tel. 360-0818); and 467 Mandalay Ave., Clearwater Beach (tel. 796-1854). For general camera supplies or repairs, contact the Southern Photo Technical Service, 1750 Ninth Ave. N., St. Petersburg (tel. 896-6141).

Post Office The main post office is at 3135 First Ave. N. (tel. 323-6516); it's open Monday through Friday from 8am to 5:30pm and on Saturday from 8am to 12:30pm.

Shoe Repairs Two handy downtown locations are Bill's Shoe Service, 454 First Ave. N. (tel. 822-3757); and Holmes Shoe Repair, 17 6th St. N. (tel. 898-7930).

Taxes A 7% sales tax is applied to all purchases and the cost of restaurant meals. The local hotel-occupancy tax is 10%, added to the cost of your hotel room. There's also a $6 airport departure tax for international flights.

Transit Information For information on the local transit system, call 530-9911.

Weather Dial 894-6666.

WHAT TO SEE & DO

THE TOP ATTRACTIONS

THE PIER, 800 Second Ave. NE. Tel. 821-6164.

The focal point of the city, this festive waterfront sightseeing/shopping/entertainment complex extends a quarter of a mile into Tampa Bay. Dating back to 1889, it was originally built as a railroad pier, but over the years it was redesigned in various formats until taking its present shape of an inverted pyramid in 1988.

Today it's the city's prime playground, with five levels of shops and restaurants, plus an aquarium, tourist information desk, observation deck, catwalks for fishing, boat docks, a small bayside beach, miniature golf, water-sports rentals, and sightseeing boats. A free trolley service operates between The Pier and nearby parking lots.

Admission: Free to all the public areas and decks; donations welcome at the aquarium.

Open: Shops, Mon–Sat 10am–9pm, Sun 11am–7pm; restaurants, daily 11am–11pm; lounges, daily 10am–midnight or 1am; aquarium, Mon and Wed–Sat 10am–9pm, Fri–Sat 10am–1pm, Sun 11am–7pm.

FLORIDA SUNCOAST DOME, 1 Stadium Dr. Tel. 825-3100.

The skyline of St. Petersburg was dramatically changed in 1990 with the completion of this $110-million slant-roofed dome, built on a 66-acre downtown site to host major concerts, festivals, and sports events. The stadium's translucent roof is the first cable-supported dome of its kind in the United States and the largest of its type in the world.

Admission: $4–$30, depending on the event.

Open: Tours, available when events are not scheduled.

SALVADOR DALÍ MUSEUM, 1000 3rd St. S. Tel. 823-3767.

Nestled on Tampa Bay south of The Pier, this starkly modern museum houses the world's largest collection of works by the renowned Spanish surrealist. Valued at over $150 million, the collection includes 94 oil paintings, over 100 watercolors and drawings, and 1,300 graphics, plus posters, photos, sculptures, and objets d'art, and a 2,500-volume library on Dalí and surrealism.

Admission: $5 adults, $3.50 seniors and students, free for children under 10.
Open: Tues–Sat 10am–5pm, Sun–Mon noon–5pm. **Closed:** Mon, Easter-Christmas.

MUSEUM OF FINE ARTS, 255 Beach Dr. NE. Tel. 896-2667.

Resembling a Mediterranean villa on the waterfront, this museum houses a permanent collection of European, American, pre-Columbian and Far Eastern art, with works by such artists as Fragonard, Monet, Renoir, Cézanne, and Gauguin. Other highlights include period rooms with antiques and historical furnishings, plus a gallery of Steuben crystal, and world-class rotating exhibits.

Admission: $4 suggested donation.
Open: Tues–Sat 10am–5pm, Sun 1–5pm; third Thurs of each month 10am–9pm.

ST. PETERSBURG HISTORICAL AND FLIGHT ONE MUSEUM, 335 Second Ave. NE. Tel. 894-1052.

Located on the approach to The Pier, this museum features a permanent interactive exhibition chronicling St. Petersburg's history. The 30,000 items on display range from prehistoric artifacts to documents, clothing, and photographs. There are also computer stations enabling visitors to "flip through the past." Walk-through exhibits include a prototype general store and post office (ca. 1880) and a replica of the Benoist airboat, suspended "in flight" from a 25-foot ceiling and commemorating the first scheduled commercial flight in the world, which took off from St. Petersburg in 1914.

Admission: $4.50 adults, $3.50 seniors, $1.50 children 7–17, free for children 6 and under.
Open: Mon–Sat 10am–5pm, Sun 1–5pm.

SUNCOAST SEABIRD SANCTUARY, 18328 Gulf Blvd., Indian Shores. Tel. 391-6211.

Of all the attractions outside the immediate downtown area, this one is well worth a detour or a special trip. Founded in 1971 by zoologist Ralph Heath, Jr., it's the largest wild-bird hospital in the nation, dedicated to the rescue, repair, recuperation, and release of sick and injured wild birds. At any one time, there are usually more than 500 sea birds living at the sanctuary, from cormorants, white herons, and birds of prey to the ubiquitous brown pelican.

Admission: Free, but donations are welcome.
Open: Daily 9am–dusk. **Directions:** Take I-275 north of downtown to Fla. 694 (Exit 15) west, cross over the toll bridge to Gulf Boulevard, and turn left; the sanctuary is seven blocks south.

MORE ATTRACTIONS

CLEARWATER MARINE SCIENCE CENTER, 249 Windward Passage, Clearwater. Tel. 447-0980.

Nestled on an island in Clearwater Harbor, this facility is dedicated to the rescue and rehabilitation of marine mammals and sea turtles. The center also operates a turtle hatchery that releases more than 3,000 hatchlings each year in local waters.

Admission: $3 adults and students, $1.75 children under 3.
Open: Mon–Fri 9am–5pm, Sat 9am–4pm, Sun 11am–4pm. **Directions:** From the mainland, turn right at Island Way; the center is one mile east of Clearwater Beach on Island Estates.

FORT DESOTO PARK, Fla. 679. Tel. 866-2484.

One of the oldest sections of St. Petersburg, and used as a fort during the Spanish-American War, this is the largest and most diverse park in the area, made up of five islands south of the mainland, all nestled between the waters of Tampa Bay and the Gulf of Mexico. With a total of 900 acres, seven miles of waterfront, and almost three miles of beaches, the islands are all connected by roads

Clearwater Marine Science Center 1
Florida Suncoast Dome 9
Fort DeSoto Park 13
Grant Field 2
Great Explorations 11
John's Pass Village & Boardwalk 4
Museum of Fine Arts 6
Salvador Dali Museum 10
St. Petersburg Historical & Flight One Museum 7
Suncoast Seabird Sanctuary 3
Sunken Gardens 5
Sunshine Skyway Bridge 12
The Pier 8

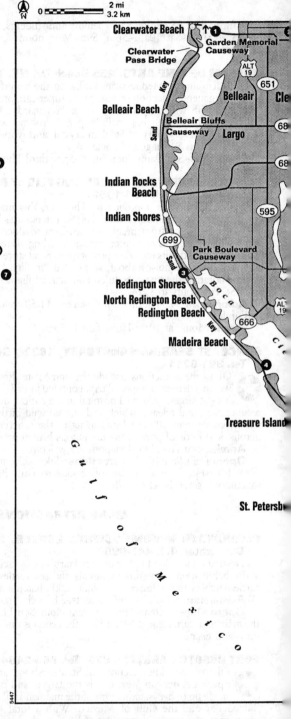

0 2 mi 3.2 km
N

Clearwater Beach
Garden Memorial Causeway
Clearwater Pass Bridge
ALT 19
651
Belleair
Belleair Beach
Belleair Bluffs Causeway
Largo
Sand Key
Indian Rocks Beach
595
Indian Shores
699
Park Boulevard Causeway
Redington Shores
Boca
North Redington Beach
Redington Beach
666
Madeira Beach
Treasure Island
Gulf of Mexico
St. Petersb

5447

ST. PETERSBURG AREA ATTRACTIONS
Courtney Campbell Causeway
60
Old Tampa Bay
275
To Tampa
19
St. Petersburg-Clearwater International Airport
Howard Frankland Bridge
686
688
92
Gandy Bridge
693
694
Pinellas Park
74th Ave.
54th Ave.
38th Ave.
49th St.
595
Coffeepot Bayou
Downtown
St. Petersburg
ALT 19
Central Ave.
375
S. Pasadena
Gulfport
22nd Ave. S.
175
Albert Whitted Municipal Airport
St. Petersburg Beach Causeway
Big Bayou
Lake Maggiore
Coquina Key
Pinellas Bayway
54th Ave. S.
Little Bayou
682
Long Key
Bird Key
Intracoastal Waterway
Bush Key
Cabbage Key
Shell Key
679
The Reefs
Madelaine Key
Mullett Key
Tampa Bay
Airport
5
6
7
8
9
10
11
12
13

and bridges. A public park for over 25 years, it also offers fishing piers; shaded picnic sites; a bird, plant, and animal sanctuary; and campsites.

Admission: Free, except for tolls totaling 85¢.

Open: Daily sunrise–sunset. **Directions:** Take I-275 south to the Pinellas Bayway (Exit 4) and follow the signs.

JOHN'S PASS VILLAGE AND BOARDWALK, 12901 Gulf Blvd., Madeira Beach. Tel. 391-7373.

Named after Juan (John) Levique, a 19th-century sea-turtle fisherman who lived here, this is a rustic Florida fishing village on the southern edge of Madeira Beach. It's composed of a string of simple wooden structures topped by tin roofs, all resting on pilings 12 feet above sea level, and connected by a 1,000-foot boardwalk. Most of the buildings have been converted into shops, art galleries, and restaurants. The focal point is the large fishing pier and marina, from which many water sports are available for visitors.

Admission: Free.

Open: Shops and activities, daily 9am–6pm or later; most restaurants, daily 7am–11pm. **Directions:** From downtown, take Central Avenue west via Treasure Island Causeway to Gulf Boulevard; turn right, go for 20 blocks, and cross over the bridge; the entrance is on the right.

SUNKEN GARDENS, 1825 4th St. N. Tel. 896-3186.

One of the city's oldest attractions, this seven-acre tropical garden park dates back to 1935. It contains a vast array of 5,000 plants, flowers, and trees. In addition, there's a walk-through aviary and over 500 rare birds and a wax museum depicting biblical figures.

Admission: $8.95 adults, $5 children 3–11.

Open: Daily 9am–5:30pm.

SUNSHINE SKYWAY BRIDGE, I-275 and U.S. 19. Tel. 823-8804.

Spanning the mouth of Tampa Bay, this 4.1-mile-long bridge connects Pinellas and Manatee Counties and the city of St. Petersburg with the Bradenton/Sarasota areas. Built at a cost of $244 million over a period of five years (1982–87), this is Florida's first suspension bridge, soaring 183 feet above the bay.

Admission: $1-per-car toll each way.

Open: Daily 24 hours. **Directions:** From downtown, take I-275 south and follow the signs.

COOL FOR KIDS

GREAT EXPLORATIONS, 1120 4th St. S. Tel. 821-8885.

With a variety of "hands-on" exhibits, this museum welcomes visitors of all ages, but is most appealing to children, especially on a rainy day. Kids can explore a long, dark tunnel; shoot a game of laser pinball; paint a work of art with sunlight; and play a melody with a sweep of the hand, to name just a few of the activities.

Admission: $5 adults, $4.50 seniors, $4 children 4–17, free for children under 4.

Open: Mon–Sat 10am–5pm, Sun noon–5pm.

SPORTS & RECREATION

SPECTATOR SPORTS

BASEBALL The **Florida Suncoast Dome,** 1 Stadium Dr. (tel. 825-3100), is St. Petersburg's sporting centerpiece. This $110-million domed stadium has a seating capacity of 43,000. As we go to press, this facility is still searching for a major-league baseball team. Exact details of schedule and prices will be announced when arrangements for a team are finalized.

The winter home of the St. Louis Cardinals is **Al Lang Stadium,** 180 Second Ave. (tel. 822-3384). They are here for spring training each February and March. The crack of the bat can also be heard at other times, with major-league exhibition games in the spring, followed by the St. Petersburg Cardinals, a Class A minor-league team (April through September). Admission is $3 to $7.

The Philadelphia Phillies play their winter training season at the **Jack Russell Stadium,** 800 Phillies Dr., Clearwater. (tel. 442-8496). The season is mid-February to April. Admission is $6 to $7. **Grant Field,** 373 Douglas Ave., Dunedin (tel. 733-0429), is newly expanded, and is the winter home of the Toronto Blue Jays for a mid-February to April season. Admission is $6 to $7.

DOG RACING Founded in 1925, **Derby Lane,** 10490 Gandy Blvd. (tel. 576-1359), is the world's oldest continually operating greyhound track, with indoor and outdoor seating and standing areas. Admission is $1 for adults, $2.50 for Derby Club level. It's open January to June, Monday through Saturday at 7:30pm. Monday, Wednesday, and Saturday races are at noon.

RECREATION

With year-round sunshine and 28 miles of coastline along the Gulf of Mexico, the St. Petersburg area offers a wealth of recreational activities.

One of the newest developments, of benefit to walkers, bicyclists, joggers, and nature lovers is the new **Pinellas Trail,** a 35-mile-long, 15-foot-wide path stretching from St. Petersburg to Tarpon Springs. So far, 16 miles of the trail have been completed, from Dunedin to Seminole, with the remaining 16 miles slated for completion by 1994. When fully open, it will be the longest linear recreation trail of its kind in the eastern United States. For more information and a brochure describing the current scope of the trail at the time of your visit, contact the Pinellas County Park Department, 631 Chestnut St., Clearwater, FL 34616 (tel. 813/581-2953 or 462-3347).

When visiting St. Petersburg, you can get up-to-the-minute recorded information about the city's sports and recreational activities by calling the **Leisure Line** (tel. 893-7500).

BICYCLING With miles of flat terrain, St. Petersburg is ideal for bikers. Among the prime biking routes are Straub Park and along the bayfront, Fort DeSoto Park, and Pass-A-Grille.

Beach Cyclist, 7517 Blind Pass Rd. (tel. 367-5001), on the northern tip of St. Petersburg beach, offers several types of bikes, from a beach cruiser (allowed on the beaches at Treasure Island and Madeira Beach) to a selection of standard racing bikes. Prices are from $10 for 4 hours, $12 for 24 hours, $39 per week, and it's open Monday through Saturday from 10am to 6pm, Sunday from 11am to 5pm.

Transportation Station, 645 Bayway Blvd. (tel. 443-3188), on Clearwater Beach, rents all types of bikes from single speed to racers, tandems, mountain bikes, and one- and two-passenger scooters. Helmets and baby seats are also available. Prices for bicycles are from $5 to $8 an hour, $16.95 to $24.95 for 24 hours, $40 to $165 per week; scooters are from $12 to $16 an hour, $42.95 to $59.95 for 24 hours, $99 to $150 per week. It's open daily from 9am to 5pm.

BOAT RENTALS If you can handle a boat yourself, **Beach Motor Sport Rentals, Inc.,** Slips 5 and 6, Clearwater Beach Marina, Clearwater Beach (tel. 446-5503), rents craft equipped with 70hp–175hp motors. Sizes range from 17 to 20 feet, with capacities of three to seven people. Eight-foot mini-boats with 6hp engines, ideal for two people, can also be rented by the hour. Prices are $85 to $145 for a half day, $150 to $230 for a full day; mini-boats are $20 an hour. Hours are daily 9am to 5pm.

Captain Dave's Watersports, 9540 Blind Pass Rd., St. Petersburg Beach (tel. 345-4336), offers waverunner and powerboat rentals, parasail rides, snorkeling trips, sailing, and shelling trips. Prices for waverunner rentals are $35 per half hour, $60 per hour; powerboat rentals are $50 and up for one hour, $70 and up for two hours, $135 and up per day; parasail rides are $40; snorkeling trips are $35; sailing and shelling trips, $25. Hours are daily from 9am to 5pm or later.

Fun Rentals, Municipal Marina, Slip 300, 555 150th Ave., Madeira Beach (tel. 397-0276), rents waverunners, pontoons, and fishing boats to sightsee, fish, or play on the waters of the Intracoastal Waterway. Waverunners cost from $35 an hour; pontoons, $35 an hour (minimum two hours); 14-foot fishing boats with motor, $15 an hour, $50 for four hours. It's open daily from 9:30am to 5:30pm.

A downtown facility, **Waterworks Rentals,** The Pier (tel. 363-0000), rents waverunners and boats from 12 to 22 feet. A second location is at 200D 150th Ave., Madeira Beach (tel. 399-8989). Prices for waverunners are from $29 for a half hour; for boats, from $20 per hour. Daily hours are 9am to 6pm or later.

FISHING One of the largest party-boat fishing fleets in the area, Capt. Dave Spaulding's **Queen Fleet,** Slip 52, Clearwater Beach Marina, 25 Causeway Blvd. (tel. 446-7666), offers trips of varying duration. Bait is furnished, but rod rental is extra. Prices are $20 for a half day, $30 for three-quarters of a day, and $40 for a full day; it will cost an extra $5 for rods.

Capt. Kidd, Merry Pier, 801 Pass-A-Grille Way, St. Petersburg Beach (tel. 360-2263), takes passengers on half and three-quarter-day fishing trips in the Gulf. Rates, including rod, reel, and bait, are $24 for adults and $21 for children and seniors on a half-day trip; $33.50 for adults and $31.50 for children and seniors on a three-quarter-day outing. Half-day trips are scheduled Monday through Friday 8am to noon and 1pm to 5pm; three-quarter-day trips, Saturday and Sunday from 8:30am to 3pm.

If you want a change from the usual fishing boat, try **Double Eagle's Deep Sea Fishing Boats,** Slip 50, Clearwater Beach Marina, 25 Causeway Blvd., Clearwater Beach (tel. 446-1653). They offer two catamarans, 83 feet and 65 feet in length. The vessels go 20 to 25 miles offshore into the Gulf, on four- or seven-hour trips, with bait provided. Prices are $20 to $30 for adults, $16 to $25 for children, and $4 for tackle. The four-hour trip departs daily, 8am to noon and 1pm to 5pm, and the seven-hour trip leaves daily at 9am lasting until 4pm.

Miss Pass-A-Grille, Dolphin Landings Charter Boat Center, 4737 Gulf Blvd., St. Petersburg Beach. (tel. 367-4488 or 367-7411), is conveniently docked in the heart of the St. Petersburg Beach hotel strip. This fishing boat offers daily trips into Tampa Bay and the Gulf. Prices are $26.95 for four hours, $37.95 for seven hours. Sailings are scheduled Tuesday, Wednesday, and Friday at 8am and 1pm, Thursday, Saturday, and Sunday at 9am.

GOLF Adjacent to the St. Petersburg/Clearwater Airport, the **Airco Flite Golf Course,** 3650 Roosevelt Blvd., Clearwater (tel. 573-4653) is an 18-hole, par-72 course, with driving range. Lessons and golf club rentals are also available. The price per person, including a cart, is $33. It's open daily, 7am to 6pm.

Bardmoor Country Club, 7919 Bardmoor Blvd., Largo (tel. 397-0483), is often the venue for major tournaments. This club offers an 18-hole, par-72 course, plus a driving range. Lessons and rental clubs are also available. Greens fees are $48 Monday through Friday, and $55 Saturday and Sunday, including carts. It's open daily, 7am to dusk.

One of the top 50 municipal golf courses in the U.S., **Mangrove Bay Golf Club,** 875 62nd Ave., NE (tel. 893-7797), hugs the inlets of Old Tampa Bay and offers 18-hole, par-72 play. Facilities include a driving range; lessons and golf club rental are also available. Prices are $19.40; $29.45 including a cart. It's open daily, 6am to 6pm.

SAILING **Annapolis Sailing School,** 6800 34th St. S. (tel. 867-8102 or toll free 800/237-0795), can teach you to sail or perfect your sailing skills. Various courses are offered at this branch of the famous Maryland-based school, lasting two, five, or eight days. Prices, depending on season and length of course, are $185 to $1,655 per person.

If you prefer to be part of the crew or just want to relax for 2½ hours, enjoying the views of the Gulf waters, sail aboard a 65-foot windjammer or a 38-foot racing yacht at the **Suncoast Sailing Center,** Slip 10, Clearwater Beach Marina, Clearwater Beach (tel. 581-4662). Rentals of small sloops and sailing lessons are also available. Reservations are required. Prices range from $19.50 to $22.50 for adults, half price for children. The boats depart daily at 10am, 1:30pm, and 4:30pm.

TENNIS **Hurley Park,** 1600 Pass-A-Grille Way, Pass-A-Grill, St. Petersburg Beach, sports just one court, and is available on a first-come, first-serve basis. The price is 25¢ for 15 minutes (quarters only). It's open daily, 8am to 10pm.

On a larger scale, the **Racquet Club of Paradise Island,** 10315 Paradise Blvd., Treasure Island (tel. 360-6062), offers 20 courts, 16 clay, 4 hard, and 6 lighted. Lessons are available at this club, which is surrounded by the waters of Boca Ciega Bay. Prices per person per hour are $5 Monday through Friday, $7 Saturday and Sunday. It's open Monday to Friday 8am to dark, Saturday and Sunday 8am to 6pm. Containing 15 Har-Tru courts, **St. Petersburg Tennis Center,** 650 18th Ave. S. (tel. 894-4378), provides lessons and clinics. Prices are $3 to $6 per person per hour; after 4pm the cost is $4 per person per hour. It's open daily 9am to dark.

WATERSPORTS **Captain Dave's Watersports,** 9540 Blind Pass Rd., St. Petersburg Beach (tel. 345-4336), offers waterskiing lessons for $35 per half-hour lesson. A 15-minute pull is $20.

BAY CRUISES

Albion Cruises, 801 Pass-A-Grille Way, St. Petersburg Beach (tel. 360-2263), offers shuttle service to nearby Shell Island, south of St. Petersburg, via a 32-passenger pontoon-style boat. The ride takes 15 minutes, and you can return on any shuttle you wish. Boats leave daily at 10am, noon, 2pm, and (summer only) 4pm, and prices are $10 for adults, $5 for children 12 and under.

Cruises around Boca Ciega Bay and the Gulf of Mexico are offered by **Capt. Anderson,** St. Petersburg Beach Causeway (tel. 367-7804). The three-deck boat operates at lunch and dinner times, with buffet meal service and dance music. On some evenings, cruises with special themes, such as Gospel music, are offered. Cruises take place from October to mid-May. The sightseeing and lunch cruises operate from Tuesday to Friday and cost $7.50 for the sightseeing cruise, $13.50 for the lunch cruise. Dinner cruises are offered on Tuesday and from Thursday to Saturday from 7 to 10pm and cost from $17.95 to $19.95; cocktails extra. Reservations are required.

The ***Caribbean Queen*** (tel. 895-BOAT) departs from The Pier, and offers one-hour sightseeing and dolphin-watching cruises around Tampa Bay. Sailings are daily at 11:30am, 1pm, 3pm, and 5pm, and cost $8 for adults and $5 for children 3 to 12.

Captain Memo's Pirate Cruise, Clearwater Beach Marina, Slip 3 (tel. 446-2587), sails on the 49-passenger motorized sailboat *Sea Hogge.* Swashbuckling two-hour daytime "pirate cruises" and evening champagne cruises are offered, under the direction of fearless Captain Memo and his all-female crew. Cruises operate on Monday from 4:30 to 6:30pm, on Tuesday through Saturday from 10am to noon, 2 to 4pm, and 4:30–6:30pm. For adults, daytime cruises cost $25, evening cruises $28; both daytime and evening cruises cost $18 for seniors and juniors 13 to 17, $15 for children 2 to 12, free for children under 2.

The ***Sea Screamer,*** King Fish Wharf, Treasure Island (tel. 367-2996), claims to be the world's largest speedboat. This 73-foot turbo-charged twin-engine vessel provides tow rides on one trip—an exhilarating spin in Gulf of Mexico waters and a leisurely narrated cruise around Treasure Island with opportunities to view birds and marine life along the way. Prices are $9 for adults, $6 for children 6 to 12, and sailings are daily at noon, 2pm, and 4pm.

WHERE TO STAY

The St. Petersburg area offers a great variety of accommodations, from posh resorts and chain properties to small family-run motels or bed-and-breakfasts. Above all, it also offers a choice of settings—downtown St. Petersburg, St. Petersburg Beach, or the "Holiday Isles," a cluster of a dozen neighboring beaches.

Price-wise, the high season is from December/January through April. The best of bargains are available in May and September through November.

DOWNTOWN ST. PETERSBURG

Expensive

STOUFFER VINOY RESORT, 501 Fifth Ave. NE, St. Petersburg, FL 33701. Tel. 813/894-1000, or toll free 800/HOTELS-1. Fax 813/822-2785. 360 rms. A/C MINIBAR TV TEL

$ Rates: $119–$399 single or double. AE, CB, DC, DISC, MC, V.

With an elegant peach-toned Mediterranean-style facade, this sprawling seven-story world-class resort has greatly enhanced the downtown area. Dating back to 1925 and originally known as the Vinoy Park, it reopened in 1992 after a total and meticulous $93-million restoration and refurbishment. It overlooks Tampa Bay and is within walking distance of The Pier, Central Avenue, museums, and other attractions.

All the guest rooms, many of which enjoy lovely views of the bayfront, are designed to offer the utmost in comfort and include three phones, an additional TV in the bathroom, hairdryer, bathrobes, and more; some units in the new wing have individual Jacuzzis and private patios/balconies.

Dining/Entertainment: Marchand's Grille, an elegant room overlooking the bay, specializes in steaks, seafood, and chops. The Terrace Room is the main dining room for breakfast, lunch, and dinner. Casual lunches and dinners are available at the indoor-outdoor Al Fresco near the pool deck and at the Clubhouse at the golf course on Snell Isle. There are also two bar/lounges.

Services: Concierge, 24-hour room service, afternoon tea service, laundry service, tour desk, child care, complimentary coffee and newspaper with wake-up call.

Facilities: Two swimming pools; 16-court tennis complex (nine lighted); 18-hole championship golf course on nearby Snell Isle; private 74-slip marina; two croquet courts; fitness center with sauna, steam room, spa, massage, and exercise equipment; access to two bayside beaches; shuttle service to gulf beaches; hair salon; gift shop.

Moderate

THE HERITAGE, 234 Third Ave. N., St. Petersburg, FL 33701. Tel. 813/822-4814, or toll free 800/283-7829. 75 rms. A/C TV TEL

$ Rates (including continental breakfast): $62–$95 single; $70–$105 double. AE, CB, DC, MC, V.

With a sweeping veranda, French doors, and tropical courtyard, the Heritage is the nearest thing to a southern mansion you'll find in the heart of downtown. Dating back to the early 1920s, it was completely restored in the late 1980s. The furnishings include period antiques in the public areas and in the guest rooms.

Dining/Entertainment: The Heritage Grille offers a creative menu of "nouveau American" light regional cuisine.

Services: Room service, valet laundry.

Facilities: Outdoor heated swimming pool, Jacuzzi.

PRESIDENTIAL INN, 100 Second Ave. S. (P.O. Box 57306), St. Petersburg, FL 33701. Tel. 813/821-7117. 30 rms. A/C TV TEL

$ Rates (including continental breakfast): $85–$130 single or double. AE, CB, DC, MC, V. **Parking:** Free adjacent covered self-parking.

Under the same management as the adjacent Hilton Hotel, this unique property occupies the fifth floor of a 12-story bayfront office complex. The bedrooms, each with a different view of the bay or city, are individually decorated with dark woods, silk wall hangings, and tasteful artworks; bathrooms offer separate phone extensions, and eight have private whirlpools. Guests have access to an on-premises living room–style lounge/reading room and to the Hilton Hotel's restaurants, room-service system, and laundry valet.

ST. PETERSBURG HILTON AND TOWERS, 333 1st St. S., St. Petersburg, FL 33701. Tel. 813/894-5000, or toll free 800/HILTONS. Fax 813/823-4797. 333 rms. A/C TV TEL

$ Rates: $65–$125 single or double. AE, CB, DC, MC, V.

Situated downtown on the bay, this 15-story tower is convenient to most major attractions. The spacious lobby reflects the tone of this hotel, with a rich decor of marble, crystal, tile, antiques, artwork, and potted trees and plants. The bedrooms are furnished with traditional dark woods, floral fabrics, a king-size bed or two double beds, and an executive desk; many have views of the bay.

Dining/Entertainment: Charmene's is a full-service restaurant specializing in continental cuisine. For light fare, try the First Street Deli, and for a quiet drink with a piano background, settle into Brandi's Lobby Bar; or for a lively evening, it's Wings, an aviation-themed lounge.

Services: Room service, concierge, valet laundry, babysitting.

Facilities: Outdoor heated swimming pool, patio deck, Jacuzzi, sauna, gift shop.

Inexpensive

DAYS INN MARINA BEACH RESORT, 6800 34th St. S., St. Petersburg, FL 33711. Tel. 813/867-1151, or toll free 800/227-8045 or 800/325-2525. Fax 813/864-4494. 157 rms. A/C TV TEL

$ Rates: $49–$115 single or double. AE, CB, DC, MC, V.

Located on the southern tip of the city, off I-275 on the approach to the Skyway Bridge, this sprawling two-story motel seems to have it all. Offering quick access to downtown, it sits in a tropical setting on 14 acres along the Tampa Bay shoreline. For good measure, it's also a year-round base of the Annapolis Sailing School. Guest rooms have an airy decor with light woods, pastel tones, ceiling fans, plants, and private balconies or patios; some units also offer kitchenettes.

For dining there's a restaurant, a beach bar, a lounge, and a snack bar. Other facilities include a private bayside beach, two outdoor swimming pools (one heated), a Jacuzzi, seven tennis courts, a fishing pier, a marina, shuffleboard and volleyball courts, water-sports rentals, a games room, a children's playground, and a coin-operated laundry.

HOLIDAY INN–STADIUM, 4601 34th St. S., St. Petersburg, FL 33711. Tel. 813/867-3131, or toll free 800/HOLIDAY. Fax 813/867-2025. 134 rms. A/C TV TEL

$ Rates: $49–$99 single or double. AE, CB, DC, DISC, MC, V.

Even though this basic two-story hotel is on the busy U.S. 19 corridor, it's set back from the main road in a convenient and quiet setting, across from a marina and south of downtown. Bedrooms are furnished in contemporary style, with dark woods, brass fixtures, and light pastel fabrics and carpeting.

Duke's Restaurant and Lounge provides meals all day as well as danceable music at night. Additional amenities include room service, valet laundry and dry cleaning, an outdoor freshwater swimming pool, a patio, shuffleboard, and a guest laundry.

Budget

BAYBORO BED AND BREAKFAST, 1719 Beach Dr. SE, St. Petersburg, FL 33701. Tel. 813/823-4955. 4 rms (all with bath). A/C TV

$ Rates (including breakfast): $55–$70 single or double. MC, V.

Situated in a residential area a few minutes south of Bayboro Harbor, this grand three-story Victorian overlooks the bay opposite Lassing Park and a small beach. An "Old South" ambience prevails here, with a wide veranda bedecked with rockers and cozy upstairs bedrooms, filled with antique beds and armoires, lace and quilts. Breakfast is served in the dining room or on the veranda.

BEACH PARK MOTEL, 300 Beach Drive NE, St. Petersburg, FL 33701. Tel. 813/898-6325. 26 rms. A/C TV TEL

$ Rates: $35–$40 single; $40–$65 double. MC, V.

Bayboro Bed & Breakfast 16
Beach Park Motel 21
Best Western Sea Stone Resort 4
Captains Quarter's Inn 7
Clearwater Beach Hotel 2
Colonial Gateway Inn 8
Days Inn Island Beach Resort 9
Days Inn Marina Beach Resort 15
Don CeSar 12
Econo Lodge 13
Heritage 19
Holiday Inn-Stadium 14
Mansion House 20
Palm Pavilion Inn 1
Presidential Inn 18
Radison Suite Resort 6
Sandpiper Beach Resort 10
Sheraton Sand Key Resort 5
St. Petersburg Hilton & Towers 17
Stouffer Vinoy Resort 22
Sun West Beach Motel 3
Tradewinds 11

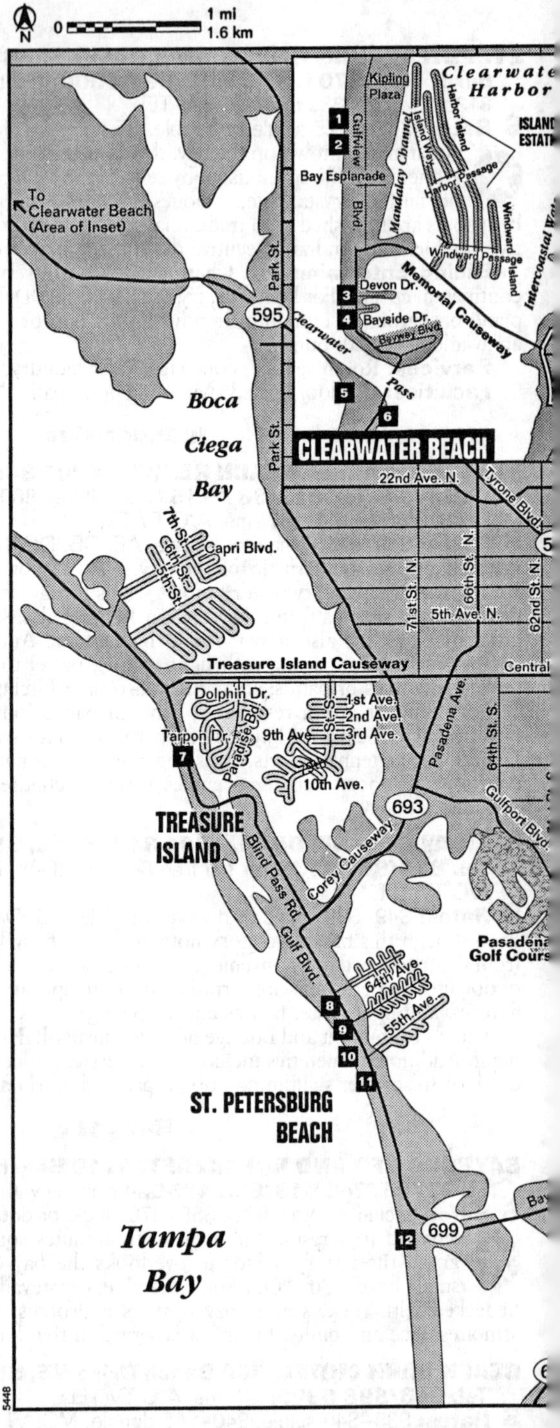

N
0 1 mi
1.6 km
To Clearwater Beach (Area of Inset)
Clearwater Harbor
Kipling Plaza
Gulfview Blvd.
Bay Esplanade
Mandalay Channel
Island Way
Harbor Island
Harbor Passage
Windward Passage
Windward Island
Intercoastal Wa
ISLAND ESTAT
Memorial Causeway
Devon Dr.
Bayside Dr.
Bayway Blvd.
Clearwater Pass
CLEARWATER BEACH
595
Park St.
Boca Ciega Bay
22nd Ave. N.
Tyrone Blvd.
7th St.
6th St.
5th St.
Capri Blvd.
71st St. N
66th St. N.
62nd St. N
5th Ave. N.
Treasure Island Causeway
Central
Dolphin Dr.
Paradise Blvd.
Tarpon Dr.
9th Ave.
1st Ave.
2nd Ave.
3rd Ave.
10th Ave.
Pasadena Ave.
64th St. S.
693
Gulfport Blvd.
TREASURE ISLAND
Blind Pass Rd
Corey Causeway
Gulf Blvd.
Pasadena Golf Course
64th Ave.
55th Ave.
ST. PETERSBURG BEACH
699
Tampa Bay
5448

ST. PETERSBURG AREA ACCOMMODATIONS

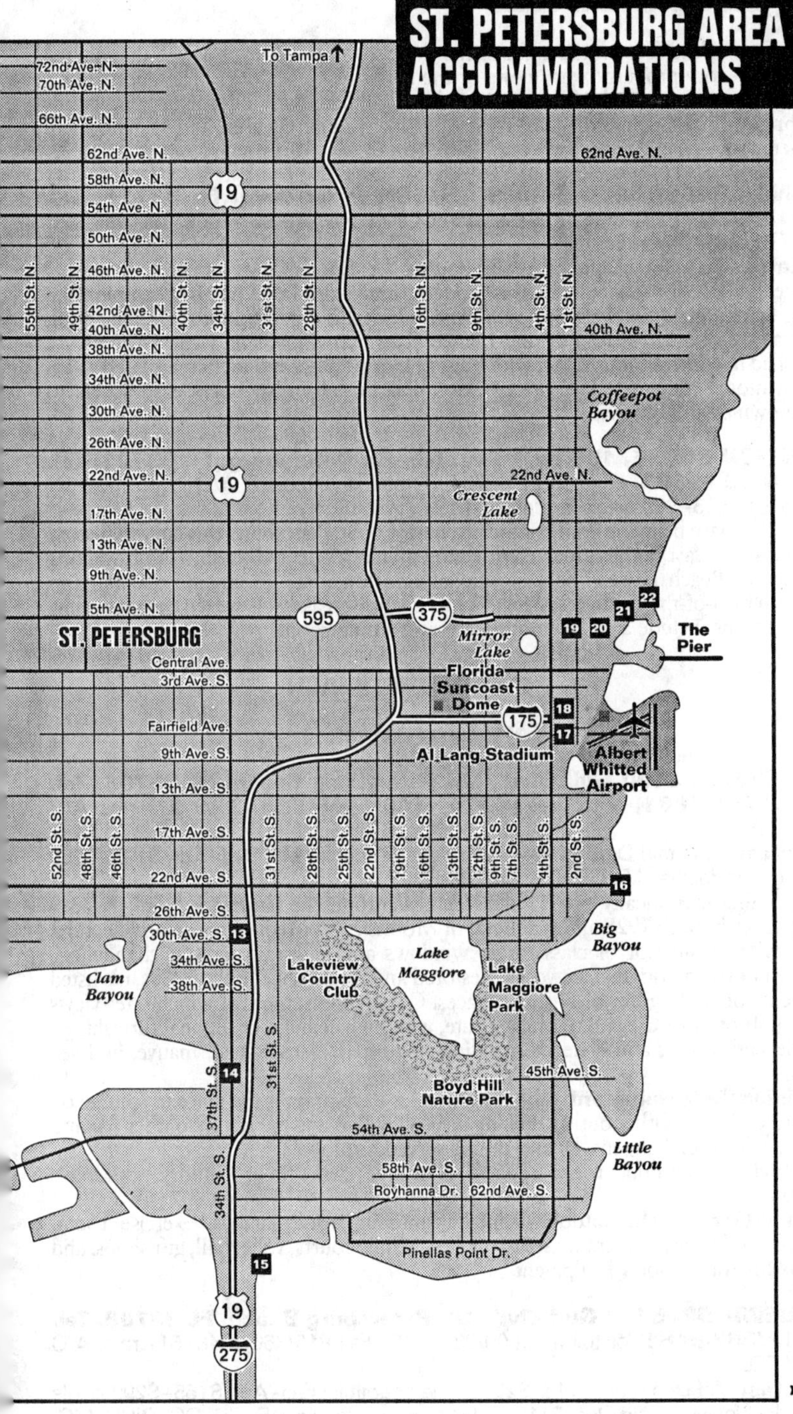

$ One of the few motels right in the downtown area, this is a well-maintained two-story property with views of the bayfront or The Pier. The guest rooms have one or two double beds, or a king-size bed, with a decor of light woods and bright Florida colors. Each has a small balcony or sitting area; and 11 have small kitchenettes.

ECONO LODGE, 3000 34th St. S., St. Petersburg, FL 33711. Tel. 813/867-1111, or toll free 800/55-ECONO. Fax 813/867-7068. 120 rms. A/C TV TEL

$ Rates: $29–$55 single; $29–$60 double. AE, DC, MC, V.

An ideal choice for tennis buffs, this modern three-story hotel has 10 championship tennis courts and an on-staff pro. Other facilities include an outdoor swimming pool, tropical courtyard, restaurant, and lounge. The public areas and guest rooms are furnished in contemporary style, with bright Florida colors and fabrics. Situated south of downtown along the U.S. 19 corridor, this hostelry also offers easy access to downtown or the beaches.

MANSION HOUSE, 105 Fifth Ave. NE, St. Petersburg, FL 33701. Tel. 813/821-9391. Fax 813/821-9754. 5 rms (all with bath). A/C

$ Rates: $55–$65 single or double. MC, V.

Reputed to have been the home of the first mayor of St. Petersburg, this cozy two-story bed-and-breakfast home is located downtown on a residential street, within walking distance of Beach Drive, The Pier, and other attractions. Rooms are decorated in southern turn-of-the-century style and a full English breakfast is served each morning. Public rooms include a screened-in porch and sitting room.

ST. PETERSBURG BEACH

Very Expensive

DON CESAR, 3400 Gulf Blvd., St. Petersburg Beach, FL 33706. Tel. 813/360-1881, or toll free 800/247-9810. Fax 813/367-3609. 277 rms. A/C TV TEL

$ Rates: May–mid-Dec, $115–$195 single or double; Mid-Dec–Apr, $195–$250 single or double. AE, CB, DC, MC, V.

Sitting majestically on 7½ acres of beachfront, the landmark "Pink Palace" dates back to 1928 and is a blend of Moorish and Mediterranean architecture, with an interior of classic high windows and archways, crystal chandeliers, marble floors, and original artworks. Restored and refurbished in the 1980s, it's listed on the National Register of Historic Places. Guest rooms, most of which offer views of the gulf or Boca Ciega Bay, are first-rate, with high ceilings, traditional furnishings, marble bathrooms, and a decor blending rich tones of rose, teal, mauve, and sea green.

Dining/Entertainment: The King Charles Restaurant is the place to splurge on a gourmet dinner. Other outlets include the Lobby Bar, and the Beachcomber Bar and Poolside Grill for light snacks and drinks served outdoors.

Services: 24-hour room service, concierge desk, valet laundry, children's program.

Facilities: Beach, outdoor heated swimming pool, Jacuzzi, exercise room, saunas, whirlpools, resident masseuse, lighted tennis courts, volleyball, gift shops, and rentals for water-sports equipment.

TRADEWINDS, 5500 Gulf Blvd., St. Petersburg Beach, FL 33706. Tel. 813/367-6461, or toll free 800/237-0707. Fax 813/360-3848. 511 rms. A/C TV TEL

$ Rates: Mid-Dec–Jan, $115–$225 single or double; Feb–Apr, $165–$299 single or double; May–mid-Dec, $115–$199 single or double. AE, CB, DC, DISC, MC, V.

An oasis unto itself, this six-story hotel sits amid 13 acres of beachfront property, sand dunes, and tropical gardens. Bedrooms, which look out on the gulf or the extensive grounds, have every up-to-date convenience, from computer-card keys to wet bars, coffee makers, toasters, contemporary furnishings, and private balconies.

Dining/Entertainment: The top spot is the Palm Court for lunch or dinner. Other outlets include the Flying Bridge, a casual beachside floating restaurant and bar; Reflections, a waterside piano lounge with fireplace and patio; the Fountain Square Deli; and Picnic Island with gas grills for guest barbecues.

Services: Room service, valet laundry, children's program.

Facilities: Three heated outdoor swimming pools, enclosed heated pool, saunas, whirlpools, paddleboats, motorized gondolas, fitness room, tennis, paddle tennis, racquetball, basketball, croquet, bicycles, putting green, hammocks, beach and water volleyball, shuffleboard, games room, general store.

Expensive

SANDPIPER BEACH RESORT, 6000 Gulf Blvd., St. Petersburg, FL 33706. Tel. 813/360-5551, or toll free 800/237-0707. Fax 813/360-3848. 159 rms. A/C TV TEL

$ Rates: Mid-Dec–Jan, $75–$175 single or double; Feb–Apr, $109–$229 single or double; Apr–mid-Dec, $75–$150. AE, CB, DC, DISC, MC, V.

A well-landscaped tropical courtyard separates the two wings of this six-story property, set back from the main road. Decorated with light woods, pastel tones, and touches of rattan, most units have two double beds, some have a king- or queen-size bed, as well as coffee makers, toasters, small refrigerators, and wet bars.

Dining/Entertainment: Piper's Patio is a casual café with indoor/outdoor seating; and the Sandbar offers frozen drinks and snacks by the pool.

Services: Room service, concierge, valet laundry, child care.

Facilities: Beachfront heated swimming pool, enclosed heated swimming pool, two air-conditioned sports courts for racquetball, handball and squash, exercise room, volleyball, shuffleboard, games room, gift shop/general store.

Moderate

COLONIAL GATEWAY INN, 6300 Gulf Blvd., St. Petersburg Beach, FL 33706. Tel. 813/267-2711, or toll free 800/237-8918, or 800/282-5245 in Florida. Fax 813/367-7068. 200 rms. A/C TV TEL

$ Rates: $89–$115 single or double. AE, CB, DC, DISC, MC, V.

Spread over a quarter mile of beachfront, this U-shaped complex of one- and two-story units is a favorite with families. Rooms, most of which face the pool and a central landscaped courtyard, are contemporary, with light woods and beach tones; about half the units are efficiencies with kitchenettes.

Dining/Entertainment: The Colonial Inn restaurant is well known for its breakfast and dinner buffets, Etchings Lounge is a popular nightspot, and the Swigwam beach bar offers light refreshments.

Facilities: Outdoor heated swimming pool, children's pool, shuffleboard, games room, and parasail and water-sports rentals.

DAYS INN ISLAND BEACH RESORT, 6200 Gulf Blvd., St. Petersburg Beach, FL 33706. Tel. 813/367-1902, or toll free 800/544-4222 or 800/325-2525. Fax 813/367-4422. 102 rms. A/C TV TEL

$ Rates: $69–$139 single or double; $79–$159 efficiency. AE, CB, DC, DISC, MC, V.

Located on the gulf beachfront, this two-story complex sits on five acres of tropical property. Guest rooms, furnished in light woods and pastel tones, have picture-window views of the beach or a central courtyard with the pool, lush greenery, and fountains. About half the units are efficiencies with kitchenettes.

Dining/Entertainment: Meals are available at Riddles, a family-style restaurant, and at Players Bar and Grille. Jimmy B.'s beach bar provides outdoor refreshment and evening entertainment.

Facilities: Outdoor heated swimming pool, volleyball, shuffleboard, games room.

Inexpensive

ISLAND'S END RESORT, 1 Pass-A-Grille Way, St. Petersburg, FL 33706. Tel. 813/360-5023. Fax 813/367-7890. 6 units. A/C TV TEL

$ Rates: $65–$85 one-bedroom unit; $155 three-bedroom unit. No credit cards.

Nestled in the quiet southern tip of Pass-A-Grille where the Gulf of Mexico meets Tampa Bay, this is a resort well named and a good choice for those who want a nonhotel atmosphere. Six contemporary cottages enjoy a shady setting on the water's edge. Each cottage has a dining area, living room with sofa bed, kitchen, bathroom, and bedroom (one unit has three bedrooms). Facilities include a lighted fishing dock, patios, decks, barbecues, and hammocks; and a public beach is less than a block away.

THE HOLIDAY ISLES

Very Expensive

BELLEVUE MIDO RESORT HOTEL, 25 Belleview Blvd. (P.O. Box 2317), Clearwater, FL 34617. Tel. 813/442-6171, or toll free 800/237-8947. Fax 813/441-4173 or 813/443-6361. 242 rms. A/C MINIBAR TV TEL

$ Rates: May–Nov, $85–$135 single, $130–$150 double; Dec–Apr, $135–$175 single, $150–$195 double. AE, CB, DC, DISC, MC, V.

Perched on a high bluff above Clearwater Bay, this massive multigabled white clapboard Victorian hotel sits amid lofty native pines, palms, and palmettos. Unlike most Clearwater hostelries, it's not on Clearwater Beach, but attracts a clientele who appreciate staying at a landmark—dating back to 1897 and listed on the National Register of Historic Places, it's the largest occupied wooden structure in the world. Although the exterior and much of the interior have been preserved over the years, there have also been modern additions, such as a futuristic glassy entrance and circular atrium-style lobby. The high-ceilinged guest rooms, for the most part, remain unchanged, decorated in Queen Anne style, with dark-wood period furniture.

Dining/Entertainment: The main restaurants are the Victorian-style Candlelight Room for dinner; the informal Terrace Café for breakfast or lunch; and the new Madame Ma's for gourmet Chinese cuisine. There is also a pub, lounge, and poolside bar.

Services: Room service, dry cleaning and valet laundry, nightly turn-down, currency exchange, transfer service from/to Tampa Airport, babysitting.

Facilities: 18-hole par-72 championship golf course, four Har-Tru tennis courts, indoor and outdoor heated swimming pools, Jacuzzi, steam rooms, sauna, Swiss showers, workout gym, jogging and walking trails, access to a private Cabana Club on the Gulf of Mexico, bicycle rentals, fishing and sailboat charters, gift shops, art gallery, newsstand.

Expensive

CLEARWATER BEACH HOTEL, 500 Mandalay Ave., Clearwater Beach, FL 34630. Tel. 813/441-2425, or toll free 800/292-2295. Fax 813/449-2083. 157 units. A/C TV TEL

$ Rates: $75–$150 single or double. AE, CB, DC, MC, V.

Dating back 80 years but revamped and updated in 1988, this is one of the few Clearwater Beach properties with an old-world ambience. The complex, which sits directly on the gulf, consists of a six-story main building and two- and three-story wings. Rooms and rates vary, according to location—bay-view or gulf-view, poolside or beachfront.

Dining/Entertainment: The Dining Room offers views of the gulf, as does the nautically themed Schooner Lounge. Outdoor service is provided at the Cabana Beach Bar.

Services: Room service, valet laundry.

Facilities: Heated outdoor swimming pool, sun deck, library.

NORTH REDINGTON BEACH HILTON, 17120 Gulf Blvd., N. Redington Beach, FL 33708. Tel. 813/391-4000, or toll free 800/HILTONS or 800/447-SAND. Fax 813/391-4000, ext. 7777. 125 rms. A/C MINIBAR TV TEL

$ Rates: May–Nov, $79–$129 single or double; Dec–Apr, $129–$189 single or double. AE, CB, DC, DISC, MC, V.

Surrounded mostly by private homes and condominiums, this six-story property edges 250 feet of beachfront. Guest rooms are decorated in pastel tones, with extra-large bathrooms and full-length-mirrored closets. Each unit has a balcony with a view of either the gulf or Boca Ciega Bay.

Dining/Entertainment: Jasmine's Steakhouse offers outdoor and indoor dining, and the poolside Tiki Bar is popular each evening for its sunset-watching festivities.

Services: Room service, valet laundry.

Facilities: Outdoor heated swimming pool, sun deck.

RADISSON SUITE RESORT, 1201 Gulf Blvd., Clearwater Beach, FL 34630. Tel. 813/596-1100, or toll free 800/333-3333. Fax 813/595-4292. 220 suites. A/C MINIBAR TV TEL

$ Rates: May–Nov, $99–$175 single or double; Dec–Apr, $129–$175 single or double. AE, CB, DC, DISC, MC, V.

Opened in 1990, this 10-story all-suite hotel is an expansive $40-million seven-acre property overlooking Clearwater Harbor, with the Gulf of Mexico just across the street. Each suite has a bedroom with balcony offering water views, as well as a complete living room with a sofa bed, wet bar, VCR, and tapedeck.

Dining/Entertainment: The Harbor Grille specializes in barbecues and buffets, and the Harbor Lounge has a piano bar, while Kokomo's offers light fare and tropical drinks.

Services: Room service, laundry, free shuttle to the beach, child care.

Facilities: Outdoor heated swimming pool, sun deck, sauna, exercise room, waterfront boardwalk.

SHERATON SAND KEY RESORT, 1160 Gulf Blvd., Clearwater Beach, FL 33515. Tel. 813/595-1611, or toll free 800/325-3535. Fax 813/596-8488. 390 rms. A/C TV TEL

$ Rates: May–Nov, $69–$99 single or double; Dec–Apr, $100–$148 single or double. AE, CB, DC, DISC, MC, V.

Situated along 32 gulf-front acres, this nine-story resort overlooks a 650-foot beach and is a favorite with water-sports enthusiasts. Guest rooms currently offer standard beach-toned decor with light-wood furniture. All units have a balcony or patio with views of the gulf or the harbor.

Dining/Entertainment: Rusty's Restaurant serves breakfast and dinner; for lighter fare, try the Island Café, or the Sundeck or Gazebo Bar. The rooftop Sky Lounge offers live music for dancing.

Services: Valet laundry, babysitting.

Facilities: Outdoor heated swimming pool, Jacuzzi, three lighted tennis courts, volleyball court, gift shop, newsstand, games room, children's pool, playground, water-sports rentals.

Moderate

BEST WESTERN SEA STONE RESORT, 445 Hamden Dr., Clearwater Beach, FL 34630. Tel. 813/441-1722, or toll free 800/444-1919 or 800/528-1234. Fax 813/449-1580. 65 rms, 43 suites. A/C TV TEL

$ Rates: $45–$88 single or double; $88–$166 suite. AE, CB, DC, DISC, MC, V.
Formerly two separate hotels, this is now one resort on the bayfront, connected by a pool and sun deck. The focus is on the Sea Stone Suites, a six-story building of classic Key West–style architecture containing 43 one-bedroom suites, each with kitchenette and living room. A few steps away, the older five-story Gulfview wing offers 65 bedrooms. Furnishings are bright and airy, with pastel tones, light woods, and sea scenes on the walls.

Dining/Entertainment: The Marker 5 Restaurant is on the lobby level of the suite complex, offering indoor and outdoor seating and a lounge.

Facilities: Heated outdoor swimming pool, Jacuzzi, boat dock, coin-operated guest laundry, meeting rooms.

PALM PAVILION INN, 18 Bay Esplanade, Clearwater Beach, FL 34630. Tel. 813/446-6777. 26 rms, 4 efficiencies. A/C TV TEL

$ Rates: $38–$95 single or double; $55–$110 efficiency. AE, CB, DC, MC, V.

A stroll along the Clearwater beachfront is bound to draw your attention to this three-story art deco building, recently restored and artfully trimmed in pink and blue. The lobby area and guest rooms are equally art deco in design with rounded light-wood and rattan furnishings, bright sea-toned fabrics, and vertical blinds. Rooms in the front of the house face the gulf and those in the back face the bay; four units have kitchenettes. Facilities include a rooftop sun deck, beach access, and complimentary coffee.

Inexpensive

ALPAUGH'S GULF BEACH MOTEL APARTMENTS, 68 Gulf Blvd., Indian Rocks Beach, FL 34635. Tel. 813/595-2589. 16 rms. A/C TV TEL

$ Rates: $52–$74 single or double. MC, V.

A long-established tradition in the area, this family-oriented motel sits beside the beach with a grassy central courtyard area. The rooms offer modern furnishings, and each unit has a kitchenette and dining area. Facilities include coin-operated laundry, lawn games, picnic tables, and shuffleboard at each location.

There's a second Alpaugh's motel at 1912 Gulf Blvd., Indian Rocks Beach, FL 34635 (tel. 813/595-9421), with similar facilities and room rates, plus a one-bedroom cottage for $64–$78 and some two-bedroom suites for $70–$90.

CAPTAIN'S QUARTERS INN, 10035 Gulf Blvd., Treasure Island, FL 33706. Tel. 813/360-1659. 6 rms, 3 suites. A/C TV TEL

$ Rates: $45–$70 single or double; $65–$95 suite. MC, V.

This nautically themed property is a real find—offering well-kept accommodations on the gulf at inland rates. Six rooms are efficiencies with new mini-kitchens (including microwave oven, coffee maker, and wet bar or sink), and three units have a separate bedroom and a full kitchen. The complex sits on 100 yards of beach, an ideal vantage point for sunset-watching. Facilities include an outdoor solar-heated freshwater swimming pool, a sun deck, guest barbecues, a library, and a guest laundry.

PELICAN—EAST & WEST, 108 21st Ave., Indian Rocks Beach, FL 34635. Tel. 813/595-9741. 8 units. A/C TV

$ Rates: $30–$50 single or double at Pelican East, $50–$70 single or double at Pelican West. MC, V.

"P.D.I.P." (Perfect Day in Paradise) is the motto at this well-kept motel complex offering a choice of two settings, depending on your budget. The lowest rates are at Pelican East, 500 feet from the beach, with four units, each with bedroom and separate kitchen. Pelican West sits on the beachfront, offering four apartments, each with living room, bedroom, kitchen, patio, and unbeatable views of the gulf.

SUN WEST BEACH MOTEL, 409 Hamden Dr. S., Clearwater Beach, FL 34630. Tel. 813/442-5008. 4 rms, 10 efficiencies. A/C TV TEL

$ Rates: $40–$61 single or double; $48–$79 efficiency. DISC, MC, V.

Overlooking the bay and yet only a two-block walk from the beach, this well-maintained one-story motel has a heated pool, fishing/boating dock, sun deck, shuffleboard court, and guest laundry. All units, which face either the bay, the pool, or the sun deck, have contemporary resort-style furnishings. The four motel rooms have small refrigerators and the 10 efficiencies have kitchens.

WHERE TO DINE

From elegant candlelit dining rooms to panoramic waterfront restaurants or casual cafés, St. Petersburg has it all—especially outstanding seafood, fresh from gulf waters and beyond.

Like many Florida cities, St. Petersburg is a great exponent of the "early bird dinner"—a three- or four-course evening meal at a set price, usually served between 4pm and 6 or 7pm. By being an "early bird," you can sample even the most expensive restaurants and rarely pay more than $10 for a complete dinner.

DOWNTOWN ST. PETERSBURG

Expensive

BASTA'S CANTINA D'ITALIA RISTORANTE, 1625 4th St. S. Tel. 894-7880.

Cuisine: NORTHERN ITALIAN/CONTINENTAL. **Reservations:** Recommended.

$ **Prices:** Main courses $13.95–$22.95. AE, CB, DC, MC, V.

Open: Lunch Mon–Fri 11:30am–3pm; dinner Mon–Sat 5–10pm.

Situated near the Dalí Museum, this classy little enclave is off the beaten track but worth a detour. The decor is a blend of art deco and Mediterranean influences, but the main attraction is the award-winning food. Specialties include seafood Porto Fino (lobster, shrimp, clams, scallops, and crab legs poached in white sauce over angel-hair pasta), and filet mignon Napoleone (filet of beef topped with mozzarella cheese, mushrooms, and herbs, and sprayed with brandy), as well as veal saltimbocca, shrimp scampi, lobster tails, steak Diane, and rack of lamb.

Moderate

APROPOS, 300 Second Ave. NE. Tel. 823-8934.

Cuisine: AMERICAN. **Reservations:** Not accepted.

$ **Prices:** Main courses $8–$15. MC, V.

Open: Lunch Tues–Sat 11am–3pm; dinner Thurs–Sat 6pm–midnight; brunch Sun 8:30am–2pm.

Overlooking the marina and The Pier, this trendy art deco–style restaurant offers both air-conditioned seating indoors and patio-style seating on an outdoor deck. The menu, which features light foods spiked with fresh herbs, includes such dinner entrees as rosemary chicken, vegetarian platters, lamb chops, pepper steak, and fresh seafood.

THE COLUMBIA, 800 Second Ave. NE. Tel. 822-8000.

Cuisine: SPANISH. **Reservations:** Recommended.

$ **Prices:** Main courses $7.95–$16.95. AE, CB, DC, MC, V.

Open: Mon–Thurs 11am–10pm, Fri–Sat 11am–11pm, Sun noon–10pm.

A branch of the Tampa landmark of the same name, this restaurant occupies the fourth floor of The Pier complex. Although it lacks the antique decor of the original Ybor City location, it excels by offering unequalled views of the Gulf of Mexico and the St. Petersburg skyline. A second location in this area is also on the water at 1241 Gulf Blvd., Clearwater Beach (tel. 596-2828). For a description of the menu, see "Where to Dine" in the Tampa section.

LEVEROCK'S, 4801 37th St. S. Tel. 864-3883.

Cuisine: SEAFOOD. **Reservations:** Not accepted.

$ **Prices:** Main courses $3.95–$6.95 at lunch, $6.95–$12.95 at dinner. AE, CB, DC, MC, V.

Open: Daily 11:30am–10pm.

Dating back to 1948 and synonymous with the freshest of seafood at affordable prices, Leverock's operates six fish houses along the Florida Gulf Coast (five in the St. Pete area and one in Bradenton). With the exception of the Pinellas Park site, all Leverock's restaurants offer lovely water views (this location, southwest of downtown overlooks Maximo Moorings marina and Boca Ciega Bay). Menu selections range from 10 different shrimp dishes to sautéed snapper, grouper Florentine, salmon stir-fry, and crab cakes. Those with hearty appetites might opt for the "captain's platter" of shrimp, scallops, fish, crab legs, and petite lobster tails. Steaks, chicken Cordon Bleu, and baby back ribs round out the menu.

Other Leverock's locations in the area are at 7000 U.S. 19 at Park Boulevard, Pinellas Park (tel. 526-9188), north of downtown; 10 Corey Ave., St. Petersburg Beach (tel. 367-4588); 565 150th Ave., Madeira Beach (tel. 393-0459); and 551 Gulf Blvd., Clearwater Beach (tel. 446-5884).

WATERFRONT STEAK HOUSE, 8800 Bay Pines Blvd. N. Tel. 345-5335.

Cuisine: AMERICAN. **Reservations:** Not accepted.
$ Prices: Main courses $6.95–$15.95. AE, CB, DC, MC, V.
Open: Daily 11:30am–10pm.

Northwest of downtown at the Lighthouse Point Marina, overlooking Boca Ciega Bay, diners can find choice western beef at affordable prices. The menu features three different cuts of prime rib, two sizes of filet mignon, and four types of steaks, plus chopped steak, beef kebabs, and four variations of surf-and-turf. Just for variety, there are baby back ribs, chicken, and two or three seafood items.

Budget

CHA CHA COCONUTS, 800 Second Ave. NE. Tel. 822-6655.

Cuisine: AMERICAN. **Reservations:** Not required.
$ Prices: Main courses $3.95–$7.95. AE, CB, DC, MC, V.
Open: Mon–Thurs 11am–midnight, Fri–Sat 11am–1am, Sun noon–11pm.

You'll feel as if you've been transported to the tropics when you enter this informal spot on the top floor of The Pier complex. While you dine, you can take in panoramic views of both the Gulf of Mexico and the St. Petersburg skyline. A second location in this area is also on the water at 1241 Gulf Blvd., Clearwater Beach (tel. 596-6040). For a description of the menu, see "Where to Dine" in the Tampa section.

FOURTH STREET SHRIMP STORE, 1006 4th St. N. Tel. 822-0325.

Cuisine: SEAFOOD. **Reservations:** Not accepted.
$ Prices: Main courses $4–$11. No credit cards.
Open: Mon–Thurs and Sat 11:30am–8:30pm, Fri 11am–9pm, Sun noon–8pm.
Closed: Mon May–Dec.

Wedged on a busy street north of downtown, this is an Old Florida–style fish market and restaurant, offering no-frills seafood at rock-bottom prices. The tablecloths, utensils, and glasses are plastic and the plates are made of paper, but the seafood is the real thing—heaping servings of fresh grouper, smelts, or frogs' legs, shrimp of all sizes, oysters, and clams. Florida crab croquettes are a specialty.

PEP'S SEA GRILL, 7610 4th St. N. Tel. 521-1655.

Cuisine: SEAFOOD. **Reservations:** Not accepted.
$ Prices: Main courses $5.95–$12.95. No credit cards.
Open: Mon–Sat 4–10pm, Sun 11:30am–9pm.

Located north of downtown is this small, almost diner-style eatery, with a cheery art deco decor. It's known for serving fresh seafood at affordable prices. The menu items vary with the local catch, but specials often include salmon and snow crab, stone crabs, and a hearty one-pound shrimp feast.

Another branch is located in St. Petersburg Beach at 5895 Gulf Blvd. (tel. 367-3550).

SHELLS, 1190 34th St. N. Tel. 321-6020.

Cuisine: SEAFOOD. **Reservations:** Not accepted.

$ **Prices:** Main courses $4.95–$12.95. MC, V.
Open: Dinner only, Sun–Thurs 4–10pm, Fri–Sat 4–11pm
Shells is a local institution. The first Shells opened in Tampa in 1985, and this location followed soon after, as have more than 20 other branches in Florida and beyond. For a description of the decor and menu, see "Where to Dine" in the Tampa section. Other branches in the St. Petersburg area are at 17855 Gulf Blvd., Redington Shores (tel. 393-8990), and 3138 U.S. 19 N., Clearwater (tel. 789-3944).

TED PETERS' FAMOUS SMOKED FISH, 1350 Pasadena Ave. S. Tel. 381-7931.
Cuisine: SMOKED SEAFOOD. **Reservations:** Not accepted.
$ **Prices:** Main courses $3.95–$11.95. No credit cards.
Open: Wed–Mon 11:30am–7:30pm.
Heading southwest of downtown toward the beach, the aromas of smoked fish tell you that you are approaching this rustic little roadside stand. The menu is limited, focusing primarily on smoked salmon, mackerel, or mullet, served with German potato salad. If you feel like something lighter, try a sandwich filled with smoked fish spread.

ST. PETERSBURG BEACH

Moderate

LUCKY FISHERMAN SEAFOOD HOUSE, 5100 Gulf Blvd. Tel. 360-5448.
Cuisine: SEAFOOD. **Reservations:** Accepted only for parties of eight or more.
$ **Prices:** Main courses $7.95–$15.95. MC, V.
Open: Dinner only, Mon–Sat 4:30–10pm, Sun 12:30–9pm.
Set back from the main road, this beach house–style restaurant overlooks the gulf and offers great views amid a decor of modern art deco furnishings with pastel tones. The menu, which focuses on seafood, includes snow crab legs, baked flounder stuffed with crab and scallops, seafood mixed grill (salmon, grouper, swordfish), baked orange roughy, and charcoal-broiled shrimp on a skewer. In addition, there are a variety of steaks and chicken dishes.

HURRICANE, 807 Gulf Way. Tel. 360-9558.
Cuisine: SEAFOOD. **Reservations:** Not accepted.
$ **Prices:** Main courses $6.95–$17.95. MC, V.
Open: Daily 8am–1am.
If you're a fan of Florida black grouper or even if you've never tasted it before, here's *the* spot to try it. Overlooking Pass-A-Grille beach, this informal indoor-outdoor restaurant is synonymous with grouper. Entrees range from Cajun grouper and grouper Alfredo, to grouper Oscar, grouper au gratin, or grouper amandine, to name a few. And if you crave something else, there's always crab legs and claws, shrimp, scallops, and swordfish, as well as barbecued ribs and steaks.

MULLIGAN'S SUNSET GRILLE, 9524 Blind Pass Rd. Tel. 367-6680.
Cuisine: SEAFOOD/AMERICAN. **Reservations:** Not accepted.
$ **Prices:** Main courses $7.95–$19.95. AE, MC, V.
Open: Daily 11am–11pm; brunch Sun 11am–3pm.
Overlooking the waters of Boca Ciega Bay at the north end of St. Petersburg Beach, this informal restaurant offers indoor and outdoor seating. The straightforward menu offers steamed seafood platters, stone crabs in season, and seafood combination pots for two people (with steamed oysters, snow crab, shrimp, corn on the cob, and more), as well as ribs, steaks, Southwest-style chicken, and pastas.

SILAS DENT'S, 5501 Gulf Blvd. Tel. 360-6961.
Cuisine: REGIONAL/SEAFOOD. **Reservations:** Recommended.
$ **Prices:** Main courses $7.95–$20.95. CB, DC, DISC, MC, V.
Open: Dinner only, Mon–Thurs 5–10pm, Fri–Sat 5–11pm, Sun noon–10pm.
With a rustic facade of driftwood and an interior of palm fronds and cedar poles, this

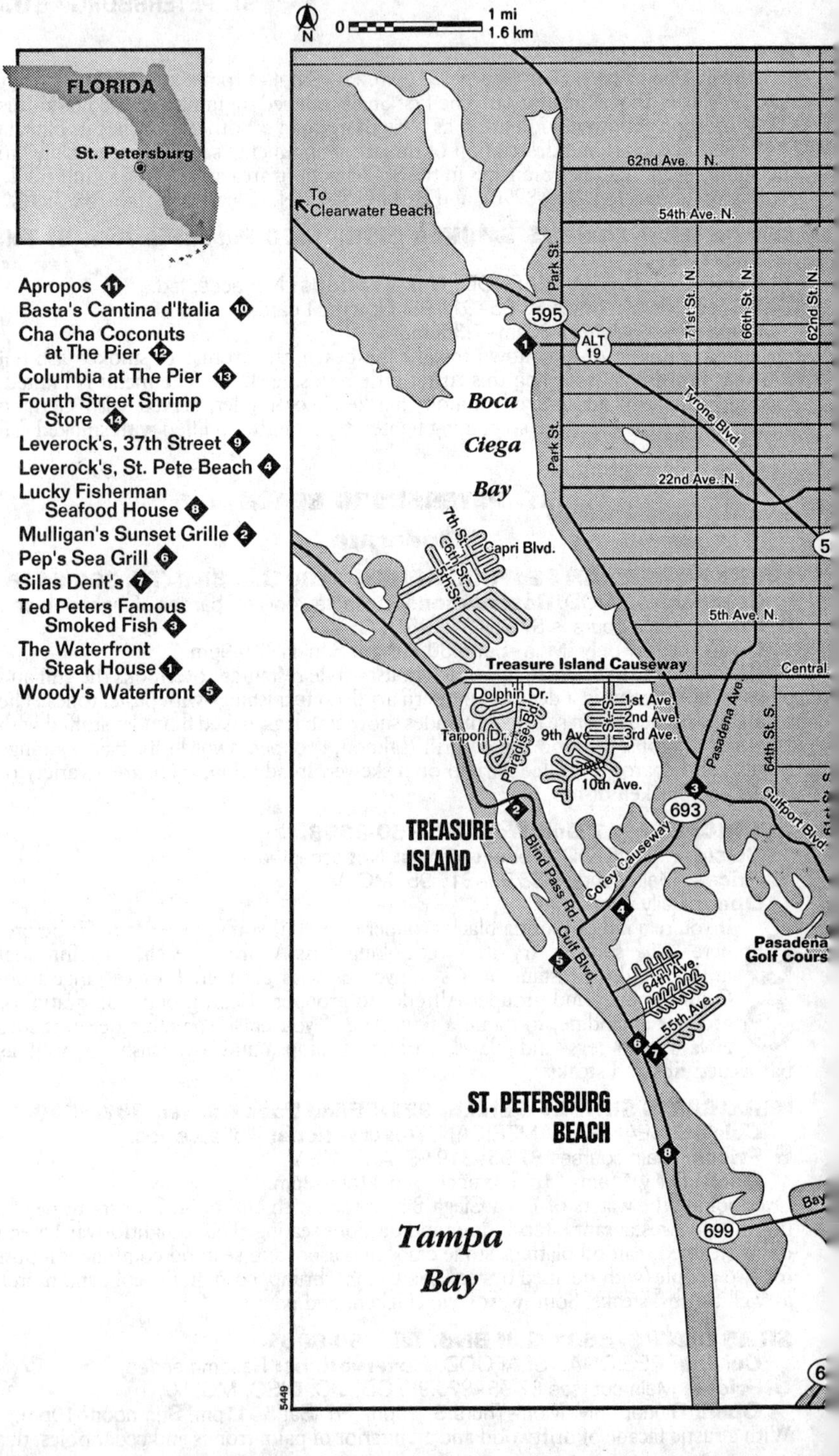

Apropos 11
Basta's Cantina d'Italia 10
Cha Cha Coconuts at The Pier 12
Columbia at The Pier 13
Fourth Street Shrimp Store 14
Leverock's, 37th Street 9
Leverock's, St. Pete Beach 4
Lucky Fisherman Seafood House 8
Mulligan's Sunset Grille 2
Pep's Sea Grill 6
Silas Dent's 7
Ted Peters Famous Smoked Fish 3
The Waterfront Steak House 1
Woody's Waterfront 5

N
0
1 mi
1.6 km
To Clearwater Beach
62nd Ave. N.
54th Ave. N.
Park St.
71st St. N.
66th St. N.
62nd St. N.
595
ALT 19
Tyrone Blvd.
Boca Ciega Bay
22nd Ave. N.
7th St.
6th St.
5th St.
Capri Blvd.
5th Ave. N.
Treasure Island Causeway
Central
Dolphin Dr.
Paradise Blvd.
Tarpon Dr.
9th Ave.
1st Ave.
2nd Ave.
3rd Ave.
10th Ave.
Pasadena Ave.
64th St. S.
Gulfport Blvd.
693
TREASURE ISLAND
Blind Pass Rd.
Corey Causeway
Gulf Blvd.
Pasadena Golf Cours
64th Ave.
55th Ave.
ST. PETERSBURG BEACH
Bay
699
Tampa Bay
5449

ST. PETERSBURG AREA DINING

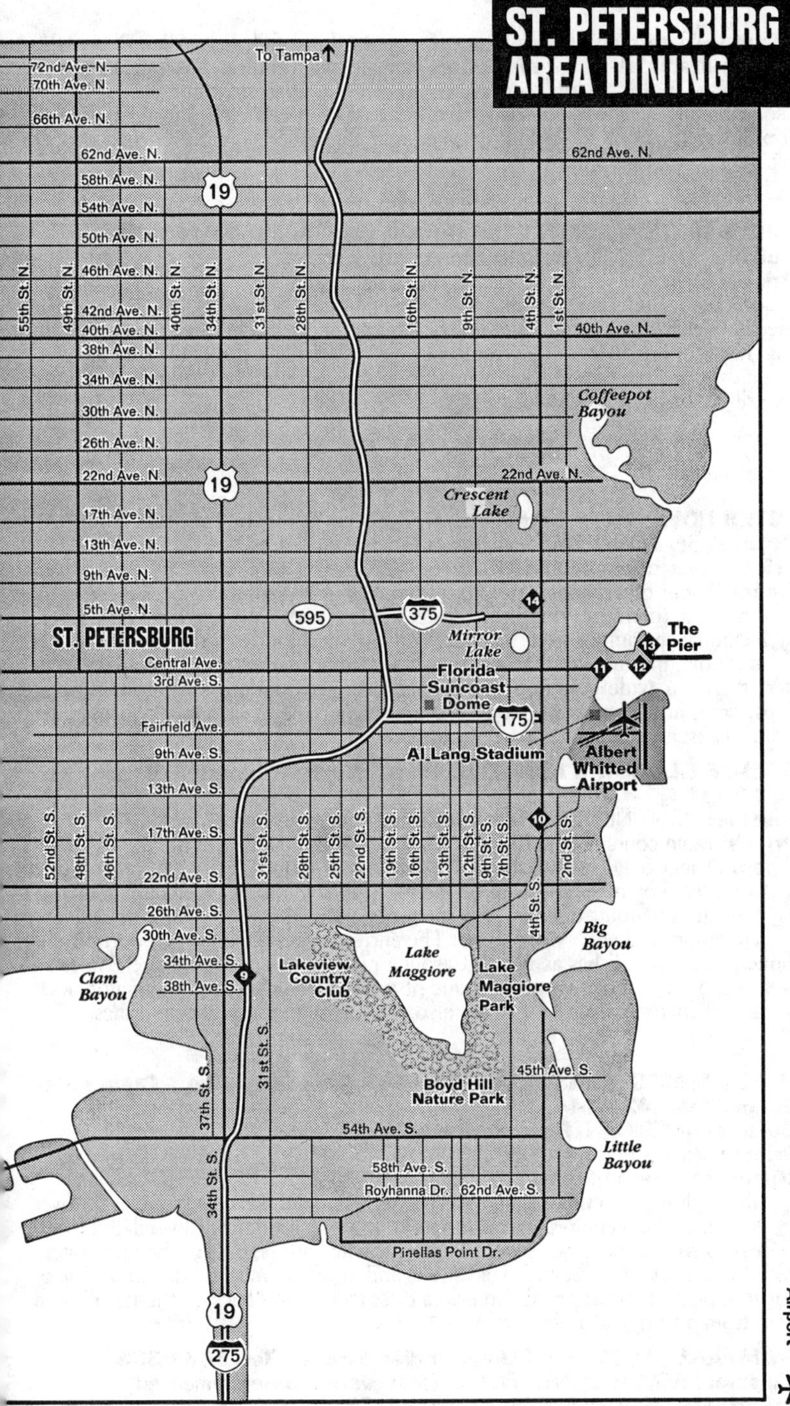

Airport

restaurant seeks to replicate the home of popular local folk hero Silas Dent, who inhabited a nearby island for many years early in this century. The menu aims to reflect Silas's diet of local fish using such ingredients as alligator, amberjack, grouper, and squid, along with such modern favorites as Dungeness crab, lobster tails, and scallops, as well as prime rib, filet mignon, and chicken Silas (with red bell pepper sauce).

Budget

WOODY'S WATERFRONT, 7308 Sunset Way. Tel. 360-9165.
Cuisine: AMERICAN. **Reservations:** Not accepted.
$ Prices: Main courses $2.95–$6.95. No credit cards.
Open: Tues–Sun 11am–2am.

Beside the beach, this casual café and beach bar offers indoor and outdoor patio seating. Ideal for lunch, a cooling tropical drink, or late-night snack, the simple menu offers sandwiches, burgers, chicken wings, fried shellfish, and the ubiquitous grouper (fried, grilled, or blackened).

THE HOLIDAY ISLES

Very Expensive

LOBSTER POT, 17814 Gulf Blvd., Redington Shores. Tel. 391-8592.
Cuisine: SEAFOOD. **Reservations:** Recommended.
$ Prices: Main courses $12.50–$26.75. AE, CB, DC, MC, V.
Open: Dinner only, Mon–Sat 4:30–10pm, Sun 4–10pm.

First and foremost, this is a lobster house, with 22 variations of lobster, including specimens from Maine, South Africa, Florida, and Denmark—tails or whole, in sauces and au naturel—all sold at market prices. In addition to lobster, there's a wide selection of grouper, snapper, salmon, swordfish, shrimp, scallops, crab, and even Dover sole, prepared simply or in elaborate sauces. Filet mignon, steaks, and chicken round out the menu.

THE WINE CELLAR, 17307 Gulf Blvd., North Redington Beach. Tel. 393-3491.
Cuisine: CONTINENTAL. **Reservations:** Recommended.
$ Prices: Main courses $10.75–$27.50. AE, CB, DC, MC, V.
Open: Dinner only, Tues–Sat 4:30–11pm, Sun 4–10pm.

Considered by many locals to be the top choice in the St. Petersburg area, this popular restaurant doesn't even sport a view of the water. With its culinary reputation, it doesn't need views. The entrees present the best of Europe and the States, with such dishes as North Carolina rainbow trout, red snapper Waleska, frogs' legs provençal, various cuts of prime rib, weinerschnitzel, beef Wellington, rack of lamb, and chateaubriand. There are also vegetarian and low-calorie dishes.

Expensive

BOB HEILMAN'S BEACHCOMBER, 447 Mandalay Ave., Clearwater Beach. Tel. 442-4144.
Cuisine: AMERICAN. **Reservations:** Recommended.
$ Prices: Main courses $10.95–$25.95. AE, DC, MC, V.
Open: Mon–Sat 11:30am–11pm, Sun noon–10pm.

Although it doesn't have water views, this restaurant has been popular for over 40 years. The menu presents a variety of fresh seafood, from Everglades frogs' legs to Maine lobsters, as well as Atlantic sole and the best of the local catch. Beef is also a specialty here, with aged steaks and prime rib much in demand. One of the most popular items on the menu is in a class by itself—"back-to-the-farm" fried chicken from an original 1926 recipe.

LE POMPANO, 19325 Gulf Blvd., Indian Shores. Tel. 596-0333.
Cuisine: FRENCH/CONTINENTAL. **Reservations:** Recommended.
$ Prices: Main courses $10.95–$22.95. AE, CB, DC, MC, V.
Open: Lunch Mon–Sat 11:30am–2:30pm; dinner daily 4–10pm.

★ Set back from the road, this modern California-style restaurant offers wide-windowed views of the Intracoastal Waterway, across from the gulf. Entrees include veal Cordon Bleu, roast duckling à l'orange, chicken Oscar, sweetbreads, chateaubriand, rack of lamb, and of course, a signature dish of filet of pompano en papillote.

Moderate

FRIENDLY FISHERMAN, 150 128th Ave., Madeira Beach. Tel. 391-6025.

Cuisine: SEAFOOD. **Reservations:** Not accepted.
$ **Prices:** Main courses $7.95–$19.95. MC, V.
Open: Sun–Thurs 7am–10pm, Fri–Sat 7am–11pm.

At the southern tip of Madeira Beach, this waterside restaurant has become the centerpiece of John's Pass Village, an outgrowth of a busy fishing business launched over 50 years ago. The menu focuses on seafood, served smoked, steamed, fried, or broiled. Choices range from amberjack and mullet to stone crabs, shrimp, grouper, snapper, and flounder, as well as lobster tails, and four kinds of surf-and-turf.

SEAFOOD & SUNSETS AT JULIE'S, 351 S. Gulfview Blvd., Clearwater Beach. Tel. 441-2548.

Cuisine: SEAFOOD. **Reservations:** Recommended.
$ **Prices:** Main courses $6.95–$16.95. AE, MC, V.
Open: Daily 11am–10pm.

A Key West–style atmosphere prevails at this indoor-outdoor eatery across from the beach. And yes, there is a Julie (Julie Nichols), who is usually on the scene, and this is indeed a great vantage point for sunset-watching. Just to make sure no one misses this spectacular sight, sunset time is posted on a blackboard every day. The menu offers lots of seafood—Florida lobsters, stone crabs, conch, grouper and other fish (prepared charcoal-broiled, blackened, fried, or broiled), as well as steaks, surf-and-turf, and chicken.

SCANDIA, 19829 Gulf Blvd., Indian Shores. Tel. 595-5525.

Cuisine: SCANDINAVIAN. **Reservations:** Recommended.
$ **Prices:** Main courses $7.95–$19.95. AE, CB, DC, MC, V.
Open: Lunch Tues–Sat 11:30am–3pm; dinner Tues–Sat 3–9pm, Sun noon–8pm.

Unique in decor and menu along the gulf coast, this chalet-style restaurant brings a touch of Hans Christian Andersen to the beach strip. The menu offers Scandinavian favorites, from smoked salmon and pickled herring, to roast pork, sausages, schnitzels, and Danish lobster tails, as well as a few international dishes such as curried chicken, surf-and-turf, roast leg of lamb, and local seafood choices—jumbo shrimp, scallops, grouper, flounder, and more.

Inexpensive

OMI'S BAVARIAN INN, 14701 Gulf Blvd., Madeira Beach. Tel. 393-9654.

Cuisine: GERMAN. **Reservations:** Recommended.
$ **Prices:** Main courses $6.95–$13.95. DISC, MC, V.
Open: Daily noon–9:30pm.

This little restaurant is a small patch of Germany on the gulf. You won't find much seafood here, but you will have a choice of various schnitzels, sauerbraten and schweinebraten (roast pork), chicken paprikash, beef goulasch, Bavarian bratwurst, and stuffed pepper.

Budget

CRABBY BILL'S, 401 Gulf Blvd., Indian Rocks Beach. Tel. 595-4825 or 593-1819.

Cuisine: SEAFOOD. **Reservations:** Not accepted.
$ **Prices:** Main courses $1.95–$9.95. MC, V.
Open: Mon–Thurs 11am–10pm, Fri–Sat 11am–11pm, Sun 1–10pm.

$ As the name implies, crabs are the specialty here—steamed blue crabs, garlic crabs, stone crab claws, snow crabs, soft-shell crabs, and crab cakes. The atmosphere is informal—plastic cutlery, paper plates, wooden mallets, and stacks of paper napkins are standard fare at every picnic-style table, while country music plays in the background. But the seafood is first-rate and people don't mind waiting or sharing a table to get in on the action. Besides crab, you can indulge in heaping platters of oysters, clams, or mussels on the half shell, fried or steamed shrimp, as well as seafood gumbo and oyster stews.

SHOPPING

SHOPPING CLUSTERS

GAS PLANT ANTIQUE ARCADE, 1246 Central Ave. Tel. 895-0368.

Housed in a former gas plant, this four-story complex is the largest antiques mall on Florida's west coast, with over 100 dealers displaying their wares. Open Monday through Saturday from 10am to 5pm, and on Sunday from noon to 5pm.

JOHN'S PASS VILLAGE AND BOARDWALK, 12901 Gulf Blvd., Madeira Beach. Tel. 391-7373.

★ Situated on the water, this converted fishermen's village houses over 60 shops, selling everything from antiques and arts and crafts and beachwear. There are also several art galleries, including the Bronze Lady, which is the largest single dealer in the world of works by Red Skelton, the comedian-artist. Open daily from 9am to 6pm or later.

THE PIER, 800 Second Ave. NE. Tel. 821-6164.

★ The hub of shopping for the downtown area, this five-story pyramid-shaped complex houses more than a dozen boutiques and craft shops. The Pier also leads to Beach Drive, one of the most fashionable downtown strolling and shopping streets. Open Monday through Saturday from 10am to 9pm and on Sunday from 11am to 7pm.

SPECIALTY SHOPS

BACK IN THE WOODS GALLERY, 242 Beach Dr. NE. Tel. 821-7999.

Across from the Museum of Fine Arts, this shop specializes in limited-edition prints of wildlife art, as well as wildlife stationery and other gift items. Open Tuesday through Friday from 11am to 5pm and on Saturday from 11am to 3pm.

EVANDER PRESTON CONTEMPORARY JEWELRY, 106 Eighth Ave., St. Petersburg Beach. Tel. 367-7894.

If you're in the market for some one-of-a-kind hand-hammered jewelry, it's well worth a visit to this unique gallery/workshop, housed in a 75-year-old building on Pass-A-Grille. Open Monday through Saturday from 10am to 5:30pm.

FLORIDA CRAFTSMEN GALLERY, 235 3rd St. S. Tel. 821-7391.

This is a showcase for the works of over 100 Florida artisans and craftspeople—jewelry, ceramics, woodwork, fiberworks, glassware, paper creations, and metal works. Open Tuesday through Saturday from 10am to 4pm.

HASLAM'S, 2025 Central Ave. Tel. 822-8616.

★ Although the St. Pete area has lots of bookshops, this huge emporium, established in 1933, claims to be Florida's largest, with over 300,000 books—new and used, hardcover and paperback, and electronic. Open Monday through Thursday and Saturday from 9am to 5:30pm, on Friday from 9am to 9pm.

P. BUCKLEY MOSS, 190 Fourth Ave. NE. Tel. 894-2899.

This gallery/studio features the works of one of Florida's most individualistic artists, best known for her portrayal of Amish and Mennonite people. The works include paintings, graphics, figurines, and collector dolls. Open Monday through Saturday from 10am to 5pm, and from September to April also on Sunday from noon to 5pm.

RED CLOUD, 208 Beach Dr. NE. Tel. 821-5824.

This is an oasis for Native American crafts, from jewelry and headdresses to sculpture and art. Open Monday through Saturday from 11am to 5pm.

SENIOR CITIZEN CRAFT CENTER GIFT SHOP, 940 Court St., Clearwater. Tel. 442-4266.

Opened almost 30 years ago, this is one of the area's most unique gift shops—an outlet for the work of about 400 local senior citizens/consignors. The items for sale include knitwear, crochetwork, woodwork, stained glass, clocks, scrimshaw, jewelry, pottery, tilework, ceramics, and hand-painted clothing. It's well worth a visit, even though it's a little off the usual tourist track. Open June to August, Monday through Friday from 10am to 4pm; and September to May, Monday through Saturday from 10am to 4pm.

THE SHELL STORE, 440 75th Ave., St. Petersburg Beach. Tel. 360-0586.

This shop specializes in corals and shells and an on-premises mini-museum illustrates how they both live and grow. In addition, you'll also find a good selection of shell home decorations, shell hobbyist supplies, shell art, planters, and jewelry. Open Monday through Saturday from 9:30am to 5pm.

THE STRAW GOAT, 130 Beach Dr. NE. Tel. 822-4456.

This shop overflows with the work of American and European artisans, with particular emphasis on Scandinavian gifts and cooking utensils. Items range from crystal chandeliers and chimes to wall hangings and decorative stationery. Hours are Monday through Saturday from 10am to 5pm.

WINGS, 6705 Gulf Blvd., St. Petersburg Beach. Tel. 367-8876.

If you forgot your swimsuit or need a new one, this huge emporium is hard to beat, for price and selection. In addition to swimwear, you'll find hats, sunglasses, T-shirts, and more. Open daily from 9am to 10pm.

Other locations are at John's Pass Village, Madeira Beach (tel. 392-9211), and 400 Poinsettia Ave., Clearwater Beach (tel. 449-2710).

EVENING ENTERTAINMENT

THE PERFORMING ARTS

Major Concert/Performance Halls

BAYFRONT CENTER, 400 1st St. S. Tel. 892-5767, or 892-5700 for recorded information.

This is the city's waterfront showplace, with the 8,400-seat **Bayfront Arena** and the 2,000-seat **Mahaffey Theater.** The schedule includes a variety of concerts, Broadway shows, big bands, ice shows, circus, and sports.

Admission: Tickets, $5–$40, depending on event.

FLORIDA SUNCOAST DOME, 1 Stadium Dr. Tel. 825-3100.

This giant arena has a capacity of 50,000 for concerts, but also presents a variety of smaller events.

Admission: Tickets, $15–$30, depending on the event.

RUTH ECKERD HALL, 1111 McMullen-Booth Rd., Clearwater. Tel. 791-7400.

This 2,200-seat auditorium is a major venue for a varied program of Broadway shows, ballet, drama, symphonic works, popular music, jazz, and country music.

Admission: Tickets, $10–$40, depending on the event.

Theaters/Dinner-Theaters

AMERICAN STAGE COMPANY, 211 3rd St. S. Tel. 822-8814.

This is St. Petersburg's resident professional theater, presenting contemporary dramas and comedies.

Admission: $10–$20.

ST. PETERSBURG LITTLE THEATER, 4025 31st St. S. Tel. 866-1973.

This is the city's community theater, presenting six plays or variety shows a year, from September through May.

Admission: $9–$10.

SHOWBOAT DINNER THEATRE, 3405 Ulmerton Rd., Clearwater. Tel. 573-3777.

Designed with a vintage showboat facade, this inland theater presents a variety of Broadway comedies and musicals, with major stars, along with buffet meals.

Admission: $26–$35 evenings, $21–$25 matinees.

STATE THEATER, 687 Central Ave. Tel. 821-9584.

Originally a movie house, this renovated theater presents a variety of live shows including blues, jazz, reggae, rock, comedy, and local performers.

Admission: $5–$25.

TIDES DINNER THEATER, 16720 Gulf Blvd., N. Redington Beach. Tel. 393-1870.

This facility presents Broadway musicals with performances by the local Seminole Players.

Admission: $25 evenings, $21 matinees.

VAUDEVILLE PALACE, 7951 9th St. N. Tel. 577-5515.

In the vaudeville tradition of yesteryear, this dinner-theater presents a rousing musical-comedy show.

Admission: $19.70–$22.40 evenings, $18.65 matinees.

THE CLUB & MUSIC SCENE

Comedy Clubs

COCONUTS COMEDY CLUB, 6110 Gulf Blvd., St. Petersburg Beach. Tel. 360-NUTS, 360-6887, or 360-4575.

One of the oldest and best-known comedy spots on the beach strip, this club features an ever-changing program of live stand-up comedy acts. Shows are Tuesday, Thursday, and Sunday at 9pm, and Friday and Saturday at 9 and 10:45pm.

Admission: $7, plus a two-drink minimum.

COMEDY LINE, 401 Second Ave. N., Indian Rocks Beach. Tel. 595-9484.

Local comedy acts perform at this club at Hamlin's Landing on the beach strip. Shows are on Friday and Saturday at 8:30pm and 10:45pm, and Sunday and Tuesday through Thursday at 8:30pm.

Admission: $5–$7.

Jazz/Blues/Reggae/Folk

CAMS—CONSORTIUM FOR ART AND MEDIA STUDIES, 5635 Park Blvd., Pinellas Park. Tel. 546-0731.

An alternative to the usual bar, this is an acoustic coffeehouse, and a showcase for poetry, storytelling, and music ranging from blues, jazz, and '50s and '60s tunes, to folk and country. Open daily from 8pm to 1am.

Admission (including coffee and popcorn): $3.

THE HURRICANE LOUNGE, 807 Gulf Way, St. Petersburg Beach. Tel. 260-4875.

Long recognized as one of the best places for jazz, this beachside spot has a varied program of jazz on Sunday, Wednesday, and Thursday from 9pm to 1am and on Friday and Saturday from 9:30pm to 1:30am. Drinks run $2–$4.

Admission: Free.

RINGSIDE CAFE, 2742 4th St. N., St. Petersburg. Tel. 894-8465.

Housed in a renovated boxing gymnasium, this informal neighborhood café has a decided sports motif, but the music focuses on jazz and blues (and sometimes reggae), on Friday and Saturday nights from 10pm to 2am.

Admission: $2 or more.

Dance Clubs/Discos/Top-40s Music

A.C.L. CLUB, 1030 Central Ave. Tel. 823-6183.

One of the oldest clubs in the city, this place is known for rock jam sessions, live rock, and rhythm and blues bands. Open Tuesday through Saturday from 9:30pm to 1am.

Admission: $2–$5.

BEACH NUTTS, 9600 W. Gulf Blvd., Treasure Island. Tel. 367-7427.

This is a quintessential beach bar, perched atop a stilt foundation like a wooden beach cottage on the Gulf of Mexico. The music ranges from Top-40s to reggae and rock. Open daily from 5pm to 1am. Drinks cost $2–$4.

Admission: Free.

BIG CATCH, 9 1st St. NE. Tel. 821-6444.

This casual downtown club features live and danceable rock and Top-40s hits, as well as darts, pool, and hoops. Open Thursday through Saturday from 9pm to 2am.

Admission: $3–$5.

CLUB DETROIT, 16 2nd St. N. Tel. 896-1244.

Housed in the landmark Hotel Detroit, this lively spot includes a lounge, Channel Zero, and an outdoor courtyard, Jannus Landing. Look for blues, reggae, and progressive DJay dance music indoors and live rock concerts outdoors. Open daily from 9pm to 2am.

Admission: $2 and up indoors, $5–$15 for outdoor concerts.

MANHATTANS, 11595 Gulf Blvd., Treasure Island. Tel. 363-1500.

Nestled on the beach strip, this new club offers dancing to live contemporary and classic rock music seven nights a week from 7pm until 2am.

Admission: $3 and up.

Ballrooms

COLISEUM BALLROOM, 535 Fourth Ave. N. Tel. 892-5202.

Dating back to 1924, this landmark Spanish-style building is *the* place to go in downtown St. Petersburg for an evening of dancing to big-band music.

Admission: $3–$11.

JOYLAND, 11225 U.S. 19, Clearwater. Tel. 573-1919.

This is the area's only country-western ballroom, featuring live bands and well-known performers.

Admission: $3–$10.

3. SARASOTA

63 miles S of Tampa, 150 miles SW of Orlando, 225 miles NW of Miami

GETTING THERE By Plane Sarasota-Bradenton Airport, 6000 Airport Circle, Sarasota (tel. 813/359-5200), is located north of downtown between U.S. 41 and U.S. 301. Airlines serving the airport include American, Continental, Delta, Northwest, TWA, United, and USAir.

By Train Amtrak trains arrive at Tampa station, with bus connections to Sarasota. For full information, call toll free 800/342-2520.

By Bus Greyhound/Trailways buses arrive at the Sarasota depot at 575 N. Washington Blvd. (tel. 813/955-5735).

By Car From points north and south, Sarasota can be reached via I-75, U.S. 41, U.S. 301, and U.S. 19. From the east coast of Florida, use Fla. 70 or Fla. 72.

Often referred to as the "circus town," Sarasota is synonymous with circus legend John Ringling, who came to Sarasota in the 1920s and left quite an imprint. He built a palatial home, Ca'd'Zan, on the bayfront, acquired extensive real estate, erected a museum to house his world-class collection of baroque paintings, and moved the famed circus winter quarters from Bridgeport, Conn., to Sarasota, where it remained until 1957 when it moved farther south to Venice.

Known as the cultural center of Florida, Sarasota is home to the Florida West Coast Symphony, the Asolo Performing Arts Center, the Van Wezel Performing Arts Hall, and many more artistic venues. A bright and thriving city of 50,000 people, Sarasota also boasts 20 miles of beach, and an average of 361 days of sunshine per year.

Like much of Florida, Hernándo de Soto is credited with being the first European to explore the area. Legend has it that Sarasota was named after de Soto's daughter, Sara, and hence "Sara Soto," or, eventually, "Sarasota."

ORIENTATION

ARRIVING

West Coast Limousine (tel. 813/355-9645) provides van transfers from the airport to hotels in the Sarasota area. Price depends on destination, but averages $6–$10 per person. Taxi services include **Green Cab Taxi** (tel. 813/922-666) and **Yellow Cab of Sarasota** (tel. 813/955-3341).

INFORMATION

For information about attractions, hotels, restaurants, events, and more, contact the **Sarasota Convention & Visitors Bureau,** 655 N. Tamiami Trail (U.S. 41), Sarasota, FL 34236 (tel. 813/957-1877, or toll free 800/522-9799).

CITY LAYOUT

Sarasota is divided into two sections. The **downtown** area on the mainland hugs the bayfront, with a modern and sleek urban skyline, edged by picturesque marinas, landscaped drives, and historic Spanish-style buildings. U.S. 41 runs through downtown Sarasota in a north-south direction.

An adjacent beach strip to the west, on the Gulf of Mexico, is composed of four islands or "keys," separated from downtown by Sarasota Bay. With white sandy beaches, lagoons, and lush vegetation, **Siesta Key** exudes a tropical ambience; the streets are narrow and shaded by overhanging branches draped with Spanish moss. The **Siesta Drive Causeway** and the **Stickney Point Road Causeway** link Sarasota with Siesta Key.

Lido Key is a lively and well-developed island with a string of motels, restaurants, and nightclubs. At the entrance to Lido Key is **St. Armands Key,** a tiny enclave named after Charles St. Amand (early spelling), a 19th-century French homesteader. It owes its development to circus-master John Ringling who built the four-lane **John Ringling Causeway** that provides access to Lido, St. Armands, and to **Longboat Key,** a narrow, 12-mile-long island which is one of Florida's wealthiest areas.

GETTING AROUND

BY PUBLIC TRANSPORTATION Sarasota County Area Transit/SCAT (tel. 951-5851) provides a regularly scheduled **bus** service for the area. Standard fare is $1; exact change is required.

BY TAXI Taxi companies serving the Sarasota area include **Diplomat Taxi** (tel. 355-5155), **Green Cab Taxi** (tel. 922-6666), **Sarasota Cab** (tel. 366-0596), and **Yellow Cab of Sarasota** (tel. 955-3341).

BY CAR Rental-car companies with desks at the airport include **Avis** (tel. 813/359-5240), **Budget** (tel. 813/359-5353), **Dollar** (tel. 813/355-2996), and **Hertz** (tel. 813/355-8848).

BY WATER TAXI Sarasota Water Taxi (tel. 813/365-5677) operates a daily scheduled service connecting Longboat, Lido, and Siesta Keys with the downtown area (boarding is available at Sarasota Quay Shopping Complex and Marina Jack's at Island Park). The fare is $3.50 one-way, $6 round-trip, and $10 for an all-day pass. Hours are 10am to 5pm.

FAST FACTS

Area Code Sarasota's area code is 813.

Dentist For emergency dental repairs, contact the Sarasota Walk-in Dental Center, 2000 Webber Rd. (tel. 365-1722).

Doctor Most hotels have a doctor on call; if not, contact the Sarasota Physician Referral Center (tel. 957-7777).

Drugstores Eckerd Drugs has over a dozen pharmacies in the downtown and beach areas, including one at the Crossroads Shopping Center, 3800 S. Tamiami Trail (tel. 955-3328), that's open until midnight.

Emergencies Dial 911.

Hospitals The Sarasota Memorial Hospital, 1700 S. Tamiami Trail (tel. 955-1111), and Doctors' Hospital of Sarasota, 2750 Bahia Vista (tel. 366-1411), are two prominent local facilities.

Library Try the Selby Public Library, 1001 Blvd. of the Arts (tel. 951-5501).

Newspapers/Magazines The *Sarasota Herald-Tribune* is published daily. *Sarasota Magazine* is a monthly magazine covering the area.

Post Office The main post office is at 1661 Ringling Blvd. (tel. 952-9720).

Taxes There's a 9% hotel tax, a 7% restaurant tax, and 7% general sales tax.

Transit Information Dial 951-5851.

Weather Call toll free 800/282-5584.

WHAT TO SEE & DO

THE TOP ATTRACTIONS

BELLM CARS & MUSIC OF YESTERDAY, 5500 N. Tamiami Trail. Tel. 355-6228.

This museum displays over 200 classic and antique autos, from Rolls-Royces and Pierce Arrows, to the five cars used personally by circus czar John Ringling. In addition, there are over 1,200 antique music machines, from tiny music boxes to a huge 30-foot Belgian organ.

Admission: $7.50 adults, $3.75 children 6–12, free for children under 6.

Open: Mon–Sat 8:30am–6pm, Sun 9:30am–6pm. **Directions:** Take U.S. 41 north of downtown and one mile south of the airport.

MARIE SELBY BOTANICAL GARDENS, S. Palm Ave., off U.S. 41. Tel. 366-5730.

A 17-acre museum of living plants, this facility is said to be the only botanical garden in the world to specialize in the preservation, study, and research of epiphytic plants ("air plants"), such as orchids, pineapples, and ferns. It is home to more than 20,000 exotic plants including over 6,000 orchids, as well as a bamboo pavilion, waterfall garden, cactus and succulent garden, fernery, hibiscus garden, palm grove, tropical food garden, and a native shore-plant community, plus a museum of botany and the arts.

Admission: $6 adults, $3 children 6–12, free for children under 6 accompanied by an adult.

Open: Daily 10am–5pm.

MOTE MARINE SCIENCE AQUARIUM, 1600 Thompson Pkwy. Tel. 388-2451.

Part of the noted Mote Marine Laboratory complex, this facility focuses on the marine life of the Sarasota area. Displays include a living mangrove swamp and seagrass environment, a 135,000-gallon shark tank, loggerhead turtles and their eggs, dolphins, manatees, and an extensive shell collection. In addition, there are many "research-in-progress" exhibits on such topics as the red tide, aquaculture enhancement, cancer in sharks, and the effects of pesticide and petroleum pollution on the coast. The aquarium is located on City Island, just south of Longboat Key.

Admission: $5 adults, $3 children 6–17.

Open: Daily 10am–5pm. **Directions:** Take John Ringling Circle north to City Island Park, at the foot of the bridge between Lido and Longboat Keys.

MYAKKA RIVER STATE PARK, 132007 Fla. 72. Tel. 924-1027.

This is a 28,875-acre "Old Florida" preserve of wetlands, prairies, nature trails, birdwalks, and dense woodlands along the Myakka River. It includes an outstanding wildlife sanctuary and breeding grounds, home to hundreds of species of plants, trees, and flowers, as well as deer, alligators, and birds such as ospreys, bald eagles, and sandhill cranes. There are two ways to get an overview of the entire park, either via one-hour tram tours or a one-hour airboat ride.

Admission: $3.25 per car (up to eight passengers); airboat or tram tours, $6 adults, $3 children 6–12.

Open: Daily 8am–sunset. **Closed:** Day after Labor Day to Oct 1. **Directions:** Take U.S. 41 south to Stickney Point Road and go 15 miles east on Fla. 72.

PELICAN MAN'S BIRD SANCTUARY, City Island Park. Tel. 388-4444.

Situated next to the Mote Marine aquarium is this shelter and rehabilitation center for injured pelicans and other wild sea birds. It's operated by Dale Shields, who has devoted his life to this cause, helping more than 22,000 birds and earning the unofficial title of "Pelican Man" from those who come to visit.

Admission: Free; donations encouraged.

Open: Daily 10am–4pm. **Directions:** Take John Ringling Circle north to City Island Park.

RINGLING MUSEUM COMPLEX, 5401 Bayshore Rd. Tel. 355-5101, or 351-1660 for recorded information.

The former estate of circus entrepreneur John Ringling, this 38-acre site overlooking Sarasota Bay offers four attractions. Foremost is the **John and Mable Ringling Museum of Art,** Florida's official state art museum, which houses a major exhibit of Baroque art as well as collections of decorative arts and traveling exhibits. Next is the 30-room **Ca'd'Zan** (House of John), the Ringling winter residence, built in 1925 and modeled after a Venetian palace, and the **Circus Galleries,** a building devoted to circus memorabilia including parade wagons, calliopes, costumes, and colorful posters. The grounds also include the **Asolo Center for the Performing Arts,** a professional theater company, plus restaurants and shops.

Admission: $8.50 adults, $7.50 seniors, free for children 12 and under.

Open: Oct–June, Fri–Wed 10am–5:30pm, Thurs 10am–10pm; July–Sept, daily 10am–5:30pm. **Directions:** From downtown, take U.S. 41 north to De Soto Road, and turn left onto Ringling Plaza.

SARASOTA JUNGLE GARDENS, 37-01 Bayshore Rd. Tel. 355-5303.

Situated on the bayfront south of the Ringling Complex, this is a 10-acre preserve featuring jungle trails, tropical plants, exotic waterfowl, and reptiles in natural habitats. In addition, there is a petting zoo, bird shows, and a shell and butterfly museum.

Admission: $8 adults, $4 children 3–12, and free for children under 3.

Open: Daily 9am–5pm. **Directions:** From downtown, take U.S. 41 north to Myrtle Street, turn left, and go two blocks.

SPORTS & RECREATION

SPECTATOR SPORTS

BASEBALL Sarasota is the winter home of the Chicago White Sox who are at the **Ed Smith Stadium,** 2700 12th St. and Tuttle Ave. (tel. 954-7699), for spring training during March and April. East of downtown, this stadium seats 7,500 fans. Admission is from $5 to $9.

DOG RACING At **Sarasota Kennel Club,** 5400 Bradenton Rd. (tel. 355-7744), you can "go to the dogs" and watch these sleek greyhounds in action. The club is located two blocks east of the Ringling Museum Complex, off of De Soto Road. Admission is $1 per person and it is open December to June, Monday through Saturday at 7:30pm; there are matinees Monday, Wednesday, and Saturday at noon.

RECREATION

With its flat, shady terrain beside the Gulf of Mexico and Sarasota Bay, Sarasota is natural turf for bicycling, walking, and many water sports.

BICYCLING **Fun Rentals of Siesta Key,** 5254 Ocean Blvd. (tel. 346-0900), rents bicycles, ranging from standard models to 10-speed, 18- and 21-speed mountain bikes, tandems, 2- and 4-passenger surreys, and duo cycles. Prices are from $3 to $18 per hour, $10 to $66 for eight hours, and $35 to $300 per week. Moped/scooters are also rented; prices are $14 to $21 per hour, $35 to $52 for eight hours, $120 to $180 per week. It's open daily from 10am to 5pm.

Situated just east of downtown, **Sarasota Bicycle Center,** 4084 Bee Ridge Rd. (tel. 377-4505), rents bikes of various types, from 3- to 10-speed, for $15 a day, $30 per week, or $50 for two weeks. It's open Monday through Saturday from 9am to 6pm.

BOAT RENTALS **All Watersports,** Boatyard Shopping Village, 1504 Stickney Point Rd. (tel. 921-2754), rents two- and three-seater speedboats from $45 to $65 per hour, and jet skis for $40 per hour. Parasail rides can also be arranged at $30 for 15-minute rides. Situated on the approach to Siesta Key, it's open daily from 10am to 7pm.

Cannons Marina, 6040 Gulf of Mexico Dr. (tel. 383-1311), on the end of Longboat Key, rents 14- to 24-foot runabout speedboats that cost $65 to $195 for a half-day and $90 to $265 for a full day. Pontoons can be rented for $100 to $140 for a half day and $135 to $175 for a full day. Open skiffs are $40 for a half day and $55 for a full day. Water skis are $25 for a full day. It's open daily from 8am to 6pm.

Mr. C. B.'s, 1249 Stickney Point Rd. (tel. 349-4400), is located beside the Stickney Point Bridge. 16- to 18-foot runabouts and pontoons can be rented for bay fishing and cruising. Runabouts are from $75 to $90 for four hours, $110 to $130 for a full day; pontoons are $100 for four hours, $160 for a full day. Bicycles are also rented from $10 a day. It's open daily from 7am to 6pm.

FISHING **Capt. Joe Bonaro,** Midnight Pass Marina, Siesta Key (tel. 349-3119), takes small groups of up to six passengers for deep-sea fishing excursions aboard the *Rumrunner*, a 29-foot custom-built fishing boat, docked across from Turtle Beach. Prices are $50 per person for a half day and $80 for a full day. It departs daily by reservation only.

For other fishing excursions, try **Flying Fish Fleet,** Marina Jack's Marina, U.S. 41 at Island Park Circle (tel. 366-3373). Docked along the bayfront of downtown, these boats offer deep-sea fishing excursions, half-day, full-day, or 6-hour trips, or a 4½-hour sunset trip. Bait and tackle are furnished. Prices for half-day and sunset trips are $20 for adults, $15 for seniors, and $12 for children; 6-hour trips are $25 for adults, $20 for seniors, and $15 for children; all-day trips are $30 for adults, $25 for seniors, and $20 for children. Monday through Saturday, half-day trips are scheduled at 8am to 12:30pm and 1pm to 5:30pm, on Sunday from 1pm to 5:30pm. The 6-hour trip is offered Sunday to Tuesday and Thursday and Friday from 9am to 3pm. The all-day trip takes place on Wednesday and Saturday from 9am to 5pm, and the sunset trip is on Tuesday and Friday, 4 to 8:30pm.

GOLF **Bobby Jones Golf Complex,** 1000 Azinger Way, off Circus Blvd. (tel. 955-8097), is Sarasota's largest public course, with two 18-hole championship layouts (par 72 and par 71) and a 9-hole executive course (par 30). Play is on a first-come, first-serve basis for tee times. Prices include carts and are $24 from November to April and $16 from May to October. It's open daily, 7am to dusk.

Rolling Green Golf Club, 4501 Tuttle Ave. (tel. 355-6620), is an 18-hole, par-72 course with wide-open fairways. Facilities include a driving range, rental clubs, and lessons. Tee times are assigned two days in advance. Prices, including cart, are $24, arriving before noon, $29 arriving before 2pm. Open daily 7am to dusk.

Sarasota Golf Club, 7820 N. Leewynn Dr. (tel. 371-2431), is an 18-hole, par-72 course that requires that tee times be arranged at least three days in advance. Facilities include a driving range, lessons, and club rentals. Prices, including carts, are $28, arriving before noon, and $22, arriving after noon. It's open daily, 7am to dusk.

SWIMMING Sarasota's beaches are known worldwide for their fine white-powdery sands and clear turquoise waters. Some of the most popular public beaches include Lido Beach, North Lido Beach, and South Lido Beach on Lido Key; and Siesta Beach, Crescent Beach, and Turtle Beach on Siesta Key.

TENNIS **Sarasota Civic Center Municipal Courts,** 901 N. Tamiami Trail (tel. 364-4605), is a downtown public facility with six Har-Tru tennis courts, available for play on a first-come first-serve basis. The price is $4.30 per person per hour. It's open daily, 8am to 9pm. If you prefer clay courts, try the **Siesta Racquet Club,** 5831 Midnight Pass Rd., Siesta Key (tel. 349-5355), which has six clay courts for public use. Equipment rentals and tennis lessons can also be arranged. The price is $8 per person for 1½ hours of play, and is open daily from 8am to 7pm. Four other hard courts are located east of downtown at **Forest Lakes Tennis Club,** 2401 Beneva Rd. (tel. 922-0660). A pro shop and lessons are available. The price is $4 per person for 1½ hours of play. It's open Monday through Saturday 9am to 6pm.

WATERSPORTS Situated on the bayfront downtown, **O'Leary's,** Island Park Marina, Island Park Circle (tel. 953-7505), rents jet skis and offers sailing lessons and other watersports activities by appointment. The price of jet skiing for two hours is from $25 to $75. It's open daily from 7:30am to 8pm.

BAY CRUISES

Le Barge, Marina Jack Marina, U.S. 41 at Island Park Circle (tel. 366-6116), offers two-hour cruises around Sarasota's waterways aboard a 65-foot two-deck vessel from October to May. The hours for the sunset cruise change with the time of sunset, and leave daily, between 5 and 7pm. The early afternoon cruise is daily, from 2 to 4pm. Both cruises cost $8.50 for adults, and $4.50 for children 12 and under.

The 41-foot 12-passenger sailboat ***Enterprise,*** Marina Jack Marina, U.S. 41 at Island Park Circle (tel. 951-1833), cruises the waters of both Sarasota Bay and the Gulf of Mexico. The 3-hour half-day cruise departs daily at 8:30am and 12:30pm and costs $35; the 2-hour sunset cruise departs daily at 4:30pm and costs $20.

WHERE TO STAY

Sarasota is a city of new hotels and motels, divided equally between the downtown area and the beach strip. Rates are at their highest from December to April and can be downright bargains from May to November. Rates are usually slightly higher along the beaches at all times, so bargain hunters flock to the downtown area and commute to the beach.

DOWNTOWN/MAINLAND

Expensive

HYATT, 1000 Blvd. of the Arts, Sarasota, FL 34236. Tel. 813/366-9000, or toll free 800/233-1234. Fax 813/952-1987. 297 rms. A/C TV TEL

$ Rates: $79–$190 single or double. AE, CB, DC, DISC, MC, V.

Located beside Sarasota Bay and boasting its own marina, this 10-story tower is the downtown area's centerpiece hotel. It sits adjacent to the Civic Center, the Van Wezel Performing Arts Hall, and the Sarasota Garden Club, and is within walking distance of downtown shops. The bedrooms, all of which have balconies and overlook the marina or bay, are decorated in contemporary style with soft beige and beach tones.

Dining/Entertainment: The main restaurant is Pompano Cay, known for seafood; the Boathouse offers casual fare and water views of the marina, and Tropics Lounge provides libations and evening entertainment.

Services: Complimentary airport shuttle, room service, valet laundry.

Facilities: Heated outdoor swimming pool, patio, health club, marina.

Inexpensive

COMFORT INN, 4800 N. Tamiami Trail, Sarasota, FL 34234. Tel. 813/355-7091, or toll free 800/221-2222. Fax 813/359-1639. 72 rms. A/C TV TEL

$ Rates (including continental breakfast): $45–$90 single or double. AE, CB, DC, DISC, MC, V.

Just half a mile south of the airport, this two-story hacienda-style motel is set back from the main road in a palm-tree-shaded setting. The bedrooms have contemporary furnishings, with light woods, pastel tones, and mica accessories. Facilities include a coffee shop, heated outdoor swimming pool, and sauna.

HAMPTON INN, 5000 N. Tamiami Trail, Sarasota, FL 34234. Tel. 813/351-7734, or toll free 800/336-9335. Fax 813/351-8820. 97 rms. A/C TV TEL

$ Rates (including continental breakfast): $50–$90 single or double. AE, CB, DC, DISC, MC, V.

The closest downtown hotel south of the airport (a quarter mile away), this three-story hostelry sits on its own grounds in a quiet garden setting. The bedrooms, offering a choice of king-size or double beds, are decorated in pastel tones, with light-wood furnishings. Facilities include a heated swimming pool and a guest laundry.

WELLESLEY INN, 1803 N. Tamiami Trail, Sarasota, FL 34234. Tel. 813/366-5128, or toll free 800/444-8888. Fax 813/951-2956. 106 rms. A/C TV TEL

$ Rates (including continental breakfast): $39–$99 single or double. AE, DISC, MC, V.

Situated just north of the downtown district on the main thoroughfare, this imposing four-story hotel overlooks a marina and boatyard. A welcoming ambience prevails in the elegant lobby area, filled with plants and comfortable seating. The bedrooms are spacious with standard furnishings of light woods and pastel tones, many with views of the marina. Facilities include valet service, an outdoor heated swimming pool, and complimentary airport shuttle.

THE KEYS/ISLANDS

Expensive

AZURE TIDES, 1330 Ben Franklin Dr., Lido Beach, Sarasota, FL 34236. Tel. 813/388-2102. Fax 813/388-3015. 34 units. A/C TV TEL

$ Rates: $105–$289 single or double. MC, V.

Set on 160 feet of private beachfront overlooking the gulf, this two- and three-story Key West–style property offers one- and two-bedroom suites with fully outfitted kitchens, sleeper sofas, and videocasette recorders. Each unit has custom-designed art deco–style furnishings of light woods, pastel fabrics, mirrored closets, and batik wall hangings. Living/dining areas have airy skylit cathedral ceilings and each unit has a patio or balcony. Facilities and services include a heated outdoor swimming pool, deck, cabañas on the beach, a beach bar, concierge, valet service, and a VCR film library.

CRESCENT VIEW BEACH CLUB, 6512 Midnight Pass Rd., Siesta Key, Sarasota, FL 34242. Tel. 813/349-2000, or toll free 800/344-7171. Fax 813/349-9748. 26 units. A/C TV TEL

$ Rates: $95–$185 single or double efficiency; $145–$250 two-bedroom condo suite. MC, V.

Enjoying a quiet setting on the gulf at Crescent Beach, this property is ideal for families or several couples traveling together. It offers two types of one- and two-bedroom apartments—condo suites facing the beach and gulf and efficiency units overlooking the pool or garden. All units are decorated in tropical teal tones with bright Florida fabrics and rattan furnishings; each has a living/dining area and a balcony. The smaller units have kitchenettes with microwave ovens and coffee makers; the condo suites have completely outfitted kitchens, with dishwasher. Facilities include a heated outdoor swimming pool and spa, picnic tables, and a guest laundry.

HALF MOON BEACH CLUB, 2050 Ben Franklin Dr., Lido Key, Sarasota, FL 34236. Tel. 813/3694, or toll free 800/358-3245. Fax 813/388-1938. 86 rms. A/C TV TEL

$ Rates: Dec–Apr, $90–$195 single or double; May–Nov, $65–$120 single or double. MC, V.

Nestled in a quiet garden setting at the southern end of Lido Key, this two-story art deco–style hotel is right on the beach. The guest rooms, each of which has a patio or balcony with views of the pool or beach, are furnished with light woods, quilted fabrics, sea art and plants, and views of pool or beach. All units have a refrigerator and coffee maker and some have kitchenettes with microwave ovens. Facilities include an indoor/outdoor restaurant, outdoor heated swimming pool, and volleyball and shuffleboard courts.

HOLIDAY INN, 233 Ben Franklin Dr., Lido Key, Sarasota, FL 34236. Tel. 813/388-3941, or toll free 800/HOLIDAY. Fax 813/388-4321. 140 rms. A/C TV TEL

$ Rates: May–Nov, $89–$123 single or double; Dec–Apr, $145–$180 single or double. AE, CB, DC, MC, V.

A stand-out along the beachfront, this modern seven-story hotel is directly across from Lido Beach and within walking distance of St. Armands Circle. Bedrooms, all of which have balconies and face the gulf or the bay, are furnished with light woods, pastel fabrics, and framed shell art.

Dining/Entertainment: For panoramic views of the Gulf of Mexico, try the rooftop Sand Dollar restaurant and lounge. Other outlets include the KoKoNuts Lobby Lounge and the casual Pool Bar.

Services: Room service, valet laundry.

Facilities: Outdoor swimming pool, sheltered crossover access to the beach.

HOLIDAY INN, 4949 Gulf of Mexico Dr., Longboat Key, FL 34228. Tel. 813/383-3771, or toll free 800/HOLIDAY. Fax 813/383-7871. 146 rms. A/C TV TEL

$ Rates: $106–$176 single; $116–$186 double. AE, CB, DC, DISC, MC, V.

This three-story hotel, sitting on a stretch of private beach, has a tropical ambience. Most of the guest rooms surround a central "Holidome" courtyard with a pool and recreation facilities. Many rooms also have views of the gulf. The decor emphasizes floral fabrics of raspberry, peach, and teal tones and light woods.

Dining/Entertainment: Choices include the Crest Dining Room, specializing in buffets; the Crest Café, for light fare overlooking the central Holidome; and the Beach Bar, Stormy's Lounge, and Crow's Nest Lounge for libations.

Services: Room service, valet laundry.

Facilities: Outdoor and indoor heated swimming pools, private beach, whirlpool, sauna, massage/tanning salon, games room, four lighted tennis courts, pro shop, water-sports equipment rentals.

LONGBOAT KEY HILTON, 4711 Gulf of Mexico Dr., Longboat Key, FL 34228. Tel. 813/383-2451, or toll free 800/282-3046. Fax 813/383-7979. 102 rms. A/C MINIBAR TV TEL

$ **Rates:** May–Nov, $85–$210 single or double; Dec–Apr, $130–$210 single or double. AE, DC, MC, V.

Surrounded by lush foliage and gardens, this five-story property, which sits directly on the gulf, is the poshest of the chain hotels on Longboat Key. The bedrooms, accessible by computer-card keys, are furnished in a Florida-style decor, with light woods, pastel fabrics, and rattan touches. Most units have a balcony or patio.

Dining/Entertainment: The main restaurant is the Sunset Bay and Grill, offering great views of the gulf and seafood.

Services: Room service, valet laundry.

Facilities: Heated outdoor swimming pool, private beach, water-sports equipment rentals, tennis courts.

Inexpensive

BEST WESTERN SIESTA BEACH RESORT, 5311 Ocean Blvd., Siesta Key, Sarasota, FL 34242. Tel. 813/349-3211, or toll free 800/223-5786. Fax 813/349-7915. 59 rms. A/C TV TEL

$ **Rates:** $55–$99 single or double. AE, CB, DC, DISC, MC, V.

Newly renovated in late 1992, this modern two-story motel is the only major chain affiliate on this island. Situated across the road from Siesta Beach, it is laid out in a two-building configuration, with 44 rooms in one and 15 in the other; each unit is decorated in pastel tones with light woods, and a few have kitchenettes. Facilities include a heated swimming pool, Jacuzzi, guest laundry, and shuffleboard court.

GULF SUN MOTEL, 6722 Midnight Pass Rd., Siesta Key, Sarasota, FL 34242. Tel. 813/349-2442. 2 rms, 15 efficiencies. A/C TV TEL

$ **Rates:** $60–$95 single or double; $63–$125 efficiency. MC, V.

Nestled in a palm-tree-shaded garden setting, this well-kept motel is not on the gulf front, but within walking distance of Crescent Beach. Bedrooms have standard furnishings with queen-size beds and refrigerators; some units are efficiencies with kitchens. Facilities include a private swimming pool and barbecue equipment.

WHERE TO DINE

DOWNTOWN/MAINLAND

Expensive

BIJOUX CAFE, 1287 1st St. Tel. 366-8111.

Cuisine: INTERNATIONAL. **Reservations:** Recommended.

$ **Prices:** Main courses $12.95–$21.95. CB, DC, MC, V.

Open: Lunch Mon–Fri 11:30am–2pm; dinner Mon–Sat 5:30–11pm.

Situated in the heart of the theater district at the corner of Pineapple Avenue, this bistro-style restaurant is bright and airy, with crisp linens, brass fixtures, floral paintings, and leafy plants. The innovative menu includes prime veal chop stuffed with Boursin cheese and sun-dried tomatoes, blackened scallops, New Orleans crab cakes, charcoal-grilled tuna, roast duckling with ruby port-orange sauce, and Black Angus peppered steak.

CHEZ SYLVIE, 1526 Main St. Tel. 953-3232.

Cuisine: FRENCH. **Reservations:** Recommended.

$ **Prices:** Main courses $12.50–$23. CB, DC, MC, V.

Open: Lunch Wed–Sat 11:30am–3pm; dinner Tues–Sat 5:30–10pm.

Under the careful supervision of Sylvie Routier, this shopfront bistro adds a touch of France to the downtown area. With classical music playing in the background and a French provincial decor, this restaurant offers an ever-changing menu ranging from rack of lamb, filet mignon, and free-range baby veal to jumbo sea scallops.

RISTORANTE BELLINI, 1551 Main St. Tel. 365-7380.

Cuisine: NORTHERN ITALIAN. **Reservations:** Recommended.

$ Prices: Main courses $12.95–$21.95. DISC, MC, V.

Open: Lunch Mon–Fri 11:30am–2pm; dinner Mon–Sat 6–10pm.

With a decor reminiscent of Venice, this midtown shopfront restaurant produces top-class cooked-to-order pastas and entrees. In addition to universal favorites such as chicken cacciatore and saltimbocca, the menu includes such creative choices as scalloppine Bellini (veal topped with asparagus and mozzarella), roasted quail wrapped in bacon, breast of chicken topped with smoked salmon and mozzarella, and snapper sautéed with fresh tomato-basil olive oil.

Moderate

CAFE ST. LOUIE, 1258 N. Palm Ave. Tel. 955-8550.

Cuisine: AMERICAN. **Reservations:** Recommended.

$ Prices: Main courses $9.95–$21.95. AE, DC, MC, V.

Open: Dinner only, Tues–Sat 5–10pm.

A theatrical atmosphere prevails at this chic downtown restaurant overlooking Cocoanut Avenue. The menu features prime rib, rack of lamb, veal sautéed with peppers and mushrooms, roast Long Island duckling, shrimp Ponchatrain (stuffed with Roquefort and cream cheese), pastas, and vegetable plates. After dinner, relax with a drink at the piano bar.

COASTERS SEAFOOD BISTRO, 1500 Stickney Point Rd. Tel. 923-4848.

Cuisine: SEAFOOD. **Reservations:** Recommended.

$ Prices: Main courses $8.50–$13.50. AE, MC, V.

Open: Daily 11:30am–1:30pm.

In the Sarasota Boatyard Shopping Village on the east side of the bay, this informal restaurant offers great water views and a variety of settings from an indoor brasserie-style dining room to an outdoor sun deck and waterfront patio. The menu includes such choices as mustard grouper, blackened tuna, broiled amberjack, baked scallops au gratin, and shrimp on a skewer, plus beef and ribs, chicken, and pastas. The raw bar is particularly noteworthy.

MARINA JACK, 2 Marina Plaza, Island Park. Tel. 365-4232.

Cuisine: SEAFOOD. **Reservations:** Recommended.

$ Prices: Main courses $10.95–$19.95. AE, MC, V.

Open: Lunch daily noon–3pm; dinner daily 5–10pm.

Overlooking the waterfront with a wraparound 270° view of Sarasota Bay and Siesta and Lido Keys, this restaurant is synonymous with seafood. The menu offers fresh native fish such as grouper, red snapper, swordfish, tuna, and dolphin, prepared charcoal-grilled, pan-seared, blackened, or sautéed. In addition, there are half a dozen shrimp selections, crab-stuffed roughy, and Caribbean lobster, as well as steaks, chicken, and pastas.

If you prefer to be on the water when you dine, this restaurant also operates the *Marina Jack II*, a paddlewheel sightseeing boat, offering lunch and dinner cruises. For information and reservations, call 366-9255 (October through August).

NICK'S ON THE WATER, 230 Sarasota Quay. Tel. 954-3839.

Cuisine: ITALIAN. **Reservations:** Recommended.

$ Prices: Main courses $5.95–$16.95. AE, DISC, MC, V.

Open: Lunch Mon–Sat 11:30am–4pm; dinner Mon–Thurs 4–10pm, Fri–Sat 4–11pm, Sun 11:30am–10pm.

One of the many fine-dining choices in the Sarasota Quay complex, this indoor-outdoor spot is really two restaurants in one—a terrace overlooking the marina, and a wine bar with a vineyard ambience. The menu offers pizzas and pastas as well as such entrees as rigatoni à la vodka, calamari or shrimp marinara, sweet or hot scungilli, steak pizzaiola, osso buco, and Nick's "chef's special" of veal medallions with melted cheese, mushrooms, and prosciutto.

CARAGIULOS, 69 S. Palm Ave. Tel. 951-0866.

Cuisine: ITALIAN. **Reservations:** Not accepted.

$ Prices: Main courses $5.95–$13.95. CB, DC, MC, V.

Open: Mon–Thurs 11am–10pm, Fri–Sat 11am–11pm, Sun 4–9pm.

Housed in the historic MiraMar Hotel in the downtown theater district, this informal street-level indoor-outdoor restaurant offers menu choices such as shrimp Fra Diavolo, chicken Florentine, veal piccata, and eggplant rollatini, plus gourmet pizzas, pastas, sandwiches, and salads.

PATRICK'S, 1442 Main St. Tel. 952-1170.

Cuisine: AMERICAN. **Reservations:** Accepted only for parties of six or more.

$ Prices: Main courses $5.95–$16.95. AE, MC, V.

Open: Daily 11:30am–midnight.

With a semicircular facade, this informal New York–style brasserie offers wide-windowed views of downtown at the corner of Main Street and Central Avenue. The decor blends brass fixtures and tiled floors with hanging plants and ceiling fans, plus a unique collection of sporting memorabilia, including sculptures of baseball players and referees. The menu offers steaks and chops, burgers, seafood, pastas, salads, sandwiches, and omelets, as well as such specialties as veal piccata, francese, or marsala; broiled salmon with dill-hollandaise sauce; shrimp de Jonghe; and sesame chicken.

OLD HICKORY, 5100 N. Tamiami Trail. Tel. 355-8757.

Cuisine: AMERICAN. **Reservations:** Accepted only for parties of 10 or more.

$ Prices: Main courses $5.95–$12.95. No credit cards.

Open: Mon–Sat 11:30am–10:30pm.

Reputed to be Sarasota's oldest restaurant (established in 1949), this casual place is situated on the main thoroughfare, north of downtown. The menu focuses on barbecued meats, cooked on hickory wood producing a genuine smoked flavor, with choices such as steaks, ribs, and chicken, as well as broiled fish, butterfly shrimp, and cornbreaded catfish.

Budget

MRS. APPLETON'S FAMILY BUFFET, 4458 Bee Ridge Rd. Tel. 378-1177.

Cuisine: AMERICAN. **Reservations:** Not accepted.

$ Prices: Lunch buffet $4.95; dinner buffet $6.95. CB, DC, DISC, MC, V.

Open: Lunch Mon–Sat 11:30am–3:30pm; dinner Mon–Sat 4–8:30pm; Sun 11am–8:30pm.

A sumptuous rotating buffet is the big draw at this restaurant, particularly popular with seniors. The selection changes daily but usually includes carved roast beef, lamb, turkey, pork, corned beef, or ham; fried chicken; barbecued beef ribs; baked fish; and lots of vegetables and salads, as well as desserts and a sundae bar.

SHELLS, 7253 S. Tamiami Trail. Tel. 924-2568.

Cuisine: SEAFOOD. **Reservations:** Not accepted.

$ Prices: Main courses $4.95–$12.95. MC, V.

Open: Dinner only, Sun–Thurs 5–10pm, Fri–Sat 5–11pm.

Synonymous with fresh seafood at low prices, this restaurant is part of a Tampa-based chain. This branch is situated on the main thoroughfare two miles south of downtown. For a description of the menu, see "Where to Dine" in the Tampa section.

YODER'S, 3434 Bahia Vista St. Tel. 955-7771.

Cuisine: PENNSYLVANIA DUTCH. **Reservations:** Not accepted.

$ Prices: Main courses $4.95–$9.95. No credit cards.

Open: Mon–Thurs 6am–8pm, Fri–Sat 6am–9pm.

It's worth a slight detour about three miles east of downtown to sample this cozy eatery. The menu emphasizes made-from-scratch Amish cooking including home-style pot roast, meatloaf, baked and southern fried chicken, cabbage rolls, and country-smoked ham, as well as filet of flounder or prime rib. Burgers, salads, soups, and sandwiches are also available. Two dozen types of homemade pies are on the dessert list, including traditional shoo-fly, strawberry rhubarb, chocolate peanut butter, and key lime.

THE KEYS/ISLANDS

Expensive

CAFE L'EUROPE, 431 St. Armands Circle, St. Armands Key. Tel. 388-4415.

Cuisine: CONTINENTAL. **Reservations:** Recommended.

$ **Prices:** Main courses $13.95–$21.95. AE, CB, DC, MC, V.

Open: Lunch Mon–Sat 11am–3pm, dinner Mon–Sat 5:30–11pm, Sun 5:30–10pm.

As its name implies, a European atmosphere prevails at this popular restaurant, with a decor of brick walls and arches, dark woods, beamed ceilings, brass fixtures, pink linens, and hanging plants. The menu offers selections ranging from steak tartare, rack of lamb, crab Dijon, roast duckling with cherry-cognac sauce, and pork piccata to bouillabaisse marseillaise, sautéed sweetbreads with wild mushrooms, and sautéed Dover sole.

CHARLEY'S CRAB, 420 St. Armands Circle, St. Armands Key. Tel. 388-3964.

Cuisine: SEAFOOD. **Reservations:** Recommended.

$ **Prices:** Main courses $6.95–$21.95. AE, MC, V.

Open: Mon–Thurs 11:30am–10pm, Fri–Sat 5–10:30pm, Sun noon–10pm.

Live piano music adds to the lively atmosphere at this informal indoor-outdoor restaurant. As you might expect, the specialty of the house is crab—particularly lump crab cakes and crab claws. In addition, the menu includes lobster, yellowfin tuna, Lake Superior whitefish, Atlantic swordfish, sautéed walleye, and lake trout, as well as steaks, veal, pork, and chicken.

CHART HOUSE, 201 Gulf of Mexico Dr., Longboat Key. Tel. 383-5593.

Cuisine: AMERICAN. **Reservations:** Recommended.

$ **Prices:** Main courses $15.95–$22.95. MC, V.

Open: Dinner only, Sun–Thurs 5–10pm, Fri–Sat 5–11pm.

Situated overlooking the Gulf of Mexico on the southern tip of Longboat Key, this restaurant offers panoramic views and a menu concentrating on eight different cuts of steak and prime ribs. In addition, there's a wide selection of seafood, including Australian lobster, swordfish, mahimahi, shrimp, and scallops. All entrees include unlimited helpings from a sumptuous salad bar.

Moderate

THE COLUMBIA, St. Armands Circle, St. Armands Key. Tel. 388-3987.

Cuisine: SPANISH. **Reservations:** Recommended.

$ **Prices:** Main courses $10.95–$16.95. AE, CB, DC, MC, V.

Open: Mon–Sat 11am–11pm, Sun noon–10pm.

A branch of the highly successful restaurant of the same name that originated in Ybor City, this place has a distinctive Iberian ambience.

Try the red snapper Alicante, baked in a casserole along with onions and peppers and topped with almonds, or the filet mignon Columbia. All entrees include Cuban bread and rice or potato. For a complete description of the menu, see "Where to Dine" in the Tampa section.

HEMINGWAY'S, 325 John Ringling Blvd., St. Armands Circle, St. Armands Key. Tel. 388-3948.

Cuisine: REGIONAL. **Reservations:** Recommended.

$ **Prices:** Main courses $6.95–$17.95. AE, MC, V.

Open: Lunch daily 11:30am–4pm; dinner Sun–Thurs 4–10pm, Fri–Sat 4–11pm.

With an airy and plant-filled Key West atmosphere, this informal second-floor restaurant overlooks St. Armands Circle, with both indoor and outdoor seating. The menu offers choices such as Key West pepper steak, lobster, Key Largo chicken (with bacon, broccoli, and cheese on linguine), southern fried shrimp, grouper Oscar, and surf-and-turf.

MOORE'S STONE CRAB, 800 Broadway, Longboat Key. Tel. 383-1748.
Cuisine: SEAFOOD. **Reservations:** Not accepted.
$ **Prices:** Main courses $7.95–$17.95. MC, V.
Open: Sun–Thurs 11:30am–9pm, Fri–Sat 11:30am–9:30pm. **Closed:** May 16–Oct 14.

Overlooking Sarasota Bay on the north end of Longboat Key, this popular 25-year-old seafood house began as an offshoot of a family seafood business established in 1927. Consequently, you'll hardly get fresher crab, since the restaurant still has its own boats and crab traps; and serves about 50,000 pounds of stone crab a year. The menu also features crab cakes and soft-shell crab as well as shrimp, scallops, Florida lobster, and other local fish. A few chicken and beef dishes round out the menu.

Inexpensive

TURTLES, 8875 Midnight Pass Rd., Siesta Key. Tel. 346-2207.
Cuisine: AMERICAN. **Reservations:** Recommended.
$ **Prices:** Main courses $3.95–$12.95. AE, MC, V.
Open: Daily 11:30am–midnight.

Located across from Turtle Beach, this informal restaurant sits on Little Sarasota Bay, offering views of the water from tables both indoors and on an outside deck. The menu ranges from steaks, barbecued ribs, salads, sandwiches, pastas, pizzas, and burgers to a selection of fresh seafood such as crab cakes, lobster and crab en casserole, and baked scallops au gratin. Foods low in cholesterol, sodium, and fats are also featured, and there's live music each night.

Budget

THE BUTTERY, 470 John Ringling Circle, St. Armands Key. Tel. 388-1523.
Cuisine: AMERICAN. **Reservations:** Not required.
$ **Prices:** Main courses $7–$10. No credit cards.
Open: Daily 24 hours.

An ideal spot for breakfast, lunch, or a snack, this informal eatery also offers light dinner entrees such as petite sirloin, chicken stir-fry, lime grouper, or lemon pepper catfish. Other items, available all day and night, include fruit-filled pancakes and waffles, omelets, burgers, sandwiches, salads, and finger foods.

Other branches are located at 5133 Ocean Blvd., Siesta Key (tel. 346-1343), open daily from 6am to 10pm; and 2833 Bee Ridge Rd. (tel. 923-5153), open 24 hours daily.

SHOPPING

Shopping in Sarasota is synonymous with **St. Armands Circle** on St. Armands Key, the "Rodeo Drive" or "Fifth Avenue" of Florida's west coast. Developed by John Ringling, it's a circle of more than 150 international boutiques, gift shops, galleries, restaurants, and nightspots, all surrounded by lush landscaping, patios, and antique statuary.

Downtown's main shopping focus is on **Sarasota Quay,** a new peach-toned and multilevel mixed-use facility housing shops and galleries amid a bayfront layout of piazzas and fountains.

Favorite shopping streets include historic **Palm Avenue** downtown and **Avenue of the Flowers** off Gulf of Mexico Drive on Longboat Key. The area's largest enclosed mall is south of downtown at **Sarasota Square Mall,** 8201 S. Tamiami Trail at Beneva Road. The city's largest and most interesting bookstore for browsers and shoppers alike is the **Main Bookshop,** 1962 Main St. (tel. 366-7653), open daily from 10am to 10pm.

EVENING ENTERTAINMENT

To get the latest update on what's happening during your visit, call the city's 24-hour **Artsline** (tel. 359-ARTS).

THE PERFORMING ARTS

Major Concert/Performance Halls

ASOLO CENTER FOR THE PERFORMING ARTS, 5555 N. Tamiami Trail. Tel. 351-8000.

An attraction in itself, this 300-seat, rococo-style horseshoe-shaped theater and educational complex located adjacent to the Ringling Museum of Art was built from the original parts of an 18th-century Italian court theater and installed here piece by piece in 1957. It provides a year-round setting for a variety of plays, concerts, educational programs, lectures, meetings, symposia, and art films. The Asolo Theatre Company is the professional company in residence, presenting eight productions a year of contemporary and classic plays.

Tours: Free tours offered Mon–Sat 10am–11:30am except on matinee days.
Admission: Tickets, $5–$30, depending on the event and time.

VAN WEZEL PERFORMING ARTS HALL, 777 N. Tamiami Trail. Tel. 953-3366.

With a lavender seashell shape, this hall is visible for miles on the Sarasota skyline. It offers excellent visual and acoustic conditions, with year-round programs ranging from symphony and jazz concerts, opera, musical comedy, and choral productions to ballet, and international performers. It's the home of the Florida West Coast Symphony, the Jazz Club of Sarasota, the Sarasota Ballet of Florida, and the Sarasota Concert Band.

Admission: Tickets, $10–$40.

Theaters

FLORIDA STUDIO THEATRE, 1241 N. Palm Ave. Tel. 366-9796.

Located downtown on the corner of Palm and Cocoanut Avenues, the Florida Studio Theatre presents innovative and experimental drama, Tuesday through Sunday from December through April, and hosts a New Play Festival each May.

Admission: Tickets, $5–$18.

GOLDEN APPLE DINNER THEATRE, 25 N. Pineapple Ave. Tel. 366-5454.

This downtown theater presents cocktails, dinner, and a professional Broadway-style show, usually a musical, year-round daily except Monday.

Admission: Tickets, $25–$26 evening, $19 matinees.

THE OPERA HOUSE, 61 N. Pineapple Ave. Tel. 953-7030.

The Sarasota Opera Association performs here in February and March. Other companies including the Sarasota Ballet present their works during the rest of the year at this downtown venue.

Admission: Tickets, $14–$40.

THE PLAYERS OF SARASOTA, 838 N. Tamiami Trail. Tel. 365-2494.

Founded in 1930, this is Sarasota's longest-established theater, a community group presenting eight plays a year—a mix of comedies, musicals, and dramas. The season runs from September through June, with evening performances Tuesday through Saturday and matinees on Sunday.

Admission: Tickets, $10–$14.

THEATRE WORKS, 1247 1st St. Tel. 952-9170.

Located downtown at Cocoanut Avenue, this professional non-Equity company presents musical revues and other works, year-round Tuesday through Saturday in the evening and matinees on Sunday.

Admission: Tickets, $15.

THE CLUB & MUSIC SCENE

CLUB BANDSTAND, 300 Sarasota Quay. Tel. 954-7625.

Reputed to have Sarasota's largest dance floor, this spot offers progressive and Top-40 dance music each evening from 9pm until 2am.

Admission: $3.

DOWNUNDER JAZZ BAR, 214 Sarasota Quay. Tel. 951-2467.

Located at U.S. 41 and 3rd Street, this club is part of the innovative Sarasota Quay shopping and entertainment complex. It offers contemporary jazz, Sunday through Thursday from 9pm to 12:30am and Friday through Sunday from 9pm to 1:30am. Drinks run $2–$4.

Admission: Free.

LIMERICK JUNCTION, 1296 1st St. Tel. 366-6366.

Situated around the corner from the Sarasota Opera House, this Irish-themed indoor-outdoor pub has an "open mike" night on Tuesday and presents a variety of music (blues, rock, bluegrass, and more) on Wednesday and Thursday. On Friday and Saturday there's comedy and on Sunday it's Irish music. Times vary, but performances usually run from 9pm to midnight or later.

Admission: $2–$3 for most music; $6 for comedy, plus a $6 drink minimum.

PATIO LOUNGE, St. Armands Circle, St. Armands Key. Tel. 388-3987.

One of the liveliest spots along the beach strip, the Patio Lounge features the Omni dance band performing high-energy dance music, Tuesday through Saturday from 9:30pm to 2am.

Admission: $3.

PARADISE CAFE, 1311 1st St. Tel. 955-8500.

This popular downtown spot presents musical cabarets on Thursday and Friday at 9pm and on Saturday at 8pm, and live piano music Monday through Saturday from 6pm.

Admission: $8 for cabaret; free for piano music.

4. BRADENTON

26 miles S of St. Petersburg, 41 miles SW of Tampa,
15 miles N of Sarasota

GETTING THERE By Plane Bradenton shares an airport with Sarasota. For full details on the Sarasota-Bradenton Airport, see the Sarasota section.

By Train Amtrak trains arrive at Tampa Amtrak Station (see the Tampa section) and bus connections are provided to Bradenton.

By Bus Greyhound buses arrive at the carrier's depot at 501 17th Ave. W., Bradenton (tel. 747-2984).

By Car Bradenton is accessible from points north via the Sunshine Skyway Bridge (U.S. 19/I-275). Other north-south routes leading into Bradenton include I-75, U.S. 41, and U.S. 301. From the east, take Fla. 64 and Fla. 70.

Bradenton is a city edged by water—Tampa Bay, the Gulf of Mexico, and Intracoastal waters lie to the west, and the city is bordered on the north by the Manatee River, on the west by the Braden River, and on the south by Sarasota Bay. It's also a city of history, explored by the Spanish in the 16th century and eventually established over 100 years ago as the city of "Braidentown." It was named for the Braden brothers, Joseph and Hector, who settled the area in 1842. The superfluous "i" was added in error and remained in the name until 1903; 21 years later the "w" was dropped, giving the city its present name.

Although it has been touched by urban sprawl in recent years, this city still maintains some links with the past such as its historic "Old Main Street" (12th Street in today's city layout), and many Spanish-style buildings. Bradenton's star attraction, however, is Anna Maria Island, west of downtown. It's a 7½-mile stretch of sandy and tree-shaded beaches that rim the Gulf of Mexico. Legend has it that early Spanish settlers were so taken with the beauty of the island that they named it "Ana-Maria Cay," in honor of Mary, the mother of Christ, and her mother, Anne.

Today Bradenton is synonymous with the sweet aroma of fresh oranges in the air. As the home of Tropicana, this city of 40,000 people is a major producer of orange juice and citrus products, as well as other agricultural products such as tomatoes and ornamental plants.

ORIENTATION

ARRIVING

Van transport from the airport to hotels in Bradenton is provided by **West Coast Limousine** (tel. 813/355-9645). The price depends on the destination, but averages $10–$15. Taxi companies in Bradenton include **Bruce's Taxi** (tel. 813/755-6070) and **Yellow Cab** (tel. 813/748-4800).

INFORMATION

For travel information about Bradenton, Anna Maria Island, and the surrounding Manatee County area, contact the **Manatee County Convention & Visitors Bureau,** 1111 Third Ave. W. (P.O. Box 1000), Bradenton, FL 34206 (tel. 813/746-5989, or toll free 800/822-2017). The county also maintains a walk-in **visitor center,** at 5030 U.S. 301, Ellenton (tel. 813/729-7040).

CITY LAYOUT

Bradenton is laid out like a rectangle, with **U.S. 41** as a line of demarcation running through the center of the city in a north-south direction. All **"streets"** are numbered and run parallel to U.S. 41 in a north-south direction; and they are designated as east or west of that route.

"Avenues," which run east-west through U.S. 41, start at the Braden River and continue southward in ascending numerical order. Like the streets, avenues are also labeled as "east" or "west" of U.S. 41.

The basic core of downtown hugs the Manatee River near 12th Street. Originally known as Main Street, 12th Street (or "Old Main Street") today contains a row of historic old buildings leading to the Manatee River and a waterfront pier.

West of downtown is the **Intracoastal Waterway** and **Anna Maria Island.** The city is traversed in an east-west direction by two state roads—**Fla. 64** (also known as Manatee Avenue), crossing the north side of the city and **Fla. 684** (Cortez Road), crossing the southern sector. Two bridges, **Anna Maria Island Bridge** (on Fla. 64) and Cortez Bridge (on Fla. 684) connect Anna Maria Island to the mainland. Situated seven miles west of downtown between the Intracoastal Waterway and the Gulf of Mexico, this subtropical barrier island is 7½ miles long and a quarter of a mile to nearly 2 miles wide. It is composed of three island cities, Anna Maria to the north, Holmes Beach in the center, and Bradenton Beach to the south, and is accessible from the mainland via Fla. 64 and Fla. 684.

Cortez Island is on the east side of the **Cortez Bridge,** on the approach from the mainland to Bradenton Beach on Anna Maria Island.

GETTING AROUND

BY PUBLIC TRANSPORTATION (BUS) Manatee County Area Transit, known locally as **Manatee CAT** (tel. 749-7116), operates scheduled bus service throughout the area. The basic fare is $1 on weekdays and 50¢ on weekends.

BY TAXI Taxi companies serving the Bradenton area include **Bruce's Taxi** (tel. 813/755-6070), **Dependable Cab** (tel. 813/749-0993), and **Yellow Cab** (tel. 813/748-4800).

BY CAR Major rental-car companies maintain desks at the Sarasota-Bradenton Airport (see the Sarasota section).

FAST FACTS

Area Code Bradenton's area code is 813.

Dentist For emergency dental repairs, contact the Dental Centre, 4630 5th St. W. (tel. 751-9020).

Doctors Most hotels have a doctor on call; if not, contact Physician Referral Services at L. W. Blake Hospital (tel. 954-7445) or Manatee Memorial Hospital (tel. 745-7575).

Drugstores There are at least half a dozen Walgreens Drug Stores in the Bradenton area, including one branch that operates a 24-hour prescription service at Cortez Commons, 5574 Cortez Rd. W. (tel. 792-3817).

Emergencies Dial 911.

Hospitals Try the Manatee Memorial Hospital, 206 2nd St. E. (tel. 746-5111), or L. W. Blake Hospital, 2020 59th St. W. (tel. 792-6611).

Library The Central Library is located at 1301 Barcarrota Blvd. (tel. 748-5555).

Newspapers The *Bradenton Herald* is published daily.

Post Office The main post office is at 824 Manatee Ave. W. (tel. 746-4195).

Taxes There's a 10% hotel tax, a 6% restaurant tax, and a local sales tax of 6%.

Transit Information Call 749-7116.

WHAT TO SEE & DO

THE TOP ATTRACTIONS

DESOTO NATIONAL MEMORIAL PARK, DeSoto Memorial Hwy., 75th Street W. Tel. 972-0458.

Nestled on the Manatee River northwest of downtown, this park commemorates the Spanish explorer Hernándo de Soto's 1539 landing in Florida. Aiming to reflect the look and atmosphere you might have found here 400 years ago, it includes a restoration of de Soto's original camp site, and a scenic half-mile nature trail that circles a mangrove jungle and leads to the ruins of one of the first settlements of the area. From December through March, park employees dress in 16th-century costumes and portray the way the early settlers lived, including demonstrations of cooking and musket-firing.

Admission: Free.

Open: Daily 8am–5:30pm. **Directions:** Take Manatee Avenue (Fla. 64) west to 75th Street West and turn right; follow the road to its end and the entrance to the park.

GAMBLE PLANTATION, 3708 Patten Ave., Ellenton. Tel. 723-4536.

Situated northeast of downtown Bradenton, this is the oldest structure on the southwestern coast of Florida, and a fine example of an antebellum plantation home. Built over a six-year period in the late 1840s by Maj. Robert Gamble, it is constructed primarily of a primitive material known as "tabby" (a mixture of oyster shells, sand, molasses, and water), with 10 rooms, verandas on three sides, 18 exterior columns, and eight fireplaces. It is maintained as a state historic site, and includes a fine collection of 19th-century furnishings. Entrance into the house is by tour only, although the grounds may be explored independently.

Admission (including the tour): $2 adults, $1 children 6–12, free for children under 6.

Open: Thurs–Mon 9am–5pm; guided tours given at 9:30 and 10:30am, and 1, 2, 3, and 4pm. **Directions:** Take U.S. 301 north of downtown to Ellenton; the site is on the left at the juncture of U.S. 301 and Fla. 683 (Ellenton-Gillette Road).

MANATEE VILLAGE HISTORICAL PARK, Sixth Ave. E. and 15th St. E. Tel. 749-7165.

A tree-shaded park with a courtyard of hand-laid bricks, this national historic site features restored buildings from the city of Bradenton and the surrounding county. It contains the Manatee County Court House, dating back to 1860 and the oldest structure of its kind still standing on the south Florida mainland; a Methodist church built in 1887; a typical "Cracker Gothic" house built in 1912; and the Wiggins General Store, dating to 1903 and full of local memorabilia from swamp root and grub dust to louse powder, as well as antique furnishings and an art gallery.

Admission: Free; donations welcome.

Open: Mon–Fri 9am–4:30pm, Sun 2–5pm. **Closed:** Sun July–Aug. **Directions:** From U.S. 41, take Sixth Avenue East east to 15th Street East at the juncture of Manatee Avenue East.

SOUTH FLORIDA MUSEUM AND BISHOP PLANETARIUM, 201 10th St. W. Tel. 746-4131.

The story of Florida's history, from prehistoric times to the present, is told in exhibits including a Native American collection with life-size dioramas; a Spanish courtyard containing replicas of 16th-century buildings; and an indoor aquarium, the home of "Snooty," the oldest manatee (or sea cow) born in captivity (1948). The adjacent Bishop Planetarium features a 50-foot hemispherical dome with arcs above a seating area, for laser light shows and star-gazing activities.

Admission: $5 adults, $2.50 children 5–12, free for children under 5.

Open: Tues–Sat 10am–5pm, Sun 1–5pm. **Directions:** From U.S. 41, take Manatee Avenue west to 9th Street West and turn right.

ANNA MARIA ISLAND MUSEUM, 402 Pine Ave., Anna Maria, Anna Maria Island. Tel. 778-0492.

Housed in a former 1920s ice house, this museum aims to present the history of Anna Maria Island. It contains memorabilia, maps, records, books, and photographs, plus collections indigenous to the island, such as shells, sand dollars, and a turtle display. It's situated adjacent to a historical landmark, the Old Anna Maria Jail.

Admission: Free.

Open: Tues–Thurs and Sat 10am–noon. **Closed:** June–Aug. **Directions:** Take Fla. 64 west to Fla. 789 (Gulf Drive) and turn right; continue north on Gulf Drive via Holmes Beach to Anna Maria, and turn right at Pine Avenue.

ORGANIZED TOURS

***CORTEZ XI*, 12507 Cortez Rd., Cortez. Tel. 794-1223.**

This two-deck boat, part of the Cortez Fleet, offers a 2½-hour narrated sightseeing cruise around Anna Maria Island, as well as a 4-hour cruise along the Intracoastal Waterway to Egmont Key, a nearby tropical island where there's an opportunity to disembark for snorkeling and shelling. In addition, there are shorter 1½-hour cruises in Tampa Bay for bird-feeding and dolphin-watching.

Price: Anna Maria Island cruise, $8 adults, $4 children under 15; Egmont Key cruise, $12 adults, $6 children under 15; bird-feeding and dolphin-watching cruise, $6 adults, $3 children under 15.

Schedule: Anna Maria Island cruise, Mon at 1:30pm; Egmont Key cruise, Tues, Thurs, and Sun at 1pm and Wed at 9am; bird-feeding and dolphin-watching cruise, Mon and Fri at 10am, and Wed at 2pm.

FLORIDA GULF COAST RAILROAD, 83rd St. E., off U.S. 301, Parrish. Tel. 776-3266.

See the sights of rural Manatee County northwest of Bradenton on a 1¼-hour narrated sightseeing tour via a 1950s steam-engine train. There is a choice of seating—in open-window coaches, air-conditioned lounge cars, or caboose. Tickets are sold on a first-come, first-served basis.

Price: $6–$9 adults, $4–$5 children 2–11.

Schedule: Departures Sat at 11am, 1pm, and 3pm; Sun at 2pm and 3pm.

SPORTS & RECREATION

SPECTATOR SPORTS

MCKECHNIE FIELD, 9th St. and 17th Ave. W. Tel. 747-3031.

Located east of downtown, this 6,562-seat field is the winter home of the Pittsburgh Pirates, for the March-April spring training season.

Admission: $8–$8.50.

RECREATION

BOAT RENTALS Situated on the east side of the Cortez Bridge, **Cortez Watercraft Rentals,** 4328 127th St. W., (tel. 792-5263), rents fishing, ski and pontoon boats, waverunners, and other equipment. Prices are $55 to $125 for fishing boats; $65 to $135 for ski boats; $85 to $155 for pontoon boats; $25 per half hour for waverunners. It's open daily from 8am to 6pm.

Perico Harbor Marina Boat Rentals, 12310 Manatee Ave. W. (tel. 795-2628), is on Perico Island between the mainland and Anna Maria Island. This facility rents 17-foot four-passenger powerboats and 20-foot eight-passenger pontoon boats.

Powerboats cost $95 for a half day, $125 for a full day; pontoon boats cost $100 for a half day, $145 for a full day. It's open daily from 7am to 6pm.

FISHING Whether you prefer to fish from a pier or a boat, Bradenton offers many opportunities. There is pier fishing at **Anna Maria City Pier** on the north end of Anna Maria Island, and at the **Bradenton Beach City Pier** at Cortez Road. Both are free of charge.

For fishing in deep-sea waters, the **Cortez Fleet,** 12507 Cortez Rd., Cortez (tel. 794-1223), offers four-, six-, and nine-hour trips, departing from the east side of the Cortez Bridge. The boats are equipped with the latest in electronic fish finders, and rod, bait, and tackle are provided. Prices for a four-hour trip are $21 for adults, $19 for seniors, and $5.25 for children under 15; a six-hour trip costs $30 for adults, $27 for seniors, and $7.50 for children under 15; and a nine-hour trip is $37 for adults, $33 for seniors, and $9.25 for children under 15.

Four-hour trips depart on Monday and Friday at 8am and 1pm; for six-hour trips, on Sunday, Tuesday, and Thursday at 9am; and for the nine-hour trips, on Wednesday and Saturday at 8am.

GOLF Situated just off U.S. 41, **Heather Hills Golf Club,** 101 Cortez Rd. W. (tel. 755-8888), operates an 18-hole, par-61 golf course on a first-come first-served basis. There's a driving range and clubs can be rented. The price, including a cart, is $16.95 per person until 3pm and $11.65 after 3pm. It's open daily from 6:30am until dark. **Manatee County Golf Course,** 5290 66th St. W. (tel. 792-6773), sports an 18-hole, par-72 course on the southern rim of the city and requires that tee times be set up at least two days in advance. They also have a driving range and golf clubs for rent. The price, including a cart, is $29 per person. It's open 7am to dusk.

Located just north of Fla. 684 and east of Palma Sola Bay, **Palma Sola Golf Club** has an 18-hole, par-72 course which requires two-day advance booking for tee times. The charge is $30 per person, including a cart. It's open daily, 7am to dusk. **River Run Golf Links,** 1801 27th St. E. (tel. 747-6331) is another possibility, set beside the Braden River. This 18-hole, par-70 course has lots of water in its layout. Two-day advance notice is required for tee times. Golf clubs can be rented. The price, including a cart, is $23 per person and it's open daily, 7am to dusk.

SWIMMING Swimming along safe and sandy beaches is a prime reason to visit the Bradenton area. There are four public beaches on Anna Maria Island—**Anna Maria Bayfront Park,** on Bay Boulevard at the northwest end of the island, fronting both the Intracoastal Waterway and the Gulf of Mexico; **Coquina Beach,** at the southwest end of Gulf Drive on Anna Maria Island, with a gulf and a bay side, sheltered by towering pines and palm trees; **Cortez Beach,** on Gulf Drive in Bradenton Beach, just north of Coquina Beach; and **Manatee County Public Beach,** at Gulf Drive, Holmes Beach, at the west end of Fla. 64.

TENNIS **Nick Bollettieri Tennis Academy,** 5500 34th St. W. (tel. 813/755-1000 or toll free 800/USA-NICK), is one of the world's largest tennis-training facilities, with over 75 championship courts, aerobic and sports training centers, video analysis, and a pro shop. Visitors can tune up on their tennis skills by enrolling in a one-day instructional program; three-day and one-week programs are also available for all age groups. The academy is open year-round and reservations are required for all activities. One-day instructional programs are $220, with overnight accommodations, $150 without boarding; full day of play alone on courts is $75.

Walton Racquet Center, 3600 59th St. W. (tel. 749-7173), is a part of the county park system. The center has eight clay and eight hard courts. It's open Monday through Thursday from 7:30am to 9:45pm, Friday from 7:30am till 7pm, and Saturday and Sunday from 7:30am to 5:30pm. Prices are $2.40 per person for 1½ hours on hard courts, $4.40 on clay courts.

WHERE TO STAY

DOWNTOWN/MAINLAND

Moderate

HOLIDAY INN RIVERFRONT, 100 Riverfront Dr. W., Bradenton, FL 34205. Tel. 813/747-3727, or toll free 800/HOLIDAY. Fax 813/7464289. 153 rms. A/C TV TEL

$ Rates: May–Nov, $74–$135 single or double; Dec–Apr, $110–$190 single or double. AE, CB, DC, DISC, MC, V.

Sporting a Spanish hacienda-style motif and overlooking the Manatee River, this five-story hotel stands out on the downtown skyline. The public areas also reflect an Iberian ambience, with dark woods, tile floors, and high beamed ceilings; an outdoor courtyard is full of palm trees, tropical flowers, lush foliage, and cascading fountains. Bedrooms are contemporary, with light woods and soft floral tones; all have balconies, with views of the river or the courtyard. Facilities include a Spanish-themed restaurant, a nautical-style lounge, a heated outdoor swimming pool, and room service.

Inexpensive

FIVE OAKS INN, 1102 Riverside Dr., Palmetto, FL 34221. Tel. 813/723-1236. 4 rms. A/C TEL

$ Rates (including breakfast): $55–$100 single or double. MC, V.

Across the Manatee River directly north of downtown, this stately Spanish-style bed-and-breakfast is surrounded by palm trees, oaks, and gardens overlooking the water. The bedrooms are individually decorated and named, offering a choice of king-size, queen-size, or twin-bed configurations. Guests enjoy use of a parlor with fireplace, and an enclosed wraparound solarium/sunporch filled with wicker and rattan furnishings.

PARK INN CLUB, 4450 47th St. W., Bradenton, FL 34210. Tel. 813/795-4633, or toll free 800/437-PARK. Fax 813/795-0808. 129 rms. A/C TV TEL

$ Rates (including continental breakfast): $50–$110 single or double. AE, DC, DISC, MC, V.

Nestled on its own well-landscaped grounds and set back from the main road along the busy Fla. 684 (Cortez Road) corridor, this three-story contemporary hotel is wrapped around a central courtyard with a patio and swimming pool. The spacious guest rooms are furnished in pastel tones with light woods. In addition to the pool, facilities include a lounge where guests are served breakfast and complimentary cocktails each evening.

ANNA MARIA ISLAND/BEACHES

Moderate

HARRINGTON HOUSE, 5626 Gulf Dr., Holmes Beach, FL 34217. Tel. 813/778-5444. 10 rms. A/C TV

$ Rates: $79–$149 single or double in main house, $59–$139 single or double in Beach House. MC, V.

In a tree-shaded setting on the beach overlooking the Gulf of Mexico, this three-story bed-and-breakfast exudes an Old Florida ambience. Built in 1925, it has been renovated and refurbished to the highest standard. The seven bedrooms are individually decorated with antiques, wicker, or rattan furnishings. Some units have four-poster or brass beds, and the higher-priced rooms have French doors leading to balconies overlooking the gulf. In addition to the bedrooms in the main house, three rooms are available in the adjacent Beach House, a 1920s captain's home recently remodeled and updated.

All guests enjoy use of the high-ceilinged living room with fireplace, an outdoor pool, patio, and complimentary use of bicycles, kayaks, and other sports equipment.

Inexpensive

CATALINA BEACH RESORT, 1325 Gulf Dr. N., Bradenton Beach, FL 33510. Tel. 813/778-6611. 31 rms. A/C TV TEL
$ Rates: $45–$90 single or double. AE, DC, MC, V.

Nestled in a shady spot across the street from the beach, this two-story Spanish-style motel offers well-kept rooms with modern furnishings and bright Florida colors, some with kitchenettes. Facilities include a restaurant, outdoor solar-heated swimming pool, barbecue grills, shuffleboard courts, guest laundry, fishing and boating dock, and water-sport rentals.

SAND & SEA MOTEL, 2412 Gulf Dr., Bradenton Beach, FL 34217. Tel. 813/778-2231. 30 rms. A/C TV TEL
$ Rates: $42–$90 single or double. MC, V.

Situated directly on the beach overlooking the Gulf of Mexico, this modern two-story motel is surrounded by shady palm trees, with under-building parking. Bedrooms, which overlook the beach or the garden, are spacious with standard furnishings and tiled bathrooms. Gulf-front rooms have balconies. Facilities include an outdoor heated swimming pool, Tiki-style beach umbrellas, lounge chairs, shuffleboard courts, and a guest laundry. Efficiency apartments are also available at higher rates.

WHERE TO DINE

DOWNTOWN/MAINLAND

Moderate

LEVEROCK'S, 12320 Manatee Ave. W. Tel. 794-8900.
Cuisine: SEAFOOD. **Reservations:** Not accepted.
$ Prices: Main courses $5.95–$17.95. AE, CB, DC, DISC, MC, V.
Open: Daily 11:30am–10pm.

Overlooking Perico Harbor at the west end of the mainland, this trilevel restaurant is known for its great views as well as the freshest of seafood at affordable prices.

Menu selections range from a variety of shrimp dishes to snapper, grouper, and crab to steaks, chicken, and ribs. For a full description of the menu, see the listing for Leverock's in the "Where to Dine" section in St. Petersburg.

THE PIER, 1200 First Ave. W. Tel. 748-8087.
Cuisine: AMERICAN. **Reservations:** Recommended.
$ Prices: Main courses $10.95–$16.95. AE, DC, DISC, MC, V.
Open: Mon–Fri 11:30am–9pm, Sat–Sun 11:30am–10pm.

With commanding views of the Manatee River, this restaurant is *the* place to dine downtown. It sits at the foot of 12th Street on Memorial Pier, housed in a stately Spanish-style landmark building. The menu offers imaginative choices such as snapper hollandaise, shrimp tempura, crabmeat-stuffed flounder, and chicken Cordon Bleu or Oscar, as well as steaks and prime rib.

SEAFOOD SHACK, 4110 127th St. W., Cortez. Tel. 794-1235.
Cuisine: SEAFOOD. **Reservations:** Not accepted.
$ **Prices:** Main courses $5.95–$19.95. AE, MC, V.
Open: Sun–Thurs 11:30am–9pm, Fri–Sat 11:30am–10pm.

A tradition in the area for over 20 years, this informal spot sits on the marina, along the edge of the mainland beside the Fla. 684 bridge (Cortez Bridge) leading to Bradenton Beach. The menu offers many different seafood combinations and at least six different shrimp dishes (from scampi to stuffed), as well as freshly caught Florida lobster, stone crabs, grouper, and snapper. The "Shack specialty" is sautéed frogs' legs, and beef and chicken are also available.

The Seafood Shack Showboat, docked beside the restaurant, offers sightseeing cruises, priced at $7–$10, which entitle participants to discounts off dinner entrees in the restaurant.

Inexpensive

MILLER'S DUTCH KITCHEN, 3401 14th St. W. Tel. 746-8253.
Cuisine: AMERICAN. **Reservations:** Not accepted.
$ **Prices:** Main courses $4.95–$8.95. No credit cards.
Open: Mon–Sat 11am–8pm.

With a sprinkling of Pennsylvania Dutch recipes, this restaurant is an oasis of home-style cooking, nestled along a busy road known more for fast food. The menu includes Dutch casserole (noodles, peas, cheese, potatoes, beef, mushrooms, and chicken soup with croutons), pan-fried chicken, and cabbage rolls, as well as prime rib, stuffed flounder, veal parmesan, meatloaf, fried shrimp, barbecued pork ribs, lasagne, and spaghetti. To top it off, there are 17 varieties of freshly baked pies.

MRS. APPLETON'S FAMILY BUFFET, 4848 14th St. W. Tel. 758-9990.
Cuisine: AMERICAN. **Reservations:** Not accepted.
$ **Prices:** Lunch buffet $4.95; dinner buffet $6.95. CB, DC, DISC, MC, V.
Open: Lunch Mon–Sat 11:30am–3:30pm; dinner Mon–Sat 4–8:30pm, Sun 11am–8:30pm.

Situated in a shopping center half a mile south of Cortez Road (Fla. 684), this restaurant is short on views or setting, but offers an unbeatable value at its rotating buffet table. For a description of the food, see the listing in the "Where to Dine" section in Sarasota.

ANNA MARIA ISLAND/BEACHES

Moderate

SANDBAR, 100 Spring Ave., Anna Maria, Anna Maria Island. Tel. 778-0444.
Cuisine: SEAFOOD. **Reservations:** Not accepted on deck; "preferred seating" policy in main restaurant.
$ **Prices:** Main courses $8.95–$19.95. MC, V.
Open: Lunch daily 11:30am–3pm; dinner daily 4–10pm.

"We are seafood" is the motto of this popular restaurant, perched on the beach overlooking the Gulf of Mexico, just off Gulf Drive. Established in 1979, it offers air-conditioned seating indoors and deck-style seating outside. The seafood choices change daily, depending on the local catch, but often include soft-shell crab and crab cakes, sautéed scallops, shrimp scampi, and stuffed grouper or flounder. Steaks and surf-and-turf, pastas, and chicken round out the menu.

Inexpensive

PETE REYNARD'S, 5325 Marine Dr., Holmes Beach, Anna Maria Island. Tel. 778-2233.

Cuisine: INTERNATIONAL. **Reservations:** Not accepted.
$ Prices: Main courses $6.95–$14.95. MC, V.
Open: Daily 11:30am–10pm or later.

Established in 1954, this dockside restaurant offers three dining rooms but is best known for its revolving 40-item salad bar. The menu includes local seafood and shellfish, as well as crab-stuffed chicken breast, pork ribs, liver and onions, roast pork loin, vegetable plate, pastas, and a "house specialty" of prime rib.

ROTTEN RALPH'S, 902 S. Bay Blvd., Anna Maria, Anna Maria Island. Tel. 778-3953.
Cuisine: INTERNATIONAL. **Reservations:** Not accepted.
$ Prices: Main courses $5.95–$15.95. MC, V.
Open: Daily 11am–10pm.

On the north end of the island overlooking the Anna Maria Yacht Basin, this casual Old Florida–style restaurant offers indoor and outdoor seating. The menu offers many seafood choices (from scallops and shrimp to crab cakes, snow crab, oysters, and grouper), as well as British-style favorites such as fish and chips and steak-and-kidney pie. Other choices include Danish baby back ribs, chicken pot pie, and Anna Maria chicken (marinated and grilled with a honey-mustard sauce).

Budget

HARBOR HOUSE, 200 N. Gulf Dr., Bradenton Beach, Anna Maria Island. Tel. 778-5608.
Cuisine: AMERICAN. **Reservations:** Not accepted.
$ Prices: Main courses $5.95–$9.95. AE, DISC, MC, V.
Open: Dinner only, Mon–Sat 4–9pm, Sun noon–9pm.

Located on the beach just south of the Fla. 684 (Cortez Road) bridge, this casual restaurant offers great water views and a choice of settings—a full-service restaurant and a patio-style oyster bar. The menu focuses on seafood platters, steaks, barbecued ribs, pastas, and southern fried chicken. In addition, all-you-can-eat buffets are available on many nights.

SHELLS, Island Centre, 3200 E. Bay Blvd., Holmes Beach, Anna Maria Island. Tel. 778-5997.
Cuisine: SEAFOOD. **Reservations:** Not accepted.
$ Prices: Main courses $4.95–$12.95. MC, V.
Open: Dinner only Sun–Thurs 5–10pm, Fri–Sat 5–11pm.

Situated in a shopping center just south of the Fla. 64 bridge, this is a fairly new branch of the Shells chain, known for fresh seafood at low prices. For a description of the menu, see "Where to Dine" in the Tampa section.

EVENING ENTERTAINMENT

THE PERFORMING ARTS

ISLAND PLAYHOUSE, 10009 Gulf Dr. N., Anna Maria, Anna Maria Island. Tel. 778-5755.

For over 45 years, the Island Players, a community theater group, have performed from October through May.

Admission: Tickets, $8–$10.

RIVERFRONT THEATRE, 102 Old Main St. (12th St. W.). Tel. 748-5875.

Situated across from the Pier on the Manatee River, this community theater features the Manatee Players, a group established in 1948. They present musicals and dramas throughout the year, as well as a summer musical revue, band concerts, and a series of nontraditional works.

Admission: Tickets, $13–$15.

THE CLUB & BAR SCENE

ACES LOUNGE, 4343 Palma Sola Blvd. Tel. 795-3886.

Situated west of downtown on Palms Sola Bay, this lounge features a variety of live music, including karaoke on Saturday and Sunday, from 9pm to 1am. Drinks run $2–$4.

Admission: Free.

CAFE ROBAR, 204 Pine Ave., Anna Maria, Anna Maria Island. Tel. 778-6969.

Located at the corner of Gulf Drive, this elegant place offers piano music and a sing-along bar each evening from 8pm until midnight. Drinks cost $2.50 and up.

Admission: Free.

D. COY DUCKS, 5410 Marina Dr., Holmes Beach, Anna Maria Island. Tel. 778-5888.

Wedged in the Island Shopping Center, this bar is known for its varied program of live Dixieland bands, jazz pianists, and guitar/vocalists. Music starts at various times (from 5 to 8pm) and usually continues until midnight or 1am nightly. Drinks go for $2 and up.

Admission: Free.

PEWTER MUG, 108 44th Ave. E. Tel. 756-7577.

Situated downtown one block east of U.S. 41, this lively lounge offers a blend of jazz bands or contemporary tunes, from 9pm until midnight Thursday through Sunday. Drinks cost $2 and up.

Admission: Free.

SCOREBOARD SPORTS PUB, 7004 Cortez Rd. W. Tel. 792-6768.

Bradenton's "only original sports pub" is an ideal place to watch football and other sports, from 8pm until midnight, depending on what's scheduled. Drinks are $2 and up.

Admission: Free.

CHAPTER 13

THE SEASHELL COAST

Thousands of years ago, life on these semitropical islands must have been idyllic for the resident Calusa tribe, who feasted on the abundant fish and shellfish from the sun-sparkled Gulf of Mexico waters and heaped tons of discarded shells into shell middens. Some shell middens, such as Mound Key, actually became new islets.

In 1513, Spanish Conquistador Ponce de León sailed along the shores of what is now Fort Myers Beach. The Calusas' paradise was usurped soon after. The Spaniards' greedy appetites were not satiated by seafood—they desired gold, land, and the souls of the natives. Eventually, notorious pirates, headed by José Gaspar, pursued their lucrative buccaneer business from the secluded coves. According to legend, Captiva derives its name from the captive women Gaspar held for ransom on this remote island. Ancient pirate maps depict buried loot on some islands, but the bounty has not been discovered. Perhaps there's truth to the legend that Gaspar's ghostly guards will frighten away any treasure hunter who comes close to the secret hiding places.

For most tourists today, the treasure is the bounty of seashells, which includes just about every variety under the sun. Should you think that you could never become avidly interested in seashells, be forewarned—picking up shells on the beach becomes addictive here. Who can resist such gorgeous specimens washed in by the tides on the white pearlescent sands?

Of course, the Seashell Coast is more than just shells. Some of Florida's most luxurious resorts, award-winning restaurants, and fancy shopping complexes are located here. Water sports, fishing, tennis, golf, and a variety of beach vacation pleasures await. Sightseeing is interesting too, including famous homes, unusual museums, outstanding parks, and the proximity to such unique wildlife sanctuaries as Ten Thousand Islands and the Everglades.

SEEING THE SEASHELL COAST

The area is served by two airports—the Southwest Florida Regional Airport in Fort Myers and the Naples Municipal Airport in Naples. By car, you can get to Fort Myers easily by taking I-75 south from the Tampa Bay area; or take Alligator Alley from Fort Lauderdale, leading directly to Naples, then drive north on I-75 to Fort Myers. From Miami, the Tamiami Trail (U.S. 41) also leads directly into Naples, from which you can continue north on U.S. 41 to Fort Myers. Sanibel and Captiva are just west of Fort Myers, via the causeway.

1. FORT MYERS

148 miles NW of Miami, 123 miles W of Fort Lauderdale, 134 miles S of Tampa

GETTING THERE **By Plane** Among the airlines serving Fort Myers's newly

WHAT'S SPECIAL ABOUT THE SEASHELL COAST

Beaches

- ☐ Sanibel, Captiva, Cayo Costa, and Marco Island beaches—some of the world's best beaches for collecting seashells.
- ☐ Lover's Key, a hideaway beach, accessible by tram from the adjoining state park.

Wildlife Sanctuaries

- ☐ Ding Darling National Wildlife Refuge, encompassing more than 5,000 acres on Sanibel, with biking, hiking, canoeing, and driving trails for observing hundreds of species of birds and luxuriant Florida flora.
- ☐ Briggs Nature Center, in the Rookery Bay National Estuarine Research Reserve, with boat excursions for exploration, canoe rides, and a nearly mile-long boardwalk.
- ☐ Corkscrew Swamp Sanctuary, owned and operated by the National Audubon Society, 11,000 acres noted for the largest virgin bald cypress forest in the U.S. and woodstork migration.
- ☐ Babcock Wilderness Adventures, with excursions led by trained naturalists to observe alligators, bison, exotic birds, wild turkey, snakes, panthers, and wild hogs in Telegraph Cypress Swamp.

Shopping

- ☐ Naples's ritzy shopping malls, particularly the super-glamorous Waterside.
- ☐ The Shell Factory in North Fort Myers, displaying zillions of seashells from everywhere in the world.

Regional Food and Drink

- ☐ Outstanding locally caught fish and seafood, locally grown citrus and tropical fruits and vegetables, as well as grapes for the regional wine produced at the Eden Vineyards and Winery.

Activities

- ☐ Abundant golf courses, some rated among the top in the nation.
- ☐ Excellent tarpon fishing—the waters between Cayo Costa and Gasparilla Island are considered among the world's best for this sport.

Buildings

- ☐ Seminole Lodge, winter home of inventor Thomas Alva Edison from 1886 to 1931, showing his talent for architecture, with Florida's first swimming pool.
- ☐ Mangoes, winter home of Henry Ford, next door to the Edison House, designed in the style of that era.

expanded **Southwest Florida Regional Airport** are Air Canada, American Airlines, American Eagle, Continental Airlines, Northwest Airlines, TWA, United Airlines, USAir, USAir Express, and international charters—even the Concorde has landed here! The cost of airport limousine service to downtown Fort Myers is $20. Yellow Cab (tel. 352-1055) charges approximately $18 ($1.35 base rate plus $1.35 per mile) from the airport to downtown.

By Train The closest Amtrak (tel. toll free 800/USA-RAIL) train station is in Tampa (see "Tampa," in Chapter 12). However, special Amtrak bus service is provided to/from Fort Myers for all Amtrak arrivals/departures out of the Tampa station.

By Bus The Greyhound bus station is at 2275 Cleveland Ave. (tel. 813/334-1011).

By Car From Fort Lauderdale, Alligator Alley leads directly west to the Seashell Coast. The Tamiami Trail (U.S. 41) or I-75 is the route to take from Miami. From the Tampa Bay area, take I-75 south.

Now a vibrant city enhanced by regal palm-tree-bordered boulevards, Fort Myers had humble beginnings as a U.S. Army outpost named Fort Harvie, built in 1844, during the Seminole Wars.

This remote area was accessible only by boat. However, a few resourceful pioneers decided to settle here when word spread about the warm climate, the excellent location on the banks of the Caloosahatchee River with proximity to the Gulf of Mexico, and the acres of untouched land suitable for farming and cattle grazing. Fort Myers grew to be a big cowtown.

It was Thomas Alva Edison, the inventor and horticulturist, who catapulted Fort Myers into the resort world. He arrived in 1885 at age 36 to regain his health and recuperate from the tragic loss of his wife. During his visit, Edison was so impressed by the scenic Caloosahatchee River area and the tropical bamboo plants growing wild along the riverbanks that he decided to establish a winter retreat. Edison discovered that the bamboo could be utilized in his inventions. In the ensuing years he established his winter headquarters in what had become Fort Myers, remarried, worked diligently in the laboratory, and invited such friends as Henry Ford and Harvey Firestone to be his guests in the new home, Seminole Lodge.

In addition to his own botanical garden, Edison found time to beautify the new city by planting the stately palm trees on what would become McGregor Boulevard. This had been cattle-grazing country and the pioneers were not too enthusiastic about Edison's beautification plans. However, newly arrived settlers from the Netherlands, Belgium, and Luxemburg planted lovely gardens where gladiolas flourished and Fort Myers eventually became the Gladiola Capital of the World.

Slowly, Fort Myers progressed, while retaining its leisurely lifestyle. A dignified resort city, handsomely bordered by the wide expanse of riverfront, Fort Myers today is experiencing a downtown renaissance, complete with a new riverwalk park. It's a serene city where you can stroll or ride a bike, stay in a comfortable hotel, dine in a variety of good restaurants (delicious seafood!), play golf on truly challenging courses, indulge in shopping at popular malls, charter a fishing boat, enjoy interesting sightseeing in and around the city, participate in water sports at Fort Myers Beach, only 15 miles away, or just relax. Reasonable prices are another advantage of a Fort Myers vacation—who could ask for anything more?

ORIENTATION

CITY LAYOUT Fort Myers's main thoroughfare is **McGregor Boulevard,** bordering the Caloosahatchee River. For 15 miles, the boulevard is lined with majestic royal palm trees. Actually, McGregor Boulevard (Fla. 867) is the scenic but slower route. The boulevard begins in downtown Fort Myers and can lead either to Fort Myers Beach by continuing on San Carlos Boulevard (Fla. 968), or to Sanibel Island by turning right onto Old McGregor or Summerlin Road (Fla. 869). Another, perhaps quicker, route is to take four-lane **Summerlin Road** from Colonial Boulevard in Fort Myers, and from Summerlin, either turn left onto San Carlos to Fort Myers Beach, or go straight ahead on Summerlin to Sanibel Island.

U.S. 41 is "The Strip," with shopping malls, shopping centers, and fast-food and chain restaurants. It's the main north-south artery for the area. Daniels Parkway, Colonial Boulevard (Fla. 884), Dr. Martin Luther King, Jr., Boulevard (Fla. 82), Palm Beach Boulevard (Fla. 80), Pine Island Road (Fla. 78), and Bonita Beach Road are the main east-west roads in Lee County.

INFORMATION The **Fort Myers Chamber of Commerce,** 2310 Edwards Dr., Fort Myers, FL 33902 (tel. 813/334-6626), open Monday through Friday from 9am to 5pm, supplies a variety of information. The free walking-tour guide of historic Fort Myers is very helpful. Good information is also available from the **North Fort**

Myers Chamber of Commerce, 13180 N. Cleveland Ave., North Fort Myers, FL 33903 (tel. 813/997-9111), open Monday through Friday from 9am to 5pm. The **Fort Myers Beach Chamber of Commerce,** 394 Estero Blvd., Fort Myers Beach, FL 33931 (tel. 813/463-6451), also open Monday through Friday from 9am to 5pm, dispenses all sorts of information to visitors.

The **Lee County Visitor and Convention Bureau,** 2180 W. 1st St., Suite 100 (P.O. Box 2445), Fort Myers, FL 33902 (tel. toll free 800/533-4753), provides free, informative brochures filled with every detail about the entire area.

GETTING AROUND

BY BUS The Lee County Transit System provides public transportation throughout the county. Rides cost $1. For route information, call 939-1303.

BY CAR The best way to get around is by car. Because taxis are expensive, it's more practical to rent a car. Most car-rental agencies are located in Fort Myers's Southwest Florida Regional Airport, including **Alamo** (tel. 768-2424), **Avis** (tel. 768-2121), **Budget** (tel. 768-1500), **Hertz** (tel. 768-3100) and also at Naples Municipal Airport (tel. 643-1515), and **National** (tel. 768-1902). All these agencies also have nationwide toll-free telephone numbers, should you want to reserve a car in advance. A local company, **Value** is located in Fort Myers at 1640 Chamberlin Rd. (tel. 768-1200). There's usually a desk at your hotel for arranging car rental.

BY TAXI Taxis are expensive, as they are everywhere. Call **Yellow Cab** (tel. 332-1055) for fare information and taxis.

BY TROLLEY The fun way to get around for sightseeing is the San Francisco–style trolley. The fare is approximately $1, and you can get off and reboard along the route for no extra charge.

FAST FACTS

Area Code The telephone area code is 813.

Dentist The toll-free Dental Referral Service number is 800/336-8478.

Doctor For physicians and medical services, call Lee Memorial Hospital (tel. 334-5900), the Southwest Florida Regional Medical Center (tel. 939-8414), or the Gulf Coast Hospital (tel. 768-8414).

Emergencies Call 911.

Food Marts Both SuperAmerica, 11225 S. Cleveland Ave. (tel. 278-1166), and 7-Eleven, 6221 Estero Blvd., Fort Myers Beach (tel. 463-3402), are open daily 24 hours.

Laundry/Dry Cleaning Try Pewett Center Cleaners, 12719 McGregor Blvd. (tel. 482-0576).

Pharmacies Walgreens, at 7070-3 College Pkwy. (tel. 939-2142), is open 24 hours daily.

WHAT TO SEE & DO

THE TOP ATTRACTIONS

BABCOCK WILDERNESS ADVENTURES, Fla. 31. Tel. 338-6367 for information, 489-3911 for reservations.

★ Explore the 90,000 acres of the working Babcock Ranch and the mysterious Telegraph Swamp during a fascinating, 90-minute swamp-buggy tour, conducted by an experienced naturalist. Visitors observe birds and wildlife in their natural habitat. Alligators, bison, panthers, wild boars, and a variety of creatures go about their daily routine. On this tour, more species of birds and animals will be seen than anywhere else in Florida. At one point, visitors dismount the buggy for the 10-minute stroll along the boardwalk in the cypress swamp, which includes a visit to the immense, natural enclosure to observe the Florida panthers.

Although no food is sold at the Babcock Ranch, complimentary lemonade is served and you may take along a picnic lunch to enjoy in the special wooded area. Tour reservations are a must, and the swamp buggies depart right on time.

Admission: $15.95 adults, $7.95 children under 12.

Open: Jan–Apr, tours Tues–Sun, on the half hour 9am–3pm. May–Oct, tours Tues–Sun, twice a day between 9 and 11am. Nov–Dec, Tues–Sun, four times a day between 9am and 3pm. **Directions:** From I-75, take Exit 26 and head east for three miles on Fla. 78, past the Lee Civic Center, until you reach Fla. 31; turn left (or north) on Fla. 31 and drive about nine miles to the marked entrance; from here, you'll be heading east, driving past two miles of Florida flora to the visitors reception center.

HENRY FORD WINTER HOME, 2350 McGregor Blvd. Tel. 334-3614.

Mangoes, the winter vacation home of billionaire industrialist Henry Ford and his wife, Clara, was purchased in 1916 so that the Fords could be neighbors to their good friends the Edisons. Decorated and furnished 1920s style, the attractive home is also notable for the tropical landscaping. Because the Fords enjoyed square dancing with the Edisons and mutual friends, a festive atmosphere prevails.

Admission: $4 adults, $2 children 6–12. Combination tickets for the Edison-Ford complex, $8 adults, $3 children 6–12.

Open: Mon–Sat 9am–4pm, Sun 12:30–4pm. **Closed:** Thanksgiving and Christmas Days.

BURROUGHS HOME, 2505 1st St. Tel. 332-1229.

To meet sisters Mona and Jettie Burroughs, all dressed up in 1918 finery for the "Living History" tour of this two-story Victorian mansion, is like a personal visit back in time. Built in 1901 by affluent cattleman John Murphy, it was later sold to the Burroughs family. The Burroughs sisters are local historians who chat about life in the mansion while escorting visitors upstairs, downstairs, and to the garden overlooking the Caloosahatchee River. The Georgian Revival mansion is listed on the National Register of Historic Places.

Admission: $3.20 adults, $1.05 children 6–12.

Open: Tours, Mon–Fri on the hour 10am–4pm. **Directions:** Take I-75 to Exit 25 to Fowler Street and turn right.

EDISON WINTER HOME AND LABORATORY, 2350 McGregor Blvd. Tel. 334-3614.

Seminole Lodge, built by inventor Thomas Alva Edison, was the winter-vacation retreat for himself, his wife, Mina, and their family from 1886 to 1931. In his laboratory here, Edison created thousands of inventions—the lightbulbs he made in 1910 are still burning. Edison also built Florida's first swimming pool on the adjoining patio. After Edison died in 1931, his wife bequeathed the beautiful 14-acre riverfront estate to the state of Florida so that everyone could enjoy touring the Victorian-furnished home, the fascinating botanical garden (with the world's largest banyan tree), and the interesting laboratory.

Admission: $6 adults, $2 children 6–12, free for children under 6. Combination tickets for the Edison-Ford complex, $8 adults, $3 children 6–12.

Open: Guided tours depart every half hour, Mon–Sat 9am–4pm, Sun 12:30–4pm. **Closed:** Thanksgiving and Christmas Days.

MORE ATTRACTIONS

EDEN VINEYARDS WINERY AND PARK, 19850 Fla. 80 in Alva. Tel. 728-9463.

This is serendipity—who would expect a winery in Florida? On the 28 acres, the vineyards produce American and French hybrid grapes for seven different kinds of wines (some have won prizes). A guided tram tour includes wine sampling. The carambola (starfruit) wine is something different. Also noteworthy are the Cypress Cathedral nature trail and the herb-spice garden. Hospitality prevails, as this is a family-owned enterprise.

Admission: $2.50 adults, free for children. It's important to call ahead for tour reservations.

Open: Daily 11am–5pm. Tours given daily 11:30am–3:30pm. **Directions:** From I-75, take Exit 25 to Fla. 80 and follow Fla. 80 east for 10 miles to the winery.

FORT MYERS HISTORICAL MUSEUM, 2300 Peck St. Tel. 332-5955.

Housed in the restored Spanish-Mediterranean–style Atlantic Coast Line train depot, this interesting museum is not just about railroads. However, one major exhibit happens to be the "Esperanza," the lengthiest and last of the plush Pullman private railroad cars, which is parked outside the museum. Rare artifacts, photographs, and exhibits present Fort Myers's history from the ancient Calusas and the Spanish Conquistadors on to the first settlers. There are photos of Colonel Myers too, who never visited the army fort named for him. Especially if you collect Carnival and Depression glass, don't miss the outstanding Cooper Glass Collection. From time to time, special displays and programs focus on a variety of subjects from art to tribal pow-wows.

Admission: $2 adults, 50¢ children under 12.

Open: Mon–Fri 9am–4:30pm, Sun 1–5pm. **Closed:** Holidays.

KORESHAN STATE HISTORIC PARK, U.S. 41. Estero. Tel. 992-0311.

Located on more than 300 acres along the Estero River, this historic landmark was the site of a now-extinct religious sect, the Koreshan Unity Movement, which believed that man lived *inside* the earth. Cyrus Reed Teed and his followers arrived from Chicago in 1894 to establish the self-sufficient settlement. Ahead of their time, the Koreshans believed in equal rights for women. Several buildings and gardens have been restored. Everything about the Koreshans is displayed in the museum.

Nature trails and canoe trails wind through the settlement and there is also a picnic and camping area. For a guided tour by rangers, a minimum of four people is required. The information center provides a free self-guided tour map. Don't forget the insect repellent.

Admission: $3.25 per automobile (maximum of eight passengers), $1 for pedestrians or bikers.

Open: Daily 8am–sunset. **Directions:** Take U.S. 41 south of Fort Myers to Estero.

LEE COUNTY NATURE CENTER, 3450 Ortiz Ave. Tel. 275-3435.

Three nature trails wind through this 105-acre nature center so that visitors can observe Florida's flora and fauna. In addition, there's an aviary, a children's natural-history museum, a live reptile exhibit, a 400-gallon saltwater aquarium, and a museum store. Also on the premises, the planetarium features star and laser-light shows (the extra admission price depends on the show being featured).

Admission: $2 adults, $1 children under 11.

Open: Mon–Sat 9am–4pm, Sun 11am–4:30pm. **Directions:** From I-75 take Exit 22, follow Colonial Boulevard, and turn right onto Ortiz Avenue.

SIX MILE CYPRESS SLOUGH PRESERVE, Penzance Crossing and Six Mile Cypress Pkwy. (between Colonial Blvd. and Daniels Rd.). Tel. 338-3300.

The 2,000-acre wetland ecosystem is interesting to observe from the mile-long boardwalk. There's a great diversity of southwestern Florida's plants and wildlife. An amphitheater is on the premises; lots of informative pamphlets are available, too.

Admission: $2 per vehicle.

Open: Daily 8am–5pm.

ORGANIZED TOURS

BY TRAIN What fun to enjoy dinner in an old-fashioned dining car on the **Seminole Gulf Railway Dinner Train** (tel. 275-8487), chugging along from Fort Myers to Punta Gorda, a three-hour trip enhanced by a glorious sunset and live music. Or you may opt for the Sunday brunch on board or a sightseeing excursion, which includes light meals and refreshing drinks. This choo-choo of nostalgic charm travels along the scenic countryside and crosses photogenic waterways.

Dinner trains leave Monday through Friday at 6:30pm, brunch trips begin on Sunday at 10am, and excursion trains leave Wednesday through Saturday at 10am, 12:30pm, and 3pm. Prices run about $50 for adults and children on the dinner train, about $45 for adults and children for the brunch trip, and about $15 for adults and children for the excursions.

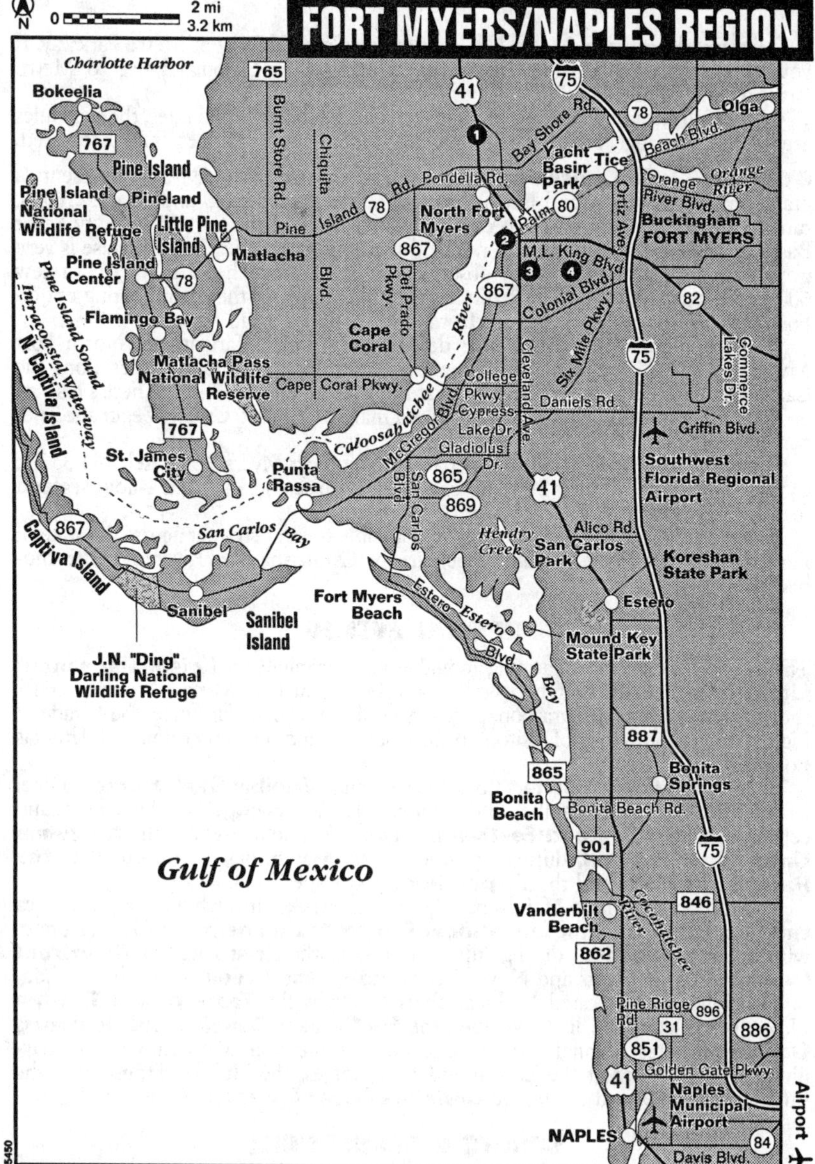
FORT MYERS/NAPLES REGION
N
0
2 mi
3.2 km
Charlotte Harbor
Bokeelia
767
Pine Island
Pine Island National Wildlife Refuge
Pineland
Little Pine Island
Matlacha
Pine Island Center
78
Flamingo Bay
Pine Island Sound
Intracoastal Waterway
N. Captiva Island
Matlacha Pass National Wildlife Reserve
767
St. James City
867
Captiva Island
San Carlos Bay
Sanibel
Sanibel Island
J.N. "Ding" Darling National Wildlife Refuge
Punta Rassa
765
Burnt Store Rd.
Chiquita Blvd.
Pine Island Rd.
78
Pondella Rd.
North Fort Myers
867
Del Prado Pkwy.
Cape Coral
Cape Coral Pkwy.
Caloosahatchee River
McGregor Blvd.
College Pkwy.
Cypress Lake Dr.
Gladiolus Dr.
865
869
San Carlos Blvd.
Fort Myers Beach
Estero Blvd.
Estero Bay
Hendry Creek
41
75
Bay Shore Rd.
78
Olga
Beach Blvd.
Yacht Basin Park
Tice
Orange River
Orange River Blvd.
Palm
80
Buckingham
FORT MYERS
M.L. King Blvd.
Ortiz Ave.
Colonial Blvd.
82
867
Six Mile Pkwy.
Cleveland Ave.
75
Commerce Lakes Dr.
Daniels Rd.
Griffin Blvd.
Southwest Florida Regional Airport
41
Alico Rd.
San Carlos Park
Koreshan State Park
Estero
Mound Key State Park
887
865
Bonita Springs
Bonita Beach
Bonita Beach Rd.
901
75
Gulf of Mexico
846
Vanderbilt Beach
Cocohatchee River
862
Pine Ridge Rd.
896
31
886
851
Golden Gate Pkwy.
41
Naples Municipal Airport
NAPLES
84
Davis Blvd.
Airport
5450

ATTRACTIONS:

Edison's Winter Home 2

Fort Myers Historical Museum 3

Lee County Nature Center 4

Shell Factory 1

All trains depart from Metro Mall Station, on Colonial Drive at Metro Parkway. If you're arriving via I-75, take Exit 22 west and follow Colonial Drive to Metro Parkway and Metro Mall.

Note: Call ahead for reservations and to recheck schedules and rates; the schedules are subject to change. From time to time, a Murder Mystery Dinner Train is featured.

BY BOAT **J. C. Cruises** (tel. 334-7494, or toll free 800/634-0449) presents a grand variety of year-round lunch, brunch, dinner, sightseeing, and theme cruises, ranging from three hours to two days. Trips depart from the Fort Myers City Yacht Basin on the Caloosahatchee River. The three-hour Everglades Jungle Cruise is very popular, via scenic waterways to observe flora and fauna. The *Captain J.P.*, a new 600-passenger paddlewheeler, is fun, evoking memories of the steamboating era on Fort Myers's waterways—trips are from three hours to a full day.

A 36-foot pontoon **catamaran** departs daily from Marinatown, North Fort Myers (tel. 574-2524). "Funtoon" itineraries range from one-hour cruises along the Caloosahatchee River to stopover visits at the Edison Winter Home. There's also an ecotour along the Orange River to observe a manatee habitat. Cruises begin at $5 per person.

Jammin' Sailboat Cruises, departing from Fort Myers Beach (tel. 463-3520), charge $30 per person for a 2½-hour champagne cruise and $45 for a 4-hour seafood feast cruise. A variety of cruises can be arranged.

Note: You might like to know that it's possible to boat straight across the state of Florida from Fort Myers to Palm Beach via the Caloosahatchee River and Okeechobee Waterway.

SPECIAL EVENTS

The Seashell Coast's most dazzling annual event is definitely the **Edison Pageant of Light,** celebrated the first two weeks of February in Fort Myers. Arts and crafts shows, a five-kilometer marathon, pageants, and the spectacular finale, the Parade of Lights, attract thousands of visitors to the festivities and the winter home of Thomas Edison.

Seashell lovers and collectors flock to the annual **Sanibel Shell Fair** on Sanibel Island in March (see "Sanibel and Captiva Islands," below). Nearby Pine Island celebrates with a **Seafood Festival** in March. A unique event is the **Koreshan Unity Lunar Festival,** during April, in Estero. May brings the **Concert in the Park** in Fort Myers and the **Tarpon Rodeo** in Cape Coral.

In addition to Fourth of July parades and fireworks throughout the area, Boca Grande is the scene for the **Invitational Tarpon Tournament** and Alva celebrates with a **Grape Festival** during July. Music is in the air at August's **Riverfront Concert** in Fort Myers and November's **Jazz-on-the-Green** on Sanibel Island.

Delicious foods created by local chefs highlight the **Taste of the Town,** a November celebration. In November, the **Fort Myers Beach Sand Sculpting Contest** inspires original artistry. December is merry and bright with holiday-illuminated splendor at the Edison and Ford homes, the Holiday House, and the Burroughs Home, and the festive **Christmas Boat Parade** in Cape Coral.

SPORTS & RECREATION

BASEBALL Great news for **Boston Red Sox** fans—the team relocated to Fort Myers for spring training in 1992. On 12 acres, the new $13.75-million complex, City of Palms Park, 2201 Edison Ave., at Broadway (tel. 334-4700 for information), includes stadium seating for 6,500. During spring training (usually from the first week in March to the first week in April), the **Minnesota Twins** play at the Lee County Sports Complex, at 14100 Six Mile Cypress Pkwy. (tel. 768-4270 for ticket information, 338-3000 for general information about the complex), with stadium seating for 7,500. Baseball has been a tradition here since 1896.

BEACHES From Cape Coral south through Bonita Beach, the 50-mile stretch of wide, white sands and Gulf of Mexico sparkling blue waters is known as the **Lee County Island Coast,** and includes **Fort Myers Beach** on Estero Island. One of the most beautiful sun-sand-and-sea playgrounds is **Lover's Key** in the Carl E. Johnson Recreation Area, about 10 miles south of Fort Myers Beach. To get there, take Estero Boulevard; the park is at the southern tip of Estero Island. A special tram shuttles across Oyster Bay to Lover's Key. Admission to the beach costs $1.50 for adults, 75¢ for children and senior citizens. It's open daily from 8am until sundown. Beautiful **Bonita Beach** is south of the Carl Johnson Park.

All sorts of beach information and the surrounding attractions, plus maps depicting how to get there, are available from the Lee County Visitor and Convention Bureau, 2180 W. 1st St., Suite 100 (P.O. Box 2445), Fort Myers, FL 33902 (tel. toll free 800/237-6444 or 533-4753, 800/LEE-ISLE in Florida).

DOG RACING They're off and running after the rabbit at the **Naples–Fort Myers Kennel Club,** 10601 Bonita Beach Rd. (U.S. 41), in Bonita Springs (tel. 992-2411). Greyhound racing is featured the year around at 7:45pm Tuesday through Saturday; matinees are scheduled at 12:30pm; on Sunday, racing starts at 1:30pm. Children are welcome, if accompanied by an adult. You can watch the races in style from the Sky Region restaurant, where cocktails, lunch, and dinner are served. Both track and restaurant are closed Monday.

GOLF & TENNIS The **Cape Coral Golf and Tennis Resort,** 4003 Palm Tree Blvd., Cape Coral (tel. 542-3191, or toll free 800/648-1475), offers an 18-hole championship golf course, open to the public. Greens fees are about $40 in summer, double that in winter. Eight Har-Tru tennis courts (five illuminated) are also part of the resort.

The **Lehigh Country Club,** 225 E. Joel Blvd., Lehigh Acres (tel. 369-2121), offers two golf courses. Greens fees are approximately $12 in summer, near $30 in winter. Tennis courts are also available.

The **Bay Beach Golf Club,** 7401 Estero Blvd., Fort Myers Beach (tel. 463-2064), is open to the public. Tee-off times are 7:30am to 5pm.

The **Eastwood Golf Course,** 4600 Bruce Herd Lane (tel. 275-4848), owned by the City of Fort Myers, is one of the top five public courses in the South. On this challenging 18-hole championship course, greens fees range from $15 (mid-April to mid-December) to $25 (mid-December to mid-April), with lower fees after 2pm.

Many other local courses welcome the public, including the **Fort Myers Country Club** (tel. 936-2457) and the **River's Edge Country Club** (tel. 433-4211).

Just south of Fort Myers Beach, the **Bonita Springs Golf and Country Club** (tel. 992-9500) and the **Pelican's Nest** (tel. 947-4600) are open to the public.

The **Sanibel Harbour Resort & Spa,** at Sanibel Causeway, Fort Myers (tel. 466-4000, or toll free 800/767-7777), features 13 tennis courts for day and night play plus a 5,500-seat stadium to observe championship teams and tournaments.

The **Fort Myers Racquet Club,** 4900 Deleon St. (tel. 278-7277), provides eight courts, open to the public for day and night play.

For detailed information about golf and tennis, call the Lee County Visitor and Convention Bureau (tel. toll free 800/237-6444, 800/LEE-ISLE in Florida).

HORSEBACK RIDING The **Hancock Creek Stables,** 865 Moody Rd., North Fort Myers (tel. 997-3322), offers hour-long trail rides. Rates are $16 for adults, $11 for children 9–13. Children must be at least 9 to ride. Rides are at 5pm Monday through Friday (or by appointment for two people or more), and on Saturday and Sunday at 9am, 11am, 2pm, and 4pm.

MINIATURE GOLF **Jungle Golf,** 4038-17710 San Carlos Blvd., Fort Myers Beach (tel. 466-9797), gives mini-golf fans a splash of exotica with jungle streams, cascading waterfalls, and tropical flora and fauna. Admission is $4.95 for adults, $3.95 for senior citizens and children under 12.

Rinky Dink Adventure Golf, 17450 San Carlos Blvd., Fort Myers Beach (tel. 466-5855), also offers a beautiful setting and a very challenging course. Admission is $5.50 for adults, $4.50 for those over 52 years old or 12 and under.

Rates are comparable at **Golf Safari,** 3775 Bonita Beach Rd. SW (tel. 947-1377), and at **Fort Adventure,** 1915 Colonial Blvd. (tel. 936-3233).

The newest place to play miniature golf in a luxuriant tropical setting is at **Mike Greenwell's Bat-A-Ball and Family Fun Park,** 35 NE Pine Island Rd., Cape Coral (tel. 574-4386). A resident of Cape Coral and a Boston Red Sox leftfielder, Greenwell frequents his amusement complex, open Monday through Thursday from 10am to 10pm, and Friday through Sunday from 10am to 11pm. Call ahead for the range of prices for mini-golf, the batting cages, go-cart track, and game arcade; there are special birthday party rates.

WATER SPORTS **Paradise Parasail Wind & Water Sports,** 1400 Estero Blvd. (tel. 463-7272), behind the Lani Kai Hotel, offers waverunner rentals, jet skis, Hobie Cats, parasail rides, waterskiing, and more. **Underwater Explorers Diving Center,** 12600 McGregor Blvd. (tel. 481-4733), rents diving equipment for $36.50 per day. **Ken's Sports,** 4600 S. Cleveland Ave. (tel. 936-7106), rents snorkeling gear at $40 per day.

Sailboat rentals are available at **Aqua Sports Ltd.,** 6890 Estero Blvd., Fort Myers Beach (tel. 463-1710). The rates are about $40 an hour on a 16-foot Hobie Cat (boat only—no captain). Arrangements can be made to rent a sailboat with a captain.

Deep-sea fishing expeditions and charter boats sail out from the **City Yacht Basin,** downtown Fort Myers (tel. 334-8271); **Getaway Marina,** 18400 San Carlos Blvd., Fort Myers Beach (tel. 466-3600); **Snug Harbor,** under the bridge at Fort Myers Beach (tel. 463-4343); **Gulf Star Marina,** Fort Myers Beach (tel. 765-1500); and **Blue Moon Charters,** 21665 Indian Bayou Dr., Fort Myers Beach (tel. 463-3939). To give you some idea of deep-sea fishing charter rates, the boats at Getaway Marina charge about $25 per person for a half-day excursion, $40 per person for a full day. Fishing bait and tackle are included, and food and drink are available on board.

WHERE TO STAY

MAINLAND FORT MYERS

Expensive

SANIBEL HARBOUR RESORT & SPA, 17260 Harbour Pointe Rd., Fort Myers, FL 33908. Tel. 813/466-4000, or toll free 800/767-7777. Fax 813/466-2150. 240 rms, 100 two-bedroom condo apts. A/C TV TEL

$ **Rates:** Dec 1–19, $105–$235 double. Dec 20–Apr 17, $220–$350 double. Apr 18–May and Oct–Nov, $135–$285 double. June–Sept, $105–$235 double. Inquire about special packages. MC, V.

This luxurious resort overlooks beautiful San Carlos Bay and is convenient to the Sanibel Island Causeway. The balconied rooms are exceptionally attractive and spacious, and have terrific views. There's plenty to do here, with the excellent sports facilities. An 80-acre nature preserve is also part of the resort.

Dining/Entertainment: For great dining and refreshments, there are four restaurants and lounges, including the intimate Toucan Room—very elegant and notable for gourmet dinners.

Facilities: Four swimming pools, whirlpools, 13 lighted tennis courts, marina with rental boats, fishing facilities, special recreational activities for children. The excellent spa and fitness center offers a variety of healthful treatments and exercise programs.

SHERATON HARBOR PLACE, 2500 Edwards Dr., Fort Myers, FL 33901. Tel. 813/337-0300, or toll free 800/325-3535. Fax 813/337-1530. 193 rms, 224 suites and penthouse. A/C TV TEL

$ **Rates:** Dec–Jan, $90–$130 double. Feb–Apr 15, $120–$170 double. Apr 16–Nov, $80–$120 double. AE, DC, DISC, MC, V.

Overlooking the prestigious Yacht Basin Marina and a Caloosahatchee River panorama, the Sheraton Harbor Place is within walking distance of the Edison Winter Home, Harborside Convention Center, and more. The indoor/outdoor Aqua Bar is unique, surrounded by waterfalls and flaunting what must be Florida's largest indoor mural (it depicts an undersea fantasy world).

Dining/Entertainment: La Tiers restaurant, offering reasonably priced meals, looks out to the photogenic harbor. Nightly live entertainment is featured in one of the cocktail lounges.

Services: Complimentary transportation to the airport (less than 20 miles from the hotel).

Facilities: Two outdoor and one indoor swimming pools, lighted tennis court, Jacuzzi, exercise room; bike and boat tours to the beaches (about a half-hour drive) and for shopping and sightseeing.

Moderate

COURTYARD BY MARRIOTT, 4450 Metro Pkwy., Fort Myers, FL 33901. Tel. 813/275-8600. Fax 813/275-7087. 149 rms. A/C TV TEL

$ Rates: Jan–Apr, $90–$100 double. May–Dec, $74–$84 double. AE, DC, DISC, MC, V.

Because this pleasant hotel is so centrally located, it's a favorite with business travelers. However, now that downtown Fort Myers has undergone a "facelift," complete with the new Riverwalk, more and more tourists stay at the Courtyard because of its proximity to interesting sights. Amenities include a swimming pool and whirlpool in the courtyard, and an exercise room. Meals and cocktails are served in the restaurant and lounge (check on the restaurant's meal schedule; it closes during certain hours). Airport transportation is complimentary.

HOLIDAY INN CENTRAL, 2431 Cleveland Ave., Fort Myers, FL 33901. Tel. 813/332-3232, or toll free 800/998-0466. Fax 813/332-0590. 126 rms. A/C TV TEL

$ Rates: Dec 16–Jan, $75 double. Feb 2–Apr, $95 double. May–Dec 15, $69 double. AE, DC, DISC, MC, V.

Calling all Red Sox fans—the hotel is only two blocks from the new Red Sox spring training baseball stadium! As you can note from the name, the hotel is centrally located for most of the city's favorite tourist sights—about four blocks from the Edison Winter Home, about half a mile from the Fort Myers Historical Museum. Movie fans will like the free HBO in the guest rooms. The outdoor pool is heated and health club privileges can be arranged. Complimentary airport transportation is another nice "extra." La Viola restaurant serves breakfast from 6:30 to 10am, lunch from noon to 2pm, and dinner from 5 to 10pm; the cocktail lounge is open until 10pm.

TOUCAN RESORT, 2220 W. 1st St., Fort Myers, FL 33901. Tel. 813/332-4888. Fax 813/334-3844. 100 rms and suites. A/C TV TEL

$ Rates: High season, $70 double; $140 Jacuzzi suite. Low season, $59 double; $110 Jacuzzi suite. AE, CB, DC, DISC, MC, V.

Located on the banks of the scenic Caloosahatchee River, the colorful Toucan Resort is as bright as the toucan birds that rule the roost in South American jungles. At a cost of $7 million, the lively resort has been completely remodeled and refurbished from its former life as a Ramada Inn. More rooms and suites will be added.

One big asset is the massive redesigned patio area with a super-size swimming pool, Jacuzzi, and plenty of comfortable chairs for sun-worshippers. The Tiki Lounge, overlooking the river, is very popular for light meals and drinks. At the end of the work day, local residents come to relax in the lounge. It's fun to fish here too, from the private boat dock and fishing pier. The resort is close to Fort Myers's main sightseeing attractions.

Inexpensive

SHELL POINT VILLAGE GUEST HOUSE, 15000 Shell Point Blvd., Fort Myers, FL 33908. Tel. 813/466-1111. Fax 813/454-2220. 39 rms. A/C TV TEL

$ Rates: High season, $70–$78 double. Low season, $35 double. Additional person $6 extra. Children stay free in parents' room. Monthly rates available. MC, V.

Less than two miles from the Sanibel Causeway, this tranquil place is a real bargain, especially should you be planning visits to Sanibel Beach, where rates are certainly much higher. Shell Point Village overlooks a marina and the Caloosahatchee River. Actually, this is not a guesthouse but a two-story motel with large picture windows and pleasant decor. There's a heated swimming pool, a putting green, and two lighted tennis courts. Inexpensively priced meals are served in the glass-enclosed Crystal Dining Room, open for breakfast from 7 to 10:30am, for lunch from 11:30am to 1:30pm, and for dinner from 4:30 to 6:30pm.

BED & BREAKFAST

DRUM HOUSE INN, 2135 McGregor Blvd., Fort Myers, FL 33903. Tel. 813/332-5668. 6 rms.

$ Rates: High season, $125 double. Low season, 20% discount. No credit cards.

In the historic downtown area, the turn-of-the-century Drum House is the Lee Island Coast's first bed-and-breakfast inn. Lovingly restored by innkeepers Shirley and Jim Drum, and decorated with antiques, the Drum House offers relaxation in the sitting parlor, music room, television room, and library. The sunny breakfast room is very pleasant for the morning meal. Every afternoon, complimentary wine and cheese are served. Artwork by local artists Marilyn and George Schaffer enhances the decor. It's a nice walk to the Edison Winter Home just down the street, or the Drums can supply bikes. No smoking is allowed in the inn.

FORT MYERS BEACH

Expensive

SANTA MARIA, 7317 Estero Blvd., Fort Myers Beach, FL 33931. Tel. 813/765-6700, or toll free 800/765-6701. Fax 813/765-6909. 60 suites, penthouse. A/C MINIBAR TV TEL

$ Rates: Jan, $95 one-bedroom suite, $625 per week, $2,355 per month. Feb–Apr 18, $125 one-bedroom suite, $825 per week, $3,145 per month. Apr 19–Sept 6, $75 one-bedroom suite, $485 per week, $1,825 per month. Sept 7–Nov 15, $65 one-bedroom suite, $415 per week, $1,565 per month. Two-bedroom suites, $75 per day in low season to $145 per day in high season; two-bedroom town-house accommodations slightly higher. Three-bedroom penthouse, $125 per day in low season to $205 per day in high season, with special weekly and monthly rates. Daily maid service $25 per day extra (penthouse rates include maid service). AE, MC, V.

The new Santa Maria is the most deluxe place to stay on Fort Myers Beach. Spacious, beautifully furnished suites can accommodate four people in the one-bedroom units, and up to six people in the two- and three-bedroom units. Every suite flaunts a screened balcony and is equipped with full-size washer/dryer, microwave, wet bar, and two television sets. In the large swimming pool, you can swim laps. There's also a Jacuzzi and a sauna. Although the complex has no restaurant, the barbecue area is available to guests who want to grill anything from hot dogs to steaks. The Santa Maria is close to restaurants, boutiques, water-sports facilities, golf, and tennis.

Moderate

DAYS INN AT LOVER'S KEY, 8701 Estero Blvd., Fort Myers Beach, FL 33931. Tel. 813/765-4422, or toll free 800/325-2525. 75 studio apts. A/C TV TEL

$ Rates: Dec 16–31, $110–$135 double. Jan, $95–$110 double. Feb–Apr, $125–$150 double. May–Dec 15, $75–$95 double. Bargain weekly rates available off-season. AE, DISC, MC, V.

What a wonderful location at the south end of Estero Island—across the road from the outstanding Lover's Key State Recreation Area! From the balconied apartments of this new hotel, the panoramic views of islands in the gulf and estuary are absolutely beautiful. A pretty swimming pool and a patio area is a popular rendezvous for guests. Fishing, water sports, boating, nature cruises, and shelling expeditions can be arranged. The coffee shop serves light meals and snacks at reasonable prices (cocktails, too).

MARINER'S PINK SHELL BEACH AND BAY RESORT, 275 Estero Blvd., Fort Myers Beach, FL 33931. Tel. 813/463-6181, or toll free 800/237-5786. Fax 813/463-1229. 170 units. A/C TV TEL

$ Rates: Apr 19–Dec 18, $525–$910 unit per week. Dec 19–Jan 3 and Feb–Apr 18, $798–$1,365 unit per week. Jan special (Jan 4–31) $616–$1,043 unit per week. Vacation package plans available. MC, V.

Secluded at the scenic north end of Estero Island, between the Gulf of Mexico and Matanzas Pass Bay, this resort complex has been named one of the best in the United States for families with children. No wonder—the daily activity schedule is action-filled, especially the supervised program for kids. Accommodations range from hotel rooms to beach cottages, apartments, efficiencies, and an executive suite. In addition to the uncrowded white sand gulf beach, the resort offers two swimming pools, a wading pool, a 200-foot private fishing pier, 21 boat slips, a water-sports center, two lighted tennis courts and a volleyball court, rental bikes, and more. Coconuts, the beachside grill and bar, is popular for refreshments.

BONITA SPRINGS

Moderate

BEACH AND TENNIS CLUB, 5700 Bonita Beach Rd. SW, Bonita Springs, FL 33923. Tel. 813/992-1121, or toll free 800/237-4934. Fax 813/992-8035. 120 studio apts. A/C TV TEL

$ Rates: Dec 15–Apr 15, $525–$575 per week double (one-week minimum stay required). Apr 16–Dec 14, $325–$375 per week double (three-day minimum stay required). No credit cards.

Located on Estero Bay between Fort Myers Beach and Naples, this attractive condominium resort is a great vacation value. There's a restaurant on the premises, three swimming pools (one especially for the kids), and 10 clay tennis courts. The beautiful Gulf of Mexico beach is just across the street.

COMFORT INN MOTEL, 9800 Bonita Beach Rd., Bonita Springs, FL 33923. Tel. 813/992-5001. Fax 813/992-9283. 69 rms. A/C TV TEL

$ Rates: Dec 21–Jan 20, $65 double. Jan 21–Apr 21, $95 double. Apr 22–Dec 20, $60 double. AE, DC, DISC, MC, V.

Spacious, pleasant accommodations here include a convenient refrigerator. Each room has a balcony to enjoy the views. In the patio area, the swimming pool and whirlpool are the fun places to be. For snacks and light meals, guests frequent the coffee shop (cocktails are also served).

CAPE CORAL

Moderate

CAPE CORAL GOLF AND TENNIS RESORT, 4003 Palm Tree Blvd., Cape Coral, FL 33904. Tel. 813/542-3191, or toll free 800/648-1475. Fax 813/542-4694. 100 rms. A/C TV TEL

$ Rates: Mid-Dec to mid-Apr, $82.50–$104.50 double. Mid-Apr to mid-Dec, $50–$62.50 double. Ask about special golf vacation packages. AE, CB, DC, DISC, MC, V.

This casual resort, a favorite with golfers and tennis enthusiasts, offers an 18-hole championship golf course and eight lighted tennis courts. Adjoining the swimming pool, the cabaña bar and grill is a popular rendezvous. A dining room and coffee shop are also on the premises. Usually, live entertainment is featured at night in the cocktail lounge. Decorated in soft pastels, many of the cozy rooms overlook the golf greens or the landscaped grounds shaded by stately palm trees.

LEHIGH

Moderate

LEHIGH RESORT, 225 E. Joel Blvd., Lehigh, FL 33936. Tel. 813/369-

2121, or toll free 800/843-0971. Fax 813/368-1660. 124 rms, 140 apts. A/C TV TEL

$ Rates: High season, \$72–\$140 double; \$80–\$140 apt. Low season, \$48–\$120 double or apt. Senior discounts and special sports packages available. AE, DC, MC, V.

This rambling, friendly resort is part of a retiree residential development, but is definitely for the sports-minded of all ages—there's also a children's program. Golfers like the two challenging 18-hole golf courses, and tennis buffs will find happiness on the courts. Volleyball, racquetball, biking, and swimming (in two pools) are also highlighted. Strolling along the woodland nature trail is pleasant. Restaurants and lounges are on the premises. From time to time, groups of square dancers come to the resort and guests are welcome to join in the fun. And if you want to go into the "big city," Fort Myers is less than a 20-mile drive away. Accommodations are in hotel rooms and efficiency and one- and two-bedroom apartments.

WHERE TO DINE

DOWNTOWN FORT MYERS

Expensive

PETER'S LA CUISINE, 2224 Bay St. Tel. 332-2228.

Cuisine: CONTINENTAL. **Reservations:** Recommended.

$ Prices: Main courses \$17.95–\$28.95. AE, DC, MC, V.

Open: Lunch Mon–Fri 11:30am–2pm; dinner Mon–Sat 5:30–9:30pm.

Chef Peter Schmid, who was born in Bavaria, masterfully blends European cuisine with local seafood, fruits, and vegetables. Among his creations are sautéed jumbo sea scallops, lightly laced with champagne sauce and served with a risotto of wild rice; broiled breast of chicken with avocado; veal à la française with avocado; and white-chocolate mousse with fresh-fruit sauce. Peter's food arrangements are always artistic. Of course, the wine list features a variety of selections to complement the cuisine. The dining room has a very refined ambience and the clientele are fashionably attired. On the upper level, a live jazz group entertains nightly in the cocktail lounge (the bar is open until 1am).

VERANDA, 2122 2nd St., at Broadway. Tel. 332-2065.

Cuisine: CONTINENTAL. **Reservations:** Recommended.

$ Prices: Appetizers \$3.25–\$7.95; main courses \$13.95–\$24.95; lunch \$2.95–\$7.95. AE, MC, V.

Open: Mon–Sat 11am–10pm (lounge stays open later).

A romantic, gracious atmosphere prevails at the Veranda, composed of two restored historic homes and a brick courtyard with a small fishpond. Shaded by tropical trees, the courtyard sports umbrella-topped tables, where it's delightful to enjoy interesting sandwiches for lunch, such as the "Carpetbagger," which upstages any mere club sandwich. Omelets, salads, soups, crab cakes, and an outstanding chicken marsala are included on the lengthy lunch menu.

The dinner menu is a gourmet delight, highlighting grilled Florida snapper, Bourbon Street filet of beef, southern sampler mixed grill of fish and seafood with saffron fettuccine, roast duckling served with a tangy raspberry sauce, and much more. Complimentary accompaniments include sweet corn muffins, just-baked honey-molasses bread, and sassy pepper jelly. Desserts are "to die for," especially the chocolate pâté with raspberry chambord coulis, peanut butter fudge pie, and southern pecan praline tart with French vanilla ice cream. The wine list is also notable. No wonder that the Veranda wins so many fine-dining awards. At night, entertainment in the cocktail lounge completes a perfect evening.

Moderate

CHART HOUSE, 2024 W. 1st St. Tel. 332-1881.

Cuisine: CONTINENTAL. **Reservations:** Recommended.

$ Prices: Appetizers \$3.25–\$7.95; main courses \$7.75–\$21.95. AE, DC, DISC, MC, V.

Open: Dinner only Sun–Thurs 5–10pm, Fri–Sat 5–11pm. (cocktail lounge, 5pm–1am.)

Attractive nautical decor is very appropriate for this friendly, popular restaurant overlooking the river panorama. At sunset, the views are splendid. Early evening dining is offered daily from 5 to 6pm, with a moderately priced menu from $8.75 to $14.95. The lengthy salad bar is one of the best anywhere, with such gourmet choices as marinated palm hearts. There's a special price for salad bar only, accompanied by hot sourdough and squaw breads; otherwise, you may make unlimited trips to the salad bar at no extra charge with dinner. Seafood selections include charcoal-broiled mahimahi, baked sea scallops, and New Orleans–style shrimp. Beef and chicken are featured also; grilled teriyaki sirloin steak is a specialty. For the devoted beefeater, the Callahan Cut is great—an extra-thick cut of prime rib. Cocktails are served too, as well as a nice selection of wines. The luscious mud pie highlights the dessert menu. The Raw Bar is a big favorite with locals.

MCGREGOR'S WOOD GRILLE & BAR, 3583 McGregor Blvd. Tel. 939-7300.

Cuisine: INTERNATIONAL. **Reservations:** Recommended.

$ **Prices:** Appetizers $3.95–$7.95; main courses $5.95–$10.95 at lunch, $9.95–$19.95 at dinner. AE, DC, MC, V.

Open: Lunch daily 11:30am–2:30pm; dinner daily 5–10pm (sunset dining menu served until 8pm); brunch Sun 11am–2:30pm. Bar, Mon–Thurs 11:30am–11pm, Fri–Sat 11:30am–midnight, Sun 11am–10pm; happy hour daily 11:30am–8pm with complimentary chef-carved buffet Mon–Fri 5–7pm.

A country club atmosphere prevails in this swanky window-walled restaurant overlooking the golf fairways. Nestled among gardens and towering palm trees, the restaurant was named for a Fort Myers pioneer, Tootie McGregor. The lounge is adorned with sepia photos of Thomas Edison, whose former winter home is a short distance away. As a connoisseur, Edison and his wealthy friends might have highly recommended the chef's innovative specialties seared on the oak grill, from seafood to steaks. The pasta dishes are also unusual, especially the oak-seared chicken breast with spinach fettuccine and the penne pasta with oak-grilled New Orleans andouille sausage, vegetables, and a Jack Daniels whiskey-cream sauce.

Lunch and dinner are also served in the friendly bar, where the leather-furnished lounge has more than a touch of class. There's nightly entertainment in the lounge, and a good jazz combo plays Thursday through Saturday. The cuisine and the congeniality have made McGregor's one of the most popular places in Fort Myers.

THE PRAWNBROKER RESTAURANT AND FISH MARKET, 13451 McGregor Blvd. Tel. 489-2226.

Cuisine: SEAFOOD. **Reservations:** Recommended.

$ **Prices:** Main courses $5.95–$26. AE, DC, MC, V.

Open: Dinner only, Mon–Sat 4:30–10pm, Sun 4:30–9pm. Fish market, Mon–Sat noon–10pm, Sun 3–9pm.

Really fresh fish and other seafood lure big crowds to the Prawnbroker, and the moderate prices provide extra bait. Fish and shellfish are prepared in so many ways that it takes time to read the menu. From peel-it-yourself shrimp to oysters crowned with caviar, it seems that everything from the briny deep is here. When stone crab claws are in season, (October to May), the Prawnbroker serves this Florida delicacy by the ton. Beef lovers, don't despair—steaks are grilled to order. As you'd expect, the restaurant is very casual, and very crowded. The Fish Market on the premises is popular with those who also like to cook seafood at home.

SMITTY'S, 2240 W. 1st St. Tel. 334-4415.

Cuisine: BEEF. **Reservations:** Recommended.

$ **Prices:** Main courses $7.95–$25.95. AE, DC, MC, V.

Open: Mon–Sat 11am–10pm, Sun 11:30am–9pm.

For over 30 years, Smitty's has been a favorite with local residents and the restaurant most tourists have heard about (Smitty's is within walking distance of the Edison Winter Home). The prime beef is always perfectly prepared, whether your choice is rare roast beef or grilled, thick, juicy tenderloin. A favorite accompaniment is the big baked potato with a variety of toppings, including Smitty's rich cheese sauce. The restaurant also features its own peppercorn salad dressing and just-baked bread. Seafood dishes are also on the menu; as you might expect, the surf-and-turf is extra-special here. For dessert, who can resist the brandy Alexander cream pie?

Budget

MARGARET'S HOME COOKING, 3209 Dr. Martin Luther King Jr. Blvd. Tel. 332-1335.
Cuisine: SOUL FOOD.
$ Prices: $1.95–$7.95. No credit cards.
Open: Tues–Sat 6am–8pm.

This modest, homey restaurant is one of the most popular in town, especially for the catfish and grits, on the menu for breakfast, lunch, and dinner. Specials Tuesday through Thursday are stew beef, oxtails, meatloaf, turkey wings, liver and onions, and chopped steak. Friday and Saturday specials are chitlings, candied yams, potato salad, oxtails, collard greens, and beef stew, all cooked lovingly as per Margaret's favorite real southern-style family recipes.

SNACK HOUSE RESTAURANT, 2118 1st St. Tel. 332-1808.
Cuisine: AMERICAN. **Reservations:** Not accepted.
$ Prices: $1.50–$9. No credit cards.
Open: Mon–Sat 7am–3pm (may close at 2pm on Sat).

A favorite breakfast and lunch rendezvous since 1949, the casual Snack House is the place to see all the city's political VIPs. In fact, the Snack House is known as *the* place for the "power breakfast." Many of the politicians and legal eagles work in the downtown office building where the Snack House is located, on the ground floor. Because of the clientele, you know that the food has to be good—and it is. Favorites are the old-fashioned country ham with red-eye gravy, two eggs, hot biscuits, and grits; the pancake sandwich with egg and bacon; the high-protein breakfast (less than 400 calories); bagel with cream cheese; steak and eggs; and much, much more. There's a kids' breakfast too, for a mere $2.65. For lunch, sandwich prices range from $1.45 for an egg sandwich to $3.50 for the hearty Cuban sandwich. And there are salads, soups, and hot dishes. Homemade cakes and pies are delicious. Prices are amazingly low.

FORT MYERS BEACH

Moderate

GULF SHORE RESTAURANT, 1270 Estero Blvd., Fort Myers Beach. Tel. 463-9951.
Cuisine: SEAFOOD/BEEF/POULTRY. **Reservations:** Recommended.
$ Prices: Breakfast from $3; lunch $4.95–$7.25; dinner $10.95–$18.50. AE, MC, V.
Open: Breakfast/lunch daily 7am–3pm; dinner daily 5–10pm.

Friendly and casual, this window-walled restaurant offers splendid views of the beach and gulf from every table. Yes, breakfast and lunch are served until 3pm, as the management believes that vacationers should be able to order these two meals as early in the day or as late in the afternoon as they wish. And if you want red beer (tomato juice with beer) with your eggs caliente for breakfast, it's on the menu. Breakfast is a veritable feast, with 16 different omelets, stacks of multigrain pancakes, eggs Alaskan (an English muffin topped with poached egg, Alaskan crabmeat, and a piquant sauce), and quiche Lorraine—just to name a few. A variety of heaped-high sandwiches, salads, and seafood plates are featured for lunch.

Favorites on the dinner menu are scallops provençal, shrimp Dijon, prime rib, baby back ribs, and boneless chicken teriyaki. There are great cocktails too, such as the Margarita and the Lazy Sunset. The Gulf Shore has become popular with European tourists. The restaurant's distinctive architecture dates back to the 1920s, when the building housed the Crescent Beach Casino.

BONITA SPRINGS

Moderate

MCCULLY'S ROOFTOP, 25999 Hickory Blvd., Bonita Springs. Tel. 992-0033.

Cuisine: CONTINENTAL. **Reservations:** Not accepted.

$ **Prices:** Appetizers $1.95–$8.95; main courses $8.50–$20. AE, CB, DC, MC, V.

Open: Lunch Mon–Fri 11:30am–2:30pm; dinner Sun–Thurs 5–9:30pm, Fri–Sat 5–10pm; champagne brunch Sun 10:30am–2pm.

For four generations, the McCully family has been in the restaurant business, beginning on Long Island, (N.Y.), and now, for almost 20 years, at the very popular Rooftop overlooking the gulf and Hickory Pass. Among the delicious specialties are grouper maison, topped with glazed bananas and laced with a tropical sauce; seafood strudel; jumbo lump crabmeat and shrimp, wrapped in phyllo dough and topped with lobster crème fraîche; tender roast prime rib of beef accompanied by traditional Yorkshire pudding; and roast pork calypso, glazed with rum and tropical seasonings. The Spa Menu highlights grilled chicken with vegetable salsa, gingered charcoal-broiled fresh salmon, Boston scrod with dilled yogurt sauce, and an exceptional vegetable plate—healthful dining can be most enjoyable. There is nightly entertainment and dancing (check the schedule).

SPRINGS GARDEN RESTAURANT & LOUNGE, 24080 N. Tamiami Trail, Bonita Springs. Tel. 947-3333.

Cuisine: CONTINENTAL. **Reservations:** Recommended.

$ **Prices:** Appetizers $1.25–$2.95 at lunch, $3.95–$6.50 at dinner; main courses $4.95–$7.95 at lunch, $9.95–$24.95 at dinner. MC, V.

Open: Lunch Mon–Fri 11:30am–2pm; dinner Mon–Sat 5–10pm, Sun 4:30–9:30pm.

Fruit plates, salads, sandwiches, and some hot specialties such as shrimp fettuccine Alfredo are popular at lunch at the Springs Garden, five miles north of Bonita Beach Road.

For dinner, the restaurant acquires a French accent with nine veal dishes that have gained fame with the clientele. However, there are many, many more dishes to choose from, such as Imperial seafood combo, red snapper Sarasota, grouper royale, Cajun chicken, New York strip steak, and a mixed grill (for hearty appetites). After-dinner coffees are concocted with liqueurs and spirits, and topped with whipped cream. You can even dance off the calories to the music of a live band, Tuesday through Saturday from 8:30pm to 12:30am; big-band/Dixieland is usually scheduled on Sunday.

SHOPPING

SHOPPING CENTERS

BELL TOWER SHOPS, 12499 U.S. 41 SE. Tel. 489-1221.

This complex flaunts a Spanish mission motif for more than 50 specialty shops in a setting of tropical gardens highlighted by an outstanding fountain-splashed courtyard. Among the classy shops is Jacobsons, a high-quality department store. Water-sports enthusiasts will like Jet Set Surf and Sport, with everything from beachwear to surfboards. Fridays, a popular bistro, is one of a dozen restaurants here—and there are 12 cinemas. Shops are open Monday through Saturday from 10am to 6pm and on Sunday from noon to 5pm.

EDISON MALL, U.S. 41 at Colonial Blvd. Tel. 939-5464.

This is southwestern Florida's largest enclosed mall, featuring at least 150 shops and such well-known department stores as Burdines, Dillards, JC Penney, and Sears. Four banks and 18 restaurants are also part of this attractive complex landscaped with colorful gardens, cascading fountains, and towering palm trees. Open daily Monday through Saturday from 10am to 9pm and on Sunday from 11:30am to 5:30pm.

METRO MALL, 2855 Colonial Blvd. Tel. 939-3132.

This mall highlights 60% savings and more on leading designer fashions and name-brand merchandise in the 70 outlet stores. Restaurants and snack bars are included in the tropical garden setting. This is definitely a bargain hunter's mall. Open daily Monday through Saturday from 10am to 9pm and on Sunday from noon to 5pm.

ROYAL PALM SQUARE, 1400 Colonial Blvd. Tel. 939-3900.

Named for Fort Myers's trademark royal palm trees, this is considered one of southwestern Florida's most beautiful shopping-dining complexes. More than 45 chic shops feature fashions, fine china, crystal, books, and unusual gifts. Gorgeous tropical gardens are enhanced by meandering streams and Spanish fountains, plus a courtyard aviary. Open daily from 10am to 6pm.

A FLEA MARKET

FLEAMASTERS, 4135 Anderson Ave. Tel. 334-7001.

Featuring hundreds and hundreds of bargain-filled shops, both indoors and outdoors, from souvenirs to serious collector's items, Fleamasters has just about everything under the sun. There are snack bars too, and live entertainment. Open on Friday, Saturday, and Sunday only, from 8am to 4pm. Admission and parking are free.

A SHELL SHOP

THE SHELL FACTORY, 2787 N. Tamiami Trail, North Fort Myers. Tel. 995-2141.

The Shell Factory claims to be the world's largest shell shop—and who could dispute this? For more than 50 years, the Shell Factory has been selling seashells from around the world, as well as the beautiful local shells. Everything made from shells is here too, from jewelry to shell-filled lamps. A variety of coral and genuine pearls are also featured. And there's more—resort fashions, fancy foods from Florida, Mexican artifacts, all sorts of souvenirs. Open daily from 10am to 6pm.

AT THE BEACH

Seafarers Village Shopping Mall, 1113 Estero Blvd., Fort Myers Beach (tel. 463-1113), located near the pier, has 16 specialty shops featuring a grand variety from shells and T-shirts to designer swimwear. Fusions has a terrific selection of beachwear for men and women in sizes from small to extra-large. There's also a good deli in this informal mall. Open daily from 10am to 5pm.

Springs Plaza, at U.S. 41 and Bonita Beach Rd. (tel. 992-7770), offers interesting boutiques and specialty shops.

IN PUNTA GORDA

Should you happen to be north of Fort Myers in Punta Gorda, about a mile west of U.S. 41 or accessible from Exit 29 on I-75 at the U.S. 17 interchange, check out the shopping-dining-entertainment complex called **Fisherman's Village,** right at Charlotte Harbor. Built on the old city fish dock pier, which extends 1,000 feet into the harbor, Fisherman's Village has 35 shops and seven restaurants.

EVENING ENTERTAINMENT

THE PERFORMING ARTS

ARCADE THEATER, 2267 1st St. Tel. 332-6688.

This historic newly renovated theater in downtown Fort Myers presents a variety of performances. Call for the schedule and prices.

BARBARA B. MANN PERFORMING ARTS HALL, 8099 College Pkwy. SW. Tel. 489-3033.

This dazzling, $7-million performing arts center on the campus of Edison Community College features world-famous celebrities. The luxuriously carpeted hall, seating nearly 2,000 people, is highlighted by a magnificent crystal chandelier and paintings by renowned artist Robert Rauschenberg. Presentations include everything from Broadway musicals to symphony concerts. Call for information on current programs and ticket prices.

HARBORSIDE CONVENTION HALL, 1375 Monroe St. Tel. 334-7637 for information, 334-4958 for the box office.

Recently opened in downtown Fort Myers, this 3,000-seat auditorium has spotlighted such entertainers as Ray Charles, the Oak Ridge Boys, Liza Minelli, and Victor Borge as well as the Red Army Chorus and Dance Ensemble from Moscow, World Cup Champions on Ice, and the Big Band Salute to Glenn Miller. Boat and auto shows are also featured here. Call the box office for schedule and ticket information.

THE CLUB & BAR SCENE

DOWNTOWN FORT MYERS The downtown is enjoying a renaissance, with evening entertainment spotlighted at several restaurants and hotels. Entertainers perform nightly at the **Victoria Pier** restaurant and pub, 2230 Edwards Dr. (tel. 334-4881). Contemporary jazz combos attract the crowds to **McGregor's Wood Grille & Bar,** 3583 McGregor Blvd. (tel. 939-7300), where different groups play Thursday through Saturday from about 8pm to 12:30am. At **Peter's La Cuisine,** 2224 Bay St. (tel. 332-2228), jazz and blues are spotlighted nightly, usually from 9pm to 1am. The **Toucan Resort,** 2220 1st St. (tel. 334-3866), provides entertainment Wednesday through Sunday. Other hotel venues in Fort Myers with nighttime entertainment are the **Sheraton Harbor Place,** 2500 Edwards Dr. (tel. 337-0300); **Edison's Electric Lounge** in Holiday Inn Airport, 13051 Bell Tower Dr. (tel. 482-2900); and the **Sanibel Harbour Resort & Spa,** 17260 Harbour Pointe Dr. (tel. 466-4000).

Because schedules are subject to change, it's a good idea to phone ahead. Also, for what's currently brightening up the night in Fort Myers and the surrounding area, inquire at your hotel's front desk or check the nighttime listings in the weekend newspapers.

ON THE BEACHES Real night owls and the 20-something crowd are at **Kokomo Joe's,** at the Lani Kai Island Resort, 1400 Estero Blvd., Fort Myers Beach (tel. 765-6500). This is the only beach restaurant open 24 hours. And there's dancing on the beach at the resort's Lani Kai Tiki Bar. The atmosphere is super-casual, even to dancing in bare feet.

At **Top O'Mast Restaurant & Lounge,** 1028 Estero Blvd., Fort Myers Beach (tel. 463-9424), good bands and disc jockeys liven up the night. On Friday and Saturday nights, **The Bridge,** 706 Fisherman's Wharf, Fort Myers Beach (tel. 765-0050), offers live music and entertainment.

On Bonita Beach, **McCully's Rooftop** (tel. 463-7010) is popular for dancing. The **Springs Garden Restaurant and Nightclub,** 24080 N. Tamiami Trail, Bonita Springs (tel. 947-3333), is another place to dance Tuesday through Saturday and spotlights special shows on Friday and Saturday.

OTHER ENTERTAINMENT

SeaKruz, docked at the Palm Grove Marina, 2500 Main St. (tel. toll free 800/688-7529), sails out for afternoon and evening cruises. Lady Luck may smile upon you in the gambling casino. Daytime cruises are usually from 10am to 4:30pm Monday through Saturday and from 11am to 5:30pm on Sunday. The evening cruises usually sail out Monday through Saturday at 6:30pm and return at 12:30am (later on Friday and Saturday). Delicious meals are served at the table. At night, the fun includes dancing to a live band and a colorful show. There's plenty of action on board, or you can just relax. Prices range from approximately $52 to $62, less for children. Inquire about the special hotel-cruise packages.

EASY EXCURSIONS

PINE ISLAND

Less than 20 miles west of Fort Myers, Pine Island is a fishermen's haven. Very quiet and very casual, Pine Island is accessible by causeway from the village of Matlacha (where the fishing from the bridge is terrific). Here you can see what Florida used to be like before resort development. Pine Island lures seafood lovers to rustic, waterfront restaurants in Bokeelia village on the northern tip and St. James City on the southern edge. Most of the locals have lived on the island since childhood. Retired residents have come here for the completely laid-back lifestyle. On the rickety piers, local fishermen are surrounded by pelicans and seagulls, hoping to share the bounty of fish.

Except for weekends, the **Pine Island Chamber of Commerce,** P.O. Box 525, Matlacha, FL 33909 (tel. 813/283-0888), supplies lots of information in its tiny office. You may also find out where to find someone with a boat to take you to the uninhabited island of Cayo Costa (with an outstanding beach) or to the private island of Useppa—it's worth a try.

There are several friendly "seafood shacks" on Pine Island; the following three will give you an idea of what to expect.

Where To Dine

BOKEELIA CRAB SHACK, Main St., Bokeelia, Pine Island. Tel. 283-2466.

Cuisine: SEAFOOD. **Reservations:** Not accepted.
$ Prices: Main courses $5–$17. No credit cards.
Open: Daily 11am–9pm.

Miles and miles of beautiful water views are part of the enjoyment of dining in the Crab Shack. Popular for its home-cookin' at modest prices, the restaurant was a rooming house in the good old days. Just about everyone begins a meal with the famous clam chowder. Baked fish, steamed shrimp, and plump oysters on the half shell are among the favorites. The home-baked key lime pie is a delightful dessert. By the way, although seafood highlights the menu, the delicious grilled hamburger on a bun is so big that you'll need both hands to lift it up to your mouth.

SNOOK HARBOUR INN, at foot of Matlacha Bridge. Tel. 283-1131.

Cuisine: SEAFOOD. **Reservations:** Not accepted.
$ Prices: Main courses $4.25–$14.95. No credit cards.
Open: Lunch daily 11am–5pm; dinner daily 5–10pm.

Whether you choose to dine indoors or outdoors on the dock, it's so relaxing to watch the boats sail by and the sea birds circling in the sky. For lunch, seafood sandwiches on a homemade Kaiser roll are heaped high with grilled grouper, or crab cakes, mullet filet, or your favorite from the briny deep. A variety of hot seafood platters include the Matlacha sampler and the Snook seafood combo. Yes, beef is served too, from big burgers to steaks. On Friday and Saturday from 5 to 10pm, the Admiral's Seafood Buffet is truly a feast for $14.95 and also includes buffalo wings, the salad bar, and hush puppies. For children under 12, the buffet costs $6.95 (there's also a children's menu daily). Imported beer is a bargain at $2 for draft. Tempting pies and cakes are baked on the premises.

WATERFRONT RESTAURANT AND MARINA, 2131 Oleander St., St. James City, Pine Island. Tel. 283-0592.

Cuisine: SEAFOOD. **Reservations:** Not accepted.
$ Prices: Main courses $7–$20.
Open: Daily 11am–8pm.

You can dine very casually on the dock, or indoors if you prefer air conditioning. If you're a boater, just tie up at the marina. In a former life, the restaurant was the island's little old schoolhouse. Among the menu favorites are lightly fried fish sandwiches and heaped-high seafood baskets with French fries. Tasty shrimp are served in a variety of ways from steamed to stuffed. For the beefeaters, steak and roast beef are on the menu. And chicken parmigiana is also a popular dish.

PUNTA GORDA

It's an interesting side trip to Punta Gorda, a former fishing village about 25 miles north of Fort Myers, where the Gulf of Mexico meets the Peace River. One of the main attractions is the new **Fishermen's Village,** flaunting 35 shops and seven restaurants on what used to be the old city pier, extending 1,000 feet into Charlotte Harbor.

The four-mile **Art Trail** starts at Fisherman's Village and leads you on to downtown shops and galleries. Historic homes add to the downtown area's charm.

Boaters can tie up right at the Fisherman's Village Marina. From the marina, **King Fisher Cruise Lines** (tel. 639-0969 or 639-2628) offers day excursions to Cayo Costa, Cabbage Key, and Useppa. Arrangements may be made for sunset cruises, nature excursions, and chartered fishing boats.

If you can't miss a day without golf, the course at the **Burnt Store Marina Resort** (tel. 639-3650) offers 27 holes. In addition to the resort, moderately priced places to stay in Punta Gorda are the Holiday Inn, Howard Johnson Riverside Lodge, and the Best Western Inn. **Salty's Harbor Side,** the waterfront restaurant and lounge at Burnt Store Marina Resort, is open daily (tel. 639-3650, or 332-7222 from Lee County).

Where To Dine

EARL NIGHTINGALE'S RESTAURANT, Fishermen's Village. Tel. 637-1177.

Cuisine: CONTINENTAL. **Reservations:** Recommended.
$ Prices: Main courses $7.95–$28.95. AE, MC, V.
Open: Daily 11:30am–9pm.

Overlooking the Charlotte Harbor panorama, this two-level restaurant is noted for fine dining. Downstairs, the atmosphere is more casual and the menu is lighter. Upstairs, elegance prevails with formally attired waiters, candlelight, lovely linens, and fresh flowers on the tables. As you might anticipate from all this sophistication, jackets are required for men. Seafood, veal, beef, and poultry are deliciously prepared, with the accent on French style. The service is excellent.

VILLAGE OYSTER BAR, Fishermen's Village. Tel. 637-1212.

Cuisine: SEAFOOD. **Reservations:** Not required.
$ Prices: Main courses $6.95–$25. MC, V.
Open: Mon–Thurs 11:30am–8pm, Fri–Sat 11am–9pm, Sun noon–8pm.

This attractive, casual restaurant has great views of the dock, where you can see the shrimp boats that deliver the crustaceans. The varied menu lists just about every fish and shellfish in the sea, and everything is prepared the way you like it. Even when there's no "R" in the month, freshly shucked oysters are in demand. There is a nice cocktail lounge, which stays open late.

---

2. NAPLES

35 miles S of Fort Myers, 110 miles W of Miami and Fort Lauderdale, 165 miles S of Tampa

GETTING THERE By Plane Airlines serving the **Naples Municipal Airport** (tel. 643-6875) are American Eagle (tel. toll free 800/433-7300), Delta/Comair (tel. 263-1101), and USAir (tel. toll free 800/428-4322). Airport transportation is provided by Affordable Limousine Service (tel. 455-6007), Airport Mini-Bus Service (tel. 263-3333), Lydon Transportation (tel. 598-1991), Maxi-Taxi of Florida (tel. 262-8977), and Naples Taxi Service (tel. 643-2148).

By Bus The Greyhound bus terminal is located at 2669 Davies Blvd. (tel. 774-5660).

By Car Alligator Alley, now a four-lane highway, leads across the state from Fort Lauderdale. From Miami, take U.S. 41 (the Tamiami Trail). From St. Petersburg and Tampa, take I-75 or U.S. 41 south.

The most glamorous city on Florida's Gulf of Mexico coast, Naples has more than just a touch of class. "Barefoot elegance" definitely applies to the highly rated beach resorts. Even budget-priced hotels are classier than their counterparts elsewhere. Although Naples could play a starring role in the television program "Lifestyles of the Rich and Famous," this sophisticated beachside city is not the least bit snobbish. Everyone in the shops (which could upstage Palm Beach boutiques), restaurants, hotels, and attractions is as hospitable to families and budget travelers as they are to the very affluent who live and vacation here.

Naples is also rich in history, which can be traced back 10,000 years. First residents were the Calusas, who left behind the towering mounds of discarded shells, some as high as 50 feet.

It wasn't until the 1860s, after the Civil War ended, that there were other footprints on the beach. Confederate Gen. John Williams of Kentucky happened to be scouting around the remote area, accessible only by boat. It was love at first sight. The general decided that this extraordinarily beautiful territory would be perfect for a winter vacation retreat for himself and his wealthy friends.

Proud of having been designated an honorary citizen of Naples by the king of Italy, General Williams named the seaside sanctuary Naples and built a beach hotel with the assistance of his Kentucky business partner. The hotel venture became a great success; affluent vacationers told their friends about the warm sunshine, tropical beach, and the luxuriant flora. For conservative millionaires and their families, who preferred privacy, Naples was the perfect winter hideaway. Eventually, the wealthy decided to build luxurious winter vacation homes along the serene beach. Hidden from view by exotic foliage and palm trees, this scintillating gulf front became known as "Millionaires' Row."

Because the wealthy, well-traveled residents are accustomed to the very best that money can buy, Naples is imbued with a special sophistication. Very much aware of its natural beauty, the city imposes strict zoning laws along the 10 miles of white sand beach. The subtropical environment is also protected by the resorts, which have preserved the mangrove jungle on their properties.

Serene and refined, Naples is a place to relax on the beach, observe Mother Nature, enjoy gourmet dining, visit art galleries, browse in high-fashion shops, play golf and tennis, and take time out to smell the roses.

ORIENTATION

INFORMATION The **Naples Area Chamber of Commerce,** 3620 Tamiami Trail N., Naples, FL 33940 (tel. 813/262-6141; fax 813/262-8374), is open from 8:30am to 5pm. The friendly, helpful staff provides free informative literature, maps, and answers to any questions.

CITY LAYOUT The **Tamiami Trail (U.S. 41)** leads into town and **Fifth Avenue,** the main street. Part of Fifth Avenue and **3rd Street South** (take a left) are considered historic Old Naples, famed for swanky shops in a tropically landscaped setting, which also extends from Broad Avenue South to 14th Avenue South. Fifth Avenue also leads to **Gulf Shore Boulevard,** ribboning the Gulf of Mexico.

For **Vanderbilt Beach,** follow U.S. 41 to Vanderbilt Beach Road (north).

GETTING AROUND

BY TAXI Taxi rides are expensive, approximately $2 at flag fall plus about $1.75 for each mile. Taxi service is available from **Yellow Cab** (tel. 262-1312), **Maxi Taxi** (tel. 262-8977), and **Naples Taxi** (tel. 775-0505). Note that Naples Taxi charges a flat rate by zones—for example, about $11 from the Registry hotel to Old Naples.

BY TROLLEY In San Francisco style, the brightly painted **Naples Trolley** (tel. 262-7300) clang-clangs around 25 different stops to shops, restaurants, sightseeing attractions, and hotels. The tour conductors are very informative. Tickets cost $9 for adults, $4 for children under 12. There's no extra charge for disembarking wherever you wish and then reboarding. Should you stay on board for the entire route, the tour takes about 1¾ hours.

BY CAR Renting a car is the best way to get around. Two of the largest agencies are at the Naples airport: **Avis** (tel. 643-0900) and **Hertz** (tel. 643-0265 or 643-1515). Nearby on Airport Road, the agencies include **Budget** (tel. 643-2212), **Sears** (tel. 643-3006), and **Thrifty** (tel. 643-4590). Hotels also make arrangements for rental cars.

BY WATER TAXI The **Naples Water Taxi** (tel. 774-7277) takes passengers along the bayfront, including restaurants, shopping malls, and hotels, via electrically operated boats. The water taxi is available upon demand rather than on a fixed schedule, and tours are also offered. Basic fares along the north bay are $4 per person one-way, $6 round-trip. Call ahead. Inquire about the "frequent floater" rates.

FAST FACTS

Area Code The telephone area code is 813.

Automobile Club AAA members needing assistance can call the AAA Automobile Club South (tel. 263-0600).

Dry Cleaner One Hour Professional Dry Cleaners is at 3050 Tamiami Trail N. (tel. 261-4324).

Emergency In an emergency, call 911.

Hospital For medical assistance, contact the North Collier Hospital (tel. 597-1417).

Pharmacy For 24-hour pharmacy information call Walgreen's toll free number, 800/925-4733.

Shoe Repair For shoe repairs, try Heel Quik in the Coastland Mall, 1900 Tamiami Trail N. (tel. 262-4335).

WHAT TO SEE & DO

SIGHTS & ATTRACTIONS

COLLIER AUTOMOTIVE MUSEUM, 2500 S. Horshoe Dr. Tel. 643-5252.

A "must see" for car buffs or racing-car enthusiasts. Inside this beautifully landscaped museum, there are at least 75 brightly polished cars, including the first Ferrari and the late Hollywood star Gary Cooper's sleek Duesenberg SSJ. Each automobile is handsomely displayed. The collection is very highly rated by major newspapers and racing-car champions. Even if you don't consider yourself an automobile aficionado, it's fun to see the antique cars and the plush Rolls-Royces.

Admission: $6 adults, $3 children 3–13.

Open: May–Nov, Tues–Sat 10am–5pm, Sun 1–5pm; Dec–Apr, Tues–Sat 10am–5pm.

COLLIER COUNTY MUSEUM, in the County Government Center, Airport Rd. and U.S. 41. Tel. 774-8476.

Insight into 10,000 years of Collier County history is offered (Collier is the largest of Florida's 67 counties). Artifacts and photos recount the major happenings from Calusa settlements to Millionaires' Row. On the two-acre grounds, an antique steam locomotive is on display as well as a re-created Seminole village. In March and November (check on the exact dates), Native American festivities take place on the museum grounds.

Admission: Free.

Open: Mon–Fri 9am–5pm, Sat 10am–4pm.

PALM COTTAGE, 137 12th Ave. S. Tel. 261-8164.

Built in 1895 as the winter residence of a Kentucky newspaper editor, this gracious home was the scene of many gala social functions through the years. In 1946 Palm Cottage was purchased by socialites Laurance and Alexandra Brown, who would raise a cocktail flag to announce another fabulous party, which might include such Hollywood stars as Gary Cooper and Robert Montgomery. Today Palm Cottage is headquarters of the Collier County Historical Society. Authentic furniture, paintings, photographs, and memorabilia adorn the 12 rooms. The $100,000 museum also houses a wildlife collection and a replica of a pioneer fishing boat. Palm Cottage is located in Naples's oldest residential area.

Open: Late autumn to late spring, tours conducted Mon–Fri 2–4pm; off-season, by appointment only. Call ahead for the current schedule and rates.

TED SMALLWOOD'S STORE, Chokoloskee Island. Tel. 695-2989.

Dating back to the rough pioneering days, this is one of southwestern Florida's oldest buildings, which has been converted to a museum that includes a gift shop. The rustic, historic store was also a Native American trading post. Usually every March, a colorful Seminole Indian Day is celebrated in the store.

If you read best-selling author Peter Matthiessen's recent book *Killing Mr. Watson,* you know that Ed Watson, the reputed killer of the notorious female outlaw Belle Star, was gunned down near the Smallwood dock. Since Watson's reputation was very unsavory, no one grieved that he met his demise in a hail of bullets. The fascinating novel comes to life when you visit Smallwood's.

Open: Call for information. **Directions:** Take U.S. 41 south, exit at Fla. 29; it's just south of Everglades City.

NATURE RESERVES

BIG CYPRESS NATIONAL PRESERVE. Tel. 695-4111 or 695-2000.

The preserve, together with the surrounding Big Cypress Swamp, encompasses more than 2,000 square miles. The preserve is a sanctuary for alligators, deer, the Florida panther, and a great variety of birds. The area helps provide water for the Everglades. During the Seminole Wars, many of the Seminoles escaped to the swamp to avoid forced emigration to Oklahoma. Their descendants still live in Big Cypress Seminole Indian Reservation and Miccousukee Indian Village.

Two highways pass through the swamp: I-75 reaches the swamp about 20 miles east of Naples. The Visitor Information Center is on U.S. 41, about 60 miles east of Naples. The center shows a short descriptive film of Big Cypress, and is open Thursday through Sunday from 9am to 4:30pm; closed holidays. Since schedules change, it's a good idea to call ahead.

COLLIER SEMINOLE PARK, Tamiami Trail (U.S. 41). Tel. 394-3397.

Adjoining Big Cypress, 15 miles east of Naples, the more than 6,000 acres offer fishing, boating, picnicking, camping, canoeing, and nature observing along special trails. Many species of birds inhabit this mangrove jungle. And for those interested in road engineering, a dredge used to build the Tamiami Trail is exhibited. The Interpretive Center has complete information about the park.

Admission: $3.25 per car.

THE CONSERVANCY BRIGGS NATURE CENTER, Shell Island Rd. off Fla. 951. Tel. 775-8569.

Along the half-mile length of boardwalk, visitors observe a great variety of birds in their natural habitat, which is actually the Rookery Bay National Estuarine Research Reserve. Arrangements may be made for canoe and boat tours. The center is south of Naples, halfway to Marco Island.

Admission: $2 adults, $1 children 6–15.

Open: Tues–Sat, but check schedule in advance.

THE CONSERVANCY NATURE CENTER, Goodlette Rd. (on 14th Ave. N.). Tel. 262-0304.

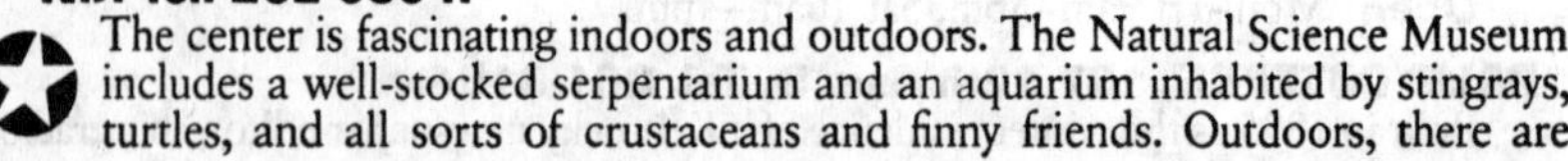

The center is fascinating indoors and outdoors. The Natural Science Museum includes a well-stocked serpentarium and an aquarium inhabited by stingrays, turtles, and all sorts of crustaceans and finny friends. Outdoors, there are nature trails, a butterfly atrium, and an aviary with bald eagles and other winged creatures. Free 45-minute boat rides are offered to observe lagoon wildlife. It's very obvious that the staff is completely dedicated to Mother Nature. Among the unique items in the Nature Store are clothes hangers adorned by bright ceramic parrots and birds (good books are here, too).

Admission: $3 adults, $1 young adults, free for children under 6.

Open: Mon–Sat 8:30am–5pm, Sun 1–5pm.

CORKSCREW SWAMP SANCTUARY, Sanctuary Rd. Tel. 657-3771.

This 11,000-acre wilderness is maintained by the National Audubon Society. Among nature's wonders are the wood storks, which build their nests atop cypress trees hundreds of feet high; nesting takes place from November through April. Two miles of nature trails lead through the largest bald cypress forest with some of the oldest trees in the United States. A great variety of migratory birds and wading birds inhabit the swamp sanctuary, where ferns and orchids also flourish. This is also "home sweet home" for alligators. It's a good idea to take along binoculars to get a real good look at the wildlife lurking here. The sanctuary is northeast of Naples, 15 miles east from I-75 via County Rte. 846.

Admission: $5 adults, $4 students, $2.50 children 6–12, free for children under 6.

Open: Daily 9am–5pm.

COOL FOR KIDS

JUNGLE LARRY'S ZOOLOGICAL PARK & CARIBBEAN GARDENS, 1590 Goodlette Rd. Tel. 262-4053.

A family favorite for many years, Jungle Larry's features guided tram tours that meander around the 52-acre preserve to observe animals and birds in a junglelike habitat. The "safari" also includes the spectacular gardens and boat tour. Visitors are captivated by the Wild Animal Show, the Tropical Bird Circus, and the Animal Training Center. Don't miss tiger-feeding time, usually at 2pm. Especially for kids, the Petting Farm, elephant rides, and a playground provide fun time. Should you want to take along a lunch, picnic facilities are on the premises, or you can buy food at the park.

Admission: $10.95 adults, $6.95 children 3–15. Inquire about special discounts.

Open: Daily 9:30am–5:30pm (last admission at 4pm). **Closed:** Thanksgiving and Christmas Days.

TEDDY BEAR MUSEUM, 2511 Pine Ridge Rd. Tel. 598-2711.

This unusual museum, featuring at least 2,000 stuffed teddy bears, is not the least bit "stuffy." Teddy bears are cleverly displayed (many are animated) descending from the rafters in hot-air balloons, attending a business board meeting, sipping afternoon tea, celebrating a wedding, hibernating in a winter den. One historic exhibit recounts the story of why the teddy bear was named for President "Teddy" Roosevelt. A vast display shows off teddy bears from almost everywhere in the world and includes a collection of antique bears. Adults enjoy the museum just as much as the kids. The outdoor sculpture of bears in a tree is outstanding. In the adjoining gift shop, you can buy a teddy bear to call your own, or all sorts of teddy-bear-related souvenirs and books.

Admission: $4.50 adults, $2.50 senior citizens and children 13–19, $1.50 children 3–12, free for children under 3.

Open: Wed–Sat 10am–5pm, Sun 1–5pm.

ORGANIZED TOURS

BY AIRBOAT Everglades City Flyer Airboat Tours, 911 10th St. S. (tel. 263-0098, or 455-9832 evenings), is the only airboat taking off from Naples (most depart from in and around Everglades City, about a 35-mile drive south). Captain Charlie Beauchamp is at the helm and also gives the interesting commentary on the two-hour wildlife trips. The itinerary includes the area between Naples, Marco Island, and the upper Ten Thousand Islands. Passengers always sight plenty of birds when the airboat goes by the Rookery, and dolphins frolic in the waters. Captain Beauchamp slows down the airboat so that passengers can enjoy observing the playful dolphins, and he also slows down around Naples Bay for a good look at the mansions. Complimentary soft drinks are on board.

Tours depart three times a day (usually at 10am, 1pm, and 3:30pm) from Turner's Commercial Dock, between Tin City and the Cove Inn. Best call ahead for reservations. The cost is $20 plus tax for adults, $10 for children 5–12, and free for children under 5.

CRUISES At Old Marine Market Place, 1200 Fifth Ave. S., a variety of boating excursions await. Certainly the most unusual boat is the Polynesian-style ***Tiki Islander*** (tel. 262-7577) with thatched roof and two carved heads highlighting the stern. Among the *Tiki*'s tours are a half day for shelling on Keewaydin Island and fishing the inland waterways of the Ten Thousand Islands. A sightseeing cruise of Naples Bay highlights the mansions, the scenic finger canals, and the northern area of the Ten Thousand Islands. Call for the exact schedule and rates.

Sailing from Old Marine Market Place, at Tin City, the **Dali Charter** (tel. 262-4545) and **Buoy One Charter** (tel. 434-0441) offer deep-sea fishing trips, an afternoon sightseeing cruise, and a sunset sightseeing cruise. The 65-foot party boat and the 40-foot deluxe fishing vessel are also available for private charter, for a full or half day. Call for rates and schedules.

The **Naples Water Taxi** (tel. 774-2722) is available for charter at about $45 an hour.

Rosie, an old-fashioned paddlewheel cruise boat, departs from 1484 Fifth Ave. S. (tel. 775-6776) and features a "Good Morning" cruise ($9.95), a lunch buffet cruise ($14.95), and a sunset supper cruise ($24.95). Call for reservations.

The interesting two-hour trips offered by **Island Nature Cruises,** 25000 Tamiami Trail E. (tel. 394-3101, or toll free 800/237-4173), leave from Port of the Islands, about 32 miles south of Naples. Passengers get an insight into the amazing ecosystems of the Everglades and the Ten Thousand Islands. Plenty of wildlife can be observed, as more than 500 types of fish, manatees, and dolphins inhabit the waters around the islands, and more than 300 species of birds live in the Everglades. Tours usually depart daily at 9:30am and 12:45pm, December to April; the schedule changes for tours May through November, so call ahead. The charge is $12 for adults, $10 for seniors over 55, and $6 for children 2–12.

Holly Sherwin, an experienced canoeist and licensed U.S. Coast Guard captain, is your guide for **Up the Creek Boat & Canoe Excursions,** 672 Hickory Rd. (tel. 261-7748). A dozen boating excursions (canoe or power) take you through Everglades National Park, Rookery Bay, Clam Pass, Mound Key, the Ten Thousand Islands, and other natural wonders in southwestern Florida. Holly is a confidante of Mother Nature and she will tell you all about the flora and fauna observed on these fascinating trips. Specialized tours can also be arranged. Half-day sojourns cost $150 per trip; full-day trips $240. The boats accommodate six people. Drinks are included on all tours, and arrangements can be made for meals at an extra fee. Don't forget to take along wading shoes. Reservations are necessary, of course.

SPECIAL EVENTS

Thanks to all the publicity on national television, the best-known annual event is the **Swamp Buggy Races** (tel. 774-2701 for information), held in March and October on the 129-acre Swamp Buggy/Florida Sports Park. Races culminate in a muddy area six feet deep, where the mud-drenched winner gets to escort the newly crowned Swamp Buggy Queen.

Naples Tropicool (tel. 262-6141), scheduled for the first two weeks in May, is a fun fiesta of art shows, concerts, and a variety of special events. **July 4th** celebrations illuminate the skies with fireworks displays. Around mid-March and also mid-November **Seminole Indian Days** are celebrated at the Collier County Museum (tel. 774-8476). During the Christmas season, there's a brilliant **Festival of Lights** in the 3rd Street area (tel. 649-6707) and a **Fifth Avenue Christmas Walk** (tel. 262-4177).

Almost every month, a variety of events are scheduled. For details, contact the **Naples Area Chamber of Commerce** (tel. 813/262-6141; fax 813/262-8374).

SPORTS & RECREATION

BOATING Sailboats, Hobie Cats, and windsurfers can be rented from the **Naples Beach Hotel and Golf Club,** 851 Gulf Shore Blvd. N. (tel. 261-2222). Water-sports lessons are arranged by appointment.

DIVING The **Under Seas Dive Academy,** 4125 Tamiami Trail E. (tel. 774-1234), sells and rents water-sports equipment and features diver certification classes in the indoor heated pool.

GOLF Naples boasts at least 35 golf courses, including private, semiprivate, and public. The following list represents most of the public courses.

The **Lely Flamingo Island Club,** 8002 Lely Resort Blvd. (tel. 793-2223), opens at 7:30am. The exciting 18-hole course, designed by Robert Trent, charges $80 in season for greens fees (including cart) and $35 off-season.

The **Marco Shores Golf & Country Club,** 1450 Mainsail Dr. (tel. 394-2581), features an 18-hole course designed by Devlin and Von Hagge. You can play Tuesday through Friday from 8am to 5pm and on Saturday and Sunday from 7am to 5pm. During high season it's necessary to call 48 hours in advance for reservations.

The **Naples Beach Hotel and Golf Club,** 851 Gulf Shore Blvd. N. (tel. 261-2222), is well known for the 18-hole championship course, a true challenge. Orchids flourish along the fairways. Greens fees (including cart) range from $70 in high season to $30 off-season.

The **Naples Shore Country Club,** 18100 Royal Tree Pkwy. (tel. 774-5931), has an 18-hole course with water play included in 17 of the holes.

In nearby Bonita Springs, the **Pelican Nest Golf Club,** 4450 Bay Creek Dr. SW (tel. 947-4600), features three 9-hole Tom Fazio–designed courses, open from 7:30am to 7pm. Greens fees (including cart) range from $90 in high season to $35 in July. At Pelican, collared shirts are required, and slacks or walking shorts but no blue jeans.

The **Quality Inn Golf & Country Club,** 4100 Golden Gate Pkwy. (tel. 455-1010), has an interesting 18-hole championship course with greens fees in the $50 range.

The 18-hole course at the **Riviera Golf Club,** 52 Marseille Dr. (tel. 774-1081), requires advance reservations during the high season.

MINIATURE GOLF **Celebrity Golf,** 9999 Tamiami Trail E. (tel. 774-7715), features two 18-hole courses that are truly a challenge, with the kind of water hazards and sand traps that would be encountered on a full-size fairway. Batting cages are also offered here. Open daily from 10am to midnight.

Coral Cay Adventure Golf, 2205 Tamiami Trail E. (tel. 793-4999), has two 18-hole miniature courses sprawling among waterfalls, streams, reefs, and caves. It's fun for the entire family.

TENNIS Open to the public, the **Cambier Park Tennis Courts,** 755 Eighth Ave. S. (tel. 434-4694), offers 14 courts (nine are hard-surface, five Har-Tru clay), 11 illuminated for night play. A USPTA pro gives lessons and conducts tennis clinics. It costs about $5 to play here. Open in high season Monday through Friday from 8am to 10pm, on Saturday to 5pm, and on Sunday until 4pm; summer hours are 8am to 10pm Monday through Friday, to 5pm on Saturday, and until 1pm on Sunday. Walk-on play is allowed.

Although a private club, arrangements can be made to play at the **Forest Hills Tennis Club,** 100 Forest Hills Blvd. (tel. 774-2442). Open daily from 8am to 10pm, the facility offers seven Har-Tru outdoor courts with four lighted for night play. The contact for nonmembers is Bob Randolf—call ahead.

The **Naples Beach Hotel and Golf Club,** 851 Gulf Shore Blvd. N. (tel. 261-2222), features four Har-Tru courts open to the public. Lessons, a tennis clinic, and a pro shop are available. Call the tennis director ahead.

The **World Tennis Center,** 4800 Airport Rd. (tel. 263-1900), is actually an all-suite resort and highlights its tennis facilities. On site are 11 clay and 5 hard courts; 10 are lighted for night play. There's a full-time teaching staff plus tennis clinics. A 2,500-seat stadium is included in the tennis facility. Tennis club privileges are free for resort guests only.

WHERE TO STAY

IN NAPLES PROPER

Very Expensive

EDGEWATER BEACH HOTEL, 1901 Gulf Shore Blvd. N, Naples, FL 33940. Tel. 813/262-6511, or toll free 800/821-0196, 800/282-3766 in Florida. Fax 813/262-1243. 124 suites. A/C TV TEL **Transportation:** The hotel can arrange airport transfers.

$ **Rates:** High season, $199–$405 one-bedroom suite; $315–$495 two-bedroom suite. Apr–May, $115–$245 one-bedroom suite; $225–$325 two-bedroom suite. Special low season and package rates available. AE, CB, DC, DISC, MC, V.

Beautifully situated on the prestigious boulevard known as Millionaires' Row, the all-suite resort is bordered by a wide ribbon of white sand gulf beach. Overlooking the beach, surrounded by luxuriant flora and centered around a garden courtyard with a swimming pool, the pastel pink seven-story building is adorned with white grillwork balconies and plantation shutters. Tastefully decorated suites, enhanced by Mexican tile floors, feature a kitchen with refrigerator, microwave, coffee maker—the works.

Dining/Entertainment: For a romantic candlelit dinner, the elegant penthouse dining room, the Crystal Parrot, looks out to Gulf of Mexico vistas. One of the chef's specialties is sautéed Norwegian salmon in a whole-wheat crust, served on mushroom polenta and laced with merlot-wine sauce. In the adjoining Crystal Parrot Sunset Lounge, libations are accompanied by live piano music and a brilliant sunset. A pianist also plays in Traditions Lounge, a lobby hideaway looking out to the gulf. In the garden courtyard, the Fountain Café is delightful for breakfast (yes, there's really a splashing fountain here). Poolside, Flippers specializes in juicy burgers and tasty salads.

Services: Friendly front-desk personnel will arrange for sightseeing tours.

Facilities: Heated swimming pool and patio adjacent to the beach; water-sports equipment, deep-sea or freshwater fishing, and bike rentals available. Arrangements can be made for guests to play on nearby tennis courts and an 18-hole championship golf course.

THE REGISTRY RESORT, 475 Seagate Dr., Naples, FL 33940. Tel. 813/597-3232, or toll free 800/833-8389. Fax 813/597-3147. 420 rms and 29 suites, 50 villas. A/C TV TEL **Transportation:** Upon request, the resort can arrange airport limousine service.

$ **Rates:** $120–$315 one-bedroom unit for two people; higher for suites; $325–$365 villa for up to four people. Rates depend on season and location. Vacation packages highlight, golf, tennis, water sports, ecology, romance. AE, CB, DC, MC, V.

Scenically located on shimmering Pelican Bay and overlooking the Gulf of Mexico (a 15-minute drive from Naples Airport, 30 minutes from Fort Myers's Southwest Florida Regional Airport, less than two hours from Miami International Airport), the handsomely designed high-rise resort radiates elegance from the splendid lobby to the penthouse. Celebrities who have vacationed here include television talk-show host Larry King. The service is excellent. It's fun to take the free shuttle, via the wildlife preserve, to the three-mile-long white sand gulf beach. Or you can stroll along the boardwalk to the gulf on the same route. Many species of birds from the nearby Clam Pass Sanctuary can be sighted.

Dining/Entertainment: The resort's restaurants are outstanding. Café Chablis is open for breakfast, lunch, and dinner from 7am to 9pm (until 10pm on weekends).

There's a children's menu and a moderately priced "early bird" dinner served from 5 to 7pm daily. The Brass Pelican, highly acclaimed for seafood, features a Raw Bar for ordering shellfish by the piece in addition to the extensive menu. Only dinner is served, from 6 to 10pm Tuesday through Thursday, to 11pm on Friday and Saturday. The very casual poolside Palm Terrace serves snacks, burgers, sandwiches, salads, and tropical drinks daily from 11am to late afternoon. Lafite, the swanky award-winning gourmet restaurant, merits a special listing (see "Where to Dine," below). If you like sweets, you'll love Scoops Ice Cream Parlour and Pâtisserie, open from 8am to 9pm daily; it has real Italian capuccino, too.

The nightclub, Garrett's, spotlights dancing on Friday and Saturday from 9pm to 2am. A pianist performs nightly in the scintillating Lobby Lounge—and if couples happen to be inspired to get up and dance to a particularly romantic song, it's permissible.

Services: At the lobby concierge desk, arrangements can be made for golf, water sports, sightseeing, nature walks, car rental, airport limousine, or for any assistance. In the lobby, complimentary coffee is served from 6:30 to 8am. Room service is offered around the clock. A babysitting service is available, and supervised programs for kids 5–12 at reasonable rates are in the Kid's Clubhouse (also a Kid's Night Out).

Facilities: Three heated swimming pools, whirlpools and a landscaped pool-patio area provide relaxation and fun. Miles of beach are accessible by boardwalk across the ecology-protected mangrove area (the Registry's "backyard"). Rentals are available for bicycles, sailboats, catamarans, aquabikes and water-sports equipment. Golf can be arranged at the nearby Pelican's Nest; a putting green is on the resort grounds. Horseshoes, putting, and shuffleboard equipment are available at the Tennis Pro Shop. The Tennis Center includes 15 courts, (5 are lighted). In the immense window-walled Health Club, high-tech workout equipment is featured, as well as a sauna, massages, facials, sea-algae body treatments, and much more; fresh fruits and juices are complimentary. There's a $5-per-day fee for use of the Health Club facility, which is open from Monday through Friday 6:30am to 8pm, on Saturday from 8am to 6pm, and on Sunday from 8am to 4pm.

Expensive

NAPLES BEACH HOTEL AND GOLF CLUB, 851 Gulf Shore Blvd., Naples, FL 33940. Tel. 813/261-2222, or toll free 800/237-7600, 800/282-7601 in Florida. Fax 813/261-7380. 239 rms, 34 efficiencies, 42 suites. A/C TV TEL

$ **Rates:** Mid-Dec to May, $150–$365 double. Apr to mid-Dec, usually 50% less. Discount packages available. AE, CB, DC, DISC, MC, V.

A family-oriented, casual resort, rambling along an outstanding white sand gulf beach and landscaped with tropical gardens, the hotel has been owned and managed by the Watkins family since 1946. Third-generation Michael Watkins maintains the traditional hospitality, dating back to the original turn-of-the-century Naples Hotel. New buildings and renovations have been planned carefully to preserve the hotel's history. Pleasantly decorated in Florida style, accommodations are not posh but comfortable. Private balconies look out to the gardens and the gulf. The exotic orchids, gracing the hotel's floral arrangements, grow on the golf course.

Dining/Entertainment: The resort has the only restaurants and bars actually on the beach, since the hotel predates Naples's strict zoning laws. Moderately priced dinners with candlelight are featured in the mural-decorated Everglades Dining Room, looking out to the gulf. HB's on the Gulf is casual for breakfast, lunch, and dinner. The carefree Sunset Beach Bar is popular for sandwiches, salads, snacks, tropical libations—and a glorious sunset.

On the fairway, golfers recharge in the Brassie Café and Lounge or grab a hot dog and frosty beer at the Tenth Tee Tent. Brassie's features live entertainment and dancing Tuesday through Saturday nights. Every Sunday, a good local band plays jazz and reggae from 4pm at the beach bar. From June to September, there's a free once-a-month performance of Jazz-On-The-Green by nationally known jazz and blues bands.

Services: The Naples Trolley stops at the resort on its regular route with shops and attractions along the way. During summer months and major holidays, the supervised Beach Klub for Kids features a variety of free activities.

Facilities: Olympic-size freshwater beachside pool, 18-hole par-72 championship course (complete with pro, pro shop, driving range, and putting green), tennis center (with four Har-Tru courts and a pro for expert instruction); biking, sightseeing, water sports, and deep-sea fishing can be arranged; sailboats rented on the beach.

Moderate

COVE INN RESORT AND MARINA, 1191 8th St. S., Naples, FL 33940. Tel. 813/262-7161, or toll free 800/255-4365. Fax 813/261-6905. 102 rms and efficiencies. A/C TV TEL

$ Rates: High season, $105 double; $120 efficiencies; $250 two-bedroom penthouse. Low season, $55–$65 double or efficiency; $175 two-bedroom penthouse. AE, DC, DISC, MC, V.

Especially if you're a boater, this is your kind of place, right at the scenic City Docks and Cove Marina. In fact, the marina offers rental and charter discounts to Cove Inn Resort guests. Each attractive room is decorated differently and looks out to the bay panorama. As for restaurants, the Cove Inn Coffee Shoppe, located in the lobby, has been rated best for home-style and unusual breakfasts seven years in a row (great pancakes!) and lunch is also served; the coffee shop is open from 7am until 1:30pm. The popular Dock Restaurant and the well-known Chart House, serving lunch and dinner, are located at either end of the Cove Inn. A heated swimming pool and lively outdoor Chickee Bar are on the premises. When you want to relax on the beach or do some shopping, you're only a few minutes' drive away.

PARK SHORE RESORT, 600 Neapolitan Way, Naples, FL 33940. Tel. 813/263-2222, or toll free 800/548-2077. Fax 813/263-0496. 156 suites. A/C TV TEL

$ Rates: Nov–Apr, $155–$180 suite. May–Oct, up to 50% less. AE, MC, V.

Overlooking a lagoon and landscaped gardens, the attractive, balconied one- and two-bedroom suites have living and dining rooms, offering much more space than just a hotel room. There's a choice of cooking in the fully equipped kitchen, grilling in the outdoor barbecue area, or dining in the resort's Island Club restaurant (open from 11am to 11pm)—and there are plenty of restaurants nearby. For fun and games, the resort offers a heated pool, whirlpool, four tennis courts, four racquetball courts, volleyball, basketball, and shuffleboard.

QUALITY INN GOLF & COUNTRY CLUB, 4100 Golden Gate Pkwy. Naples, FL 33999. Tel. 813/455-1010, or toll free 800/4-CHOICE. Fax 813/455-4038. 153 rms, efficiencies, and suites. A/C TV TEL

$ Rates: High season, $85–$120 room or efficiency for two. Low season, $50–$85 room or efficiency for two. Year-round, $96–$200 suite for up to eight people. Weekly and monthly rates, and vacation packages with meals, available. AE, DC, DISC, MC, V.

A place right on the golf course—what could be more convenient for the avid golfer? In addition to the 18-hole championship course, there's a pro shop, rental equipment, golf lessons, and a driving range. For tennis buffs, there are two courts. Resort amenities also include a heated swimming pool and poolside bar designed like a Seminole chickee. The restaurant and lounge are open until 10pm (for early-risers, breakfast is served at 7am).

WORLD TENNIS CENTER & RESORT, 4800 Airport-Pulling Rd., Naples, FL 33942. Tel. 813/263-1900, or toll free 800/292-6663. Fax 813/649-7055. 148 two-bedroom/two-bath apts. A/C TV TEL

$ Rates: High season, $150 apt for up to four people. Low-season, $75–$125 apt for up to four people. Weekly and monthly rates available. MC, V.

Although you really don't have to be a tennis buff to stay at the resort, tennis is definitely in the limelight here. Club privileges are extended to all resort guests.

Facilities include 16 tennis courts (11 clay, 5 hard-surface, 10 lighted for night play), a USPTA staff offering instruction, a full-service pro shop, and a tennis activities calendar for all age and ability levels. There's a heated swimming pool and La Petit Café and Bar poolside. Whirlpool spas and Jacuzzis are located indoors. If you like to fish, bass-stocked fishing lakes are on the premises.

The comfortable accommodations, with complete kitchen, living room, dining room, and washer/dryer, are in Mediterranean-style white stucco buildings, most with balconies, surrounded by 82 tropically landscaped acres. Beaches, shops, and restaurants are within a five-mile drive.

AT VANDERBILT BEACH

Very Expensive

RITZ-CARLTON NAPLES, 280 Vanderbilt Beach Rd., Naples, FL 33963. Tel. 813/598-3300, or toll free 800/241-3333. Fax 813/598-6690. 463 rms and suites. A/C TV TEL

$ Rates: High season, $300–$550 double; $800–$2,300 suite. Low season, $130–$350 double; $780–$2,300 suite. AE, DC, DISC, MC, V.

An opulent vacation retreat, the grandiose 14-story hotel is a favorite of affluent foreign visitors. Most of the rich and famous book suites on the Ritz-Carlton Club floor, where the amenities are very special. A well-known New York newspaper columnist has stayed at the resort "to get away from it all." The lobby is high luxe, from the imported marble floor with Oriental rugs to the sparkling Waterford crystal chandelier—a royal ambience for the afternoon British-style tea served daily. The splendid collection of 18th- and 19th-century art adorning the walls requires a special curator. All guest rooms look out to the gulf panorama; most have balconies. Four-poster beds with expensive quilted spreads add a traditional touch, in keeping with the Ritz reputation for elegance. Guests let down their hair to stroll along the mangrove-surrounded boardwalk to the miles of gulf beach.

Dining/Entertainment: The casual Beach Pavilion on the boardwalk is relaxing for breakfast, snacks, and refreshments. For dinner, you can "put on the ritz" in the wood-paneled Grill Room, reminiscent of a British private club, or the Dining Room, notable for the superbly prepared gourmet specialties. Be prepared to spend at least $160 for dinner for two (including wine) in the Dining Room, but worth it for fine food, the best wines, and the epitome of service. Both the Grill Room and Dining Room are open from 6 to 10pm nightly. Usually, Sunday brunch is served in the Dining Room from 11am to 2:30pm. In high season, a live band plays for dancing nightly in the Club.

Services: Ritz-Carlton hotels pride themselves on their services so there's no problem with arrangements for water sports, sightseeing, car rental, bikes, or whatever your vacation needs. A supervised children's program is offered and a social program for adults who wish to participate. Room service is around the clock.

Facilities: Uniquely shaped, heated swimming pool and patio, six tennis courts (lighted for night play), fitness center (with sauna and massages); adjoining three miles of white sand beach (with rentals available for catamarans, windsurfers, and water-sports equipment); golf privileges arranged at a nearby 18-hole championship golf course.

Moderate

LA PLAYA BEACH & RACQUET INN, 9891 Gulf Shore Dr., Naples, FL 33963. Tel. 813/597-3123, or toll free 800/237-6883, 800/282-4423 in Florida. Fax 813/597-6278. 178 rms, efficiences, and suites. A/C TV TEL

$ Rates: High season, $120–$325 for two people. Low season, $78–$185 for two people. AE, MC, V.

Sweeping views of the bay or gulf can be admired from every room in this attractive beachfront resort. Sliding glass doors in all the guest rooms lead to private balconies.

Pleasantly decorated in a variety of color schemes, accommodations are very spacious. There's plenty of action on the premises—six tennis courts, a volleyball court, shuffleboard, and two heated swimming pools. Gulfside Café La Plaza, with a dining patio and bar, is especially delightful at dinner, when candlelight lends a romantic glow. The café, also open for breakfast and lunch (from 7:30am to 10pm), features continental cuisine. From January to May, a special restaurant named La Casba serves French-style specialties. Open year-round, La Tasca offers casual dining, a deli-style take-out and bar. Shoppers will like the resort's beachwear boutique.

VANDERBILT INN ON THE GULF, 11000 Gulf Shore Dr. N., Naples, FL 33963. Tel. 813/597-3151, or toll free 800/643-8654. 147 rms, 16 beachfront efficiences. A/C TV TEL

$ Rates: High season, $135–$240 for two people. Low season, $80–$140 for two people. AE, DC, DISC, MC, V.

Cheerful tropical decor in the accommodations and public rooms sets the tempo for a casual, fun vacation. In addition to the resort's lengthy stretch of wide white sand gulf beach, there's more beach at the neighboring 166-acre Del-Nor Wiggins State Recreation Area, offering shelling and turtle-watching in season, and fishing, boating, and strolling along the boardwalk nature trail. Of course, rental boats and rental water-sports equipment are available on the resort's beach. Sun worshippers surround the heated, free-form swimming pool; kids love to splash in the wading pool. The beachside Chickee Bar and Restaurant is the place for an alfresco lunch or dinner, or refreshing drinks. Sunset-watchers flock to the Chickee for the Sunset Happy Hour, and the scene is exceptionally lively when entertainment is featured here on weekend afternoons until about 9pm. In the Seabreeze Lounge, popular for lunch, a live band plays for dancing on Thursday, Friday, and Saturday from 9pm to midnight. The Jasmine Court serves breakfast from 7 to 11:30am and romantic candlelight dinner from 5 to 10pm. There's a good wine list, too. Many European vacationers have discovered the resort.

Budget

DAYS INN, 1925 Davis Blvd., Naples, FL 33942. Tel. 813/774-3117, or toll free 800/272-0106. Fax 813/775-5333. 158 rms and suites. A/C TV TEL

$ Rates (including continental breakfast): High season, $85–$110 for two people. Low season, $70–$95 for two people. Low season (Apr 29–Dec 18), $40–$60 for two people. AE, DC, DISC, MC, V.

This is certainly not your everyday Days Inn. The attractive building is surrounded by landscaped gardens and the pool area is outstanding, complete with whirlpool. For kids, the playground is fun. Barbecue grills are supplied in the pleasant picnic area. Among the amenities are a free refrigerator and personal safe in the room, and free HBO and Disney television channels. A moderately priced restaurant is also on the premises. The location is convenient to the beach (about a five-minute drive), shopping malls, and golf courses. Even the wallet-friendly accommodations in Naples have a touch of class.

HAMPTON INN, 3210 Tamiami Trail N., Naples, FL 33940. Tel. 813/261-8000, or toll free 800/732-4667. Fax 813/261-7802. 93 rms, 14 deluxe rms. A/C TV TEL

$ Rates (including continental breakfast): High season, $85–$95 double; $125 deluxe double. Low season, $62–$80 double; $99–$109 deluxe double. AE, DC, DISC, MC, V.

Friendly hospitality prevails, especially every morning when a complimentary continental breakfast is served. Another plus factor is that there's no charge for local calls or for HBO. Deluxe rooms have king-size beds, a pull-out sofa in the living room, and a kitchen with a microwave and a refrigerator. For keeping in trim, a heated swimming pool and exercise center are on the premises. There's no restaurant or lounge, but the hotel is only a hop, skip, and a jump from the huge Coastland Mall shopping-restaurant complex, and it's also close to the great shops and eateries on Fifth Avenue. As for swimming and water sports, Naples Beach is less than two miles away and Vanderbilt Beach less than three miles. This attractive hotel is a real bargain.

BED & BREAKFAST

INN BY THE SEA, 287 11th Ave. S., Naples, FL 33940. Tel. 813/649-4124. 6 rms. A/C TV TEL

$ Rates (including continental breakfast): Dec 21 to mid-May, $90–$130 double. Mid-May to Dec 20, $55–$95 double. MC, V.

A pleasant stroll to the beach, this charming inn has delightfully furnished bedrooms with brass headboard beds covered with old-fashioned floral spreads. The art on the walls is by local artists. Listed in the National Register of Historic Places, the inn retains the original pine floors. Comfy wicker furniture emphasizes the Old Florida ambience. The delicious breakfast includes fresh orange juice, fruit, just-baked muffins and breads, cereals, and a nice variety of imported coffees and teas. If you need a bike or water-sports equipment, just let your hosts know and everything will be arranged.

WHERE TO DINE

VERY EXPENSIVE

LAFITE, in The Registry Resort, 475 Seagate Dr. Tel. 597-3232.

Cuisine: CONTINENTAL/REGIONAL AMERICAN. **Reservations:** Required.

$ Prices: Appetizers $7.75–$13.50; main courses $22–$35. AE, DC, MC, V.

Open: Dinner only, Mon–Thurs 6–10pm, Fri–Sat 6–10pm.

In this magnificent dining room, the superbly prepared food is on the level of France's finest restaurants. Even restaurant critics become ecstatic—Lafite is the recipient of several distinguished dining awards. For starters, the lobster bisque garnished with truffle is considered one of the best anywhere. Or your prelude might be broiled quail breast with pancetta, or sautéed goose liver in Calvados. Innovative main dishes include Parma ham–wrapped grilled sea scallops; rack of lamb with Boursin crust and minted apple chutney; ahi tuna loin in black-and-white sesame-seed crust; poached salmon with Blue Point oyster dressing. And there's more—venison chops, veal tenderloin, crisply roasted duckling, and steamed Maine lobster. For every dish, the presentation is exceptionally artistic. The wine list is very select and the maître d' and sommelier offer expert assistance (for years, the maître d' presided over the famous Plaza Hotel's restaurant in New York). Sublime desserts are presented on the trolley. Service is excellent without pretense. In this super-sophisticated ambience, men are required to wear jackets.

SIGN OF THE VINE, 980 Solana Rd. Tel. 261-6745.

Cuisine: INTERNATIONAL. **Reservations:** Required.

$ Prices: Appetizers $7–$10; main courses $25–$38. AE.

Open: Oct 16–May 3, dinner only, Mon–Sat 6–10pm. Aug 1–Oct 15, dinner only, Fri–Sat 6–10pm. **Closed:** May 4–July.

Ever since owners-chefs Nancy and John Christiansen opened the Sign of the Vine in this gracious, old-fashioned house in 1985, their gourmet restaurant has been a great success. Flickering candlelight, a real wood-burning fireplace, nostalgic fresh-flower bouquets, antique dinnerware, and hand-lettered menus presented in a silver picture frame contribute to the very romantic ambience. If you prefer, dinner is also served on the pretty porch, overlooking the garden. Dinner is leisurely, as though you're dining in a friend's lovely home. Appetizers are indeed sublime—lobster and crab springroll, tempura clams and mussels (battered and fried in the shell), and pasta with duck sausage and Brie, just to mention a few. With an authentic Bellini cocktail, who could ask for anything more?

But the main dish is yet to come, with complimentary selections from the relish cart, home-baked French bread, special salad, a fresh-fruit sorbet, and a hot popover with tangerine butter. Among the menu highlights are Jack's creation of lobster chunks with mushrooms and artichokes in a sassy Pernod-cream sauce accompanied by vegetable baklava. Another favorite is Tuscan scaloppine of veal with white beans and polenta. Should you prefer a light main dish, the grilled fresh Florida pompano is delicious. Nancy likes to make grandmother-style desserts. Her pies, homemade ice creams, baked fruit compotes, and the warm bread pudding with a whisky/brown-sugar sauce are superb. Although the wine list is small, the choice of domestic and imported wines would please any connoisseur. Of course, the Sign of the Vine is listed among Florida's best restaurants.

EXPENSIVE

CHARDONNAY, 2332 N. Tamiami Trail. Tel. 261-1744.

Cuisine: FRENCH. **Reservations:** Recommended.

$ **Prices:** Appetizers $5.75–$15.50; main courses $15.50–$25.25. AE, MC, V.

Open: Mid-Dec to Apr, dinner only, 5:30–10pm. May to mid-Dec, dinner only, Mon–Sat 5:30–10pm.

"Tres chic" describes the glass-enclosed dining pavilion, where the table linens are mauve and the dinnerware is Villeroy & Boch. The ambience is definitely romantic. One of the favorite appetizers is pâté de canard aux pistaches (duck pâté studded with pistachio nuts). For the main dish, delicious choices include fricassée de homard St-Jacques au safran (lobster-and-scallop ragoût laced with saffron sauce), poulet chardonnay (breast of chicken sauced with chardonnay wine), and côte de veau des gourmets (sautéed veal chop with mushrooms). An outstanding green salad is complimentary. Wines may be ordered by the glass or bottle from the fine selection. Who could resist the individual baked-to-order luscious soufflés for dessert? No wonder that Chardonnay has received so many restaurant awards through the years.

CHEF'S GARDEN/TRUFFLES, 1300 3rd St. S. Tel. 262-5500.

Cuisine: AMERICAN/INTERNATIONAL. **Reservations:** Required at Chef's Garden.

$ **Prices:** Main courses $16.95–$27 at Chef's Garden, $4.95–$20 at Truffle's. AE, CB, DC, DISC, MC, V.

Open: Chef's Garden, lunch Mon–Sat 11:30am–2:30pm; dinner daily 6–10pm. Truffles, daily 11am–11pm; brunch Sun 11am–2pm. **Closed:** Lunch at the Chef's Garden June–Sept.

Located on the first level, the Chef's Garden looks out to the screened tropical garden patio. It's relaxing to sip before-dinner drinks by candlelight in the garden (or to dine here). The dining room indoors is romantic, with soft lights, tropical foliage, and sparkling table settings. The gourmet clientele frequenting the award-winning restaurant are fashionably dressed, befitting the refined ambience. An award winner for over 20 years, the Chef's Garden is rated as one of Naples's very best restaurants. Among the intriguing dinner selections is a mixed grill of large shrimp and andouille sausage accompanied by ratatouille risotto with sun-dried tomato-basil butter. The restaurant has also won many awards for its fine wine list. For lunch, the menu lists hearty soups, salads, sandwiches, and chef's specialties. Live entertainment, especially jazz-in-the-garden, is scheduled very often.

Upstairs, casual Truffles serves delicious pastas, a grand variety of sandwiches, interesting salads, light main dishes, and extraordinary desserts. All menu items are available for take-out at Truffles.

This outstanding restaurant duo is part of Cuisine Management's galaxy of culinary superstars.

ST. GEORGE AND THE DRAGON, 936 Fifth Ave. Tel. 262-6546.

Cuisine: BEEF/SEAFOOD. **Reservations:** Not accepted.

$ **Prices:** Main courses $11–$32. AE, DC, MC, V.

Open: Lunch Mon–Sat 11am–4pm; dinner Mon–Sat 4:30–11pm. **Closed:** Christmas Day.

A favorite since 1969, the restaurant's club atmosphere is heightened by hand-carved wood beams on the vaulted ceiling. The collection of marine antiques is outstanding. Lanterns provide the dim lighting, but remember that St. George and the dragon existed before electricity. Just about everybody orders the famous conch chowder to begin lunch or dinner. The restaurant also excels in succulent roast prime rib of beef; thick, juicy steaks; grilled filet of locally caught fish; and other seafood dishes. Unusual salads appeal to the lunch bunch. In the dining room, jackets are required at dinner for the men. However, there's no need for a jacket when dining casually in the cocktail lounge (but no shorts, please, after 4pm). Because the cocktail lounge is such a friendly place, no one complains when it's necessary to wait here for a table in the dining room.

MODERATE

BAYSIDE, A SEAFOOD GRILL AND BAR, 4270 Gulfshore Blvd. N. Tel. 649-5552.

Cuisine: CONTINENTAL. **Reservations:** Required upstairs only.

$ **Prices:** Main courses $3.95–$11.50 downstairs, $13.50–$25 upstairs. AE, DC, MC, V.

Open: Downstairs, Jan 1–May 1, daily 11am–11pm; May 2–Dec, daily 2–11pm. Upstairs, lunch daily 11am–2:30pm; dinner daily 5:30–10pm.

Looking out to the scenic bay, this interesting, two-level restaurant in the Village on Venetian Bay features casual, moderately priced dining downstairs and more formal, expensive dining upstairs (the water views are especially spectacular here). Downstairs the menu is lighter, offering such international specialties as quesadilla with spiced chicken and guacamole, angel-hair pasta with shrimp and vegetables, and Cuban black beans with chorizo. Soups, salads, sandwiches, "finger foods," and pizza are featured, too. On the second level upstairs, the gourmet menu highlights are Bayside bouillabaisse, oak-grilled chicken breast, oak-grilled strip steak with porcini-mushroom butter, sautéed calves' liver with pancetta and glazed onions, grilled jumbo sea scallops, and more. Desserts are deliciously different, such as chocolate polenta cake laced with white-chocolate sauce, apricot baklava topped by cinnamon ice cream, and cappuccino ricotta cheesecake in a hazelnut crust. Nightly entertainment is usually presented in the lively downstairs bar. Bayside is a Cuisine Management restaurant, well known for classy ambience and very creative chefs.

VILLA PESCATORE/PLUM'S CAFE, 8920 Tamiami Trail N. Tel. 597-8119.

Cuisine: NORTHERN ITALIAN/AMERICAN. **Reservations:** Recommended for Villa Pescatore; not accepted at Plum's.

$ **Prices:** Main courses $15.95–$20.95 at Villa Pescatore, $4.50–$15.95 at Plum's Café. AE, CB, DC, DISC, MC, V.

Open: Villa Pescatore, dinner only, daily 6–10pm. Plum's Café, Mon–Sat 11am–11pm, Sun 5–11pm.

Sharing the same address, these two highly acclaimed restaurants offer a choice of elegant dining in Villa Pescatore or dining lightly and casually in the Plum Café. For lunch especially, the sandwiches, salads, and pastas are favorites in Plum's (try the chicken carbonara for something different). All menu items in Plum's are available for take-out or delivery.

The recipient of dining awards, Villa Pescatore is notable for Umbrian specialties such as spiedini mixti (grilled chunks of lamb, Italian sausage, pork, and chicken on a skewer served with balsamic-vinegar glaze). One of the most delicious appetizers is baked cherrystone clams putanesca. Salads are a meal in themselves, such as the panzanella Umbria, a crusty bread salad with sliced vegetables, plum tomatoes, and raddichio in a basil vinaigrette. The pastas and risottos are outstanding. Grilled fish and grilled meats are also on the menu, plus a pizza margherita. Villa Pescatore is also noted for its extensive wine list. Both restaurants belong to prestigious Cuisine Management, so now you know to "save room" for the luscious desserts.

BUDGET

THE DOCK AT CRAYTON COVE, 12th Ave. S. on Naples Bay. Tel. 263-9940.

Cuisine: SEAFOOD. **Reservations:** Not required.

$ **Prices:** Main courses $5–$15. AE, MC, V.

Open: Mon–Sat 11:30am–midnight, Sun noon–midnight.

Right on the waterfront, fringed with fishing boats and yachts, this very casual restaurant looks out to all the action on the bay—and to brilliant sunsets. The friendly owners, Phil and Vim De Pasquale, and the pleasant, nautically dressed staff contribute to the warm hospitality. You can be very sure that the fish and seafood on the menu are as fresh as can be. From hearty clam chowder served in a mug to peel-and-eat shrimp, there's a delicious variety of appetizers (hot wings for non-lovers of seafood). The selection of interesting salads includes grilled seafood Caesar salad. As for sandwiches, you can get anything from a hot dog or hamburger to a grilled tuna-steak sandwich or a grilled swordfish club sandwich. Main platters feature fish or seafood sizzling from the grill, plus barbecued baby back ribs and Jamaican-style chicken. Of course, fish and chips is on the menu. At the Raw Bar, shellfish can be selected by the piece. The De Pasquales emphasize that cholesterol-free, 93% saturated-fat-free Nutra-Fry shortening (made with canola oil) is used for frying in the kitchen. Beers, wines, and cocktails are available. At the bar, the late-night scene is especially lively and often continues to 1am on weekends.

MICHELOB'S—RIB CAPITAL OF FLORIDA, 371 Airport Rd. Tel. 643-RIBS.

Cuisine: BARBECUED SPARERIBS. **Reservations:** Not accepted.

$ Prices: $5–$15. AE, DC, MC, V.

Open: Sun–Thurs 11am–9pm, Fri–Sat 11am–10pm; brunch Sun.

The name of the restaurant says it all by this winner of national and international cook-off competitions for the best ribs and best barbecue sauces. The big specialty is the super-tender, lean baby back ribs, imported from Denmark (the hogs are tulip-fed!). Great coleslaw and baked beans, too—platters are heaped with hearty portions. There's also a children's menu. The Sunday brunch presents a true "groaning board." Cocktails are served too, in this very friendly, very casual restaurant. By the way, Michelob's has a delivery service.

SILVER SPOON CAFE, in the Waterside Shops at Pelican Bay, 5395 Tamiami Trail. Tel. 591-2123.

Cuisine: AMERICAN/ITALIAN. **Reservations:** Recommended.

$ Prices: $3–$8.70. MC, V.

Open: Sun–Thurs 11am–10pm, Fri–Sat 11am–11pm.

Situated in the swanky Waterside Shops complex, the Silver Spoon Café flaunts sophisticated black-and-white high-tech decor. Window walls look out to the action in the mall and the extravaganza of cascading waterfalls in the meandering streams. As an innovation, the piled-high sandwiches are accompanied by southwestern-style black beans, unless you prefer french fries. The tomato-dill soup has become a favorite, and the gourmet pizzas and the pasta dishes are highly recommended. Calorie-watchers will be pleased with the interesting salads, including grilled fish salad of the day. If you like old-fashioned chicken pot pie, the Silver Spoon's recipe is topped with calorie-conscious puff pastry. Desserts are a delight, from the cappuccino freeze to the peanut butter ice-cream pie. There's a kids' menu, too. Beer, wine, and champagne are served. Because the café is so popular, it's a good idea to reserve ahead.

PUBS

THE ENGLISH PUB, 2408 Linwood Ave. Tel. 774-2408.

Owned and managed by hospitable Brits, this pub recalls "merry olde England" with an authentic British menu featuring the ploughman's lunch, fish and chips, Yorkshire pudding, steak-and-kidney pie, bubble and squeak, bangers—the lot. Draft ales, lagers, and stout are dispensed. Lots of action at the dart board.

Open: Lunch daily 11am–5pm; dinner daily 5–9pm. AE, DC, MC, V.

OLD NAPLES PUB, 255 13th Ave. S. Tel. 649-8200.

More of an American-style pub, the Old Naples serves soups, sandwiches, salads, burgers, and pizza after 4:30pm. Beer and wines-by-the-glass are available. On weekends, a pianist entertains.

Open: Mon–Sat 11am–12:30am. AE, MC, V.

PATE'S PICCADILLY PUB, 625 Fifth Ave. S. Tel. 262-7521.

Here the pub atmosphere is of paneled wood walls and brass fixtures with softly glowing lights. Dining is cozy in any of the five rooms, and the cocktail lounge is romantically dim. In this upscale pub, the menu highlights prime rib, steak, and seafood, including oysters Rockefeller. One of the favorites is the Hot Brown, a roast-turkey sandwich crowned with sharp Cheddar cheese and broiled until golden brown. Pate's is especially lively during the happy hour from 4:30 to 7pm nightly.

Open: Lunch Mon–Fri 11:30am–3pm (lunch is seasonal so check ahead); dinner daily 5–10pm. AE, DC, MC, V.

DESSERTS & PICNIC FARE

Cheesecake lovers shouldn't miss the **Naples Cheesecake Company,** 8050 Trail Blvd. (tel. 598-9070). The flavors, such as Bailey's Irish cream, amaretto, and blueberry swirl, are sensational.

At the gourmet **Pelicatessen** at Waterside on Pelican Bay at the West Boulevard entrance (tel. 597-3003; fax 813/597-3087), take-out and catering services are available. The deli specializes in imported cheeses, freshly sliced meats, unusual salads, prepared entrees, desserts, imported wines and beers, fresh fruits, and much more.

SHOPPING

COASTLAND CENTER, 1900 Tamiami Trail N. Tel. 262-7100.

This enclosed air-conditioned mall boasts more than 100 stores plus food courts and eateries. Among the big department stores are Burdines, Dillards, JC Penney, and Sears. Everything is here, including fast shoe repairs at Heel Quik, near Dillard's. And if you wish you could afford jewelry from Tiffany, Winston, or Cartier, your dazzling dreams come true at Impostors, where stunning designer-jewelry look-alikes have been created at very affordable prices. Coastland is open Monday through Saturday from 10am to 9pm and on Sunday from noon to 5pm.

CORAL ISLE FACTORY SHOPS, Fla. 951 en route to Marco Island. Tel. 775-8083.

The shops offer more than 50 designer outlet stores, featuring such well-known names as Geoffrey Beene, Van Heusen, Capezio, London Fog, Polly Flinders, Anne Klein, and Adolfo, with discounted fashions for men, women, and children. For the home, the bargains are in Fieldcrest Cannon, Dansk, and Mikasa. If you want a good read, stop in at the Publishers' Warehouse. Should you shop until you're ready to drop, recharge in the Yogurt House Eatery. Coral Isle is open Monday through Saturday from 9am to 8pm and on Sunday from 10am to 6pm.

OLD MARINE MARKETPLACE AT TIN CITY, 1200 Fifth Ave. S.

Recalling the turn of the century, when Naples was a remote fishing village, the marketplace conjures up the adjectives "quaint" and "picturesque." Historic boathouses have been restored to house 50 interesting shops and restaurants. It's fun to stroll along cobbled and planked riverwalks and browse in boutiques that sell everything from avant-garde resortwear and clever T-shirts to ornate imported statuary from Bangkok. And when you want to take time out for lunch, dinner, or refreshments, the Riverwalk Fish and Ale House and Merriman's Wharf are two popular, very casual restaurants—and inexpensive, too. Both eateries stay open until midnight, attracting a lively crowd. By the way, charter boats are available at the marina.

OLD NAPLES, along 3rd St. and the avenues.

This nine-square-block historic area is in the southern section of the city between the Gulf of Mexico and Naples Bay. Beautifully landscaped with towering palm trees, gardens, fountains, and courtyards, this nostalgic district combines handsomely restored old balconied buildings with the dramatically new.

Streets and avenues are lined with more than 100 swanky shops, 11 distinguished art galleries, an array of top restaurants, and historic sights. This elegant shopping district is Naples's answer to Worth Avenue in Palm Beach and Rodeo Drive in Beverly Hills, California.

Art lovers should not miss the **Arsenault Gallery,** 385 Broad Ave. S. (tel. 263-1214), showcasing paintings of Naples by local artist Paul Arsenault. For shell collectors, there's a wonderful world of shells at the **Blue Mussel,** 478 Fifth Ave. S. (tel. 262-4814).

Along 3rd Street South, upscale shops include Johnston of Florida, the Mole Hole of Naples, Robert of Philadelphia, Bake's Precious Jewels, and the Beach House of Naples. Among the excellent restaurants are the Chef's Garden/Truffles, the Third Street Café, and the Old Naples Pub.

In the good old days, world-famous pilot Charles Lindbergh utilized Fifth Avenue as a runway when he visited his fiancee on nearby Sanibel Island.

THE VILLAGE ON VENETIAN BAY, 4200 Gulf Shore Blvd. N. Tel. 261-0030.

Along the old-world–style red-brick walkways here are more than 50 exciting shops, art galleries, and waterfront restaurants. Overlooking scenic Venetian Bay, the Mediterranean-inspired village deserves the architecture awards it has received.

Among the high-fashion women's boutiques are Chico's, Zora's, and Regina's. Men actually enjoy shopping in the Captain's Shoppe, Mark Chrisman, and Terruzzi. On and Offshore sells good-looking clothes and unusual accessories for the family. Captain Kid's Toy Treasures is a favorite with the children. Wm. Phelps Custom Jeweler is notable for artistically designed gold jewelry set with precious stones.

Top restaurants include the Bayside Seafood Grill & Bar and Maxwell's on the Bay. And there's a Ben & Jerry's Ice Cream Shop, too.

Throughout the year, festive events are presented in the Village; call the above telephone number for the current schedule and the current shopping hours.

WATERSIDE SHOPS AT PELICAN BAY, Seagate Dr. and Tamiami Trail N. Tel. 598-1605.

Naples's newest and most glamorous shopping-dining oasis has ornate Mediterranean architecture enhanced by gorgeous tropical landscaping that flaunts three cascading waterfalls and meandering streams. Among the 50 prestigious shops and boutiques are Saks Fifth Avenue, Jacobson's, Polo/Ralph Lauren, and Crabtree & Evelyn. Rick Moore Fine Art of Naples, an outstanding gallery, showcases world-class glass sculptors.

For dining, the Silver Spoon Café is notable for Italian specialties. The Pelicatessen Deli will delight gourmets and wine connoisseurs with a tempting array of delicious take-out foods, a variety of wines, a fresh produce market, a grocery department, and a sidewalk café. Waterside is open Monday through Saturday from 10am to 9pm and on Sunday from noon to 5pm (on Sunday the Pelicatessen opens at 10am, two hours ahead of the mall).

EVENING ENTERTAINMENT

THE PERFORMING ARTS

PHILHARMONIC CENTER FOR THE ARTS, 5833 Pelican Bay Blvd. Tel. 597-1900.

This impressive mega-million-dollar center is one of the most splendid performing and visual arts centers anywhere. Beautifully landscaped with gardens and fountains, the complex includes art galleries and a courtyard adorned with statuary. The center is the home of the **Naples Philharmonic.** The year-round schedule is filled with cultural events such as the Bolshoi Ballet, and concerts by celebrated artists such as soprano Kathleen Battle and violinist Itzak Perlman, and internationally known orchestras. Opera is also featured. On the lighter side, Tony Bennett and Marcel Marceau, as well as Broadway shows, are highlights. Call ahead for the schedule.

Admission: Varies with performance.

NAPLES DINNER THEATRE, 1025 Piper Blvd. Tel. 597-6031.

The theater calls itself "Broadway by the Sea." Ornately decorated in turn-of-the-century style, the theater has a four-tiered horseshoe-seating arrangement that provides good views for such shows as *Guys and Dolls, Driving Miss Daisy,* and *Steel Magnolias.* The candlelight buffet is included with the show. Also on the schedule are Big Band and Cabaret Nights. Men are required to wear jackets. Call ahead for reservations. Performances are Tuesday through Saturday, with the buffet beginning at 5:30pm and the curtain at 8:15pm.

Admission: Tickets, $30–$40, including buffet.

THE CLUB & BAR SCENE

BAYSIDE SEAFOOD GRILLE & BAR, in the Village on Venetian Bay. Tel. 649-5552.

A pianist, featured every night except Monday, plays soft music from 7 to 11pm.

THE CHEF'S GARDEN LOUNGE, 1300 3rd St. S. Tel. 262-5500.

This place in Old Naples often spotlights Jazz in the Garden on certain nights. Best to check ahead.

BRASSIE'S, at the Naples Beach Hotel, 851 Gulf Shore Blvd. N. Tel. 261-2222.

"Oldies but goodies" are played for dancing. This is one of Naples's most popular nighttime places.

CHICKEE HUT, in the Vanderbilt Inn, 11000 Gulf Shore Dr. N. Tel. 597-3151.

Sunset attracts the crowds to this bar on the beach. On weekends, there's entertainment at this beachfront rendezvous.

THE ENGLISH PUB, 2408 Linwood Ave. Tel. 774-2408.

Early evening brings the dart players to this pub where Brits and Anglophiles can recharge their batteries with steak-and-kidney pie, fish and chips, and other traditional dishes after a game. Of course, British beers are on tap. A fun place to be. Open Monday through Saturday from 11am to 9pm (closed major holidays).

GARRETT'S, in the Registry Resort, 475 Seagate Dr. Tel. 597-3232.

Night owls wing it to Garrett's, open weekends from 9pm until 2am (schedules do change so check ahead). Beamed ceilings, tropical plants, great spectrum lighting, and a 16-foot-wide video screen enhance the multilevel club, where a disc jockey presides. The variety of music keeps everybody on the dance floor, other than time out for drinks (there's a good bar here, too).

TIN CITY, 1200 5th St.

A lively place to be in the evening. Merriman's and the Riverwalk Fish and Ale House have lounges open until 10 and 11pm.

OTHER ENTERTAINMENT

Clip-clop around Old Naples aboard a **Naples horse-and-carriage evening tour** (tel. 649-1210), leaving from the City Dock. The Third Street South route is especially interesting, with prestigious art galleries, historic buildings, and splendid shops. The around-the-town ride costs about $30 for a half hour, and up to four adults can be seated. The **town and beach tour** costs approximately $40 for 45 minutes; an hour's tour costs about $50. And a romantic ride to the beach can be arranged. Since the horse-and-carriage rides are seasonal and rates change, it's best to call ahead.

AN EXCURSION TO MARCO ISLAND

Less than a half-hour drive south of Naples, Marco Island has retained a get-away-from-it-all atmosphere, despite three beach resorts (Marco Beach Hilton Resort, Marriott's Marco Island Resort and Golf Club, and the Radisson All-Suite Beach

Resort). What a culture shock these would be to the Calusas, the island's ancient residents. In addition to Calusa shell mounds (one is 40 acres wide!), archeologists have discovered many artifacts. The Calusas would have been great basketball champions, as they towered to nearly seven feet tall. Marco Island, the largest of the Ten Thousand Islands chain, abounds in history, from the Calusas to the Spanish conquistadors to the first pioneers who arrived around 1870. The village of Goodland, about a ten-minute drive east from the Marco Island hotels, is still rather remote and has a year-round population of 400.

Should you want to know more about the island, hop aboard a **Marco Island Trolley** (tel. 394-1600 for rates) at any of the 22 different stops; the tour guides are very informative. Sightseeing cruises are featured by Captain Quinn (tel. 394-2511) and cost less than $40 for 2½ hours. Information is also available at the Marriott Marco Island Resort's beach chickee hut.

For golfers, there's a new 18-hole championship golf course, a real challenge with its lagoons and cypress swamps, at Marriott's Marco Island Resort and Golf Club (tel. 394-2511).

Tiger Tail Beach State Park (outstanding beach!) offers swimming, water-sports rentals, windsurfing instruction, changing rooms, and showers. Todd's also serves snacks and refreshments (tel. 642-8414).

Shoppers will enjoy exploring the Shops of Marco, the Port of Marco Shopping Village, Pelican Plaza, and the Town Center, all with dozens of boutiques, art galleries, and casual eateries. And the Coral Isle Factory Shops, lined with boutiques (see "Shopping," above) is halfway between Naples and Marco Island.

WHERE TO DINE

In addition to the dining variety at the Radisson Suite Resort, Marco Beach Hilton, and Marriott's Marco Island Resort, there are many good restaurants.

BLUE HERON INN, 387 Capri Blvd., Isles of Capri. Tel. 394-6248.

Cuisine: INTERNATIONAL. **Reservations:** Required.

$ Prices: Fixed-price multicourse dinner $25.50–$31.95. DISC, MC, V.

Open: Dinner only, Mon–Sat with seatings at 6:30 and 8:45pm (two tables for 7 and 7:30pm seating). **Closed:** Aug–Sept.

★ One of the 10 best restaurants in southwestern Florida, this elegant inn has won an award for its lobster Caribe. Since the menu changes every two weeks, it's best to call owner-chef Peter Thorpe and order this delicious dish ahead. Another highlight is the nine-ounce lobster tail. For the fixed-price dinners, there are choices from chicken to rack of lamb; the only extra charges are for wine or cocktails and the tip, as soup, salad, vegetables, dessert, and coffee or tea are included.

OLD MARCO INN, 100 Palm St., Old Marco Village. Tel. 394-3131.

Cuisine: INTERNATIONAL. **Reservations:** Recommended.

$ Prices: Main courses $16.95–$35. AE, DC, DISC, MC, V.

Open: Dinner only, daily 5:30–10pm. **Closed:** Usually mid-Aug to mid-Sept.

Built as a private residence in 1883, the inn retains a gracious formality, from the crystal chandelier to the rich furnishings, and is perfect for a quiet dinner. Seafood, beef, chops, and poultry are prepared with an international flair. Austrian-style wienerschnitzel is just one of the specialties. Before dinner, it's relaxing to enjoy a drink in the popular piano bar, open nightly from 8pm.

SNOOK INN, 1215 Bald Eagle Dr., Marco Island. Tel. 394-3313.

Cuisine: SEAFOOD. **Reservations:** Not accepted.

$ Prices: Main courses $5–$20. AE, MC, V.

Open: Daily 11am–10pm.

Looking out to the scenic Marco River, the very casual Snook Inn offers indoor or outdoor seating at lunch and dinner. Usually, a seafood buffet is featured on Thursday and Friday from 5 to 9pm, for less than $15. Although fish and shellfish are the specialties on the menu, tasty burgers, steaks, and chicken are also among the choices. The Chickee is a fun place, offering a happy hour Monday through Friday from 4 to 6pm and on Sunday from 10pm until night owls go home. Live entertainment is spotlighted, but call ahead for the schedule. If you wish, there's free shuttle service to and from Snook Inn from anywhere on Marco Island—just call AAnytime Taxi (yes, that's double "A") (tel. 860-9393).

STAN'S IDLE HOUR SEAFOOD RESTAURANT, downtown Goodland, Marco Island. Tel. 394-3041.

Cuisine: SEAFOOD. **Reservations:** Not accepted.

$ Prices: Main courses $4.50–$9.95. No credit cards.

Open: Lunch Tues–Sun 11am–2pm, dinner Tues–Sun 5–9pm.

For food, fun, and games, this rustic restaurant is well worth the trip. Owner Stan Gober, an Ernest Hemingway look-alike, keeps the action going with all sorts of activities, from the Men's Best Legs Contest to the Buzzard Lope Celebration and the annual Goodland Mullet Festival (always the weekend before the Super Bowl). When frogs' legs are in season, fresh from the nearby Everglades, these are a treat, accompanied by at least three-inch-wide fried onion rings. Stone crab (in season) is another delicacy here. Fresh grouper sandwiches and fried oyster sandwiches are terrific. If you like buffalo chicken wings, try Stan's delicious version. Should you arrive by boat, you can dock just a few steps from the bar. The outdoor patio with its thatched huts is delightful for lunch or dinner at this unconventional eatery, a favorite with "characters." Goodland is less than a 10-minute drive east from the center of Marco Island.

3. SANIBEL & CAPTIVA ISLANDS

15 miles W of Fort Myers

GETTING THERE By Car From Fort Myers, take Fla. 867. Should you be driving from the south via U.S. 41, keep a sharp lookout for the barely visible sign (about four miles south of Fort Myers) pointing west to Sanibel. Round-trip toll to the islands across Sanibel Bridge is $3 (payable in full upon access).

Seashells on Sanibel and Captiva have intrigued visitors ever since Ponce de León discovered the islands in 1513. The Spanish conquistador christened the coast Costa de Caracoles (Coast of Seashells). One version of how Sanibel got its name claims that José Gaspar was so enchanted by the island's beauty that he named it for his queen, Santa Isabella of Spain. Mispronounced through the years, the name became "Sanibel." As for Captiva, another legend claims that the same notorious Gaspar kidnapped wealthy women from the Spanish galleons he looted and held them captive for ransom on the remote island. Nobody knows what the Calusas called the islands when the tribe lived here thousands of years ago. Diseases acquired from the Spanish and pirate invasions made the Calusas extinct by the 17th century, but their impressive shell mounds remain.

A New York investment group attempted settling on Sanibel around 1833, but they didn't stay very long. A few farmers settled on Sanibel around 1892. Two years later, the Bailey family arrived and eventually opened what is now Bailey's General Store. During this time, early settler Clarence Chadwick started a 300-acre key lime plantation on Captiva, which prospered. But his copra business did not, although thousands of coconut-palm trees were planted on his vast property.

After Chadwick's brother-in-law concluded that fishing was more profitable than farming, many of the plantation workers' cottages were converted to fishing camps. Fishing was so terrific—and still is—that affluent fishing enthusiasts flocked to Captiva and didn't mind taking the mail ferry from the mainland. From a rustic fishing camp, Chadwick's progressed to a beach resort, which is now the super-deluxe South Seas Plantation total resort. Until ferry service began in 1926, private boat was the only access to the islands. Everything changed drastically after the Sanibel Bridge and Causeway opened in 1963, linking the islands to the mainland three miles away. Fortunately, the once-isolated islands maintain the hideaway atmosphere because of strict zoning laws. Homes have been built so far back from the roads and the roadsides are so thick with trees and foliage that no signs of civilization are visible for miles in some areas.

What's the difference between the two islands? Sanibel is the larger, about 12 miles long and about 3 miles wide. Connected to Sanibel by a bridge, Captiva is almost 6 miles long, and narrower. At least 40% of the islands' land area is protected as wildlife sanctuaries. Both islands are beautifully wooded with pines, giant banyan trees, and flamboyant tropical flora. The wide, white sand beaches, adorned with sea oats, are outstanding, and the gulf waters are as clear and iridescent as the Caribbean. Being larger, Sanibel could be considered livelier, as it has more shopping centers, more restaurants, more hotels, and more attractions (such as the historical museum and Lighthouse). Strict zoning laws apply to both islands, where no building can be more than four stories high.

Among the celebrities who visit the islands frequently are television journalists Ted Koppel and Roger Mudd and television weatherman Willard Scott. The world-famous artist Robert Rauschenberg maintains a home here. Their privacy is always respected by residents. In the past, the *New York Times* Pulitzer Prize–winning cartoonist J. N. "Ding" Darling was a very frequent visitor. He was one of the island's earliest conservationists, and the wildlife refuge bears his name. Edna St. Vincent Millay, the poet, also visited often. And inspired by her vacations on the beautiful islands, Anne Morrow Lindbergh, the wife of renowned aviator Charles Lindbergh, wrote *Gift from the Sea,* a tribute to the almost-magical tranquility experienced by every visitor.

The reminder on the official map of Sanibel and Captiva says it all: "Respect our speed limit; if you are in a hurry, you don't belong on Sanibel and Captiva."

ORIENTATION

INFORMATION The very helpful **Sanibel/Captiva Chamber of Commerce Visitor Information Center** is right at the island entrance on Causeway Road, Sanibel, FL 33957 (tel. 813/472-1080). Racks of free informative brochures give every detail about the islands. If accommodations are required, the staff offers assistance, and there's no charge to call local hotels, motels, or condominium apartments. This is Florida's busiest tourist information office; it's open Monday through Saturday from 9am to 7pm and on Sunday from 10am to 5pm (until 6pm in peak season).

GETTING AROUND

BY TAXI **Airport Shuttle** (tel. 472-0007) is also a local taxi service. Transportation for up to three persons from Southwest Regional Airport in Fort Myers costs approximately $26 (plus gratuities).

For getting around the island, the cost is $3 and up. **Sanibel Taxi** (tel. 472-4160) operates around the clock on the island (usually charging a $5 minimum) and their cabs can take you to the airport in Fort Myers.

BY BICYCLE **Finnimore's Cycle Shop,** 2353 Periwinkle Way (tel. 472-5577), offers current-model bikes in the size and speed you prefer, and adjustments are made to fit you. They have good weekly rates, and there's free delivery and pickup on multiday rentals. The shop is open every day from 8:30am to 5:30pm.

Island Moped, 1470 Periwinkle Way (tel. 472-5248), rents mopeds and bikes. The shop is open daily from 8:30am to 5:30pm.

BY CAR **Avis** is located at 1015 Periwinkle Way (tel. 472-8180) and **Budget** is at 2353 Periwinkle Way (tel. 472-0088). Should your car require towing, **Island Garage,** 1609 Periwinkle Way (tel. 472-4318), can be contacted around the clock. For repairs, the garage is open Monday through Saturday from 8am to 5pm.

BY TROLLEY The **Sanibel Trolley** (tel. 472-6374) offers transportation. The schedule varies according to season, so it's best to call ahead.

The **Sanibel Route,** a one-hour round-trip of approximately 16 miles, stops at or near restaurants, the post office, library, shopping centers, beach accesses, sightseeing attractions, and more. There are five round-trips daily from the Chamber of Commerce Visitor Information Center. The ticket costs $2 and you may board or disembark at any of the scheduled stops; reboarding is free. The **Captiva Route,** a two-hour, 36-mile trip costs $4 (there's a twice-daily round-trip from Sanibel). Children under 5 are charged half price. Tickets can be purchased after you hop aboard.

The narrated **Sanibel Trolley Tour** costs $8 and is usually scheduled at 10am and 12:30pm November through April on Monday, Wednesday, and Friday. The two-hour tour is the fun way to learn island lore and history from a very knowledgeable guide.

FAST FACTS

Area Code The area code for Sanibel and Captiva is 813.

Convenience Stores 7-Eleven stores are located on Sanibel at 1521 Periwinkle Way (tel. 472-9197) and 2460 Periwinkle Way (tel. 472-8696). The one-stop Bailey's Shopping Center, 2477 Periwinkle Way, Sanibel, has most convenience stores and services, including Bailey's General Store (tel. 472-1516), open from 8am to 9pm seven days a week.

Drugstores Eckerd Drugs is at 2331 Palm Ridge Rd., Sanibel (tel. 472-1719). The Corner Pharmacy is in Bailey's Shopping Center.

Emergencies For emergencies, dial 911. For medical assistance, contact Doctors Clinic/Sanibel, 695 Tarpon Bay Rd. (tel. 395-1800), or the Wegryn Medical Center, 4301 Sanibel-Captiva Rd. (tel. 472-4131).

Hairdressers/Beauty Shops The Sanibel Beauty Salon and Sanibel Barber Shop are in Bailey's Shopping Center. Hair, Skin & Nails Day Spa of Sanibel, upstairs in the Periwinkle Place Shopping Center, 2075 Periwinkle Way, Sanibel (tel. 395-2220), offers everything from facials to remineralizing wraps; open Monday through Saturday and evenings by appointment.

Laundry Island Cleaners/Wash House (tel. 395-0055) in Bailey's Shopping Center offers fast dry cleaning and laundrette service.

Photographic Needs Arundel's Hallmark Card and Party Shop, in Heart of the Island Plaza, 1626 Periwinkle Way, Sanibel (tel. 472-0434), offers one-hour photo processing. The Captiva branch is at 220 Chadwick's Sq. (tel. 395-0434).

Rentals Child Care Rentals (tel. 482-8129) rents high chairs, strollers, and other equipment, with free delivery and pickup.

Telegrams There's a Western Union office in Bailey's General Store (see "Convenience Stores," above).

WHAT TO SEE & DO

NATURE & CONSERVATION

The environment and ecology are top priorities on Sanibel and Captiva. On these tropical island retreats, there's a devoted appreciation of Mother Nature—no glitzy theme parks or amusement parks mar the natural beauty and tranquility.

C.R.O.W. [CARE AND REHABILITATION OF WILDLIFE], Sanibel-Captiva Rd. Tel. 472-3644.

More than 1,800 "patients" are treated every year at C.R.O.W.'s three-story headquarters. Wildlife shelters simulate natural habitats for recuperating hawks, owls, brown pelicans, otters, bobcats, foxes, and more.

Admission: Free.

Open: Oct–Mar, open house on the last Sun of each month 1–3pm (a great way to learn about wildlife); otherwise, by appointment only.

DING DARLING NATIONAL WILDLIFE REFUGE. Tel. 472-1100.

The refuge encompasses approximately 5,000 acres, at least one-third of Sanibel Island. The refuge is home to hundreds of species of birds and migrating waterfowl, among them roseate spoonbills, white ibis, blue herons, snowy egrets, ospreys, and anhingas. Alligators, raccoons, and otters inhabit the refuge.

Along the five-mile drive through untouched mangrove swamp, much wildlife can be observed. At present, the five-mile drive is closed on Friday due to environmental concerns. Biking and hiking trails and canoeing also offer fascinating observation. For example, the two-mile Indigo Trail, starting at the visitor center, abounds in birds feeding and resting. Along the nearly two-mile walking trail at Baily Tract on Tarpon Bay Road, which winds around a freshwater pond, you can see alligators as well as herons, egrets, and a variety of other birds. Canoe rentals are available at the Tarpon Bay Recreation Area, off Tarpon Bay Road, where you can also watch birds feeding on the oyster beds when the bivalves are exposed at low tide. Don't miss naturalist "Bird" Westall's canoe excursion to observe the profusion of wading birds fishing for their seafood breakfast. At the visitor center, you can obtain a list of the hundreds of species of birds in the refuge, details about the observation tower, and information for the various trails. A slide presentation is usually shown at 10am, noon, and 2pm.

Inquire about the new two-hour guided/narrated tram tour, which leaves from the Tarpon Bay Center at the end of Tarpon Bay Road.

Admission: Free; the Wildlife Drive (Sun–Thurs sunup–sundown), $3 per vehicle, $1 for hikers and bicyclists (current Federal Duck Stamps, Golden Age, Golden Access, and Golden Eagle Passports are accepted).

Open: Refuge, daily dawn–dusk. Visitor center, Nov–Apr, daily 9am–5pm; May–Oct, daily 9am–4pm. **Closed:** Major holidays.

SANIBEL/CAPTIVA CONSERVATION FOUNDATION, 333 Sanibel-Captiva Rd. Tel. 472-2329.

Here, environmental workshops, the library, exhibits, guest lecturers, and a variety of brochures will help you learn more about the islands' unusual ecosystem. Native plants, birdhouses, books, and nature-oriented gifts are for sale. Guided and self-guided tours are offered so that visitors can observe wildlife and native vegetation. The 247-acre wetlands tract features four miles of nature trails along the Sanibel River. During peak season, guided trail tours begin at 10am, 11am, and 2pm.

Admission: $1.

Open: Winter, Mon–Sat 9:30am–4:30pm; summer, Mon–Fri 9:30am–3:30pm.

MORE ATTRACTIONS

The **Island Historical Museum,** 850 Dunlop Rd. (tel. 472-4648), was formerly a private home and is typical of "Florida Cracker" architecture. Constructed with hard Florida pine and embellished with "beaded" woodwork and large antique-glass windows, the museum is furnished pioneer style. Among the displays are the islands' prehistoric history, old photos from the pioneer days, old-fashioned clothing, and a variety of memorabilia. Museum hours are usually 10am to 4pm on Thursday, Friday, and Saturday. Best to call ahead. Admission is free; donations are accepted.

Dating back to 1884, **The Lighthouse,** at the east tip of Periwinkle Road, is one of the few still operational in Florida. The Lighthouse marks the entrance from the Gulf of Mexico into San Carlos Bay and the light beams assisted cattle transports sailing from Punta Rassa to Key West and Cuba. Now operated by remote control, the flashing white lights emitted from the 98-foot tower still assist shipping traffic. Since 1950, the U.S. Coast Guard property at the Lighthouse has been a wildlife refuge. The cottages at the foot of the tower belonged to the lightkeepers, who trudged up the countless stairs every day to fill the giant lantern with oil.

The **Sealife Learning Center** at the Fantasy Island Center, 2353 Periwinkle Way (tel. 472-8680), features a 100-gallon touch tank, 15 aquariums, and other sea animal displays to introduce nature enthusiasts to sealife in the Gulf of Mexico. Visitors come in contact with local sea plants and myriad creatures. The center serves as a marine laboratory, classroom, and departure point for beach walks on Sanibel Island and is affiliated with Aqua Trek Nature Tours.

ORGANIZED TOURS

CANOE TRIPS A resident of the islands for many years, Mark "Bird" Westall (tel. 472-5218) is well known for his memorable three-hour canoe expeditions along the Sanibel River, along the Ding Darling Refuge canoe trails, and around Buck Key (where once Calusas lived and pirates lurked). "Bird" Westall offers a variety of nature trips. His excursions depart from Tarpon Bay, located in the Ding Darling Wildlife Refuge. But whatever you do, don't miss "Bird" Westall's canoe trip at dawn to observe the birds feeding in the wildlife refuge. He never takes out more than 12 people at one time (in three canoes). You're so close to wading birds that binoculars aren't necessary—ibis, roseate spoonbills, and great blue herons are just an oar's length away, patiently waiting to catch their fish breakfast in water less than a foot deep. Call for prices.

CRUISES **Adventure Sailing Charters,** sailing from the South Seas Plantation Marina for 20 years, features half-day, full-day, and sunset excursions on the *Adventure,* a 30-foot sloop, accommodating up to six passengers. The company also owns *Starship,* a 21-foot professional racing catamaran. Captain Mike McMillan welcomes children, also. For information, call 472-7532 days, 472-4386 nights.

Captain Dick Barnes and Nancy are hosts aboard ***Lady,*** a 32-foot custom Downeaster with enclosed cabin and restroom, cruising to Cabbage Key, Upper Captiva, and Boca Grande for lunch and dinner or just sightseeing tours. *Lady* departs from the 'Tween Waters Marina on Captiva (tel. 472-3788).

Captiva Cruises (tel. 472-7549) sets sail with the 150-passenger *Jean Nicolet,* a 65-foot-long, 24-foot-wide vessel with two decks. Island cruises to either Cabbage Key or Useppa Island are featured, and also a variety of breakfast, dinner, and sightseeing excursions.

NATURE WALKS **Caretta Research** takes its name from the scientific name for the enormous loggerhead turtle, *Caretta caretta.* The turtle comes ashore to the island beaches during the nesting period of May through August. At night, beach patrols are on duty to protect the turtles and their eggs. Should you want to participate in the Beach Walk or would like more information about the turtles and their nests, call 472-3177; if there's no answer, just leave a message and your call will be returned.

The **Audubon Society** sponsors morning walks to observe the many species of birds on the islands. The society also presents movies, lectures, and courses to identify the local birds. Contact the chamber of commerce (tel. 472-1080) for the schedule.

SHELLING EXCURSIONS For the ultimate shelling experience, **Mike Fuery's Charters** (tel. 472-1015 or 994-7195) sail out of 'Tween Waters Inn Marina, usually around 7am, and take you to veritable treasure troves of shells on the isolated beaches of Johnson Shoals and Cayo Costa islands. (By the way, the Cayo Costa beaches, rated among the best anywhere, are accessible by boat only.) Mike Fuery is a real malacologist—his knowledge of shells and island lore is absolutely fascinating. Half-day shelling tours usually cost about $160 for up to six people. Who knows—you may find the rare, elusive brown-speckled junonia.

SPECIAL EVENTS

The main event is the annual **Sanibel Shell Fair,** a four-day celebration held since 1937 in early March. The seashell extravaganza takes place in the Sanibel Community Center, 2173 Periwinkle Way (tel. 472-2155), from 9am to 5pm. Admission is free to the Shell Fair, but there's a $2 admission to the Shell Show. Exhibits include seashells from around the world and unusual shell art is for sale. Fun activities are part of the event. Arts and crafts fairs are also on the March schedule, featuring wood carving, weaving, making fish nets, and leather embossing.

The **Island Road Rally,** a treasure hunt on wheels, is held in July. October's highlight is the **Island Luau,** presented around the pool at the Dunes Golf & Tennis Club, 949 Sand Castle Rd. (tel. 472-3355). The Dunes also hosts an annual **Taste of the Islands** in May and **Jazz-on-the-Green** in November.

One of the most spectacular sights is the **Luminary Trail,** the first week in December, featuring miles of glowing luminaries along Periwinkle Way and the Sanibel-Captiva Road.

Check with the Sanibel-Captiva Chamber of Commerce (tel. 472-1080) about events presented throughout the year.

SPORTS & RECREATION

BIKING Leave your car in your hotel parking area and go biking to enjoy the slow-paced, tropical atmosphere. Since there are no hills, biking is easy and there's no problem getting around the relatively small islands. From Lighthouse Point at Sanibel's eastern tip, a major bike path leads to Blind Pass at Sanibel's western end. Actually, there are approximately 25 miles of safe, very scenic biking (the chamber of commerce supplies maps of bike routes; tel. 472-1080). From the main route, it's fun to take the side routes on Casa Ybel Road, Gulf Drive, Tarpon Bay Road, and more. Where there's no bike route, state law requires cyclists to ride single file on the right side of the road, with the traffic. Moped riders are not allowed on bike paths—they must use the roads. Bike rentals are easily arranged, but prices vary; call for information.

BOATING Rentals are available at **The Boat House,** Sanibel Marina (tel. 472-2531), and include 15- to 21-foot powerboats. **Club Nautico** (tel. 472-7540) rents powerboats from 20 to 28 feet. **Jensen's Twin Palms Resort and Marina** (tel. 472-5800) offers boat rentals. You can rent a canoe at **'Tween Waters Inn** on Captiva (tel. 472-5161).

One of the most famous sailing schools, Steve and Doris Colgate's **Offshore Sailing School** (tel. 454-1700) features three- to seven-day programs every week at South Seas Plantation on Captiva. It's fun to take instruction aboard the 27-footer.

FISHING Arrangements for fishing charters can be made at any one of the many marinas on Sanibel, including **Castaways** (tel. 472-1112) and **Sanibel** (tel. 472-2531), and on Captiva at **'Tween Waters Inn and Marina** (tel. 472-2531) and the **South Seas Plantation Resort** (tel. 472-5111). Most of the captains have 20 years' experience and more. Both salt- and freshwater fish are caught and the big-game fishing challenge is for tarpon.

Without a boat, fishing is still terrific at the **Sanibel/Captiva Bridge** and the pier at Sanibel's tip near the Lighthouse. In season, the lucky place for snook is **Redfish Pass.**

GOLF & TENNIS Golfers can tee off on the 6,000-yard, par-70, 18-hole championship course at the **Dunes Golf and Tennis Club,** 949 Sandcastle Rd. (tel. 472-2535). For information about playing on the Dunes's seven tennis courts, call 472-3522. Instructions can be arranged for golf and tennis at the Dunes. The **Beach View Golf Club** (tel. 472-2626) also has an 18-hole course. On Captiva, the **South Seas Plantation** (tel. 472-5111) is proud of its beautiful 9-hole course, which can be played twice for par-72. Several hotels and resorts have tennis courts for guests.

SHELLING Just about every visitor becomes afflicted with the "Sanibel Stoop," the position acquired from constantly looking down at the sand in the enjoyable search for seashells. Along Gulf of Mexico beaches and the bay, the tides bring in so many shells that Sanibel is considered among the top three places in the world to collect seashells. Every hotel posts a listing of tide tables. Low tide is the time to go to the shoreline with the shell bucket. The best months are December, January, and February, but many beautiful specimens have been found at other times of the year. High tides, storms, and high winds bring in the greatest abundance of shells—and shell-seekers.

Location is the reason for Sanibel's shell bonanza: It's right in the middle of a productive area in the gulf so that the winds and tides combine to bring in live shells from the tremendous beds that have built up offshore. The winds and tides also sweep the sea bottom of empty shells, which arrive by the ton on the beaches.

In addition to beachcombing along the shore for empty shells, many expert collectors go wading or snorkeling for live specimens. However, shell beds could be depleted and the law states that only two live shells per species per person may be taken (in the Ding Darling Wildlife Refuge, no live shells may be taken).

A closed shell signifies that a live creature is still inside. If you're not sure, it's best to leave the shell on the beach. It's a good idea to wear sneakers when shell hunting along the shoreline—you might happen to step on broken shells.

Before taking your bounty home, the shells should be boiled in water and dipped in a bleach-water solution for thorough cleaning and to prevent odors. Most motels have such supplies. For the finishing touch, rub a little baby oil on the shells.

WATER SPORTS Snorkeling equipment rentals and a variety of diving gear is available at the **Pieces of Eight Dive Shop,** 3600 South Seas Plantation Rd. (Chadwick's Square), Captiva (tel. 472-9424). The cost is approximately $40 for equipment only, $90 for equipment and a dive.

Windsurfing begins at **Windsurfing of Sanibel,** 1554 Periwinkle Way (tel. 472-0123), where windsurfers are rentable, and lessons are offered at the **South Seas Plantation** (tel. 472-5111) on Captiva. Board rentals are approximately $40 for a half day, about $50 for a full day. The instructions are necessary and a group lesson costs around $25.

Para-Sail, based on Captiva (tel. 472-1296), claims that anyone of any age can be a parasailor. **Super-Feat** has a 24-hour ParaSail Hot Line (tel. 283-2020), or you can call them on the boat phone (tel. 851-7700). Parasailing is at the north end of Captiva Road, just past the post office at the public beach.

Waterskiing lessons are also offered by Super Feat; the instructor is a barefoot waterski champion.

Holiday Water Sports, at the South Seas Plantation on Captiva (tel. 472-2938), features waverunners, waterskiing, and parasailing.

WHERE TO STAY

In addition to the beautiful beach hotels on Sanibel and Captiva, a variety of accommodations are available in condominiums, cottages, and villas. Prices will vary, but will run about $550–$750 a week in summer, about double that in peak season. The chamber of commerce provides a list of realtors (tel. 472-1080), including **Priscilla Murphy Realty,** 1019 Periwinkle Way (tel. 472-1511), and **VIP Realty Group,** 1509 Periwinkle Way (tel. 472-1613, or toll free 800/237-7526).

SANIBEL ISLAND
Very Expensive

POINTE SANTO DE SANIBEL, 2445 W. Gulf Dr. (at Tarpon Bay Rd.), Sanibel Island, FL 33957. Tel. 813/472-9100, or toll free 800/824-5442. Fax 813/472-0487. 140 condominium apts. A/C TV TEL

$ Rates: Feb–Apr, and Dec 16–31, $1,200–$2,500 apt per week. Jan, $972–$1,800 apt per week. May–Dec 15, $575–$1,155 apt per week. AE, DISC, MC, V.

The highest rates for these luxurious apartments are for gulf-front villas, some large enough for six people. Rates are lower for apartments not overlooking the gulf. The landscaped swimming area is very attractive, with a little bridge leading to the Jacuzzi. A glass floor in the clubhouse allows fish-watching in the lagoon below. In addition to the ornately decorated one-, two-, and three-bedroom villas, the penthouse is perfect for the lifestyle of the rich and famous.

SUNDIAL BEACH & TENNIS RESORT, 1451 Middle Gulf Dr., Sanibel Island, FL 33957. Tel. 813/472-4151, or toll free 800/237-4184. Fax 813/472-1809. 260 apts. A/C TV TEL

$ Rates: High season, $245–$400 apt. for up to four people. Low season, $150–$270 apt for up to four people. Children under 14 stay free in parents' apt. Vacation packages available. AE, DC, MC, V.

An outstanding beachfront resort, where many television celebrities come to relax, Sundial is tropically landscaped, complete with fountain-splashed garden courtyards. Very spacious, tastefully decorated accommodations with party-size balconies overlook the beach or gardens. In addition to one or two bedrooms, the apartments have large living rooms, dining areas, and complete kitchens (some have an extra den). Beachside lanai apartments offer screened porches and large patios with spectacular gulf views.

Dining/Entertainment: The Sundial's award-winning restaurant, Windows on the Water, offers a delicious culinary experience with "Gulfshore cuisine" (see "Where to Dine," below). The adjoining Sunset Lounge is relaxing for drinks and offers a bountiful complimentary buffet. From 5:45 to 8:45pm, popular pianist and chanteuse Helen Skelton entertains ("The Today Show" weatherman, Willard Scott, and his wife often relax here). Every night except Monday, a dance band plays Top-40 hits from 9pm until very late.

At Noopie's Japanese Seafood & Steakhouse (open to the public), master chefs, cooking at the tables on the built-in grills, put on quite a show as they prepare delicious steak, chicken, and seafood dishes. Wines and exotic drinks are served (also sake and Japanese beers). Open 5:30 to 9:30pm Tuesday through Saturday—dinner is by reservations only (tel. 395-6014) and there are eight different seating times.

The Deli (at the Gift Shop) is open from 7am to 12:30am daily, offering piled-high sandwiches, snacks, and picnic foods. Sprinkles Sweet Shop, next to the Game Room, dishes up ice cream and pastries. Lively Crocodial's Patio Bar and Grille, a poolside rendezvous, serves hot dogs, hamburgers, salads, and overstuffed sandwiches. The frozen libations are refreshing. Live music entertains the sun worshippers every Saturday and Sunday afternoon (this is one of the largest pool bars in southwestern Florida).

Services: Limited room service (cold foods only) until 10pm, babysitting, supervised recreational program (Children's Club) daily for kids 3–12, aquacise for teens and adults, daily adults' activities (from beach walks to shell jewelry making), complimentary slide shows and lectures (marine biology, manatees, history; open to the public), daily maid service. Taxi or limousine service at a nominal charge to the Southwest Florida Regional Airport in Fort Myers.

Facilities: 13 tennis courts, five swimming pools, 2,400 feet of white sand beach, jogging trail, fitness room with the latest equipment, gift shop, convention facilities; shuffleboard, croquet, putting, and Ping-Pong equipment, and board games available; bike and boat rentals from the bike/boat center; movie and VCR rentals. Golfers can arrange to play at the nearby Dunes Golf & Tennis Club (guest privileges).

Expensive

CASA YBEL RESORT, 2255 W. Gulf Dr., Sanibel Island, FL 33957. Tel. 813/472-3145, or toll free 800/237-8906. Fax 813/472-2109. 114 apts. A/C TV TEL

$ Rates: High season, $270–$325 apt. Low season, $200–$235 apt. MC, V.

On the historic site of Sanibel's first resort, beachfront Casa Ybel is imbued with turn-of-the-century charm. Recently, the resort completed a $550,000 refurbishment and the spacious one- and two bedroom apartments are bright with a new color scheme, tropical rattan furniture, pastel carpeting, and ceramic tile. Each apartment has its own big screened-in porch, where it's so relaxing to look out to the beautiful beach. The landscaped swimming pool area is a popular rendezvous. Children congregate in the special playground. Six tennis courts get lots of action. Rental bikes are available. At the water-sports center, rentals are arranged for sailboats, Sunfish, and windsurfers. For guests who wish to participate, there's a social program. Truffle's, the famous restaurant at Casa Ybel's, merits a separate listing (see "Where to Dine," below).

GALLERY MOTEL, 541 E. Gulf Dr., Sanibel Island, FL 33957. Tel. 813/472-1400, or toll free 800/831-7384. 32 units. A/C TV TEL

$ Rates: Mid-Dec to mid-Apr, $150–$215 for two people. Mid-Apr to mid-Dec, $100–$185 for two. MC, V.

Nestled in tall palm trees overlooking the Gulf of Mexico beach, the Gallery Motel has a tranquil location on the island's southeastern tip. All accommodations (motel rooms, efficiencies, cottages, and apartments) have open-air balconies or porches, refrigerators, and fully equipped kitchens. The cottages are very spacious and very attractively furnished. The palm-surrounded swimming pool and suntanning patio are next to the wide expanse of white sand beach. Barbecue grills are available for a fun picnic. Shuffleboard is on the premises and rental bikes are available.

RAMADA INN RESORT, 1231 Middle Gulf Dr., Sanibel Island, FL 33957. Tel. 813/472-4123, or toll free 800/228-2828, 800/443-0909 in Florida. Fax 813/472-0930. 98 units. A/C TV TEL

$ Rates: High season, $158–$210 double. Low season, $120–$155 double. AE, DC, DISC, MC, V.

Swaying palms, flamboyant flowers, and the long stretch of white sand beach emphasize the tropical island atmosphere at this friendly gulf-front resort. Spacious, attractively decorated accommodations include suites and two efficiences; there are refrigerators in about 35 rooms. The freshwater swimming pool and poolside snack bar are nestled in a garden landscaped area adjoining the beach. For the sports enthusiast, there are two lighted tennis courts and rental bikes. Arrangements can be made to play golf on a nearby course, within walking distance. The very popular J. Todd's Restaurant and Lounge serves breakfast, lunch, dinner, cocktails—and a great Saturday-night buffet in peak season. In the lounge, there's a lively happy hour from 4 to 7pm, where Frank the bartender is known for his very special drinks.

SANIBEL INN, 937 Gulf Dr., Sanibel Island, FL 33957. Tel. 813/472-3181, or toll free 800/237-1491. Fax 813/472-5234. 48 rms, 24 condos. A/C MINIBAR TV TEL

$ Rates: High season, $220–$340 double. Low season, $145–$240 double. AE, DISC, MC, V.

Situated on acres of gulf beachfront, the inn includes two- and three-story buildings. The spacious rooms are attractively furnished, complete with mini-refrigerator and coffee maker. Elaborate condo units have separate bedrooms, living rooms, dining areas, and kitchenettes. The swimming pool area is tropically landscaped and a boardwalk leads to the beach. There's a putting green, two tennis courts, rental bikes, and a water-sports center. Portofino's, the inn's popular restaurant, is notable for northern Italian cuisine, as well as fresh seafood and steaks; it's open for breakfast from 7:30 to 10:30am and for dinner from 4:30 to 10pm. If you like breakfast outdoors, the poolside café opens early.

THE SEA SHELLS OF SANIBEL, 2840 W. Gulf Dr., Sanibel Island, FL 33957. Tel. 813/472-4634, or toll free 800/533-4486. 44 condominiums. A/C TV TEL

$ Rates: High season, $925–$975 condo weekly. Low season, $495–$545 condo weekly. Jan rates lower.

The handsomely decorated two-bedroom/two-bath, completely furnished condo apartments here can accommodate four people. Screened porches look out to the landscaped tropical gardens (the larger apartments have two porches). A swimming pool and tennis and shuffleboard courts are on the premises. The beach access leads to the gulf, where the shelling is excellent along the white sands. Managers Haskel and Revonda Cross are very hospitable and will give you very good tips about what to see and do on the islands. If you like tranquility, this is your kind of place.

WEST WIND INN, 3345 W. Gulf Dr., Sanibel Island, FL 33957. Tel. 813/472-1541, or toll free 800/824-0476, 800/282-2831 in Florida. Fax 813/472-8134. 104 rms and efficiencies. A/C TV TEL

$ Rates: High season, $160–$200 double. Low season, $105–$140 double. AE, MC, V.

Decorated in tropical pastels, the attractive rooms have balconies or patios overlooking the gulf, the wide expanses of green lawns, and beautiful gardens shaded by palm trees. The large swimming pool and thatch-roofed refreshment hut are but a few steps from the outstanding beach. Children like to splash around in the wading pool. Two tennis courts and a putting green are on the premises (an 18-hole championship golf course is only minutes away). Bikes, sailboats, and windsurfers can be rented. Grills are available for barbecues. Although many rooms have kitchenettes, there's also a small restaurant for when you don't feel like cooking.

Moderate

KONA KAI, 1539 Periwinkle Way, Sanibel, FL 33957. Tel. 813/472-1001. 20 rms and efficiencies. A/C TV TEL

$ Rates: Dec–Apr $75–$155 double. May–Nov, $40–$85 double. Lower weekly rates available. AE, MC, V.

A Polynesian motif is the theme, especially at the large swimming pool surrounded by luxuriant foliage. Guests can use the poolside barbecue grills. Although the motel is not on the beach, you can stroll along the Sanibel River, a few steps away. Shops and restaurants are within walking distance. This is a good buy for the money, offering choices of motel rooms, efficiencies, or two-bedroom efficiencies, completely equipped with kitchen utensils.

Kona Kai's management company, the **Sanibel Resort Group** (tel. 813/472-1833 or 813/472-1001) also rents one- and two-bedroom apartments a block from the beach or across the street—all clean, comfortable, and very moderately priced. These include the Blue Heron (tel. 472-1206), complete with canal fishing docks; the Driftwood (tel. 472-1852), a block from one of the best shelling beaches; the Tahiti Resort Apartments (tel. 472-1001); the Periwinkle Resort Apartments (tel. 472-1880), adjacent to a 35-acre wildlife sanctuary; Villa Capri, with chalet cottages; and the Blue Dolphin (tel. 472-1600), on the beachfront, notable for a 10-foot-wide sun deck.

CAPTIVA ISLAND

Very Expensive

SOUTH SEAS PLANTATION RESORT AND YACHT HARBOUR, P.O. Box 194, Captiva Island, FL 33924. Tel. 813/472-5111, or toll free 800/237-6000, 800/282-6158 in Florida. Fax 813/472-7541. 600 rms, condominiums, cottages, town houses, and private homes. A/C TV TEL

$ Rates: Jan–May, $250–$750 double. June–Jan, $150–$550 double. Many vacation packages available. AE, DC, DISC, MC, V.

Many celebrities come here to unwind amid the 330 acres of tropical island beauty on Captiva's northern tip. This was actually a 19th-century working key lime and coconut plantation owned by Clarence Chadwick. He would be amazed to see today's mega-million-dollar total resort, flaunting a grand variety of accommodations, some with private pools and private tennis courts. There are hundreds of gardenside and seaside villas; one-, two-, and three-bedroom condominium apartments; beach cottages on stilts with screened porches; and beach villas with two to four bedrooms. Clever landscaping and miles of woodland have retained a languid plantation atmosphere. Guests can take long walks on the beach or stroll through the pine woodland, where several species of birds can be sighted.

Dining/Entertainment: The winner of many awards, Chadwick's is open to the public. The tropical atrium setting is romantic and the Caribbean cuisine with the chef's innovations is a taste treat every night. Chadwick's, open for breakfast, lunch, and dinner, features a Caribbean Celebration buffet on Tuesday, a sumptuous seafood buffet on Friday, and the delicious champagne brunch on Sunday. Chadwick's lounge spotlights entertainment from 8:30pm to 12:30am every night except Tuesday (dancing, too).

The elegant King's Crown, exclusively for guests, was formerly the plantation workers' commissary. The handsome wood beams and the impressive fireplace remain. In this sophisticated dining room, lobster in sorrel sauce is a gourmet specialty, and the rack of lamb is noteworthy. Of course, the luscious key lime pie is made from local limes. The King's Crown is open for dinner only; reservations are necessary and men must wear jacket and tie.

For a very casual breakfast, lunch, or dinner, Cap'n Al's Dockside Grill serves indoors or outdoors. And Mama Rosa's Pizzaria is the place for pizza. Uncle Bob's Ice Cream Parlor satisfies the sweet tooth. When you want to create your own feast, C.W.'s Market & Deli and the Ship's Store Deli are on the premises.

Services: Room service, babysitting, children's activities, teenagers' activities, shuttle to the resort's different areas.

Facilities: Touring pro Virginia Wade presides over the 22 tennis courts. The nine-hole gulfside golf course is exclusively for guests. There are two marinas, one with Steve and Doris Colgate's Sailing School. In addition to 2½ miles of private beach, there are 18 swimming pools (many with poolside bars). A water-sports center also arranges parasailing, windsurfing, boat rentals, and more; bikes can also be rented. Chadwick's Shopping Center includes high-fashion boutiques, jewelry stores, and gift shops (all open to the public). Resortwear is featured in Reflections Dockside Boutique.

Expensive

'TWEEN WATERS INN, 15951 Captiva Dr., Captiva Island, FL 33924.

Tel. , or toll free 800/223-5865, 800/282-7650 in Florida. Fax 813/472-0249. 126 cottages. A/C TV TEL

$ Rates: High season, $150–$250 cottage. Low season, $80–$175 cottage. Ask about vacation packages. MC, V.

Although the 'Tween Waters Inn has been a favorite since 1926, the very casual resort gained fame from a frequent guest, J. N. "Ding" Darling, the Pulitzer Prize–winning *New York Times* cartoonist for whom the nearby wildlife refuge is named. Scenically located between the Gulf of Mexico and Pine Island Sound, the inn has a very appropriate name. Actually, the resort is mostly composed of cottages, a couple with fireplaces—nothing fancy, just simple white furniture and terrazzo floors—just what beachcombers would want. The private strip of beach is secluded by palm trees, Australian pines, and bushy sea grape trees. There's a very large swimming pool complex, complete with poolside bar and grill. Tennis courts are lighted for night play. At the full-service marina, there are charter captains to take you fishing, shelling, or sailing. Canoes and bikes can be rented.

Casual meals are offered at the bayside Canoe Club café and bar (good pizza). The casual gourmet will like the Old Captiva House, where seafood, pastas, and beef and veal dishes are among the specialties; it's open for dinner only from 5:30pm. During the peak season, reservations are recommended. Live entertainment is spotlighted nightly in the Crow's Nest and Lounge, from 9pm to 1am; happy hour is celebrated daily from 4 to 6pm.

Anne Morrow Lindbergh spent a winter vacation here writing *A Gift from the Sea.*

WHERE TO DINE

SANIBEL ISLAND

Expensive

JEAN-PAUL'S FRENCH CORNER, 708 Tarpon Bay Rd. Tel. 472-1493.

Cuisine: FRENCH. **Reservations:** Required.

$ Prices: Appetizers $6–$7; main courses $21–$25. $19 minimum per adult. MC, V.

Open: Dinner only, Mon–Sat seatings at 6 and 8:30pm. **Closed:** Usually May–Nov.

A favorite since 1979, this chic bistro is enhanced by large pots of beautiful flowers, French prints on wood-paneled walls, terra-cotta floors, and an unusual birdcage on the bar. Candlelight on the tables and the recorded soft music of a French chanteuse provide the right romantic touches. There's nothing pretentious here—no stiffly formal atmosphere, and the waiters are gracious. A welcoming treat, usually an eggplant tapenade dip, is presented as soon as customers are seated. If you've been craving authentic French onion soup, search no more—Jean-Paul's onion soup is a classic. The soft-shell crab à la provençale is deliciously crisp, adorned with a tangy tomato-based sauce, which is tasty spread on the accompanying just-baked French bread. Roast duckling in fruit sauce is a big favorite. Other excellent choices include veal medallions with mushrooms and sauce, filet mignon in a piquant green-peppercorn sauce, breast of chicken in a sassy lemon sauce, and daily fresh seafoods. For dessert, Jean-Paul's pecan pie and chocolate mousse can be described as "divine."

THE MAD HATTER, 6460 Sanibel-Captiva Rd. Tel. 472-0033.
Cuisine: NEW AMERICAN. **Reservations:** Required.
$ Prices: Appetizers $6–$10; main courses $18.95–$28. AE, MC, V.
Open: Dinner only, daily 5–10pm.

Beautifully located on the tip of Sanibel just before Blind Pass Bridge, this small waterfront restaurant (only 12 tables) has great views of the gulf and an exciting menu. Of course you'd expect fantastic food from a restaurant named for one of the characters in Lewis Carroll's *Alice In Wonderland.* Indeed, the food is a fantasy of cuisines, based on California, the Southwest, and the South with exotic accents. For example, one of the most interesting appetizers is fried wontons, stuffed with home-cured salmon, shiitake mushrooms, and pickled ginger, served with wasabi and sweet ginger-soy dipping sauce. Among the notable main dishes are spicy grilled shrimp, scallops, and vegetables on skewers with an orange-tequila and chive glaze, served with key lime orzo and black-bean quesadilla; and grilled grouper with roasted green pumpkin seed sauce, brown basmati rice, and honey-glazed string beans. Prime New York strip steak is also on the menu, accompanied by three-peppercorn butter, julienned sweet potatoes, roasted eggplant, crimini mushrooms, and onions laced with a soy-prune sauce. And you don't have to be a vegetarian to enjoy the garlic linguine with summer vegetables. Warm apple tart with homemade cinnamon ice cream is a favorite dessert. The wine list is highlighted by California estate wines. Sunsets are absolutely glorious when viewed from the large picture windows.

Moderate

HARBOR HOUSE, 1244 Periwinkle Way. Tel. 472-1242.
Cuisine: AMERICAN. **Reservations:** Recommended.
$ Prices: Appetizers $3.50–$7.50; main courses $11–$20. MC, V.
Open: Dinner only, daily 5–9:30pm.

This family-owned, casual restaurant claims to be the island's first seafood restaurant. "Olde Island" atmosphere prevails in a nautical setting. Among the favorite appetizers, listed under "Anchors Aweigh," are the "Captain's Stuffed Clams" and the deep-fried veggie combo accompanied by a creamy dill dip. If you have your sights set on seafood, the Florida lobster stuffed with crabmeat and the Sanibel scallops sautéed in garlic-butter sauce are favorites. Landlubbers are tempted with grilled Cajun-style chicken breast, filet mignon, New York strip steak, and barbecued spareribs. There's a children's menu also. Homemade key lime pie is prepared with the limes from the family's own trees. Cocktails and beer are served. For a delicious bargain, "early bird" special dinners, costing under $10, are featured daily from 5 to 6pm. Menu items are available for take-out.

THE JACARANDA, 1223 Periwinkle Way. Tel. 472-1771.
Cuisine: SEAFOOD/BEEF. **Reservations:** Recommended.
$ Prices: Appetizers $3.75–$6.95; main courses $11.95–$17.95. AE, MC, V.
Open: Dinner only, daily 5–10pm.

Named for the Brazilian purple-flowered jacaranda tree, this friendly, casual restaurant features a raw bar and dining in the screened patio. Or you may want to relax with one of the specialty cocktails, such as a Sanibel Sunrise or Island Lemonade. Recipient of several dining awards, the Jacaranda is best known for expertly prepared fish and seafood, which the chef will bake, broil, grill, or blacken according to your preference. However, the Black Angus strip steak, prime rib of beef, and chicken marsala are also very popular. Vegetarians will like the vegetables en papillote (julienned veggies baked in parchment paper). One of the most frequently ordered pasta dishes is the linguine combined with a dozen littleneck clams, tossed in a piquant red or white clam sauce. If you can't make up your mind between the seafood and the beef, why not order surf and turf? The Jacaranda version features a four- or eight-ounce filet mignon served with either five jumbo shrimp or an eight-ounce lobster tail. For dessert, the chef's key lime mousse pie is refreshing. Or for something delightfully gooey, the turtle pie is piled high with ice cream and crowned with caramel, fudge sauce, chopped nuts, and whipped cream. In the Patio Lounge, a happy hour is celebrated from 4 to 7pm, and there's dancing nightly plus live entertainment. Call ahead for the schedule.

TIMBERS RESTAURANT AND FISH MARKET, 703 Tarpon Bay Rd. Tel. 472-3128.

Cuisine: SEAFOOD/STEAK. **Reservations:** Not accepted.

$ Prices: Appetizers $3.95–$6.95; main courses $12.95–$20. AE, MC, V.

Open: Dinner only, daily 4:30–10pm. (Fish Market, Mon–Sat noon–10pm, Sun 2–10pm).

Newly located in the Timbers Center, this casual restaurant is very proud of being the winner (eight years in a row!) in the annual Taste of the Islands Awards for their seafoods and steaks. In fact, Timbers's sister restaurant, the Prawnbroker in Fort Myers, is rated as one of the best in southwestern Florida. Timbers prints a new fresh-fish menu every day and some of the selections might include red snapper, grouper, yellowtail, salmon, sole, scrod, swordfish, yellowfin tuna, mahi mahi, and blacktip shark. The chef will charcoal-broil or blacken your choice or steam the shellfish. Tasty Captiva crab cakes or soft-shell crabs can be selected sautéed or fried. Other favorites include pompano en papillote, fish 'n sirloin (with a six-ounce steak), and barbecued jumbo shrimp. Steaks are aged and cut on the premises, grilled exactly to your preference. Timbers even has a Fresh Fish Hotline (tel. 395-CRAB) if you want to know the fresh seafood selections of the day.

By the way, another member of the Timbers family is nearby: **Matt & Harry's Steak House,** at 975 Rabbit Rd. (tel. 472-TNDR).

TRUFFLES, at Casa Ybel, 2255 W. Gulf Dr. Tel. 472-9200.

Cuisine: AMERICAN/CONTINENTAL. **Reservations:** Recommended for dinner.

$ Prices: Appetizers $3.25–$6.95; main courses $11.75–$18.50. AE, DC, MC, V.

Open: Daily 11am–10pm; patio breakfast mid-Dec to mid-Apr daily 8:30–11am; jazz brunch Sun 10am–3pm.

Re-created from an elaborate Victorian mansion, Thistle Lodge, Sanibel's first resort on this site, Truffles combines gracious charm with casual island atmosphere. Windows look out to the gulf waters, or you can dine on the patio, weather permitting. A consistent award winner, Truffles is known for creative cuisine, especially such pastas as shrimp carbonara and chicken and sausage cannelloni. The menu also features "perfect prime rib," an apt description. A garlic, lime, and olive oil marinade adds exceptional flavor to grilled breast of chicken. Tomato-corn salsa is a tasty accompaniment to sautéed pompano. A variety of sandwiches, burgers, salads, and fried jumbo shrimp are available for lunch or light dinner. There are marvelous desserts too, such as cappuccino/white-chocolate pie, raspberry Grand Marnier cake, and chunky chocolate-chip cheesecake. Libations may be sipped in the Turtle Watch Lounge Patio, where the happy hour is celebrated from 5 to 7pm on Wednesday and Friday. On Sunday, tropical drinks and casual fare are delightful on the patio, when a guitarist entertains from 3 to 6pm.

Truffles belongs to the same Cuisine Management company as the Truffles in nearby Naples.

WIL'S LANDING RESTAURANT, LOUNGE AND FISH MARKET, 1200 Periwinkle Way. Tel. 472-4772.

Cuisine: AMERICAN. **Reservations:** Not accepted.

$ Prices: Appetizers $3.95–$9.50; main courses $13.95–$22. AE, MC, V.

Open: Lunch daily 11:30am–2pm; dinner daily 5–10:30pm (lounge and fish market open at 11:30am; early-bird dinner 5–6pm).

It's very evident that fish and shellfish are really fresh in this attractive restaurant, as their own fish market on the premises attracts so many customers. At the raw bar, just-shucked oysters can become glamorous when topped with diced red onion, sour cream, and caviar—ask for oysters Romanoff. Bahamian conch chowder is one of the specialty soups, homemade in Wil's kitchen. The interesting menu also features poultry, beef, and pastas, in addition to the fish and shellfish. One of the favorite dishes is chicken and shrimp piccata, a delicious combination. For the kids, there's a special menu, inexpensively priced. Among the delectable desserts are Kahlúa chocolate-chip cheesecake and a fresh-fruit fondue with white- or dark-chocolate dipping sauce. Check Wil's entertainment schedule for the special nights, when bands play for dancing from 9:30pm to 1am, and the karaoke fun nights.

WINDOWS ON THE WATER, 1451 Middle Gulf Dr. Tel. 472-5151.

Cuisine: GULF SHORE/CONTINENTAL. **Reservations:** Recommended.

$ Prices: Appetizers $3.95–$6.95; main courses $13.95–$19.95. AE, MC, V.

Open: Breakfast daily 7am–10am, lunch daily 11am–2pm, dinner daily 5–10pm; brunch Sun.

Relaxed elegance prevails in this handsomely decorated dining room, enhanced by floor-to-ceiling Palladian windows that look out to glorious views of palm trees extending to the beach and gulf, all beautifully reflected in the mirrored back wall. Executive Chef Peter Harman, who trained with famous Paul Prudhomme, is well known for his innovative culinary expertise. His gulf shore cuisine blends foods representative of southwestern Florida with his own mixture of intriguing seasonings and tropical fruits. Among the favorites are Sanibel crab cakes with mustard sauce; seafood ravioli laced with lobster sauce; snapper Casa Ybel, garnished with blue crabmeat; Sanibel Sampler, a combination of bronzed mahi mahi, cedar-planked salmon, and snapper; and grilled filet mignon accompanied by caramelized onions and sautéed mushrooms. His key lime pie and the chocolate bayou cake are delectable desserts. No wonder that Windows on the Water has won so many awards! The wine list offers excellent choices by the glass or bottle. And you can purchase Chef Harman's seasonings in the gift shop.

Budget

BUD'S ANY FISH YOU WISH, 1473-C Periwinkle Way. Tel. 472-5700.

Cuisine: SEAFOOD. **Reservations:** Not required.

$ Prices: Main courses $4–$12. AE, MC, V.

Open: Breakfast daily 8–11am; lunch/dinner daily 11am–9pm (early-bird dinner specials 4–6pm; dine in only).

You can wear your most casual attire in this rustic restaurant, featuring an under-the-sea motif with papier-mâché fish mobiles. Fish and shellfish are deliciously prepared to your preference—select your seasonings, too. Meals include salad, fresh-made bread, Louisiana beans and rice or homemade pasta topped with Alfredo, marinara, or clam sauce—a bargain. The bayou combo, a platter of assorted steamed seafood, appears to be stacked a foot high; allow a good half hour to eat everything on the plate. If you don't want fish, Cajun chicken with beans and rice, New York strip steak, and pasta are other menu choices. "Skyscraper" club sandwiches are big favorites. Seafood in baskets is served crisp and hot. Homemade desserts are highlighted by Vestal Virgin Cake and Georgia Mae's Cousin's Divorced Sister's Brother-in-Law's Mud Ball. Bud's homemade ice cream and milkshakes are delicious. Cappuccino and espresso are prepared Italian style. The bakery sells hot-from-the-oven breads and goodies. Special cakes can be ordered 48 hours in advance. All menu items can be packaged for take-out.

CALAMITY JANE'S CAFE, 630 Tarpon Bay Rd. Tel. 472-6622.

Cuisine: AMERICAN. **Reservations:** Not accepted.

$ Prices: $4.95–$10.95. AE, DC, DISC, MC, V.

Open: Breakfast Mon–Sat 7–11am, Sun 8am–noon; lunch Mon–Sat 11:30am–3pm; dinner Mon–Sat 5–9pm (early-bird specials after 3pm).

One of the island's most popular restaurants for breakfast, lunch, dinner, and refreshments, this friendly café was formerly a post office. Among the eye-openers for breakfast are the poor boy (bacon, egg, and cheese on a hoagie) and the thick cinnamon-raisin French toast. Great sandwiches, tacos, salads, burgers, grilled fish, seafood, jambalaya, "finger food" baskets, pasta, chicken, and homemade pies are on the varied menu. Beer, wine, and champagne splits can also be ordered. But the all-time favorite here is the savory New England clam chowder, which frequent customers say is "the best." Anything on the menu can be ordered to take out.

ISLAND PIZZA, 1619 Periwinkle Way. Tel. 472-1581.
Cuisine: ITALIAN. **Reservations:** Not accepted.
$ Prices: Main courses $5–$14. No credit cards.
Open: Daily 11am–9pm.

Ever tried Crusty Curl Pizza? This is the place for a new treat. Sicilian pizza is another favorite. In addition to pizzas, which have made this restaurant popular for many years, the menu also features veal, chicken, and eggplant parmigiana; calzones; and salads, pastas, steaks, burgers, ribs, homemade soups, hot submarines, and all sorts of deli sandwiches. Beer and wine are served. You can eat in, take out, or have delivery service (after 5pm).

THE LAZY FLAMINGO, 1036 Periwinkle Way. Tel. 472-6939.
Cuisine: AMERICAN. **Reservations:** Not accepted.
$ Prices: $4.50–$14.95. AE, DC, MC, V.
Open: Daily 11:30am–1am.

What could be more laid-back than a lazy flamingo? In this very casual, very friendly restaurant, T-shirts and shorts or jeans are the dress code. At the raw bar, oysters are shucked to order. One of the favorites is "The Pot," about two dozen select oysters or clams, or a combination, steamed in beer and spices. Beer-steamed peel-and-eat shrimp is also popular. Conch chowder, conch fritters, and conch salad are reminiscent of the Bahamas (where conch is considered an aphrodisiac). The flamingo-pink menu also offers buffalo wings, burgers, salads, grilled grouper platters, grilled chicken breast sandwiches, steak sandwiches, mussels marinara, and much more. Beer, wine, and champagne are also served. Try chocolate key lime cheesecake for dessert. Food can be ordered to take out.

LIGHTHOUSE CAFE, 362 Periwinkle Way. Tel. 472-0303.
Cuisine: AMERICAN. **Reservations:** Not accepted.
$ Prices: $3.75–$10. MC, V.
Open: Breakfast daily 7am–3pm; lunch daily 11am–3pm; dinner daily 5–9pm.

When you're on vacation and don't have to care about schedules, isn't it nice to know that you can order breakfast up to 3pm? The Lighthouse omelets are actually meals, especially the ocean frittata with delicately seasoned scallops, crabmeat, shrimp, broccoli, and fresh mushrooms, crowned by an artichoke heart and creamy Alfredo sauce. Seafood Benedict is another delight—or select a turkey Benedict, if you prefer. For a romantic eye-opener, the Lighthouse mimosa consists of freshly squeezed orange juice, chilled champagne, and fresh-fruit garnish.

One of the busiest on the island, this casual restaurant also features an interesting lunch menu, including seafood topped off with melted Swiss cheese on a grilled croissant, Philly cheese steak, a tangy seafood salad, and tasty soups. Usually, Tuesday through Thursday, kids can eat for free when their parents dine here.

McT's SHRIMP HOUSE & TAVERN, 1523 Periwinkle Way. Tel. 472-3161.
Cuisine: SEAFOOD. **Reservations:** Not accepted.
$ Prices: Main courses $9–$26. AE, DISC, MC, V.
Open: Dinner only, daily 5–10pm in the Shrimp House, 4pm–12:30am in the Tavern.

An Old Florida atmosphere prevails in this very casual restaurant, where budget dining is fun in the lively tavern. You can select your preference in seafood from the abundant raw bar or enjoy steamer baskets, burritos, sandwiches, and a variety of munchies. Usually on Sunday and Thursday the Tavern features a Maine lobster special for under

$10. The Tavern is also famous for the key lime daiquiri, a very refreshing cocktail. For fun and games, the dartboard is popular—and so is the large-screen TV. Every night, "wannabe" singers attend the karaoke party.

In the adjoining Shrimp House, crowds line up for the early-bird dinners, served to the first 100 people (seating from 5 to 6pm only). For approximately $8, the selections include prime rib, steamed shrimp platters, barbecued beef ribs, seafood Créole, and fish and chips. If you want to spend more, order one of the award-winning jumbo shrimp dinners or all-you-can-eat shrimp-and-crab platters. There's a kids' menu, too. The wickedly rich Sanibel mud pie is just one of the homemade desserts.

QUARTERDECK RESTAURANT, 1625 Periwinkle Way. Tel. 472-1033.

Cuisine: AMERICAN. **Reservations:** Not accepted.

$ Prices: Main courses $3–$18.95. MC, V.

Open: Breakfast daily 8am–noon; lunch daily 11am–2:30pm; dinner daily 5–9:30pm.

The Quarterdeck is a sister restaurant to the Lighthouse Café. Here you'll find the same well-prepared bacon and eggs, pancakes, omelets, and more, but the menu is more ambitious. One of the favorite specialties here is San Francisco eggs, consisting of freshly ground beef, chopped spinach, and scallions sautéed with eggs and served with hash-brown potatoes and sourdough bread. The luncheon menu features hearty sandwiches, a variety of burgers, many salads, and soup-and-salad combinations. From the lengthy dinner menu, you can choose grilled duckling, seafood, steaks, or baby back ribs. Although the Quarterdeck is casual, the appetizers are sophisticated and include baked Brie, fried calamari rings, seafood-stuffed mushrooms, quesadillas, and Cajun shrimp on a skewer. Irresistible desserts are highlighted by key lime cheesecake and the chocolate pecan pie.

SANIBEL GRILL, 703 Tarpon Bay Rd. Tel. 472-HIKE.

Cuisine: AMERICAN. **Reservations:** Not accepted.

$ Prices: $2.95–$8.95. AE, MC, V.

Open: Mon–Fri 11:30am–midnight, Sat–Sun 4pm–midnight.

Adjoining the famous Timbers restaurant, the Sanibel Grill is part of the Timbers "family." A rendezvous for sports fans, who frequent the Sports Bar, this casual eatery is always lively. And you don't have to be a sports fan to know that the charcoal-grilled burgers are probably the best on the island. And where else could you get charcoal-grilled pizza? The overstuffed sandwiches are delicious, especially the grouper Reuben on rye. Soups, salads, quesadillas, and shrimp basket are also luncheon choices. A $5 lunch special is usually featured. There's lots of late-night action, when fans watch sports on the 100-inch satellite TV. A lively happy hour is featured daily from 4 to 7pm and 10pm to midnight.

CAPTIVA ISLAND

Expensive

BUBBLE ROOM, 15001 Captiva Dr. Tel. 472-5558.

Cuisine: BEEF/SEAFOOD. **Reservations:** Not accepted.

$ Prices: Appetizers $4–$7; main courses $16.95–$26.95. AE, DC, DISC, MC, V.

Open: Lunch daily 11:30am–2:30pm; dinner daily 5:30–10pm.

At the first sight of the restaurant's exterior, painted in bubblegum-ball colors of purple, green, pink, and yellow, you just know that an outrageous decor awaits inside. But who could imagine this amusing blend of the '30s, '40s, and '50s with a "Hooray for Hollywood" motif and bubbles everywhere? Puppets suspended from the ceiling, statues of great movie stars, Christmas decorations, multicolored bubbling lights, toy trains, and thousands of movie stills add to the circus atmosphere. Big Band–era music sets a nostalgic tempo from antique jukeboxes. Everyone loves the Bubble Room, which began in 1979 with 28 seats and has expanded to a 150-seat restaurant and bar.

Aside from the fun and games, the Bubble Room receives many dining awards. The amusing menu features specialties named for old-time movie stars. Food is served in King Kong portions but there's the "Tiny Bubble" for smaller appetites. Friendly

Bubble Scout servers first bring out a basket of warm "sticky" buns and the wonderful Bubble Bread baked with Roquefort cheese and oregano. For the happy ending, the cappuccino cheesecake or fudge nut brownie pie merit much applause. At night, the pink piano and piano-key bar attract a fun crowd and visiting celebrities.

CAPTIVA INN, 11509 Andy Rosse Lane. Tel. 472-9129.

Cuisine: CONTINENTAL. **Reservations:** Required.

$ Prices: Prix-fixe seven-course dinner $37.50. No credit cards.

Open: Dinner only, Tues–Sat from 7pm.

Now under the new management of host Liam Drummond, the Captiva Inn's tables are elegantly adorned with crystal, lace, and linen. When the reservation is made, guests will be advised about the evening's choice of entrees and details about the preparation. Everything will be perfect, as executive chef Bill Yourell was formerly with the Mad Hatter and is very well known for his culinary expertise.

Upon arrival, guests are welcomed with a complimentary champagne crème cassis drink, which is refilled through the appetizer course. The gourmet feast includes a choice of appetizers, homemade soup, fresh salad with avocado dressing, fruit sorbet, the entree, tempting desserts, and European coffee. Should you have any special food requests or are a vegetarian, just consult with chef Bill or host Liam in advance. Among the entrees to choose from are aged beef, lamb, duck, veal, pork, Florida grouper, shrimp, and snapper. You can order ahead from the wine list, if you wish. In the near future, the Captiva Inn hopes to serve dinner on Sunday also and to expand with an additional à la carte menu. No smoking in the dining room, please.

THE GREENHOUSE, Captiva Village Sq. Tel. 476-6006.

Cuisine: CONTINENTAL. **Reservations:** Recommended.

$ Prices: Appetizers $7.25–$9.25; main courses $21–$30. MC, V.

Open: Dinner only, daily 5:45–10pm.

Unusual culinary creations attract local gourmets and vacationers alike to this cozy 12-table restaurant. Decorated with plants and art, the dining area shares space with the open kitchen. Among the innovative specialties are lobster, tasso, and pozole tamale in tomatillo sauce; grilled Florida quail with mascarpone cheese and tomatoes in lentil sauce; nutty duck breast atop tasso grits and green-corn sauce; and vegetarian lasagne layered with grilled vegetables and four cheeses. The Gulf Coast cioppino, brimming with seafood, is just as delicious (if not more so) than San Francisco's cioppino. Should you merely want a grilled New York strip steak, that's on the menu too. Don't expect the mundane from pastas, salads, and sandwiches—each selection is prepared and garnished very creatively. You just know connoisseurs dine here, when Russian caviar headlines the menu. Wines can be ordered by the bottle or glass.

Moderate

BELLINI'S OF CAPTIVA, Andy Rosse Lane. Tel. 472-6866.

Cuisine: NORTHERN ITALIAN. **Reservations:** Recommended.

$ Prices: Appetizers $5.50–$7.95; main courses $10.50–$21.50. AE, MC, V.

Open: Dinner only, daily 5:30–10pm (cocktail lounge, 7pm–late).

Bella, bella (beautiful!) describes the indoor dining room. When weather permits, romantic dining is in the garden courtyard's tropical setting. Indoors or outdoors, the favorite prelude to dinner is the frozen peach Bellini cocktail, a version of the world-famous Bellini served at Harry's Bar in Venice, Italy. Intriguing choices from the antipasti list are carpaccio of beef tenderloin, prosciutto fantasia (Parma ham, melon, and mozzarella), crisply fried calamari, and cozze posillipo (steamed mussels with a marinara sauce). Highlighting the pasta dishes is penne Captiva, pasta in a vodka-mascarpone-cheese sauce, tossed with julienned smoked salmon. Veal is a specialty, of course, and the Don Andrea Combo is very different (veal, peppers, and shrimp sprinkled with parmesan cheese). Fresh fish, lobster tail, and roast duckling are presented with that special Italian touch. The superstar of the menu is "Bellini's Romantic Adventure," featuring two Maine lobsters and a bottle of Dom Perignon champagne (the price is $150, but isn't a wonderful romantic adventure worth a million?). On the wine list, you will find excellent wines from Italy, France, and California. There's usually nightly entertainment from 7pm in the cocktail lounge.

MUCKY DUCK, Andy Rosse Lane. Tel. 472-3434.
Cuisine: SEAFOOD/PUB FOOD. **Reservations:** Not accepted.
$ Prices: Appetizers $3.25–$7.95; main courses $8.95–$17. MC, V.
Open: Lunch Mon–Sat 11:30am–2:30pm; dinner Mon–Sat 5–9:30pm.

This well-known British-style pub is so close to the gulf that the views are great for sunset-watching. Because tables are so limited and the pub is so popular, expect to wait before being seated. But the friendly owner makes the rounds and keeps everybody in good humor. Fish and chips and the ploughman's lunch are menu favorites. For dinner, Avalon shrimp is a special treat, with deep-fried crabmeat-stuffed shrimp. Charcoal-grilled Polynesian chicken, steaks, broiled fish, and a vegetarian platter are also on the dinner menu. For dessert, the Mucky Duck homemade key lime pie is among the temptations. Imported bottled beers represent six countries. Wine can be ordered by the glass or bottle. The Mucky Duck has been such a success on Captiva that a second one was opened in Fort Myers Beach, but the atmosphere there is more subdued. Mucky Duck T-shirts and other Mucky Duck souvenirs are for sale at both locations.

OLD CAPTIVA HOUSE, in the 'Tween Waters Inn, Captiva Rd. Tel. 472-5161.
Cuisine: SEAFOOD/STEAK. **Reservations:** Recommended.
$ Prices: Appetizers $3.95–$6.95; main courses $12.95. MC, V.
Open: Breakfast Mon–Sat 7:30–10:30am; lunch Mon–Sat noon–3pm; dinner daily 5:30–10pm; brunch Sun 9am–1pm.

In the good old days, when New York cartoonist "Ding" Darling stayed at the 'Tween Waters Inn, he was a regular in the Old Captiva House. The dining room and piano lounge are decorated with his cartoons. Recently, the restaurant has experienced a popularity boom, thanks to good reviews from restaurant critics, who have applauded the Captiva bisque, mussels marinara, veal saltimbocca, coq au vin, shrimp scampi, and grilled fresh tuna with pecan-butter topping. The children's menu features pastas, burgers, chicken fingers, and grouper fingers. Although the restaurant is casual, nostalgia lends a touch of class. You can reminisce with a slice of old-fashioned Black Forest cake or crème caramel for dessert.

SUNSHINE CAFE, Captiva Village Sq. Tel. 472-6200.
Cuisine: CONTINENTAL. **Reservations:** Recommended.
$ Prices: Main courses $7.25–$31.95. No credit cards.
Open: Daily 11:30am–9:30pm.

All in all, this friendly café has only 10 tables (five inside and five outdoors) but the food is worth the wait. Specialties have a New Orleans accent, such as the hearty gumbo, "Po' Boy" sandwich, and grilled chicken breast with spicy tasso ham. And if you like pasta Italian style, you'll love the sauté of fresh shellfish served over linguine with fresh herbs, roasted garlic, and imported cheese. Grilled prosciutto-wrapped jumbo shrimp accompanied by tropical fruit chutney is deliciously different. Or you can order light dishes, such as a plate of black beans and rice or a Caesar salad. The wine list is very impressive, especially for such a small café. For dessert, tempting choices change daily, but the favorites are white-chocolate cheesecake in an Oreo-cookie crust and banana rum cake on a berry compote. Anything on the menu can be ordered to take out for a scrumptious picnic.

SHOPPING

Tropically-landscaped ✪ **Periwinkle Place,** 2075 Periwinkle Way, flaunts 36 swanky shops and boutiques. This is Sanibel's largest shopping center and includes **Chico's** (tel. 472-0202), where local designer Helene Garlnick has created dramatic casual fashions and accessories. Chico's is also located in upscale Chadwick's Square on Captiva (tel. 472-6101 or 472-4426). **Congress Jewelers** in Periwinkle Place specializes in gold and precious stones. Their specially designed gold jewelry, inspired by seashells and sea creatures, is unique. Call for a free catalog (tel. toll free 800/882-6624).

For shells galore, visit **She Sells Sea Shells,** 1157 Periwinkle Way (tel.

472-3991), and **Neptune's Treasures,** at Tree Tops Center, 1101 Periwinkle Way (tel. 472-3132). If you're interested in crafts or would like to make your own shell gifts, visit **Three Crafty Ladies,** 1446 Periwinkle Way (tel. 472-2893).

In Olde Sanibel Plaza on Tarpon Bay Road, the **Sanibel 5 & 10** is a fun place to buy comical cards, joke gifts, beachwear, Disney toys, and more. The **Island Book Nook,** 2330 Palm Ridge Place (tel. 472-6777), stocks more than 10,000 new and used books and is the islands' paperback exchange.

Among the interesting art galleries are **Jungle Drums,** 11532 Andy Rosse Lane on Captiva, and on Sanibel, **Matsumoto Gallery,** 751 Tarpon Bay Rd.; **Sagebrush Gallery,** 2340 Periwinkle Way (tel. 472-6971); **Island Wildlife Gallery,** 2353-A Periwinkle Way (tel. 395-1100); **Sagebrush Gallery,** 2340 Periwinkle Way (tel. 472-6971); **Whale and the Bird Nature Gallery,** 1560 Periwinkle Way, (tel. 472-8333); **Sanibel Gallery,** 1628 Periwinkle Way (tel. 472-3307); and **Dolphin Waters Marine Life Art Gallery,** on Tarpon Bay Road in Timbers Center (tel. 472-4688).

Handcrafted stoneware, porcelain, and Raku are featured at **A Touch of Sanibel Pottery,** 1544 Periwinkle Way (tel. 472-4330). The **Lion's Paw,** 1025 Periwinkle Way (tel. 472-0909), is notable for a wide array of gifts, fashions, jewelry, and fashionable accessories.

On Captiva, the **Captiva Discount Liquor Store,** 11500 Andy Rosse Lane (tel. 472-5668), and **Captiva Liquors,** across from the South Seas Plantation (tel. 472-5366), are well stocked with spirits.

As previously mentioned, Bailey's Shopping Center has a variety of stores for one-stop shopping, including **Bailey's General Store,** 2477 Periwinkle Way (tel. 472-1516), dating back to 1899, which sells everything from fishing tackle to groceries.

EVENING ENTERTAINMENT

THE PERFORMING ARTS

THE PIRATE PLAYHOUSE, 2200 Periwinkle Way, Sanibel. Tel. 472-0006.

From December through April, excellent professional theater is performed six nights a week (Monday through Saturday) with curtain time at 8pm. Since 1984 the renovated playhouse has featured such productions as *Same Time Next Year, Lend Me a Tenor, I'm Not Rappaport, Jacques Brel Is Alive and Well and Living in Paris,* and other Broadway hits. On Wednesday a matinee performance is usually scheduled.

Admission: Tickets, approximately $20.

OLD SCHOOLHOUSE THEATER, Periwinkle Way (across from the Pirate Playhouse), Sanibel. Tel. 472-6862.

Professional productions are presented during the winter months and the community theater group performs in the off-season (call for the current schedule and prices).

THE CLUB & BAR SCENE

You won't find glitzy lounges on the islands, but night owls will enjoy the fun places to roost. And if you want to get an early start, early-evening happy hours are very popular, especially if complimentary hors d'oeuvres are served.

BELLINI'S OF CAPTIVA, 11521 Andy Rosse Lane, Captiva. Tel. 472-6866.

Good nightly entertainment is spotlighted in the lounge from 7pm until late. Just about everyone orders a peach Bellini cocktail.

CHADWICK'S LOUNGE, in Chadwick's Restaurant (at the entrance to the South Seas Plantation Resort), Captiva. Tel. 472-5111.

Each night except Tuesday different entertainment is scheduled from 8:30pm (call ahead for the program). There's a nice, large dance floor to trip the light fantastic. If you get hungry, a limited menu is served until 11pm. The daily happy hour is from 4:30 to 7:30pm with complimentary hors d'oeuvres.

CROW'S NEST LOUNGE, in the 'Tween Waters Inn, Captiva. Tel. 472-5161.

Considered the islands' number-one nightspot, the Crow's Nest features live entertainment nightly from 9pm to 1am. It's fun to dance to the live bands, too. Every Monday from 6 to 9pm, kooky crab races are scheduled. During the daily happy hour (from 4 to 6pm), drinks are half price. There's a new Sports Pub here too, with a happy hour on Saturday and Sunday from 11:30am to 6pm.

McT's TAVERN, 1523 Periwinkle Way, Sanibel. Tel. 472-3161.

In this very informal tavern, you can play darts or video games, watch the large-screen TV, and participate in "Karaoke Kraziness." The tavern is open daily from 4pm to 12:30am.

MULLIGAN'S LOUNGE, at the Dunes, 949 Sandcastle Rd., Sanibel. Tel. 472-3355.

Should you plan to play on the golf course or tennis courts here (open to the public), you might like to know that the happy hour is celebrated from 3 to 6pm with reduced drink prices and complimentary hot, buttered popcorn. It's a good opportunity, also, to take a look at this attractive resort.

PATIO LOUNGE, at the Jacaranda, 1223 Periwinkle Way, Sanibel. Tel. 472-1771.

At this island "hot spot," listen to or dance to great live bands every night of the week. Until midnight, a special raw bar menu and light menu are available. Entertainment usually begins at 7pm. Happy hour, from 4 to 7pm, offers reduced prices on most drinks.

SANIBEL GRILL, at the Timbers Restaurant, 703 Tarpon Bay Rd., Sanibel. Tel. 472-HIKE.

Open from 11:30am until midnight seven days a week, the big lure here is the lively Sports Bar, flaunting a 100-inch satellite TV. Charcoal-grilled pizza and burgers are also attractions. Happy hours are daily from 4 to 7pm and 10pm to midnight. You can't get happier than that.

SUNSET LOUNGE, at the Sundial Beach and Tennis Resort, 1451 Middle Gulf Dr., Sanibel. Tel. 472-4151.

Sunsets seem to be more splendid from the window wall of this very attractive, classy lounge. Dancing to a live band and entertainment are featured nightly from 9pm. The happy hour, from 5:45 to 8:45pm, is not to be missed, when well-known islander Helen Skelton performs at the piano—she has been a favorite here for a long time. NBC television weatherman Willard Scott and his wife often come to listen to Helen's songs. The complimentary hot and cold happy hour buffet features such goodies as buffalo wings, veggies to dip, and more. Domestic wines and draft beer are discounted.

TARWINKLE'S LOUNGE, at the Tarwinkle Seafood Emporium, Periwinkle Way and Tarpon Bay Rd., Sanibel. Tel. 472-1366.

Fishwatchers have fun observing the more than 500-gallon aquarium from the bar. The lounge happy hour is from 3:30 to 7pm daily—and all day Sunday. In season, football fans have their eyes glued on the 61-inch TV. Reduced prices are offered on most drinks, and special prices on light food. On Friday night, the tacos are complimentary. Karaoke is in the spotlight on Tuesday and Friday. The lounge opens every day at 11:30am and is open until 1am—a friendly hangout for night owls.

TRUFFLES TURTLE WATCH LOUNGE AND PATIO, at Truffles Restaurant, Casa Ybel, 2255 W. Gulf Dr., Sanibel. Tel. 472-9200.

Every Wednesday and Friday from 5 to 7pm the "attitude adjustment" hour attracts residents and vacationers for relaxing, live guitar music, and complimentary light food. At Truffles Sunset Pool Bar, Sanibel's Danny Morgan performs from 3 to

6pm on Sunday. The pool bar is open daily from 11am to sunset, offering a menu of appetizers, light foods, and tropical drinks.

WIL'S LANDING, 1200 Periwinkle Way, Sanibel. Tel. 472-4772.

The daily happy hour begins when the restaurant opens at 11:30am and continues until 7pm. From 5 to 7pm, free hors d'oeuvres are served. There's usually dancing to a live band on Monday and Saturday from 10pm. Karaoke is featured twice a week. Call ahead for the entertainment schedule.

EASY EXCURSIONS

Island-hopping is part of the fun during a Shell Coast vacation. Fascinating barrier islands, imbued with ancient history and legends, are accessible only by boat, and trips usually last about a half hour. You may want to linger longer after shelling on Robinson Crusoe–style beaches, and enjoy a delicious meal in a cozy inn or revel in the luxury of tropical tranquility. Cruising the scenic waters between the barrier islands is similar to taking a back country road rather than the superhighway. What a thrill to watch playful dolphins diving in and out of the waters and to observe countless cormorants, egrets, and frigate birds on the mangrove keys. A captained boat can be arranged from a Sanibel marina or on Captiva at the 'Tween Waters Inn Marina or the South Seas Plantation Marina. Of course, you can rent a boat and be your own skipper. Tour boats also leave from Pine Island (accessible by bridge), such as the *Tropic Star* at the Four Winds Marina (tel. 283-0015), offering cruises to Cabbage Key for lunch or dinner. If there's an inn on an island which piques your interest, just call to find out how boat transportation is arranged.

CABBAGE KEY

Scenically located at Mile Marker 60 on the Intracoastal Waterway, Cabbage Key must have been a favorite seafood eatery for the ancient Calusas. Their shell mounds have given the 100-acre key one of the highest elevations in the area. Tall coconut palms are everywhere, but the island derives its name from the profusion of cabbage palms. There are special walking trails on the island for nature lovers.

Where to Stay and Dine

CABBAGE KEY INN, Cabbage Key. Tel. 813/283-2278. 6 rms, 4 cottages.
$ Rates: $70 double; $145 cottage. MC, V.

One of the few signs of civilization on the islet is the rustic, white house built in the 1930s by mystery novelist Mary Roberts Rinehart and her son. Eventually the home was converted into a cozy inn with guest rooms, a dining room, and a bar. Certainly the dining room wallpaper is the most expensive anywhere—signed one-dollar bills completely cover the walls and ceiling for a total of perhaps more than $25,000. You, too, may autograph a dollar bill and tape it on the wall if you're able to find the space. According to legend, fishermen would leave their names on a dollar bill before going out for the day, to make sure that a beer and sandwich would be available upon their return. Jimmy Buffet is a frequent visitor and some fans claim that the popular singer was inspired here to write his hit song "Cheeseburger in Paradise" (yes, the burgers are juicy and thick).

Since this is an island, with no supermarket in sight, the Cabbage Key Inn features mainly local specialties on the lunch and dinner menus, such as grilled grouper, charcoal-broiled shrimp, seafood with pasta, and key lime pie. At dinner, grilled New York strip steak can be ordered. Prices range from about $10 to $25. The dining room is open from 7:30am (a delicious breakfast is served) to 9pm Monday through Saturday and from 6:30am to 7pm on Sunday. At night, the bar is often lively, especially when there are visiting celebrities, and when talented guests play the piano and guitar.

Yes, the inn now has electricity and indoor plumbing. As for telephones, there's one in the owner's office and a pay phone at the dock. Oh, yes, there is a TV, and it's in the bar. Especially on weekends, the Cabbage Key Inn is very popular with boaters and tourists who come for breakfast, lunch, or dinner. For reservations write to P.O. Box 200, Pineland, FL 33945.

CAYO COSTA ISLAND STATE PARK

This could be the closest one can get to a deserted tropical island paradise. In fact, the beach is rated one of the nation's best. Cayo Costa State Park encompasses most of the island, which is the largest in the unspoiled barrier-island chain. There are miles of deserted white sand beaches, perfect for finding at least 50–60 different kinds of shells. And the swimming is delightful. The island contains acres of pine forest, mangrove swamp, oak palm hammocks, and grassy areas with palm trees (there are no paved roads). In addition to a bonanza of shells, many species of birds and wildlife can be observed. Fishing, boating, picnicking, and primitive camping are allowed.

The state maintains primative cabins on the northern portion of the island, near Johnson Shoals, where the shelling is extra-special. The island's only full-time resident is the park ranger. For cabin rentals or information, contact Cayo Costa State Park, P.O. Box 1150, Boca Grande, FL 33921 (tel. 813/964-0375).

Access is by boat only. Captain Mike Fuery offers fishing and shelling excursions from 'Tween Waters Inn Marina on Captiva Island (tel. 472-5161). The *Tropic Star* sails out to Cayo Costa daily at 9:45am from Four Winds Marina (tel. 283-2278) on Pine Island. The cruise stops at Cayo Costa first, then proceeds to Cabbage Key for lunch, and stops again at Cayo Costa on the return, arriving back at Pine Island at 4pm. Lunch is on your own, of course. Or you can stay on Cayo Costa (take a picnic lunch) and return on the afternoon boat.

GASPARILLA ISLAND

According to legend, the infamous pirate José Gaspar lived in style on this seven-mile-long barrier island, which he named for himself. From this home base, Gaspar would sail out with his pirates to plunder ships and kidnap any wealthy women who might be aboard. In one year alone, his log book recorded the looting and burning of 40 Spanish galleons. During his 25-year career, José Gaspar was "Super Pirate." His buried treasure chests have never been found, though legend claims that his pirates buried their personal wealth on nearby Cayo Pelau and that the area is haunted by the pirates' ghosts to discourage treasure seekers.

Gaspar would not be pleased to know that these days most people refer to Gasparilla Island as **Boca Grande,** which is actually the name of the island's town, founded by the affluent DuPont family in the 1880s. By the 1920s the charming town had become a popular place for wealthy tourists to escape the harsh northern winter weather. In addition, the tarpon fishing was, and still is, the best in the world. The island became the vacation hideaway for such millionaires as John Jacob Astor, J. Pierpont Morgan, and Barron Collier (for whom Collier County is named). Elegant mansions were built on the island, but these are hidden from view by luxuriant foliage and high stucco walls. Dead-end lanes lead to the gulf. You get a glimpse of these magnificent mansions while driving or biking in the 29th Street area, a neighborhood belonging to some of the richest families in the country.

Park Avenue is considered the island's downtown. Railroad Plaza, formerly the railroad depot, is a handsome turn-of-the-century pink-brick structure with a rose-colored tile roof, housing a cluster of classy boutiques and the Loose Caboose ice-cream parlor. Evidently the late Hollywood actress Katherine Hepburn had a sweet tooth, as she frequented the ice cream parlor whenever she visited the island. It's not known if former President George Bush and his wife, Barbara, stopped in for ice cream during their five-day vacation on the island after the 1992 elections.

A seven-mile paved bike route goes through downtown to the white sand gulf beach; rental bikes are available. One of the prettiest streets for biking or strolling is **Banyan Street,** lined with huge, very old tangle-limbed banyan trees. If you're interested in shells, don't miss the **DuPont Shell Collection** in the Johann Fust Community Library, an unusual pink stucco building which used to be a millionaire's residence. Shutterbugs like to photograph the **Boca Grande Lighthouse** in a gulf-front park, where you can picnic. And it's fun to photograph the street signs with such amusing names as Dam-If-I-Will and Dam-If-I-Care.

Among the interesting **restaurants** are the casual Lighthouse Hole Restaurant, the popular Laff-A-Lot, and the swanky Pink Elephant. Miller's Marina, where pelicans like to rendezvous, and Whidden's Marina can give you information about **fishing charters or sightseeing excursions.**

Tarpon fishing is one of the island's big lures. Gasparilla Island is "the tarpon fishing capital of the world," thanks to the greatest feeding and breeding grounds in Boca Grande Pass. The **World's Richest Tarpon Tournament,** usually the first weekend in July, features a $100,000 prize. On the charter boats, most fishing captains are third-generation experts and members of the Boca Grande Fishing Guides Association. For a free informative tarpon-fishing brochure, write to the association at P.O. Box 676, Boca Grande, FL 33921. For information about the island, write to **Boca Grande Chamber of Commerce,** P.O. Box 704, Boca Grande, FL 33921 (tel. 813/964-0568).

Gasparilla is accessible both by boat and from the mainland via U.S. 41. About four miles beyond Port Charlotte, turn west onto Fla. 771, leading to the Boca Grande causeway (toll: $3.20); from there, follow the signs to Boca Grande. Depending on traffic, the drive from Fort Myers is about two hours, and about three hours from Naples (less than 20 miles from Port Charlotte).

Where to Stay

GASPARILLA INN, Fifth Ave. at Palm, Boca Grande, FL 33921. Tel. 813/964-2201. Fax 813/964-2733. 150 rms, suites, and cottages.

$ Rates: Mid-Dec to mid-Apr, $340–$456 double (three meals included). Mid-Apr to mid-June, $220–$263 double (two meals included). No credit cards (but personal checks and traveler's checks accepted). **Closed:** Usually mid-June to mid-Dec (inquire in advance).

The elegant Gasparilla Inn is the quintessential Boca Grande experience. Built in 1912, the inn is an architectural beauty with stately pillars, southern-style verandas, handsome wood floors, and a high-ceilinged aristocratic dining room. This is the home-away-from-home for affluent vacationers. When the island's social season is at its height in December, February, and March, it could be difficult to book a room, because the management protects the privacy and security of their wealthy clientele.

Actually, the Gasparilla Inn is a resort, complete with 18-hole golf course, tennis courts, a croquet court, two swimming pools, and a Beach Club. The Pink Elephant, a separate restaurant in the complex, also features fine dining but is less expensive than the inn's dining room. A drugstore and small grocery store are on the premises, as well as bicycle rentals.

When President and Barbara Bush vacationed on the island after the 1992 elections, they stayed at the waterfront mansion of Bayard Sharp, owner of the Gasparilla Inn.

WATERFRONT MOTEL, Railroad and 11th Sts., Boca Grande, FL 33921. Tel. 813/964-2294. Fax 813/964-0382. 32 rms and efficiencies.

$ Rates: Feb–June 15, $85–$125 double. June 16–Nov 20, $75–$115 double. Nov 21–Jan, $105–$125 double. MC, V.

In this unpretentious motel, rates vary according to where you stay. Water-view accommodations with fully equipped kitchens in the newly renovated building are, of course, more expensive than standard rooms without a water view in the older building. If you arrive in your own boat, there's docking here. And a swimming pool is on the premises. No restaurant, but eateries are nearby.

Where to Dine

THEATER RESTAURANT, Fourth and Park Aves., Boca Grande. Tel. 964-0806.

Cuisine: CONTINENTAL. **Reservations:** Recommended.

$ Prices: Main courses $4–$8 at lunch, $12.95–$20 at dinner. MC, V.
Open: Lunch Mon–Sat 11:30am–3pm; dinner Mon–Sat 5:30–10pm. **Closed:** Aug–Sept.

At dinner, the curtain goes up in this former theater with delicious productions, starring roast pork tenderloin glazed with marsala wine and herb jelly, lobster chunks tossed with fettuccine Alfredo, grilled lamb chops laced with chardonnay wine and mint sauce, and grilled steak accompanied by big, garlic-flavored mushrooms. The paintings and sketches on the paneled walls are by local artists. As for the large saltwater aquarium, it almost steals the show.

NORTH CAPTIVA

After a 1921 hurricane split this piece of land from Captiva, it was born again as an island named North Captiva or Upper Captiva. One of the area's best hideaways, thanks to the complex channels leading into the harbor, North Captiva is a beachcomber's dream come true. At the harbor entrance, the **fish house** on stilts dates back to the turn of the century, when commercial fishermen lived here. The house is listed on the National Register of Historic Places. Boaters, but not too many, come here for the day with family and friends.

When the refreshing salt air whets the appetite, there are three delightful, small restaurants. Near the harbor entrance and all but hidden by mangroves, **Barnacle Phil's** is known for grouper sandwiches, juicy hamburgers, and savory black beans with rice to eat outdoors or at one of few inside tables. **Grady's,** on a canal bank near the harbor, serves breakfast, lunch, and dinner—pompano is a specialty. Close to the boat dock, the **Over the Waterfront** restaurant offers lunch daily and outstanding dinners (the menu, listing at least 10 entrees, is changed nightly).

Should you decide to spend more than a day, overnight arrangements must be made in advance with **Upper Captiva Property Management** (tel. 813/472-9223) and the minimum stay is three days. They rent privately owned houses and condos, the only accommodations on the island. When you do make your reservations, inquire about transportation from the dock to your accommodations; also ask about supplies that might be needed. You will want to bring your own food and groceries—there's a little general store, but prices are very high as everything is "imported" from the mainland.

To get to North Captiva water taxis are available on Pine Island at Pineland Marina. One-way fare is $5 for stay-over guests and $10 for day-trippers (tel. 283-1113 for schedules). Or you can rent or charter a boat at the 'Tween Waters Inn Marina (tel. 472-5161). Other than the tricky channel, the good news about renting your own boat is the pleasure of exploring all the islets so close to North Captiva. There is an airstrip for private planes.

PALM ISLAND

Just off the village of Cape Haze, Palm Island and the Palm Island Resort are accessible by boat only. However, the reception center is on the mainland in Cape Haze and the resort's launch shuttles over on the hour from 8am to 10pm (to 11pm on Friday and Saturday). If you're not a guest of the resort, free round-trip boat passes are available at the reception center to go to the resort only, where you can look around and enjoy lunch or dinner at the resort's Rum Bay restaurant.

On the seven-mile-long barrier island, the Palm Island Resort occupies two miles; the rest belongs to the beautiful **Don Pedro Island State Recreation Area.** Ferry transportation to the area is usually arranged by the Ship's Lantern restaurant on Fla. 775, just a few minutes from the Palm Island Resort's reception center. Bordered by a long stretch of white sand beach, the park offers swimming, excellent shelling, fishing, nature trails, and picnic facilities. Florida's state parks are usually open from 8am to sunset daily. For pedestrian visitors, the admission fee is usually $1. For more information about the ferry and park, contact Don Pedro Island State Recreation Area, c/o Barrier Islands, GEOPark, P.O. Box 1150, Boca Grande, FL 33921 (tel. 813/964-0375).

Where to Stay and Dine

PALM ISLAND RESORT, 7002 Placida Rd., Cape Haze, FL 33947. Tel. 813/697-4800, or toll free 800/824-5412. Fax 813/697-0696. 160 villas. A/C TV TEL **Directions:** See below.

$ Rates: Mid-Dec to mid-Apr, $200–$325 one- to three-bedroom villa. Mid-Apr to mid-Dec, $135–$200 one- to three-bedroom villa. Children under 6 stay free with parents. AE, MC, V.

On a gorgeous stretch of white sand beach, the villas offer outstanding gulf views, and screened porches overlook the beach. The attractively decorated villas offer a spacious living room, dining room, fully equipped kitchen (some also have laundry rooms), and comfortable bedrooms. Although being a lazy beachcomber seems like the best idea, the resort features 11 tennis courts and five heated swimming pools, plus golfing privileges at three 18-hole championship courses only five minutes away on the mainland. A little tram shuttles around the resort to take you wherever you wish. And when you want to go to the mainland for shopping or exploring, the resort's boat is at your service. For purchasing groceries to cook in your villa, there's a small store on the premises and a supermarket on the mainland, a few minutes away from the reception center.

From U.S. 41, take Fla. 776 (north of Englewood); follow Fla. 776 for about 15 miles to Fla. 775 and follow the signs to Cape Haze. Or from Port Charlotte, take Fla. 776, then Fla. 771, and exit at Fla. 775.

Dining in the Rum Bay restaurant, the chef has a flair for subtle seasoning and wine sauces. Delicious seafood treats include barbecued bacon-wrapped shrimp and broiled local fish. The grilled steaks are thick, tender, and juicy; veal and poultry are also on the menu. There's a good wine list to enhance a romantic dinner. If key lime pie is on the menu, do indulge in this tangy, creamy dessert.

Main courses are priced at $10.95–$15.95, and the restaurant is open daily for lunch from noon to 2pm, and for dinner from 3 to 9:30pm. The restaurant is open to the public, but reservations are suggested if you're not a guest of the resort (tel. 697-0566). The restaurant accepts MasterCard and VISA.

INDEX

GENERAL INFORMATION

DESTINATIONS

Key to abbreviations: *B* = Budget; *B&B* = Bed & Breakfast; *CG* = Campground; *E* = Expensive; *Hs* = Hostel; *I* = Inexpensive; *M* = Moderately priced; *VE* = Very Expensive; * = Author's favorite; *$* = Super-value choice.

Please Send Me the Books Checked Below:

FROMMER'S COMPREHENSIVE GUIDES

(Guides listing facilities from budget to deluxe, with emphasis on the medium-priced)

	Retail Price	Code
☐ Acapulco/Ixtapa/Taxco 1993–94	$15.00	C120
☐ Alaska 1994–95	$17.00	C130
☐ Arizona 1993–94	$18.00	C101
☐ Australia 1992–93	$18.00	C002
☐ Austria 1993–94	$19.00	C119
☐ Belgium/Holland/ Luxembourg 1993–94	$18.00	C106
☐ Bahamas 1994–95	$17.00	C121
☐ Bermuda 1994–95	$15.00	C122
☐ Brazil 1993–94	$20.00	C111
☐ California 1993	$18.00	C112
☐ Canada 1992–93	$18.00	C009
☐ Caribbean 1994	$18.00	C123
☐ Carolinas/Georgia 1994–95	$17.00	C128
☐ Colorado 1993–94	$16.00	C100
☐ Cruises 1993–94	$19.00	C107
☐ DE/MD/PA & NJ Shore 1992–93	$19.00	C012
☐ Egypt 1990–91	$17.00	C013
☐ England 1994	$18.00	C129
☐ Florida 1994	$18.00	C124
☐ France 1994–95	$20.00	C131
☐ Germany 1994	$19.00	C125
☐ Italy 1994	$19.00	C130

	Retail Price	Code
☐ Jamaica/Barbados 1993–94	$15.00	C105
☐ Japan 1992–93	$19.00	C020
☐ Morocco 1992–93	$18.00	C021
☐ Nepal 1994–95	$18.00	C126
☐ New England 1993	$17.00	C114
☐ New Mexico 1993–94	$15.00	C117
☐ New York State 1994–95	$19.00	C132
☐ Northwest 1991–92	$17.00	C026
☐ Portugal 1992–93	$16.00	C027
☐ Puerto Rico 1993–94	$15.00	C103
☐ Puerto Vallarta/Manzanillo/ Guadalajara 1992–93	$14.00	C028
☐ Scandinavia 1993–94	$19.00	C118
☐ Scotland 1992–93	$16.00	C040
☐ Skiing Europe 1989–90	$15.00	C030
☐ South Pacific 1992–93	$20.00	C031
☐ Spain 1993–94	$19.00	C115
☐ Switzerland/Liechtenstein 1992–93	$19.00	C032
☐ Thailand 1992–93	$20.00	C033
☐ U.S.A. 1993–94	$19.00	C116
☐ Virgin Islands 1994–95	$13.00	C127
☐ Virginia 1992–93	$14.00	C037
☐ Yucatán 1993–94	$18.00	C110

FROMMER'S $-A-DAY GUIDES

(Guides to low-cost tourist accommodations and facilities)

	Retail Price	Code
☐ Australia on $45 1993–94	$18.00	D102
☐ Costa Rica/Guatemala/ Belize on $35 1993–94	$17.00	D108
☐ Eastern Europe on $30 1993–94	$18.00	D110
☐ England on $60 1994	$18.00	D112
☐ Europe on $50 1994	$19.00	D115
☐ Greece on $45 1993–94	$19.00	D100
☐ Hawaii on $75 1994	$19.00	D113
☐ India on $40 1992–93	$20.00	D010
☐ Ireland on $40 1992–93	$17.00	D011
☐ Israel on $45 1993–94	$18.00	D101

	Retail Price	Code
☐ Mexico on $45 1994	$19.00	D116
☐ New York on $70 1992–93	$16.00	D016
☐ New Zealand on $45 1993–94	$18.00	D103
☐ Scotland/Wales on $50 1992–93	$18.00	D019
☐ South America on $40 1993–94	$19.00	D109
☐ Turkey on $40 1992–93	$22.00	D023
☐ Washington, D.C. on $40 1992–93	$17.00	D024

FROMMER'S CITY $-A-DAY GUIDES

(Pocket-size guides with an emphasis on low-cost tourist accommodations and facilities)

	Retail Price	Code
☐ Berlin on $40 1994–95	$12.00	D111
☐ Copenhagen on $50 1992–93	$12.00	D003
☐ London on $45 1994–95	$12.00	D114

	Retail Price	Code
☐ Madrid on $50 1992–93	$13.00	D014
☐ Paris on $45 1994–95	$12.00	D117
☐ Stockholm on $50 1992–93	$13.00	D022

FROMMER'S WALKING TOURS

(With routes and detailed maps, these companion guides point out the places and pleasures that make a city unique)

	Retail Price	Code
☐ Berlin	$12.00	W100
☐ London	$12.00	W101
☐ New York	$12.00	W102
☐ Paris	$12.00	W103
☐ San Francisco	$12.00	W104
☐ Washington, D.C.	$12.00	W105

FROMMER'S TOURING GUIDES

(Color-illustrated guides that include walking tours, cultural and historic sites, and practical information)

	Retail Price	Code
☐ Amsterdam	$11.00	T001
☐ Barcelona	$14.00	T015
☐ Brazil	$11.00	T003
☐ Florence	$ 9.00	T005
☐ Hong Kong/Singapore/ Macau	$11.00	T006
☐ Kenya	$14.00	T018
☐ London	$13.00	T007
☐ New York	$11.00	T008
☐ Rome	$11.00	T010
☐ Scotland	$10.00	T011
☐ Sicily	$15.00	T017
☐ Tokyo	$15.00	T016
☐ Turkey	$11.00	T013
☐ Venice	$ 9.00	T014

FROMMER'S FAMILY GUIDES

	Retail Price	Code
☐ California with Kids	$18.00	F100
☐ Los Angeles with Kids	$17.00	F002
☐ New York City with Kids	$18.00	F003
☐ San Francisco with Kids	$17.00	F004
☐ Washington, D.C. with Kids	$17.00	F005

FROMMER'S CITY GUIDES

(Pocket-size guides to sightseeing and tourist accommodations and facilities in all price ranges)

	Retail Price	Code
☐ Amsterdam 1993–94	$13.00	S110
☐ Athens 1993–94	$13.00	S114
☐ Atlanta 1993–94	$13.00	S112
☐ Atlantic City/Cape May 1993–94	$13.00	S130
☐ Bangkok 1992–93	$13.00	S005
☐ Barcelona/Majorca/ Minorca/Ibiza 1993–94	$13.00	S115
☐ Berlin 1993–94	$13.00	S116
☐ Boston 1993–94	$13.00	S117
☐ Cancún/Cozumel 1991–92	$ 9.00	S010
☐ Chicago 1993–94	$13.00	S122
☐ Denver/Boulder/Colorado Springs 1993–94	$13.00	S131
☐ Dublin 1993–94	$13.00	S128
☐ Hawaii 1992	$12.00	S014
☐ Hong Kong 1992–93	$12.00	S015
☐ Honolulu/Oahu 1994	$13.00	S134
☐ Las Vegas 1993–94	$13.00	S121
☐ London 1994	$13.00	S132
☐ Los Angeles 1993–94	$13.00	S123
☐ Madrid/Costa del Sol 1993–94	$13.00	S124
☐ Miami 1993–94	$13.00	S118
☐ Minneapolis/St. Paul 1993–94	$13.00	S119
☐ Montreál/Québec City 1993–94	$13.00	S125
☐ New Orleans 1993–94	$13.00	S103
☐ New York 1993	$13.00	S120
☐ Orlando 1994	$13.00	S135
☐ Paris 1993–94	$13.00	S109
☐ Philadelphia 1993–94	$13.00	S113
☐ Rio 1991–92	$ 9.00	S029
☐ Rome 1993–94	$13.00	S111
☐ Salt Lake City 1991–92	$ 9.00	S031
☐ San Diego 1993–94	$13.00	S107
☐ San Francisco 1994	$13.00	S133
☐ Santa Fe/Taos/ Albuquerque 1993–94	$13.00	S108
☐ Seattle/Portland 1992–93	$12.00	S035
☐ St. Louis/Kansas City 1993–94	$13.00	S127
☐ Sydney 1993–94	$13.00	S129
☐ Tampa/St. Petersburg 1993–94	$13.00	S105
☐ Tokyo 1992–93	$13.00	S039
☐ Toronto 1993–94	$13.00	S126
☐ Vancouver/Victoria 1990–91	$ 8.00	S041
☐ Washington, D.C. 1993	$13.00	S102

Other Titles Available at Membership Prices

SPECIAL EDITIONS

	Retail Price	Code		Retail Price	Code
☐ Bed & Breakfast North America	$15.00	P002	☐ Marilyn Wood's Wonderful Weekends (within a 250-mile radius of NYC)	$12.00	P017
☐ Bed & Breakfast Southwest	$16.00	P100	☐ National Park Guide 1993	$15.00	P101
☐ Caribbean Hideaways	$16.00	P103	☐ Where to Stay U.S.A.	$15.00	P102

GAULT MILLAU'S "BEST OF" GUIDES

(The only guides that distinguish the truly superlative from the merely overrated)

	Retail Price	Code		Retail Price	Code
☐ Chicago	$16.00	G002	☐ New England	$16.00	G010
☐ Florida	$17.00	G003	☐ New Orleans	$17.00	G011
☐ France	$17.00	G004	☐ New York	$17.00	G012
☐ Germany	$18.00	G018	☐ Paris	$17.00	G013
☐ Hawaii	$17.00	G006	☐ San Francisco	$17.00	G014
☐ Hong Kong	$17.00	G007	☐ Thailand	$18.00	G019
☐ London	$17.00	G009	☐ Toronto	$17.00	G020
☐ Los Angeles	$17.00	G005	☐ Washington, D.C.	$17.00	G017

THE REAL GUIDES

(Opinionated, politically aware guides for youthful budget-minded travelers)

	Retail Price	Code		Retail Price	Code
☐ Able to Travel	$20.00	R112	☐ Kenya	$12.95	R015
☐ Amsterdam	$13.00	R100	☐ Mexico	$11.95	R128
☐ Barcelona	$13.00	R101	☐ Morocco	$14.00	R129
☐ Belgium/Holland/ Luxembourg	$16.00	R031	☐ Nepal	$14.00	R018
			☐ New York	$13.00	R019
☐ Berlin	$13.00	R123	☐ Paris	$13.00	R130
☐ Brazil	$13.95	R003	☐ Peru	$12.95	R021
☐ California & the West Coast	$17.00	R121	☐ Poland	$13.95	R131
			☐ Portugal	$16.00	R126
☐ Canada	$15.00	R103	☐ Prague	$15.00	R113
☐ Czechoslovakia	$15.00	R124	☐ San Francisco & the Bay Area	$11.95	R024
☐ Egypt	$19.00	R105			
☐ Europe	$18.00	R122	☐ Scandinavia	$14.95	R025
☐ Florida	$14.00	R006	☐ Spain	$16.00	R026
☐ France	$18.00	R106	☐ Thailand	$17.00	R119
☐ Germany	$18.00	R107	☐ Tunisia	$17.00	R115
☐ Greece	$18.00	R108	☐ Turkey	$13.95	R027
☐ Guatemala/Belize	$14.00	R127	☐ U.S.A.	$18.00	R117
☐ Hong Kong/Macau	$11.95	R011	☐ Venice	$11.95	R028
☐ Hungary	$14.95	R118	☐ Women Travel	$12.95	R029
☐ Ireland	$17.00	R120	☐ Yugoslavia	$12.95	R030
☐ Italy	$18.00	R125			